Childhood and Children

A Compendium of Customs, Superstitions, Theories, Profiles, and Facts

by
Joan Bel Geddes

Oryx Press
1997

The rare Arabian oryx is believed to have inspired the myth of the unicorn. This desert antelope became virtually extinct in the early 1960s. At that time several groups of international conservationists arranged to have 9 animals sent to the Phoenix Zoo to be the nucleus of a captive breeding herd. Today the Oryx population is over 1,000, and over 500 have been returned to the Middle East.

© 1997 by Joan Bel Geddes
Published by The Oryx Press
4041 North Central at Indian School Road
Phoenix, Arizona 85012-3397

Published simultaneously in Canada
Printed and bound in the United States of America

Excerpts on pages 549–53 are from *Anne Frank: The Diary of a Young Girl* by Anne Frank. Copyright 1952 by Otto H. Frank. Used by permission of Doubleday, a division of Bantam Doubleday Dell Publishing Group, Inc.

∞ The paper used in this publication meets the minimum requirements of the
American National Standard for Information Sciences—Permanence of Paper
for Printed Library Materials, ANSI Z39.48-1984.

Library of Congress Cataloging-in-Publication Data
Bel Geddes, Joan.
    Childhood and children : a compendium of customs, superstitions,
theories, profiles, and facts / by Joan Bel Geddes.
        p. cm.
    Includes bibliographical references and index.
    ISBN 0-89774-880-8 (alk, paper)
    1. Children. I. title.
HQ781.B45 1996
305.23—dc21   96–48258
                                                            CIP

Dedication

It is natural in life
that birth should lead to death;
that that which has been shall pass
as that which is to be emerges.

Our task is to do the most we can
to ensure that death does not follow birth too closely
and that life lived long is lived well.

The above lines were on the last Christmas card I received from James P. Grant, executive director of the United Nations Children's Fund (UNICEF) from 1980 to 1995. It was his idea that I should write this book, and he was going to write an introduction to it, but he died early in 1995 before being able to do so. His life was lived unusually well. He inspired many people and prolonged and improved many lives through his tireless work on behalf of the world's children. I gratefully dedicate this book to James Grant's memory as a substitute for his intended introduction.

Contents

Preface

Why, how, and for whom was this book written?

Children and childhood are almost completely ignored in most history books, encyclopedias, anthologies, and almanacs, which concentrate on the achievements of the adult half of the world's population—and until fairly recently, when the women's movement began to delve into neglected "herstory"—primarily on the male half of that half.

Children and Childhood: A Compendium of Customs Superstitions, Theories, Profiles, and Facts is different. It aims to fill that gap by focusing on childhood. It was not written *for* children, however, but *about* them, for all adults who care for them: parents, doting aunts, uncles, grandparents, pediatricians, child psychologists, teachers, and social workers, and for historians, anthropologists, and sociologists—as well as for the general public. Trivia buffs will find intriguing little-known anecdotes and information in its pages. Even people not particularly interested in children may find, to their surprise and pleasure, much that interests them in this book because it contains so many surprising and even startling observations.

The information in the book was gathered over many years. In the 1950s, I was the editor-in-chief of a monthly magazine for parents and began collecting so many anecdotes about children and childhood that my husband said I should write a book on the subject. A publisher agreed, and in 1965 the book appeared, entitled *Small World: A History of Baby Care from the Stone Age to the Spock Age.* It was like a dress rehearsal for this new book, though it was much shorter and did not cover nearly as much ground.

Later, after my own children were launched in school and college, I worked full-time at the United Nations Children's Fund (UNICEF) and became head of its editorial and publications section. My awareness of the world's children soon took on a global geographic dimension to supplement my interest in their history, which was buttressed by UNICEF's sending me, in 1970, on a fact-finding trip around the world. I worked in Africa, Asia, the Middle East, Canada, England, Ireland, Scotland, and Europe, as well as in many regions of the United States. Although my travels did not include Australia, New Zealand, or South America, I also leaned about children in those areas, from experts in the field as well as from children themselves, when they visited the United Nations or wrote to me.

Thus, although this book contains many facts acquired through research, it also includes observations and opinions of my own based on more than 30 years of personal conversations, interviews, and letters. My large collection of memories and notes made over those decades have now been gathered and packed into a necessarily limited number of pages. Much interesting material has had to be left out of the resulting book because the subject matter is so vast that no one volume could contain it all. Readers can get a good idea of the variety of subjects that are included by looking through the detailed index and by reading the tables of contents that appear on the opening pages of each chapter.

Socrates once said, "If I could climb to the highest place in Athens, I would lift up my voice and shout, 'Fellow citizens—why do you turn and scrape every stone to gather wealth and take so little care of your children to whom one day you must relinquish it all?'" I hope that some of the information in this book may cause at least a few readers to ponder the still-relevant wisdom of those words.

But do not expect to find the book solemn. It contains not only wise exhortations and some inspiring facts but also some that are strange, even outrageous, and some that are funny. I hope readers will not merely learn useful things from these pages but that they will have a good time as they explore the world of childhood and children.

ACKNOWLEDGMENTS

I would like to thank Doubleday & Company for permission to quote from *The Diary of a Young Girl* by Anne Frank and UNICEF for generously granting blanket permission to use any of their published reports, books, magazines and illustrations. I have made diligent inquiries in a conscientious effort to find out if any other material used in this book is under copyright and apologize if I have overlooked any copyright holders who can substantiate their claims. Some quotations and information in this book were taken from informal personal conversations of interviews or letters, and I thank these people for the information they gave me.

Every book is a collaboration between its author, editors and publisher, and a book like this, filled with comments by and information about so many people, is particularly beholden to a great many individuals, so the traditional author's list of acknowledgments would be almost as long as the book if it were complete (some of my thanks are implicit in the bibliography). But a few individuals must be singled out for special thanks.

First of all, at UNICEF there was James P. Grant, its Executive Director from 1984 to 1995, who was such an ardent advocate for the world's children and who first introduced to me the idea of compiling a book about them. Secondly, my dear friend and mentor Jack Charnow introduced me to important records, documents and publications and guided and encouraged me whenever I felt swamped. The inspired and inspiring Tarzie Vittachi took special interest in this project and with his enthusiasm and wisdom gave me many useful ideas on how to develop it. Then there was Eduard Specscha who gave me an important warning about how much information I was trying to include, when he said, "I think this will be an extremely interesting and important book, but if you don't watch out, you'll still be working on it when you're 120."

It is literally true that *everyone* I worked with at the United Nations, at headquarters and in the field, in National UNICEF Committees and in nongovernmental organizations, contributed in one way or another to this book, but a few people were especially important: Lisa Adelson, John Balcomb, Maggie Black, Jim Breetveld, Bob Brennan, Doug Brunner, Horst Cherni, Ole Dich, Joan Dydo, Paul Edwards, Adhiratha Kevin Keith and his helpful assistants, and Mehr Khan, Hala Kitani, Henry Labouisse, Jack Ling, Elfi Lunkenheimer-Maclay, Beryl Menon, Marilee Reiner, Mary Sawiki, Rhonwen Searle, Judy Spiegelman, Ellen Tolmie, Nico Van Oudenhoven, and Jeanne Vickers.

I am also indebted to the following people who made my life easier with their efficient and cheerful clerical and secretarial assistance from time to time: Alex Allard, Marjorie Camisuli, Chandika Kapalika, Athar Khan, Laura Lopez-Lising, Khurram Mirza, Sirramatta Ndow, Ann Prendergast, Tui Promakul, Nikolle Solomone, and Martine Villedrouin.

Among other friends to whom I feel very grateful for their encouragement and advice during the book's preparation are Gemma Biggi, Noreen Drukker, Rachel Rephan Ginsberg, Margaret Green and her daughter Sayers, Peter Grenquist, Joan and Dean McClure, Rosemary Ostergren, Lee Pattison, William L. Thourlby, and Mary Taylor.

Individuals who gave valuable help with research were Ruth Steinkraus Cohen, Gerry Cornez, Elizabeth Small Davis, Rajinder Garcia, Herman Gordon, Lydia Marcus, Bill Tracy, and Barry Ulanov.

Above all, extra gratitude is due to my hard-working agent Ed Knappman; the helpful people at Oryx Press, Anne Thompson, Karla Olson, and Pat Cattani, Sandi Bourelle, Linda Vespa, Tom Brennan, and Natalie Lang; and my children, Anne, Nicholas and Kate, for their very generous help and for patiently putting up with me during the crises that arose during various stages of the book's preparation. Kate's cover design was an especially appreciated contribution.

To one and all, many, many thanks!

Introduction

Children are small in size when compared to adults, but they are not smaller in importance. And, although there is a proverb that says, "the chicken does not teach the hen," there are many important things that adults can learn from children.

A few children have had a big influence on history, even if they do not usually get much credit for doing so. It was adventurous schoolboys who stumbled into an unexplored cave in Lascaux, France, in 1940 and discovered a collection of murals and engravings from the sixteenth century BC, thus opening up to archaeologists a source of fascinating and previously unsuspected knowledge about prehistoric people. In 1994, another boy discovered additional magnificent art from the Stone Age in caves near Vallon Pont-d'Asc, France. It was a Bedouin shepherd boy who first stumbled onto an urn in another cave at Qumran near the northern end of the Dead Sea in 1947, making what the head of the Israel Antiquities Authority has called "the most important find in the twentieth century," the Dead Sea Scrolls. And at a time when Egypt's Pharaoh had ordered all newborn Israelite males to be killed, his young daughter disobeyed him and secretly rescued a baby boy, whom she eventually adopted and named Moses. Without her courage we might never have had the Ten Commandments.

Countless children, often anonymous, have made major contributions to linguistics, to advertising and industry, to art and music, to mythology and literature, to philosophy, to medicine and the other sciences, and to politics. The son of the Catholic King James II of England helped overthrow his father's government and dynasty, merely by being born. Some children have brought about, unwittingly, important changes in law. For example, after 19 persons in Salem, Massachusetts, were executed for witchcraft in 1692 on the testimony of a group of hysterical girls, a repentant judiciary made legal reforms about rules of evidence. And the grief universally felt for the kidnapping and murder in 1932 of the Lindbergh baby caused the U.S. government to make kidnapping a federal crime.

Despite the claim that necessity is the mother of invention, it is usually curiosity, observation, and imagination that produce new things. The major portion of useful inventions, knowledge, and achievements have been brought about by inventive, childlike, creative observers of the world around us, whose vision is unclouded by judgments about what is "practical" or "possible" or "impossible" or "good" or "bad."

For example, the first compound microscope was invented in the sixteenth century by Zacharia Janssen, a maker of spectacles, when he was only 10 years old, and the telescope was invented in principle by some Dutch children who were playing one day outside his spectacle shop with defective lenses that he had discarded. The children found out that when the lenses were held one in front of the other, which everyone knew was not supposed to be done, distant objects appeared closer. News of their discovery somehow spread to Italy, and to the attention of a man named Galileo Galilei (1564–1642) who proceeded to construct the world's first astronomical telescope in 1609 on the basis of the children's discovery—and of course he, not the children, got all the credit for this wonderful invention. (It turned out to be an unlucky discovery for him, however, because what he saw by looking through his telescope disproved ancient notions about the solar system and the earth's supposedly central place in it, and so the Inquisition threatened him with torture unless he denied the evidence of his own eyes. In 1637, he became totally blind and could never again look into the heavens through his beloved telescope. And it was more than 380 years before the Church finally issued an official apology admitting it had been mistaken and unjust in persecuting him.)

Three centuries before Freud lived, the poet John Dryden wrote, "Men are but children of a larger growth." And in our post-Freudian era we have learned what a powerful influence childhood experiences play in forming our characters as adults. Maria Montessori, the Italian educator who was a contemporary of Freud, explained the significance of childhood in these words from her book *The Secret of Childhood:*

> None of us has always been a grownup; it was a child who constructed each personality. Before we became the important adult personages we are now, the respected members of society, we were another personality—very different, very mysterious—but not considered by the world at all, not respected, of no importance whatever, with no say in the running of things. Yet all that time we were really persons capable of doing something that we cannot do now. He who is the constructor of man can never be a person of no importance. He is capable of

doing something great, like a seed. It is only when we realize the wonderful way in which the child creates the man that we realize, at the same time, that we hold in our hands a secret by which we can help in the formation of a better humanity.

Another thing readers will discover from this book, which tells about how children lived centuries ago as well as how they live today, is that "the good old days" were never entirely good and the bad new days are not entirely bad in comparison. It is helpful to gain that perspective on current events, a good antidote against both euphoria and despair.

People often tell children, "These are the best years of your life." Many children ponder that statement, thinking of their various woes and frustrations (and even the happiest child has had at least a few of these) and may think, "gee, if this is the best life gets, why go on?" Most children are remarkably resilient, however. Their tendency to short attention spans usually means that they have an enviable knack for quickly compensating for unhappiness. Most of them can bounce back from sorrows and find ways to have fun even in appalling circumstances. In the midst of war's rubble in Lebanon or Bosnia or Rwanda, they play hide-and-seek and tag. In crowded and drenched refugee camps during the monsoon season in India, slogging through mud, they make mudpies.

Both sentimentalists and cynics are wrong about children and childhood. Few children are either angels or brats—most are a mixture of the two. Childhood is also a mixture, neither an Edenic period of innocence and bliss nor a period of unrelieved pain, although both bliss and pain are frequently parts of it. Childhood contains, as does adult life, diverse experiences: many delights and many woes. But childhood is different from adulthood in that most of its experiences have never been known before. As we get older we tend to lose our naive sense of awe and even become bored by repetition of many life events, but in childhood most experiences are to some extent fascinating just because they are new. Adults who can hold onto a child's sense of curiosity, enthusiasm, wonderment, and adventure are the world's greatest people—its artists, poets, philosophers, and geniuses.

There is still another value to be gained by looking closely at children. In a time when many individuals seem intent on stressing the differences among races, nationalities, cultural backgrounds, classes, gender, and ages, it is helpful to be reminded instead of the basic similarities that unite all human beings. Like flowers, children come in many different colors and speak different languages and wear different kinds of clothes, but the differences between them are not nearly as fundamental as the ways in which they are alike: All children cry when hurt, sulk when annoyed, yell when angry, tremble when frightened, giggle when amused, smile when happy, and unfailingly respond to love with love. Even in these days when a distressingly large number of children are performing criminal acts, it may be reassuring to learn from statisticians that the number who do is only 7 percent. But you will not find out much about the other 93 percent in newspapers because, as Betty Allen, president emeritus of the Harlem School of the Arts, put it: "If a kid were out here holding everybody hostage with a machine gun, that would get publicity. But you can't show nice kids learning. That's boring." I think that in this book you will discover that finding out about that majority of children is not at all boring.

The one basic thing every adult has in common with everyone else in the world is that he or she was once a child, and it is also true that inside every adult a child is still there, hidden but alive. Readers of this book may be reminded of their own childhoods and as a result feel a closer kinship with all other children and therefore with all members of our human family, past, present, and future.

1

The History of Childhood

FIRST OF ALL—WHAT IS A CHILD?

At first glance what it means to be a child seems simple enough to explain. Childhood is seen as a long, protracted and protected period of dependence, in which going to school is a dominant feature. But one only has to look into the past, or to shift one's view to other parts of the world, to see this concept of childhood begin to dissolve.

The most obvious way to define a child would seem to be in terms of age. "The United Nations Convention on the Rights of the Child" (adopted by the UN in 1989) defines a child as "every human being to the age of 18 unless, under the law of his or her state he/she has reached his/her age of majority earlier." But that is rather vague.

Childhood is in many ways a modern invention. In Europe in the Middle Ages there was no such thing as privacy. Children lived, worked, played, ate, and slept with their parents and knew the facts of life at an early age. Then, in Europe from around the seventeenth century, children of wealthy families began to be treated differently. They began to receive a long period of careful training. And in the eighteenth century, with the introduction of laws making education compulsory, this view of childhood was gradually extended, at least in theory, to all children. Nevertheless, lower-class children still lived in the adult world. In Victorian London and in other cities, many children drank, gambled, were active sexually, worked hard to support themselves, and never saw the inside of a school.

Today, most of the world's children live in the earth's poorer parts, in Africa, Asia, and South America, or in the slums and impoverished rural sections of the so-called developed countries. For poor families in these areas childhood is much shorter than it is for children in well-to-do families, because poor children usually have to go to work from a very early age to help support their families. In some undeveloped countries children as young as three may be sold to well-off families for lifelong servitude as domestic servants. Many as young as five toil all day long on plantations, and the International Labour Organization estimates that more than 50 million children between the ages of seven and 15 work in factories, mines, offices, and shops. And the majority of children in poor countries either never go to school or, if they do, never have a chance to go beyond elementary school.

> Even in developed countries children can feel confused about exactly when it is that they become adults. Is it at puberty? Or at 16, 17, 18, or 21? When is it okay to drive a car? To drink liquor? To vote? To have sex? And to get married?

In ancient Egypt and Rome and at other times and places, marriage in the early teens was normal and many girls (alias young women) had babies before they were 15. In Elizabethan and Jacobean England the average age of brides was about 24 and 27 for bridegrooms. The primary reason for delayed marriages was to limit births among poor people, and the higher the social status, the younger was the age of marriage.

In our century marriage is legal at age 12 in Bolivia, Chile, Cuba, Ecuador, Honduras, India, Ireland, Panama, Paraguay, Peru, Spain, Venezuela and in the Canadian province of Quebec. And it is legal at 14 in Argentina, El Salvador, Greece, Guatemala, Guyana, Hungary, Italy, Malaysia, Malta, Mexico, Nicaragua, the Philippines, and Portugal. In China girls can actually be legally married even earlier, when they are one year old. In any country, children of the Baha'i faith, both boys and girls, can marry at age 15—

2

although never at any age without the consent of all living parents. India has the world's lowest average ages for marriage, 20 years for males and 14 for females.

In the United States the minimum age for marriage with or without parental consent is 18 in most states, 21 in Mississippi and Puerto Rico. With parental consent, it is legal for girls at 13 in New Hampshire, and for both boys and girls at 14 in Alabama, New York, Texas, and Utah. For boys it is also legal at 14 in New Hampshire.

In 1970 the U.S. Census Bureau found 2,983 males who were already widowers at age 14, and 289 females who, at that same age, had been widowed or divorced. Such figures would be most unlikely today, because more and more young people are postponing marriage or not getting married at all—which doesn't mean they are not cohabiting or having children. The number of young girls in the United States who are sexually active and often become mothers when they are still too immature to cope well with the responsibilities involved has increased enormously.

So it seems that the question "What is a child?" is debatable. Some young people are precocious and mature early. Others are late bloomers. As one old saying put it, anyone who thinks everyone develops at the same time may know a lot about raspberries but nothing about grapes.

Two things we do know for certain about children, however. They are almost half of the world's population. And they are the world's future. According to the Indian poet Rabindrinath Tagore (1861–1941), "Every time a child is born it brings with it the hope that God is not yet disappointed with man."

CHILDREN—PRO AND CON

Attitudes towards children have varied through the centuries from saccharine, almost idolatrous, love and reverence to indifference or intense dislike. Here is a sampling of opinions.

In Praise of Children

Blessed be childhood, which brings down something of heaven into the midst of our rough earthliness.   —*Henri Frederic Amiel (1821–1881)*

Children and young people are our greatest treasure . . . . To me children are worth more than all my music . . . . We should say to each of them: Do you know what you are? You are a marvel. A miracle. You are unique. Since the beginning of the world there hasn't been and until the end of the world there will not be another child exactly like you. And look at your body—what a wonder it is! Your legs, your arms, your cunning fingers, the way you move! . . . . And when you grow up, can you then harm another who is, like you, a marvel? You must cherish one another. You must work—we all must work—to make this world worthy of its children.   —*Pablo Casals (1876–1985)*

In praise of little children I will say / God first made man, then found a better way / For woman, but His third way was the best: / Of all created things the loveliest / And most divine are children. Nothing here / Can be to us more precious or more dear. / And though, when God saw all His works were good, / There was no rosy flower of baby-

3

hood, / 'Twas said of children in a later day / That none could enter Heaven save such as they.   —*William Caxton (1422–1491)*

I love these little people; and it is not a slight thing when they, who are so fresh from God, love us....It is one of my rules in life not to believe a man who may happen to tell me that he feels no interest in children.
—*Charles Dickens (1812–1870)*

God sends children for another purpose than merely to keep up the race—to enlarge our hearts; and to make us unselfish and full of kindly sympathies and affections; to give our souls higher aims; to call out our faculties to extended enterprise and exertion and to bring round our firesides bright faces, happy smiles, and loving and tender hearts—my soul blesses the great Father, every day, that He has gladdened the earth with little children.
—*Mary Howitt (1799–1888)*

Truly I tell you that unless you become like a little child, you cannot enter the kingdom of heaven.   —*Jesus of Nazareth*

The utmost reverence is due to a child.   —*Juvenal (c. 60–130)*

Ah! what would the world be to us / If children were no more? / We should dread the desert behind us / Worse than the dark before. / For what are all our contrivings, / And the wisdom of our books, / When compared with your caresses, / And the gladness of your looks? / Ye are better than all the ballads / That ever were sung or said; / For ye are living poems, / And all the rest are dead.   —*Henry Wadsworth Longfellow (1807–1882)*

I seem, for my own part, to see the benevolence of the Deity more clearly in the presence of very young children than in anything in the world
—*William Paley (1743–1805)*

Each child has something to teach us, a message that will help to explain why we are here.   —*The Talmud*

Children are our greatest wealth.   —*Josip Broz Tito (1892–1980)*

If men do not keep on speaking terms with children, they cease to be men, and become merely machines for eating and for earning money.
—*John Updike (1932–)*

A dreary place would this world be / Were there no little people in it; / The song of life would lose its mirth, / Were there no children to begin it. / No little forms, like buds to grow, / And make the admiring heart surrender; / No little hands on breast and brow, / To keep the thrilling love chords tender. / The sterner souls would grow more stern, / Unfeeling nature more inhuman, / And man to stoic coldness turn, / And woman would be less than woman. / Life's song, indeed, would lose its charm / Were there no babies to begin it; / A doleful place this world would be / Were there no little people in it.

—*John Greenleaf Whittier (1807–1892)*

On the Other Hand...

The newborn babe is full of the stains and pollution of sin, which it inherits from our first parents through our loins.

—*Richard Allestree (1619–1681)*

The life of children, as much as that of intemperate men, is wholly governed by their desires....Children cannot be happy, for they are not old enough to be capable of noble acts.   —*Aristotle (384–322 B.C.)*

The innocence of little children lies in their limbs, not in their will.

—*Saint Augustine (354–430 B.C.)*

Children are holy terrors—in both the figurative and literal sense of the term.

—*G. K. Chesterton (1874–1936)*

All children are essentially criminal.   —*Denis Diderot (1713–1784)*

Childhood and youth are vanity.   —*Ecclesiastes*

All children are by nature children of wrath, and are in danger of eternal damnation in hell.   —*Jonathan Edwards (1703–1758)*

A child is a curly headed, dimpled lunatic.

—*Ralph Waldo Emerson (1803–1882)*

Anyone who hates dogs and small children can't be all bad....I never met a kid I liked.   —*W. C. Fields (1880–1946)*

Of all the pestilences dire, / Including famine, flood, and fire, / By Satan and his imps rehearsed, / The neighbor's children are the worst.

—*Stoddard King (1889–1933)*

Children are overwhelming, supercilious, passionate, envious, inquisitive, egotistical, idle, fickle, timid, intemperate, liars and dissemblers; they laugh and weep easily, are excessive in their joys and sorrows, and that about the most trifling subjects; they bear no pain, but like to inflict it on others....Children are without pity.   —*Jean de La Bruyere (1645–1696)*

We rejoice in the spontaneity of small children. But, in truth, children are all born liars, cheats, thieves and manipulators who don't know how to delay gratification. . . .   —*M. Scott Peck (1936–)*

Children, after being limbs of Satan in traditional theology and mystically illuminated angels in the minds of educational reformers, have reverted to being
little devils—not theological demons inspired by the Evil One, but scientific
Freudian abominations inspired by the Unconscious.

—Bertrand Russell (1872–1970)

I feel the same about kids as I do about adults. Some are delightful, some are
dreadful. A person's a person, no matter how small. Most writers of children's
books will tell you all children are wonderful, but they're not.　　*—Dr. Seuss
(1904–1991)*

I must have been an insufferable child; all children are.

—George Bernard Shaw (1856–1950)

Children are torment and nothing else.　　　　　*—Leo Tolstoy (1828–1910)*

Parents of young children should realize that few people, and maybe no one,
will find their children as enchanting as they do.

—Barbara Walters (1931–)

CHILDREN THROUGHOUT HISTORY

You may think children have no history. They did not create the laws and wars that fill our
history books.They were "born yesterday" and represent the world's future, not its past,
inspire prophecies rather than reminiscences. Yet, although individually every child's
history is short, as a species they have been around a long, long time.

Despite a few dissenting voices, love for children is so universal that some biologists
and sociologists think it was the origin of human altruism, hence of the development of
cooperation, socialization, and civilization. But a long look backwards into history makes
one think the mother and father instinct must frequently have been dormant or else
frustrated for thousands of years.

Traditionally children have been considered by law the property of their parents,
with no real value of their own except as potential workers or transmitters of family
property. Therefore parents were allowed, until recently, to do whatever they wished with
and to their children. In many cases what they did was appalling. In some cases this is still
true, but the difference is that child abuse is no longer approved by the majority of people,
nor is it sanctioned by law.

Today abortion is legal, although bitterly opposed by many people who believe it is a
crime to kill an unborn child. In the ancient world medical science had not advanced far
enough to make abortion safe for mothers, so infanticide was used instead as a form of
birth control. It was widely practiced by families that could not afford to support more
children; or to get rid of handicapped children; or twins, who were often considered
unlucky; or to reduce the number of girls, who were considered less desirable than sons;
or to propitiate the gods via child sacrifice. Not only have children through most of history
had no "right to life" but no right to protection either before or after birth.

6

Violent whippings, mutilation, and sex abuse have been socially acceptable in many cultures. For example, "the glory that was Greece" had brothels where men legally had sex with babies and children of either gender, and little boys were frequently castrated to make them more amenable.

Disease, malnutrition, and early death—the norm for most children throughout both ancient and modern history—has usually been due more to ignorance and poverty than to malevolence, however. Even the killing of girls was not always due to cruelty or lack of parental love; fathers sometimes killed their daughters *because* they loved them, to save them from rape or starvation, their usual fate in times of war or famine. And not all parents who exposed unwanted children to the elements instead of keeping them did so because they wanted them to die. On the contrary, they often did so in the hope that someone would come along, find the children, and adopt them.

> We are accustomed these days to startling revelations about the true history of all sorts of things, but few histories have been so completely ignored as that of children and of childhood itself. Children by and large did not appear in the history books we read in school. They scarcely appeared in our literature until the nineteenth century.
>
> —Henry F. Smith, M.D., clinical instructor in psychiatry at the Massachusetts Mental Health Center, 1984

Child slavery and child labor have been common until recently and still exist in many parts of the world. In England during the industrial revolution there was a law that said "anyone old enough to stand up" was old enough to do manual labor for 14 hours a day.

Religious and civil leaders attempted from time to time to change social attitudes and curb harsh treatment of children, at first with reproofs and condemnation, later with mild punishments, and still later with severe penalties. Jews, after Abraham (c. 2000 B.C.), outlawed child sacrifice. Christians were taught to respect children because even they had souls, although unbaptized babies would be excluded from heaven. Mohammed (c. 570–632) tried to prevent the killing of daughters. Some civil leaders also tried occasionally to curb mistreatment of children. However, most of the laws passed that helped children were motivated by a desire to protect society's welfare or families' property rights, not by a humanitarian concern for children's rights. Such rights did not exist. For all these reasons, psychohistorian Lloyd De Mause claims that "the history of childhood is a nightmare from which we have only just begun to awaken."

Children's rights are still nonexistent in many areas, but at last and at least most governments now acknowledge them in theory. An amazing change has taken place in the past two centuries, due to a convergence of ethical, social, and scientific factors. The explosion of scientific knowledge in regard to medicine and nutrition has made health care for all a feasible goal. Improvements in transportation and communication now make it possible to send aid to remote areas. Deeper understanding of child psychology has made people aware of the crucial importance of education and child care.

Humanitarianism applied to children came to a peak after World War II when an intergovernmental fund to help needy children was created: The United Nations International Children's Emergency Fund (UNICEF). This marked a unique step forward, an unprecedented example of international cooperation on behalf of children.

The twentieth century is deservedly scolded for its violent crimes, injustices, and wars, but these do not distinguish it. All centuries have had these. What is new in our time, as historian Arnold Toynbee (1889–1975) has pointed out, is that this is the first time since the dawn of mankind in which people have dared to think it possible to make the benefits of civilization available to the whole human race.

Including its smallest members.

CHILDREN IN THE MIDDLE AGES

At the Bibliothèque Nationale in Paris in January 1995, childhood in the Middle Ages was the subject of an exhibition drawing on the library's extensive collections as well as loans and photographic reproductions. The intention of the exhibit was to show what home and school life were like and, according to the author of its catalogue, Pierre Rich, to counteract the long-accepted view of historian Philippe Ariès that in the Middle Ages children were seen simply as shrunken adults. Among the documents presented as evidence were pediatric manuals including the best-selling encyclopedia on childhood by Barthélemy l'Anglais, the medieval Dr Spock; accounts of the lives of medieval saints; records of convicted child killers; and recently excavated toys.

Life back then was undeniably hard. It was short, and so was childhood. In the countryside, children began working in the fields at the age of eight or nine. Poor children were apprenticed to artisans at age 12, with the artisans supplying clothes, shoes, food, and lodging and the parents paying a fixed sum and guaranteeing reimbursement for anything broken by the child during the learning period. By canon law girls could marry at 12, boys at 14. There was also plenty of danger: plague, evil spells, bandits, kidnappers, horses' hooves. For most people life was brutish and short. One in three children died before reaching the age of five. However, those who survived usually had childhoods as happy and loving as their parents could provide. Life was rigorous, as was that of adults, but it was far from joyless.

Not everyone loved children, any more than everyone does today. For example, when Abelard (1079–1142) asked Héloise to marry him, she turned down his proposal, explaining that for a man the noise and messy digestive habits of an infant would be difficult to tolerate. But some people revered children as holy.

Children were breastfed until age two or three. Wet nurses were used by all except the very poor, and they were carefully chosen for their morality, cleanliness, good temper, sweet breath, and the size of their breasts; it was thought that large breasts might result in a bent nose for the child. After weaning, children were given carefully chosen bland diets. Teething problems were soothed by rubbing the gums with chicken fat or the brain of roast hare or by letting children suck on the roots of gladiolas.

Children were not allowed to crawl, but they were urged to walk very early. They were the mother's responsibility until they were seven years old, although fathers cuddled them when they were little and took a more active role later. As an example of how important a father's role in raising children was considered, the exhibit cited the case of a father who laughed when his small son stole things; when the boy ended on the scaffold, as a last act he was asked to kiss his father's hand but instead bit his father and pulled his nose to reproach him for having allowed him to fall into evil ways.

Education was considered important as an opportunity to improve. Medieval French had 60 words for education or upbringing. At school the children wrote on wax tablets, although writing was considered less necessary than reading. Even Charlemagne (742–814) could not write. Most children learned to count and do their ABCs on their fingers. Girls were, when social rank permitted, taught to read and when they went to convent schools at the age of seven or eight they were taught not only needlework but Latin, Hebrew, and Greek.

Recreation wasn't neglected either. There were plenty of toys, according to the financial condition of the parents: dolls, model boats, swords, tops. And the entire month of December was devoted to the child, with the festivities not ending until Epiphany on January 6.

A Chronology of Changing Attitudes towards Children

2650 B.C.: In Egypt Ptah Hotep, a sage who lived in the Fifth Dynasty (2750–2625 B.C.), wrote what is now the oldest surviving example of Egyptian literature, *The Precepts of Ptah Hotep;* it laid down rules regarding children, stressing above all their duty to obey their fathers.

2300 B.C.: In China, Emperor Yao (2357–2258 B.C.) established the attitude that children owed total obedience to their fathers. For centuries Confucianism has reinforced this concept.

2250 B.C.: In Babylon, King Hammurabi (c.1955–1913 B.C.), the sixth king of the first dynasty of Babylon in its golden age, established the *Code of Hammurabi*, a set of laws and edicts discovered in 1901. The code included rules regarding children's lifelong subservience to their fathers, with severe punishments for disobedience. It also made rules regarding adoption; however, these were to protect the rights of the adopters, not of the children.

1155 B.C.: In China, the legal code stated that "a child possesses nothing while its parents are living."

753 B.C.: A city on seven hills had existed for some time, but according to tradition this was the year when it became Rome, named after its first king, Romulus. He and his twin brother Remus were the children of Rhea Silvia, a Vestal Virgin who had broken her vow of chastity. She claimed she could not help it because her lover was the god Mars. Vestal Virgins were aristocratic girls given away by their families when they were 10 or 11 years old to live in the Temple of Vesta, goddess of the hearth, where they tended a sacred fire and a shrine containing holy objects. After Rhea's babies were born she abandoned them, as was then customary among parents of unwanted children, placing them in a basket which she threw into the river Tiber. Tradition says they were rescued by a she-wolf who nursed them and became their foster mother.

c. 730 B.C.: In Rome, the Government established the *Potestas Patriae*, a law that gave absolute power to fathers to whip, imprison, sell into slavery, or even kill their children.

c. 680 B.C.: In Rome, its second King, Numa Pompilius (715–673 B.C.) modified this power slightly, but not much.

146 B.C.: Following their victory in the Punic Wars, the Romans destroyed the Phoenician city of Carthage. Historian Diodorus Siculus wrote that when the Carthaginians "saw their enemy encamped before their walls, they were filled with superstitious dread, for they believed that they had neglected the honors of the gods that had been established by their fathers. In their zeal to make amends for this omission, they selected 200 of the noblest children and sacrificed them publicly."

34 B.C.: In Rome Emperor Augustus Octavius (63 B.C.–A.D. 14) established the *Lex Julia* and *Lex Papia*, laws that raised the status of children. Childless people were limited in what they could inherit; politicians with the most children were to be elected; financial awards were provided by the state to adopters of orphans.

c. 69–125 A.D.: Gaius Suetonius Tranquillus, who became a secretary to several Roman emperors, was born. He wrote a number of books about Roman society, including *Lives of Famous Whores* and *The Twelve Caesars*. In the latter he described how the elderly Emperor Augustus (63 B.C.–A.D. 14) relentlessly deflowered virgins, some of them procured for him by his wife, and how Emperor Tiberius (42 B.C.–A.D. 37) trained young boys whom he called his minnows to nibble at him lasciviously during his swims.

90 A.D.: In Rome, Emperor Domitian (51–96) passed a law prohibiting castration of infants. Castrated boys were favorite voluptuaries in the brothels of imperial Rome.

97: In Rome, King Nerva (30–98) had the government subsidize poor parents; 5,000 children were receiving state aid by the year 100.

c.100: In Rome, Emperor Trajan (53–117) taxed landowners to provide maintenance for 300 poor children; he also gave freedom to foundlings.

306: In Spain, the Council of Elvira excommunicated for 10 years mothers who killed their children; two of the years were to be spent weeping!

314: Another Church Council decreed that a woman who had killed her child was not allowed to enter a church for the rest of her life.

315: The Roman Emperor Constantine I, the Great (c. 280–337) forbade infanticide and allowed adopters of foundlings to enslave them. Ten years earlier he had not allowed this but found adoptions so rare that he permitted them in order to give people a financial incentive to save abandoned children. Constantine also passed a law against castration of little boys, but the practice was still widespread.

325: Article 10 of the Council of Nicaea decreed that asylums for travelers, the sick, and the poor, including orphaned and runaway children, were to be established in every village.

350: The King of Sparta established a law requiring mothers to breastfeed.

374: Roman law for the first time defined killing of infants as murder. The Emperors Valentinian I (321–375), Valens (328–378), and Gratian (359–383) of Rome issued edicts establishing punishments for both child exposure and murder.

391: Roman Emperors Valentinian II (372–392) and Theodosius the Great (346–395) issued edicts declaring that a child sold into slavery by his father could become free after a short term, without having to reimburse his owner for expenses.

409: Roman Emperor Honorius (384–423) issued an edict limiting the period of child slavery to five years.

419: The above edict was revised to limit child slavery to three years.

438: Emperor Theodosius II (401–450), second Emperor of the Eastern Roman Empire, established fines for parents who sold their children and provided further protection for foundlings and adopters.

529: Emperor Justinian the Great (483–565) of the Eastern Roman Empire proclaimed liberty for all foundlings.

553: Emperor Justinian formulated a comprehensive body of civil law for the Roman world; among its provisions were punishments for people who tried to enslave abandoned children. Also, the Council of Constantinople equated infanticide with homicide and Pope Gregory I (540–604) established capital punishment for it.

591: *Al Hidana*, a Muslim law, used public funds to help foundlings and to encourage adoptions.

c. 650: Mohammed (570–632) outlawed the killing of children, which was widespread, particularly of girls, among Arabs. He especially deplored the practice of burying girl children alive, saying that if it was necessary to kill a child it should be done with kindness.

c. 689: Theodore, the Archbishop of Canterbury (c. 602–690), in England ruled that a man could not sell his son into slavery after age seven. If the boy was younger then it was acceptable.

787: Bishop Datheus of Milan established the first foundling home in Italy for abandoned children.

1140: The *Decretum of Benedictine Monks*, which became the basis of the Catholic Church's canon law when it was confirmed by the *Decretals* of Pope Gregory IX (1147–1241) in 1234, established a basic universal law punishing infanticide.

c.1200: Pope Innocent III (1161–1216), appalled at the sight of "countless" infant bodies floating in the Tiber river, encouraged the spread of foundling homes in Italy but without much response.

1445–1471: In England, Canterbury court records show that parents were prosecuted for abortion and for infanticide; no distinction was made between the two. Also, parental negligence was punished as well as intentional killing, with public penances or whippings. This was church law only, however; the condemned were not turned over to the secular courts.

1527: A priest in Rome recorded that "the latrines resound with cries of children who have been plunged into them."

c.1625: Saint Vincent de Paul (1581–1660) established the first foundling hospitals in France.

1650–1700: In the American Colonies, where land was available to divide among many heirs and children were desired to help work on farms, the practice of abandoning or killing children was modified—only illegitimate children were killed.

1661: In France, the criminal code, based on ancient Roman law, permitted a father to kill a son or daughter who annoyed him, even after they were adults.

1719: In England, for the first time, a child was employed in a factory, in a silk mill in Derby.

1720: In China, Houses of Pity for Homeless Children were established.

1741: In London, philanthropist Thomas Coram (1668–1751) opened a Foundling Hospital to rescue dying babies lying in gutters and rotting in dung heaps.

1780: One of the world's first progressive schools for poor children, founded by the Swiss educational reformer Johann Heinrich Pestalozzi (1746–1827) failed. However, he later established other schools and his methods of instruction strongly influenced elementary schools through Europe and America.

1807: The slave trade was abolished in Britain. Slavery had existed almost as long as human beings had, but by now it had grown into a profitable international trade. It was helped along by Africans who sold slaves to the Portuguese in the sixteenth century, the Dutch in the early seventeenth century, and the British, Danes, French, and Swedes later in the seventeenth century. It is estimated that 12.5 million slaves were sold by Africans between 1650 and 1850. The trade spread to America and reached its peak in the eighteenth century, particularly in the rural South and in the Caribbean where large plantations needed many laborers. In many cases women and child slaves were treated benignly, as house servants, and many black women were affectionately regarded as "Mammies" entrusted with the care of their owners' children. Nonetheless slavery was harmful to black children because men were frequently sold away from their families. Thus began what became pervasive, millions of black children being raised by single mothers with absentee fathers.

1816: In Austria the first school for mentally handicapped children was opened.

1823: In England the Society for the Prevention of Cruelty to Animals was established 60 years before one regarding cruelty to children, but it occasionally intervened in court to protect abused children on the grounds that "children are animals."

1833: In England social reformer Lord Shaftesbury (1621–1683) sponsored a *Child Labour Act*, which was passed, regarding children working in factories; it permitted employment of children as young as six years old and for as many as 14 hours a day. As a Tory member of Parliament he introduced further legislation in 1842 and 1847 improving children's working conditions.

1837: Friedrich Froebel (1782–1852), a German educator who had worked under Pestalozzi (see 1780, above) and then decided to concentrate on preschool children, founded the world's first kindergarten ("children's garden") in Blankenburg, Switzerland. He invented a series of educational games for children. He introduced kindergartens throughout Germany, but as an educational and political reformer he was considered so radical that he was condemned to death in 1848—though he was later pardoned.

1854: From this year until the late nineteenth century Protestant ministers in the eastern part of the United States transported over 100,000 children from orphanages in "Orphan Trains" to find new homes in the Midwest where they would work on farms or as maids or companions to invalids. Often they were separated forever from their siblings.

1862: In Canterbury, Connecticut, the first private school for black girls in America, the Academy for Young Ladies of Color, was opened. It was declared illegal and abolished, and the teacher who founded it was put in jail. However, the ruling was later overturned on appeal. The state apologized to its founder and granted her a pension.

1867: The first volume of *Das Kapital* by Karl Marx and Friedrich Engels was published, containing horrifying examples of legal child labor.

1870: The International Committee for the Red Cross was founded in Geneva, Switzerland, and during the same year the *English Education Act* established compulsory education for children in England.

1871: In India, Infanticide Act #366A of March 4 forbade the killing of girls. And in New York City protective services were provided for an abused child named Mary Ellen by the Society for the Prevention of Cruelty to Animals (founded in 1866), using the same rationale as English predecessors had used, namely that children are animals.

1872: In Japan, universal education was introduced.

1873: The first kindergarten in the United States was opened.

1875: In New York the world's first Society for the Prevention of Cruelty to Children was founded.

1882: In Concord, Vermont, the first U.S. normal school to train teachers opened.

1883: In England the Liverpool Society for the Prevention of Cruelty to Children was founded—the first one in Europe.

1891: In England free elementary education began. And in India, a March 17 law prohibited cohabitation before age 12.

1899: In Germany a child labor law was passed.

1908: In England, Lord Robert Baden-Powell (1857–1941) founded the Boy Scouts. In the United States the Supreme Court upheld a Kentucky law establishing separate schools for white and black children.

1909: In the United States the first White House Conference on Children and Youth was convened by President Theodore Roosevelt (1858–1919), with notes handwritten by him inviting 200 people to serve as delegates; the President also established the U.S. Children's Bureau as an official part of the federal government.

1910: Lord Robert Baden-Powell and his sister Agnes founded the Girl Guides and the Boy Scouts of America.

1913: The Girl Scouts of America was founded by Juliette Low (1860–1927).

1916: The first Child Labor Law in the United States set the minimum working age at 14, but in 1919 the Supreme Court declared the law unconstitutional.

1918: World War I ended. It was called "the war to end all wars," so U.S. President Woodrow Wilson (1856–1924), looking forward to a peaceful future, proclaimed that 1918 was to be known as "The Children's Year."

1919: A second Child Labor Law was passed in the U.S. but it too was declared unconstitutional.

1920: In London the Save the Children Fund was founded by Eglantine Jebb (1876–1928). In the United States the Second White House Conference on Children and Youth met. From then on one has been held every 10 years, with steadily increasing participation.

1921: Eglantine Jebb moved to Geneva, where she founded the International Union for Child Welfare (IUCW), with Save the Children Funds as national branches in many countries.

1923: The IUCW drafted the *Geneva Declaration* specifying five Rights of the Child, the first document in history to state that children have rights.

1924: The League of Nations adopted the *Geneva Declaration.*

1945: In August the first atom bomb was dropped, killing and maiming thousands of Japanese including children, but also decisively ending the most destructive war in history, World War II, in August. In October the United Nations (UN) was founded in San Francisco. At the request of its Relief and Rehabilitation Association (UNRRA), the U.S. Army produced a motion picture called *Seeds of Destiny*, a documentary film depicting the horrifying plight of children in postwar Europe. The film was used to influence people to support emergency relief for Europe's thousands of orphaned, hungry, ill, and homeless children and to raise money for a United Nations Emergency Appeal for Children.

1946: In December the United Nations International Children's Emergency Fund (UNICEF) was established. Founding Executive Director Maurice Pate (1894–1965) insisted on political neutrality for the Fund. He and his former boss, Herbert Hoover (1874–1964), on their fact-finding tour of Europe in 1945 agreed that they could not look in the eyes of a starving child and ask its politics. UNICEF provided food, medicines, blankets, clothing, and shelter for children of both Axis and Allied nations and was credited with saving an entire generation of Europe's children.

1948: The United Nations General Assembly passed the *Universal Declaration of Human Rights* with a special clause regarding protection of women and children.

1950: The emergency work of UNICEF in Europe was finished so its mandate was due to expire. However, at the pleading of Third World delegates who said children in their countries lived in a state of "permanent emergency," it was made permanent and its mandate was extended to provide help to needy children in Africa, Latin America, and the Middle East.

1952: In England the first-ever international seminar on mental health and infant development was held, with 51 people from 30 countries.

1954: The U.S. Supreme Court in its unanimous ruling on Brown v. Board of Education ended legal racial segregation in the nation's public schools. Segregation under the supposedly "separate but equal" Jim Crow laws—America's apartheid—had existed since the 1890s. The court upheld the view that "in these days it is doubtful that any child may reasonably be expected to succeed in life if he is denied the opportunity of an education. Such an opportunity. . . is a right which must be made available to all on equal terms." Enforcement proved difficult, however, and many schools continued to be segregated de facto because of housing patterns and opposition to busing children into different neighborhoods.

1959: The UN General Assembly passed unanimously a *Declaration on the Rights of the Child* after a two-year debate. One major point of contention was when these rights begin, at or before birth. The compromise final draft said "before birth" but did not specify how long before, so the controversy continues about the conflicting right of a woman to have an abortion if she wishes and a child's right to prenatal care from the moment of conception.

1960: In the United States the 6th White House Conference on Children and Youth was held, to recommend legislation and other governmental actions to promote children's welfare. It involved an entire year of preparation by 500 child care experts. It was attended by more than 7,500 people representing almost 600 national organizations engaged in work on behalf of children, as well as delegates from seven other nations. Reports on its deliberations filled nine volumes.

1962: The UN held its first debate on family planning in December, at the urging of the Swedish government. It called for international cooperation in family planning programs, both to help control the global population explosion and to improve maternal and child health.

1963: On September 16, four young black girls were killed while singing in the choir of the Sixth Street Baptist Church in Birmingham, Alabama, when it was bombed by fanatical white supremacists. Their murder galvanized public opinion and, instead of intimidating black children, it strengthened their resolve to assert their rights as American citizens. Over and over again children rode on buses in spite of the frightening jeers and sneers they faced from many white folks and walked into schools where they were greeted with hostility. Eventually, after the long nonviolent struggle led by Martin Luther King, Jr. (1929–1968), southern youngsters won the right to attend good schools and to eat in restaurants, and their parents at last won the right to vote.

1973: The Children's Defense Fund was established in Washington, D.C., to lobby on behalf of children. This was also the year when the U.S. Supreme Court made a seven-to-two decision in the case of Roe v. Wade. The decision states that every woman has a legal right to abortion. The decision resulted in intense controversy and the birth of a Right to Life movement to protect the unborn. Many state laws have been passed to modify a woman's "absolute" right to abortion by requiring parental consent in the case of young girls, or by limiting the reasons for abortion to cases where the mother's health is endangered or the pregnancy is due to rape or incest, or by confining abortions to the first trimester of pregnancy, or in some cases by denying public funds to hospitals that perform abortions. A few of these modifications have been upheld, but the battle is far from over. Confrontations between right-to-lifers and clinics have sometimes erupted in violence. The right to life of doctors who perform abortions has been threatened and in at least one instance was taken away; a doctor's killer lost his own right to life when he was sentenced to death for murder. Most advocates for the unborn are nonviolent, however. Groups such as Birthright, founded in Canada, whose motto is "It is the right of every pregnant woman to give birth and the right of every child to be born," offer free guidance and referral services including child care and adoption as alternatives to abortion for pregnant women.

1979: The UN sponsored the International Year of the Child (IYC), with active participation by governments and nongovernmental organizations in 170 countries.

Reprinted from the Edmonton Committee for International Year of the Child Report of Oct./Nov. '79.

1980: One important result of IYC was a survey of legislation affecting children in 60 countries, with recommendations for improvements.

1983: UNICEF declared a "Child Survival and Development Revolution" to mobilize governments to save the lives of children by concentrating on low-cost health measures capable of broad implementation.

1984: An international agreement to promote breastfeeding was signed by 114 nations.

1985: The civil war in El Salvador ceased for three days when both the Government and rebels dropped their arms and the only shots fired were those used to immunize the nation's children. This was the first time in history a truce had ever been declared for the explicit purpose of helping children.

1989: Governor Mario Cuomo of New York declared the "Decade of the Child." And the United Nations General Assembly unanimously approved a Convention on the Rights of the Child, which would give the force of law to the 1959 Declaration on Children's Rights in all countries that ratified it.

1990: A World Summit for Children was held on September 29 and 30 at the United Nations headquarters in New York. This was the largest gathering in history of world leaders in one place, with 71 heads of state—premiers, presidents, prime ministers, a king, a grand duke, a cardinal, and their entourages from every continent—meeting in an unprecedented effort to improve the lives of the majority of the world's children. The world leaders signed two documents: *The World Declaration on the Survival, Protection and Development of Children,* a moral commitment on behalf of their governments and an exposition of the challenges, tasks, and opportunities that lay ahead, and a *Plan of Action* setting seven specific goals for implementing the declaration by the year 2000.

1991: One out of eight U.S. children under 12 is hungry, according to a 1991 report of the Food Research and Action Center, a nonprofit organization, in Washington, DC. According to their survey, 5.5 million U.S. children suffer from hunger, and 6 million more are at risk.

1992: For two weeks in June, in Rio de Janeiro in Brazil, 114 heads of state and 20,000 members of nongovernment organizations from all around the world attended the United Nations Conference on Environment and Development—otherwise known as the Earth Summit. Building on the achievements of the 1990 World Summit for Children, as well as those of a World Conference on Education for All in Thailand, also held in 1990, it placed children at center stage. The tragic sight of Rio's hundreds of abandoned street children added to the participants' intense concern for children.

In November a "Week of Tranquility" sponsored by UNICEF was held in Sarajevo, featuring exhibits of children's art about the war. Food, clothing, and other supplies were provided to nearly 200,000 children during the week.

1993: The U.S. Environmental Protection Agency announced that passive smoking (breathing smoke from another person's cigarette) is a serious threat to public health. Especially alarming were findings of the severe effects of passive smoke on the health of infants and children, which were linked to respiratory diseases, ear infections, and even, possibly, learning and behavioral problems.

1994: Swarms of refugees fled from brutal civil wars in Rwanda and Burundi, and a special camp for unaccompanied children who had lost their parents was set up in Ziare.

In June a centuries-old ritual that had destroyed the happiness and lives of a majority of Islamic girls came to the attention of immigration officials in America when Fauziya Kassindja, a 17-year-old girl from Togo, escaped to the U.S. and applied as a refugee, because if she were to be returned to her country she would be subject to compulsory genital mutilation. This ancient Muslim custom evidently arose as a way to ensure wives' fidelity and destroy sexual pleasure. In June, 1996 Fauziya was at last granted asylum and in fact received a book contract with a New York publisher. This one girl's struggle to protect herself had inspired such widespread concern that now, at last, there is a real possibility of abolishing this ancient abuse of girls.

The U.S. infant mortality rate dropped to 7.9 per 1,000, a record low, in 1994. Yet officials expressed concern at the continuing gap in mortality rates between white and black babies, with black babies having a mortality rate 2.2 times as high as white babies (recorded in 1991).

1995: A week-long World Summit for Social Development was held in March in Copenhagen. Its goals included the regulation of child labor to prevent dangerous work, reduction of inequality between boys and girls, and measures to reduce the epidemic of violence that is now afflicting our societies.

1996: President Bill Clinton signed a welfare reform law, which created more stringent regulations in order for parents and children to receive welfare assistance. The Republican-sponsored legislation, which had some bipartisan support, including President Clinton's, angered many children's activitists, notably Marian Wright Edelman, the head of the Children's Defense Fund, who said that it would push one million children into poverty.

ROYAL CHILDREN WHO WERE MONARCHS

If you have ever envied people born to the purple you may change your mind after reading about some of the world's youngest heirs to thrones.

Alexander III (1241–1286) became King of Scotland at age eight upon the death of his father Alexander II. At 10 he married Margaret, 11-year-old daughter of England's King Henry III (see page 20) who had succeeded King John. Young Alexander's marriage at first was not popular with the Scots, who suspected Margaret of having undue English influence over him, and he and she were confined under guard in Edinburgh Castle until her father managed to win their release. Later, in his twenties, Alexander defeated a

Norwegian invasion and added the Hebrides and the Isle of Man to his kingdom. When in his forties peace was secured, and his daughter Margaret married a Norwegian. He had his grandaughter, also named Margaret, who became known as "the Maid of Norway," acknowledged as heir to his throne. She was titular Queen of Scotland after he died, but she too died four years later, under mysterious circumstances. Alexander is the subject of "Lament for Alexander," one of the earliest Scottish poems.

Alexander Obrenovich (1876–1903) became King of Serbia at age 13 when his father Milan, who had won Serbian independence from Turkey, abdicated to become chief of the Serbian army. For four years Alexander was titular king under a regency, not assuming full power until he was 17. When 18 years old, he abolished the country's constitution. After several other arbitrary acts and an unpopular marriage, he and his wife were murdered by a group of his officers when he was 27.

Caesarion (See Ptolemy XV, page 26.)

Charles II (1661–1700) became King of Spain at age four, with Queen Mother Marlana de Austria as regent until he was 14 when he assumed full control. He inherited a nation exhausted from many wars and left it still demoralized when he died at 39. Having never married, he had no legitimate heir and his death became the signal for the War of Spanish Succession which lasted for 13 years.

Charles III, The Simple (879–929) became King of France at age 14. His reign was tempestuous and at age 44 he was sent to prison.

Charles VI, The Well-Beloved (1368–1422) became King of France at 12 under the regency of four uncles until he assumed control of the government at age 20. He ruled well for four years until he became subject to attacks of insanity. Plagued by jealousy among Charles's regents, France suffered civil strife for years and in 1415 was invaded and met a humiliating defeat at Agincourt by King Henry V (1387–1422) of England. After the armistice, Charles's daughter Catherine de Valois married Henry, thus uniting France and England in peace—temporarily.

Charles VIII (1470–1498) became King of France at seven, with his 23-year-old sister Anne de Beaujeu ruling ably as regent until he was 21. He had a tumultuous reign and died childless.

Constantine VI (770–797) became Emperor of the Eastern Roman Empire at age nine under the guardianship of his mother Irene. He quarreled with her and she had him put to death at age 16, thereupon usurping his throne.

Constantine VII, called "Porphyrogenitus" meaning "Born to the Purple" (905–959) became Emperor of the Eastern Roman Empire at age seven under the regency of his brother Alexander, who lived only one more year, and of his mother and stepfather Romanus I who practically excluded him from actual government. He became a distinguished classical, scientific, and legal scholar and patron of the arts, and led a successful campaign against the Arabs in Syria. His career came to an abrupt end when he died at 55, having been poisoned by his son and successor Romanus II.

Edgar, The Peaceful (944–975) became King of Northumbria and Mercia at age 15, appointed by nobles discontented with the rule of his elder brother Edwy. On Edwy's death in 959 Edgar became King of a united England, pacifying Northumbria and allowing the Danes a degree of self-government. At age 29 he received a deferred coronation and the homage of eight British princes including the King of Scotland. He was the father of Edward the Martyr (see below).

Saint Edmund, The Martyr (841–870) became King of the Anglo-Saxon kingdom of East Anglia at 14. During an invasion by the Danes that began in 866 he was bound, scourged, and beheaded for refusal to renounce Christianity. He was 29.

Edward, The Martyr (962–978), son of Edgar the Peaceful (see below),was crowned King of the English at age 13. He defended churches and monasteries against their enemies. When 15 years old he was assassinated at the instigation of his stepmother who was ambitious for her son Ethelred II (see below).

Edward III (1312–1377) became King of England at 15. At 18 he took control of the government away from his mother Isabella, putting her under restraint, and having her paramour Mortimer, who had been ruling with her, drawn, quartered, and hanged because he had connived at the death of his father Edward II. As King Edward III led magnificent tournaments and revels and established the Order of the Garter, but he also waged wars against France and Spain which resulted in financial ruin.

Edward V (1470–1483) became King of England at age 12 but was promptly deposed on grounds of illegitimacy by his uncle who declared himself Richard III. With his younger brother, the Duke of York, Edward was thrown into the Tower of London. Neither was ever seen again and rumors said that "the little Princes of the Tower" were smothered to death at the order of King Richard. Shakespeare thought this was true and wrote a play about it, but there is today a society in England determined to exonerate Richard. The fate of the little Princes remains unknown.

Edward VI (1537–1553), the only son of Henry VIII, became King of England and Ireland at age nine. His mother, Jane Seymour (c. 1509–1537), died when he was less than two weeks old after an exceptionally difficult childbirth, and Edward was always a frail child. He died from tuberculosis at the age of 15. But he is immortal as a result of the great painting of him as a little boy by Hans Holbein (1497–1543).

Elagabulus (204–222) became Roman Emperor at 14. He was notorious for imposing worship of Baal on the Roman world and for his extravagant homosexual orgies.

Ethelred II, The Unready (968–1016) became King of England at age 10 after his mother arranged for the death of his half-brother Edward, "The Martyr" (see above). She did her favored son no favor, because during his tumultuous reign there was constant conflict with Norwegians and Danes. After a massacre of Danes in 1002, the Danes retaliated under the leadership of their King, Sweyn Forkbeard, by plundering England annually from 1003 to 1014, ravaging the land and demanding tribute. Upon Ethelred's death Sweyn's son Canute (c. 995–1035) became King of England and a year later married Ethelred's widow. Ironically, Canute turned out to be a popular and just king not only of Denmark but of England, and became known as "Canute the Great."

Francis II (1544–1560) became King of France at 15. He married Mary Queen of Scots when he was 14 and left her a widow when he was 17.

Frederick II (1194–1250) became King of Sicily when he was three years old. At 14 he was declared of age and assumed control of the Government. Within months he married the much older Constance of Aragon, the first of three wives, and with her help tightened his grip on the country and soon spread his power farther afield. At 21 he also became King of Germany and at 26 was crowned Holy Roman Emperor. In spite of the fact that he was excommunicated three times (in 1227, 1239, and 1245) he led the fifth Crusade in 1228. He captured Jerusalem in 1229, made a 10-year truce with the Sultan of Egypt and was crowned titular King of Jerusalem. One of his unusual claims to fame was that he produced the world's first great study of bird behavior and falconry.

Harold I, The Fair-haired (850–933) became King of Norway at age 10. The first 12 years of his reign were marked by continual civil war. He forced those he conquered to leave Norway and established a strong kingdom for many years until his power was weakened by dissension among his sons. He abdicated in the year 930, at age 80.

Henry I, Henry the Child (1244–1308) became the first male ruler of Hesse (a German duchy) at the age of three. Little is known of him except that he was the grandson of Saint Elizabeth of Hungary.

Henry III (1207–1272) became the Plantagenet King of England at age nine. Son of King John Lackland, he inherited and reciprocated the animosity of the barons who compelled him to accept a series of reforms called *Provisions of Oxford* in 1258. He repudiated the agreement as his father had repudiated the Magna Carta, thus causing another rebellion known as the Barons' War which lasted six years. He was defeated in 1264 and held prisoner for a year until his son Edward rescued him, and he took little part in government thereafter. Edward succeeded him eight years later as King Edward I.

Henry IV (1050–1106) became King of Germany and Holy Roman Emperor at age six. He had a contentious reign, feuding with Pope Gregory VII who twice excommunicated him and the second time, in 1084, deposed him, after which Henry had himself crowned by an antipope. His last years were marked by the rebellion of his sons and in 1105 he was de-throned and imprisoned by his youngest son.

Henry VI (1421–1471) became King of England when less than nine months old and was crowned King of France at age 10. He was expelled from France in 1453 by Charles VII (Joan of Arc's dauphin) when France finally managed to oust the English, ending the Hundred Years War. After age 34 his reign was marked by periods of mental derangement and by economic and political unrest culminating in the War of the Roses between the houses of Lancaster and York. The Yorkists won and Henry was deposed in 1461. He was imprisoned for five years, rescued, and reinstated as king but soon recaptured and impris-oned again, this time in the Tower of London where it is said he was murdered.

Hsüan T'ung (1906–1967) became Emperor of China at age three, upon the death of his uncle, Emperor Kuang Hsu, in 1908. The last political act of Dowager Empress Tzu Hsi (1835–1908), his great aunt, was to name him emperor. He was the last emperor of the Manchu Dynasty, but reigned only three years, abdicating at age six in 1912, when China became a republic. (Later, in private life, he took the name of Henry, in honor of Henry VIII!)

Ivan IV, The Terrible (1530–1584) became ruler of Russia at age three under the regency of his mother. At age 14 he assumed control and had himself crowned Tsar ("Grand Prince"); he was the first Russian ruler to use this title. He conducted long wars, was defeated by Poland and Sweden but acquired Siberia. He was driven partially mad by the deaths of his wife and his son Dmitri and other causes, and in a fit of anger killed his son Ivan in 1580.

Ivan VI (1740–1764) became Tsar of Russia when only eight weeks old but was forced to abdicate at age two and spent the rest of his life, 22 years, in prison.

James I, El Conquistador (1208–1276) became King of Aragon at age five. A great organizer and warrior, he won the Balearic Islands and Valencia, signed a peace treaty with France, and spent the last 20 years of his life in wars against the Moors.

James II (1430–1460) became King of Scotland at age six. His childhood was marked by bitter conflicts among great Scottish families. When he assumed control of government at 19 he executed his former guardian for having expelled his mother from joint guardianship. He continued his father's policy of suppressing the great feudal lords, and he stabbed to death the Earl of Douglas who had conspired against him. At age 30 he was killed by the accidental bursting of a cannon during his siege of Roxburgh Castle.

James III (1452–1488) became King of Scotland at age eight when his father James II (see above) was killed, but he did not assume control of government until he was 28. He continued his father's policy designed to break the power of great nobles. His brothers Alexander and John were captured and held in custody by the nobles, but Alexander escaped to England; Alexander favored peace between England and Scotland. and obtained recognition from King Edward IV of England as King of Scotland. He then marched to Edinburgh with the aid of English troops to try to overthrow his brother. A rebellion resulted. James was defeated in battle and murdered shortly afterwards.

James IV (1473–1513) became King of Scotland at age 15, following the death of his father James III (see above). He married Margaret Tudor, daughter of England's Henry VII and their union led ultimately to the succession of members of the Stuart family to the English throne. After disputes with Henry VIII James gathered an army and led an unsuccessful invasion of England, during which he was killed at age 30.

James V (1512–1542) became King of Scotland when one year and five months old, under the regency of his mother when his father James IV (above) died in battle. When he was 12 she proclaimed him competent to rule, but for three years he was held prisoner by nobles so was unable to assume control until he was 16. He introduced reforms intended to protect people from oppression by nobles, and also waged war with England, which ended in his defeat. He died soon after this and was succeeded by his six-day-old daughter Mary Stuart (see page 23).

James VI (1566–1625), son of Mary Stuart, became King of Scotland when only 11 months old, upon the forced abdication of his mother, who left Scotland the following year and never saw him again. In 1603, after the death of "Good Queen Bess" who had beheaded his mother in 1587, he became King James I of England. Despite his mother's staunch Catholicism he was raised a Protestant and initiated the English translation of the Bible known as the King James version, which has been called the only great literature ever written by a committee.

Jane, Lady Jane Grey (1537–1554) was proclaimed Queen of England at age 16, on July 9, 1553. She was imprisoned 10 days later and beheaded along with her husband, thus ending the shortest reign in English history. This tragic great-granddaughter of Henry married against her will at age 16 as part of her father's plot to wrest the royal succession from Henry's VIII's daughters Mary and Elizabeth.

Jigme Singye Wangchuk (1955–) became King of Bhutan at age 12 and as of the printing of this book was the world's youngest reigning monarch.

John II (1405–1454) became King of Castille at age one, ruling under regents until he was 13. The last 35 years of his reign were marred by civil war.

John IV (1250–c. 1261) became Emperor of the Eastern Roman Empire at age eight. He was dethroned a year later, imprisoned, and blinded by Michael Palaeologus, a member of a Greek Byzantine family that furnished the next and last eight rulers of the empire.

John V, Palaeologus (1332–1391) became Emperor of the Eastern Roman Empire at age nine. The third Emperor installed by his family, he had a troubled reign character-ized by the gradual weakening of imperial power and by encroachments of the Ottoman Turks, but the family managed to hang on through five more reigns.

Kuang Hsu (1871–1908) at age four became the ninth Manchu Emperor of China, following the death of the 19-year-old Emperor T'ung Chih (page 27). His aunt, the Dowager Tzu Hsi (1835–1908), was regent until he assumed full power at age 17. All went well until 1898 when he had a falling-out with her over political reforms which she opposed. The name Tzu Hsi means "motherly and auspicious" but this "motherly" aunt had him killed, just before her death in 1908, and appointed his three-year-old nephew Hsüan T'ung (aged three; page 20) as the new Emperor.

Louis I, The Great (1326–1382) became King of Hungary at 16. Later, when he was 44, he also became King of Poland. He engaged in a long series of wars with Venice between 1342 and 1381 for control of the Adriatic coast, finally achieving a successful treaty a year before he died.

Louis II (1506–1526) became King of Hungary at age 10. He lost Belgrade to the Turks in 1521, and was killed in battle when he was 20.

Louis III (863–882) became King of France at age 16, jointly with his brother Carloman until Louis's death at age 19. Louis ruled the north of France, and in 881 he defeated invading Norsemen. After Louis died, his brother became ruler of all France.

Louis IV, The Child (893–911) became King of Germany at age six. His country was overrun by Hungarians in the year 900 when he was seven, and he died when only 18.

Louis VII, The Young (1121–1180) became King of France at 16. That same year he married Eleanor of Aquitaine. The marriage lasted 15 years (two of which he spent on the second Crusade), but they divorced in 1152 and two years after that he gave up Aquitaine. He had a long struggle with Eleanor's second husband, England's Henry II, because many parts of France were held by England.

Louis IX, Saint Louis (1214–1270) became King of France at age 12, with his mother as regent until he was 22. He had a relatively peaceful reign, but at 30 took the crusader's vow and went on the sixth Crusade in 1248. He was defeated and captured in Egypt, and remained in Syria for four years; during his absence his mother again became regent. He was canonized in 1297 because he was exceptionally pious, kind and just to his subjects, and honorable in his personal life.

Louis XIV, The Great, and **The Sun King** (1638–1715) became King of France at age five. He was a king who really enjoyed being king. He was a despot. "L'état, c'est moi" (the state is me) he proclaimed and his personal life was far from exemplary. He persecuted the Huguenots, causing thousands to flee from France. He waged a series of wars, creating huge debts, and the condition of the poor worsened during his reign. Nonetheless, he accomplished many things. He built the palace of Versailles and his court there was the most magnificent in Europe. Due in large part to his sponsorship, French arts and letters were in their golden age. He had three mistresses and fathered a number of children, both legitimate and illegitimate, treating them all well and raising them together. His third mistress, Mme de Maintenon, was the children's governess; she was an enlightened educator—even of the king, getting him interested in charities and other good works. He married her after the queen died. His 73-year reign was the longest in European history.

Louis XV, The Well-Beloved (1710–1774) became King of France at age five. Actually, he was not very well loved. Animosity and even hatred of him developed over the years as he was involved in a series of wars and discord over finances that were never resolved. He had several mistresses including the most famous, the glamourous Madame de Pompadour, who was not a good influence politically except that she was a lavish patroness of architecture, the arts, and literature.

Louis XVII (1785–1795) became King of France at age eight. He was imprisoned with his parents, Louis XVI and Marie Antoinette (see below), during the French Revolution and died in prison at age 10.

Malcolm IV (1141–1165) became King of Scotland at age 12, but by the time he died at 24 he had lost much of it. He succeeded his grandfather David I to the Scottish throne; David was the youngest son of Malcolm III who killed Macbeth. Malcolm IV was forced to surrender to Henry II of England the areas of Northumberland, Cumberland, and all the fiefs Henry's mother Queen Matilda had given to his grandfather.

Marie Antoinette (1755–1793) married the future King Louis XVI of France when she was 15 and became Queen of France at 19. When she was a child she met Mozart who was so charmed by her that he proposed to her; she would perhaps have had a happier life if she had accepted. She was much disliked by the French masses for her frivolous and extravagant ways and her lack of concern for the poor, which helped to ignite the anger that led to the French Revolution. In 1793 she was arrested, along with her husband and children, found guilty of treason, and guillotined. But her courage, honesty, and dignity during her trial and at her death did much to redeem her reputation.

Mary Stuart (1542–1587) became Queen of Scots when only six days old, on the death of her father James V. When she was seven months old she was betrothed to Edward VI of England but later the engagement was broken. When she was six years old she became betrothed to the five-year-old dauphin of France. She married him at 16. He was crowned Francis II the following year so at 17 she became Queen of France as well as of Scotland.

Francis died a year later, thus at 18 she was a widow. At 19 she returned to Scotland to take control of the Government. At 23 she married a cousin, Lord Darnley, and became a mother at 24. Darnley was an unscrupulous and vicious man, despised by the Scots. He was murdered, so at 25 she became a widow for the second time. After his death she made another unpopular marriage, to Lord Bothwell, which caused a revolt. The people loved Mary but would not tolerate her husbands; she was forced to abdicate in favor of her 11-month-old son, who became King James VI (see page 21).

She fled to England and tried to persuade her cousin Queen Elizabeth to acknowledge her right to be named as the childless queen's legitimate heir, basing her claim on the fact that her grandmother, Margaret Tudor, had been a sister of Elizabeth's father, Elizabeth denied her claim and had her put in prison. Mary was kept in prison for 19 years, despite many attempts by loyal followers to rescue her, until she was 45 and Elizabeth had her beheaded.

Nero (37–68 A.D.) became Emperor of Rome at age 17. He was tutored by the great philosopher Seneca. When 13 he was adopted by his stepfather Emperor Claudius and at 16 married Claudius's daughter Octavia. Ten years later his mother poisoned Claudius so that her son could become Emperor. With this start Nero began one of the most wicked reigns in history. He instituted cruel persecutions of Christians, having many of them put to death, but he was an equal-opportunity murderer. When 22 he had his mother murdered and later murdered his wife and sister-in-law. At 25 he married again, and later had this wife murdered too. At 27 he was accused of starting a fire that destroyed a great part of Rome. At 28 he discovered a plot against him and had many Romans put to death, including his former tutor Seneca. At 31 he completed his career by killing himself.

Saint Olaf II (995–1030) became King of Norway at age 11. After taking part in Viking expeditions, he became a Christian and tried to achieve the conversion of Norway. He made many enemies and at 33 had to flee to Sweden. Later he tried to reconquer Norway but was defeated and killed. Paradoxically, after his death he was acclaimed a national hero and the patron saint of Norway. In 1164 he was canonized.

Olaf III (1370–1387) became King of Denmark at age six and of Norway as Olaf IV at age 10, but he never ruled either country. His father was Norwegian and his mother Danish. She ruled as regent of both countries. After Olaf's death at age 17 she seized control of both countries and in 1397 also became Queen of Sweden, uniting the three nations in a dynastic union that lasted for 176 years.

Olaf IV (1100–1115) became King of Norway at age three, jointly with his two brothers, 19-year-old Eystein and 14-year-old Sigurd. After Olaf died at age 12 and Eystein at 33, Sigurd ruled alone for eight more years until his own death. He is considered a good king who brought peace and prosperity to his country.

Otto III (980–1002) became Holy Roman Emperor at age three, under the regency of his mother until her death and then of the Archbishop of Mainz, until he was 16. At 18 he moved to Rome, hoping to make it the Empire's capital, but he died at 22, failing to achieve his goal.

Peter I, The Great (1672–1725) became Tsar of Russia at age 10, at first officially co-ruling with Ivan, his one-year-old half-brother, from 1682 until Ivan died in 1689 at age seven; thereafter ruling alone. At 17, at the command of his mother, he married Eudoxias, and had a son, but she bored him with her piety and after nine years of marriage he asked for a divorce. When she refused he sent her to a convent. Four years later he became enamored of a most unlikely girl: a peasant who was a serf. She became his mistress a year later, exerted great influence over him, and in 1711 saved his life during a campaign against the Turks. A year after that he married her, and 12 years later had her crowned empress. One year afterwards he died and she succeeded him as Catherine I. Her reign lasted only two years before she too died, but in the short time given her she did well. Among other things she established the Russian Academy of Sciences. In contrast, Peter's reign had been long and at times turbulent. He waged a 21-year war against Sweden through which he expanded Russia's territory. He founded a new city, the beautiful St. Petersburg, as Russia's capital in 1703. And he traveled widely throughout Europe, bringing back to his previously isolated and backward country many aspects of Western culture and at the same time establishing Russia in European minds as an important country.

Peter II (1715–1730), Peter the Great's grandson, became Tsar of Russia at age 11 but reigned for only three years, dying at age 15.

Peter II (1923–1970) became King of Yugoslavia at age 11, under a regency headed by his uncle Prince Paul. This was a new and unstable nation created by the Treaty of Versailles after World War I, which tried to unite ancient enemies, the Croats, Serbs, and Slovenes. Peter assumed sovereignty in March of his 18th year, just one month before Hitler invaded the country. He fled to London where he set up a government-in-exile and lived during World War II, but when the war ended his exile continued. He was forced from the throne because Yugoslavia had become a republic under the Communist leader Marshal Tito (1892–1980). Through autocratic but efficient methods, Tito kept the country together while he lived but, when the Iron Curtain collapsed in 1991, the old animosities resurfaced and the nation was split apart in a vicious civil war. Peter offered to return to try to restore peace and order, but the people were too busy fighting to pay much attention.

Philip I (1052–1108) became King of France at age eight. During his six-year regency the kingdom was at a low ebb, but the royal domain increased after he took over. His private life was less triumphant. At age 43 he was excommunicated for disowning his first wife Bertha of Holland and marrying Bertrada, who was the wife of the Count of Anjou.

Philip II (1165–1223) became King of France at age 15. He persecuted Jews, fought several long wars against England and Flanders, and went on the third Crusade in 1190–1191. At the start of this crusade he and King Richard The Lionhearted of England were allies, but they quarreled in Sicily and in Syria. When they returned home he joined up with John, Richard's brother and enemy and also, if the legend is true, the wicked foe of Robin Hood, in a six-year war to seize possessions in France, after which he turned on John and deprived him of the lands John had helped him win. Philip was equally disloyal in love, marrying three times and then repudiating his wives. However, to his credit, he built many fine institutions and churches, encouraged trade, and gave the first charter to the University of Paris in the year 1200.

Philip IV (1605–1665) became King of Spain at age 16. His reign was a disaster for Spain; its industry and commerce declined and the country was impoverished by a series of wars with France, Germany, Holland, and Portugal; and the Spanish province of Catalonia revolted and seceded to France.

Ptolemy V, Epiphanes, the Illustrious (210–180 B.C.) became King of Egypt at age seven. He had been declared of age at four and betrothed to his sister Cleopatra I (not her famous namesake) at five, and married her when he was 17 in accordance with Macedonian tradition. At 15 his concessions were listed in a decree inscribed by Egyptian priests on the Rosetta stone. But at 19 members of his court killed him with poison.

Ptolemy VI, Philometor "Loving His Mother" (186–145 B.C.) became King of Egypt at age five but was not crowned until he was 13. In the meantime the mother he loved was his regent. He married a sister named Cleopatra II. Three years after being crowned he was put in prison, but later that year was restored to the throne. At 41 he died in battle.

Ptolemy XIII (67–47 B.C.) became King of Egypt at age 10. He co-ruled with his 19-year-old sister and wife Cleopatra VII (69–30 B.C.) (the famous Cleopatra). But when he was 11, he decided he wanted to rule alone and expelled her. She was imprisoned until Julius Caesar (c. 100–44 B.C.) arrived in Egypt and restored her to the throne, deposing Ptolemy, who then drowned in the Nile during a vain attempt to escape from Caesar's soldiers.

Ptolemy XIV (58–44 B.C.) became King of Egypt at age 11. He was the younger brother of Ptolemy XIII and the second husband of their sister Cleopatra VII. Caesar, although he was openly living with Cleopatra, insisted on her marrying this brother, after the older one had died, so that she would continue to fulfill the will of their father that required co-regents. She married him the same year she gave birth to Caesar's son, when she was 22. For three years Ptolemy XIV ruled along with her, and then without her when she went to visit Rome with Caesar. Caesar hoped to become Emperor, marrying her and naming their son as his heir, but this infuriated the Roman Senate and they had Caesar killed, so she and the boy returned to Egypt. Shortly after that, her 14-year-old brother/husband died and she appointed her son as the new co-regent. Since Cleopatra was almost as notorious for her ruthlessness as for her beauty, many people suspect that she had Ptolemy XIV killed in order to put her son on the throne in his place.

Ptolemy XV, Caesarion (47–30 B.C.), the son of Caesar and Cleopatra, became King of Egypt at age three. He had a glamorous infancy during which his parents lavished luxuries on him while training him to become a future Emperor of Rome, but after his father's assassination when he and his mother returned to Egypt, he was installed as her new co-regent. He had a 10-year-reign, that ended abruptly and tragically when he was 17 and his mother and stepfather Anthony committed suicide. They were defeated in battle by Rome's Emperor Augustus (63 B.C.–A.D.14). Cesarion was also captured and viciously tortured, dragged through the streets, and then killed by Roman soldiers.

Richard II (1367–1400) became King of England at 10. When he was 14 economic distress in England resulted in rebellion. He gained control eight years later and confiscated the estates of Henry of Bolingbroke (who, unfortunately for Richard, later became King Henry IV). He was defeated by Henry, captured, deposed by Parliament at age 32, and imprisoned. He died, probably murdered, in jail at 33.

Sheng-tsu (1654–1722) became Emperor of China at age eight. He was a patron of scholars, at 23 founding the College of Inscriptions and ordering compilations of many books of Chinese classics. He traveled all over the empire, added provinces in the north, conquered Formosa at age 29, concluded a treaty on boundaries with Russia, reorganized Mongolia, and secured control of Tibet. He was friendly to the Jesuits, giving them responsible scientific posts at the imperial court, but he also issued an anti-Christian decree in 1717 refusing to allow them to propagate their faith.

T'ung Chih (1856–1875) became Emperor of China (the eighth of the Manchu dynasty) at age six. His mother, who had become a concubine of his father Emperor Halen Feng when she was 17, became regent after his death in 1861 and ruled as the Dowager Empress Tzu Hsi until T'ung Chih was 17 years old. His own reign was very brief. He died of smallpox at 19.

Tutankhamen (c. 1339–1321 B.C.) became King of Egypt when he was nine years old. He lived only 18 years. The tomb in which he was buried was discovered and unearthed by archaeologist Howard Carter in 1922 in the Valley of the Kings. In addition to Tutankhamen's mummy with his handsome boyish face, it contained a unique and perfectly preserved trove of beautiful treasures including elegant furniture with whimsical carvings, magnificent clothes and jewels, great sculptures of animals and goddesses, and games and toys. He died young but will always be remembered by people who cherish youth and beauty.

Valentinian II (373–392) at age three became Emperor of Rome jointly with his younger brother Gratian (359–383). He had a short and sad life. His brother died, when Valentinian was 10. At 12 he was driven from Italy by an enemy but returned later and gave promise of being a good ruler. When 18 he established a law that a child whose father had sold him into slavery could become free after a short term without having to reimburse his owner for expenses. But at 20 he was murdered by the Frankish commander of his own army.

THE MUSEUM OF CHILDHOOD IN EDINBURGH, SCOTLAND

This museum claims to be the first museum in the world devoted solely to the history of childhood. It was founded in 1955 by Joseph Patrick Murray (1908–1981), a bachelor who claimed he did not like children. He said he had "a rooted conviction that children are only tolerable after their baths and on their way to bed."

He told a newspaper reporter that he was spurred into establishing the museum when he read of two dolls in Scotland, once owned by Queen Victoria, which were sent to a museum in London because there was no place to display them in Scotland. He persuaded his colleagues on the Edinburgh town council to make space available to display dolls and other objects reflecting all aspects of the lives of children in the past.

The first exhibits were "a pitiful handful of toy soldiers, building blocks and railway stuff of my own," he said, but the idea immediately attracted public interest and donations of treasured childhood possessions soon poured in. By 1957 the collection had become so large that it was moved to its own building in Edinburgh's Royal Mile on High Street.

Murray provoked controversy and much amusement by displaying a design for a proposed memorial window to "good" King Herod in the museum's entrance hall. It showed a benign-looking monarch surrounded by children lying higgledy-piggledy at his feet, accompanied by the caption: Modern research suggests that the exact number of 'Innocents' massacred could not have been more than 12 or 13. To a museum curator, when distracted by noisy or aggravating children, this seems a very disappointing total, and one well within his capacities to improve.

The building has been renovated several times over the years, to make room for its constantly growing collection. In July 1986 the extended museum was opened by 10-year-old Susan Gibson, the winner of a competition held by the *Edinburgh Evening News*. It had 70 percent more display space than before and an elevator to accommodate disabled visitors. Its five floors now accommodate hundreds of amusing and beautiful examples of several centuries of toys: push, pull, and riding toys; toy trains; model vehicles; toys that move; mechanical toys; farms, zoos, and circuses; Noah's Arks and other Sunday toys; musical toys; optical toys; puppets; toy theatres; dolls; dolls' houses; teddy bears; board games; card games; outdoor game equipment; children's pastimes such as samplers and scrapbooks; as well as many exhibits of children's feeding dishes, spoons, and bottles; medicines; clothing; school supplies and books—all with informative and entertaining captions.

In the museum's first guidebook, Murray maintained that this was an institution devoted to a special aspect of social history and was not aimed at children: "This is not a children's museum; it is a museum about them." Even so, over the years, vast numbers of children, along with adults, have visited it and loved it. It soon gained a worldwide reputation, so that it now has many imitators in many countries.

2

Children in Folklore, Mythology, and Religion

FOLKLORE ABOUT CHILDREN

Child Folk Heroes

In Greece

Hercules (or Heracles): Once upon a time when the little Heracles was 10 months old, Alemene of Midea took him and Iphicles, his younger brother, and laid them, washed both and suckled full, in the fine brazen buckler Amphitryon had gotten in spoil of Pterelaus, and setting her hand upon their heads, said 'Sleep my babes, sleep sweetly and light; sleep sweethearts, brothers twain, goodly children. Heaven prosper your slumbering now and your awakening tomorrow'.

And as she spoke, she rocked them until they feel asleep.

By that time the Bear swung low towards her midnight place over against the uplifted shoulder of mighty Orion. Then sent the wily Hera two dire monsters of serpents, bridling and bristling and with azure coils, to go upon the broad threshold of the hollow doorway of the house, intending the devour the child Heracles. And there on the ground they both untwined their ravening bellies and went writhing forward, while an evil fire shone forth from their eyes and a grievous venom was spewed out of their mouths.

But when, with tongues flickering, they were come where the children lay, suddenly Alemene's little ones (for Zeus knew all) awoke, and there was a light in the house. Iphicles straightway cried out when he spied the evil beasts and their pitiless fangs above the target's rim, and kicked away the woolen coverlet in an agony to flee; but Heracles made against them with his hands, and gripping them where lies a baneful snake's fell poison hated even of the Gods, held them both fast in a sure bondage by the throat. For a while the two wound their coils about that young child, that suckling babe at nurse who never knew tears; but soon they relaxed their knots and loosed their weary spines and only strove to find enlargement from out of those irresistible bonds.

—as told by Theocritus, Greek poet of the third century BC.

In America

The pioneers who built America had no comic books or television sets to entertain them and help them relax after the long, back-breaking days they spent in exhausting manual labor. In the evenings, around campfires and in their bunkhouses, they usually just talked, reminiscing and exchanging stories about men like themselves. The many trades and callings all had their own heroes, generally working men trying to do the nearly impossible. Over the years they embroidered the stories, with humor and imagination, turning some of these men into larger-than-life supermen, and they passed the stories down to their children and grandchildren. Two of the greatest of these legendary heroes were Paul Bunyan, a logger, and John Henry, a black railroad track laborer. There are countless tales about their exploits, but in this book we will concentrate on what is said about their childhoods.

Paul Bunyan: They say Paul Bunyan was the mightiest logger who ever lived, and so big that people could not agree as to his exact size. His parentage and birth date are not definitely known. Some claim he was French Canadian, others that he was Irish, still others Swedish or Norwegian. Anyway, he was a healthy baby, and grew so fast that it soon became a great problem for his parents to take care of him.

According to the legend about him, Paul had outgrown everything in his home by the time he was three weeks old. So his father built a large cradle of logs in a clearing which had the sky for a roof. The very first night in this new cradle, Paul rolled around so much in his sleep that he knocked down four square miles of standing timber. So Paul's father then made a big floating cradle and anchored it off the coast. But when Paul rocked, it caused a tidal wave that threatened to flood the villages along the entire coast of Maine. To try to stop this, the British Navy, lying off the coast of Nova Scotia, fired broadsides for seven hours before the child woke up and started wading ashore. This made matters still worse because the waves from each stride caused several of His Majesty's ships to founder. Proof of this happening, it is said, is that the tides in the Bay of Fundy are still the highest in the world.

Soon Paul's mother and father decided they would have to move to an uninhabited area where Paul could have lots of room, with plenty of good fresh air. In the tall, uncut forest they built a cabin big enough to stage a three-ring circus, and here Paul went right on growing by leaps and bounds. He tore around all day and then, unlike most boys, was fast at getting to sleep. In fact, he could blow out a candle at the far end of the cabin and be in bed before the room got dark.

Paul showed great promise of becoming one of the creative geniuses of all time when, at age two, he dug and built Niagara Falls so that he could take a shower. Up to that time nobody had ever heard of a shower bath.

John Henry: The legend says that on the night John Henry was born the sky was black. Stars wouldn't shine and rain fell hard. Forked lightning lit the sky and the earth trembled like a leaf. John Henry at birth weighed 44 pounds, and he came into the world with a cottonhook for a right hand and a river song on his tongue.

They didn't know what to make of him when he was born. "He's got a bass voice like a preacher," said his mama. "He's got shoulders like a cotton-rollin' roustabout," his papa said. "He's got blue gums like a conjuring man," the nurse woman said.

"I might preach some," said John Henry, "but I ain't gonna be no preacher. I might roll cotton on the boats, but I ain't gonna be no cotton-rolling roustabout. I might got blue gums like a conjuring man, but I ain't gonna get familiar with the spirits. 'Cause my name's John Henry and when folks call me by my name, they'll know I'm a natural man."

About that time John Henry rose up and stretched. "Well," he said, "ain't it about supper time?"

"Sure it is," said his mama. "And after," said his papa. "Long after," said the nurse woman.

"Well," asked John Henry, "has the dogs been fed?"

"Yes," said his mama. "Sure they has," said his papa. "A while ago," said the nurse.

"Well then," roared John Henry, "ain't I as good as the dogs?" And when John Henry said that he got mad. He reared back in his crib and broke out the slats. He opened his mouth and yowled, and it blew out the lamp. He spat and it put out the fire. "Don't make me mad," said John Henry, and the thunder rumbled and rolled. "Don't let me get mad on the day I'm born, 'cause I's scared of my own self when I gets mad."

And then John Henry told them what he wanted to eat. "Bring me four ham bones and a pot full of cabbages. Bring me some turnip greens treetop tall. Bring me a pone of cold corn bread and some potlicker to wash it down. Bring me two hog jowls and a kettleful of whippoorwill peas. Bring me a skillet full of red-hot biscuits and a big jugful of cane molasses. 'Cause my name's John Henry!"

Many years later John Henry was driving steel on a tunnel in West Virginia when the first automatic steel drill was brought into the mountains. A contest was held to see whether the best steel driver in the world could outdo the new machine. John Henry won, but the effort broke his heart and he soon died, proving that no man working with his hands can beat a machine. It was the end of an era.

In Japan

Kintoki, the Golden Boy: His legend dates from medieval Japan. It is said that Yorimitsu, a great warrior hero, was out hunting one day in the mountains when he came across a child with the physique of an infant Hercules and a skin that was brick-red, playing with a bear cub. Yorimitsu asked the boy to introduce him to his mother. She was a tall woman of wild appearance, with long black hair falling to her waist, dressed only in leaves, although she spoke the language of the court. She was Yama-Uba, the Mountain Mother, and she told him that the boy's father was a great general of the Minamoto clan who had been killed in battle, and she was bringing up the boy by herself in hardship, with the intention of making a hero of him.

Yorimitsu asked Yama-Uba to put the boy Kintoki in his care. She assented and when the boy grew up he became one of Yorimitsu's principal officers, taking the name of Sakata-no-Kintoki. He is the hero of a number of legends which recount feats of bravery and strength similar to the Twelve Labors of Hercules.

Kintoki is a particularly popular subject with Japanese artists, especially as a young boy. Invariably he is depicted as an infant with chubby limbs of brick-red, accompanied by an immense axe which he carries as an emblem of his strength and courage. A great Japanese artist, U tamaro, in the eighteenth century produced many delightful prints concentrating on the relationship between this mischievous little boy and his mother. In some we see the impotent annoyance of the child who is conscious of his supernatural gifts but whose mother treats him as an ordinary baby, fondling and breastfeeding him, dressing him, shaving the crown of his head in keeping with a Japanese custom regarding children below the age of four or five, cleaning his ears, and scolding him. We see him belligerently making faces at her, pulling her hair and having tantrums, but also there are many tender scenes of them playing games together and kissing each other affectionately.

TRADITIONAL SUPERSTITIONS ABOUT CHILDREN

- It is good luck to be born on Christmas Day.

- It is bad luck to cry on Christmas Day.

- A child who finds a coin and an orange in the toe of his or her stocking on Christmas morning is lucky; a naughty child will find only a stick or a rock.

- A child who cries on his or her birthday will cry every day of the following year.

- Regarding days of birth:

  Monday's child is fair of face,

  Tuesday's child is full of grace,

  Wednesday's child is sour and sad,

  Thursday's child is merry and glad,

  Friday's child is loving and giving,

  Saturday's child works hard for a living,

  While the child that is born on the Sabbath Day is blithe and bonny and good and gay.

- One should wish on the candles of one's birthday cake, then try to blow them all out with one breath. If one doesn't, one's wish will not come true. Also, one won't get one's wish if one tells anyone what it was.

- Children will have bad luck if they are not spanked on their birthday. They should receive one spank for each year of age and then:

  One to grow on,

  One to live on,

  One to eat on,

  One to be happy on,

  One to get married on.

- Fortunes can be told by putting a coin, a button, a ring, and a thimble in a birthday cake. A child who gets the coin will be rich. One who gets the button will be poor. One who gets the ring will marry, and one who gets the thimble will be an old maid or a bachelor.

- The seventh child of a seventh child will be brilliant and become famous.

WHERE DO BABIES COME FROM?

Knowledge of the behavior of birds and bees is not enough to answer this question, which, at some point, every child asks his or her parents. A well-known joke tells about a twentieth century American father whose tiny son asked him where he came from. The father, wanting to be modern, truthful, and scientific, set the child upon his knee and gave an elaborate, up-to-date explanation of birds, bees, hormones, ovaries, eggs, sperm, genes, Fallopian tubes, chromosomes, and wombs, only to have the child look more and more skeptical and bewildered. Finally, when the father had run out of information and breath, the small seeker after knowledge sighed, "Thank you. I just wanted to know because Charlie told me he came from Chicago." Another father managed to be truthful without going into so much detail. When his little boy asked him where he was when his parents were on their honeymoon, the father said: "You arrived with me and you left with your mother."

> Apart from man, no creature wonders about its own existence.
>
> —Arthur Schopenhauer (1788–1860)

Many children are very curious about their origin and about the origins of everything. Jean Piaget (1896–1980), the eminent Swiss psychologist who spent a lifetime chatting with and eavesdropping on children, said all children seem to assume that they were found by their parents and that they pre-existed somewhere before being found. He said the basic assumption children spontaneously make is that everything, including the universe itself, has to have been made by some creative being. "Who made the sun?" one two-year-old asked him. In this respect, their speculations agree with those of adult philosophers, myth-makers, and theologians. As Australian theologian Frank Sheed (1897–1981) once put it: "If there is a meal there has to have been a cook."

Joseph Campbell (1904–1987), in his famous four-volume book about mythology, *The Masks of God* (1959–1967), goes so far as to attribute the arrival of babies as the basic mystery that inspired all the world's myths and primitive religions as well as the earliest art. Childbirth, he says, is what made people become philosophers:

> In mythology, the image of birth from the womb is an extremely common figure for the origin of the universe. In the earliest ritual art the naked female form is extremely prominent. The mystery of the woman is no less a mystery than death. Childbirth is no less a mystery, nor the flow of the mother's milk, nor the menstrual cycle in its accord with the moon. The creative magic of the female body is a thing of wonder.

George MacDonald (1824–1905), the Scotsman whose vocation was theology and whose avocation was writing for children, wrote a poem called "Baby" that appeared in his famous children's book, *At the Back of the North Wind.* In the poem he said that babies come "out of the everywhere into the here" and he was quite right, judging by the world's folklore. In Austrian folklore babies are said to spring forth from lakes, ponds, rivers, and trees. In China they grow in gardens. In Denmark they come from the sea. In England they bloom on rose bushes or are unearthed from parsley beds. In France they pop up from under cabbage leaves. In Germany they seem to have a wider choice. In addition to the ocean, lakes, ponds, rivers, and trees, they have come from moors and sand hills, or from underneath rocks and stones. Still another German theory is that unborn babies live in a very beautiful house where everything they see is gold, and a golden glow remains on everything they look at until they are one year old or until they first look into a mirror.

And How Do They Get Here?

In Guatemala it is said that a snake brings the infant. In Malaysia people have said that birds transport children from soul-trees in another world to this one. In Siberia the Kamchadales say it is the spider who carries the child to its new home.

The two main theories in Western European tradition, however, are storks and swans. In America and England, babies have traditionally been transported from their point of origin to their familial destination in a diaper (or nappie, if the baby is English) held in a stork's beak.

In northern Germany storks fetch babies from the ocean and bring them to rocks near the seashore where they dry them out before bringing them to their mothers. Other versions describe the seacoast rocks as "swan stones" and hold that before being born babies are shut up inside these stones to wait until a swan swims by and opens one of the stones with a special key and takes out a little child. Some folklore authorities think the swan myth is older than the stork myth, but the stork story is more persistent and so old that its origin is unknown. It is considered probable that it began in Germany or Switzerland where people have traditionally regarded the stork as a sacred bird.

In some places, storks are believed to be human beings who have been enchanted; therefore no one must harm them in any way. The stork is known by various pet names, including *adebar* (luck bringer) in German and *ole vaer* (old father) in Dutch. When a stork nests on the roof of a house, a close relationship is believed to be established between the stork's family and that of its human neighbors. If a stork is seen lighting on a rooftop, a baby will be born in that house during the coming year unless the stork lays no eggs.

A more prosaic explanation of how babies get here is the one given by Oscar Wilde (1854–1900) in his play, *The Importance of Being Earnest.* They arrive in a doctor's little black bag.

Gods and Goddesses of Motherhood and Childhood

The world's earliest myths viewed the birth of the universe and the earth and the individual person as analogous aspects of one great creative process attributed to fertile mother goddesses: the Great Mother Cybele in ancient Phrygia; Inanna, also called Ishtar, in Mesopotamia; Gaea, the "deep breasted", Isis and Artemis, represented as having a multitude of breasts, in ancient Greece; and Partavi and Kali in India.

Later, as society became patriarchal instead of matriarchal and as people became aware of the male role in procreation, these goddesses were often replaced by gods. In ancient Egypt the source of creation and fecundity was considered to be the god Khnum, the "molder" who shaped the "world-egg" on his potter's wheel and also shaped children in their mothers' wombs. In China, the god Kuan-Yin was the giver of children.

The relationship between physical love and fertility was exemplified and encouraged by a number of amorous gods and goddesses. The Egyptians venerated Bast, "the Cat Goddess," who was depicted with the head of a lioness and the body of a woman. She was a goddess of love, pleasure, and birth and was honored by wild orgies as a practical way of promoting births. In ancient Greece the god of both pleasure and fertility was Dionysius, who also encouraged procreation through orgies. The Greek goddess of love and fertility was Aphrodite. Her son, the child-god Eros, enouraged romantic love as he still does, by shooting his arrows through people's hearts.

Of Childbirth and Childrearing

In Babylonia the goddess Belit-Ili, sometimes called Nintud, "The Lady of Childbirth," watched over the birth process, and a goddess appropriately called Mama or Mammitu determined, at the moment of birth, the newborn's destiny.

In Egypt a god named Bes presided over both marriage and childbearing. He was the protector of expectant mothers, and many mothers named children after him. Egyptian goddesses who helped women during childbirth included Heket, a frog-headed goddess who was also a midwife who assisted every morning at the birth of the sun, and Meshkent, who personified the two bricks on which, at the moment of delivery, Egyptian mothers

35

crouched. She went from house to house bringing relief to women in labor, and appeared beside the mother at the exact moment of the baby's birth, when she also played the role of a fairy godmother, predicting the newborn's future. Nephythus was another Egyptian goddess who aided women during childbirth. Also the Egyptian goddess Hathor, the embodiment of motherhood, music and joy, represented as a cow, sometimes appeared at a birth to prophesy the newborn's future. And Shai ("destiny") was a sort of guardian angel who was born at the same time as the baby, grew up along with the child and kept track of his or her sins and virtues, and after death reported to Osiris (the king god of the afterlife) so that he and his heavenly jury could render judgment regarding the person's deserved punishment or reward in the next life.

In Greece Ilithyia, a daughter of Hera, presided at every childbirth, bringing women in labor both pain and deliverance on the theory that no child could be born unless both of these were present. She arrived at the birth scene accompanied by Moerae, the Fates: Clotho, the spinner, who personified the thread of life that was cut off at the moment of death; Lachesis, who represented luck or chance; and Atropos, inescapable destiny. These three were present at everyone's birth and later in life, when one married, they had to be invoked for the union to be happy.

Some goddesses gave mothers and children additional help. In Mesopotamia, Gula, the goddess of health, had to be propitiated because she inflicted either illness or health depending on her whim. The goddess Namtar was more dependable; she protected the health of boys.

In Egypt there were three goddesses who helped nursing mothers. Apet (or Opet or Tauret) "the Great" was a popular one who symbolized maternity and breastfeeding and was represented as a hippopotamus with large breasts. Nekhebet presided over the suckling of infants, and is often shown in Egyptian art nursing the pharoah and other royal children. Renenet also presided over the suckling of babies; she nourished them herself and also gave them their names, personalities, and fortune.

In Greece Hera was the goddess who presided over all phases of feminine life, during childhood and marriage and motherhood.

A Slavonic goddess, the Kikimora, helped mothers with household tasks, but only if the mistress of the house was diligent. If she was lazy, the Kikimora gave her trouble and woke up her children during the night by tickling them.

Many Roman gods and goddesses helped mothers and children. The Romans' mythology was as systematic as their well-organized society. By 400 B.C. they had adopted and renamed the great gods and goddesses of Greece. Aphrodite became Venus, Artemis became Diana, Eros became Cupid, Gaea became Tellus, Hera became Juno. These continued to perform the functions they had performed for the Greeks, aiding lovers, married couples, mothers, and children. But for centuries before that the Romans had already developed their own detailed mythology.

Each family had a general supervisor, the Lar, whose image had a place of honor at the family altar and who was invoked on all important family occasions. Families were also protected by the Penates, especially in regard to their food supply, and at every meal their images were placed between the dishes and they were offered the first helping of food. Quarrels between husbands and wives were placated by the god Viriplaca.

In addition, the Romans had the largest and most specialized staff of divine baby sitters in history. At the moment of birth the intervention of three divinities, Deverra,

Intercidona, and Pilumnu, drove away evil spirits. Newborns were taught to utter their first cry by the god Vagitanus.

The creative force that guided the individual, appearing at the birth of a boy, watching over his development, forming his personality, protecting him, and remaining with him until the hour of his death, was the Genius. Juno performed for girls the functions that the Genius did for boys. On the day of a birth an image of the Genius or of Juno was offered wine and flowers as part of a family celebration. The infant's purification, a spiritual and physical cleansing ceremony which took place shortly after a birth, was presided over by the goddess Nundina.

Breastfeeding was supervised by the goddess Rumina. Babies' cradles were watched over by Cuba, a goddess who helped keep the babies quiet and protected them while they were asleep. After weaning, children were taught to eat and drink by two goddesses, Educa and Potina. Children's growth was watched over by two other goddesses: Ossipaga helped their bones to grow and Carna their flesh. Children's intellectual faculties were awakened by the god Sentinus. Children were taught to speak by the goddesses Abeona and Adeona and the god Febulinus. Whenever children were out of their parents' sight they were guarded by the goddess Domiduca. Even orphans were not neglected. They were protected by the goddess Orbona.

DEVICES TO PROTECT CHILDREN FROM THE EVIL EYE

Before the era when germs were recognized as a child's most dreaded enemies, most mothers feared the "evil eye," a mysterious force that could harm children by looking into their eyes. Parents also feared mischievous fairies who could change their children, and gypsies who might kidnap them. If a hitherto healthy child took sick or a previously sweet child began to be naughty, mothers were told this wasn't their child; it was a "changeling" who had been put in place of the child by a malevolent spirit. Many real natural dangers as well as imagined ones always threatened the lives of newborns, so the need for powerful supernatural protection was universally felt.

Special Charms

In addition to invoking gods and goddesses, parents used many magical devices to protect their children. In many countries amulets, charms to ward off evil, are still hung around children's necks or pinned onto their clothes or placed in their beds.

The ancient Egyptians used scarabs, dark-shelled beetles considered sacred or carved representations of them, for this purpose. Many jewels worn by Hindu and Muslim children have traditionally been regarded as potent charms against the evil eye. Many ancient charms from Thebes, Athens, and Ephesus have been preserved. Usually these were made of gold or silver but some were of shells or ivory or stone, in many shapes, sometimes images of gods or birds or beasts.

In the Middle Ages, among good luck charms which lacked charm were bits of skull or "finger of birth-strangled babe ditch-delivered by a drab."

In Latin countries amulets are almost as common today as they were in ancient Rome. One old Italian charm against the evil eye is a sprig of rue. In Naples this is often placed on an infant's breast while it is sleeping. One of the oldest and still most frequently used amulets in Italy is the *mano in fica* (in Portugal and Brazil it is known as the *figa*), a small model of part of an arm topped by a hand, with the thumb held between the index and middle fingers. It is worn by children of all classes and may be made of almost anything: bone, cornelian, gold, horn, lead, or wood.

Other religious or superstitious jewelry includes small crosses, crowns, crucifixes, hearts, palms, and round and oval saints' medals. Little girls usually wear earrings as well as finger rings, bracelets, necklaces, and anklets. The original intention in piercing a child's ears, which in Spain was traditionally done to infants of both sexes, was to preserve the eyesight. Spanish babies' ears were customarily pierced, and gold wire inserted in the small holes soon after birth. The wire was removed from the holes when boys reached manhood. In Portugal the piercing of babies' ears traditionally was done when they were three months old, in France at the age of three years.

In Turkey, as soon as a child is born, even today, it is loaded with amulets, and a piece of soft mud is also stuck onto its forehead. This is done to distract the evil eye away from the baby's eyes.

In Iran for this same purpose a baby's head is smeared with soot, preferably while the rest of its body is still inside its mother. Iranian mothers also divert the attention of the evil eye by hanging blue beads around a child's neck; often these same beads have been used earlier, tied to the mother's braids early in her pregnancy.

Spitting

Even today in Greece and several other countries, before someone looks at a baby the mother may ask the person to spit on it three times, as a preventive in case the person possesses the evil eye. In parts of Ireland, too, as soon as a baby is born, the nurse takes the precaution of spitting on it.

Salt

In the second century the Greek physician Galen taught that salt was strengthening to newborns, so for centuries in many countries, wherever this eminent doctor's vast influence reached, newborn babies were sprinkled with salt before being swaddled for the first time.

In Scotland it became traditional to give a newborn baby's first bath in salted water, for both medicinal and superstitious reasons. Salt was considered to be obnoxious to anyone possessing the evil eye. To make babies doubly obnoxious to possessors of the evil eye, salt was put into every young Scot's mouth as soon as he was born, and also sprinkled over the baby's cradle.

Other Devices

In ancient Greece a newborn baby, after a brief ground-touching ceremony, was immediately wrapped up carefully and carried ceremoniously around the household altar, to let all the household gods see it so they would know it and give it their protection.

In eighteenth-century England cradles were made of ash or elder wood whenever possible, because these woods were holy and therefore protective. The ash tree had been regarded as sacred since the days of ancient Scandinavian sagas, and it was afterwards made even holier by the fact that Jesus as a baby had reputedly been bathed in front of a fire of ash wood. And the elder was holy because the cross on which Jesus died was believed by some people to have been made of elder wood. Still another way to protect a baby was to place an open Bible in its cradle.

Chinese mothers, as readers of the novel *The Good Earth* by Pearl Buck will remember, used to try to fool the evil eye by boasting in reverse about their children, vying with each other in describing them as ugly, miserable, and sickly so that people with the evil eye would think they were not worth looking at. They also prevented their children from being stolen by malignant powers and replaced by changelings by painting crosses on their children's foreheads with a mixture of banana-skin ashes and water.

Other traditional methods of protecting babies against fairies and the evil eye were toadstone rings made of fossil teeth, pine cones, the skin of a hyena, the kernel of the fruit of a palm tree, a man's coat spread across the infant's cradle, and anything made of metal. Because of a belief in the power of metal, a needle or pin was sometimes stuck in the baby's cap or clothing, or a key or knife or pair of scissors was placed above or in the cradle. These customs are still practiced in Iran and some other countries.

A horseshoe hung over the front door was also used to help keep evil spirits away from a child's home. We still see horseshoes used to bring good luck, but most users do not realize why they are supposed to be lucky. Saint Dunstan, an English monk and Archbishop of Canterbury in the tenth century, once shod the devil with red-hot horseshoes, according to his followers, and the spirit of evil has been afraid to go near horseshoes ever since.

Another method used in England to protect children from the evil eye was simply to keep their faces hidden from it so they would be overlooked. The small piece of muslin or lace which many English nannies, even in the early years of the twentieth century, placed over babies' faces whenever they took them out for an airing, was a survival of this ancient device, even though most nannies had no idea why it was customary. Habits live on long after the reason for them has been forgotten.

CHILD SACRIFICE TO GODS AND DEMONS

Killing children in order to offer them to gods was practiced by Ammonites, Assyrians, Aztecs, Babylonians, Franks, Gauls, Incans, Mayans, Moabites, Phoenicians, and Saxons, and in certain periods by Germans, Greeks, Israelites, Romans, and Scandinavians. Thousands of bones of sacrificed children have been dug up by archeologists, often with inscriptions identifying the victims as first-born sons of noble families, reaching back to 7,000 B.C.

Among the Phoenicians (c. 1100–322 B.C.), the primary god was Elioun, the "All Highest," whose son Uranus, the Sky, married Gaea (or Gaia) the Earth. Uranus was often violent and tried to destroy their children. Two of his sons were Atlas and Cronus. According to Greek mythology, Atlas was punished for disobedience by having to hold up the world on his shoulders, which is why books of maps are called atlases. Cronus is said to have founded Byblos, which claims to be the world's oldest continuously inhabited city, in

Lebanon. Cronus was as vicious as his father; among other things, he cut off the head of one of his daughters. People feared such gods and took drastic measures to appease them.

The Phoenicians' religious rites were performed by priests called Magi. To escape from the Romans who were waging war against the Phoenicians and who finally conquered them, some of these priests migrated to Ireland where, like the Druids in England, they continued offering human sacrifices to propitiate their gods. They required followers to offer the gods the first fruits of their crops and the first-born children of their families.

Plutarch described child sacrifice in Carthage, the city established by the Phoenicians around 810 B.C. and destroyed by the Romans after their victory in the Punic Wars in 146 B.C. In *The Parallel Lives of the Noble Greeks and Romans*, he wrote:

> With full knowledge and understanding they offered up their own children, and those who had no children would buy little ones from poor people and cut their throats as if they were so many lambs or young birds; meanwhile the mother stood by without a tear or moan, but should she utter a single moan or let fall a single tear, she had to forfeit the money, and her child was sacrificed nevertheless; and the whole area before the statue was filled with a loud noise of flutes and drums so that the cries of wailing should not reach the ears of the people.

According to Greek mythology, Athens was once under siege and its attacker King Minos of Crete asked the god Zeus to help him avenge the death of his father Androgeus by inflicting a plague on Athens. To rid themselves of this plague the Athenians agreed to send Minos an annual tribute of seven boys and seven girls. The children were to be fed to the Minotaur, a monster with a human body and the head of a bull that Minos kept confined and that was fed exclusively on human flesh. The Minotaur was finally slain by Theseus, one of the Athenian boys being delivered to him as a sacrifice, with the aid of Ariadne, a daughter of Minos.

In Rome the practice of sacrificing children to gods persisted, off and on, from 900 to 200 B.C., despite periodic efforts to outlaw it. In his *Lives of the Caesars,* the historian Suetonius (c. A.D. 120) wrote that because of an evil portent one year the Roman Senate decreed that no male born that year would be allowed to live. Dio Cassius (A.D. 155–230), another Roman historian, said that Didious Julianus, Roman Emperor for two months in A.D. 193, "killed many boys as a magic rite" until he too was murdered.

Among the Israelites, the most famous individual example of child sacrifice is the one that did not happen: When Abraham was convinced that God wanted him to offer his only and beloved son Isaac as a burnt offering, he set out to obey. Just as he was lifting a knife to slay his son, however, an angel of the Lord called to him and said, "Abraham, lay not thine hand upon the lad," and then told him that "in thy seed all the nations of the earth shall be blessed, because thou hast obeyed my voice." From this time on, the descendants of Abraham forbade child sacrifice; nevertheless, some of them lapsed from time to time into worship of evil idols who demanded it of them.

Psalm 106 in the Old Testament of the Bible describes how some of them

> hearkened not to the voice of the Lord [but] joined themselves to worshippers of Baal, and ate of the sacrifices of the dead. Thus they provoked the Lord to anger, and a plague broke in upon them. Others mingled among the heathen and learned their works, and served their idols which were a snare unto them. Yea, and they sacrificed their sons and their daughters unto devils, and shed

innocent blood, even the blood of their sons and of their daughters whom they sacrificed to the idols of Canaan, and the land was polluted with blood....therefore was the wrath of the Lord kindled against his people.

The Old Testament prophet Jeremiah (in Chapter 19, verse 5) also told how some built altars and killed their sons as burnt offerings to the idol Baal and "therefore, saith the Lord, this place shall be called the valley of slaughter." And Ezekiel (Chapter 22, verse 39) described God's anger at two "wicked sisters" who "caused their sons to pass through the fire, to devour them, and when they had slain their children to their idols then they came the same day into My sanctuary to profane it."

Among the Aztecs (1325–1521) in what is now Mexico, numerous children and babies were sacrificed to their god Tlaloc. Ironically, his wife Chalchiuhtlicue was the goddess invoked for the protection of newborn children. For the festivals in Tlaloc's honor the priests looked for large numbers of babies whom they bought from their mothers. After killing them, they cooked and ate them. If the children cried and shed many tears the spectators rejoiced, saying this was a sign that rain was coming.

Among the Incans (c. 1400–1533) in what is now Ecuador and Peru, children were sacrificed to Catequil, the god of thunder and lightning. Human sacrifices also occurred yearly at festivals in honor of the gods Inti, the Sun, whose sister-wife, the Moon, called Mama Quilla, was the goddess who protected married women; to Pachacamac, the supreme god of fire; and to Viracocha, the god of rain and water and, by extension, of fertility and procreation. Viracocha's sister-wife was Mama-Cuna who educated the Acllas ("Virgins of the Sun"), girls chosen at the age of eight and shut up in cloisters which they could not leave until they were 14 or 15 and then only to marry high-ranking chiefs. If an Aclla was convicted of relations with a man before marriage, she was buried alive unless she could prove that she was pregnant, in which case it was considered to be due to the Sun.

When the Spanish explorer Francisco Pizarro arrived in Peru in 1531, he was greeted warmly by the Incans, who thought he was a god whose coming had been predicted. At first he was friendly in turn, but one day Atahualpa, the Incan ruler, took him to visit an Incan temple and Pizarro discovered that their gods demanded human sacrifices. He was appalled and told Atahualpa that his gods were not gods but devils. After that they became mortal enemies. Pizarro marched on Cuzco, the Incan capital, in 1533, killing Atahualpa and capturing the city and with it immense amounts of gold. He founded a new capital city, Lima, while waging war with another Inca chief, Almagro, whom he also defeated and killed. But Pizarro could not enjoy his victories or his gold, because he was slain in revenge by Almagro's followers.

Child Sacrifice and Bridges

The game of London Bridge has given immortality to an extremely grisly aspect of history. London Bridge keeps falling down and the only way to build it up again is to capture someone. When the real London Bridge was first built (c. 963), it kept falling down, supposedly until the workmen decided to capture some small children and bury them alive under its foundation stones.

This is a reminder of an ancient worldwide belief that bridges could be safely built only if someone was first captured and his or her life was offered as a sacrifice. Small children were usually considered the best offering because they were innocent and therefore fit to act as redeemers, specifically as a bridge's guardian, protecting it against the capricious forces of nature or the malicious mischief of river demons.

Another bridge, in Brittany, legend says, also kept falling down until a four-year-old boy was buried alive in its base, after which the structure stood firm. In this case it is said that the young guardian was buried with a candle in one hand and a piece of bread in the other, so that the poor little thing would be able to see in the dark and would not go hungry after they walled him in.

In 1843, a new bridge was being built at Halle in Germany, and people in the area were frightened because they heard that a child was going to be built into the foundation. Even more recently, in 1872, the same fear arose when a bridge was being built across the Ganges, in India. And when a bridge gate at Bremen in Germany was demolished in the nineteenth century, the skeleton of a child was found embedded in the masonry.

The Sacrifice of a Nursing Mother

For determination to nurse one's baby in spite of serious difficulties, the all-time championship probably belongs to the unfortunate young consort of a King of Albania. Her story is one of the grimmest tales of Jacob Grimm (1785–1863) in his *Teutonic Mythology*. She breastfed her baby while being buried alive.

Some 300 masons had been working for three years at foundation stones in the town of Scutari, but whatever they built by day a demon named Vila tore down every night. Finally, the vile Vila is supposed to have agreed to stop this sabotage if a king's wife was walled up in the foundation. The next day a king's consort, not knowing about this decree, brought some food out to the workmen and was promptly rewarded for her kindness by being walled in by the masons, who dropped their stones around her. She was a new mother and worried more about what would happen to her baby than about what was happening to her, so she succeeded in persuading the workmen to leave a small opening in the wall so that she could continue to nurse her baby. The baby was brought to her and held up to her once a day every day until she died.

THE CHILDREN'S CRUSADES

In France

Two of the strangest and saddest episodes in the history of religion occurred in the thirteenth century. The religious fervor that engulfed Europe during the period of the Crusades, when Christians tried to capture Jerusalem from "the infidels," inspired 50,000 children to leave their homes to go to the Holy Land, with tragic results.

In the spring of 1212, a 12-year-old shepherd boy named Stephen left his flocks to preach in the countryside and attracted large crowds by his extraordinary eloquence. He told his listeners he would lead them to Jerusalem and that they would succeed in capturing the Holy Sepulcher from the infidels and bringing it to Christendom, where their elders had failed. Not only children but many grown men and women were inspired by this child. By the end of June 30,000 children under the age of l2 were camped outside the town of Vendome, ready to follow Stephen to Jerusalem. King Philip II of France had taken part in the third crusade (in ll90) and had returned without victory. Knowing what these children would be up against, he ordered them to disband and go home, but they refused.

Impressed by their piety and the almost miraculous quality of this spontaneous movement, priests and friars joined the procession when the children set out to walk across France. As they entered different cities they were enthusiastically greeted and provided with food and lodgings. As a result, vagrants and prostitutes gradually joined them in order to share in their gifts and to corrupt the children.

It was an unusually hot summer. There was a drought, and many children died. When asked to pray for rain, Stephen explained that the drought presaged the drying up of the seas that would enable them to cross the Mediterranean on dry land as the Israelites had crossed the Red Sea.

Some children got disillusioned and tried to go back home but got lost and fell among thieves. The majority maintained blind faith in Stephen. However, by August they were no longer radiant with hope, but sick and weak, dragging themselves on crutches and pushing each other in handmade carts and wheelbarrows. Only a small number of those who had started out reached the port city of Marseilles, and when they did, they saw that the Mediterranean was not dried up after all.

In Marseilles, while they were wondering what to do, two merchants, known to us and to iniquity as Hugh the Iron and William the Pig, offered to transport the children to Palestine by ship, free of charge. They trustingly set sail on seven ships.

For more than l8 years nothing was heard of them until a pilgrim returned from the East, saying he was one of the young priests who had accompanied the children. He said that Hugh and William were not ordinary merchants but slave traders. Two of their ships had foundered at sea off the coast of Sardinia and all their passengers had drowned.The rest of the children were taken captive on the coast of Africa. Some were sold in slave markets at the first port of call, others shipped to Egypt where they earned a better price, and 400 of the healthiest were taken to Baghdad to be enrolled in the service of the Caliph; l8 of these died as martyrs for refusing to convert to Islam. A few who were literate, including this priest, were bought by the governor of Egypt, who was interested in studying French language and literature; they were used as teachers and interpreters, and were treated well.

Many years later Pope Gregory IX (1227–1241) built a chapel on the island of San Pietro to commemorate the children who lost their lives in the shipwreck; its ruins can be seen today.

In Germany

Another children's crusade also began in the spring of l2l2 when another peasant boy, named Nicholas, started preaching outside the cathedral in Cologne, also attracting thousands of disciples. Although the French children had expected to conquer the infidels by force, the German ones were urged to convert them by their faith. These children were older than their French counterparts, and their number included many boys of noble birth and a large percentage of girls. The enthusiasm aroused by Nicholas was so great that any priests who disapproved of his project were accused of jealousy.

Of the 20,000 children who left Germany with Nicholas only a few ever returned home. On their travels they met hardships and dangers, many collapsing and dying from exhaustion or starvation. Soon the remainder were also joined by vagabonds and prostitutes, so that what had begun as a holy procession disintegrated into an unruly mob. Half the children were missing before they reached the Alps. It is believed that 7,000 of them arrived at Genoa in August, 1212. Most were permitted to stay only overnight because city authorities suspected that they might be part of a plot by the German Emperor to invade the city. However, those children willing to stay permanently in Genoa and who could prove they were of noble birth were offered citizenship, and to this day some families in Genoa claim to be descended from these children.

Nicholas and his few still faithful followers moved on and visited Rome to ask Pope Innocent III (1161–1216) for his blessing and help. Although touched by their piety, the Pope firmly told them to go home, absolving them of their vows. Nicholas and some others refused to be absolved, however, and boarded a ship sailing for Palestine. It is recorded that he fought bravely at Acre and later returned home unharmed. But most of the children trudged northwards. Some, who lacked the courage to face the long, dangerous and exhausting trip back home, became aimless vagrants, and many of the girls became prostitutes. Some are believed to have been sold into slavery.

Those who made it back to Germany faced still further disillusionment and suffering. They were taunted and stoned by people who had originally considered their crusade the work of God but now saw it as the work of the Devil and considered the children possessed by evil spirits. Nicholas's father was publicly hanged as an instrument of evil.

This story helped to inspire another strange tale which is still one of the most popular of German legends. It is said that in July 1376, a man arrived in the town of Hamelin and struck a deal with its magistrates to get rid of its many rats. When he played his pipe the rats followed him straight into the river until not one was left. The ungrateful townsmen refused to pay the piper, so he again played his pipe and this time all the town's children followed him out of town and never returned. The famous poem by Robert Browning (1812–1889), "The Pied Piper of Hamelin," ends with the children's disappearance into a playground, but in the legend they reappeared dancing and singing along the route of Charlemagne, the traditional road on which crusaders set forth for the Holy Land. At noon, every Sunday in the summer, the town of Hamelin reenacts this story, and tourists from all over the world come to watch and to wonder.

RELIGIOUS FESTIVALS INVOLVING CHILDREN

Every religion singles out certain days of the year as special occasions for penance or celebration, or to commemorate events of historical signifance in their tradition. Some holy days are of no interest to young children because they are solemn with long sermons, and youngsters tend to squirm or fall asleep. Others fascinate children because of their colorful pageantry or because they emphasize juvenile participation.

The following descriptions of special days that appeal to Buddhist, Christian, Hindu, Islamic, and Jewish children are unequal in length; there are more examples in some traditions than in others. But this survey reveals an interesting fact about rituals that evolved separately. The Jewish Bar Mitzvah resembles the Hindu boy's second birth. Long periods of penance are important in both Buddhism and Christianity and have an equivalent in Islam's Ramadan and the Jewish Days of Atonement. By recognizing the universal human needs and aspirations met in varying degrees by these religions, instead of being put off by what may seem strange details in the ways in which these find expression, we discover how much people in every culture have in common.

Buddhist Festivals

The Buddhists calculate the New Year according to the position of the sun and by the months of the moon based on a Hindu calendar. The *Solar New Year* is based on the sun's position in relation to the 12 signs of the Zodiac and begins when the sun enters Aries, in April. The *Lunar New Year* usually is in December, except in Burma (officially called the Union of Myanmar since 1989, but still popularly known by its traditional name) where the 12 lunar months begin in April.

The Flower Festival: On April 8 in Japan, this celebrates Buddha's birthday (c. 563 B.C.). Buildings and streets are decorated with colorful paper flowers to represent the showers of petals and sweet rain that are said to have fallen from the heavens when Buddha was born in a grove of blossoming trees. In Japan's cities processions of thousands of children march to Buddhist temples, carrying lotus blossoms. A statue of the child Buddha stands in each temple in a flowery shrine, and a metal basin nearby is filled with sweet tea made from hydrangea leaves. The children pour the tea over the statue with a ladle, recalling the story of Buddha's miraculous birth.

New Year's Day: On April 13–18 in Thailand, the new year arrives after months of hot weather, so it is celebrated with cool water. In the temples people bathe statues of Buddha. Children pour perfumed water into their parents' hands as a sign of respect. They also wade in ponds, rivers, and canals, carrying pots and pails to scoop up water which they spray on each other in mock battles. There are parades with bands and dancers, and the paraders spray water on the spectators.

Vesak or Wesak: In April during the full moon of the year's sixth lunar month, this holiday is observed in Kampuchea, Laos, Sri Lanka, Thailand, and Vietnam. On this day Buddha's birth, enlightenment, and death are all celebrated together, because it is believed that all three events occurred on the night of the full moon. In some countries such as Thailand, where Wesak is called *Visakha Buja,* it is observed as a holy day without entertainment, except for processions of people visiting monasteries, carrying candles and colored lanterns. In Laos, although the morning is devoted to religious solemnities, the afternoon is a time of gaiety and fun, with the *Boun Bang Fai* (Rocket Festival) when many rockets, often 20 to 30 feet long, decorated with flowers and streamers, are fired from the shores of the Mekong River, and parades of dancers and musicians entertain everyone.

Khao Phansa: In mid-July the night of the full moon of the eighth lunar month in Southeast Asia marks the beginning of the Buddhist penitential, a season when monks may not leave their monasteries for three months. Buddha chose this period, which is the rainy season, as a time of retreat, study, and prayer because he didn't want monks walking across the fields during this time when they might kill farmers' newly planted rice seedlings. On the first day of the season worshippers bring food to the monks as well as gifts of the eight things Buddha allowed monks to own: a robe, a belt, an undergarment, a begging bowl, a blade, a needle, a mat, and a sieve. In Thailand Buddhists believe that no boy will ever be fully mature unless he spends some time as a monk, and Khao Phansa is the time when many Thai boys enter a monastery to spend three months serving the monks, praying, and studying Buddhist teachings. On the evening before they "take the yellow robe" their families hold large feasts accompanied by gongs, drums, and flutes. During the feasts the boys are honored but must sit in complete silence with their eyes lowered. The next day their families give them a delicious meal before shaving their heads and eyebrows, and they are then led to a monastery in a procession bright with banners and flags.

Dhammsetkya: In Burma, the first day of the season of penance begins in the month of Waso (or Wazo) on the night of the full moon and commemorates the day when Buddha preached his first sermon in which he revealed the *Dhamma* (the Great Truth) that enlightened him as he meditated under the bo tree. This is the traditional season for boys to seek admission to the Sangha, the Buddhist order of monks; the specific day is chosen by an astrologer and based on the boy's horoscope. The *Shinbyu* (novitiation) is the most important ceremony in the life of a Burmese boy, a symbolic reenactment of the day when Buddha renounced his royal life. Boys of 12 or 14, and sometimes as young as four, are dressed like princes in elaborate turbans and silk robes. They are the center of attention at a banquet; afterwards they are led through the streets on white horses, accompanied by bands of musicians and their families and friends carrying food, robes, candles, and flowers. When they reach the monastery the boys are presented to the monks, who shave their heads and replace their elaborate clothing with yellow monastic robes. Before the boys enter the monastery they solemnly chant the *bo dang* prayer signifying their willingess to accept the strict discipline of monastic life for the next three days to three months, during which time they will eat only one meal a day.

Oban: In July, in Japan: Also known as "The Feast of Lanterns for the Dead," this is a solemn yet joyful three-day Buddhist holiday. Families visit their ancestors' graves, clean and sweep them, leave lanterns and offerings of food. Homes are scrubbed in preparation for visits from the ancestors' spirits; lighted sticks or lanterns are placed in front of each house, and places are set for the ancestors at the holiday feast. Afterwards families give their ancestors a sendoff by launching little wooden boats filled with food, colored lanterns, incense, and memorial tablets on which the ancestors' names are written. On the last night of the holiday teenage boys and girls perform a special dance called the *Bon odori.*

Full Moon in the 11th Lunar Month: This day signifies the end of the penitential season in Southeast Asia. It coincides with the end of the rainy season, when monks are again free to take part in events outside their monasteries. It is observed in different ways in different countries: In Burma it is celebrated not only as the end of the rainy season but also as the anniversary of Buddha's return to earth after visiting his mother in heaven. For three days homes and buildings are lit with colored lamps, and in the evenings processions are made to pagodas.

Ho Khao Slakand: In Laos, this is the last day of the penitential season when Laotian Buddhists bring offerings to the monks who are now ending their retreat. People draw the name of an individual monk to whom they bring a present of food or one of the eight articles Buddhist monks are allowed to own. Parents also give their children toys and candy on this day.

Tazaungdaing: On November l9 in Burma, this holiday, also known as Weaving Day, is observed in memory of the robe that Buddha's mother is said to have once woven for him. Weaving competitions take place at pagodas all over the country. At 5 P.M. in Rangoon girls sit down at looms in the Shwe Dagon Pagoda and keep weaving until each girl has completed one entire robe. The girl whose robe is judged the most well made receives a prize. At dawn, the next day monks lead a procession around the temple and offer one robe to each of the five statues of Buddha.

Christian Holidays

The Christian year is a cycle of seasons and days commemorating the life of Jesus, the history of the Church, and the lives of saints. The Eastern Orthodox year starts in September; the Catholic and Protestant church year begins in November. Many of the days are special for children.

The Season of Advent: Advent is observed the four weeks before Christmas. The word *advent* means "coming" and the purpose of this period is to prepare for Christ's coming on Christmas with suitable reverence and eagerness. In many homes people set an Advent wreath of pine needles and holly surrounding four candles on a table; one candle is lit on the first Sunday of Advent, a second on the second Sunday, and so on. Children are also often given Advent calendars which show snow scenes and pictures of children, each on a little numbered tab which they lift up each day, finding underneath each one a picture of an appropriate pre-Christmas activity, until on Christmas Eve they find a picture of the Holy Family.

Saint Catherine's Day, November 25: This is the feast day of Catherine, patron saint of girls, unmarried women, students, and people who work with wheels, such as drivers, spinners, wheelwrights. This is why whirling fireworks are called Catherine Wheels.

In France and Belgium, this is a day-long time of special merrymaking for children. French settlers brought this festival to Canada where a unique custom, *la tire* (taffy pull), was added to the day's pleasures in the seventeenth century when Marguerite Bourgeoys, a beloved teaching nun who founded the first school in Quebec, used to make taffy for her pupils to encourage them to attend school. French Canadians still use her recipe.

Klopfelnachte (Knocking Nights): On the last three Thursday evenings before Christmas in Germany, children wear masks and go from house to house making up and chanting rhymes that begin with the word "knock." They also make noise by ringing cowbells, cracking whips, and banging pots and pans, in order to drive away evil spirits. As a "reward" they receive fruit, candy, or coins.

The Nuremberg Christmas Fair: On December 4 in Germany since l639, the city of Nuremberg has held a yearly pre-Christmas fair starting on this date. A girl dressed as the Christ Child who, according to German folklore, brings children presents on Christmas Eve, steps onto the balcony of the church in the town's main square and announces the opening of the fair. Everyone sings holiday music and thus begins a three-week period of shopping for holiday gifts, foods, and decorations.

Saint Nicholas Day, December 6: This feast is celebrated in honor of Nicholas, patron saint of children, sailors, thieves, and virgins. In the fourth century Bishop Nicholas of Myra, in what is now Turkey, once took pity on three girls in a poor family and secretly threw a bag of gold for each of them through their bedroom window on three successive nights. This was to provide them with dowries, which in those days were necessary if girls were to find husbands. Having thus been saved from shame and lives of loneliness, the grateful girls learned who their benefactor was and ever since then his name has been associated with gift giving.

In Holland where Saint Nicholas is nicknamed "Sinterklaas," he arrives every year from Spain by ship a week before his feast day, dressed in a bishop's robes. Church bells and booming cannons greet his arrival, and he rides down the gangplank and through town on a white horse, accompanied by his Moorish helper, Peter, leading a parade with floats, brass bands, and marching, cheering children. This sets off a whole week of preparations for his feast day: Children write humorous poems, buy and wrap gifts and hide them around the house, and hold parties on December 5, the eve of his feast. During these parties, suddenly the doorbell rings and a man dressed as Peter dashes in, scatters candies around the room, and leaves a basket filled with presents. The children take turns unwrapping the presents and reading their poems aloud. Before going to sleep that night, when Dutch children believe the saint will ride over rooftops delivering still more presents, they leave carrots and hay in their shoes for Saint Nicholas's horse by the fireplace or on a window sill. Next morning the carrots and hay are gone and gifts are there instead: switches for naughty children but chocolate letters (their initials in chocolate) and gingerbread cookies called "speculas" for all good children.

In Venezuela, Saint Nicholas rides on his white horse to visit schools, hospitals, and orphanages where he hands out toys and sweets.

In America, Saint Nicholas is honored not on December 6 but on December 24. Here he is known as Santa Claus, a jolly stout fellow in a red suit and white beard who lives at the North Pole but travels around the world on Christmas Eve, carrying large bags bulging with toys, riding through the sky in a sleigh pulled by reindeer, and climbing down chimneys to deliver his toys. This image of him dates from 1823 when a poem called "A Visit from Saint Nicholas" was first published. It was written by Clement Moore, an Episcopalian minister, rector of the parish of St. Luke in the Fields in Greenwich Village, New York City, when he was a concerned and worried father trying to amuse and cheer up a beloved child whose happiness as Christmas approached was endangered because she was seriously ill. He never expected to publish this personal and private poem, but friends who saw and enjoyed it secretly published it. When it appeared in public it received immediate and undying popularity.

His portrayal keeps getting embellished: A crew of little elves that work in Santa's toy shop at the North Pole and a Mrs. Claus have been added to the cast, along with a song immortalizing one of his helpers, Rudolph, "The Red-Nosed Reindeer."

The following editorial about Santa, by Francis P. Church, is one of the most famous editorials ever written. *The New York Sun* published it annually before Christmas from 1897 until 1949, when the paper went out of business. It was written in response to a child who wrote the paper asking if there really is a Santa Claus.

"Yes, Virginia, there is a Santa Claus"   —Editorial page, *New York Sun*, 1897

We take pleasure in answering thus prominently the communication below, expressing at the same time our deep gratification that its faithful author is numbered among the friends of *The Sun*:

Dear Editor,

I am 8 years old. Some of my little friends say there is no Santa Claus. Papa says, "if you see it in *The Sun*, it's so." Please tell me the truth, is there a Santa Claus?

—Virginia O'Hanlon

Virginia, your little friends are wrong. They have been affected by the skepticism of a skeptical age. They do not believe except they see. They think that nothing can be which is not comprehensible by their little minds. All minds, Virginia, whether they be men's or children's, are little. In this great universe of ours, man is a mere insect, an ant, in his intellect as compared with the boundless world about him, as measured by the intelligence capable of grasping the whole of truth and knowledge.

Yes, Virginia, there is a Santa Claus. He exists as certainly as love and generosity and devotion exist, and you know that they abound and give to your life its highest beauty and joy. Alas! how dreary would be the world if there were no Santa Claus! It would be as dreary as if there were no Virginias. There would be no childlike faith then, no poetry, no romance to make tolerable this existence. We should have no enjoyment, except in sense and sight. The eternal light with which childhood fills the world would be extinguished.

Not believe in Santa Claus! You might as well not believe in fairies. You might get your papa to hire men to watch the chimneys on Christmas eve to catch Santa Claus coming down; what would that prove? Nobody sees Santa Claus, but that is no sign that there is no Santa Claus. The most real things in the world are those that neither men nor children can see. Did you ever see fairies dancing on the lawn? Of course not, but that's no proof that they are not there. Nobody can conceive or imagine all the wonders there are unseen and unseeable in the world.

You tear apart the baby's rattle and see what makes the noise inside, but there is a veil covering the unseen world which not the strongest man, nor even the united strength of all the strongest men that ever lived, could tear apart. Only faith, poetry, love, romance, can push aside that certain veil and picture the supernal beauty and glory beyond. Is it all real? Ah, Virginia, in all this world there is nothing else real and abiding.

No Santa Claus! Thank God! He lives and lives forever. A thousand years from now, Virginia, nay 10 times 10,000 years from now, he will continue to make glad the heart of childhood.

Saint Lucy's Day, December 13: In Sweden, this feast day is called *Lucladagen*. Held on the winter solstice, the darkest day of the year, it marks the beginning of Sweden's Christmas season. It is a festival of lights honoring Lucia, a Sicilian saint; her name means light. For more than 60 years Swedish girls have observed her feast with elaborate rituals. Before dawn the eldest daughter in a family acts as Lucia, rising and preparing the family's breakfast: coffee and specially shaped saffron buns with raisin eyes called *Lussekattar* (Lucy's cats). At sunrise Lucia puts on a long white robe with a red sash and on her head sets a crown of evergreens decked with candles. Her sisters and brothers also dress at dawn, each girl in a white robe and with a candle to carry as a *Lucia maiden*, each boy in a white robe and a tall, pointed cap decorated with silver stars, as a *star boy*. Then the candles are lit and Lucia and her companions go to their parents' room to wake them up, singing a Swedish version of the song "Santa Lucia." Lucia then serves coffee and buns to each member of the household. Later during the day a girl who has been chosen as the village Lucia, Queen of Lights, carries food and drink to every house and to stables to feed the animals, in memory of the girl who, in the early fourth century, gave away her dowry to feed the poor.

Posadas: December 16–24 in Mexico are the nine nights before Christmas in which the journey of Mary and Joseph to Bethlehem in search of lodgings (*posadas*) are reenacted. For days the markets are full of toys and sweets, little clay figures for making nativity scenes, and *piñatas* (pottery or *papier ache* figures decorated with colored paper and filled with small toys and candies). On each night a party is held and a new piñata is given to the children. After dark, families form processions, carrying lighted candles. Two children lead the march, each carrying a nativity scene on a tray. The procession ends at the house where that night's posada is to be held. Inside, a manger is set up for the Christ Child. Everyone kneels before it to pray. There are good things to eat and a dance with guitar music, then all eyes turn to the piñata hanging from the ceiling. One child is blindfolded, whirled around three times, and given a stick to smash the piñata with. If he or she fails to break it, other children are given tries until one finally hits the jar and a shower of nuts, fruits, sweets and tiny toys comes tumbling down.

This procession and party is repeated every night until *Noche Buena* (The Good Night) which is Christmas Eve, when little children dressed as shepherds stand on either side of a nativity scene and two people acting as godparents lay a figure of the baby Jesus in the manger. Then everyone sings a cradle song to the baby, and this last posada is followed by Midnight Mass, with even the littlest children attending, after which there are fireworks and clanging church bells and everyone goes home to enjoy a big supper. In some villages, this final posada is held in church, and boys and girls do shepherd dances to the music of violins. The figure of the baby Jesus stays in church until Epiphany on January 6, which is when the Wise Men will bring presents to Mexican children.

In Venezuela during this period, many churches hold a *Miss de Aguinaldo*, a daily morning Christmas Carol Mass. In the capital city of Caracas many streets are closed to traffic before 8 a.m. because it has become the custom to rollerskate to these masses. Before bedtime on the previous night children tie one end of a string to their big toe and hang the other end out the window, and in the morning skaters tug on any strings they see, to wake up their friends so that nobody will miss the fun. After Mass they all enjoy breakfast together.

The Christmas Season

Christmas Eve, December 24: In Austria, Germany, and Switzerland, children are not allowed to help in decorating the Christmas tree, which is done on this night. They stay outside the room while it is being done, excitedly awaiting the opening of the door when they will discover what *Kriss Kringle* has brought them.

In Canada, the United Kingdom, the United States and other countries, however, this is usually the night when families decorate their trees together with baubles, tinsel, and strings of lights, and children hang up stockings for Saint Nicholas or Santa Claus or, in England, Father Christmas (a dignified but benign man with a long white beard) to fill with presents during the night. Many families also attend candlelight carol-singing services in the early evening or at midnight, and in some churches children are dressed as shepherds and angels surrounding the Christmas cribs, with two especially priviliged children dressed as Joseph and Mary.

In Ecuador, people choose "godparents" for the Christ Child, who arrange a nativity scene at their house and invite friends and neighbors to a meal. After Vespers at church, fireworks and balloons entertain the children, and at midnight all go to Mass. In the church a life-sized nativity scene is set up, and one of the village's newborn babies is chosen to play the part of the infant Jesus. After church people dance and feast.

In Ireland, there is a tradition of lighting a candle and placing it in front of one's house on Christmas Eve, just before sunset. The father sets the candle in place and either the youngest child or a daughter named Mary lights it. This is to welcome travelers who, like the Holy Family, may need shelter for the night. After the evening meal on Christmas Eve, an extra loaf of bread, a pitcher of milk and another candle is placed on the kitchen table, and the door is left unlocked. To symbolize Christ's manger, mince pies are sometimes baked in cradle-shaped tins. The manger scene is a very popular decoration in Irish homes, schools, and churches. Children receive their presents the next day when a large dinner is served, usually with turkey and plum pudding.

> Christmas is forced on a reluctant and disgusted nation by the shopkeepers and the press.
>
> —*George Bernard Shaw, in 1897*

In Norway during the two weeks before Christmas, people make hectic preparations. Fourteen kinds of cookies, a different kind for each day after Christmas, are made and everything must be ready by 4 P.M. on Christmas Eve when church bells ring in "Christmas peace." The Christmas Eve dinner includes bowls of rice porridge, in one of which the mother has put an almond; whoever finds the almond in his or her bowl will get a special gift. After dinner the Christmas tree is adorned with tiny candles, flags, and other decorations. These often include a marzipan pig, a symbol of the Norse goddess Friea who was worshipped in Norway centuries ago.

In Sweden, the *tomte*, a good-hearted Christmas gnome, arrives with a bag full of presents on Christmas Eve.

Christmas ("Christ's Mass"), December 25: Christmas is often observed more as a secular holiday than as a holy day, and some think its emphasis on giving presents fosters greed more than love and generosity in children. But there is a saying that it is possible to give without loving but impossible to love without giving.

The day is celebrated in different ways in different parts of the world because in each nation people merge local conditions and traditions with their observance of Christ's birthday. For example, in Zaire, where whole villages take part in pageants reenacting the Christmas story, a palm-thatched shelter decorated with flowers represents the stable in Bethlehem and a real baby is laid in the manger, visited by "shepherds" who bring along flocks of goats, not sheep, and on Christmas morning drums, rather than church bells, summon the people to church.

The actual date of Christ's birth is unknown, but in the fourth century the Church decided it would be fitting to observe it around the time of the winter solstice, superseding the ancient Roman winter festival called the *Saturnalia* which began on December 17 and culminated in *Natalis Solis Invicti* (the Day of the Birth of the Unconquered Sun).

> There seems a magic in the very name of Christmas. Petty jealousies and discords are forgotten.... Would that Christmas lasted the whole year through.
>
> —*Charles Dickens, in 1843*

On this day people exchanged greetings and gifts and rejoiced that the darkest days of the year were over. Thus the birthday of the Sun was transformed into the birthday of the Son of God.

Puritan reformers in England and America banned the celebration of Christmas as a "Popish" innovation without scriptural basis, and some sects, such as Jehovah's Witnesses, still forbid its observance because of its pagan origin and commercialism. Most people, however, children particularly, enjoy both the secular and religious aspects of the day: the singing of carols; the indoor and outdoor decorations including the crèche, or crib, which has been popular ever since 1224 when Saint Francis of Assisi conducted an outdoor Christmas service around a manger with a live ox and ass; and the Christmas tree, which originated in Germany. According to one account Martin Luther (1483–1546) was so struck one Christmas Eve, while walking in the woods, by the beauty of the stars shining above some fir trees, that he cut down one tree, brought it home and placed candles on it and a star above it. The Christmas tree was internationalized in 1841 when the German-born consort of Queen Victoria, Prince Albert, brought it to England.

Twelfth Night, January 5: Twelve nights after Christmas, this holiday commemorates the night when the Three Kings or Magi (Wise Men) came to Bethlehem in search of the infant Jesus.

In Italy, according to an ancient legend beloved by Italian children, the Magi asked an old woman named Befana (her name is an abbreviation of Epiphany) to help them find Jesus, but she was so busy sweeping her floor that she didn't join them. Later she set out alone in search of the Christ Child but never did find him, She still searches for him every year on this night, flying around on her broomstick, visiting every home and leaving presents for all good children.

In Norway, the night is celebrated with a mixture of ancient pagan, Christian, and secular features as *Julebukk* (Yule Buck), harking back to the days when the Vikings worshipped the god Thor and his pet goat. Yuletide revelers dressed up in buckskins and danced with goats' heads mounted on poles. In the Middle Ages adults gave up this custom but children still dressed up in costumes on this night, some as devils carrying poles topped by goats' heads and some representing angels or biblical characters carrying large transparent paper stars mounted on poles with lighted candles inside. They would go from house to house singing folk songs and hymns and be greeted with gifts of sweets or money. Since 1966 Norwegian Boy Scouts and Girl Guides have given a more serious purpose to the tradition. They still go from door to door in groups singing and asking for handouts, but instead of a goat's head or star they place a UNICEF poster on top of their poles and carry leaflets about its work plus empty milk cartons in which they ask people to place donations for UNICEF. This *Julebukk Aksionen* has grown bigger every year, with thousands of children taking part, raising money for UNICEF, and helping to spread information about what it does for children.

Epiphany, January 6: Also known as the Day of the Three Kings, this holiday commemorates the Three Kings who brought gifts to the baby Jesus. In France, families have a party on this day at which a round flat cake (*galette*) is served. Inside the cake is hidden a coin and a tiny china doll representing the baby Jesus, and the child who receives the piece containing the coin or doll becomes king or queen for the day. In Latin America and Spain, children put hay for the kings' camels in their shoes and set them beside their beds or by the front door of the house on the eve of Epiphany. When they wake up the next morning they find the hay gone, replaced by candies and other gifts.

Saint Knut's Day, January 13: In Denmark, Norway, and Sweden, this holiday is named in honor of King Knut (or Canute), who ruled Scandinavia from 1080 to 1086. He decreed that the festive Yuletide season should last for 20 days. Parties are held on this final day, and in Sweden it is called *Julgransplundering* (Yule plundertime) because this is when decorations are taken off the Christmas trees; children eat up the cookie ornaments and then throw the trees out the window.

Lent

The Saturday before Lent: In Trinidad and Tobago, a special carnival is held on this day, exclusively for children. Well ahead of time children have joined masque bands, groups which choose themes from popular fairy tales or children's stories and make costumes illustrating the themes. On this Saturday they hold parades dressed in costumes, and sing and dance the jump-up, a free-style dance. Children's steel drum bands compete for prizes, and a prize is also given for the best children's masque band.

The Monday before Lent: On this day, called Festelavn in Denmark, children start the day by poking their parents awake with willow or birch twigs that they have covered with crepe paper or silk ribbons. This custom probably dates back to the Vikings, who used to beat each other with switches to drive out evil. Parents stop the beatings by giving the children special buns. Later in the day, children in masks and costumes go from neighbor to neighbor and receive coins, candy, and more buns.

The Last Tuesday before Lent: In the Middle Ages everyone went to church on this day to be *shriven* (to confess and have their sins forgiven), in preparation for Lent. The day became known in English as *Shrove Tuesday.*

In England, the day is also called "Pancake Tuesday" because housewives made pancakes in order to use up their supplies of meat, eggs, or butter, which were forbidden during Lent. And it is said that in America the doughnut was invented on a Shrove Tuesday by a mother, to give her children a combined pre-Lenten food treat and toy.

In Latin countries, this Tuesday, and often several days before it, is called *Carnival* from the Latin *carnem levare*, meaning the removal of meat. It is the year's major holiday, a boisterous festival dating back to the times when Lent was observed with great austerity. This was the last chance for people to have fun and be festive before the 40 days of the Lenten fast. People spend weeks ahead of time learning songs, practicing dances, and making elaborate costumes and floats in preparation for the day's big parades and parties.

In Colombia, in preparation for Carnival, children make papier-mâché images of Joselito Carnaval (The Spirit of Carnival). The day's festivities begin with La Gran Parada

(The Big Parade). Thousands throng the streets with elaborate floats decorated with masses of flowers, led by groups of dancers and musicians including *cumbiamberos*, children who twirl lighted candles as they dance. In the afternoon there is a *Batalla de Flores* (Battle of Flowers) when the floats are dismantled and people toss the flowers at each other. Finally, just before dawn the next morning Joselito Carnaval is buried in a mock funeral, and the children who made the best papier-mâché likenesses of Joselito get prizes.

In France and French-speaking areas throughout the world, this day is called *Mardi Gras* (Fat Tuesday). In southern France it is the climax of 12 whole days of celebrations with a great parade of floats made of flowers. As in Colombia and other countries, it ends with Battles of Flowers when everyone starts throwing flowers at everyone else until they are all knee-deep in blossoms.

In Germany the day is called *Fastnacht* (The Eve of the Fast) and it and the days preceding it are celebrated so enthusiastically that they are known as the fifth season of the year.

In Greece, Carnival begins on a Sunday before Lent and lasts for three weeks. There are a great many parties and dancing in the streets. The Monday after the last Sunday of Carnival is a special holiday called "Clean Monday" when people go on picnics, eating only foods without olive oil or butter.

In Haiti, for weeks and even months before Carnival, boys make *Lamayotes*, wooden or cardboard boxes decorated with tissue paper and paint. When Carnival begins they put a "monster" inside—a lizard, bug or mouse—and run around in masks and costumes offering a peek inside to anyone who will pay them a penny.

In Spain, at Carnival time boys and girls play a special game, *el Pelele*, where they make a dummy stuffed with straw and dressed in old clothes to symbolize some unpopular person and place it on a sheet or blanket and toss it in the air. (In ancient times there was a Shrovetide sport of tossing a dog, but today people are more merciful.) One painting by Goya shows Spanish girls tossing a pelele.

Ash Wednesday, the First Day of Lent: This is a day of fast and abstinence, though young children are exempted from fasting. The devout go to church where a priest puts a smudge of ashes on their foreheads, to remind them of their mortality and of their obligation to do penance for sin and to renew themselves spiritually through prayer and good works. Children wear their ashes proudly all day, refusing to wash them off.

Saint Patrick's Day, March 17: The austerities of Lent are relaxed for this day when Irish people all over the world dress up in green and wear shamrocks, the little three-leafed plants used by Saint Patrick to illustrate how the Holy Trinity—God the Father, Jesus the Son, and the Holy Spirit—are three distinct but equal persons in one God. Along with church services and parties, big parades are a feature of the day, with bands of school children marching and twirling batons, dancing, and waving little green silk or paper flags.

Good Friday, the Friday before Easter: In most countries this is a very solemn day commemorating the crucifixion of Christ, but children in Bermuda observe it in a unique way, by filling the skies with what they call "headstick" kites made with brightly colored tissue paper and newspapers. This custom dates back to an imaginative Sunday School teacher in the early nineteenth century, who explained the Ascension of Christ into heaven after his death and resurrection by taking his class on Good Friday to the top of the island's highest hill and launching a kite. When all the string was played out, he cut the string and the kite soared higher and higher until it disappeared into the heavens.

The Easter Season

The date of Easter varies each year because it is based on the lunar calendar, and Easter Sunday is celebrated on different dates by different Christian sects. Roman Catholics and most Protestants celebrate Easter on the first Sunday after the first full moon that occurs on or after March 21.

Holy Saturday, the Easter Vigil: This is a serious time, but in Mexico it is observed less solemnly, with many people making ugly effigies of Judas, who betrayed Jesus for 30 pieces of silver. They stuff them with candies and little gifts and firecrackers and then hang them up outside. When they set fire to them they explode and children scramble for the treats that burst forth from them.

Easter Sunday: This, the most joyous day of the Christian year, celebrates Christ's Resurrection three days after his death. In the eighth century the Venerable Bede, an English monk who was an eminent historian, speculated that the word *Easter* may have come from *Eostre*, the Anglo-Saxon name of a Teutonic goddess of spring and fertility whose symbol was a rabbit. This may explain the origin of the Easter Bunny. Eggs may have become a special Easter symbol of rebirth because for centuries they were among the foods forbidden during Lent. Coloring and decorating eggs, and taking part in Easter egg hunts and races, in which children roll eggs with spoons, are three very popular traditions among children at Easter.

In Hungary, Easter is called *Husvet* (The Feast of Meat) and the long Lenten fast is broken with a meatloaf made of chopped pork, ham, eggs, bread, and spices. Decorated Easter eggs, prepared in advance, are exchanged by children as a token of friendship.

In Poland, children and mothers make beautifully decorated Easter eggs called *pisanki* and on the Saturday night before Easter families take the eggs, along with bread, salt, and sugar, to church to be blessed. On Easter Sunday church bells, which have been silent during Lent, ring out to call families to church. After the service families gather for a holiday meal which starts when the blessed eggs are sliced and shared. The traditional Easter feast includes ham, sausages, salads, *babka* (the national cake) and *mazurki* (sweet cakes filled with nuts, fruit and honey). In the afternoon, friends and families go visiting.

Easter Monday: In Hungary, children put on old clothes to play *amigus*, an exuberant water-throwing game in which boys drench girls with water.

Forty Days after Easter, Ascension Day: In Florence, Italy, this day is celebrated with the *Festa del Grillo* (The Cricket Festival). Children catch or buy a cricket which they put into a little cage and take into the park along the Arno River. Afterwards they hang the cages outside their windows, and if they are lucky the crickets will sing.

Fifty Days after Easter, Pentecost: This is the anniversary of the day when the Holy Spirit inspired the apostles to begin preaching the Gospel (The Good News).

In Czechoslovakia, a special celebration called The Riding of the Kings is held on this day. Boys and girls are selected as kings and queens for the day, to ride in parades through their villages on horses decorated with flowers.

In Denmark, Pentecost is called *Pinse* and marks the coming of spring. Young people ride into the woods on bicycles and gather branches from the budding trees to decorate their homes.

In England and Commonwealth countries, the day is called Whitsunday (White Sunday) because traditionally this was the day on which people were baptized, usually wearing white clothes (white symbolizing purity). The following day, *Whitmonday*, is also a holiday in many countries, and in some English towns festive parades of children and adults are held, with the children wearing white and carrying flowers and banners.

In Germany, Pentecost marks the opening of the outdoor eating season. Families have picnics, and people with pet canaries hold contests to see which bird is the best singer; the winning canary has its cage decorated with flowers.

In the Netherlands, an old tradition of children bringing pet doves and pigeons, symbols of the Holy Spirit, to church on this day is observed.

Other Special Days

San Antonio's Day, January 17: Saint Anthony is known as the protector of animals. In many Latin American countries on his feast day both children and grownups take their pets and other animals to church to be blessed and guarded against accidents and disease for the coming year. In Mexico, children dress up their pets for the occasion. Church plazas are riotous with swarms of cows and donkeys painted with stripes or polka dots, rabbits wearing bonnets, parrots sporting neckties, hens and chickens, dogs and puppies, cats and kittens wearing dresses and coats. The barking, braying, meowing, mooing, quacking, and squealing throng in front of the church is blessed by a priest and sprinkled with holy water.

Santa Cruz: For three days in May in the Philippines, this fiesta commemorates the finding in 324 by Saint Helena, the mother of Constantine, of the cross on which Christ died. The star of the pageants featured during the celebration is a girl chosen to represent Empress Helena. She is escorted for three nights by her son Constantine, played by a little boy, leading processions of children. After each procession the *pabitin* (a large trellis made of bamboo, laden with fruits, candies and toys) is slowly lowered until it is within the children's reach and they grab for the prizes.

Children's Day: On the second Sunday in June in Protestant churches in America children sit together in the front pews and participate in church services, singing in the choir and reading scripture. This is an outgrowth of a European tradition when this was the day on which children joined the church. First observed in the United States in 1856 in Chelsea, Massachusetts, as "Rose Sunday," it was officially designated as a church holiday in 1868 by the Methodist Episcopal Church. Later it was adopted by the Presbyterians and other denominations.

Saint John's Day, June 24: This is the day on which the birthday of John the Baptist is celebrated. In French Canada, Saint Jean is the patron saint of the province of Quebec, which celebratres his feast day with parades, carnivals, bonfires, and street dancing. In Paraguay, this is the day to predict the future. On St. John's Eve each girl dreams of the man she will marry, and on the day itself people jump over bonfires for good luck, and young girls plant corn, believing its color will tell them whether their husbands will be dark or fair.

Buhé, August 10: In Ethiopia on this day the church celebrates the transfiguration of Christ which it considers the first sign of Jesus's supernatural powers. Families bake special breads on this day, small oval loaves reserved for groups of children who go from house to house singing. When they have collected a good supply of the Buhé bread, the children go off to eat it together and enjoy contests and games.

Saint Bartholomew's Day, August 24: In Germany, a race is held which originated centuries ago, to show that shepherds could run faster than any sheep that might go astray. Boys and girls race barefoot, and the winning "shepherd" and "shepherdess" each receive a sheep. After the race there are dances and games. In one traditional game each contestant balances a pail of water on his or her head and tries to carry it to the tub at the finish line; whoever pours the water into the tub first is the winner.

Saint Sergius of Randonezh Day, September 25: In Russia this feast day honors Sergius, who at the age of 20 was living as a hermit in a forest north of Moscow. He shared his food with all, even with a bear cub that used to visit him daily, and his feast day is a favorite among Russian Orthodox children because he enjoyed making toys for children.

Cosme e Damiao Day, September 27: In Brazil, Cosmos and Damian are considered patron saints of children. They were twin brothers from Syria, doctors who accepted no pay and who, while still very young, died for their faith. On this feast day people give their children candies and special dinners.

White Sunday, in October in Samoa: This is one of the best days of the year for children in Samoa. Parents give them new books and new clothes, usually white ones, which they wear to church in the morning. Starting with the church service, which the children lead, all traditional roles are reversed for the day. At home, where Samoan girls and boys normally begin cooking meals for their parents at the age of 10, the parents cook a special feast and do not eat until after the children have finished.

Halloween, October 31: Originally known as All Hallows' Eve, this was a serious time, the Eve of All Saints' Day when people would venerate all saints, especially those who have no special feast day of their own. For most people the idea of honoring dead saints through prayer has given way to that of remembering the dead by dressing up in costumes resembling skeletons and ghosts or witches and devils, and it has become an evening for children to break loose from the constraints of good behavior and play pranks, some harmless, some not. In recent years a much less harmful version of the evening has been primarily associated with "Trick or Treat" when youngsters in costume go door to door asking for handouts, threatening to play some "trick" on anyone who doesn't give them a "treat." Also, since the 1950s, millions of children have generously asked for contributions to UNICEF on Halloween rather than for cookies or candy as their "treat" and have raised more than $2 million to help children in developing nations. In 1967 U.S. President Lyndon Johnson, and every President since then, proclaimed October 31 as National UNICEF Day.

All Souls' Day, November 2: On this day Christians all over the world pray for and honor all those who have died and many visit cemeteries to put flowers on their families' graves.

In parts of England, children still follow an ancient custom, going from house to house "souling," asking for the "soul cakes" that in times past were offered to the dead.

In Sicily, children believe that if they pray for their ancestors at bedtime, the souls of the dead will bring them toys and candies during the night.

Hindu Festivals

There are several Hindu calendars. Most of them share 12 lunar months that range from 27 to 31 days in length, with an intercalary month approximately every 3 years. Each month is measured from full moon to full moon and is divided into a dark half, that of the waning moon, and a bright half, that of the waxing moon. The names of the months are:

- Chaitra (March–April)
- Vaisakha (April–May)
- Jayestha (May–June)
- Ashadha (June–July)
- Shravana (July–August)
- Bhadrapada (August–September)

- Asvina (September–October)
- Kartika (October–November)
- Marga or Mangsir (November–December)
- Pausa (December–January)
- Magha (January–February)
- Phalguna (February–March)

New Year's Day, in the Spring: In many parts of India, this is called Diwali (The Festival of Lights) and is celebrated on the first day of the bright half of Chaitra, but in northern India people celebrate it in the autumn (see page 59). In some areas Diwali is a day of exuberant mischief for children. Grownups are warned to wear old clothes when they go outdoors because children run around throwing colored powders at them.

In the Punjab and Bengal people celebrate the Solar New Year, when the sun enters the sign of Aries in mid-April. In Nepal the New Year also begins in the spring but is observed on the first day of Vaisakha.

Ram Navami (Rama's Birthday): This is observed on the ninth day of the bright half of Chaitra. According to Hindu belief Rama was the seventh incarnation of the god Vishnu. He is the hero of the *Ramayana*, one of India's greatest epics. On his birthday people retell stories from it and decorate themselves, buildings, and streets with designs made with colored powder, and hang garlands of flowers around the necks of friends. School children decorate the floors of their classrooms and themselves, especially their foreheads and cheeks, with pretty powder designs, and give garlands of fresh flowers to their teachers, visitors, and friends.

Teej: Starting on the third day of the bright half of Shravana, this honors Parvati (another name for Siva's wife) and also celebrates the coming of the monsoon rains in most parts of India. It is a traditional festival for girls and women, and the one time of year when women can leave their duties in their husbands' homes and return to their childhood homes to visit their parents, brothers, and sisters. Parvati is worshipped for two days and then her statue is taken through the streets in a parade with richly decorated elephants, camels, dancers, and singers. Swings are hung from trees and walls, and girls and women, in bright green costumes, swing and sing songs in praise of Parvati.

An especially festive observance of Teej takes place in Brindavan, where the child-god Krishna lived for a while. Statues of him and of Rhada, the milkmaid who was his first love, are placed on a huge swing made of silver and gold, stretched from one side to the other of the temple's inner courtyard. Crowds of pilgrims throw coins at the swing, and priests reciprocate by spraying holy water on the people. Plays reenacting events in Krishna's life are performed and the sacred roles of Krishna and Rhada are traditionally portrayed by children.

Janmashtami (Krishna's Birthday): On the eighth day of the dark half of Shravan, the eighth incarnation of Vishnu as Krishna is celebrated. This is one of the favorite festivals of Indians, especially of children. Many families put a plaster, brass, or ivory image of the baby Krishna in his cradle, surrounded by flowers, in their homes. They go to a temple where priests chant the story of Krishna's birth and childhood. People never tire of hearing about the pranks and games of this lovable little boy, and about how he enchanted milkmaids by playing his flute, the sound of which was so sublime that when he played it the reeds from which the flute had grown wept tears of delight, rivers slowed down to listen and grew lotuses for him, and the deer in the forest stood still attentively, ears erect.

At midnight, the hour of his birth, priests bring out a statue of the baby in his cradle and worshippers cry "*Vijay!*" (Victory!) and bathe Krishna in a nectar of milk, butter, honey, and sugar. People perform the dances that Krishna and the milkmaids used to dance by moonlight, and statues of Krishna are paraded through town in torchlight processions. The next day people throng to fairs for music, dancing, storytelling, and plays about his life. Boys dressed as Krishna compete in sports to win dishes of his favorite foods. One of their traditional games is to shimmy up a tall greased pole while people squirt water at them as they try to reach a pot of yogurt at its top. Another is to scramble on top of each other to try to break a pot that hangs high above them. These games are inspired by tales of how Krishna, as a little boy, loved milk and butter so much that they had to be kept in a pot high out of his reach.

Ganesh Chaturti: On the fourth day of the bright half of Bhadrapada, this festival honors Ganesh, the kindly Hindu god of good luck and prosperity, who is another favorite of Indian children. He was the son of Siva and Parvati, and one day he so provoked his father that Siva cut off his head! His mother begged her husband to replace it and, since an elephant was nearby, Siva gave him an elephant's head. An image of the elephant-headed god appears above many doors in India and many people ask for his help before beginning any new project. For his festival they decorate images of him and offer him foods he is supposed to like.

Pushkar Fair: For 10 days preceding the full moon in the month of Kartika this takes place in Pushkar, a desert village in the northwestern state of Rajasthan, one of the holiest places of pilgrimage in India. The name "Pushkar" means "full to the brim" in Sanskrit, and the lake is believed to have been created from a lotus petal that fell from the hand of Brahma, the Creator. Every year thousands of pilgrims come to bathe in its sacred waters and to worship in the only temple in India dedicated to Brahma. People set up tents around the lake to sell, buy, and trade camels, cattle, horses, goats, sheep, and donkeys. Children cram the streets, watching puppets enact stories from the *Ramayana*, eating *chappaties* (flat round pieces of whole-wheat bread), chewing on strips of sugar cane, playing games such as tug of war and musical chairs, and watching camel races. A contest called "camel rush" is held, in which as many men as possible pile on top of a camel, with a prize going to the camel that can hold the greatest number. There are about 10,000 camels at the fair, and fashionable ones receive fancy haircuts and perfumed shampoos.

Diwali, in Autumn: In northern India on the 15th day of the dark half of Kartika, "Ka Lakshmi," the Hindu goddess of wealth and prosperity, visits and blesses every home that is lit up to greet her. This "Festival of Lights" is celebrated in the spring in other parts of India (see page 58). In preparation for the goddess's visit, families clean and whitewash their homes, make beautiful paintings with colored powders on their floors and walls, and prepare *diyas* (little clay lamps). Flowers are hung over the front door, and special foods are cooked. On the morning of Diwali the family rises early. They visit relatives and exchange gifts. For the children there are gifts of candy, and in the afternoon fairs with rides and fireworks. At sunset the diyas are lit and the whole family joins in stringing row after row of lights along the roof, windows, and courtyard and on the road leading to their house, to guide Ka Lakshmi to their home.

Special Hindu Ceremonies Involving Children

Welcoming Newborns: When boys are born into Rajput families in northern India, they receive a noisy greeting. For 10 days there is drumming and singing outside the house. On the sixth day after a boy's birth, or the fifth day after a girl's, the baby is dressed for the first time.

On *Bahari*, the first Sunday after the birth, women gather in the family's courtyard to praise the goddess Bhamata, who brings children. The walls of the room where the baby was born have been painted with designs of gods and goddesses, and the mother now leaves this room for the first time, to present her baby to the assembled household and guests. After the tenth day, the baby can be named. The mother chooses her children's names, but until she has decided a son is called *lala*, meaning jewel, and a baby girl is called *lali*.

The first cutting of the baby's hair is a solemn event that occurs during the baby's first year. Relatives gather and the baby is taken on its first trip outside, to a temple, where the hair is offered at a family shrine.

Among Brahmins of Gujerat in northwestern India, the 12th day after birth is the time of name giving. Relatives come to the house and everyone eats a sweetmeat made of millet seed, coconut, and sugar. The baby's father's sister ties scarlet threads to the cradle and around the baby's waist, to ward off the Evil Eye, and then for the first time the baby is carried from the room where he was born into the main room of the house, where the floor has been reddened with clay and spread with green leaves. He is laid on a red silk sari, and four of his brothers and sisters or other close relatives take hold of the corners and swing him in it gently, while singing the naming song. The aunt announces the baby's name which she has chosen in accordance with strict rules. The first letter depends on what stars were in the sky when the child was born, and the name must also include the name of one of the gods. The baby also receives a second name which will be that of his father, and a third name, that of the father's family.

Birthdays: Hindu children celebrate their birthdays only until they are 16 years old, but before then, birthdays are festive. They start with early rising to dress in new clothes, to receive their parents' blessings, to say prayers at the *Puga*, the family shrine, and to go with the family to a temple bringing an offering of flowers, all before breakfast. At the temple the birthday child kneels before a priest who marks his or her forehead with a red or black dot. Then the child has the whole day off from school. Usually friends and relatives come for a midday dinner, after which there are games and presents. And sometimes a child of wealthy parents gives a party for orphans who have no family.

Upanayana, "the Beginning of Wisdom": This is a Hindu boy's second birth, a ceremony celebrated by those who belong to the three highest castes of Hindu society: Brahmins, who are priests and teachers; Kschatriyas, who are soldiers and rulers; and Vaisy, who are farmers, shopkeepers, and merchants. A Brahmin boy is usually eight years old when he goes through this ceremony; boys of the other two castes are usually ll or l2. An astrologer decides on an auspicious day for the ceremony.

The boy must spend the previous night in complete silence. In the morning he takes his place with his parents under a canopy in the courtyard outside his house. A barber arrives to cut his nails and shave his head, except for one long lock of hair on top, and the boy bathes and puts on clean clothes. Then he eats with his mother for the last time, because after the upanayana he will be a man and not allowed to eat with women.

If he is a Brahmin, after the meal he receives a sacred cord from his *guru* (teacher). It is a white cotton thread of three strands twisted together, the symbol of second birth. He holds this between the thumb and little finger of each hand while the guru recites a prayer for his strength, long life, and spiritual illumination. At the last words the boy slips the cord over his head and lets it hang from his right shoulder across his body to his left hip. He will wear this cord all his life as the sign that he is *dvija* (twice born), a full member of his people's religious community. Now his teacher pours water into the palms of the boy's hands, and then both the boy's and the guru's heads are veiled with a silk scarf while the guru whispers into his pupil's right ear the verse, "Let us meditate on the most excellent light of the Creator; may he guide our intellects." For the rest of his life the boy must repeat these words every day.

He is now no longer a child. That evening he performs the ritual of evening prayer, one of the daily duties of a Brahmin. And every year thereafter he will observe the anniversary of his rebirth.

Islamic Holidays

The Islamic calendar consists of l2 lunar months which alternate between 29 and 30 days. Because the moon's orbit is just over 29 days long, a leap day is added to the l2th month. There are no intercalary days to make the Islamic year of 354 days conform to the solar year of 365 days, so every solar year the calendar moves back ll days, which means that all Islamic holidays sooner or later occur in every month of the Gregorian year. The day begins at sunset, so holidays start on the eve of the date on which they are celebrated.

Ashura, the Tenth Day of the First Month: This commemorates the death of Imam Hussein, Mohammed's grandson, and is the major festival of the year for Shi'ite Muslims, who consider Hussein's father, Ali, Mohammed's legitimate successor. After Ali died, his son was on his way to claim leadership of the Muslim community when he and his party were surrounded by rivals and cut off from water. They refused to surrender and were killed on this day. In Iran, the Shi'ites observe the day with dramatic performances depicting Hussein's last days. A less solemn tradition is also associated with the day, which is enjoyed by children, commemorating the safe landing of Noah's ark. According to tradition, *Ashura*, a sweet pudding, filled with nuts and fruits, was made by Noah's wife for a family celebration when the flood ended. It is still eaten on this day.

Mulid (Mohammed's Birthday), the Twelfth Day of the Third Month: This, the most joyful day of the Muslim year, is observed as a national holiday in all Muslim countries. The minarets of mosques and domes of public buildings are illuminated with electric lights and decorated with banners, and in most cities there are fairs, parades, and feasts. Mohammed was born around A.D. 570 in Arabia in the town of Mecca. His birthplace was a small, humble house. It is said that 7,000 angels brought heavenly dew in a golden pitcher for the mother to wash the baby, and all living creatures of earth, air, and water greeted the birth with joy and cried out the creed that was to become the foundation of the Muslim faith: "There is no god but Allah and Mohammed is his prophet."

In Egypt cannons and firecrackers announce the birth at sunrise. People wear new clothes, visit their families and friends, and exchange gifts. In Indonesia celebrations last for almost the whole month. Festivities in Java start on the sixth day of the month with the opening of a fair, announced by the playing of gamelin orchestras in the courtyards of mosques. People gather to listen to stories about Mohammed's life and to sing songs of praise. In Libya, school children prepare a special decoration for the day, called *Khumasa*, a paper cone adorned with tinsel, bells, and ornaments topped by a hand, a symbol of protection and good luck. In Pakistan, big parades, with marching bands and troops of Boy and Girl Scouts, are held. Food is given away to the poor, sermons are preached, and passages of scripture are read through loudspeakers in the streets.

Nisfu Sha'ban, the Fourteenth Day of the Eighth Month: In some areas this is called *Lailat al Bara'a* (Night of Repentance) and in some called *Shab e Barat* (Night of Record). It is a night of spiritual preparation for the next month of Ramadan and is the time to settle old quarrels, to forgive, and to be forgiven. Tradition holds that on this night Allah approaches earth calling people to repent of their sins, and He records the deeds of each person that will shape his or her destiny during the coming year. In some countries this night is a solemn time to pray for the dead, and it is customary to visit cemeteries and to put fresh flowers on family graves, and to place oil lamps and candles at shrines. Although primarily an evening of prayerful vigils, in some parts of the world it is also a merrymaking festival, with fireworks, illuminated mosques, and friends and relatives gathering to exchange *halawinat* (sweets), some of which are exquisitely decorated with gold and silver leaf. Alms and sweets are also distributed to the poor.

Ramadan, the Ninth Month: This entire month is a time of fasting. An hour before sunrise, drumbeats or a call from the minaret of a mosque alert people to prepare a light morning meal. From the moment at dawn when a white thread can be distinguished from a black thread until sunset, when one can no longer distinguish between them, Muslims, except for children and the very old, may not eat, drink, or smoke. In Bahrain and Dubai, during this month, children go from house to house singing special songs in praise of those who fast. In return they receive handfuls of nuts and sweets which they collect in long cloth bags called *kees*.

The twenty-seventh night of Ramadan is called *ailat al Qadr* (The Night of Power). It is said that on this night the gates of paradise open and angels descend to bestow God's blessings on those who are at worship. This holiday commemorates the night when Mohammed received the first of many revelations from Allah, through the angel Gabriel. These revelations form the *Koran* (Reading), the Islamic scriptures, which children begin to study when they are young. A big celebration, *Khatma*, is held when children have read all 114 chapters of the Koran for the first time. Parents and friends take them from house to house and at each house they read some verses and receive congratulations, sweets, and other presents. Teachers also receive gifts on this day, in appreciation of their work with the children.

Eid Al Fitr, the First Day of the Tenth Month: This holiday signifies the breaking of the fast. On the first day of the tenth moon, cannons and drums announce that Ramadan is over, and three days of celebration begin. Children get presents, including new clothes.

After the family has gone to the mosque for prayer, they return home for a feast, their first midday meal in a whole month. Special foods, *saiwiyan* (thin noodles cooked with milk, sugar, and coconut) and *halvah* (a sweet made with ground nuts, sesame seeds, and honey) are served. In the afternoon friends and relatives visit each other, saying *Eid mumarak* (Blessed Eid) in greeting, and bringing coins and candy for the children. Usually a fair is also held, with magicians and jugglers, music, a miniature circus, fireworks, and camels and elephants to ride.

In Iraq, often puppet shows are given, and merry-go-rounds or ferris wheels are set up in town squares. In Nigeria, the celebrations begin with the Damask dance, in which the dancers, accompanied by drummers, wear colorful robes and carved wooden masks decorated with beads. In Pakistan, fireworks and feasts are given. In the Sudan, children receive red dolls holding paper fans made of candy. In Turkey, people call the day *Seker Bayrami* (the Candy Holiday). They dress up in traditional costumes and children are given money wrapped up in pretty embroidered handkerchiefs in addition to candy.

Eid Al Adha (the Feast of Sacrifice), the Tenth Day of the Twelfth Month: On this day Muslims sacrifice a cow, ram, or lamb, donating part of it to the poor and using the rest in a family feast. It commemorates the day when Ibrahim, about to sacrifice his son Ishmael as an offering to Allah, heard a voice from heaven telling him to sacrifice a ram instead. This is the Muslim version of the Old Testament story about Abraham and Isaac. Arabs believe they are descendants of Ishmael.

In Bahrain, children on this day follow a custom known as the Children's Sacrifice. Several weeks before, they have planted seeds of barley in little baskets which are hung on a wall and watered every day. By this day the seeds have sprouted, and after dinner the children feed their *hiya biyas*, as the sacrificial plants are called, with some food left over from the family's feast. Then, in groups, they walk along the beach singing songs and swinging their baskets until they finally toss them into the sea.

In Gambia, Mali, Mauritania, and Senegal, this day is called *Tabaski*. Children dress up in new clothes, usually miniature versions of those worn by their parents. Blue is the favorite color. Then families go on excursions. In front of every home a hole is dug to receive the parts of the lamb or goat that will not be eaten at the holiday feast. At least once during the holiday, boys are taken by their fathers to a mosque to pray.

Jewish Holidays

The year A.D. 2000 will be the Jewish year 5760. The Jewish calendar calculates years by the sun and months by the moon. Ten months alternate between 29 and 30 days, and two vary in length. A 13th intercalary leap month (Adar II) is added seven times to the lunar calendar in a 19-year cycle on the third, sixth, eighth, eleventh, fourteenth, seventeenth, and nineteenth years. Days are considered to begin at sunset, and the seventh day of every week, Saturday, is the *Sabbath*, a holy day of rest, on which Jews may not do any work because the seventh day was the one on which the Lord rested after completing His creation.

Rosh Hashanah (Head of the Year), **the First Day of the First Month:** This is the first of the *High Holy Days* or *Days of Awe*, a 10-day period of penitence and spiritual renewal that mark the beginning of the Jewish New Year. It is traditionally considered the anniversary of the creation of the world and a time to begin a better life as a partner in God's divine plan. According to rabbinic legend, God opens three books on this day. In the first are inscribed the names of the righteous, in the second the names of the wicked, and in the third the names of the average people who comprise the bulk of humanity. People are given 10 days to determine their own fate in the coming year, because the record is not sealed until twilight on the last day. Jews celebrate Rosh Hashanah by eating a special round loaf of *challah* bread, to remind them that the year always comes round to a new beginning, and apples dipped in honey, to make the New Year sweet.

Yom Kippur (the Day of Atonement), **the Tenth Day of the First Month:** This is the last and most solemn of the High Holy Days. Many Jews fast from sundown the day before until sunset on Yom Kippur. They pray to be forgiven the sins they have committed during the past year, and resolve to live well during the New Year. Some Jews act out their repentance dramatically by wearing rags on this day, weeping and tearing their hair and throwing possessions into the sea, to symbolize their discarding of bad habits.

Succoth (the Feast of Booths or Tabernacles), **the Fifteenth Day of the First Month:** This is the beginning of a seven-day harvest festival of thanksgiving which also commemorates the temporary shelters in which the wandering Israelites slept at night in the desert for 40 years after their Exodus from Egypt. To celebrate this festival, children help their parents and teachers build a *Succah*, a little hut, outside their home or on the roof or in front of their school or synagogue. They build it out of tree branches and decorate it with leaves, flowers, fruit, and paper designs. Inside the succah they put a table and chairs and four special plants—citron fruit, date palm, willow, and myrtle—which are held in both hands while a blessing is said. On each day of the festival people gather in the succah to recite prayers and to eat. The family may have wine and cakes there or, if weather permits, eat all their meals and even sleep there during the next week. The first two days of the festival are also celebrated in synagogues with special services in which worshippers carry young palm tree shoots tied together with twigs.

Simhat Torah ("Rejoicing in the Law"), **the Twenty-Third Day of the First Month:** This is the last day of Succoth, celebrated with parades and dancing. Every synagogue has hand-lettered scrolls of the *Torah*, the first five books of the Bible, and during a year of weekly Sabbath services the entire Torah is read. On this day the final book is completed and the cycle begins again. In celebration, people dance joyfully around the synagogue singing and passing the scrolls to each other. Children join the processsion, waving flags printed with miniature scrolls.

Hannukah (Feast of Lights), **the Twenty-Fifth Day of the Third Month:** This is the first of eight days commemorating a miracle said to have occurred more than 2,000 years ago. When the *Maccabees*, a small group of Jews fighting for religious freedom, gained control of their Temple in Jerusalem, they found only one day's supply of holy oil. They used it to light the *Menorah*, an eight-branched candelabra, and to their amazement the one day's supply of oil lasted for eight days, until a new supply arrived. Since then Jews have recalled this miracle by gathering around menorahs and lighting one candle on the first night, two on the second, and so on for eight successive nights. Special foods on these days include *latkes* (potato pancakes served with sour cream and applesauce), and there are prayers and songs, presents and stories for the children.

The evenings are a traditional time for games: cards, chess, and the children's favorite, a game played with a spinning top called a *dreidel*. It is played by Jewish children all over the world during the eight nights of Hannukah each year. Dreidels are four-sided tops that originated in medieval Germany. Traditionally they are made of wood or lead, but elaborate examples in silver also exist. On each of the four sides there is a Hebrew character or a Roman letter (N, G, H, and S). Two or more children gather around a table, with the dreidel in the middle. Each child has an equal number of coins or counters and each contributes two of them to the pot. Lots are drawn for the first spin. If the dreidel comes to rest with N uppermost, that player wins nothing and the player to his or her left then spins. If H is uppermost, the player wins half of the pot. If S lands uppermost, the player must contribute another counter to the pot. But if G comes up, the player wins the entire contents of the pot. Each time a player hits the jackpot, he or she scores one point, and the winner is the one who has the highest score out of 10 games.

Tu Bishvat ("The New Year for Trees"), **the Fifteenth Day of the Fifth Month:** On this day families in ancient Palestine used to plant a tree for each baby born during the year: cedars for boys and cypresses for girls. When a child married, his or her tree was cut down and used as a post for the traditional wedding canopy. Today, dressed in white and crowned with sprigs of evergreens, Israeli children plant trees that will grow almonds, dates, figs, lemons, oranges, or pomegranates, and they hold dances to celebrate spring-time.

Purim, the Fourteenth and Fifteenth Days of the Sixth Month: King Ahasuerus of Persia had a wicked adviser named Haman who wanted to kill all Jews, and who persuaded the King to draw a lot (*pur*) to decide the day for the slaughter. But the King's Queen Esther, who was Jewish, begged him to save her people, and because she was good and beautiful and the King loved her, he spared the Jews and instead had Haman hanged on the gallows that he had built for Mordecai, Esther's uncle. In memory of the brave Esther, who had risked the King's displeasure by defending her people, Mordecai commanded that the days of the Jews' deliverance should be remembered and celebrated forever in every generation, every province, every city, and every family. Jews do this by reading aloud the book of Esther in the Bible and children delight in drowning out every mention of Haman with noisemakers and stomping feet.

Pesach (Passover), **the Fourteenth Day of the Seventh Month:** On this evening, the first day of Passover, which lasts for eight days, Jews recall their escape under the leadership of Moses from Egypt where they had been slaves. The Pharaoh refused to let them go, even though God punished Egypt with many plagues. Finally Moses warned the Pharaoh that a tenth and final plague would kill all the Egyptians' firstborn sons if he would not let the Jews go. To protect their own firstborn sons, Jewish families sacrificed a lamb and sprinkled some of its blood on their doorsteps as a signal to the Angel of Death that these were Jewish, not Egyptian, homes. The Angel "passed over" their homes. After this dreadful prophecy had come true, the Pharaoh was finally convinced of the power of the Jews' God, so he relented and allowed the Jews to leave. In gratitude for their freedom Jewish families have ceremonial dinners every year called *seders* at which they serve special foods including *matzohs*, flat unleavened bread which recalls the haste with which the Jews had to leave their homes; they couldn't wait for their bread to rise. At these dinners, prayers are said and songs are sung, and the youngest boy present asks four questions beginning with, "Why is this night different from all other nights?" and his father retells the dramatic story of the Exodus.

Shavuot or Pentecost, the Sixth Day of the Ninth Month: This festival takes place seven weeks (Shavuoth) or 50 days (Pentecost) after Passover. In Biblical times it was an early summer festival during which the first fruits of the harvest were offered up to God at the

Temple in Jerusalem. Today green plants and flowers decorate synagogues and temples on the day, recalling its agricultural origin and also symbolizing the eternal greenness of the *Torah* (the Law), which has been described as the "tree of life." It is believed that on this day Moses returned from the top of Mount Sinai and brought his people two stone tablets containing God's Ten Commandments and the Israelites accepted these, the *Torah*, as their Covenant with God. In the Middle Ages Jewish boys first began *cheder* (Hebrew School) on this day, and there is a custom of placing a drop of honey on the page when a Jewish child first starts religious studies. Dishes made from milk and honey are eaten on Shavuoth, to symbolize the great joy of studying the Torah which is called "as nutritious as milk and as sweet as honey." Scholars are the most respected members of the Jewish community, and the study of the Torah is the highest ideal held before every Jewish boy.

Other Special Ceremonies for Jewish Children

Bar Mitzvah: In Israel and in Jewish communities all over the world a boy's childhood officially ends on his thirteenth birthday. He then becomes Bar Mitzvah (a Son of the Commandment) and is responsible for a man's religious duties of prayer, fasting, and attendance at synagogue. To prepare for this day, boys are trained in the Jewish faith and learn to recite prayers and to read the Hebrew scriptures.

When the day arrives a boy's father gives him a full-sized prayer shawl, with which he is to cover his head from now on when he prays, and the *tephillin*, two narrow strips of black leather with a square box attached, containing Bible texts from the books of Exodus and Deuteronomy on small pieces of parchment which he is supposed to wear from now on when he says his daily prayers. One of the tephillin must be bound around his left arm near his heart, the other to his forehead near the brain, before he starts to pray, to remind him that he should both love and study the holy words.

On the Sabbath following his thirteenth birthday the boy goes to the synagogue and during the service is called to the desk to give a short speech he has written in which he thanks his parents and teachers and promises to follow in the ways they have taught him. Afterwards. his family gives a gala feast in his honor, with many invited friends and relatives, who bring him lavish presents. This is the biggest day in a Jewish boy's life.

In recent years some Jews have added a corresponding ceremony for girls called **Bat Mitzvah.**

CHILD SAINTS, VISIONARIES, AND MARTYRS

From ancient times to the present there have been amazing instances of children who have had an intense prayer life, have reported seeing visions, and have made heroic sacrifices for their faith. A remarkable thing about these children is their insistence on the reality of their religious experiences even when facing ridicule and severe punishments, including threats of death and death itself, for their "stubborn lying." These have been children who otherwise were not disobedient or mentally unbalanced. They have demonstrated a remarkable unity spiritually, with their trust in and love for God and belief in miracles, and psychologically, showing exceptional independence, courage, and determination that transcend differences in creeds and cultural influences. Also surprising has been the strong and enduring influence they have had on adults.

Adele Roncalli: In 1944, when seven years old in Bergamo, Italy, she reported seeing the Virgin Mary 12 times and "the miracle of the sun," an apparition in which the sun appears to spin and hurl itself towards the earth at a frightening speed. After her visions, 200 miracles were reported in Bergamo, 70 of which were accepted by officials of the Catholic Church as authentic.

Agnes: In A.D. 304 at the age of 12 or 13 this Roman girl was put to death, for refusing to marry and to deny her faith, by the Roman Emperor Diocletian who had outlawed Christianity. Her grave in Rome was marked "Agne Sanctissima" which means Most Holy Lamb. Her feast day is January 21 and she is the patron saint of young girls and of Catholic Girl Scouts.

Bernadette Soubirous (1844–1879): At 11 A.M. on February 11, 1858, this frail, shy, and illiterate 14-year-old girl of a poor family was gathering firewood when she suddenly saw a beautiful lady in a grotto near the village of Lourdes, in France. The vision returned to her 17 more times between February and July and talked to her, identifying herself as The Immaculate Conception, a term Bernadette did not understand (she had flunked her catechism class). She said the Lady instructed her to tell the parish priest to have a shrine built on this spot, but when she did he ridiculed and scolded her, and her parents beat her for making up such an absurd story.

During one of the visions the Lady told Bernadette to dig in the ground. Observers, who could not see or hear the Lady but who were transfixed by Bernadette's ecstatic expression, feared she had gone mad when she began scratching the ground, but suddenly a spring of fresh water gushed up. A mother dipped her ill baby in the icy water, against onlookers' advice, and the baby was immediately cured. The spring has never ceased to flow, yielding 22,000 liters of water a day, and every year three million people come to Lourdes from all over the world to bathe in this water, many of them reporting cures of serious illnesses and infirmities. A medical bureau made up of physicians of all creeds and of none has amassed immense documentation of inexplicable cures. Despite the fact that people with open sores and contagious diseases have been bathing together in this water for almost 40 years, there has never been an epidemic, something of a miracle in itself.

> To those who believe in God no explanation is necessary; to those who do not believe in God no explanation is possible.
>
> —*Franz Werfel in* The Song of Bernadette *(1941)*

In 1866 Bernadette joined the Sisters of Charity at St. Gildard in Nevers and thereafter lived a quiet humble life as a nun. One day after being told to describe her childhood experiences to a visitor who said, "I can't believe it," she rather saucily replied, "I am only required to tell you what happened, not to make you believe it."

Her visions were declared genuine by the Pope in 1862 and she was canonized in 1933. Her feast day is April 16. Her body, which has not decomposed, lies in her convent in a glass coffin, and she has a sweet, peaceful expression on her lovely face. Franz Werfel wrote her biography, *The Song of Bernadette*, which was translated into English in 1941. In 1943 it was made into an impressive film starring Jennifer Jones, who received an Oscar for her portrayal of Bernadette.

Brigid (c. A.D. 450–525): An Irish girl, also known as Bridget (which means bride), was born a slave and later was influential in abolishing slavery in Ireland. She spent her childhood and much of her adult life as a dairymaid, even after she founded a religious order and became the Mother Abbess of a community of 13,000 nuns in Kildare, the first convent built in Ireland. She eventually founded three other monasteries.

Although a dairymaid, she was intellectual and is often depicted with a shepherdess's staff in one hand and a book in the other. The Irish call her "sweet Saint Bride of the yellow, yellow hair." While still a young child she became renowned for her beauty, as well as for her charity and many miracles. Among the popular stories about her is one about when she was sent to a dairy to bring home some butter. On the way home from the dairy she gave it all away to the poor. To protect her from being scolded, the Lord rewarded her kindness and the pail was miraculously refilled with the sweetest butter anyone had ever tasted. She was reputed to cure the sick and the insane, to heal lepers, and to give sight to the blind. But she was a real child, also known for falling asleep while Saint Patrick was preaching. Along with Saint Patrick and Saint Columba, she is a patron saint of Ireland, as well as of people in the dairy industry. Her feast day is February 1.

Children of Fatima: On May 13, 1917, three Portuguese youngsters, ten-year-old Lucia de Jesus, and her cousins, nine-year-old Francisco Marto and seven-year-old Jacinta Marto,

> Thou hast hidden these things from the wise and prudent, and hast revealed thrm unto babes. Out of the muths of babes and sucklings hast thou perfected praise.
>
> *—St. Matthew's Gospel (21:16)*

were looking after their parents' flock of sheep at the Cova da Iria, a mile from the village of Fatima where they lived, when they saw a mysterious Lady. Francisco saw her but did not hear anything, but the two girls heard her say she was from heaven and that she would return on the thirteenth day of each month until October 13 when she would tell them who she was and send a sign so that people would believe them. In the meantime they were to say the Rosary every day. When they told their parents about this they were scolded and beaten for lying, but they stuck to their story and went back to the Cova on the 13th of each month. More and more curious people joined them, none seeing anything except a light around the rapt faces of the children. The crowds finally became so great that the Government was concerned about the public health hazard, since there were no roads or accommodations or water in the Cova. (Later a spring appeared, which now provides drinking water for the never-ceasing flow of pilgrims.) So the children were arrested and separated, each being told that the others had admitted they made the story up, and that they would be killed unless all of them admitted it. In spite of how terrified they were, none of them recanted, and they were finally released.

On October 13 enormous crowds, including skeptical newspaper reporters from Lisbon, gathered, even though it was raining heavily. Suddenly the rain stopped and the assembled people saw "the miracle of the sun," whirling in the sky like a Catherine wheel and then descending towards them. Many people got hysterical, thinking it was the end of the world, but after 10 minutes, just as it seemed about to crash onto them, the sun returned to its normal place in the sky. The strange phenomenon was described in the press, along with the message given to Lucia and Jacinta from the Lady, that she was the Queen of Heaven and that everyone should pray for world peace and that they should particularly pray for the conversion of Russia. World War I was in its second year and the United States had just entered it. This message was delivered to unsophisticated children who knew nothing about world politics, in the very month when the Bolsheviks took power, so a great many people took it seriously as a supernatural warning.

After a seven-year canonical investigation, the Catholic Church authorized devotion to Our Lady of Fatima, and she became the Patron Saint of Portugal. Today the Cova is no longer the serene, quiet, and isolated rural pastureland it was in 1917; the area now contains roads, hotels, restaurants, souvenir shops, a convent and retreat house, and a basilica that is a beautiful example of Portuguese architecture. On either side of its main altar are two tiny graves perpetually decorated with flowers; Jacinta and Francisco died two years after the visions. Lucia became a nun and has lived into her late seventies. Pope John Paul II attributed his survival after an assassination attempt which occurred on an anniversary of the children's vision, to the intercession of Our Lady of Fatima and in gratitude and obedience to one of her supposed requests, he consecrated Russia to her in the 1990s. A large international organization of devotees called the Blue Army believes that the collapse of Communism in Russia was due to the intervention of Our Lady of Fatima.

Children of La Salette: Two French peasant children, Melanie Mathieu, 14, and Maximin Giruad, 11, said they saw a vision of Mary as a sorrowful, weeping figure on September 19, 1846, on a mountain in the French Alps, near the town of La Salette. She gave them a message, they said, about the need for penance to atone for the world's many sins. The Bishop of Grenoble decided the apparition was credible, and five years later her message was delivered to Pope Pius IX. Devotion to Mary under the title of Our Lady of La Salette was authorized, and a missionary order of priests of La Salette was established. The shrine's church became a basilica in 1879.

Children of Medjugorje: Since 1981 in this village in Bosnia-Herzegovina in the former Yugoslavia, seven boys and girls have reported having daily or weekly visions and conversations with the Virgin Mary. In every other respect the children, some of whom are now young adults, are normal; they are attractive, intelligent, articulate, and friendly. Pilgrims from all over the world began thronging to the village and many have returned home to report inspiring and even miraculous experiences. When Yugoslavia was still Yugoslavia, its Communist and officially atheist government did not discourage believers from coming, because it welcomed the prospect of a profitable increase in tourism. And religious authorities did not discourage them either. The local Bishop

> Children and fools speak the truth.
>
> —*French Proverb*

did not believe in the revelations, and some other church authorities consider them out-and-out frauds; but the Franciscan priests who have been the children's spiritual directors do believe in them, so despite his skepticism the Bishop allowed curiosity seekers and believers to visit. The village became a major site of pilgrimages, attracting more than 10 million visitors in the 1980s, and people continued to come even after civil war broke out in 1991, making it not only a difficult place to get to but a dangerous one. Several books have been written about Medjugorje, with interviews and photos of the young seers, by both supporters and denouncers.

Children of Pontmain: On January 7, 1871, in Pontmain, Belgium, the Virgin is alleged to have appeared to several children: Eugene Barbedette, the 12-year-old son of a farmer living in the village, his 10-year-old brother Joseph Barbedette, and Francoise Richher and Jeanne Marie Lebosse, children from neighboring cottages who were called in to witness the sight. They all said she was very tall, wearing a blue robe studded with stars. A crown of gold was on her head and a red line ran around it, which they said symbolized the blood shed by Christ for the sins of the world. There was a scroll beneath her feet on which was written, "Pray, my children. God will hear you, and in a little while my Son will be moved." The parents, pastor and other adults present at the time could see nothing. Only these four children, one sick child, and a baby in its grandmother's arms reacted— the baby smiled and reached out towards the apparition.

Clare of Assisi (1194–1253): When she was a beautiful and rich 15-year-old, Clare horrified her family by running away from home and from an ardent suitor to join her friend Francis, who had left his own wealthy family to live as a beggar and to found the Franciscan Brothers in the year 1209. When she was 19 Clare founded an associate order for women, the Poor Clares. Her mother at first strongly disapproved of Clare's unconventional life style, but later she and Clare's two sisters joined her order. Clare was canonized two years after she died. Her feast day is August 12.

David (c. 1060–962 B.C.): A shepherd boy in Bethlehem, David spent his days tending sheep, playing the harp, composing psalms of great beauty, and "dancing before the Lord." He was unexpectedly annointed by the prophet Samuel who prophesied that he would be the successor of Saul, the first King of Israel. The boy showed extraordinary courage by volunteering to confront the Philistine giant Goliath, who was terrorizing Jewish soldiers, and to everyone's astonishment slaying him with a slingshot. He was brought to serve in King Saul's court, where he formed a deep friendship with Saul's son Jonathan and later married Saul's daughter Michal. His enormous popularity, however, aroused Saul's jealousy and he was exiled until after Saul's death in 1010 B.C. when he became the second King of Israel and made Jerusalem (The City of David) his capital. He has been immortalized by great sculptors such as Donatello and Michelangelo, and the Catholic Church has made him the patron saint of poets.

Guru Nanak (1469–1539): The founder of the Sikh faith, Nanak as a young boy was put to work by his father tending cattle. One day, overcome by heat, he fell asleep. A cobra slithered out of a nearby hole and spread out its hood to shade his face from the sun. A few minutes later Rai Bular, the Muslim landlord for whom Nanak's father worked, happened to pass by. Seeing the cobra near Nanak and thinking the boy was in danger, he walked cautiously towards him, but as soon as the cobra saw him it slid back into its hole. Rai Bular took this as a sign that the boy was a favored saint who should not be treated as an ordinary child. When Nanak was in his late teens he married. He led an exemplary family life and had two children. His followers believe he was demonstrating that the family is a school in which self-love is exalted into love for others and that to earn an honest living is a prerequisite of godliness. There is no divorce among Sikhs.

Guru Har Krishan (1656–1664): The youngest of all the Sikh gurus, he was just over five years old when he became Guru, but he fulfilled his duties seriously for three years until he died of smallpox at age eight. His father, the seventh Guru, had chosen him as his successor over his older brother Ram Rai, who refused to accept their father's decision and placed his case before the Muslim Emperor Aurangzeb. Har Krishan went to Delhi at the Emperor's command, meeting many people along the way and explaining to them the principles of Guru Nanak's religion, and blessing and curing the sick. The Emperor was impressed and decreed that Ram Rai's claim was false. There was a severe outbreak of cholera while Guru Har Krishan was in Delhi, and many died. People prayed to him to save them. He sent for a jug of water, touched it, said a short prayer and then said, "Mix this water with the water from the reservoir; everyone who takes a sip of it will be cured," which proved to be true.

Jakob Bohme (1575–1624): A happy little boy, born near Gorlitz in Germany, Jakob in later life compared the life of angels to the life of children in May gathering wild flowers. He became apprenticed to a shoemaker and one day a stranger, "with a severe but friendly countenance," after buying some shoes from him, said: "Jakob, thou art little but shall be great, such a one as at whom the world will wonder." He began thinking a lot about God and once, for seven days, was "surrounded with a divine light," the first of his many mystical experiences. The poet Angelus Silesius wrote of him:

> Nearer the gate of Paradise
> than we, Our children
> breathe its air, its angels see.
>
> —*Richard Henry Stoddard (1825–1903)*

> Fish in water live, and plants in earth,
> And fowl in air, and sun in firmament,
> Fire is a salamander's rightful home
> And God's own heart is Bohme's element.

After Bohme grew up he wrote a number of books which got him in trouble. The minister of Gorlitz considered him a heretic and ordered him to write no more. But he did, and his philosophical writings became known and admired in many countries.

Jeanne d'Arc or **Joan of Arc** (1412–1431): A French peasant girl, Joan was born and reared in Domremy, a small village in Lorraine, a peaceful rural section of France, during a period when most of the nation was torn by civil war and by English invaders. As a child she tended her father's sheep, helped to plough the family's 50-acre farm, and became a skilled seamstress. She played in the fields, singing and dancing with her three brothers and little sister. One summer morning when she was 13 she was picking flowers when a dazzling light shone by her right hand. She was frightened because from the midst of the light a voice came telling her she should seek the Dauphin, the un-crowned King of France, rescue him from his foes, and crown him at Rheims. Years before she was born there had been a prophecy that France would be restored by a Maid. She told no one about this experience, but she became more pious, helping the poor and praying so much that her neighbors thought her ridiculous. For three years she continued to hear voices from Saint Catherine, Saint Margaret, and the archangel Michael, sometimes two or three times a week. Later she said, "I saw them with the eyes of my body, as plainly as I see you now; and when they went away, I would cry."

In 1428, when she was 16, she finally got up the courage to follow their instructions and left home, telling people that "within the year" the king would be crowned at Rheims.

She managed to persuade some soldiers to follow her and was given a horse and a suit of armor. She amazed people by making prophecies that proved accurate and leading her soldiers to victories in Orleans and other cities against great odds. She finally met the Dauphin and gave him a secret sign that to him proved she was from God. On July 17, 1429, she led him into the cathedral at Rheims where he was crowned king.

After that Joan heard no more voices and everything she did was on her own unaided judgment. She began to make mistakes, eventually getting captured, chained around her neck, arms, and legs, tried by a church court as a heretic and a witch and finally, at age 19, burned at the stake. Her ashes were thrown into the Seine along with her heart, which the fire had not consumed.

At a retrial held 17 years after her death, she was declared innocent. She was canonized in 1920 and is now the patroness of France. Her official feast day according to the Church is May 30, but the city of Orleans honors "the Maid of Orleans" on May 8, the anniversary of the city's liberation by her. The rest of France celebrates her life on May 2. She has inspired many works of art, including a novel by Mark Twain, which he considered the most important book he ever wrote, and a great play by George Bernard Shaw.

Joseph Smith (1805–1844): This American farm boy born in Vermont, the fourth of nine children, who had very little education, for a long time wondered if "a Supreme Being did exist" but he developed a strong faith resting, as he wrote, on the beauty of the created universe: "the sun the glorious luminary of the earth and also the moon rolling in their magesty [sic; this and all other misspellings and punctuation in quotes are left as they were in his writings]. through the heavens and also the Stars shining in their courses and the earth also upon which I stood and the beasts of the field and the fowls of heaven and the fish of the waters. All these bespoke an omnipotent and omniprasant power a being who makith Laws and Decreth and bindeth all things in their rounds."

At 12 he came across the Bible verse that said, "if any of you lack wisdom, let him ask of Him that giveth to all men liberally," and for the next three years he studied the scriptures seriously, "Believing as I was taught that they contained the word of God." But he remained confused by the failings of Christians he knew and "this was a grief to my Soul. I pondered many things in my heart concerning the sittuation of the world of mankind the contentions and divisions the wickedness and abominations and the darkness which pervaded the minds of mankind my mind became exceedingly distressed . . . by searching the Scriptures I found that mankind did not come unto the Lord that they had apostisised from the true and liveing faith and there was no society or denomination that built upon the Gospel of Jesus Christ in the new testament and I felt to mourn for my own Sins and the Sins of the world."

At 15 he had his first vision. He had gone into a clearing in the woods and a "pillar of light" came down and rested on him and he was "filld with the spirit of God." Later he understood this to be the opening event in a new dispensation of the Gospel. It convinced him that all Christian sects were man-made and that God had chosen him to restore the Church.

At 22 he received further visions, including very special visitations in 1827 from an angel who called himself Moroni and who, Joseph said, gave him a book written in strange hieroglyphics on golden plates, telling the early history of the true church in America. He claimed it was written by a prophet named Mormon who said Christ appeared after His ascension and established a church in the New World.

Joseph also claimed to have translated this book with miraculous aid. In 1830 when he was 25 he published it in Palmyra, New York, as *The Book of Mormon,* and that same year he became the founder, first prophet, and elder of the Church of Jesus Christ of Latter-day Saints (Mormons). He acquired followers rapidly, but when he was 39 he was arrested by non-Mormons in Illinois and killed by a mob. Nevertheless, the church he founded has thrived and is now one of the fastest growing religions in the world.

Maria Goretti (1890–1902): An unusually pretty and pious Italian peasant girl, Maria Goretti was murdered at age 11 while resisting the sexual advances of a 19-year-old boy who was the son of her father's business partner. As she was dying she forgave the boy. He later served a long prison term for rape and murder, during which he had a vision of Maria and repented. He was present at her canonization by Pope Pius XII in 1950. She is upheld to the young as a model of purity. Her feast day is July 6. In 1987 a movie, narrated by Malcolm Muggeridge, was made of her life.

Martin de Porres (1579–1639): A mulatto son of a Spanish knight and a colored freed woman who lived in Lima, Peru from his earliest days Martin was gentle and loving, but these traits were not always appreciated by his mother. When she sent him out to buy food, he too often could not resist giving it to someone he thought was needier than he was. He would return home empty-handed to get a severe scolding. He also had as strong a love of animals as St. Francis of Assisi, including those most people consider pests, such as mice and rats, and would protect and feed them (as well as talk to them).

He and his younger sister Juana were parted from their mother for a while during their childhood, living in Ecuador with a wealthy great-uncle who wanted to educate them. They learned to read and write, and when Martin returned to Lima he became an apprentice to a man who was a doctor, druggist, and barber surgeon. Martin studied hard, reading all the books about medicine that he could find in order to help poor sick people.

When Martin grew up he went to live in St. Dominic's monastery in Lima where he served the monks as a doorkeeper and barber. At first he annoyed the friars as much as he had annoyed his mother, because he treasured even the vermin that nibbled at the monastery vestments, excusing their behavior on the grounds that "the poor little things are insufficiently fed." But gradually the monks accepted Martin's eccentricity because after he had talked to the little creatures and kept them well fed, they stopped bothering anyone.

After a while Martin opened a hospital at the monastery so that he could care for people who were sick or hurt or hungry. Phyllis McGinley, in her book *Saint Watching,* said Martin constituted himself as a one-man Humane Society, also keeping a hospital for dogs and cats at his sister's house. Strangely, it seems that in addition to helping people and animals in Lima, he helped others. After his death thousands of people came from far and near, even from foreign lands, to pay tribute to him, claiming they had seen him caring for the sick and helping the poor in other parts of the world, even while other people had seen him in the monastery in Lima. This is one of the very few instances in history when the Catholic Church has claimed that someone could bilocate.

Phyllis McGinley also tells us that Martin was a friend of Rose of Lima (see below) and that he performed more "miracles of love" than she did. However, unlike her, he was not an ascetic, and his gentle approach to life was so much less dramatic than hers that it had less appeal to people in the violent sixteenth century than Rose's "heroic" approach to sanctity did, so that it was many centuries before "this gentlest of holy men" was canonized in 1962.

Rose of Lima (1586–1617): A beautiful girl born to a wealthy family in Peru, Rose disappointed her mother greatly as a child because she did not want to live a high-society life and went to bizarre lengths to avoid it. She was so afraid flattery would make her proud that she cut her hair in an unbecoming style, wore a hair shirt under her ball gowns, pierced her flesh with pins under her elegant white gloves, and slept on a bed on which she sprinkled broken glass. She wanted to become a nun but her parents wouldn't allow it, so instead she persuaded them to let her turn their garden house into a chapel, and she spent most of her time there in meditation and prayer. It was said that mosquitoes swarmed around the place and often bit her visitors but wouldn't bite her. She refused to marry, and spent most of her time when she wasn't in prayer visiting and helping the poor, not considered a seemly activity for an aristocratic young girl in those days. Later her family lost its money and she tended them with the same devotion she had bestowed on other poor people. When she died there was an outpouring of the entire population of Lima, and she became the patron saint of South America and of the Philippines, as well as of schoolgirls. She was the first person born in the Western Hemisphere to be canonized, in 1671. Her feast day is August 23.

Solomon (c. 973–c. 933 B.C.): The son of David and his favorite wife Bathsheba, Solomon became King of Israel after his father's death. He was noted for his wealth and wisdom; even as a child his wisdom was legendary. When 13 he managed to settle amicably a bitter property dispute. His father had decided the treasure in question should be divided between the claimants, but Solomon discovered that the plaintiff had a son and the defendant a daughter, so he said, "If you will adjust your strife so as to do no injustice to the other, unite your children in marriage and give this treasure as their dowry." This was a precursor of his famous decision described in the Bible (1 Kings 3: 16–20) in the case of two women each claiming to be the mother of the same baby. He proposed that the baby be killed so that each could have half. When one of the women cried out, "No, no, no, let her have the child!" he said, "This is the real mother" and gave it unharmed to the woman who preferred giving up child's life to giving up her own claim on it.

Tekakwitha (1656–1680): Later known as Kateri, the Lily of the Mohawks, Tekakwitha was an American Indian girl born in a log cabin in a small village called Ossernenon (today Auriesville) in the Mohawk Valley in New York State. As a papoose she napped tied to a cradle-board swinging from a tree or carried on her mother's back. As a toddler she wore fur coats provided by her hunter father, and slept in a bed made of fur. until her parents, aunt, baby brother, and she all fell sick and she was the only survivor. She got better but her eyes never got quite well and pained her all the rest of her life. She was then taken to a village where her uncle was Chief Great Wolf of the Indian tribe, the Turtles. Almost every day she went into the woods standing very still listening for God, loving Him, and trying to find ways to please Him. She never went to a school but learned to plant and grow corn, to cook it into corn pudding, to embroider and make her clothes out of leather, decorating them with shells, beads, and porcupine quills.

Eventually some Blackrobes (Jesuit priests) came to visit her village. Tekakwitha did all the cooking and serving for them and they said they had never seen such a sweet girl. She watched the fathers when they were praying and tried to pray like them, learning to kneel and make the sign of the cross. In the woods she cut down a little birch tree, tying two sticks together with the band of wampum from her forehead to make a white cross, then planting it upright with some red berries placed at the foot. She often went there to pray. Then, a few years later, some more Blackrobes arrived in a canoe to stay, building a little church out of logs. She came there every day, and told Father Jacques de Lambertville that she longed to be baptized. He baptized her that Easter, giving her a new name, Kateri, which means white, or pure.

One day her uncle told her he had found a handsome husband for her. Crying, she said, "Thank you, but I am never going to be married. I want to be like the Blackrobes with only God to love and work for. I have promised God I will not marry." Other children in the village began to hiss at her and taunt her for being a Christian, but she never answered back. One boy once ran after her waving a tomahawk, saying, "Give up being a Christian or I'll kill you." He meant it, but when she bowed her head and answered, "You can take away my life, but you cannot take away my faith," he admired her courage so much that he spared her.

Sorry to see she was being persecuted for her faith, Father de Lambertville decided to help her go to live in another village, La Prairie in Canada, where other Blackrobes and Christian Indians lived. He sent her a young Christian Indian named Hot Ashes to be her guide. They walked for many miles until Kateri's feet were scratched and bleeding and her eyes hurt. They ate wild grapes, berries, and nuts, and caught fish to roast, following the Hudson River to Lake George (then called the Lake of the Blessed Sacrament) where Hot Ashes had left his canoe. At last they came to the St. Lawrence River, following it to the village of La Prairie, which looked very much like the one she had left, but it was clean and the people were different, going to Mass every day and not fighting or stealing from each other. She loved it there, and the priests used to find her in church every day even in the bitter cold winter, at four o'clock in the morning. She lived there for three years until she died.

After her death miracles were reported by people who prayed to her. A little boy named Rocco who was blind and sick got well and able to see again after his mother prayed to Kateri, and a three-year-old girl who was blind gained her eyesight and lived for many years as a teacher. Today there are two large shrines dedicated to Kateri at Auriesville, New York, and at Caughnawauga, Canada, near Montreal. She was beatified on June 22, 1980, and her feast day is July 14.

Teresa of Jesus, or **Teresa of Ávila** (1515–1582): At the age of seven this daughter of a noble family in Spain was so inspired by reading dramatic tales about Christian martyrs that she ran away from home with her four-year-old brother in order to die for Christ in the land of the Moors. Fortunately, the two were soon found and brought home. When she was 12 her mother died. Teresa was grief-stricken. She asked the Blessed Mother to be her mother from then on, and she was convinced that this prayer was decisive for her life. She entered the Carmelite convent in Ávila at 19 and later founded 17 other convents and 15 monasteries. She was a reformer of the Carmelite Order, ruling strictly and with great executive ability, but also with humor (once she said, "God deliver us from sad saints") and with common sense (at another time, when a novice fainted after receiving Holy Communion, she told her it happened not because of anything mystical but because she was hungry from too much fasting, and ordered her to eat).

She went from success to success, explaining that "by myself I can do nothing, but God and Teresa together are a majority." Yet her life was not always smooth sailing. She compared life to "a night in an uncomfortable inn" and once, when things had gone particularly badly, she raised her fist and cried out to God, "If this is how You treat Your friends, no wonder You have so few of them!"

She was, above all, one of the greatest mystics who ever lived, having many visions, and she wrote extensively: many poems, both whimsical and serious; meditations on prayer and on scripture; an autobiography; and her two masterpieces, luminous guides to the spiritual life, *El Camino de la Perfeccion* (The Way of Perfection) and *El Castillo Interior* (The Interior Castle). She was canonized in 1622 and occupies a unique place in Christian history. She was such a profound teacher of mystical theology that in 1970 she was officially proclaimed a Doctor of the Church, the only woman ever to have received this honor. Her feast day is October 15.

Thérèse of Lisieux, also known as **Thérèse of the Child Jesus, the Little Teresa,** and **The Little Flower** (1873–1897): Born in Alençon, France, the youngest of nine children, Thérèse had a happy childhood in a loving and deeply religious family. Her mother was an energetic, affectionate, witty, and bright woman who suffered through the deaths of several of her children, and who was one of the first working mothers, helping to support her family as a maker of lace. She held her children to high standards but never scolded them for an unintentional fault or mistake. She died when Thérèse was not yet five, but Thérèse's father and older sisters took over the mother role very well, until the sisters left home to become nuns in the town's Carmelite convent. From an extremely early age Thérèse was exceptionally devout yet spirited and independent. She aspired to be a saint and to save souls. Reading about a murderer who was to be executed, she wrote him comforting letters and was thrilled when she learned he had repented.

She had lots of delightful toys, which are preserved in her childhood home, but her favorite was a miniature altar where she pretended to be a priest and say Mass. She seriously wanted to be a missionary priest but since church rules made that impossible, she "adopted" two missionary priests, becoming their lifelong correspondent and benefactor, and for herself decided the next best thing was to become a nun like her sisters. "Not being able to be a missionary in action," she explained, "I wished to be one through love and penance; I understood that Love encompasses all vocations...that it embraces all times and all places . . . in a word, that it is eternal." After her death and canonization, the Pope named her Patron of the Missions, so in a way she eventually got her first wish after all.

At 14, on her one trip abroad, a pilgrimage to Rome, she took part in a public audience with the Pope and shocked people by audaciously breaking through the crowd and asking for and getting the Pope's permission to enter Carmel before the prescribed age. She became a Carmelite nun at 15.

In her autobiography, *The Story of a Soul,* written at her sisters' request, she noted down her childhood memories and thoughts, describing her "Way of Spiritual Childhood" or "The Little Way," a way to be holy even if one has no great opportunities for heroism or great talent, intellect, or influence. In it she said, "I rejoice in being little, because only children and those who are like them will be invited to the heavenly banquet." Recalling her childhood, she wrote, "I understood that to become a saint, there is only one single thing to do during the night of this life. . . .we must see life in its true light; it is an instant between two eternities. . . .to love Jesus with all the strength of one's heart . . . Prayer and sacrifice are the invincible weapons Jesus has given me." Her "little way" to holiness meant that the smallest thing done for love of God and neighbor would do, from not complaining if someone splashed one's clothes to being gracious and kind to someone one disliked:

> I understood that each soul is free to respond to the calls of Our Lord, to do little or much for Him, in a word to select among the sacrifices He asks. Then I cried out 'My God, I choose everything! I will not be a saint by halves; I am not afraid of suffering for Thee'....Prayer is an eagerness of the heart, a simple glance towards Heaven, a cry of recognition and love thrown with joy; finally, it is something of grandeur, of the supernatural, which expands and nourishes the soul.

Her book, which she had thought was only for her sisters' eyes, was published in a number of languages soon after her death of tuberculosis at age 24. It surprised people by immediately becoming one of the most popular and influential spiritual books of the twentieth century. In it one of the things she said was: "I want to spend my heaven doing good on earth," and she promised to send down "showers of roses." Ardent devotion to her became worldwide and many people after praying to her for favors reported receiving not only what they prayed for but an unexpected gift of roses at the same time. Understandably, she has been named the patron of florists, as well as of France and of the Missions. She was canonized in 1925, and her feast day is October 3rd.

Zorawar Singh and Fateh Singh: These were the two youngest sons of Guru Gobind Singh (1666–1708), who was the tenth and last Guru of the Sikhs. They became martyrs for the faith during a period of religious persecution, when they were aged nine and seven. They and their aged grandmother were captured and imprisoned in Sirdhind Province. Unusually handsome, bright, and fearless boys, they were sent to the governor's court where they were offered fabulous rewards if they would renounce their faith. After persuasions and temptations failed, threats and tortures were tried, but the boys remained unwavering. They passed cold winter nights in prison without any bedding or cloth in which to wrap themselves. Again they were brought to the court and the choice of death or acceptance of Islam was offered to them. They preferred death. The viceroy of the province ordered that they be bricked up while alive. The wall of the city was knocked down for a length of three yards and the boys were made to stand a yard apart from each other. The wall was then rebuilt brick by brick on their tender limbs until it reached the height of their shoulders. Then the executioners slit the boys' throats with butcher knives.

This atrocity took place on December 27, 1705, and is a significant date in Sikh history. Their grandmother died in prison upon hearing of the tragic fate of her two little grandsons. But when Guru Gobind Singh heard about their deaths, he was calm. He closed his eyes and thanked God for the triumphant end of their lives, saying, "My sons are not dead. They have returned to their Eternal Home."

Since all his sons had died during his lifetime Gobind Singh did not nominate a successor. Instead he installed the *Guru Granth Sahib* (Holy Book) as guru. From then on the concept of guru became not only that of the message contained in the Holy Book but of the *Guru Panth* (the Spirit of the Guru), which is present wherever members of the *Khalsa* (pure ones) gather to deliberate and make decisions in the presence of the Holy Book. From that time on, all male Sikhs have taken *Singh* (meaning lion) as their surname.

REINCARNATED CHILDREN

Buddhists, Hindus, and many other people regard babies as reborn, rather than merely newborn. Reincarnation involving a cycle of birth-death-rebirth is not a myth in the sense of being a fanciful story in which imaginary characters personify natural forces and thus explain mysteries of life in a way that is more poetic than scientific. It is, according to the people who believe in it, a logical explanation of what truly happens to the souls of living beings, and they believe they have solid evidence based on observation to demonstrate its truth. As the *Bhagavad Gita*, the ancient Hindu scriptures, puts it: "Never was the spirit born; never shall the spirit cease to be. Never was there no time; End and Beginning are dreams; the spirit remains birthless and deathless and changeless forever; Death has not touched it at all, though the house of the spirit seems dead. . . .The end of birth is death; the end of death is birth; this is ordained."

According to the Greek historian Herodotus, writing in the third century B.C., the Egyptians were the first people to hold the doctrine that the soul is immortal and that after death it enters another creature at the moment of that creature's birth. He said the Egyptians believed that the soul makes the round of all living things before finally, after a period of transmigration taking about 3,000 years, it again enters the body of a newborn human being. He also said this theory had been adopted by certain Greeks.

Marco Polo (1254–1324), after observing the people of Cathay, described in his memoirs *The Travels of Marco Polo*, written in c. 1296, a variant on the idea of reincarnation. Life as they saw it is not an endless cycle of births and rebirths, but a purposeful journey:

> They hold that as soon as a man is dead he enters into another body; and according to whether he has conducted himself well or badly in life, he passes from good to better or from bad to worse. That is to say, if he is a man of humble rank who has behaved well and virtuously in life, he will be reborn after death from the womb of a noblewoman and will become a nobleman; and so he will follow an ever upward path culminating in assumption into the Deity. But if he is a man of good birth who has behaved badly, he will be reborn as the son of a peasant; from a peasant's life he will pass to a dog's and so on continually downward.

This idea that we are punished or rewarded in one life for deeds committed in an earlier life is part of the doctrine of *Karma* (the law of cause and effect by which everything one does is the cause of everything else one endures). This is the philosophical basis of the Hindu caste system, in which poverty and misfortune are not regarded as inexplicable ills or matters of chance but as just punishments for previous sins, even though the person suffering may be an infant unaware and incapable of having committed any sins. Some babies are born to high caste parents, and this good luck is proof that they have deserved good luck. Others are born at the lowest level of society, so low that they are "untouchable;" nothing they do can alter the miserable condition fixed for them at birth, although if they are virtuous they can improve their lot in their next life. Even to permit their shadow to fall on you will make you untouchable too, so you dare not go near them to help them unless you are a *Mahatma* (Great Soul) like Gandhi whose love for all people casts out all fear of castes. He called the untouchables *Haridans*, meaning Beloved of God.

Buddha did not speculate about the afterlife, concentrating instead on how one should live in this life, but most of his followers firmly believe in reincarnation. A charming story tells about a little child who wanted to make an offering to Buddha but had nothing in the world to give him, so he collected some dust and, joining his open hands, childishly offered it to the Blessed One. Buddha was touched by this gesture of faith and smilingly accepted the gift in the spirit in which it was given; later this innocent child was rewarded by being reborn as the great Indian Emperor Asoka.

Two famous men alive today are believed by millions of people to be reincarnations of two other famous men who lived centuries ago: the Dalai Lama, born in 1935, held to be a reincarnation of Buddha, and the Aga Khan IV, born in 1936, whose followers consider to be a reincarnation of Mohammed.

In central Africa, the Bambara people believe that a recognizable physical mark on a baby's body is evidence of the reappearance of an ancestor who was similarly marked. Some of them take the initiative in identifying reincarnated souls and make special marks on corpses so that when people are born again they will be clearly recognized. When an infant dies, the gravedigger may mark its cheek or forehead with ashes or fold the dead baby's little finger; then when another baby is born with the same mark or with a bent finger, people will know who that baby is.

In Zambia a newborn child is often placed at its mother's breast while the names of its ancestors are said aloud. Then, if it begins to suck at the mention of a particular name they consider this a sign of its identity.

A variation on the idea of transmigration of souls is found among the Bakongos in the Congo, who believe that the spirit of a person still alive may enter the body of a baby. It would, therefore, seem tactless to compliment a Bakongo grandmother on her grandchild's strong resemblance to her because such a resemblance would be a sign that she is now soulless and will soon die.

BUDDHA

The great philosopher and teacher revered throughout Asia as the Buddha, meaning the Enlightened One, was born sometime around 560 B.C. He was the son of Suddhodana, King of the Sakyas, who reigned in Kapilavatsu, a province in northern India near the border of Nepal. Some Buddhists believe him to have been the ninth incarnation of Vishnu. Almost all Buddhists believe he had passed through many existences to prepare himself for his mission to teach the world how to attain enlightenment and serenity.

Religious traditions and legends have embellished the story of his life, particularly of his birth and childhood. There is a folk tradition that his conception was miraculous and that his mother, Queen Maya, saw in a dream before he was born that he would enter her womb in the shape of a lovely little elephant as white as snow, bearing a white lotus in his trunk. The next day the queen's dream was interpreted by 64 Brahmins, who predicted the birth of a boy destined to become a great universal ruler.

The queen was traveling when the time for the birth grew near and was not able to reach home, so she went into a garden where he was born while she was standing and holding onto a branch of a tree. He came forth from her right side without causing her the least pain. At this moment the whole universe showed its joy by miracles: musical instruments played without being touched, trees and plants burst forth with flowers, and lakes with lotuses, and rivers stopped flowing to contemplate the newborn child.

At once the baby began to walk, and a lotus appeared on the ground as soon as his foot touched it. He took seven steps in the direction of the seven cardinal points, and thus took possession of the entire world. And on that same day Yasodhara Devi, who was to become his wife, the horse Kantaka which he would later ride when he left his palace in search of knowledge, his squire Chandaka, his friend and favorite disciple Ananda, and the Bo tree under which he would many years later achieve enlightenment, were all also born.

Five days after his birth the young prince received the name Siddhartha; 108 Brahmins were invited to his name-giving ceremony, among whom were eight specialists in interpreting bodily marks. Seven of them predicted two possibilities: if the child remained at home he would become a universal monarch, but if he left home he would become a buddha; the eighth predicted that the baby would definitely become a buddha.

Seven days after his birth his mother is said to have died of joy and her sister Mahaprajapati took care of him after that as a devoted foster mother. When she took him to the temple, the statues of the gods bowed down before him and a saintly old man from the Himalayas told her that he observed in him 80 signs that were pledges of a high religious vocation.

Siddhartha was raised in great luxury and comfort. When he was 12, a council of Brahmins told his father that if the prince ever beheld the spectacles of old age, sickness, and death he would devote himself to asceticism, so the father had his sumptuous palace with its vast and beautiful gardens surrounded by a well-guarded triple wall, and any mention of the words death or grief were henceforth forbidden.

However, as with many overprotective parents, the father's efforts on behalf of his child did not produce the results he had hoped for. One day, about 10 years after the young prince's happy marriage that had produced a son, he announced that he wanted to visit the town outside the palace walls. Later on as the Buddha he taught that it is the duty of every man to have a son before going out on his own to seek enlightenment. The king ordered that the town be swept and decorated and that every ugly or depressing sight be hidden. But the prince, riding through the streets, noticed a wrinkled and trembling old man and with astonishment learned that decrepitude is the fate of the very old. He was shocked and immediately began to wonder about the meaning of existence.

He went home, renounced his throne, shaved his head, donned monk's robes, and set out in search of spiritual knowledge. After seven years of wandering, practicing asceticism and mortification, he decided this was not the road to wisdom. He reached the town of Uruvela, where he sat down beneath a sacred Bo tree, vowing never to move or eat again until he had achieved enlightenment. For the next 28 days evil spirits tried to distract him from his vigil, but he resisted all forms of earthly temptation including Discontent, Delight, and Thirst.

After this spiritual test, he began to find disciples, and during the next 45 years his fame and his teachings about the Middle Way and the Four-Fold Path to Truth spread all over India, and later into Burma, Cambodia, China, Japan, Nepal, Sri Lanka, and Thailand.

KRISHNA

Hindus worship many gods, yet they are essentially monotheistic, considering these gods as representing different aspects of the Godhead, a trinity consisting of Brahma, Siva, and Vishnu. But among their pantheon of other gods, some are special favorites, and none is more popular than Krishna. For more than 2,000 years he has been worshipped as the eighth avatar, or incarnation, of Vishnu.

Krishna was the author of the Hindu scripture, the *Bhagavad Gita* (the Song of the Lord), and the hero of the great epic, *Mahabharata* (c. 400). Although revered as an incomparable teacher, lover, and hero, his most popular representation is as a child. The Hindu poet Surdas (1478–1581) composed over 800 poems on Krishna's childhood, and in sculpture and paintings Krishna is often depicted as a plump, beguiling infant crawling on all fours.

The many legends and cults that have developed around him have their basis in a historical character born in Mathura, of the Yadavas tribe. It is said that he was the eighth son of Vasudeva and his wife Devaki, who was the aunt of the then reigning King Kamsa. It had been prophesied that Kamsa would be killed by Devaki's eighth son, so Kamsa determined to destroy Krishna. But his mother arranged to hide him and his elder brother Balarama by giving them to a cowherd, Nanda, and his wife Yasoda, who raised them as their own.

When Kamsa learned that the boys had disappeared, he ordered all male children in his kingdom slaughtered, but again Krishna and his brother escaped. Nanda smuggled them away, first to Vraja and then to Vrndavana, villages which are still sacred to Hindus because Krishna lived there.

Krishna was a beautiful, appealing, jolly, impish, adventurous child. He wore a garland of wild flowers around his neck and bells around his waist and wrists. He played with his own shadow, rolled in the dust, danced to make his bangle jingle, sang, played the flute, and passed almost all his time in merriment. He had an insatiable love of butter and was always on the prowl in search of some, so much so that the villagers nicknamed him the butter thief. He also loved sweets so much that his foster mother was constantly trying to hide them from him.

Why is this strange, rambunctious child the favorite incarnation of the deity both among many ordinary simple people and profound mystics? Describing and analyzing the devotion to the child Krishna in his book *The Sword and the Flute*, scholar David R. Kinsley says Krishna's childish pranks express both the power and the freedom of the divine united with that of the typical behavior of young children who are uninhibited and impulsive.

> For the divine to become embodied as a child is eminently suitable, for they behave in similar ways. Each belongs to a realm of energetic activity that is imaginative and rich and therefore creative. . . .Krishna's play makes the world around him sparkle with aliveness.

This theophany, says Kinsley, also clearly reveals a second aspect of deity. As an infant and child, God Himself is approachable, allowing us to dispense with formality. Another characteristic of Krishna which Kinsley points out in *The Sword and the Flute* is his astonishing divine beauty that transcends the ordinary world.

He is irresistible to those who know him—or who hear his music. . . .Krishna expresses the delightful and complex nature of the divine-human relationship that unfolds itself in ecstatic devotion. . . .while lordship and awesome power certainly belong to the Godhead, its most essential nature is to infuse and taste bliss in the intimacy of love. . . .The notes of Krishna's flute represent the Voice of God, calling man to leave earthly things and turn to the joys of divine love.

Krishna's childhood was said to be threatened from time to time by horrendous demons sent by his evil uncle to destroy him. But they were powerless to harm the miraculous child and could not even interrupt his fun. They simply became new sources of amusement for him, and he disposed of them as if it were all a game.

The demoness Putana, the first fiend sent by Kamsa, disguised herself as a lovely woman who pretended to dote on the infant and asked his mother if she could feed him from her own breasts. Yasoda allowed her this privilege, so Putana poisoned her nipples in an attempt to kill him. But the poison was ineffective, and the baby turned the tables on the demoness by sucking the life from her. The people of Vrndavana then chopped up her corpse and burned it, and it gave off the sweet odor of sandalwood; she had been redeemed by her physical contact with Krishna.

A many-headed serpent Kaliya, that lived in a nearby stream, poisoned its waters causing the death of many cattle, so Krishna arrived on the scene, climbed a tree, and leapt into the poisonous waters, proceeding to bait the monster by swimming and playing there. Enraged, Kaliya emerged from its lair beneath the waters and gripped Krishna in its coils, but Krishna easily freed himself and proceeded to circle the demon until its many heads began to droop with exhaustion. Then Krishna jumped onto the heads and danced, rhythmically stamping his feet on them until the heads were torn and bleeding and the monster admitted defeat and begged for mercy. Krishna granted it its life but banished it to an island in the ocean.

The mighty Krishna, in the form of a child, was obviously fearless and invincible. His only weak spot was his heel, and after a long life he finally died when a hunter mistook him for a deer and shot an arrow into his foot.

RAMAKRISHNA

Born in Bengal in the village of Kamarpukur to a devout Brahmin family, even before his birth Ramakrishna (1836–1886) was marked out for unusual holiness. His father said that in a dream the god Vishnu appeared to him saying, "I bless you and will be born as your son, and will receive your loving care." At about the same time, his mother had a vision at a Siva shrine: she saw a divine light emanating from the holy image, filling the entire place and engulfing her, whereupon she lost consciousness and fell to the ground. Soon after this incident she conceived the wonder child, who today is widely regarded as a universal saint. Gandhi described Ramakrishna's life as "a story of religion in practice," and the French critic Romain Rolland called it "the consummation of 2,000 years of the spiritual life of 300,000,000 people."

Ramakrishna's childhood days were happy. He was merry, jovial, and popular with all the children of his village, although he often retired into solitude and meditation. From the age of six he frequently experienced ecstasies. He never went to school, gaining instruction instead from itinerant monks. He enjoyed modeling images of gods in clay and enacting divine roles in amateur plays. At nine he was invested as a Brahmin and initiated into the ways of worship of the family deity Raghuvit.

At 16 Ramakrishna was summoned to Calcutta to help his elder brother Ramkumar, who had assumed his father's duties after their father died in 1849, starting a Sanskrit school and performing priestly functions in Calcutta households.

At 20 Ramakrishna began his own priestly career with due ceremony, but shortly after this found himself in a spiritual storm of supernormal experiences. Many people thought he had gone mad. His mother decided he needed a wife, and at 23 he married Sarada Devi, who was only six years old. Later she became his first and most devoted disciple and the Holy Mother of a large group of young people who were attracted to Ramakrishna as his fame grew. She formed the Ramakrishna Brotherhood to spread his mission of the universality of religion through service to mankind.

The universalism of his religious experiences led him to say,

> I have practiced all religions, Hinduism, Islam, Christianity, and I have found that it is the same God toward whom all are directing their steps, though along different paths. . . .He who is called Krishna is also called Siva and bears the name of Primitive Energy, Jesus and Allah as well—the same Rama with a thousand names. A tank has several ghats; at one Hindus draw water in pitchers and call it Jal; at another Muslims draw water in leather bottles and call it Pani; at a third Christians, and call it Water. Can we imagine that the water is not Jal but only Pani or Water? How ridiculous! The substance is one under different names and everyone is seeking the same substance; nothing but climate, temperament and name vary. Let each man follow his own path. If he sincerely and ardently wishes to know God, peace be unto him! He will surely find Him."

THE DALAI LAMA

Lhamo Thondup, born in Tibet in 1935, was a year old he was declared to be a direct descendent of Buddha and the fourteenth incarnation of the Dalai Lama, the traditional leader of Tibet before he was a year old.. The process by which this was decided was observed by reporters from all over the world. Astrologers in Tibet scanned the starry skies for signs while saffron-robed Buddhist monks in gem-studded temples prayed hard for them, until they determined the place where the soul of the recently departed thirteenth Dalai Lama would reappear. State officials then traveled to the designated area and inquired about recent births. Kyetsang Rimpoche, a representative of the thirteenth Dalai Lama, traveling incognito, went to the homes of several possible candidates to investigate them, and asked for lodgings for the night. One evening he and his companions played for a long time with Lhamo Thondup.

Thubten Jigme Norbu, a Tibetan monk and older brother of Lhamo Thondup, wrote an autobiography, *Tibet Is My Country,* in which he described what happened. Kyetsang Rimpoche had a number of things with him that had belonged to the thirteenth Dalai Lama, and the normal procedure was to bring them quite casually to the notice of children who might conceivably be the long-sought-for reincarnation, to see if they recognized any of these objects. No sooner did the baby Lhamo catch sight of the dead thirteenth Dalai Lama's rosary than he indignantly took it, declaring that it was his. According to his brother, Lhamo was an unusually lively and high-spirited child, and he insisted that Kyetsang Rimpoche should give him this rosary. Not only that, but he told the disguised Kyetsang Rimpoche that he knew he was a lama from Lhasa (where the Dalai Lama's palace was located). And the visitors could hardly believe their ears when the child addressed them in Lhasa dialect. Then the same thing happened with a walking stick and a damaru (a small double drum), both of which had previously belonged to the thirteenth Dalai Lama. Lhamo grabbed them, saying they were his, and he refused to be parted from them any more. He was so excited that he was near tears. His mother found this extremely embarrassing and tried to soothe the boy with promises of a much bigger drum at the first opportunity, but it was this drum the child wanted, and he insisted on taking it to bed with him. Later, while he was sleeping, it was removed from his fingers and given back to the person his mother considered its rightful owner.

Kyetsang Rimpoche was deeply impressed, he but did not reveal the secret of his visit that evening. Instead he left the house early the next morning, later returning with his assistants, but this time no longer incognito. He handed Lhamo's parents presents and explained that he was an ambassador from Lhasa. Lhamo Thondup was now subjected to a very thorough examination. In addition to the rosary, the walking stick, and the damaru, the delegation this time had with them the thirteenth Dalai Lama's silver pencil, his spectacles, and his eating bowl, together with clever imitations of them. Kyetsang Rimpoche now greeted the little boy while wearing the real rosary around his neck and holding the imitation one in his hands in prayer, but the child did not hesitate, immediately trying to take the rosary from Rimpoche's neck by force, once again insisting it was his. This time he was allowed to have it. The oral examination of the child was also completely satisfactory, and the delegation went away firmly convinced that in Lhamo Thondup they had found the fourteenth incarnation of the Dalai Lama.

From that moment on, this child was revered throughout his nation as its ruler and spiritual head. He was enthroned at the age of six-and-a-half after having received many hours of religious instruction and having learned to read and write. He was dignified on all official occasions, although still a lively and even impudent child with a sense of humor. He romped in the monastery gardens, played pranks, and occasionally disobeyed his teachers, and he missed his family and cried when his parents' visits ended, as he has recounted with charm and frankness in his own autobiography.

He spent his unique childhood enclosed in a temple, studying and praying for many hours a day, presiding over innumerable lengthy and elaborate ceremonies, his small fingers endlessly raised in blessing to crowds of worshippers, until he was 21. Then, disguised as a humble peasant, he undertook a long and dangerous journey on foot, enduring cold and hunger, fleeing for his life with 100,000 other Tibetans into India from Chinese invaders who wanted to dethrone and imprison him.

The rest of his life has been spent in exile, but he has magnificently fulfilled the destiny he chose—or which was chosen for him—while he was still a baby. He has become one of the most loved and admired spiritual leaders in the world by members of all religions and of none, in 1989 receiving the Nobel Prize for Peace in response to his persevering but consistently nonviolent efforts to uphold human rights, end torture, and restore independence to Tibet.

Postscript: The Littlest Lamas

The word "lama" means monk, and although Dalai Lamas are the primary ones there are a great many others in Tibetan Buddhism.

The second most important religious official is the Panchen Lama. The last one to be indisputably acknowledged died in 1989, and in 1996 there were two six-year-old candidates for his position, one installed by the Chinese and one recognized by the Dalai Lama. His choice, Gendun Choekyi Nyima, disappeared in 1995, apparently under house arrest in Beijing along with his parents and 50 monks associated with his nomination. The Chinese have heaped scorn on the boy, asserting that he once drowned a dog, a serious crime in the eyes of Buddhists, and that his parents are "notorious for speculation, deceit and scrambling for fame and profit." In contrast they have presented their own nominee, Gyaltsen Norbu, as a paragon of virtue.

In spite of China's efforts to change Tibetan society, the religiosity that has always been a major part of the country's mystique has so far survived. Lamas are still major influences on all Tibetans, and they are still chosen as reincarnations of their predecessors, but since the Chinese overran the country in 1950 and closed or destroyed more than 6,000 monasteries, a great many monks have gone into exile. Their searches are no longer confined to their native land.

In 1987 a Spanish boy named Osel Ita Torres, whose parents converted to Buddhism, was selected as the reincarnation of Lama Yeshe. Lama Yeshe had left the Himalayas to found 30 Buddhist meditation centers around the world, and had died two months before Osel was born. Lama Zopa Rimpoche, a Tibetan monk who had been searching through several countries for Lama Yeshe's reincarnation, decided he had found him when the boy chose the dead Lama's prayer beads from a group of objects in front of him and began to dance with them. The Dalai Lama confirmed the identification on March 12, 1987, and Osel became the youngest ever Buddhist monk when he was installed at the age of three as head of the Kopan monastery in a solemn ceremony in Dharmasala, India.

His family's adjustment to Osel's new life was not as harmonious as that of the Dalai Lama's. In February 1996, his mother said she wanted her son back, complaining that the monks "are spoiling him rotten."

In February 1996, another young boy, Somam Wangdu, living in Seattle, was declared to be the spiritual heir to the exiled Tibetan monk Deshung Rinpoche. He was welcomed to Nepal where he traded his American "monster" sweatsuit for maroon robes and a monastic life in a remote setting outside Katmandu. He was four years old.

And in February 1996 the Dalai Lama recognized as a reincarnation of a Buddhist teacher a two-and-a-half year old boy.

Bahái Buddhism Christianity Hinduism Islam Judaism Sikhism Taoism

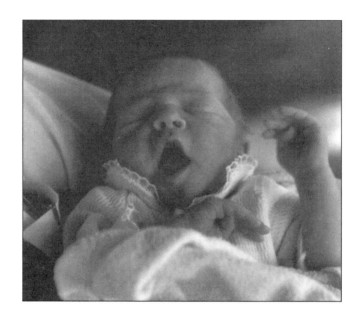

3

Childbirth and Newborns

PREGNANCY AND CHILDBIRTH

An extremely mysterious relationship exists between the mother's menstrual cycle and the baby's life in the womb are both measured in lunar months of 28 days. That is how long it takes for the moon to complete its cycle of waxing and waning, and it takes 10 lunar months on the average for a one-celled egg to develop

> "In a world without women," Mark Twain was once asked, "what would men become?" "Scarce, sir," he replied. "Mighty scarce."

into a newborn baby. In other words, the moon waxes and wanes 10 times while a baby is inside its mother's womb. We speak of pregnancy as nine months long, but calendar months are measurements devised by humans; they vary and differ slightly from the regular months established by nature. Pregnancy is really "10 moons long"—280 days.

Hippocrates (c. 460–377 B.C.), a Greek physician, has been called the Father of Medicine, revered for his pioneering work and high standards of professional conduct embodied in the Hippocratic Oath still taken by doctors today. His code of medical ethics, which he imposed on his disciples, contained, among other things, a promise never to take human life, which sometimes presents a dilemma for today's advocates of abortion and assisted suicide. He was a general practitioner, however, not a child specialist. Soranus of Ephesus, who practiced medicine in Alexandria and Rome in the late first and early second century, was the first and foremost expert on childbirth and child care in the ancient world. His writings dominated medical opinion in these matters for almost 1,500 years. He established rules about how babies should be cared for, bathed, dressed, and fed, and he advised on weaning, teething, and methods of teaching. For example, he taught that breastfeeding should not begin until the third day of life; at first, he said, a baby should be fed on diluted and boiled honey. We now know this method to be harmful for children.

Aristotle (381–322 B.C.) was the first embryologist. The *embryo* is what a baby is called from the time of conception until it is eight weeks old; then it is called a *foetus*, or *fetus*, until it is nine months old and emerges as a newborn baby. Aristotle's day-to-day account of how a chicken develops inside an egg was the foundation of the science of embryology, but he was never able to observe a human embryo.

Leonardo da Vinci (1452–1519), the great painter, sculptor, inventor, and scientist, was the first person we know of who observed the human embryo. He began a notebook devoted to embryology around A.D. 1512 that contains one of the first, and unquestionably one of the most beautiful, drawings ever made of a child in the womb. This notebook was one of over 100 that Leonardo filled with anatomical sketches; they were in part an artistic project, exercises to help him achieve accuracy in his finished paintings of people, and in part a scientific project, as he hoped to publish an atlas of human anatomy but never finished it.

Leonardo personally dissected more than 30 human bodies in order to make his drawings. Dissection is the only way in which certain anatomical knowledge can be acquired, but at this time it was widely regarded as a dreadful sin. Leonardo therefore kept his notebooks a secret, and they were not published until 200 years after his death.

Complaints about the "sin" of dissection grew until Emperor Charles V (1500–1558) asked the theological faculty of the university at Salamanca for an opinion on the matter. Their decision was that "dissection of human cadavers serves a useful purpose, and is therefore permissible to Christians."

Andreas Vesalius (1514–1564), a less gifted artist but the first great anatomist in history, continued Leonardo's studies. He published a major book on anatomy entitled *De humani corporis fabrica* in 1543.

Gabriel Fallopio (1523–1562), one of Vesalius's pupils, made an important discovery about anatomy. He was the first person to see and describe the *Fallopian tubes*. He acquired immortality by having these two pencil-thin tubes about three to five inches long, which connect a mother's womb to her abdominal cavity—the corridors through which every egg passes on the beginning of its journey from conception to birth—named after him. Their function, however, was not learned for another three centuries, when the mammalian *ova*, or maternal egg cells, were discovered.

Prejudice against dissection remained great in the average person's mind, regardless of theological opinion. Many people considered it an insult to the dead. It therefore continued to be so difficult to obtain bodies for use in medical schools that one professor in the seventeenth century in Montpellier, named Guillaume Rondelet, dissected the body of his own dead child in his class.

Grave robbing was the least of the evils that resulted from this difficulty. In 1752 two nurses committed murder to obtain a body for a group of medical students. Unable to find a corpse, they enticed a woman and her small son into their house, got the woman drunk, and then smothered the little boy with a mattress; they were paid "two shillings, sixpence" for his body, and were later hanged for the crime. Others committed these types of murders until adequate laws were passed providing medical schools with a regular method of obtaining bodies. But the fear and suspicion that dissectors had obtained their bodies wickedly, or even that they had dissected living bodies, cropped up from time to time, to give the latest accused medical student a close kinship with Leonardo, who had also been accused of doing that.

The Gradual Growth of Knowledge

The Hippocratic school of medicine in ancient Greece had thought that the male semen was the formative activating agent or "soul" that produced a new person, and that there was female semen which provided the material or "soil" to be fertilized, and a baby-to-be was a mixture of "soul" and "soil." Male spermatozoa were not discovered until 1677, and female ova were not discovered until 1821. The union of a male sperm and a female egg cell was seen for the first time in 1843, in a rabbit.

The female ovum, or egg cell, is the largest cell in the human body—yet it is only about 1/180 of an inch in diameter. The smallest cell in the human body is the male sperm; about 175,000 sperm cells weigh as much as a single egg cell. Wilhelm His of Basel, Switzerland, a professor at the university there from 1857 to 1872, was the first person to study the development of the human embryo and show the origins of its tissues, using specimens obtained in operations after miscarriages. He made the first three-dimensional models showing the human embryo at different stages.

In 1819, the stethoscope was invented by a French physician, René Théophile Hyacinthe Laënnec (1781–c. 1817). This modest but useful invention was inspired by the gallant doctor's desire to help a lady in distress: A shy patient of his was embarrassed when he applied his ear to her chest, so he made a cylinder of paper to listen through. A student of his, Jean Alexandre Lejumeau, the Vicomte de Kergaradec, soon afterwards applied the stethoscope to the abdomen of a pregnant woman, because he had a theory that the fetus moves about in the womb's *liquor amnii* (amniotic fluid) and he wanted to find out if he was right. He hoped to hear the sound of splashing. He didn't, but he was the first person in the world to hear an unborn baby's heartbeat; he heard "double pulsations," the mother's heart and her baby's heart beating twice as fast. This discovery was of great importance because it enabled doctors to tell whether a baby was developing normally and warned them when special steps might be necessary. It also made it possible to find out if twins were on the way.

With our new sensitive scientific instruments, and the legacy of information which has been passed down to us, we now know quite a lot about how a baby develops during those 280 days when it is inside the womb.

The Incredible Adventure of Conception

By the time an infant is born it has gone through a remarkable series of experiences on a journey far more amazing than anything it will ever do again. And it has all been done according to a detailed and intricately organized timetable. The small egg which begins human life is one of several thousand that are in the mother's ovary. When an ovary has released one of these eggs and sent it traveling down a Fallopian tube toward the uterus, where it will arrive in four or five days, it is such a small dot that it would take 175 others just like it to fill up one inch.

At the instant when an even tinier tadpole-like sperm enters this small egg, thus fertilizing it, the future child's sex and all the traits it will inherit from its mother (in the egg) and from its father (via the sperm) are now already determined. About 60 hours after this small one-celled egg has been fertilized by a sperm, it contracts and then divides into two cells. This process is repeated in another spasm of activity, and it becomes four cells. With continuous repetition, it becomes a cluster of tens, hundreds, thousands, and millions of cells until nine months later, when the baby emerges into the outside world, its body will contain 200 billion cells! And each cell will have about 10,000 times as many molecules as the Milky Way has stars.

Scientists estimate that they could fill a 1,000-volume encyclopedia with the coded instructions in the DNA (deoxyribonucleic acid inside every single human cell), if the instructions could be translated into English. They also estimate that there are 3 million to 4 million genes inside each human cell. Astoundingly, they are now able to identify one particular gene among these millions, produce an image of that gene, and examine it for abnormalities and determine whether or not the human being to whom it belongs is missing certain parts of his or her genetic blueprint. This is done through a process called *amniocentesis* in which cells are taken from the fluid around the embryo and their chromosomes are examined.

The cells of the embryo specialize. Some grow into different parts of the body, forming tissues, muscles, and bones. Others separate from surrounding tissue, forming a bag of waters and small tubes through which the fetus will receive nourishment and a soft wall that will enclose it and protect it from injury during the coming months.

The Timetable of the Embryo and Fetus

The beginning of a spinal cord appears two weeks after conception. The embryo is now a quarter of an inch long. A heart is already formed at one end, and a tail at the other.

During the third and fourth weeks, the heart begins to beat even though its beat is not able to be heard until several weeks later, and the blood starts to circulate. Arms and legs have begun to form.

By the fourth week, the brain, backbone, and muscles are forming. The eyes, ears, and nose have begun to develop. The embryo can now be seen, through ultrasound, without a microscope. He or she is now about a half-inch long and looks like a grain of puffed wheat.

By about the eighth week (second month), the embryo has grown to 175 times its original length, a stupendous increase, though it is only an inch long. Even at this small size, all its features are now recognizably human and it already has all its organs. The embryo has now grown into a fetus, and its body is 20 percent complete.

By the third month, the fetus possesses complete genital organs, eyes, nose, mouth, arms, legs, hands, and feet—and even tiny finger and toe nails. It is now about three or four inches long and weighs one ounce. It has lost its tail. By about the tenth week, its heartbeat can be heard with a microphone. It is at this time, according to Hinduism, that the child's soul enters the body.

By the fourth month, all the nerve cells the baby will ever possess have been formed and are ready to function. The teeth are forming. Eyebrows and lashes begin to grow. The body is now 40 percent formed. The fetus is six to eight inches long and weighs half a pound. It is about now that the mother begins to feel it move its arms and legs; this process is called *quickening*. This is when Saint Thomas Aquinas (1224–1274) thought the soul is infused.

By the fifth month, it is exercising vigorously and its mother feels strong flutters and twitches.

Was the Mona Lisa an expectant mother?

An entertaining explanation was given in 1958 by Dr. Kenneth Keele, an English medical historian, of the mysterious smile of the Mona Lisa, which for many generations has intrigued and tantalized art lovers. In a lecture he gave at the Yale School of Medicine, he said it was obvious to him that the famous smile is just the contented glow of a pregnant woman.

By the sixth month, it is about 12 inches long, weighs about 1½ pounds, and the doctor can hear its heart beat with a stethoscope. By now it has fingerprints. The body is about 60 percent formed.

By the seventh month, its eyes have opened, and hair may have appeared on its head unless it is one of the many babies who are born bald or with only light fuzz. It is now about 14 inches long and weighs about 2½ to 3 pounds. If it should be born now, it could probably survive with special care.

By the eighth month, it is about 18 inches long and probably weighs four or five pounds. It is about ready to turn in the womb to a position preparing it for birth, and the mother will soon feel the process called lightening, and less kicking.

By the ninth month, it is about 20 inches long and usually weighs six or seven pounds. The body is now 80 percent formed and ready for delivery.

To the mother the past nine months may have seemed like a long time, but when you think of all that has been happening during those months it seems a remarkably short time. While the baby was in the womb, 30 generations of cells accumulated in its body. The rest of its life span from birth on will add only five more generations of cells to complete the body. From now on the process will be so much slower that it will take another 20 years for this to happen and for the body to become mature and 100 percent formed.

A human baby is in the womb a month longer than a chimpanzee, the smartest of all its rivals, and stays infantile three years longer. Biologists consider the first six years of human life as the infantile period. To quote biologist Desmond Morris: "Monkeys and apes appear to race through all the same cycles as man. But for both brain and intelligence to grow, man needs more time for learning. Biologically, it takes more time to become human. Obviously, too, it is the human brain and human learning which gain particular advantages by this biological slowdown."

WHEN DO MOST BABIES ARRIVE?

Parents have the distinct impression that babies pick the most inconvenient possible moment, say from 3 A.M. to 5 A.M., to announce their arrival, thus showing from the very beginning just who is boss. And apparently there is some scientific evidence that babies like to turn night into day. A few doctors have studied hospital birth records to see if old wives' and husbands' tales are true.

Their Favorite Hours and Months

A study made in Pennsylvania in 1957 of more than 38,000 births showed more babies arriving during the eight hours between 3 A.M. and 11 A.M. than during the next eight-hour period from 11 A.M. until 7 P.M. This and another study of over 33,000 births both showed that 5 A.M. was the most popular time of arrival. In this second study, 3 A.M. was the next most frequent time, and 8 A.M. the third. The least busy hour of the day on the babies' timetable was 7 P.M..

Another physician who kept records also found that babies usually arrive at night: 62 percent of his mothers went into labor between 9 P.M. and 9 A.M. And a placard at a Birth Exhibit in the Health Museum in Cleveland, Ohio, stated that most births occur between 9 P.M. and midnight.

Another study of 600,000 births presented to an international scientific conference in 1962 reported that more babies are born around 3 A.M. than at any other hour, and that labor usually begins just after midnight and least often around noon.

So, although the evidence is scanty and the findings differ slightly, all seem to agree that babies avoid daylight, preferring night life. As far as the time of year is concerned, records at the United States National Office of Vital Statistics indicate that more babies are born during August than in any other month.

The Influence of the Moon

Until the eighteenth century, doctors believed the moon's birth, growth, decline, and death affect human lives, and that most births occur at the time of the full moon. This is still a worldwide popular belief. The first modern scientific report on the subject was published in 1938, in Germany. It confused the question by stating that more babies are born between seven and nine days after either a full or a new moon. In 1950 another medical study found no connection whatever between phases of the moon and the daily birth rate. But that same year another research project showed a slight correlation over a five-year period.

The investigation made by a Pennsylvania obstetrician published in 1957 was over a 10-year period, and it reported that more babies were born close to the new moon than to the full moon. In 1959 a doctor in New York contradicted this with his findings over a nine-year period, covering 510,000 births. He said most babies arrive around the time of the full moon and the fewest at the time of the new moon. In New York City alone, he said, 1,000 more babies are born every year during the full moon cycle than during the new moon cycle. He concluded that the moon's influence on the human birth rate is small but nonetheless statistically significant.

Do Babies Decide When to Emerge?

The ancients thought so. Hippocrates and many others thought labor starts when the unborn child gets hungry and begins to search for food. They theorized that when it has grown to a point where the mother can no longer provide enough food to satisfy it, it starts a series of violent (indignant? panicky? exploratory?) movements, which rupture the membranes around it and thus initiate the process of delivery. As long as knowledge of embryology was based primarily on observations of the chicken and the egg, as it was for centuries, this explanation seemed logical: an unborn chick does peck vigorously at its shell until it succeeds in breaking it and emerging triumphant.

The first person to theorize that a human baby behaves differently from a baby chicken was Soranus, mentioned above. He was the first obstetrician, and also the first person to think and teach that the human baby is a passive partner in childbirth while the mother's muscles do all the work. Another great obstetrician, Mauriceau, in France in the seventeenth century, also taught this. In spite of those doctors, most people before, in between, and since them, still have believed that the human baby actively struggles to come out of the mother's womb. We now know, or think we do, that this is not true. But to this day no one knows exactly what mechanism initiates labor. Doctors give explanations that do not really explain. They simply speak of "sudden," "automatic," "spontaneous," "involuntary," exertions, contractions, and dilations of the muscles of the uterus which push the baby down the birth passage and at the same time widen the passage to let the baby go through it, until it is suddenly propelled into the outside world.

"The Savior of Mothers": A Doctor Who Made Childbirth Safer

Childbed fever, or puerperal infection, was the scourge of maternity hospitals throughout Europe in the mid-nineteenth century. Most women in this period delivered their babies at home, but those who had to seek hospitalization because of obstetrical complications or for other reasons faced death rates ranging from 25 to 30 percent. Some people thought the infection was caused by overcrowding or poor ventilation or physical weakness, and few had any idea that it was contagious.

In 1844 Ignaz Semmelweis, a doctor from Hungary who had received his degree at the University of Vienna, was appointed assistant at the obstetrics clinic in Vienna. He proceeded to investigate the cause of maternal deaths, over the strenuous objections of his chief who considered this a waste of time because he had reconciled himself to the idea that these deaths were unavoidable.

There were two divisions in the clinic, one where student doctors were taught and a second that was serviced only by midwives, and Semmelweis noticed that the death rate from childbed fever was two to three times higher among the patients in the students' division than it was in the midwives' section. He speculated that perhaps the students, who often came directly from the dissecting room where they examined mothers who had died, were carrying infection to healthy mothers when they examined them. So he ordered the students to wash their hands in a solution of chlorinated lime before each examination. His order was ridiculed as a pointless nuisance, but he enforced it, and mortality rates in the students' division dropped from 18.27 percent to 1.27 percent. In March and August of 1848 not a single woman in this division died in childbirth. One would think this was convincing proof of his theory, but logic does not always prevail against entrenched prejudice.

In 1848 a revolution swept through Europe and Semmelweis took part in it. After the revolution was put down in Vienna, he found that his political activities had further increased the antipathy of his superiors at the clinic. In 1849 he was dismissed from the staff.

He left Vienna in 1850 and for the next six years worked at the St. Rochus Hospital in Pest, Hungary. When an epidemic of puerperal fever broke out in its obstetrics department, he was put in charge, and again his measures promptly reduced the mortality rate. During his years there it averaged only 0.85 percent, while in Prague and Vienna the death rate was still between 10 and 15 percent.

In 1855 he was appointed professor of obstetrics at the University of Pest. He married, had five children, and developed a private medical practice. His ideas were now accepted in Hungary, but this did not satisfy him because in the rest of Europe doctors continued to reject his "nonsense" about washing hands. In 1861 he published a major work on the subject, which he sent to all the prominent obstetricians and medical societies abroad, but again his ideas met with nothing but scornful rejection. He sent open letters to professors of medicine in several countries, but both individually and in conferences physicians and natural scientists still refused to take his views seriously.

More and more frantic, angry, depressed, and frustrated, he became obsessed. He took to passing out pamphlets in the streets, where he met with jeers and was regarded as a wild-eyed fanatic. His obsession and depair brought on a severe nervous breakdown. He was taken away to a madhouse, and he died there in August 1865.

After his death, his doctrine was eventually accepted universally by medical science, largely as a result of the influential support of the English Dr. Joseph Lister (1827–1912), the father of modern antiseptic surgery. Dr. Lister said, "I think with the greatest admiration of him and his achievement and it fills me with joy that at last he is given the respect due to him." Alas, this respect came too late to fill Semmelweis with joy, but it has earned him the honorific of "the savior of mothers" and greatly reduced the fear of childbirth.

COMMENTS ON NEWBORNS

In every child who is born, under no matter what circumstances and of no matter what parents, the potentiality of the human race is born again, and in him too, and in each one of us, our terrific responsibility toward human life.
—*James Agee (1909–1955)*

It is as natural to die as to be born, and to a little infant, perhaps, the one is as painful as the other. —*Francis Bacon (1561–1626)*

Talk of Columbus and Newton! I tell you the child just born in yonder hovel is the beginning of a revolution as great as theirs. . . . There is nothing in the world so serious as the advent of a child with all his possibilities to parents with good minds and hearts...the overflow of fondness and wonder, your love is the soft pillow prepared for him. —Ralph Waldo Emerson (1803–1882), to his daughter on the birth of her baby in 1865.

Babies are such a nice way to start people. —*Don Herald (1917–)*

I believe that each newborn child arrives on earth with a message to deliver to mankind. Clenched in his little fist is some particle of yet unrevealed truth. . . . He must be treated as top sacred. Our mission is to exercise the kind of loving care which will prompt the child to open his fist and offer up his truth, his individuality, the irreducible atom of his self. We must provide the kind of environment in which the child will joyfully deliver his message through complete self-fulfillment. . . . I have seen the lifeless faces of children whose selves have never been revealed even to themselves, whose unique message will never be delivered. We should hold annual services at the grave of the Unknown Child to remind us of the millions of living children who never really come alive, whose souls remain in limbo in spite of our humanitarian declarations about the sanctity of the individual.
—*Sam Levenson (1911–1980), in a letter to his children in his autobiography* Everything But Money

The baby, like a sailor tossed up by fierce waves, lies speechless, deprived of all vital support, naked on the ground where first nature has sent it forth with pain from its mother's womb into the regions of light; and it fills the air with a mournful

94

wail, as is fitting for one for whom so many sorrows remain to be passed through in life.   —*Lucretius (96–55 B.C.) in* On the Nature of Things

Had God consulted me about it, I should have advised Him to continue the generation of the species by fashioning human beings out of clay, as Adam was made.   —*Martin Luther (1483–1546) in* Table Talk

To my embarrassment I was born in bed with a lady.
                              —*Wilson Mizuer (1876–1933)*

Nature obliges man alone, of all living beings, to clothe himself while to all the others she has given various kinds of coverings, such as shells, crusts, spines, hides, furs, bristles, hair, down, feathers, scales, and fleece. The very trunks of the trees she has protected against the effects of heat and cold by a bark which is, in some cases, doubled. Man alone, at the very moment of his birth, thrown naked upon the earth, she abandons to cries. . . . Introduced thus to the light, man has wrappings immediately put on all his limbs, something which happens to none of the beasts born among us. Born to such singular good fortune, there lies the animal destined to rule all the others, bound hand and foot and weeping aloud, this being the penalty he has to pay on starting life, and that for the single fault of being born. Alas for the foolishness of those who can think, after such a beginning as this, that they were born for the display of vanity!
                              —*Pliny the Elder (A.D. 23–79)*

Do not be born good or handsome, but be born lucky.   —*Russian Proverbs*

Never will a time come when the most marvelous recent invention is as marvelous as a newborn baby. The finest of our precision watches, the most supercolossal of our supercargo planes, don't compare with a newborn baby in the number and ingenuity of coils and springs, in the flow and change of chemical solutions, timing devices and interrelated parts that are irreplacable.
                              —*Carl Sandburg (1878–1967)*

When we are born we cry that we are come / To this great stage of fools.
                              —*William Shakespeare (1564–1616) in* King Lear

I cried the minute I was born, and every day since has explained why.
                              —*Spanish Saying*

All appeared new, and strange at first, inexpressibly rare and delightful and beautiful. . . . My knowledge was Divine. . . . My very ignorance was advantageous. . . . All things were spotless and pure and glorious. . . . I knew not that there were any sins, or complaints, or laws. I dreamed not of poverties, contentions, or vices. . . . Is it not strange that an infant should be heir of the whole world, and see those mysteries which the books of the learned never unfold?
                              —*Thomas Traherne (1620–1674), describing his own birth*

I feel there is no right more basic to humanity and more important to each individual than the right to enter this world as a wanted human being who will be fed, sheltered, cared for, educated, loved and provided with opportunities for constructive life.
—*U Thant (1909–1974)*

MULTIPLE BIRTHS

In 1996 the National Center for Health Statistics released its latest information about the number of multiple births in the United States, showing that they had risen by about 2 percent a year between 1980 and 1993, and in 1993 had topped 100,000 for the first time.

Parents of multiples are usually thrilled at first, but soon find themselves overwhelmed with problems. More than half of all multiples arrive prematurely and weigh less than 5½ pounds, which is considered the bottom of the normal range for newborns. Premature, underweight infants are 40 times more apt to die during their first weeks than full-term normal babies, and multiple preemies are seven times more likely to die during their first 28 days than are "singletons." Birth defects are also more likely to occur in cases of multiple births than of single ones. According to one study, the rate of cerebral palsy is six times higher in multiple births than it is for singles.

All these problems create other problems, such as enormous medical bills, worries, and an exhausting workload for the parents, and recent studies reveal that child abuse is more common in families of multiples, as are marital difficulties that lead to more frequent divorce.

Dr. Louis Keith, an obstetrician-gynecologist who with his identical twin brother Donald founded the Center for Study of Multiple Births in Chicago, says "these problems are not going to go away because more and more women are over 35 when they have their first babies" and older mothers are more likely than younger ones to give birth to multiples. This natural tendency is increased if they have taken fertility drugs to help them conceive, as more and more would-be mothers are doing these days. Such drugs greatly increase the likelihood of multiple fetuses. The latest figures for this phenomenon are that fertility treatments are responsible for 25 to 30 percent of multiple births.

Dr. Keith works with a support organization called Twin Services, founded in 1979 by Patricia Malmstrom, the mother of identical female twins. When her twins were preschoolers, Malmstrom decided multiples needed a group to lobby on their behalf. "The issues related to multiple births," she has said, "medical, financial, social, are bigger than the families themselves. But society doesn't seem ready to deal with that fact. We're being a Paul Revere on this topic: Awake! Awake! Twin Services provides expertise and resources for any family expecting or rearing multiples. It runs Twinline (510-524-0863), a national phone service that provides counseling and referrals, and TWIN, which provides recorded information.

In 1996 Twin Services completed a three-year federally funded program to train educators, health care workers, and social service providers in the special needs of multiple-birth children.

Twins

Twins account for about 98 percent of multiple births. In some cultures they are looked at with awe as wonderful beings with special powers such as the ability to predict the future and to cure diseases. In others they are considered evil omens, and the smaller and weaker twin is sometimes abandoned or killed, in the false belief that a mother cannot provide enough milk to nourish two babies at a time. Even worse, in some primitive societies it is believed that the mother must have been unfaithful because one man could not have fathered two children at the same time, so both of the twins are put to death.

The Likelihood of Having Two Babies at a Time

The least likely mother to give birth to twins is one in her twenties, having her first pregnancy. Twins apparently occur about once in every 87 births, and registration statistics show that twins occur about 87 times for every one set of triplets. There is a principle known to biologists as Hellin's law, which states that twins occur in this ratio, triplets occur about once every 87 x 87 births, and quadruplets once every 87 x 87 x 87, and so on.

American blacks appear to have the highest twin birth rate of any racial group, and the Japanese have the lowest, with only 33 pairs of twins for every 10,000 single births.

A 10-year study made between 1946 and 1956 of 3,000 pairs of twins indicated that the most likely mother to have twins was a married woman between the ages of 35 and 39 who already had a family of eight children! The next most likely was a woman between ages 35 and 39 who already had seven children. A woman between 30 and 35 who had six children came next, then one with five, and so on. These findings applied only to fraternal twins, however; with identical twins occurring about once in every three sets of twins, and a mother having an equal chance at any age of having them.

According to more recent information, Bradford Wilson and George Edington, authors of *First Child, Second Child* (1981), a woman of 40 is three to four times more likely to produce twins than one aged 20. Also, twins usually grow up with at least one older sibling because women have usually given birth to at least one child before having twins.

Fraternal Twins

The tendency to produce fraternal twins seems to be inherited solely through mothers, never through fathers. A woman who herself is a fraternal twin is much more apt to give birth to fraternal twins than anyone else, but a man who is a fraternal twin has no more chance to father such a pair than any other man.

More male twins are born than female, and more mixed twins than either. Fraternal twins, who are born of two separate eggs, are often of both sexes and usually no more alike than ordinary brothers and sisters.

Identical Twins

Identical twins are always of the same sex. Unlike fraternal twins, they are born of one egg and are often so much alike that even their parents have trouble telling them apart. The remarkable affinity that exists between identical twins is usually lifelong. They often get the same illnesses at the same time, and their teeth come in and later decay at the same time, even if they are raised in different families and environments.

One of the most unusual examples of the affinity between identical twins was a case of two identical boys in the United States who were adopted as young babies by two quite different families. When the twins were eight years old, one of the foster families moved, and the boys were separated by 1,000 miles and did not see each other again until they were in their twenties. They discovered then they had both married girls of the same age, had both become electricians, they worked at different branches of the same company, and coincidentally owned terriers with the same name.

Sir Francis Galton (1822–1911), a British scientist who made a lifelong study of heredity and wrote a book called *Hereditary Genius*, coined the word "eugenics" as "the science which deals with all influences that improve inborn qualities." This new science got an evil reputation when the Nazis in its name tried to do away with "inferior" people by sterilizing and killing them. However, when used responsibly this science has helped biologists, clinicians, demographers, sociologists, and other professionals work together with the aim of increasing understanding of the human species and improving the quality of life. Galton studied a great many twins, and he knew of one case where a girl twin thought she was talking to her twin sister when she was actually speaking to her reflection in the mirror. However, even identical twins have differing fingerprints and may have different handwriting. Galton found only one pair of twins among 85 who could not tell their handwriting apart.

Here are additional facts about twins and other multiple births, gleaned from magazines, newspaper reports, television news programs, and TV documentaries, as well as from *The Guinness Book of World Records* and other reference books.

The Most Sets of Twins Ever Born to One Mother

The record is held by Mrs. Feodor Vassilyev in Russia, who bore 16 pairs of twins between the years 1725 and 1765. (She also had seven sets of triplets and four sets of quadruplets.)

Mrs. Mary Jonas of Chester, England, who died in 1899, comes next, with 15 pairs of twins, all of them mixed boy-and-girl sets.

The Heaviest Pair of Twins at Birth

A woman who must have had one of the most uncomfortable pregnancies ever was Mrs. J. P. Haskin of Fort Smith, Arkansas, who gave birth in February 1924 to twins, one weighing 14 pounds, the other 13 pounds and 12 ounces, a total of 27 pounds and 12 ounces.

Runners-up were two boys born in April 1995, to 22-year-old Mrs. Ferrel Maycroft of Michigan. Jeff weighed 10 pounds and 5 ounces, and Danny weighed 10 pounds and 5½ ounces, for a combined weight of 20 pounds and 10½ ounces.

The Lowest Recorded Birth Weight for Surviving Twins

This record belongs to a pair born to Florence Stimson of Peterborough, England, in August 1931. Their combined weight was only 2 pounds 3 ounces, with Mary weighing only 16 ounces and her sister Margaret 19 ounces.

The Shortest Interval between Twins

Anna Steynvaait of Johannesburg, South Africa, produced two sets of twins in record time—within 10 months—in 1960.

The Longest Interval between Twins' Births

In Rome, Italy, Mrs. Danny Petrungaro, who had been on hormone treatments after suffering four miscarriages, gave birth normally to a girl, Diana, on December 22, 1987, but her twin sister Monica was not born until 36 days later, when she was delivered by a Caesarean on January 27, 1988.

The Longest-Lived Pairs of Twins

Eli and John Phipps were born in February 1803, in Affington, Virginia. Eli lived to the age of 108 years and 9 days, and when he died, in 1911, his twin brother John was still living.

Runners-up were Mildred Widman Philippi and Mary Widman Franzini, identical twins born in St. Louis, Missouri, in 1880; they celebrated their 104th birthday together in 1984. They beat long odds, because the chances of identical twins both reaching the age of 100 are estimated at 1 in 50 million. Mildred died in May 1985, just 44 days short of the twins' 105th birthday.

The Area with the Greatest Number of Twins

This is said to be Chunsgchon, South Korea. In September 1981, 38 pairs of twins were born there among only 275 families, the highest ratio ever recorded.

The Largest Gathering of Twins Ever Held

In Twinsberg, Ohio, 1,181 sets of twins met together in August 1985.

Longest Parted and Reunited Twins

Iris and Aro Haughie, born on January 13, 1914, were raised separately and never knew each other until April 27, 1989, when, through the help of a New Zealand television program called *Missing*, they were reunited after 75 years. Fraternal twins Lloyd Earl Clark and Floyd Ellsworth Clark, born in Nebraska on February 15, 1917, were parted when only four months old, and lived under their adopted names: Lloyd as Dewayne William Gramly, and Floyd as Paul Edward Forbes. Both knew they had been born twins but it was not until June 16, 1986, that they finally met each other, after having been apart for over 69 years.

The Most Unusual Family of Twins

This, perhaps, is the Collister family in England. It consists of two pairs of identical twins and their children. Twin sisters Pat and Pauline married twin brothers John and Peter on the same day in 1980, and each wife gave birth to a baby within an hour of the other in September 1984. Their children have trouble telling their parents apart, so they call their mothers "Auntie Mummy" and their fathers "Uncle Daddy."

The Mothers of Twins Clubs

This was founded in 1960 as a national organization "to broaden the understanding of those aspects of child development and rearing which relate especially to twins, through the interchange of information between parents, educators, doctors and others with a direct interest and appropriate experience." From its base in Albuquerque, New Mexico, it publishes a newsletter that reports the latest news on research projects and other articles of interest to mothers of twins. It advises parents about decisions to be made in connection with twins' upbringing, such as whether it is desirable to encourage their individuality by separating them in school or to keep them together at all times. The national organization of Mothers of Twins Clubs is against a set policy on this question, saying most of its members prefer a case-by-case approach. Studies of twins have indicated that only slightly more than half prefer to be separated, although in fact more than three-quarters are, and some elementary schools make separation mandatory, believing this is in the best interest of the children because it reduces competition and rivalry between them.

Conjoined Twins

Called by the unscientific name of "Siamese twins" because the first famous pair was born in Thailand when it was called Siam, these are twins whose bodies have not totally separated while in the womb. In times past, such babies were regarded with horror or morbid curiosity as hopeless freaks, but since the advancement of surgical techniques in our century many have been able to be separated and to live normal lives afterwards. Even those who cannot be separated because they share vital organs are now viewed with more compassion than in the past.

The first so-called Siamese twins were Chang and Eng Bunker (the names mean "Left" and "Right"), born in Meklong, Siam on May 11, 1811. They were joined by a cartilaginous band at their chests. In spite of this they became successful and wealthy, having a long vaudeville career in the United States, and when they were 32 years old both actually got married, to sisters Sarah and Adelaide Yates of North Carolina. Chang fathered 10 children and Eng fathered 12. They lived to be 62, dying within three hours of each other on January 17, 1874.

Another famous pair who reached maturity were Daisy and Violet Hilton, born in Brighton, England, in February 1908. They were joined at the buttocks. But they were pretty and were able to have long careers as singers and dancers in vaudeville. They died from Hong Kong flu in Charlotte, North Carolina, in January 1969 when they were 60 years old.

The earliest successful separation of conjoined twins was performed in December 1952, by Dr. Jack S. Geller at Mount Sinai Hospital in Cleveland, Ohio, on two girls who were joined at the sternum. Also during the 1950s, in a clinic in Turin, Italy, a team of 24 doctors managed to separate two six-year-old girls, Santina and Giuseppina Foglia, who had been joined since birth at the base of their spines with a six-inch patch of bone. They had been frail physically and for a time seemed feeble mentally; they learned to walk and talk late. The operation was risky because the same blood coursed through both girls. Each body had grown dependent on the other and their lungs were weak, but it was a success. When they woke up afterwards, Giuseppina reached out toward her sister in a nearby crib and exclaimed, "You're so far away!"

The oldest surviving unseparated twins known are Yvonne and Yvette Jones, born in Los Angeles, California, in 1949. Their heads are fused together at the crown, but they have turned down offers of an operation to separate them.

Triplets

In 1939 multiple births—twins, triplets, and so forth—accounted for about one in 90 deliveries, but now they account for one in 40. The incidence of triplets rose seven times faster than single births between 1973 and 1990. About 2,500 sets are born each year.

Maureen Boyle, a mother of triplets and the executive director of Mothers of Supertwins, a national organization based in New York, has said, "Those expecting triplets and above may get better treatment than those with twins, because at least there is usually the recognition of high risk." In her own case, she was saved from losing her triplets when her early contractions were detected, and she was ordered to bed. But in a case in California in 1995, another woman's insurance company denied coverage for an at-home uterine monitor, which Mrs. Boyle said can be crucial. The California woman delivered two girls and a boy at 26 weeks and her babies had to stay a long time in intensive care, where the average room charges for triplets totals $255,000.

The Most Sets of Triplets Ever Born to One Mother

Madelena Granata gave birth to 15 sets of triplets between 1839 and 1886, in Nocera Superiore, Italy. And Mrs. Feodor Vassilyev of Shuya, Russia, gave birth to seven sets of triplets in the eighteenth century.

The Fastest Births of Triplets

Three boys, Bradley, Christopher and Carmon, were born within two minutes to Mrs. James E. Duck of Memphis, Tennessee, in March, 1977.

The Heaviest Triplets

These are said to be two boys and a girl who together weighed 26 pounds and 6 ounces, born in March 1968, in Iran.

The Longest-Lived Triplets

The Cardwell triplets were born on their parents' cotton farm near Waco, Texas, on May 18, 1899. For six months their parents could not decide what to name them. They were local celebrities and this dilemma got written up in the newspapers, reaching the eyes of Frances Cleveland, the First Lady of President Grover Cleveland. She suggested they be called Faith, Hope, and Charity—which was done. They were always close: Charity once sent look-alike Faith on a date in her place "and [the boy] never did know the difference." After living through 18 presidencies and a total of six husbands and six children, they were living together, in a retirement home, in 1994, when they were 95 years old.

Talented Identical Triplets

Triplet brothers Perry, Phil, and Paul Johnson, born in 1965, all went to the University of Kansas where they shared the same major (chemistry) and by graduation in June 1985 won matching Phi Beta Kappa keys for academic excellence. All three then went on to medical school together; ever since the age of eight they had all wanted to be doctors. They are so much alike that Perry once said, "Our common enemy is people who think we are all the same person. Once a girl asked me, 'When you wake up in the morning and look in the mirror, do you know which one you are?'"

Quadruplets

The Most Sets Ever Born to One Mother

Mrs. Feodor Vassilyev (1707–1782), who lived in Shuya, Russia, gave birth to four sets of quads. She also holds the record for having the most sets of twins and triplets.

The Heaviest at Birth

These were born to Mrs. Ayako Tsuchihashi in Kagoshima, Japan, in October 1978. She had four girls whose combined weight was 22 pounds and 13 ounces.

The Longest-Lived Quads

Adolf, Anne Marie, Emma, and Elizabeth Ottman were born in Munich, Germany, in May 1912. The first to die was Adolf, in March 1992, at the age of 79 years and 316 days.

Quintuplets

The Most Sets

Quintuplets occur once in 48 million births. There is no recorded case of more than one set of them in one family.

The Heaviest at Birth

This is a tie between those born to Mrs. Lui Saulian in Zhejiang, China, in June 1953, and those born to Mrs. Kamalammal of Pondicherry, India, in December 1956. Both sets of quints had a combined birth weight of 25 pounds.

The Longest-Lived

Until the twentieth century there were no known cases in which all five babies survived past infancy. But with the aid of modern medicine there are now several. Among the most prominent are:

The Andersons: Scott, Roger, Owen, Audrey, and Diane, born to Karen Anderson of Portland, Oregon, on her twenty-eighth birthday, April 26, 1973. (See page 107).

The Dilegentis: Franco, Maria Fernando, Maria Ester, Maria Cristina, and Carlos Alberto, born to Vallotta de Dilengenti in Buenos Aires, Argentina, on July 15, 1945.

The Dionnes: Emilie, Yvonne, Cecile, Marie, and Annette, born to Mrs. Oliva Dionne in Callander, Ontario, Canada, on May 20, 1934. Emilie died at age 20 and Marie at 36, but the others outlived them. (See page 104).

The Fischers: Mary Ann, Mary Magdalene, Mary Catherine, Mary Margaret, and James Andrew, born to Mary Ann Fischer, who already had five other children ranging in age from eight to three, in Aberdeen, South Dakota, on September 14, 1963.

The Jacobssens: Alan, Brett, Connor, Douglas, and Edward, born to Linda and Bruce Jacobssen in London, England, on April 26, 1985.

The Klavers: On February 6, 1996, Paula and Shmuel Klaver of New York City greeted three girls and two boys delivered by Caesarean section about one minute apart, with a team of 26 doctors and nurses assisting. The babies, who each weighed less than two pounds, were born 13 weeks prematurely. All of them required treatment for immature lungs, but all were listed in stable condition. The mother, who already had two sons, aged 12 and 10, had wanted more children because her sons "had shown me how wonderful children can be." She had been taking a fertility drug under a doctor's supervision for four years. When these new babies arrived, both the parents and their older children were thrilled. The father, a musician, canceled an engagement in order to stay at the hospital until 4 A.M. after the births, alternately comforting his tired wife and cooing at the infants. Steven, their 12-year-old, said, "My whole life is going to change. I don't think I will be ready but I'll have fun as I'm trying to get to know them." And David, the 10-year-old, said, "I'm very ecstatic and very shocked that we have three sisters."

The Klaver babies are the forty second surviving set of quintuplets to date in the United States, only two of which are believed to have been conceived without fertility therapy, according to Maureen Boyle of Mothers of Supertwins.

Sextuplets

The Greatest Known Number of Surviving Sextuplets

The Gianninis: Francesco, Fabrizio, Giorgio, Roberto, Letizia, and Linda, born to Rosanna Giannini in Florence, Italy, on January 11, 1980.

The Rosenkowitzes: David, Jason, Grant, Nicolette, Emma, and Elizabeth, born to Susan Jane Rosenkowitz in Mowbray, Cape Town, South Africa, on January 11, 1974.

The Waltons: Six girls born to Janet Walton in Liverpool, England, on November 18, 1983.

(Intriguing coincidence: Two of these three sets of sextuplets were born on January 11.)

Longest-Lived Sextuplets

In 1866 in Chicago, Illinois, sextuplets were born to the Bushnell family. Two boys and two girls survived infancy; the last survivor was Alicia who lived until age 85.

Septuplets

There have been six cases of septuplets in the twentieth century: in 1907 in Nigeria; in 1920 in East Africa; in 1931, in Portugal; in 1933 in British Guiana; in 1937 in India. And on May 21, 1985, Patti Jorgenson Frustaci, 36 years old, of Orange, California, who had been taking a fertility drug, gave birth to septuplets. They were born by Caesarean section 12 weeks prematurely, each weighing less than two pounds. One little girl was stillborn, two boys and another girl died a few weeks after birth, but three survived.

Octuplets

Two known cases of octuplets have occurred in this century. In 1921 Enriquita Ruilba in Tampico, Mexico, gave birth to eight babies on the same day, and in 1934 Mrs. Tam Sing in Swoom Yam Sha, China, gave birth to seven boys and one girl in one day.

Nonuplets

Geraldine Brodrick of Sydney, Australia, gave birth to nine children—five boys and four girls—on a day in June 1971. Two of the boys were stillborn, and none of the other babies lived more than six days.

Two other sets of nine babies were also born in this century, one set in Philadelphia, Pennsylvania, in May 1912, and another set in Bagerhat, Bangladesh, in May 1977. All these babies died in infancy.

Decuplets

The largest number of babies ever reported in a single birth is 10. In 1924 there was a report from Spain of 10 babies born at once, and in May 1936, a similar report came from China. In April 1946, two boys and eight girls were born together in Bacacay, Brazil, but none survived.

Quindecuplets

In July 1971 Dr. Gennaro Montanino in Rome, Italy, announced that he had removed the fetuses of 10 girls and 5 boys from the womb of a 35-year-old housewife. A fertility drug she had taken was responsible for this unique instance of multiple conceptions.

THE MOST FAMOUS BABIES IN THE WORLD IN THE 1930s

The birth of the Dionne Quintuplets in 1934 received the kind of intensive newspaper, radio, and magazine coverage usually reserved for wars, disasters, and national elections. They were the first known quintuplets to survive and soon became international celebrities.

Five Births in 30 Hectic Minutes

The quintuplets' mother was a 24-year-old French Canadian named Elzire Dionne. She had married at 16 and already had had six children: three boys (one of whom had died) and three girls. The family lived in a four-room farmhouse, with no electricity. Mrs. Dionne, who usually felt well during pregnancies and never had prenatal medical care, was tired during her pregnancy. Five active children to take care of were five reasons, and another was financial worry: her husband, Oliva Dionne, was unemployed and on the dole.

On May 28, 1934, at 2 A.M., labor began, two months early. Mrs. Dionne and her husband thought she might be having twins, so they sent for a doctor, even though she had two midwives.

In a newspaper interview the next day, the parents said the midwives had efficiently prepared for the doctor, but three babies arrived before the doctor got there at 4:30 A.M. By then Mrs. Dionne was in convulsions and hemorrhaging internally, so the doctor concentrated on her while the midwives looked after the babies. The fourth and fifth babies arrived only 30 minutes after the first one, and Mrs. Dionne fainted.

The midwives, said the Dionnes, tended to the new arrivals even though the doctor told them, "You're wasting your time; they won't live." Mr. Dionne baptized the babies as the doctor passed them to him. Then the doctor left, noting that he was expecting another delivery later that day and needed to rest.

Dr. Dafoe's version of what happened was different. In August he wrote a series of newspaper articles and a report for the *American Medical Association Journal* in which he said he arrived at 4 A.M. "to find the home in confusion, no preparation made for confinement except for a kettle boiling on the stove. Two babies had already been born, a third was arriving. . .The father had disappeared. I scrubbed up. . .and took over."

According to Dafoe, he washed his hands, then passed a third little girl to the dumbfounded midwives, and another, and another. He recalled that he, not the father, baptized the babies. Mrs. Dionne was in shock and he thought she might be dying, he wrote, so he went to get a priest. Three hours after the births the mother was out of danger. "During this time of great worry the five babies were almost forgotten," he wrote, "but their kitten-like cries reminded me of their presence. . . . "

The total birth weight for all five babies was only six pounds. Later the mother named them Yvonne, Cecile, Marie, Emilie, and Annette.

The Struggle to Keep the Preemies Alive

Mr. Dionne called the local paper to place an announcement there, and within a few hours the Dionne home was inundated with reporters, photographers, nurses, an amusement promoter, and gifts. Most important and welcome was a 10-year-old incubator sent from the *Chicago American* and the *New York Evening Journal* and delivered by an escort of Royal Canadian Mounties.

When the incubator arrived, Dr. Dafoe gave the three weakest babies two drops of rum each and popped them into the incubator, which was too small to hold all five. A graduate nurse was hired that afternoon. Every two hours a trained nurse fed the quints two medicine droppers of milk, corn syrup, and water. The feedings took so long that as soon as she had finished with Baby No. 5 she had to start over again with Baby No. 1.

By the third day, the babies were the longest living set of quintuplets. Dr. Dafoe announced that he would not charge for his services, and the premier of Ontario instructed the Public Welfare Department to provide all necessary care for the babies and Mrs. Dionne. The Dionnes received five complete layettes, and other gifts poured in.

On the fifth day, the weakest of the three incubator babies again turned blue, but she was revived with two more drops of rum. These babies then developed colic and constipation, and were submitted to the indignities of milk of magnesia and warm water enemas. Then, on the eighth day, all five babies turned yellow from jaundice. The doctor was not alarmed, however, as jaundice is not unusual in week-old infants.

By the second week, the babies were getting plenty of milk. Neighbors who were nursing their own babies arrived to donate their extra milk. A Toronto child specialist promised 20 ounces of milk a day from mothers in Toronto, and the A.M.A. in Chicago also sent milk.

For the first few weeks the babies were fed every 2 hours, then 2½, and then 3 for a considerable time. In December 1934, seven months after their birth, they were still being fed every four hours. The babies in incubators were kept there until they weighed six pounds. All the babies were somewhat anemic and showed signs of rickets, and in the early autumn they developed severe intestinal toxemia, which gave Dr. Dafoe "many anxious moments."

The Family in Conflict with the Government

A promoter from Chicago, as soon as he read about the quintuplets, contacted Mr. Dionne about exhibiting them at the Chicago's World's Fair, and Mr. Dionne signed a contract with him. Unwittingly, he signed away his miraculous babies, for, as *Life* magazine wrote, "his pathetic attempt to ease the financial burden he foresaw in the quints touched off a high-powered campaign to protect the babies from heartless exploitation." The terms offered by the promoter were $100 a week until the babies were moved to Chicago. Once on exhibit, they were to get $250 a week plus 10 percent of the receipts. However, Dr. Dafoe said he would not consent to this arrangement.

Dr. Dafoe said the Ontario government was a great friend to these babies. It had a tiny hospital constructed for the babies only 100 yards away from the family's home. It provided food for the entire Dionne family and for the staff of the hospital. It repaired the roads into town to accommodate the swarms of curious visitors, it constructed a new power line for electricity, and it appointed a Board of Guardians to prevent exploitation of the babies. When there was an attempt to kidnap the babies in August, the government set up special police protection for them and, finally, took custody of them.

In September the babies were moved into the Dafoe Hospital, as it was called. The building had nine rooms, and it was fireproof, electrified, and heat-controlled by thermostat. Money to build the hospital had been raised by Canadian businessmen. But the parents were so indignant at having their babies taken away from them that they refused to attend the gala arrival ceremony.

Dr. Dafoe was put in charge of the hospital, and he taught the girls to call him "Papa Dafoe." He hired a large staff of nurses who enforced a rigid daily schedule that included two-hour periods during which the girls were displayed to the public through glass walls.

The doctor and his nurses enforced strict discipline, with solitary confinement and beatings common punishments for disobedience. When one staff nurse complained to Dr. Dafoe that the head nurse was cruel, he fired the staff nurse for insubordination. The staff spoke only English to the children, whose parents spoke French, further isolating them from their family. The Dionnes were so upset by the way the children were being raised that they hired a lawyer to help them regain parental control.

The eminent psychiatrist Dr. Alfred Adler (1870–1937) agreed that separating the quints from their parents was harmful and on a radio program said the girls were "suffering from emotional starvation." Thus began a lengthy and intense struggle between two irreconcilable attitudes, the parents holding that the children were an intrinsic part of a private family and that it was wrong to separate them from their parents and siblings, the government holding that the children belonged to the government.

Papa Dionne went on tour to raise money for his family, explaining that he would use it to restore parental control. He also wanted a share in the Quintuplet Fund, money being held in trust by the government and not to be drawn on until the babies were 18 years old. Mr. Dionne wanted to use some of the money to support the older brothers and sisters. He appealed to the pride and prejudice of all French Canadian Catholics, saying the quints were being deprived of their language and religion. "We do not like the way the Government is splitting up our family. . . . The other children are not being treated right. That's why we are on this tour."

The Canadian government replied that it had taken Dionne off the dole when the quints were born and given him $75 a month from the trust fund. They denied that he had been forced to sign away parental rights and said they were protecting the quints because "a lot of American showmen want to get control of the babies."

Time magazine explained the controversy thus: "For a man to beget quintuplets seems to Father Oliva Dionne a private and personal achievement whose profits properly belong to him. On the contrary, thinks the Liberal Government, it is a public achievement of society, as represented by Dr. Allan Dafoe, who delivered and reared them, the U.S. newspapers that sent a hot water incubator and saved their lives, the Northern Ontario businessmen who built the modern Dionne nursery heated against Northern Ontario's minus-30-degree winter weather."

After a furious debate in Parliament, the *Dionne Quintuplet Guardianship Act* of 1935 was passed. The quints were made wards of King George VI with Dr. Dafoe as their guardian, and control of the babies' estates was given to the minister of welfare.

The struggle was still not over, however. Private investigators found that Dr. Dafoe was not the saint most people considered him. He had profited personally from commercial endorsements and had illegally spent thousands of dollars from the quints' funds for the expenses of his self-promoting lectures. He was dismissed as the girls' guardian, though he was still in charge of the hospital.

Meanwhile the government, which had made millions of dollars from the quints, found there was a drop in tourism and sales and royalties from quint-related products; people were losing interest in the girls now that they were six years old. But they enjoyed one last moment of glory: they were invited to England to meet King George VI and Queen Elizabeth, who also invited their parents, brothers, and sisters, as well as their doctor.

In 1944 when the quints were 10, the Government finally turned control of them back to their father, announcing that the special care once needed was now deemed "no longer necessary," and that Dr. Dafoe was resigning "due to health reasons." He died the following year.

The family was now wealthy; the trust fund had grown to $1 million. They built a new house with 10 bedrooms, 5 bathrooms, and a security fence, and there were no more public viewings. All the quints lived to adulthood, although Emilie died after an epileptic seizure at age 20. Annette, Cecile, and Marie each got married and had children, later divorced and lived together again, with Yvonne who wanted for a while to be a nun but never took final vows. An unhappy aftermath of their life story is that in 1995, the surviving quints accused Dionne of having sexually abused them when they were young.

THE ANDERSON QUINTUPLETS

Scott, Roger, Owen, Audrey, and Diane Anderson were born two minutes apart in Portland, Oregon, on April 26, 1973, their mother's twenty-eighth birthday. She had never before been able to carry a baby to full term and had had six miscarriages. However, she had two other children, Eric, Jr., and Paul, whom she had adopted when she thought she would never be able to be a "natural" mother.

Like most people, when I thought of quintuplets, I thought of the Dionnes, and I had a deep fear of repeating that tragedy. Their story was freshly engraved in my mind because my mother had just brought me a September 1940 copy of *Life* magazine that had a long article about the family. She and I flipped through the pages, horrified by what had happened to the five little girls. Taken away from their parents by a well-intentioned doctor and raised by a staff of governesses and nurses, they were kept in a glass-walled compound so that they could be viewed by curious onlookers. On a typical Sunday, people stood patiently in line to watch them play. To prepare the girls for the viewing, a governess spent two hours a day grooming them. I was determined that nothing like that would ever happen to our children. More than anything else, I wanted them to have a "normal upbringing," and to me that meant being raised by a mother and a father.

Karen Anderson and Jo Robinson, Full House: The Story of the Anderson Quintuplets *(1986)*

The Andersons stunned everybody by choosing to raise their quints without any help, even though Diane had a weak heart and lungs and their oldest boy, Eric, was deaf and asthmatic, giving them an already challenging parental workload. There were then only four or five other sets of quintuplets in the United States, and in those cases the parents had hired governesses or nurses and enlisted teams of volunteers to help them cope.

In 1975 *Redbook* Magazine ran a series of three articles on the Anderson family by pediatrician Dr. Benjamin Spock, mother-of-three Judith Viorst, and child psychologist Dr. T. Berry Brazelton. All marveled at the children's and parents' strong personalities, poise, happiness, and good health. Dr. Brazelton wrote:

> I spent an earthshaking week with the Andersons when the quintuplets were two years old. I learned more from that one visit than I've learned in any other week of my life, medical school be hanged! I had expected to find bedlam—tantrums, negativism, constant demands. But I was wrong. Karen and Eric were remarkable parents, compassionate, firm, able. They had individualized those quintuplets from the first, and each one had a firm sense of his/her identity and a fabulous self-image. Every mother and father should read *Full House*, this remarkable account of the stress, and the coping strengths to meet it, which Karen and Eric found to raise this group of secure individuals. I fell in love with them.

UNUSUAL BIRTHS
The World's Smallest Babies

The smallest surviving infant ever reported in the United States was Jacqueline Benson, born in Palatine, Illinois, on February 20, 1936. She weighed only 12 ounces.

In 1938 the *American Medical Association Journal* contained a report about another baby who weighed only 1 pound and 4 ounces when she was born in 1920, and who had set a record by living to adulthood. The affidavit signed by the nurse who weighed her at birth said: "Ruth Thomas was so small in size that she could almost lie in the ordinary retail cigar box. Her fingers were not bigger than darning needles and her legs were no bigger than a lady's second finger."

The smallest surviving baby ever born in the world is believed to be Marion Chapman, who weighed only 10 ounces when she was born six weeks prematurely on June 5, 1938, in South Shields, England. She was fed hourly for the first 30 hours with brandy, glucose, and water, through a fountain pen filler. At three weeks she weighed one pound 13 ounces, by her first birthday 13 pounds 14 ounces, and on her twenty-first birthday 106 pounds. She later got married and lived to age 45.

The Most Premature Babies

The most premature baby born in the United States was Ernestine Hudgins, born on February 8, 1983, in San Diego, California. She was premature by about 18 weeks and weighed only 17 ounces.

The nurses at St. Vincent's Hospital in New York City gave a vivid account of their experiences with a baby born 12 weeks prematurely in 1986. She was Jennifer Fernandez, weighing less than a pound and a half at birth, and who looked, they said, more like a miniature old woman than a baby. Her skin was transparent. Beneath matchstick ribs her tiny heart beat rapidly. The chances of survival for a baby born three months prematurely were extremely slim, so extra-special care was needed around the clock, and there were many complications. Enclosed in an incubator, her tiny body was obscured by tubes and tape. There were sensors attached to her little belly which monitored her heart rate and temperature. A tube fed her intravenously through her tiny hand. The nurses could check the placement of tubes and change her diapers through portholes in the side of the incubator. But none of these machines, nor any of the doctors or nurses, could make Jenny well. They could only help to keep her alive. They said the rest was up to her.

She seemed to want to live. Certainly every hour she was alive defied the odds. "Our Jenny," said one of the nurses, "she's a fighter!" Maybe it was the attentive doctors. Or the nurses who talked to her and stroked her back. Or perhaps it was her mother's vigil that gave her the will to live. Whatever it was, 14 weeks after being admitted to the hospital's Neonatal Intensive Care Unit, Jennifer went home a healthy 5 pounds 2 ounces. And during those weeks all who knew her said they felt she had taught them a powerful lesson about the value of life without ever uttering a single word.

Another extremely premature baby was born in Ottawa, Canada, on May 20, 1987. He was James Elgin Gill, 120 days ahead of schedule, weighing 1 pound 6 ounces.

The Heaviest Newborns

The heaviest viable baby on record born normally to normal parents was the son of Carmelina Fedele of Versa, Italy, born in September 1955, weighing 22 pounds and 8 ounces.

A boy named Sithandive, weighing 22½ pounds at birth, was delivered by Caesarean section on May 24, 1982, at Sipetu Hospital, Transkei, South Africa.

Coincidental Births

Four generations of boys in a family in Wilmington, North Carolina, were all born on the Fourth of July: (1) Ralph Bertram Williams in 1876, exactly 100 years after the Declaration of Independence; (2) his son, Ralph Bertram Williams, Jr; (3) his grandson, Ralph Bertram Williams III; and (4) his great-grandson, Ralph Bertram Williams IV, in 1982.

The only verified example of a family producing five single children with coincidental birthdays is the Cummings family of Clintwood, Virginia. All five children of Ralph and Carolyn Cummings were born on February 20: Catherine in 1952, Carol in 1953, Charles in 1956, Claudia in 1961, and Cecelia in 1966. Random odds against five such births occurring singly on the same date are estimated to be 1 to 17,797,577,730.

Leap Year Births

The Henricksen family of Andenes, Norway, has three children who were all born on February 29, Leap Year Day: Heidi in 1960, Olav in 1964, and Lief Martin in 1968. Thus as of February 29, 1996, Heidi, who had lived 36 years, had celebrated only nine birthdays; Olav, who was 32 in 1996, had had eight, and Lief Martin, who by 1996 was 28 years old, had had only seven birthdays.

109

Babies Born with Teeth

According to Britain's Royal Society of Medicine, about one of every 2,000 babies is born with teeth. Pliny (A.D. 23–79) mentioned a child named Marcus Curius Dentatus because he was born with teeth. Shakespeare said King Richard III was born with teeth and "could gnaw a crust when two hours old." In France and Italy there is an ancient belief that such babies will grow up to attain eminence, a belief supported by three toothy French tots who grew up to become King Louis XIV, The Great (1638–1715), Cardinal Richelieu (1585–1642), and Napoleon (1769–1821). King Louis was born sporting two strong teeth and the wet nurses who took over his feedings which his mother, Anne of Austria, in the fashion of fashionable ladies of that day, refused to provide, complained bitterly about being bitten.

Nowadays, babies born with teeth do not usually get a chance to sink their teeth into anyone. It is modern dental practice in these rare cases to pull out all the teeth when the baby is just a few days or weeks old, because of the danger that they might become loose and lodge in the baby's throat. A boy was born in Pittsburgh, Pennsylvania, in 1957 with eight teeth, a good head start on the teething process, but this gave him no advantage; he was relieved of them at the age of three days.

It is understandable that mothers prefer nursing babies to be toothless, but dislike of baby teeth can go too far. In some parts of Africa, babies born with teeth have been put to death.

According to Chinese folklore it is much better for the parents if a baby delays a while before cutting his first teeth, because if he is an early teether he will grow up to eat his parents, but a late teether will support them in their old age.

Test Tube Babies

Modern medical technology has made it possible for some would-be mothers who find it difficult to conceive in the normal way to conceive babies outside the mother's body. Such children are called "test-tube babies" and the technique used is called in vitro fertilization (IVF). It provides hope to many couples; more than 25,000 attempts are made every year, though only about 13 percent are successful.

The world's first test-tube baby was Louise Brown, externally conceived in November 1977. She was born by Caesarean section to her 31-year-old mother, Lesley Brown, in Oldham General Hospital in Great Britain, on July 25, 1978, and weighed 5 pounds 12 ounces at birth. A great deal of publicity followed this extraordinary birth, which one might think would have puzzled and embarrassed Louise, but she apparently took the whole subject in stride and grew up as a normal, healthy, well-adjusted, and attractive child. In 1994 she attended a large gathering of other children who had been born by this process and enjoyed meeting them, saying it made her feel as if she had hundreds of siblings.

The first test-tube baby in the U.S. was Elizabeth Jordan Carr, who was conceived externally in April 1981 and delivered by Caesarean section at Norfolk General Hospital in Virginia, weighing five pounds 12 ounces on December 28, 1981.

The World's First Test-tube Twins

At the Queen Victoria Medical Centre in Melbourne, Australia, on June 5, 1981, Stephen and Amanda Mays were delivered by Caesarean section to 31-year-old Mrs. Radmila Mays.

Amanda weighed five pounds and six ounces, and Stephen weighed five pounds and three ounces.

The World's First Test-tube Triplets

Two girls and a boy were born through in vitro fertilization in Adelaide, Australia, on June 8, 1983. (At the request of the parents, no names were published.)

In Vitro Quads

Three years after they were married, Keith and Karin Screws, who owned a small ranch in Swainsboro, Georgia, learned that Keith had cancer. A doctor told them that his chemotherapy might render him sterile, so they might consider storing some of his semen in a sperm bank, which they did. They both wanted to experience parenthood very much, so when Keith was feeling better they decided that in spite of their uncertain future they would try to bring new life into the world. Their doctor told them their best chance would be with in vitro fertilization. Because there is only a 20 percent chance of achieving pregnancy that way, to improve the odds the reproductive endocrinologist decided to implant five fertilized eggs, not expecting more than one or two to survive. But four did. In November 1992, Keith's cancer reached his liver, and his one desire now was to live long enough to see his babies born. On December 17, 1992, they were delivered by Caesarean section while their father sat beside their mother in the operating room. Only the largest one weighed as much as four pounds, but they were all healthy. They lived in incubators in the hospital for about a month, while their father was also there for more chemotherapy, and the nurses took the babies into his room for visits.

After they returned home, Keith's health continued to deteriorate, but he was happy with the babies, and the family learned how many people cared for them. Local businessmen raised enough pledges to begin building them a new, larger house. Finally, in June 1993, Keith, only 32 years old, died peacefully. But life went on. Ground was broken for the new house in December in a ceremony with many friends and neighbors present. The town's mayor said, "We hope that when these babies are grown, they will look at this house and understand how much their father was respected and admired by everyone who knew him." Instead of being bitter about her husband's death, Karin says without it she never would have realized the amazing goodness that lies in people. His death took one life away from her but four other lives were given to her to sustain and comfort her, and this made her realize gratefully how precious life is.

Babies Born from Frozen Embryos

Another medical advance has made it possible to remove eggs from the mother's womb, have them fertilized outside the womb, then frozen and stored, and at a later date implanted in the womb for a "normal" pregnancy.

The first birth achieved by this method occurred in Melbourne, Australia, on March 28, 1984. The baby was delivered by Caesarean section and the birth was announced by scientists from Monash University, but the names of the family were kept secret.

In the U.S. a boy conceived by this method was delivered by Caesarean section on June 4, 1986, to a 36-year-old mother at Cottage Hospital in Santa Barbara, California, and a second child was born to the same mother by the same procedure on October 23, 1989. This is believed to be the only case so far of siblings born from frozen embryos. Again, the names of the family were withheld from the public.

Ethical, Medical, and Financial Problems about In Vitro Fertilization and Frozen Embryos

Ever since the 1980s, in vitro fertilization and the freezing of embryos have proliferated without monitoring or regulation. The fertility industry is very competitive and lucrative, so that some facilities will do almost anything, including the implanting of as many as eight embryos, in order to increase the chances of conception.

Some women beg their doctors to implant lots of fertilized embryos, especially if they are over 35 with declining odds of achieving pregnancy. But in England doctors can lose their licenses if they implant more than three at a time, and in 1996 the American Society for Reproductive Medicine decided it was necessary to do some self-policing. They planned to issue new IVF guidelines to limit the number of implanted embryos to three or four. Dr. Alan DeCherney, the chief of obstetrics and gynecology at Tufts University, explained that the goal is to prevent creating quintuplets and to reduce triplets in assisted pregnancies from 5 percent to 1 or 2 percent. Fewer multiple births would spare mothers some of the risks they face, such as Caesarean deliveries, anemia, hypertension, and post-partum hemorrhaging.

Another important consideration is that by implanting a smaller number of embryos, doctors and parents would less often have to face the ethical problem of "selective reduction," the aborting of some of the multiple but viable fetuses.

In 1994 in the U.S. a lawsuit was brought by a man who had donated sperm when he was married to his ex-wife. The issue in question was which parent should have custody of frozen embryos. Though the couple had divorced six months after the husband donated sperm the mother wanted to give birth. The father, however, said he no longer wished to have children by his former wife, and he wanted the embryos destroyed. The case created a great deal of controversy, with different judges deciding differently, and as of this writing the issue is undecided.

A Woman Who Gave Birth to Her Own Grandchildren

When she was 14 years old Christa Schweitzer learned that she had no uterus and therefore would never be able to bear a child. She was devastated, but her mother, Arlette Schweitzer, tried to console her, saying, "Never mind. By the time you're ready, they'll have something. Science moves fast." She was right. On Arlette's nineteenth wedding anniversary she and Christa drove from their home in Aberdeen, South Dakota, to Rochester, Minnesota, to consult a doctor at the Mayo Clinic. He looked at Christa's healthy mother and said, "All she needs is a carrier." Christa's eggs could be implanted in her mother.

Four years later Christa met Kevin Uchytil; on their third date she told him about her problem and about the possible solution. They got married in 1989, and in 1991 Christa and her mother began treatments at the University of Minnesota. A few months later four of Christa's eggs, fertilized by Kevin's sperm, were implanted in Arlette's uterus. Eight months later, the 42-year-old Arlette, with Christa at her side, gave birth—to twins.

This was the first time in the United States that a grandmother had borne a daughter's babies, and the event received lots of publicity. Arlette did not think it was particularly astonishing. "Parents donate their kidneys for their children," she said. "A lot of mothers would do this. They'd do it for love. . . . When your child needs something, you do everything you can to help. . . .I sat on the nest, but they were Christa's eggs."

Since then she has heard from other grandmothers who carried babies for their children. One woman in South Africa gave birth to triplets for her daughter in 1987. And soon more will be able to help their daughters in this way, now that doctors have begun to implant embryos in women even in their fifties.

FAMOUS PARENTS OF ILLEGITIMATE CHILDREN

Saint Augustine (A.D. 354–430): Philosopher and convert to Christianity who became Bishop of Hippo in North Africa. His eloquent writings, his autobiographical *Confessions* (397–401) and *The City of God* (413–426), had such a profound spiritual and theological influence that he was named a Doctor of the Church. Before his conversion he had a long relationship with a mistress and they produced a "love child" whom he named Adeodatus (Latin for "Gift of God"). Augustine wrote that "though children be against our wills begotten, yet being born they even compel us to love them," and he described his son as "most excellently made, though born in sin, and of rare wit and talents, surpassing those of many learned men."

Phineas Taylor Barnum (1810–1891): American showman and owner of a popular circus. He promoted this as "The Greatest Show on Earth" after merging it with his most successful competitor in 1881 to form the still incomparable Barnum and Bailey's Circus. He had four legitimate daughters and one illegitimate son, who grew up to become a doctor.

Mikhail Baryshnikov (1948–): The great Russian expatriate ballet dancer. He has fathered three children, Peter, Anna, and Sofia Luisa by ballerina Lisa Rinehart, as well as an older daughter, Alexandria, whose mother is the actress Jessica Lange.

> There are no illegitimate children—only illegitimate parents.
>
> —Lern R. Yankovich, Judge's opinion in Zipkin v. Mozon, June, 1928

Rodrigo Borgia (1431–1503): Italian, better known as Pope Alexander VI. He had five illegitimate children before becoming Pope. Two of them, Cesar and Lucretia Borgia, became as notorious as their father. An enthusiastic lover of art as well as of power and of women, he condemned the puritanical Savonarola to death and was a patron of Michelangelo and Raphael.

Fidel Castro (1927–): Ruler of Cuba since 1959. In 1952, when he was a charismatic young revolutionary striving to oust the hated dictator Batista, he met Mrs. Natalia Revuelta, a wealthy, socially prominent married woman. She fell in love with him, and in 1955 they had a daughter, Alina Fernandez Revuelta, given her mother's surname. Castro never publicly acknowledged or denied his fatherhood but it was widely known. The daughter grew up to denounce her father as "a tyrant" and described his regime as "a dead end street," with economic collapse, food shortages, and political and cultural repression. She regularly applied for visas so she could leave the country, but they were always denied. Finally, in 1993, she secretly obtained a Spanish passport, gained weight, donned a wig and applied makeup so she would look like the woman whose identity she assumed.

In December, pretending to be a tourist, she boarded a flight to Madrid, and from there flew to the United States which granted her political asylum.

Not long ago, Castro was asked how many children he had. He replied, "Well, I don't have a tribe. Not that much. Fewer than a dozen I think."

Alexandre Dumas père (1802–1870): French author. He was prolific in more ways than one. Writer of short stories, essays, plays, historical works, and novels including *The Three Musketeers, The Count of Monte Cristo,* and *The Man in the Iron Mask*, he acknowledged and adopted three illegitimate children. The first was Alexandre Dumas fils, born when Dumas père was 22 years old, who followed in his father's footsteps and became an author. Towards the end of his life Dumas père estimated that he had 500 children in various parts of the world.

Isadora Duncan (1877–1927): American dancer: She had two children by Gordon Craig, and English stage designer, producer, actor, and author, who was himself illegitimate. The children died at a very early age in an auto accident when Duncan was driving. She was devastated and decided she must have more children. She wrote George Bernard Shaw asking him to be their father, saying, "With your brains and my beauty imagine what wonderful children we could have." But Shaw declined, replying, "Yes, but what if they inherited my looks and your brains?"

Benjamin Franklin (1706–1790): American statesman, printer, journalist, scientist, diplomat, and inventor. He had three sons including one illegitimate one.

John Harvey Kellogg (1852–1943): An American surgeon and nutritionist. He altered America's eating habits forever by inventing peanut butter, zwieback, shredded wheat, cornflakes, and other breakfast cereals. He claimed to have 42 children "acquired in Providential ways."

Karl Marx (1818–1883): German father of Communism. He had seven legitimate children and one illegitimate son, Frederic Demuth (1851–1929), whose mother was the maidservant of Marx's wife; he was a lover of the proletariat in more ways than one. Marx never acknowledged his paternity; the boy was raised by Marx's close friend and collaborator, Friedrich Engels (1820–1895), who, on his deathbed 12 years after Marx's death, revealed that "Freddy is Marx's son."

François Mitterand (1916–1995): Socialist president of France in the 1980s and 1990s. In November 1994 the magazine *Paris Match* caused a sensation by publishing photographs of a young woman identified as the president's 20-year-old daughter, named Mazarine, born out of wedlock. Many people had long known he had an illegitimate daughter in addition to two sons by his long-standing marriage to Danielle Mitterand. Most French people believe the only reason to meddle in the private life of a political figure is if the disclosure reveals a deceitful practice in conflict with his public position or if it seems to influence his public performance, and they felt that these criteria did not apply in the case of Mitterand. In 1984 he told a group of journalists in private, "Yes, I have a natural daughter. So what?" *Paris Match* reported that "the President is very proud of this child, who shares his passion for books." When the French taboo on revelations about her was broken by *Paris Match,* more people were scandalized by the fact that her name had been dragged into the French press, in imitation of the scandal-mongering practices of British and American tabloids, than by the knowledge of her parentage.

Benito Mussolini (1883–1945): Italian Fascist dictator. He had six children, five legitimate and a sixth, Benito Albino, born in 1915, who was illegitimate. When the child was two years old Mussolini denounced the mother, Ida Daiser, as "dangerous, unbalanced, and criminal" and had her interned as an enemy alien; she spent the last 10 years of her life in a mental institution. The boy grew up under the supervision of guardians and died of unknown causes on an unknown date, some time during World War II.

Jean Jacques Rousseau ((1712–1778): French philosopher. He had five children, all illegitimate, by his mistress Thèrése le Vasseur, an illiterate girl who remained faithful to him in spite of his refusal to marry her and his insistence on putting each of their children, immediately after birth, into a foundling home. This unparental attitude did not prevent him from writing *Emile, ou Trait, de l'Education* (1762), in which he told parents how children should be raised and which had a great influence on modern education.

Ellen Terry (1894–1928): Terry was a renowned English actress whose son Gordon Craig (1872–1966) was an almost equally famous stage designer, producer, actor, and author. Among his books was one about his mother called *Ellen Terry and Her Secret Life*. He was not only illegitimate but in turn became a parent of illegitimate children (see Isadora Duncan on page 111).

Charles Wesley (1707–1788): English co-founder with his brother, John Wesley, of Methodism and composer of more than 6,000 hymns. He had three sons: one, Samuel Sebastian, was illegitimate. This son became a famous cathedral organist and, like his father, a composer of church music.

Royal Fathers

For centuries it was the custom in Europe for kings to have wives in order to produce legal heirs to the throne but to keep, quite openly, mistresses as objects of affection. If more people today were familiar with history, there would not have been such a brouhaha in the 1990s over the fact that Charles, the Prince of Wales, had a mistress; he was simply following an ancient royal tradition that was once widely known and condoned. In many cases kings' illegitimate children were openly acknowledged, lived, and were educated in the palace along with their royal half brothers and sisters, the legitimate children. It was also customary for kings to bequeath hereditary estates and titles to their illegitimate children, and many aristocratic families are proud of, rather than ashamed of, being thus descended from royalty. There are too many instances to list but some outstanding examples follow:

Charlemagne (Charles the Great) (742–814): Also known as King Charles I, King of the Franks and Holy Roman Emperor. He had 10 illegitimate children in addition to 8 legitimate ones, all raised together. He was a zealous promoter of education and the arts, and founded a palace school where his children and others were educated. He believed in the education of girls as well as boys and was reported to be so fond of his daughters that he would not permit them to marry because this would mean they might leave home.

King Charles II of England (1630–1685): Known as The Merry Monarch. His reign was distinguished more by his many liaisons with mistresses and the illegitimate children these produced than by political achievements. He died without leaving any legitimate children but had at least 14 illegitimate ones by 13 mistresses, whom he publicly acknowl-

115

edged and financially supported (in style) and ennobled. His most famous mistress was "pretty, witty" Nell Gwynne (c. 1650–1687), who was so upset after their son Charles was born and had not yet been given a title that one day when the King was coming to visit her, as he approached her house she leaned out a window and held the baby up, looking as if she was about to toss him out, whereupon King Charles cried out, "Nelly, don't kill the Duke of Albans!"

King Henry I of England (1069–1135): The youngest and only English-born son of William the Conqueror who himself was illegitimate. He was called Henry Beauclare (meaning scholar) because he was unusually learned for a king in this period. He didn't live in a scholarly ivory tower, however. His reign was plagued by wars with France, and in 1120 his only legitimate son, William, drowned on his way from Normandy to England. He had one other legitimate child, his daughter Matilda. In addition he publicly acknowledged 20 illegitimate children, nine sons and 11 daughters, by 6 mistresses.

King Louis XIV of France (1638–1715): Known as "Le Roi Soleil" (the Sun King), Louis was a despotic ruler. His reign was distinguished by great prestige and cultural glories but also sullied by military defeats which, by the end of his life, had nearly ruined the country financially. Almost annually his mistresses presented him with children, most of whom he acknowledged, giving them royal titles and estates. The two youngest he kept secret for many years, having them live separately and raised by his friend Mme de Maintenon, but after his queen died he moved them all into the palace, acknowledging the children and marrying their governess.

King Philip IV of Spain (1605–1665): He impoverished his country with unsuccessful foreign wars but managed to produce 32 children, all illegitimate, and did not abandon any of them.

King William IV of England (1765–1837): Called "Silly Billy" and later "The Sailor King," he was a son of King George III (1738–1820). He had a long connection with an actress, Dorothea Jordan, which he finally was forced to break off in order to marry Adelaide of Saxe Meiningen. He became heir to the throne, and in 1830 succeeded his older brother, George IV (1762–1830), as King of Great Britain and Ireland. He was an unimpressive ruler who opposed emancipation of slaves and caused political crises by obstructing the passage of reform bills, but he had two redeeming features: he was a devoted father to his 10 illegitimate children, and he had a niece who succeeded him to the throne and became Queen Victoria.

There have been many illustrious people who started life as illegitimate children, including Sarah Bernhardt, Frederick Douglass, Alec Guinness, Alexander Hamilton, Billie Holiday, Jesse Jackson, Leonardo da Vinci, Marilyn Monroe, and William the Conqueror.

DIFFERENT OPINIONS ABOUT ILLEGITIMACY

In societies and social classes where marriage was not primarily the result of a romance but a practical way of begetting legal heirs, illegitimacy bore no great stigma. "Love children" were generally accepted on their own merits. In recent times, especially among celebrities, many people have opted to have children without bothering to go through the legal process of marriage.

There was a huge furor in the United States over the popular television show "Murphy Brown" when the unmarried title character gave birth to a baby, and Vice President Dan Quayle attacked the show as setting a bad example to its many viewers and undermining traditional family values. Moralists faced a dilemma: If a woman conceives an illegitimate baby, would they not prefer her to have it and raise it on her own rather than to abort it?

> Discrimination and various other forms of injustices suffered by children as a result of being born out of wedlock still exist in most countries and greatly reduce the possibility for happy and successful lives. These injustices are usually supported not only by social customs but also by law. The enactment of legislation embodying the principle of equality is the first prerequisite of ensuring social justice to children born out of wedlock. However, outmoded concepts and deep-rooted social prejudice might still persist and should be eliminated by educating the public to adopt a just attitude towards these persons.
>
> —*International Year of the Child Secretariat, 1979*

In Sweden no such dilemma exists, because there are no longer any illegitimate children in Sweden. A law was passed in 1979, the Year of the Child, outlawing the term and outlawing any distinction in status between children born to unmarried or married parents, stating that every child has the same legitimate status. Every child has the right to adopt either the paternal or maternal surname, the right to receive maintenance from both parents, providing that paternity has been established. It has been reported that in about 90 percent of all cases paternity is established, with most Swedish fathers voluntarily coming forward. The law allows both parents to share custody of and to act as guardians for their children if they want to, a departure from the past, when the mother automatically became the child's custodian.

Even before this new law, Swedes were inclined to look tolerantly on illegitimacy. They passed a law in 1917 that substituted for the term *bastard*, the terms *born inside marriage* and *outside marriage*. This is the same ultraliberal country that since 1979 has made spanking a child a criminal offense and that permits a child to divorce its parents.

Special Concerns in the United States

A population explosion has occurred in out-of-wedlock births in the United States in recent years. Between 1960 and 1990, illegitimate births increased more than 400 percent. In 1960, 5.3 percent of all births were out of wedlock but by 1990 the figure was 28 percent, and, by 1995 it was 31 percent.

Between 1983 and 1993, the number of children under age 18 who were living with a parent who had never married soared by more than 70 percent. The U.S. Census Bureau reported 243,000 American children living with one never married parent in 1960, and by 1993 that number had climbed to 6,300,000.

A worrisome aspect of this increase was that much of it was attributable to teenage pregnancies, which nearly doubled between 1970 and 1990. Rare in the 1960s, by the late '80s nearly one unmarried teenage girl out of 10 got pregnant. Not merely eyebrows but

117

howls of outrage would have been raised in the 1950s at the fact that 72 percent of American high school seniors have engaged in sex, according to the Centers for Disease Control and Prevention, and the results are over 1,000,000 teenage pregnancies a year, leading to 406,000 abortions, 134,000 miscarriages, and 490,000 live births, according to the American Enterprise Institute.

Sexual permissiveness and parenthood have not brought teenagers happiness. For one thing, not all pregnancies among unmarried girls are due to consental sex; the Alan Guttmacher Institute has reported that 74 percent of girls under 14 have been victims of rape, and "date rape" has become an increasingly frequent problem among teenagers. Approximately 3 million teens every year get a sexually transmitted disease, and since 1960 the teen suicide rate has more than tripled. Suicide has become the third leading cause of death among adolescents, following motor vehicle accidents and all other accidents. In 1960 only 1 percent of teenagers tried to take their lives, compared with more than 5 percent in 1990. The strains of single parenthood have also led in many cases not only to nervous breakdowns but to increased cases of child abuse and even to infanticide.

Problems associated with unmarried parenthood also have had disastrous results in terms of poverty. In 1994 the Census Bureau reported that 66.3 percent of children who were living with only their mothers lived in poverty, compared with 38.4 percent of children in one-parent families where the mother was divorced and only 10.6 percent of those who lived with married parents. The median annual family income in households where two parents were present was $43,578, in contrast to $17,814 for one-parent families where the mother was divorced and, if the mother had never been married, the median income was only $9,272.

What Is to Be Done?

U.S. Conservatives believe that welfare support for children of dependent families indicates that pregancies out of wedlock are socially acceptable and that they therefore increase the willingness of young girls and women to do nothing to avoid single parenthood, although some fear that withdrawing or reducing aid to unmarried mothers would have the adverse effect of increasing the already high number of abortions in this country. Liberals tend to agree that the welfare system has become too expensive for government to afford, and that some kind of reform is necessary, but that withdrawal of aid to dependent children would be cruel to the innocent victims of their parents' actions, and increase the number living in severe poverty.

Various proposals have been made. One is to stop attacking welfare mothers and increase pressures on absentee fathers to make them accept responsibility—by various means, such as taking away their drivers' licenses—for the children they beget. Another suggestion is to deprive unmarried mothers of welfare benefits unless they take training to go to work and earn a living so that they will not stay dependent on welfare. (Paradoxically, an opposite trend would force working mothers of young children not to go to work but to stay home and take full-time care of their children; in 1995 one divorced mother who took a job lost custody of her child because she wasn't staying home with it all day.) Yet another suggestion has been to encourage unmarried mothers to give their children up for adoption or to revive the use of orphanages. Those institutions have often had bad reputations, but with proper management they can and have offered safe havens to many children deprived of their parents through death or abandonment.

One point on which most people can agree is that illegitimacy is not the fault of the child, and therefore whatever measures are taken to reduce their number should not harm children. As is increasingly decided in custody cases, whatever is done should be "in the best interests of the child."

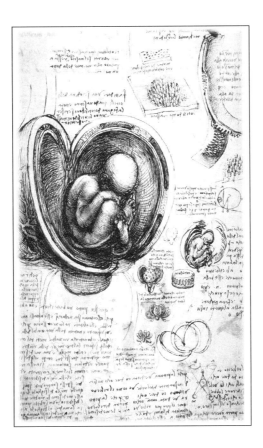

The world's best medicine

UNICEF

4

Health Care and Children with Disabilities

LIFE EXPECTANCY IN PREVIOUS CENTURIES

Edmund Halley (1656–1742), the great English mathematician and astronomer of Halley's comet fame, originated the science of vital statistics and prepared the first detailed mortality tables in 1693. Life and death could now be studied statistically, and the life insurance industry was born.

While most children born in developed countries today can expect to live out the biblical span of three score and 10 years, to age 70, and the fastest growing group in the United States today is people over 100 years old, average life expectancy was never anywhere near that high in the past. The following life expectancies in different historical periods have been estimated for the average male at age 15, once he had survived the early years when childhood diseases snuffed out many lives. These estimates were based on examinations of skeletons, tombstones, legal documents, and census records. Infectious diseases were the most frequent cause of death.

- Neanderthal: 33 years
- Bronze Age: 40 years
- Ancient Greece and Rome: 36 years
- Medieval England: 49 years
- United States at the end of the nineteenth century: 60 years

The commonly held notion of family life in Colonial America—that several generations lived together and shared farm and household chores—is far from the truth. Few people lived long enough to see their children grown, let alone their grandchildren. Average life expectancy at birth for Americans was 34.5 years for males and 36.5 years for females when George Washington became president in 1789. Data compiled in 1790 by the prominent American physician, Dr. Benjamin Rush, indicated that out of 100 babies born in a given year in Philadelphia more than one-third died before age six and only one-fourth lived beyond age 26.

PRE-TWENTIETH CENTURY "CURES" FOR CHILDREN'S AILMENTS

For aches and "pynes": Apply a salve made of swallows mashed to a jelly.

For bruises: Spread an ointment of crushed earthworms on them.

For colic: "The Collicke," as the English used to spell it, has inspired some of the most revolting medicines in history. In A.D. first century the Roman scholar Pliny the Elder (A.D. 23–79) in his famous encyclopedia *Historia Naturalis* (*Natural History*) recommended what he claimed were some "excellent" remedies:

- Roasted lark, including the feathers, burned to ashes and pulverized, taken in doses of three spoonfuls in water for four days.
- The intestine of an ossifrage (a type of hawk), worn as an amulet.
- Transferring the ailment from the sick person to blind puppies, by suckling the puppies with milk from the patient's mouth.

121

- Touching the patient's abdomen with a bat's blood.
- Having the colic victim drink water in which his feet have been washed.

Among other mixtures prescribed for colic over the centuries were powdered guts of a wolf in white wine; "hot water, oil and pepper"; "horse dung, erratic poppy water, and spirits of wine." This last one was a seventeenth-century English prescription, and the doctor recommending it admitted that it was "loathsome and will not go down with the delicate." In Elizabethan times things had been more palatable: mint was recommended as a cure for colic. And American pioneer babies with colic were given peppermint sticks to suck. This was the first candy made in America.

For eye troubles: Hang an amber necklace around the child's neck. Or pierce the ears. For a stye: Apply a poultice of crushed snails, or rub the stye with a cat's tail.

To bring down fevers: Sit by the child saying "abracadabra" or tear up some live pigeons and place their palpitating bodies on the child's feet.

To prevent fits or convulsions: Have the child wear a necklace of orris root (or peony root according to Shakespeare's physician son-in-law). Or have the child wear a ring made from the handles, nails, or screws of coffins, or of money offered in church collections, which have been melted down into rings. As a sedative, give a drink that contains hares' brains. To alleviate difficult breathing, according to a medieval recipe, put the lung of a fox into sweetened wine, and have the patient drink the mixture.

To stop hiccups, or *yexing,* as they used to be called: Have the victim cross the front of the left foot with the forefinger of the right hand while saying the Lord's Prayer backwards.

To cure jaundice: In the ninth century, according to records, jaundice afflicted more than 30 percent of all children a few days after birth. Pliny recommended having the children drink wine mixed with:

- Ashes of a stag's antlers.
- The blood of an ass's foal.
- The dung of a newborn colt, especially the very first dung voided by a foal after its birth (he claimed that if the dung was taken in pieces the size of beans, this drink would effect a cure in three days).

To cure measles: Have the child drink a mixture of sheep's dung, sulphur, porter, and water. (Dr. Courtney Dunn, author of a book published in 1919 called *The Natural History of the Child,* wrote sadly about this ancient Irish remedy, saying that "in 1878 a great many young children were permanently relieved from all further ills by the above prescription.")

To cure scarlet fever: Place some of a child's hair in a piece of bread and give it to an animal to eat. The idea was that the illness could be taken away from the child and transferred to the animal. Sandwiches made of children's hair between two slices of bread were often given to dogs when children were sick, and if they made the dogs cough that was proof that the disease had been transferred.

For smallpox: Feed the patient 30 or 40 dried toads ground into a fine powder.

For stomachaches, known in England as the gripes: The ancient Egyptians were firm believers in emetics and purgatives on a regular three-times-a-month basis to prevent constipation and nearly all other illnesses. Senna and peppermint were widely used in

Europe and America as stomachics for both constipation and its opposite, diarrhea. In the nineteenth and early twentieth centuries, castor oil was widely used as a purgative. The Egyptians also used this vile-tasting stuff, incredibly, for anointing their bodies and as a cooking oil.

For swollen glands: Have the patient touched by the hand of a man who has been hanged. This prescription was easier to fill than one might suppose, because there were people who attended the frequent public executions for the precise purpose of obtaining such items and later selling or renting them.

For teething babies: Give them necklaces of large round seashells or strings of roots to chew on. In Bali a teething baby traditionally bit on a silver box hung around its neck, which contained a piece of the baby's own umbilical cord. Or have the mother or baby nurse wear a strong necklace and invite the baby to bite on it. In Russia, *nyanyas* (nannies or baby nurses) for centuries wore teething necklaces of bright red unbreakable beads as part of their uniforms. In the seventeenth and eighteenth centuries the rage in England was the famous Anodyne Necklace, invented and marketed by Dr. Paul Chamberlen. The word "anodyne" means sedative or painkiller, and something in this necklace did soothe babies whose teeth and gums were sore, when they sucked on it. But its manufacturer evidently did not think the truth was dramatic enough and advertised it as a guaranteed miracle rather than a mere prescription. One advertisement claimed that "after wearing them but one night, children have immediately cut their teeth with safety who but just before were on the brink of the grave, with their fits, fevers, convulsions, gripes, looseness, etc. all proceeding from the teeth, and have miraculously recovered."

For toothache: Rub the child's gums with a wedding ring or a thimble. Or attach a wolf's tooth to the child's clothing. Or drive a nail into an oak tree. Or, in medieval Bulgaria, hold a bit of iron between the teeth while the Sabbath church bells are ringing. Or have the sufferer drink tortoise blood, or take pills made of garlic, horseradish seeds, and milk.

For prevention of toothache, rather than cure: Wash your babies' mouths with holy water immediately after they are baptized. Avoid washing on Fridays. Or bite off the first fern that appears in the ground in the springtime. Or, in France, take a bath on Christmas Day, to prevent both toothaches and fevers during the coming year.

In England, to help a baby get good strong second teeth: The mother should swallow the first baby tooth to come out.

To cure thrush: In Scotland, put a frog's head or a small fish in the child's mouth to transfer the disease to it, and/or recite the second verse of the eighth Psalm on three consecutive mornings.

To cure whooping cough: Feed the patient a fried mouse. Or hang a spider sealed inside a goose quill around the child's neck. Or stuff onions inside his boots.

Additional all-purpose cures: In 1688 in England, when the son of King James II was born, the obstetrician was Dr. Hugh Chamberlen of the famous Chamberlen family, and he had the court apothecary take two drops of blood from the baby's umbilical cord and add them to black cherry water, to be used as a general remedy against all future ailments. In the eighteenth century a stock remedy for all infantile and childhood sicknesses was Daffey's Elixir, a mixture of herbs, caraway seeds, and juniper berries in alcohol, treacle, and water; this was recommended by the king's physician and was standard nursery equipment in England. In the nineteenth century, terrible-tasting concoctions called "cleansing powders" were given to all ill children, no matter how slight or serious their ailments were.

DR. BENJAMIN RUSH (1745–1813)

A history of medicine called *Magic, Myth and Medicine* by Donald T. Atkinson, published in 1956, included a vivid account of the life of Dr. Benjamin Rush (1745–1813) and his fight for medical sanity in the early years of America. He wrote that in 1745, a great event in American medicine occurred in Philadelphia. A lusty boy, Benjamin Rush, was born. From his first wail as he lay in the arms of the midwife until the time of his death in 1813, Benjamin Rush continued to raise his voice so it could be heard by all. That the voice was to be long remembered is evidenced by the fact that he transformed the care of the sick in early America, a practice then filled with superstition and crude and irrational ideas which had been responsible for many deaths among the early pioneers, into a science which saved and is still saving many lives."

The infant mortality rate in Philadelphia when Rush was alive was high. Mothers usually nursed their babies, but often the mothers were themselves ill-nourished , and many of them could not provide milk for their offspring. When babies were fed by bottle, the bottles used were unsterilized and because of lack of ice, the milk frequently was spoiled and became another source of intestinal infection. In this period one out of every 10 children succumbed to intestinal disease before its first birthday.

In 1769 Rush was appointed professor of chemistry in the Medical College of Philadelphia. Through experiments in his chemical laboratory, he learned that boiling milk for a short period reduced the likelihood of its becoming sour. He concluded that boiling milk that was to be given to infants would probably decrease their high death rate.

He presented a thesis, *On the Cholera Infantum,* to a Philadelphia medical society, but his recommendations were skeptically received and seldom acted on. If at that time the medical profession had accepted his proposal to heat milk to the boiling point before feeding it to children, as it was later, without any doubt it would have saved thousands of infants' lives.

Unfortunately, Rush was a prophet without honor in his own country and, although everyone now knows that his idea was correct, it did not gain acceptance until seven decades after his death, when the French chemist Louis Pasteur (1822–1895) verified and popularized it in the 1880s. This is a sad example of the all-too-familiar story of entrenched establishments refusing to heed the advice of innovators.

BRAILLE: THE BOY, THE MAN, AND THE SYSTEM

One day in 1812 a three-year-old boy named Louis Braille (1809–1852) was playing happily in the shop of his father, a saddle maker in the village of Coupvray in France, a few miles from Paris. The boy was trying to carve a piece of leather. He tried to drive an awl through it, but the sharp instrument slid across the leather and went into his left eye. He screamed, his father dropped his work, saw blood streaming from the eye, and raced with the boy to the only doctor in the village, a veterinarian who could do nothing more than try to staunch the flow of blood. Next morning, a lawyer in the village drove Louis and his father to Paris to consult a famous doctor; he too could do nothing. He had to tell the father that nothing remained of the left eye to work with and, still worse, he feared that the optic nerve of the other eye had also been destroyed.

In a week the fierce pain had left but not the tragedy. The little boy would never be able to see again.

In this era people were fatalistic, and blind children were often cast from their homes as accursed. Some joined troupes of the blind and traveled from fair to fair to be exhibited as freaks. Some were hired for menial tasks as beasts of burden, shoveling coal all day or sweeping piles of fertilizer, in return for just enough food to keep them alive, and sleeping on the bare ground. Most of them became permanent beggars. Few received any education. But when he was seven, Louis's parents sent him to the village school, where his teacher was amazed at his intelligence. Louis's neighbors scratched out grooves on the road so that he could find his way to school, and indented the road to the town pond so that, with the cane his father made him, he could find his way there and sit in the sun listening to other children playing. The tapping of his cane gave Louis some security, and later in life became a clue that enabled him to tap out a code of letters to help himself and other blind people to read and write.

When Louis was 10 he was sent to the *Institute Nationale des Jeunes Aveugles*. This was a special school for blind children in Paris founded in 1784 by Valentin Hauy, who in 1780 had made up his mind to devote his life to improving the lot of the blind. He was considered an eccentric when he started the school, which was not much of a school even by the standards of that day. From 12 to 20 students lived in cramped quarters in a ramshackle building, and the instruction was meager. Out of painfully fashioned twigs, letters of the alphabet were formed some six inches high, and to write a simple sentence with these twigs required a great deal of time and space. Even when the children learned to write their names, there was nothing for them to read, until M. Hauy developed a method of embossing books for the blind. The embossed, or raised, letters were an inch high, which was an improvement, and within two years the Institute proudly acquired a library of three books. Pupils could now learn to read a little but still could not write easily, and their books were incredibly cumbersome; each was divided into 20 parts, and each part weighed almost 20 pounds.

After Louis had been at this school a while, he was fortunate to be introduced to a famous pianist, Thérèse von Paradis, who had a theory that the blind could be taught music. She herself had been blinded when young, and her enlightened and wealthy father had encouraged her to continue the musical career for which she had shown great promise. At the age of 14 she made her debut in Vienna and left her audience spellbound. She continued her musical studies in the only way then possible for the blind: by employing other pianists to play for her by the hour and memorizing what she heard. She was impressed by Louis and paid the organist at the church of St. Anne money to defray the cost of a year's tuition for him. He proved to be such a promising pupil that the organist taught him without fee after the year was up, and for two years Louis continued to tap his way to the church twice each day to be instructed on the organ. He began playing so well that his teacher, who later became a prominent organist and violincellist, a composer and performer, said he was envious of Louis because of his talent.

Then, in 1822, when Louis was 13, M. Hauy suddenly died of a heart attack, and the new head of the school thought it was ridiculous to try to teach the blind anything cultural; he thought they should just learn a useful trade. For five hours a day Louis and the other pupils now had to work in a small shop where bullets were made.

Within the next few months both of Louis's parents and the only close friend he had made at school died too. And then his music teacher moved from Paris. However, life soon improved again. The canon asked Louis to take over as the church organist. With money left him by his parents and the stipend paid by the church, he was able to support himself and even to subsidize the tuition of two other blind students, and at age 17 he became one of the teachers at the Institute.

One day a friend read him a newspaper item about a former army captain, Charles Barbier, who wondered if a system of nightwriting he had invented could be made available to the blind for development. It was a code made of shapes punched in thick paper that left a bulge, and by tracing one's finger along its indentations simple messages could be read in the dark. Using Barbier's method as a basis, Louis spent the next three years trying to work out a simpler and more versatile code, while continuing to teach from five to seven hours a day and to play the organ. Finally, after much experimentation, he devised a practical code with 43 symbols made of perforated dots that could be used for arithmetic and musical notation as well as for reading and writing words. He was thrilled as he transcribed many books, and the whole previously unknown world of literature became available to him.

Then came endless frustration and discouragement. The Institute refused to let him teach his new method to its pupils because this would make its own system obsolete and ruin its reputation as an educator. He tried to interest the French Royal Institute of Science, also in vain.

At the early age of 43, in 1852, Louis died of tuberculosis without knowing that his invention would ever be accepted. But once again a girl named Thérèse affected his destiny: Thérèse was a young blind girl talented at the piano and organ, whom he had instructed in his dot method of writing and reading music. With his help, she had set up a Braille music library that she used whenever she performed. Two years after Louis's death she gave a series of concerts which attracted the attention of Louis Napoleon, the new Emperor of France, who was planning the Paris International Exposition scheduled for the following year. He ordered that the Braille system be included in an exhibit with Thérèse demonstrating how it worked, as part of the evidence that France was developing culturally and scientifically under his rule.

Visitors at the Exposition were tremendously impressed, and news of Braille spread around the world. From that point on, Braille began to liberate blind people everywhere. Today there is not a single country where the blind are not taught with the Braille method. Countless books and magazines and newspapers and even greeting cards are printed in Braille. The blind can now not only read and write but can go to college and work in almost any occupation, thanks to this boy who lost his eyesight at age three and to two blind friends of his named Thérèse.

ALEXANDER GRAHAM BELL (1847–1922)

In his childhood, Alexander Graham Bell's parents thought he might become a professional pianist, but he was more interested in following in the footsteps of his grandfather and father who both worked with the deaf. His father had developed a system called

"Visible Speech," a physiological alphabet of pictures that showed how the lips, tongue, teeth, palate, throat, and lungs move in forming sounds. By imitating these pictures, deaf people could learn to make audible words. Alexander was fascinated by this process, and by using it, he himself helped to teach a young deaf girl to speak while he was still a child. This was the beginning of his life work.

Alexander was born in Scotland but when he was in his twenties, he and his family moved to the United States. In Boston he opened his own school to train teachers of the deaf, building on his father's methods, and he became a professor of vocal physiology at Boston University.

Later he worked at the Horace Mann School for the Deaf where he devised an apparatus for transmitting sounds by electricity, to show deaf children how vibrations in the air affect our ears as sound. This led to his invention of electric hearing aids, which was the forerunner of a patent he received for a method of "transmitting vocal or other sounds telegraphically by causing electrical undulations similar in form to the vibrations of the air accompanying the said vocal or other sounds." It was also the technical description of what we now call the telephone, the hitherto inconceivable invention that made it possible for people to hear from each other even when they were separated by long distances. It was first shown to an amazed public in 1876, the one hundredth birthday of the United States, at the Centennial Exhibition in Philadelphia.

The following year Bell married a deaf woman, Mabel Hubbard, who shared another of his interests, the possibility of flight. She later founded the Aerial Experiment Association, the first research organization ever established and endowed by a woman.

The couple later moved to Washington, D.C., where Alexander continued experiments in communications, medical research, and techniques for teaching speech to the hearing and speech impaired. In 1893 he was joined by one of his former patients, the 13-year-old deaf and blind Helen Keller, whose life he had helped to salvage from utter despair seven years earlier when she had come to him as a patient. He had recommended her contacting a school for the deaf, which sent her a full-time teacher who found a way to enable her to communicate with people. Together he and she participated in ground-breaking ceremonies for the opening of the Volta Bureau, an international study and information center concerning deafness. They also participated in the opening of the American Association to Promote the Teaching of Speech to the Deaf, which, since 1956, has been called The Alexander Graham Bell Association for the Deaf.

The range of Bell's inventive genius and his enormous influence on the world is represented only in part by the telephone, for which he is now primarily remembered. He held 18 patents granted in his name and 12 others that he shared with collaborators. These included 14 for the telephone and telegraph, five for aerial vehicles, four for hydroairplanes, four for the photophone, which transmitted the first wireless telephone messages, two for a selenium cell, and one for the phonograph.

All of these have proved useful and have helped not only deaf people, but everybody, to communicate more freely with each other. Everyone anywhere in the world can now communicate with friends, colleagues, doctors—anyone they wish or need to speak to, no matter where they are. Today we blithely take this ability for granted, yet it involves inventions so extraordinary that they permanently transformed society. And it is fascinating to realize that we might still not have this ability if the means to do it had not evolved from the work of this one man who, while still a boy, wanted to find a way to help deaf children.

Two Disabled Girls Who Became World Famous

Helen Keller (1880–1968)

Helen Keller was born in Tuscumbia, Alabama, in June 1880, a healthy, happy, bright baby who started to talk when only a year old. When she was 19 months old an attack of what was diagnosed as brain fever suddenly left her permanently blind and deaf. In her isolation and frustration she became a wild, unruly child, throwing and breaking things, spilling food, pinching, kicking, scratching, biting people, and uttering the choked howls of the deaf-mute when she was angry, which was most of the time. Some people thought she must be an idiot. As she later described her condition at this time, she was "a Phantom in a world that was no world."

When she was six, her desperate parents went to Washington, D.C., to consult the famous Dr. Alexander Graham Bell, whose invention of the telephone 10 years earlier, in 1876, had developed out of his and his father's work as teachers of speech to the deaf. Dr. Bell recommended that they contact the Perkins Institution for the Blind in Boston, Massachusetts. A Dr. Samuel Gridley Howe (1801–1876) there had taught Laura Bridgman, a deaf-blind child like Helen, to read, to write and to communicate with people by using a finger alphabet invented in the Middle Ages by monks who had taken vows of silence. In 50 years no other doctor had been able to do for other deaf-blind children what Dr. Howe had done for Laura, but at the Perkins Institution they were still hoping and trying. The Director of the Institution, Michael Anagnos, sent 20-year-old Annie Sullivan, who had just graduated from Perkins, to the Keller home to work as a governess and see if she could help the child. Annie needed a job, so she took up this offer, though without much hope of success.

Annie Sullivan (1866–1936)

As a child Annie gave no indication that she would grow up to become a great teacher, receiving acclaim and honorary degrees from other educators. She was a handicapped daughter of impoverished Irish immigrants, born in squalid poverty in Feeding Hills, Massachusetts. As far back as she could remember she had had trouble with her eyes as a result of trachoma. When she was eight her mother died of tuberculosis. Two years later her alcoholic father abandoned her, her younger sister, and seven-year-old brother Jimmie Sullivan. Their father later hanged himself in a Chicago flophouse. Annie was sent to the State Infirmary, an almshouse, because she was difficult to manage and too blind to work, and Jimmie was sent with her because he was becoming helplessly lame with a tubercular hip.

Jimmie died three months after they entered the almshouse, leaving Annie lonely, miserable, and trapped for four years until the stench of the filthy house grew so great that the State Board of Charities ordered an investigation. When its committee arrived, Annie threw herself down in front of them, crying out, "I want to go to school!"

In October 1880, at the age of 14, this illiterate, nearly blind girl was sent to the Perkins Institution and began her education. She learned the manual alphabet in order to be able to talk with Laura Bridgman, who was in her sixties and still living at Perkins. A doctor then performed nine operations on Annie's eyes, after which she could see well enough to read for limited periods of time, but not well enough to merit transfer to a school for the sighted. She remained at Perkins for six years until her high school graduation, when this girl who at 14 had not even been able to write her own name became valedictorian of the senior class.

Annie arrived in Tuscumbia on March 3, 1887, a date that Helen cherished all her life as her "soul's birthday." The first thing Annie did was to insist on full authority, refusing to permit the indulgence of bad behavior that Helen's parents had put up with. She refused to let Helen eat with her fingers, firmly placing utensils in her hand and removing food if Helen would not use them. When Helen threw food, Annie removed her from the table and made her go without the meal. If she broke a toy, Annie took it away and refused to mend or replace it. When she screamed and hit people, Annie took her into a separate room, locked the door, and stayed there with her until she finally calmed down. Her parents were aghast, thinking Annie was much too hard on "the poor child," but Annie stuck to her guns and gradually made Helen realize it was useless to fight her.

The other thing Annie did, from the day she arrived, was to spell into Helen's hands, continually signing words that described actions and objects. Helen was curious about this and began to respond by imitating the finger motions, though without understanding what they signified. It took a month before Helen awakened, when Annie one day pumped water over her hand while making the sign for the word "water" in the hand, and the child suddenly realized what the sign meant. In that thrilling moment Helen found the key to make contact with other people, realizing that everything and everyone has a name and the name she gave Annie Sullivan was "Teacher." Helen later wrote that in her teacher's fingers "words rang, twinkled, rippled, danced, buzzed and hummed, making every word vibrant to my mind."

Their Astounding Achievements

The combination of an unusually gifted and imaginative teacher and an eager, intelligent pupil produced amazing results. Annie was a strict and demanding teacher but also great fun. She started teaching Helen through play. Helen had not laughed since she became deaf and blind, until one day when Annie tickled her.

In the next three years Helen learned the alphabet, both manual and Braille, and to read and write. Then she learned that somewhere in Norway a dumb child had been taught to talk with her mouth, and she would not rest until arrangements were made for her to take speech lessons. At 10 she started speech classes with Sarah Fuller, the principal of the Horace Mann School for the Deaf in Boston, and after 11 lessons she was able to say, though haltingly, "I am not dumb now." Determined now to go to college, she spent the next four years at the Wright Humason School for the Deaf in New York, studying arithmetic, geography, French, German, and typing, always with Annie's help.

In 1900 she entered Radcliffe College, promptly making many friends, and was elected vice president of the freshman class. For four years Annie helped her with her studies, in spite of her own weak eyesight, reading hour after hour, week after week, and transcribing with her fingers all the lectures and the texts that were not available in Braille, even those in Greek and German, languages she did not know. When Helen was graduated cum laude it was a joint triumph. Helen was always sickened and angry when people praised her brilliance, explaining that she would still be "a Phantom in a world that was no world" without Teacher's constant devotion.

After her graduation, Helen and Annie moved to Wrentham, Massachusetts, to live for the first time in a home of their own. A year later they were joined by John Albert Macy (1877–1932), a distinguished author, editor, and literary critic whom Annie married. He helped Helen work on articles and books, including *The Story of My Life*, published as a serial in the *Ladies' Home Journal* in 1902 and in book form in 1904. This book became a classic, continuously in print and translated into 50 languages. In 1903 Helen published another book, *Optimism (An Essay)*, and a third one in 1908, *The World I Live In*, in which she described the joys she experienced despite lack of sight or hearing. There were many: she said she loved her family and friends, kittens and dogs, gardening, swimming, horseback riding, sailing, fishing, hiking, picnics, bicycling, music (which she "heard" through vibrations penetrating through the floor and furniture), literature, philosophy, and God. In 1913 she wrote another book, *Out of the Dark,* and in 1927 still another, *My Religion.*

Helen became a celebrity, giving lecture tours in the United States and abroad. In spite of the fact that her guttural speech was not easy to understand, a handicap she considered worse than her "lesser" ones of deafness and blindness, with Teacher by her side helping to explain and interpret, and with her own vitality, sense of humor, and warm smile, she charmed audiences, enjoying success in a career that became increasingly necessary to make money, as Teacher's eyesight steadily darkened and her health began to fail. The financier Andrew Carnegie (1835–1919) helped them out by giving Helen an annuity, and in 1914 they added Polly Thompson of Glasgow, Scotland, to their household, to work for them in a secretarial capacity. Polly lived with them until Teacher's death 22 years later, and then stayed on as Helen's companion for 31 more years until Helen's own death in 1967.

Bringing Light to the Blind

Neglect of the blind was nearly universal in the years when Helen Keller was growing up. For example, the medical profession had known since 1887 that *ophthalmia menatorum* was preventable but it was never discussed publicly because it was connected with venereal disease. Helen daringly started campaigning for the prevention of this ailment, which causes blindness in newborn children, in 1902 while she was still a junior in college, and in 1907 she wrote several articles on the subject for the *Ladies' Home Journal.*

She continued her advocacy after she was 43, when she began what she later called her real lifework, joining the American Foundation for the Blind. She was an active member of its staff and its leading spokeswoman for 44 years, going on speaking tours on its behalf at the request of many governments and other organizations. She was greeted by crowds of thousands, appeared before legislatures and educators and the press, inspired people by her presence, and gave tough-minded realistic advice to leaders of rehabilitation programs not only for the blind but for other handicapped people as well. In 1932 she started the Helen Keller Endowment Fund of $2 million, designating its money for the use of those who were both deaf and blind.

After Annie died in 1936 Helen determined to spend all the rest of her life in service to others "so that on each 3rd of March to come I can look back upon some achievement that has justified Teacher's faith in me." She published two more books after Annie's death: *Helen Keller's Journal* in 1938, and *Let Us Have Faith* in 1940. She and Polly traveled to Africa, Asia, Europe, Latin America, and the Middle East as well as all over the United States, encouraging improved services for the handicapped. Helen was exhilarated by the pioneering schools she visited and the progress being made in just a few decades, for the first time in history, in social welfare and rehabilitation services. By 1937, 30 states had established commissions for the blind since she had served on the first one, in Massachusetts.

Always she warned that there is no one way to help handicapped children, because each person is unique, but that it is destructive to pity them. Instead, as Teacher had told her, "treat them as normal human beings who, using the resources of the soul, can fill out physical deficiencies" and "clear away the rubbish of obstructing pessimism and blinding optimism" and "treat a problem as an opportunity for courage." What handicapped children need, she said, is "discerning love" and hard work to encourage them to achieve because "achievement is the most satisfying of all pleasures, but it is won only at the price of valiant fight."

> It must have pleased Helen when Annie Sullivan was honored as the heroine of an extremely moving and successful play called *The Miracle Worker* by William Gibson, which was adapted into an equally successful movie in 1962. The starring role of teacher was portrayed by Anne Bancroft and the part of Helen was played by child actress Patty Duke. They both won Academy Awards, for best starring and best supporting actress.

As for herself, she said: "My life has been happy because I have had wonderful friends, and plenty of interesting work to do. I seldom think about my limitations, and they never make me sad. Perhaps there is just a touch of yearning at times, but it is vague, like a breeze among flowers. The wind passes, and the flowers are content."

BLIND CHILDREN AND ART

Blind children love to dance and sing and play musical instruments. They also enjoy visual arts, in their own way. There are museums that allow them to touch sculpture, and they can model clay as well as children who can see what they are doing, as was demonstrated in a booklet called *Sculpture by Blind Children* published by the American Foundation for the Blind. The booklet showed the work of 18 blind children between the ages of 8 and 11, some of whom were multiply handicapped (blind and retarded, or blind and cerebral palsied).

Under the guidance of their teacher, Jeanne Kewell, at the California School for the Blind, they had produced truly beautiful art: statuettes of charming birds and animals and of people engaged in various vigorous activities—fighting, skating, horseback riding, playing. Some were of subjects the children had personally experienced, others of things they imagined from books they had read. For instance, one sixth-grade girl, who was studying King Arthur in her English class, described why she enjoyed modeling knights in armor:"Because in clay you can feel the way they come thundering across the field and strike each other in the middle." These children could not see, but they could feel, and we have Helen Keller's word that those of us who use our eyes and ears have no idea of the marvels one can discover with one's hands and nose, because most of us do not bother to cultivate these "minor" senses.

This remarkable blind and deaf woman, whose life was a glorious reproof to those who think life could not be worth living if one were so severely handicapped, wrote an essay in this booklet in which she listed among her joys "the delicate tremble of a butterfly's wings in my hand, the soft petals of violets curling in the cool folds of their leaves or lifting sweetly out of the meadow grass, the clear, firm outline of face and limb, the smooth arch of a horse's neck and the velvety touch of his nose."

"My world is built of touch sensations," Keller wrote,

> it breathes and throbs with life. . . . With my hands I can feel the comic as well as the beautiful in the outward appearance of things. Remember that you, dependent on your sight, do not realize how many things are tangible. All palpable things are mobile or rigid, solid or liquid, big or small, warm or cold, and these qualities are variously modified. The coolness of a water lily rounding into bloom is different from the coolness of an evening wind in summer, and different again from the coolness of the rain that soaks into the hearts of growing things and gives them life and body. The velvet of the rose is not that of a ripe peach or of a baby's dimpled cheek. . . . What I call beauty I find in certain combinations of all these qualities, and is largely derived from the flow of curved and straight lines which is over all things.

The beauty and eloquence of these words should convince us that we who are "touchblind" or "smellblind" are, in our own way, handicapped.

Blind Children Who Became Outstanding Musicians

Ray Charles (full name: Ray Charles Robinson) (1930–): Born in Albany, Georgia, Charles started to go blind at the age of five. At seven his right eye was removed and shortly thereafter he became totally blind. He was sent to the St. Augustine School for the Deaf and Blind in Florida, where he learned to read Braille, sang in the school chorus, and learned to play and write for piano, organ, saxophone, and every other brass and wind instrument. When he was 15 his mother died, and he left school to become a professional musician. Playing and singing in many styles—ballads, blues, country, gospel, jazz, rock and roll, and soul—he soon became well known, and five times was voted America's top male singer in the International Jazz Critics poll conducted by *Downbeat* magazine.

The emotional appeal of Charles's vigorous music transcended language barriers; he has performed to many sell-out concerts in Europe, Africa, and Asia, as well as in the United States. He appeared in a motion picture based on his life, called *Light Out of Darkness,* and has said, "Seeing people or not seeing them, life is still life. I don't need to see to play or sing the way I do." He was a great inspiration to another fantastically successful blind musician, Stevie Wonder (see page 134), whose first record album, made when he was 12, included a song called "A Tribute to Uncle Ray." In 1986, Ray Charles won the Life Achievement Award, the highest honor the United States Government gives to an American artist. He once said, "I never spent any time wanting to be famous but I always wanted to be great." He succeeded in being both.

George Shearing (1920–): Born in London, England, Shearing was blind since birth. He has played the piano and composed music almost all his life. One of a family of six children, he was allowed to play with empty bottles, tossing them into the air and listening with delight to the sound of breaking glass; his mother reasoned that the world of sound was George's life. At age five, he began to study classical music, later receiving encouragement from a music instructor at the Linden Lodge School for the Blind in London. In his teens he became interested in the recordings of Art Tatum (also blind; see below) and other jazz musicians, and at 17 he decided to become a jazz pianist. His first job was playing piano in a pub for a pound a week plus tips. When he was 18, jazz critic Leonard Feather heard him playing as a swing accordionist during a jam session at London's Rhythm Club and, impressed, arranged to have him make records. He wrote arrangements, played piano and accordion with jazz orchestras, and had a series of radio broadcasts on the BBC, the British Broadcasting Company. He was chosen as England's most popular jazz pianist by *Melody Maker* magazine four times in its annual poll. In 1941 he married, and he and his wife had a daughter.

In 1945 he visited the United States and, urged to stay, formed a trio, then a quartet, then a quintet, and in 1950 went on a transcontinental tour playing before full concert halls everywhere. In 1956 he became a U.S. citizen. Success continued: his quintet was seven times voted as the best musical combo in both *Downbeat* and *Metronome* magazines' polls. In an article he wrote for the *American Weekly*, entitled "I Turned Down the Gift of Sight," he told how he had refused offers of people who wanted to will him their eyes, because "I am a completely happy man."

Art Tatum (1910–1956): Born in Toledo, Ohio, Tatum was blind from birth and the child of a poor family in a black ghetto. He found consolation by playing the piano at a very early age. He spent most of his 46 years perched on a piano stool, mesmerizing audiences with his extraordinary and inventive virtuoso technique. He had a greater influence on more jazz musicians than any other pianist.

Alec Templeton (1910–1963): Born in Cardiff, Wales, Templeton was blind from birth. His mother once said that "when I first got over the shock that I had a little boy who would never see, I decided I would never let him realize he was handicapped. We treated him exactly as we treated his sisters." He had to put his toys away himself and was often sent on errands. This early training made him self-reliant. At the age of two he imitated perfectly on the piano the sounds of the bell in a nearby church. At four he composed a lullaby that his mother used to put him to sleep. At five he directed a choir of his playmates. When he was six, his mother said, "he was so far advanced musically that the rest of the family practically gave up playing; he made us all feel silly." He was eight years old before he ever heard the word *blind*. He was playing in the lobby of his apartment house one day when he heard a woman say, "Oh that poor little blind boy." He went upstairs and asked his mother why he was called poor, and what blind was. She tried to explain, but never having seen he could not understand what he was missing, so he decided then and there not to worry about it.

At 12, Alec was enrolled as a student in the Royal Academy of Music, learned to read music in Braille, and auditioned for the BBC, which hired him; for more than 12 years he presented novelty musical acts almost daily on radio. At 16 he won a piano contest in which 20,000 pianists competed. He graduated from Oxford University and then studied for four more years at the Royal College of Music. His success on radio, in recordings, concerts, and recitals, both as a serious pianist and as a musical satirist, was unique; he could improvise in any composer's style so brilliantly that he could fool most listeners. With an uncanny memory he could play long compositions after hearing them only once. His delicious sense of humor and obvious delight in life charmed audiences for decades, with improvisations on the piano in which he combined audience requests, played familiar songs in different tempos, mixed classics with pop, and kept up a witty commentary. One of his favorite tricks was to take a popular tune and play it in the style of Mozart, Puccini, Debussy, Strauss, or Bach. Married and happy, he once said, "I adore people, and jokes, and music, and the fresh feeling of the wind. What I can't have, I don't think about."

Lennie Tristano (1919–1978): Born in Chicago, Illinois, during the disastrous flu epidemic that followed the First World War, Tristano's eyesight was weakened at birth by influenza. He started school at the age of four and spent a year and a half in the first grade: "They just didn't think I learned easily, and I just didn't think I wanted to stay in the first grade forever, so I moved to another school." For three or four years he went from school to school, his progress hampered by increasing physical difficulties. But from his fourth year he was able to sit down at the piano and work out simple tunes. Then, at age six, he suffered a serious attack of measles and his already weak eyesight grew dimmer. When he was nine his parents sent him away for the pivotal years of his life, from 9 to 19, to a state institution for the sightless.

The only qualification for entrance to the institution was eye trouble, but many of the children were in addition severely retarded, crippled, even psychotic. The atmosphere was prisonlike, and the education sparse. Yet Lennie flourished, thanks to a sympathetic music teacher; he was able to study piano, saxophone, clarinet, and cello. By the age of 10, his second year there, his eyesight was almost totally gone, but he had developed a very good memory. He could do long and complicated math problems in his head as well as memorize music. Starting at 10, he led a band that played occasional dates at local taverns.

By the time Lennie was ready for college, his musical talent was so obvious that his music teacher took him to the American Conservatory in Chicago where he got a scholarship. He became interested in jazz as a result of listening to Art Tatum records; this disappointed his teachers who had hoped he would become a classical pianist. He developed into a phenomenal jazz pianist and composer, who produced many dazzling musical innovations, including playing one tempo with his left hand while simultaneously playing in another tempo with his right hand. Later he became the teacher and mentor of many other outstanding jazz musicians. In addition to his musical gifts he had a formidable intellect and was a voracious reader of Talking Books for the Blind; to save time, he played them at fast-forward speed, which made the words an unintelligible blur to listeners with less acute hearing.

Stevie Wonder (real name: Steveland Judkins Morris) (1950–): Born in Saginaw, Michigan, Stevie was a premature baby, blind at birth. Despite his disability he had a fairly normal childhood, running and climbing trees; he showed a musical aptitude very early. At two he pounded a tin pan with a spoon to the rhythm of music on the radio. At four he began playing the piano, and soon after that learned the harmonica. He wore out several sets of drums. By age nine he was singing solos at the services of the Whitestone Baptist

Church in Detroit, but he was expelled from the choir after a church member heard him singing and playing rock'n'roll with some other children. When he was still nine he began hanging around a recording studio every day after school, playing every instrument he could get his hands on and writing songs; his first was called "Lonely Boy." At 12 he had his first big hit, "Fingertips," a harmonica number that sold over a million copies. Among his early albums were "Little Stevie Wonder: The Twelve Year Old Genius," which contained "Fingertips" and "A Tribute to Uncle Ray", a vocal salute to Ray Charles (see page 133), whose style he imitated during his early years as a performer. For a time he continued to attend public school but then transferred to the Michigan School for the Blind in Lansing; while traveling on music tours he studied for several hours a day with a private tutor. He made nine other successful albums before he was out of his teens.

He received his high school diploma at the age of 19, the same year in which he made his concert debut. By age 21 he had made $1 million, having moved successfully from the role of child prodigy to that of a most original and popular musical performer. He produced music that bridged the gap between soul and pop, with a remarkable series of one-man record albums, for which he wrote all the music and most of the lyrics, performed the vocals, prepared the arrangements, and played most of the musical instruments, jumping from piano to drums to synthesizer. In 1985 he co-wrote "We Are the World" for the African famine relief program launched by rock musicians around the globe.

HEARING-IMPAIRED CHILDREN

Which is harder on a child, being hearing impaired or blind? Dr. Samuel Johnson wrote that deafness is "the most desperate of human calamities." Helen Keller said deafness was a much greater handicap than blindness, that it isolated her more than lack of eyesight did. And therapists have learned that the hearing impaired do seem to have a harder time than the blind, partly because their handicap is invisible; people who are sympathetic and considerate when they see a blind child tend to be puzzled and impatient when a deaf child fails to answer them or "do as it is told."

Nobody knows exactly how many hearing impaired children there are in the world, but census studies estimate that 2 million people in the United States are profoundly deaf, more than 18 million have hearing impairment, and about 250,000 of these are deaf from infancy.

Of the millions of children who suffer hearing loss, many are totally deaf. Deafness, of course, will not kill them. It is not fatal. It is not even painful. It is merely an invisible, insidious crippler. The future for many hearing impaired children may be tragically different from that of their hearing counterparts; 90 percent of all deaf people 16 years old or older are either functionally illiterate or have fifth-grade or lower reading levels, and there is no way to measure the degree of their frustration and loneliness.

Children born deaf or who become deaf before they learn to talk have traditionally suffered from a dreadful stigma. Because they could not talk normally they were called *deaf and dumb* and although the word *dumb* in this context was a synonym for *mute* rather than a description of their mental powers, it was associated in people's minds with stupidity. But in our century great progress has been made in helping the deaf communicate, both by teaching them lip reading and by developing their own language of pantomime.

135

ASL, American Sign Language, is in fact the fourth most widely used language in the United States, the first three being English, Spanish, and Italian. And it is extremely beautiful and eloquent, expressing emotions and concepts through graceful hands that dance and fly. People who are fluent in it often joke that the people who do not know it are handicapped.

While sign language isolates the hearing impaired from the rest of society, it has one great advantage over lip reading: greater comprehension. Even expert lip readers can read only about a third of what is said to them, according to Lou Ann Walker, author of *A Loss for Words: The Story of Deafness in a Family*, because vowels are formed in the back of the mouth, so that words such as *laps, lapse, leaps, lips, lops, loops,* and *lopes* all look alike on the lips.

Ms. Walker's book is a memoir of growing up as a hearing person who was the child of two deaf parents, both of whom had lost their hearing before they were two years old. As she explains, "until the age of 2, babies are tape recorders, taking in everything that is being said around them. The brain uses these recordings as the basis of language . . . . For those who become completely deaf during infancy, using the basics of language becomes a task as difficult as building a house without benefit of drawings or experience of carpentry."

However, the lives of deaf children and of children of deaf parents are not necessarily unrelievedly grim. As the essayist George Will has put it, "the triumphant adaptations of people who cannot hear take us to the heart of the glory and mystery of what it is to be human."

Children of Silent Parents

Lou Ann Walker, who says she could sign before she could talk and whose first "word" was a crooked index finger in the dimple of her cheek signifying an apple, says she and her two sisters had to be parents to their parents. "It's hard for kids of deaf parents to feel totally relaxed. You are part of deaf culture, yet not a part of it. You're part of nondeaf culture, and not a part of it."

Such children have to contend with the intolerance and ignorance of unhandicapped people. For example, 90 percent of children born to deaf parents can hear normally, and they have to interpret for their parents in restaurants and shops. In itself this is not too upsetting. "Like all children," Walker says, "I loved feeling important." But the dark side is the obscenities, ridicule, and insults they hear, from which they try to protect their parents. "Children need to look up to their parents, even if it means doing some rearranging . . . . What I admired about my father was his dignity, and my mother her joy . . . . Our family was proud and hardworking and self-sufficient." When strangers' questions revealed bigotry and ridicule, "I reworded questions if I had to interpret them. And I never allowed myself to think about the underlying meaning."

Another well-known child of hearing impaired parents is the actress Louise Fletcher who won an Academy Award in 1976 for her performance in the movie, *One Flew Over the Cuckoo's Nest*. As she received the Oscar she waved it in the air, beaming and looking directly into the TV camera, and said to her parents in sign language (which she interpreted aloud for the rest of the TV audience), "Thank you for teaching me to have a dream; you have seen my dream come true." She is a member of the board of the Deafness Research Foundation (DRF), engaged in studies to determine causes of different types of hearing impaired. Her two sisters and her brother also work with the hearing impaired, in gratitude to their parents who, she says, "were a constant inspiration to us."

Parenting a Deaf Child: Louise Treadwell Tracy and Her Son John

The son of Louise Treadwell Tracy and Spencer Tracy was born in 1924 in Milwaukee, Wisconsin. Spencer Tracy had married Louise in 1923 when she was his leading lady in the theater, but she gave up her acting career after John's birth. He was a happy baby but cried so seldom that when he was three months old she consulted a doctor, who told her he was incurably deaf. After that she consulted virtually every leading ear specialist and explored all the theories of education for the hearing impaired, in the process becoming an expert herself. She took a $100 correspondence course for mothers of deaf children, conducted by the Wright Oral School in New York City and, after learning the Wright method, combined it with other approaches. She taught John to talk and to lip read. Hearing impaired children need lots of attention, consideration, and love, she said, and "the child's progress depends largely on the mother, who is like a god to a little deaf child. She must make the child as attractive and likeable as possible, and teach him good habits."

Not all parents are able to accept so peacefully and constructively the knowledge that they have a child with a disability. Knowing he would take it badly, Louise was afraid to tell her husband, and he did not realize their son was deaf until John was two years old. A friend later commented, "When Louise discovered John was deaf she worried and took him to a doctor; when Spencer discovered it he worried and went out and got drunk." Having a son who was not normal made him feel both guilty and inadequate, although John's deafness was not due to any defect in the father but had apparently been caused by an illness the mother had during her pregnancy.

In every respect except his deafness, John was a healthy child: emotionally, mentally, and physically. He became a good athlete and went on to college where he was popular and an honor student. After college he worked as an artist with the Walt Disney studios, got married, and at 29 had a normal son.

Spencer Tracy always gave his wife full credit for their son's happiness and success. In *Spencer Tracy, A Biography*, by Larry Swindell, he said,

> I wanted to help but was no damn good at it. I would come home after she had been working with the boy for hours and start undoing the good Louise had done. Maybe she had been working with him all day on a word like "shoe," showing it to him and saying the word over and over, trying to get him to read her lips. So I would pick up the damn shoe and throw it across the room and scare the poor kid half to death. I had no patience, and it's just amazing how much she had, and has. All I could do was pray for a miracle.

He didn't realize it, but the miracle was already there—Louise was the miracle.

In 1930, when Spencer Tracy began his phenomenal career in motion pictures, the family moved to California where Louise began forming study groups, bringing parents of deaf children together and teaching them what she had learned about different types of deafness and their causes and treatment. She offered family counseling and personally trained many instructors. In 1942 she established the John Tracy Clinic in a wooden bungalow at the University of Southern California. The clinic provided free assistance to parents and children and was an immediate and lasting success. It was supported entirely by voluntary contributions, becoming one of Hollywood's favorite charities. Louise Tracy won four honorary degrees and an award from the Save the Children Foundation for her important and useful work.

SHHH

"SHHH", is the acronym for an organization in the United States called Self-Help for Hard of Hearing People, established in 1966. Howard E. Stone, head of the organization, who became hearing impaired as a result of an accident at the age of 19, works to raise awareness of the approximately 20 million people in the United States who are hearing impaired, and to promote programs encouraging people to prevent deafness by early diagnosis and other means.

He is particularly disturbed about the fact that "the roar of contemporary life" hastens hearing loss. He says that a 75-year-old shepherd in the Sudan has the hearing acuity of a 15-year-old in America in the days before amplified rock music. Today 30 to 60 percent of college freshmen in the United States have hearing deficits, and amplified rock music is blamed for much of this.

CHANGING ATTITUDES TOWARD CHILDREN WITH DISABILITIES

People's attitudes toward children with disabilities have undergone a great and wonderful evolution in the past hundred years. For centuries, such children have been ostracized, scorned, neglected, and hidden away—even murdered by people unwilling to care for them or unaware of how to do so. For example, ancient Greece was in many ways a great and civilized state, but children born deformed were left to die of cold and starvation on the streets. And Aristotle, though a great and wise man, thought deaf children unteachable and therefore that deaf adults should be disenfranchised. Most people justified their laziness, ignorance, and coldness by convincing themselves that children with disabilities were beyond help and not worth trying to help. But thanks to the enormous advances in medicine and physical therapy, there is less defeatism today and we have now learned that even severely challenged people can actually add greatly to our world. Many famous artists, musicians, educators, scientists, social workers—people in all fields—have overcome their disabilities, inspiring us and making our world richer than it would have been without them.

Of course, not everyone in past centuries neglected the sick or scorned the weak, but the help given them used to be primarily custodial, self-sacrificing care given from a kind heart with little or no hope that the lives being saved could ever be happy or useful. Today we have learned that even hard-to-train children may be capable of real accomplishments when given encouragement to develop skills within their capabilities.

Parents cannot create talent in their children if it is not there, but they can create opportunities and incentives to develop whatever talent *is* there. Even nongeniuses can accomplish a lot, when given enough intelligent, loving, individualized attention and encouragement. In fact, even severely brain-damaged or psychotic children can make progress and become happy people, as the inspiring work of many doctors and therapists working in this century's new field of rehabilitation have proved. Brilliant and stubborn parents and psychiatrists who refused to admit the word "hopeless" into their vocabulary have rescued psychotics who had lost almost every resemblance to human beings. Some children so subnormal they were considered "vegetables" have responded to the loving labors of therapists who believe there is no such thing as a worthless person.

Religion for centuries has taught that we should love and serve the least among us, and in our time people have finally begun to practice what preachers have preached, and modern science is showing how to love in such ways that the "least" are no longer inevitably doomed to remain the least.

1981, The International Year of Disabled Persons

December 16, 1976, marked an important moment for the United Nations and the world. At that time, the General Assembly declared 1981 as the International Year of Disabled Persons (IYDP), the first worldwide attempt to deal with the needs of disabled people. To get the year off to a productive start, the UN made a broad range of recommendations for international, regional, and national activities. National Committees for IYDP were established. Mass media campaigns were organized. Legislation to eliminate discrimination against disabled persons was reviewed. And preventive measures and rehabilitation services for the disabled were promoted as an integral part of national planning.

As part of the UN's efforts, UNICEF focused on the needs of handicapped and disabled children. To call attention to how widespread the problem of disability among children is, it issued the following paper:

Facts about Child Disability

ONE OUT OF EVERY 10 CHILDREN IN THE WORLD is born with an impairment or acquires one early in life. Such a child may be partially or totally blind or deaf, mentally retarded, physically limited, or having a learning problem. All such children need special help: timely treatment, education, and training to overcome the difficulties created by their impairment. They also need understanding and encouragement from parents, family, and the people around them. In many cases timely help can correct the problem and prevent any disability. In most others, it makes the difference between a happy and a tragic life. But far too often such children get neither help nor encouragement. And so they lose their chance of becoming useful and happy citizens.

Throughout the world, the problems of disabled children have been aggravated by longstanding ignorance and superstition regarding the causes and treatment of many disabilities.

This fact sheet included the following shocking statistics:

- There are more than 500 million persons who go through life with a disability, and this number is growing.

- Blindness affects some 10 million to 15 million people worldwide, and 70 million have a significant hearing impairment.

- One out of 10 persons suffers from a mental illness at some stage during a lifetime, and mental patients occupy one quarter of all hospital beds; 40 million people are affected by mental retardation, another 40 million by functional psychiatric disorders.

- Malnutrition is closely linked with disability. The most severe form affects 100 million children under age five in the developing world, and can permanently stunt mental and physical growth. Every year at least 250,000 children go blind for lack of vitamin A; and iodine deficiency, which causes endemic goiter and can lead to cretinism, affects 200 million.

- There are around 75,000 cases of polio each year and the incidence is increasing in many developing countries.

- Each child in a rural area in a developing country is likely to suffer from 5 to 10 times the disease episodes of a child living in an industrialized country.

- There will be at least 150 million disabled children in the developing world by the year 2000 unless preventive measures are taken now.

Fortunately, the future for many disabled children promises change. Due to the success of both IYC (International Year of the Child), and IYDP, new antidiscrimination laws and impressive medical advances, their lives will change for the better. The United States is one country that has been leading the way, with passage of the ADA (The *Americans with Disabilities Act*) in 1994, a federal law that requires most public buildings (libraries, museums, office buildings, restaurants, stores, schools) and public transport to provide access to people in wheelchairs via lifts, ramps, wide doors, and aisles, free hearing aids in theaters and lecture halls, and many other devices that give new freedom to people who formerly were homebound. The days of ostracism and loneliness are at long last coming to an end.

PHYSICALLY CHALLENGED CHILDREN WHO BECAME HIGH ACHIEVERS

Aesop (620–560 B.C.): A Greek slave, born deformed and ugly but so brilliant and witty that he was given his freedom. His name is still renowned as the inventor of the fable, and his stories are still popular after more than 2,600 years.

Association of Handicapped Artists: A group of American painters, founded in 1961, whose members are crippled by illness, accidents, or birth defects. They paint by holding their brushes or pencils with their mouths or feet instead of their hands, proving that even severely disabled people can enjoy life, become self-reliant, and earn their living as contributing members of society. They produce quality greeting cards, note paper, gift wrap, and art calendars.

Lyman Frank Baum (1856–1919): American author of children's books. The seventh of nine children, he was a shy, sickly child, unable to play games with other boys, spending most of his time acting out fantasies with imaginary playmates and toys. Once, during a walk, he saw a scarecrow that frightened him, and for months after that he repeatedly dreamed that it was chasing him. This scary ogre made of straw was transformed years later into the beloved scarecrow of the *Oz* books. When he was 12, his parents decided this sentimental boy needed to be shaken out of his dream world, so they sent him to a military school. The tough discipline was too much for the delicate youngster; he had a nervous breakdown and from then on detested the military. After that he was educated by private tutors.

His childhood habit of fantasizing continued into adult life, and his main fatherly occupation with four sons was to make up fairy tales to amuse them. It was his mother-in-law who suggested that he publish them, which he finally did in 1897 under the title *Mother Goose in Prose* followed by the phenomenally successful *Wizard of Oz* series. (For more information about Baum, see page 464.)

Christy Brown (1932–1981): Irish artist and author. He was the ninth child in a family of 21 children, all of the same mother. When he was four months old she noticed there was something wrong with him. He was examined by many doctors and labeled a hopeless case, mentally defective. What he had was cerebral palsy, but at the time this condition had not yet been diagnosed and understood. But his mother refused to accept the advice to "put him away or it will just break your heart." She said he was her child and a part of her family, and even though he seemed to have learned nothing by age five, she maintained, "I know my boy is not an idiot; it is his body that is shattered, not his mind." She kept talking and singing and reading to him, as to a normal child even though there was no visible response. He later described his reactions:

> I used to lie on my back all the time, a little bundle of crooked muscles and twisted nerves, surrounded by a family that loved me and hoped for me and that made me a part of their warmth and humanity. I was lonely, imprisoned in a world of my own, unable to communicate with others, cut off, separated from them as if a glass wall stood between my existence and theirs . . . and then suddenly, it happened! In a moment everything was changed, my mother's faith in me rewarded.

What happened was that one day he saw a piece of yellow chalk and "as though by its own volition my left foot reached out and very impolitely took the chalk out of my sister's hand." He held it tightly between his toes. His mother brought him a slate and taught him how to write the letter A with the chalk. He did it with great difficulty, but he did it, and from then on was on the road to a new world of mental freedom, learning the alphabet and then words, and then drawing pictures, gradually becoming skilled enough to have a one-man show in a Dublin art gallery. Laboriously he began also to write poetry and, with the aid of a skillful speech therapist, learned to talk. He was even able, after he grew up, to have a happy marriage.

In 1955 Christy published his beautifully written and powerfully moving autobiography, *My Left Foot,* which became an international best seller. After his death, the book was made into a magnificent motion picture. The role of Christy was played by Daniel Day Lewis, who won an Academy Award as the best actor of the year (1989) for his brilliant performance. To help him understand Christy's frustrations, humiliations, and determination, the actor lived in a wheelchair during all the months of filming and insisted on being carried into restaurants for his meals. The Irish actress Brenda Fricker also won an Academy Award as the year's best supporting actress for her portrayal of Christy's mother.

Karel Capek (1890–1938): Czech author. He suffered all his life from a spinal disease. Writing seemed to compensate him for the lack of ability to engage in physical activity. His first writings were published when he was 14 and he became a distinguished and prolific journalist, playwright, essayist, short story writer, and novelist. His most famous play was *R.U.R. (Rossum's Universal Robots)* produced in 1920, one of the first imaginative treatments of the then new scientific invention of robots.

Peter Falk (1927–): American actor in theatre, films, and television. When he was three years old surgeons removed his right eye along with a malignant tumor. Although he was self-conscious about his glass eye, he became a three-letter athlete, an excellent student, and president of his class in high school. He caught the acting bug at age 12 when he made his first stage appearance in a production of *The Pirates of Penzance* at summer camp, but he did not act professionally until he was 28. Finally he quit his job and moved to New York City to become a full-time actor.

Despite successes on the stage, he was advised not to expect much work in movies because of his glass eye. Nevertheless, he made a name for himself both in films and on TV, in both comedy and drama, and won a number of awards. He used the squint caused by his false right eye to advantage in his acting, contributing to an air of menace or of benevolent detachment, as befitted the occasion. And the series *Columbo,* in which he starred in the title role as a shrewd but eccentric detective, was a smash hit and continued year after year in one of the longest runs ever on TV. In 1995, he received many accolades for his role as a grandfather in the movie *Roommates.*

Samuel Johnson (1709–1784): English critic, essayist, conversationalist, satirist, and lexicographer. He was a sickly child. His eyes were weak and at the age of two he suffered from a tubercular infection in the glands of the neck, commonly known at that time as "The King's Evil." It was believed that the disease could be cured by the monarch's touch, so his mother traveled with him to London in 1712 where Queen Anne duly touched him and hung a gold amulet around his neck, which he wore for the rest of his life.

Karen Killilea (1940–): This American girl was born so severely crippled that her doctor told her mother to "put her on a mountain top and let her die." Her parents, Jim and Marie Killilea, were horrified by this callous suggestion and spent many years working hard to give Karen warm love and to help her live as normal a life as possible. To pay for the enormously expensive medical treatments, her father held down two full-time jobs for many years. Her mother wrote a best-selling book in 1953 called *Karen,* which described their efforts and the heroic struggles of Karen herself to overcome her birth injuries. The book helped to publicize cerebral palsy, about which little was known at that time, and helped to bring about a real revolution in the attitudes of both parents and doctors towards this birth defect. It inspired many parents who had previously kept such children locked up or hidden away in attics to bring them out in the open. It also helped persuade schools to accept these children, and to teach other children to accept them too, with understanding, respect, affection, and admiration instead of ridicule and revulsion.

Karen's mother followed this book with two others: *Wren,* the story of Karen told for children, and *With Love from Karen,* in which she told what happened to Karen during her teen years.

For many years Karen patiently put up with constant pain. In order to be able to walk she wore braces that increased the pain, but she did learn to walk, as well as to talk, sing, swim, and ride horseback. She became an excellent student and, through her valiant spirit and charm, brought joy to many friends. When she grew up, she discarded the hated braces, preferring to stay in a wheelchair, but she did not stay idle. She had always loved animals and became a professional dog trainer for a few years, after which she was able to support herself as a private secretary.

Edward Lear (1812–1888): English artist and poet. As a child he was often ill, had bad eyesight, was asthmatic and epileptic, and slightly deformed physically. But in spite of all this he had a wonderful sense of humor and enjoyment of nature. At 18 he made drawings of most of the animals in the London zoo, and he painted pictures of all the animals in the private menagerie of the Earl of Derby, making up delightful nonsense rhymes for the Earl's grandchildren. For a time he taught drawing to Victoria, the Queen of England. He was happiest when amusing children with his "nonsenses," which were later, in 1846, published. As a result, he became famous as the inventor of the limerick.

Alfred Nobel (1833–1896): Swedish manufacturer, inventor, and philanthropist. In his childhood he endured great poverty as well as illness. Just before he was born his father had to file for bankruptcy, and the family had a narrow escape during a fire that destroyed their home and all their possessions. When he was six his father left home to escape arrest and debtors' prison, and his mother struggled to support herself and three young sons with a small milk and vegetable shop. They lived on the verge of destitution for many years. From his very first day, Alfred was weak and sickly, and everyone except his mother gave up hope that he would live. He spent his first years in her constant care, and at 18 wrote a long autobiographical free-verse poem in English called "A Riddle" describing his childhood:

> My cradle was a deathbed, and for years a mother watched with ever anxious care, so little chance to save the flickering light. I scarce could muster strength to drain the breast, and then convulsions followed, till I gasped upon the brink of nothingness my frame a school for agony with death for goal . . . . We find him now a boy. His weakness still makes him a stranger in the little world wherein he moves.
>
> When fellow boys are playing he joins them not, a pensive looker on; and thus debarred the pleasures of his age his mind keeps brooding over those to come . . . .

At eight he was finally considered well enough to attend school. He gained top marks in all subjects, as well as in diligence and conduct, and was among the top three of the school's 82 pupils, but his family moved to Russia to join his father, who had found work in St. Petersburg, and that one year was all the formal schooling he ever had. His brilliance, however, won out over poverty, sickness, and lack of education, and by the time he died he was a successful and very wealthy man as a result of his invention of dynamite and more than 100 other patented items. He left a will directing that the interest on his fortune should be divided annually among those who had done the greatest services to mankind in chemistry, medicine, physics, literature, and peace to promote brotherhood among nations, thus establishing the Nobel Prizes which have been awarded every year since 1901.

Itzhak Perlman (1945–): American citizen born in Israel, a virtuoso violinist. When he was four years old he became a victim of polio, which left him permanently disabled, but he did not allow this affliction to end his ambition to become a violinist. He kept practicing during a year-long convalescence and later continued studying. Despite the fact that walking is difficult for him—he has to use crutches and must play the violin sitting down—he has not let either discomfort or embarrassment keep him from having a stunning concert career ever since his debut at age 13. He makes more than 100 concert appearances a year and also spends some time in private teaching. He is married to Toby Lynn Freidlander, also a violinist and a Juillard graduate as he is, and they have four children. He is loved by audiences not only for his warm, rich musicality but also for his informality and sense of humor. Asked about his physical handicap, he says simply, "Nothing bothers me." Actually, however, one thing does: neglect of handicapped children. During the United Nations' International Year of Disabled Persons (1981) he worked especially actively on their behalf. (For more about his early career, see pages 393–94.)

Alexander Pope (1688–1744): English poet: Pope was physically deformed with curvature of the spine as a result of a tubercular infection at age 12, and what he called his "tender crazy little carcass" was never to grow taller than four feet, six inches. His physical weakness was in marked contrast to the force with which he expressed his strong opinions. A man named Ray Smith described him this way when Alexander was 14 years old: "Egad, that young fellow will either be a madman or make a very great poet." He became the latter, making his name at age 16 with his first published verses, and in later life translating *The Iliad* and *The Odyssey*, as well as composing his own immortal poems. Lines from his *Essay on Man, Essay on Criticism* and *Moral Essays* have been quoted more often than any other writings except those of the Bible, Shakespeare, and "Anonymous."

Dinah Shore (1917–1994): American popular singer. Her real name, on her birth certificate in Tennessee, was Frances Rose Shore. When she was two years old, she caught polio, which seriously affected her right leg and foot. Their natural appearance and functions were gradually restored through a strenuous regimen of massages, swimming, tennis, and dancing lessons. She learned to sing and play the ukelele, and at 14 she borrowed her sister's party dress, lied about her age, and won a singing engagement at a local nightclub. In high school she was a cheerleader and was voted "Best All Around Girl" by her graduating class of 1934. She went on to Vanderbilt University, graduating in 1938 as head of women's government and president of her sorority. Her first big start in show business was during her sophomore year, on a 15-minute weekly Nashville radio program. This launched one of the longest and most successful singing careers on radio and TV, and for many years she was also a popular hostess and gracious interviewer on an afternoon TV talk show as well as being a talented photographer, painter, gourmet cook, and tennis player.

Robert Louis Stevenson (1850–1894): Scottish author: If he had not been a sickly boy having to spend a lot of time in bed playing with toys, pretending that the bed was a battlefield or a series of hills and valleys or a boat sailing to faraway places where he had imaginary adventures, the world's children might have been deprived of one of their greatest literary treasures, *A Child's Garden of Verses*. He also wrote other great books, not all for children but eagerly adopted by them: *Black Arrow, Dr. Jekyll and Mr Hyde, Kidnapped,* and *Treasure Island.*

Henri de Toulouse-Lautrec (1864–1901): French artist: He was seemingly a fortunate child, born to a wealthy and distinguished family. His grandfather, father, and uncle were all talented artists and sportsmen, so it is not surprising that he began riding horseback at an early age and started painting at the age of 10. But his luck ran out when he was 14, when he fell from a horse, breaking his left thighbone. A year later, in a second accident, his right thighbone was fractured. These accidents required long periods of painful treatments and, because of a congenital bone defect, they left his legs atrophied and made walking difficult. He never grew more than five feet, one inch tall, and as an adult his fully developed torso resting on dwarfish legs gave him an unusual appearance.

To pass the lonely hours during his convalescence, Henri spent more and more time on art, and at 17 decided to become a professional artist, offending his father who was repelled by his son's deformity as well as by his decision to paint professionally, considering this beneath the dignity of an aristocrat. Besides, Henri's first two art teachers disliked his work; one of them actually called it "atrocious." So in the mid-1880s Henri left home and moved to the Montmartre section of Paris. The work he did there, portraits of popular entertainers, led to his first public acclaim. He began to receive commissions to illustrate publications and exhibitions and, instead of producing conventional oil paintings on canvas, he created many posters and produced more than 300 lithographs.

Unfortunately, his health never improved. He suffered a mental collapse in 1898, was committed to a sanitorium, and died at the early age of 36. Despite his suffering, his life cannot be considered a failure because he is recognized as a major figure in late nineteenth-century art. His work has brought great pleasure to many and its originality has influenced the art of decades to come.

Andy Warhol (1928–1987), American artist. As a child Andy was frail and had three nervous breakdowns before the age of 11. All his life he exhibited a strange mixture of extreme shyness and avid publicity seeking. He became the inventor and foremost popularizer of Pop Art. Nobody was ever quite sure when he was spoofing and when he was serious, but his posters and films and photomontages were immensely popular, as was he. It was hard to know whether he himself or his work was more celebrated during his lifetime.

Chick Webb (1902–1939), American jazz drummer and swing band leader. Born crippled in Baltimore, Maryland, into a poor but close family, Chick was indomitably cheerful and never seemed to let his physical handicaps bother him, although they were considerable. He was a hunchback and for 16 years suffered with tuberculosis of the spine. But his spirit was as large as his body was small. An incredibly talented, incomparable drummer, he played with all the jazz greats, and in the swing era his own band was one of the tops. He also became famous as the patron of the great singer Ella Fitzgerald, who sang with his band after Chick discovered her in 1934 when she was in her teens. He and his wife adopted her, and she became the featured and popular singer for the enormously popular Chick Webb band.

The Remarkable Neil Marcus

Many handicapped children have shown enormous courage and, in spite of great pain and frustration, have grown up to make impressive achievements in adult life. One of the most inspiring examples is Neil Marcus, a worthy role model not only for other disabled children but for anyone who has to cope with serious problems. His example seems especially important today when "the culture of victimization" has overtaken the world.

Neil was born in January 1954 and until he was seven years old his mother says, "he was just like any other darling boy, happy and adaptable." Then, when he was in fourth grade he suddenly could not hold his pen in his right hand, so he shifted to the left. A month or so later he had trouble throwing a ball; his right arm would no longer do what he wanted it to do. His parents sent him to summer camp, hoping his health would improve there, but when he returned home it was a great deal worse: his right foot was curled up, his right hand useless, and his speech somewhat slurred.

He was taken to see a bone specialist, then a neurologist, then a psychologist, then a psychiatrist. The psychologist thought his family was too happy and did not fight enough. The psychiatrist found him quite normal. Neil was the youngest of five children; the others were in their teens when his troubles began, and all of them were close, none seeming to resent the extra attention Neil had to get—in fact they seemed to enjoy giving him special attention themselves.

Discovering What His Strange Illness Was

Neil was finally diagnosed as having *dystonia musculorum deformans*, a neuromuscular affliction. A doctor explained that it was very rare and, as happened in Neil's case, many victims of it were misdiagnosed at first. Today its cause is still unknown. Its symptoms resemble those of cerebral palsy, but that involves brain damage and children are either born with it or get it as the result of an accident. In dystonia, the brain seems to be intact, but muscles are damaged, and the harder one tries to make certain motions the more resistance is set up in the muscles. Hardly anybody in the lay world had ever heard of dystonia until it was featured in the 1993 movie *Resurrection,* in which the central character cured a patient afflicted with it.

An Agonizing Childhood

Eventually Neil's problems became so severe that they were totally disabling, so he underwent surgery. Doctors had discovered that freezing a small spot at the back of the brain could relieve at least some of the symptoms; it seemed to slow down the electrical flow that overstimulates the muscles and puts them into spasm. Doctors also tried innumerable relaxing medicines, including one often used to stop tremors in Parkinson's patients, but this did not help Neil.

The first operation was temporarily successful; his right side became perfect again. But the improvement was short-lived. Then the spasms jumped to the left side. And a second operation seemed to make both speech and movements even worse. Finally, he was helped enormously by a third operation, performed by Dr. Irving Cooper at St. Barnabas Hospital in New York, which brought him to a higher plateau that has stayed fairly constant through the years, enabling him to function on his left side, albeit clumsily and with a degree of difficulty that would make most people give up. Many simple tasks require him to spend as much energy as normal people would climbing a mountain.

In adjusting to his uncooperative limbs, Neil went through many stages during his childhood. For a while he did not want anyone to see him and was horribly embarrassed at school if his classmates saw him in a wheelchair. But one day when Neil was absent his father created a breakthrough by going to the school and discussing Neil's illness with the whole class, answering their questions frankly and explaining what Neil's difficulties were. From that day on, the children were on Neil's side and no longer shunned him. Soon they were taking rides in his wheelchair and kidding around with him, and he belonged. Then he had a period when he did not want to associate with other disabled people; he wanted to be in the mainstream.

By the time he graduated from high school, he was the valedictorian of his class. And he then went on to college.

His Adult Triumphs

In college he began writing a column for the college newspaper, at first typing with one finger but eventually learning to use computers. Nowadays he writes daily on a word processor, taking a laptop with him on his travels. He writes and edits publications devoted to improving the public perception of the disabled. He has also written what he called a "disabled fable," *The Princess and the Dragon*, with a wheelchair-bound princess as its heroine.

Soon he had a backlog of humorous vignettes, some about people he had met, some just whimsy, all in an original style. One day his brother Roger, who was an actor, singer, and comedian, got hold of these and recorded a group of them. Roger knew Rod Lathim who ran the Access Theatre in Santa Barbara, California, which has produced plays with handicapped actors since 1979. He played the tape to Lathim who suggested that Roger work with him and Neil to make it into a stage piece. The play that resulted was *Storm Reading,* and Lathim gambled $30,000 on its production, with the two brothers performing together, Neil as himself, Roger as his voice. Actor Michael Douglas, a longtime backer of the Access Theatre, and screen writer David Seltzer were so impressed that they brought the play to Hollywood, where it was performed to rave reviews. Jean Kennedy Smith, a sister of John, Robert, and Ted Kennedy, also got interested and helped to promote it. She runs another organization that sponsors plays, dance, music, and art for the handicapped, The Special Arts Foundation. In 1989 the foundation held a festival at the Kennedy Center in Washington, D.C., bringing together many big stars who performed along with children—some blind, some deaf—from all over the world. This show was later made into a one-hour NBC Special that included an appearance by Neil and Roger.

Neil always loved the theater, as did everyone in his family. Although he has difficulty doing the same thing twice the same way, he has no trouble being relaxed on stage. It is hard for him to go through prescribed words and motions, but he was elated to discover that audiences liked him. An understatement: audiences love him, once they get over the first shock of seeing his deformed body. His quirky sense of humor and contagious good cheer make his show so popular that every performance ends with a rousing standing ovation, not just because the audiences feel sympathy and admiration for someone so severely handicapped but because they have been caught up in Neil's humorous view of the world. *Storm Reading* has become the Access Theatre's most successful work, with both nationwide and international tours every year between 1987 and 1995, when it was permanently preserved on a video.

Even offstage Neil lives an extraordinary life, made possible in large part by his supportive family His parents were unusually well equipped to help him cope, and not only because they are both endowed with an uncommon amount of common sense. His mother contributed to him her acting and writing talent; for six years as Lydia Perera she was the star and author of a one-woman radio program for children. And his father, Wil Marcus, contributed not only writing ability but a lot of the courage and patience needed

147

to endure physical pain and frustration; he was bedridden for two years with tuberculosis. And the affection and rapport among Neil and his siblings were delightfully in evidence when he and Roger performed together.

His parents have never been overprotective. Their advice to all parents is to realize that although children may do things clumsily, the parents should resist the strong temptation to say, "Never mind, I'll do it for you," because children like to learn how to be self-sufficient. For instance, Neil loves to cook, and his mother says he is a great cook, but when he chops onions and other vegetables "unless you are made of steel, you can hardly refrain from taking the knife away from him; you are convinced he is going to cut off all his fingers and fall over backwards at the same time. But don't interfere unless he wants help. He can do it—not prettily, but he'll get it done if you let him. Clumsiness is not really a major limitiation."

Neil wants to try everything. He was exhilarated to find out that he could be a painter, a dancer, and a friend to every minority group in the world. He participates in all kinds of causes and activities, and can hardly say no to any challenge. He goes camping and white-water rafting, and takes an interest in every kind of experimental theater group. He loves new experiences and has traveled as far away as Laos.

One of his most unusual traits is his ability to laugh at himself, as well as at the people who stare at him. His parents did not shield him from criticism or make special rules for him, and they all learned to laugh sympathetically at his awkwardness. Even he could see the humor in the way strangers avoided him or treated him as if he were a child. It did not hurt him because he realized their reactions were only natural given the fact that they simply did not understand.

So his play contains funny imitations of how strangers view him and hilarious episodes such as his attempt to order a cheeseburger with onion rings at a Burger King drive-in window despite his nearly unintelligible speech. There are also dramatic and poignant scenes such as one when his wheelchair was stolen. But whether he is depicting his adventures and misadventures through humor or drama there is not a trace of self-pity or desperation. He simply lets people share the experience of what it is like to be different and thus expands their understanding of how many humans have some sort of difference.

But the most unexpected and remarkable thing about Neil is not his wit or energy or the variety of his interests. It is his enormous *joie de vivre* and his gratitude for being alive. The high point of his play is a moving declaration of how genuinely happy he is, which puts his viewers' own problems into perspective as they are swept up into a realization of how much there is in life to be thankful for. Instead of the play being depressing or harrowing, it fills the audience with joy.

In 1994 *Storm Reading* was included as part of the United Kingdom's City of Drama Festival in Manchester. The company provided audio description and, for the first time, dual sign language translation, American Sign Language and British Sign Language. The play was presented by the New Breed Theatre Company, a resident group of artists with disabilities. *The Manchester Evening News,* reviewing the play, called it "a remarkably honest and entertaining experience... educating and breaking barriers, widening horizons and [Marcus] doing his all with a gentle good humor that must inspire everyone who sees him." People from London, including directors of Graeae Theatre, another company of actors with disabilities that tours throughout the UK and internationally, attended as well. The review in London's newspaper, *The Guardian,* summed up everyone's reaction, saying Neil Marcus "captures the audience defiantly, unsentimentally for two hours of wildly funny, sharp philosophical musing on his—and the human—predicament. It's an astonishing celebration of life. It's an exhilarating, liberating experience."

Ruthie and Verena Cady

Ruthie and Verena Cady (1984–1991) brought great happiness to their parents Marlene and Peter Cady, to their sister Maria, and to all their friends and neighbors in Cranston, Rhode Island, during their seven years of life, even though their birth was considered a horrible tragedy.

They were conjoined twins, and when the doctor who delivered them first saw them he almost did not spank them to get them crying, because he thought it might be better if they died immediately. But they promptly started crying on their own, and as their mother said, "he realized they had a little oomph." She felt numb when told the twins she had been expecting were joined to each other from the sternum to the waist but, as she wrote in a fascinating article in *People* magazine, she thought, "Oh well, okay, let's just pull them apart. Just unsnap them or unzip them or whatever you do." She cried later when told they shared vital organs, a heart and some of their intestines so that it might not be possible to separate them and that anyway they would probably live only a few months. Afterwards, as she got to know them and discovered that they were actually two very lovely little girls, she decided that for some reason they were meant to be together.

At first taking care of them was hard. Until they were four months old, they needed extra supplies of oxygen continually. They could not turn themselves or move well, so they got bed sores. They were so close together they would hit each other sometimes and wake each other up—in fact, for two whole years they woke up every hour all night long. And when they were nine months old, they got pneumonia and had to be hospitalized.

But as they grew, the sense of tragedy was replaced by a realization that these were exceptional children in every way. They were extremely pretty, friendly, full of fun, and ingenious in learning how to do things. When people first saw them and said, "Oh, how tragic!" their mother's comment was, "the only tragedy is in your interpretation of the girls' situation, because obviously Ruthie and Verena are happy kids." They were allowed to explore, and the parents did not set limits for them. They found their own limitations and learned to cope with them. "When they were younger," their mother said, "I would try to teach them the 'best' way to walk or sit or go to the toilet, but invariably, when I left them alone, they found better ways of doing things."

They learned to walk using a special four-wheel walker, and were getting around on their own by age two. Since they faced each other, they were always hugging. They could not both walk straight ahead, but they figured out how to walk sideways, almost like dancing. They even learned to roller skate. And after they got the hang of a new specially designed tricycle that allowed one to pedal while the other was a passenger, they took turns steering and rode it up and down the street for three whole days, knocking on doors and ringing bells to make sure everyone knew about their new treasure.

They had very distinct personalities. Verena was the more serious and practical one, and she was talkative, insisting on answering the phone and chatting. Ruthie had artistic talent and loved to paint and draw and make things with her hands. Ruthie was more mischievous than Verena, who checked up on her and taught her not always to demand

149

her own way. They early mastered the art of compromise and if they had a disagreement, they were usually good about talking it over and resolving the dispute quickly. They figured out how to solve the problem of who is in charge by agreeing that each of them got to make important decisions, such as what games to play, on alternate days.

The twins attended preschool from age three to five, at age six went to kindergarten, and at seven entered first grade. They both loved school, and the other children accepted the twins completely, some even envying the fact that Ruthie and Verena always had a friend and playmate with them and were never lonely. Their sister Maria expressed a similar thought when she was seven, telling her mother, "I like being Ruthie's and Verena's sister because they really love me and they're special. Maybe I'm not as special because it seems sometimes people don't even notice me. Sometimes I feel sorry for my sisters being attached, because they don't always want to do the same thing. But when they aren't arguing I think they're very lucky to be together."

The photographs that accompanied the cover story about them in the July 3, 1989, issue of *People* gave convincing proof of how delightful these smiling and giggling little girls were, but they did have serious health problems. The heart they shared was an imperfect one, which made them tire more easily than other children and recover more slowly when they got sick. Because they were more susceptible to infection than most children, they took daily doses of antibiotics. In January, 1991, Ruthie developed pneumonia again and both girls had to be confined to a hospital oxygen tent. Though they returned to school, Ruthie's lungs remained weak, and she needed oxygen tubes.

The twins had never been told that they might not live to adulthood, but on their seventh birthday in April, 1991, Verena stunned her mother by calmly remarking, "Wouldn't it be surprising if we lived until we were nine? But I don't think it's going to happen. I think that pretty soon we're going to die. But don't worry, Mom. God told me he'll make sure everything's all right." The following month Verena, like Ruthie, needed extra oxygen, and their nights were disturbed by episodes of painfully rapid heartbeats. Verena, astonishingly, began to make plans for their deaths, while Ruthie listened. She gave her mother a list of friends she wanted at their funeral, and friends to be sent flowers, and said she would need to have her and Ruthie's names put somewhere so they would be remembered. Her mother said the children were both totally calm, and that Verena's self-possession seemed almost otherworldly. Her father said, "I don't know where she got it. I have 29 years on her, and I'll never have that kind of wisdom."

On the morning of May 19, Verena said to her mother, "We're dying now, Mommy. You'd better get Daddy now." Minutes later, after Peter and Marlene had told her how much they loved her, Verena joined Ruthie in death. At their funeral service, the girls' father told the hundreds of friends and relatives assembled, "Inhale Ruthie's and Verena's spirit, and exhale any sorrow you may feel at their passing." And their mother said, "They could find happiness in things you'd never even think of looking at. That's the big message I hope people get from their lives. Appreciate what you have. Ruthie and Verena taught us so much. They were a perfect example of sisterhood and unity. It would make a pretty neat world if we all lived the way they did."

PHYSICALLY CHALLENGED CHILDREN WHO BECAME ATHLETES

Anthony Burton (1939–): Anthony was an English child, who from the age of 20 months until was seven he spent four months of every year in hospitals, enduring long, painful operations and illnesses. He was born with an incredible number of deformities. Bones in both hands were missing. "Your baby will never use his thumbs, and probably never his hands," doctors warned his mother. The hands were lifeless, turned in at right angles, and his forearms, which could not move, were only an inch long. One side of his face was paralyzed; a perpetual stream of water flowed from one tear duct, and the roof of his mouth was convex, a condition that invariably impedes speech and causes the teeth to come in late and malformed. His second teeth grew in horizontally as if they were going to push through his lips, and it took eight and one-half years of orthodontics to straighten them.

For the first few weeks of his life he could suck very little and had to be fed every hour and a half through a small tube. His mother tried to strengthen and stretch his arms, massaging each one in turn until her own arms ached, and twisting, bending, and rubbing his fingers, trying to move the bones, which lacked joints. She repeated the process three times a day for two or three hours each time. She also cleaned his bad eye with a saline solution twice a day, and mopped his face to wipe away the stream that ran continually down his cheek.

When he was six months old, an eye specialist agreed to operate on Anthony's bad eye. The operation was an ordeal, but it was a success; afterwards, his mother said Anthony's eyes were "as clear as stars." But his other problems were not over. He could not take solid food. He was too weak to sit up. And he still could not move his arms or hands. His mother invented exercises they did together for several hours every day, which he enjoyed as if they were games. At 13 months he still could do nothing without help. It took years to improve his paralyzed face, which his mother massaged every day. But when he grew up he was handsome.

Shortly before his eighth birthday he and his mother went to Lourdes, where they believed a miracle occurred because after the visit Anthony was able to move his fingers and was now able to write. Fortunately, he had a very happy disposition despite his physical problems, and he had many, many interests. He loved music and books, and when he was old enough to go to school was a good student. In his teens, in spite of continued clumsiness and sloppy table manners, due to his high marks he got a scholarship to a boarding school. He could now dress himself, except for buttons, and he learned Latin and Greek, joined the debating club, got a leading role in a school play, and began enjoying many games: billiards, bridge, even ice skating, ping-pong, squash, and track, and then developed a passion for tennis. This worried his mother: How could he possibly serve, holding his racket and at the same time throwing a ball? He solved that difficulty ingeniously by holding the racket between his knees and throwing the ball high in the air with both hands, then as it came down grasping the racket, again with both hands. He got so good that he received the prize for the doubles finals on the school's Prize Day, as well as the prize in French.

In 1956 his mother wrote a book about him called *Crippled Victory.* The foreword, by a psychiatrist said, "Anthony, who has required the skilled help of so many different medical and surgical specialists, has at no time needed psychiatric assistance. A more stable and cheerful individual does not exist . . . .Many pagan culture patterns sanction the destruction after birth of imperfect babies . . . . In Anthony's case, however, love and the Christian ethos governed the situation, with the result that an unusually gifted and happy individual has survived to enrich society and give pleasure to his friends and loved ones."

On the book jacket the publisher summed up his story saying, "The moral is unmistakable: if Anthony Burton can play tennis, no one of us has the smallest right to despair about anything."

Glenn Cunningham (1909–1988): Born in Atlanta, Kansas, Glenn was so badly burned when he was eight years old that he was told he would never walk again. It took him more than two years simply to straighten out his right leg. But he went on to become one of the greatest all-time mile runners, holder at one time of five world track records, and in 1974 he was made a member of the U.S. Track and Field Hall of Fame.

Raymond (Clarence) Ewry (1873–1937): Born in Lafayette, Indiana, Raymond was partially paralyzed by polio as a boy. He was advised by a doctor that jumping from a standing position would help to restore strength to his withered legs. His therapy became his sport, launching him on a triumphant athletic career. He made his Olympics debut in Paris in 1900 and in one afternoon won the standing high jump, setting a world record of 5 feet, 5 inches, plus the standing long jump and the standing triple jump, and finishing third in the running high jump. Four years later in the 1904 Olympic Games in St. Louis, Missouri, he won three more gold medals, successfully defending all three of his titles.

Dawn Fraser (1937–): An Australian child who suffered from bronchial asthma, Dawn became one of the immortal heroines of swimming. She started her unique collection of medals at the Olympics in Melbourne, Australia, in 1956, winning the 100-meter freestyle and sharing in the 4 x 10 meter freestyle relay victory, and also winning a silver medal in the 400-meter freestyle. She became the only swimmer to have won an Olympic title in the same event at three successive games when she won victories in the 100-meter freestyle in Rome in 1960 and in Tokyo in 1964. All in all, she won 23 national championships, 39 world record plaques, six Commonwealth Games gold medals, four Olympic gold medals, and four Olympic silver medals.

Jahangir Khan (1963–): Born in Karachi, Pakistan, into an athletic family, Jahangir had a hernia that doctors said condemned him to a sedentary life. He was operated on twice, once at age 3 and again at 13. Even after the operations, doctors advised him to avoid any physical stress. But while the rest of his family took afternoon naps, Jahangir was out in the neighborhood, hitting balls against a wall. At 15 he tried out for the Pakistan International Squash Team but failed to qualify. However, his brother Hasan, a squash coach with Pakistani International Airways, persuaded PIA to sponsor Jahangir in the World Amateur Singles competition in Australia. Jahangir surprised squash circles by winning the championship. At 17 he was crowned world champion. After that he won 40 consecutive tournaments without losing a single match. His name Jahangir was appropriate and prophetic: it means "Conqueror of the world".

Edward (Teddy) M. Kennedy, Jr. (1961–):Teddy is a nephew of Eunice Shriver, founder of the Special Olympics, and son and namesake of U.S. Senator Ted Kennedy. At the age of 12 in the mid-1970s, while trying to make his school football team, he received a bad bruise on his right knee, which would not heal. It was discovered that he had a bone cartilage cancer found only in young people, which has a survival rate of only 25 percent. Doctors recommended an immediate amputation of the leg above the knee. The operation was only the first step in a treatment that lasted for years and included extensive chemotherapy. His brave response to his condition was in the true Kennedy tradition of *Profiles in Courage* and with his father's encouragement he refused to act like an invalid, and instead became an expert skier. In 1986 a television biography of him was produced, which ended with his making an impassioned appeal for the rights of the disabled and the opportunities that should be opened to them. He said he disliked being called *handicapped* or *disabled*, preferring to think of himself simply as *physically challenged,* a term he coined that has become widely used since then.

Greg Louganis (1960–): Greg is an American boy who started diving because he had a learning disability. He also suffered from race prejudice because he was dark skinned as a result of Samoan parentage; he was frequently humiliated by being called "nigger." Finding it hard to make friends and not being good in academic subjects at school, he decided to go in for a solitary sport. It was a wonderful decision. He was the most magnificent diver at both the 1984 Olympics in Los Angeles and the 1988 Olympics in Seoul, Korea, winning gold medals in both springboard and platform diving at both Games. His diving was poetry in motion and some people consider him the finest diver there ever was. In 1994 he published an unusually candid autobiography revealing that he was gay and had AIDS.

Wilma Rudolph (1940–1994): Born in Clarksville, Tennessee, the 20th of 22 children, Wilma contracted double pneumonia, scarlet fever, and polio at age four and almost died. The illnesses left her left leg paralyzed. Once every week, on her mother's day off from work, she and her mother made the 90-mile round trip to Nashville for heat and water treatment on the leg, and every night her brothers and sisters took turns massaging her leg. At age six, she started to hop on one leg. At eight, she was able to walk with a leg brace; later an orthopedic shoe replaced the brace and she wore this special shoe until she was 11 years old and able to move well enough to play basketball in bare feet. At 13 she went out for the high school basketball team. Her sophomore year she set a single-season scoring record, and she won all-state honors all four years. She also took up running and won the state high school titles in the 50-, 75- and 100-foot dashes. She loved sprinting so much that sometimes she would skip school to run on a track across the street. When she was 15, Ed Temple, the coach at Tennessee State University, saw her run and invited her to attend his summer track camp.

At 16 Wilma won a place on the Olympics' sprint relay squad and shared in its bronze medal at the 1956 games in Melbourne, Australia. She went to Tennessee State University to continue being coached by Ed Temple. An injury kept her off the track for most of 1958, but in 1959 she won the first of her four consecutive American Athletic Union (AAU) 100-meter titles. Early in 1960 she became violently ill after a tonsillectomy but soon resumed training for the 1960 Olympics in Rome. Two months before traveling there, she set a world record in the 200 meters, and won both the 100-meter and 200-meter AAU titles. At the Rome Olympics she created a sensation, becoming the first woman since Babe Didrikson a generation earlier to win three gold medals in track and field, and the first ever to win them in one Olympics. She was also the third woman since World War II to win both the 100- and 200-meter races and to share in the 4 x 100-meter relay victory, which set a world record of 44.5 seconds.

153

She achieved all this in spite of serious problems. On the day before the l00-meter race she stepped into a hole in the ground and sprained an ankle. Even so, she managed to race the next day in the semifinal, winning it in ll.3 seconds to equal the world record. The following day she won the final easily in ll.0 seconds. And in the record-setting relay race, where she was the last runner, her team was behind by two yards, but she ran so fast that she turned the deficit into a three-yard victory.

She was promptly mobbed and hailed as America's greatest female sports heroine since Babe. French journalists called her *La Gazelle* and *La Perle Noire* (the Black Pearl). She was not only a fast runner but an amazingly graceful one; when she ran she seemed to float airborne almost effortlessly rather than to be confined to the ground, and she never looked tired or out of breath at the end of a race.

She toured Europe after the Olympics, competing in invitational track meets and drawing throngs of admirers everywhere she went. In l96l, back in the United States, she was also idolized. In February of that year she competed in the Millrose Games at Madison Square Garden in New York, the first woman in 30 years invited to participate in this prestigious indoor track event racing against men. She won the 60-yard dash there, tying her own previous world record, and two weeks later set another world record in the same event. That summer she set still another women's world record in the l00-meter race, firmly establishing her status as the finest female sprinter of her time.

The Associated Press named her Female Athlete of the Year twice, in l960 and l96l, and in l96l she was also voted the Sullivan Award for outstanding amateur athlete, male or female, in America. Later she was also voted into the National Track and Field Hall of Fame, and the Helms Hall of Fame, the Women's Sports Foundation Hall of Fame, the Black Athletes Hall of Fame. In l990 she became the first woman to receive the National Collegiate Athletic Association's Silver Anniversary Award.

Wilma retired in l96l, returned to college, and received a degree in education. She became a teacher and high school basketball and track coach, as well as a spokeswoman for a movie studio. Her dramatic life story was made into a prime-time television movie, written, produced and directed by Olympic historian Bud Greenspan in l977. She also established the Wilma Rudolph Foundation in Indianapolis to help disadvantaged children through sports and education. The foundation works with thousands of young people every year, teaching them discipline and hard work. "I wanted to leave behind a legacy, and I thought this would be ideal," she said before her death in November l994.

O. J. Simpson (Orenthal James, "The Juice") (1947–): O.J. was born in San Francisco, California, and grew up in a housing project in a slum that he described as "your average black ghetto." He was so late in learning to walk that his parents took him to San Francisco General Hospital, where his mother worked the night shift as an orderly, to be examined. The doctors found that the boy had a severe case of rickets as a result of malnutrition (a deficiency of Vitamin D and calcium) that had weakened his legs. They said that if he was to be able to walk, they would have to break and reset his legs, or fit him with braces. The family could not afford either treatment, so they created a set of homemade braces with his shoes placed on the opposite feet. The result was that he ended up bowlegged, but not only strong and able to walk but to run with great speed. His mother said that when he was still in braces he was watching the Rose Bowl on TV and told her that one day he would play in that game. She said, "How could I believe him, when he did not even have his shoes on the right feet?"

In addition to his physical problems, O.J. had others. When he boasted that "someday people will read about me," his sister said, "Yeah, in the police records." He frequently picked fights, stole, and was a poor student. But he had such an exceptional talent for football that he soon became a star in the local playgrounds. He also had great charm and was a born leader. At Galileo High School he became the leader of two gangs, one known as The Superiors, which organized dances and community events, the other known as the Persian Warriors, which stole food and liquor for these events. O.J. bragged that he was the "baddest" of the guys. At 15, after several minor scrapes with the law, he was arrested and had to spend a weekend in jail. On Monday when he got home, instead of having to face an irate father, he was stunned to see one of his heroes, Willie Mays, star center fielder of the San Francisco Giants. Mays had heard about the great young athlete with a bad attitude and offered to try to help him. They spent the day together, a day that changed O.J., making him determined to work hard in order to become successful and wealthy.

Galileo's football team was one of the worst in the city, but when O.J. was a senior, the team was playing one day against the St. Ignatius team, which had won 23 straight games. Galileo's team was trailing St. Ignatius by 25–10 when suddenly Simpson took over and scored touchdowns of 90, 80, and 60 yards for the biggest upset in the city's high school history. The St. Ignatius coach was so awed that he telephoned the University of Southern California the next day, recommending that O.J. receive a football scholarship. His C-minus school marks were too low for him to qualify, so he went instead to City College for a year, brought his grades up, and switched to USC, where he went on to win the Heisman Trophy in 1968, running on a world record relay team. He became the No. 1 draft choice in the National Football League in 1969.

Later he became a professional football player and a member of the Football Hall of Fame, and in 1973 he won the Jim Thorpe Trophy for most valuable NFL player, pro football's highest award. For 20 years he was one of the nation's most popular celebrities until the tragedy of his wife's murder in 1994. His trial, at which he was charged in the murders of Nicole Brown Simpson and her friend Ron Goldman, and the "not guilty" verdict have been two of the most controversial events in America's legal history.

Tony Volpentest (1963–): His parents' sixth child, Tony was born with deformed arms and legs. He had no feet or hands, yet he started walking before he was a year old, on his stumps. In 1985 his parents sent him to the Shriners' Hospital for Crippled Children in Portland, Oregon. He was given flexible bars that emulate feet, providing 70 to 90 percent of a foot's normal action. Having always loved sports, he played football and became a runner. When people were amazed, he said it was no big deal: "Everyone has a handicap; mine happens to be my feet." At the Barcelona Olympics in 1992 he competed in the Paraolympic Games in which 55,000 people in the stadium watched 1,000 physically challenged athletes from 85 countries. Tony won the 100-meter race, with a new world record time of 11.63 minutes, becoming the fastest amputees printer in the world.

In 1996 at the Paraolympics in Atlanta, in which 4,000 disabled athletes from 110 countries competed, Tony again ran his race and again broke his own world record, completing the 100-meter dash in 11.36 seconds, a mere second and one-half behind the world's fastest able-bodied runner.

THE SPECIAL OLYMPICS

Eunice Kennedy Shriver (1920–), sister of President John Kennedy and of Robert and Ted Kennedy, and wife of Sargent Shriver, the first director of the U.S. Peace Corps, founded the Special Olympics for the physically and mentally challenged in the l960s. Her combined interest in sports and children with disabilities was spurred by the fact that she and her brothers and children were all athletic and that she had a mentally challenged sister, Rosemary Kennedy. Mrs. Shriver was awarded an honorary degree by Princeton University in l978 for her work in organizing and promoting these sports competitions and for her work as the Executive Vice President of the Joseph P. Kennedy Jr. Foundation.

When the President of Princeton conferred the degree of Doctor of Humane Letters on her, the citation read:

> An imaginative leader of efforts to improve the lives of the mentally handicapped, she has been largely responsible for increased scholarly research in this field, changes in government policies, and a fundamental reversal of public attitudes. Through her inspired foundation and continuing administration of the Special Olympics program, she has made available to thousands of handicapped children and adults the priceless gift of the opportunity to compete, to succeed, and to gain pride and confidence in themselves. Their gains, through her efforts, have enriched us all.

Rafer Johnson (1935–), winner of the Decathalon in the 1960 Olympic Games in Rome, was a close friend of Robert Kennedy and was with him when he was murdered. Since that year he has devoted himself full-time to working with physically challenged child athletes as the national head coach and president of the California branch of the Special Olympics. In a recent promotional campaign for the organization, he explained why in these words:

> When I saw how handicapped people had the chance to enjoy themselves in competition and how well it was received, I knew I wanted to be involved. . . . . It makes me feel good when I can see a child able to feel proud about what he can accomplish. As national head coach, I have seen how far some have come. I have seen blind athletes run the 50-yard dash at the sound of their coach's voice or down a rope or line that marks off the lanes. I have seen young people in wheelchairs compete in a way that's inspiring to any athlete. We've had athletes stop before the finish line to wait for his or her friend and cross together—you'd never see that in any other kind of competition.

Since this program began as a local event involving just a few children it has grown every year into what has become an international televised event, with enthusiastic participants and their sponsors from every continent. Special Olympics have enabled more than 3 million athletes with developmental or other disabilities to come together to experience the spirit of competition and camaraderie. This has been made possible through the active participation of many prominent individual volunteers such as Arnold Schwarzenegger, donations from national and local charities, and from generous contributions by corporations such as Procter & Gamble and Toyota.

When Mrs. Shriver was 73, she retired from active participation in the organization she had started, and her son took over the leadership of the Special Olympic World

Games. In 1995, in New Haven, Connecticut, more than 7,000 athletes from all around the world participated.

CHILDREN WITH LEARNING DISABILITIES WHO BECAME SUCCESSFUL

Hans Christian Andersen (1805–1875): Andersen was a Danish writer of fairy tales, a poet, a novelist, and a dramatist. He made extreme spelling errors of a bizarre nature all his life, clear evidence of dyslexia, and was also a very frail and shy child, without play-mates. In his solitary play he invented stories to amuse himself, which he later turned into his famous fairy tales that have amused everyone else ever since. His story of the poor little ugly duckling who turned into a beautiful swan seems symbolic of his life.

Winston Churchill (1874–1965): Winston was born two months prematurely and so unexpectedly and suddenly during a ball at Blenheim Palace that there was no time to bring his mother to a bedroom; he was born in a cloakroom off the ballroom. He was a sickly and accident-prone child. At five he was thrown by his pony and suffered a concussion. Soon afterwards he developed chest problems, respiratory tract disorders resembling asthma. At nine he had double pneumonia (the first of eight bouts he suffered during his life). At 18 he fell 30 feet from a tree and lay unconscious for three days. He also had a slight speech impediment, which did not prevent him from becoming a great orator in later life.

Winston's father had hoped his son would become a lawyer, but his school record was too poor. He started school at age seven and hated it. He was always at the bottom of his class and was considered an untalented, backward child by his disappointed father, his governess, and most of his teachers. At 12 he was admitted to Harrow School as a favor to his prominent parents, in spite of the fact that he turned in a blank paper in his Latin entrance exam. It took him three full terms to get promoted from the lowest form.

When he finally managed to graduate, he applied to Sandhurst, Britain's West Point, but flunked the entrance exam three times. Yet once he got there he distinguished himself at last, and graduated with honors, eighth in a class of 150. He then went on to an illustrious career in government, became Prime Minister and was the inspiring and revered leader of his nation and the entire free world during World War II. After retiring, he became an excellent landscape painter and a distinguished author, living to age 88.

Tom Cruise (1962–): An American boy who was severely dyslexic, as were his mother and three sisters, Tom compensated for poor school performance by excelling at sports, and in his senior year in high school landed the leading role in his school's production of the musical *Guys and Dolls*. He skipped his graduation and plunged into theater work, waiting on tables at night and going to auditions all day for months, before finally getting small stage roles and eventually leading roles in motion pictures and becoming a popular movie star.

Harvey Cushing (1869–1939): Harvey was noted as the worst speller in his grammar school classes. He nonethless obtained a Bachelor of Arts degree from Yale and a Doctor of Medicine degree from Harvard, then became the most eminent brain surgeon in America and a Pulitzer Prize-winning author of many books on medicine.

Thomas Alva Edison (1847–1931): An American child who was physically delicate, Edison was diagnosed as retarded and mentally ill by his teacher when he entered shool, and he was always at the bottom of his class. His father thought him hopelessly stupid. His mother, however, disagreed; she took him out of school and taught him herself, and encouraged his interest in science by letting him use their home's basement as a laboratory for his many experiments. While still a child, Thomas became deaf as a result of being boxed on his ears for naughtiness by a neighbor. At 12 he was a newsboy on a railway when, as a reward for saving the life of the stationmaster's child, he was given lessons in telegraphy and became an operator. He went on to invent many telegraphic devices. The mimeograph, microphone, phonograph, incandescent electric lamp, alkaline storage batteries, and talking motion pictures are among the more than 1,000 inventions that he patented during his lifetime.

Albert Einstein (1879–1955): As a small German child Albert was so late in learning to talk that his parents feared he was subnormal. He was also slow in physical development and considered himself a weakling, hating games and athletics. When he was five, his parents hired a private tutor for him, but lessons stopped when, in a tantrum, he threw a chair at the tutor. When Albert was sent to school he was very unhappy and managed to get a doctor's certificate stating that he was suffering from a nervous breakdown, thus gaining his objective of being dismissed from school.

He had a generally poor academic record up to the age of 15; had a very poor memory, was mentally slow, unsociable, and a "dreamer." He had no gift for languages and, although he was brilliant in physics and mathematics, he failed his entrance examination the first time he applied to the Federal Institute of Technology. Yet his theory of relativity, published in 1915, revolutionized physics and led to the splitting of the atom and the beginning of the space age. He won the Nobel Prize for physics in 1921. After the atomic bomb was dropped on Hiroshima, he became a pacifist and said, "If I had known they were going to do this I would have become a shoemaker."

Susan Hampshire (1942–): A British child, Susan was ridiculed by her classmates and considered stupid because she suffered from dyslexia, so her school years were painful. From the age of nine she wanted to be an actress, but her mother discouraged her because of her reading problems. However, at 16 she quit school and joined a small repertory company as an assistant stage manager. She taught herself to read moderately well and to memorize parts, but her auditions were unsuccessful because first readings aloud continued to be too difficult. Once she got a few parts, however, her beauty, charm, sensitivity, and comic and dramatic skills resulted in a triumphant career on the stage, in movies, and on television. Her stardom did not interfere with volunteer work, which she undertook over the years: She worked with Albert Schweitzer in Africa shortly before his death, contributed financially toward the education of children in Biafra, maintained a strong continuing interest in helping dyslexic children, and developed improved reading materials to help them learn to read.

William James (1842–1910): Born in New York City into an intellectually distinguished family, William had difficulty reading and writing all his life. He said, "I'm a very poor visualizer and find that I can seldom call to mind even a single letter of the alphabet in purely retinal terms. I must trace the letter by running my mental eye over its contours in order that the image of it shall leave any distinctness at all." In spite of this unusual handicap he graduated from Harvard University's medical school in 1869 and became a popular teacher of anatomy, physiology, and hygiene; he later branched out to become a revered professor of philosophy. He was also the author of distinguished and still influential books on both philosophy and psychology.

Bruce Jenner (1949–): An American decathlete, Jenner suffered from learning disabilities as a child, but he compensated for poor school work with sports. He became an outstanding and versatile athlete, winning a gold medal in the demanding Decathlon at the 1976 Olympics in Montreal. He followed that triumph with a lucrative career as a television sportscaster.

James Earl Jones (1931–): In 1993 this American, whom many people consider the world's greatest black actor, published his autobiography called *Voices and Silences*. It astounded many people to learn that this poised, and articulate man, whose deep and distinctive voice is a major part of his commanding presence, had endured a parentless childhood in the Mississippi delta living in squalor, and was so traumatized that he counld not even speak. He was mute off and on for years until he discovered the theater and studied acting. He then mastered his craft so successfully that after his Broadway debut at age 26 he went on to triumph in starring roles in the theater, movies, and television.

King Karl XI (1655–1697): Karl was a Swedish royal child with lifelong reading and spelling problems characteristic of dyslexia; these were so severe he often held documents upside down when pretending to read them, and whenever possible he relied on interviews instead of written reports. Yet he reorganized his country, improving the army, the navy, and economic conditions. He is considered one of Sweden's wisest kings.

Leonardo da Vinci (1452–1519): This Italian artist believed to have been dyslexic because he had a strange, almost illegible, handwriting. Yet he was a genius: architect, painter, sculptor, poet, musician, scientist, engineer, inventor, mathematician, and meteorologist. His lifetime achievements have never been equalled.

George S. Patton (1885–1945): An American child, George could write script but could never learn to read print. He had an extraordinary memory, though, and is said to have managed to graduate from West Point by memorizing entire lectures and texts. He went on to an outstanding career as an army commander and general in World War II.

Nelson Aldrich Rockefeller (1908–1979): Although he had severe dyslexia, with the aid of an unusually intelligent and devoted mother who carefully supervised his education, Nelson grew up to have a distinguished career in public life. He was U.S. Assistant Secretary of State, then Governor of New York, and finally Vice President. He was also a great patron of the arts and a generous philanthropist.

Auguste Rodin (1840–1917): Auguste was a French boy who was described as the worst pupil in his school. Baffled by arithmetic and spelling, he was thought to be an idiot by his father and his uncle, who considered him uneducable. Even so, he enriched his and succeeding generations through his art, becoming a world-famous sculptor. At the age of 67 he was awarded an honorary degree from Oxford University.

Woodrow Wilson (1856–1924): This American boy was considered dull and backward. He did not learn the alphabet until he was 9 and could not read until ll. This did not keep him from becoming a professor of history, jurisprudence, and political economy, the author of books on government, the President of Princeton University, the Governor of New Jersey, and the President of the United States. In recognition of his assistance in bringing about the armistice at the end of World War I and his contributions to the creation of the League of Nations, he received the Nobel Peace Prize in 1919.

CHILDREN'S HEALTH: PROGRESS AND SETBACKS IN OUR CENTURY

In the 1970s, 1980s, and 1990s the annual child death toll was reduced by more than 25 million, largely due to the widespread use of penicillin and other antibiotics, and to inoculations against polio, pneumonia, and measles. AIDS has become a new worldwide plague, but some of the worst diseases have been conquered. For example, smallpox for centuries was a children's disease as common as the much milder chickenpox. It scarred, blinded, and killed millions, and in 1968 it was still common in 30 countries. But in 1973 South America was declared free of it, and in 1974 the World Health Organization (WHO) announced that only four countries were still afflicted. By 1975 special campaigns in those four countries had wiped this centuries-old disease off the face of the earth. A new vaccine for chickenpox may soon eliminate that disease as well.

Leprosy, another much dreaded disease throughout history, is no longer always a sentence of despair and death; it is finally being brought under control by modern medicine and lepers need no longer be shunned and ostracized in leper colonies. There is a horrible side effect of some of their medicine, however. Thalidomide is often prescribed to lepers because it has an almost miraculous ability to treat the disease's complications. It is also a highly effective painkiller and is valuable against some potentially fatal side effects of bone marrow surgery; macular degeneration, a common cause of blindness; tuberculosis; and even AIDS. But this is also the medicine that, in the 1960s, became synonymous with tragedy. It was prescribed to many pregnant women as a sleeping pill. No one at the time knew it could cause harm to the fetus, but when these mothers' babies were born they were appallingly deformed. Approximately 12,000 thalidomide babies were born around the world. Some countries promptly made strict rules governing its use, but controls are much laxer in other parts of the world. Consequences are now apparent in Brazil, a large producer of thalidomide because it is home to perhaps 300,000 people with leprosy. At least 46 new instances of birth defects caused by it occurred there in 1994.

Only two companies in Brazil are authorized to produce the drug, but there are several greedy underground laboratories that reportedly sell it to people without a prescription or warning. The Thalidomide Victims Association was formed by members of Brazil's first thalidomide generation who are now adults, to start an intensive education campaign. Thalidomide, as these people show, does not kill children or reduce their life expectancy, and the resilience of the human spirit is clearly demonstrated by the fact that many first generation thalidomide babies have grown up to lead successful and happy lives. Nevertheless, they do not want others to have to go through what they did.

Progress in life expectancy is a significant indicator of social progress, and analysts have discovered that the progress being made today in developing countries is proceeding at a faster rate than that which improved and extended lives in Europe during its own industrial revolution. A convergence of factors has made this possible. The communications and transportation revolutions in our century have transformed the developing world over the past 50 years, putting radios in a majority of homes and television sets in most villages, thus enabling health workers to reach even isolated communities and families. Developing societies now have an immeasurably greater ability to exchange information and to contact and mobilize their people than was available to industrialized nations when they were at a comparable stage of development. These technological breakthroughs have made it possible to put knowledge of today's medical advances into practice on an unprecedented scale. The time has come when parents everywhere can be given the knowledge and means of "death control."

Nutritional Progress

Although our world still contains vast areas where children are malnourished and food shortages and deadly famines exist, a great many children are today eating more varied and more nutritious food than any children ever did in the past.

Today everyone knows how important vitamins are for maintaining good health, yet no one had ever even heard of them until 1911 when Polish chemist Casimir Funk announced his discovery that some foods contained a substance he called "vita-amine." Later this was called vitamin B. Vitamin A was not discovered until 1913 and was not chemically synthesized until 1936. Vitamin B-1 was discovered in 1915 and synthesized in 1945. And vitamin D, the antirickets vitamin, was not known until 1922.

The existence of what we now call vitamin C was suspected as early as 1757 but was not chemically analyzed until 1918 or synthesized until 1933. Today many baby foods are fortified with vitamin C because it is not present in milk and is a great aid in the development of strong bones, teeth, blood vessels, and tissues; it also increases resistance to infections and colds. Orange juice has been a popular drink all over the world ever since the Portuguese discovered oranges in China in the sixteenth century, but even after its nutritional value was discovered in the 1930s it was usually not given to babies because some were allergic to it, and also because it was difficult, if not impossible, to strain it to a consistency that would flow freely through a nipple without clogging. The modern baby food industry has developed a special infant juice that solves this problem and removes the substances that caused allergic reactions in some infants.

In the first (1914) edition of the U.S. Government's booklet, *Infant Care*, no solid foods were recommended until a child was over a year old, but nowadays vegetables and fruits can be safely introduced by about the sixth month, if not earlier. The commercial baby food industry is what has made this possible. It was started in 1927 by Daniel Gerber (1898–1974), a new father who one day was watching his wife struggling as she tried to mash and strain peas for their baby. He was employed in his father's canning factory and said, "Here, let me take the peas over to the factory where they can be easily processed." Mr. and Mrs. Gerber began testing batches of strained food on their daughter Sally and other babies, and by 1941 the company had a full line of baby foods that were outselling their adult products.

Another type of food is also now available even if it is out of season. From 1912 to 1917, Clarence ("Bob") Birdseye (1886–1956) was engaged in the fur trade in Labrador. He noticed how well the natives preserved fish and other foods by freezing them so that they could last during their harsh winters, and he began experimenting with quick-freezing foods. When he returned to his home base in Gloucester, Massachusetts, he perfected his quick-freezing and packaging process during the 1920s and in 1927 established the General Foods Company with his line of frozen food products. By the 1940s the term "Birds Eye" had become a household word, and the days when a wide range of fruits,

161

vegetables, and other foods were available only at certain times of the year were gone forever.

The Child Survival and Development Revolution

According to the World Health Organization (WHO), four low-cost actions can save the lives of 20,000 children a day within a decade:

- breastfeeding
- growth monitoring
- treatment of diarrhea through newly invented oral rehydration tablets (ORT)
- inoculations against diphtheria, pertussis, polio, tetanus, tuberculosis, and measles

Breastfeeding is hardly a revolutionary suggestion; from time immemorial it has been the normal way to feed infants. It gives babies a healthful head start in life because breast milk contains antibiotics that protect nursing babies from illness.

However, there have always been some women who refuse to nurse, worrying that it will ruin their figures (which is not true) or is inconvenient. In recent decades breastfeeding diminished greatly, due in part to the development of the baby food industry. This was especially unfortunate in poor communities where many mothers were spending money their families could ill afford instead of taking advantage of what nature provides free. Because many of the parents were illiterate, they could not read instructions for sterilizing bottles and incorrectly prepared formulas that made babies sick. An international effort has been launched to encourage hospitals to teach mothers to breastfeed.

In 1980 UNICEF and WHO together declared a "Child Survival and Development Revolution" to promote these life-saving actions, and the response in many countries was tremendous. For example, in Brazil 400,000 volunteers took part in an immunization campaign that reached 20,000,000 children. In the Dominican Republic 20,000 volunteers, many of them students, visited almost every home in the country to vaccinate children against polio and measles. And in Pakistan the immunization rate jumped from 5 to 50 percent of all children by 1985.

One of the most dramatic responses was from Colombia, which in 1984 launched a five-year vaccination crusade. It focused on protecting the country's nearly 4 million

children under five, who annually accounted for more than a quarter of all deaths in the nation. Calls to join in the effort went out from the president, provincial governors, and mayors, from newspapers and broadcasting stations, from the Catholic Church, and from school teachers. In the first year nearly 60,000 volunteers helped to operate over 10,000 vaccination posts set up in marketplaces, at street corners, in clinics, and in schools, and the vaccination rate of Colombia's children under five was raised to over 60 percent. By the time the plan was in full operation in 1989, there were 362,000 active volunteers from the ranks of the Red Cross, the Colombian Institute for Family Welfare, the Girl and Boy Scouts, national police, priests, nuns, and lay people, even owners of canoes who went into jungles in the most remote areas of the country to transport childen from isolated tribes to health centers. They vaccinated over 80 percent of the children under five, halved child deaths from diarrhea, prevented complications of pregnancy and childbirth, and through a new nutrition program reduced the chronic malnutrition that had afflicted one in four Colombian children.

An interesting detail of the comprehensive five-year plan was that the majority of health monitors were high school students. By a presidential decree, all ninth-graders were given 20 hours of training and then did 80 hours' work in their communities. The Minister of Education also revised the school curriculum so that students in every grade would learn 16 proven measures to protect children's growth and development.

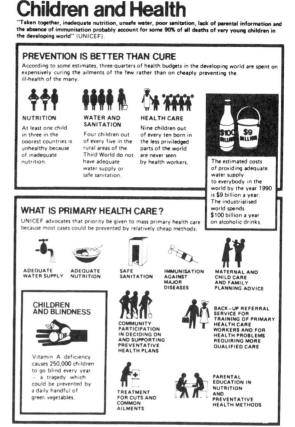

Children and Health

"Taken together, inadequate nutrition, unsafe water, poor sanitation, lack of parental information and the absence of immunisation probably account for some 90% of all deaths of very young children in the developing world" (UNICEF).

PREVENTION IS BETTER THAN CURE

According to some estimates, three-quarters of health budgets in the developing world are spent on expensively curing the ailments of the few rather than on cheaply preventing the ill-health of the many.

NUTRITION
At least one child in three in the poorest countries is unhealthy because of inadequate nutrition.

WATER AND SANITATION
Four children out of every five in the rural areas of the Third World do not have adequate water supply or safe sanitation.

HEALTH CARE
Nine children out of every ten born in the less priviledged parts of the world are never seen by health workers.

The estimated costs of providing adequate water supply to everybody in the world by the year 1990 is $9 billion a year. The industrialised world spends $100 billion a year on alcoholic drinks.

WHAT IS PRIMARY HEALTH CARE?

UNICEF advocates that priority be given to mass primary health care because most cases could be prevented by relatively cheap methods:

ADEQUATE WATER SUPPLY

ADEQUATE NUTRITION

SAFE SANITATION

IMMUNISATION AGAINST MAJOR DISEASES

MATERNAL AND CHILD CARE AND FAMILY PLANNING ADVICE

CHILDREN AND BLINDNESS
Vitamin A deficiency causes 250,000 children to go blind every year – a tragedy which could be prevented by a daily handful of green vegetables.

COMMUNITY PARTICIPATION IN DECIDING ON AND SUPPORTING PREVENTATIVE HEALTH PLANS

TREATMENT FOR CUTS AND COMMON AILMENTS

BACK–UP REFERRAL SERVICE FOR TRAINING OF PRIMARY HEALTH CARE WORKERS AND FOR HEALTH PROBLEMS REQUIRING MORE QUALIFIED CARE

PARENTAL EDUCATION IN NUTRITION AND PREVENTATIVE HEALTH METHODS

As dramatic as this response was, something even more unprecedented occurred in El Salvador: a cease fire was declared during that country's civil war, and for three days the only shots were vaccinations.

Even before this "revolution," life expectancy was rising in most parts of the world. In almost every country birth rates have fallen since 1950, and the proportion of children born who survive beyond their first or fifth year has risen, as has life expectancy. Other important developments are that nearly 60 percent of the people in the developing world now have access to clean water, compared to a mere 29 percent in 1970. This is important, since WHO says that nearly four out of five of the diseases and disabilities that afflict children in developing nations are related to contaminated or inadequate water. Safe drinking water and sanitation could cut infant mortality by as much as 50 percent.

Food production has also increased; several countries that used to have to import food are now self-sufficient. Between 1955 and 1975 the people of Africa, Asia, and Latin America doubled irrigation and brought over 375 billion acres of new land into production—more than the entire crop land of Canada, Japan, the United States and western Europe combined.

Large areas of famine and environmental pollution still exist, but it is important to acknowledge the real achievements that have taken place. Literally millions of babies born in the late 1990s can look forward to much longer and healthier lives than they could have if they had been born in earlier centuries or even as recently as 1970.

One cautionary note, however: sometimes once-conquered diseases make a come-back, either because viruses may become immune to antibiotics or because people who no longer see any cases of a once-feared disease become overconfident. For example, mothers who have never experienced the annual terror that plagued previous generations may think it is no longer necessary to take their children to the doctor to get shots of anti-polio vaccine. In 1994 and 1995 there was a sudden resurgence of polio in some parts of the world because too many children were not being immunized against it. Tuberculosis, also no longer considered a threat in the developed world, reappeared unexpectedly too.

Another problem is that with the widespread travel prevalent in our increasingly interdependent world, devastating plagues once confined to a few locales can now easily cross international borders, quickly spreading from one country to others. Germs do not need passports.

Although new drugs are very effective for a while in combatting disease, it does not take long for parasites to become resistant to them. In 1996 there was a highly alarming resurgence of malaria, which was thought to have been conquered. The drug resistance began in Cambodia, spread to the Thai-Myanmar border, and then was transmitted through Bangladesh to India and finally to Africa.

AIDS has captured the world's attention, but many doctors say that malaria may be the most deadly disease in the world. Health experts estimate that 300 million people are infected with malaria every year, and that more than 2 million die. Quinine used to be a potent fighter against malaria, but it has lost its effectiveness. Now researchers say that the parasites infecting the refugee population along the Thai-Myanmar border are showing a 50 percent resistance to the latest drugs, and an 80 percent resistance among children.

"The parasite has developed resistance to all antimalarial drugs that are thrown at it," says Dr. Nicholas White, director of the Wellcome-Mahidol University Oxford Tropical Research Program in Bangkok. Every day thousands of infected refugees come in for testing and treatment at the small clinics run by the Shoklo Malaria Research Unit. Its doctors are financed by the Wellcome Trust, the World Health Organization, the United States Army, and other groups. But as the disease becomes more deadly, research has been slowed because malaria is seen as an ailment of the poor and therefore does not offer the potential market that would justify huge expenditures by drug companies. "The most effective antimalaria measure in the world is money," says Dr. White. "You spray money at malaria and you tend to get rid of it. A few GIs got malaria in Somalia. . .every GI that gets it is jolly good for the world because that means more money for malarial drug research."

As Dr. Michele van Vugt, a young Dutch doctor working in a refugee camp in Thailand, says, "The parasites are very, very clever, much more clever than us. We don't know why, but this area is where the resistance begins. And then it spreads all over the world."

AIDS AND CHILDREN

Few people had ever heard of AIDS, an acronym for Acquired Immune Deficiency Syndrome, when doctors started describing it in 1981 as the result of infection with a *human immune deficency virus (HIV)*. This ghastly disease, which has since become a worldwide plague, is spread solely through the exchange of blood and other body fluids. In Africa the virus is transmitted almost exclusively through heterosexual contacts. In Thailand, where the number of infected people shot up from 1,000 to roughly 50,000 in just three years, the epidemic apparently started among intravenous drug users before it spread among heterosexuals. In Eastern Europe, AIDS spread primarily through unsafe medical practices. In the United States the epidemic was at first concentrated in major cities, almost always among gay men and drug users, but later its incidence rose nearly four times as fast in the nation's smallest cities as it did in its largest ones, and it increased by 36 percent or more among heterosexuals and among newborn babies.

By 1989 newborns were getting AIDS at a faster rate than gays or drug users. Many got it prenatally. In some areas, such as Romania, unsanitary medical conditions caused hundreds of infants to become infected.

American teenagers are also special targets for AIDS; there were already 2.5 million cases in 1989. Today people in their twenties are among the greatest number of new AIDS cases, which means that most of them actually got the HIV virus while in their teens.

RyanWhite (1971-1990)

Ryan was a boy who became famous as a result of getting AIDS, the way he was treated as a result, the courageous way he faced his problems, and how his response changed the way other people have since reacted to the disease's victims.

He lived in Kokomo, Indiana, where he and his sister, his parents, and grandparents had all been born, a friendly town that they never wanted to leave. But he had a different destiny.

Ryan was a hemophiliac. This condition causes excessive loss of blood from the slightest scratch and must frequently be treated through blood transfusions. He was just 13 in December 1984 when he was diagnosed with AIDS, which he had acquired as a result of a blood transfusion. At that time no one realized that this new and deadly virus could be transmitted that way. Blood transfusions are now carefully monitored.

Doctors told Ryan's mother the disease was still so new they could not predict how long he would live; he might have only six more months. When he heard what was the matter with him, he did not cry or even seem frightened. He just wanted to know how soon he would be able to go back to school.

By summer he was well enough to get a paper route and hang out with his friends. But when September came, the school board refused to let him return. Everyone was afraid of him. Despite overwhelming, well-publicized medical evidence that AIDS is not contracted through casual everyday contact, the board claimed it could not guarantee the health of Ryan's fellow students. Later, a court forced the board to relent, and Ryan returned to school, but only for one day. A group of parents promptly brought suit to bar him, and he was sent home until arguments could be heard in court, which took months. Finally a judge affirmed Ryan's right to attend school, after what his mother has described as "more than a year of bitter legal combat in the center ring of a national media circus." He returned to school but faced humilating regulations: He had to drink from a separate water fountain and use a separate bathroom; he was forced to use paper plates and disposable utensils and was not allowed to take gym or use the locker room or pool. Ridiculous rumors spread. People said he spat on food and tried to bite people. Parents would not let their children associate with him. When he walked down the school hall kids ran away screaming.

Not only his family and neighbors but people all over the country had learned through newspapers and appearances of Ryan on TV that Kokomo was no longer a friendly town. Even old friends who secretly sympathized with him would not shake his hand, and then one Sunday while he and his family were at church, a bullet shattered their home's picture window. Ryan anounced: "Mom, it's time to get out of Kokomo."

She sold their house, at a tremendous loss because it was called "the AIDS house," and moved 20 miles south to a town called Cicero. Here, to their amazement, his new high school accepted him with open arms. The students got together for AIDS awareness classes, inviting expert speakers, and counseling was offered to anyone who was afraid. The entire country was aware of what was going on. Ryan appeared on "Nightline" and the "Today" show and made hundreds of new friends. In spite of increasing weakness, he traveled around the country speaking about AIDS, and everywhere he went AIDS patients told him that because of his public struggle he had eased the way for them.

Ryan was not bitter or unforgiving about the way he had been treated in Kokomo. He told his mother, "People were just doing what you were trying to do—watching out for their kids. They were scared to death, and that's why they acted so crazy. In a way, I really can't blame them—though they were wrong."

In the spring of l990 Ryan's health began slipping, and while in Los Angeles for an AIDS benefit he became very ill. He was rushed back to Cicero and put in the hospital, where he often became unconscious. He died on Palm Sunday. After his death his mother learned that the repentant churches in Kokomo had been praying for him.

Mrs. White created the Ryan White Foundation, a nonprofit group with headquarters in Indianapolis that works to increase public awareness of how to combat HIV infections and to fight discrimination against people who are already infected. The foundation places a particular emphasis on reaching teenagers with the message that the surest way to protect themselves against AIDS is through sexual abstinence and a drug-free life. Mrs. White is very proud to have been Ryan's mother, convinced that "God chose this average boy from an average town in Middle America to do His work, to be an example in the face of ignorance, prejudice and fear and to sow compassion in people's hearts. How else could Ryan have survived for nearly six years when the doctors had given him only six months?"

NICHOLAS GREEN: A SEVEN-YEAR-OLD BOY WHO SAVED MANY CHILDREN'S LIVES

Nicholas Green (1987–1994) was a handsome, delightful, lively seven-year-old who was interested in practically everything, from tap dancing to history and mythology. He was thrilled to visit places like the Roman Forum, the Colosseum, the ruins of Pompeii, and beautiful temples in Italy during September 1994 on a vacation trip with his parents, Margaret and Reg Green, and his four-year-old sister Eleanor. But suddenly disaster struck, though he never knew it. A bullet shattered the rear window of his family's rental car, entering his brain as he was sleeping in the rear seat. Nicholas never woke up again he died two days later.

The entire world heard about the tragedy. Italians were appalled and shattered by what one newspaper called "our shame."

Nicholas's parents immediately decided that since their son had been in perfect health they should donate his organs to sick people in need of transplants, and their decision created another nationwide sensation. As one newspaper columnist said, "Perhaps they do not realize how rare that gesture is in our country. . . . .Half the children with heart ailments in Italy do not make it and die while awaiting a transplant."

To the Greens the decision was spontaneous and heartfelt. "Our little guy was going to have a great future," said his father. "That's been taken away. Now somebody else has the right to have a shot at it. We thought it very important to give his future to someone who had lost theirs."

Newspapers and TV stations throughout Italy carried their story and the family was "flooded with kindness," Nicholas's mother said. Their refusal to be embittered and to blame Italy for the tragedy drew even more sympathizers. Letters and telegrams poured in. Strangers on the street, hard-boiled police officers, even the prime minister of Italy, hugged them and wept with them and gave them gifts. Schoolchildren wrote stories and poems about Nicholas, musicians composed songs about him, towns named streets and schools after him. After a ceremony in Rome, Italy's president presented the Greens with a medal of honor. He also arranged for them to be flown home to California in an Italian air force jet.

In their small home town they continued to receive overwhelming expressions of sympathy via telephone not only from Italy but from as far away as England and Australia. Dozens of letters arrived daily, some addressed simply to "Parents of Nicholas, Bodega Bay, California."

A few months later the Greens were invited back to Italy for a ceremony in honor of Nicholas. Wondering if they could bear to return, but feeling obliged to, they were well rewarded. They met a beautiful 19-year-old who had been just days away from death when she received Nicholas's liver. A 14-year-old was alive because she had received one of his kidneys. An 11-year-old had been on dialysis for a year until he was given the other kidney. Two people, a school teacher and a salesman, had had their eyesight restored when each of them received a cornea from Nicholas. And a 30-year-old woman had received cells from Nicholas's pancreas to help her body produce insulin. The only beneficiary the Greens did not meet was a boy still recovering from a transplant operation after receiving Nicholas's heart.

Italian doctors told the Greens that Nicholas had changed the entire country, which had been so moved by the boy's killing and the grace of his parents that, although Italy had one of the lowest rates of organ donation in Europe the willingness to donate had gone up 400 percent since Nicholas died. This enormous progress they gratefully designated as "the Nicholas effect."

At his funeral in California, attended by classmates and fellow Boy Scouts, Nicholas's teacher said, "I never dreamed that this friendly little boy who entered my classroom would have a higher purpose."

Nicholas had been particularly fond of the myth about Persephone, who was kidnapped into the lower world but was reborn every spring, "and he seemed to get the idea of rebirth in an adult way," said his father in his eulogy at the funeral. "He has saved the lives of many children and if that's not immortality it's close." On the eve of the funeral his father, blinking back tears, said, "All the human sympathy that's come our way has changed into something more profound, more spiritual. The main lesson of all this is the goodness that we've seen, rather than the badness. Nicholas has struck a spark of love in the hearts of millions of parents and children around the world . . . . I have a vision of millions of parents all over the world giving their chiildren just a slightly longer hug before sending them off to school, and reading one extra page before they go to bed at night . . . . He has already helped save the lives of other children. He could have lived to 100 and done less."

HELPING CHILDREN WITH DISABILITIES

Obviously, children with physical or mental disabilities encounter more frustrations than other people do, and therefore need extra help. But custodial care is only part of what they need. The most important help one can give them is that which increases their self-esteem. People who always feel inadequate become more than merely discouraged; they become self-pitying, or feel guilty, and depressed, or resentful and hostile. And if the person taking care of them interprets their hostility as lack of gratitude and becomes resentful in turn, little progress is possible.

The modern world's increased knowledge of how the mind works has made people more understanding when patients resist help and repay kindness with nastiness. They recognize this as often an unconscious cry for more help, rather than an indication that help is being "wasted" on people who do not appreciate it. It is very hard for a chronic patient to stay patient, and what looks like anger may really be disguised shame. So it is the caretaker who needs to be patient, and to realize that trying to "shame" someone who is already ashamed of his inadequacies into acting less obnoxious may just make him or her worse. Sincere compliments, about anything one can find to praise, will not spoil a child, and scornful or angry scoldings may not improve him. In fact, it may be quite the other way around. Paradoxically, the less there seems to be to praise in a child, the more praise he or she probably needs.

Avoid Comparisons

Among other things that psychologists working with these children have learned is that holding up role models of people who have done remarkable things despite severe handicaps will inspire and bring new hope to some children with special problems, but sometimes such stories do just the opposite. Children who are less challenged may feel resentful and embarrassed that they cannot do as much as others who have faced even greater obstacles. So they become more discouraged than ever. Not everyone can emulate great feats: a child may be weak physically but extremely strong mentally or emotionally, or the other way around. These are simply different types of problems, each deserving of understanding.

Concentrate on Abilities, Not Disabilities

This admonition, which was one of the slogans for the International Year of the Disabled, is one of the most important pieces of advice that can be given to anyone trying to help a child with disabilities. None of us can do everything that everyone else can do, so in that sense all of us have some disabilities. But at the same time, there is almost always something that even extremely challenged children can learn to do if they are given help and opportunity. Helen Keller wrote in her book *Teacher*, "Every human being has hidden away in him capabilities waiting to be discovered."

However, when children are severely disabled, parents are often kept so busy with their physical care that they often forget or are unable to provide the extra things that could aid intellectual and social growth and perhaps even decrease the children's need for constant care. But children's attitudes toward themselves are just as important to their progress as their physical condition. A deep sense of inadequacy will make it impossible for them to do even those things that are well within their capabilities, which are often far greater than they—or anyone else—realizes.

Education and recreation for children with disabilities should not be regarded simply as ways to (1) help them pass the time, (2) assuage loneliness, or (3) provide a little pleasure to try to make up for a lot of unhappiness. Those are important, but even more important is the need to stimulate the children and to help them accomplish something that will enable them to feel a genuine sense of achievement.

At whatever level a child is, progress and hope and satisfaction are possible if we simply compare what the child can do today with what he or she could do last week or last year, instead of focusing on what someone else can do. The proud smile of triumph on the face of a palsied child who has finally learned to crawl or walk across a room or say "hello" is as radiant as the smile of a young gymnast who has just received a score of 10 in an Olympics competition. And deserves just as enthusiastic congratulations.

Ray Charles told an amusing story about how his mother taught him self-reliance and self-respect when he was a self-pitying little boy who had recently lost his eyesight. He expected his mother to do everything for him, and she did a lot, but one day she refused to tie his shoelaces for him. He felt helpless but she said firmly, "Just because you're blind don't mean you're stupid! Figure it out." He did, after a struggle. And he said this was the most important lesson he ever got.

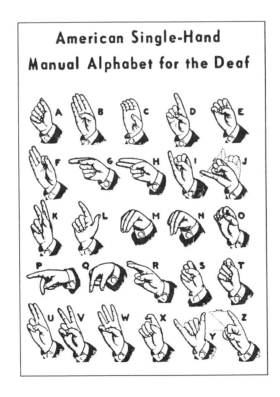

American Single-Hand Manual Alphabet for the Deaf

UNICEF

5

Child Development

INFANCY, BABYHOOD, CHILDHOOD, AND YOUTH

The ability to talk is such a fundamental aspect of human nature that the development of this one skill is used to define the early stages of human development. Semantically, an infant is someone who is speechless, and a baby is someone who babbles.

Different authorities, however, define infancy and babyhood differently. An infant may be anyone:

- under two, if you are a pediatrician
- under six, if you are a biologist or child psychologist
- under seven, considered below "the age of reason," if you are a theologian
- under 21, if you are a lawyer

In law books one comes across sentences which strike nonlegal minds as funny and startling, such as: "In common law, if the infant was over 14, he had the right to choose the person whom he would like as guardian." In a dictionary of legal terms you may read: "Every person is by the law styled an infant until he has attained the age of 21 years."

According to some child psychologists, infancy lasts until age five. But Lucy Sprague Mitchell (1878–1967), a founder of the Bank Street College of Education, said: "In spite of all the startling changes which a child has gone through by the end of his fifth year, he is still so immature that psychologists commonly refer to this whole period as 'the infancy period.'"

Most pediatricians and psychiatrists, however, regard infancy as a shorter period than that. Dr. Alan F. Guttmacher says, "In general, 'infant' describes the young human being during the first two years after birth. He becomes a 'child' as he achieves mastery over such basic skills as walking, talking, feeding himself, and controlling elimination."

Psychologist Harry Stack Sullivan (1892–1949) defined infancy as the "epoch" of personality development from birth to the "maturation of the capacity for language," and called childhood the "epoch" of personality development from infancy to "the maturation of the capacity for living with compeers."

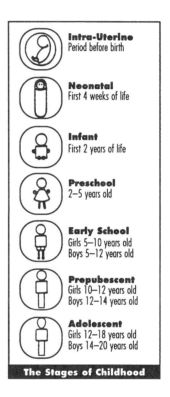

Intra-Uterine
Period before birth

Neonatal
First 4 weeks of life

Infant
First 2 years of life

Preschool
2–5 years old

Early School
Girls 5–10 years old
Boys 5–12 years old

Prepubescent
Girls 10–12 years old
Boys 12–14 years old

Adolescent
Girls 12–18 years old
Boys 14–20 years old

The Stages of Childhood

What Is a "Youth"?

Legal definitions of "child" and "youth" vary from place to place. For example, in Guyana, Iceland, and Malayasia, a child is a person under age 14; in the Falkland Islands and Mauritius, under 15; in Austria, a minor who has not completed compulsory schooling; in the Netherlands, a person whose compulsory education has not yet begun or ended. A youth, or young person, in Bahrain and Malaysia is in the age range 14 to16; in Iceland, 14 to 17; in Nepal, 14 to 18; in the Falkland Islands, Mauritius, and Poland, 15 to 18; in St. Kitts-Nevis-Anguilla, 16 to 18; in Switzerland, under 20.

THE IMPORTANCE OF HELPING CHILDREN IN THEIR EARLY YEARS

Children are the most fragile, defenseless, innocent and wretched victims of our collective neglect and indifference. Their survival in conditions of physical or emotional deprivation is no less than a miracle, a testimony to the strength of human endurance and resilience. Yet this phenomenon cannot absolve us of our shared responsibility for the shocking numbers of children who needlessly succumb to starvation, malnutrition, and disease before age five.

—Estefania Aldaba Lim, Assistant Secretary-General of the United Nations for the International Year of the Child, 1979

Children neglected in their tender years become like unto a garden, which in the springtime...where there is nothing sowen, there is like to be nothing reaped but weeds. *—William Batty, Elizabethan childcare authority, 1581*

It is in the early years that hope and faith are born, that the ability to give and receive love grows its first tender roots. It is also the time, the seed bed, for alienation, hatred and despair to develop. Both are things the results of which we recognize a generation later simply as peace and war, love and hatred, happiness and unhappiness....

—John Grun, Director of the United Nations Secretariat of the International Year of the Child, 1979

Many of the things we need can wait. The child cannot. He is building up his bones and his blood right now, and he is training his senses. The answer we give him cannot be 'tomorrow'; his time is NOW. After the age of seven, whatever is done for the child will be no more than partial repair of the damage; it may remedy, but not cure . . . . In some crafts, when something is spoiled at the beginning, it cannot be mended. The same occurs in the case of the child: tardy repairs are not of any more use. And thus we destroy the divine pattern of the child.

—Gabriela Mistral (1889–1957), Nobel prize winner for Literature from Chile

Granny is sitting by the fireside knitting a stocking. She is very old, and her eyesight is failing, and every now and then she drops a stitch without noticing it. But she goes on knitting just the same, and in due course the stocking is finished. But, on account of the dropped stitches, it is not so strong or so perfect a garment as it might have been. Similarly, if the child misses some of his sensitive periods during his development, he will still grow up into an adult, but that adult will not be so strong nor so perfect an individual as he would have been if he had been able to avail himself of their constructive power.
—Maria Montessori (1870–1952), Italian physician and educator

There is reason to believe that the capacity for innovation, for experimentation, the acquisition of new knowledge, and invention are necessary to development.

To develop these capacities requires that children be exposed to an atmosphere where their curiosity is stimulated, their right to ask questions insured, where they have ample opportunity to play that gives free expression to imagination as well as to physical skills, and where their health is protected. If these conditions do not exist, economic and social development is retarded. It is important, however, that we do not exclusively emphasize these grounds of social utility in order to justify greater investment in the child, particularly the young child, and so fall into a variant of the conception of the child as a servant of society. We should pay heed to enhancing the joys and wonders of childhood as objectives in their own right.

—Herman Stein, *Special Consultant to the*
International Year of the Child, 1979

The Origin of Speech

People have often wondered about how human beings first learned to speak and what word was the first ever uttered. Two main theories, informally dubbed the *bow-wow theory* and the *babble-babble theory*, have been developed by linguists. The first one surmises that people began speaking by imitating sounds made by animals. The second, more widely held view, is that people babbled meaninglessly, as babies do, and gradually began to connect their babbling with their experiences, as babies also do. According to this theory, babbling is as natural to humans as barking is to dogs and quacking is to ducks. The second theory seems confirmed by observation of newborn babies.

The conscious, intentional use of sound is a later and different type of activity, requiring a degree of observation and control, whereas the first spontaneous sounds, called *nature sounds* or *nursery sounds* by linguists, are made without any thought. Once noises become imitative, we have the creation of *onomatopoeias*, words that sound like what they describe (as the word *babble* itself does); this is how many words originated.

We know little about primitive man's first attempts to speak, because we cannot know about something of which there is no existing record, and people learn to speak long before they learn to write. The oldest language of which we have any written records is Sumerian, spoken around 3500 B.C.

The ancient Egyptian hieroglyphic inscriptions are almost as old as the Sumerian. Chinese and Sanskrit records go back to about 2000 B.C. The earliest Greek writings date from about 1500 B.C., and the earliest Latin we know of goes back to about 500 B.C. To put these dates in perspective with the history of mankind, the following comparison will be helpful: if the total history of mankind had taken place in one day, this would mean we have written records going back about five minutes.

In their curiosity about the origins of human speech, linguists have carefully studied the origin of speech in babyhood on a systematic, wide-ranging basis in modern times, but we also know of several intriguing early research projects on the subject.

Herodotus, the "father of history" (c. 484–late 420s B.C.), wrote that Egyptians used to think their society was the most ancient in the world. Psammetichos, an early Egyptian ruler, decided to try to find out if this was so and thought of an ingenious way. He took at random, from two ordinary families, two newly born infants and gave them to a shepherd to be brought up among his sheep, under strict orders that no one should ever utter a single word in the babies' presence. They were to be kept all by themselves in a lonely cottage. The shepherd was to bring in goats from time to time, to see that the babies had enough milk to drink, and to look after them physically in any other way necessary, but never to say a word to them.

"All these arrangements were made by Psammetichos," explained Herodotus, "because he wanted to find out what word the children would first utter, once they had grown out of their meaningless baby talk." Evidently Psammetichos was one of those who believed that the ability to use sounds meaningfully to communicate ideas is an inherent, instinctive aspect of human nature rather than an activity that must be acquired by learning from teachers. "The plan succeeded," wrote Herodotus in his *Histories*:

> Two years later the shepherd, who during that time had done everything he had been told to do, happened one day to open the door of the cottage and go in, when both children, running up to him with hands outstretched, pronounced the word 'bekos'. The first time this happened the shepherd did not mention it; but later, when he discovered that each time he visited the children to take care of their needs the same word was constantly repeated by them, he informed his master. Psammetichos ordered the children to be brought to him and when he himself heard them say 'bekos' he decided to find out what language the word belonged to. His inquiries revealed that it was the Phrygian word for bread, and in consideration of this the Egyptians gave up their claims and admitted the superior antiquity of the Phyrgians. That this was what truly happened I myself learned from the priests of Hephaestus at Memphis although the Greeks have various improbable versions of the story, such as that Psammetichos had the children brought up by women whose tongues he had cut out. The priests' version, however, is the one I have given.

Another experiment of the same type was conducted by King Charles II (1630–1685) of England. Curious to know what babies would first say if they had no adult examples to influence them, he had two infants taken to an uninhabited island to be raised by deaf and mute nurses. Unfortunately, there seems to be no record of what happened to them.

How Children Learn to Speak

All babies, no matter what language their parents and neighbors speak, make the same sounds. The sounds have been analyzed by speech experts into four basic types:

- crying
- babbling
- lalling
- echolalia

Crying

All newborns come into the world, as Longfellow said, "with no language but a cry." Crying is the very first thing every newborn baby does. The medical term for a baby's first cry is *vagitus*. This comes from the Latin word *vagire*, meaning to squall. Also, the Roman god Vagitanus was the one who taught them to cry, according to Roman mythology. It was another god, Fabulinus, who later taught them to speak.

At first, a baby's crying is a simple monotonous bleat or quack, but soon it becomes sufficiently differentiated to express different needs. A loud scream communicates fear or anger. A sharp, fretful moan expresses pain. A low whimper, discomfort. A weak whine, sickness. A strong and lusty roar, a demand for food or attention. Even in young babies crying becomes a conscious means of communication.

Babies whose needs are attended to promptly seem to cry differently from babies less efficiently cared for. Those whose mothers are promptly attentive tend to cry as an announcement but to stop quickly, as if having once delivered their message, they know it will be attended to. In contrast babies whose mothers are neglectful or busy or less competent will usually cry longer and with much more anguish.

On the other hand, babies even less fortunate, those who have no mother taking care of them and who live in large institutions where it is impossible for anyone to give them much individual attention, seem to give up altogether. Such babies cry far less often than babies in private homes. Apparently they soon learn the sad fact that it is no use crying because it brings no results, so they suffer in comparative patience or apathetic silence. So when a mother finds it annoying that her child cries, she should actually be glad: it is a demonstration that the baby has those most valuable of all possessions, hope and trust.

Babbling

A few weeks or months after birth, a baby's voice begins to be used for more than crying. It starts to produce a new type of sound: babbling, or cooing, or gurgling begins. This differs from crying both in its sweetness of tone—its only rival in musical charm is the trill of songbirds—and in its purpose. It does not express any need to be helped. It is a recreational activity, indulged in simply for the baby's own pleasure, a joyful playing around with sounds. We might call it the beginning of musical improvisation. The jazz composer Billy Strayhorn (1935–1967) called it "liquid music." Perhaps it corroborates the theory of Charles Darwin (1809–1882) that singing preceded the invention of speech.

Vowels

Cooing consists of vowel sounds only at first, starting with *a*, and then branching out into other sounds, some of which are common to languages other than the baby's "mother tongue," and some of which actually belong to no known language and defy attempts to spell them. Every baby is an experimenter who starts off making far more sounds than exist in any one language, and then gradually narrows them down by concentrating on those spoken around him, until eventually the baby even forgets how to make the unpracticed, unused sounds.

For example, some African babies of san-speakers are encouraged to practice clicking because many of Bantu words are made up of clicks. Children learning other languages soon lose the ability to make clicks.

Consonants

After babies have played around with vowels for a while, they start in on consonants, by smacking their lips together. The first three consonants practiced are almost always *m*, *p*, and *b*, called the *labials*. They begin by putting a consonant in front of a vowel, as in ma, pa, and ba, and then learn to put it on the other side too, as in mama. After these tricks are mastered, the babies go on to try out new consonants. Usually the next ones are *t* and *d*, called the *dentals*. Then the baby places its tongue against the roof of its mouth and

175

produces *k*, *g*, and *ng* sounds, called the gutturals. It is often years before *r* and *s* can be mastered, which is why we hear babies call a rabbit a *wabbit* and a pussy cat a *putty tat*. About 10 percent of children are still fairly unintelligible at the age of three and a half.

Lalling

When the typical baby is between six and nine months old, infancy's *lalling* stage usually begins. This is when babies repeat certain sounds they like over and over again such as *baba, mama, papa,* and *dada*. And this is when parents start to get really excited and the mother says proudly, "She actually said Mama" and the father, equally delighted, jumps at hearing *Papa* or *Dada*.

A word that originates in a physiological process common to the whole human race is called a *physonym* by linguists. The word *mama* is one of these because it is formed by sounds every baby makes naturally. The nature sounds or nursery sounds of *m* and *a* are so natural in every nursery, as a baby moves its tongue and lips, that they form the basis of the word for *mother* all over the world. It is not surprising that for words describing the most fundamental human relationships, the most universal sounds are selected. The words for *mother* and *father* are alike in a great many languages which otherwise have little in common.

Two psychologists at the University of Louisville in Kentucky, Ray H. Bixler and Harold C. Yeager, Jr., wrote in *Psychological Reports* in September, 1958, that human speech may have begun with the word *mama*. It is the most universal of all words. It was used in the earliest civilizations and can still be found in almost every culture. Dr. Yeager said all babies everywhere cry "ma ma" and that it means a different thing to them than any other sound they make.

It is amusing that the Babylonian goddess of childbirth, who was also regarded as the protector of children, was also called *Mama*, but this was not just a funny coincidence. The goddess probably got her name in the same way individual mamas receive theirs—when babies made the mama sound as almost their first recognizable attempt at speech, the doting women who hovered over them, rejoicing at this early sign of progress, pounced with delight on the sound, repeating it and getting the babies to repeat it as often as possible. In most cultures, these proud and happy women appropriate the sound to themselves. Since they show pleasure every time the baby says it, the baby soon begins to say it every time it sees the nice lady who likes it so much, and soon both lady and baby identify her with the sound. Babylonian mothers were evidently more devout, more humble, and more generous than most. They offered the precious sound to the motherly deity who could give their babies the best protection.

The consonant *m* is part of the word for mother almost everywhere. In Anglo-Saxon the word for mother is *Modor*. In Arabic it is *Am*. In Celtic, *Mathair*. In Danish, *Moder*. In Dutch, *Moeder*. In England a mother is formally *Mater* and informally *Mummy*; in the American version of the English language, she is *Mother* and *Mommy* or *Ma* or *Mom* or *Mama*. In French, she is *Mère*, with *Maman* the affectionate form of address. In German, *Mutter*. In Greek, *Metera*. In Hebrew, *Em*. In Italian and Spanish, *Madre* (and *Mama*). In Latin, *Mater*. In Persian, *Madr*. In Russian, *Mater*. In Sanskrit, *Matr* (or *Matar*). In Swahili, *Mama*. In Swedish, *Moder*.

Among other names for mother we also find *Nana* and *Ana* (or *Anna*) and these names, along with *Nanny* and *Mammy* are also sometimes applied to fathers, aunts, grandmothers, nurses, big sisters, or even uncles in cultures where much of the mother's role in baby care is taken over by mother substitutes. In other words, the nursery sounds *ma* or *ama* or *mama* or *nana* universally stand for whatever person is most closely connected with the nursery. Examples: Among the Bontok people of Luzon in the Philippines, where children are raised by fathers instead of mothers, the word for *father* is *Ama*. In China, where babies are usually cared for by a nurse, it is the nurse who is known as *Amah*. In the American south, during the period when slaves took care of their masters' children, the caretakers were called *Mammy*.

The nature sounds a baby makes after that first basic one of *ma* are used all over the world to name other people and items that are important in a baby's life. *Da* is usually one of the next sounds uttered by infants, with *pa*, *ta* and *na* as close rivals. Thus we find *dada* meaning mother in Togo, turning into *dad* and *daddy* in English and into *sister* in Swahili in East Africa where the eldest girl is active in baby care, into *nurse* in some languages and into *breast* in others. *Dada* has many variations. *Adda* means *little father* in some languages. *Atta* means *father* in Latin and in the oldest Teutonic dialects; Atilla (or Atli) the Hun got that name because his followers called him *little father*. It means *eldest sister* or *mother* in Sanskrit. *Atti* is the word for *father* in some Swiss dialects.

Papa is also often selected to name parents. The Latin word *pario*, which means, "I bring forth," is the source of the words *parent* and *paternal*. French, German, Greek, Italian, and Spanish-speaking children all say *papa* for *father*, with *pater*, *pitar*, *padre*, or *père* as variants used for formal designations. These are paralleled by *fata*, *fader*, *foter* and *father*, and by *vater* (German) and *vadar* (Dutch). In some languages *baba* means *father*. In Hebrew the word for *father* is *Abba* and in Gothic it is *Aba*.

Nana has protective and affectionate connotations. It becomes *Nanna* and the pet name for *grandmother*, or *Nanny* for the English child's devoted nurse, and Nyanya for the Russian baby's nurse. *Nanna* was also the name of another Babylonian god who protected people, and *Anna* was the name of a Mediterranean mother goddess and also the name of the revered grandmother of Jesus.

Echolalia

Differences in language develop as babies concentrate on the particular sounds they hear most frequently. Language is produced not merely by our ability to make sounds but by the selective process through which we choose out of the almost infinite number of possible sounds a few to be used as symbols. Observant infants gradually begin to catch on to this concept. Echoing the sounds they hear most often, sooner or later they learn to associate them with the ideas and objects they represent.

Eight to Nine Months

This is when babies usually pay closer attention than before to the sounds other people are making and start to imitate the sounds consciously. In this stage of speech development, called *echolalia*, meaning the echoing of sounds, they now may really begin to mean it when they say "Mama" and "Dada", having observed that when they repeat these sounds they get a special reaction from special people.

Twelve to Eighteen Months

By this time most babies are using a number of one or two syllable words purposefully. They have learned to be able to control their lips and tongue movements so they can intentionally produce a sound they want to make. This is a tremendous physical accomplishment. They have also learned to connect some of these sounds with certain objects; they are mastering the arts of observation, of analysis and identification, of symbolism and communication which they began practicing when they first smiled and gestured. These are tremendous intellectual accomplishments.

Twelve to Twenty-four Months

Most babies understand the meaning of some of the words said to them before they are able to pronounce them, and they can actually say a few words fairly clearly by the time they are a year old. By the time they are a year-and-a-half old, they usually have a vocabulary of about l0 words. By age two, most children have a vocabulary that has grown to about 200 or 300 words, and they can put these together into short sentences.

and beyond...

By age three, this vocabulary has usually tripled. By four, it contains about 1,500 words, and by five about 2,000. Few adults use more than 3,000 or 4,000 words. Usually children are about seven or even older before they acquire enough physical control to master all the complicated blendings of sounds required by their native language.

Of course, there are always babies who break these general rules. No two babies' minds are identical any more than their faces or personalities are. Children born with special handicaps, particularly the blind or deaf, need extra special help and progress more slowly. But even children without these disadvantages vary in the speed with which they start talking. Albert Einstein (1879–1955) did not speak at all until he was three. The Scottish essayist and historian Thomas Carlyle (1795–1881) was another late talker. It is said that he had not uttered a single word until he was two years old, but then one day, when he saw another child crying, he unexpectedly called out, "What ails thee, Jock?" And Victoria Lincoln, an American author, wrote in the *New Yorker* magazine about how worried she had been because her charming daughter was as speechless as Harpo Marx, until one day, when she was four, she suddenly pointed to an electric socket and said very distinctly, "Those are dangerous for babies." In short, some children start speaking early, one word at a time, while others seem to prefer to wait until they feel confident enough to say whole sentences correctly.

SUPERSTITIONS ABOUT LEARNING TO SPEAK

In view of the fact that almost every human baby sooner or later learns to speak, it seems odd that many people have believed in the necessity of strange precautions to protect the ability to talk. In Bohemia, for example, for many generations it has been believed that neither a baby nor a nursing mother must ever eat fish because fish are mute and will pass on their muteness to children. In Serbia, in times past, babies were not allowed to eat any fowl unless it had been heard crowing or clucking, for fear that if they did they would remain dumb for a long time. In ancient Germany, two babies not yet able to speak were never allowed to kiss each other in the belief that if they did each would transmit his or her muteness to the other.

Many people have believed it necessary to cut the *frenum*, or bridle, the small piece of flesh underneath every newborn infant's tongue, in order to make articulate speech possible. It is true that in a small number of cases, a doctor will find it necessary to do this, but it is rarely needed. The expression *tongue-tied* to describe people who are slow in speaking, and the term *an unbridled tongue* to describe very free speech, are both heritages from the days when this belief was widespread. In many parts of France the operation was regularly done at birth, performed routinely by nurses and midwives with the nail of the little finger, which was allowed to grow extra long for this purpose. In Germany, the *speech band* used to be cut in the case of any baby who did not speak easily by the end of the first year.

Speech difficulties have been explained in various ways. In Prussia, tickling the soles of a baby's feet was regarded as the cause of stuttering. In Italy, it was thought that all babies would stutter unless they had their first drink out of a hand bell. Serbian babies, however, when weaned, had to have their first drink of water out of a cowbell when they were weaned. In Bohemia, mothers used to wean their babies on Holy Saturday and after a baby's "last supper" on Good Friday, when the mother nursed him for the last time, she would breathe into his mouth to encourage him to speak. In Austria, a person returning from Holy Communion used to breathe into a baby's mouth to grant him the gift of speech.

In parts of Germany other techniques were also practiced to speed up the process of learning to talk. When a baby was going to be baptized, one of its relatives would prepare a "christening letter" containing money or a poem and with it would draw three crosses through the baby's mouth. Or when a baby, carried by its mother, paid its first visit to neighbors or friends, it would be presented with three eggs, pressed to its mouth three times with the words, "As the hens cackle, the child learns to prattle."

Tongue Twisters

To improve children's babyish pronunciation, it used to be the fashion to make them memorize lengthy articulation exercises or tongue twisters, and speech therapists still use these to help children who lisp or stutter.

The famous "Peter Piper" who "picked a peck of pickled peppers" is the only surviving member of a once famous alphabetful of characters who appeared in a book written to teach small children clear articulation. The Peter Piper rhyme was also highly thought of in the nineteenth century as a cure for children's hiccups; the child was to say it quickly three times in one breath. An early version of Mr. Piper's activities, published in an early American reader, was "Peter Piper picked a peck of prickly pears from the prickly pear trees on the pleasant prairies."

Another popular sentence of this type was "Up the high hill he heaved a huge round stone; round the rugged riven rock the ragged rascal rapid ran." Almost every English-speaking child has struggled strenuously to say "She sells sea shells on the sea shore" clearly, but most of them do not attempt to pronounce "I scream for ice cream" too clearly, because they are so amused by the intentional ambiguity of the sounds.

Such tongue trippers, intentionally difficult to pronounce, have been used to teach children to speak clearly and to dissolve them in giggles in many other languages as well as English.

Should Children Be Seen and Not Heard?

Most parents eagerly encourage their children to speak and are proud of every new word until the children are well launched as verbalizers. Then parents tend to reverse themselves and try, usually in vain, to persuade them to keep quiet.

> God gave us two ears and one mouth, to show us that we should listen twice as much as we speak.
>
> —*Arab Proverb*

The idea that children should be seen rather than heard was strictly practiced in ancient Sparta. Spartan youngsters were taught to be terse in speech. They were supposed to act rather than talk; if they really had to talk, the less said, the better. The district surrounding the city of Sparta, and the first area Sparta came to dominate, was named Laconia. To be terse in speech, therefore, we still say today is to be *laconic*.

Plutarch (c. 46–120) much admired the fact that Spartan children were habitually silent. He said that as a result of this training they learned to say accurately and briefly whatever they wanted to say, and he commented approvingly that "as loose and incontinent livers are seldom fathers of many children, so loose and incontinent talkers seldom originate many sensible words."

> Teach your child to hold his tongue; he'll learn soon enough to speak.
>
> *Benjamin Franklin (1706–1790) in Poor Richard's Almanac, 1734*

MYTHS ABOUT THE ORIGIN OF LANGUAGES

The universal babble of babies that precedes the development of separate languages accords with the mythological idea that a blissful Golden Age when everyone lived in universal harmony preceded mankind's development of separate languages. The Sumerian epic of the Golden Age describes the pre-Babel times in the appropriately named city of Babylonia:

> Once upon a time, there was no snake....
> There was no fear, nor terror....
> Once upon a time, the lands Shuber and Hazai,
>
> Many tongued Sumer,
> The whole universe, the people in unison,
> In one tongue gave praise to Enlil.

This ancient description of a happy time when people of different countries all lived together in peace, all worshipping the same deity in one tongue, indicates that the Sumerians, like the Hebrews of later times, believed a universal type of speech existed before the development of separate languages.

According to the biblical story of the Tower of Babel (Genesis 2: 19), when men grew too proud and ambitious for their own good, God caused a tumult among them which resulted in their starting to speak in a multitude of languages so they could no longer understand each other.

Flavius Josephus (c. A.D. 37–c. 93) the Jewish historian, commented on this: "The place wherein they built the tower is now called Babylon because of the confusion of that language which they readily understood before; for the Hebrews mean by the Babel, Confusion."

Ontology and phylogeny thus parallel each other, microcosm and macrocosm show the same development, history and biography evolve in the same way, society and psychology operate by the same laws, and both the Sumerian and Hebrew myths teach the eternally inescapable truth that failure to understand and communicate with one's neighbors produces discord and wars which result in still greater failure to communicate and understand each other. Every baby, as he abandons the language of baby talk that he shares with every other baby in the world, giving it up in order to learn one of the world's thousands of different languages instead, is unfortunately exchanging babble for Babel.

HOW CHILDREN CAN LEARN FOREIGN LANGUAGES

The ability of children to learn a language is so marked in their early years that modern educators are often criticized for wasting precious time by not teaching foreign languages at the nursery school and kindergarten levels.

The English parents of John Milton (1608–1674) did not make this mistake. He knew both Greek and Latin before he was seven.

A bizarre experiment was conducted in the twentieth century by the Berlitz family, famous international language teachers. One of the Berlitz babies was taught several languages at once. Each member of the family was assigned a particular language, and whenever that person saw the baby he or she spoke in that language only. The child soon learned to talk to each of them in what he assumed was their own tongue. Later, when asked if this had been very confusing and difficult, he said no, he simply thought everyone has different ways of speaking, just as they each have different names, and that if you want to communicate with anyone you have to learn that person's particular use of words.

It should perhaps not be so surprising that he was able to learn several languages at once, because uncountable numbers of other children have demonstrated this ability on a smaller scale, growing up from the beginning with two languages at once. French Canadian toddlers acquire French and English vocabularies simultaneously as a matter of course, hardly realizing which is which. Many Irish youngsters are introduced to Gaelic before they learn English, and by school age have mastered both languages.

Children with foreign relatives often find it no harder to learn two languages at once from the beginning than it is to learn one. They talk as soon, as painlessly, and eventually as incessantly, as other children do, proving over and over again how bright the average child is and how easily he or she can become an above-average linguist if exposed to several languages while still receptive and eager. Furthermore, if a foreign language is learned early in life, which the Italian educator Maria Montessori (1870–1952) identified as the language-sensitive period, children will retain the authentic accents they have learned, whereas when older people learn a new language they will rarely be able to speak it without a foreign accent.

It is common in homes where parents are of different nationalities for each of them to address their children in his or her native tongue. Many children of foreign-born parents, when they enter school, can pick up a third language without too much difficulty if they are allowed to mingle freely with the other children instead of being segregated in special education classes where they are taught English only as a "second language," a special academic subject. Children learn language faster by being exposed to the new language in a natural way, through playing games, hearing stories, learning songs, and overhearing jokes and gossip. English and American children, after all, have no difficulty learning to sing "Sur le pont d'Avignon" or "Frère Jacques," for example.

Trying to teach a child a language by stuffing its head with rules of grammar, conjugations, and spelling makes the learning a chore. As Frank Toritz, an outstandingly successful language teacher in the 1950s and 1960s pointed out, it is boring and confusing. It would be almost impossible for a youngster even to learn its "mother tongue" if the mother constantly corrected its grammar. When little children say "I sitted" we know what they mean and it would be foolish and rude to interrupt what they are about to tell us by saying, "You mean you sat." This would stifle a child's spontaneity and squelch his or her natural desire to tell us something, producing shyness and a feeling of inadequacy. Children will soon enough catch on to the right way to say a word when they hear others repeating it correctly.

LEFT-HANDEDNESS

Most babies are born ambidextrous, although recent ultrasound studies of fetuses in their mothers' wombs have indicated that 8 percent suck the left thumb and 92 percent suck their right thumbs. This ratio of preference is usually shown after birth as well, with only about 10 percent of children preferring to use their left instead of their right hand. This is true only of humans, however; most animals show about a 50-50 split in left or right dominance, and chimpanzees, gorillas, monkeys, and orangutans are all ambidextrous.

No one is sure why some people are left-handed or why male lefties outnumber female ones by two to one. Plato, who was right-handed, had a theory that the position of an infant in its mother's arms while nursing, with one hand restrained while the other is free, determined hand preference. Observing that most mothers and nurses were right-handed and carried their infants in their left arms in order to keep their right hands free for other work, he feared they would produce an entire new generation of "lefties," but his prophecy has never been fulfilled.

In recent years there have been a few studies, but they are inconclusive. A survey of 1,117 people in Boston found that blondes were twice as likely to be left-handed or ambidextrous as people with dark hair. Another study, of mothers over 30 years old, found that their firstborn children were more apt to be left-handed than those born to younger mothers.

Attitudes Towards "Lefties"

Languages reflect the ancient and widespread prejudice against left-handed people. The left has traditionally been associated with evil or error. In French the word for left is *gauche*, meaning clumsy, inept, or incorrect, and rebels and revolutionaries have been called *leftists* ever since the French Revolution when moderates in the French Assembly sat in front of the speaker with conservatives on his right and radicals on his left. In German the word for left is *link,* meaning clumsy or awkward. A Hebrew colloquialism for clumsiness is "two left hands." Italians have several derogatory terms for left-handedness including *stanca,* which also means weary or mentally exhausted, and *zona sinistrata*, the term for a disaster area. In Japanese the term *hidari maki* means counterclockwise and strange; and the expression "a move to the left" means that you've been demoted. In ancient Japan, a man could divorce his wife if he found out she was left-handed; in modern Japan, however, the ancient prejudice against left-handers has diminished since baseball is now such a popular sport there and so many excellent players are *southpaws,* alias lefties. The Latin word for left is *sinister,* which means corrupt, harmful, or menacing. The Portuguese word for left is *canhoto* which means naughty or mischievous. In Spanish the word *izquierdo* means not only left but crooked, and an expression "ne se zurdo" means "don't be left-handed," a euphemism for "don't be stupid."

In fact, the one exception to the word *left* being some kind of a linguistic insult seems to be in Greek, where the word for left is *aristera* meaning the best. This is the root of the English word *aristocratic,* but the English word *left* comes not from Greek but from the Anglo-Saxon word *lyft* meaning weak or broken. In English, a "left-handed compliment" is an insincere one, flattering but at the same time containing a veiled insult. An able assistant is called a "good right hand." And the right is, of course, right, i.e., correct. The *Oxford English Dictionary* defines *left-handed* as awkward, crippled, defective, characterized by underhanded dealings, questionable, inauspicious, illegitimate.

Speaking of illegitimacy, a "left-handed honeymoon" used to be an expression that meant an adulterous escapade, and a child born out of wedlock was called a "child of the left hand."

Superstitions, Myths, and Religious Symbolism about the Left

Superstitions and myths have reinforced fear and dislike of leftness. One ancient superstition says that if you see a shooting star it means someone has died, and if the star shoots to the right that person has gone to heaven but if it shoots to the left he has gone to hell. The custom of throwing salt over one's left shoulder for good luck grew out of the belief that the devil hovers over one's left, or weak, side, and tossing the salt would scare him away. The left side of the body was considered susceptible to the powers of witchcraft and temptation, which is why wearing a wedding ring on the left hand became customary as a way to protect fidelity in marriage. At a banquet it has been considered bad luck to pass wine with your left hand or to toast someone with a glass held in the left hand; a left-handed toast is an insincere one. A widespread superstition among gypsies and in Morocco and Scotland is that an itch in the right palm foretells money coming to you, while an itch in the left hand means you are about to lose money. Another old superstition is that if your right eye twitches you will soon see a friend, but if your left eye twitches you will meet an enemy.

In religion, too, where dualism contrasts right versus wrong, good versus evil, and the divine versus the demonic, the left has usually been chosen to symbolize the wrong side. Not always, however. Michelangelo, originally a lefty who taught himself to be ambidextrous, portrayed in the Sistine Chapel ceiling the creation of man by having God reach out and touch Adam's left hand. And God himself placed the heart on the left side of the body. Hebrews and Arabs write from right to left. And Boy Scouts, those trustworthy, loyal, brave, clean and reverent boys, shake hands with each other with the left hand. Also, of course, there is the city of Paris, where the Left Bank is the creative cultural hub.

But because God is said to have made Eve from a rib taken from Adam's left side, some theologians used to theorize that since the rib came from the left, or evil, side, women were symbols of sin, or at the least the "weaker sex." Some were not even sure women had souls. Kinder and later theologians, however, held that since the rib was next to the heart, this meant women were to be loved.

At the Crucifixion "the bad thief" who did not repent was the one on Christ's left, whereas the one on His right was "the good thief" who did repent and was therefore told he would be with Christ in paradise. On Judgment Day, saints are expected to be placed on Christ's right side and sinners on His left to be cast into hell, and He himself is seated at the right hand of God the Father in Heaven. Also, according to the Koran, on Judgment Day when everyone will receive a "Book of Deeds" containing the record of each one's life, if the book is placed in the right hand they are blessed, but if it is placed in the left hand they are damned. The Ayatollah Khomeini (1900–1989) claimed that the Shah of Iran, Mohammed Reza Pahlavi (1919–1980), was cursed by Allah, and the proof was that the Shah's firstborn son was left-handed.

Because of these and similar beliefs, it used to be the custom to force all left-handed children to shift to the right hand. Native American mothers would often tie the left arms of their babies to their cradle-boards, to force them to use their right hands. Indonesians used to tie an infant's left arm to its side to force right-handedness. Left-handed handwriting was forbidden in schools in East Germany, the former Soviet Union, and the Eastern European countries behind the Iron Curtain. It seems ironic that Communists, considered left-wingers by other people, should have wanted to discourage leftness, but they did. A slang expression in the Soviet Union for "acting like a sneak" was doing something "on the left" and in Russia if you operate *nalyevo*, on the left, you're working in the black market.

Why Attitudes Are Changing

Not all the reasons for wanting children to favor their right hands are irrational. In countries with primitive sanitation facilities, the left hand is traditionally used to take care of bodily wastes and garbage disposal, so it is actually unclean, and therefore it is customary and cleaner to eat, write, and shake hands with the right hand. However, where such precautions are unnecessary and when people realize that legends and figures of speech are imaginative metaphors not to be taken too literally, the ancient taboos against using the left hand are no longer relevant. The great American statesman, author, and inventor Benjamin Franklin (1706–1790) was way ahead of his time in defending the "right" of left-handers to receive respect. As a child he was often accused of clumsiness and sometimes beaten for insisting on using his left hand, but he fought all attempts to force him to switch to the right one. As an adult he wrote an impassioned *Petition to Those Who Have the Superintendency of Education,* pleading with them to let left-handed children develop naturally and signed it, "Your obedient servant, THE LEFT HAND." Two centuries later, when the future American novelist Jessamyn West (1902–1984) started school and teachers tried to force her to write only with her right hand, her mother wrote a note to the school saying, "God intended this child to use her left hand."

Forcing a child who is naturally left-handed to switch to right-handedness can be very harmful. It usually creates physical problems such as poor coordination and therefore in in many cases reduced athletic ability. This in turn may increase a child's shyness and make it harder for him or her to make friends, reducing his or her popularity at school and lowering self-esteem. The resulting frustration may cause sleep disorders and behavioral problems, making a child belligerent and prone to tantrums, and it can lead to other serious psychological problems which reveal themselves in speech impediments such as lisping and stammering.

A famous example of this was King George VI of England (1895–1952), who was agonizingly shy and embarrassed all his life by an uncontrollable stutter developed when his mother insisted on forcing him to be right-handed. The confusion, stress, and anxiety caused by making children switch handedness can also interfere with success in school work, interfering with concentration and making it harder for them to learn to read and write; they may have poor penmanship or develop mirror writing, forming letters backwards, or become dyslexic, transposing numbers and scrambling the letters in words. It is rare for children born left-handed ever to become fully switched anyway; they will almost always continue to find it easier to do some things with the left hand even though they may have learned to write with the other one, thus never establishing the complete dominance that enables one to achieve maximum physical coordination and mental powers.

The folly of efforts to abolish left-handedness is accentuated by the fact that there is no real reason to consider it a handicap. Many left-handed people are high achievers and greatly admired (see below for a list of some of them.) There is even evidence that being left-handed can in some ways be an advantage. Results of SAT tests show that left-handed boys average much higher scores in mathematics than their right-handed schoolmates. As a rule lefties are also faster and more accurate typists and perform better than righties in the arts. And 20 percent of the members of Mensa, the organization for people with exceptionally high IQs, are lefties. Some famous left handers include Astronaut Buzz Aldrin, President George Bush, Billy the Kid, Lewis Carroll, England's Prince Charles, President Bill Clinton, Jimmy Connors, Tom Cruise, Leonardo da Vinci, Henry DeSalvo (the Boston Strangler), Senator Bob Dole, President Gerald Ford, Henry Ford, Benjamin Franklin, President James A. Garfield, Judy Garland, Cary Grant, President Herbert Hoover, Jack the Ripper, John McEnroe, Michelangelo, Martina Navratilova, Ross Perot, Pablo Picasso, President Ronald Reagan, Babe Ruth, and President Harry S. Truman.

So in recent times, more and more parents and teachers try to leave it up to children to decide which hand they find easiest to use. There are simple ways to do this.

How to Help Left-handed Children

While babies are still young, objects like toys, cups, and spoons should be placed in front of them without favoring either side, and the mother or baby sitter should watch to see which hand they use to pick them up. At first they will use their hands interchangeably, but gradually one hand will be used more often than the other, and once it is clear that they consistently favor that hand, objects should be placed regularly on that side. This may not happen until age two or three and sometimes even later.

Today lefties are finally coming into their own. In 1900 only 2 percent of the population wrote with their left hands, but the number has risen to over 12 percent, almost certainly due to more parents and teachers allowing lefties to stay that way. There are 30 million of them in the United States alone. Organizations to help them now exist, among them Lefthanders International, founded in Topeka, Kansas. This organization formulated a "Bill of Lefts to protect the needs and interests of lefthanders everywhere." Among its Articles was Article 2, which stated that "All persons shall have the privilege of diminishing the use of the word 'right' to mean 'correct' by substituting 'ok', 'true' or similar affirmatives." Article 7 said, "All lefthanded persons shall enjoy the freedom, encouragement and instruction to develop their talents and skills to the fullest." Article 8 said, "Lefthanders shall have the freedom to refrain from apologizing for their handedness in social situations." It helps if at a dinner party the host or hostess places left-handed guests at the end of the table so their hands will not collide with those of the person sitting on their right.

Article 4 said, "All lefthanded persons shall be entitled to make their product needs known to manufacturers and retailers." They might have added "to parents," who often become impatient when a left-handed child finds it hard to wind a watch or to handle certain tools. One way a parent can help if children have trouble learning how to tie shoelaces or button shirts, for example, is to use the "mirror image technique," having them face you and mimic your actions as if looking into a mirror where images of right and left are reversed.

People should realize that clumsiness is often caused by the fact that most products are made only for the convenience of right-handers: belt buckles, buttonholes, cameras, can openers, clocks and watches, corkscrews, gloves, musical instruments, nutcrackers, power drills, scissors, screwdrivers, slot machines, sporting goods like baseball mitts, fishing reels, and golf clubs, stick shifts on cars, thermometers, windup toys, even drinking fountains in playgrounds. And think of how frustrated a left-handed child must feel riding on a merry-go-round and never being able to catch the ring! Therefore, Lefthanders International puts out a catalog offering more than 100 products especially designed for lefties.

Also most major cities now have companies specializing in products for lefties. Among these are left-handed versions of musical instruments that usually frustrate children. Left-handed violinist Charlie Chaplin had a special violin made for him with strings and chin rest reversed so that he could bow with his left hand; he performed with this in his film *Limelight* (1952). A book, *Left-Handed Guitar*, by Nicholas R. Clarke, contains charts showing chord positions for guitars with strings that are reversed for left-handed players. The left-handed guitarist Jimi Hendrix (1942–1970) could not afford to buy a special guitar when he first began playing, so he taught himself to play the guitar upside down. Eventually he did buy left-handed instruments, but he never lost his early ability to play upside down.

SOME THOUGHTS ABOUT GENIUSES

Children are all born with the equipment and capabilities of what is called *genius*. They become subgeniuses or degeniused by virtue of the progressive frustrations of so-called *growing-up* (there being neither *up* nor *down* directions in the universe!).
                                                    —*Buckminster Fuller (1895–1983)*

The secret of genius is to carry the spirit of the child into old age.
—*Thomas Huxley (1825–1895)*

Every child is, to a certain extent, a genius, and every genius is, to a certain extent, a child. —*Arthur Schopenhauer (1788–1860)*

Erroll Garner (1923–1977) a great jazz pianist, from the first time he ever put his fingers on piano keys at the age of three, was tremendously gifted. Once in an interview he was asked when he had learned to play the piano and replied, "I never learned; I always knew. It was God given." But then he quickly added, "But even though it was God given to me I had to *develop* it. That part was up to *me*."

Inborn talent is of no use if it remains undeveloped either through lack of opportunity or lack of determination. Even geniuses must nurture their gifts or they don't stay geniuses. Mental muscles like physical ones shrivel up if they are not exercised. Thomas Edison (1847–1931) defined genius as "one percent inspiration and 99 percent perspiration." Once, when Ignace Paderewski (1860–1941) was praised as a genius, he said, "Now I am a genius, but before that I was a drudge."

Late Bloomers

Not all geniuses reveal their genius in the first few years of life. Some are actually even considered developmentally disabled during their early childhoods. For example, these great men were considered slow as children: Winston Churchill (1874–1965); Thomas Edison (1847–1931); Mahatma Gandhi (1869–1948), who said in his autobiography that he had great difficulty learning anything when he was a small child, which "would strongly suggest that my intellect must have been sluggish, and my memory raw"; and Richard Wagner (1813–1883), who showed no talent for music until he was in his teens.

Among 1,500 gifted children studied by Dr. Lewis M. Terman (1877–1956) of Stanford University in California, one of the most brilliant had not managed to learn the alphabet by the age of eight.

Studies of Gifted Children

Dr. Terman's 30-year study of gifted children from infancy to adulthood is one of the most comprehensive yet made. Among the many theories it has exploded are several that seem to have been invented by average people to console themselves for not being more brilliant; for example, it is not true that

- all infant prodigies end up unhappy and maladjusted in later life
- most infant prodigies peter out fairly soon until they are no longer outstanding
- children with more-than-average brains suffer from under-average health and social ability

The Stanford University studies have shown, on the contrary, that most gifted children grow up to be healthy and emotionally stable, with better jobs and longer life expectancy than most normal children.

187

INTELLIGENCE TESTS

Ever since 1575 when a Spanish physician Juan Huarte defined intelligence as the ability to learn, exercise judgment, and be imaginative, psychologists have been trying to decide just exactly what intelligence is and how to measure it. In 1904 Alfred Binet (1857–1911), a French psychologist, developed the the first intelligence test involving analogies, patterns, and reasoning skills for measuring the intelligence of schoolchildren. In 1912 a German psychologist W. Stern proposed the "intelligence quotient" as a way of measuring mental age compared to chronological age. And in 1916 the American psychologist Lewis Terman (see page 187) built on his predecessors' work, coining the term "I.Q.," and he developed intelligence tests for the army during World War I. In 1916 he published his Stanford-Binet IQ Tests in *The Measurement of Intelligence.* These tests were named in honor of Alfred Binet and of Stanford University where Terman was a professor. This distinguished university, incidentally, might never have existed if a 15-year-old boy had not died in 1884. The following year his grieving parents founded and endowed it as Leland Stanford, Jr. University.

Dr. Terman invented the IQ (Intelligence Quotient) test to measure intelligence. A child's IQ is considered average when it is within 10 points of 100. If a five-year-old, for instance, answers no more questions correctly than most four-year-olds can answer, that child's IQ will be 80. If he or she answers as many correctly as most children a year older, his or her IQ will be 120. These figures are reached by dividing the *mental age,* in these examples four or six, by the real age (in this case, five) and then multiplying the result by 100.

To rate as *gifted,* a child would have to score 130 or higher on an IQ test. Only about 1 percent of all children can do that.

Long-range studies have shown that intelligence as measured by IQ tests fluctuates from one age to another much more than used to be supposed. The greatest decline in IQ usually takes place before the age of five or six.

It is believed that the main factors in determining whether a child will be a *riser* or a *downer* is his or her emotional health. If small children find new experiences challenging and fun, if they are self-confident and eagerly try to learn new things because they are curious and not afraid of failure, their IQ will keep on rising. But if they are fearful about losing approval because of failure, or too tense to get fun out of learning, or nervous and fidgety and therefore find it hard to concentrate, they will be downers. Often, however, downers become risers again after the age of eight, so parents of slow preschoolers need not get overanxious.

Physical factors, such as the rate at which muscular and neurological coordination develop, can also produce *learning blocks* in small children. For instance, the stabilizing of *handedness* and achieving *cerebral dominance* occurs much later in some children than in others. Neurologists say this explains why many extremely bright children have great difficulty in the beginning with reading and spelling.

IQ Tests for Babies

In the 1920s many adoption agencies gave IQ tests to babies before placing them in homes, hoping to give unusually bright babies to unusually intelligent parents, average babies to average parents, dull babies to less intellectual parents. But since then it has been learned that **IQ** fluctuates greatly and that many things other than native intelligence can affect it, this is done less frequently today.

Dr. Nancy Bayley (1899–), a psychologist at the child development section of the American National Institute of Mental Health, did a number of studies measuring mental and motor development from infancy to adulthood and found that the ability of a baby to accomplish certain tasks before or after the "normal" age for these activities had no relation to his or her later intelligence. Bayley also found that increases and decreases of 20 to 30 points over a person's development from infancy to adulthood were not uncommon.

Intelligence Tests of Adopted Children

In 1960 two bitter battles were fought over children with exceptionally high IQs. In New Jersey the Board of Child Welfare tried to take away a four-year-old girl from foster parents with whom she had been living since infancy, who wanted to adopt her permanently. She had a near-genius **IQ** and the foster parents were not intelligent enough to develop her to her full potential, the Board maintained, saying they preferred TV to books. The parents claimed that love is as important as brains, that the little girl would be deeply hurt if she were taken away from them, and that they would do their best to see that she received all the training she could use, including college. They said they would not give her up unless they were legally forced to do so, whereupon the Board of Child Welfare took them to court. After several suspenseful days in which thousands of people got into thousands of heated arguments on the case, the court decided in favor of love.

After the battle was over, a child psychologist said the whole dispute had been ridiculous, because an **IQ** measures present not potential intellectual ability, and if the child had not been receiving more than adequate stimulation from her home and foster parents she would not have been able to score so high on the **IQ** test.

In Baltimore, Maryland, the parents of an adopted girl applied to adopt a baby sister for her. They were refused on the grounds that the girl they had already adopted had such a high **IQ** that they would not be able to find a sister of equal intellectual ability and therefore the relationship between the children would be a poor one. Again many people rallied to the parents' cause, asking if bright children were to be penalized for being bright by not being allowed to have sisters. Certainly the variations that exist among natural siblings indicate that God is not as squeamish about matching parents and children as adoption agencies try to be.

Limitations of IQ Tests

Today most psychologists concede that, although **IQ** tests are useful in evaluating a child's current mental condition, they are not useful for making accurate predictions about later life. Another limitation, which increasingly has bothered educators and psychologists, is that only one type of intelligence is measured by them. They reveal little, if anything, about a child's creativity, sense of humor, friendliness, originality, imagination, or understanding of values. Many child psychologists have been hard at work trying to devise tests that would measure some of these less tangible but very important qualities.

DR HOWARD GARDNER'S THEORIES ABOUT "MULTIPLE INTELLIGENCES"

Dr. Howard Gardner, a developmental psychologist at the Harvard Graduate School of Education, a MacArthur Fellow, and winner of the Grawemeyer Award in Education, is noted for his theories about multiple intelligence. He has broadened the concept of what "counts" as intelligence and included such factors as personality, emotions, and the cultural context in which all mental processes necessarily unfold.

Early in his career Gardner developed a lifelong interest in studying artistic thought and how creative talent develops. A few psychologists such as William James (1842–1910), Sigmund Freud (1856–1939) and his daughter Anna Freud (1895–1982), who was the first psychiatrist to specialize in child psychiatry, and Jean Piaget (1886–1980) whose work with young children Gardner greatly admired, had studied creative processes and how humans can fashion comprehensive theories in science or powerful works of art. Most later psychologists and educators focused primarily on intellectual development, paying less attention to children's social, moral, emotional, and aesthetic development. One outstanding exception was Erik Erikson (1902–1994), whom Gardner was fortunate to have as a tutor in college.

Gardner has examined the components of artistic production from numerous vantage points: that of the normal child, the gifted child, the child who exhibits pathology, the normal adult, the brain-damaged adult, individuals from different cultural backgrounds, and the childhoods of several "exemplary creators" such as Einstein, T.S. Eliot, Freud, Martha Graham, Mahatma Gandhi, Picasso, and Stravinsky, and of many child prodigies who may someday join the ranks of these famous people. In addition he has examined the creative processes and products of Mozart, the poet Charles Baudelaire, who had an unhappy childhood and wrote after sustaining brain damage, and Nadia, and English autistic girl who became a graphic artist.

Based on what he learned about these lives, Gardner identified certain attributes that seem to hold true across gender and culture: a deep disdain and mistrust of mainstream thought; a significant amount of independence from an early age; a childlike, idealistic vision; and 10-year productivity cycles often followed by lulls and/or depression.

Gardner's primary approach has been to study the working activities of the young child who is in the process of developing artistic competence. He became fascinated by the seemingly casual production of young children and the masterworks of accomplished artists, and says that if there is any single theme that permeates his scholarly life, it is the similarities and the differences between "child art" and art.

In 1991 Gardner published *The Unschooled Mind: How Children Think and How Schools Should Teach Them,* which inspired a great deal of controversy by criticizing educational methods and materials and showing how ill-suited most institutions and teachers' minds, patterns of learning, and practices are to develop children's creative gifts. Gardner maintained that, despite formal schooling, people remain heavily influenced by practices and beliefs they develop at a very early age. All children, he said, arrive at school with theories about themselves, others, and the world around them. Then, rather than challenging and building on these theories, schools ignore them and proceed to teach an altogether new set of rules. The two sets of coping skills, which may be contradictory, continue to coexist, often unhappily, for decades.

Gardner also said that little is actually understood by pupils about subjects such as physics, history, and art as they are taught in school, because the teachers have ignored the full-blown, though primitive, theories children have developed before starting school. He claimed that "in nearly every student there is a five-year-old mind struggling to get out and express itself." And he asked, "How can we help students move beyond rote learning of academic subjects to enable them to achieve genuine understanding?"

In 1983 Gardner had published a book called *Frames of Mind: The Theory of Multiple Intelligences*, and he immediately became famous and even more controversial for vigorously attacking IQ tests and for offering new definitions of intelligence. His objections to the tests were not unfamiliar, since many critics had already said that instead of measuring a child's innate intelligence they really measure only a child's previous exposure to cultural experiences, leaving children who lack such experiences at an unfair disadvantage, and furthermore that they measure only one type of intelligence.

What did surprise readers, however, was that he claimed there are seven separate forms of intelligence. He defined them as:

- *Linguistic:* Ability to read, write, and talk well.

- *Logical-mathematical:* Ability to discern patterns and categories quickly, and speed at learning and excelling in chess, checkers, and bridge. (He said these two have been the dominant kingpins since the dawn of "rational thought.")

- *Musical:* Sensitivity to all kinds of sounds, not just formal musical notation, and ability to hear patterns and rhythms within these sounds.

- *Spatial:* Interest in color, shape, use of space; and ability to visualize clearly without aids.

- *Bodily-kinesthetic:* quick learning of motor skills. Excellence in independent lab work and other hands-on projects. Leadership in team work. Athletes with interest in mind-plus-body and sports that involve strategy.

- *Self-intelligent:* Self-taught, self-motivated. The ability to learn without books, peers, or other expert guidance. Quiet self-assurance.

- *Other-intelligent:* Intuition, sensitivity to others' moods, body language, and sub-textual messages.

While not everyone agrees with his categories, Gardner's theories have stimulated a lot of new ideas and have had a great influence on recent education. Among his other books are *The Arts and Human Development; The Mind's New Science: A History of the Cognitive Revolution;* and *To Open Minds.*

An example of the new thinking about types of intelligence is a book by Daniel Goleman called *Emotional Intelligence,* which describes factors other than IQ that can contribute to a successful and happy life. It was published in 1995 and snapped up by so many readers that, by May 1996, it had been on the *New York Times* best seller list for 34 weeks.

CHILD PRODIGIES IN THE PAST

Alexander Graham Bell (1847–1922): A Scottish teacher of the hearing impaired, a researcher, and an inventor, Bell moved to the United States when he was in his twenties. In his childhood his musical talent was so exceptional that he was expected to become a concert pianist, but he was more interested in following in the footsteps of his grandfather and father who worked with the deaf. He had only three years of formal schooling; his father was his main educator. Bell was deeply interested in his father's inventions. One was a system of marks which he placed over the letters in books to help children learn how to pronounce words correctly. Another was a system called "Visible Speech," a physiological alphabet of pictures that showed how sounds are formed; by imitating these, the hearing impaired could learn to pronounce words.

While still under school age, Bell used this system to teach a young deaf girl to speak, and he actually taught his dog to speak by opening and closing its mouth and moving its throat muscles with his fingers. When he was 12 he and a friend invented a "talking machine" by constructing a head with a big open mouth through which could be seen a red rubber tongue stuffed with cotton. Under the head was a box that formed its neck, with rubber vocal cords inside it. It rested on another box that held a pair of bellows that were the machine's lungs. His friend pumped the bellows while Alexander pulled the strings and levers that made the tongue and lips move, and the machine then distinctly said "Mama." This was a precursor of his lifelong inventiveness culminating in his major inventions of hearing aids, the telephone, and 28 other patents. (For additional information about his work, see page 126.)

Nathaniel Bowditch (1773–1838): An American mathematician and astronomer, Bowditch left school at age 10 but taught himself algebra, French, German, Italian, Latin, and Spanish.

John Dalton (1766–1844): An English chemist and physicist, at age 12 Dalton was already a teacher in charge of a Quaker school in Cumberland. In 1794 he wrote the first detailed description of color blindness, from which both he and his brother suffered, a condition thereafter called Daltonism. He has been called a father of modern science because he arranged the table of atomic weights and was the first scientist to give a clear statement of atomic theory.

Huig de Groot or Hugo Grotius (1553–1645): A Dutch jurist, statesman, dramatist, poet, and author of the first great work on international law, by five Grotius was proficient in astronomy and mathematics. He wrote poetry at age seven, and at eight was writing Latin elegies. At 11 he was a law student at Leiden University, and so brilliant that he was taken on an official diplomatic mission to Henry IV of France at age 13. By the time he was 15 he had written three plays in Latin, and at 15 the first of his political studies was published. At 20 he was appointed historiographer by the Dutch government.

In later years Grotius's life was equally remarkable. In 1619 his theological and political writings were considered so heretical that he was arrested and sentenced to life imprisonment, but with the courageous and ingenious help of his wife, who hid him in a trunk, he escaped two years later, to France. There Louis XIII gave him a pension for a while and he finished and published in 1625 his masterwork *De Jure Belli et Pacis (On the Law of War and Peace)*, which analyzed international relations and foresaw the need for an International Court of Justice three centuries before one was finally established in 1913 at the Hague. Legal authorities believe that if statesmen had followed his teachings rather than the more cynical political tactics advocated by Machiavelli. we would now enjoy a much more peaceful world.

Christian Heinrich Heinecken (1721–1725): A famous German child; when only 10 months old, Heinecker could repeat every word spoken to him. At the age of one year he could recite the principal stories of the Old Testament. At two he was already versed in the history of both the Old and New Testaments. At three he could speak French and Latin and, it was said, "reply to most questions on universal history and geography." At four he not only read religious and church history but rationally commented and expounded his own theories. After a visit to the King of Denmark he was pronounced a "wonder." But upon returning home he became ill; he died while still only four years old. His story makes one recall an inscription on a young child's grave in a cemetery in Boston, Massachusetts: "It is so soon that I have been done for, That I wonder what I was begun for."

Thomas Henry Huxley (1825–1895): A prominent English biologist, physician, lecturer, and author of books on science, as a child Huxley received only two years of formal school. He hated it so much that he set about educating himself, so successfully that by age 12 he had taught himself German and was reading advanced works on geology and logic. He studied medicine in his teens and became a professor at the Royal College of Surgeons. He was the foremost advocate in England of Darwin's theory of evolution through natural selection and survival of the fittest, to which he added in 1863 an anthropological perspective in his book, *Zoological Evidences as to Man's Place in Nature*. He wrote many essays on theology and philosophy from the viewpoint of an "agnostic"—a term he invented to describe the view that God's existence can neither be known (theism) nor denied (atheism), and that all we can really know for certain is what is perceivable by our senses. He also wrote many books on science and had a great influence on the teaching of science in schools.

Carl von Linné (Carolus Linnaeus) (1707–1778): A Swedish botanist, physician, and professor of medicine, at age eight Linnaeus was already called "the little botanist" because of his obsession with collecting and studying plants. He never lost this interest and through his constant studies and influential books he invented and established a revolutionary new system of classification based on plants' sex organs, with names consisting of generic and specific elements, and plants grouped hierarchically into genera, classes, and orders. His system of botanical nomenclature is still in use among scientists today.

Thomas Babington Macaulay (1800–1859): An English writer, historian, and statesman; Macaulay began to read incessantly at age eight and developed a photographic memory. At seven he started a compendium of universal history which developed in later years into eight volumes of writings, including a highly popular book, *Lays of Ancient Rome* (1842) and a five-volume *History of England from the Accession of James II* (1848–1861). He became a lawyer and member of Parliament, and in 1857 was raised to the peerage. His nephew wrote a two-volume biography of him.

John Stuart Mill (1806–1873): A British philosopher, at three Mill was already learning Greek. He wrote a history of Rome when only six-and-a-half. He spoke and read Latin fluently by age five and at eight his favorite book was Ovid's *Metamorphoses*.

Blaise Pascal (1623–1662): A French mathematician, physicist, essayist, and philosopher; at 11 Pascal taught himself geometry without the aid of books or teachers, in the room where he passed his hours of play. He took a piece of charcoal and drew diagrams on the floor, trying to make perfectly round circles, triangles with equal sides and angles, and so forth. He advanced in these experiments, with one discovery leading to another until, without ever seeing a mathematical work, he reached the 32nd proposition of Euclidean geometry. While still a child he also built a calculating machine and a slide rule and laid the foundation for the modern theory of probabilities.

William James Sidis (1898–1944): An American scholar; Sidis's parents believed that "a baby is never too young to start learning anything" and hung alphabet blocks over his crib. At 18 months he began reading the *New York Times* regularly. By his second year he was spelling, reading, and counting. At age three he taught himself Latin and Greek. Before he was nine he learned a series of additional languages, invented an Esperanto-like one of his own, wrote textbooks on grammar and astronomy, and devised a new table of logarithms. He passed the anatomy exam of the Harvard Medical School at nine, but Harvard refused to admit him until he was 11, when he became the youngest student ever to enroll there. At 11 he gave a famous two-hour lecture on four-dimensional bodies to the Harvard Mathematical Club. After graduating from Harvard, where he was ostracized and the butt of practical jokes, he was appointed mathematics professor at the Rice Institute in Houston, Texas.

Unfortunately, for the rest of his life he was increasingly unhappy. He hated the publicity surrounding his achievements and sought privacy to the extent of becoming a recluse. In 1986 a biography of him was published: *The Prodigy* by Amy Wallace.

William Thomson (1824–1907): An Irish mathematician and physiologist, later knighted for his scientific achievements and known as Lord Kelvin, Thomson was six when his mother died. His father, a teacher of mathematics, took over his education, so well that at age 11 he entered the University of Glasgow and finished second in his class in mathematics. His first paper on mathematics was written during his teens but was not read to the Royal Society of Edinburgh until he was an elderly professor because they thought it unseemly to have it read by a schoolboy.

Thomas Young (1773–1829): An English Egyptologist, physician, and physicist, Young helped to decipher the hieroglyphics on the Rosetta stone, and he also worked out the wave theory of light in 1803. He could already read at age two and by four had read the entire Bible twice. He studied a dozen languages during his youth and could play a variety of musical instruments. At Cambridge University his nickname was Phenomenon Young.

Manya Sklodowska (1867–1934), A Reluctant Prodigy

An infant prodigy whose parents tried to hold her back, not because they did not appreciate her but because they wanted her to enjoy a normal childhood in a happy family, Manya Sklodowska grew up to become the world-famous Marie Curie (changing her name to

Marie when she went to study in Paris). With her husband Pierre Curie she was co-discoverer of radioactivity and of the chemical elements polonium and radium. Unlike many scientists, they refused to make profits on their discoveries by taking out patents on them, because they felt that if they were of value they should belong to the whole world.

Manya was born in Warsaw, Poland, in November 1867 and showed early signs of the genius and the sweetness that later resulted in her being the first woman ever appointed to teach at the Sorbonne in Paris; the first person ever unanimously elected to the French Academy of Medicine because every other candidate for the vacant chair voluntarily stepped down when they learned she was a candidate; the first person ever to receive two Nobel prizes; and the person whom Einstein once described as "of all celebrated beings, the only one whom fame has not corrupted."

She learned to read in one night at age four when one of her older sisters was in first grade and struggling over her homework. She thought it would help if she did it aloud, so she pretended that baby Manya was the first grader and that she was the teacher, and showed her the book with the letters in it. Manya's memory was so prodigious that, having once been shown the letters, she remembered them for good. Later that evening when her parents were checking on the bigger girl's homework, the younger one piped up with the answers. Big sister was embarrassed at being outdone by the baby, so the baby promptly burst into tears of shame at having humiliated her sister and thereafter pretended she had forgotten how to read.

Her parents saw her secretly reading books whenever she thought nobody was watching, but until her sister learned to read the baby bookworm loyally stuck to her story that she didn't know how either. And the parents pretended they did not know she was pretending because, like her, they had no desire for her to outshine the rest of her close and happy family to a singular extent. Eve Curie, Marie's daughter, wrote in her mother's biography (1937) that the parents "treated their infant prodigy with the amazing memory as if she wasn't in the least prodigious."

Incidentally, Eve Curie was born in the year when her parents received the Nobel prize for their discovery of radium. Ironically and tragically, Marie later became the first person known to die of radium poisoning. Eve later became Eva Labouise, the wife of UNICEF's second Executive Director, and was with him when he too received a Nobel Prize, on behalf of UNICEF.

Modern-Day Prodigies

Balamurali "Bala" Krisna Ambati (1978–) "Bala" was born in India, but when he was three his family moved to New York; where he became the youngest medical doctor in the United States, perhaps in the world. His achievement is not too surprising when one reviews his early academic records. When he was an infant his father, Murali Ambati, an industrial engineer, and his mother Gomathi Ambati, a math professor, recited numbers to him instead of nursery rhymes, and at age four he mastered calculus. He became interested in medicine at four as the result of getting badly burned when a pot of boiling water spilled on his legs and he had to undergo three operations. "After that, I started to think about assuaging human suffering," he said.

He started school at age six and within two weeks had finished first grade; two months later he finished second grade, and completed third grade later that same year. He continued to excel in every class and kept skipping grades. When he was 10 he applied to college and scored 750 on the math and 620 on the verbal Scholastic Aptitude Test; the average twelfth grader scores 500. By then he had a large collection of scholastic awards, trophies, and certificates of merit, and on his college application form he described himself as "a prodigy with a purpose." The purpose he had in mind was to become the world's youngest physician.

By age 11 he and his brother had written a book on AIDS, aimed at students, that was acclaimed by the American Medical Association. He also became a freshman at New York University at 11, where he again did accelerated work, completing his junior year as a premedical student the following year, and at 14 he became the youngest graduate in the university's history.

Bala was accepted by the State University of New York at Buffalo where he awed his fellow students. As one of them told *People* magazine, "teenagers think they know everything, but he kind of *does* know everything." And not only about medicine; he also enjoys basketball, chess, and ping-pong.

At 16 he transferred to Mt. Sinai Medical School in New York City, and in May 1995, when he was 17, he attained his long-standing goal. He was among the school's top-ranking graduates and a certified medical doctor. That year he also got his driver's license, so that he could make house calls. He planned to do his internship in Manhasset, New York, before moving on to Boston to take his residency at the Massachussets Eye and Ear Infirmary, affiliated with Harvard.

Adragon Eastwood DeMello (1988–): An American prodigy named after the Chinese Year of the Dragon in which he was born, and after the film star Clint Eastwood, a relative, DeMello spoke his first word, "Hello," at seven weeks, and graduated from the University of California at age 11.

Sam Hirschman (1957–): An American bridge champion, this boy from Southfield, Michigan, was taught to play bridge by his father, and entered his first bridge tournament when he was seven. When he was 11, his ambition was to achieve the rank of life master. He played in five regional tournaments that year before finally, in July 1988, in Calgary, Alberta, he succeeded. He was then 11 years, 9 months, and 5 days old, and had broken by one month the record set seven years earlier by Douglas Heath of New York City, to become the youngest ever life master in bridge.

Masoud Karkehabadi (1981–): Masoud is an American boy of half Iranian and half Mexican parentage. Karkehabadi's parents had no idea their baby was unusual when he was born. He was their firstborn, so they did not know what to expect and were not surprised when he started talking in complete sentences at 12 months. But they were when, at age two, he was devising programs on their home computer, and when, at three, he started giving his father highway directions from his baby car seat.

When he was four, his favorite game was listening to his father's heartbeat with a toy stethoscope, and he decided then and there that he wanted to become a doctor.

His parents became more and more awestruck by him. The father says, "We've had doctors and engineers in our family, but never any geniuses," and the mother says, "I didn't do anything special during my pregnancy, but people somehow think it was something I ate!"

When Karkehabadi started school, no class could keep up with him, as he devoured encyclopedia articles and remembered everything he read. With permission from the local school, his parents hired tutors and had him taught at home. When he was seven, and would normally have been in second grade, he passed the high-school equivalency test with a perfect score.

He then went to Mount San Antonio College, a community college in California. He finished its hour-long math placement exam in 10 minutes. At first his classmates considered him a freak, but he won their friendship by helping them with their homework. The college issued a press release about their remarkable pre-med student, calling him "the real-life Doogie Howser" and reporters from as far away as Japan came to interview him, with questions like, "Do you have enough time to play?" His answer to that was, "Yes, but sometimes I'd rather read a book." However, he often does play when not in class; he enjoys climbing trees, playing Nintendo with his younger brother Ahmad, and petting his foot-long iguana. Los Angeles's TV Channel 9 News program wanted to see if the stories about him were exaggerations, so they had a medical professor quiz him. He asked the boy, "Where is the proximal humerus?" and Masoud calmly replied, "the upper arm," thus ending their doubts.

In January 1991 he transferred to Orange Coast College, graduating at age 10, and then went to the University of California as an 11-year-old premedical student with an A average, doing laboratory work on Parkinson's disease with the goal of becoming a neurosurgeon. He said, "God gave me a gift and made me smart. I want to help people."

Psychologist Linda Kreger Silverman, head of the Gifted Child Development Center in Denver, Colorado, praised Masoud's parents for encouraging his education. She said being in college when so much younger than the other students would not necessarily hurt his social development because it is "utter nonsense" to think gifted people can make friends only with people their own age. However, she warned that he still had the body and emotional needs of an 11-year-old. During his first week at university he demonstrated that by losing one of his baby teeth. "They must continue to let him indulge in boyish pursuits like video games," she said, and "because gifted children are often perfectionists," he should be given opportunities to relax, perhaps expressing himself through art or music. She also said too much media attention could be destructive "if it makes him think he's valued only for doing remarkable things. Bright children need to feel they're cherished regardless of whether or not they are superachievers, or else they'll live in fear of making mistakes." Her comments could be helpful not only in Masoud's case, but for all parents of gifted children.

Michael Kearney (1983–): An American genius, at the age of 10, in June 1994, Kearney graduated with honors from the University of South Alabama, becoming the youngest college graduate in American history. This was his third title in the *Guinness Book of Records*; he had already held the records for the youngest high school graduate and the youngest college student. He had only seven years of formal schooling, four of them in college. His parents, Kevin and Cassidy Kearney, wrote a book about raising him. The mother says, "Having kids like Michael and Maeghan [his younger sister Maeghan Kearney, also with a very high IQ] is hectic and tiring. It's physically and emotionally draining." The book, called *The Accidental Genius,* was published in Japan and in November 1994 the family went on a two-week tour of Japan to promote it.

Martha Morelock, a researcher in the child study department at Tufts University, disagreed with the book's title. She thought there was nothing accidental about the boy's gifts. Both his parents have IQs of more than 150. "All gifted children I've studied," she said, "have very bright parents and come from families with long histories of high achievement. I believe there is a heavy genetic influence." There was also a strong environmental one, since both parents actively encouraged Michael's gifts. They taught him to read very early, though the father says, "It was never our intention to push him, but Michael had a raging desire to learn."

His brilliance was evident before he could walk. He spoke his first words at four months. "He'd say, 'What's for dinner?'" recalls his mother. At eight months he started reading product names on TV commercials and "before we knew it," says the father, "he could spell with 100 percent accuracy, and his command of English soon exceeded mine." By the time he was four he had finished fifth-grade material. When he was five he enrolled at NOVA, an alternative high school in Marin County, California, which he completed in a single year. The family then moved to Mobile, Alabama, when Michael was accepted by the university there.

Michael told *People* magazine that "higher learning is a lot of fun. But sometimes college was tough because people kept calling me Doogie Howser [after the TV program about a fictional medical prodigy]. I didn't like that. But I like being smart. There really aren't disadvantages to it." One big advantage is that he had to spend only a few hours a week doing homework, and the rest of his time was spent playing video games, baseball, and the piano.

Read Stowe, a professor at the University of South Alabama, says, "He's one of the most intelligent people on earth. There isn't a word for his brilliance." He asked Michael what he planned to do after graduation, and Michael said he was thinking about getting a graduate degree in anthropology. Professor Stowe asked what he would do if he had a Ph.D. by the time he was 14, and Michael said he'd go back to high school. Why? "Because," he said, showing that in some ways he was a pretty normal young boy, "that's where the girls are."

Seth Kinast (1992–): An omniverous reader from Hutchinson, Kansas, Kinast has parents who believe so strongly in early education that they started reading aloud to him when he was still in the womb. By the time he was three years old he could say the alphabet in Greek, count in German and Spanish, was reading at the third-grade level, and had read most of the 1,200 books in his bedroom.

Ruth Lawrence (1971–): An English mathematician Lawrence passed her Oxford University entrance exam at the age of 11, gaining top marks, and became Oxford's youngest ever undergraduate. She achieved this without ever having attended school, being taught at home by her father.

Nicholas MacMahon (1988–): A remarkable student from Betchworth, England, MacMahon was already studying at a university when he was four years old. He learned to read before he could even speak, when he was less than a year old. He never enjoyed typical toys for babies, but was enthusiastic about a set of flash cards that had pictures on one side and the words for them printed on the other. His mother would say, for example, "cat" and he would promptly point to the word cat. When he was a year old he began correcting his mother's spelling with words like *caterpillar*. He started talking at age one, and one of his first words was "Mozart." He loved classical music and could identify composers just by hearing their works. At 18 months he enjoyed answering the phone and taking messages for his parents. At two his mother, who speaks French, started talking French to him, and soon he was speaking it fluently. Then his parents bought him a small violin, and he taught himself to play it like a virtuoso. When he was three he began reading encyclopedias and memorizing the information in them, such as the Latin names for insects and animals.

In an effort to satisfy their son's insatiable hunger for learning, his parents enrolled him in an elementary school when he was four, but he was asked to do "babyish" things like coloring, which he did not enjoy. They contacted Brunei University for advice and were told he could study there under the private tutelage of Valsha Koshy, an expert in teaching gifted children. Koshy placed him in computer classes along with students training to be teachers, and said that "within 20 minutes he was completely familiar with the keyboard." He was soon writing fluently on the computer and started doing problem-solving with numbers. Koshy said Nicholas was the most gifted child he had ever met.

Kim Ung Yong (1936–): A Korean mathematician and poet; at the age of four Ung Yong had composed and published poetry, spoke English, German, and Japanese as well as Korean, and performed integral calculus on a live television program in Tokyo, "The World Surprise Show." His IQ was estimated to be around 210.

United States Team at the 1994 International Mathematical Olympiad: Six American high school students astonished judges at this world mathematics competition in Hong Kong when, for the first time in its 35-year history, everyone on the team achieved perfect scores on a nine-hour examination. Their flawless performance on the test of algebra, geometry, and numbers theory gave them victory over 360 other students from 68 countries. The test consisted of six questions, each worth seven points, so a perfect individual score was 42 and the Americans' perfect team score was 252. China placed second with a team score of 229; Russia was third with 224; Bulgaria was fourth with 223; Hungary fifth with 221; and Vietnam sixth with 207. For years these competitions have been dominated by China and Russia, and this was the first victory for the United States since it tied with the Soviet Union in 1986.

The six winners were Jeremy Beam of Ithaca High School in Ithaca, New York; Alexandr L. Khazanov of Stuyvesant High School in New York City; Jacob A. Lurie of Montgomery Blair High School in Silver Spring, Maryland; Noam M. Shazeer of Swampscott High School in Swampscott, Massachusetts; Stephen S. Wang of Illinois Mathematics and Science Academy in Aurora, Illinois; and Jonathan Weinstein of Lexington High School in Lexington, Massachusetts. They qualified to represent the United States by scoring higher than 350,000 other teenagers on the American High School Math Exam in February 1994 as well as on a series of followup tests, and by attending a month-long math seminar at the U.S. Naval Academy in Annapolis, Maryland, before leaving for Hong Kong on July 8. The Army and Navy helped pay for their training and travel. They were coached by Walter E. Mientka, professor of mathematics at the University of Nebraska, who commented on their success by saying, "These are students of exceptional ability who were helped to develop by good public schools and who enjoyed lots of parental support."

Some of their ecstatic parents, in newspaper interviews, recalled how they first noticed their sons' prodigious abilities. The mother of Jeremy Beam, who is a professor at Cornell University, said she noticed her son's interest in math at an early age, when she was still reading aloud to him at bedtime, saying, "He was more interested in the page numbers than in the stories; he liked abstract symbol systems." The mother of Jacob Lurie said her son began asking her questions about infinity when he was three years old; "he wanted to know what is the largest number." And the mother of Noam Shazeer said her son taught himself to do arithmetic calculations when he was three, using a rubber puzzle formed in concentric circles that could be divided into various fractions.

No American team at this competition has ever included any girls, although girls are common on other countries' teams, and two girls achieved perfect scores on the 1994 test: Theresa Eisenkoibel of Austria and Catrin Maclean of the United Kingdom.

Rohan Varavadekar (1983–): An American preschooler born of Indian parents living in Texas, Rohan attained a sudden moment of fame at age four in newspaper and television interviews when he was eliminated from a spelling bee which he seemed about to win. He had defeated all but 3 of 200 contestants, all older than he was, by spelling with ease words like *bioengineering* and *scrumptious*. The sponsors of the contest made him step down because they suddenly realized that if he won and became the city's champion he would not qualify to represent them in the national championship contest to be held in Washington, D.C., where contestants had to be at least in kindergarten and five years old.

He had been reading newspapers and books since he was three. At four he could name all 50 of the United States and their capitals. His memory for numbers was as remarkable as his memory for words and letters, and he worked as "a walking telephone book" for his parents. He told reporters he wanted to be a lawyer when he grew up. "He says he wants to save the good guys from the bad guys," his mother explained.

Thomas Dewey Watson (1928–): Born in Chicago, Illinois, this American biochemist shared the 1962 Nobel Prize for Physiology and Medicine with Britain's geneticist Francis Crick for their work which led to the discovery of the molecular structure of DNA. As a child he was a regular participant on the "Quiz Kids," the television show in the 1940s that featured child prodigies, and his later career was sure proof that child prodigies do not necessarily lose their special talents when they get older.

6

Children and Family Life

Different Types of Families

The family is the first social unit a child discovers upon entering the world. It is impossible to exaggerate the predominant and unique role the family plays in every child's physical, emotional, mental, and moral well-being, and in the way in which the child will gradually move out into society, which in our century is changing in so many ways so rapidly that it often causes adjustment problems. Whatever might be the nature or extent of such problems, there will almost certainly be no lasting or valid solutions without the family's active participation. This shows that the family should be a major concern of all those who want to help children have happy lives.

But granting this, what exactly do we mean by *the family*? Many people who are full of praise for *family values* and who fear and resent anything they think threatens the sanctity and authority of the family, do not realize how many different types of families there are and how their values differ. The one word *family* is used for many varieties of living arrangements, depending on the historic context and geographical milieu, as well as on personal choices.

The following terms describe these diverse types of families.

Clans and Septs

Clans are groups of families that claim to be descended from a mutual ancestor; they have distinctive clothing (such as tartans in Scotland), which identify them as members, and they band together for protection and companionship. Septs are families not related to clans by blood but who become affiliated to clans, and in return for various services each offers the others protection. This inter-family arrangement arose in the highlands of Scotland at a time when there were frequent wars between rivals or with England, and the mutual support of scattered clans and septs was important for survival. Clans also exist in other parts of the world, particularly in Africa, where they band together to help each other and to protect each other from real or perceived enemies. Today, however, they often fight each other and disastrous civil wars result.

Egalitarian Families

Egalitarian families were rare in ancient times but have become the ideal in Western countries since the women's movement has raised the status of women. In this type of family, women are no longer expected to be meekly subservient to men, and modern fathers are expected to cooperate with mothers rather than to domineer over them. In this type of marriage, decisions and responsibilities are not the perogative of either the mother or father; both parents are expected to participate through discussion and cooperation.

Extended Families

Extended families consist of parents, children, grandparents, uncles, aunts, nieces, nephews, cousins, and perhaps step-parents and in-laws, all living together or near each other and taking care of each other. This type of family is common in rural Africa, in India, and in many other parts of the so-called Third World. It provides little privacy to individuals but guarantees close companionship as well as comforting security to needy members. It also frequently places great burdens upon stronger members who must take care of their weaker brethren.

Foster Families

In foster families, parents' children are not related to them by birth, but take care of them as if they were. Some do it because they receive financial compensation from social agencies which place orphans or abused or neglected children with them for protection. Others take care of unwanted or handicapped children out of the generosity of their hearts even though, unless they successfully go through the legal processes involved with formal adoption, they have no assurance that the children will be allowed to remain with them indefinitely.

Gens

A *gens* is a group of several families all descended through the male line from one male ancestor. All members of the gens have the same middle or last name. The gens takes care of orphans and other members who are unable to earn a living on their own; it is also responsible for its members' debts. In ancient Rome each gens had its own separate gods and priests and its own burial place. The leader of the gens was the high priest until he died and was replaced. Rules and disputes among families were settled by the gens tribunal.

Interracial Families

In times past most people married people who belonged to their own social class, clan, or tribe. However, because of today's greatly increased travel and chances to meet many other types of people, members of different religions, nationalities, and races are getting to know each other—and some of them fall in love. Until recently, in South Africa and the United States marriage between blacks and whites was illegal, but this is no longer true, and the number of interracial marriages has tripled in the past decade. In 1992 the U.S. Census bureau reported that there were 246,000 black/white couples in the U.S. They often face strong hostility, at least at first, from other members of their families, and insults and ostracism, and sometimes violent threats, from racist strangers, but most of these marriages are strong, enduring, and happy. The couples and their children must have great determination, self-respect, courage, patience, independence, loyalty, and a sense of humor.

Matriarchies

In matriarchal families the mother is the head. In ancient times there were many such families, but gradually patriarchies (see page 204) became more common. Nonetheless, because today so many women choose to have children even though they are unmarried or the fathers are absentees, there is now a growing number of matriarchal families.

Matrilineal Families

These are families in which women own all the property, inherited through the mother's line. If a boy receives property he has to give it to a sister or to the mother of his cousins, nephews, or nieces. Daughters, not sons, have the obligation to support aged parents. The mother also passes on her surname to her children. This form of family existed in the centuries before the father's role in procreation was clearly understood; it still exists in a few remote parts of the world.

Monogamy

Under this system, husbands and wives can have only one spouse, unless one of them dies, when it is then legal for the survivor to take another. In traditional Christian families, this exclusive relationship lasts "for better or worse until death do us part," but today divorces and remarriages have become so common that some people call modern monogamous marriages *serial polygamy*.

Neolocal Families

These are families that set up a new home for themselves upon getting married, not living with either set of parents although the new home may be right next door, as it usually is in Kenya, for example.

Nuclear Families

This is the term for families that consist of one or two parents and their children, physically isolated from other relatives. It is a comparatively new type of family, but has become typical today in the United States and some other Western countries. It provides couples with welcome independence but also leaves them vulnerable if they find themselves in need of support.

The Paterfamilias

This is the name for the head of a patriarchal family (see immediately below). He is the man who begins an ancestral line and is the primary god of the *gens*. In each generation he has absolute power over his *familia*. No other member of the family owns any property during his lifetime, and in ancient China and Rome he could order the death of any family member who disobeyed or displeased him. When he dies, his power and wealth are usually divided among his male descendents and each of them begins a new familia. This was the standard type of family in ancient Rome and still is in traditional Islam.

Patriarchies

Patriarchies are families in which the father is the head, and his word is law. For consolation, the mother is described as the *heart* of the family. It has been the predominant type of family in America, China, Japan, and Europe for centuries, and in a slightly modified form still is, though fathers no longer have the life-and-death power or exclusive property rights, except in Islam, that they had in ancient times.

Patrilineal Families

In this type of family the father owns all the family's property and hands it down to his sons along with his name and status. If he has no sons, which is considered a tragedy, it goes to brothers or, if there are none, to nephews. Daughters and wives inherit nothing. Mothers and wives rarely own any property. If a woman does own property she is expected to turn it over to her husband upon getting married. However, women may act as guardians over their sons' property until the sons are grown up. This was the family form not only in ancient China, Japan, among the Mayans, in the Roman Empire, and in most royal families, but until the twentieth century it was also the form in the United States.

Patrilocal Families

In this kind of family, when a bride and groom marry, they move to the home of the groom's father, where they remain all their lives. The wife no longer owes obedience or allegiance to her own mother but to her mother-in-law. This is the usual form of family life in China and India, as it also was in ancient Rome.

Polyandry

Under this system women are allowed to have more than one husband at a time. It occurs in areas where men greatly outnumber women—in parts of Africa, Eskimo communities, India, Siberia, and Tibet.

Polygamy

Polygamy is the opposite of polyandry, allowing men to have more than one wife at a time. It usually occurs in areas where women greatly outnumber men. It is a way to protect women rather than to exploit them, to insure that no girls will end up as lonely "old maids." It was practiced in Old Testament times, and in China, and in America in the territory of Utah among Mormons until their church agreed to give it up. The Mormons did not disapprove of it, but they wanted to become a state and the U.S. government did not permit the practice. There are still, however, some Mormons who defy both their church and U.S. law, living in large polygamous families.

Polygamy has always been widely practiced among Arabs and throughout Africa. Mohammed accepted the custom but regulated its practice among Muslims by establishing rules that limited a husband to only four wives at a time, and even then allowing them to have only the number they could support financially. Theoretically they must treat them all equally, but it is extremely easy for a man to divorce one if he would like to take on another wife instead. Mohammed himself had nine wives.

Primogeniture

This is a system of inheritance in which all a family's property is inherited by the eldest son. It may seem unjust to the younger children, but it protects property from being divided up in each generation into equal but smaller and smaller segments that eventually are too tiny to support a family, as happens in rural India. Also, in countries such as Norway where ruling families did not practice it, the death of a noble or king was almost invariably followed by an uncivil civil war among his sons, each of whom wanted all their father's estate and power instead of just a small part of it. For many generations primogeniture has been the practice in England, where the eldest son inherits the family's home, land, and title, if any; the second son is destined to serve the church; and the third one is expected to go into business or government or military.

Same-Sex Families

Not only do many men and women live together in lasting relationships, but many men live with other men and women live with other women. In some of these unions the couples are as devoted and committed to each other as traditional married couples are expected to be, "until death do us part," and more and more of them choose to go through a formal religious marriage ceremony. Many wish to go further and have such marriages legally recognized, so they can be protected by civil law. As Laurie McBride, executive director of the Lobby for Individual Freedom and Equality, who has shared her life with her partner for 11 years, explains, they want their marriages "to be treated with the respect and dignity given every other marriage."

In 1993 Hawaii's Supreme Court ruled that denial of marriage licenses to three homosexual couples amounted to unconstitutional discrimination on the basis of sex unless the state could show a compelling reason for the denials. This alarmed opponents of same-sex marriages in 20 other states because the U.S. Constitution says "full faith and credit shall be given in each state to the public acts, records and judicial proceedings of every other state. So if Hawaii's court should decide there is no compelling reason to forbid such marriages, then all states would have to recognize Hawaii's same-sex marriages.

Traditionalists point out that for thousands of years marriage has been defined as a union between a man and a woman. Even so, says Andrew Sullivan, the conservative editor of the *New Republic* magazine, because "marriage promotes mainstream ideals, social cohesion, emotional security and economic prudence" same-sex marriages should also be encouraged.

Until recently, homosexual couples could not have children, but this is changing in countries where laws increasingly let them adopt, or when they take advantage of modern medical technology and one or both partners get inseminated artificially by using sperm and eggs donated by relatives or friends. Many people look with disfavor on families where children have "two mommies" or "two daddies" but tolerance for these families is growing and the fact that they now can have children adds urgency to the desire of same-sex couples to legalize their unions. For example, a man named Russell Reish and his partner of 25 years, Albert Masse, are proud of having successfully raised two of Mr. Reish's nieces who were abandoned by their own parents (both girls are now married with children of their own), but Reish worries that he cannot be legally certain that when he dies he can leave his partner his estate. Another serious problem for same-sex couples with children is that they have the double expense of both having to adopt the children, so that if one parent dies the survivor will not lose custody.

> Although none of these different types of families can guarantee happiness, or even justice, for all their members, none can fairly be dismissed as wrong or immoral because underlying all their variations there are certain basic family values they share. They have all evolved as attempts to provide people with needed protection, security, stability, and lifelong companionship, even if their definitions of those things differed greatly at times, under widely differing social and economic circumstances. And in every case, whatever bizarre form it takes, the family has the strongest lifelong influence on the children whom it creates, feeds, clothes, guides, and shelters.

Evidence that many people have a live-and-let-live attitude toward such unions was pointed out in February, 1996, by the *New York Times* editorial writer and former drama critic Frank Rich, who noted that two of the most popular sitcoms on television, "Friends" and "Roseanne," had recently presented "sincere, even sentimental, gay weddings to sky-high ratings and mere ripples of protest" and the *The Birdcage,* a movie celebrating "a gay couple's 20-year bond as an enclave of familial stability in a country full of broken homes" sold $18 million worth of tickets in its first weekend. This does point out how ironic it is that in an era when more and more heterosexual marriages are collapsing, there should be this strong movement among homosexuals to wish to enter stable and lasting marriages. Rich Tafel, head of the Log Cabin Republicans, argues in debates with opponents in his party, "You can't have it both ways—accusing gays of being promiscuous and then denying us the right to incorporate into monogamous, legally recognized relationships."

HOW EUROPE'S FAMILIES LIVED 1,000 YEARS AGO

In 1992 *Time* magazine in its Fall Special Issue ran an article by Howard G. Chua-Eoan that contained an interesting comparison of life in A.D. 999 as the world approached the first millenium of the Christian era with life today as the second millenium approaches. This was 1,000 years ago, a mere blip in time if measured by the age of the earth, but hugely different from 1999 in human terms. Time moved slowly, at the speed of an oxcart or a sturdy pair of legs, and Europe was one of the earth's most unpromising places, the Third World of its age. It had some villages and cities, but it was mostly a collection of untamed forests. They were dangerous places where wild animals and bandits roamed, but they also sustained life. Trees and shrubs provided firewood, berries, and nuts, and animals provided food.

Lords lived in large wooden structures, and peasants in small huts with mud walls and thatched roofs. Everyone, including the families' animals, slept together around the hearth. Straw was scattered on the floors to collect scraps and animal waste, and the only housecleaning was periodic sweeping out of the straw.

The seasons came and went, punctuated mainly by frequent church holidays, which provided brief relief from life's labors. The calendar year began at different times in different regions; only later would Europe settle on the Feast of Christ's Circumcision, January 1, as the year's beginning.

The population was growing faster than it had in the previous five centuries. Nevertheless, there was still a shortage of people to cultivate the fields, clear the woodlands, and work the mills. Therefore, taxes were levied on youths who did not marry upon reaching puberty, abortion was considered homicide, and a woman who terminated a pregnancy was expelled from the church.

Illness and disease were endemic, particularly skin diseases and tuberculosis. Lepers were an especially unfortunate caste of pariahs living on the outskirts of villages. Constant famine, with rotten flour and vitamin deficiencies, afflicted huge segments of society with blindness, goiter, paralysis, and bone malformations that produced hunchbacks and cripples. Many women died in childbirth, and few people lived past age 30. Fifty was old age.

Although the pace of life was slow as far as transportation was concerned, it was speeded up in one way compared to our lives today. There was no time for what we now call childhood. Children had to grow up quickly and do useful work as soon as possible. This was true for all classes. Emperors were leading armies when they were just teenagers, and Pope John XI was only 21 when he became Pope.

The approaching apocalypse and subsequent end of the world, which many people expected the millenium to bring about, could hold few terrors for people whose ordinary lives already contained so many.

MARRIAGE AND FAMILY LIFE TODAY

Marriage is no longer "until death do us part." In the United States the divorce rate is the highest in the world, with nearly 60 divorces per every 100 marriages. In Canada, Czechoslovakia, Denmark, and France, the number of divorces skyrocketed between 1970 and 1990.

Another notable change in family structure has been the greatly increased number of people who are bypassing marriage altogether, opting for independence rather than togetherness, even if they have children. The never-married set has more than doubled betwen 1970 and 1996. Single parents are not just welfare mothers or other women who have been deserted by husbands or boyfriends who fathered their children, but many self-supporting women voluntarily opt to have children without the encumbrance of a husband. This trend is most notable in the United States and northern Europe, but it is evident in almost every developed country except Japan.

Why? In the past marriage provided security for women, but nowadays they can and do have jobs so that they need not depend on a husband to provide them with a home. So if their marriage turns out to be unhappy, they no longer are forced to remain in it. They can support themselves and their children, even if not quite as well as their husbands could—because most women tend to have to work longer hours for less pay than men do. But the freedom of women to work outside, instead of inside, the home also has had its disadvantages. It often causes new family tensions and in many cases a less close bond not only with their husbands but with their children. If they are not home to look after them, someone else must do it, so a large part of the family income has to be spent on housekeepers and child care, cutting deeply into earnings. So they are on a treadmill. Their freedom to hold a job may actually reduce their actual freedom.

Marriage has always had its detractors. "Wedlock—a padlock," says an English proverb.

Francis Bacon (1561–1626), in an essay in 1625, *Marriage and Single Life*, described the lot of married women: "Wives are young men's mistresses, companions for middle age, and old men's nurses."

George Bernard Shaw (1856–1950), even though he himself had a long and stable marriage, said, "No man dares tell the truth about marriage while his wife is alive, unless he hates her. . . .Home is the girl's prison and the woman's workhouse."

Hippolyte Taine (1828–1893), a French historian and literary critic, described marriage in 1867 saying, "We study ourselves for three weeks, we love each other three months, we squabble three years, we tolerate each other 30 years, and then the children start all over again."

Mark Twain (1835–1910), who was happily married, once said, "Familiarity breeds contempt—and children." But later he made a more serious comment: "Love seems the swiftest, but it is the slowest of all growths. No man or woman really knows what perfect love is until they have been married a quarter of a century."

Marriage has also had many defenders throughout the centuries. Confucius (551–479 B.C.) said, "the first bond of a society is marriage." Cicero (106–43 B.C.) said, "Marriage lies at the bottom of all government."

Broneslaw Kasper Malinowski (1884–1942), Polish anthropologist, said, "the family is not a product of culture; it is the starting point of all human organization."

John Stuart Mill (1806–1873) believed in marriage, but not in the traditional patriarchal type. A strong advocate of rights for women, in his book *The Subjection of Women* he wrote,

> The moral regeneration of mankind will only really commence when the most fundamental of the social relations—marriage—is placed under the rule of equal justice, and when human beings learn to cultivate their strongest sympathy with an equal in rights.

In our century, despite the increasing number of failed marriages and breakdown of the family, marriage is still upheld as an ideal.

William C. Menniger (1899–1966), the eminent American psychiatrist, wrote that in the ideal home and the ideal marriage capacity to care for others grows. "From being in love, we mature to loving. We grow from getting to giving—and, may I say, giving in, often. Not giving in 50 percent, but at times giving in 100 percent."

Bertrand Russell (1872–1970), the English philosopher, was denounced in his lifetime as an immoral proponent of *free love* because he believed unions between men and women should be voluntary without needing laws to make them respectable, yet he was one of the most eloquent defenders of lifelong marriage in his book *Marriage and Morals*, published in 1929. He said,

> Most wholesomely constituted people desire, and will continue to desire to have children; they will go on feeling that the best guardians of children are their parents living together in a permanent union. And when we put aside the question of children. . . and consider only the facts of personality, a permanent union is still required for development. In a series of transitory unions no two people can really ever know each other and the possibilities each holds; they only take the first step on a road which beyond all others leads to the heart of life. . . . Moreover, the view that romantic love is essential to marriage is too anarchic, and . . . forgets that children are what make marriage important. But for children, there would be no need of any institution concerned with sex, but as soon as children enter in, the husband and wife, if they have any sense of responsibility or any affection for their offspring, are compelled to realize that their feelings toward each other are no longer what is of most importance.

Despite today's antimarriage trends, it seems that being married is actually good for people. Isaac Asimov (1920–1992) in his *Book of Facts* in 1984 cited a finding that those who have never married are seven-and-a-half times more likely to be hospitalized in a psychiatric facility than those who are married. According to the National Institute of Mental Health, the rate for such admission in 1975 for Americans 14 years of age and older was 685.2 per 100,000 unmarrieds, compared with 89.9 per 100,000 marrieds. Since so many people are health conscious nowadays, even to the point of fanaticism, perhaps it is time for a major campaign to be launched, like the one against smoking, warning the public that "not getting and staying married can be dangerous to your health."

FAILED MARRIAGES, DIVORCE, AND CHILDREN

Dorothy Dix (1861–1951), an American journalist who wrote a nationally syndicated column of advice to the lovelorn in the early 1900s, had a simple explanation for marital problems, described in *Dorothy Dix: Her Book,* published in 1926: "The reason husbands and wives do not understand each other is because they belong to different sexes."

Despite this pessimism, Dix did not believe in divorce. In the same book she said, "So many persons who think a divorce a panacea for every ill find out, when they try it, that the remedy is worse than the disease."

In her day divorce was difficult to obtain. (Adultery was the only allowable reason for it in the U.S. and many people perjured themselves in order to get one.) It was also relatively rare and a stigma was attached to divorcees, often causing them to be ostracized, so it was not surprising if they were even unhappier after divorce than while still unhappily married. But since the 1960s when divorce law began to be liberalized, and after "no fault" divorce was permitted if a couple mutually wanted to part, it has become so common that it is no longer socially unacceptable. People who would like to be divorced may decide to stay together "for the sake of the children," but in cases where the marriage is full of unpleasant tensions, many now conclude that the children are better off after the quarelling parents separate.

In 1989 a best-selling book called *Second Chances: Men, Women and Children a Decade after Divorce* was published. The authors were Judith S. Wallerstein, Ph.D., founder and executive director of the Center for the Family in Transition in California, which counsels more divorcing families than any other agency in America, and Sandra Blakeslee, a free-lance science and medical writer. In 1971 Wallerstein began the California Children of Divorce Study, the only study of divorcing families conducted over the course of a decade, on which this book was based. It examined the long-term effects of divorce on 60 middle-class families, in order to find out whether divorce changes lives for better and for worse.

"Divorce has two purposes," Wallerstein says. "The first is to escape the marriage, which has grown intolerable for at least one person. The second is to build a new life." And her landmark study also had two purposes: to find out how divorced men and women have succeeded or failed in translating their hope for a better life into a reality, and to learn how their children have fared during the post-divorce years.

One mother told Wallerstein that getting divorced was "the best thing that ever happened to me." She had rushed into her first marriage as a pregnant teenager, and "grew up" after her divorce six years later, becoming confident enough to handle raising her children, complete her education, get a good job, and become happily remarried. The divorce was good for her children, too, she said, because they discovered as she did that "you can survive anything as long as you know people care about you and love you."

Not all the stories Wallerstein heard were that reassuring. By observing their behavior and listening sympathetically to their frank revelations, Wallerstein learned that the effects of divorce on many children are long-lasting and may in later life make it more difficult for them to form their own happy relationships. A 16-year-old said she had drifted into promiscuity after feeling abandoned by "a mom that works all the time and a dad who never comes to see me." And a 21-year-old child of divorce said that "all those years I denied feelings. . . .That's how I coped with the unhappiness in my parents' marriage. And that's why I didn't get upset at the divorce. . . . Only this past year, when I met Frank, did I become aware of how much feeling I was sitting on all those years. I'm afraid to love him because I'm afraid I'll lose him, afraid he won't stay mine. Before I met Frank I always said to myself that I would never let anyone or anything hurt me. But it didn't work when I fell in love. You see, it takes practice to let pain happen. I'm able to cry now for the first time."

Dr. Wallerstein has drawn certain conclusions about how to cope with the demanding experience of divorce. It is important, she says, to resolve feelings of anger and betrayal and lingering resentment if an ex-spouse is happy in a new marriage, as well as to avoid depression and despair over your own failure if you do not have child custody and you realize how distant you have become from your own children who no longer seem to want or need you. She has learned that it is vital for children that their divorced parents maintain strong parenting roles through visitation or joint custody arrangements.

A book like this can be very useful for people who are divorced or are thinking about divorce, as well as for the older children of divorced parents. Since divorce has reached a point where it threatens 50 percent of all recent marriages and has been "silently altering the fabric of the entire society," as Dr. Wallerstein says, the book "is intended for us all."

Fighting for Child Support

Of course there are a shocking number of cases of irresponsible divorced parents who stop caring for their children. In New York State, Governor George Pataki is doing something about that. He has instituted a law to assure that parents pay what they owe in financial child support, even though it is not in governmental power to insist on the emotional support they should also give.

State officials are now permitted to randomly compare Department of Motor Vehicle records to lists of parents (mostly fathers) who have fallen more than four months behind in child support payments. The licenses of delinquent parents remain suspended until they either pay the arrears or agree to a payment schedule. State courts know of 380,000 cases of child support payment orders. In 350,000 of these cases, or 91 percent, parents are behind in child support. In 170,000 cases, or almost half, no payments have ever been made. In September, 1995, the New York State Department of Social Services sent notices to 1,400 people warning them that their drivers' licenses would be revoked if they did not begin making child support payments. By February, 1996, New York had mailed such notices to 380,000 delinquent parents. State officials announced that this policy had resulted in collection of nearly $2 million in child support payments since it began suspending drivers' licenses on chronic nonpayers, and they expect the policy to increase

211

child support payments by $30 million in 1996. They hope the policy will reduce welfare costs by enabling some families who begin getting the child support payments to pull themselves out of poverty.

"Children need the financial and emotional support of both parents," the governor said in a statement in February, 1996. "It's important that people get the message that abandoning your children violates a fundamental human value."

To add clout to this policy, on February 26, 1996, the governor distributed a list of the 10 most delinquent parents, who together owed about $750,000 in support for 24 children, and displayed "Wanted" posters with their names, addresses, and photographs. He hoped to embarrass the parents and to issue a warning to other delinquent parents.

MOTHERS—QUOTES

Any mother could perform the jobs of several air traffic controllers with ease.
—Lisa Alther (1944–)

The crow thinks her own bird the fairest.   *—Anonymous*

God can't be always everywhere; and so, He invented mothers.
—Sir Edwin Arnold, (1832–1904), "Mothers"

My opinion is that the future good or bad conduct of a child entirely depends upon the mother.   *—Napoleon Bonaparte (1769–1821)*

The darn trouble with cleaning the house is it gets dirty the next day anyway, so skip a week if you have to . . . . the children are the most important thing.
—Barbara Bush (1924–)

Cleaning your house while your kids are still growing is like shoveling the walk before it stops snowing.   *—Phyllis Diller (1917–)*

If there were no schools to take the children away from home part of the time, the insane asylum would be filled with mothers.
—Edgar Watson Howe, Country Town Sayings, 1911

Children are what the mothers are. No fondest father's fondest care, Can fashion so the infant heart.   *—Walter Savage Landor (1775–1864), "Children"*

One mother is more venerable than a thousand fathers.
—Laws of Manu, ancient writings of the man whom Hindus regard as the forefather of the human race

God knows that a mother needs fortitude and courage and tolerance and flexibility and patience and firmness and nearly every other brave aspect of the human soul. But because I happen to be a parent of almost fiercely maternal nature, I praise *casualness*. It seems to me the rarest of virtues. It is useful enough when children are small. It is important to the point of necessity when they are adolescents.   —*Phyllis McGinley in* McCall's *magazine, May, 1959*

Newton's discovery of the law of falling bodies is all very fine, but that doesn't mean that a mother's discovery of how to hold her baby isn't important too . . . . Women should put the right value on things, and realize that their washing is just as important as the Constitution of the German Empire.
                              —*Pierre Auguste Renoir (1842–1919)*

Children are the anchors that hold a mother to life.
                              —*Sophocles (c. 496–406 B.C.)*

I remember my childhood when the sunrise would burst into my bedside in the daily surprise of morning; when the faith in the marvelous bloomed like fresh flowers in my heart every day, looking into the face of the world in simple gladness; when insects, birds and beasts, the common weeks, grass and the clouds had their fullest value of wonder; when the patter of rain at night brought dreams from the fairy land, and mother's voice in the evening gave meaning to the stars.
                              —*Rabindranath Tagore (1861–1941), "The Crossing"*

The bearing and the training of a child is woman's wisdom.
                              —*Alfred, Lord Tennyson (1809–1892)*

SOME PROLIFIC MOTHERS

Leontina Albina (1925–): Born in Argentina in 1925), Albina married in 1943 and produced five sets of triplets, all boys, before she and her husband and children moved to San Antonia, Chile, where she gave birth to her 55th child in 1981. An eathquake killed 11 of her children, but 40 (24 boys and 16 girls) were still living as of 1992.

Queen Anne (1665–1714): Stuart Queen of Great Britain and Ireland from 1702 until her death, Anne had a tragic maternal history. In 1683 she married and in the next 19 years, before coming to the throne, she conceived 18 children. Only five were born alive, and all but one of the others died in infancy; he died at 11 years of age.

Rose Fitzgerald Kennedy (1890–1995): She was the long-lived matriarch of one of the most famous families in the world. During the early years of her marriage she had nine children: Joseph, Jr. (Joe), John (Jack–later President of the U.S.), Eunice, Robert (Bobby), Patricia, Edward (Ted–later U.S. Senator), Jean, Kathleen, and Rosemary. She kept her figure so well in spite of all her pregnancies that when her husband was the U.S. Ambassador to Britain and she was introduced at a reception, the Prime Minister looked admiringly at her and said, "You have made me believe in the stork."

Inna Prigozhy (1944–): Mother of 17 children, the largest family in Byelorussia. She married her husband Mikolai when they were both 18, and they never planned to have so many children but, as he has said, Inna has "a real talent for motherhood." Before World War II the town they lived in, Vitebsk, where Marc Chagall was also born, had 180,000 inhabitants, but they were almost totally annihilated during World War II. By 1944 there were only 118 residents, and the town held the sad record for the largest number of aging widows in the Soviet Union. There is an old Russian saying, "God, do not send us riches, send us children." In today's world this may not be how many people feel, but in post-war Vitebsk big families became the norm, viewed as compensation for the losses of the past. Many families boasted 10 children, but the Prigozhys held the town record. . . and were warmly rewarded. Their 16–room house was provided to them by the City Soviet. They also got free shoes and clothing from local factories. Workers at the town's refrigerator factory, on their own time, built an especially large refrigerator for them. Workers at the local television factory donated a color TV set. And the factory where the father worked gave them a minibus and paid their rent and utility bills. They also received monthly allowances from the State for each child under eight, plus free day care, medical care, summer camp, education, school books, and lunches for each school-age child. The father, afraid the children would get spoiled by all this generosity, organized a family cooperative to get the children to help with household chores. And twice every month of the year they have celebrated with gala birthday parties!

Queen Charlotte Sophia (1744–1818): In 1761 she married King George III, King of Great Britain and Ireland (who lost the American colonies). She gave birth to 15 children.

Maria Theresa (1717–1780): Empress of Austria and the Holy Roman Empire. She had 16 children. She was remarkable; in addition to raising a large family and ruling a vast empire, she founded in Vienna the then largest maternity hospital in the world, was a patroness of Haydn and Mozart, founded the Viennese School of Music, and instituted many major social reforms, such as abolition of torture for criminals.

Mrs. Feodor Vassilyev (1707–1782): A Russian peasant who in 27 confinements between the years 1725 and 1765, gave birth to 69 children: 16 pairs of twins, 7 sets of triplets, and 4 sets of quadruplets; 67 of them survived infancy. The case was reported to Moscow by the Monastery of Nikolsky in 1782. Empress Catherine the Great was said to be duly impressed, and Mrs. Vassilyev was later presented at Court.

Queen Victoria (1819–1901): Queen of England and Empress of India. She had nine children, the largest number ever born to a reigning English queen. They all married European royalty and produced heirs, and she became known as the Grandmother of Europe.

P.S. The average married woman in seventeenth-century America gave birth to 13 children. But no prolific human mother has ever equalled the record of a cat named Dusty, who gave birth to her 420th kitten in June 1952, in Texas, according to the *Guinness Book of World Records*. And even Dusty is outdone by the average cockroach. A female roach can produce 400,000 descendants in a year.

FATHERS—QUOTES

The words that a father speaks to his children in the privacy of home are not heard by the world, but, as in whispering galleries, they are clearly heard at the end and by posterity.
—*Jean Paul (1763–1825)*

Lo, children are a heritage of the Lord. As arrows are in the hand of a mighty man, so are children for the youth. Happy is the man that hath his quiver full of them.   *—Psalm 127*

Let thy time of marriage bee in thy young, and strong yeares; for believe it, ever the young wife betrayeth the old Husband, and shee that had thee not in thy flower, will despise thee in thy fall, and thou shalt bee unto her, but a captivitie and sorrow; thy best time will be towards thirty, for as the younger times are unfit, eyther to chuse or to governe a wife and family; so if thou stay longe, thou shalt hardly see the education of thy Children, which being left to strangers, are in effect lost, and better were it to bee unborne than ill bred, for thereby thy posterity shall either perish or remayne a shame to thy name, and family.
        —Sir Walter Raleigh (1552–1618) in
        Instructions to His Son and to Posterity

Without progeny a man is not complete.   *—From* Rig-veda *(Hindu scripture)*

He who is not childless goes down to his grave in peace.
        —George Santayana (1863–1952)

If children were brought into the world by an act of pure reason alone, would the human race continue to exist? Would not a man rather have so much sympathy with the coming generation as to spare it the burden of existence, or at any rate not to take it upon himself to impose that burden upon it in cold blood?
        —Arthur Schopenhauer (1788–1860)

Tis a happy thing
To be the father unto many sons.
        —William Shakespeare (1564–1616),
        in King Henry VI, Part III, Act II)

SOME PROLIFIC FATHERS

Johann Sebastian Bach (1685–1750): A German organist and composer, Bach was the father of 20 children, all of whom received musical training. Four of his sons, William Friedemann (1710–1784), Karl Philipp Emanuel (1714–1788), Johann Christoph Friedrich (1732–1795), and Johann Christian (1735–1782), and one grandson, Wilhelm Friedrich Ernst (1759–1845), became distinguished professional musicians. Counting cousins, uncles, and grandparents, there were 52 musicians in the Bach family.

Adam Borntrager (1888–1984): An Amish farmer in Medford, Wisconsin; when Borntrager died at age 96, he was the progenitor of 107 direct descendants; a total of 675 descendants were still living: 11 children, 115 grandchildren, 529 great-grandchildren, and 20 great-great-grandchildren.

Cain: Cain was the eldest son of Adam and Eve, and the world's first murderer, but also, according to ancient tradition, the inventor of agriculture, of weights and measures, of domestication of animals, and the builder of the world's first city. The historian Josephus (37–100 A.D.), author of *Antiquities of the Jews,* wrote that after killing his brother Abel, Cain fled from his family, and then "was solicitous for posterity, and had a vehement desire for children, he being 230 years old; after which time he lived another 700 years, and then died. He had indeed many children . . . it would be tedious to name them." Tradition says he had 33 sons and 23 daughters. But who were their mothers, since scripture gives no indication? As one witty Jesuit priest quipped: "For the creation of you and me, Incest was a necessity."

Peter Chamberlen the Elder (1560–1631): An English obstetrician who invented the forceps, he had 14 children, and for generations in the seventeenth and eighteenth centuries many Chamberlens became renowned doctors famous for their undeniable and outstanding skill in midwifery, and infamous because they kept this important life-saving invention a family secret for almost a century instead of letting other doctors and midwives know about it. Also their greed for money turned some of them into extremely wealthy quacks.

K'ung Futzu (Confucius) (c. 551–c. 479 B.C.): A Chinese philosopher and social reformer; his family tree can be traced both back and forward farther than that of any other family, to his great-great-great-great-grandfather in the eighth century B.C.. and forward to his 85th lineal descendents Weiyi (born in 1939) and Weining (born in 1947), both of whom live in Taiwan.

Edward I (1239–1307): A King of England, Edward had 18 legitimate children, more than any other monogamous king, by his two queens, Eleanor of Castile, whom he married in 1254 and who died in 1290, and Margaret of France (1282–1318), whom he married in 1299.

Francisco Goya (1746–1828): A Spanish painter and etcher, during his busy life and many travels, Goya managed to find time to produce 20 children.

Captain Wilson Kettle (1851–1963): A father from Port Aux Basques, Newfoundland. When he died at the age of 112, he left 11 children, 65 grandchildren, 201 great-grandchildren and 305 great-great-grandchildren, a total of 582 living descendants.

Charles Willson Peale (1741–1827): A famous American portrait painter; thrice widowed, he had 17 children of his own and adopted three more who were orphaned children of one of his sisters. He had a theory that it was possible, if one wanted to, to train all of one's children to excel in art. He did not know that his father, from whom he had undoubtedly inherited his own skill with his fingers, had been arrested in England as a skillful forger. To inspire his children he named them after great artists, and five of them did indeed become talented artists themselves: Raphaelle (1774–1825), Rubens (1784–1865), Rembrandt (1778–1860), Titian (1780–1798), and Titian II (1799–1895).

Isaac Singer (1811–1875): Singer is credited with inventing the sewing machine; some people think his wife was the inventor, but because women at that time could not own copyrights, he got the credit. He had 24 children, including one illegitimate, and 54 grandchildren.

Glynn de Moss ("Scotty") Wolfe (1908–): A former American Baptist minister, at age 76 he married his 24th wife, aged 38, who divorced him after 11 months. His previously oldest wife was 22 years old, and he claimed that he had 41 children.

Polygamous Fathers

Abdal-Aziz Ibn Saud (1880–1953): Founder and king of Saudi Arabia from 1932 until his death, he had 300 wives, and his royal house in the twentieth century is estimated to have as many as 5,000 princes and 5,000 princesses.

Fatah Ali Sha (c. 1762–1835): Ruler of Persia from 1797 to 1835, he was said to be the father of 154 sons and 560 daughters.

Moulay (The Bloodthirsty) Ismail (1645/46–1727): The emperor of Morocco, he was reputed to have fathered a total of 525 sons and 342 daughters by 1703, and a 700th son in 1721.

Mongkut (1804–1868): Mongkut was the 43rd child of King Rama II of Siam, who reigned from 1809 to 1824, but as the first son born to Queen Suriyem he was favored to succeed to the throne. When he was 19 he had his first child. From age 20 to 47, during the reign (1824–1851) of his older half-brother King Rama III, he was a celibate Buddhist monk and became Abbot of a monastery in Bangkok. Following his half-brother's death he became King Rama IV in April 1851, and acquired 30 wives in the next four months. In all, he had 27 royal wives who were the mothers of his royal children, 34 concubines, and 82 children, 66 of whom were still living at the time of his death.

Ramses II (1292–1225 B.C.): The fourth king of the XIXth Dynasty in ancient Egypt, who reigned for 67 years. He had a half-dozen wives, including his first one, the beautiful Queen Nefertiti, and numerous concubines. He is known to have fathered 100 children, of whom 52 were sons. Twelve sons died before he did, so on his death he was succeeded by the 13th. As was customary for pharaohs, this son was buried in Egypt's Valley of the Kings. Historians know the names of 30 of his daughters and all of the sons, and they got extremely excited in May 1995 when another mausoleum 3,200 years old containing at least 62 rooms laid side by side was discovered in the Valley. The names of some of Ramses's sons, including that of Amonherkhepesjef, the firstborn, were inscribed on the tombs in which they were buried. It was particularly interesting to find the firstborn son there, because it is believed that Ramses II was pharaoh at the time of the Exodus of the Israelites from Egypt. According to the Bible's Book of Exodus, the first son of the Pharaoh was killed by God to prove the power of the Israelites' God after Moses had warned the pharaoh that all the firstborn sons in Egypt would die if he continued to enslave the Israelites. It was this son's death that finally convinced Ramses II that he had better listen to Moses's warnings and set the Israelites free.

Ramses III (1198–1166 B.C.): An Egyptian pharaoh, he was said also to have had 100 children.

Brigham Young (1801–1877): Young was a Mormon leader; according to official church records he had 27 wives, but there is evidence that he actually had at least 70. He was the father of 59 children; 3 died in infancy, but 25 sons and 31 daughters survived.

SOME FAMOUS CHILDREN WITH MANY SIBLINGS

Christy Brown (1932–1981): An Irish artist and author, he was the ninth in a family of 21 children, all of the same mother.

Luther Burbank (1849–1926): An American botanist whose experimental work created the modern science of cross-pollination, he was his father's thirteenth child by a third wife.

George Burns (real name Nathan Birnbaum) (1896–1996): Comedian and writer, Burns was the ninth of 12 children.

Catherine of Sienna (1347–1380): A Catholic saint, she was her father's 25th child.

Céline Dion (1968–): An internationally popular French-Canadian singer and TV star, she is the youngest of 14 children.

Edward Lear (1812–1888): An English writer of nonsense verse for children, he was the youngest of 21 children, all by one mother.

Marie Antoinette (1755–1793): The fifteenth of 16 children of Emperor Francis I and Maria Theresa, Archduchess of Austria.

William Phipps (1651–1695): The first person born in the American colonies to be knighted by the British crown. Phipps was one of 26 children; he also had the distinction of being appointed royal governor of Massachusetts in 1692.

Wilma Rudolph (1940–1994): An American Olympic champion runner, she was the seventeenth of 19 children.

Margaret Sanger (1883–1966): Best known American birth control pioneer. Margaret was one of 11 children.

John Wesley (1703–1791) and **Charles Wesley** (1707–1788): The English founders of Methodism, were the fifteenth and sixteenth of 19 children, all born of the same mother.

BOYS AND SONS—QUOTES

The fact that boys are allowed to exist at all is evidence of a remarkable Christian forbearance among men.
—Ambrose Bierce, in The San Francisco News Letter, *1869*

He dies only half who leaves an image of himself in his sons.
—Carlo Goldoni, in Pamela Nubile, *1757*

If a man sets his mind to disinherit his son and says to the judges, "I will disinherit my son," the judges shall inquire into his past, and if the son has not committed a crime sufficiently grave to cut him off from the sonship, the father may not cut off his son from sonship.   —Code of Hammurabi, *c. 2250 B.C.*

There must always be a struggle between a father and son, while one aims at power and the other at independence.
—Samuel Johnson (1709–1784), in
James Boswell's The Life of Samuel Johnson, *1791*

Boys are capital fellows in their own way, among their mates; but they are unwholesome companions for grown people.
—*Charles Lamb (1775–1834), in*
The Old and the New Schoolmaster, *1821*

A son can bear with complacency the loss of his father, but the loss of his patrimony may reduce him to despair.
—*Niccolò Machiavelli (1469–1527), in* The Prince, *1513*

A boy is, of all wild beasts, the most difficult to manage.
—*Plato, (c. 427–347 B.C.) in* Laws, *c. 360 B.C.*

Preachers' sons always turn out badly.   —*American proverb*

A wise son maketh a glad father.   —*Proverbs X: 1*

A foolish son is a grief to his father, and bitterness to her that bare him.
—*Proverbs XVII: 25*

A stupid son is better than a crafty daughter.

The ungrateful son is a wart on his father's face; to leave it is a blemish, to cut it off is painful.   —*Chinese proverbs*

One boy is more trouble than a dozen girls.   —*English proverb*

The son who does not look like his father shames his mother.
—*French proverb*

Sons are the props of a house.   —*Greek proverb*

A virtuous son is the sun of his family.   —*Sanskrit proverb*

What greater ornament to a son than a father's glory, or to a father than a son's honorable conduct?   —*Sophocles (c, 496–406 B.C.), in* Antigone, *c. 450 B.C.*

GIRLS AND DAUGHTERS—QUOTES

As is the mother, so is her daughter.   —Ezekiel *16: 44*

Thank heaven for little girls, they grow up in the most delightful way.
—*Maurice Chevalier, (1888–1972), in the film* Gigi

My son's my son till he gets him a wife,
But my daughter's my daughter all of her life.
—*Dinah Maria Mulock Craig, in* Young and Old

To a father, growing old, nothing is dearer than a daughter! Sons have spirits of higher pitch, but less inclined to sweet, endearing fondness.
—*Euripides, (fifth century B.C.) in* The Suppliants

Girls we love for what they are; young men for what they promise to be.
—*Johann Wolfgang von Goethe (1749–1832),*
in Dichtung und Wahrheit, *1831*

What are little boys made of?
Snakes and snails and puppy dogs' tails.
What are little girls made of?
Sugar and spice and all that's nice.
That's what little girls are made of.

—*Mother Goose*

A girl is worth only a tenth of a boy.   —*Chinese proverb*

Brilliant daughter, cranky wife.

A house full of daughters is like a cellar full of sour beer   —*Dutch proverbs*

Daughters and dead fish do not keep well.   —*English proverb*

They who are full of sin beget only daughters.   —*Hindu proverb*

Daughters pay nae debts.

A dink [neat] maiden aft maks a dirty wife.   —*Scottish Proverbs*

All meat's to be eaten, all maids to be wed.   —*Spanish Proverbs*

Better give birth to a stone, for it could be used to build a wall.
—*Uzbek proverb, often quoted at the birth of a girl*

The woman should be weak and passive, therefore girls should be early accustomed to restraint...they must be trained to bear the yoke from the first....Cunning is the natural gift of woman...she should early learn to submit to injustice and to suffer the wrongs inflicted on her by her husband without complaint.
—*Jean Jacques Rousseau (1712–1778), in* Emile, *1762*

You cannot hammer a girl into anything. She grows as a flower does, she will wither without sun; she will decay in her sheath as a narcissus will if you do not

give her air enough; she may fall and defile her head in dust if you leave her without help at some moments of her life; but you cannot fetter her; she must take her own fair form and way.
—*John Ruskin (1819–1900), in* Sesame and Lilies, *1865*

ADOPTION

The following derives from a 1995 report by Gerald H. Cornez, national executive director of WAIF.

With the close of World War II dramatic change came in the process of adoption and in attitudes towards alternative methods of forming families. Prior to that time, adoption was regarded as a service to adults who could not have children biologically, rather than as a service for children who desperately needed families.

Mass media attention in the late 1940s focused on the plight of children orphaned by war or abandoned during the ensuing military occupation. The U.S. Government enacted legislation to allow for adoption of related children born and living overseas, but for children whose paternity was not known or acknowledged, this was not enough.

Founding of the First International Adoption System

In the early 1950s an American film star, Jane Russell, began to search for three children she would eventually adopt. That search grew into a mission that has resulted in the adoption placement of more than 38,000 children.

Russell visited overcrowded orphanages of post-war Germany, Italy, France, and England. She saw many children living pitifully in bombed-out basements, meagerly fed and clothed, inadequately supervised. Some children as old as five had not learned to walk, not because of physical defects but because no one was available to care for them or teach them. And these were the luckier children. In Korea and Japan, similar children were fighting in the streets over food, dying from malnutrition, their bodies rolled into gutters and forgotten except by other children who watched them die.

Russell returned home determined to lift these children out of that misery. She had neither the political, legal, nor social work training to negotiate the resistance she would encounter, but her determination led to the passage of the *Orphan Adoption Amendment* of the *U.S. Migration Act of 1953.* This began the process of intercountry adoption as it exists today. She then founded the first international adoption program, called WAIF. It began with 4,000 children bypassing the immigration quotas and entering the United States for adoption.

WAIF believed that the best answer for homeless children, however, was adoptive placement in their own countries, where language and culture would not add to the adjustment factors of adoption. Therefore, it also supported, through the International Social Service, education to strengthen adoption programs wherever possible and to introduce the concept in countries where adoption did not previously exist. For children who could not find families in their own countries, however, international adoption developed as a viable alternative. In the process, many dramatic changes were begun.

Adoption Loses Its Stigma

Before WAIF, adoption was often kept secret, and parents would go to great lengths to conceal the fact that the child in their home had been born to someone else. They lived in constant dread that some relative or neighbor might suspect the truth or that their adopted child would somehow find out. Some families picked a significant birthday or other special occasion to reveal the facts to their adopted children, often with disastrous results.

"Baby" used to be the word associated with adoption, but because of WAIF adoption has become an open solution to the loneliness of a child: a child of any age, any race, any handicap. Far from demanding an infant who looks just like them, many recent adoptive parents have proudly welcomed children in need into their families, raising them with the love all children deserve. Of all the accomplishments WAIF can point to, this change in society's attitude is the most far-reaching and satisfying.

New Questions and Progress

Social service agencies began to question why children could not be placed from state-to-state, so the Child Welfare League of America established the Adoption Resource Exchange of North America which matched waiting children with waiting families. This model program served the development of local, state, and regional adoption exchanges and interstate compacts for adoptive placement of children across state and provincial borders. Its concept has proven successful in Great Britain and other countries as well. Today children and families are listed on computers and featured in photo listing books updated monthly.

The 1960s and 1970s also brought new legislation enabling single parents to adopt, both domestically and internationally.

Developing nations, too, have seen the need to protect and serve homeless children, who once were viewed as a low priority for the minimal social services available. Immediately following the East Pakistan war in 1971, Bangladesh was the first such country to meet the needs of unwanted children. With reports of thousands of women who had been brutally raped, the Bengali government turned to international agencies to serve the children who had not yet been born but who would not be accepted by their cultures. Canada and the United States quickly responded to their call.

Adoption information and training have been exchanged freely. National adoption conferences have been held in Australia, Great Britain, Israel, South Africa, and the United States, and several international forums have been held, including a delegation of adoption workers sent from the U.S. to Russia.

Children with Special Needs

With increased birth control, abortion, and more unwed mothers deciding to raise their children, far fewer babies are available for adoption today than in the past. Waiting time for healthy infants can be as long as 5 to 10 years, with 40 couples waiting for every child available.

Adoption organizations have, therefore, changed their focus. WAIF no longer works overseas, now concentrating on the 300,000 American children who live in foster care.

These are older, handicapped, or of minority race. They are called children with special needs but, like all children, they share the common need of a permanent, nurturing family.

Because those wishing to adopt do not usually seek out older and handicapped children, adoption agencies now vigorously recruit appropriate families. They do so through public service advertising and weekly newspaper and television features. WAIF developed Project Adopt, an innovative series of adoptive parent recruitment events. Parties are held in cities where children available for adoption are introduced to prospective adoptive families. They are brought together in a nonthreatening atmosphere of games, entertainment, and refreshments where children are seen for their potential rather than for their handicaps. WAIF finds families for an average of 65 percent of the children at these events. Newspaper and television feature stories have similarly encouraging statistics.

In response to the success of Project Adopt, the United States Department of Health and Human Services awarded a grant to WAIF to develop additional Project Adopt sites as well as a guide to distribute to all the 2,000 adoption agencies in the United States.

New Adoption Laws in the 1990s

Thus far this decade has brought about additional significant changes and challenges to the adoption system. In spite of the media attention devoted to several exceptional, unsettling, and controversial cases in which children wanted to "divorce" their birth parents and in which adoptive parents, who had lovingly raised children for several years, were forced to give up these children to hitherto unknown birth parents, adoption continues to be a viable alternative method of creating families.

Jane Russell continued her advocacy efforts and saw the realization of the first federal adoption law in the United States. The *Adoption Assistance Act* mandates that states develop a case plan for each child entering the foster care system, judicially reviewing each case until the child is able either to return home to a restrengthened family or else is placed for adoption. A federal adoption subsidy is provided for all children with special needs, and an interstate compact has been implemented which enables such children to be placed for adoption across state lines while ensuring the continuance of medical, therapeutic, and educational benefits. Far less costly than continuing foster care, the Adoption Subsidy Program has enabled more than 50,000 children to be adopted by parents who could not afford the medical and education costs of a child with physical, emotional, or mental disabilities.

Other major changes in adoption in the United States are the emphases on preventive services to strengthen or reunite families through a variety of services and counseling. Similarly, recent legislation provides housing subsidies to families that are at risk of losing their homes and children for lack of financial resources. And Independent Living Initiatives are long overdue services to children who outgrow the foster care system without having been adopted or reunited with their birth families. Services begin at age 14 and include counseling, training, forced savings, and rent subsidies in group living situations.

New Relationships between Adoptive and Birth Parents

Each of the United States has developed an adoption registry involving all members of the adoption triad: the adoptees, biological parents, and adoptive parents. All of them can now register and gain access to identifying information about the other parties if these are also registered. This process has eased the search process for many adoptees who want to obtain information about their birth parents as well as for birth parents who decide they want to know what has happened to the children they gave up.

The evolution of open adoptions, in which the adopting and biological parents meet and usually relate closely during pregnancy and delivery and establish a mutually acceptable ongoing relationship, has changed the rights of birth mothers especially. And children appear to be faring well with the inclusion of the birth mother in their lives as a natural situation. Contacts range from minimal to regular but usually infrequent visits; the adopters are clearly established as the child's functioning parents, limiting the child's confusion while providing friendly access to his or her birth family and encouraging the biological parents to go on with their lives without the wound caused by abandonment of their child.

Initial reluctance of many people in the adoption system to accept this process has ebbed somewhat as they have begun to adjust to a variety of structures, such as single, divorced, and step-families that have increasingly become the norm rather than the exception. Admittedly, registries and openness have frightened and mobilized those who fear contact with their biological children or contact between their adopted children and birth parent(s). Traditional adoptions still provide confidentiality, although more and more people now question the fairness to the child to be forever denied birth parent information, and no one can predict whether agreements of confidentiality will still be honored when a child reaches the age of majority. But the tides have turned against secrecy; Concerned United Birth Parents, long thought of as a minority position organization, has successfully forged the key position of birth mothers to have the right of involvement and choice in the selection of adoptive parents for their children.

Increasing numbers of foster parents are adopting the children placed in their temporary care, and family members are increasingly undertaking foster care to children related to them, a process known as Kinship Care. Nevertheless, economic conditions will continue to erode the quality and breadth of care regardless of legislation because the foster care program has become so overburdened. New York City is not an isolated example, and it has seen the foster care population grow from 17,000 to over 50,000 children in just a few years. It is hoped that continuing budget and staffing cuts will provoke a response from the private sector to avoid recent disservices, such as the reality of children coming into the system having to sleep on the floor of the department of children's services, or being placed each night with a different family on an emergency basis.

Interracial Adoptions

Much attention has been focused on the placement of children with adoptive families of different races. The system has emphasized same-race placement for many years, following the initiative of the Association of Black Social Workers. It is widely believed that the African American community does not have the resources or the information necessary to adopt all the children of color who are in need of permanent families. By stopping transracial placements, it was hoped that services to the black community and to the black children waiting to be adopted would be improved and increased. Unfortunately, however, not enough has been done, in spite of some inroads made by the continuing success of programs such as One Church, One Child, begun in Chicago by Father George Clements, a black priest who adopted a child in order to set an example.

Conversely, movements such as the Child Care System of the National Coalition to End Racism in America have effectively advocated the placement of children both in foster care and adoption in the earliest available home that is qualified to meet a child's needs. While all child advocates who do not want placement significantly delayed still work toward the goal of a same-race placement, the l03rd U.S. Congress passed the *Multiethnic Placement Act of 1994* aimed to ensure timely adoptive placement regardless of race. However, it is anticipated that the intent of the law will be stronger than its actual impact once it filters through the maze of state laws, systems, and agency policies.

International Developments

Adoption today crosses all boundaries, be they national, racial, or cultural. This was never true in the past. Internationally, adoption has continued to gain acceptance, even in countries where it was formerly almost unknown. Some countries, such as Brazil, still do not encourage or permit foreigners to adopt their children. Others, such as Romania, actively welcomed American would-be adoptive parents because of their many internal problems caused by recent political and economic upheaval. When suitable resources in a child's country of origin are unavailable to ensure the best interests of children, the desirability of intercountry adoption is increasingly recognized.

The Most Important Point about Adoption

As controversy continues about all facets of adoption policy and practice, we are drawn back to the necessity of adoption as a service to and for children. When people focus, incorrectly, on adoption as a service to adults wishing to adopt, they fail children by not protecting their right to be reared by their biological families, if possible and suitable, or to be assured that they are placed permanently with qualified, nurturing, and loving families. Only time will prove our success in the light of media attention to unfortunate isolated cases and of the ravages of addiction and abuse on the future of a significant number of children in the adoption system.

No one in the system sets out to hurt children. They are helpers working against difficult circumstances and pressures. But if our eyes remain focused on the best interest of the child first and foremost, we will continue to change lives positively, one child at a time.

As long as there are children anywhere who remain without families, countries and agencies and individuals will be called upon to respond to the cry of the lonely and vulnerable child.

> Grisly footnote to the history of adoption: The first woman ever hanged in New Zealand was Minnie Dean in August, 1895. Her crime was "baby farming." She adopted unwanted babies for a fee, a "service" she began in 1889, and then she disposed of them. She was found guilty after police dug up bodies of three infants in her flower garden.

DO CHILDREN BRING THEIR PARENTS HAPPINESS?—QUOTES

Yes!

He knows not what love is who has no children.   —*Anonymous*

A child is the very sign and sacrament of personal freedom. He is a fresh will added to the wills of the world; he is something that his parents have freely chosen to produce and which they freely agree to protect. They can feel that any amusement he gives (which is often considerable) really comes from him and from them, and from nobody else.   —*G. K. Chesterton (1874–1936)*

Here all mankind is equal: rich and poor alike, they love their children....All men know their children mean more to them than life. If childless people sneer, well, they have less sorrow, but what lonely good fortune.
                              —*Euripides, (fifth century B.C.)*

Other people's harvests are always the best harvest, but one's own children are always the best children.   —*Chinese proverb*

Who has not children knows not why he lives.   —*German proverb*

A house without children is only a cemetery.   —*Sanskrit proverb*

Romance fails us and so do friendships, but the relationship of parent and child, less noisy than all others, remains indelible and indestructible, the strongest relationship on earth.   —*Theodore Reik (1888–1969)*

Children endow their parents with a vicarious immortality.
                              —*George Santayana (1863–1952)*

The only things that count in life are the imprints of love which we leave behind us after we are gone.   —*Albert Schweitzer (1875–1965)*

People who really love each other fully and truly they are the happiest people in the world, and we see that with our very poor people. They love their children. They may have very little, they may have nothing, but they are happy people."
                              —*Mother Theresa of Calcutta (1910–)*

No!

The wise man, whoever he may be, if he intends to have children, must turn to me [to folly]....Tell me, I beg you, what man is there who would submit his neck to the noose of matrimony if, as wise men should, he first truly weighed its

inconvenience? Or what woman is there who would ever enter it if she seriously considered either the dangers of childbirth or the troubles of bringing children up?"
　　　　—Erasmus of Rotterdam (1466–1536), in his satire In Praise of Folly

The childless escape much misery.　　*—Euripides (fifth century B.C.) in* Medea

When I consider how little of a rarity children are, that every street and blind alley swarms with them, that the poorest people commonly have them in most abundance, that there are few marriages that are not blest with at least one of these bargains, how often they turn out ill, and defeat the fond hopes of their parents, taking to vicious courses which end in poverty, disgrace, the gallows, etc. etc. I cannot for my life tell what cause for pride there can possibly be in having them. If they were young phoenixes, indeed, that were born but one in a year, there might be a pretext. But when they are so common—I do not advert to the insolent merit which they [mothers] assume with their husbands on these occasions. Let them look to that. But why *we*, who are not their natural born subjects, should be expected to bring our spices, myrrh, and incense—our tribute and homage of admiration I do not see.
　　　　　　　　　—Charles Lamb (1775–1834), in
　　　　　A Bachelor's Complaint on the Behavior of Married People

This is sent merely to inform you that a short time ago I received a letter from you from which I learned that you have an heir, which circumstance I understand has afforded you a great deal of pleasure. Now in so far as I had judged you to be possessed of prudence I am now entirely convinced that I am as far removed from having an accurate judgment as you are from prudence, seeing that you have been congratulating yourself on having created a watchful enemy who will strive with all his energies after liberty, which can only come into being at your death."
　　　　—Leonardo da Vinci (1452–1519), in a letter to his half-brother
　　　　　　　　　Domenico, 30 years his junior

Insanity is inherited . . . we get it from our children.
　　　　　　　　　—Sam Levenson (1911-1980)

　　　　To get the whole world out of bed
　　And washed, and dressed, and warmed, and fed,
　　　　To work, and back to bed again,
　　　Believe me, Saul, costs worlds of pain.
　　　—John Masefield (1930–1967), in The Everlasting Mercy

How sharper than a serpent's tooth It is to have a thankless child!
　　　　—William Shakespeare (1564–1616), in King Lear

Providence frequently punishes the self-love of men with children very much below their characters and qualifications, insomuch that they transmit their names to those who give daily proofs of the vanity of the labor and ambition of their progenitors.　　　*—Richard Steele (1672–1729), in* The Spectator

The laws promulgated by Emperor Augustus (63 B.C.–A.D. 14) which rewarded fathers and penalized bachelors did not succeed in producing more marriages, as the government desired, because the childless state is so attractive.

—*Tacitus (55–117 A.D.)*

Children are a torment, and nothing else.

—*Leo Tolstoy (1869–1945), in* The Kreutzer Sonata, *1889*

If they realized in advance the cares and sorrows that children cause their mothers, women would be sore afraid of them as death...and hate them like cruel, wild beasts or venomous serpents.   —*Juan Luis Vives (1492–1540)*

Children are certain cares and uncertain comforts.

Children suck the mother when they are young and the father when they are old.   —*English proverbs*

Little children, headache; big children, heartache.   —*Italian proverb*

Maybe!

It is a great happiness to see our children rising round us, but from that good fortune spring the bitterest woes of man.
—*Aeschylus (525–436 B.C.), quoting an old adage in* Agamemnon, *c. 490 B.C.*

The joys of parents are secret, and so are their griefs and fears; they cannot utter the one, nor they will not utter the other. Children sweeten labors, but they make misfortunes more bitter; they increase the cares of life, but they mitigate the remembrance of death. The perpetuity by generation is common to beasts; but memory, merit and noble works are proper to men: and surely a man shall see the noblest works and foundations have proceeded from childless men, which have sought to express the images of their minds when those of their bodies have failed; so the care of posterity is most in them that have no posterity....He that hath wife and children hath given hostages to fortune, for they are impediments to great enterprises, either of virtue or mischief.
      —*Francis Bacon (1561–1626), in* Of Marriage and the Single Life

It is horrible to die without children...[but] Children are always ungrateful.
      —*Napoleon Bonaparte (1769–1821)*

Deceive not thyself by overexpecting happiness in the married estate. Look not therein for contentment greater than God will give, or a creature in this world can receive; namely, to be free from all inconveniences. Marriage is not like the hill Olympus, 'wholly clear' without clouds. Yea, expect both wind and storms sometimes, which when blown over, the air is clearer and wholesomer for it. Make account of certain cares and troubles which will attend thee. Remember the nightingales, which sing only some months in the spring, but commonly are silent when they have hatched their eggs, as if their mirth were turned into care for their young ones. Yet all the molestations of marriage are abundantly recompensed with other comforts, which God bestoweth on them who make a wise choice of a wife. —*Thomas Fuller (1608–1661), in* The Holy and Profane State

Soldier, robber, priest, atheist, courtesan, virgin, I care not what you are, if you have not brought children into the world to suffer, your life has been as vain, and as harmless, as mine has been."
    —*George Moore (1852–1870), in* Confessions of a Young Man

Special Days Enjoyed by Families Worldwide

The following descriptions of days on which children and families are honored is just a small sample of some of the most popular and colorful occasions. It would be impossible to include all of them.

January 15 in Japan, *Seijin-No-Hi* (**Adults' Day**): This is a 1,000-year-old national holiday honoring boys and girls who have reached the age of 20, with ceremonies, banquets, films, games, parades, and sports events. Age 13 is usually regarded in Japan as the dividing line between childhood and youth, but the twentieth birthday is special because that is when the government confers full legal rights and responsibilities.

January 20 in Bulgaria, **Grandmother's Day**: Midwives in this country are traditionally older women and because they help bring babies into the world, they are affectionately called *babas* (grandmothers). Every year children honor their babas by bringing them flowers on this day. Nowadays most babies are born in hospitals but the custom has survived: children now bring flowers to the doctors and nurses who helped bring them into the world.

February 29 worldwide, **Leap Year Day**: Under the Gregorian calendar now used by most countries the year consists of 365 days, but because it actually takes 365 days, 5 hours, 48 minutes and 45 seconds for the earth to revolve completely around the sun, there is one extra day every 4 years. It is called Leap Year Day because for a long time English courts did not recognize February 29 and the day was "leaped over" in their records. Children born on February 29 get a chance to celebrate their birthdays only every four years, so parents try to make it a very special day.

229

The last Sunday in Lent in England, **Mothering Sunday**: In the seventeenth century on this day people held family reunions and went *mothering* to bring their mothers flowers and cakes. The custom died out in the eighteenth century but was revived during World War II.

March 19 in Spain, **St. Joseph's Day**: This is when fathers are honored. Fathers are also honored on **Father's Day** on the third Sunday in June in Canada, England, and France and since 1909 in the United States, where the holiday was established in memory of William Smart, a Civil War veteran whose wife died in childbirth but who successfully brought up five sons and a grateful daughter on his own. It began as a religious observance but is now an official holiday in many states.

March 21 in Mexico, **The Day of the Indian Child**: This is a national holiday celebrating the birthday of Benito Juarez, Mexico's first President, who was a full-blooded Indian. Special exhibits are held of paintings and handicrafts by Indian children.

April 7 in Mozambique, **Mother's Day**: This is also celebrated all over the world: on the first Sunday in May in Spain; on May 10 in Guatemala; on the second Sunday in May in Brazil, Canada, Germany, Norway, Switzerland, and the United States; on the last Sunday of May in France; on June 28 in the Central African Republic; on December 8 in Panama. In the United States it was proclaimed as an official national day to honor mothers after a seven-year campaign by Anna Jarvis, and because her mother's favorite flowers were carnations it became customary for people on this day to wear carnations in their lapels: red ones for living mothers and white ones for those who had died.

April 23 in Turkey, **Children's Day**: This is the anniversary of the opening of the nation's first Grand National Assembly in 1923; 400 students are elected by their classmates to take seats in national and local governments for the day to learn how government works. Ice cream and movies and free transportation are offered, and visiting foreign children are also invited to participate in parades, shows, and balls.

May 5 in Japan, **Children's Day**: From the seventeenth century this was celebrated as Boys' Day. Every family that had a son flew a kite over its house, in the shape of a carp, a symbol of strength and courage, qualities parents want in their children, especially boys. The carp was chosen because of its stamina in swimming upstream. But since world War II May 5 has become a day on which girls are honored as well as boys. They go to Shinto shrines where priests bless them and wish them health and happiness, after which the family eats a special meal together.

May 27 in Nigeria, **Children's Day**: Schools are closed and children take part in ceremonies, parades, and rallies. There are special radio and TV broadcasts, and prayers are offered in mosques and churches. Other activities include exhibitions of children's art, movies, sports events, and dances.

June 1 in Byelorussia, China, Czechoslovakia, Mongolia, Poland, Russia and Ukraine, **International Children's Day**: This usually begins with formal official ceremonies and awarding of prizes to children for moral, intellectual, physical, and aesthetic excellence. During the day special performances are staged by and for children, and there are relay races, tugs of war, ping-pong matches, marbles, and other games, plus gymnastic demonstrations and dances.

August 16 in Paraguay, **The Day of the Child**: This is a holiday celebrated with special programs for children: puppet shows, games, dances, and songs. Girl Guides stage publicity campaigns in connection with the day to make people more aware of the needs of children.

October 2 in India, **Gandhi's Birthday**: In some parts of the country this is celebrated as **Universal Children's Day**; in other areas, Universal Children's Day is observed on November 14, Nehru's birthday. Schools, children's museums, and other cultural centers hold special programs in which children fly kites, play games, and take part in painting and sculpture workshops.

The Second Monday in October in Canada, and the **fourth Thursday in November** in the United States, **Thanksgiving Day**: This is a traditional time for big family gatherings and big feasts. The traditional Indian celebration was adopted by the Pilgrims in 1621 in Plymouth, Massachusetts, in gratitude for a successful harvest, as only half of the original settlers had lived through their first harsh winter. They celebrated with the neighbouring Indians who had befriended them and introduced them to new crops: cranberries, corn (maize), pumpkins, and turkey. It is still almost obligatory in the United States to eat those foods on this day.

Other Harvest Festivals take place in other countries too, all over the world. Dates vary as much as the crops do, with corn festivals among Native Americans, yam festivals in Africa, rice festivals in Asia, grape and wine festivals in Europe. Many such festivals are centuries old and feature offerings to ancient gods, giving thanks to those who are (or used to be) considered protectors of crops or propitiating evil spirits who might cause famines. Formal rituals and prayers are followed by informal family fun. At town and state fairs children are an important part of the festivities, proudly displaying their pet animals and prize-winning flowers and vegetables, and enjoying pony and train rides, swings and carousels, ball games, races, horse shows, and picnics.

October 31 in Canada, Ireland, the United Kingdom, and the United States, **Halloween (All Hallows Eve)**: In Ireland this is an official national holiday. Centuries ago it was the date of a Celtic harvest festival when it was believed that spirits of people who had died during the year came back to earth, so people wore frightening masks and costumes to scare them away. The custom of dressing up as skeletons, ghosts, witches, goblins, and devils has survived, especially among children, and for many years this evening was a favorite among them as an excuse to be impish. Their pranks were often so destructive (slitting tires, breaking windows, etc.) that grownups took measures to introduce more benign customs.

Many shops allow children to paint their windows and give prizes to the best pictures. Some families decorate their front doors with corn stalks and fruits, celebrating the autumn harvest. Some set up humorous stuffed figures in fancy costumes on porches and lawns, and put Jack-o-Lanterns in their windows (a pumpkin hollowed out and carved with open spaces for eyes, nose, and mouth so that when a lighted candle is placed inside a smiling face glows forth). Jack-o-Lanterns originated in Ireland, but instead of using pumpkins children carved turnips or potatoes.

The popular custom of children going from house to house saying "Trick or Treat" (give me a treat such as candy or coins or I'll play a trick on you) took on a benevolent aspect in 1950 when a group of Sunday School children in Pennsylvania decided to contribute the financial "treats" ($17) they had received on Halloween to UNICEF. This modest beginning launched a multimillion-dollar custom. The idea caught on and since then literally millions of children have joined annual "Trick or Treat for UNICEF" campaigns in Canada, Denmark, Finland, Ireland, and the United States, raising more than $100 million to help children in the Third World by collecting coins in orange boxes or by holding fund-raising (and fun-raising) events such as face-painting contests, monster movie festivals, raffles, and parties in churches, community centers, and schools where children bob for apples, play games, tell ghost stories, and get prizes for the best costumes. In 1967 President Lyndon Johnson declared the day National UNICEF Day in the United States, as has every U.S. President since then,

In November in India and Nepal, **Bhai Doj** (Brother and Sister Day): During the Hindu Festival of Lights the bond between brothers and sisters is honored in family celebrations. A sister draws a mandala, circular symbol of the universe, on the floor with rice powder. In the evening her brother sits on a stool in its center and she puts some vermillion powder on his forehead to ward off evil and sprinkles rice over his head to wish him a long and happy life. In return the brother gives her a piece of jewelry, a sari, or money, as a sign of his promise to look after her needs always. In families which have only boys or girls, children ask cousins or best friends to be their "brothers" or "sisters."

November 15 in Japan, **Schichi-Go-San** (Seven-Five-Three): This day honors all Japanese children who are seven, five or three years old. Dressed in kimonos, they visit shrines with their families, carrying paper bags printed with good luck signs. Priests drop *thousand year candies* into the bags, and parents fill them with other presents.

December 31 worldwide, **New Year's Eve**: For many young children this is a particularly exciting occasion because it is the only night of the year when they are allowed to stay up after midnight. And since the invention of television much of the fun has been to see New Year's Eve celebrations move around the world as they cross time zones. In Ecuador families sew old shirts and trousers together to make an *Año Viejo*, a figure of the old year, which they stuff with straw. These are displayed in windows, and on New Year's Eve everyone walks around town admiring them. Some children dress in black as the Año Viejo's widows, and beg for contributions for his funeral expenses. When the clock strikes midnight people light matches to Año Viejo and as he burns his "widows" scream while everyone else breaks into a dance to welcome the New Year. In Spain there is a tradition of taking a bunch of grapes and having to eat 12 of them between the first and last chimes of the clock at midnight. If you succeed they say you are sure to have prosperity during the New Year.

7

Child Rearing and Education

COMMENTS ON CHILD REARING AND EDUCATION

Those who educate their children are more to be honored than those who produce them; the latter gave them life only, but the former give them the art of living well. —*Aristotle (384–322 B.C.)*

Education commences at the mother's knee, and every word spoken within the hearing of little children tends towards the formation of character.
—*Hosea Ballou (1771–1852)*

You cannot teach a child to take care of himself, unless we let him try. He will make mistakes, and of these mistakes will come his wisdom.
—*Henry Ward Beecher (1813–1887)*

There is so much to teach and the time goes so fast.
—*Erma Bombeck (1927–1996)*

The first duty to children is to make them happy. If you have not made them so, you have wronged them. No other good they may get can make up for that.
—*Charles Buxton (1875–1942)*

The biggest business in the world, and the most important business in the world, and the business that outweighs all other values in the world is the business of raising children.
—*Brock Chisholm, First Director-General of the
World Health Organization, in 1958*

Ignorance is the night of the mind, a night without moon or stars.
—*Confucius (c. 551–479 B.C.)*

Raising children is an uncertain thing; success is reached only after a life of battle and worry. —*Democritus (fifth century B.C.)*

To insure good mothers, there must be a means of a good education provided for young girls. Better leave the boys of a generation without learning than the girls, if one sex must be doomed to ignorance.
—*Godey's Lady's Book, in 1890*

Treat people as if they were what they ought to be and you help them become what they are capable of being. —*Johann Wolfgang von Goethe (1749–1832)*

Almost every child, on the first day he sets foot in a school building, is smarter, more curious, less afraid of what he doesn't know, better at finding and figuring things out, more confident, resourceful, persistent and independent than he will be again in his schooling—or, unless he is very unusual and very lucky, for the rest of his life. . . .In he comes, this curious, patient, determined, energetic, skillful learner. We set him down at a desk, and what do we teach him? Many things. First, that learning is separate from living. 'You come to school to learn,' we tell him, as if the child hadn't been learning before, as if living were out there and learning were in here, and there was no connection between the two. Secondly, that he cannot be trusted to learn and is no good at it. Everything we teach about reading, a task far simpler than many the child has already mastered, says to him, 'If we don't make you read, you won't, and if you don't do it exactly the way we tell you, you can't.' In short, he comes to feel that learning is a passive process, something that someone else does *to* you, instead of something you do for yourself.

—*John Holt (1923–1985), in the* Saturday Evening Post, *1969*

I looked on child rearing not only as a work of love and duty but as a profession that was fully as interesting and challenging as any honorable profession in the world and one that demanded the best that I could bring to it.

—*Rose Fitzgerald Kennedy (1890–1995)*

Children are travelers newly arrived in a strange country, of which they know nothing; we should therefore make conscience not to mislead them. They are strangers to all we are acquainted with, and happy are they who meet with civil people, that will comply with their ignorance, and help them to get out of it . . . A child's mind is not a pot to be filled, but a fire to be kindled.

—*John Locke (1632–1704), in* Some Thoughts Concerning Education

If you bungle raising your children, I don't think whatever else you do will matter very much. . . .The personality of the child guides you. If you start with love, security and discipline, and just work from there, the raising will be rewarding all around, and fun . . . . I never want a home in which you have to say to children, 'Don't touch.'   —*Jacqueline Kennedy Onassis* (1929–1994)

The principal goal of education is to create men who are capable of doing new things, not simply of repeating what other generations have done—who are creative, inventive, and discoverers. The second goal of education is to form minds which can be critical, can verify, and not accept everything they are offered. The great danger today is of slogans, collective opinions, ready-made trends of thoughts. We have to be able to resist individually, to criticize, to distinguish between what is proven and what is not. So we need pupils who are active, who learn early to find out by themselves, partly by their spontaneous activity and partly through material we set up for them; who learn early to tell what is verifiable and what is simply the first idea to come to them.

—*Jean Piaget (1896–1980)*

Do not train boys to learning by force or harshness, but direct them to it by what amuses their minds, so that you may be the better able to discover with accuracy the peculiar bent of the genius of each.   —*Plato (427–347 b.c.)*

See everything; praise most things; overlook many things; correct a few things.

—*Pope John XXIII (1861–1963)*

I used to have six theories about how to raise children, and no children; now I have six children, and no theories. —*Lord Rochester (1612–1658)*

Child rearing is a long, hard job [but] taking care of their children, seeing them grow and develop into fine people, gives most parents—despite the hard work—their greatest satisfaction in life. This is creation. This is our visible immortality. Pride in their worldly accomplishments is usually weak by comparison.
—*Dr. Benjamin Spock (1903–)*

The child is entitled to receive education, which shall be free and compulsory, at least in the elementary stages. The child shall be given an education which will promote his general culture, and enable him on a basis of equal opportunity to develop his abilities, his individual judgment, and his sense of moral and social responsibility, and to become a useful member of society. . . .He shall be brought up in a spirit of understanding, tolerance, friendship among peoples, peace and universal brotherhood and in full consciousness that his energy and talents should be devoted to the service of his fellow men. . . .The best interests of the child shall be the guiding principles of those responsible for his education and guidance. —*United Nations Declaration on the Rights of the Child,* 1959

Historical footnote: It is interesting to see that even the most enlightened and progressive theorists about education, not only in previous eras but even in the twentieth century, almost always referred to the child who was to be educated as "he."

PROVERBS ABOUT CHILD REARING

Educate a man, you educate one person; educate a woman, you educate a nation.

Knowledge is better than riches.

Knowledge is like a garden; if it is not cultivated it cannot be harvested.
—*African proverbs*

Train up a child in the way he should go; and when he is old he will not depart from it. —*Biblical proverbs*

Before fathers and mothers, uncles and aunts, itch as you may, you dare not scratch. —*Chinese proverb*

An idle brain is the devil's workshop

Ill examples are like contagious diseases. —*English proverbs*

Children are what we make them.

Keep a tight rein on your son. —*French proverbs*

Better unbred children than ill-bred ones.   —*German proverb*

Learning is treasure no thief can touch.

Unplowed fields make hollow bellies; unread books make hollow minds.
                                                              —*Asian proverbs*

THE "PRESCHOOL" YEARS

There is really no such thing as a preschooler, because every child enters school at birth. The fact that all her/his work is "homework" and that she does not sit at a desk in a classroom does not alter the basic fact that she (or he) must study constantly and learn rapidly a great many complicated subjects, observing, memorizing, analyzing, and evaluating them. It has been said that a child in the first three or four years of life works as hard and learns as much as a student in four years at a university.

William James (1842–1910), an affectionate father as well as an observant psychologist, said the world is a "big, booming, buzzing confusion" to a newborn baby, but almost immediately, each infant begins to sort out some of the confusion and to notice individual things with special interest. Alert babies examine their environment with intense curiosity and appreciative concentration that almost no one else, except dedicated artists and scientists and philosophers, ever applies to the commonplace.

As a later psychoanalyst, Ernest Schachtel, put it in *Metamorphosis: On the Development of Affect, Perception, and Memory:*

> Everything is new to the newborn child . . . . No Columbus, no Marco Polo, has ever seen stranger and more fascinating and thoroughly absorbing sights than the child that learns to perceive, to taste, to smell, to tough, to hear and see, and to use his body, his senses, and his mind. No wonder that the child shows an insatiable curiosity. He has the *whole world* to discover.

Children of all races and social classes start off on a fairly equal footing as far as knowledge and ability are concerned, knowing instinctively how to sleep and how to cry, and also promptly learning how to suck. Thereafter, inequalities set in and some learn faster than others, depending primarily on their health and on the demands made upon them and the opportunities given to them by the culture into which they were born.

The brain inside a baby's head is a truly remarkable thing. It has been compared favorably with the most advanced modern machines. Though mass produced by unskilled labor and weighing only a few ounces, it is a nonlinear computer containing more than a billion binary decision units (called brain cells).

Some baby-care practices, however, seem designed to sabotage the functioning of this magnificent machine, according to brain specialist Glenn Doman, director of the Institute for the Achievement of Human Potential in Philadelphia. He explains that "at the root of all learning are stimulation of the senses and organization of the nervous system, because the brain learns how to be brainy by building its experience on a foundation of early sensations and certain very basic body movements." Therefore, he maintains, from the very earliest days of life, the brain and the five senses should be stimulated with the sounds of music and speech, the sights of colors and shapes, the smell of flowers, the taste of milk, and the touch of textures and kisses and hugs. He believes it is wrong to darken a child's room at nap time, or even at night, or to surround babies with a "soothing," quiet atmosphere, or to confine them to playpens instead of encouraging them to crawl as a preparation for walking. He also thinks parents should give little children a head start by teaching them to read and to count with the aid of flash cards, and he conducts a "Better Baby Institute," where parents are taught these techniques.

Not everyone agrees with him, however. Some claim that by "pushing" babies so soon you deprive them of the right to develop "naturally" and enjoy a more peaceful preparation for future active years.

When Should a "Preschooler" Stop Being One?

Opinions on how soon a preschool child should begin getting some education outside the home have differed widely from time to time and from place to place.

In Elizabethan England, the age of four was generally considered the best age to start formal education.

Heinrich Bullinger (1504–1575), the Swiss Calvinist reformer whose suggestions were followed by many Puritans, objected to any set age for starting formal instruction, but he believed that in most cases a child was ready for it between the ages of five and seven.

Some children, among them Benjamin Franklin (1706–1790) and Jean Renoir (1841–1919)—were preschoolers until the age of eight, while others started going to school at the early age of three. Maria Montessori (1870–1952), the great Italian educator, believed that *all* children should start going to school at three, if a school is available that has educational methods and equipment that are properly adapted to small children's capacities and interests.

In undeveloped and developing countries, where most of the world's children live, the term "preschool" may not have much meaning, since so many children never get a chance to go to school; they are "preschoolers" all their lives. In advanced countries, the term may also be unrealistic because many very young children, particularly the growing numbers of those whose mothers have jobs that take them away from home during the day, are sent to day care centers. Some centers are merely custodial, but others perform elementary educational functions.

Home Schooling

In most countries with universal education, six or seven is the age at which children are legally required to go to school, unless their parents insist on educating them at home, in which case they must apply for and receive special permission from school authorities.

An example of parents who have defied such authorities is the Amish, a pacifist religious sect founded in the fifteenth century that emigrated to America to escape persecution in Europe. They believe that farming is "the good life" and they have helped make Lancaster County in Pennsylvania a garden spot with their beautiful and prosperous farms. They do not believe in education beyond the elementary grades, considering the "3 Rs" sufficient for a simple rural community, so for many years they were in constant conflict with education officials over compulsory school laws. After a long struggle, however, they finally were given the right to run their own schools and their children are no longer required to go to high school.

Most parents who do not want to send their children to schools feel that way because they think schools give too little rather than too much education. An example of this attitude is that of Laszio Polgar, a former teacher in Budapest, Hungary, who prepared for fatherhood by studying the biographies of 400 great intellectuals from Socrates to Einstein. Before getting married he told Klara, his future wife who was also a teacher, "We both agree that the school system produces the gray average mass. But give me any healthy newborn and I can make a genius." They decided they would not send their children to school but instead would teach them at home, believing that "true learning only passes between loved ones."

How well did Polgar's theories work out? He proved he was a man of his word. When his first daughter Zsuzsu was born in 1969, he quit his job in order to stay home and teach her. By age four she could speak English, German, and Russian as well as Hungarian. At six she was studying university-level mathematics. By 16 she had written three books on chess in German.

Her two younger sisters, Zsofi and Judit, have had the same upbringing and are equally remarkable. All three had devoured a huge library of books, most of them on chess—for which they developed a passion—by the time they were five. Ever since they gained worldwide admiration in 1986 as a result of their spectacular performances in two international chess tournaments in Puerto Rico and New York (see page 318) they have continued to dazzle people, entering and winning chess competitions in Europe and America.

The Polgar sisters are members of the chess club of Budapest and work with masters there when not traveling to foreign competitions, and they spend at least four hours a day at the game. Judit actually became a grandmaster at the age of 10. She says that "sometimes chess feels like a sport, sometimes it feels like art, and sometimes it feels like a job."

Some people might think these girls have a hard life, studying so much all year long, but Zsuzsu thinks it is average families that have a hard life. "It's disgusting," she says, "a man educating himself and sending a woman into the kitchen, and then calling her stupid and not on his own level."

During the rare moments when she and her sisters are not studying or playing chess they enjoy jogging, table tennis, and soccer. Also, for fun, they challenge each other to blindfold matches, playing without boards or notes.

Most definitely, few parents would have either the ability or the desire to give their children such an intensive education and would much rather turn over the teaching to schools. But Mr. Polgar has certainly proved that teaching at home can, in some cases at least, produce prodigies.

In 1996, according to the U.S. Department of Education, more than 500,000 American parents were now teaching their children at home. All states now allow home schooling. And the president of the National Home Education Research Institute said that more than 65 studies have shown that home-schoolers perform at average or above average levels.

HISTORICAL PERSPECTIVES ON CHILD REARING

Lloyd deMause, the well-known and influential psychohistorian and publisher of the magazine *Psychohistory,* considers the relationship between parents and children "the main dynamic of history." He regards with horror the way most children have been treated throughout history, yet he is basically an optimist because he sees a continuing improvement, at least in Western civilization, as each generation of parents tries to avoid mistakes made by previous ones.

In his writings he has described the evolution of child rearing from the period when infanticide was common, a practice that he believes led to Christianity and the worship of "the dead son."

The next child-rearing mode, which prevailed from the fourth to the thirteenth centuries, he says, featured "abandonment." Parents sent their children off to "a wet nurse, to the monastery or nunnery, to foster families, to the homes of other nobles as servants or hostages," or subjected them to "severe emotional abandonment at home." He thinks this stage led to the development of feudalism, which is exemplified in the way a feudal lord knighted a person by slapping him on the face and kissing him on both cheeks and taking his hand: all fatherly gestures symbolizing the promise that "I will not abandon you if you will be loyal to me," the essence of the feudal oath.

Parents gradually overcame their abandoning ways in the eighteenth century, he says, and began to be "intrusive" instead. They kept their children, but took over their minds and trained them to do the parents' will. This trend progressed through the nineteenth and twentieth centuries in a milder form that he calls "socializing," and rigid child-rearing methods produced children who became a corps of workers and industrialists.

During all these centuries parents gradually began to show greater empathy for their children and, as a result, punished them less severely. Infanticide gave way to beatings with cat o' nine tails, which in turn gave way to spanking.

That even today some parents treat their children viciously, he has explained by saying such parents are "arrested" psychologically at a previous stage of development. Many parents alive today are the last generation of parents who are still at the "intrusive" or "socializing" stage, but many others have reached the "helping" stage, in which they have such a high degree of empathy for their children that they realize children do not exist for the parents' benefit but actually have rights of their own.

That many couples today have decided not to have children at all deMause sees not as rejection of children but as an increased awareness that children need a great deal of love and attention and actually have a right to those things. "In the past," he says, "you could have five kids and forget about them," but nowadays some people are honest enough to realize and admit that they simply do not want to make the necessary sacrifices, or that they may be unable to support children.

EDUCATION IN NONINDUSTRIAL SOCIETIES

A Hindu sage named Vatsyayana in the first century A.D. wrote rules for domestic life, and said parents should allow children "all indulgence and freedom" until they are five years old. American Indians, however, differ from India's Hindus by expecting a great deal of hard work from their small children. This is not considered punitive, however. It is merely another aspect of the self-reliance they encourage in their children.

An observer of two three-year-olds, one in a European city and one in an African village, might think both children were doing the same thing, playing with dolls, miniature tools, or clay. In one case, however, the activity is done simply because it is fun, while in the other case it is serious training to carry out real duties. Whichever it is, play or work, the same psychological fact about tiny children is in operation. Little people love to imitate big people, and in one culture this trait is enjoyed as a source of entertainment while in another it is quickly turned into useful activity.

Early Rearing of Girls

The Dakota Indians present little girls with dolls or, as they call them, "made children," but these are not mere playthings. They are deliberately used to train babies to take care of other babies; as soon as another real baby joins the family, the next youngest girl turns into a baby sitter. She already knows how to carry the baby on her back while walking and working because she has practiced with her doll. Traditionally she is also given, while still a little girl, a small work bag with materials for making tiny moccasins while she imitates her mother who makes larger ones.

In Malaysia, girls as young as three have always helped their mothers cultivate the fields hulling rice while they were still so tiny they could hardly lift the pestle.

Among the Seminoles in Florida girls as young as four were traditionally responsible for stirring the soup while it boiled, kneading dough for the family's bread, washing vegetables, watching the fire and keeping it stoked. These activities were not regarded as "playing house." They were real responsibilities that the girls were expected to accept as their part of maintaining their home.

UNICEF/Mariantonietta Peru

Throughout South America, most little Indian girls are given small water jugs even while they are still being carried in their mothers' arms, and when the mother collects water the baby does too. As soon as she is big enough to climb down from her mother's arms and start walking, she begins to carry her own little water jug on her head. She also has a toy spindle from babyhood and learns to spin and weave early by imitating her mother.

In Sumatra, among the Battas, a girl's size used to be measured not in inches or pounds but by the number of *gargitis* (water vessels made of a bamboo stalk) she could carry.

In many countries, children as young as six or seven regularly carry babies on their backs, and not just tiny infants but babies one or two years old. Among other regular duties that little girls all over the developing world share are going to the brook or lake or village pump every day to fetch water, and to the woods to gather kindling.

Early Rearing of Boys

Little boys everywhere love to go boating or fishing with their fathers. In Brazil many boys learn canoeing on outings with their parents, and the youngsters are equipped with small but real paddles.

For centuries Native American boys have played with bows and blunt-pointed arrows. In many cases the play soon became as assignment. They were expected to kill small game for the family's meals.

The tiny wooden spears with which young Australian aborigines still play are also used both as toys and as tools, for the real job of digging up small roots and the larvae of insects.

In New Guinea, at four years of age boys already know how to make fires for cooking, how to fetch wood, wash dishes, and peel fruit. They are also encouraged to play and work with tiny nets, fishing spears, and small canoes.

South American Indian boys also play with small traps with which they catch leaves, as practice for trapping game.

IMITATION

Despite the fact that so much has always been expected of small children in primitive cultures, such societies often give their children comparatively little formalized training. "No one teaches the smith's son his trade; when he is ready to work God shows him how" is an old proverb of the Tschi tribe in West Africa. It explains that little boys watch their fathers and imitate them so often that they gradually know how to do what they have been watching without ever being aware of having to learn it. Since it is God who gave the children their curiosity and desire to imitate, it is in truth God who teaches them.

Anthropologists and other observers who have lived among primitive people have often been amazed at the extreme precocity of their small children, despite the fact that they are on the whole unguided, unguarded, undisciplined, and unadmonished. These people, who live closer to nature than more sophisticated people, have always known intuitively what progressive educational theorists have been saying for the past 200 years in Europe, that children learn by doing and by imitating adult role models better than by hearing lectures and getting scoldings. As one exasperated modern child said to her mother, "I'd understand it perfickly if only you wouldn't explain it!"

Wordsworth (1770–1850) wrote that a small child acts "as if his whole vocation were endless imitation."

While imitation works well in cultures where the work is comparatively simple and physical, it has its limitations as a teacher in cultures where tasks are more complex, varied, and intellectually demanding and where parents are less frequently observed at work. The length of time it takes a society's children to learn what will be required of them as adults has been said to be a measure of how advanced that society is. The prolongation of infancy, which some people criticize as a sign of an infantile culture, is therefore in reality a sign of an unusually advanced culture. Children growing up in a highly complex society stay childish a long time, not because too little is expected of them but because so much is expected of them. There is so much for them to learn that the learning process is inevitably extended.

SOCRATES' OPINION ON EDUCATION AND CHILD REARING

The philospher Socrates (469–399 B.C.) believed that all wrongdoing is based on ignorance because no one desires bad things and that, therefore, the proper training of children in the moral virtues is enormously important. His method of teaching, called the "Socratic method," was unorthodox: Instead of pretending that the teacher knows everything and that the pupils' task is simply to repeat his words by rote, he asked the pupils questions instead of giving them answers, in order to encourage independent thinking.

It seems as strange to us today as it did to his devoted followers that these views got him in such trouble that he was condemned to death for perverting the young. Yet he willingly submitted to this sentence, instead of trying to escape as his friends and pupils urged him to do, because he believed it is a citizen's duty to submit to legal authority and that it is worse to do injustice than to suffer it.

Although his educational method was considered subversive, his opinions about raising children were certainly not. "Children are your riches," he told parents, "and upon their turning out well or ill depends the whole order of their father's house." And evidently he thought most fathers' houses were quite disorderly, because he complained about the behavior of the younger generation in conventional terms that sound remarkably like those many parents and teachers would use more than 2,000 years later. "Children now love luxury," he said,

> have bad manners, contempt for authority, disrespect for elders, and they love to chatter in place of exercise. Children are now tyrants and not servants of the household. They no longer stand up when an older person enters the room, they contradict their parents, they chatter in front of company, they gobble up the food on the table, they cross their legs and they tyrannize their teachers.

PLUTARCH ON CHILD REARING

An eloquent representative of the comparatively permissive school of discipline was Plutarch (c. 46–c. 120), the Greek biographer and moralist. In his essays, *Opera Moralia,* he stated that he was vehemently opposed to "uncontrolled and brutish" anger and spanking. "I say," he wrote,

> that children should be persuaded to gentlemanly behavior by admonition and reasoning, not, in heaven's name, by blows and torments. It must be obvious that such treatment is appropriate to slaves rather than to free people. People who are treated harshly become lethargic and recoil from the degradation. For the freeborn, praise and blame are more effective than any kind of abuse; praise incites them to excellence, blame deters them from shameful behavior.
>
> But reproof and approval must be in alternation and in varied ways. Whenever children grow bold, they should be reduced to modesty by reproof, and then again be encouraged by commendation. We should imitate the practice of nurses who, after they have made their babies cry, offer the breast to them again, to comfort them. But neither should we exalt and puff them up with compliments; excess of praise inflates conceit and enervates.

Plutarch was rather progressive in his views on the danger of expecting too much of small children. He criticized fathers who, in their eagerness to see their children excel, imposed "disproportionate tasks upon them," saying

243

Children cannot perform these, and therefore fail, whereupon they are depressed by their unhappy experience and therefore no longer receive instructions with docility. Just as plants are nourished by moderate applications of water but are choked by excess, so the mind grows by proportionate assignments but is submerged by too many. We must therefore give children respites from unrelieved toil, remembering that all human life is divided between intensity and relaxation. . . .To put the matter briefly, rest is the sauce of work. We may observe that this principle applies not only to living creatures but also to inanimate objects: bows and lyres we unstring, in order that we may be able to tighten them again.

CHILD REARING IN FIFTEENTH THROUGH EIGHTEENTH CENTURY EUROPE

Harshness of discipline and constant "belashing" of children and even of servants was normal until the fifteenth century. Agnes Paston, for instance, a highly religious and respectable English lady, mother of a large family, stated without embarrassment or apology in the Paston family's letters that she responded to the disobedience of her daughter Elizabeth by having her "beaten once in the week or twice, sometimes twice in one day, and her head broken in two or three places."

By the sixteenth century, parental severity was decreasing but still existed in many "good families." Poor little Lady Jane Grey (1537–1554) said that her parents expected her to do everything "even so perfitely as God made the world" and that if she failed to be "perfite" they punished her with "pinches, nippes, and bobbes." Sir Thomas Elyot, writing on child care in 1530, confirmed her complaint and said her parents frequently slapped and even kicked her.

Elizabeth Tanfield, an Elizabethan lady who married at age 15 and had 11 children, was known as a tenderhearted, affectionate, lenient mother. Yet when she felt it necessary to punish one of her children, she made the wrongdoer kiss the rod with which she whipped him, in order to show thorough penitence and submission. This was a common practice at this time. Shakespeare referred to it in *Two Gentlemen of Verona* when Julia compared the varying moods of love to those of a "testy babe" who will "scratch the nurse and presently all humbled kiss the rod."

Ben Jonson (1572–1637), the playwright and poet, who was an extremely devoted father, came out on the side of freedom and love against severity and sternness in his play *Every Man in His Humor* (1598), where he had a father advocate gentle means of correction for wayward conduct. He echoed the argument of Plutarch, saying:

> There is a way of winning more by love
> And urging modesty than fear.
> Force works on servile natures, not the free.
> He that's compelled to goodness may be good,
> But 'tis but for that fit; where others, drawn
> By softness and example, get the habit.
> Then, if they stray, but warn them; and the same
> They should for virtue have done, they'll do for shame.

Thomas More on Raising Children

Sir Thomas More (1478–1535) was another example of a devoted father who did not believe in using the rod. He managed to raise five children and 11 grandchildren without severity. Sir Thomas, known as Saint Thomas since he was canonized in 1935, believed strongly in authority, whether religious, civil, or parental, but he believed equally strongly in kindness. He stood against the prevailing brutal discipline of his era as firmly as he stood up for his religious principles even at the cost of his life when his former friend and patron King Henry VIII had him beheaded for refusing to approve of Henry's divorce from Queen Katherine and later marriage to Anne Boleyn.

More's son-in-law William Roper wrote a biography of Sir Thomas in which he told how More's training of his children began in their infancy. He set high standards for their conduct and learning and was one of the first people in England to advocate education for girls as well as boys. His children learned the Greek alphabet by shooting bows with arrows at the letters, and the rod was barred. His favorite method of persuasion was encouragement via frequent rewards for goodness: gifts of cake or fruit, many kisses, and words of warm praise. It was a merry household. Erasmus of Rotterdam used to come to visit. He described how much he enjoyed being taken into their garden to see a monkey, rabbits, a fox, a ferret, and a weasel in the children's private zoo.

Away on business trips, More whiled away the hours in a saddle writing his children, often in Latin verse:

In one of these letters he told the children how much he loved them, saying

> It is not so strange that I love you with my whole heart, for being a father is not a tie which can be ignored. Nature in her wisdom has attached the parent to the child and bound them spiritually together with a Herculean knot. This tie is the source of my consideration for your immature minds, a consideration which causes me to take you often into my arms. This tie is the reason why I used to dress you in silken garments and why I could never endure to hear you cry. You know, for example, how often I kissed you. My whip was invariably a peacock's tail. Even this I wielded hesitantly and gently so that sorry welts might not disfigure your tender seats. Brutal and unworthy to be called a father is he who does not himself weep at the tears of his child.

How Spanking Affected One Child
—Martin Luther

Without the parental harshness that was customary in the fifteenth century, the Protestant Reformation might never have occurred. Martin Luther (1483–1546) began to resent authority in early childhood. His parents, although they were "good" people, punished him so severely that he remembered it many years later and even said their harshness was what had made him leave home to become a monk. "My father once whipped me so that I ran away and felt ugly toward him until he was at pains to win me," he said once. At another time he said, "My mother beat me for stealing a nut, until the blood came. Such strict discipline drove me to the monastery, although she meant it well." Yet his parents' roughness was by no means extraordinary or excessive by the standards of the time. When young Martin went to school he encountered worse: "I was caned in a single morning fifteen times for nothing at all."

Tudor Conduct Books

In Tudor England, a large number of *conduct books* were written to guide married couples, especially parents, and almost all were best sellers. Some of them, such as *A Work for Householders* (1530) by Richard Whitford and *The Golden Grove* (1599) by William Vaughan, advocated severe strictness. But most of them, including *De Civilitate Morum Libellus* by Erasmus (translated into English in 1532), *Rules of a Christian Lyfe* (1534) by Pico de Mirandola (translated by Sir Thomas Elyot), *The Christian State of Matrimony* (1546) by Henry Bullinger, *The Christian Man's Closet* (1590) by Bartholomew Batty, *Christian Economie* (1590) by William Perkins, and *The Court of Good Councell* (1607), an anonymous English translation of *Civil Conversation* by Stephano Guzzo, advocated moderation, encouraging children with praise and gifts and, in Perkins's words, using "the rod only when words did not prevail."

Bartholomew Batty quoted from Cicero, Seneca, Socrates, and Saint Augustine, to show that intelligent and moderate discipline was an important parental duty. Henry Bullinger said that good example is the best form of discipline; parents should "act before their little ones as they would act before God." However, children should not go uncorrected, because it is "better that children weep than old men." Although spanking with "the rod of correction" is sometimes necessary, said Bullinger, it should always be done "with love and not in a way that would cause fear."

In response to a widow's request for advice on how to select a husband to help her bring up her children, the poet and statesman Sir John Davies (1569–1626) wrote verses about parental discipline:

> The parcels of thyself (thy children) strike
> When they misdo; yet, not so often as then:
> Sometimes to wink at what we do mislike
> Is well to see to do, like prudent men;
> That is, when sweetness, more than sharpness, will
> Their proper good, keep from improper ill.

Sir Thomas Elyot (c. 1490–1546) had a balanced view. He objected to parents being too harsh and using "strypes" but also objected to parents being too indulgent. He said "too much love is not love at all."

Erasmus (1466–1536) told parents they should let their children "drink the seeds of love" before disciplining them. He laid down strict rules though, about the good manners children should practice, even in bed. In those days when it was customary for several people, both family members and their guests, to sleep together. Erasmus said children should learn to be considerate by lying still so as not to disturb those in bed with them, never turning over unless the others did, and they should take the spot nearest the wall so that their guests or elders would be able to get out of bed easily if they wished. The cranky morning-after mood of a child who has had to endure a night like that may be the origin of the phrase about "getting up on the wrong side of the bed."

Stephano Guzzo, in his conduct book *Civil Conversation,* published in 1607, said wise parents could "keep their children in awe with only shaking their heads at them or using some such sign."

Richard Whitford disagreed. He published the sternest of all the conduct books, *A Work for Householders.* It became a favorite parental guide not only in Tudor England but also in Colonial America. This puritanical author urged whipping with the rod if a small child was "stiff hearted, stubborn, and froward" and said older children who misbehave should be put on a diet of brown bread and water. He proposed a list of commandments for children and suggested that they recite the following verse if they were guilty of breaking them:

If I lie, backbite, or steal,
If I curse, scorn, mock, or swear,
If I chide, fight, strive, or threat,
Then I am worthy to be beat,
Good mother, or mistress mine;
If any of these nine
I trespass to your knowing,
With a new rod and a fine,
Early, naked, before I dine
Amend me with a scourging.

Montaigne's Condemnation of Violence in Child Rearing and Education

Michel de Montaigne (1533–1592) spoke fluent Latin by the age of five. He enjoyed reading classical literature at an age when most children are still struggling with "c-a-t spells cat." He claimed that this precocity was due to his father's "peculiar" educational experimenting and not to any intellectual superiority of his own. His father hired a Latin-speaking tutor for him and also forbade anyone in their house to speak to the boy in any other language.

Montaigne found his first literary delight in the fables of *Metamorphoses* by Ovid. "Though only seven or eight years old," he wrote, "I slipped away from every other pleasure to read it" because "it was the easiest book I knew and, by reasons of the matter therein contained, most agreeing with my young age." He greatly preferred it to adventure tales and fairy stories "and such idle time-consuming and wit-besotting trash of books wherein youth commonly amuses itself."

However, Montaigne tells us that the head start in "grandeur of soul and knowledge" that his father hoped to give him by exposing him early to the cultures of ancient Greece and Rome did not last long. "My peculiar education served no purpose," he wrote many years later. "There is not a schoolboy in the middle grades who cannot call himself more learned than I." After starting school at the age of six and hating it, "my Latin quickly sank . . . . By disuse I have since lost all power to wield it. I have not spoken it, and scarcely written it, in 40 years."

Montaigne loved his father and was grateful for his preschool educational experiment, saying "he is not to be blamed for failing to reap the fruits appropriate to such excellent culture." He blamed himself primarily for his failure to sustain his head start. The problem, said this former child prodigy, was that he was not really a prodigy at all, but actually a rather slow child with a "weak memory" whose native language just happened to be Latin:

Though I possessed a sound and healthy constitution and a tolerably gentle and amenable nature I was, with it all, so heavy, lumpish and drowsy, I could not be roused from my laziness—even to get me out to play . . . . under this sluggish disposition I nourished bold imagination and opinions beyond my age. But I had a slow wit that would go no faster than it was led, a delayed grasp of things, a slack inventiveness, and, to top it off, an incredibly poor memory. It is no wonder that out of all this my father was able to extract very little of worth.

Montaigne's Indictment of Sixteenth-Century Schools

In addition to blaming himself, Montaigne blamed the schools he went to for failing to develop the early skills and interests he had acquired, saying "there is nothing more charming than the little children of France. But they generally deceive our hopes and grow up showing no particular excellence." French schools, he claimed, "turn them into dullards."

In angrily describing the elementary schools of his day, he gave a wistful description of what they should have been like, a description that may have seemed ridiculously fanciful when he wrote it but quite normal to the many children of later generations who have been able to go to good schools since the benign concepts of the kindergarten and progressive education have been established. In his *Essays* he wrote,

> The strict discipline of our schools has always displeased me. They are little else but jails for our imprisoned youth . . . . Enter one of them when the lessons begin, and you will hear nothing but the cries of tortured children and the noise of teachers drunk with wrath. A pretty way this to awaken in tender and timorous souls an appetite for learning! How much more decent it would be to see the classroom strewn with greenery and posies than with the bloody stumps of birch and willow! If I had my way I'd paint the walls . . . with pictures of Joy and Gladness, of Flora and the Graces. Where children go for profit, let them also find their pleasure.

Despite these strong feelings about his own and his schools' failings, Montaigne grew up to become one of the most admired, wittiest, and wisest essayists of all time, so it seems that his father's ambition for him won out in the end. Neither his own "laziness" nor poor schooling were able to turn Michel de Montaigne into a "dullard."

Perhaps this was because his family life was happy enough to counteract his experiences in school. It was not only teachers he condemned but other children's parents who were less loving than his own. He opposed spanking with a passion and eloquence rarely if ever equalled by anyone else writing on the subject. In one of his essays he wrote:

> They tell me that in all my childhood I never tasted the whip but twice, and then lightly enough . . . . Passing along our streets, how many times I have wanted to stage a violent row in order to avenge boys I have seen attacked, beaten, and flayed by some father or mother insane with wrath! You see them rush forth, their eyes blazing and their throats roaring, often against a baby just off the breast. And behold, the little fellow is lamed and stunned with blows, while our courts pay no attention to it—as though these wounded and crippled victims were not members of our commonwealth . . . . Such behavior is no longer correction, but revenge. Punishment is a medicine for the young, and would we tolerate a doctor who raged against his patient?

248

I condemn all violence in the education of a young soul which is meant for honor and freedom. There is I know not how much servility in rigor and constraint, and I believe that what you cannot accomplish by reason, prudence and skill, you will never be able to do by force. I was brought up in that manner, and I used it with Leonor, my only daughter. [Actually, Montaigne had five children, but all except one died in early infancy.] Up to the age of five or more she had never been corrected for her childish faults (her mother's indulgence agreeing readily with mine), except by words, and those very gentle. Even if my method should not succeed, I would place the blame somewhere else, because I know it to be natural and just. I would have followed it even more scrupulously toward boys, since they are destined for even less subjection. I would have made it my business to fill their hearts with frankness and freedom. I have never noticed that whipping does anything to children but make them either cowardly or stubborn.

Fortunately, primary schools have improved enormously since the era when Montaigne indicted them. He would be delighted and stunned if he could visit a good modern kindergarten with its small and brightly painted chairs and tables, large windows, plants and aquariums, easels and musical instruments, picture books and pictures on the walls, and well-equipped play corners and playgrounds.

Royal Child Rearing

Variations between indulgence and severity and reliance on "the rod of correction," even by fond parents, was common in France in the seventeenth century among the aristocracy as much as among the "common" people. The fascinating diary kept by M. Heroard, a pediatrician to the children of the King of France, contains many entries noting the frequency with which the heir to the throne was beaten.

The first occasion was in October 1603 when the dauphin was two years old: "Waked at 8 o'clock; was naughty; whipped for the first time." Another time the diary says: "Went off to his room; screaming at the top of his voice, and was soundly whipped." Then again: "Naughty, whipped (for refusing to eat). Calming down, he asked for his dinner and dined."

M. Heroard must have been almost as distressed as the little prince at these beatings, because he believed in gentler methods of training. He wrote a treatise on education that expressed his ideals of discipline:

We should lisp with little children, by which I mean we should accommodate ourselves to their weakness and teach them rather by means of gentleness and patience than by harshness and hastiness. . . .We ought to reward them by little gifts appropriate to their rightdoing, and only punish them in such a manner as will make them feel a small sense of shame at their naughtiness rather than by terrifying them with the fear of punishment.

The king, however, disagreed with his pediatrician. When the dauphin was six years old, the king wrote the dauphin's governess saying, "I am annoyed that you have not whipped my son. I order you to whip him every time he is willful or naughty, knowing by my own experience that nothing else did me so much good. At his age I was well whipped, and I know I profited."

Such reminders would have seemed unnecessary because by the time the future king was four years old he was already having nightmares as the result of whippings. It was customary in the seventeenth century, when children had been seriously naughty, not to whip them promptly after the misbehavior but to save up such punishment for the following morning, perhaps to remind the children the next day not to repeat the performance. The result of this in the dauphin's case was to prolong fright: fear of what was going to happen to him in the morning often kept him awake at night or, if he slept, gave him nightmares.

The whippings and nightmares continued even after he became King Louis XIII at the age of nine. In 1611, after he had been king for a whole year, his doctor's diary contains an entry saying, "The king waked at midnight in a fright because he expected to be whipped in the morning." Why? Surely nobody other than a seventeenth-century boy-king was ever whipped for such a reason: it was "because he had been obstinate in learning the reply he was to make to the deputies of the reformed religion meeting at Saumur."

This very rough treatment of a sovereign majesty is quite a contrast to the hands-off policy regarding children in many other royal families. In Spain it was an offense punishable by death to lay a hand for any reason whatsoever on an heir to the throne—an *infante* (male) or an *infanta* (female). This rule was enforced so literally that once, when two courtiers saved the life of an infanta by pulling her away from a horse about to trample her, they had to flee the country in order to avoid the death penalty for having touched her.

In Tudor England, young princes and princesses were reared along with playmates called *whipping boys* who acted as stand-ins when disciplinary action was thought necessary. If a prince was naughty enough to deserve a whipping, this was duly given but not to the culprit because his body was considered too sacred to suffer such an indignity. Instead, he had to watch while his innocent friend got beaten for what he had done.

Child Rearing in the Age of Enlightenment

In the seventeenth and eighteenth centuries, often called the Age of Enlightenment, parental affection for children continued to coexist with cruelty to them in the name of discipline.

Susanna Wesley, mother of the famous John Wesley who grew up to become the founder of Methodism in 1738, was a devoted mother, but she was also strict. She gave birth 19 times but raised only 6 children because 13 died while still very young. John, her fifteenth child, wrote of her, in admiration, that she taught her babies "of a year old and even less to fear the rod and cry softly. . . .The odious noise of the crying of children was rarely heard in the house."

Two philosophers, one from England and the other from France, were the most influential educational theorists of this era. Both of them rejected the Calvinist idea that all infants are born desperately wicked and must be rigidly tamed to become civilized. Yet some of their actions and theories might seem suitable only for the desperately wicked.

John Locke (1632–1704)

Locke was a distinguished scholar, but his book, *Thoughts on Education*, published in 1690, contains a strange mixture of sensible and unsound advice on child rearing. He believed in hardening the young, and the many mothers who faithfully followed the advice in his extremely popular and influential book sometimes carried it to amazing extremes, with disastrous effects on their children. He recommended icy baths for infants and young children at a time when many adults would wash no more than their faces and hands for fear of catching cold, and he thought children should wear shoes with thin soles so that water could leak in, thinking such procedures would inure them against the cold. He cautioned against feeding children meat and fruit, and recommended having them drink warm beer instead of water, which was, in fact, often polluted. His advice was influential, for even in nineteenth-century America beer was recommended for children rather than water.

Mary Martha Sherwood (1775–1851), a writer of popular children's books, was brought up according to Locke's theories and reminisced unnostalgically about her childhood. In *Mrs. Sherwood and Her Books for Children*, "it was the fashion," she said, "for children to wear iron collars round the neck, with blackboards strapped over the shoulders." This was supposed to insure good posture. She continued,

> To one of these I was subjected from my sixth to my thirteenth year. I generally did all my lessons standing in stocks with this same collar round my neck; it was put on in the morning and seldom taken off till late in the evening . . . . At the same time I had the plainest possible food; dry bread and cold milk were my principle food, and I never sat in a chair in my mother's presence.

Sometimes the practices advocated by Locke weakened, instead of strengthening, children. The poet Robert Southey (1774–1843) never forgave Locke for having advocated long, ice-cold baths every morning for children, which he blamed for the early death of his delicate young sister. This severity was intended to strengthen children physically, not to punish them for misbehavior. Like primitives who put children through physical torture in order to teach them courage yet considered it an outrage to spank them as punishment for a moral lapse, Locke stood for moderation in regard to discipline. He was anti-indulgence but also, vehemently, antiwhipping. He predicted future regrets for parents who spoil their "fondlings" by letting them have whatever they cry for and do whatever they please, saying that when the children are "too big to be dandled, and their parents can no longer make use of them as playthings, then they complain that the brats are untoward and perverse." Yet he also strongly protested against violence toward little ones and blamed such parental behavior for the children's misbehavior. He said parents teach children to be violent, vengeful, and cruel by using violence themselves, "a lesson which most children every day hear." Furthermore, he said, another result of parental violence is to turn a child into "a low-spirited moped creature. . .with his unnatural sobriety, he may please silly people who commend tame inactive children, because they make no noise nor give them any trouble" but that, having had his spirit broken, he will probably be "all his life an useless thing to himself and others."

Jean Jacques Rousseau (1712–1778)

This tremendously popular writer was a most unlikely person to set himself up as an expert on child rearing. He was mentally unstable, warped by an extremely unhappy childhood; his mother died immediately after his birth and his father bitterly resented him and mistreated him. At age 16 he ran away. For years he lived in poverty with Thérèse le Vasseur, an illiterate servant girl whom he refused to marry. They had five children, but he also refused to let her raise them. As soon as each one was born he took it from her and sent it away to a foundling hospital, never seeing any of them again. He was also paranoid, with a violent temper, and quarreled with almost everyone he knew. Yet he wrote many books, two of which, published in 1762, were important: *The Social Contract* and *Emile*. Each contained a combination of wisdom and nonsense, and they incurred the condemnation of leading members of both church and state, institutions he despised. The first book proclaimed the doctrines of liberty, equality, and fraternity that inspired the French Revolution, but the second one, named for a fictional boy, a "noble savage" raised in an idealized natural environment, struck a forceful blow against "civilized" society's treatment of its children, advocating a more natural and less pedantic way to train and develop children's mental, physical, and moral capacities. His theories were a great influence on many parents and educational reformers like Friedrich Froebel (1782–1852), who established the first kindergarten, and Johann Pestalozzi (1746–1827), a pioneer in providing free education for orphans and the poor, and a founder of progressive education.

Child Rearing in Plymouth Colony

The whipping post and "a paire of stocks" were standard architectural features of every "Constablerick" in the Plymouth Colony in Massachusetts founded in 1620.

The Pilgrims believed that Sunday was a day to keep holy by lengthy worship and by lengthy lashings. Church services lasted from 8 A.M. until noon and then again from 2 P.M. until 6 P.M. and even small children were required to attend. For eight hours every single Sunday the youngsters remained in the upstairs gallery, along with Indians and Negroes. Near them stood an "anciente widow" over 60 who was to be "obeyed as a mother in Israel." This deaconess stayed "in a conveniente place...with a little birchen rod in her hand" and it was her job "to keep little children in great awe, from disturbing the congregation."

Downstairs, the theoretically undisturbed congregation was under similar surveillance: a deacon, also armed with a rod, was on the prowl for adult sinners who might doze off during the long services. If anyone should be unfortunate enough to snore, he would promptly receive a sharp rap on the skull.

The children, watching from upstairs, are said to have "larfed out loud" when the tithingman used his rod on those elders who were caught napping. And "larfing" was only one of the many "indecencies" that Plymouth's stubbornly spirited young children committed during the services. "Boys will be boys," evidently, despite the omnipresence of a Puritan deaconess. Jonathan Edwards (1703–1758), one of Plymouth's sternest preachers, said that "ye wretched Boys" were "young vipers, yea, infinitely more hateful than vipers to God." They were charged with fidgeting, stamping their feet, pinching each other, giggling, sitting down during two-hour prayers, "frequently passing and repassing by one another in the Galleries," sneaking outdoors during the lengthy sermons, and even "running out of ye meeting house before prayer be done and ye blessing pronounced."

Even the little girls were naughty. They too fidgeted, stamped their feet, giggled, and furthermore pulled each other's hair, "larfed out loud" at the boys' "indecencies" and made eyes at the boys. The behavior of both girls and boys was so terrible, in fact, that it brought the horrors of war down upon them in chastisement, according to Pastor John Cotton (1584–1652), known as the Patriarch of New England. He said the Indians' attacks on the colony during King Philip's War in 1675 were the sign of God's anger at the behavior of these children.

Finally, the ineffective deaconesses were replaced by *inspectors of youth*, also armed with birch rods, appointed by the parishes to keep order "in ye pue of ye wretched boys." These were instructed "to see that they behave comlie, and to use such raps and blows as shall be meet." They were to put an end to all "Smiling and Larfing and Intiseing others to the same evil." Despite their switches, however, "whispering and Larfing in the meeting house" continued, and the inspectors of youth were ordered to strike harder and more often, and were specifically instructed "that the same course be pursued with the girls."

Thus the Plymouth Colony should have learned something that many a parent has learned since: children who are spanked too frequently become so used to it that it becomes necessary to spank them harder and harder and more often.

Even when these children got home after the eight-hour church services were over, they were not allowed to relax. No socializing or visiting was allowed in New England on the Sabbath. The only traveling permitted on that day was to and from church, unless there was an emergency justifying payment of a fee to obtain a special travel permit or passport. There was even a law in Connecticut that "No Woman shall kiss her child on the Sabbath." And "female children," or "church children," alias adult female members of the church, knew they would be severely scolded by the pastor if they should ever suffer their children "to play on Sabbath evenings."

All in all, *suffer* seems an appropriate word to use in connection with these little children of the Pilgrim Fathers, though not by any means in the sense of *allow*, which is the meaning of the word in Jesus's famous phrase, "Suffer the little children and forbid them not to come unto unto me." He had been indignantly reproving the apostles for trying to restrain the noisy freedom some small childen were displaying in his presence, but his permissive message certainly got lost in translation from Aramaic into English.

If this Sabbath day severity toward childish high spirits bothered any kind-hearted parents, it is unlikely that they argued about it, unless they felt so strongly that they considered it worthwhile to pay a 40-shilling fine (equivalent to over $100 today), because another rule about Sabbath observance was that married couples were forbidden to quarrel on the Lord's Day.

VIEWS ON PUNISHMENT

The Puritans' severity towards the young was in great contrast to the way children were treated by their neighbors, Native Americans.

John Frost, author of a book called *Historical Sketches of the Indians,* published in 1854, wrote that "corporal punishment is seldom used for the correction of children . . . . They think that corporal punishment breaks the spirit of the child, and in this they appear to be wiser than their white brethren. Parental love should persuade and guide the bold of spirit, not destroy their courage."

Most American Indian tribes, for example, enjoy having wild, obstreperous children. And they are deeply shocked at the idea of spanking a small child.

Among the Winnebago Indians there is a saying: "If you have a child, do not strike it. If you hit a child, you will merely drive more naughtiness into it."

In Guyana, punishment has traditionally been considered something suitable only for a dog, not for a child.

In Borneo physical punishments are almost unknown; the most a parent will normally do is to tweak a disobedient child's ear and ask if he is deaf.

Physical and moral toughening-up is considered a necessary part of growing up in primitive societies, in view of warlike neighbors and/or harsh weather and living conditions. This often involves a certain amount of cruelty, but physical punishment in order to correct childish misbehavior is rare in nonliterate cultures.

There are several reasons for this. For one thing, children hardened to endure the many physical discomforts of primitive existence would probably not be greatly impressed by blows and cudgels. Other methods of discipline make more of an impact. For another thing, frequent discipline is less necessary in a simple society than in a complex one. Fewer things are regarded as wrong, and there is apt to be less temptation to deviate from behavior considered right. These societies change very slowly, and the mere fact that something has always been done a certain way and that a child hardly ever sees or can even imagine a different way of behaving is usually sufficient, in a simple, homogeneous culture, to produce conformity in the young. The moral force of unanimous disapproval, and in unusually severe cases of misbehavior, ostracism by the entire community, also compels obedience in most matters.

It is usually only when children are leaving childhood via puberty rites (which are sometimes held long before physical puberty, as early as six or seven) that brutal treatment occurs. Throughout the years of infancy and early childhood, except for the simple and usually quite painless tasks expected of them, primitive children are normally treated with permissiveness, kindness, affection, tolerance, and respect. Much behavior that other people would consider "naughty" is encouraged or amusedly tolerated. Unrestrained behavior is considered a sign of health and vigor.

For serious misbehavior, however, every society has some type of punishment; some mild, some harsh. Many Native Americans use ridicule as punishment. Blackening of the face, tying a child to a post, or immersion in a river have been among corrective measures used, as well as sending the child out of the lodge; sometimes a child might be kept a whole day in this situation as punishment for grave misconduct. Among some tribes in India and Africa, a father's or mother's solemn curse (which could later be ritually lifted) on an unusually disobedient child has sometimes been a device used.

Another dire method has been warnings or threats about the supernaturally evil results of evil-doing. A very naughty child might be told that horns would grow on his forehead, or that he would turn into a dog or a raccoon or at the very least become ill. Since little children everywhere tend to believe trustingly whatever their parents tell them, such warnings and curses would be, of course, extremely frightening.

PUNISHMENT OF CHILDREN—QUOTES

The fault no child ever loses is the one he was most punished for.
—*Cesare Baccarias (1738–1794)*

Being human we are all liable to err. It is our duty to be understanding and kind towards one who has committed an error and is repentant. . . .Punishment does not purify; if anything it only hardens children.
—*Mahatma Gandhi (1869–1948)*

Correction accomplishes much; encouragement accomplishes more.
—*Johann Wolfgang von Goethe (1749–1832)*

I would not have little children much tormented about punctilios or niceties of breeding. Never trouble yourself about those faults in them which you know age will cure.　　　　　　　　　　　　　　　　　—*John Locke (1632–1704)*

Distrust all in whom the impulse to punish is powerful.
—*Friedrich Wilhelm Nietsche (1844–1900)*

Children are never too tender to be whipped—like tough beefsteaks, the more you beat them, the more tender they become.
—*Edgar Allan Poe (1809–1849)*

Lacking all sense of right and wrong, a child can do nothing which is morally evil, or which merits either punishment or reproof.
—*Jean Jacques Rousseau (1712–1778),* Emile, *1762*

Children should be led into the right paths not by severity, but by persuasion.
—*Terence (185–159 B.C.)*

He that spareth the rod hateth his son.　　　　　　　　—*Proverbs 13: 24*

Beat your child once a day. If you don't know why, the child does.
—*Chinese proverb*

Spare the rod and spoil the child.　　　　　　　　　—*English proverb*

One who loves well, chastises well.　　　　　　　　　—*French proverb*

THE EDUCATION OF JOHN STUART MILL

In his autobiography, John Stuart Mill (1806–1873) denied that he was a prodigy, just as Michel de Montaigne had done. However, the all-time record in IQs, based on research by Stanford University into past geniuses, appears to be a figure of over 200 for Mill.

He began the study of ancient Greek language and literature, starting with Aesop's Fables, at three. By age seven he had read Herodotus, Xenophon, Socrates, and the dialogues of Plato in Greek; English philosophers and historians, among them David Hume and Edward Gibbon; and an English translation of Plutarch, which he said he read "with great delight."

In his autobiography, he attributed his intellectual powers entirely to his father's "unusual and remarkable" educational experiment which gave him "during the years of childhood an amount of knowledge in what are considered the higher branches of education which is seldom acquired (if acquired at all) until the age of manhood."

The result of this experiment, he claimed in his *Autobiography,* shows

the ease with which this may be done, and places in a strong light the wretched
waste of so many precious years.... If I had been by nature extremely quick of
apprehension, or of a remarkably active and energetic character, the trial would
not be conclusive, but in all these natural gifts I am rather below than above par;
what I could do, could assuredly be done by any boy or girl of average capacity
and healthy physical constitution.

Unprejudiced judges may question Mill's opinion that this education was obtained
with "ease." His father, he said, "exerted an amount of labor, care and perseverance rarely,
if ever, employed for a similar purpose." The father demanded much of himself but
required even more of his little boy: "My father, in all his teaching, demanded of me not
only the utmost that I could do, but what I could by no possibility have done."

These excessively high standards prevented the prodigy from becoming conceited.
He was kept

> with extreme vigilance, out of the way of hearing myself praised . . . . I was
> not at all aware that my attainments were anything unusual at my age . . . . If
> I thought anything about myself, it was that I was rather backward in my stud-
> ies, since I always found myself so, in comparison with what my father expected
> from me.
>
> I grew up healthy and hardy, but I could do no feats of skill or physical
> strength, and knew none of the ordinary bodily exercises . . . . Though no
> holidays were allowed, lest the habit of work should be broken, and a taste for
> idleness acquired, I had ample leisure in every day to amuse myself; but as I had
> no boy companions . . . my amusements, which were mostly solitary, were in
> general of a quiet, if not a bookish, turn . . . .
>
> My father's health required considerable and constant exercise, and he
> walked habitually before breakfast . . . . I always accompanied him, and with
> my earliest recollections of green fields and wild flowers is mingled that of the
> account I gave him daily of what I had read the day before . . . . I made
> notes on slips of paper while reading, and from these, in the morning walks, I
> told the story to him . . . . In these frequent talks about the books I read, he
> used, as oppportunity offered, to give me explanations and ideas respecting civi-
> lization, government, morality, mental cultivation, which he required me to re-
> state to him after in my own words . . . .
>
> Of children's books, any more than of playthings, I had scarcely any, except
> an occasional gift from a relation or acquaintance: among those I had, *Robinson
> Crusoe* was preeminent and continued to delight me through all my boyhood. It
> was no part however of my father's system to exclude books of amusement,
> though he allowed them very sparingly.
>
> The element which was chiefly deficient in his moral relation to his chil-
> dren was that of tenderness . . . . He resembled most Englishmen in being
> ashamed of the signs of feeling, and by the absence of demonstration, starving
> the feelings themselves. If we consider further that he was in the trying position
> of sole teacher, and add to this that his temper was constitutionally irritable, it is
> impossible not to feel true pity for the father who did, and strove to do, so much
> for his children, who would have so valued their affection, yet who must have
> been constantly feeling that fear of him was drying it up at its source.

Most people today reading these lines would probably feel far less pity for the father
than for the small boy, frightened of his constantly irritable, demanding father, deprived of

toys, playmates, holidays, physical exercise, games, praise, and affection. It seems small wonder that when John Stuart Mill grew up he became estranged from his family and had a nervous breakdown at age 20 that resulted in a pathological depression lasting five years, and that when he matured as a philosopher he "never, indeed, wavered in the conviction that happiness is the test of all rules of conduct and the end of life."

The unhappy boy nonetheless felt lifelong gratitude to his father and praised his training, saying,

> If I have accomplished anything, I owe it . . . to the fact that through the early training bestowed on me by my father, I started, I may fairly say, with an advantage of a quarter of a century over my contemporaries . . .
>
> Most boys or youths who have had much knowledge drilled into them, have their mental capacities not strengthened, but overlaid by it. They are rammed with mere facts, and with the opinions or phrases of other people, and these are accepted as a substitute for the power to form opinions of their own . . . . Mine, however, was not an education of cram. My father never permitted anything which I learned to degenerate into a mere exercise of memory. He strove to make the understanding not only go along with every step of the teaching but, if possible, precede it. Anything which could be found out by thinking I never was told, until I had exhausted my efforts to find it out for myself.

And he concluded: "A pupil from whom nothing is ever demanded which he cannot do, never does all he can."

LITERACY AND ILLITERACY
Learning to Read in Eighteenth-Century England
Hornbooks

The earliest books in England intended solely for children were *hornbooks*. These were of ancient origin and by the eighteenth century had, in many cases, been superseded, but for a long time, particularly in schools for young children called Dames' Schools, they were still used as primers. They were especially popular in these schools because expenses were a major consideration and they could be bought for a penny or twopence each. Also they were very durable; they could not be torn or dog-eared or defaced like paper books, and they outlasted many generations of children. The traditional hornbook was a sheet of vellum mounted on a wooden paddle and covered with transparent horn. Its edges were bound with metal and, in the case of the well-to-do, with embossed or gilded leather. On the back there was sometimes a colored picture. On the front was the alphabet and the Lord's Prayer, and generally Roman numerals were put at the bottom.

On some of the later printed sheets, a few two-syllable words were given, and even some short edifying verses, such as:

He that ne'er learns his A B C
For ever will a blockhead be.

The hornbook's handle contained a hole for a cord, and when children went to school, they carried the hornbooks attached to their waists or swinging from their necks. If a child got into a squabble he could use the hornbook as a weapon. Teachers often used it too, as a weapon of discipline; hence the term paddling, meaning spanking.

Gingerbread Books

There were even cheaper forms of these books produced by gingerbread bakers. "Hot spiced gingerbread!" was one of the common street cries in old London, and for youngsters a slice imprinted with the letters of the alphabet was sold in the streets at a halfpenny. Of course, these were not durable like the hornbooks they imitated, but they were enormously popular among the young because children were allowed to eat each letter as they named it.

Printed Books

As the printing process gradually expanded, printed books began to replace hornbooks and gingerbread slices. Stationers started including little books for instructing children among their wares. Booksellers abandoned expensive leather bindings for these and instead produced small volumes of 16 or 32 pages, with stiff paper covers and wood-block illustrations. These books were the very first paperbacks. Thus today's large and successful paperback industry owes its origin to young children.

Alphabet Books

For the youngest children, the alphabet was also taught through books, which were merely a few pages of rhymes. For instance, quite early in the eighteenth century a certain "T.W." in London published a famous alphabet rhyme that began with the following couplet:

A was an archer who shot at a frog
B was a butcher who had a great dog.

It ended with the short anouncement that:
Z was one Zeno the Great but he's dead.

Another rhyming alphabet book, entitled *Reading Made Easy*, was published in 1786 and sold for sixpence. It featured a picture of a studious lad seated at a desk reading, and opened with the lines:

A was an acorn that grew on an oak.
B was a boy who delights in his book.

Learning to Read in America

In Colonial America there were virtually no public schools for almost two centuries. Wealthy Americans sent their sons away to boarding schools in England, or arranged for private schooling, but most children remained illiterate.

The Pilgrims in New England announced their intent to establish a "common school" in 1624 but were delayed by "want of a fitt person or hithertoo means to maintain one." What little instruction their children received was given at home. A few families got together and provided small private schools for their sons, but daughters and nieces were not allowed to attend, because education of girls was thought to be "a vain and idle thing." Even the boys got little learning; it was considered enough if they knew how to write, count and read the Bible.

Finally, in l690, *The New England Primer* was published, and in l693 the town fathers hired a teacher and decreed that "every scollar that Coms to wright or syfer or to lern latten, shall pay 3 pence pr. weke; if to Read onlie, then to pay 3 half pence pr. weke."

Then, in l705, a law was passed in Massachusetts requiring all towns with 70 or more inhabitants to maintain a grammar school or be fined five pounds a year. However, many towns preferred to pay the fine rather than have the expenses of maintaining a school and a teacher.

The New England Primer became one of the two basic books used to teach reading, not only in New England but all over the country, for more than a century. The other, published in l783, was Part I of *Grammatical Institute of the English Language* by Noah Webster (l758–l843), who later became a professor, a college president, and an author of adult dictionaries. His *Grammatical Institute* was renamed as *Webster's Elementary Speller,* though it was far from elementary by today's standards. Its word lists ranged from *bag* and *cat* to such mouthfuls as *equiponderant.* Later it was renamed again as *Webster's Spelling Book* and also known as *The Blue-Backed Speller.* Part II, on grammar, was published in 1784, and Part III, a reader, was published in l786. This three-volume set sold millions of copies and was the standard schoolbook throughout the United States until l836 when the first and second of *McGuffey's Eclectic Readers* were published.

McGuffey's Readers

William Holmes McGuffey (l800–l873) was one of ll children. He was raised on a farm and became a Presbyterian minister, college professor, and college president. As a young schoolteacher he was dissatisfied with both *The New England Primer* and *Webster's Spelling Book,* so he produced a series of readers of his own filled with stories and pictures of children at play, at work, and at school, to make it fun for children to learn to read.

The series began in 1836 with the *First Reader* and *Second Reader,* in which he confined himself to teaching the alphabet, penmanship, simple spelling, and basic rules of conduct, using only words of one or two syllables. In *McGuffey's Primer* and his *Third* and *Fourth Eclectic Readers* (published in l837), he introduced children to a wider range of stories and poems and taught advanced vocabulary, spelling, and character training.

His younger brother, Alexander McGuffey, compiled an anthology of English and American literature called *McGuffey's Rhetorical Guide;* it was published separately in l844 and added to the series in l853 as *McGuffey's Fifth Eclectic Reader.* With its many selections from great historians, orators, novelists, essayists, and poets, this set of schoolbooks was a literary storehouse for family reading, cherished long after school days were over. By l860 sales were exceeding 2 million copies a year. They became the basic schoolbooks in 37 states from the time of their publication until the l920s. Ten publishers got rich on them, but all William McGuffey got from them, aside from satisfaction, was $1,000 for the entire series, and Alexander was paid only $500 for his *Rhetorical Guide.* Altogether more than l25 million copies of *McGuffey's Readers* have been sold, and in 1993 the Smithsonian Institution reissued them 60 years after they had gone out of print.

In the Twentieth Century

Since the l930s, controversies have raged in the United States about how to teach reading. No one textbook is widely accepted any more. Publishers print lavish books filled with color illustrations, but the books' texts are criticized by many parents, historians, sociologists, and representatives of special interest groups.

Academics eliminated from texts all words considered hard for children at different grade levels to understand, although Robert Louis Stevenson, Rudyard Kipling, Dr. Seuss, and other successful writers for children maintained that putting "big" words in a children's book intrigues children and expands their intellect. This simplification resulted in eliminating serious literature from elementary schoolbooks.

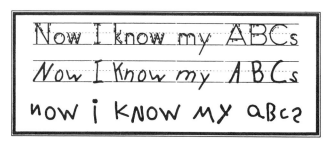

Dick and Jane and similarly bland fare replaced the classics in the 1940s and 1950s. In turn, *Dick and Jane* fell out of favor in the 1960s and 1970s for promoting suburbia and its middle class values that offended many feminists and ethnic minorities.

In the 1950s, spelling was de-emphasized and children were taught to read by the "whole word method" instead of through phonetics. It was considered wrong to push children or to let them experience the trauma of failure, so if they showed no aptitude for or interest in reading they got promoted from grade to grade anyway. As a result of this practice, a great number of high school graduates were discovered to be functionally illiterate, that is, unable to read well enough to follow directions on a map or to understand instructions in a document. Finally, this discovery culminated in a national scandal, and a book called *Why Johnny Can't Read* by Rudolf Flesch became a best-seller in 1953.

The cultural consensus that made *McGuffey's Readers* so popular all over the country no longer exists, and diverse groups now inveigh against each other to control what children are allowed to read in school. In an effort to avoid offending anyone—for example, the many different religious groups in the country—publishers began to eliminate all references to religion in schoolbooks, thus seriously distorting history. However, this effort to avoid offense itself created offense, and starting in 1986 several religious groups actively campaigned to ban all schoolbooks that, by eliminating references to religion, teach secular humanism, which they maintain is another, offensive religion. A heated battle developed between parents who wanted "creationism" to be taught instead of the theory of evolution.

In the 1990s still another group of censors arose. Textbooks that were trying to teach children more than earlier ones had done about minorities and about the achievements of women and of people in other parts of our "one world," in what was called *multicultural* education, came under fire from the very people who were trying to teach more respect for them. Ethnic, linguistic, racial, and sexual minorities became increasingly militant and vocal, insisting that their history and culture was not only deserving of respect but of more attention and admiration than other groups. So instead of increasing understanding of all groups, multiculturalism became a field of rivalry among groups vying with each other, increasing bigotry instead of tolerance. And *political correctness* became the new slogan under which only certain things could be taught. Thus a new wave of censorship made the work of textbook publishers even more difficult than before.

According to Lynne Cheney, chairwoman of the National Endowment for the Humanities in the Reagan and Bush administrations, the national guidelines for teachers of American history present a "warped view" because they contain 17 references to the Ku

Klux Klan and 19 to McCarthyism but neglect the nation's "white heroes," for example, giving no mention of Paul Revere or Thomas Edison. As a result of such criticism, the guidelines were being revised in 1996.

Also in 1996 a long-awaited report setting national standards for teachers of English was released in Washington in response to growing complaints from parents and employers that too many high school graduates cannot read or write effectively, use poor grammar, and have little knowledge of literature. The 70-page report offered no reading lists and avoided recommending particular teaching methods. Instead it set goals. By the time children finish high school, it said, they should have read a "wide range of literature" and should be able to use a library and write and critique texts. And even students who speak another language at home should be competent in "standard English." It did make some specific recommendations, including support for bilingual education for non-English speakers, and for the study of both classic and contemporary literature. Students should also, it said, be able to apply knowledge of language structure, language conventions (e.g. spelling and punctuation), media techniques, figurative language, and genre, and be able to create, critique, and discuss both print and nonprint texts.

A number of people criticized the report, including Christopher Cross, president of the Council for Basic Education, a national nonprofit group, as too vague. He said several states, including Colorado, Delaware, Illinois, Ohio, and Virginia, had already done a more thorough job in setting English standards for their schools. But Beverly Ann Chin, president of the National Council of Teachers of English, which developed the report along with the International Reading Association, welcomed such state initiatives, saying, "We believe that decisions about specific curriculums—which books are read and studied, for example—should be made at a local level."

The United Nations named 1990 "International Literacy Year," hoping to stimulate a worldwide movement for literacy as part of a vigorous plan of action extending to the year 2000. At that time over one quarter of the world's adult population (and two-thirds of the world's women) could not read or write and more than 100 billion children between the ages of 6 and 11 were not in school.

It is only recently that illiteracy has been recognized as a problem, however. Many Americans in the eighteenth century could read but did not know how to write. While religious and political ideals dictated that all children should learn a smattering of history and read the Bible (and many did), writing was not considered essential. In addition, writing was time-consuming and expensive to learn, given the high cost of paper and ink and the difficulty of keeping a quill pen in repair.

The education of girls has long been particularly neglected, all over the world. In most prominent families it consisted only of needlework, music, and dancing. Aaron Burr (1756–1836) was one of the few prominent people during his lifetime to insist that his daughter, Theodosia, should learn serious subjects rather than merely ornamental ones.

President Andrew Johnson, who became president in 1865 after President Lincoln's assassination, never went to school and did not learn to read or write until his wife undertook the task of teaching him.

In our century another president's wife, Barbara Bush, also taught literacy, and not just to her own family. In 1984 she wrote a book on the subject that raised around $100,000 for Literacy Volunteers of America and Laubach Literacy Action, two national programs she was working with, and when her husband became president one of the first things on her agenda was a literacy conference followed by an honors dinner, which was broadcast on TV. Several famous people entertained at the dinner, and a film was shown honoring 17 "learners of the month," all of whom had worked hard to learn to read.

That night was also the birth of the Barbara Bush Foundation for Family Literacy, which has an entirely volunteer board of directors that awards millions of dollars to literacy programs all over America. It also encourages illiterate parents not to be embarrassed about learning to read along with their children. Its stated goal is to establish literacy as a value in every family in the nation, understanding that the home is the child's first school, and the parent is the child's first teacher and reading is the child's first subject.

Mrs. Bush has also helped a program called RIF (Reading Is Fundamental), whose volunteers work in schools, homeless shelters, migrant workers' camps, soup kitchens, and public housing projects, reading aloud to children and encouraging parents to do the same. She enjoyed her job as First Lady but complained that although she worked hard all year long on literacy campaigns the only times the media gave her publicity was when she did something less consequential, like climbing a ladder to put the star on top of the White House's Christmas tree. In a way, though, she was mistaken, because she also received huge press coverage for a speech she made in 1990 at Wellesley, a women's college in Massachusetts. She told the graduating class she hoped they would consider three very special choices in their lives: "the first is to believe in something larger than yourself . . . . to get involved in some of the big ideals of your time." The second is to "find joy in life." And the third is to realize that while careers are important for women as well as men, "you are a human being first, and human connections of friends and family are the most important investments you will ever make."

"We are in a transitional period right now," she said, "fascinating and exhilarating times . . . learning to adjust to the changes and choices men and women are facing." She brought the predominantly female house down by saying, "Who knows? Somewhere in this audience may even be someone who will one day follow in my footsteps and preside over the White House as the president's spouse . . . . I wish him well!" But, she added, "whatever the era, one thing will never change: fathers and mothers; if you have children, they must come first. Your success as a family, our success as a society, depends *not* on what happens at the White House, but on what happens inside *your* house."

Explaining why she had chosen literacy as her cause, she said it was "because I honestly believe that if more people could read, write, and comprehend, we would be that much closer to solving many of the problems plaguing our society."

There are only two places in the world where literacy is between 99 and 100 percent. Everyone in Iceland must have completed eight years of school in order to get a job, and also must be able to speak three languages including Icelandic (Islenska), which is 1,000 years old and is spoken in no other country. Icelanders read more books per capita than any other people in the world.

The other place is the state of Karala in southern India. In spite of extreme poverty—its per capita income is less than $350 a year—it is the most remarkable success story in the Third World. One of the most crowded places on earth, it has a population the size of California's squeezed into a state the size of Switzerland. Furthermore, its population is mixed (60 percent Hindu, 20 percent Muslim, 20 percent Christian), yet they all live peacefully together. Among its people's achievements, which include good health care, a low birth rate (achieved without any legal coercion), and an average life expectancy in the seventies, after a long series of literacy campaigns the United Nations in 1991 certified it as 100 percent literate.

As if to prove Mrs. Bush's point about the social value of literacy, both Iceland and Karala are very stable societies and in both of them crime is almost non-existent.

Modern Experts on Child Rearing

Parenthood is the only important profession for which no prior training is required. The mother instinct is assumed to be so powerful that it makes up for lack of training—and in most cases it does. Yet it is quite understandable that many mothers feel an occasional need for advice and are relieved when they can find some in a book.

Of couse not all advice by so-called experts is useful or correct. One has only to read the advice given by the Tudor Conduct Books (see pages 246–47) to realize how opinions about child rearing can differ, and how absurd and even harmful some advice can be. But today's child experts are refreshingly humble. They emphasize that mothers should follow only advice they feel comfortable with, advice consonant with their own values. The opening words in Dr. Spock's famous book, *Baby and Child Care* (1946), which for many years was *the* authority on how to raise children, were "Trust yourself. You know more than you think you do."

Specialists in Different Aspects of Child Rearing

The most prominent child care experts in recent times have all been well qualified, although the information one of them gives that is extremely useful to one mother may not be as important to another one. Yet all of them are worth knowing about.

Maria Montessori (1870–1952) on Education

Dr. Maria Montessori the first woman doctor in Italy, entered the education field as a result of discoveries she made when practicing medicine with retarded children. She found that even severely handicapped, disturbed, and deprived slum children considered hopeless could learn a great deal if they were given the means to "teach themselves."

The basic secret she discovered was that even little children and slow children and "naughty" children enjoy learning if given real work suited to their level of development, and that they will go on rapidly to the next stage and the next, by themselves, if they are given appropriate and gently graduated tools and tasks.

In fact, she said, they enjoy work more than play. *Work* she defined as purposeful activity that gives a sense of accomplishment when performed, whereas *play* is aimless activity. An indefinite amount of play, she found, produced boredom and restlessness and, therefore, behavioral problems. In contrast, gradually more and more challenging work produces continually expanding interests, skills, and satisfaction.

She studied children in different situations to find out what activities and degrees of difficulty were appropriate for developmental learning: what steps followed what, in what order. She discovered that there are definite stages at which children are particularly sensitive to colors, or to music, and when it is easy for them to learn languages. And she designed graduated learning tools to help them make progress (at their own pace, without coercion) with drawing, writing, mathematics, and other subjects.

She trained many teachers to expose children to these teaching aids at appropriate times but not to insist on their use. They were to act as friendly guides and supervisors rather than dictatorial instructors. It was impressed upon them that their role was not to teach the children but to help the children teach themselves. The quiet, busy, free, and happy atmosphere in Montessori classrooms all over the world attest to her remarkable wisdom.

In 1995 the government of South Africa hired David Kahn, a leading American Montesorri teacher, to teach in the slums where almost everyone was illiterate because of having been deprived of education under apartheid.

Dr. Arnold Gesell (1880–1961) and His Colleagues

In 1911 Dr. Gesell founded the Yale Clinic for Child Development and remained affiliated with Yale's medical school until he retired in 1948, after which Yale established the Gesell Institute of Child Development to carry on his work.

A pioneer in establishing normal ranges of children's behavior, Dr. Gesell introduced an observation room with a one-way window so that researchers could unobtrusively watch and learn about children's spontaneous behavior. Later he also used movie cameras to record their actions.

Gesell trained several generations of students, and the many books he wrote both on his own and in collaboration with colleagues were very reassuring to young mothers. They pointed out that much childish behavior that might seem naughty is merely a normal phase. For example, children are able to remove objects from a box or drawer or pocketbook before they are capable of putting things into them, so it is futile to scold children for being "messy" when they do not pick up after themselves. Soon enough they will be able to put things back and be "neat."

He also explained that very young children are possessive and cannot happily share toys. Instead of trying to force them to do so, scolding them for being "selfish" and probably making them cry, if one calmly waits a few months they will learn not to feel so threatened and will discover that it is fun to share things. The lives of a lot of mothers and children became much more peaceful once the mothers understood more about the natural stages of child development, thanks to Dr. Gesell.

Dr. Benjamin Spock (1903–)

This pediatrician was a popular professor of pediatrics at Cornell University's medical college from 1933 to 1943 while also maintaining a thriving private practice. It was in 1946 that he became world famous by publishing his book *The Common Sense Book of Baby and Child Care*, later retitled *Baby and Child Care*. It was updated as recently as 1992 (cowritten with Michael B. Rothenberg, M.D.) and was translated into 39 languages, selling more than 40 million copies—more than any other book except the Bible.

Spock had an uncanny ability to describe children's ailments and to explain how to cope with such distressing things as colic, how to recognize and differentiate between symptoms of measles and chickenpox, what to do about conditions such as croup, earaches, or mumps, how to reduce fevers or the anguish of poison ivy, etc. At moments when these problems arose, turning to his book would help a mother decide if she should take her child to the doctor or attempt to treat her at home.

Dr. Spock also dealt with behavioral problems, but here he was more controversial. Due to his political activism in opposing the Vietnam War, he got blamed for the rebellious behavior of so many youngsters. People called the rebels in the 1960s "the Spock-marked generation" and said they had been spoiled because he had taught their parents to be too permissive. However, a rereading of his book proves he had not advocated an "anything-goes" approach to child rearing. He urged gentleness in discipline rather than severity and hoped parents would let their children develop their own views and interests, but he never advocated rudeness or promiscuity or use of drugs. However, he and "the Spock generation" unfortunately lived during a turbulent and distressing era in history.

Dr. Haim Ginott (1922–1873)

In the 1950s and 1960s Dr. Ginott was a prominent child psychiatrist who specialized in helping troubled families. He had his own private practice, as well as a weekly television program on which he answered questions from worried parents. He was exceptionally kind and understanding in the way he helped parents see things from their child's point of view. He wrote several useful books, including his best-known *Between Parent and Child*. Among his advice was that a mother's love, while essential, is not enough to enable her to cope with a difficult child. He said she needed to learn tactics, and those he taught were, quite literally, lifesavers in many cases where well-meant tactics used by parents were making things worse instead of better.

One example Ginott gave concerned a clumsy child who often spilled milk. The old adage about not crying over spilled milk should have been applied, but an annoyed parent was baffled because in spite of being scolded and/or punished for being careless, the child spilled again and again. Dr. Ginott explained why scoldings just made the child, who was already embarrassed and humiliated, more nervous so that she was more apt than ever to spill again, whereas calm sympathy, combined with giving her a constructive way to make amends—asking her to clean up the mess—would have eased the situation.

Another example was of a boy who was in constant fights with other boys. When his mother tried to find out what he might have done to antagonize the boys, he sulked and stopped telling her about the continuing problem, but after Dr. Ginott told her to "be on his side" and offer sympathy instead of seeming to sympathize with his opponents, the boy "miraculously" changed his attitude and by himself began to act more friendly.

These are but two examples of Dr. Ginott's empathy and uncommon common sense, which can help to solve what begin as small behavioral problems that, if mishandled, can escalate into serious psychological ones.

Dr. Bruno Bettelheim (1903–1990)

Bettelheim was another psychiatrist who specialized in emotional problems. For 29 years he headed the University of Chicago's Sonia Shankman Orthogenic School, a treatment center for severely disturbed children, and he wrote more than 20 books on psychotherapy, including in 1950 *Love Is Not Enough: The Treatment of Emotionally Disturbed Children*.

In later life Bettelheim also published advice on raising normal children. In one of his books, called *A Good Enough Parent* (1987), he summed up his lifelong effort to discover and test what is required for successful child rearing. He said:

> The best preparation for parenthood is to realize that there will be problems. Nobody is faultless, so people should forget about trying to be a perfect parent who will raise a perfect child. There are no perfect children. And there is not one perfect formula to use because each parent-child relationship is unique.

He claimed that, with effort, anyone can become a reasonably good parent, but that the only sure thing about raising children is that it is demanding work with no guarantees. He said:

> Raising children is a creative endeavor, rather than a science, a journey of exploration for both parent and child, and if a parent is too anxious about making mistakes anxiety will be passed on to the child as well. . . . The best way to raise responsible, self-assured children is to be that kind of person oneself, because children learn more from their parents' examples than from anything their parents tell them.

To help reassure parents Bettelheim drew on case studies and on his own childhood in discussing how to get children to open up and confide in you, why reasoning with children does not always solve a problem, why praise works and punishment does not, what is really behind temper tantrums, why play is serious business to children, and how to enrich your time together.

T. Berry Brazelton (1918–)

This psychiatrist and pediatrician agrees that nobody should worry about not being a perfect parent. "It isn't possible," he says, "you learn only by mistakes." Dr. Brazelton has been called the father of no-guilt parenting and "Dr. Feelgood." He consoles parents by saying, "It is impossible not to blow up sometimes. Toddlers will see to that. They have a marvelous capacity for finding your weakest points."

He shows compassion for both bewildered parents and misbehaving children, saying, as did Dr. Ginnot, "It helps if you learn to see things from the child's side."

Brazelton is the author of 22 books. The first one, called *Infants and Mothers* (1969), explained that "normal babies are not all alike." He had followed the first year's development of three very different types of normal babies whom he labeled as active, average, and quiet. In one of his latest books, called *Touchpoints* (1992), he urged parents to relax, because children's tantrums, nightmares, and fussiness are often signs of healthy development that can signal growth spurts. He told how to recognize crucial regressive behavior, such as nail biting and emotional manipulation, as markers of progress toward developmental milestones like walking, talking, and toilet training.

After many years with the Harvard Medical School, Dr. Brazelton retired and became its clinical professor emeritus of pediatrics, and Harvard established a Brazelton chair in child development. Now in his seventies he talks to parents in different cities once or twice a week with a mix of humor and serious advice, offering insights into the behavior of infants and young children. He is also a political activist, urging people to fight for decent child care services and for a four-month parental leave after their children are born. (In Sweden, 18 months off are provided for either parent, at 90 percent pay.) He also has a cable television program and a weekly syndicated newspaper column.

For a long time Brazelton held the firm belief that mothers should stay home full-time with their children instead of going out to work. Now, he says, "I have three militant daughters and they said, 'Dad, you are out of this century,'" and many of his patients convinced him that they had to be "working mothers." So he finally accepted that but says they must learn to concentrate on the job when at work and then on their children when at home. "It's up to parents today to realize that if they have less time with their kids, they damn well better make it count. When they come home they should really attend to the child and not have other things distracting them, and on weekends they ought also to have very special times with the child, when they are really paying attention to him, and the child knows it.

Dr. Robert Coles (1929–)

This distinguished child psychiatrist has long been affiliated with the Harvard University Medical School, becoming professor of psychiatry and medical humanities there in 1978. An astoundingly prolific and Pulitzer prize-winning author, he has spent his adult life studying the psychology of children and putting what he has learned into practice by helping child patients and advising parents.

In his early years Coles was the student and colleague of two other eminent psychologists. The founder of child analysis, Anna Freud (1895–1982), Sigmund Freud's daughter, was his inspiration, mentor, teacher, and a friend with whom he corresponded for nearly 30 years. He also studied with Erik Erikson (1902–1994), a pioneer in child psychoanalysis with Anna Freud in Vienna. With Erikson, Coles was a faculty member of the Harvard Medical School, where a research center has been established in his name, as well as at Yale and the University of California at Berkeley, even though he had no college degree and neve studied medicine but became renowned through his influential books on human (not just child) development. (See also pages 600–01.)

Penelope Leach (1937–)

This English child expert has one qualification these other experts lack: she is a mother. "I have been there," she says. Her other qualifications include a B.A. from Cambridge University, an early career as a social worker, a Ph.D. in psychology from the University of London, and service as a senior fellow on a medical research team at the London School of Economics. She held that post for a number of years until her young son became ill and she felt he needed her full time so she decided to stay home with her children. She then began her writing career, training herself to write amid family chaos.

> Not a single one of these experts believes in spanking. All of them say it gives wrong messages: fear of getting caught rather than self-discipline; anger at parents and resentment of their authority; and that it is all right to hit someone (thus laying the groundwork for future child and spouse abuse.)

During the 1980s and 1990s Penelope Leach became the world's best-selling advisor to mothers, translated into 28 languages and being read by more mothers than any expert since Dr. Spock. But in spite of having written many books and magazine articles on child rearing, she says one should raise a child "by the baby, not by the book." She does not believe in rules, saying you know your own child best so that even if you feel that other people know more than you do about children in general, not even the most expert of them knows as much as you do about your child in particular, so if general advice does not seem to apply to your child, don't take it.

Dr. Leach strongly believes that parenting should be *fun* and that if you make your child happy, the child will make you happy. She says you should savor each stage, instead of hurrying and trying to rush your child into the next one. Patience, not pushing, is the surest route, she stated in one of her columns in *Child* magazine, to your child's feeling loved, respected, and celebrated.

> Child development is a process, not a race. In the first year each infant recapitulates the evolutionary stages that produced humanity, so major landmarks like walking and talking are important and exciting. But that does not mean that it is necessarily better to reach them faster and pass them sooner.

Leach says children can thrive in any kind of family where they receive security and unlimited love and in no family where they do not. She emphasizes that love is not spoiling, and discipline is not the same as punishment. "Well-behaved children and principled adults are made by influence, not through force."

Her own children are grown up, and she says,

> That's the thing about raising children. You're always aiming to put yourself out of a job. I always wanted to end up with people, rather than babies. It doesn't happen overnight and it isn't easy. But one day you look at your baby and realize he's turned into a child. You look at your baby and realize he's turned into a child. You look at your child and discover he's become an adult. And if you like the adult he's become, that's the greatest thing in the world.

SEX EDUCATION

In the United States in recent years sex education has become a subject of intense controversy. Many parents think sex is so personal and intimate that it should be discussed only in the privacy of the home, not openly in elementary or high schools. They believe that having kids talk frankly about the subject encourages premature curiosity and promiscuity.

On the other hand, teachers of the subject and many parents maintain that curiosity about sex is natural and inevitable and that too many parents fail to teach their children anything about it. When they do not, this group claims youngsters simply talk and experiment among themselves, often picking up wrong and even harmful information, with teenagers not knowing how to take precautions against pregnancy or protecting themselves from transmittal of the AIDS virus and other sexually transmitted diseases, and girls giving birth when they are too young for the responsibility of parenthood. Therefore, educators feel that the task of sex education devolves upon them.

However, many of their efforts have produced indignant outcries from parents and many religious leaders who are appalled at teachers describing birth control methods and dispensing condoms to students as part of "safe sex." Those objecting contend that the only totally safe way to avoid pregnancy and disease is abstinence. In some schools that point is stressed in sex education courses, and abstinence is no longer ridiculed or considered impossible to maintain. In some cities girls have decided to be proud of abstaining, and have set up special clubs to proclaim the fact. Yet in February, 1996, the Roman Catholic clergy in France surprised people by endorsing the use of condoms as a lesser evil than impregnating teenage girls or transmitting AIDS.

Many of today's parents and teachers, both liberals and conservatives, would undoubtedly be shocked at some of the bawdy jokes, rowdy and blunt demonstrations that people in primitive, classical, and medieval societies used to introduce small children to knowledge of sex. In fact, many "play" activities that used to be considered normal during those periods would today be considered sexual abuse of children.

For centuries males and females, both adults and children, married and unmarried, all slept in cozy togetherness on the floor. When people began to use beds, they climbed in together—often sleeping six to a bed. Furthermore, in warm weather they slept stark naked except for nightcaps, which for centuries people thought necessary to prevent head colds.

In the sixteenth century, however, things changed, at least in England. Stern sexual discipline became the rule. Parents were admonished to protect their daughters' chastity vigilantly, starting in the cradle. Little girls must be kept away from all male company, even that of relatives. This school of thought held that laughing, kissing, and hugging have nothing to do with the "right" way to treat children, in strong contrast to those who hold that children thrive best when they experience much warm affection.

It was not only sixteenth-century English parents who accepted these warnings against all physical expressions of love. They crossed the Atlantic Ocean, where the Puritans in New England agreed. In Massachusetts it was once against the law for a married couple to have sexual intercourse on Sunday. Lacking in accurate sex education, the Pilgrims assumed that babies were always born on the same day of the week on which they were conceived. If one arrived on a Sunday it meant it had been conceived on a Sunday, and its disgraced parents were punished by being placed in the town stocks.

Also, in Connecticut a law remained on the books clear into the twentieth century making it illegal for a mother to kiss her children on the Sabbath.

HOW COMPUTERS ARE CHANGING EDUCATION

Nowadays every school that can afford to buy computers promptly does so. Students need to be prepared for success in the electronic world of e-mail and the Internet that is rapidly replacing the paper work that has characterized education and communications ever since Johannes Gutenberg (1400–1468) invented movable type and the printing press.

An interesting side effect of this is the discovery that many children who have been labeled learning disabled may not actually be after all. They may have trouble learning to read simply because they are not "linear" thinkers, so trying to read and write frustrates and confuses them. But computers are not limited to a linear approach. They are flexible and interactive, and the freedom this gives users to explore facts and ideas from many different angles releases their hitherto unrecognized intelligence. Instead of staying at the bottom of the class and getting to hate school, they can now shine.

This is confirmation of the theory of "multiple intelligences" developed by Dr. Howard Gardner (see page 190).

Just as it is now generally accepted that there is more than one type of intelligence, sensible teachers and wise parents are no longer upset at the fact that every child does not progress in every subject at exactly the same rate. They have also begun to be realize that some teaching methods are more effective with certain types of children than with others.

Some children use sensory modes to receive and process information most efficiently and easily. Acronyms used for these modes are VAKT, for Visual, Auditory, Kinesthetic, and Tactile, and HAPTIC for physical hands-on learning, combining kinesthetic and tactile. Some children are able to use all these modes of learning in a process often called integration.

Children whose intelligence is primarily visual need to see something to understand it. They have a strong sense of color and may have artistic ability but have difficulty with spoken directions and trouble following or remembering lectures. They are obviously very different from "auditory" children who prefer to get information by listening, who have difficulty following written directions and problems with reading and writing; they have to hear something in order to understand it.

Both these types of children have different strengths and needs from the HAPTIC children who prefer hands-on learning and can assemble parts without reading directions, for example. They may be very well coordinated and have athletic ability, but have difficulty sitting still and will learn best if physical activity is involved.

But how can the most well-meaning teachers manage to meet the very different needs of these different types of children? Unless they have very small classes, they do not have time to tailor their teaching to the contradictory needs of each individual student. This is where audio-visual aids and computers can come to the teacher's (and the childrens') rescue.

For the visual child, graphics (films, slides, diagrams, and illustrations, even doodles) can reinforce learning; notes on different subjects can be organized with color coding; directions can be written down and saved on disks; flow charts and diagrams help with note-taking; facts and spelling that are to be memorized can be visualized on the computer screen.

For the auditory child, test questions and directions can be put on tape and then read aloud; the child can participate in interviews and discussions that can also be preserved on tapes; and class and lecture notes and facts to be memorized can all be taped and listened to as often as necessary without bothering anyone else.

The HAPTIC child needs frequent breaks in study periods but can use these to memorize or drill while walking or exercising. The experiential learner can make models, do lab work and role playing, trace letters and words to learn spelling and remember facts, and express abilities through dance, drama, gymnastics, lab projects, and other group activities. And the use of computers can reinforce learning through the sense of touch.

Problems with Computers

One of the main difficulties about computers in the classroom is that few schools can afford to supply enough computers for a whole class, so one child usually "drives" while several others watch, goof off, kibbitz, etc. The brightest or most aggressive student now tends to commandeer the computer, and in coed schools girls, unfortunately, rarely get a chance to drive.

There are ways to get around this problem, however. Teachers can establish rotating schedules so that all the children get to take turns driving, and they can encourage the teamwork necessary to complete complex problem-solving programs, with the students learning to work together, sharing ideas, and producing an agreed-on end result. Solving electronic puzzles together and doing joint online research encourages both more cooperation and more learning.

Schedules should also provide time for each child in a class to have some reserved periods to work alone, because (for reasons that will be described below) individual work in privacy is one of the computer's most valuable educational contributions.

Another problem is that many teachers, particularly older ones, actually feel threatened by computers. They do not understand them without some special training, and they have the erroneous notion that they are going to be replaced by machines, so they are reluctant to encourage their use. Accustomed to thinking linearly and verbally, they fail to take advantage of the varied, exploratory, inductive, visual, creative processes the computer makes possible and the ways these can help students grasp ideas through pictures and images.

This problem is certainly, however, only temporary. As younger teachers enter the profession it will become as obsolete as today's computers rapidly become obsolete, replaced by improved, more "user-friendly" ones. Furthermore, experience has proved that, far from replacing teachers, computers can be enormously helpful teachers' aides. This is well demonstrated by:

"Dreary Drill" and "Tireless Tutor"

These are teachers' slang for electronic workbooks, which both teachers and pupils can use to take care of the drudgery and practice involved in memorizing multiplication tables, parts of speech, spelling and rules of grammar, names of oceans, lakes, rivers, cities, planets in the solar system, etc. These boring tasks can now be introduced by the teacher with great enthusiasm because they can all be delegated to computers. Students as well welcome this new development because they would rather keep their long struggles with such things as times-tables, chemistry formulas, and irregular verbs private instead of having to face a teacher's annoyance or a classmate's ridicule.

Computer Assisted Instruction (CAI) lets students progress at their own pace while still drumming all the essentials into their heads. With traditional paper workbooks and homework, you have to wait for your teacher to go over your work with a red pencil, but with a computer you immediately see the right answer and can move on or you can keep reviewing until you know it. Unlike a human teacher, a computer never embarrasses a slow learner by getting tired or impatient.

The Children's Television Workshop, which developed *Sesame Street* was the first educational organization to realize that children can learn numbers and letters more quickly when these are presented along with music, color, and variation. But the notion that "A" and "6" can be packaged with glitz and introduced in lots of different ways—the more the merrier—still bothers many teachers. And the idea that children may learn "H" before "A" and "9" before "6" many still consider heretical.

For the most part, schools and school personnel, have not yet figured out that children are *not* terrified by nonlinear thinking, that they enjoy learning and can best express themselves and understand abstract concepts in other ways, and in fact find it far easier and more interesting to explore a subject from many angles. To illustrate how this works, one can compare studying a subject via a computer to visiting a house. One can go through the front door and move directly in a straight line from the hall to the next room, proceeding "linearly" from one room to the next, but another person may choose to wander, exploring the upstairs first, while another may head for the kitchen or the back yard first. This personal freedom of choice makes learning more fun. However, this does make it harder for teachers to plan, control, and test, so it is understandable that many teachers are doing a poor job of incorporating these new ways of learning into their curricula. It is very, very different from anything our educational system has had to grapple with in the past.

The Future of Education

Advances in computer technology are occurring so rapidly that what is innovative today will be obsolete by tomorrow, so there is no way to predict what is ahead.

An enthusiastic and brilliant pioneer in designing computer materials for schools, Ann-Byrd Platt has described her work in lectures, saying,

> Much depends on how educators and parents choose to change schools and their own views about what constitutes both intelligence and learning. If they decide to acknowledge that we can see and hear and process information differently than we used to, schools will continue to be a vital part of any child's training for life. If they don't and schools remain stuck where they are now then formal academic institutions will become increasingly ineffective and even irrelevant.
>
> We must let go of the notion that only linguistic and logical intelligence 'count' in real life. If we can't open our minds a bit more, the hand-wringing about the appalling decline in test scores, teaching credentials, and the youth of tomorrow will become ever more frenzied.
>
> Huge tomes of written text are dead, and huge computer databases of unremitting text will also undoubtedly expire shortly. Pithy captions amplifying photos, computer-generated graphics, hand drawings and other visual representations are alive and well and exciting. So is great radio or 'audio' writing and recording. And all the right music or sound effects to go with them. After e-mail will be mobile phones . . . . How well you talk and the mood you create with sound will matter as much as how well you wrote and the paper you wrote on have in the past . . . .
>
> There's no reason schools can't change to accommodate these new ways of sharing knowledge and ideas . . . . New is not bad; it's just scary. If we can accept what is unnerving and unknown and integrate it into the schools, education will be a lot better in 50 years for many, many more children. If we don't, it will just get worse. We have to move beyond initiating a logical, linguistic elite to really, truly teaching as many children as much as possible in as many different ways as we can dream up.

In spite of their cost, which may come down in the future, computers can be especially useful in inner city schools, with large classes and overworked teachers, and in rural areas, where children may have limited or no access to libraries and museums.

There is no doubt that computers are making learning much more exciting, but skeptics point out that a decade of computers in schools has not resulted in any marked improvement in children's learning basic skills. A professor of math at the University of Washington, Neil K. Blitz, thinks computers should be kept out of math classes until students have finished calculus. "To be inundated with visual stimulation and a machine that does things for you is not the best way to learn," he says. "It isn't science simply because they are punching a keyboard on a computer."

The Internet

In 1996 an enormous number of schools were using their computers to sign on with the Internet. The U.S. Department of Education reported that 50 percent of American schools now had access to the Internet, up from 35 percent in 1994. The number of individual classrooms connected with it had jumped from 3 percent to 9 percent nationwide in just two years. Furthermore, President Clinton announced in February, 1996, that the Federal government was going to invest $2 billion toward getting every classroom in the U.S. connected by the year 2000.

This worries many people. "The basic problem with the Internet is that no one runs it," explains Susan Vezzia, editor of *Multi-Media Schools* magazine. "People think because information is on the computer it is right." But anything anybody wants to enter into it stays there, and children can pick up a bewildering number of "facts" that simply are not true. For example, if a computer is asked to search for information on the word "biology" it will come up with 400,000 entries, and no teacher can dig through all of them to verify their accuracy.

Kids absolutely love the Internet because it enables them to contribute their own ideas, and hundreds of students' poems, drawings, and newspapers are now entered. It thrills children to realize that their work will be on display all around the world. It also excites them to be able to exchange ideas with other people; there was one instance where three 11-year-olds were arguing with a noted astrophysicist about the size of the explosion that would occur if a comet hit Jupiter.

John B. Gage, chief scientist at *Sun Microsystems* in California, which has set a goal of getting all 13,000 schools in its state to connect their classrooms and libraries to the Internet on "Net Day" during 1996, says, "the old model of the teacher absorbing physics, biology, and other sciences and then pouring it into kids' brains is gone. Now what is happening is that the kids do the exploration; the kids are in control."

That is the stuff of nightmares for many educators and parents. "A fifth-grader is an inappropriate teacher," says the author of *Silicon Snake Oil: Second Thoughts on the Information Highway,* published in 1995 by Doubleday. "I don't want my children to learn from other students. I want them to learn from competent teachers."

There can no longer be any reasonable doubt that despite a few skeptics technological literacy is becoming necessary for everyone, and in the future it will be even more so. But here is a thought to comfort those of us who still love books. Computers are going to supplement books, not replace them. You can curl up with a good book more comfortably than with any computer, even a laptop. But reading books will be only one aspect of the new literacy that our children must acquire in order to enjoy productive lives and careers in the next century.

"If a Child . . ."

If a child lives with criticism, he learns to condemn.

If a child lives with hostility, he learns to fight.

If a child lives with fear, he learns to be apprehensive.

If a child lives with pity, he learns to feel sorry for himself.

If a child lives with ridicule, he learns to be shy.

If a child lives with jealousy, he learns what envy is.

If a child lives with shame, he learns to feel guilty.

If a child lives with encouragement, he learns to be confident.

If a child lives with tolerance, he learns to be patient.

If a child lives with approval, he learns to like himself.

If a child lives with recognition, he learns that it is good to have a goal.

If a child lives with honesty and fairness, he learns what truth and justice are.

If a child lives with security, he learns to have faith in himself and in those about him.

If a child lives with friendliness, he learns that the world is a nice place in which to live.

If a child lives with sharing, he learns about generosity.

If you live with serenity, your child will live with peace of mind.

—*Bhavan's Journal, 1979*

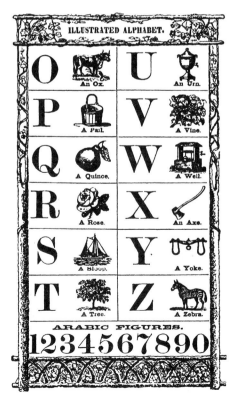

8

Child's Play and Toys

CHILDREN LEARN THROUGH FUN

The first thing the average baby does of its own accord, after the first few days on earth when it wholly concentrates on the primary necessities of life such as sleeping and eating, is to look around at the world and then to smile. Animal babies also eat and sleep and observe the world, but only human babies really smile.

Not long after the first smile, contented chortles and gleeful gurgles begin and, if the baby is unswaddled, joyful wriggles. Soon baby discovers the ability to play and starts reaching out to grasp and taste whatever is at hand: the blanket, the rattle that harmonizes so pleasantly with cooing, the small stuffed animals that are almost as cuddly as babies themselves, and if baby has a cradle gym, the colored shapes that dangle from it.

In short, infants learn to play long before they learn to sit, crawl, talk, or do anything else. Joy is their natural response to life if their basic physical needs have been satisfied, and it is through joy that they grow and move on to other experiences. The happier they are the more rapidly they develop. So play, sometimes considered a trivial aspect of life, is in a way the most serious and fundamental, because it is the stimulant that awakens every infant from a comparatively passive, self-centered, animal-like existence into the fullness of a truly human, social, and active life. Throughout childhood, child's play continues to be important in teaching physical and mental and social skills.

COMMENTS ABOUT CHILD'S PLAY

You can do anything with children if you only play with them.
—*Otto von Bismarck (1815–1898)*

Play is the highest form of research. —*Albert Einstein (1879–1955)*

The plays of children are the germinal leaves of all later life.
—*Friedrich Froebel (1782–1852)*

The chief art is to make all that children have to do sport and play.
—*John Locke (1632–1704)*

I seem to have been only like a boy playing on the seashore and diverting myself in now and then finding a smooth pebble or a prettier shell than ordinary whilst the great ocean of truth lies undiscovered before me.
—*Isaac Newton (1642–1727)*

Play is the first poetry of the human being. —*Jean Paul (1762–1825)*

Behold the child,
by Nature's kindly law,
Pleased with a rattle, tickled with a straw.

—*Alexander Pope (1688–1744)*

All work and no play makes Jack a dull boy.   *—English proverb*

Child, how happy you are sitting in the dust playing with a broken twig all the morning; I smile at your play with that little bit of broken twig. I am busy with my accounts adding up figures by the hour. Perhaps you glance at me and think what a stupid game to spoil your morning with. Child, I have forgotten the art of being absorbed in sticks and piles. I seek out costly playthings and gather lumps of gold and silver. With whatever you find, you create glad games.

                                        —Rabindranath Tagore (1861–1941)

A Survey of Children's Toys, Past and Present

When children in ancient Greece put away their "childish things," it was customary for them to give them up to appropriate gods and goddesses as devotional offerings. Girls usually gave their balls, dolls, dolls' clothes, and tambourines to Artemis, goddess of the heart, moon, and nature. Boys in most cases dedicated their toys to the god Hermes, messenger of the gods and patron of thieves! A poem by Leonidas of Tarentum, a Greek writer in the third century B.C., records a gift to Hermes of a ball, a top, and some rattles, by a boy named Philocles.

> When I was a child I played as a child, but when I became a man, I put away childish things.
>
> *—Saint Paul*

Even after we grow up and discard childish toys, however, we should not look back on them as mere frivolities. The word *toy* is related to the word *tool* and toys are literally the tools with which children imitate adults, practice skills, and gradually learn to turn into adults themselves.

A survey of toys is a survey of humanity's history, its customs, manners, and styles, because toys show us the world in miniature.

Animal Toys
Clay Animals

Among prehistoric toys that have been discovered in archaeological excavations are many clay animals, and on ancient gravestones of children in Greece are pictures showing children playing with toy animals. In India clay birds and animals are still made for children from molds that are many generations old. Clay birds, which often double as whistles or ocarinas, have been popular toys in Russia and Scandinavia for many centuries.

In addition to having children donate their toys to gods and goddesses when they grew up, there was an ancient custom of burying toys with children who had died. This custom had a significant influence on the history of art if the following story told by Vitruvius, author of a 10-volume treatise on architecture in the first A.D. century is true:

In the late fifth century. B.C., a little girl in ancient Corinth died, and her nurse gathered all her toys into a basket, covered with a large tile to protect them from rain, which she placed on the ground next to the grave. An acanthus seed happened to be underneath the ground at that spot, and the plant grew, eventually lifting the basket of toys high into the air. One day a Greek architect and sculptor named Callimachus passed by the tomb and noticed the basket upheld by a tall column topped by leafy branches. The attractive sight inspired him in the design of columns in his future architecture, and thus the classic Corinthian column with its capital formed of acanthus leaves entered the world, becoming one of the main elements in Greek, Roman, and Renaissance architecture.

Noah's Arks

These were features of most Victorian nurseries in England. They were collections of toy animals assembled in commodious wooden toy chests in the shape of Noah's ark, and because of the ark's connection with religion these were in many families the only toys children were allowed to play with on Sundays. The arks originated in Germany in the eighteenth century . Some contained as many as 200 pairs of ingeniously carved figures ranging from glowworms to giraffes and including Mr. and Mrs. Noah, their three sons, and their sons' wives. Charles Dickens (1812–1870) affectionately recalled his own Noah's Ark in *A Christmas Tree.* Among the animals in it that he cherished were "the noble fly, a size or two smaller than the elephant; the ladybird, the butterfly—all triumphs of art!"

Other collections of toy animals also were popular in the nineteenth century when live traveling menageries inspired toy makers to produce zoos with exotic animals such as leopards and pelicans. The success of the famous Barnum and Bailey Circus, "The Greatest Show on Earth," that toured the world in 1871, gave circus animals a great boost. And in the 1920s, after the first World War, when the demand for toy soldiers declined temporarily, model farms with miniature animals, fences, trees, and haystacks became popular.

Stuffed Animals

Margarete Steiff (1847–1909), born in Würtemberg, Germany, where she lived all her life, was the originator of soft, huggable, plush, felt-stuffed animals. She was a seamstress who in 1880 began making toys for children she knew, out of remnants from her dressmaking materials. Her first animal was a felt elephant. He was a precursor of many marvels to come: life-sized frogs, geese, giraffes, lions, mice, monkeys, owls, rabbits, tigers, walruses, zebras, and huge dinosaurs. One of her most amazing creations was a velvety, handmade, life-sized (210 pounds) elephant stuffed with wood shavings, which has mingled with and rivaled real elephants as an attraction at the Bronx Zoo in New York.

Teddy Bears

Margarete Steiff has been called the inventor of the teddy bear because she made the world's first stuffed bear in 1902. However, International Doll Collectors, Inc., says the original teddy bear was made and named in that same year by Morris Michtom, a Russian immigrant to America, in honor of President Teddy Roosevelt (1858–1919). The president had recently been on a bear hunt during which a cub had wandered into his camp; the president refused to shoot it and instead adopted the cub as a pet, and it became known as "Teddy's bear."

After seeing a newspaper cartoon about the incident, Michtom, who ran a stationery shop in Brooklyn and with his wife made toys as a sideline, cut out a small cub of stuffed brown plush, with button eyes, and displayed it in his shop window along with newspaper clippings about the president. By the end of the first day 12 passersby had requested copies of the toy, so the Michtoms began making them in quantity. They sent the original one to the White House with a letter asking permission to name it "Teddy Bear." The president replied, "Dear Mr. Michtom, I don't think my name is likely to be worth much in the bear business, but you are welcome to use it." The president turned out to be a poor prophet, and Michtom turned out to be a shrewd toy maker. He founded the Ideal Toy Corporation, one of America's largest toy manufacturing firms, and he and his sons during the next 50 years produced many other best-selling toys.

The teddy bear was an instant and lasting worldwide success. In 1907, Steiff's teddys, which have the manufacturers' identifying metal button in one ear, attracted much attention at the Leipzig Fair, and 3,000 were immediately ordered. Steiff's bears have continued to outsell all others.

Year after year teddy has been modernized. An antiseptic teddy bear named Algy appeared on the market in the 1950s for the benefit of children allergic to house dust; henceforth it would no longer be necessary to tear beloved but dust-collecting bears away from sneezing children. And a talking teddy appeared in 1963, with a microphone in his tummy that served as an intercom system. At night when this teddy lay in a sleeping child's arms his owner's mother could hear her child's slightest whimper, and she could even talk to the child through the microphone and make teddy murmer soothing messages.

According to the Museum of Childhood in Edinburgh, Scotland, teddy bear lovers are called arctophiles and they have abounded since the toy's invention. Among the most famous are the late British Poet Laureate John Betjeman with his "Archibald" and Prime Minister Margaret Thatcher with her "Humphrey."

In 1984 a new spurt of interest in teddy bears was produced by the appearance of *Aloysius,* the teddy who went to Oxford University in the television series based upon Evelyn Waugh's novel, *Brideshead Revisited* (1945). Aloysius was played by a vintage teddy named Delicatessen. Delicatessen had sat on a shelf in a deli in Maine for 50 years before being given to the late British actor Peter Bull, who was famous for his collection of over 300 toy bears. At Bull's death his collection was bequeathed to the Toy and Model Museum in London, except for Delicatessen, which the actor left to a friend.

An International Teddy Bear Club was founded with headquarters in London to organize events for collectors, including auctions. Scores of octogenarian teddy bears have been auctioned. One 1905 Steiff version sold at Sotheby's in October 1985 for $4,488; its owner had bought it eight years earlier for what he then considered a ridiculously high price of $42.

The craze for collecting teddy bears shows no signs of abating. In Ireland, on June 24, 1995, one of the largest picnics ever held was attended by 33,573 teddy bears and their owners, at the Dublin zoo.

Toy Horses

"Hobby horses" were known in ancient China and in Greece around 500 B.C. The first ones were just sticks topped by carved horses' heads, but before long they evolved into "rocking horses."

The first rocking horses stood on rockers like chairs and cradles. Riding them introduced the skills of horsemanship and gave a child a sense of balance; if ridden too hard they could throw the rider. Usually wooden horses were painted dapple grey, but more expensive models were covered with pony skin.

In the nineteenth century the rocking horse was a favorite toy in England and America. In 1877, in London alone, 11 manufacturers produced elaborately carved and realistically painted rocking horses. These evolved into carousels or "merry-go-rounds"; in England ostriches, peacocks, swans, and other animals joined the horses; in France the merry-go-rounds featured pink pigs.

The swing bar type of rocking horse was patented in America in 1884 and gave a safer but less exciting ride. Fine horses were made in large numbers in Britain, and variations that developed were velocipedes or tricycle horses and push-along chariots. In the twentieth century metal horses appeared. An example is the Bronco, which contains metal springs. Children squeal in combined terror and delight, feeling like cowboys as they learn to stay on while the horses buck.

Psychologist William James (1842–1910) once said he disagreed with biologists who say humans acquire their knowledge entirely through education because they lack the inborn instincts that nature gives to animals and birds. He cited as an example of a human instinct as basic as that of a kitten that cannot resist chasing its tail or playing with a dangling string the fact that a little boy is incapable of seeing a rolling ball without wanting to run after it.

BALLS

These are perhaps the most universal of all toys. Balls made of braided string or leather or plain animal skins stitched together after being stuffed with wads of feathers, bran, husks of corn, rushes or grasses, seeds, or even human hair were among the earliest types. In ancient Egypt balls were also made of papyrus, pottery, and wood. Glazed clay balls were used for rolling and throwing; lighter and softer balls were made of reeds or leaves, especially palm leaves, and rattan, braided together to form a circular mass. Such balls are museum pieces now in many parts of the world but are still playthings in active use in developing countries. Ancient Romans played with two main types: a "follis," a large ball filled with air, and a "paganica," a small soft ball stuffed with feathers.

The rubber ball originated in Mexico. It was one of the things Columbus discovered on his second trip to South America in 1493, where he found Indian children playing with a heavy black ball made of vegetable gum. But the modern type of rubber ball did not appear until the 1870s, when India rubber toys of all types became popular with children. Rubber balls containing whistles, and with "colored raised Japanese figures that do not fade" were advertised in England in 1876, and for babies at that time there were rubber balls made with rattles inside, covered with netted wool and hanging from rubber strings so that the babies would not lose them.

In Victorian England, babies played decorous parlor games with balls of velvet or wool yarn or silk, made of cloth remnants and filled with cardboard stuffing or hair.

Construction Toys

Blocks and bricks are basic toys that vividly demonstrate the link between the word *toy* and the word *tool*. From babyhood through adolescence, boys and girls learn to observe and create with building blocks.

In 1913 H. G. Wells published a book called *Floor Games* in which he lashed out at toy shops for "trifling with great possibilities," indignantly complaining about the "skimpy, ridiculous bricklets" they sold that were too small to make decent constructions. For his own children he said he hired an unemployed carpenter to make large blocks that could be used in "imaginative games." Since his time many companies have produced blocks that would have pleased him.

In the 1920s, "Meccano Erector Sets" with interlocking shapes gave thousands of children endless hours of pleasure. And in the early 1930s, in London, Paul and Marjorie Abbatt opened a toy shop that specialized in large wooden bricks: whole bricks, half bricks, and quarters. These could become elements of toy towns and helped to pioneer the popularity of safe, well-made, and durable playthings that can stimulate the imaginations of children, as Wells had wanted.

Also in the early 1930s, Ole Kirk Christiansen, a carpenter in Jutland, Denmark, began making wooden toys in his workshop and formed a toy company called Lego, a contraction of the Danish term *leg godt* meaning play well. He peddled his toys on a bicycle through the countryside, and a few years later his 14-year-old son Godtfred Christiansen dropped out of the village school to join him. After World War II Godtfred stopped making wooden toys and invented a line of construction toys of colored plastic blocks, beginning full production in 1952. The business prospered and soon became international. By the end of the 1960s, sales in Canada and the United States alone amounted to $8 million a year.

Lego blocks are so versatile they can be used to build miniature cars, locomotives, large houses, and whole towns with roads and harbors, even musical instruments. Their versatility was demonstrated in 1968, in Billund, Denmark, when Godtfred Christiansen opened Legoland, an 11-acre park featuring, in addition to a children's theater and playgrounds, a miniature city built entirely from Lego blocks.

In 1978, as a prelude to the UN's International Year of the Child, UNESCO sponsored an impressive exhibit in Paris of "Children's Games and Toys throughout the World." It demonstrated that ingenious people can construct objects out of almost any materials. Included among more than 900 toys from 56 countries were many constructed by children, parents, teachers, and local craftsmen using simple tools and local or waste materials. There were animals from Brazil made of feathers; race cars from Denmark made of clothespins; a dragon from Italy made by a 12-year-old boy out of egg cartons, with ping-pong balls for eyes; airplanes from the Ivory Coast made of wire; trucks from Sierra Leone made of bamboo. Tin cans and bottle caps had been turned into automobiles and wagons, cigarette boxes had become boats, a simple gourd and rudimentary banana-fibre figure made by a six-year-old in Tanzania was a doll, and stilts were made from tin cans.

Another exhibit of toys made by children was held in New York in the 1980s in which one of the most spectacular examples was a large, astonishingly accurate, and detailed suspension bridge made by a young boy entirely out of tongue depressors.

IBM sponsors annual contests for children who make toy airplanes, many from nothing more elaborate than sheets of paper. The ultimate in paper constructions, however, are unquestionably the *origami* toys made by children in Japan.

KITES

Among adults as well as children, kites are favorite toys in many countries. They have been flown since before recorded history in Asia, where they were first made, originating in China over 3,000 years ago. They then spread to India, Indonesia, Japan, Korea, Malaysia, Singapore, Sri Lanka, and Thailand before flying westward in the seventeenth century when they became particularly popular in Holland where the flat countryside provides uninterrupted wind.

Paper pinwheels, which also move in the wind and are easier for small children to fly than kites are, appear to have been modeled on windmills and may have originated in Holland.

In early times, kites were used not as toys but for signals and messages and to keep away evil spirits. Even today in Japan kites are sometimes kept flying all night over houses to scare away unfriendly spirits, and a kite in the shape of a carp is flown over the house of a newborn boy to bring him good luck and long life. In Korea the origin of kite flying is attributed to a general in ancient times who is said to have once inspired his troops to victory by sending up a kite with a lantern attached, which the soldiers thought was a new star, a sign of divine help. In both Korea and Malaysia people sometimes write down their misfortunes on a kite and then, after it is up in the air, cut the string so their troubles, carried away on the kites, will disappear forever.

Kites are made in many shapes, some extremely fanciful and beautiful. In China they are often in the form of fierce-looking dragons. In Indonesia they may be shaped like birds and butterflies as well as dragons, with long string tails. The design of Japanese kites varies in different parts of the country; they may be geometrical or in the shape of humans, animals, birds, or fish, and some have more than one tail (the Japanese name for kite is *tako*, meaning octopus). Korean kites are usually rectangular. Some Thai kites are diamond-shaped and some are star-shaped. There are also musical kites with whistles and metal strings attached that hum when they vibrate in the wind. In Sri Lanka on Sunday afternoons the skies over the beaches become multicolored, with hundreds of children's bright-colored kites in all shapes and sizes flying through the air.

In some places children hold competitions with their kites. For example, in Indonesia, especially during the windy weeks before the rainy season, children hold kite-flying contests with kites attached to lines coated with powdered glass; the object of the competitors is to cut loose the other players' kites. About 10 competitors launch their kites simultaneously and as their lines cross each other the kites break free and disappear into the sky. The child whose kite flies the longest is the winner of the contest.

In Singapore there is a kite festival for three or four weeks during January. *Hari Raya,* a joyous Muslim holiday, is also a special day on which children fly kites. Kite flying has also become a big sport in Thailand, with teams, umpires, official rules, and a national championship. The competitions involve fighting between kites controlled by teams with as many as 20 players on each side.

MOVABLE TOYS

The simplest, oldest type of movable toy is one that works by pulling a string. Among ancient examples that have been preserved in Egypt are a dancing pygmy that spins in circles, a toy rat that bites a toy snake, a tiny mouse whose jaw opens when its tail is yanked, and an ivory hound dog that bites when a lever is pulled.

Some early movable toys included human figures, such as a diminutive peasant who grinds corn on a stone when a string is pulled. And one of the weirdest is a wooden one from the nineteenth dynasty of Egypt (c. 1250 B.C.), a prostrate, bound slave who is evidently receiving the death penalty, for he is being chewed by a wild animal.

The Greeks had a word for jointed figurines with movable arms and legs. They called them *neurospastons,* meaning drawn with strings. The Romans called them *sigillaria* because they were originally images used at Roman festivals of the same name. Some Greek neurospastons were animals. More elaborate types were like puppets, made so they could do special things, such as wash clothes or knead dough, by the tug of strings attached to their arms. The Romans also made toy crocodiles and tigers that snapped their jaws and wiggled their tails.

The earliest movable toy we know of that worked on a principle more complicated than that of a pulled string was one made by Archytas of Tarentum around 400 B.C. It was a wooden dove that flew when its body was filled with air, and then gently returned to the ground as the air escaped.

Toys that moved by water power, steam, or mercury were made later in China, Egypt, and Greece. Still later, in Nuremberg, Germany, toys were invented that moved by the weight of sand rather than water. There have also been many other techniques employed to make toys move: falling weights, twisted elastic and string, and metal springs. Most wooden mechanical toys were invented by woodcarvers in Germany, making their industry the oldest in Europe, dating back 500 years. Their folk toys with movement were made long before, and also after, the coming of steam, clockworks, and electricity.

Louis XIII of France as a child in the fifteenth century owned several delightful movable toys, including a ship with a crew that rowed by means of shifting sand, a marionette peepshow, and a toy glass fountain that sprayed real water. He also owned and loved a drum that played when he wound its spring. And he had a toy coach pulled by two tiny horses, so made that after it started moving toward him across a table its small coachman cracked his whip, and as it came to a stop, a page stepped down to open its door and then a little lady stepped out to curtsy to the charmed little prince.

The most skillful makers of mechanical toys in history may have been the Swiss Pierre Jacquet Droz (1721–1790) and his son Henri Louis Droz, who made such amazing mechanical toys for the King of Spain that they were almost condemned by the Spanish Inquisition as sorcerers.

The seventeenth and eighteenth centuries were the great heyday of toys moved by water, wind, sand, mercury, and clockworks. A toy duck that, when placed in water, would swim around, plume its feathers, and nibble breadcrumbs, was mentioned by Pierre Larousse in the encyclopedia he published in France in 1874. Joséphine Bonaparte (1763–1814) loved mechanical toys, and when petitioners came to see Napoleon with their children she gave them a miniature tree full of singing birds or a monkey that played a violin.

Clockwork toys, still popular throughout the nineteenth century, became plentiful when machine-produced tinplate toys appeared. Again Germany was a great center for their manufacture, especially from 1890 to 1910. Tin toys were also made in America, England, France, and Japan. Later, sharp edges and chemicals in the paint gave cause for concern about the safety of tin toys, but they remained popular because they were inexpensive, well made, long lasting, and they worked.

After clockwork toys, music boxes were soon invented too, and they were combined with other toys to produce tiny peepshows in which mechanical dancers moved to music. These became enormously popular.

The first toys to work by electricity appeared in 1889 at the Paris Exposition, when the experiments of Thomas Edison were first publicized.

Toy evolution has not, however, been a straightforward process of simple playthings gradually being replaced by more and more complicated ones. No matter how inventive people become, simple devices continue to amuse children. A permanently beloved toy that works by a simple spring was invented in the sixteenth century, when the first jack-in-a-box popped up and began to play peekaboo with children. In the nineteenth century the jack-in-a-box was one of a large group of popular "penny toys" in England. Other simple animated marvels available for a mere penny were twirling carousels, boats on wheels, small rocking horses, toy soldiers, walking birds, and jumping jugglers. From the Austrian Tyrol in the eighteenth century came little wooden acrobats that jump up and down on a crossbar as the toy that holds them is pushed along, with its wheels making the bar revolve. Tyrolean clowns, wrestlers, and bears still jump up and down and pound hammers at each other on the same ancient principle. And pecking birds operated by a short string or pendulum have continued to delight German, Russian, and Scandinavian children.

Other types of movable toys are discussed below.

Spinning Tops

These have been spinning around our spinning planet for many centuries. They are mentioned by Aristophanes (448–c. 388 B.C.), Plato (427–347 B.C.), and Virgil (70–19

B.C.), and the Roman statesman Cato (234–149 B.C.) recommended them to parents as a more suitable game than dice for children.

Tops were common in England by the fourteenth century, where they were connected with church ceremonies. Each parish had its own top, and on Shrove Tuesday every year top-spinning contests were held among parishes. Once a top stopped spinning it was put away until the following year and was said to be "sleeping"; hence the expression "to sleep like a top."

In some African countries, hollow tops that hum or whistle are popular. African children also spin tops made from forest nuts. In South America children spin the fruit of the calabash. American Indian children in the Southwest of the United States call tops *dancers* and keep them spinning by striking them with thongs made of buckskin.

In Asia tops come in many shapes and sizes. In some rural areas they are made from conch shells, their pointed tips ground flat. The Japanese make many kinds, including a "childbearing top," which contains smaller tops that are released as it spins. In Malaysia after the rice harvest, top-spinning competitions begin. Some Malaysian tops are six inches in diameter and weigh more than five pounds. Each player sets one spinning, then lifts it onto a thin post about eight inches high, where it may spin for as long as two hours. Both top spinning and top making are traditions requiring great skill, and are passed down from father to son. In Sri Lanka, children play *smitti*, a game in which one player sets his top in motion and another tries to knock it over with his own spinning top. If the child succeeds he or she wins a point.

Swings and Seesaws

No list of movable toys would be complete if it did not include those that rock and roll, swing or twirl, on which children can be pushed and pulled. As soon as they can sit upright with a little help, children are blissful when placed on a swing or seesaw and pushed back and forth and up and down.

The swing is an inheritance from ancient Athens, but among the Athenians, as in Asia today, swings were used by big girls and grown women rather than by babies. There was even a special swinging festival of youth, the *Aiora*, celebrated by girls swaying on swings and by boys jumping up and down on seesaw-like contraptions made of skins filled with wine. The ropes for the swings were made of strong vines, as they still are today in many countries, and these ropes were also used for jumping rope, another still popular childhood activity worldwide.

In Korea today there are traditional swing festivals where two girls together on a swing push each other and sometimes compete to see who can swing the highest. They also jump up and down on a *noltwigi*, a springy wooden seesaw board balanced on a pillow made of rice straw, to see who can jump highest, most gracefully, and stay on the board the longest.

In Elizabethan England seesaws were called "wild mares" and "titter-me-trotters," shortened to "teeter-totters" in the eighteenth century. The song "See saw, Margery Daw" is thought to have originated earlier with sawyers using a two-handed saw, who found its rhythm helpful in synchronizing and speeding up their work. It was not turned into a nursery rhyme game until about 1700, but its later popularity eventually caused the term *seesaw* to replace the other names.

Whirligigs and Sleds

Another type of movable toy, popular among American farm children in the days of the pioneers, was the "whirling-gig," later named the "whirligig," a revolving device made from a horizontal pole attached to a tree stump with a pin. Two children at each end of the pole raced around in circles, giving rides to other children perched on the pole. In the summer this was a homemade carousel, and in the winter it was used for lively games of "Snap the Whip," where instead of sitting on the pole children tied their sleds to it and tried not to fall off while being whirled around.

Sleds were among the earliest vehicles for children, and there was a special type in early America called the "jump scooter," which had a flat seat on top of a barrel stave attached to a sled, with a rope handle in front. Steering it took a lot of skill.

Yoyos

These toys that move up and down on a long string are said to have originated in ancient China, and there are pictures of yoyos on classical Greek pottery from around 450 B.C. Like many children's toys, they are also enjoyed by many adults.

In the sixteenth century, large yoyos weighing up to four pounds, with 20-foot-long thongs, were used as weapons in the Philippine jungles. In the eighteenth century, the yoyo was the rage among British and French aristocrats. In Britain it was known as the "bandalore" or "The Prince of Wales's toy." The Duke of Wellington (1769–1852) was one of the toy's most prominent fans. In France during the Revolution it was called *l'emigrette* because it was a favorite pastime of the emigré nobles in prison or driven from Paris by the Reign of Terror.

In 1926 an American named Donald F. Duncan marketed the yoyo commercially and it became a worldwide craze. Yoyo clubs sprang up all over the globe, with players competing in championship contests and stunt-playing exhibitions. The longest individual continuous endurance record is 120 hours, achieved by John Winslow of Gloucester, Virginia, in 1977.

RATTLES

Along with toes, fingers, and thumbs, the first toys in the average baby's life were also among the earliest toys in mankind's life. Rattles over 3,000 years old, of clay and earthenware and wood, have been found by archaeologists. They have small pebbles inside, to produce a rattling noise, and they vary in shape: some are round, some pear-shaped, some barrel-shaped, some egg-shaped. Some are elaborately decorated, carved, and painted. A clay rattle shaped like an owl, made around 1200 B.C., was discovered in a tomb in Cyprus and can be seen today in the British Museum. Some ancient Greek rattles shaped like ducks, rabbits, turtles, and even mother apes with offspring have been found in children's graves.

The Greek philosopher Archytas of Tarentum (400–365 B.C.) praised the rattle as "an admirable invention which people give to their children to amuse them and prevent them from breaking anything in the house, for a young person cannot be quiet."

At one time, all rattles were called "babies' bells." Toy bells have been discovered in the tombs of children of the first Christians in the catacombs of Rome. It is pleasant to know that, even when they were hiding out from their persecutors, parents saw to it that their children had toys to play with. Children's rattles were also found among the ruins of Pompeii. Some of them were shaped like pigs, because pigs used to be sacrificed for the preservation of children. Obviously these pigs were sacrificed in vain, for their young owners died with them when the volcano erupted and destroyed the city.

Ornate silver rattles involving groups of little bells linked with rings around tiny figures of birds, mermaids, monkeys, and other creatures, sometimes with a silver whistle as an added attraction, appeared in noble families' nurseries in Spain during the Middle Ages. Medieval rattles, known in England as *baubles*, were quite elaborate. Sometimes they were made in the shape of a knight's helmet, sometimes in the forms of birds or other animals. In country districts during the Middle Ages, rattles containing small bells were often made of wicker. To amuse wealthy babies there were silver rattles, many adorned with tinkling bells and often attached to gumsticks of coral or agate for teething infants to chew on. Such "rattels" were still popular in Elizabethan times and in Georgian England.

Native American mothers have traditionally made their babies' rattles from gourds filled with seeds and pigs' bristles and decorated with birds' feathers. Small shiny bright-colored objects, often exquisitely embroidered, are hung to the hoods and awnings of most Native American cradles, so that the tinkling sound and twinkling sight will divert the baby. Little bracelets of porcelain, beads, and bits of shells are also used to ornament the mother's hood or headdress and at the same time to entertain her papoose as she carries it around.

Mothers' necklaces serve the world over as babies' rattles also, though that is not usually a necklace's main function. An exception is the case of the baby nurses in Russia who used to be required to wear big red beads for the babies to pull and chew on. The bubble-shaped *bulla*, which babies in ancient Rome wore around their necks, may also have been a kind of rattle because Plutarch (c. A.D. 46–120) described it as both "an ornament" and "a child's toy."

In the twentieth century few babies play with silver rattles. Most of them wave mass-produced plastic rattles, if their parents have access to a store, or gourds filled with seeds if they live in remote and poor rural areas. But almost every baby in the world has a rattle of some kind.

WHEEL TOYS

Hoops

The simplest possible type of wheel toy is a wheel attached to nothing. It rolls along merrily all by itself, with a happy child racing alongside and catching it just before it falls.

Children in Greece used to roll hoops from an early age, both historically and biographically speaking. They used hoops on long handles for push toys and also enjoyed the noise of spoked hoops from which small disks dangled and clattered. The Greeks regarded hoop-rolling as a healthful exercise for children and also for adults with weak constitutions. The physician Hippocrates recommended it in one of his medical treatises written about 300 B.C. And the Greek sage Artemidorus in the A.D. second century wrote: "If you dream about rolling a hoop, it means that you have come to the end of your troubles, and abundant happiness will follow."

Games with hoops were also important to American Indians, to train boys in marksmanship. A screen of fiber or rawhide netting was woven into the center of a hoop after which it was rolled along the ground between two lines of players, who hurled darts at the rapidly moving target. This form of darts is still played today in some countries (see page 00).

Bowling with wooden hoops was a regular pastime among European children in the nineteenth century, and hoop races often involved older boys as well as little girls.

The hula hoop craze in the 1950s and 1960s added another chapter to the hoop's history. This time a large lightweight plastic hoop was spun around the player's waist in fast and elegant gyrations. Naturally, it inspired many contests to see who could keep it going the longest. Again, doctors recommended this activity as good exercise. Although for a while the fad faded and one could no longer find hula hoops in stores, it is revived from time to time and has never really died out entirely. In 1990 there was a 24-hour relay with 2,010 participants in St. John, New Brunswick, Canada, which was written up in the *Guinness Book of World Records* by setting a world record for simultaneous hula hooping.

Wheeled Vehicles

Little children in ancient Corinth, Rome, and Thebes liked wheels attached to boxes. They used to pull small wooden carts and tiny chariots with wooden horses on wheels, which they steered with reins. These still exist in toy museums, where the whole history of transportation is reproduced in miniature, starting off with simple toy boats and carts and concluding with airplanes and rockets.

A common feature of child life from the fifteenth to the eighteenth centuries was a sort of playpen on wheels. The six-year-old dauphin of France in 1607 had a go-cart he used to roll around his garden, and he also had a red and gilt coach large enough for him to sit in while he was pulled around the room by his pages. But another royal child had something even more delightful: the infant Napoleon II (1811–1832), named the King of Rome by his father, used to ride around in a tiny carriage pulled by real lambs.

Pedals were invented in the nineteenth century and they resulted in the appearance of a new type of wheeled toy, the "manumotive vehicle." At first these were called "walkalongs" and then became identified as bicycles, tricycles, or quadricycles, depending on how many wheels they had.

James Kenward in his book, *The Suburban Child*, published in 1955, reminisces about the toys and joys of his own childhood in England at the beginning of the twentieth century. He tells about the many types of vehicles that were then omnipresent. He and his playmates did not graduate directly from their strollers onto tricycles, like the children of today whom he describes as "brought up in the saddle." In those days, he explains, there was an intermediate period during which toddlers went walking every day. On these walks they were accompanied by convoys of nursery toys, so that from 3:00 to 4:30 P.M. every day, that is, from "after rest" to tea time, "the characteristic noise of Suburbia was of tiny wheels scraping along the pavements—a noise which combined with the jangling of the toys themselves to produce something like the chirruping of crickets."

The daily ritual of the walk began officially when the grownup in charge made a loop at one end of a string and slipped it over a small child's finger or wrist. At the other end of the string was the trailing convoy, sometimes "an orthodox train of locomotives and carriages but more often a mixed assortment." His own favorite grouping consisted of a locomotive towing a small elephant on brass wheels, which in turn towed a truck, which in turn towed an acrobat, which in turn towed a rabbit who "lolloped" because his front feet were attached to a crank, which in turn towed a naval gun.

Among the many types of large wheeled toys he played with were beadwheels, flying Dutchmen, handlecarts, handlewagons, hobby horses, hoops, pedal horses, pedal motors, scooters, tricycles and urchincars. But "the prince of pavement toys," says Kenward, was then, as it still is, the tricycle.

Miniature Model Vehicles

In 1934 Meccano began large-scale production of small-scale vehicles: buses, cars, trams (alias streetcars), and trucks, launching a new major toy industry. Its series of "Dinky Toys" was followed by the appearance on the market of rival products of competitors from Britain and other countries. The 1950s and 1960s are regarded by collectors as the heyday of these tiny die-cast vehicles, although enormous numbers are still produced.

In Britain the most popular rivals to Dinky Toys were "Corgi Toys" and the "Lesney Matchbox" and "Models of Yesteryear" series. Corgi Toys first appeared in 1957 and incorporated such new features as clear plastic windows, jewelled headlights and bonnets (hoods to American), and boots (trunks to Americans) that opened—glamorous features that were rapidly introduced to the Dinky range as well. The accuracy of details and the variety of these well-made models deserved and guaranteed their enduring popularity.

Toy Trains

Steam powered the industrial revolution and the machine age in the nineteenth century. The earliest passenger-carrying locomotives ran in Europe and the United States in the late 1820s and early 1830s, but it was a while before toy makers began to imitate them.

The first toy trains were fine models made for children of the rich, but later simple pull-along "floor" or "carpet trains" became available. The oldest known toy train still in existence is one made about 1840 in England. It is a gay little rainbow-colored wooden one with yellow wheels and coaches adorned with painted daisies, and it carries 12 extremely tiny passengers along a wooden track only 30 inches long, lined with tiny trees. Toys like this were fun but the real excitement of toy trains did not enter the nursery until model steam trains with water-filled boilers heated by spirit burners were produced. These were realistic—noisy and smelly. They were sometimes called Birmingham "dribblers" or "piddlers" because of the sprays of steam that emanated from them.

By the 1880s French and German manufacturers of tin toys began producing accurate, up-to-date models of clockwork trains, which were safer for children and less messy than those powered by live steam. A set of model tin plate toy trains made in Germany established a record in 1984 when it was sold at a Sotheby's auction in London for 25,000 pounds ($35,700).

In 1891, at the Leipzig Fair, Gebruder Marklin and Company of Gopingen, Germany, showed a much-admired clockwork railway set that could be added to with extra features and sets of railroad tracks. This probably marked the beginning of the "gauge system" for model railways. The gauge is the distance between pairs of wheels or rails. Gauge "1" equaled 1.75 inches; Gauge "0" equaled 1.25 inches, and Hornby Dublo "00" equalled 0.65 inches. By 1914, Gauge "00" was the most popular scale; using it a realistic layout could be built on the floor or a large table. Gauge "00" trains were popular because most families could afford a small set, a beginning that could grow and give increased pleasure to both children and parents over the years.

The first miniature electric trains were displayed in New York City in 1890, and by the 1930s electric power replaced clockworks. It allowed different speeds and greater realism. The Hornby Dublo system, announced in *Meccano* magazine in 1938, could be set on a table and easily dismantled. During World War II in England it was described as "the ideal blackout hobby for boys and their fathers," an absorbing occupation to keep one's mind off the frightening bombings going on.

DOLLS

The History of Dolls

Dolls, like other toys, have almost as long a history as children do. They have been found in ancient Egyptian tombs, some of which are 3,000 years old. The most primitive types were made of thin flat boards, sometimes with faces consisting only of raised dabs of clay, with strings or wooden beads for hair, while others were made of stuffed linen and had flax or fur hair stuck on with tar. They were usually "paddle dolls," with legs joined together in one piece to form a handle, but some had movable, joined arms and legs. There is a little Egyptian doll in the British Museum who has a glorious head of hair made from mud beads. And the daughter of an Egyptian Pharaoh of the nineteenth dynasty (1315–1200 B.C.), who died at the age of two or three, was buried at Thebes with a lovely doll made of painted wood with movable arms, wearing a short white dress.

Many of the earliest dolls were puppets. Greek ones painted in bright colors were often made with movable limbs attached to their bodies by strings and pins, and some could be made to jump about by means of a string through the top of the head. In the fourth century B.C., clay dolls of this type were made in quantity; archaeologists have found them in fragments of what appear to be toy shops.

Other ancient dolls were made of pottery or metal, and there were also rag dolls, some made flat like silhouettes, others woven of wool in the round. The Greeks also made some fragile dolls of plaster and wax and baked clay with painted faces and hinged arms and legs, which were remarkably like later Victorian dolls. The Romans had similar dolls, and for the children of wealthy families there were exquisite ones of wood and ivory. In Etruscan children's tombs, dolls have been found that still show traces of pretty dresses of woven cloth embroidered with flowers.

Plutarch said that many girls in the first century in Greece kept their dolls until the morning of their weddings, which usually arrived when they were 12 or 13 years old, before relinquishing them and offering them to a goddess. His own daughter Timoxena gave up her dolls on her seventh birthday, offering them at the altar of Venus. Until then she had cherished them and played with her baby dolls so realistically that she frequently begged her nurse to put them to her breast and feed them.

Not all early dolls were playthings, however. There were, for example, the *Ushabti* (or Answerers) of ancient Egypt, small clay or terra cotta figurines meant to represent slaves and friends of the dead and buried in tombs to accompany the dead on their trip to the next world. This was a humane custom that replaced an older less amusing one of burying live slaves and friends to take care of the dead members of royal families and to keep them from being lonely in the world beyond.

Dolls have been used as fetishes throughout the centuries. Some have been used to receive any disease or misfortune that otherwise would threaten the owner. When someone was sick a doll representing the invalid was often cast into a fire to destroy the disease. In an unpleasant tradition of voodoo, dolls have been named for enemies and then cursed and stuck with pins to bring misfortune to the people they represented. This and other unplayful uses of dolls are still made in some countries. In Austria, there is an ancient tradition of giving dolls to brides to assure fertility. In Ghana, young girls tie around the waist an *akwaba*, a flat doll carved of light wood, about nine inches high, with a string of beads around its neck and waist, to indicate that they are single. In New Zealand, Maori women wear a *tiki doll* around the neck to insure easy childbirth or large families. In the Sudan, fertility dolls are used to induce pregnancy. They are made of clay and decorated in scraps of fabric or beads.

Facts such as these are sometimes cited as evidence that dolls were invented as religious symbols or ceremonial objects long before they were designed as toys. According to some archeologists and historians, ancestor dolls, spirit dolls, votive dolls, talismen, and fetish dolls credited with occult powers preceded dolls as playthings. But perhaps these scholars who have peered into ancient tombs have failed to lift their eyes and look around at living children, and do not realize that the desire of a little child to mother a doll and of a parent to give a child a doll are universal impulses that can coexist with the use of dolls as sacred or magical objects.

Among the Pueblo Indians, for instance, the same small objects (sometimes carefully carved of wood, at other times just bundles of rags or sticks with bits of cloth wrapped around them), serve as both idols and toys. They are treated with reverence during religious ceremonies and at other times are wrapped up in blankets and carried around tenderly by motherly little girls, just like any other baby doll.

Other examples of how dolls can simultaneously be playthings and part of religious or semi-religious ceremonies are given every springtime in Japan, when the annual Doll's Festival is held. Also in Japan, *daruma* dolls are playthings while they are also used to bring good luck. Some are sold to farmers who use them as scarecrows to protect their crops. [See the section on Japanese dolls starting on page 301.]

In the Middle Ages

There is evidence in the writings and paintings of the Middle Ages that dolls were common toys, although they were sometimes considered dangerous because magicians and witches used them for sorcery. Perhaps for this reason many mothers in the Middle Ages would not allow their children to play with any doll unless it had first been blessed by a priest.

Professional doll makers appeared in the fourteenth century in the cities of Sonneberg and Nuremberg in Germany, making wooden dolls with movable arms and legs. This became a leading home industry. Rural families carved them during the winter and brought them to the cities in the spring to be exported all over the world. These dolls became famous because they were so well carved and no two were ever exactly alike.

Some early German dolls were made without legs, the bodies ending in handles to make it easy for a child to hold them, as had been done in ancient Egypt. Dolls like this still exist in France, where they are called *poupards*.

The Nuremburg Museum in Germany has examples of clay dolls from the fourteenth century, stiff but richly ornamented little figures. By the fifteenth century elaborate and expensive dolls were made for the daughters of the aristocracy. Since it was then customary for girls to be married at a very early age, many of these seem to have been made as wedding gifts.

Dolls in the Sixteenth, Seventeenth, and Eighteenth Centuries

During the sixteenth century, references to the human image as a child's toy turned up in English literature but not under the term "doll." Doll, at that time, was a nickname for Dorothy (as "Moll" was for Mary, or "Hal" for Harry) and was used also as a general term for a pet or a mistress. Toy images were called *babes* or *babees*. The term "babies" was not used for human infants until later. It seems a little strange to us to read about an excise tax that was levied in England in 1656 on "babies with heads of earth," and to see what look to us like tiny copies of adults referred to as "babes." However, in this era both adults and children dressed alike, so what look to us like miniature adults may have seemed like replicas of children to children of that time.

Few dolls have been preserved from the sixteenth century other than some expensive aristocratic types. The oldest English doll still in existence is believed to be one surviving from the reign of King Henry VIII. She has a wooden head covered with plaster and wears an elaborate red velvet dress. The Englishwoman who first owned her was so fond of her that in 1548 she willed her to her granddaughter with the request that she be passed down to future descendents. This was done for several centuries, but she now resides in a museum in Leeds.

Elizabethan "babies" once served as goodwill ambassadors. Sir Walter Raleigh (1552–1618), when he set forth on his expedition to America, took along some wooden ones for his sailors to give to Indian children, hoping in this way to make friends of the natives.

Wooden dolls, many whittled by fond fathers and uncles, and "babes of clouts" (clouts meant rags) were the most common types in the sixteenth and seventeenth centuries, but few of these humble types of dolls have been preserved.

By the seventeenth century, better-class dolls in Europe were made of cloth or leather bags stuffed with sawdust or bran, and there are some magnificent dolls that were made for King Gustavus Adolphus in 1630, still preserved at Uppsala in Sweden.

The oldest dressed wooden doll in the Victoria and Albert Museum in London is one from 1690 who has a pink satin dress with much trimming, an elaborate headdress, and black beauty patches on her face. Another English wooden doll made in the year 1690 brought the highest price ever paid so far for a doll, in an auction at Sotheby's in London in May 1984: 16,000 pounds ($36,000).

In the late seventeenth century, professional doll makers began to produce elaborately costumed sophisticated ladies with dark glass eyes, and hair nailed to the tops of their heads. Doll dressing became such a fine art by the eighteenth century that it has preserved an accurate record of contemporary fashions.

There is a record of a court trial held in England in 1733, during the reign of King James I, of some dolls stolen from their owner, a turner by trade, who made furniture and toys. The dolls he said had been stolen were "14 naked babies and two dozen dressed babies and one jointed baby." The mention of the jointed baby implies that the others were simple turned figures, so perhaps even well into the eighteenth century jointed dolls may have been in the luxury class. Some cute wooden dolls of the period were made of clothespins and potato mashers, and clothed in simple cotton dresses.

Around 1750 the industrial revolution resulted in mass-produced dolls. These were called "penny woodens" and were made entirely of wood, but they were less primitive than earlier handmade wooden dolls. They were jointed and ranged in size from a half-inch to four feet tall.

The major wooden toy producers during the seventeenth and eighteenth centuries were those in the Austrian and Bavarian Tyrol, southeast of Nuremberg. At first people of these areas marketed their toys through peddlers and independent agents, but by about the end of the eighteenth century wholesale houses dealing solely in toys became established in Nuremberg, solidifying its position as the toy distribution center of the world.

Wax, a material that had been used in ancient times to make dolls, was forgotten about until it reappeared in the eighteenth century, when it became another popular material for dolls. Most of the few wax dolls that have survived were in great doll houses, or "baby houses" as they were then called. These wax "babies" were skillfully and naturalistically molded on stuffed linen bodies. Often they were made without legs, with their bodies resting on stiff petticoats. Some dolls wore seven petticoats apiece. Others had glass eyes and real hair, even on eyelashes and eyebrows.

Most eighteenth-century dolls were made in Austria, but England also became famous for the realism of its wax dolls. They were forerunners of the life-sized figures of Mme. Tussaud. Most of these dolls were not entirely wax but had only wax faces on top of calico bodies stuffed with sawdust.

Luxury dolls from the eighteenth century are now known by collectors as "Queen Anne" dolls, although they were made both before and after the reign of Queen Anne (1702–1714). They reached a high level of splendor and costliness and were used more as status symbols by the aristocracy than as children's toys. Those that still exist show little evidence of having been played with.

A less expensive type of doll made of paper also became available in the eighteenth century. These first paper dolls, made of thick cardboard, appeared around 1700. Both America and England claim to have invented them, but in France, around 1790, they became known as "English dolls." They wore the latest ladies' fashions, including lingerie and corsets, and they often had as many as six sets of dresses.

In the Nineteenth Century

With the spread of the industrial revolution and the growth of the middle class, better quality dolls became more widely available. Doll making was a thriving industry by now, especially in England, France, Germany and Holland, and early in the century new materials began to be used and new types of dolls appeared.

Wooden dolls were still in evidence, however. Many of them were imported to England from Holland and were therefore called "Dutch dolls" or "Flanders babies." Some wooden dolls were made with crude, scooplike hands, but others had shoulders, elbows, hips, and knees. The famous dolls of Princess Victoria, as she was known until she became Queen of England at the age of 18 in 1837, were of this type. She had 132 dolls and for 32 of them she made the clothes herself. Taking care of so many dolls must have been good practice not only for mothering nine children in later years but also for ruling an empire. Her dolls can still be seen today, in Kensington Palace in London.

"Pedlar dolls" became well liked in the first half of the century. These were replicas of the era's street hawkers who were one-woman department stores that sold wares from door to door. These dolls came equipped with little baskets carrying varied wares: tiny umbrellas, lanterns, candlesticks, dishes, and so forth.

Early in the nineteenth century a new type of doll was born in England. For the first time many "babies" were made to look like actual human babies. In the Victoria and Albert Museum there is one with a lovely lace dress and equipped with a minute powder puff, hairbrush, and other accessories. Another baby doll from this period is equipped with "nappies" (diapers to Americans).

The artist Kate Greenaway (1846–1901), who had a great influence on the clothing of several generations of dolls as well as of children through her exquisite drawings, herself as a child had only one doll to play with. It was almost four feet tall and wore full-sized baby clothes.

The "shut-eye doll" was born in 1826, soon after the hollow china head was invented. In the earliest ones the eyes closed and opened in response to a tug on a string, but in later models a lead weight was placed inside the doll so that it shut its eyes, apparently naturally, when it was laid down.

The first "talking dolls" appeared around 1830, "Mama dolls" and "Papa dolls" who spoke when their arms were moved. Later, Thomas Edison marketed for $20 a doll with a larger vocabulary than most; it was called "Edison's Phonographic Doll" and recited, rather squeakily, "Mary Had a Little Lamb."

An "eating doll" also appeared in the 1880s. She ate candy that emerged for reuse at the bottom of her foot.

Some dolls in this century had papier mâché heads, molded, painted, and glazed. Their hair was shaped in the elaborate styles of the period and they wore elegant costumes. The bodies were sometimes made of wood, sometimes of stuffed calico. They were first produced primarily in Germany and later in America by Ludwig Greiner, a German immigrant in Philadelphia who, in 1856, took out the first doll patent in the United States. His dolls, made for 25 years, were similar to those then being made in Germany except that his had painted eyes, while most of the German dolls had glass ones. These dolls became known as "milliners' models" because they were sent around the countryside to display the latest in feminine finery topped by chic hats.

"Wax dolls" were popular too because their features could be molded more realistically than wooden or papier mâché dolls. They looked more lifelike and the wax gave them a pretty, translucent complexion. Most collectors today prize the early ones known as "slit heads" from the technique used to insert wigs of mohair in the tops of their heads, and also those called "squash heads" or "pumpkin heads" because of the shapes of their molded coiffures. Their arms were usually made of white, pink, or tan kid attached to a stuffed calico body.

The world's loveliest wax dolls were made in London between 1850 and 1900 by the Montanari, Chierotti, and Marsh families. The first two used molded thick wax, while the Marsh dolls were made of a wax layer over composition, an inexpensive mixture of many materials such as crushed paper, plaster of Paris, bran, sawdust, and glue that, though malleable when wet, hardens into a durable form. Heads of composition dolls were often cast in the same molds designed for costlier dolls, but they were within the financial reach of many more people. Soon composition came to be used for dolls' arms and legs as well as heads, and eventually to mold their bodies.

The first "china dolls" were made in Germany, with heads of glazed porcelain on top of calico bodies, and with china limbs. Many china heads were sold separately, however, because these dolls were a great luxury and it therefore became common practice for many people to buy only the head and then to mount it on a homemade body. For many little girls, china dolls were such special gifts that they were received only once and they were played with extremely carefully because they were breakable and could not be repaired. Children today, who are used to comparatively inexpensive plastic dolls, have no idea what a real tragedy it was in those days to break a loved and irreplaceable doll.

When clay comes from the kiln it is in a hard form known as "bisquit" or "bisque" which can either be glazed to produce glossy china or left in its unglazed state. Some of the world's most beautiful dolls in the 1850s had heads made of bisque. They were mass produced in porcelain factories both in France and Germany.

In France in the 1860s, a family of toy makers, the Jumeau family, revolutionized the industry with dolls whose heads and shoulders were made of bisque and their bodies made from intricately cut and carefully stitched stuffed white kid, even to the fingers and toes. M. Jumeau's son patented a swivel neck for these dolls. Their eyes, made of enamelled glass, were realistic. Their clothes were *haute couture* and they were lavishly supplied with accessories such as boots, slippers, parasols, furs, jewels, gloves, and fans, all contained in leatherbound trunks complete with locks and often with the dolls' initials. They were so exquisitely made that they set a standard of beauty and excellence that has never been surpassed. Little girls were thrilled when they were allowed on special occasions to open the trunks, dress up the dolls, and play gently with them.

In addition to baby dolls and fashion dolls and gentleman dolls, there were specialty dolls— for example, mechanical dolls who could perform feats ranging from smoking to swimming. After clockwork toys were invented, walking dolls joined the doll population. Walking dolls of 1862 vintage worked with concealed clock mechanisms that propelled them smoothly and rhythmically. Dancing dolls, which have survived from 1872, had lively footwork that sounds like tap dancing, caused by a hidden clock mechanism. England's Princess Victoria owned a toy theater where she used to put on shows for her dolls, with tiny mechanical dancers whirling to the tunes of a music box. And there is a walking doll that was born in 1870, when it was known as an *autoperipatetikos*, on display in the Victoria and Albert Museum in London.

Another type of specialty doll in the nineteenth century was the fortune doll. Paper fortunes were sewn onto the doll's costume or placed in a circle around her. A spindle inside her enabled the doll to spin around, and when she stopped spinning her cane pointed to one of the fortunes.

The idea of merchandising dolls and other toys to capitalize on the fame of a fashionable craze did not originate in our century with Davy Crockett, Peter Pan, Mickey Mouse, Raggedy Ann, Babar, Winnie the Pooh, or Shirley Temple. When *Uncle Tom's Cabin* was a best-selling novel and a hit play that toured America in the 1850s, a double-doll called "Eva Topsy" was manufactured. Wrapped cozily in a large blanket, when held in one position little Eva, haloed by soft blond curls, lay sleeping peacefully; when turned upside down and around, bright-eyed dark-skinned Topsy suddenly "growed," complete with gaily printed hair ribbon, nightie, and coverlet.

One would imagine that Beatrix Potter (1866–1943), the English author-illustrator who created Peter Rabbit and his sisters Flopsy, Mopsy, and Cottontail, must have cuddled and loved soft floppy bunnies as a tiny girl. However, the only toy she ever owned was a dilapidated black wooden doll called Topsy.

Modern Dolls

Humble, old-fashioned rag and wooden dolls continue to be cherished in the twentieth century, although they are now a minority of the doll population.

In 1914 a comic strip artist, Johnny Gruelle (1880–1938), painted a face on an old rag doll and named it "Raggedy Ann." She was soft and cuddly, with bright red wool hair and a big painted smile. She was dressed in red striped stockings, a flouncy white apron, and flowered red dress. She had the words "I love you" written on the red heart on her chest. She was the heroine of Gruelle's much loved books about her and her brother "Raggedy Andy," another rag doll with equally red wool hair, a huge smile, and the words "I love you" over his heart. He was clad in a red checked shirt, blue trousers, a blue cap, and bow tie. These two dolls became so popular that during the half-century after their birth there were approximately 10 million of them. They have stayed the same friendly, jolly, huggable little creatures for more than 80 years in spite of all the more glamorous dolls now surrounding them. Only one change has been made over the years: in the 1960s one manufacturer added a music box to Raggedy Ann's innards.

In the 1920s there was a delightful children's book called *Rackety Packety House* about a shabby and neglected dolls' house. It contained a family of bedraggled rag dolls with faded wooden heads, who were ignored by the snobbish young English princess who owned them because she preferred her big, new, fancy dolls' house filled with beautifully clad china dolls. The author Frances Hodgson Burnett (1849–1924) explained that it is only when you are sound asleep that your dolls can move around on their own. At night, when their owner was asleep, all the dolls got together and became good friends and finally the young princess realized how sweet and jolly and lovable the rackety ones were. She had their faces repainted and sewed new clothes for them, and thereafter the humble and aristocratic dolls lived as good neighbors and playmates, husbands and wives, happily ever after. This seems like a parable of what has happened in the modern world, where old-fashioned cloth and wooden dolls still exist even though the most sophisticated dolls ever seen are now vying for the attention of children.

In 1930 another children's book called *Hitty: Her First Hundred Years*, by Rachel Field, told about the adventures of a small wooden doll who went to a party and was humiliated at first by the big, beautiful wax and china dolls there. She immediately won the hearts of sympathetic children, and the book became a best seller.

Fashion dolls and other specialty dolls also have continued to be made today. Mme. Alexander was one of the leading American manufacturers and designers of fashion and costume dolls in the middle of this century. She was born in 1925—appropriately in a doll hospital that her parents ran. In the 1930s, specialty dolls enjoyed a special boom. Some were advertisement dolls, such as Aunt Jemima, who advertised pancakes. Most of them were modeled after famous personalities: Sonja Henie, Mickey and Minnie Mouse, Shirley Temple. Today this tradition is still carried on, with Peanuts dolls, the Simpsons, and others. Even though Shirley Temple has not appeared in movies since the 1930s, she still holds her own in the doll world: A Shirley Temple "Stand Up and Cheer" doll made of fine bisque porcelain, wearing a red-and-white polka-dot dress and frilled petticoat, with a red bow in her hair and Mary Jane shoes with white anklets, plus dimples, eyebrows, eyelashes, and ringlets, was produced and promoted in 1986.

Yet the twentieth century has brought as many changes in the world of dolls as it has in everything else. Developments in the plastics industry, starting with celluloid but soon moving on to durable and flexible materials like vinyl, have resulted in a completely new type of doll: soft, washable, virtually unbreakable, incredibly realistic, inexpensive, and manufactured in enormous quantities.

With so many kinds of dolls to choose from, novelty became all-important, and every few months there seemed to be a new fad. Dolls became more and more realistic every year and yet, in the constant search for novelty, weird dolls also took center stage in spurts, when realism began to pall and the desire for fantasy prevailed.

For instance, in the 1960s there was a rage for "good-luck trolls" made by Thomas Dam, a woodcarver in Denmark. They were promptly described as "those Dam things from Denmark." They had soft hair made of Icelandic sheeps' wool and glassy popeyes. After a hiatus, the popularity of trolls was revived in the 1990s.

Also, 12,000 "Poor Pitiful Pearl" dolls a day poured forth from the Horsman Doll Factory in South Carolina during the 1960s. These were strangely appealing, wistful little ragamuffins.

Baby Dolls

Today's realistic baby dolls not only open and shut their eyes and say "Mama," but many also drink and eat, burp and cry, crawl or walk. Their skin is soft, their hair looks and feels real, and it can be brushed, combed, cut, shampooed, and set in curlers.

In the 1920s a doll known as the "Bye LoBaby" was created in California. Its face and figure were modeled accurately on a real three-day-old newborn, undoubtedly one of the youngest professional models in history.

Another extremely realistic baby doll was the "DyDee" doll originated by Marie Wittman, a schoolteacher, who brought the idea to Hugo Baum of the American Effanbee Toy Company in the early 1960s. Mr. Baum, who has been called the Ziegfield of the doll industry, fell in love with the DyDee doll at first sight. She had lots of what today's doll makers call play value. Her little mother could bottle feed her, after which she wet her diapers, after which the child-mother could bathe, powder, and change her. Her manufacturers were ingenious: the water she drank emptied into a tube through which it was pulled by suction, and the exit valve held the water back for a decent interval, so that the young mother would not become confused about the timing relationship between a baby's two natural functions.

When first introduced, the DyDee doll was not greatly admired. People thought she was vulgar. But after about a year she became a big hit. In England her respectability and popularity dated from the day when the Duchess of Kent went to Harrod's department store and bought one.

In the 1960s there was also a doll called "Baby Brite" who had two magic belly buttons. When one was pressed she turned her head, shut her eyes, and went to sleep; when the other was pressed, she opened her eyes and lifted both arms to be picked up.

There was a furor in the 1960s when some realistic baby boy dolls were introduced complete with penises. And along with this sex revolution in the doll industry came the movement for racial equality. There had been popular black dolls before, notably "Topsy" and "Little Black Sambo," a cloth doll that many children in the 1920s dearly loved, as they also loved the humorous short story in which he played the title role. However, these were comical rather than glamorous, and many blacks resented the image they portrayed of their race. Black families began to demand attractive and realistic black dolls for their little girls, and the law of supply and demand soon provided some.

And then other races and nationalities also wanted representation. With the growing internationalism of society in this century, geographic costume dolls have become increasingly popular. UNICEF has periodically produced sets of Festival Dolls, attractive paper dolls clothed in traditional costumes of many countries and accompanied by little booklets giving information about each country. In New Delhi, India, an International Doll Museum features what it claims is the world's largest collection of traditional costume dolls, from over 65 countries.

Today there are three "baby doll collections" produced by the Pleasant Company in Wisconsin designed for children three years old and up: an African American Collection, an Asian American Collection and a Caucasian Collection. Each doll is dressed in a lace-trimmed cotton sleeper with a matching undershirt and cloth diaper. It can be ordered alone or with a pop-up book called *Our New Baby*, which is particularly useful to give young children expecting a sister or brother. Letting the older child take care of her own baby while Mother takes care of hers can help prevent jealousy over a new sibling. Among optional accessories are a cuddly little bunny that squeals; a diaper bag containing a washcloth and towel, bottles of make-believe lotion and bath powder, several diapers, and a changing pad; baby clothes including bootees and socks, a sweater, bonnet, party dress with matching bib; and a book of lullabies and a beribboned lullaby basket with a mattress, blanket, pillow, and bumper pad that has a musical heart that softly plays "Brahms' Lullaby" when it is pressed.

Other New Types of Dolls

Of course, babies tend to grow up and so do baby dolls. Some nowadays are not only lifelike but life-sized, so specifically that they come in three-month, one-year, two-year, and three-year sizes.

The first really big doll to become widely popular in the United States was "Patti Play Pal" in the early 1960s. She was a plastic three-year-old that looked very much like a flesh-and-blood one. She owed her popularity to the fact that she was the first large doll to be made light enough in weight not to be a burden to her playmate owner. Patti was three feet tall and could wear her three-year-old owner's clothes, yet she weighed only four-and-a-half pounds.

There were teenage dolls too, as everyone knows because of the immense popularity of "Barbie" and her boyfriend "Ken," who have been teenagers for more than 50 years. Clearly the mother instinct of little girls is not the factor that has made these dolls so popular; rather, they are perceived as teenage role models. Mattel Toys, the company that produced Barbie, also had good sales with a dark-skinned version of her, and later went further, introducing "Shani," a black doll whose facial features and slightly fuller figure more accurately reflected the way many African American girls actually look (less anorexic than the fashion model Barbie).

Another twentieth-century development has been activism on behalf of the disabled, and in response to this there are now "sick" and "disabled" dolls. Little girls have for many generations enjoyed playing nurse and doctor, but never before have they had so much medical equipment. There are now dolls that come supplied with eyeglasses, bandages, braces, crutches, slings, arm and leg casts, thermometers, wheelchairs, wooden legs, even removable spots so that they can recover from chicken pox and measles. Some actually respond to mouth-to-mouth resuscitation.

One of the modern developments in dolls has made its appearance with the assistance of the computer industry: the interactive doll. Several of these, with vocabularies larger than "Mama," were introduced in the 1960s, but most of them could not speak very distinctly. One that could, however, was "Charmin' Chatty," who was truly charming. She was introduced by Mattel in 1963, and advertised as "the doll that plays with you." She was a lanky little girl, two feet tall, with an appealing face and big eyes behind a pair of black wire-rimmed glasses, dressed in a neat little sailor suit, and she came in two versions, one blonde and one auburn haired, with optional accessories. She could sit down or stand, move her arms, open her eyes or shut them, but above all she could speak, extremely clearly, and in foreign languages.

She was provided with a series of five record disks to be inserted in her back, and they contained 120 varied words. One record was called "Let's Play"; it came with two sets of games, "At the Fair" and "Skate and Slide." Another one was about going shopping; others were about birthday parties or pajama parties, and one called "Travels around the World" introduced seven different languages: English, French, German, Italian, Japanese, Russian, and Spanish. And the pièce de résistance was that she had her own Golden Book in which her owner could read all about her. She is no longer on the market but has become a coveted collectors' item.

Another younger type of talking doll, introduced before Christmas in 1986, was appropriately named "Baby Talk." Still another was named "YakketyYak." Baby Talk was an infant-size doll programmed to respond to specific situations and vocal promptings. She could move her lips and cheeks and flutter her eyelashes, giggle, and say such things as "hug me" and "let's play." If a child put her on her back she would say, "I'm tired; I want to go to sleep." After this, if the child continued to make noise, Baby Talk repeated this message every 20 seconds, but if the room was quiet she would say, "Nighty night, I'm going to sleep," and her electronics would shut off.

Dolls have become increasingly big business. In the 1980s manufacturers, retailers, and parents were stunned by the passion with which children took to the "Cabbage Patch Kids," cuddly dolls who were loved, it seemed, not in spite of the fact that they were not pretty but because of that fact. Evidently their pathetic looks brought out little girls' mothering instinct. The craze went so far that stores were continually sold out and in 1984 summer camps even had to provide accommodations for them. Children were not content to own just one, either; they demanded whole families. In 1985 these dolls earned Coleco Industries, their manufacturers, more than $597 million. This equaled briefly the phenomenal annual sales of Barbie, who is sold in 140 countries at the astonishing rate of two dolls every second, according to Ruth Handler, cofounder of Mattel and the creator of Barbie. Incidentally, she named Barbie and Ken after her daughter and son, but neither of them was fond of their namesakes. But according to Mrs. Handler, the typical American girl between the ages of 3 and 10 is so smitten that she owns an average of eight Barbie dolls.

Startling innovations in the doll population continue to appear. Following a special survey of the qualities young girls find appealing, the American Greetings Corporation created a pink-cheeked doll dressed all in pink. They christened her "Strawberry Shortcake." In 1980 they introduced her to American children as the star of a series of animated TV specials on over 100 stations; she quickly became the nation's favorite doll for a while. Via an avalanche of related commercial products featuring replicas of her, along with pink doll furniture and accessories, foods, and candies, she earned the staggering sum of $1 billion for her creators. This was almost, but not quite, as much as Mattel Toys has earned over the years from Barbie.

Among other innovations, there is now a "pregnant doll" that can give birth to a tiny baby doll and then get back her slim figure. And one ingenious manufacturer, in an effort to dissuade teenage girls from having babies, has made a baby doll that screams constantly all night long. These dolls are produced for educational purposes and are expensive, but they are also proving to be quite effective.

The American Girls Collection

The ultimate in attractive African American dolls is "Addy Walker," a porcelain doll with long black hair that can be brushed and braided, and who has lovely clothes and many accessories. She is part of a recreational and educational collection made and distributed by Pleasant T. Rowland, founder and president of the appropriately named Pleasant Company in Middleton, Wisconsin. The Pleasant Company specializes in historic American dolls, made for girls over eight years old, "old enough to read who still love to play," as its catalog says. Each of these dolls comes with one or more books with stories about the period the doll represents, and replicas of items from that period.

GUYS AND DOLLS

It seems hard to understand why the desire to play with, protect, feed, and be fond of a small person should frequently be regarded as something to be squelched in future fathers while it is considered admirable and enthusiastically encouraged in future mothers. Only today, when it is increasingly common for fathers to share child care and other household responsibilities, the fact that some boys enjoy playing with dolls is no longer considered disgraceful, and psychologists actually encourage parents to allow their sons to play with dolls.

Raggedy Andy, in the 1920s, helped to break the taboo against boys playing with dolls because he was such an undeniably boyish and jolly doll that there could be no possible disgrace in a boy's enjoying his company. But actually there were many masculine dolls longer ago than this. Before the creation of the baby doll in the seventeenth century, male and female dolls were made in almost equal numbers.

It is lucky for future generations of children that one little boy who loved to play with dolls was allowed to: Hans Christian Andersen (1805–1875) in Denmark. His father was a cobbler and a skillful woodcarver, and he liked to make ingenious toys for his son. He made Hans a peepshow with many characters, and he put plays on for him. He made him a mill with a miller who danced. He made pictures that changed when Hans pulled a string. And he made wooden dolls who nodded their heads. Hans himself made a little playhouse in his back yard by taking a broomstick and stretching one of his mother's aprons from a wall to a nearby gooseberry bush. In this "house" he played for hours with his wooden dolls, and even made clothes for them; his mother hoped he would be a tailor when he grew up. And the first Hans Christian Andersen fairy tales were stories he made up to tell his dolls.

As a young boy in Scotland the future inventor of the telephone, Alexander Graham Bell (1847–1922), showed a sign of things to come by inventing a talking doll that said "Mama."

A famous cutter-out of paper dolls was Victor Hugo (1802–1885), who made them for his children. He used to tell stories to them and other enthralled groups of children while keeping his fingers busy cutting out paper dolls, swans, and castles.

George Bernard Shaw (1856–1950) also admitted that he had enjoyed playing with dolls when he was a boy. And the French composer Maurice Ravel (1875–1937) was another boy who loved dolls and who continued to love them even after he had grown up. He had an enormous toy collection that spilled out from shelves and glass cases all over his piano, and in addition to collecting toys he made them for small children he knew. When we listen to his musical tribute to childhood, "Ma Mére l'Oye" (Mother Goose), we have to be glad that he was this childish.

JAPANESE DOLLS

Dolls are important in Japan. Japan takes them so seriously that it even holds a three-day Doll Festival every year, in the spring.

The art of doll making is handed down in families. One family in Tokyo has been making dolls for 10 generations. Several types of dolls have been made in Japan for more than 300 years:

- *The daruma:* Referring to this doll a Japanese proverb says, "If he falls down seven times, he will come up eight times." The doll is constructed with a weighted round base so that whenever it is pushed over it will roll around for a few seconds but always return to an upright position. It is named after Bodhidharma, a sixth-century priest credited as the founder of Zen Buddhism, who stressed the importance of acquiring inner serenity and a balanced life.

  There are many kinds of darumas. "Bean dolls" are constructed in the same way as traditional darumas, are decorated in dark blue and bright red, and made in pairs to keep each other company; they are regarded as symbols of a happy couple. Many darumas are made for the celebration of the Japanese New Year. In the winter Japanese children build snowmen in the shape of the daruma. In parts of Japan woman darumas are thrown into the homes of friends to bring happy new year wishes. Some darumas are considered charms against illness and for the healthy growth of children.

  An amusing tradition associated with darumas is the "wishing daruma" made without eyes. When a child makes a wish he or she paints in one eye and only after the wish has come true does the daruma receive its second eye.

- *The gosho:* This is a fat doll with a round face meant to look like that of a baby.

- *The okeshi:* This doll has a wooden cylinder for a body and a painted ball on top for the head. It makes a sound like a baby crying when its head is turned. Peasants in the northern provinces of Japan make these dolls, spending their winter evenings painting them in bright colors.

- *The hina:* This is an ancestral ceremonial doll that is displayed in March during the annual Dolls' Festival. A pair of these hina dolls is bought at the birth of every girl. Each year a new one is added for each daughter, and the whole doll family is handed down from mothers to daughters for many generations. When a girl grows up and gets married, she takes her hina dolls with her to her new home.

These dolls are the ultimate in delicacy, both as to charm and breakability, so little Japanese girls are trained from an early age to play with them lovingly but extremely carefully, even reverently.

During the three days of the yearly Doll Festival, girls wait on their hina dolls with loving care. Doll families are taken to visit each other, carried on the backs of their little mothers just as Japanese babies are carried on their mothers' backs. Each doll sleeps at night under a green mosquito netting, with a tiny wooden pillow. The little girls cook real food for the dolls, red and white rice cakes and sweets shaped like fruit and fish, and serve them on toy dishes. The food is offered first to the dolls and later to the children who brought them to visit.

This kind of play is very formalized and has several serious purposes. It is intended to teach girls from an early age to be gentle because the dolls are so fragile, to be good cooks and neat housewives, to be cordial hostesses and gracious guests, and to appreciate beauty. Not only are the dolls exquisitely made and clothed, but the shelves that hold them are covered with attractive red cloth and decorated with paper peach blossoms and lanterns and with miniature orange and cherry trees on either side. The Festival is also meant to encourage respect for the traditions of their ancestors and the leaders of their country. On the top shelf, in the place of honor, dolls representing the Emperor and Empress sit, with little ladies in waiting, musicians, guards, and footmen, all dressed in the rich court costumes of ancient Japan and arranged on either side or below them.

When the ceremony of *O-Hina-sana* (Honorable Miss Doll) is over, the dolls are carefully put away along with other family treasures and left untouched until the next year, when they will again be taken out and arranged on shelves in the family's best room.

THE ARMS RACE IN THE NURSERY

War games have been played throughout history and every real war has had its fighting men and weapons reproduced in miniature to add to the unending armament race that goes on in the world's playrooms and playgrounds. The ancient Egyptian equivalent of a toy gun was a miniature battle ax. Children in ancient Greece and Rome played with toy soldiers made of baked clay or wood or metal. The ancient Etruscans left behind them in Italy many metal toy soldiers, horsemen and horses, and wrestling boys, found inside their children's tombs.

In every primitive society little boys, almost as soon as they can hold anything in their fists, are given small spears made of sticks, or bows and blunt-tipped arrows, miniature tomahawks, or clubs. Bows and arrows have always been favorite toy weapons in China and Japan. Japanese boys have played for centuries with bamboo water pistols and blow-arrows, and in China small bamboo popguns that shoot pellets of paper, blowguns that shoot pebbles, and guns that shoot water have also been popular for centuries.

Gunpowder burst into Chinese nurseries in the tenth century, even before it was used in real wars. The Chinese at that time allowed it to be used only for making firecrackers.

England was where the peashooter originated, in l500. Realistic little pistols made of brass were other sixteenth century toys in England. Toy armies were not sold in shops until the eighteenth century, but little figures of medieval knights in armor with lances and maces, made of glazed stone or metal, were made before that privately. Tiny knights who joust when worked by strings have survived from the year ll80, and in the Elizabethen era toy soldiers were marching on movable slides.

The first flat painted army of tin soldiers was made by Andreas Hilpert, a tin founder and pewterer in Nuremberg, Germany, around 1730 during the war-filled reign of Frederick the Great. These tiny soldiers immediately conquered the world. Soon small armies dressed in the uniforms of almost every country were made, and a standard height, called the Nuremberg scale, of one-and-one-half inches or less was agreed on by the manufacturers, so that no children meeting other children in battle with their tin soldiers would have an unfair advantage or disadvantage by having giants fight against midgets. With advancing technology, tin soldiers advanced from flat to semiflat and then to rounded shapes. In the nineteenth century fully three-dimensional solid military battalions appeared for the first time. The appropriately named Britain family in Great Britain produced the first set of light-weight rounded metal soldiers in l893. Less expensive plastic armies began to appear in the late l950s.

Although the trend toward ever more lethal weapons, which has been such a distressing aspect of the history of war, has always been imitated in the nursery, there has been one major difference. Even though there has been no peace, there has been coexistence. New weapons have not rendered older ones obsolete. Ancient Vikings and medieval knights, American cowboys and Indians still fight battles today along with their more sophisticated successors, both modern armies and aliens from outer space.

In real war, bows and arrows and daggers were replaced by the crossbow in the Middle Ages. It was considered such a horrifying "improvement" over its predecessors that at first soldiers who used it in battle had to do a year's penance before they could be absolved in the confessional and allowed to receive Holy Communion. Later the crossbow gave way to cannons and modern guns, and even these seem almost benign in comparison with today's latest weapons, both real and "pretend": death-ray guns and atomic bombs. Among the variations offered for sale at recent toy fairs have been replicas of 30-caliber machine guns, hand grenades, rocket "satellite destroyers," realistic bombers carefully designed to teach future bombardiers how to sight on target, aim, and release their deadly loads, remote-control jet bombers, jet air moon rocket launchers, ICBM-missile launching stations, and Frankenstein-like robots, which will destroy anything at a child's command.

Keeping Guns—Toy or Real—Away from Children

Many parents excuse the presence of these realistic lethal weapons in their children's hands by saying the children demand them, but there are several things wrong with this alibi. For one thing, children cannot be given everything they want. Parents deny their children poisonous food and try to protect them from dangers of which they are aware even when the children are not, such as playing with knives or matches and crossing the street against traffic. "The egg does not teach the hen," says an old Russian proverb. And there is a famous Chinese story about a child's nurse who was scolded by the parents for letting him cry for an hour instead of giving him whatever it was that he wanted; the nurse replied, "You give it to him; he saw the moon shining in a bucket of water, and he wants the moon."

Secondly, children are often shown these things and made to want them long before they have asked for them or even heard of them. Many mothers give toy guns to little boys while they are still in baby carriages, thinking it's "cute" to teach them to say "bang, bang, you're dead!"

Thirdly, if children do see these destructive things on TV, in newspapers, magazines, movies, and elsewhere does it follow that it is a good idea to let them see even more of them than is inevitable and to treat them as fun and show them in detail how to use them? Shakespeare said, "The sight of means to do ill deeds makes ill deeds done." And the frightening increase in recent years of children who have killed other children with real guns, often because they do not make a clear distinction in their minds between real life and play, bears this out.

If war is an inevitable necessity, perhaps it is sensible to train little boys and girls through play to perform their future part in it courageously by putting guns in their hands and gas masks on their faces. However, since everyone, including soldiers, claims to hate war, it would seem more tasteful to do so with a bit of reluctance rather than with uncritical enthusiasm.

In the early days of America, when pioneers who lived in isolated areas needed guns for hunting and protection, children were carefully and firmly taught that guns are weapons, not toys, and they were never to play with them. The American poet Henry Wadsworth Longfellow (1807–1882), when he was a little boy, liked to play soldier and started out loving guns but later changed his mind. He was five years old when the War of 1812 started. He actually saw the battle between the American brig *Enterprise* and the British schooner *Boxer*, and was so excited that he wanted to take his toy gun and go off right away to be a soldier in the war. Later, however, he went hunting one day with his brother and shot a robin by mistake; with tears in his eyes, he resolved never to fire a gun again.

The Impact of Real War on War Games

In 1955, when the English writer James Kenward recalled his childhood in his book *The Suburban Child*, he described with relish the elaborate war games he used to play on cold or rainy days. His entire nursery became a battlefield, with rivers marked in chalk across the floor, railway lines and bridges, roads, towns, farms, and clusters of trees carefully laid out, and cavalry, infantry, and guns set into opposing positions. Sometimes the battles, which he usually played with his uncle, took all day, and sometimes even all weekend. He said these battles were exciting but not really bloodthirsty; the soldiers did not kill each other; they "took" each other as in chess.

But then, suddenly, real war arrived and took the fun out of this fascinating game:

> When I was seven, there came the First World War. . . .Many of the fathers [and uncles] who found themselves soldiers at the beginning of the war were caught in the act of playing. They were like children snatched out of their game into this reality. Their soldierhood was a nightmare developed out of a dream. They had enjoyed their uniforms and their summer camps as children enjoy dressing up and acting, and then it happened to them as children are told that it will happen to people who persist in making faces—they got stuck like that. The troop trains that whistled their way into the tunnel were filled with children in uniform.

Incredulity and panic swept through families, affecting even the smallest members.

Since this war, he says, "even little wars have seemed out of place in the nurseries." He points out that the word *civilization* contains the word *civil*, as opposed to the word *military*. And he suggests an interesting challenge to future toy makers:

> Civilization, as I see it, begins where the instincts necessary to win humanity through the jungle of competing animals can be translated into terms of games and play; and world peace, as I see it, involves the playing of international games besides the keeping of international law, for games, which depend upon rules for their existence, are nurseries of law.

In most centuries children were not directly involved in battles outside the nursery. In wartime they suffered from food shortages and from the deaths of fathers and uncles, but they themselves were considered innocent noncombatants. It is far different today. Napalm has been invented, which produces sheets of fire that rip off children's skin. There is saturation bombing of cities by bombs unable to distinguish between combatants and noncombatants. And there are the fiendish new explosives housed inside what look like bars of soap or fountainpens or dolls, which are scattered around mine fields, so that when children pick one up, because they are curious and attracted by the sight of this little object on the ground, their fingers and hands are blown off.

Even that is not all. There is the current practice among terrorists of holding children as hostages or making them watch while their parents are tortured and/or killed, raped, bayoneted, disemboweled, decapitated, burned alive, or beaten to death right in front of them. And there is the new practice in some countries of actually recruiting boys as young as 9 or 10 to kill or to be killed as real soldiers in real battles.

Truly, it is hard nowadays to think of war as suitable and enjoyable child's play.

During the Vietnam War a group of elementary school pupils in New York City came to that conclusion and decided to picket Macy's in the pre-Christmas season because its toy department sold war toys. Then Nicholas Ulanov, one of the children, got a better idea. He said picketing tends to annoy people; many Christmas shoppers would feel guilty if they crossed a picket line and other people would dislike seeing angry protesters interfering with the joyful Christmas spirit. So he suggested, instead, "positive picketing" to get their message across, having heard that F.A.O. Schwartz, the big toy store on Fifth Avenue, had recently dropped war toys from its wares. The group of children were seen on the evening news a week later marching up and down in front of the store carrying large signs that said, "Thank you, Schwartz, for not selling war toys." They were smiling instead of scowling, and so were the passersby and shoppers.

P.S. During 1979, the International Year of the Child, the government of Sweden passed a law making it illegal to sell war toys.

9

Children's Games
and Sports

GAMES FOR BABIES

Shortly after babies discover that it is fun to play with their fingers and toes, they make another enjoyable discovery: they have playmates eager to share their interest in these fascinating things. Their parents or caregivers show them how to use them in games like Little Bo Peep, Pat-a-Cake, Peek-a-boo, Pease Porridge Hot, This Little Pig Went to Market, and Two Little Dicky Birds. According to *The Oxford Dictionary of Nursery Rhymes*, the rhymes that accompany such infant amusements are probably among the most ancient verses in the English language. But time has not diminished their charm, and when the newest baby in the world is introduced to the oldest poems and games in the world, the result is instant delight.

These verses have been handed down from one generation to another orally, so we cannot trace their origins accurately. But even though they are undoubtedly older than any existing written records of them, we can trace part of their lives through old manuscripts.

The nursery rhyme about Little Bo-Peep apparently dates, in the form in which we know it, from the nineteenth century, but there are references to "bo-peep" in manuscripts as far back as A.D. 1364. A hide-and-seek game called *bo-peep* gradually became known as *peep-bo* and then as *peek-bo*, finally becoming the Peek-a-boo game now known to all mothers and babies.

The rhyme and accompanying infants' game of Pat-a-cake originated around 1698.

The most common toe or finger rhyme for the past century, "This Little Pig Went to Market," was already known in Elizabethan times. The Chinese, incidentally, have their own version of "This Little Pig"; it starts, "This little cow gives good milk."

The popular hand-clapping game Pease Porridge Hot, which used to be played in cold weather to warm up tiny hands as well as to arouse laughter, was published in the form known today in 1797. A riddle version of it is even older, dating from 1765:

> Pease porridge hot,
> Pease porridge cold,
> Pease porridge in a pot,
> Nine days old;
> Spell me that without a P,
> And a clever scholar you will be.

The finger game Two Little Dicky Birds ("sitting on a wall, one named Peter, the other named Paul; fly away Peter, fly away Paul; come back Peter, come back Paul!") originated around 1765. At first it concerned two blackbirds who sat on a hill, one named Jack and the other named Jill, but their names were changed to those of the two apostles during the nineteenth century when all influences on the infant mind were supposed to be edifying.

GAMES PROVIDE A MIRROR TO HISTORY

More than 700 years ago, in the year 1283, the King of Castille, Alfonso X (1226–1284), compiled the first book of games in European literature: the *Libro de Juegos*. The king was a brilliant scholar, and he was to go down in history as *Alfonso El Sabio* (The Learned). He personally supervised a group of writers whose task it was to produce a series of books on the most vital subjects of the day. These included history, law, religion, astronomy, magic, and games. The fact that games were included in this company shows how important play was in the medieval scheme of things. "God has intended men to enjoy themselves with many games," the king declared in the book's introduction, pointing out that these entertainments would "bring them comfort and dispel their boredom."

The principal board games discussed in Alfonso's manuscript had already traveled nearly halfway around the world, and some had histories going back 1,000 years or more. Chess, the king's personal passion, had been developed centuries earlier and had traveled from India to Spain where its elephants, maharajas, and chariots were replaced by castles, kings, and bishops. The Morris Games Alfonso described dated back to ancient Egypt, where they were popular among the common people. Backgammon, one of the great entertainments of the thirteenth-century nobility, had evolved from the Roman game *Tabula*, though Alfonso's subjects probably learned the game from the Arabs, who called it *Nard*. The impulse to play games, in other words, is a universal one that has bypassed cultural and linguistic boundaries.

Just as the ancient and primitive religions of the world show profound similarities in their fertility rites and their sun and moon worship, many games appear to be common property to human beings everywhere. Many of those now thought to be mere children's pastimes are, in fact, relics of ancient rituals, historical events, and legends, often dating back to the dawn of mankind. Tug of war, for example, is a dramatization of real struggles between opposing forces; knucklebones (or dice) were once part of the fortune teller's equipment; hopscotch was related to ancient myths about labyrinths and mazes, later adapted to represent the Christian soul's journey from earth to heaven.

In an ancient palace at Thebes in Upper Egypt there is a wall painting showing Ramses III (1198–1156 B.C.) engaged in a board game with the goddess Isis, the wife of Osiris, Lord of the Dead. Herodotus, the Greek historian of the fifth century B.C., reported that the Pharaoh sometimes won these matches, but not always. In the seventeenth chapter of the Egyptian *Book of the Dead* there is a reference to a game played after death: the players are spirits of the departed, enjoying themselves in the next world.

Casting lots, as in dice or knucklebones, gave human beings an opportunity to consult the gods when making difficult decisions, while the results of games played by champions were interpreted by priests and others skilled in reading the future. These practices may seem strange today, but who is there who has not tossed a coin to make a decision?

Certain kinds of games undoubtedly originated as a training ground for the young, or as a means of maintaining acquired skills. Chess was an imaginative reconstruction of a battlefield, and the strategy and foresight demanded by the game are still thought to provide excellent intellectual training. More mundane but no less useful skills were involved in such games as darts, hoops, foot races, and virtually every other game that demands strength, speed, or dexterity. Japanese soldiers were once required to play shuttlecock in order to acquire agility and speed.

Ancient Children's Games

Children playing tag would be surprised to hear that they are getting a history lesson, but historians say that all circle games are descendants of ancient tribal dances once used in religious ceremonies, and all games involving chasing and hiding and capturing are based on primitive hunting and warfare.

As far as we know, the oldest children's game still played today is King of the Castle, in which a child jumps up on a sand castle or other height and dares others to pull him down. Horace (65–8 B.C.) refers to this game several times, which means that it goes back at least to 20 B.C.

Children owe many of their favorite games to the fact that a severe famine occurred one year, thousands of years ago, in Libya, if the historian Herodotus was right. He said the starving Libyans thought of an ingenious way to alleviate their misery and at the same time conserve food: they ate and played on alternate days! One day they would play so continuously and actively that they had no time to think about food, and the next day they would rest and enjoy their food and invent new games to play the day after that. According to Herodotus, all ball games were invented by the Libyans, as well as all the other games, except checkers, which they and the Greeks commonly played. These included Pitch and Toss, Tug of War, Blind Man's Buff, Hide and Seek, and Hopscotch.

Every small child loves to play ball and to ride piggy-back, and these activities were also enjoyed by the youth of ancient Greece. They were encouraged to throw and catch balls, to run and jump, as soon as small legs could manage, because the Greeks were great believers in physical fitness and vigorous exercise. Homer (c. 850 B.C.) described one Greek ball game played by two people, which was sort of an energetic version of jacks, using feet as well as hands. One player tossed a ball as high as possible, and the other had to jump up and catch it before it or his feet touched the ground.

Another game the Greeks invented combined both ball and piggy-back. A player who failed to catch a ball was penalized by having to carry another player on his shoulders; this second player stayed up there until he too missed a ball thrown at him by an opposing player who was also mounted on someone's shoulders. This game was popular with grown men and women as well as with children. The ladies played a ladylike version that must have been quite difficult because they sat side-saddle on their human horses.

Games in the Middle Ages

If we could put ourselves back in time and pay a visit to the era we call the Dark Ages, we would find the darkness brightened by much gaiety. The average medieval adult shared many qualities with children: a naive and trusting faith, physical ruggedness that made sleeping on the floor and eating with one's fingers perfectly normal, and noisy exuberance that found outlets in boisterous, rowdy play. Grownups and children together romped and sang and danced on village greens, skipped around maypoles, and played tag and other rough-and-tumble games. There was much more constant togetherness among age groups then than there is today. Adults did not join in childish activities because it was their parental duty, but because they really enjoyed playing as much as the children did, and it helped to pass the time. After all, books, magazines, movies, and TV were not yet available.

309

Among the games medieval adults and children enjoyed were Hide and Seek, called at that time Hoop and Hide (or, for some reason, Harry Racket); Hoodman's Blind, which we today call Blind Man's Buff ("buff" referring to the three taps or buffets that the blind man is supposed to give when he catches a player); Hot Cockles, in which one player was struck by another and had to guess which; Hunt the Slipper; King of the Castle; Prisoners' Bars, which today is called Prisoner's Base; and an early version of Cops and Robbers called French and English; who were the good guys and who the bad guys of course depended on the nationality of the players. In the eighteenth century a variation on this last game was called Hare and Hounds, and American Indian children had a similar game based on the hunt, called Deer and Wolf.

The romping games played on the village greens by both adults and children together during the Middle Ages included a wild version of football, then called foteball, and "leapfrogge." One version of leapfrog was Jumping the Candlestick, which has come down to us in the nursery rhyme, "Jack be nimble/Jack be quick/Jack jump over the candlestick." Candle-leaping was a sport in England for several centuries, but it did not mean that children were encouraged to play with fire; adults and infants together played a game based on it in which one small child represented a candle, a circle of still smaller children around him made up the candlestick, and "Jack" had to jump over all of them.

Pick-a-back or piggy-back nowadays is primarily a method of transportation, a way to keep on walking with a tired child who refuses to take another step, or a device to raise children high enough so they can see parades over taller people's heads. But it was still a real game in the Middle Ages. From the eleventh to the fourteenth century it was played by children as a variation of Tournament, a game in which youngsters imitated the jousting of knights. In Pick-a-back two big children or adults acted as horses and held on their shoulders two tiny knights who tried to knock each other off. Variations of this are still played in some countries.

Children's Games in the Renaissance

A famous picture called "Children's Games" was painted in 1560 by the Flemish artist Pieter Bruegel the Elder (1520–1569). It is now a proud possession of the Kunsthistorisches Museum in Vienna. It shows a large number of children in an outdoor square playing 71 games. They are certainly all having a good time: playing blind man's buff, follow the leader, leapfrog, London Bridge, piggy-back, and tag, and also climbing trees, making sand castles, racing, somersaulting, standing on their heads, swimming, and playing with balls, blocks, dice, dolls, hobby horses, hoops, marbles, musical instruments, pop guns, rackets, rattles, sticks, stilts, and tops.

Across the English channel, in Elizabethan homes at this time, games were slightly more restricted. Indoor games were usually played in the long central gallery, which often had fireplaces and was the most comfortable and popular room in the house. Here children played at skittles and blind man's buff while their elders strolled up and down for exercise and conversation. Both boys and girls also played with great hilarity a game called Drop the Cap, ancestor of the modern Drop the Handkerchief. Caps were more available back then than handerkchiefs; people wiped their noses on their sleeves, but everyone wore a cap both indoors and out. The game ended in a wild chase, as the child behind whom a cap was dropped ran after the child who had dropped it.

Other games mentioned by Shakespeare, and probably played by him as a child, were hide and seek, football, tennis, handball, and armball. But ball playing in sixteenth

310

century England got a bad reputation. Ball games were played so roughly that they were not considered suitable for children, especially for well-bred ones. The scholar Sir Thomas Elyot (1490–1546) warned noblemen against playing them, and King James I (1566–1625) of England forbade his son ever to play with a ball. For almost a century the only ball players were peasants.

However, ball playing is not inherently rough and dangerous, as it was in some of the peasants' rowdy games, and could not stay exiled from aristocrats' children forever. There is a painting of King George III (1738–1820) that shows a benign side to his character unknown to his angry American colonists; he is playing ball with his daughter the Princess Amelia.

Eighteenth-Century Games

Games that go back at least to the eighteenth century include Follow My Leader; Forfeits, originally called Questions and Commands; Here We Go Gathering Nuts in May; Here We Go 'Round the Mulberry Bush; and Puss in the Corner. All of these have survived through the nineteenth and twentieth centuries.

Games in the Nineteenth Century

In the Victorian era, games became much more sedate. In the cozy quiet of the typical parlor, the parlor game was born, invented by house-proud mothers who ingeniously found ways to allow their children to play without messing up their neat houses.

A popular pull toy of the period was a wagon mounted on low, wide wheels like furniture castors, so that the children could pull it around without injuring carpets. Swings were designed that could be attached to any doorway by rubber pads, without nails or screws to mar the woodwork. Marbles became popular with the very young and the very old. So did jack straws and Magic Hoops, the latter played by throwing hoops of different sizes onto hooks attached to a gaily striped pole. And an indoor ball game was invented wherein a Mother Goose, hidden at first, was knocked into sight by a properly thrown soft ball.

Of course Victorian children were not confined to the parlor. In fact, they probably saw much less of it than modern children see of the accurately named *living room*, which has replaced the formal parlor of that era. Pre-TV children played outdoors as much as possible and, in addition to romping in parks and gardens, they were taken on long walks almost daily.

RECREATIONAL REMINDERS OF SOME BAD OLD DAYS

Some games that innocent young children find delightful might terrify them if they thought about the games' meanings, which, fortunately, they do not. Aside from the obvious example of London Bridge, which is based on the ancient practice of capturing a child and placing its body inside a bridge's foundation in order to keep the bridge from falling down (see page 41), there are other games based on gruesome historical facts.

Eeney, Meeny, Miney, Mo

Probably everyone has, at one time or another, used this counting-out formula to settle disputes between two small people, as well as to start off a game. Great antiquity is attached to these syllables, and variations of them are invoked all over the world.

- An eighteenth-century English version was *Ena mena mona mite.*
- A nineteenth-century German variation was *Ene, tene, mone, mei.*
- And the twentieth-century Austrian version is: *Eine, meine, meine, mu.*

These apparently come from ancient numerals now forgotten. Kipling wrote:

> Eenee, Meenee, Mainee and Mo
> Were the first Big Four of the Long Ago.

Some people believe that such counting-out rhymes are remnants of formulas used by the ancient Druids for choosing human sacrifices.

An unpleasant reminder of racial bigotry appears in the line added to "Eeny Meeny Miney Mo," which originated in New England during the nineteenth century and was still chanted by white children in America in the early years of the twentieth century: "Catch a nigger by his toe / But if he hollers, let him go." A more ruthless version of this used to be "If he hollers make him pay / Fifty dollars every day."

Earlier English versions said, "Catch a tinker" or "Catch a chicken" or "Catch a rooster." Today's children usually ask for nothing more vicious than to "Catch a tiger by the toe, / And if he hollers let him go."

Ring a Ring of Rosies

> Ring a ring of rosies,
> A pocket full of posies,
> Tishshoo! tishshoo!
> We all fall down!

This is an earlier version of "Ring around the Rosie," a game small children still love to play.

Some people think it dates back to the days of the Great Plague of London in 1665. "A pocket full of posies" is said to refer to bouquets of herbs that people at that time carried as protection from the "rosy" rash, and sneezing ("tishshoo!") was the first symptom that showed when people caught the disease, after which they all fell down—dead.

In the nineteenth century a less deadly and more decorous version of the game came into favor. It became a dance rather than a romp, and "fall down" was not a signal to collapse on the floor but to make a deep curtsey or bow.

Oranges and Lemons

This is an ancient game that is still popular among English children. It is similar to London Bridge and even more explicitly ferocious, with its lines:

> Here comes a candle to light you to bed.
> Here comes a chopper to chop off your head.

These words are recited as the taller children form an arch with their arms and the littler ones pass underneath in a row. Then comes the refrain, "Chop, chop, chop, chop!" with the arms coming down to capture the child who is under the arch at the moment of the final "chop." Some people believe that the head-chopping part refers to the period when public beheadings were frequent and the condemned were led through the streets while church bells tolled for them in mourning.

Another theory is that the head-chopper referred to was Henry VIII, with his nasty habit of chopping off his wives' heads. If so, the reference was evidently tactfully withheld until Henry himself was safely dead, because the earliest known versions of the jingle (c. 1740) do not contain the so-called "execution formula" and are just a set of rhymes that match the names of London's churches, to accompany a jolly square dance.

A VERY SPECIAL GAME: CHESS

More books have been written about chess than about all other games combined; there are more than 15,000. No one knows for certain when or where the game was invented, though many think it originated in the second century in Babylon, Egypt, Greece, India, or Persia.

It is amazing that such a complex game has so many devotees, particularly among children. Yet it has been called a child's game because nearly all excellent players achieve a high standard of play before reaching their teens. Many learn the game at the age of four or five, with little or no formal instruction, by watching adults play.

This, however, is a recent phenomenon. When nine-year-old Samuel Reshevsky began touring Europe in 1919, simultaneously giving displays and holding his own against strong adult players, the public was not merely astonished at his extraordinary ability but at the fact that a child could play chess at all. But two years after his tour ended in 1919, an annual chess tournament for boys under 18 was inaugurated in England, and other countries soon followed suit.

According to analysts, by the tenth move of a chess game, players have selected 20 out of some 169,518,829,100,544 trillion possible moves! And, as Harold Schonberg, a music critic who describes himself as a "chess nut," has said, "Knowing the moves does not make one a chess player any more than knowing the alphabet makes one a Shakespeare."

To play chess exceptionally well requires alertness, concentration, an excellent memory, logic, calculation, imagination, the ability to visualize and organize, courage, perseverance, stamina, patience, calmness under stress, and discipline, as well as a ferocious will to win and a passion for the game. There is a strict hierarchy among skilled players: Class C, Class B, Class A, Expert, Master, Senior Master, Grandmaster, and International Grandmaster.

Alexander Ilyin Zhenevsky (1894–1941), a Russian chess master, used his position as chief commissar in the headquarters of the Soviet General Reservists' Organization to have chess included in all training programs for army conscripts. He explained: "The chief value of sport is that it develops in a man mental qualities which are of supreme importance in a soldier. Here a parallel with chess involuntarily suggests itself. After all, chess too—and in some ways even more than sport—develops in a man boldness, presence of mind, composure, a strong will and, more important, something which sport cannot, a sense of strategy."

He certainly was persuasive; in the mid-1920s the government began to invest heavily in the game, and it became the favorite Soviet indoor sport. Soon at least 7 million registered chess players in the Soviet Union played in chess clubs, in schools, Young Pioneer camps, communes, trade unions, and community centers, and it is estimated that there were at least 40 million additional unregistered players. The area has produced many outstanding players, including seven world champions.

In recent years, especially in Russia, chess has become a popular spectator sport. Most people think of it as an agonizingly slow game, with world championsip matches that take weeks, even months, and the players sometimes losing from sheer exhaustion. However, variations of the game are fun for expert players to play and for other people to watch: speed or lightning chess, where players must make their moves in specified brief periods of time, even instantaneously, or lose the game; exhibitions where one player takes on a group of others simultaneously; and games where one expert plays while blindfolded.

Shelby Lyman, who had been the top player at Harvard University, represented the United States in the 1956 Students Chess Olympiad and became the eighteenth ranked player in the United States, suggested televising the Fischer-Spassky match in 1972, and he became the host of TV's highly successful "World Championship Chess Program." With his witty comments and expert analyses of the moves on a wall-sized board, Lyman made the chess board seem as exciting as a ball field. He became an overnight celebrity and turned chess into a popular spectator sport in the United States, not followed by nearly as many people as watch it in Russia but eagerly followed by growing numbers of fans.

In 1986, during the Karpov-Kasparov World Championship match, he added two children to his panel of consulting experts, known as "Kibitzers' Korner": Julia Sarver, 10 years old, and her brother Jeff Sarver, the World Under-10 Champion.

Chess has been booming in America even among children as young as third-graders, ever since Chess-in-the-Schools, a program sponsored by the American Chess Foundation, was founded in New York City in 1986, through which pupils receive weekly chess lessons in a 12-part program. First tried on a voluntary, experimental basis in Harlem, it soon proved its value.

What accounts for the huge popularity of this ancient game among today's children? One reason is that it is computer-compatible, with software that has made it a game that can be played alone or with distant opponents. David McEnulty, the only full-time chess teacher in New York's public schools, explains that "It's an aggressive game, and children are aggressive. This is really an elegant way of beating people up." One eight-year-old obviously agrees; she started a class essay, "Chess is a cool combat game." But as McEnulty adds, it provides combat with rules, and so feels safer to children than the combat of the streets.

Child Prodigies in Chess

José Raul Capablanca (1888–1942): A Cuban prodigy who earned the nickname of The Chess Machine, was the most spectacular chess player in the world at the beginning of the twentieth century. He learned to play at age 4 by watching his father play, and at 12 he had already defeated Cuba's reigning champion. From 1916, when he was 18, until 1924 he never lost a single game, setting an unparalleled record. During his entire lifetime he lost only four of approximately 700 tournament games he played and was World Champion from 1920 to 1927. Unlike most great chess players, he never really studied the game and claimed he had read only one chess book during his life; however, he wrote several.

Surprisingly, he was not a good student. He attended Columbia University briefly but dropped out at age 18. As one of his classmates said, "He never learned to learn and lacked the pertinacity to apply himself to a task which did not come easily to him." However, chess did come easily to him; as Alexander Alekhine, who succeeded him as World Champion in 1927, said: "I have known many chess players but only one chess genius, Capablanca, a very great genius whose like we shall never see again. Neither before nor after have I ever seen such flabbergasting quickness of chess comprehension." At 54 Capablanca died from a stroke while watching a chess game at the Manhattan Chess Club in New York. After his death a chess club in New York was named for him.

> Every 10 years or so it seems a new child is acclaimed as a chess prodigy. Most of them fade out after a few years of early glory, but some have risen through the ranks to the highest category of players, International Grandmaster. The following are among the most outstanding prodigies in the history of the game.

Lew Cohen (1960–): Born in New York City, Cohen was taught chess by his father when he was five and played in his first tournament at seven. He also swam, bicycled, played baseball, basketball, and ping-pong; he was gifted at math and enjoyed music. At 12 he won a prize in the U.S. Open and gave a 16-board simultaneous exhibition at the Jamaica Chess Club, winning 11 of 16 games. In 1972, when still only 12, he appeared on the CBS-TV program *Sixty Minutes* playing the 29-year-old soon-to-be World Champion Bobby Fischer (see below). They played five five-minute games, one of them a five-seconds-a-move game; Fischer won them all. At 13 in another simultaneous exhibition Cohen won 21 games out of 24. And by age 14 he had 35 chess tournament trophies.

Bobby Fischer (1943–): Born in Chicago, Fischer was six when his sister Joan bought him a chess set and he immediately became fascinated by the game. A fabulous linguist, while still a child he read and studied books on chess for 5 to 10 hours a day in Dutch, English, German, Russian, Serbo-Croatian, and Spanish. He was not, however, fanatically one-sided. He was a healthy, happy boy who enjoyed many activities, especially baseball, billiards, boating, hockey, jai alai, ping-pong, swimming, and tennis. He also enjoyed music and was a good student near the top of his class, though he had only two-and-a-half years of high school. He entered his first chess tournament when eight years old. The first tournament he won was four years later. At 13 he gave a 12-board simultaneous exhibition at New York's Capablanca Chess Club in which he won 10 games and drew two. The first national tournament he won was the U.S. Junior Championship in 1956, at age 13; he received the first prize of a portable typewriter and a trophy for becoming the youngest ever Junior Champion, in what was written up as "the game of the century." A year later at 14 he won the U.S. Junior Championship again and another typewriter. While still 14 he also tied for first place in the U.S. Open Championship, becoming the youngest player in history to win it, beating more than 200 adult contestants, and he won this eight more times in future years. When 16, in 1959, he earned the title of International Grandmaster in Yugoslavia, again the youngest person in the history of chess to do so. At age 29, in 1972, he went to Reykjavik, Iceland, and defeated Boris Spassky (see page 319), thus becoming the Champion of the World. But three years later he refused a rematch and forfeited the title.

Afterwards Fischer retired from professional chess for 20 years—until 1992, when he scheduled a return match against Spassky in Yugoslavia. The two rivals were to play until one won 10 games, the winner to receive $3,350,000 and the loser a consolation prize of $1,650,000. Because of the civil war then raging in Yugoslavia, the U.S. Government forbade Americans to go there, but Fischer defiantly went anyway, and after the match was unable to return to the United States without getting arrested. He won the match and became a multimillionaire in exile.

Anatoliy Karpov (1951–): Born in the city of Zlatoust in the Chelyabinsk district of the Soviet Union, Karpov learned to play chess from his father at the age of four; he played in chess matches at his school and at the local Young Pioneers clubhouse. At seven he won a third-category chess rating, at eight the second-category rating and the district's Regional Scholastic Championship, and at 11 tied for second place in the first-category rating for the region's Men's Championship, becoming the nation's youngest Candidate Master. At 13 Karpov enrolled in a chess correspondence school headed by former World Champion Mikhail Botvinnik, and studied with him for four years. At 15 he became the Soviet Union's youngest Chess Master and began his international career early in 1967. By accident the Soviet Chess Federation sent him to take part in a tournament in Czechoslovakia intended exclusively for adults, but he was permitted to compete even though he was only 15, and he won first place. That winter he also went to the Netherlands, where he won the European International Youth Tournament.

In August 1969, at age 18, Karpov won the World Junior Championship and was designated an International Master. The next year he competed for the U.S.S.R. Championship and as a result of his dazzling performance won the designation of International Grandmaster. During these years he also performed brilliantly in school, and his name is enrolled on the list of his school's top honor students. In 1975 while an economics student at Leningrad University, he became World Champion after Bobby Fischer's forfeiture of the title. He held the title for 10 years.

Gary Kasparov (1963–): Born in Baku, Azerbaijan, in the Soviet Union, Kasparov amazed his chess-playing parents at the age of five by suggesting the solution to a baffling chess problem they had been puzzling over, although they had not yet even taught him the rules of the game. At seven he joined the Young Pioneers chess circle, where his first trainer immediately noticed his exceptional memory. At age nine he reached the finals of the Baku lightning chess championship for seniors. At 10 he was invited to enter the chess correspondence school of Mikhail Botvinnik, the Soviet Union's greatest player. A good student, he graduated with top honors and was also so outstanding at sports, particularly swimming, that for a while he was undecided about choosing between chess and a swimming career. At 11 he participated in the U.S.S.R. Junior Chess Championship. When he was 12, Botvinnik commented: "In the hands of this young man lies the future of chess." He won his first international rated tournament at 15, placing ahead of several Grandmasters. At 16, in his first international super-tournament in Yugoslavia, he placed ahead of

316

the established Grandmasters, and himself became a Grandmaster at 17. In 1984 when he was 21, he gained the title of Challenger to the World Champion Anatoly Karpov (see above) and was the youngest chess player ever to compete in a world title match. The match ended without a decision, after 48 grueling games lasting from September 1984 to February 1985. A new match between the two rivals was held the following September in Moscow and lasted until November. Kasparov won and became the new World Champion.

In February, 1996, Kasparov won a still greater triumph, which had even people who do not care about chess holding their breath in suspense. This time he was playing six games not against a human rival but a computer. IBM had had a team of research scientists working for six years to develop Deep Blue, a computer programmed to be a Grandmaster chess player. The machine is equipped with such powerful processing technology that it can search more than 100 million chess positions a second.

Throughout the match Kasparov squirmed nervously. His fellow humans everywhere were rooting for him, but they were pretty nervous too, especially after the shock they received when in the first game Deep Blue humbled humanity by besting its best player in only 36 moves.

In the end Kasparov did win the match, but he warmly congratulated the programmers, telling them that the machine had been "a serious opponent" and that the match had been "as tough as the world championship." And many scientists no longer doubt that eventually a computer will become the world chess champion.

However, even the smartest computer will never be able to do its job without human commands and input. And as a man who said he was inspired by a seven-year-old friend who had "recently discovered the deep pleasures of chess" wrote on the Op Ed page of the *New York Times*, why should our self-esteem be more threatened by losing a game from mental projection than proud to realize we are capable of building a device able to do that? As he said, the fact that we can assemble an artifact able to beat us at our own game is "a stunning triumph for human ingenuity."

Bill Lombardy (1937–): Born in New York, Lombardy was at the top of his class all through school. He was good at math but liked music and languages more, and learned French, German, Greek, Latin, Russian, and Spanish. He won his first chess tournament, the Marshall Chess Club Junior Championship, in 1952 when he was 15, and was on the Marshall Junior Team, winning against every master he encountered that year in interclub matches. His first major adult tournament was the 1954 New York State Championship, at age 16. At 19 he became the World Junior Champion, and later became an International Grandmaster. In 1967 at age 30 he was ordained a Catholic priest, and in 1991 he received an honorary degree from Princeton University for outstanding work with disadvantaged children.

Paul Morphy (1837–1884): Born in New Orleans, Morphy learned chess at the age of eight by watching a member of his family play; he went on to become the outstanding chess genius of the nineteenth century. He could not find anyone to match him in his home town but at age 12 had a chance to play two games against J. Lowenthal, a famous Continental Master who was passing through New Orleans, and he won both. His parents did not allow chess to interfere with his studies, and it was therefore not until 1857 when he was 20 that he played in an important tournament, the American Chess Congress, in which he came in first. He then went on a tour of Europe where he challenged and defeated the best players of England, France, and Germany and became world famous.

When attending the Paris Opera he was spotted by two well-known chess enthusiasts who invited him into their box for a game; he handily beat both of them during the performance of *The Barber of Seville*. When he returned to America, a hero's welcome awaited him; there were Morphy cigars, Morphy hats, even a Morphy ball club.

Nevertheless, Morphy gave up playing chess in public because his mother considered playing games in public an undignified activity unworthy of a gentleman. He became an unsuccessful lawyer and died at the early age of 47 after suffering from acute melancholia. He has been called "both the pride and sorrow of chess." He, Capablanca, and Fischer are generally considered the greatest natural chess players of all time, and 35 books have been written about Morphy.

The Polgar Sisters: Zsuzsu (1969–), **Zsofi** (1975–), and **Judit** (1977–): Born in Hungary, the Polgar sisters entered a World Youth Chess Festival held in 1986 as part of the United Nations "International Year of Peace" in San Juan, Puerto Rico. There were six simultaneous tournaments composed of age groups ranging from 10 to 26 years. Zsofi, 11, came in second in her age group. Judit, though only nine, was allowed to play in the 14-year-old group because of her exceptional ability; she came in third. Later in the year the three girls took part in a New York International Open Chess Tournament. This time 16-year-old Zsuzsu competed against 89 adult players in the Grandmasters section of the tournament, and tied for second place as the strongest woman player in the world; one of the adult players she defeated was a six-time U.S. Champion. Zsofi won six out of seven games in her section and took second place in the section. But Judit most amazed the spectators. She won all of the seven games she played against adult opponents and in informal games also played and won blindfold chess. As Jeffrey Naier, the chief arbiter of the New York tournament, said, "The secret of the sisters' skill is discipline—it's not only talent, which of course they have. But these three sisters work at chess. They are at it sometimes eight, nine hours a day." The tournament organizer, José Cjuchi, said, "I've never seen anything like this. It's incredible." (See also page 239.)

Arturo Pomar (1931–): Born in Spain, Arturo was shown the chess moves by his father when he was five years old, and within a few months he was playing regularly at the local chess club in Palma. His first big success was at the age of 10 when he was runner-up in the Championship of the Balearic Isles. The champion was unable to represent the region in the Spanish Championship that year, so Arturo was sent in his place. In the preliminary contest he finished third in a field of 12 and was hailed as a prodigy, interviewed on the radio, filmed, and given a grant to assist in his studies by the Department of Education. He was also presented with a chess board by the president of the Spanish Chess Federation and a bicycle by some fans in Madrid. In the actual championship match he came in last, but he had already made his name and fame. The following year at the age of 11, he became Champion of the Balearic Isles. At 15 he became an International Master.

Samuel Reshevsky (1911–): Born in Poland, Samuel was the sixth child of an Orthodox Jewish family, who was taught the chess moves at the age of four. A few days later he astonished his parents, after watching a game between his father and a friend, by demonstrating how his father could have saved the game. By age eight he could play blindfold and was being acclaimed as a child prodigy. His father took him to Berlin where, after giving a successful simultaneous display against some average players, he was tried out against 20 players of second-class club strength; he won 10 games, drew nine, and lost only one. He was then taken on a tour of England, France, Germany, and the Netherlands, playing from 15 to 20 players at a time, and rarely lost a game. He and his family were invited to the United States in 1920 when he was nine, and for nearly two years he toured the country giving exhibitions. At 11 he competed in his first tournament in which masters were playing. When he was 12 his parents decided that chess must give way to education and his chess activities were limited after that to just a few tournaments. Later, as an adult, he returned to the game and at 25 became the U.S. Champion, and up to 1964 when he was 53 years old, he was never beaten in a match.

Elaine Saunders (1926–): Born in England, she was one of the few girl prodigies in the history of chess. She was taught the moves by her father when she was five and started to play in tournaments at seven. She met David Pritchard, her future husband, who became Malayan Champion in 1955 when he was stationed in Singapore with Britain's Royal Air Force, when she was about seven. He said she was so small she was unable to reach the far side of the chess board. When she was 10 she won an under-21 girls' tournament and at age 13 she won the British Championship for the first time; she won it again in 1946, 1956, and 1965.

Boris Spassky (1937–): Born in Leningrad, Spassky learned to play chess during the siege of that city in World War II, in the Kirov region Children's Home to which he had been evacuated. When he returned home in 1946, at age nine, he joined the chess club of the Young Pioneers and in the following year won the prize for the best game in the Russian Federation Junior Championship competition. In 1948, at age 10, he came in fifth in the Leningrad Junior Championship and second in the Russian Federation Junior Championship. At 11 he won the Leningrad Junior Championship, and at 15 came in second in the Leningrad Championship. At 16, playing in Bucharest in his first international tournament in 1953, he came in fourth. The year 1955, when he was 18, was a milestone in his career. In addition to winning the World Junior Championship, he came in third in the U.S.S.R. Championship and represented his country in the Interzonal Tournament in Gothenburg, his first appearance in a World Championship qualifying tournament. In 1961 he became Champion of the Soviet Union and in 1969, World Champion, a title he held until 1972, when he was defeated by Bobby Fischer.

COMPUTER GAMES

In recent years books, toys, games, television, and computers have joined forces. We now consider it perfectly normal to walk into a toy store and see Babar, the stuffed elephant, in different sizes and outfits, next to Babar the book, next to Babar the jigsaw puzzle, and a Babar doll house (his palace) surrounded by Babar videos and cassettes and occasionally even an interactive CD-ROM.

There is now a cultural common ground among virtually all children in North and South America, Europe, many parts of Asia and, increasingly, in Eastern Europe and Russia. Music serves as a cultural bridge all over the world for youngsters without a common language, and many people believe that the children who are growing up today with so many of the same toys and songs and visual images via TV and computers will be part of a very different and more culturally cohesive whole in tomorrow's global village than we can even imagine at present.

In the early 1970s, a few people who loved gadgetry hooked up a primitive electronic game called Pong to their TV monitors and enjoyed a version of ping-pong. In the late 1970s, the first video games appeared: electronic poker, Pac Man, Space Invaders, Donkey Kong.

In the early 1980s, newspaper and magazine publishers and TV stations, alarmed at the potential competition of personal computers in homes, introduced teletext and videotext, slow and unwieldy combinations of text and cartoon-like graphics delivered over cable and phone lines. People enjoyed the games, but today Prodigy, an IBM online service, is the only real survivor from that period.

Also in the early 1980s, software publishers began springing up in northern California and around Boston to feed the home computers that publishers were so alarmed about. The "edutainment" games these companies developed usually worked only with a tiny memory—the equivalent of a car that can go only seven miles per hour—and limited graphics, but many of them are still considered classics: Rocky's Boots, Snooper Troops, Where in the World Is Carmen San Diego?, and the Children's Computer Workshop, an offshoot of the Children's Television Workshop with all its *Sesame Street* characters.

During this same formative era, adventure games were born. The important one was Zork, a quest through endless narrow twisting tunnels via a complex and arcane Command Language. The other big seminal work was Dungeons and Dragons. This was not at first a computer game, but it later became one. It mattered because it too was a quest, with lots of strategy and not a lot of rules, and it inaugurated the medieval/Arthurian genre that remains hugely popular today.

In the mid-1980s, videodiscs enjoyed their first fame. They were like compact discs, only bigger and more complex in that they can digitally compress video as well as audio. Their appeal is that they can replicate real pictures and film footage that looks less good than TV but far better than cartoony graphics or text-only programs. But drawbacks included expensive production costs and expensive laser hardware to make them run. Nonetheless, the Aspen Disc and Mystery Disc I and II are still wonderful after a decade, which for this constantly changing industry is the equivalent of a novel still being fresh and readable 100 years later.

In the mid-to-late 1980s and 1990s, video games were still going strong and arcades were popping up in malls across America. Ms Pac Man, The Mario Brothers, Teenage Mutant Ninja Turtles, endless flight simulators, and Indianapolis 500 simulators were produced. This was the advent of Atari and home game sets. But Ataris were soon replaced by Nintendos and Sega Game Boys. Arcades began to wane, though like movie theaters they still attracted a lot of teenagers and encouraged game sales for home use, so they continued to survive.

On the cusp of the 1990s, virtual reality (VR) became a reality. This defies description; it has to be experienced to be understood. With very elaborate computer graphics programs and new digital movie cameras, extremely believable three-dimensional, 360-degree environments can now be created. One can either walk into a dark circular booth with a wrap-around movie screen or put on a special helmet that covers one's eyes, and then literally feel transported to another place. Every detail you see around you can look completely real. The potential for these games is breathtaking. They currently cost a fortune to produce, but if you must single out the most exciting new development in electronics for children (and for adults) VR is the indisputable choice.

The Internet and the World Wide Web have ushered in yet another wave of information, education, and entertainment. If you have a modem attached to your computer, you can connect the computer to your phone line and both send and receive information almost anywhere in the world. To do this you must stop thinking of a phone as just a device that transmits sounds; it can also transmit and receive digitized text and even pictures. The Internet is like a giant bulletin board for everyone with a computer modem, where you can post notes and leave personal messages for friends or groups of people. You can also post queries about information you need and get responses from anyone who happens to see your notice. Grownups use the Net for research, but increasingly schools and educational publishers are figuring out ways to become involved. It is all new enough and intriguing enough that teachers can probably get kids to read the encyclopedia and foreign newspapers and other reference material just because the text is online and not in a heavy book.

The Net is how children in the near future will communicate not just with their nearby friends but also with kids around the world. E-mail (electronic mail) also allows discussion groups, clubs, and special interest groups to get together for the cost of a local phone call. It is an informal way of communicating, but most English teachers are waxing rapturous about the dramatic improvement in literacy that it helps foster. If you cannot be clever and funny with words or spell or punctuate properly you are clearly less attractive to your peers. So e-mail may be an educational device in addition to providing children with companionship and fun.

Parental Concerns about Technology

When children stay indoors hour after hour with their man-made gadgets, are they inevitably going to be deprived of simpler pleasures? Not necessarily. Fascinating as modern technology is, parents can make room in every child's life for other things, too. Not just for the latest thing but for some of the oldest, timeless things. Not just for communication with others but for real privacy, contemplation, and solitude as well. It may be harder nowadays to get chances to appreciate nature, but if we do not find ways for children to do it, the fears of worried environmentalists will come to pass. We will have raised a generation that thinks an astrodome is more remarkable than the sky it merely illustrates.

Fortunately, however, that need not happen. Technology can be used not to compete with nature but to teach its importance. Computer games and TV programs like *Nova* can show children beauties on our planet from faraway places they cannot visit otherwise, and children can get together with other children all over the world via their computers and e-mail to exchange ideas and organize joint environmental projects, as a great many of them are already doing.

Technology is not necessarily an enemy of nature. It can be a strong ally, promoting peace and progress. It is not a matter of either/or but of and/and. A balanced mental diet is just as important as a balanced diet of food, and an appreciation of the wonders of Virtual Reality can lead to a deepened appreciation of the marvels of Real Reality.

THE WORLD'S YOUNGEST ATHLETES

There is actually little danger that all children from now on are going to sit day in and day out in front of television sets or computers, no matter how fascinating those technological marvels are. Millions of children are bursting with so much energy that they cannot sit still for long, and they prefer active games to computer games. Among these millions, some play so hard and so well that they become outstanding athletes. Here are some examples.

In Basketball

Laniesha Butler (1981–): From New York City, Laniesha has played basketball since she was seven years old, and at age 10 she also became an excellent tennis player. In 1993, at age 11, she headed a New York basketball team called the Liberty Belles, who entered the girls' 11-and-under division of the Amateur Athletic Union (AAU) in a nine-day tournament, with 27 teams from all over America competing. The Belles did not win the championship, but they had a lot of fun and won third-place medals.

So many remarkable athletes have achieved fame and fortune in their teens that there are too many to list. The following list, therefore, only mentions outstanding ones whose talents were notable at age 15 or younger. It may serve to inspire some youngsters but will probably just give many other people an inferiority complexes.

At age 12 Laniesha broke her ankle during a game but kept on playing. And at age 13 in 1995 she was the star on the girls' varsity basketball team at Columbia Prep in New York. She was hailed by sports commentators as a prodigy, both for her running and for shooting baskets (63 points in one game). She was heralded as the player who would finally put the city, which had not produced a major college star since the 1970s, back on the women's basketball map. Coaches explain that girls have it tougher than boys; in the inner cities, they often do not have high enough SAT scores to get college scholarships; they have lost some girl players to pregnancy; and girls are also burdened with responsibilities of housework and caring for siblings usually spared the boys. But Laniesha is a good student as well as an outstanding athlete, and while still only in eighth grade, in 1994, she was nicknamed "Future."

Breezy Stephenson (1980–): Born in Topsfield, Massachusetts, by the time Breezy was nine years old she was an ace pitcher and home run slugger for a Little League baseball team made up mostly of boys. She was also a center forward on a soccer team and a national champion sprinter in track. But her favorite sport was basketball, and by age 12, when in seventh grade, she received permission from the Massachusetts Interscholastic Athletic Association to play for the Masconomet (Masco for short) girls' high school varsity basketball team. By the fifth game of the season she had become the team's starting point guard and helped Masco win its league championship. Breezy averaged 12.8 points and 9 assists per game, and Masco finished the season 24–2, advancing to the finals of the state tournament where Breezy became one of the youngest players ever to compete in the home court of the Boston Celtics.

In Biking

Betsy Edmunson (1982–): Betsy was born in Temecula, California. When she was eight years old she entered her first race, and from then on continued to practice bike racing by sprinting up a hill every morning before school, five or six times, always wearing a motorcycle helmet, before catching her school bus. She also practiced regularly out of a starting gate her parents set up for her at home, and rode her bike on roads and on a track near her home. When she was 10 she became national champion in the 10-year-old girls' division of the American Bicycle Association Grand Nationals in Oklahoma City, Oklahoma, held on Thanksgiving weekend in 1992. It was a hard race, on a 1,100-foot hilly course with five hairpin turns and 12 bumps and jumps, and she won it by about 45 seconds. Betsy and seven other girls had been earning points at races all season, but now she had more points than any other girl in any age group, and she was crowned National Number 1 at age 10.

Tiffani Glowacki (1982–): A native of Racine, Wisconsin, Tiffani was a straight-A student who relaxed by playing classical music on the piano, but she also developed strong legs by lifting weights and riding her bicycle as many as 150 miles a week. By 1994, at age 12 she was the fastest young bike racer in America. She won all four events in the girls' 10-to-12 age group at the U.S. national cycling championships: the 20-kilometer (12.4 mile) time trial; the 15-kilometer (9.3 mile) road race; the 15-kilometer criterium, and the sprint, held on a 333-meter banked track called velodrome and consisting of 500-meter, 1,000-meter, and 2,000-meter races. Her favorite event is the 15-km criterium, which she describes as "like playing chess at 30 miles per hour."

In Camel Racing

This is a popular sport in Arab countries. In 1985 Saudi Arabia held its eleventh annual camel races as the outstanding feature of a week-long National Heritage and Folk Culture Festival, with 487 camels running in the first race and 2,350 more in the second; each camel was identified by large red numerals painted on its neck. Contestants came from all over the kingdom, and everyone who completed the course, including a young boy who finished in the two-thousandth place in the second race, was given $275 just for competing. The races were held on a two-mile track. The winners were:

Muslat Sahmi Aloteiby, 12 years old, on a camel named Lattamah, who completed the race in 42 minutes and 29 seconds, winning the first prize of nearly $10,000 and a 2,000-gallon water tank.

Salem Salim, riding on al-Ghizail from the royal family's stables, who completed the race in 42 minutes and 30 seconds—only one heartbreaking second behind the first place.

In Croquet

Jacques Fournier (1983–): From Phoenix, Arizona, Jacques plays basketball at school, but he is not talking about that when he says, "You're in trouble if you stuff a hoop." He's talking about his favorite sport, which is tournament croquet, and "stuffing a hoop" means your ball does not go all the way through a hoop, or wicket. Tournament croquet is different from the game most people play in their back yards. The balls are larger, fitting through a wicket with only about an eighth of an inch to spare; the grass court is perfectly flat and smooth; and there are only six wickets, which are set up in a rectangle. Players must hit two balls through all six wickets twice, then hit a stake in the center of the court. In tournaments Jacques mostly plays with and competes against adults. In May, 1994, when he was 11 years old, Jacques and Tom Dunker, 42 years old, won the doubles event in the top amateur division at the San Francisco Open. Jacques was the youngest player ever to win a major event in croquet.

In Diving

Troy Dumais (1980–): Born in Ventura, California, Troy began diving off springboards (bouncy aluminum boards that propel a diver as high as seven feet into the air) when he was four years old and started competing at age five. When he was nine, he began diving off platforms placed at heights of three meters, then at five meters (about 16 feet) and then at seven-and-a-half meters (about 24½ feet). At age 11, he started to win championships in his age group. When 13 years old he won national age-group championships in both springboard and platform events, and at age 14, when he was old enough to be allowed to start diving from the 10-meter platform, the platform used in the Olympics, he again won both events. All in all, by age 14 he had won eight national championships.

Marjorie Gestring (1922–): A California native, Marjorie won an Olympic gold medal for springboard diving in the Berlin 1936 Olympics at age 13 years and 267 days. She was the youngest female ever to win an Olympic gold medal in any sport.

Fu Mingxia (1978–): Born in China, Mingxia left home when she was 10 years old to study at a diving school in Beijing and after that was able to see her parents, who were laborers, only twice a year when they came to visit her. At age 13 years and 11 months she set a new standard for divers at the Barcelona summer games in 1992 when she became the second youngest person ever to win an Olympic gold medal. As graceful as a bird in flight, she easily surpassed all her older competitors, doing more difficult dives than anyone else and finishing with a margin of almost 50 points because the DD (degree of difficulty) is a major factor in scoring divers.

Dorothy Poyton (1915–): Originally from Salt Lake City, Utah, Dorothy made her diving debut in Olympic competition at age 13 years and 228 days in Amsterdam in 1928, where she won a silver medal for springboard diving. At age 17 she won the gold medal in the high-board diving event at the Los Angeles Olympics in 1932, and four years later in the 1936 Olympics in Berlin she retained that title under her married name, Dorothy Hill.

Aileen Riggin (1906–): Aileen was an American girl who won the silver medal in the springboard diving competition at the age of 14 at the 1920 Olympics in Antwerp, Belgium. Four years later at the Paris Olympics, she won the bronze medal in the 100-meter backstroke, thus becoming the only Olympic competitor to win medals in both diving and swimming.

In Figure Skating

In 1996, with 200 hours of programming on the four major television networks, figure skating ranked second in ratings behind professional football as TV's most popular sport, and five prominent skaters had become millionaires. Many people date the public's immense interest in the sport to January 6, 1994, when Nancy Kerrigan was hit in the leg with a metal bar. The Harding-Kerrigan showdown at the Lillehammer Olympics a month later was the sixth most watched TV event of all time.

Oksana Baiul (1977–): This Ukrainian girl received her first pair of skates when she was three-and-a-half years old because she was chubby and her mother and grandfather thought ice skating would be a good exercise for her. She was a natural, learning jumps, spins, and other moves seemingly without effort, and by the time she was seven years old she was winning local figure skating events. When she was 13 her mother died and she no longer had a family, as her father had disappeared when she was two and both her grandparents died by the time she was 10. Viktor Petrenko, who won the men's figure skating championship at the 1992 Olympics, persuaded his mother-in-law, Galina Zmievskaya, who was also his coach, to help her, and she took Oksana into their home in Odessa, Ukraine, as another daughter. Soon after moving there Oksana entered her first senior level competition, at age 15, and became the Ukrainian National Champion. After that came the 1993 World Championship games in Prague, Czech Republic. Skaters rarely win a world championship the first time they try, but Oksana did.

After that she and other champions performed in the United States for two-and-a-half months, in a different city almost every night. When the tour ended Oksana began training hard for the Olympics, most days skating from 8:00 to 9:30 A.M., then going to school, and training for another 90 minutes each evening. At age 16 she became the youngest Olympic female figure skating champion since Sonja Henie (see page 327), in the 1994 Olympic Games in Lillehammer, Norway, where she again like Sonja Henie performed an exquisite "Dying Swan" to the music of Tchaikovsky. She won the gold medal in spite of a leg wound received in practice the day before and a fine performance by Nancy Kerrigan, who won the silver medal.

An ecstatic welcome was organized for Oksana in Ukraine where the president gave her a bonus for her gold medal: a check for $15,000, an enormous sum in a country where the average person earns less than $20 a month. She loved her homeland, but she and her coach's family left it because its skating facilities were poor. They now live in Simsbury, Connecticut, where a superb skating complex and home were built for them. Her skating in professional shows on ice has made her a millionaire.

Kurt Browning (1966–): This Canadian skater said he could not remember the first time he skated, but his sister Dana did. He was three years old and she was 12 when she took him skating on a frozen swimming hole, and that night she wrote in her diary that Kurt had "natural ability." His mother signed him up for skating lessons when he was six years old. He became the fastest skater on his ice hockey team but decided he was better at figure skating and dropped hockey. He was a natural jumper and could do a double axel by the time he was 10 years old, and triple jumps by age 13. In 1988 he got into the *Guinness Book of World Records* for landing the first quadruple jump in international competition. By 1996, when he was in his thirties, he had won the men's World Championship in figure skating four times.

Connie Chang (1981–): At age 13 this Korean girl participated in the 1994 Olympics in Lillehammer, Norway, and was on the team that won a speed relay race. She was the youngest person there to win a gold medal.

Chen Lu (1977–): One of China's youngest female sports stars, since age six Chen Lu's daily schedule was a one-and-one-half hour afternoon period of skating and another hour and a half at night, with the mornings reserved for an hour of exercise and rest. When she was nine years old she made the triple jump. At that time no one else in China could do this and, in fact, it was not considered good to teach that kind of complex movement to young skaters because they could easily be hurt. But by the time she was 10 years old Chen had learned five types of the aerial triple jumps that distinguish champion figure skaters. She performed three of them in her routine to win the Chinese National Championship in 1987 at age 12, a title she won each successive year afterwards. She was also the first Chinese figure skater to place in international competition, and in 1992 and 1993 she performed in a 45-city tour in the United States.

Peggy Fleming (1948–): Born in San Jose, California, Fleming started skating at age nine. At 15 she became the youngest U.S. figure skating champion up to that time, and she held the title for five years. At 17 she became the world champion, and she held that title for three years. And at age 19 she won a gold medal at the 1968 Olympics in Grenoble-Chamrousse where her elegant style won her worldwide acclaim. She then had a highly successful career skating in professional revues, and after that she served as a sports commentator on ABC television. Her charming personality made her one of the most lastingly popular of all American athletes.

Yekaterina ("Katya") Gordeyeva (1971–): Katya and her partner **Sergei Grinkov** won gold medals at the 1988 Olympics in Calgary, Canada and at the 1994 games in Lillehammer, Norway, where they were deemed unbeatable after a flawless performance. When first paired in 1982 by their Soviet coaches, Sergei was 15 and Katya was a skinny 11-year-old. She literally grew up in his arms. By the time they won their first Olympic gold medal at Calgary their relationship had blossomed and they were soul mates on ice and in life. In 1991 they married, and a year later had a beautiful daughter, Daria. They moved to Simsbury, Connecticut, becoming neighbors of Oksana Baiul and Viktor Petrenko in the International Skating Center complex that had been built for the Ukrainian skaters.

Then, in November, 1995, their happy lives abruptly changed. While rehearsing in Lake Placid for a forthcoming performance scheduled for "Stars on Ice," Sergei suddenly collapsed and died in Katya's arms. Doctors found that an artery that carried blood from his heart had been completely blocked, the result of undiagnosed heart disease. A funeral was held four days later in Moscow at the Red Army Club arena where they had spent so many years training. While there Katya stayed in the tiny flat where she and Sergei had lived when they first got married, which she had kept even after moving to Simsbury. "That little room is very close to my heart," Katya said. "I feel his spirit there."

In December some of the world's finest skaters, including Katarina Witt (see page 328), decided to dedicate their "Stars on Ice" show in February in Hartford, Connecticut, to Sergei, with the proceeds going into a trust fund for Katya and Daria. They asked her if she would take a bow at the end. She decided she had a better idea; she would skate. She began training in January. At first, never having skated alone, she was shaky but gradually felt stronger, and Marina Zueva, her long-time coach, told her, "Remember that Sergei will help you; try to feel that he is around you."

Almost as soon as her performance began, her fears vanished. "It was like I had double strength," she said later, and she began a series of lovingly choreographed gestures, her hand searching for another hand, her body arcing to the shape of another invisible body that made it seem as if she was still pairs-skating. At the end she skated with joy, her fingers reaching toward the sky. The tearful audience rose to its feet and then she told them, "I skated not alone; I skated with Sergei." Then she moved to the edge of the rink and picked up their daughter. The little girl's arms wound around her mother's neck, and she gently patted her mother's back as she was carried around the arena. Since then the now three-year-old Daria has also embraced skating. "I a good skater," she tells visitors, then adds, "but my mom is a *very* good skater." Katya smiles proudly, saying, "This is my life, and this is my future."

Tonya Harding (1971–): Born in Portland, Oregon, Tonya became the most famous near success in the history of sports. Suffering all her life from asthma and growing up in poverty, with five different stepfathers, her only real pleasure was ice skating, which she fell in love with the first time she saw ice in a rink in a shopping mall. She learned to skate before she could read, and later began training at the mall where she worked afternoons at a potato stand to raise money for the training. With little money to spend, her mother hand-sewed Tonya's skating costumes when she began entering competitions. At age 15 she met Jeff Gillooly, whom she married three years later, after which he managed her career although she divorced him less than a year after their wedding.

At age 16 she won the U.S. Championship in figure skating, having completed a triple axel, which only one other figure skater had ever succeeded in doing. She was enormously popular with local fans; in 1994 her fan club had 2,000 passionately devoted members who admired not only her skating but viewed her as a working-class heroine spunkily struggling against illness, accidents, poverty, and snobbish discrimination. But her lifelong ambition ended in disgrace after the 1994 Olympics, in which she skated poorly due to nervousness and injuries while training. Her ex-husband, with whom she lived even after their divorce, was convicted of having hired people to make a physical attack on her main skating rival, Nancy Kerrigan, whacking her right knee with a metal club, and Tonya was convicted of complicity in the crime.

Nancy recovered from the attack and gave an excellent performance, winning the silver medal, while Tonya was banned for life from the U.S. Figure Skating Association, stripped of the National Championship title she had won in January 1994, forbidden to participate in future Olympics, and sentenced to three years of supervised probation. In 1996 she was still struggling to pay off over $400,000 in fines and legal costs.

Sonja Henie (1912–1969): This Norwegian girl began one of the most spectacularly successful careers in sports, first competing as a figure skater in the Paris Olympics of 1924 at age 11, when she came in last. Unfazed, she made up for it later. At age 15 she won the world title in figure skating, the first of her still unequaled record of 10 individual world titles, winning one every year between 1927 and 1936 when she retired from amateur competition. At 15 years and 316 days, she was the youngest gold medalist at the Olympic winter games in St. Moritz, Switzerland, in 1928. Her exquisite interpretation of the "Dying Swan" from Tchaikovsky's *Swan Lake* ballet began a whole new era for figure skating, turning it from just a sport into an internationally popular sport-plus-art form. At 19 she again won the gold medal with her daring routines in the Los Angeles Olympics of

1932, and in 1936 at the Olympic games in Berlin she captured the gold medal for the third time. No Olympic figure skater has ever won more than three golds.

Sonja then turned professional and became a movie star. At first she was considered a movie oddity, but producer Daryl Zanuck had faith in her and paid her $125,000 for her first film, aptly called *One in a Million*. It was a huge hit, and by 1938 she was the second largest attraction in movies, right behind Shirley Temple. By 1939 she was the highest paid woman in show business. After making her last film, in 1948, she starred in the first ice show ever performed in a Broadway theater. It was produced by stage designer Norman Bel Geddes, who defied people who said it would be impossible to cover a stage floor with ice. Over the years she earned an estimated $47 million. There is now a Sonja Henie Museum in Oslo, Norway, which exhibits, among other aspects of her remarkable life, a collection of paintings by her.

Michelle Kwan (1980–): Michelle is a native Californian whose parents were Chinese but moved from Hong Kong to the United States before Michelle was born. She started skating lessons at age six. When she was seven she knew she wanted to skate in the Olympics someday, and at age 11 she moved to Lake Arrowhead, California, two hours away from home so that she could train at a skating center there; her parents visited her every weekend. When she was 12 she took and passed a skating test that moved her from junior to senior level, thereafter competing against skaters in their late teens and twenties. At 13 years of age in 1993, Michelle won her first major senior title at the U.S. Olympic Festival in San Antonio, Texas. She finished second to Tonya Harding at the U.S. Figure Skating Championships. The top two finishers were supposed to make the 1994 U.S. Olympic Team, but skating officials instead named star Nancy Kerrigan, who had missed the chance to compete in the national event because of the knee injury she suffered as a result of the assault she had received. Michelle was named an Olympic "alternate challenger," someone to fill in if Tonya or Nancy could not skate. So she went to Norway and kept training during the games but did not get to compete.

She was disappointed, but kept her hopes up for the next Olympics to be held in the summer of 1996. In the meantime she competed in the World Championships in Birmingham, England, and skated beautifully but came in fourth. Her coach said, "The only thing I could think of was that she looked very young. The judges were looking for the ladies' champion of the world, not the girls' champion." He must have been right, because 10 months later at the U.S. Nationals she appeared transformed, with a sophisticated hairdo, rouge, mascara, and lipstick, and became at 15 the youngest national champion since 15-year-old Peggy Fleming in 1964.

Marina Toherkasova (1965–): Both from the Soviet Union, Marina and her partner **Sergei Shakrai** performed the first quadruple twists in pair skating, in the Olympic games in Innsbruck, Austria, in 1977, when she was 12 years old. They were able to achieve this difficult feat because of the unusual difference in size between the tiny girl and her tall male partner. They also won silver medals in pair skating during the Lake Placid Olympics of 1980, when she was 15.

Katarina Witt (1965–): An East German girl, Katarina started skating at age 10. She was outstanding so quickly that she became a pampered athlete, sponsored by the state, with many special privileges. Her behavior was closely monitored by the Stasi, the East German secret police, as was that of all prominent athletes in the country, until the Berlin

Wall and the Communist government fell in 1989. Because of this she was sometimes accused of being a Communist spy, which she heatedly denied, and some of her early skating performances were greeted by boos as well as applause. She won the first of four World Championships in 1984, when she was 19, as well as the first of her two Olympic gold medals at the winter games in Sarajevo, Yugoslavia. In 1988 at the Olympics in Canada she won the gold medal again, becoming the first figure skater since Sonja Henie to win golds in two successive Olympics. She turned pro later that year and then starred in stage shows such as "Stars on Ice," and on television her version of *Carmen* won an Emmy.

When she appeared at the 1994 Olympics in Lillehammer, Norway, she was welcomed as the grande dame of the sport and her freestyle performance won tumultuous applause. It was performed with passion that critics called "fire on ice" in a blood-red costume to the music of the anti-war song, "Where Have All the Flowers Gone?" The song intended to deliver a "message of peace" for war-torn Sarajevo, the once beautiful, gaily bannered city where she won her first Olympic gold. "Now," she said, "when you see the pictures on television of the people killed there, and houses bombed and children crying in pain, it breaks your heart."

This spectacular performance was followed in 1995 and 1996 with a series of professional appearances on stage and television, in each of which Katarina seemed to skate better than ever.

In Football

Troy Aikman (1966–): Born in Cerritos, California, Troy always dreamed he would be a pro athlete. When he was seven years old he began to play football, baseball, and basketball at local parks and soon was one of the best all-round athletes in the area. At age 10, he began practicing his autograph, telling his mother he needed to get it right for the future. When he was 12 his family moved to Henryetta, Oklahoma, where he played baseball and basketball, but football became his number one sport. In high school he played quarterback for three years with a team that was not very good; its players were teased because of their nickname, the Fighting Hens; fans laughed and threw rubber chickens onto the field. However, he played well and was named All-State Player as a senior, earning a football scholarship to the University of Oklahoma.

Later he transferred to the University of California at Los Angeles (UCLA) and became its all-time leading passer, finishing his college career as the third-highest rated passer in NCAA history. By 1992, at age 25, he was playing pro ball with the Dallas Cowboys and was named Most Valuable Player. His team won two Super Bowls.

In 1991 Troy helped raise $225,000 to build a health and fitness center for kids in his hometown of Henryetta. He also sponsored a college scholarship for financially needy kids from Henryetta High School.

Brett ("Country") Favre (1969–): Brett was born in Gulfport, Mississippi, part Chocktaw Indian and an honorary member of the Mississippi Band of Chocktaws. At age 11, when he was in sixth grade, he wrote in a class essay that he was going to play pro football someday and promised to give his teacher free tickets once he got to the NFL. His prediction came true and he kept his promise. He learned about football from his dad, who was his high school football and baseball coach. At age 13 he was equally good at baseball, and played at baseball, and played third base for the high school varsity team, leading the team in hitting with a .325 average, though he decided to focus on football. During school from third grade through twelfth, he set his first record: he never missed a single day of school. "My parents were teachers," he laughed, "so it was tough to play hooky."

After high school Brett went to the University of Southern Mississippi, where he made 10 passing records. Then he went on to become a quarterback on the Green Bay Packers where he broke two team records in his second season, passing for more than 200 yards in each of 11 straight games; the Packers finished the season with a 9–7 record and Brett was then picked to play in the Pro Bowl.

Joseph ("Joe") Clifford Montana, Jr (1956–): A native of New Eagle, Pennsylvania, Joe was a good all-round athlete as a youngster. In Little League baseball he pitched three perfect games, and he was an all-state forward in basketball. He began concentrating on football at age eight. But when he was 15 years old and a sophomore in high school he was so slender that the coach knicknamed him "Joe Banana" and thought he was not strong enough to play, so he was kept on the bench all season. He did not give up, though; as a junior he made the starting lineup, and as a senior became quarterback and led his high school to an 8–2 record.

Later Montana became a living legend as the highest rated passer in NFL history. In college he led Notre Dame to the national title in 1977. Afterwards he led San Francisco to four Super Bowl titles, and he was the only Super Bowl player ever to be named Most Valuable Player three times. After having to miss most of two seasons due to elbow surgery, he was traded to Kansas City, entering the 1993 season ranked first in all-time passing efficiency, fifth in yards passing, and sixth in touchdown passes. He led his teams to fourth-quarter comeback wins 29 times. Joe Namath called him "the best I've ever seen; I'm an average Joe compared to him."

Ty Page (1986–): From Keyser, West Virginia, Ty was only five years old when he had his first football season. During it he rushed for 1,184 yards and scored 17 touchdowns. In 1993 and '94, he played quarterback for the Keyser Mini Steelers, a team for kids aged six, seven, and eight. In 1993, at age seven, he scored 25 touchdowns in eight games. He rushed for an amazing 964 yards on 49 carries, an average of 19.7 yards each time he carried the ball. The Mini Steelers won all eight of their games that year. In one game Ty scored five touchdowns. In another, he carried the ball four times and scored four touchdowns. The Steelers played on an 80-yard field and Ty's longest touchdown run was 76 yards. On defense, he played middle linebacker and led the Mini Steelers with 66 tackles. The team gave up only one touchdown all season. Five of the eight teams they played against could not even get a first down.

In addition to playing such outstanding football, Ty competed in another sport starting when he was four years old: wrestling. He won 20 of 22 matches against boys his own age and size. In school, where his favorite subject was math, he was outstanding again, getting mostly As.

Tiaina ("Junior") Seau, Jr. (pronounced Tee-eye-EE-nuh SAY-ow, 1969–): Born in San Diego, California, to Samoan parents, Tiaina played quarterback at age 13 on a Pop Warner football team, winning from his older brother Savaii, who attended every game, a cheeseburger for each touchdown he made. In high school he was on the basketball and track teams as well as the football team. He led Oceanside High School to the city's championship, playing tight end and linebacker. In 1987, at 18, he received a football scholarship to the University of Southern California, and in 1990 was named the PAC-10 Defensive Player of the Year and was hired by the San Diego Chargers as inside linebacker.

In 1993 he started the Junior Seau Foundation which helps youngsters by supporting programs that fight drugs, alcohol, and child abuse.

O. J. Simpson (See page 154.)

In Golf

Patty Berg (1918–): From Minneapolis, Minnesota, Patty Berg was already active in sports by the time she was 12 years old. She quarterbacked the Fiftieth Street Tigers football team to an undefeated season, and played sandlot baseball. She also took part in the national junior speed skating championships and ran the 30-yard dash for the track team at the John Burroughs elementary school. But she found golf particularly intriguing and wanted to learn more about it, having read about Bobby Jones (see page 00) who had won the U.S. Open at the Interlachen course near her home. When she was still 12 her father gave her and her younger brother memberships in the Interlachen Country Club, where she proceeded to take golf lessons and to practice regularly. After she became a top golf champion she attributed much of her success to playing at Interlachen, saying,"I think that did more for my golf game than anything because it was so great a test of golf. The course required every conceivable kind of golf shot."

At age 15 Patty qualified for the Minneapolis City Championship but did not win. She then resolved, "I'm going to go home and practice 365 days and see if I can't improve," which she did. At age 17 she won the Minnesota State Championship, a title she won again at age 18 and at 20, when she also won the U.S. Amateur title and 10 of the 13 tournaments she entered. The Associated Press named her Outstanding Female Athlete of 1938. She won more than 40 tournaments before deciding to give up her amateur status at age 22, when she signed with a sporting goods company at a salary of approximately $7,500 a year. In addition to playing in exhibitions she made appearances at summer camps for girls and offered golf clinics and schools.

At that time there were only about five women golf professionals and very small prizes. At the 1941 Women's Western Open, Patty's first prize reward was merely a $100 savings bond. So in 1949, she and Babe Didrikson (see page 348) founded the Ladies Professional Golf Association (LPGA), to legitimize and popularize golf as an acceptable sport for women. The number of professional tournaments increased from three to nine, with a total purse of about $45,000. Patty served as president of LPGA from 1949 to 1952. She also won 39 tournaments during its first decade. Among the many honors she received were the Women's Sports Hall of Fame, the Associated Press Female Athlete of the Year Award (three times), the Humanitarian Sports Award from the United Cerebral Palsy Foundation, and the 1963 Bob Jones Award "honoring the person whose contribution to the game is most completely described by the term distinguished sportsmanship."

Robert ("Bobby") Tyre Jones (1902–1971): From Atlanta, Georgia, Bobby was the youngest person ever to qualify for the U.S. Amateur Golf Tournament, in 1916 at age 14. He won three junior amateur titles and became undisputably the greatest golfer of his time and perhaps of all time. From 1922 to 1930 he won the British Open three times, the U.S. Open four times, and the U.S. Amateur title a never-equalled record of five times. And in 1930 he won the U.S. and British Open Championships plus the U.S. and British Amateur titles, thus becoming the only person ever to win a Grand Slam in golf. In 1934 he created a special course at the Augusta National Golf Club in Augusta, Georgia, and founded the prestigious Masters Championship Tournament that has been played there every year since then.

Patty ("Scooter") Sheehan (1956–): Patty was born in Middlebury, Vermont. She first played golf at age four and at four also started ski racing, learning both sports from her father who had been the men's Alpine coach of the 1956 U.S. Olympic Ski Team and who coached golf, skiing, baseball, and football at Middlebury College. By age 13 she was one of the best junior skiers in the country in slalom, giant slalom, and downhill; but when her family moved to Reno, Nevada, she switched to golf because there was a golf course only one block from their new house. After finishing high school she played golf for the University of Nevada and then at San Jose State University in California.

Patty became such a successful professional golfer that she earned more than $4,000,000 in prize money, and after winning her thirtieth tour event she was made a member of the Ladies Professional Golf Association Hall of Fame.

Eldrick ("Tiger") Woods (1976–): From Cypress, California, "Tiger" began playing golf with his father when he was only two years old and started winning world titles at age eight. His father says, "Tiger has never been disciplined, never even been told what to do," and the two of them have always had a very close relationship. Asked by journalist Peter de Jonge, interviewing him for an article in the *New York Times Magazine*, what he respects so much about his father, Tiger replied, "Everything. . .we're best friends." At age 15 he was the youngest winner ever of the U.S. Junior Amateur Championship, and he won two more junior titles that same year, becoming the only golfer since Bobby Jones to have won three junior amateur titles. Also he was the only player since Jones to have won both the Junior Amateur and the Amateur titles. At 18 Tiger won three tournaments against adults, then entered the U.S. Amateur Gold Championship in Ponte Verda, Florida, and became its youngest ever winner, as well as the first black player in the 99-year history of this prestigious amateur golf tournament. He accomplished this in an extremely dramatic game, making what the U.S. Golf Association called the greatest comeback in U.S. Amateur history, battling back from six holes down to a 1-up victory through a 30-foot birdie putt on the seventeenth hole. In the late autumn of 1994, as a freshman at Stanford University, which recruited him vigorously and gave him a full scholarship, he competed in four collegiate tournaments, winning two of them.

Tiger's performance in the Jerry Pate National Intercollegiate championship, one of the most important tournaments in college golf, at Shoal Creek golf club near Birmingham, Alabama, was another spectacular one. On the fifty-fourth hole he was tied for the lead with just one more hole to play. He had to sink a putt from 60 feet away, which he managed to do in spite of the tensions caused by two members of a black activist organization standing at the golf club's iron gates to protest Tiger's refusal to boycott this tournament because Hall Thompson, the 71-year-old founder of Shoal Creek, had told a reporter that the club "don't discriminate in every other area except the blacks." Actually, although Tiger's father told him that "in America if you have one drop of black blood in you, you're black," Tiger, who has American Indian, Chinese, Thai, and white blood in him as well, does not think of himself as black, and does not think of himself as a role model for blacks, although others may. It is the only thing about which he and his father disagree. Whether or not he is a role model, golfer Tom Watson calls Tiger Woods "potentially the most important player to enter the game in 50 years." Tiger Woods delayed his final year at Stanford University and went pro in August 1996, enticed by a $40 million endorsement contract from Nike.

In Gymnastics

Nadia Comaneci (1961–): This Romanian girl made Olympic history at age 14 during the 1976 summer games in Montreal, Canada, as the first gymnast ever to be awarded a perfect score of 10. Furthermore, she won an amazing total of seven perfect 10s, four on the uneven parallel bars and three on the balance beam. Altogether Nadia won a total of three individual gold medals that year, including one as the best all-around woman athlete there, plus a silver medal as a member of her team. And four years later, at age 18, she won two more golds at the 1980 Olympics held in Moscow, putting her in the select company of the Olympics' all-time leading gold medal winners.

Dominique Dawes (1976–): Born in Silver Spring, Maryland, Dominique took her first gymnastics class at age six and began competing in national and international events at age 12. On a typical school day she got up at 4:30 A.M. and trained at a gym from 6 to 8 A.M., then attended school from 8:30 to 2:00 P.M. She then went back to the gym again from 3:00 P.M. until 7:00 or 8:00 P.M. When she was was 15, Dominique became a member of the U.S. National Gymnastics Team. At 16 she scored a perfect 10 on her floor routine in a meet between the United States and Japan; she was a member of the 1992 U.S. Olympic Women's Gymnastic Team that won a bronze medal in Barcelona, Spain; and she also took home two individual silver medals from those games. At 18 she won all four individual events and the all-around award at the 1994 U.S. national championships. When she did her floor routines Dominique seemed to have springs in her feet; nobody could bounce higher or more quickly off the mat, which was one reason she earned the nickname "Awesome Dawesome."

At the 1996 Olympics, she did not earn an individual medal but was a member of the U.S. Women's gymnastic team, which did win a hard-fought gold medal for team performance. Teammates included 14-year-old **Dominique Moceanu, Shannon Miller, Amanda Borden, Jaycie Phelps, Amy Chow,** and **Kerri Strug**, who made a courageous and spectacular vault on a badly sprained ankle, which had been injured in her immediately preceding attempt. All these gymnasts had started the sport as young girls.

Olga Korbut (1955–): After years of practice, this tiny Soviet gymnast entered the 1972 Olympics in Munich and stunned the audience and confounded the judges when she turned a back flip on the balance beam. Critics declared that this feat was too dangerous and belonged in a circus rather than in a world-class competition, but the judges could not help but give her a 9.8 score with this athletic and innovative balance beam routine performed with the grace of a ballet dancer. They also gave her a 9.8 score in the floor exercises, but mistakes she made in the uneven parallel bars earned only a 7.5, and she fell to seventh place overall. The next day, however, she dominated the individual competitions and took the gold medal in the floor exercises. Once again defying gravity and tradition with her trademark backward flip, she also won the balance beam competition. Her final medal count at Munich included a team gold and an uneven bars silver. (The audience booed the judges when they gave her a score of "only" 9.8.) Her three gold medals and one silver were the most won by any gymnast that year. She thanked the crowd of onlookers, saying, "I cried a little yesterday but today the audience really spurred me on, and now I'm very happy." She was named the Associated Press Female Athlete of the Year.

At the next Olympics in 1976 Olga won one gold and one silver, and she was inducted into the Women's Sports Foundation Hall of Fame in 1982. She will always be remembered as the person who first popularized gymnastics and made it into a major sport.

Mary Lou Retton (1968–): Originally from Fairmont, West Virginia, Mary Lou began taking dance lessons when she was four years old, learning the basics of ballet, tap, jazz, and acrobatics, and at age seven enrolled in gymnastics classes for youngsters at West Virginia University. In 1976, at age eight, she won the beginners' title at a statewide meet in West Virginia and continued to progress rapidly. At 12 she entered the 1980 Class I nationals, competing against girls much older and more experienced than she was; she won the vault event, was second in the floor exercise, and finished seventh in the all-around competition. That same year she won the West Virginia state gymnastics title. At 13 Mary Lou was named to the U.S. Junior National Team and traveled to Canada for her first international meet where she won the all-around title. When she was 14, at a competition in Las Vegas she met world-renowned gymastics coach Bela Karolyi who invited her to train at his Gymnastics Center in Houston, Texas. She moved there in December 1982 to study with him, to sharpen her skills, adding power and difficulty to each of her events. After only two weeks with him, she received her first perfect 10 on the vault, and two months later defeated America's top gymnasts at another meet in Las Vegas. At the McDonald's American Cup, the premier U.S. international meet, she bested two world champions, Natalia Yerchenko of the Soviet Union and Boriana Stoyanova of Bulgaria, winning the vault, the floor exercise, and the all-around, and tied for first place on the uneven parallel bars.

At age 15, in 1983, Mary Lou traveled to meets around the world. She won every individual event in the South African Cup competition. Later, at the U.S. Championships in Chicago, she suffered a stress fracture in her left wrist, forcing her to skip the World Championships that year. But in December she returned to competition and became the first ever American to win the Chunichi Cup in Japan.

Her big year was 1984, when she was 16. She defended her American Cup all-around title, scoring 39.50 points out of a possible 40.00. To prepare for the summer Olympics in Los Angeles she undertook an arduous training schedule, practicing 8 to 10 hours a day. Her coach Bela Karolyi said, "I have been teaching gymnastics 25 years, and had many World and Olympic champions, but I have never coached anybody more positive and dedicated than this little girl." She won a place on the eight-member American women's Olympics team, but her chance to participate was threatened by a torn cartilage in her right knee that required surgery. Just two days after the surgery, however, she resumed her training schedule and was able to lead the U.S. Women's Gymnastics Team to a silver medal at the games, the first Olympic medal won by American women gymnasts since 1948. This was followed by her becoming the first American female ever to win an individual medal in gymnastics. She was the youngest winning gymnast at these Olympics and yet she won five medals, the most won by any athlete at the 1984 games, and they included the all-around gold medal.

Even before the Olympics, Mary Lou was already one of America's favorite athletes because of her earlier achievements, her outgoing personality, and engaging smile. After the games she quickly became the darling of corporate America, which featured her in magazines and on TV with ads for their products. She also toured, giving speeches to promote physical fitness. She was named 1984 Female Athlete of the Year by the Associated Press and 1984's Sportswoman of the Year by the magazine *Sports Illustrated*. In 1985 she became the only person to win the American Cup all-around title for a third time, and she became the first gymnast and youngest athlete ever inducted into the U.S. Olympic Hall of Fame.

Mary Lou retired from full-time gymnastics in 1986 and enrolled at the University of Texas to study communications. In 1988 she served as an NBC sports analyst for the summer Olympics in Seoul, South Korea, and in 1992 she was a columnist for *USA Today* at the Barcelona Olympic Games.

In a 1993 survey to determine America's most popular athletes, Mary Lou tied with the skater Dorothy Hammill in the top spot, even though she was no longer active in sports. Her influence on gymnastics was also lasting. She had helped to revolutionize it, changing it from traditionally graceful balletlike movements to those requiring power, speed, and agility, and she increased its popularity, inspiring thousands of youngsters to take up gymnastics.

In Ice Hockey

Mario Lemieux (1965–): From Montreal, Canada, Mario was only three when he learned to skate, developing balance by pushing a chair around the ice as he skated. He and his older brothers used to practice in the hallway of their house, which their dad packed with snow to make an indoor rink. When Mario was six he began playing on ice hockey teams. He was always the best in his age group. By the time he was 15, pro scouts were coming to his midget hockey games; and when he moved up to Juniors, an amateur league for kids aged 16 to 20, more scouts and reporters showed up. When he was 18 he was picked by the Pittsburgh Penguins and became a superstar. He was named Rookie of the Year in 1985, was four times the National Hockey League (NHL) scoring leader, twice the regular season's Most Valuable Player, and three times the All-Star Games' Most Valuable Player. He led the Penguins to consecutive Stanley Cup titles twice, in 1991 and 1992, and was named Most Valuable Player both those years. He won the scoring title in 1993 despite missing 24 games to undergo radiation therapy for Hodgkin's disease.

In Motorcycling

Robbie Reynard (1977–): This Oklahoman started riding a motorcycle at age three, and at age eight was a national champion in his age group. By age 12 he was spending most of his time riding a motorcycle around dirt tracks, flying 15 feet into the air off jumps and sliding aound corners, and he had already won 26 national championships and six world titles. He said his goal was to earn enough money from motorcycle racing to pay for college. When he turned 16 in May 1993, he was finally allowed to get his pro license, meaning he could enter races against the best riders in the world and earn prize money if he won. No one expected him to win right away. Most top pro riders are 20 to 30 years old. But in September, in his seventh pro race, Robbie became the youngest rider ever to win a professional national championship. By 1994, when he was 17, he had won enough money to pay his college bills, and he decided to pay for his sister Cherie to go to college, too.

In Mountain Climbing

Ian Spencer-Green (1980–): Born in 1980 in Colorado Springs, Ian was three years old when his father Stewart Green took him bouldering, a sport in which climbers scale huge boulders without using safety ropes. By age five Ian was scaling tall cliffs at the Garden of the Gods, a climbing area near Colorado Springs. While growing up he continued to climb more and more difficult peaks in Colorado, Arizona, California, and Utah. When he climbed he snapped metal rings called quickdraws onto bolts that had been hammered into the rock along the climbing route. A quickdraw has a gate that allows one to slip a safety rope into it; the other end of the rope drops to the ground where it is held by one's training partner, in his case Eric Harp. If Ian should slip and fall, Eric would pull the rope tight to catch him before he fell more than a few feet. Ian said, "You have to be willing to fall. You might fall 20 or 30 times figuring out how to make a hard move. Climbing is like solving a puzzle, though it challenges your physical ability, too."

By age 13 Ian was training four days a week for as long as five hours a day at the Sport Climbing Center in Colorado Springs, one of the largest indoor climbing gyms in the country, where he climbed up and down man-made walls and did as many as 15 pull-ups using only his fingertips. In the summer of 1992 he decided to undertake the challenge of climbing "the Example," a climbing route up a cliff in Canon City, Colorado. Outdoor climbing routes are rated from 5.0 (easiest) to 5.14 (most difficult), and few climbers in the world can climb a 5.14 wall. Ian could climb a 5.12 route on his first try, but the Example, a bulging chunk of limestone about 65 feet high and full of edges, pockets, and holes for climbers to hold, has a 5.13 rating. Climbers from all over the world come there to test their skills, and Ian was trying to become one of the first 13-year-olds from the United States to complete a 5.13 climb. In November 1994, one week before his fourteenth birthday, after three failed attempts, he finally managed to do it.

Asa Thomas-Train (1983–): Keene Valley, New York, is the original home of this young climber. At age 11 Asa became one of the youngest members of a group known as the Adirondack 46ers. This meant that he had climbed all 46 mountains in the Adirondack park region of upper New York State that are 4,000 feet or higher. Some of the trails are well marked, as Asa has explained: "When you get lost, you find a swamp or stream or another feature that shows up on your map; then you use your compass to guide you back to the trail." He saved some of the most difficult trails for last. "I was going to make sure I finished before school started. I did a 20-mile hike up one mountain on Monday and an 18-mile hike on Tuesday. When I got home from the second one, I was so tired that I went right to bed."

In Roller Skating

Bryce ("The Iceman") Jagel (1981–): A native of St. Petersburg, Florida, Bryce started roller skating when he was five. He won national championships in his age group 10 times: seven titles in the division for quad skates (traditional four-wheel roller skates), one outdoor title in the newer in-line skating division, and two indoor championships. In these national matches, held in July and August every year, skaters race at 300 meters, 500 meters, and 1,000 meters; the fastest six skaters in each event qualify for the final of that event and the skater with the most points from all three events wins the overall gold medal. Starting at age seven, at six national championship meets, the Iceman (called that because he is so cool under pressure) won all three races and the overall gold medal each year, and by age 13 had set six national records. To accomplish all this he trained all year long each year, working out for six hours a day seven days a week, skating every day and lifting weights, and he rode a bike 150 to 200 miles a week.

Jennifer Rodriguez (1976–): Born in Miami, Florida, at 15 Jennifer won the overall title at the Junior World Roller Skating Championships. The next year, at age 16, she won gold medals in the 500 meters, 5,000 meters, and women's relay at the 1993 World Speed Championships. She could skate as fast as 32 miles an hour.

In most cities kids play baseball, basketball, or football in their free time but in St. Louis, Missouri and nearby St. Ann, roller hockey is the king of sports, played almost anywhere that has a flat, hard surface on playgrounds, parking lots, tennis courts, dead end streets, or in bad weather indoors on roller skating rinks. Most players use in-line skates, which have four wheels in a row; but some use standard roller skates. "Roller hockey is more fun than ice hockey," explains David Leadbetter, one of the many enthusiastic young players, "because you don't get hurt as much." In roller hockey games, the penalty for checking (slamming into an opponent) is two minutes in the penalty box, and a player is kicked out of the game for fighting.

In Skiing

Parker Schmidt (1981–): Born in Steamboat Springs, Colorado, Parker went to a freestyle skiing camp at age 12 to learn "inverts" or "flips," skiing off man-made ramps and flipping into a swimming pool. Landing in water helps to keep skiers from getting hurt while they are learning to flip; before they are allowed to flip above snow, aerial skiers must perform 200 flips into a pool and then do 5 to 10 perfect flips before a panel of coaches; this is to make sure they will land on hard snow on their skis, not on their heads. By the end of the summer Parker had become one of the youngest skiers in the United States ever certified to do inverts.

At age 13 he was not only a straight A student in seventh grade, a player of baseball, football, and golf, and a mountain biker, but outstanding in his favorite sport, freestyle skiing, competing in three events: aerials, ballet, and moguls. In aerials he flew off a ramp and did tricks in the air, including a "daffy," in which the skier kicks one leg forward and the other backwards at the same time, and a "helicopter," in which the skier spins in a circle. In ballet, he performed acrobatic moves on a gentle slope. In moguls he skied as fast as he could down a 250-yard slope covered with snow bumps called "moguls."

Picabo Street (1971–): A native of Triumph, Idaho, this young skier's name is pronounced "Peek-a-boo"; for three years after her birth her parents could not decide on a name for her but they nicknamed her "Peek-a-boo" because this was her favorite game, and later they changed the spelling to Picabo, after the name of a town in Idaho. Her father introduced her to skiing at Sun Valley, about 12 miles from their home, when she was six years old, and she won her first race that very year. She was fearless and energetic, and by age seven was regularly beating older children in competitions. When she was 12 Picabo informed her parents that she intended to win a gold medal in downhill skiing in the Olympics.

She trained hard, but had several bad breaks, once seriously injuring her knee, which kept her off skis for six months. At age 19, after years of faithfully following strenuous training schedules and coaches' orders, she rebelled; she showed up out of shape at the U.S. team's summer training camp, and was suspended. After that, and some soul-searching, she decided to clean up her act; one of her unusual self-imposed training methods to improve her balance was to walk barefoot on a rope tied between two trees. In the next two years she won the North American Championship series, the U.S. super-giant slalom title, and the combined downhill and slalom at the World Alpine Champion-ships in Japan. She also placed second in a World Cup downhill race in Norway. In 1994 at the Norwegian Olympics she won the silver medal in the women's downhill race; her second-place finish was achieved in a time of 1:36:50, only 66/100ths of a second behind the winner. Her family was content with the silver, saying it seemed fitting because Picabo is an Indian word meaning "silver stream."

But Picabo was not content to settle for second place, and at the end of the 1994–1995 season she won six of the nine women's downhill races at the World Cup competi-tion, becoming the first U.S. skier ever to win a World Cup downhill title. The 1994–1995 season made her a prime-time star, and she appeared on several television shows.

In Soap Box Derby Racing

Danielle Del Ferraro (1980–): Danielle was born in Glen Cove, New York, but was raised in Stowe, Ohio. When she was 10 years old she got interested in Derby cars, after sitting in one that was on display at a mall in Akron, Ohio. Soap box racers have to help build their own cars each year, so she and her father, Ed Del Ferraro, a carpenter, built her first car that winter, and in the spring she began competing in local races. More than 200 boys and girls aged 9 to 16 compete in the Derby finals in Akron each August, coasting down a 953-foot hill two or three at a time to the finish line in their homemade cars constructed of wood and fiberglass or plastic. Racers control the engineless cars with a steering wheel and a brake. They go as fast as 32 miles per hour.

At age 12 years and 11 months, in August 1993, Danielle won the National Champion-ship of the All-American Soap Box Derby, and the next year at age 13 and 22 days on August 6, 1994, she made history by becoming the first person ever to win it twice. The soap box car she made and raced in that year, which she named "Double D" after her initials D.D., was promptly shipped from her home 10 miles away to the Soap Box Derby Hall of Fame in Akron.

In Soccer

Pelé (real name **Edson Arantes do Nascimento**) (1940–): Born in Bauru, Brazil, Pelé is acknowledged to be the world's greatest soccer player and is a beloved national hero in Brazil. He grew up in a slum. Almost as soon as he could walk he began kicking balls around empty lots. His prowess was so phenomenal that he soon found himself sponsored by people who wanted to pay to train him for competitions. His career began in earnest when he was 15 and was assigned to play the inside left position on Brazil's national team in September 1956. When he was 18, in 1958, he led Brazil to the World Cup, and did so two more times between then and 1970. He had his greatest year when he was 19 and scored 127 goals. By the time of his retirement in 1974 at age 34 he had scored 1,281 goals in 1,263 games, the most ever scored by anyone in a comparable period of time. Since officially retiring he has played in many special exhibition games, including international all-star matches for the benefit of UNICEF.

In Speed Skating

Bonnie Kathleen Blair (1964–): Originally from Cornwall, New York, Bonnie Blair is the greatest female speed skater in U.S. history. She grew up in Champaign, Illinois, the youngest by seven years of six children, all of whom skated. She began skating when she was only two years old and could barely walk, according to her mother; her older sisters and brothers carried her to the rink and put skates on over her shoes. On most winter weekends the family piled into their station wagon and traveled to races in Chicago and Milwaukee. Four of her siblings won national speed skating titles. Bonnie herself skated in her first races at age four.

She got really serious about racing when she was 14 and decided to go to Europe for intensive training if she could raise enough money. The Police Benevolent Association in Champaign wanted to help and held bake sales, raffles, and candy drives. They even sold a bumper sticker proclaiming "Bonnie—the Champaign Policemen's Favorite Speeder." They raised enough money to get her to Europe to train for the 1982 Olympics in Sarajevo, Yugoslavia, where she made the U.S. team and placed eighth in the 500-meter race.

From 1985 to 1992 she was the U.S. sprint champion, winning and setting a world record in the 500-meter speed skating race and a bronze medal in the 1,000-meter race at the winter Olympics in Calgary, Alberta, Canada, in 1988. At the 1992 winter Olympics in Albertville, France, four years later, Bonnie won two more golds, one again for the 500-meter and this time also winning the 1,000-meter race. She was named the U.S. Olympic Committee's 1992 Sportswoman of the Year and also won the Sullivan Award as the best amateur athlete in the United States. Then, in 1994, she thrilled the sports world at the winter games in Lillehammer, Norway, by winning two more gold medals, setting a record as the first American woman to win gold medals in three successive Olympics and the first ever in speed skating history to win five gold medals.

Kin Yoon Mi (1981–): Born in South Korea, at 13 Mi was the youngest female competitor at the Olympics in Lillehammer, Norway. She won a gold medal in the speed skaters' 3,000-meter relay race.

In Surfing

Kelly Slater (1972–): From Cocoa Beach, Florida, Kelly began surfing at age five and at six he entered and won his first surfing contest. He went on to win more than 200 amateur events, including U.S. championships, before turning professional in 1990 at age 18. In 1992, at age 20, Kelly became the youngest man ever to win the Association for Surfing Professionals' world title.

In Swimming

Ben Davidson (1980–): About this young Mississippian, *Sports Illustrated for Kids* has written, "It seems as if Ben has been setting swimming records from the first moment he jumped into a pool. If swimming were any more natural for Ben, he would be a fish." He began racing at age six, and by 14 in 1994 he had set 76 state age-group records in Mississippi in freestyle, butterfly, and backstroke events. By that age he had also set four U.S. national records in his age group in his specialties: the 50-yard, 50-meter, and 100-meter freestyle events.

Gertrude ("Trudy") Ederle (1906–): From New York City, Trudy was 12 years and 296 days old when she became the youngest person to break a non-mechanical World record, winning the 800-yard freestyle in the record time of 13 minutes and 19 seconds, in Indianapolis, Indiana, on August 17, 1919. At age 15 she won New York's junior 100-meter freestyle championship, and followed that with a record-setting performance in a 500-meter swim at Brighton Beach, New York. At age 16 she won a three-and-one-half mile international race, defeating more than 50 world-class swimmers and setting a course record. She continued winning races and by the time she was 17 had made 18 world distance records. At the 1924 Olympics in Paris she won three medals: bronze in the 100- and 400-meter freestyle events and a gold as part of the U.S. winning 400-meter relay team.

Trudy became interested in swimming longer distances and at age 17 announced that she was going to swim across the English Channel. The publisher of the *New York News* agreed to sponsor her and supplied her with a coach. She became a tourist attraction as admirers came to cheer her on and watch her practice in a pool at the Park Central Hotel. However, her first attempt to swim the Channel, in August, 1925, failed; after 8 hours and 46 minutes she lost control of her stroke in the strong current and had to be rescued. But one year later, on August 6, 1926, she entered the water at 7:09 A.M. heading for England from Cape Gris Nez on the coast of France. For the next 14 hours the 19-year-old girl battled high winds and rain, shifting tides and seasickness, then stepped onto British soil in triumph as the first woman ever to swim across the Channel. Her time was 14 hours and 31 minutes, nearly two hours faster than the best previous male time.

Trudy became a big celebrity, welcomed back to New York with a ticker-tape parade equaled only by the one staged for Charles Lindbergh a year later; newspaper headlines called her "America's Best Girl" and "Queen of the Waves." She received hundreds of commercial, movie, and vaudeville contracts estimated at more than $200,000. She toured Europe and the United States giving swimming exhibitions. Her accomplishments convinced people that women were capable of achieving feats equal to those of men, and she was responsible for making swimming one of the leading women's sports in the United States during the 1920s and 1930s. She was inducted into the International Swimming Hall of Fame and the Women's Sports Hall of Fame in 1980. After retiring from professional swimming, she went on to teach swimming to deaf children in New York.

Krisztina Egerszegi (1974–): Born in Budapest, Hungary, at age 14 Krisztina became the youngest swimmer ever to earn an Olympic gold medal for the 200-meter backstroke at the 1988 Olympics in Seoul, South Korea. At 18, in the 1992 Olympics in Barcelona, Spain, she won three more gold medals: in the 100-meter and 200-meter backstroke events and the 400-meter individual medley. Her training routine was to get up at 5:30

A.M. and train on exercise machines from 5:45 to 7:15 A.M. After a short break she swam for two hours, and in the afternoon she again swam laps for two-and-one-half hours.

Kornelia Ender (1959–): An East German, Kornelia won two silver medals in swimming at age 13 at the Olympics in Munich in 1972. By age 17 she was considered the greatest woman swimmer in the world, winning four gold medals, one more than any other woman competitor in Olympic swimming history had ever won in one year—and all in world-record time—plus one silver medal, at the Montreal Olympics in 1976. She set world records in the 100-meter and 200-meter freestyle and in the 100-meter butterfly. She also won the 200-meter freestyle by the stunning margin of three meters. Her fifth medal was a silver for her part in the 4 x 100-meter freestyle East German relay team.

Marcus Hooper (1967–): When he was 12 years and 53 days old this English boy became the youngest conqueror of the English Channel, swimming from Dover, England, to Sangatte, France, in 14 hours and 37 minutes.

Kusuo Kitamara (1918–): Kusuo was born in Japan. At age 14 he was the youngest competitor at the Los Angeles Olympics in 1932 and won a gold medal in the 1,500-meter freestyle swimming race.

Albina Osipowich (1914–): When she was 14 years old this American girl was the youngest ever double gold Olympic medalist. She won the 100-meter freestyle and also shared in the American relay team's victory in the 4 x 100-meter relay race, in the Olympics in Amsterdam in 1928.

Mark Spitz (1950–): From California, Mark could swim before he could walk, and at age six he was taking coaching lessons to prepare him for competitions. He set his first world record at age 17. At 18 he won four medals (two gold, a silver, and a bronze) at the 1968 Olympics in Mexico. His greatest fame came at age 22 when, in a dazzling "Spitz blitz" at the 1972 Munich Olympics, he won a never-equaled record of seven gold medals. That gave him a total medal collection of 11, the largest number ever won by one person, and 8 of his golds were won in world-record time. During his six-year swimming career Mark set a total of 26 world records. In 1990 he went back into action training for the 1992 Olympics. Although he was still a very strong swimmer, he gave up, concluding that he was no longer strong enough.

Franziska ("Franzi") Van Almisick (1978–): When this German girl was five years old her 10-year-old brother gave her advice that changed her life; he told her she must learn how to swim, and a star was born. By age seven Franzi was the best in her training group. When she was 11 years old she was enrolled in a special sports school where she could practice swimming and also attend classes. At 14 she became a member of the East German Olympic swim team, and she won four medals at the 1992 summer Olympics in Barcelona, Spain: two medals in relay events, a silver in the 200-meter freestyle, and a bronze in the 100-meter freestyle. She promptly became a celebrity in Germany, and even more so the following year at age 15 when she won six gold medals in freestyle events and relays at the 1993 European Championships. In 1994 at age 16 she was a star on her own TV show. She worked hard to win her accomplishments, swimming from 7 A.M. to 9 A.M., then going to classes and swimming again from 5 P.M. to 7 P.M., but as she said, "You're willing to do it for something you love."

In Tennis

Andre Agassi (1970–): Agassi started smacking tennis balls at age four. Although Las Vegas had been his home, he spent five of his childhood training years at the Nick Bolletieri Tennis Academy in Florida where Jim Courier and Monica Seles also studied. He became a professional player at age 16. For years most people did not take him seriously as a pro because he broke dress codes by wearing flamboyant clothes, including jewelry, a pony tail, a mustache, and a beard. But many youngsters who had not previously shown great interest in tennis enjoyed his eccentricity, and he gradually gained respect. It was later learned that his jewelry was not a sign of defiance; he was a born-again Christian and the pendant and earring, which he had worn since he was 18, featured three interlocked circles within a gold triangle symbolizing his belief in the Holy Trinity.

In 1990 Andre helped the United States win the Davis Cup and in 1992 did that again and also won his first Grand Slam title at Wimbledon. In 1994, after wrist surgery and a career crisis involving a five-month layoff that began with a humiliating first-round loss in 1993, he became a born-again champion deciding once and for all to devote himself to tennis seriously. Under the guidance of a new coach, Brad Gilbert, in September 1994 he won his second Grand Slam and the U.S. Open, even though he was seeded twentieth. His win surprised everyone, even himself. When he won match point in the final game he dropped to his knees in prayer, staying there until the loser, fourth-seeded Michael Stich of Germany, came over, picked him up, and gave him a hug. Sputtering "But...uh... wow!" he recovered sufficiently to rush over to the stands and give his sweetheart Brooke Shields, whose grandfather Frank Shields was the number one player in the United States in 1933, a big kiss, then returned to the court to be handed his victory cup, with the donor beaming and calling him "the most popular player in tennis."

Tracy Austin (1962–): In 1979 at age 16, this pigtailed American girl, displaying an iron will and a lethal two-handed backhand, became the youngest U.S. Open champion ever. First she defeated the great Martina Navratilova in the semifinals and then beat Chris Evert (see pages 343) 6-4, 6-3 in the finals. At age 18 Tracy won her second U.S. Open and was named Female Athlete of the Year for two years by the Associated Press, at ages 18 and 19. In 1992 she became the youngest player ever inducted into the Tennis Hall of Fame, although her spectacular career had been cut short at age 21, in June 1983, as a result of recurring neck and back injuries.

Jennifer Capriati (1976–): An American, Jennifer held her first tennis racket at age three, and by the time she was 10 loved the game so much that no one could pry her off the court. At age 13 she was a happy, healthy, bubbly girl who played such superb tennis that she and her family decided she should turn professional, which she did when she was only 13 years and 11 months old. At age 14, in the 1990 French Open, she became the youngest ever Grand Slam semifinalist. Also in 1990 she was the youngest player to win a match at Wimbledon. Businesses paid her lots of money to represent their products and she was soon rich and famous. In 1991, at age 15, Jennifer became the youngest female ever ranked in the Top 10 and was earning $6 million a year in endorsement deals. At 16 she upset the German star Stefi Graf to win the gold medal in the 1992 Olympics in Barcelona, Spain.

But the year 1993 was difficult for her, both on and off the court. Suffering from tendinitis and bone chips in her elbow for much of the year, she won only one tournament and lost a first-round match at the U.S. Open in September, after which she stopped playing. Then, on December 19 she and some friends were shopping in a mall in Tampa, Florida, when a security guard stopped her and found her wearing a ring she had not paid for. She said she was not stealing it but had just forgotten to pay for it, but the police gave her a citation and ordered her to go before a judge in juvenile court. The news quickly appeared in papers all around the world, and she felt deeply humiliated.

The year 1994 was even worse. In January Jennifer announced that she was going to take an extended leave from the women's tour to finish high school. At the end of March, however, she dropped out of Saddlebrook High School and then came her second arrest.

Many people have not blamed Jennifer for her fall from grace, but instead have blamed the intense pressure of professional sports and parents, coaches, and the media. The proprietor of the Palmer Preparatory School in Wesley Chapel, Florida, which Jennifer attended until 1992 and where she was an A student, said, "It has to do with how we position young athletes in our society, what we overlook if there is money changing hands." And CBS sports commentator Mary Carillo said, "I don't think children should be allowed to play professional tennis before the age of 18. There ought to be child labor laws to prevent it. Jennifer was always yearning, always looking over her shoulder at what she'd left behind. It was like she knew she was paying some kind of price for all that early success."

> Tennis is 90 percent head and 20 percent legs. There are 200 great young players with the skills to be Number One. Out of them, maybe 50 have the dedication and spirit of sacrifice to be really good. Out of them, 10 might have the mentality of a winner and, out of them, two or three have the charisma and ability of a born champion that can be molded into a superstar.
>
> —*Ion Tiviaz, Boris Becker's Coach*

Jim Courier (1970–): Born in Sanford, Florida, Jim learned to play tennis from his great aunt, a former women's coach. When he was 11 years old he went to a tennis camp, and by age 13 was one of America's top junior players. He loved baseball and wore a baseball cap when playing tennis, but he realized he was better at tennis so decided to focus on it. At age 14 he moved 65 miles away from home to live at the famous Nick Bolletieri Tennis Academy in Bradenton, Florida. For three years Jim spent his weekdays there, returning home on weekends. His roommate for a while at the academy was future tennis rival Andre Agassi. Kids at the academy went to school on weekdays until 12:30 P.M. and had tennis instruction in the afternoons.

While there Jim played in more than 25 national junior tournaments a year. In 1987 when he was 17 he reached the U.S. Tennis Association's boys' final. In 1988, at age 18, he became a professional player, and during the next five years won 12 national tournaments, two Australian Opens and two French Opens and became the biggest money maker in tennis, earning more than $11 million. At age 22 he was rated the number one player in the world, but by 1996 Pete Sampras was number one, Andre Agassi number two, and Jim had slipped to number 13.

Christine Marie ("Chris" or "Chrissie") Evert, (1954–): From Fort Lauderdale, Florida, Chris was the second of five children, and the entire family played tennis. Chris began hitting tennis balls against the walls at municipal courts at age six, and James Evert, her father, who was the professional coach at Fort Lauderdale's Holiday Park Tennis Center, decided to give her lessons, after which she spent two to three hours daily and eight hours on weekends practicing. She was not strong enough to hit backhands with one hand, so she became one of the first players to use a two-handed backhand. She won her first tournament at age 10, and at 16 she upset the world's fourth-ranked player, Francoise Durr, 6-1, 6-1, and then stunned the tennis world by defeating the top-ranked player Margaret Court 7-6, 7-6 in the semifinals. While still 16 she won the $100,000 Virginia Slims Master's tournament, her first tournament victory. In August of that year she was the youngest woman ever to play for the American Wightman Cup team; she won both her matches. The next year she played in her first U.S. Open.

Chris graduated from high school in 1972 and turned professional on her eighteenth birthday. By 1974 she had attained number one ranking, after winning the Wimbledon championship, which she won again in 1976 and 1981, and the French Open singles championship, winning this six more times between 1975 and 1986. In 1975 Chris won the U.S. Open women's singles title, winning five more times between 1976 and 1982. The Associated Press named her Female Athlete of the Year four times (in 1974, 1975, 1977, and 1980) and *Sports Illustrated* selected her as Sportsman of the Year in 1976. In 1981 she was named the Women's Sports Foundation Sportswoman of the Year and was inducted into the International Women's Sports Hall of Fame. In 1985 the Women's Sports Foundation named her the Greatest Woman Athlete of the last 25 years. In her tennis career spanning two decades, Chris led all professional players with 157 singles championships, including 18 Grand Slam titles and more than 1,300 match wins. From 1972 to 1989 she never ranked lower than the top four in women's tennis.

She was admired not only for this fabulous record but for the generous contributions she made to her sport off the courts. She was elected president of the Women's International Tennis Association (WITA) a record nine times, winning its Service Award in 1981, 1986, and 1987. And since her retirement after the 1989 U.S. Open she has remained active in the sport and in continued community service. In 1989 she hosted a Celebrity Tennis Classic to benefit the Drug Abuse Foundation of Palm Beach County in Florida, which raised over $350,000. In 1991 George Bush appointed her to the President's Council on Physical Fitness and Sports. Believing that "sports are a way to express the best in yourself," she inspired thousands of youngsters to play games the way she did, with excellence and style and proving that competitiveness need not flourish at the expense of graciousness. Twelve books have been published about her life.

Maria Jose ("Mary Joe") Fernandez (1971–): Mary Joe's parents emigrated from Santo Domingo, Dominican Republic, to the United States and settled in Miami, Florida, when she was six months old: She said that when she was three years old, "I picked up tennis by hitting tennis balls against the kitchen walls and my bedroom door. I was driving my parents crazy. There was something about the feeling of hitting the ball that I just really loved, even at that age." She began taking tennis lessons when she was five and played in her first tournament at age six. She won in her age division at the Orange Bowl junior tournament four times. When she was 13 years old she beat a top-ranked player and was urged to turn pro, which she did at age 14. At age 14 years and 1 month, she became the youngest player to win a U.S. Open match. She continued to stay in school, though, recognizing that "school keeps me down to earth," so she did not join tours full-time until after graduating from high school at 18 in 1989.

In 1992 at the summer Olympics in Barcelona she won a gold medal in doubles and a bronze medal in singles. In June 1993 at age 21 she reached the finals of the French Open and was ranked number six female tennis player in the world. She reminded some people of Chris Evert because she used a two-handed backhand, moved so smoothly around the court, and rarely lost her temper when playing. Martina Navratilova called her "one of the nicest players on the tour; she's a great fighter on the court, and a great thinker as well." Among her thoughts was the idea that she did not want to let tennis take over her life and that she intended to go to college someday, because "I have always wanted to be a teacher. I like kids a lot."

Martina Hingis (1990–): Martina was born in Czechoslovakia but moved to Switzerland at age 10. She was destined from birth to play tennis. Her mother, former Czech tennis star Melanie Hingis Zogg, named her after that other Czech-born tennis star, Martina Navratilova, put a racquet in her hands when she was only two years old, and became her coach. "I have played tennis for as long as I can remember," she has said. "I like everything about it. It's such a beautiful sport. I compete often. I like playing in front of a crowd." By age 12 she already had an amazing tennis career. In June of that year she won the junior tournament for players 18 and under at the French Open, a Grand Slam event, and was the youngest person ever to win a junior Grand Slam title. In July, in England, she reached the semifinals in junior singles and doubles at Wimbledon, another Grand Slam event. And at age 13 she won the French Open a second time.

Only three days after turning age 14 she turned pro in 1994. In 1996 the minimum age for becoming professional was to be raised to 16, so that younger girls would not face the kind of pressure that bedeviled Jennifer Capriati (see page 342), but this was still allowed in 1994. Although Martina had just started eighth grade and was wearing braces on her teeth, she already had commercial endorsement deals for clothes, shoes, and racquets, and she won her first professional game. She soon experienced growing pains, however. Playing in her second match as a professional she was beaten 6–4, 6–0 by 19-year-old Mary Pierce, ranked number five in the world, in the second round of the $750,000 European indoor tournament. Still, Pierce praised her playing, saying Martina had "made me run." And Martina said, "At least I've now experienced how fast the game is at the top; it was great to see how fast and powerful the game can be." By 1996 she proved that she had stamina and increased skill, winning many important matches.

Suzanne Lenglen (1899–1938): This young French athelete won the world's hard court women's singles championship in Paris in 1913, at age 14. She went on to win championships in women's singles and doubles and in mixed doubles, in France and England. In her twenties she dominated women's tennis, winning both Wimbledon and French titles six times. In fact, she lost only one match from 1919 until 1926 when she retired. She was a colorful personality, not only in spite of, but even because of the fact that she was given at times to throwing her racquet forcefully on the ground in tantrums when she made a bad shot during games. People were, nonetheless, fascinated by her outstanding skill, forcefulness, and individuality.

Gabriela ("Gaby") Sabatini (1970–): Originally from Buenos Aires, Argentina, Gaby later made her home in Key Biscayne, Florida. When she was six years old she took an old racquet and began hitting tennis balls against a wall. Her father enrolled her in a tennis club the next year, at age seven. "Tennis was like a toy to me," she once said, "instead of having dolls, I was playing tennis." At age 14 she won the junior championships at the

345

Italian and French Opens. At 15 she became a pro, left school, and moved from Argentina to Florida to concentrate on tennis. She won the U.S. singles in 1988 and kept moving up in the rankings; she was rated the world's number two in 1990 when she won her biggest victory so far, the U.S. Open, and in 1991 and 1992 she won her third and fourth Italian Opens.

In 1994, in the opening round of the Virginia Slims Championships in New York, Gaby played against Martina Navatilova, the 39-year-old, which in tennis is almost old age. Martina had collected a total record of 167 titles in a career that spanned 22 years, and she was widely regarded as the finest woman athlete to grace her sport. She was now retiring and this was to be her last-ever singles match in New York, where she had earned a record of 18 titles. On this final time she lost to the much younger Gabriela who had competed with Martina in 20 previous games, with Martina winning 15 of them. This time Gabriela's top spin forehands, devilish backward lobs, and searing passing shots were delivered so fast that Martina could hardly get a shot in, and Gabriela won by 6–4, 6–2. Martina said, "I was blown off the court, but if I had to lose my last match, I'd probably rather lose it to Gabriela Sabatini than anyone else."

Monica Seles (1973–): As a Yugoslavian pre-teenager Monica was already a spectacular player, with ambidextrous and two-handed forehands and backhands and what has been described as a demonic squint as her eye met the ball. Her cartoonist father, who was also her coach and mentor, inspired this squint by painting mice on her practice tennis balls and encouraging her to pretend to be a cat.

At age 16 she won the French Open for women's singles in 1990, and later in the year she became the youngest player in this century to win a Grand Slam title. At 17 and 18 she was ranked the number one woman player in the world after winning the Australian, French, and U.S. Opens both years. By now she was a millionaire and had traded her ponytail for an elegant grownup hair style; she was the first athlete ever to endorse hair and skin products for a beauty products company, a role hitherto reserved for models and movie stars. Despite her new fame, glamor, and wealth, Monica remained an unsophisticated youngster, with a huge collection of cherished stuffed animals in her new apartment in Los Angeles and another new home in Sarasota, Florida.

By 1993 she had won eight Grand Slam titles, but her career came to an abrupt halt on April 30, 1993, when she was 19. She was stabbed in the back with a kitchen knife during a changeover in a quarter-final match in Hamburg, Germany. She was so badly injured that she had to retire from tennis. Her assailant was a mentally disturbed man, a fanatical fan of her rival Steffi Graf. Monica, along with Steffi and the rest of the tennis establishment, was outraged when the assailant received only two years' probation for the crime. She underwent rehabilitation at a clinic in California and was physically healed, but for two years she still felt too vulnerable emotionally and mentally to return to competition, where mental toughness is needed. However, in July 1995, she began a triumphant comeback with a 6–3, 6–2 victory over Martina Navratilova in an exhibition match in Atlantic City, playing as well as ever.

Venus Williams (1981–): From Compton, California, Venus was only 10, a fifth-grader practicing tennis on pockmarked public courts in a ghetto, when she was hailed as the next great tennis prodigy by recruiting agents who work for tennis's marketeers. Nick Bolletieri, whose intensive training camps have gained worldwide attention for the young stars they have produced, said, "The sporting goods companies are looking for the rarity, and being a minority athlete, Venus could have it made. She's unbelievable, and very bright." Zina Garrison, then America's foremost black tennis player, said Venus was "the best 10-year-old I've ever seen."

When Venus was 12, people were still raving about her, while experiencing qualms about pushing her into prominence. Slade Mead, a tennis talent scout, said, "It's gotten to the point where it almost seems pedophilic to be sitting there telling a 12-year-old and his parents about the money you can make them." Patricia Apey, another tennis scout, said, "I don't think we're vultures. But there's a lot of parents, especially outside of North America, who aren't considering college as an option, who see tennis as a way for their kid to make a million dollars. The next thing you know, we'll be running into each other in the maternity ward at the hospital outside the incubators."

Robin Finn, in an article in the *New York Times* in April 1991, quoted some of the thoughtful comments of Richard Williams, the father of Venus and her primary coach:

> He was exhilarated but cautious about all the attention Venus was receiving, saying, "It could be a ghetto Cinderella story for Venus. We've been offered millions of dollars from homes to cars to anything you can name. I've talked to everybody, but I've signed with nobody. Venus is like a rose, and right now she's only budding. There's still a lot of ifs here. I've been broke all my life, and Venus doesn't want to be poor, but nobody is going to push our daughter into anything. I know she wants to be a role model for what a girl from this kind of background can achieve if she works hard enough. But we put God first, then comes the family, her education, and her tennis. . . .Who wouldn't want a million dollars? But I need a healthy daughter more than I need a million dollars. We want to handle this right. . . .I don't want to see her standing on some street corner, broke, and with no education to save her, when she's 17, which is what you see happen to a lot of the black kids who don't make it.

When Venus was 14 years old she managed to override her father's caution and became a professional, but she planned to play in only four to six tournaments in 1995. She received enthusiastic worldwide attention, with her height (she is six feet tall), her long legs, and her winning smile, and she said she was not worried about pressure and burnout and that she intended to go to college someday as she was interested in paleontology. On Halloween night in 1994 she played her first pro match and won it, beating 25-year-old Shaun Stafford, who was ranked fifty-ninth in the world. But three days later she got "stung by reality," as a sports commentator put it. She played against Arantxa Sánchez Vicario, the reigning French and U.S. Open champion and the world's second-ranked player. After winning the first set, she was defeated. But not in spirit. Undaunted, after the game she thanked the crowd and her sponsors for making the tournament "so much fun." And her father said he hoped his family would not turn out to be deserving of criticism. "This is a wild frontier," he said. "I know it can be a little like a drunk person taking that first drink, and then that leads to two or three more. All of a sudden you're on the tournament merry-go-round and you can't get off. I know so many parents are so greedy, but we're hoping we're not. We're hoping we can resist the pressures."

Kevin Davis, the family's lawyer, said "Richard wasn't here to do deals. This is not a business venture. It's her debut. She plays and then they go home. But for the business people who wanted to know what they'd be getting in Venus it's become more visible. She proved she can play."

In Track and Field

Mary Decker (known after her marriage as Mary Decker Slaney) (1958–): Originally from Bunnvale, New Jersey, Mary's family moved to Huntington Beach, California, when she was 10. She began running and at age 11 entered a local cross-country race on a whim and won it easily. The next year she knew she wanted to run in the Olympics. During one week when she was 12 she competed in a marathon one day, ran 400- and 880-yard races the next day, competed in three more races on Saturday, and underwent an emergency appendectomy on Sunday! By age 14 she had set her first world record in the 1,000-meters and was ranked as a world-class runner. At 15 she set three world records, in the outdoor 800-meters and the indoor 880-yards and 1,000-yards, and was hailed as the best middle-distance runner in the United States.

But all this running took its toll. She suffered an ankle injury and developed several shin breaks so severe that sometimes she could not even walk. For almost three years she took treatments on her legs to relieve the constant pain, and at 18 she was unable to compete in the 1976 Olympics and had to watch runners she had beaten at age 16 take home medals.

As an adult, Mary's whole career was a mixture of triumphs, frustrations, and amazing perseverance. In 1980 she set an American record in the 800-meter race and world records in the 880-yard and 1,500-meter races—but again could not go to the Olympics because they were held that year in Moscow and the U.S. Government boycotted them. For the next four years she won every race she entered. In 1982 she set seven world records, was the first woman to receive the Jesse Owens Award, and was named Female Athlete of the Year by the Associated Press. In 1983 she received the Sullivan Award as America's outstanding amateur athlete and was the Women's Sports Foundation's Sportswoman of the Year. In 1984 she at last got to the Olympics . . . but did not win a medal because, in the finals of the 3,000-meter race, with three laps to go, she and Zola Budd, her chief rival, bumped into each other; Decker lost her balance and fell, damaging her hip. She was unable to run again that year, but in 1985 returned to racing and set another world record in the indoor 2,000 meters, defeated the 1984 Olympic medalists in the 3,000 meters in England, and set a new world record for the mile. Altogether, during two decades of competition, Mary racked up 36 American and 17 world records, and many awards. Her regime of practicing 70 miles a week exacted a heavy price, however: 20 operations, nearly one a year, to repair injuries.

In 1994, knowing she could not afford further medical problems if she was to be ready for the 1996 Olympics in Atlanta, she asked her friend Alberto Salazar, a world-class marathoner, to help devise an injury-free training program. He limited her to 50 miles a week, some to be run on a treadmill, which is easier on the feet than roads. He explained that athletes at her level tend to push themselves to the brink and often fail not because they did not train hard enough but because they trained too hard. So she started running more slowly and carefully, saying "I dream about being healthy; that's all I need to be." In June of 1996 Mary qualified for the Olympic team despite a near-repeat of her 1984 collision with another runner.

Mildred Ella ("Babe") Didrikson, known after her marriage as Babe Didrikson Zaharias) (1911–1956): Born in Port Arthur, Texas, Babe was the sixth of seven children of Norwegian parents. While still a young child, she could kick a football farther than any of the boys she played with in a neighborhood park. She also could throw a baseball harder and hit so many home runs that her playmates began calling her Babe after their idol Babe Ruth; she was known by this nickname all her life. She also played basketball in elementary school and made the girls' team in junior high, and in high school played on every girls' team: baseball, basketball, golf, swimming, tennis, and volleyball. She became the school's star basketball forward, in one game scoring 104 points. Babe also enjoyed running and began training for the hurdles by running and leaping over neighbors' hedges on her way to and from school each day. At age 15½ she was recruited by the Employers Casualty Company in Dallas, Texas, to play on its basketball team, the Golden Cyclones, sanctioned by the Amateur Athletic Union (AAU).

She quit high school and moved to Dallas, taking a job in the company's typing pool. Just after her sixteenth birthday she entered her first track and field meet, only one month later winning two national titles and setting two new American records at the national AAU meet; she hurled the javelin 133 feet 5 inches and threw a baseball 268 feet 10 inches. At 16 she also led the Golden Cyclones to the national finals, as she did again at 17 and 18.

When she was 18, Babe was the only employee sent by the Employers Casualty Company to the AAU's national meet, which doubled that year as the qualifying meet for the 1932 Olympics. She entered 8 of 10 events and in one day, within 3 hours, won 5 of them (baseball throw, javelin throw, long jump, 80-meter hurdles, and shot put), tied one (high jump), and finished fourth in one (discus), single-handedly winning the team title for her company's team with 30 points. The runner-up was the University of Illinois with a 22-woman team, which won 22 points. Olympic rules, however, limited her to only three events, so she chose those at which she had set world records: the high jump, 80-meter hurdles, and the javelin. At the 1932 Olympics in Los Angeles she won gold medals in the javelin throw and hurdles and finished second in the high jump, but officials ruled her jumping style illegal because she dove over the bar using a new western roll style instead of the usual scissor kick.

Babe became an instant celebrity, but before the end of the year the AAU barred her from further amateur competition because she let an automobile company use a photograph of her in their ads. She became a professional in December 1932 and toured with a vaudeville act playing the harmonica and featuring a newly formed "Babe Didrikson All American Basketball Team." Thousands of curious people came to see her exhibitions, many admirers but also people who considered her a freak; there were even nasty rumors that she must be a man in disguise, because there were so few outstanding women athletes at this time. And, in fact, there has never been such a versatile and successful one at any time: As a baseball player she once hit three home runs in one game and made an incredible 313-foot throw from center field to the plate. In basketball she was twice selected for the All American team. She was also an expert at diving, lacrosse, and billiards, and one of the greatest women golfers of all time.

Babe had learned the basics of golf in high school and could already drive a golf ball more than 250 yards when, at 18, she decided to become a golf champion. Three years later she succeeded, winning the Texas Women's Golf Association Amateur Championship. The U.S. Golf Association (USGA) disallowed her win, saying she was not an amateur because of her years of touring in theaters, so in 1936 she signed a contract for $1,000 a week to do another exhibition tour with male golfer Gene Sarazen. In 1938 she was the only woman contestant in the Los Angeles Open Golf Tournament, during which she met George Zaharias, a professional wrestler, whom she married that December. From

1940 to 1943 she played in professional tournaments but refused the cash prizes because she really wanted to regain her amateur status so that she could take part in the major women's tournaments, and in 1944 the USGA reinstated her as an amateur. In 1945 she won the Western Open, the Texas Open, and the Broadmoor Invitational, and during the 1946–47 season she won 17 amateur tournaments in a row, including the 1946 U.S. Amateur and the 1947 British Amateur, becoming the first American woman to win the British title in its 54-year history.

Taking another ride on her confusing seesaw between pro and amateur, in August 1947 Babe announced she would again turn professional. She joined the Women's Professional Golf Association (WPGA) and helped found the Ladies Professional Golf Association (LPGA) in 1949. She had 31 LPGA victories, was the leading money winner in women's golf for four consecutive years from 1948 to 1951, and won three U.S. Women's Open titles.

In 1952 she was diagnosed with colon cancer and underwent emergency surgery. Less than four months after the surgery she returned to the LPGA tour and the USGA honored her with the Ben Hogan Trophy for the greatest comeback of the year. In 1954 she won the U.S. Women's Open by a record 12 strokes. In 1955 she competed in several other tournaments and finished her autobiography, *This Life I've Led.* She died in 1956.

Janet Woolum, author of *Outstanding Women Athletes: Who They Are and How They Influenced Sports in America*, described how Babe

> loved sports from an early age and had an obsession to be the best in whatever she tried and in the sports world that was nearly everything. . . .Babe dominated the sports scene and brought women's sports to the masses before women were involved in competitive athletics. . . .she propelled women's sports into society's mainstream. . . .The greatest woman in the history of American sports, she had a tremendous influence on American women.

Marion Lois Jones (1975–): A native of California, this is another versatile athlete, who has said, "I don't sit down very easily." She spent her preschool days playing outdoors, following her older brother around, and "I got exposed to a lot of different sports and learned to love them all." She played baseball and softball and was a gymnast and ballet and tap dancer, and at age five started running track. When she was 11 years old she started playing organized basketball, and one day track coach Jack Dawson saw her play; "she was dribbling and running faster than the other girls could run, and I felt confident that she could be an Olympian." He invited her to join his track club, and she began winning races easily.

In her first year in high school, she set a national record in basketball for steals by a freshman and her team won the NCAA title. At age 15, she became the first freshman ever to win California state titles in both the 100-meter and 200-meter dashes, and was named the national high school girls' Player of the Year for track and field. She received this award three years in a row, although no other athlete has won it more than once. As a sophomore she won both 100- and 200-meter dashes again, and in basketball she averaged nearly 25 points per game for the girls' varsity team. In her junior year she set a U.S. high school record in the 200-meters, and won five state titles, including one in the long jump, an event she had taken up only three months earlier. When she was a senior, she averaged 22.8 points and 14.7 rebounds per basketball game.

Many colleges were interested in recruiting Marion; she chose the University of North Carolina because its coaches said they would allow her to continue competing in both track and basketball. At age 16, in 1992, she tried out for the U.S. Olympic track team and qualified to go to the 1992 Summer Games as an alternate but decided to wait for the 1996 Games. At college she became a great sprinter and long jumper for UNC's track and field team, and won All American honors in four events at the NCAA track and field national championships, also helping UNC win the NCAA women's basketball title.

Wilma Rudolph (See page 153)

In the Triathlon

Katy Radkewich (1981–): When this Ohioan was five years old she joined a swim team, but when her older brother and sister won in their age groups at the Iron Kids Triathlon National Championship, she decided swimming was not enough. Triathletes compete nonstop in three events: swimming, cycling, and running, and she liked the variety. She entered her first triathlon when she was seven years old, finishing fifth at the National Championships in the girls' 7- to 10-year-old division. She did well in the swim and run but was slow on the bike, so she got a new racing bike and began competing successfully in about five triathlons every summer, never having lost to a girl in her age group since she was eight years old. She crashed her bike in the national finals but, although cut and bruised, still finished third. Since then she won in her age group at the National Championships five times. At ages 12 and 13 she won in the senior division for kids aged 11 to 14—who swim for 200 meters, bike for 10 kilometers (6.2 miles), and run for two kilometers (1.2 miles)—in 1992 and 1993. Her year-long training schedule consisted of swimming three or four days a week and running as often as six days a week in the autumn and winter, and in spring and summer also biking 12 miles every other day. She became a particularly good runner, and in 1994 had won two national cross-country championships by age 13.

In Water Skiing

Boofy Koser (1983–): This amazing Texas girl could at age 11 water ski at about 40 miles per hour without skis. She could ski barefoot both frontwards and backwards, dropping onto her back, spinning 360 degrees, and then bouncing back onto her feet. In 1993 she won the junior girls' division for water skiers age 13 and under, at the Barefoot National Championships. She competed in three events: in slalom, scoring points each time she crossed the wake behind the boat; in jumping, skiing up an 18-inch ramp and flying more than 30 feet; and in tricks, doing as many as she could in two 15-second runs. She also learned a front flip, in which she flipped forward and then landed on her back. As if all this were not enough action to suit her, she also played baseball, basketball, and football, and was proficient in gymnastics, ballet, and tap dancing when only 11 years old.

PUSHING CHILDREN INTO SPORTS

It is important to realize that the young athletes described here are not typical children, and that no child should be expected to equal or surpass their achievements in order to gratify a parent's ego or vicarious ambition. These young stars are to be much admired but not envied. In most cases they were not forced to accomplish what they did. The children pushed themselves, because they had exceptional natural ability and love for their sport(s). They were remarkably determined and made many sacrifices along the way to success. To some children it would be sheer torture to live as they did. And for most parents the horrendous costs of paying for coaches, equipment, and travel, not to mention medical bills, would also be torture.

Many people live very happy lives without having any interest in sports, and if a child is not athletically inclined he or she should not be made to feel inferior. Too many

parents turn what should be pleasant activities like Little League games into work instead of fun. Sports should be something a child wants to engage in, a way of promoting physical health, having friendships with teammates, and enjoying oneself, not fostering undue aggression. Above all, children and their parents should learn to be "good sports," happy if and when they play well, but not ashamed, depressed, or embittered if they don't.

Child magazine, in its September 1994 issue, ran an excellent "Parent's Guide to Organized Sports" warning against the physical and psychological injuries that can result from premature or excessive competitiveness in athletics. It provided a stage-by-stage, age-by-age guide for what activities are appropriate and wholesome for normal children as they develop physically and emotionally. Actually, however, if parents are attentive, observant, and sympathetic, their children's own inclinations will usually provide sufficient guidelines. And just as a child who is unusually interested in mathematics, science, or the arts deserves to be warmly encouraged to develop those interests even if the parents do not share them, young athletes can be given helpful encouragement without being forced or made to lose self-esteem if they fail to excel and live up to a parent's dreams for him or her. Every child is unique, with the right to be cherished and appreciated for his or her own individuality.

Two interesting books have been published on this subject: *Boys Will Be Boys: Breaking the Link between Masculinity and Violence,* by Myria Miedzian, 1991, and *The Stronger Women Get, the More Men Love Football: Sexism and the American Culture of Sport,* by Mariah Burton Nelson, 1992. Miedzian's book attacks long-standing assumptions that sports teach children cooperation, teamwork, and respect for achievements. She says sports have become so competitive that the old adage "it doesn't matter if you win or lose, it's how you play the game" no longer applies. She urges parents, grandparents, peers, teachers, coaches, and the media to stop glorifying violence and letting boy athletes turn into bullies who enjoy inflicting damage on rivals, by returning sportsmanship to sports.

Nelson claims that "sports is a woman's issue because on playing fields, male athletes learn to talk about and think about women and women's bodies with contempt." She cites statistics showing that on high school and college campuses basketball and football players have been involved in more rape incidents than any other group. But she seems to place more blame on athletes than on movie stars and other celebrities who also often let the adulation they receive go to their heads. We live in a hero-worshipping society that includes fraternities and rock stars and other groups also guilty of violence. The problem is extremely serious, but athletes are by no means the only culprits.

Ira Berkow, a sports commentator for the *New York Times*, reviewed Nelson's book, criticizing its sweeping generalizations and citing other authorities on the subject. He said the FBI estimates that 30 to 50 percent of all women in America are abused by their husbands or boyfriends at some time during their relationships and certainly not all these men are pampered athletes in the "manly sports." Laura Crites, in an article for the NOW Legal Defense Fund, said "up to 80 percent of men who abuse their wives were themselves victims of violence or have witnessed the abuse of mothers; and abused children grow up to abuse their own children; violent homes breed violent crimes." Lynn Hescht Schafran, senior staff attorney and director of the National Judicial Education Program, said, "domestic violence is a phenomenon that crosses the lines of race, ethnicity, religion, age, economic status and sexual orientation."

The ideals of sports are to play by the rules, to be creative, to strive to improve oneself. Not all athletes live up to those ideals, but as a Georgia Tech football coach, Bobby Dodd, once told a mother who hoped sports would teach her son discipline, "You give me a good boy, and I'll give you a good boy back." Harmonious family life is the best protection against bad behavior, and raising a happy, loving child is more important than trying to raise a star athlete.

10

Children, Art, and Music

SOME THOUGHTS ABOUT CHILDREN'S ART

Art is a road on which getting to your destination is less important than what you discover—and what you become—along the way.
—*Albert Dorne (1904–1965)*

Art is the bread of the soul.   —*Charlton Heston (1924–)*

Our schools have not given sufficient attention to the fine arts as essential to the full development of the human being. . .the cultivation of man's aesthetic nature is crucial to our survival in a technological world. Music, art, and the dance have as much to say about the human condition as the sciences, yet the arts are generally offered only as a minor subject.   —*Sam Levenson (1911–1980)*

Adults should not teach children to draw; they should learn from them. . . .When I was their age, I could draw like Raphael, but it took me a lifetime to learn to draw like them.
—*Pablo Picasso (1881–1973), when visiting an exhibition of children's art*

Fine art is the only teacher except torture.
—*George Bernard Shaw (1856–1950)*

First I have a think, and then I put a line around it.
—*A little girl's response when asked how she set about drawing*

When I draw, it makes me feel like I have a best friend.
—*A 13-year-old boy student at the Children's Art Gallery in New York City*

I closed my eyes and seen an angel and made one like I seen it.
—*A young boy in an art class in San Francisco*

THE HISTORY OF CHILDREN'S ART

Children's art used to be considered by most people, except for doting parents, nothing more than meaningless globs and smeared colors. At best it was "cute." But, as the folk song says, "The times they are a-changing."

- The first well-known art critic to take children's art seriously was John Ruskin, in 1857.
- The first children's art exhibit was held in 1897, when an Austrian teacher, Franz Cisek, stuck his neck out.
- The first museum to introduce art courses for very young children (three-year-olds) was the People's Art Center of the Museum of Modern Art in New York City, in 1950; since then, many museums in many countries have followed its example.

- The first Children's Art Gallery was opened in New York City in 1956; today, museums in many cities display and sell children's art.

After World War II

The end of the war brought about the first big boom in children's art. The world needed cheering up. Under the Marshall Plan, art by children was collected from every country in Europe and exhibited, and Munich celebrated the arrival of peace with an exhibition of self-portraits by children of many nations. The United Nations International Children's Emergency Fund (UNICEF) received a thank-you card for the life-saving postwar aid it was giving children who were injured, homeless or malnourished as a result of the war, from one of the children it had helped: a seven-year-old girl in Czechoslovakia, Jitka Samkova. She drew a group of happy children playing around a maypole wreathed with flowers, and underneath the picture she wrote that it showed "joy going round the world—the wreath shows that the line of children being helped is endless." Her drawing was both charming and prophetic. It won a prize in an exhibit of children's art in Prague and UNICEF officials chose it as a poster design and later printed it as a greeting card. It was so popular that it started a multimillion-dollar industry: a few years later UNICEF cards were being sold all over the world. They have become the main private source of funds for this branch of the United Nations, helping to finance its work in over 100 countries. This shows what one small child's drawing can inspire!

The Internationalism of Children's Art

Another branch of the UN that considers children's art important is the United Nations Educational Scientific and Cultural Organization (UNESCO). In 1954, the first UNESCO Seminar of Visual Arts in Education was held at the University of Bristol in England. Reports on art education in many countries were given, along with exhibits of representative examples of children's paintings. And UNESCO's monthly magazine, *Courier*, has devoted many pages to art by children.

As part of cultural exchange programs, many schools have traded children's paintings about their countries, to acquaint children in other countries with different ways of life and to make international friends.

Governments today proudly sponsor children's art, and international diplomats ceremoniously exchange it with the solemnity once reserved for gifts of costly jewels.

In India, every two years an international children's art competition is conducted by the Children's Book Trust, under the supervision of Shankar Pillai, an artist in New Delhi. In 1964, 50 paintings from the Book Trust's collection were used in a UNICEF calendar; these were so enthusiastically greeted by the public that the calendar's sales jumped more than 46 percent over sales of the previous year when adults' designs were featured. In 1966, the National Geographic Society in Washington, D.C. presented a special exhibit from this collection, which was so acclaimed that the Smithsonian Institution acquired it to send around the United States on a two-year tour of museums, before adding it to its permanent collection.

UNICEF has also been involved with other children's art exhibits, including one in 1984 called "Children's Art—Treasures from Children's Civilization." After a successful tour of Europe, it opened at the UN General Assembly public lobby for a months's run. The 2,000 art works from 80 countries, collected by Alla and Rafael Goldin, from Oslo, were part of an international children's art museum at Oslo's Norwegian Foundation of Children's History, Art, and Culture. UNICEF sponsored its showing at the UN in cooperation with the Hermann Gmiener Foundation in Vienna, the SOS Children's Villages International, and Friends of the SOS Children's Villages. The traveling exhibition was under the auspices of the Royal Norwegian Ministry of Foreign Affairs, in cooperation with the Permanent Mission of Norway to the United Nations.

The collection featured art materials and themes as diverse as the cultures they represented. The pictures were of various sizes and done on different materials, including textiles, ceramics, wood, glass, paintings, collages, and jewelry. The wide range of subjects included family relationships, "my country," war, violence and peace, religion, illustrations from literature, animals, flowers and trees, music and dance, books written and illustrated by children, art by handicapped children, and drawings of children by well-known artists.

Opening the exhibition at the UN, UNICEF's Executive Director James Grant said,"Take note of what these children are saying in their picture language—the oldest of mankind's languages. Observe how the complex problems of our troubled world have impacted on their minds and hearts and how vividly they are reflected in their art."

Nations and Cities Now Sponsor Children's Art

Many countries' most handsome and most valuable commemorative postage stamps have been designed by children. In 1960, Monaco issued a set of stamps designed by children in honor of UNICEF's fifteenth anniversary, and in 1965 Guinea issued a series in honor of UNICEF's twentieth anniversary, also executed by children. Stamp collectors should take note that a more beautiful set of commemorative stamps was never issued anywhere.

Cities also use children's art to enhance their prestige. When Paris celebrated its two-thousandth birthday in 1951 with a mammoth cultural festival, a highlight was "Paris Seen by Its School Children," an exhibit of collective paintings by children. In the same year, the Norwegian Government issued a picture book about the city of Oslo, made up entirely of children's watercolors. In New York City an annual exhibit called "Art in the News" has been sponsored annually by one of the city's newspapers, with more than 3,000 works by children in the city's public schools. Some of these paintings have been sent to other countries to serve as ambassadors of good will.

Also, one of the most handsome buildings in New York owes its handsomeness to children's art: the exterior walls of the Henry Street Settlement House are made of tiles on which children's drawings were baked; an interesting movie called *The Mural on Our Block* was made about this art project.

Other Uses of Children's Art

Children's art is now used to illustrate and decorate adult books; it is frequently featured in advertising campaigns, and not only when things for children are being advertised. It has been used as a tool for social progress, as in Peru where a U.S. Peace Corps volunteer created a whole new industry for a small, impoverished village by encouraging the children there to make pictures in embroidery; the town's child artists have received huge prices for their work, sought after by collectors all over the world.

Children's art has also been used as a potent propaganda weapon to promote good causes and charities. For example, a children's art contest was held in postwar Germany on the subject of peace and freedom: 80,000 eloquent paintings were submitted. And children's art has also been used to make people more aware of the needs and neglected talents of so-called *backward* people: retarded children, children in ghettos, tribal children, children in mental hospitals. The impressive quality of such art has often melted prejudices and softened hearts where sermons and sociologists' studies have been ineffective.

It has been a startling, almost unbelievable, transition, in a little over a century, from no status whatever to worldwide admiration.

HOW CHILDREN'S ART DEVELOPS
It Starts with Scribbles

Most children between the ages of two and three enjoy scribbling, over and over again. If you think their "messy" and repetitious scrawls are nonsensical, this is because you cannot remember what it feels like to be that young. Infant scribbles are a nonverbal language by which important concepts are examined, expressed, and communicated—or would be communicated if most adults had not forgotten how to read them. Biologists, psychologists, philosophers, educators, and artists have all found much to ponder in these markings and from them have learned significant things about human nature and art.

For one thing, it is a surprising fact that infantile scribbles and childish drawings are strikingly similar all over the world, no matter how different the objects children see around them are. There seems to be a basic quality of the infant mind that contemplates reality in a certain way, regardless of surrounding culture or intellectual ability. Environment, intelligence, and materials provided affect productivity and speed of development but not, as a rule, developmental sequence.

Until the age of four, few children's drawings are representational, not simply because very young children lack the skill to make what we consider a realistic drawing, but because that is not what they are interested in doing. They appear to start out by depicting underlying realities rather than surface appearances. They are imaginative and meditative, not superficially imitative. Very young children are nonobjective artists.

Rhoda Kellogg, a nursery school supervisor in San Francisco who studied children's art for more than 40 years, gathered the world's largest known collection of preschool art. In several pioneering studies of the subject, including a handsome book called *The Psychology of Children's Art*, written in collaboration with Scott O'Dell and published in 1967, she classified children's earliest drawings by type, to help adults learn how to understand them.

First, Kellogg says, come 20 basic scribbles: dots, lines (vertical, horizontal, diagonal, curved or roving, both open and enclosed), zigzags (both sharp and undulating), single and multiple loops, spirals, crosses, and circular lines in various combinations. These are, in fact, all the basic shapes ever used by any artist, and the average child, given enough opportunity, will have mastered them all by the age of two.

Only when children have learned all of these, and not before, by doing them singly and in combinations over and over again, do they move on to combine these elements into definite forms, which Kellogg classifies as six diagrams. These are the Greek cross; the square or rectangle; the circle or oval; the triangle; the odd-shaped area, or what a modern artist would call a free form; and the diagonal cross. These too are practiced over and over again, singly and in various combinations. Often they are so overlaid with scribbles that it is hard to see them, but they are there, part of the young artists' compositions.

The Universality of Children's Designs

By the age of three or three-and-a-half almost all children who have been given enough art materials to play with and many opportunities to use them, have taught themselves to make all 20 basic scribbles and all six diagrams. They then go on to develop these basic structural forms into patterns, which Kellogg calls *combines*, in which two diagrams are put together, and *aggregates*, in which three or more are put into one drawing.

Theoretically, 36 combines can be made from the six diagrams. However, children seem to concentrate on just a few, and some never make combines at all but go straight from diagrams to aggregates. There are hundreds of possible aggregates, but again most children select just a few as basic themes, and as a result some aggregates appear more commonly than others.

The cross and the circle are two of the most universally popular diagrams in children's art, and, significantly, they also frequently appear as basic motifs in the folk and religious art of adults.

A favorite combine is the mandala, a circle and cross (or crosses) superimposed. *Mandala* is a Sanskrit word meaning "magic circle." As Kellogg points out, a circle denotes limited or contained movement and a cross denotes open or unlimited movement in all directions, so this combination of the two forms is "a perfect integrating symbol" with "dynamic equilibrium." It is easy to see, therefore, why the mandala is a satisfying design for human beings, young and old, aesthetically, emotionally, and symbolically. It is a good example of what is called a "biological aesthetic principle," a quality that makes a design pleasing to people everywhere at a fundamental, pre-rational level because it is "a spontaneous product of normal physiological movement," thus even more basic in appeal than something that interests us only at the intellectual level. Such a design satisfies an inborn universal desire of human beings for balance, order, contrast, and completeness.

Young children, if not guided by adults, almost always place paper in the same position, like a flag, with the wide side horizontal to them if the shape of the paper being drawn on is considered part of the design. The mandala combines all six diagrams into one, so it becomes a perfect structure, a design that contains all other designs, a finite rendition of infinity. The Christian cross combined with the halo, the British flag with its superimposed crosses, the Japanese rising sun in the center of a rectangular flag, the United Nations flag with its round globe segmented by straight black lines—these, among many examples, may owe some of their emotional appeal to the fact that they are designs in harmony at a basic biological level.

Enjoyment of Colors

Maria Montessori (1870–1952), the specialist in early education, believed that child development proceeds in definite stages, "sensitive periods" in which children are particularly able to acquire different skills such as learning languages, counting, reading, and constructing. If her guidance is followed about taking advantage of the "color-sensitive period" in a child's life, we can help inexperienced eyes discern many shades and derive great pleasure from variations. According to her, if a wide range of colors is introduced at the right time, a strong appreciation of color will stay with the child throughout life and will heighten the sense of visual observation. Notably, she claimed that children who are deprived of the sight of varied colors during the period when they are especially color sensitive are those who later on are color blind.

According to experimental findings, the most color-sensitive period for most children is between the ages of three and four. But since every child is unique, growth rates are not the same for all. The safest thing, if we want children to appreciate color, is to surround them with an attractive and wide range from their earliest days.

It is not necessary, however, to try to teach children distinctions between violet and purple, pink and rose, turquoise and aquamarine, and all the other lovely gradations in the spectrum. When varied shades are there, children's natural curiosity will cause them to ask the names of what they notice when they feel ready and able to remember them. Continual exposure to beauty is important. Explanations and labels are not.

The Beginnings of Representational Art

By the age of four, most children have experimented with so many of the almost infinite possibilities of combinations of shapes that they begin to move on to a new type of art: representational or pictorial drawing. Many, but not all, children do their first pictorial drawings as early as three-and-a-half, but never before they have mastered the basic scribbles and diagrams.

The first supposedly representational drawing that most children make is of the sun. They usually begin to draw this at about the age of three. But the drawing is not really a representation of the real sun. It seems to evolve out of the mandala design, rather than as a result of looking at the sky. All children draw the sun as a circle, usually with straight lines radiating from it, even though the real sun does not look like that to the naked eye. After a while this "sun" evolves further, decoratively rather than realistically, and a "face" is often given to it. The world over, a sun with a smiling face is a favorite symbol in children's art, which they draw for years.

Often the most recognizable representational objects drawn are trees, flowers, and houses, and it is interesting to note that all over the world, no matter what type of house a child lives in or what flora and fauna surround it, these drawings are similar: a house usually shown as a rectangle with a symmetrical arrangement of square windows and rectangular doors, and a flower or a tree as a straight line with a circle on top.

Young Children's Portraits

The next basic type of children's drawings is the human being. Most children begin to draw people by the age of four. This new feat, as with the sun, does not begin representationally or realistically. Any child with clear eyesight can see that a human being has a small roundish head on top of a longer and larger body and that arms and legs come out from the body, not from the head. Even so, almost invariably a child starts drawing "people" by making circles for faces with lines inside them for mouths, and then adding vertical lines (legs) coming out of the bottom of these circles and/or horizontal lines (arms) at the sides of the circles.

For years and years, through most of childhood, most human figures that children draw, even after they have learned to add details of anatomy and clothing, have disproportionately large heads. Children's art is conceptual, not literal, a commentary, not unimaginative imitativeness.

Children do not normally draw people or things by looking at them and carefully copying their shapes. So, when still not skilled enough to depict people and objects with detailed accuracy, they sensibly concentrate on what seems most important about them. The most obvious and important features of a person are the head and face and, within the face, the mouth, so these are what children tend to draw first. The usual sequence after that is like this:

After faces come legs, first as straight vertical lines descending from the head, forming what another student of drawings by children, Dr. Joseph Di Leo (see page 364), described as "the universal tadpole figure," and later as longer loops. Then come arms, usually drawn at first as short sticks emerging on each side of the head, later as winglike loops. Later a rather lumpy body is added, making a "potato man," but even after this the arms for a while usually extend from the head rather than the torso. Feet, short horizontal sticks at first, are then added to the legs. After that, hands, with fingers shaped like forks or rakes, are added to the arms. Then, sometimes, come ears as single loops at first, then as double loops.

Only when clothing is added do sex differentiations appear. Until this point the "person" is genderless and ageless. Girls usually draw females first, boys males. Clothing is abstracted and symmetrical: trousers are rigid rectangles, extensions of a rectangular torso; dresses are straight-lined triangles. Later, details appear such as buttons, always in a straight vertical row of dots down the middle of the body.

The only type of clothing that sometimes appears earlier in this sequence is hats; these often appear even before legs and arms, each as a square box underlined with a straight line for a brim, perched on top of a disembodied head. This is seemingly due to a desire for symmetrical balance, certainly not to depict the way "Mommy" or "Daddy" is normally seen by the child.

Some theorists say arms come out of a head at first because babies are more aware of their mothers' heads and arms while they are held than of any other part of the human body, and thus those two parts of the body make such a strong emotional impact that they are merged in a child's consciousness. But why are no breasts or laps drawn? People are always drawn standing up straight and facing forward; hardly any children draw profiles or seated figures for years to come.

And why do legs sometimes appear before arms? People have speculated that young children often draw humans with legs but no arms because at the toddler stage they are surrounded by adult legs and feet at their eye level. But what seems mistaken about this hypothesis is that legs are usually shown short in relation to the size of heads. One might expect small children to think of tallness as a major trait of most people.

Some artists have speculated that children draw only features they consider essential, and since they are busily trying to learn to observe and talk and walk, they concentrate primarily on eyes and mouths and legs.

The Relationship between Children's Art and Modern Art

Concepts of art have changed in our era almost as much as machines and transportation and communication methods have. Artists have been liberated from the task of recording accurately what things and people look like; machines have been invented that can do

this: cameras, photocopiers. So now, for the first time in history, professional artists are really able to enjoy "art for art's sake." Instead of concentrating on reproducing what already exists, they are concentrating on personal inventions, using colors, shapes, and textures in combinations and with an experimental boldness their ancestors were unable to enjoy and never dreamed of. They view and interpret the world subjectively and imaginatively without being confined by rules that apply to the "real" world. In other words, they have become as uninhibited as young children.

When abstract artists first came on the scene many people ridiculed their paintings by saying, "It looks as if a child had painted it. " Nowadays, people are apt to reverse matters and compliment a child's painting by saying it looks as if a modern artist had done it. Neither remark is insulting, even if meant to

UNICEF/94–01401/Laura Lorenz Hess

be. There are clear differences between children's art and the abstract art of adults, as anyone who bothers to look closely can discover, but there are also undoubtedly things they have in common: exuberance and splashes of bold colors in unusual combinations, lack of concern about imitating literal surface appearances of objects. Grownup artists and children are both busy all the time making new discoveries about the relationships and qualities and meanings of things. What young artists lack in technique and dexterity they make up for in vigor and imagination. Since the whole world is new to young children, wonder seems almost always to be an element in their art, along with spontaneity and intensity, and often a delightful sense of humor, all qualities that adult artists strive for and which children possess naturally. Art has been described as the demonstration that the ordinary is extraordinary, and great artists as people who never lose that naive sense of wonder with which all of us are born.

Commenting on Children's Art: Be Careful!

Mrs. Maud Shaw, the English nanny who took care of the children of President John Kennedy (1917–1963) when they lived in the White House, told in her book of reminiscences about a "fearful blunder" she made once when President Kennedy's son John was painting. Meaning to encourage him, she asked if he was painting the beach, and said, "It's very good." With great dignity the boy replied, "It's not the beach! It's you." She was thoroughly startled but made a quick recovery. "Oh," she said, "I can see it now. I must have been looking at it from the wrong angle."

Mrs. Shaw was lucky that she looked as attractive as a beach in John's eyes. Some people, seeing the gargoyles and monsters and witches that many children love to draw, might burst into tears if they realized the children were portraying them.

THE PSYCHOLOGICAL IMPORTANCE OF CHILDREN'S ART

In the history of the human race, drawing preceded language. Drawing dates back to 30,000 B.C., whereas written language did not appear until 25,000 years later. Similarly, in the evolution of individual human beings, the ability to express oneself through drawing precedes fluency in words.

It is harder for small children than for adults to find constructive ways to express their strongest feelings and thoughts, which are often so vague, jumbled, and confused anyway that even if they already knew enough words they would find such things hard to describe. But the more ways people have to express their feelings, the happier and healthier they are. Little children need more outlets to let them show how they feel about things than just giggles, hugs, tears, and tantrums. There is a wide range of emotions in between the extremes of joy and rage. Art helps them get these out where they can examine, share, and manage them. It is a nonverbal way to meditate and contemplate as well as to communicate.

Psychologists have learned that children who have experienced traumas, through warfare or the death of a friend or parent, may find it impossible to talk about their emotions, but when crayons and paper are put in their hands they can reveal and deal with their grief or terror with fewer inhibitions.

These are some of the reasons child psychologists, in addition to artists and art lovers, find children's art so fascinating. It gives them a way to look inside a child's mind, to see if a child is developing normally, and to diagnose emotional or neurological problems. However, one need not be a psychologist to find the symbolic structures in children's art fascinating. As we know from abundant data provided by psychology, an enormous amount is revealed about people even in the most casual doodling all of us do.

One of the standard ways child psychologists recognize emotional disturbance in children is by seeing how they portray parents in drawings and models. If a piece of clay is identified as Mother and the child pounds and whacks it viciously, or frantically tears it into hundreds of little pieces, that obviously expresses a different attitude from the one shown if it is stroked smoothly and patted fondly. If a child draws a family and Father is a great hulk towering over all other figures, that means one thing; if Mommy or one of the children is a great deal larger, or drawn in much more detail, than a small sloppy speck of a Daddy, that obviously means something different. If one is not a trained psychologist, however, it is not advisable to try to analyze children's art too closely, because one might jump to alarming and incorrect conclusions. Even experienced analysts can make mistakes, like one in London who analyzed the bold and somewhat wild abstractions painted by a happy young chimpanzee and thought they were the work of a schizophrenic eight-year-old girl!

A Doctor Who Used Children's Drawings in Diagnosis

One of the most internationally respected pediatricians to study interpretation of children's drawings was Dr. Joseph Di Leo (1902–1994). His higher education was received mainly in Italy; he earned an M.D. at the University of Bologna in 1927, then took advanced studies at the University of Rome. After returning to the United States where he was born, he took more training at Yale's Clinic of Child Development, and in 1945 became the first director of the Developmental Clinic of the New York Foundling Hospital, a post he held for 33 years until his retirement in 1978. During those years he studied thousands of children, conducting tests to appraise their mental and physical development, and helping to spot neuromuscular dysfunctions and sensory handicaps. And during these years he became increasingly impressed by a growing realization of how studying children's drawings aided his work as a pediatrician and psychologist.

Di Leo published four books on his findings, which were translated into many foreign languages. The first one, entitled *Young Children and Their Drawings*, published in 1970, described in detail his analyses of the sketches and doodles of three- and five-year-olds. It provided scientific confirmation of the observations of the art teacher, Rhoda Kellogg, whose book on children's art had been published three years earlier. Whereas her interest had been primarily aesthetic, his was medical, but both had made the same discovery: that the art of children reveals the "universality of childhood" in that all children's drawings show similar tendencies and sequences, whether they were drawn in 1885 or a century later, in America or in other countries.

How Art Affects Child Development

Drawings are more closely related to chronological age than most other types of behavior, so it is extremely useful, in studying child development, to study children's art, if this is allowed to evolve in its own way. When parents or art teachers try to guide it along their notions of what art should be, however, it cannot perform this function. The rules will get in the way of nature. They will distort and thwart the child's visual and manual and conceptual development, making it impossible to gain as much knowledge of the child's inner life as one would have if freedom of expression were allowed. This is one of the most important reasons to let children draw as they wish.

When children are encouraged to do things their own way they grow more rapidly in independence than when someone else tries to do everything for and with them. There are so many occasions when a parent must help children that it is important to provide at least one area of activity where they can do things on their own. Children who learn to teach themselves will be much less of a nuisance than those accustomed to constant guidance. They will ask for less help, start things more easily and eagerly, pursue them more perseveringly and be less easily distracted. They will work with greater sureness and satisfaction, with a richer flow of ideas, learning self-reliance and trusting their own initiative.

This does not mean there can be no ground rules. Letting children draw what they want does not mean allowing them to make a mess by throwing paints and crayons on walls and floors. A child who still throws food on the floor instead of eating it or keeping it on a dish is too young to be ready to draw or play with clay. But by age two that kind of behavior is probably a thing of the past. If a normally well-behaved child reverts and has a tantrum, starting to make a mess, the art materials should be removed promptly, to make the young "artist" know that such behavior is inappropriate. It is time then for a nap or for going out to the park, with an explanation that when he or she again feels like creating instead of destroying, the materials will be returned. From the beginning a child should be made to realize that if he or she enjoys making scribbles or, later, pictures, this is to be done on a table or easel with a smock to protect clothing and a cloth to protect furniture.

There are several other reasons we should try not to influence what our children do with clay and colors. What they produce has meaning to them, whether or not it does to others. Children must learn to have self-respect if they are ever going to achieve anything important, and how can they learn to have it unless they are given it? They are usually eager to please adults but often do not know how. When a grownup expresses appreciation of something they make for no other reason than that they made it, this helps them feel valuable. On the other hand, if their expressions and creations are always being corrected and belittled, they become chronically dissatisfied or discouraged with themselves. And this, incidentally, is one of the main reasons that so many children who at first got great joy from art lose interest in it as they approach their teens; they become their own severest critics and, realizing they will probably never be Michelangelos, they give up. If respect for their own individuality and originality has not been firmly, convincingly, implanted when they were young, the damage will be irreparable.

On the other hand, when children are allowed to experiment freely, their awareness of what materials are, of what colors and forms and textures are, will increase more rapidly than if they are spoon-fed predigested knowledge. Such children will become more alert, more observant, more sensitive, more interested in the world, and thus more capable.

By being allowed to work and play in their own way, without constant interference, they will learn many important things in a way that really sinks in. They will learn how to select and invent, for instance. They will learn that choices have consequences and that causes produce results that they can, to some extent, control. Grownups already know how to mix red and yellow to make orange, but children do not; if one tells them, instead of letting them find out one day for themselves, one takes away some of their fun. One teaches them a fact but at the same time deprives them of a more important kind of knowledge: the realization of what it feels like to make a discovery. By learning to draw or paint or mold clay by themselves, they can learn to love learning, and this attitude will help them all through their school years and afterwards.

How Important Is Art in Children's Education?

Plato (c. 427–347 B.C.) made the arts the basis of his ideal educational system. When exposed to the beautiful and graceful, he wrote in his *Dialogues*:

> then will our youth dwell in a land of health, amid fair sights and sounds. . .and beauty, the effluence of fair works, shall flow into the eye and ear like a health-giving breeze. . .

Plato considered musical training the most important of all

> because rhythm and harmony find their way into the inward places of the soul, on which they fasten firmly, imparting grace, and making the soul of one who is correctly educated graceful and because he who has received this true education of the inner being will most shrewdly perceive omissions or faults in art and nature, and with a true taste, while he praises and rejoices over and receives the good into his soul and becomes noble and good, he will justly blame and hate the bad, now in the days of his youth even before he is able to know the reason why; and when reason comes, he will recognize and salute the friend with whom his education has made him long familiar.

In the *Republic*, Plato claimed that all grace of movement and harmony of living and even all morality is determined by aesthetic feeling. The same qualities, he claimed,

> enter largely into painting and all similar workmanship, into weaving and embroidery, into architecture, as well as the whole manufacture of utensils in general; nay, into the constitution of living bodies and of all plants, for in all these things, gracefulness or ungracefulness finds a place. And the absence of grace and rhythm and harmony is closely allied to an evil style and an evil character, whereas their presence is allied to, and expressive of, the opposite character, which is brave and sober minded.

If this is so, supreme importance should be given to that part of education that encourages a sense of rhythm and harmony. But the vast majority of people have so little understanding of the nature and importance of art, because of their own inadequate art education, that they cannot see the intimate connection Plato saw between art and goodness and a peaceful society.

From Plato to today, the plea to understand the need for art in education has often been reiterated. A UNESCO report described art's educational value this way:

> Art discovers, heightens and refines life experience. . . .Art is a selection and examination of the physical and social world in order that we may apprehend in ideal simplicity the selected properties and values usually evident only obscurely, if at all, in ordinary experience. Art serves to clarify our feelings.

The British poet, art critic, and teacher Sir Herbert Read (1893–1968) in his book *Education Through Art,* forcefully echoed Plato:

> The aesthetic principle is all pervading, the very principle of coherence in the universe and the organic wholeness of man and of his mental faculties, so that as we pass from childhood to adulthood, from savagery to civilization, we can retain the unity of consciousness which is the only source of social harmony and individual happiness. By means of such education, we make the child aware of that "instinct of relationship" which, even before the advent of reason, will enable the child to distinguish the beautiful from the ugly, the good from the evil, the right pattern of behavior from the wrong pattern, the noble person from the ignoble.

The cause of society's collective ills, according to Sir Herbert, in his book *Education through Art*, is lack of spontaneity in education and in social life, which produces disorganized economic, industrial, and cultural developments. He maintained that coercive discipline, authoritarian morality, social convention, and mechanical toil cause a thwarting of personalities,

> until instead of the wholeness of the expansive tree, we have only the twisted and stunted bush. But man is more complex than a tree and the effects of repression are far more disastrous. Man not only turns against himself, but against his fellows. The forces of his destructiveness are social as well as individual: when the individual is not bent on destroying himself, he attempts to destroy the weight of oppression, which he will identify with some specific group or nation. . . .It is only education in its widest sense, as guided growth, encouraged expansion, tender upbringing, that can secure that life is lived in all its natural creative spontaneity, in all its sensuous, emotional and intellectual fullnesss.

> Art, widely conceived, should be the fundamental basis of education, for no other subject is capable of giving the child not only a consciousness in which image and concept, sensation and thought are correlated and unified, but also at the same time, an instinctive knowledge of the laws of the universe and a habit of behavior in harmony with nature.

If art is so important, then why do so many children, most of whom genuinely enjoy it when they are little, lose interest as they get older, and what difference does that make, anyway? Sir Herbert thought it makes a tremendous difference not only to individual children but to society. He said:

> The art of the child declines after the age of 11, because it is attacked from every direction—not merely squeezed out of the curriculum, but squeezed out of the mind by the logical activities which we call arithmetic and geometry, physics and chemistry, history and geography and even literature as it is taught. The price we pay for this distortion of the adolescent mind is mounting up: a civilization of hideous objects and misshapen human beings, of sick minds and unhappy households, of divided societies and a world seized with destructive madness. We feed these processes of dissolution with our knowledge and science, with our inventions and discoveries and our educational system tries to keep pace with the holocaust; but the creative activities which could heal the mind and make beautiful the environment, unite man with nature and nation with nation—these we dismiss as idle, irrelevant and inane.

Many people would disagree with this diagnosis of modern society's ills. For one thing, Plato and Sir Herbert assumed that art is an expression of harmony, a desire to celebrate and reproduce the good, the true, and the beautiful, but today many artists are not interested in doing that. Many consider self-expression and originality more important than contemplation of truth, goodness, and beauty. Such excesses have given art a bad reputation among many people in the second half of the twentieth century.

Perhaps it is necessary to remind everyone of the noble concept of art that has existed from early times. Today, as a whole, environmentalists are more united than the art world is in trying to help everyone see and enjoy and revere the wondrous beauties in our universe, but this was traditionally the role of artists. Just as we now need environmentalists to show us the importance of protecting our social and physical environment, it now seems more urgent than ever to teach young artists to join them in appreciating the world's beauty and enhancing it.

PRODIGIES IN ART

William Blake (1757–1827): English painter, engraver, poet, and mystic. At the age of 13 Blake was apprenticed to an engraver and learned to employ a then-new process of printing from etched copper plates. At age 14 he began to produce watercolor figures and to engrave illustrations for magazines and books. He also began writing lyrical poems, hand-illustrated and colored by him. He became the author of many mystical and meta-physical works, which combined his own deep spirituality and delight in beauty, and his furious outrage at hypocrisy or injustice such as child labor, with a gentle sense of humor. Among his most famous written works were *Songs of Innocence, Songs of Experience,* and *Jerusalem*; among his most famous illustrations, those for the *Book of Job*. At the time of his death at age 70 he was occupied with engraving designs to illustrate Dante's *Divine Comedy*. In addition to his published works Blake enjoyed writing personal letters to friends which he decorated in the margins with his exquisite watercolors; though fragile, some of these fortunately have been preserved—in the art collection at the University of Texas in Austin, for example.

George Cruikshank (1792–1878): English caricaturist and illustrator. George was the son of a caricaturist and watercolorist, Isaac Cruikshank, and though he never had any formal training in art both he and his elder brother, Isaac Robert Cruikshank, picked up their father's skills and interests through a combination of heredity and example. George became the most popular and famous of the three. At the age of 12 he had already pro-duced and sold his first etching. His caricatures made fun of eminent persons, including political leaders, churchmen, and courtiers, as well as commoners. In his cartoons "The Bottle" and its sequels "The Drunkard's Children" and "Worship of Bacchus" he also crusaded against drunkenness. Among the books he illustrated, usually with colored etchings, were some for children, including *Peter Schlemihl, Grimms' German Popular Stories,* and Charles Dickens's *Sketches by Boz* and *Oliver Twist*.

Leonardo Da Vinci (1452–1519): Florentine painter, sculptor, architect, engineer, inventor, and scientist. He was an illegitimate son and somewhat neglected in his childhood, but at age 14 his career in art was launched when he had the good fortune to become a protégé of the wealthy patron of arts and letters, Lorenzo the Magnificent (1449–1492). At 18 he entered the studio of Andrea del Verrocchio (1435–1488), and then settled in Milan where he painted his superb "Last Supper" on the refectory wall of Santa Maria delle Grazie; the wall miraculously survived the bombing of the church in World War II. Very few of his other paintings have survived, except for the most famous one of all, the "Mona Lisa." In later life he entered the service of Cesare Borgia (1476–1507) in Florence as an architect and engineer, and at one time he collaborated with Michelangelo in decorating a room in Borgia's palace.

As he got older Leonardo became increasingly interested in science, filling note-books not only with drawings but with much information on biology, physiology, hydrody-namics, and aeronautics where he was far ahead of his time (see page 87).

His last years, from age 64 to 67, were spent in a chateau in France where his host and sponsor was the art-loving King François I (1494–1547), who was deeply interested in Leonardo's art and in his scientific experiments. But the king, who also had a frivolous side, enjoyed throwing elaborate parties and appreciated the fact that Leonardo contrib-uted ideas to enliven them. For one of these parties he created an automated lion that, when pounded on the chest, gushed fleur-de-lis. Leonardo also once covered the court-yard of the king's castle with sky-blue sheets that had the sun and moon painted on them, and in the evening he lit the yard with 400 two-branched candelabras, illuminating it so that, according to a letter that has been preserved, "it seemed the night had been driven away." So even in old age Leonardo retained some of the fun-loving spirit of a child.

Salvador Dali (1904–1989): Spanish surrealist painter. From the moment of his birth, Salvador played an unusual role. He was named for a brother who had died three years before he was born. His parents said he looked exactly like that brother, but they soon found out that he did not have his brother's gentle disposition. The second Salvador was rebellious, rambunctious, conceited, and flamboyant. He started life as a spoiled brat and remained one throughout his life and career. But his remarkable talent and passion for art were evident when he was young, and his mother forgave him for being a difficult child because he was so talented. She pronounced him a genius, an opinion with which he was in hearty agreement. In his autobiography, called *The Secret Life of Salvador Dali*, in which he claimed he could remember being in his mother's womb, he said, "Aside from being forbidden the kitchen, I was allowed to do anything I pleased. I wet my bed until I was eight, for the fun of it. I was the absolute monarch of the house." "At the age of seven," he once said, "I wanted to be Napoleon, and my ambition has been growing ever since."

His parents encouraged his early infatuation with art. His father wanted him to have a secure career as an academic painter and enrolled him in the Academia de San Fernando in Madrid, but he was kicked out after refusing to take an exam, saying his examiners were incompetent to judge him. In his early career, he devoured what he saw by other artists. He produced work in the style of each of them and learned from all of them, imitating many different styles before finally finding his own unique one. He was chameleonlike, metamorphosizing himself into one after another artistic guise—a feat that depended on great manual dexterity, which he had in abundance, plus a sense of careerist calculation. In 1994 an exhibit was held in London and New York that focused entirely on these early years, with more than 170 paintings, drawings, letters, postcards, manuscripts, photographs, and other documents on display. Some of them, such as the beautiful "Girl's Back," are untypical of his later work and truly lovely.

As he grew older, he not only found a personal style for his art that was unmistak-able, but also for his theatrical appearance, always with an oversized curved waxed mus-tache, and he cultivated notoriety and money so avidly that one of his surrealist col-leagues, André Breton, rearranged the letters of his name into an anagram, "Avida Dol-lars." As a mature artist Dali had incomparable technique and originality and became extremely famous, particularly after exhibiting his strange landscape, which he called "Persistence of Memory," with limp watches hanging over various objects. It was hard for people to decide which intrigued them the most, his work or his eccentricity and bizarre behavior. In his latest years he quieted down a little, became religious, and surprised people by painting some serious, moving portrayals of the Last Supper and the Crucifix-ion.

Thomas Gainsborough (1727–1788): English painter of portraits and landscapes: At age 13 Thomas persuaded his father to let him leave his home in Suffolk to go to London to study art, on the strength of the extremely impressive beginning he had already made at landscape painting. At age 14, in London, he studied Dutch landscapes and learned the art of rococo decoration. He was soon so much admired that he became one of the original 36 members of the Royal Academy of Arts. His landscapes are among the finest in English art, and his portraits were equally notable; many were of famous people, including the actress Mrs. Siddons, King George III, and Queen Charlotte, but he also painted pictures of children including "The Shepherd's Boy," "Girl with Pigs," and "The Blue Boy." The latter is now the star attraction at the Huntington Museum in Pasadena, California. According to the museum's brochure, no other painting by a British artist enjoys its enduring popularity and few paintings have been more reproduced, although it does not seem to have attracted much attention during the artist's lifetime. In the nineteenth century its fame became established through national and international exhibitions.

A persistent story concerning this painting's origin is that Gainsborough undertook it to prove that his great rival, Sir Joshua Reynolds (1723–1792), was wrong when he stated that a cool color like blue should never be dominant in a painting. Gainsborough seems to have won the argument. "Blue Boy" is a portrait of young Jonathan Buttall, the son of a close friend of Gainsborough's, and in accordance with a fashion at the time the artist dressed the boy in a costume dating from about 140 years before the portrait was painted. This type of costume was familiar through the portraits of the great seventeenth-century Flemish artist Sir Anthony Van Dyck (1599–1641), for whom Gainsborough had unbounded admiration. The museum's brochure says he seems to have planned the portrait as an affectionate tribute to a good friend and in the style of "an artist he admired above all others. This combination of circumstances may help to explain the special strength and hence the great appeal of this most famous of all English portraits."

Angelica Kauffmann (1741–1807): Swiss painter of portraits and historical subjects. Angelica was already famous at the age of 11. She painted all her life and her paintings hang in almost all the great museums in Europe. For 15 years she lived in England, where she was much admired and was made one of the original members of the Royal Academy of Arts. Sir Joshua Reynolds, the first president of the academy, painted two portraits of her. Her achievements were remarkable in an era when few women artists were taken seriously enough to attain fame.

Paul Klee (1879–1940): Swiss genius of modern abstract art. Paul was already drawing at the age of four, creating fantastic designs inspired by the patterns in the marble tabletops of his uncle's cafe, but he was drawing so vividly that he became frightened of his pictures, which seemed to him like devils come to life. When he became a professional artist, his early work consisted of bright watercolors, but later he worked in oils, producing small-scale abstractions. Like an outgrowth of his earliest scary drawings, he developed an individual way of expressing the subconscious mind and fantasy in art. From 1920 to 1932 he worked and taught at the influential Bauhaus School of Arts and Crafts in Germany, but after Adolf Hitler came to power in 1933 the school was closed and many of Klee's works were confiscated. He moved back to Switzerland, where he died during World War II, but fortunately many of his works have outlived him.

David (Alexander Cecil) Low (1891–1963): British political cartoonist. David was contributing cartoons to a local newspaper in New Zealand, where he was born, at age 11. This was the start of a distinguished career. In his twenties he moved to London and joined the staff of the *Evening Standard*, for which he drew many of his most successful cartoons, including his creation of the pompous "Colonel Blimp." During World War II Low's cartoons earned him the special hatred of Hitler whom he ridiculed mercilessly. They also earned him a knighthood in 1962. Several collections of his cartoons have been published in book form, including *A Cartoon History of Our Times* (1938), *Europe Since Versailles* (1939), *Europe at War* (1940), and *A Cartoon History of the War* (1994).

Michelangelo, full name **Michelangelo Buonarroti** (1475–1564), incomparable Italian Renaissance painter, sculptor, architect, and poet. He once said, "If I have anything of genius, it came to me from being born in the subtle air of the country of Arezzo, while from my nurse I got the chisel and hammer with which I make my figures." Giorgio Vasari (1511–1574), the famous art historian who wrote *Lives of the Greatest Italian Painters, Sculptors and Architects* (1550), described the beginning of Michelangelo's career in childhood in the following words:

> His inclination to the arts of design being strong, he spent all his time in drawing, as far as he could do so secretly, for he was often scolded by his father and those who were over him, and sometimes beaten for it, they supposing, perhaps, that it was a low thing, and unworthy of his ancient house . . . [but] the desire grew stronger every day in Michael Angelo, and Lodovico [his father], seeing there was no help for it, by the advice of his friends determined to put him with Domenico del Ghirlandajo (1449–1498) who was esteemed not only in Florence but through all Italy as one of the best masters then living, to learn painting.
>
> Michael Angelo was at this time 14 years old, and he made such progress that he astonished Domenico who saw that he not only surpassed his other pupils, of whom he had a great number, but often equalled the things he did himself. It happened once that one of the boys who was learning there had copied with a pen some women out of one of Ghirlandajo's works, and Michael Angelo, taking the paper, with a thicker pen, outlined one of the women again, as she should have been drawn; and it is a wonderful thing to see the difference, and consider the courage of the youth who was daring enough to correct his master's things. I have this drawing still, as a relic, having received it from Granaccio; and in the year 1550, when he was in Rome, Giorgio showed it to Michael Angelo, who recognized it and was glad to see it, saying modestly that he knew more of the art when he was a boy than now he was old.

He was wrong, however, as his magnificent later achievements proved: the marble statues of David, Moses, and the Pietà, the paintings on the ceiling of the Sistine Chapel, and the architecture of St. Peter's Cathedral to which he devoted the last 27 years of his life, are merely the most famous of his uniquely beautiful works of art, which are far too numerous to list here.

Claude Monet (1840–1926): French Impressionist painter. Monet had his first commercial success as an artist at age 15 when he sold some of his caricatures, but he soon gave up caricatures for serious paintings. He is considered one of the greatest of all the impressionists, and it was one of his paintings, which he called "Impression: soleil levant" ("Impression: rising sun"), that gave the name to this new artistic movement. He was constantly experimenting with different aspects of light, trying to capture them on canvas, by painting the same subject in a series, such as "Haystacks," to show how different they looked at different times of the day and the year. He loved flowers and created a large private garden at his home in Giverny, where he lived until his death and where he painted another famous series, of "Water Lilies." His home and its glorious garden have been preserved as he left them and are now among the major tourist attractions in France.

Alexandra Nechita (1986–): This girl paints for three to four hours a day and some of her paintings have actually sold for as much as $80,000. In 1995 she sold about 250 paintings for more than $2 million, but she does not live like a millionaire. Her earnings, minus her agent's commissions, go into a trust fund and like many normal children she is restricted to a five-dollar-a-week allowance. The daughter of Romanian immigrants to the U.S., Alexandra began to show an artistic flair in the usual way, with coloring books and crayons. But when her parents took away her coloring books she started drawing her own shapes and coloring them in. Enrolled in art classes at age seven, she soon was exhibiting in libraries and local galleries. She had never seen a painting by Picasso until she was eight, when she went to an exhibit at the Los Angeles County Museum, where she said, "Finally I've found somebody who paints similar to my style."

Samuel Palmer (1805–1881): English landscape painter and etcher. At age 14 Palmer was already an exhibitor at London's prestigious Royal Academy of Arts. Strongly influenced by the mysticism of William Blake, his landscapes were idealized rather than naturalistic. Later he became well known for his book illustrations.

Pablo Picasso (1881–1973): Spanish genius of modern art—painter, sculptor, and ceramist. Never known for modesty, he once said, "When I was a child, my mother said to me, if you become a soldier, you'll be a general. If you become a monk, you'll end up as Pope. Instead I became a painter and wound up as Picasso." He was a gifted draftsman before the age of 10, and when he was 14 and studying at the School of Fine Arts in Pontevedra, Spain, he painted pictures that already displayed a mastery of realism and fully adult technique. He applied for advanced training at the art school in Barcelona but was rejected on the grounds that his paintings showed he already knew more than the teachers there could teach him. According to Howard Gardner, author of *Creating Minds*, he was "by his late adolescence painting with as much finesse as any other artist of his time." He moved to Paris at age 19 where his fantastically innovative, prolific, and successful career, which he maintained with inexhaustible energy until his death at age 92, really took off, stimulated by the creative ferment of the city and by friendships with other artists, such as Gertrude Stein, who were experimenting with new forms of art.

Actually, Picasso's was not just one career but many, because every few years his work changed almost unrecognizably. For two years there was his "blue period" with striking studies of gaunt and sad figures, followed for another two years by his "rose period" featuring happy harlequins, acrobats, and circus people. Then he turned to brown and also began to do sculptures. And then came cubism, which provoked as much bewilderment as admiration. People could not undertand pictures of faces with profiles and front views superimposed. His retort was that everyone wants to understand painting, but people don't try to understand the song of the birds or a flower, or other things that surround them. So why do they have to "understand" a painting?

In 1937, during the Spanish civil war, Picasso painted what is perhaps his most famous picture, "Guernica," to depict the horror of the bombing of that town. As a youngster his only interest had been art, but the civil war turned him into a Communist sympathizer and his politics became as controversial as his art often was.

Picasso was egocentric, mercurial, arrogant, beastly at times to the adoring women who lived with him, and often neglectful of his children, but at the same time his charisma, his genius, and his gigantic productivity made him the major artist of the twentieth century.

Benjamin West (1738–1820): Self-taught American-born painter who immigrated to England. His first attempt at drawing occurred when he was only seven years old. His mother had asked him to watch her baby in its cradle while she was engaged in some work about the house. As the boy sat looking at his baby sister, she smiled in her sleep, and instantly Benjamin was seized with a desire to sketch what he saw. Taking up pens and a piece of paper he drew the sweet picture before him, as well as he could, in red and black ink. When the mother returned and picked up the piece of paper, she instantly recognized the infant's face and was astonished at the accuracy of the likeness. Benjamin continued sketching and painting portraits as he grew up.

At age 21 he moved first to Philadelphia, then to New York, then to Rome, and finally to England, where he opened a studio in London in 1763. In 1772 King George III appointed him the court's official historical painter and a charter member of the newly founded Royal Academy of Arts. King George remained his patron for 40 years, and he painted many portraits of the royal family as well as historical scenes, in which he became an innovator in English painting by portraying historical figures in realistic contemporary dress instead of classical costumes. He became a close friend of Sir Joshua Reynolds (1723–1792), whom he later succeeded as the second president of the Royal Academy, a post he held from 1792 until his death 28 years later.

How Children Have Been Portrayed in Adults' Art

The history of art records the history of childhood in rare but vivid flashes. Sculptures and bas reliefs of charming children playing, swinging on swings, throwing a ball or a discus, or racing have come down to us from ancient Egypt, Greece, and Rome. However, after the classical period children are strangely absent from art. Many beautiful paintings and sculptures of infants have graced the world's churches and museums since Jesus and John the Baptist were born and sat on their mothers' laps or played together, but for several centuries these were the only children portrayed by artists, except for heavenly cherubs, and in many renderings they looked solemn and dignified, not like real-life children. It sometimes seems hard to believe that any real, lively, playful, plump, mischievous children existed during the Middle Ages. Ordinary children apparently were just not considered worthy of portraiture. In Islamic countries nobody is considered worthy; Muslims are forbidden to make "graven images" because this is considered idolatry, so Islamic art has always been confined to abstract designs and calligraphy.

In European art in some group scenes a few little people can be seen along with big ones, though they are dressed so much like the larger people that you hardly notice them. There were some exceptions among artists, among them Andrea Della Robbia (1435–1525), who made exquisite ceramics of infants, and Leonardo da Vinci (1452–1519), who made beautiful drawings of them.

Then came the Renaissance, when things began to change. It produced many fine portraits of children, usually of family-proud aristocrats wealthy enough to be able to afford an artist's fees, and therefore expensively dressed. They often wore heavy jewelry and elaborate clothes made of thick embroidered fabrics that look more as if they belong on furniture than on children. These costumes must have weighed down their small wearers both physically and mentally, so it is no wonder that the expressions on many of their faces are solemn.

In the sixteenth, seventeenth, and eighteenth centuries, some great artists painted great pictures of children: Court artists, notably Hans Holbein the Younger (1497–1543) in England, and Velasquez (1599–1660) and Goya (1746–1828) in Spain, painted lovely realistic portraits of the children of royal families. And the Flemish painters Breugel the Elder (1520–1569) and Frans Hals (1580–1666) produced delightful pictures of peasant children, both individual smiling portraits and in group scenes showing them sharing in family festivities and playing. These children look like real children.

Another innovation in the seventeenth century that made children in portraits look less like adults than they did in the paintings of previous centuries was that some children began to wear distinctive clothes, not just smaller versions of adult clothing. And portrait painting became less formal after the Dutch painters of the seventeenth century introduced genre painting, with realistic scenes of everyday life; now, instead of standing formally or sitting still, children were depicted playing with toys and pets and even helping their parents with chores.

In the eighteenth century Thomas Gainsborough (1727–1788) was one of several painters of official portraits of the British royal family, but he also did charming ones of lower-class boys and girls engaged in lively activities. He is best known for "Blue Boy," the world's most famous formal portrait of a child (see page 369).

It appears to have been in England, France, and Holland that the delicacy and daintiness of young children gradually became appreciated and adorned by costumes designed to emphasize childishness rather than to disguise it. The rise of romanticism led to a new emphasis on emotional qualities. Pastels began to predominate in pictures of young children, and gaiety, gentleness, sweetness, and softness became characteristics of their portraits. Painters stressed the pinkness and whiteness of baby skin and emphasized it with correspondingly delicate backgrounds and clothing. Whether these painters were merely reflecting new juvenile fashions or helped to create them, it became standard to dress children so that they looked like children instead of diminutive adults. The exception was among Puritans and in rural areas of some countries where children have continued to wear smaller versions of adult clothing. Although you could now estimate the age of a young child from a picture, you still could not tell whether a baby was a boy or a girl because both wore dresses and long curls for the first five years of life.

Across the Atlantic, in Colonial America, there were at first no art schools, so most painters there were called "primitives" because they were self-taught and lacked sophisticated technique; the names of most of them are unknown because they were so humble they did not sign their paintings. Nonetheless, their work often had great charm, and the naïveté of their pictures of children was well suited to convey the naïveté of childhood. They portrayed children with affection and appreciation, and although their work was belittled for a long time, in the twentieth century it became much admired as folk art. It has a place of honor in homes where it has been handed down and in many museums.

In the nineteenth century, the French impressionists Edgar Degas(1834–1917) and Pierre Renoir (1841–1919) and the American Mary Cassatt (1845–1926) followed the example of the genre painters by depicting children realistically and informally in natural settings both indoors and outdoors. Degas specialized in drawing young girls and his best-known pictures and sculptures are of them in ballet classes. Renoir's pictures were usually outdoor scenes showing families together. In Mary Cassatt's case, the dominant theme was motherhood, and her pictures of mothers taking care of their little children, dressing them and giving them their baths, are vividly human, completely unlike traditional idealized madonnas and angelic cherubs. She was the first great woman etcher; when Degas, who later became her close colleague, first saw her etchings he exclaimed, "I refuse to admit that a woman can draw that well!" She became one of the most widely admired of the impressionists, although when she started out Cassatt and the others were ridiculed and denounced. Most critics at first did not even think Cassatt was worthy of scorn, and she was 46 years old before she won her first solo art exhibition. But she really revolutionized the art world with her pictures, paving the way for twentieth-century artists who have depicted normal life instead of thinking that art must deal only with rarified elegance.

Even while these new developments in art were taking place, formal portraiture continued to coexist with them, with traditional portrait painters like John Singer Sargent (1856–1925). And artists who were not known for depicting children occasionally relaxed and did lovely portrayals of them, for example, the sculptor Auguste Rodin (1840–1917), known primarily for his monumental statues, in his early years made a terra cotta bust of a "Girl with a Flowered Hat" in which he magically captured the subject's youth and innocence. On the whole, however, neither these artists nor art critics considered such works to be as "important" as their "major" work.

In the twentieth century a few painters, especially the popular illustrator Norman Rockwell (1894–1978) and other illustrators of children's books, continued to portray children with humor and realism, but on the whole painters have been replaced by photographers. From now on the faces and activities of children will be preserved for families' pleasure not merely once or twice in their lives but at every stage in their development.

The World-Famous Hummel Children
The Origin of the Figures

"For most of us, our childhood days are our most memorable times," said Franz Goebel in 1933 when he decided he wanted his family's factory in Bavaria, whose craftsmen followed a 300-year-old tradition of German porcelain and ceramic making, to produce a new type of figurine. He wanted to produce "a series of small ceramic figures that everyone could afford and enjoy," that would make people smile and think back on their own childhood days. Until then the image of the child in porcelain, which had developed largely as a result of Renaissance religious art, was that of angels and cherubs. There were few if any depictions of real-life contemporary children.

Searching for an artist whose work would be suitable, Goebel one day saw some art cards in a shop in Munich, with printed color reproductions based on sketches of children drawn by a Franciscan nun—exactly what he was looking for. The little children were a blend of the real and the ideal, with humor and sentiment, animation and emotion, and exuding charm and happiness. He introduced himself to the artist and, after guaranteeing high-quality control in the manufacturing process, he received her permission to produce statuettes based on her drawings and paintings.

The Artist

Berta Hummel was born in 1909 in the Bavarian village of Massing an der Rott. She started sketching as a young child, and her mother nicknamed her *das Hummele* (German for the bumblebee) because she was always buzzing with creative energy. She was a very pretty, clever little girl, with a sense of humor and quick wit, and her family encouraged her interest in art. She studied it in school and at age 16 was sufficiently proficient to become an assistant art teacher for the younger children. After graduating, she attended the Akademie der Angewandte Kunst (Academy of Applied Arts) in Munich, where she studied figure drawing with Professor Max Dasio, a well-known illustrator of children's books. She also studied color and composition, watercolor, nature drawing, and art history, and received Grade One, the highest mark attainable, in each of her subjects.

When she was 22 Berta entered a convent at Siessen, where art was one of many subjects taught by the sisters. Here she taught young children and frequently sketched her pupils. Her work was first published while she was still a postulant. In 1934 she received the habit of the Sisters of the Third Order of Saint Francis, and the bishop gave her a new name: Sister Maria Innocentia.

That same year Ars Sacra, a publishing house, began to distribute Hummel greeting cards, and the Emil Fink publishing house in Stuttgart distributed *Das Hummelbuch*, a children's book illustrated by her, which was an immediate success. And then came the meeting with Franz Goebel.

Early History—and Problems

Translating these drawings into three-dimensional figures without losing their delicacy, humor, nuances of facial expression, and subtle use of color was a great technical challenge. The sculptors and painters in the Goebel factory worked endless hours experimenting with different materials and glazes, and special paints had to be prepared. But the challenge was met with enthusiasm, and the first group of figures was displayed at the Trade Fair in Leipzig in March of 1935. Sales and export business were brisk for several years until the rise of Nazism, when an economic embargo was instituted against Germany and World War II began.

Sister Maria Innocentia's work soon came under direct attack, with the comment that it did not uphold the values of the Nazi state. It was called "Heresy in Pictures." The Nazis forbade Ars Sacra to publish her work in Germany, though they continued to allow it to be available in certain other countries. Next, the Nazis expropriated the Siessen convent, broke up its school, and sent most of the 290 nuns away, allowing only 40 (including Hummel) to remain. Substandard food and living conditions, particularly lack of heat in the buildings, and lack of medical supplies, took a toll on her health, and for the rest of her life Hummel suffered from respiratory ailments, including pleurisy and tuberculosis, of which she died in 1946 at the early age of 37.

The Postwar Revival

Less than a year after the war ended the Goebel factory, which was in the U.S. zone of occupied Germany, received permission to manufacture and export M. I. Hummel figurines again. Shortages of materials needed for their production, as well as food short-ages, made the work very difficult for a while, but American soldiers stationed in the occupation zone began to notice these little figures and to buy them to send to their families back home. By 1950 the factory was thriving again, in fact, better than ever. It added a day-care center for children, a swimming pool, a sauna, and a multipurpose sports field for its "family" of 800 employees. Tourists from other countries discovered the figurines in the 1950s and 1960s and began collecting them in large quantities.

In 1957 the U.S. Treasury designated M. I. Hummel figurines as works of art, qualifying for reduced tariff status. In 1964 the factory had a booth in the German Pavilion at the New York World's Fair, and in 1969 it opened Hummelwerk, a distribution company in the United States. It also promoted a look-alike contest in which parents dressed their children to resemble favorite Hummel figures. By 1969 the factory's work force had grown to 1,500 people.

Their Continuing Universal Appeal

In 1971, to mark its hundredth anniversary, the Goebel factory entered the collector plate market and introduced an annual Hummel plate, an extremely popular series. In 1977 the Goebel Collectors' Club was established. The first organization of its kind, it pioneered in educating collectors through a quarterly newsletter, sponsored tours of Goebel craftsmen, and also produced films. The club soon had a membership of nearly 200,000 collectors. Columns about Hummel collecting started to appear in hobby magazines and Sunday sections of newspapers, and weekend festivals drawing thousands of visitors were held. In the late 1970s several premier auction houses began featuring Hummel figurines in their sales. Under the leadership of Wilhelm Goebel, the sixth generation of his family to serve as chairman of the factory, its products were now being distributed in 88 countries.

In a speech given in 1975 Dr. Ulrich Gertz, a noted art historian and specialist in porcelain, ceramics, and sculpture, paid the following tribute to Sister Maria Innocentia Hummel:

> The uninterrupted popularity of this artist's work over the past four decades leaves little question as to its appeal. The key to this broad-based appeal is the universality of the child and of the free spirit we have all had as children, which remains locked deep inside each and every one of us. . . .If we put her work into a time capsule for 100 years, when that capsule is opened her images will still be as strong and as valid as they are today.

LULLABIES AND SONGS

The song is one of the main means by which every society passes on its heritage to the next generation. Mothers and fathers sing to their infants continually about the history of their tribe or nation and about their heroes, fictional and real. Babies hear the same songs so often that they memorize many of them without effort. They gradually learn what the words mean and absorb their society's basic values through the pleasant medium of entertainment.

Rhymes and rhythms amuse happy babies and soothe cross ones, and nurses, mothers, fathers, and other caregivers for centuries have used that fact to advantage, crooning meaningless syllables to them and encouraging babies to practice their own nonverbal vocalizing.

Poetry has been called the mother tongue of mankind. The speech of primitive people is alive with metaphors, and their myths, as well as the way they form words and invent names, all show that a poetic approach to life precedes a literal, factual one. This helps to explain the universal appeal of nursery rhymes and lullabies.

> **What will a child learn sooner than a song?**
> —*Alexander Pope (1688–1744)*, Epistle I, Book II

Every tribe in the world has its own poets and storytellers, and in some cultures every important incident is recorded in dance and song. Dances, songs, poems, and stories help relieve interpersonal tensions and bind the group together, as well as serving as vehicles for traditional lore, myths, ballads, and magic formulas. For these purposes many communities provide opportunities for dramatic ceremonies and plays, in which every member of the community may play a part.

It is no accident that preliterate people emphasize rhythm and repetition, which is a form of rhythm, in their stories, and frequently express them through dance and music. Expressing themselves nonverbally, they are revealing their kinship with all the other people in every land who are also preliterate: namely, infants, who also love music and rhythm and repetition, showing how much they do by their delighted response when they are rocked and bounced; they demand to hear the same old lullabies and nursery rhymes over and over again. Long before they can understand any words, let alone know how to read or write words, babies communicate through music, with their sing-song cooing, gurgling, chortling, and giggling. Thus the life story of the human race in its earliest, most ancient, stages is recapitulated in the life story of each of the newest people on earth.

Lullabies

Few of the lullabies mothers sing today date from antiquity. A Roman nurses' lullaby has been preserved for us, however, from the first century A.D. in a scholarly commentary on the satirist Persius: "*Lalla, lalla, lalla, aut dormi, aut lacte,*" which means "Hush, hush, hush, either sleep or eat." The Roman word *lalla* is, obviously, a close relative of the *lallai* of an Anglo Irish lullaby sung around 1315, in the reign of Edward II: "Lollai, lollai, litil child, Why wepistou so sore?" Both are related to the *lullay* of an English nursery song in a 1372 manuscript of John de Grimstone,"Lullay, lullay, litel child, softe slep and faste."

The word *lullaby* itself comes from this early word used to quiet, or to *lull*, crying babies, and the word *lulling* grew out of the *lalling* stage of baby talk, imitating the vocalizing that babies invent for themselves. Thus, in a sense, we could say that babies invented this art form that combines poetry and music, and that adults simply followed their example, imitating the sounds the babies made, which, as Tigurinus Chelidonius said in 1571, give those who listen to them "much pleasure and contentation of mind."

Some Elizabethan lullabies have come down to us via the concert stage and the music box. Of those used in today's nurseries, however, most are no older than the seventeenth century. *Tommy Thumb's Song Book*, printed in 1789, underneath a picture of a mother rocking her baby in its cradle, gave the following version of one of the most famous lullabies to have spanned the centuries and comforted 200 years' worth of babies:

> Lulliby Baby Bunting,
> Your Father's gone a hunting,
> To catch a Rabit for a Skin
> To wrap the Baby Bunting in.

And beneath the verse was the kind-hearted, schedule-defying instruction: "Encore 'till the Child's asleep."

Although a fourteenth-century writer said that the mother of a baby unable to sleep "singeth to it low and crooningly," not all lullabies have been tender and soothing. Some have expressed the despair of a mother or nurse over the fact that a child refuses to be quiet. One woeful song of this type was composed around 1780, evidently by a mother who was suffering from a financial crisis that resulted in a servant shortage:

> Bye, O my baby,
> When I was a lady,
> O then my baby didn't cry;
> But my baby is weeping
> For want of good keeping,
> O I fear my poor baby will die.

> Nouryces use lullynges and other cradyl songes to pleyse the wittes of the chylde.
>
> —*John de Travisa, 1398*

Another type of lullaby born of apparent desperation tried to make a baby go to sleep by threatening terrible things if it did not. Of course, if babies understood the words they would probably be so frightened they could never possibly go to sleep. An example of this type is:

> Baby! Baby! naughty Baby!
> Hush, you squalling thing, I say.
> Peace this moment, or it may be
> Wellington will pass this way.
> Baby! Baby! he's a giant,
> Tall and black as Rowen steeple;
> Breakfasts, dines and sups, rely on it,
> Every day on naughty people.
> Baby! Baby! if he hears you
> As he gallops past the house,
> Limb from limb at once he'll tear you
> Just as pussy tears a mouse;
> And he'll beat you, beat you, beat you,
> And he'll beat you all to pap;
> And he'll eat you, eat you, eat you,
> Gobble you, gobble you snap! snap! snap!

In addition to being warned about the Duke of Wellington, other versions threatened the baby with Napoleon Bonaparte; with Menshikov, the Russian commander in the Crimean War; and with "Black Old Knoll," Oliver Cromwell.

The illogical device of trying to scare a screaming child into going to sleep has produced a whole parade of "bogeymen." The name *bogey* comes from Bo, said to have been the name of one of the fiercest of the Gothic warriors, whose name spread instant panic among his enemies whenever it was mentioned. Practically every famous warrior and/or criminal in history has served, at one time or another, as the bogeyman of a naughty or sleepless child. Imaginary ones have also done duty. In the west of England nannies used to threaten their small charges with the arrival of John Cuthead, who cut off children's heads and carried them off in a sack.

In addition to lullabies whose authorship is unknown, a few famous poets have composed lullabies of a soothing, rather than a fearsome, nature. For example:

> Sleep, babie mine, Desire's nurse, Beautie, singeth:
> Thy cries, O babie, set mine head on aking. . . .
> Lully, lully, my babe.
> —*Sir Philip Sidney (1554–1586), "Child-Song"*

> Golden slumbers kiss your eyes,
> Smiles awake you when you rise.
> Care is heavy, therefore sleep you,
> You are care, and care must keep you;
> Sleep, pretty wantons, do not cry,
> And I will sing you a lullaby,
> Rock them, rock them, lullaby.
> —*Thomas Dekker (1570–1650), "Patient Grissel"*

> . . . .hush thee, my darling, take rest while you may,
> For strife comes with manhood, and waking with day.
> Oh! rest thee, babe; rest thee, babe; sleep on till day!
> Oh! rest thee, babe; rest thee, babe; sleep while you may.
> —*Sir Walter Scott (1771–1832),"Lullaby of an Infant Chief"*

All "Well Brought Up" Children Used to Be Musicians

According to Philippe Ariés, author of the much admired book *Centuries of Childhood*, we no longer have any idea of how big a part music, singing, and dancing used to play in everyone's life in Europe from the fifteenth century into the nineteenth. He quotes from a book published in 1597 called *Introduction to Practical Music*, which describes how the author decided he had to become a musician. He was dining out one evening when, at the end of the meal, "according to custom music books were brought to the table and the hostess presented me with a part, asking me to sing it, but when I explained that I could not, everyone wondered at this, and asked how I had been brought up." The ability to sing a part or play an instrument was so universal in England, France, Germany, Italy, and Spain that he was deeply embarrassed.

Among all social classes, children enjoyed music from an early age. Aristocratic and middle-class families played chamber music together and gave concerts for friends, and children took part in these, as is shown in many family portraits displayed in European museums. They also made music among themselves, and many paintings showed children holding musical instruments. Even among peasants and beggars, whose instruments were the hurdy-gurdy or the fiddle, children were active players and delighted listeners to music in their everyday lives.

PRODIGIES IN MUSIC

Johann Sebastian Bach (1685–1750): German organist, pianist, violinist, and composer. He could hardly help being a musical prodigy, surrounded as he was by music as soon as he was born. His great-grandfather, grandfather, father, brother, three uncles and two cousins, and, later, his father-in-law, four sons, and a grandson were all professional musicians. His father was his first music teacher, but when Johann was 10 his father died and his 24-year-old brother Johann Christoph Bach (1671–1721) took over. During their lifetimes the older boy's music was more admired than the younger one's. It is said that the older boy was possessive about his music and used to hide it, so his young sibling rival would creep downstairs at night to study it by moonlight. At 15 Johann Sebastian became a pupil and chorister at a school in Lüneberg. He used to walk 30 miles to Hamburg to hear organists play German composers, and 60 miles to another city, Celle, to hear a court orchestra play a different kind of music. At 18 he became church organist in Arnstadt but soon got into trouble for improvising and embroidering hymns.

Bach died at age 65, after going blind, but he left an indelible imprint on the world through his huge output of church, vocal, and instrumental music. As Beethoven once said of him, "*Das is nicht ein Bach, das ist ein Meer*" ("That's not a brook, it's an ocean").

Béla Bartók (1881–1945): Hungarian composer. He began composing dance pieces at age nine and was soon playing them in public. A growing interest in folk song led him to study folk music. He published a collection of 6,000 Arabic, Hungarian, and Romanian folk tunes, and these traditions greatly influenced his own compositions. He became professor of pianoforte in Budapest Conservatory and was known throughout Europe as a composer, but he was driven into exile by World War II and settled in the United States.

Ludwig von Beethoven (1770–1827): German composer, conductor, and pianist. His mother died when he was a child and his father was an alcoholic whose family was getting steadily poorer, so Ludwig had to leave school at 11 in order to earn money. He immediately became a professional musician and at 11½ was assistant to the court organist Christian Neefe; he was soon working on his own compositions. He wrote sonatas at 13 and from then on held various positions as assistant court organist and conductor. At 16 he attained the position of court organist in Cologne. At 17 he went to Vienna to study with Mozart, who told friends, "This young man will make a great name for himself in the world." However, he was not a "child wonder" in the way Mozart was. He is said to have wept at first at his enforced music lessons. His father, eager to exploit the boy's musical talent, lied about his age; in the concert tour Ludwig made at 11, audiences were told he was nine. At 28 he began to go deaf and by 49 was completely deaf but, incredibly, he continued to conduct and compose great music for 8 more years.

Joshua Bell (1968–): American violinist. Bell started playing the violin at five, but before that invented a prototype: he collected rubber bands and found that by stringing them on the knobs of a chest in his bedroom and opening the drawers to different degrees, he could make them play at different pitches. He would sit there for hours playing tunes like "Mary Had a Little Lamb." At 11 he began to take the violin seriously. He went to a summer camp for string players, where he was the second youngest of 150 students. Never before had he practiced more than an hour a day, but while at the camp he practiced eight

381

hours daily for four weeks. At camp he met Josef Gingold, a violin teacher at the Indiana University School of Music, who became his full-time teacher, advisor, and inspiration, introducing him to the music of Heifetz. Joshua went to high school through twelfth grade but spent half-days at the university's music school.

"Music was, and is, the most important thing in my life," he told a reporter, "but it wasn't everything." At 12 he won a state tennis tournament and placed fourth in the national finals, and he almost blew his first violin recital because the day before he was playing with a boomerang that hit his chin, requiring stitches. At 14 he won a music competition sponsored by *Seventeen* magazine, which led to his becoming the youngest soloist ever to play in a subscription series with the Philadelphia Orchestra. And at 17 he began playing 100 concerts a year.

Louis Hector Berlioz (1803–1869): French composer. He taught himself harmony and was composing for local chamber music groups by age 12. He studied medicine, not music, however, until he was 20, when he returned to music, writing symphonies and operas, and several books including a treatise on orchestration and an autobiography.

Georges Bizet, real name **Alexandre César Léopold Bizet** (1838–1875): French composer. At age nine he was a student at the Paris Conservatoire where he won prizes, and in his teens he won the prestigious Prix de Rome. In later life he wrote operas, the most famous of which is *Carmen,* and many songs and piano compositions.

James Herbert ("Eubie") Blake (1883–1983): American jazz pianist and song writer. When nine years old he took a manual labor job to help his financially strapped family, but he found he could make much more money by playing piano in a brothel. Instead of being pleased at the extra money, his mother beat him and forbade him to go back there. In cahoots with his father he began sneaking out of his bedroom window at night to continue his musical career. He became one of the world's most beloved jazz musicians and lived to be honored on his one-hundredth birthday.

Victor Borge, real name **Borge Rosenbaum** (1909–): Danish-born pianist and composer and comic. He started piano lessons at five. By eight he was hailed as a prodigy. At nine he  won a scholarship to Copenhagen Conservatory. He made his concert debut at 13 and started composing at 17. But he gave up his ambition to be a classical musician because his sense of humor got in the way. He found that his talent for making people laugh was even greater than his talent for piano playing and composing, so he combined the three gifts. Borge became Denmark's highest paid star, acting, writing, and directing stage, screen, and radio shows that combined comedy routines with his music.

He moved to America after Hitler invaded Denmark in 1940 and became equally successful there, known as the "Great Dane." In 1953 he won the record for the most one-man shows on Broadway: 849. He had five children, including a son Ron who worked with him on some of his shows as a "stupid" page turner. On one of his programs he performed all the vocal parts in his zany "Salieri Opera." His hilarious "Inflationary Language" was topped only by his inimitable "Phonetic Punctuation," with which he closed his laugh marathons. All his shows included enchanting piano solos, giving people a chance to catch their breath between laughs. He was knighted by all five Scandinavian countries and has continued to perform before delighted audiences in his late eighties, with as much energy and wit as ever.

Johannes Brahms (1833–1897): German pianist and composer. By age 10 Brahms was taking part in chamber music concerts. Until he was 20 he made his living as a pianist, but after that concentrated on composition. His main works include four symphonies, two piano concertos, a violin concerto, chamber, piano, and organ music, and many songs, Hungarian dances, and waltzes.

Sarah Chang (1980–): American violinist. Sarah's Chinese parents settled in Philadelphia after moving to the United States in 1979. She started playing the violin at age four when her father bought her a violin. Even before that she had wanted to play on his violin, but he would not let her touch it because "little kids have sticky fingers." He was her first teacher. Then she studied at the Curtis Institute in Philadelphia and while still a student was already becoming famous, playing with major orchestras. When she was eight years old, conductor Zubin Mehta asked her to guest solo with the New York Philharmonic on just one day's notice after a scheduled performer had canceled, and her rendition of Paganini's "Violin Concerto No. 1" earned her a standing ovation. At age 11 she began studying with Dorothy DeLay, the renowned teacher of violin prodigies at the Juilliard School in New York. At 12 she recorded an album, called "Debut," which hit the classical music charts a month after its release. Her concert dates at age 12 included the New York Philharmonic, the Philadelphia Orchestra, and the Chicago Symphony, plus engagements in seven European cities, while she continued as a school girl at the Germantown Friends School, faxing her homework to her teachers when on the road. Yet she is still a normal girl. Though she practices violin four hours a day, she also watches TV and enjoys roller skating and sleep-overs with friends. How does she manage to do all this? "I think performing is part of me," she says, "and I really love what I'm doing."

Frederic Chopin, full name **Frédéric François Chopin** (1810–1849): Polish-born son of a French father; organist, pianist, singer, and composer. At age seven, Chopin composed "Polonaise in G Minor." He played in public at eight, before the Tsar at 12, and made his professional debut as a piano virtuoso in Vienna at 19. He was noted for his lyrical piano compositions. His works include 55 mazurkas, 27 etudes, 25 preludes, 19 nocturnes, 13 waltzes, 12 polonaises, 4 ballades, 4 scherzos, 3 impromptus, 3 sonatas, 2 piano concertos, a number of songs, and a funeral march.

Van Cliburn, full name **Harvey Levan Cliburn, Jr.** (1934–): American concert pianist. His mother, a piano teacher who gave private lessons, discovered her son's ability when at the age of three he went to the piano after one of her students left and played by ear the piece he had just heard. She was her son's adviser, inspiration, and manager until she died in 1994. When Van was 24 he traveled to Russia to play in Moscow's International Tchaikovsky Competition. This was in 1958, the first year that what has since become a quadrennial event was held. Pianists, violinists, and cellists come from all over the world to compete in the three main categories for which the first prize is $5,000 and a gold medal—and fame. All piano finalists must play Tchaikovsky's "Concerto No. 1." Nobody in 1958 expected an American to win, but Van Cliburn's performance was so dazzling that he did and he became an overnight celebrity. He was no flash in the pan, however, continuing to be much in demand as a concert pianist.

Bob Dylan, real name **Robert Zimmerman** (1941–): American singer, guitarist, and composer. At age 10 he taught himself to play the guitar and by 15 had also mastered the piano, autoharp, and harmonica. He had also written a ballad dedicated to the French starlet, Brigitte Bardot. Between the ages of 10 and 18 he ran away from home seven times, yet he managed to finish high school and attend college on a scholarship at 19. During his student days he was a member of a folk-singing group at a coffee house near the campus. He stayed in college only six months, however, then spent years roaming across the country as a folk singer. He changed his name in 1962 in honor of the late poet Dylan Thomas (1914–1953). He has composed more than 200 songs, many of them comments on current issues but some in a light vein. Almost all of his records are best sellers, and he became the *de facto* poet laureate of his generation.

Duke Ellington, real name **Edward Kennedy Ellington** (1899–1974): American jazz composer, pianist, and orchestra leader. Duke began piano lessons at age seven, with his mother as his teacher, but he started out to be a painter and was good enough to win a scholarship to the Pratt Institute in New York. However, he loved jazz and often played piano in local night spots in his native city of Washington, D.C. His enjoyment of music soon won out over his interest in painting. He left high school before graduation to join a local ragtime band as its pianist, but shortly afterwards moved to New York and formed his own band. Over the years he became one of the most renowned jazz musicians of all time, expanding and deepening jazz with new forms of concert works, operas, and sacred music.

Ella Fitzgerald (1918–1996): American jazz singer. Bing Crosby called Ella "the greatest of them all, man, woman or child." She first performed on stage at 16 on a dare from some schoolmates in an "amateur hour" at the Apollo Theater in Harlem. She meant to dance but was so nervous she could not move, so she sang instead. She was a born singer, and an assistant of the bandleader Chick Webb, who was in the audience, was so wowed by her that he persuaded Chick to audition her. When Chick heard her he hired her on the spot. Learning she was an orphan, he and his wife also adopted her. For the next five years, until his death, she was his featured solo vocalist, delighting listeners with the ingenious ways she played around with melodies, improvising and "scat" singing. After Chick died she led his band for years and after that continued to sing in theaters, nightclubs, concerts, and on television and records even in her late seventies.

César August Franck (1822–1890): Belgian-French organist and composer. Franck entered Liege Conservatory at the age of eight and studied there until he was 15 when he became a professional musician. He went on international concert tours and later had a notable career as a church organist, music professor, and composer in Paris.

Evelyn Glennie (1966–): Scottish percussionist. Glennie gives as many as 120 concerts a year, seated amid more than 50 instruments, including a five-octave marimba, a snare drum, a Balinese gamelan, and a vibraphone, creating what has been called "a stunning spectrum of sound." Critics rave about her as a major artist. The *New York Times*, after she made her debut with the New York Philharmonic in March, 1996, said she is "quite simply, a phenomenon as a performer." But the astonishing fact is that she cannot hear the music she creates, though she can feel its vibrations through her feet and lower body and through her hands. "Sometimes," she says, "I see music in colors."

The youngest of three children, Evelyn grew up on a farm in northeast Scotland. Her mother played the organ in the local church and her father played the accordion.

384

When Evelyn was eight she took up the piano, and later added clarinet and recorder. That same year she began to lose her hearing. Doctors diagnosed nerve damage as the cause, and gradually it continued to deteriorate. She says, "I didn't worry too much about what was happening. It was part of me, and it developed in a natural way." She was fitted with a hearing aid but disliked it because it distorted sound, so she stopped using it. Instead, she learned to lip read, and because she has perfect pitch she has no trouble speaking clearly.

Evelyn continued to study music at her local secondary school, and one day when she was 12 she saw a schoolmate playing percussion and thought it looked interesting. She asked for lessons, and says, "It felt right."

For three years Evelyn studied at the royal Academy of Music in London, but she realized that her deafness would keep her from participating fully as a player in an orchestra, so she decided to become a soloist. In 1986, after giving a number of concerts and recitals in England, she went to Japan where she spent another year studying the marimba. She has produced seven CDs, one of which, released in 1995 and called "Wind in the Bamboo Grove," is made up completely of music by Japanese composers.

After returning to England Evenlyn met Greg Malcangi, a recording engineer who has normal hearing. They married in August, 1994, and live about 90 minutes north of London, with a barn on their property that houses the 600 or more percussion instruments Evelyn has collected from around the world. She is president of the Beethoven Fund, based in London, a charitable organization that provides music-based therapy for hearing-impaired children. However, Evelyn adamantly insists that she not be described as a deaf musician, saying, "I'm a musician who happens to be deaf."

Edvard Grieg (1843–1907): Norwegian composer. At 13 he wrote "Opus l, Variations on a German Melody for the Piano," the first of his many piano works. He also wrote choral works, Norwegian folksongs, and dances, as well as his famous *Peer Gynt* orchestral suite.

Hilary Hahn (1980–): American violinist: At l0 Hillary started studying at Philadelphia's Curtis Institute. While still there she performed with the Philadelphia Orchestra. At l4, in October l994, she made her New York debut as the soloist for four days with the New York Philharmonic. "She's 14 going on 15, not 14 going on 25," said Elizabeth Ostrow, the Philharmonic's artistic administrator, "a self-possessed youngster; there's no false sophistication about her." The New York debut was so successful that for her fifteenth year she had bookings for l7 major concerts.

George Frederick Handel, born **Georg Friedrich Handel** (l685–l759): German-born composer who in his twenties became a British subject. He received royal recognition at ll, wrote a mass at l3, was a director of opera at l9, and composed the first of 40 operas at 20. In composing his oratorios, the best-known of which is "The Messiah," he worked with such obsessive dedication that he would forget to eat for days.

Coleman ("Bean") Hawkins (l904–l969): American tenor saxophonist. Hawkins started studying piano with his mother at age four. At five he began studying the cello, and at nine took up the tenor saxophone. Music became his whole life. He studied harmony, counterpoint, and composition and while still in his teens joined the great Fletcher Henderson jazz band. He created ingenious alterations of the progressions of familiar tunes, a distinctive style, and rich, deep tones, not unrelated to his early lessons on the cello, according to music critic Barry Ulanov. His performances on fast swing tunes and on slow ballads altered forever the way the tenor sax is played.

Joseph Haydn, full name **Franz Joseph Haydn** (1732–1809): Austrian composer. Haydn began to play the organ at four, but his parents did not encourage him; he used to sneak up to the attic, where the family's organ was kept, to play it against their orders. Evidently they gave up their attempts to discourage his passion for music, because they let him move from home to be a singer in the Vienna Boys' Choir from age 8 to 17. After leaving there he made his living at first by playing in street orchestras. In his twenties he began composing and went on to become one of the most prolific composers in history.

Jascha Heifetz (1901–1987): Born in Lithuania, Heifetz was one of the greatest violinists of all time. He began studying the violin with his father at age three, first played in public at five, graduated from music school at eight, and at nine went on for advanced study at the St. Petersburg Conservatory. In 1912, when he was 11, he made his Berlin debut, astonishing everyone with his technical prowess. Fritz Kreisler, who was there, was so stunned that he told a colleague, "We might as well take our fiddles and break them over our knees!" At 12 he went on a highly successful concert tour through Germany, Russia, and Scandinavia.

After the Russian Revolution he moved to the United States and became a citizen. He made his American debut at Carnegie Hall in New York at age 16, creating even more amazement, as indicated by some words overheard between two members of the audience. One was the violinist Mischa Elman, who asked his pianist friend Leopold Godowsky, "Don't you think it's awfully hot in here?" Godowsky laughed and said, "Not for pianists." At the end of the concert, the cheering audience ran onto the stage in what was described as a stampede.

Events like this gave Heifetz an aura that lasted throughout his career. His astonishing achievements have been recorded for posterity in the Gold Seal "Heifetz Collection," a set of 65 compact discs issued in 1994 by RCA Victor that document his career over the course of 55 years. His performances remained breathtaking, continuing to fill other violinists with both awe and despair. Critics agree that the level of his accomplishments did not flag from his first recording to his last, and he was admired not just for his unparalled technique; he united virtuosity with lyricism and tenderness.

One of his solo pieces, "La Ronde des Lutins," designed to display a violinist's facility with runs, almost disappeared from the violin repertoire after Heifetz had played it, because no other violinist could bear comparison. But he expanded the violin repertoire beyond Bach, Beethoven, and Brahms with hundreds of transcriptions from unexpected sources such as Irving Berlin and George Gershwin, and even with a pop tune that he himself wrote under the pseudonym of Jim Hoyle—it was recorded by Bing Crosby. He championed contemporary composers and increased interest in chamber music. He retired at the top of his profession, devoting the remaining 15 years of his life to teaching, writing, and performing privately for his own pleasure.

Billie Holiday, real name **Eleanora Fagan** (1915–1959): American blues singer. Billie had to quit school in fifth grade to help support her family, which she did by cleaning some of Baltimore's famous white marble stoops. But her beauty, charm, and remarkable voice got her better work by the age of 15, singing in New York clubs and on the road with Artie Shaw and other bands. Her distinctive style put its stamp on everything she sang, and she is still popular through many recordings of which the most loved is the song "God Bless the Child."

Helen Huang (1982–): Pianist. Born in Japan of Taiwanese parents who moved to the United States in l985, Helen took up the piano at five, and within the year won her first competition and performed in public. She has played with several orchestras, including the Leipzig Gewandhus Orchestra on a European tour, and she made her New York Philharmonic subscription debut in February l995, at age l2. She was scheduled for l2 other performances that season, even though she was still so small she needed a special device to operate the pedals, and her repertory was limited because, she giggled, "my hands aren't big enough for Liszt or Brahms; I just started to reach an octave." Yet when she plays Mozart or Beethoven she is "an insightful and compelling performer whose skills would be envied by someone twice her age," said critic K. Robert Schwarz. She is never nervous on stage. She practices for three hours each evening and five on Sundays, and she does not need forcing because "it's something I want to do."

José Iturbi (l895–l990): Spanish pianist, conductor, and movie actor. Iturbi was already teaching pupils three and four times his own age when he was seven. At 24 he became head of the piano department of the Geneva Conservatory; later he toured Europe and North and South America with great success. Then, settling in the United States, for eight years he conducted the Rochester Philharmonic Orchestra. In the l940s he played piano and acted in several major movies.

Leila Josefowicz (1978–): Canadian violinist. She gave her first performance at three. One day when she was five, her father was running the vacuum cleaner and she said to him, "That's an F sharp." This was when her parents realized she had perfect pitch. At seven she began studying with Robert Lipsett and her career was launched. She has soloed with symphonies and other groups near her new home in California. She did a duet with Dudley Moore at a star-studded tribute to Leonard Bernstein in Los Angeles. And when she was l0 she performed for President Reagan at the gala opening of the Bob Hope Cultural Center in Palm Desert. Van Cliburn shared the bill with her and said, "She has the world at her feet." By the time she was l7 she was booked for 31 concerts for the year 1995, and that year signed an exclusive recording contract. Critics regularly say she is a joy to hear. Speaking of joy, she enjoys all music except rock, saying, "That's just a lot of banging and crashing."

Jordy Lemoine (1988–): French popular composer: At age five, this preschooler had sold 1.5 million records of a rap tune he composed called "It's Hard to Be a Baby."

Liberace, full name **Wladziu Valentino Liberace** (l919–l987): American pianist. Born in a suburb of Milwaukee, Wisconsin, Liberace began piano lessons at four. The pianist Paderewski heard him play and was impressed by his ability enough to help arrange a scholarship for him at the Wisconsin College of Music. Liberace made his debut as a classical pianist with the Chicago Symphony Orchestra at l6. But during the Depression, as he recalled in his autobiography, *The Wonderful Private World of Liberace,* paying money to hear serious music was one luxury the public gave up, so he began playing lighter music in bars and nightclubs under the name of Walter Busterkeys. In l939 he started combining pop and classics in his programs, mixed with self-parody and outrageous glitz. He featured a large candelabra on his piano and gaudy jewel-studded costumes, which intrigued so many fans that he earned an average income of $5 million a year for more than 25 years. His money enabled him to indulge a bizarre childish fantasy: he had an architect build a big house for him in Palm Springs, California, in the shape of a grand piano.

Franz Liszt (1811–1886): Hungarian virtuoso pianist and composer. Liszt began playing piano at five and composing at eight. His first concert appearance was at nine, and the performance was so impressive that the audience raised money for his musical education for the next six years. At 11 he gave a recital in Vienna; Beethoven was in the audience and so moved that he went up on stage at the end and kissed the boy on his forehead. At 12 Liszt gave concerts in England, France, and Germany. His opera *Don Sanche* was performed in Paris when he was 14. At 15 he gave concert tours in France and Switzerland. His career continued from success to success until his death and included not only playing and writing music, some of it so difficult that only he could perform it, but also writing essays and books. By the end of his career he had composed more than 700 works.

Gustave Mahler (1860–1911): Austrian composer, conductor, pianist, and accordionist. Mahler began composing at four, having become fascinated by military and folk music and reproducing them on both the accordion and piano. Though creative, he was a tormented child. As Jews, his family suffered from prejudice, and his self-made father frequently beat his delicate, cultured mother. And among his 11 brothers and sisters there was much illness and several deaths. The impact of these experiences on the child may partly explain the intense emotionalism of much of his music. Among his compositions are 10 symphonies, a cantata, and many songs.

Felix Mendelssohn, full name **Jakob Ludwig Felix Mendelssohn-Bartholdy** (1809–1847): German composer and conductor. Mendelssohn had a rigorous education at home, beginning daily at 5:00 A.M. with studies of languages, literature, drawing, painting, and music. He could sight-read music before he was eight. His first public performance was in Berlin at age nine. At 12 he composed a "Piano Quartet in C Minor." He also composed concertos, fugues, sonatas, five operas, and 11 symphonies before and during his teens. His mother was his only music teacher.

Yehudi Menuhin (1916–): Virtuoso American violinist. Menuhin later became a citizen of Switzerland and of the United Kingdom, where he was knighted. He started playing the violin at four. His first public performance was at eight. At 15 he was the youngest person in *Who's Who*. His father traveled with the world-famous prodigy, signed his contracts, gave him the ice cream cone that was his reward for a good performance, and made sure the boy did not see newspaper reviews because they might make him conceited. Not until he was 20 did Yehudi get to read how critics praised him. Long hours of practice and concerts all over the globe kept him separated from other children and his sisters, also kept isolated, were his only child companions. "It made awful fools of us when we faced our first life situations," his sister Hepzibah has written. But it did not embitter him against his parents or music. He founded a School for Young Musicians in London, "to guide not only fingers but minds for music as a way of being," and he has sponsored and befriended other child prodigies.

Midori, real name **Midori Goto** (1971–): Virtuoso Japanese violinist. Setso Goto, her mother, a chamber musician, orchestral concertmistress, and music teacher, recalls that when Midori was two "she often slept in the front row of the auditorium when I rehearsed, but one day I heard her humming a Bach concerto, the very piece I'd been practicing two days before." On her third birthday she was given a small violin, and her lessons began. She started playing in concerts at six. When she was eight and living in America she sent a tape of her playing to Dorothy DeLay, violin teacher at the Juilliard School, hoping she might be accepted as a pupil. DeLay said, "It was absolutely extraordinary; I thought a mistake had been made and that she was not eight but 28." DeLay accepted her as a scholarship student and invited her to attend the Aspen Summer Music Festival. Pinchas Zukerman, who gave a master class there, vividly remembers Midori's participation: "Out comes this tiny thing, not even 10. . .and then she played the Bartok concerto, and I went bananas . . . tears started coming down my cheeks . . . . I was absolutely stunned. I turned to the audience and said, 'I've just witnessed a miracle!'"

Nathan Milstein (1904–1992): Virtuoso Russian violinist ranked with Jascha Heifetz and Fritz Kreisler. Milstein started studying violin at four, later saying his mother made him study it to keep him out of mischief. He had several teachers, and soon outstripped all their other pupils. He performed in concert at age 10, at 11 was admitted into the Odessa Conservatory, and from age 12 to 16 attended the St. Petersburg Conservatory. In those days it was not easy for a child from a Jewish ghetto to attend these schools, but his teachers, who were convinced of his genius, used their influence to get him in. He made his recital debut at 11, accompanied on the piano by his sister. Soon he was giving recitals all over Russia.

At 17 Milstein met a young Russian pianist named Vladimir Horowitz (1904–1989), and they started giving concerts together. At 22 he moved to Paris and made a sensational debut, which launched him as an international star. Three years later he made another recording with the Philadelphia Orchestra, directed by Leopold Stokowski. In 1987 he received a Kennedy Center Honors award for lifetime achievement in the arts. He proved how well he deserved it by continuing to perform well into his eighties.

Wolfgang Amadeus Mozart (1756–1791): Austrian composer, violinist, harpsichordist, pianist, and organist. (See page 394.)

Jacques Offenbach, real name **Jakob Eberst** (1819–1880): German-born composer who later became a naturalized French citizen. By age six Offenbach played both piano and violin and had written the first of many songs that eventually led to his writing many lively operettas and opera bouffe for the Comédie Française and other theaters, including his own, in Paris. He also wrote one grand opera, *The Tales of Hoffmann.*

Nicolo Paganini (1782–1840): Italian composer and violin virtuoso. His first public performance was when he was 10, and he began professional tours at 14. He made a two-year European concert tour starting at 16. With his technical brilliance he acquired an almost legendary reputation. Unfortunately, his success went to his head. In his teens he indulged excessively in love affairs and heavy gambling, and at one point had to pawn his violin to pay gambling debts. But as he grew older he became more responsible. In his late twenties he made another highly successful international tour and became wealthy again. His technical innovations revolutionized violin playing. He also composed six violin concertos and other works for the violin.

Adelina Patti (1843–1919): Coloratura soprano. She was born in Madrid, Spain, of Italian parents. She started giving concerts in New York at age seven and later became a famous opera star.

Les Paul, real name **Lester William Polfus** (1916–): American guitarist. He began his career at age 13, in Waukesha, Wisconsin, using the show biz name Red Hot Red. He invented the solid-body electric guitar, which enabled him to create richer sounds than he could with acoustic instruments. He also originated multitrack recording and was a tireless experimenter with sonic feedback and amplification. One of his admirers said his tinkering with technology made everything he played sound so effervescent it was as if it was spilling from a champagne bottle or had been spun through a cotton candy machine.

For decades Paul was a radio and TV host and composer of song hits, performing these as well as standards on records that often reached the top of the pop charts. He played the accompaniment as he and his wife Mary Ford sang together. When he was in a bad automobile accident and had to wear a body cast, he had his right arm set in guitar-playing position. Mary died in 1977 but he continued to make club appearances in the 1990s as a "living legend."

Itzhak Perlman (1945–): Israeli-born American virtuoso violinist. When three years old Itzhak heard a violin recital on the radio and immediately wanted to become a violinist. He began practicing on a toy fiddle, and then on a standard-sized violin his parents bought second-hand for six dollars; he now plays on a $60,000 Stradivarius. When he was four he got polio, but during his convalescence he kept practicing the violin, and then enrolled in the Tel Aviv Academy of Music on a scholarship. In a few years he was appearing regularly with orchestras, and at 10 he gave his first solo recital. At 13 he came to New York for two highly successful appearances on TV, then toured to 20 cities in the United States and Canada. He stayed in New York after that, and for five years studied at Juilliard on scholarships. He made his Carnegie Hall debut at age 18, and the next year was the youngest of 119 contenders in the twenty-third annual contest of the Edgar M. Leventritt Foundation, a prestigious and demanding international musical competition. He emerged in first place, winning $1,000 and guaranteed solo appearances for the next two years with the New York Philharmonic and symphony orchestras in six other cities. He continued to triumph, playing throughout the United States and Canada and in Denmark, England, France, Holland, Israel, Italy, Portugal, Scotland, Spain and Switzerland. (For information on Perlman's later years, see page 144.)

Cole Porter (1893–1964): American composer of popular songs and musical comedies. He was 11 years old when his first song was published. When he attended Harvard, he wrote many songs, some of which are still unpublished, but 862 of his songs were published, and most of them were big hits. To this day his estate earns over $2,000,000 a year in royalties.

André Previn (1929–): German-born pianist, composer, arranger, and conductor. At six he was enrolled on a full scholarship in the Berlin conservatory, Hochschule fur Music, but at nine, in 1938, was kicked out because he was Jewish. His family, realizing life was no longer safe for Jews in Germany, escaped to Paris by pretending to be taking a weekend trip, packing only one bag and leaving everything else they owned behind. After nine months they moved to California because an uncle lived there. André's father was a lawyer but could not practice law in the United States because of immigration rules, so he became a piano teacher. His most brilliant pupil was his son. The father was a demanding teacher, training André to become a classical concert pianist. André once told a friend, "Sometimes people ask if I resented not having a normal childhood. I didn't know it wasn't normal. I thought everyone practiced eight hours a day."

At 14 he heard jazz for the first time, a record of Art Tatum playing "Sweet Lorraine." He loved it and began to practice improvising and composing jazz pieces. He got a job playing jazz on radio. Someone at MGM heard him and hired him to write some jazz for José Iturbi (see page 387) to play in a film. Previn could sight-read anything and was soon put on the staff of MGM's music department, to compose and orchestrate for movies and to work as a rehearsal pianist. He was still in high school. At age 19 he was assigned his first complete original score, for a movie starring Lassie and Jeanette MacDonald. Over the years he won four Academy Awards for his musical scores. His father was upset that he had become a "commercial" musician instead of a "serious" one, but later Previn became internationally respected as a serious conductor with major symphony orchestras, even though he also still loved and continued to play jazz in concerts.

Sergei Prokofiev, full name **Sergei Sergeyevich Prokofiev** (1891–1953): Russian pianist and composer. Prokofiev began composing at age five. His first piece was called "Indian Gallop" and was written down by his mother, his first piano teacher. He composed an opera, *The Giant,* using only the white keys, at age seven. Later he studied at the St. Petersburg Conservatory and won a reputation as a virtuoso pianist. During World War I he lived in London, and then in the United States, before returning to the Soviet Union in 1934. Two years later he wrote *Peter and the Wolf,* the internationally popular musical story for children. This was written at the request of Natalya Sats, head of the Children's Music Theater in Moscow, who wanted a piece that would teach children about the different instruments in an orchestra. He achieved this ingeniously and entertainingly by having each character in the story portrayed by a different instrument. His other works include ballets, cantatas, concertos, operas, sonatas, songs, symphonies, and suites.

Charles Camille Saint-Saëns (1835–1921): French composer, organist, pianist, and music critic. Saint-Saëns began to compose at five, gave his first recital at 10, and wrote the first of his five symphonies at 18. He became a distinguished pianist and organist, and in addition to symphonies wrote 13 operas, plus chamber music, church music, concertos for cello, piano, and violin, songs, and symphonic poems. As an adult he did not forget his childhood; he wrote a delightful orchestral piece for children: "Carnival of the Animals."

Franz Schubert, full name **Franz Peter Schubert** (1797–1828): Austrian composer. At age 11 he was a member of the chapel choir at the imperial court in Vienna, and with little formal training, when he was 14, he began to compose the first of approximately 600 songs. He is recognized as one of the greatest masters of German songs (*lieder*) in history. During his short life, only 31 years, he also wrote chamber music, 16 sonatas, and two symphonies (one unfinished but still performed).

Robert Schumann, full name **Robert Alexander Schumann** (1810–1856): German composer. He wrote his first composition, a setting for the 150th Psalm, at age 11. He was a promising pianist but after injuring a finger when he was 22, he gave up performing in favor of writing and composing. He wrote plays and poetry and translated the odes of Horace, as well as composing chamber music, four symphonies, and a large number of songs. He is regarded as the greatest composer of German songs after Schubert. He married Clara Wieck (1819–1896), the daughter of his piano teacher. She was a concert pianist, composer, and music teacher who had also been a child prodigy, giving her first concert at 11, publishing four polonaises at 12, and later writing many piano and chamber works, including a concerto. As Clara Schumann she was noted for her interpretations of her husband's piano works and those of Chopin. Apparently they had a good marriage for a while, but it was marred by his mysterious attacks of melancholia, and at age 44 he was committed to a lunatic asylum for the last two years of his life.

Andrés Segovia (1893–1987): Virtuoso Spanish guitarist. Segrovia was a musical pioneer who transformed the guitar from a mere member of the rhythm section of a band into a solo instrument for the concert stage, not only through his brilliant playing but by virtue of his many arrangements of classical pieces for the guitar. He developed a revolutionary guitar technique that permitted the performance of a wide range of music, and many modern composers wrote works for him. Largely self-taught, he made his public debut at 14 and quickly gained an international reputation. He was named Marquis of Salobrena by royal decree of the Spanish King in 1981.

John Philip Sousa (1854–1932): American bandmaster and composer. Known as the March King, Sousa wrote 140 military marches, including the famous "Stars and Stripes Forever" and "Semper Fidelis." The latter was his own favorite which, being a talented musician but a poor businessman, he sold to a music publisher for $35. He also invented the sousaphone, a musical instrument resembling the tuba but with the tubing encircling a player's body, designed to be played while marching. His career began quite differently, however, as a violinist in a dance band, when he was 11 years old. He was classically trained on the violin, and a prolific composer of songs, waltzes, and operettas in addition to the marches for which he is famous. He was also dedicated to taking music to the masses, for years traveling with concert bands to wherever railroads went, playing twice a day in each town, this endeavor thriving until the inventions of the phonograph and the radio doomed the live concerts.

Johann Strauss (1804–1849) and **Johann Strauss II** (1825–1899): Austrian composers. This father-and-son pair were both musical prodigies. Johann senior was surrounded by music all through his childhood, and by age six he was playing both piano and violin and had already produced his first composition, "Christmas Song." When he was 15 he founded an orchestra, which he conducted, while continuing to compose many works. Among them were 14 polkas, 19 marches, 35 quadrilles, and ballets, chamber music, choral works, operas, songs, symphonies, and tone poems. He is also credited with having invented a new dance form: the waltz. He composed 150 waltzes and became known as the Waltz King.

Johann senior also produced six children, but later deserted them and their mother and set up house with someone else, with whom he had four other children. Anna, his wife, resolved to challenge her prolific and profligate husband by establishing his namesake as pretender to the title of "The Waltz King." The boy fit the role well. He was expelled from school for bursting into song during class, offended his music teacher by playing waltzes on the church organ, and became an equally well-known composer. He wrote even more waltzes than his father—over 400, including the immortal "Blue Danube" and "Tales from the Vienna Woods." At 19 he got a license to perform in public with an orchestra of his own. Rivalry between the elder and younger Johann and their orchestras lasted until the elder one died at age 45, whereupon his rival, then 24 years old, combined and conducted the two orchestras. Later two of his younger brothers, Josef Strauss (1827–1870) and Eduard Strauss (1835–1916), who were also conductors and composers, continued the tradition, in turn successfully taking over their father's and brother's combined orchestra.

Suzuki-Trained Children: In Japan, many musical prodigies on the cello, piano, and violin have been developed by the Suzuki Music School, which claims it can make any child into a good musician with its special teaching method. It has exported its theories to other countries through international concert tours featuring musicians aged 6 to 16, and Suzuki schools have been established in a number of these countries.

Guiseppe Verdi, full name **Guiseppe Fortunino Francesco Verdi** (1813–1901): Italian composer. Verdi's first symphony was performed when he was 15. He continued composing for almost 75 years, and wrote 18 major operas. Among those most often performed today are *Aida*, commissioned for the new opera house in Cairo built in celebration of the construction of the Suez Canal in 1871; *Il Trovatore*; *La Traviata*; *Rigoletto*; and two based on Shakespeare plays, *Otello* and *Falstaff*, written when he was 80. In his final years he also wrote magnificent sacred music.

Dalit Paz Warshaw (1975–): American pianist and composer. When Dalit was about a year old, in bed with a fever, her Israeli aunt put on a record of Israeli songs. According to her mother, the baby listened and "perked right up, and then she sang half the record back on pitch and remembered all the Hebrew words." The mother, Ruti Warshaw, was born in Israel of a musically gifted family, but she realized this performance was truly exceptional and wondered if the baby girl was a genius. When she was three years old, Dalit demanded piano lessons, and since her mother was a concert pianist and a piano teacher, she obliged; she is the only music teacher the child has ever had. At seven, Dalit composed an eight-minute suite for orchestra. At eight, she began winning composition prizes, among them the Broadcast Music Incorporated (BMI) Award for Student Composers. At nine she composed a tone poem called "In the Beginning," about the Creation, and when she was 13, New York Philharmonic conductor Zubin Mehta presented it in a concert, with her doing the narration. Before the performance he told the audience, in a voice tinged with awe, "I want you to know she wrote all the parts for the musicians herself, and the score from which I conduct."

About half a dozen other works composed by her before she was 10 have also been performed by major orchestras, including the Cleveland Symphony and the Israel Philharmonic. At age 10 she also set to music, for piano and voice, an epic poem about the battle of Gettysburg, written by her seven-year-old brother Hilan, a violinist. Their father, an American executive vice president of a life insurance company, said, "I'm the only one who's normal around here."

Karl von Weber, full name and title **Baron Karl Maria Friedrich Ernst von Weber** (1786–1826): German composer, pianist, and opera conductor. Called the creator of the German romantic opera, Weber wrote his first opera at age 13, another at 14, and a third at 17, followed by five more. Evidently he acquired his musical talent and interest in the stage from his father, a violinist and theater manager. But he also received misfortune from him. Karl was sent into exile in his early twenties due to his father's alleged embezzlement. Nothing but death could prevent his creativity, however; he continued to compose many works of music until his death in London at age 40.

Mary Lou Williams, maiden name **Mary Lou Winn** (1910–1981): American jazz pianist and composer. She started to play when she was so small that "people had to hold me on their laps so I could reach the piano at church affairs and family parties. I would play for an hour and then rest and then come back and play some more." At six she started playing professionally. She studied music in high school and played one-nighters until age 15 when she joined the Orpheum vaudeville circuit with the Syncopaters, a jazz band led by saxophonist John Williams, whom she later married. In 1929, when she was 19, she and her husband joined the Andy Kirk band and she stayed with it until 1942, gaining a worldwide reputation both as a pianist and composer for the big bands of the swing era. In the 1960s and 1970s she switched to writing church music, but still in the jazz idiom.

Stevie Wonder (See page 134.)

Olga Zarankina (1985–): Russian composer. *Brush Squirrel*, an opera based on a fairy tale by Finnish writer Usko Laukannen, premiered to great acclaim in Moscow in 1993. The astounding thing about it was that the music and verses had been written by a five-year-old girl. When her father, journalist Yuri Zarankin, told producer Nikolai Kuznetsov, the head of the Kompositor musical theater, about his daughter's opera, the producer was understandably skeptical. But when he heard the music and verse, he was so impressed that he agreed to stage it. The Children's Musical Theater at the Berendei Cultural Center provided its choir and ballet troupe for the performance, and composer Yuri Averin arranged and conducted the score.

On opening night the house was full and enjoyed a real opera with solo parts, duets, a chorus, and ballet. It had a dynamic story line, with journeys, chases, and romance, although its characters were forest animals. The main character was "Brush," a little squirrel who was played by Natasha Alfyorova, a nine-year-old soloist with the Bolshoi Theater chorus.

Olga turned eight on March 4, 1993. She was then attending the Central Music School at the Moscow Conservatory and was writing a second opera, *The Snow Maiden*. She was already listed in *Divas*, the Russian equivalent of the *Guinness Book of Records*, as the author of 100 songs and the composer at age five of an opera she had seen performed on stage.

MOZART (1756–1791)

An infant prodigy whose achievements have added much happiness to the human race was a youngster christened Johannes Chrysostomus Wolfgangus Amadeus Mozart, born in Salzburg, Austria, in 1756. When he was three years old, he showed such interest in the music lessons of his eight-year-old sister Maria Anna (nicknamed Nannerl), that his father, Johann Georg Leopold Mozart, a violinist, conductor, composer, and music teacher, began to give him regular music lessons, too. No special coaxing or forcing was ever necessary to stimulate the little boy's extraordinary interest and ability in music.

At three he was playing the harpsichord and had memorized musical passages after listening to them once.

At four and five he began composing music, including some minuets.

By six he had composed a clavier concerto that only an expert musician could play. Also at six, playing the violin and clavier, he and his sister, playing the piano, began four years of concert tours of the royal courts of Europe.

By seven he was accomplished on the piano and organ as well as the harpsichord, violin, and clavier, and two sets of his sonatas for harpsichord and violin were published in France that year.

By eight he had composed two symphonies, the first of 14 that he wrote by the time he was 15.

At 10 he mastered counterpoint, studying it with his father.

At 12 he received an imperial commission in Vienna to compose and conduct an opera, the first of his eight operas, and he also wrote the first of his 15 orchestral masses.

At l3 he received an honorary appointment as the concertmaster to the Archbishop of Salzburg and also traveled with his father to Italy where he was knighted by the Pope.

At l4 he composed his second opera, and year after year his astonishing creativity kept increasing.

His Concert Tour Starting at Age Six

When he and his ll-year-old sister embarked on their first international concert tour, Wolfgang was already a highly accomplished musician and composer, but he was still an ingenuous little boy. As his father said, "Wolfgang is extraordinarily jolly, but a bit of a scamp as well."

Mozart was a prolific letter writer, and his informative and entertaining letters were translated and published after his death, including this one found in *Letters of Mozart and His Family* by Emily Anderson. Leopold wrote to his wife during their first concert tour, giving enchanting glimpses of their remarkable six-year-old:

> My children, the boy especially, fill everyone with amazement....The children are merry and behave everywhere as if they were at home. The boy is as intimate with everyone as if he had known them all his life...in spite of our irregular life, early rising, eating and drinking at all hours, and wind and rain, he has, thank God, kept well . . . . Everyone is amazed, especially at the boy, and everyone whom I have heard says that his genius is incomprehensible.

In Austria, where they began the tour as the guests of Empress Maria Theresa (1717–1780) and her family, "Their Majesties received us with such extraordinary graciousness that, when I shall tell of it, people will declare that I have made it up. Suffice it to say that Woferl (the father's nickname for Wolfgang) jumped up on the Empress's lap, put his arms round her neck and kissed her heartily."

Not everything went well on the tour. In Prussia the King's sister Princess Amalia showered the little boy with kisses, causing the boy's financially struggling father to comment wryly, "If the kisses which she gave to my children, and to Wolfgang especially, had all been new louis d'or we should be quite happy; but neither the innkeeper nor the postmaster are paid in kisses." Wolfgang and his sister received many presents, such as snuff boxes, costumes, swords, laces, toothpick holders and other trinkets, on this trip, but little money.

There were also, in spite of Leopold's cheerful remarks early in the tour, health problems. The tour was interrupted in October when the young star caught scarlet fever (Leopold said this was "a fashionable complaint for children in Vienna") and, as if to remind everyone what a very little boy he still was, he also felt miserable as the result of cutting a new tooth. Furthermore, the family was exposed to smallpox and the Princess Joanna, Maria Teresa's eleventh child, caught typhus and died of it during their visit. Not only health problems but bad weather and impossible traveling conditions caused concerts to be delayed or cancelled. Expenses as well as discomforts and sickness mounted, and the tour ended in financial disaster.

Yet there was always joy amid the Mozarts' troubles, as indicated in this note from the father to his wife:

> The latest news is that in order to amuse ourselves we went to the organ and I explained to Woferl the use of the pedal. Whereupon he shoved the stool away

and played standing at the organ, at the same time working the pedal and doing it all as if he had been practicing it for several months. Everyone was amazed. Indeed this is a fresh act of God's grace. . .which many a one only receives after much labor.

"Everyone was amazed" is the phrase repeated most often through all the letters. After more than 200 years, everyone is still amazed.

The Later Years

When Wolfgang was 26 he married a 19-year-old singer, Constanze Weber, and they had two sons, Karl Thomas Mozart, born when Wolfgang was 28, and Franz Xavier Mozart, born in 1791, the year of Wolfgang's death (this son later changed his name, in honor of his dead father, to Wolfgang Amadeus Mozart). Both sons followed in their family's musical tradition: Karl was a gifted pianist, and Franz/Wolfgang became a pianist, composer, and music conductor. So little "Woferl" lived long enough to leave the world a worthy human legacy as well as a magnificent musical one, having composed more than 600 works before death claimed him at the early age of 35.

There are two theories about why Mozart died so young. A medical hypothesis is that he lived so intensely, working so hard under so much stress from his constant worries about money, that his body simply gave out from exhaustion and he actually died of accelerated old age. The other theory is based on a rumor that he was poisoned by Antonio Salieri (1750–1825), a less talented but very ambitious musician who envied Mozart's effortless ability to produce great music and who coveted Mozart's prestigious, though nonpaying, position as royal chamber musician in the court of Emperor Joseph II of Austria; this seems unlikely, however, because Salieri's career was more financially successful than Mozart's.

Whatever it was that caused his death, it is a sad commentary on how the world treats many of its artists that he who had given so much to the world and whose gifts had been acknowledged with so many honors during his life was so penniless at the end of it that he had to be buried in an unidentified paupers' burial ground.

MUSICAL ORGANIZATIONS FOR CHILDREN

Vienna Boys' Choir
(Verein Wiener Sangerknaben)

This is a unique organization founded in 1496 by the Austrian Hapsburg Emperor Maximilian I. For five centuries it has proved how exquisitely young boys can sing. The boys are aged 8 to 14. Their concerts include music of earlier centuries, excerpts from operas and operettas, folk songs, hymns, and carols. The choir's two most famous members were Joseph Haydn (1732–1809) and Franz Schubert (1797–1828). In the late eighteenth and early nineteenth centuries the conductor of the choir was Antonio Salieri (1750–1825), teacher of Beethoven, Liszt, and Schubert and intriguer against Mozart at the Vienna court. He was the jealous villain of the popular but probably libelous play and movie *Amadeus*.

When the Austrian Empire was dissolved in 1918, the choir was left without financial support and was disbanded, but in 1924 it was reestablished by Joseph Schnitt, rector of the Court Chapel. To support themselves the choir began touring in 1926 and became world famous. Then, when Hitler reached Vienna the rector was arrested and the castle the boys lived in was seized. In 1945 after Hitler's defeat Schmitt returned, but no sooner had he begun to rebuild the organization than the Communists seized it as Nazi property.

In 1940 the Austrian government turned over to him the bomb-damaged Augarten Palace, which was the royal palace where Mozart, Liszt, and Wagner had performed for the nobility in the eighteenth and nineteenth centuries, and reorganization of the choir began again, along with more foreign tours.

Rector Schnitt died in 1955, but he had made arrangements establishing a nonprofit organization, the Verein Wiener Sangerknaben, to manage affairs after his death. There are now four choirs: three of them go on tour every year, so each boy is able to visit every country on the worldwide itinerary before his voice changes. Half a million people hear at least one concert from them every year, in drum-beating African jungles and sophisticated concert halls in New York and other major cities. They give only one formal concert each year in Vienna, to overflow audiences, but they also sing at the State Opera in *Carmen, The Magic Flute,* and other operas that call for children's voices, and at official city and state affairs and special religious services. At least two of the four choirs are always in Vienna at any one time, while two are on tour. The two in Vienna perform at the Hofberg Kappelle and at St. Stephen's Cathedral on alternate Sundays so that they can all be with their parents every other Sunday.

Each of the choirs has only 22 boys, and their average singing life is only about three years. Replacements occur when the voices of the choir boys change at age 13 or 14; the rate of change is about two per month. Officials hold auditions for eight-year-olds every year and standards are so high that few of the hundreds of young applicants are selected. Those who are chosen then take a two-year training course, which they must pass in order to be put on a reserve choir of 40 voices. Even then they are not full-fledged Sangerknaben. They still live at home.

When they finally are selected, their hard work really begins. They move to Augarten Palace and live with the 21 other members of their particular choir, eating, sleeping, practicing, and playing with them. They spend six months in school, with intensive individualized instruction, rising at 6:30 A.M. and going to bed at 9 P.M. and in between spending four-and-a-half hours on school work, two-and-a-half hours on vocal training and rehearsals, one hour on study of a musical instrument, and three hours of play. They are supervised by a 50-member staff. In the summer they take turns visiting their own resort in the Tyrolean Alps, where the organization operates a first-class hostelry for some 60 paying guests. The boys are then on vacation, with a less rigorous schedule, but they also give frequent informal concerts for the guests.

When Haydn was there, in his mid-teens his voice changed and he was thrown out with no provision for his livelihood. This was no doubt cruel, but less so than the ancient custom in some countries when young choir boys used to be castrated so that their voices would never change. This cannot happen today. Now, when a boy's voice changes he graduates to the *Mutanten* and can continue to live in a house set aside for these older boys until he finishes high school. If he then decides to go to the University of Vienna or the Music Academy, he can stay on. If his parents die while he is a member of the organization he is adopted by the administrative director and stays at the house until he is 21.

The rules are so strict and the work so demanding that it may seem surprising that so many boys want to be members of the Vienna Boys' Choir, and that parents are willing to let them leave home for so many years. However, for boys who love music and who want to see the outside world this provides a unique and free educational opportunity. Great prestige is attached to belonging to the choir. The fact that its work is demanding and that it is known for high standards is the very thing that makes it such an honor to belong and that makes

it appealing to boys who want to do something special with their lives. Also the packed schedule and close companionship with other boys their own age who share their interests give them two other advantages: they are never lonely and they have no time to be bored.

In 1962 Walt Disney made a beautiful full-length film in Austria about the Vienna Boys' Choir. It was called *Almost Angels*, and it cast a spell that made it seem as if that is exactly what these boys are.

The Boys' Choir of Harlem

In 1969 Dr. Walter J. Turnbull, a professional singer and public school music teacher, decided to found a boys' choir in Harlem, to provide ghetto children with the opportunity to build self-discipline and self-esteem through music. At first the idea was met with some skepticism, because many people thought that black kids, growing up in a culture in which rock and roll was the main musical taste of the younger generation, would not be interested, and would not have enough stick-to-it-iveness to keep at it. But Dr. Turnbull is a brilliant teacher who knew how to capture and hold their interest. His own enthusiasm is contagious, and he included pop music, jazz, and Negro spirituals along with classical music in their repertoire. He also included tap dancing and jitterbugging in their performances.

He gathered a group of 25 boys and combined their work in the choir with regular school work. From the beginning he insisted on discipline, good manners, good posture, and a dress code. If a boy did not behave himself and keep up with his regular studies, in addition to practicing music for two hours every day, he could not remain in the choir. This threat provided a sufficient incentive for them to obey him because they soon found being in the choir so much fun.

Dr. Turnbull is strict and demanding, but he treats the boys with respect, affection, and a sense of humor. He teaches them to set goals for themselves and to stick to them, explaining that to be able to sing a wide range of music requires discipline, and that this discipline is transferable to everything else they do. The boys enjoy the music and the well-deserved praises they receive when they perform, as well as the free travel on concert tours every summer. They realize it is an honor to be in the choir and they become proud of being able to live up to a high standard.

Since its shaky start the choir has been expanded and has grown into an internationally recognized organization. There are now two preparatory choirs, a concert choir, and a girls' choir, which was formed in response to pleas from sisters of members of the boys' choir. And every year approximately 2,000 youngsters audition, hoping to join one of the choirs.

In 1987 Dr. Turnbull established the Choir Academy of Harlem as an alternative preparatory school for fourth-graders through high school. The Academy has around 500 students who combine music with academics. It is part of New York City's regular public school system and, in contrast to the dismal record of so many inner city public schools, 98 percent of its students go on to college. As Dr. Turnbull explained to a reporter, "We're an institution that's dedicated to helping children be successful. It gives them a chance in life and it starts with how they feel about themselves. Music has the power to build their self-esteem."

During their annual summer vacations the choir goes on concert tours sponsored by Baldwin Piano, Pepsi Cola, and other companies. It has frequently appeared on television, in Broadway theaters, at Carnegie Hall, in Washington's Kennedy Center and other concert halls and auditoriums, and at World's Fairs both in the United States and abroad. In 1995 the choir released a record album, and a major motion picture deal was arranged for a Christmas movie in 1996.

The choir's high artistic standards, the quality of the boys' voices, and their demeanor have won unamimous praise. Their only problem is financial. It costs $1 million a year to run the choir, so Dr. Turnbull, in spite of his and the boys' enormous success, is always in need of more money and hoping for more corporate sponsors.

UNICEF/94-0876/Roger Lemoyne

11

Children and the Entertainment Arts

Amateur Performers

Imaginative, energetic children can have fun playing even when there are no toy shops, as long as they have legs and arms and loud voices. In the Middle Ages both children and adults loved to sing and dance and dress up, and all loves were combined when they put on masks and costumes and performed in plays and ballets. Theatrical productions became the most popular features of the most well-liked fairs and the seasonal holidays that brought good cheer throughout the year to children and adults alike.

The Morris dances, which were and still are frequently performed on the village greens in England in colorful costumes covered with little bells, were named for the Moors of southern Spain where they originated. These and other dances were a regular part of all holiday recreation, and gradually were combined with songs they called "caroles," and these in turn were combined with stories in "mummings," later called "mimes" or "pantomimes," that people enjoyed putting on, especially at Christmas and New Year's. This is one medieval custom that has survived into the twentieth century.

Before this century with its powerful cars and paved roads, traveling was so slow and uncomfortable that many people preferred to create entertainment at home instead of going out to theaters and concerts. Every girl of refinement learned to sing and play the piano, so children often put on recitals and pageants and plays both for their own enjoyment and for that of their families and neighbors.

Among those who enjoyed producing, painting scenery and performing in plays was young Thomas More (1478–1535). We know many stories about his life, including his earliest years, from his own letters and essays that have been preserved, memoirs by his many friends and the biography by his son-in-law William Roper. There is a description of a play he produced when he was a young boy, for which he painted a picture of a boy his age playing and gave him the following words:

> I am called Chyldhod; in play is all my mynde. . . myght I lade my lyfe alwayes
> in play, which lyfe God send me to myne endying day.

He did maintain a playful sense of humor to his "endying day," although in several letters to his own children, he told them that "play is the sauce only—not the meat—of lyfe."

Puppet Shows and Toy Theaters

Puppets and marionette shows were introduced to Europe in the thirteenth or fourteenth century when troops of Italian puppeteers traveled across the continent, generally accompanied by monkeys who delighted the audiences almost as much as the clever marionettes did. By 1703, a puppet show was a regular and popular feature of the annual Bartholomew Fair in England: the first one was an ambitious production about the Creation of the World, climaxed with a scene of the Flood, and the character of Punch was introduced dancing in Noah's Ark with his wife Judy.

Ever since then puppet shows, especially those featuring the rascally Punch and his long-suffering wife, have remained immensely popular with both young and old. Alexander Pope (1688–1744), Jonathan Swift (1667–1754), Henry Fielding (1707–1734), and Lord Byron (1788–1824) were among eminent writers who all wrote in praise of puppetry.

In his early years Punch associated with world-famous historical characters. He not only danced in Noah's Ark but also sat on the lap of the Queen of Sheba, gave advice to King Solomon, and socialized with many other kings and queens. But even when the show's theme was as dramatic as the story about Solomon offering to cut a baby in two in order to give half of it to each of the two women who claimed it, Punch's part in the play was always welcomed with much more enthusiasm than the rest. Swift wrote about one of the shows featuring Punch:

> Observe the audience in pain
> When Punch is hid behind the scene
> But when they hear his rusty voice
> With what impatience they rejoice
> And then they value not two straws
> How Solomon decides the cause,
> Which the true mother, which pretender.

So gradually puppeteers took the hint: Punch and Judy and their baby, who did not get cut in half but who took so much abuse that he might almost have wished he had been, ousted the other more serious characters and became a theatrical attraction on their own.

Of course many people thought that shows children watched should be more educational and edifying, and they complained about Punch and his violent treatment of Judy and the baby. However, Punch was a fellow who just could not be kept down, and he could not do educational harm because his outragious behavior was so exaggerated and hilarious that children could not possibly take him seriously.

Despite the fact that in the beginning Punch and other puppets were not specifically designed to entertain children, the children enjoyed them so much that they claimed them for their own. In Victorian England, the Punch and Judy theater came indoors and was sold as a toy large enough for small children to get inside to work the puppets themselves. Their popularity with children remains unabated in spite of other changing tastes over the years, and in England a Punch and Judy show is a feature of most children's birthday parties.

In the seventeenth century, peepshows, shadow pictures, and an assortment of inventions based on the magic lantern all joined together to become to children what TV is to their young descendants.

Toy theaters became extremely popular in both England and France, so much so that they ceased to be mere toys and became an art form. Their golden age was during Queen Victoria's reign. William Makepeace Thackeray (1811–1863), Charles Dickens (1812–1870) and Robert Louis Stevenson (1850–1894) all loved toy theaters when they were little, and the French poet Paul Valéry (1871–1945) made one for his children. Gilbert Keith Chesterton (1874–1936), who also had one when he was a little boy, wrote, "I will say positively that the toy theater is the best of all toys."

While lighter moments were provided for by casual homemade puppet shows, serious artistic productions were put on by ambitious parents and children in their toy theaters. William Blake (1757–1827) designed sets for them at one time, and later Sir Walter Scott (1771–1832) and Charles Dickens (1812–1870) wrote plays for them.

Though toy theaters are no longer such an important part of childhood, British publishers still produce designs and scripts for toy theaters with elaborate scenery and costumes that children can cut out, paste onto sticks, and thereby become theatrical producers in their own living rooms.

HARRIET BEECHER STOWE, LITTLE EVA, AND UNCLE TOM

Harriet Beecher Stowe (1811–1896) was the wife of a professor at Bowdoin College in Maine and mother of six children. One day she read a pamphlet by a runaway slave from Maryland, Josiah Henson, describing the degradation of a slave's life. It aroused her sympathy to such an extent that she poured forth her indignation in a long, eloquent, and passionate book. It was written on her kitchen table on saved scraps of brown wrapping paper while she took care of her children, including the newest baby who was deposited in a clothes basket at her feet, between doing the laundry and cooking meals; at the same time her husband worked on a scholarly book on the top floor of their house in order not to be disturbed.

Her book, called *Uncle Tom's Cabin, or Life among the Lowly*, was first published in 1851 as a serial in *National Era*, an antislavery magazine, and the following year it came out in book form. It was immediately popular, not only as a book but as a play.

This was a period when an American mother had to bear 13 children if she hoped to see six reach puberty. Diphtheria, pneumonia, scarlet fever, and other unchecked plagues carried off thousands of children every year, and others perished from accidents, drowning, lockjaw, scalding, and snakebite. There was hardly a home in America where death had not visited a child, and the scenes in this book depicting a sad mother whose child had died, and two lovely children, angelic little Eva who also died too young, and her lively slave friend, Topsy, were appealing and moving.

George Howard, a theatrical producer, decided to make a drama out of the book, bringing the fondness of Americans for their children and the anguish of infant mortality to the stage, enabling parents who repressed their grief at home to be able to express it vicariously in a darkened theater. He thought *Uncle Tom's Cabin* was a perfect vehicle to bring Americans into the theater in droves, as it indeed did.

The first "Tom show" opened in September 1852 and went on to nationwide fame. Howard's daughter, Cordelia, was so charming and such a genuinely talented actress that she and the play toured the nation for many years, and succeeded in breaking down the long-standing American prejudice against "Satan's Palace" as the theater was then described by pious Christians. Attending a performance of *Uncle Tom's Cabin* suddenly became an obligation of conscience for thousands of the devout who had previously viewed the proscenium arch as the gate of Hell. Entire congregations paid for the privilege of seeing on stage what was all too common at home, namely grown men brought to their knees in tears by the edifying death of an "angel child."

The emotions stirred up by the book and the play did much to convince people, including many who had not previously been particularly aware of or concerned about the issue, that slavery was inexcusably immoral and vicious, thus polarizing opinion on the subject between North and South and contributing to the outbreak of the American Civil

War. In 1862, when Mrs. Stowe visited President Lincoln at the White House, he greeted her by saying, "So this is the little lady who wrote the book that started the big war!" She claimed she had not written it, saying, "God wrote it. I merely did his dictation."

Despite its enormous popularity and great historical importance in helping to end slavery, this book is rarely read today and has been removed from many school libraries. People who have not read it do not realize that its saintly hero was a very brave and intelligent black man who struggled against cruel slave owners and helped to protect other slaves from unjust punishments, saving lives and helping some to escape. It seems almost inexplicable that calling someone an "Uncle Tom" is nowadays considered an insult instead of a compliment.

CHILD STARS

The following lists of famous children who have lit up the silver screen and the stage are very long, yet they are woefully incomplete. Like the stars in the sky, there are too many to count. As a species, children seem to be born performers, unselfconscious about expressing emotions freely, quick to break into giggles or tears, responsive to the people around them, and used to accepting directions. Acting is, after all, a form of play and "pretend," and almost all children are spontaneously good at that.

Some children have known only a few minutes of fame. They did not go on to become professional actors in adult life, which is not to say that they are all has-beens by age 12. It is true that a sad number of them have found life a terrible letdown after their years in the limelight, and have taken to drugs, and even to crime, by not being able to adjust. But more of them have gone on to successful lives in other fields, such as one of the earliest child stars in silent films who grew up to have a spectacular career as a writer, editor, playwright, politician, and diplomat: Clare Booth Luce (1902–1987).

Vaudeville and the Golden Age of Child Stars

For approximately a century, from the 1830s to the 1940s, a cult of childhood made some children into their families' breadwinners, and even millionaires, before they had reached school age. The myth of childhood innocence was the basis of many plays and movies, both comedies and tragedies, and the real lives of these child stars had both comic and tragic aspects as they were catapulted into unbelievable fame and adored by a vast public.

Traveling Performers

Like "Little Tommy Tucker" who "sang for his supper," some children's careers often resulted from their extreme poverty. Destitute mothers, deserted or widowed, discovered that their cute and talented children could help them pay the rent. There were traveling companies of families who performed in saloons and town halls, on showboats and in mining camps. The "wild west" was an overwhelmingly male society made up of lonesome frontiersmen, loggers, gold diggers, coal miners, and cowboys starved for entertainment and loaded with cash, and they eagerly threw money onto the stage, the piano, or the bar where the children performed.

Gradually towns grew up and vaudeville houses were built, and for many years these provided America's favorite entertainment. Many of the children worked a punishing schedule, giving three shows a day on weekdays, four on Saturdays, and five on Sundays and holidays, spending their lives on the road and in hotels, trains, and basement dressing rooms.

"The Human Mop," Buster Keaton

Buster Keaton, real name Joseph Frank Keaton (1895–1966), the great comic actor who caused audiences to collapse helplessly in laughter as he endured woes with a bland deadpan expression, had a most unusual childhood. His acting career began when he was only two years old, and he had only one day of school in his life, when he was six.

Long before he was born his parents were performers in a vaudeville act with the famous magician Harry Houdini (1874–1926), who gave Buster his nickname. He was born in Pickway, Kansas, while his parents were touring; later the town was destroyed by a cyclone and in his autobiography he deplored "the humiliation of having my birthplace blown off the map."

"Having no baby sitter," he once said, "my mother parked me in the till of a wardrobe trunk while she worked on the stage with Pop. According to him, the moment I could crawl I headed for the footlights." His father added, "When Buster learned to walk there was no holding him. He would jump up and down in the wings, make plenty of noise, and get in everyone's way. It seemed easier to let him come out with us on the stage where we could keep an eye on him."

He was soon featured in *The Three Keatons* as "The Human Mop." This, he said, was when he first developed his famous deadpan, because he discovered that his audience laughed harder if he did not laugh. Even in their early days their act got a reputation as the roughest one in vaudeville. Buster's father carried him out on the stage and dropped him on the floor, and then started wiping the floor with him. He threw him through scenery, out into the wings, and dropped him down on the bass drum in the orchestra pit. "The people out in front were amazed because I did not cry," recalled Buster. "There was nothing mysterious about this. I didn't cry because I wasn't hurt. All little boys like to be roughhoused by their fathers. They are also natural tumblers and acrobats."

But the New York Society for the Prevention of Cruelty to Children was not amused. In Keaton's autobiography, *My Wonder World of Slapstick,* he told what happened. "It started its campaign the day I made my debut at five at Tony Pastor's Theater. The New York law then barred child actors under seven years old." At five he had become the featured performer of the Keatons' act and, as his father complained:

> There were dozens of other popular family acts in vaudeville at the turn of the century. But reformers in New York, Massachuetts and Illinois, among other states, were tireless in their efforts to stop us all from going to hell via the stage. I guess they meant well, but like so many other sincere do-gooders they were a pain in the neck, particularly to those they were attempting to rescue. I doubt that any kid actor had more attempts made to save him than did our little Buster. The reason, of course, was our slam bang act.

Phony affidavits about age could get around the law, but Buster's father was accused of mistreating him. The mayor of New York, R. A. Van Wyck, ordered Buster to his office where he undressed him, so that he could personally examine him for bruises; but when he saw there were none, he had the charges dismissed.

During the next summer the Society for the Prevention of Cruelty to Children again tried to prevent Buster from performing this time in Coney Island. Seth Low, a reform mayor who had succeeded Tammany's Van Wyck, took up the cause and again Buster was stripped of his clothes and examined by a mayor, and later, as well, by a New York governor. But the family finally licked complaints on the grounds that the law barred children from performing on high or low wires, trapezes, or bicycles, but "there was not one word that made it illegal for my father to display me on stage as a human mop or to kick me in the face."

Keaton added:

> What most burned up Pop was that there were then thousands of homeless and hungry abandoned children of my age wandering around the streets of New York, selling newspapers, shining shoes, playing the fiddle on the Hudson River ferryboats, and thousands of other small children working with their parents in tenement sweatshops on the Lower East Side. Pop couldn't understand why the SPCC people didn't devote all of their time, energy, money to helping them.

In any case, Buster Keaton had no complaints. He said in his autobiography, "My parents were my first bit of great luck. I cannot recall one argument during the years I was growing up."

He began making movies in 1917 when he was 22, producing, directing, writing, and starring in them. He made 115 films in all, most of them silents that are today cherished as classics. Bosley Crowther, when he was film critic for *The New York Times*, called Keaton "the greatest of the great comedians. . .the most subtle and suggestive satirist—the keenest comic ridiculer of our social system and our mechanical age."

CHILDREN IN THE MOVIES

By 1920 most theaters had begun to run movies, and in 1933 when talking films arrived, vaudeville died. The cult of the child continued to thrive for a while, though, in motion pictures. This was due to several factors: the high death rate of children, which made people cherish children with extra fervor and pathos; the enormous influence of Charles Dickens with his touching tales of childhood suffering, which aroused people's passionate sympathies; and the loneliness of those men in the West who lived for so many years without families and therefore longed for and idealized children. And then in the 1920s and 1930s there was the Great Depression, when people needed cheering up. President Franklin D. Roosevelt once called Shirley Temple a valuable national asset and morale booster in those hard times, saying, "It is a splendid thing that for just 15 cents [sic!] an American can go to a movie and look at the smiling face of a baby and forget his troubles."

World War II, however, proved to be a global trauma that dramatically changed the tastes of the movie-going public. Sentimentalists turned into hardened realists, and the saccharine waifs of Hollywood films lost their appeal when compared to the real victims of war: children maimed, burned, abandoned, orphaned, starved, or killed. Margaret O'Brien was one child actress who managed to bridge the gap, movingly portraying a war orphan in *Journey for Margaret* in 1942. Other young stars such as Patty Duke, Hayley

Mills, and Tatum O'Neal came along later, scoring individual acting triumphs, but attitudes toward children had changed and the great era of child stars drew to its close.

While the child movie star craze was at its height, between 1935 and 1945, an estimated 100 children arrived in Hollywood every 15 minutes, looking for jobs, even though the ratio of children who, in a whole year, earned as much as one week's expenses from movie work was reckoned at less than one in 15,000. Probably half of those who arrived gave up after a few weeks and the majority after a year, but a hard core of unusually determined or lucky mothers and children remained. The gossip columnist Hedda Hopper once said, "I used to wonder if there wasn't a special sub-human species of womankind that bred children for the sole purpose of dragging them to Hollywood."

Though the lives of those children who did achieve stardom seemed glamorous to their adoring public, they were actually child laborers working to support their families, with more obligations than privileges, "doing the chores" like many other children. Sometimes their parents or so-called guardians even cheated them out of their earnings.

Famous Names in the Child Star Era

Here is a list of some of the most famous children who were propelled into fame during the child star era (the 1830s to the 1940s), both those on the stage and in movies:

Freddie Bartholomew (1924–1992): This child actor born in London, England, made his stage debut there at age three. When he was 10 his "Aunt Cissie" took him to Hollywood and he won the juvenile half of the title role in the movie *David Copperfield*. This was followed by starring roles in film versions of other classic children's books, *Little Lord Fauntleroy* at age 12 and *Captains Courageous*, a superb film in which he costarred with Spencer Tracy and Mickey Rooney, at 13. Freddie's years in Hollywood, despite his enormous success as an actor, were not very happy. He was not allowed to have any playmates for fear he would lose his British accent and, although he earned $1 million in five years, most of the money was lost in lawsuits between his parents and his Aunt Cissie. He left Hollywood when World War II broke out, returning to England, and later he became an advertising executive.

William Henry West Betty, known as **"Little Betty"** (1791–1874): This English actor made his debut in London at age 11 and was such a success that the military had to be called to restore order among the huge crowds. When he was 14 the House of Commons adjourned to witness his Hamlet. He made an enormous fortune before retiring at age 33.

Charlie Chaplin, full name **Charles Spencer Chaplin** (1889–1977): This renowned actor and film producer, born in London, England, made his first stage appearance at age seven as one of eight "Lancashire Lads" touring in vaudeville. His second, at age nine, was a clog-dancing act in the children's pantomime *Babes in the Woods* at the London Hippodrome. At age 10 he played a cat in another children's pantomime, *Cinderella*. And at 14 he got his first parts in regular stage productions as a street Arab in *Jim, a Romance of Cockayne* and as Billy the page boy in the William Gillette production of *Sherlock Holmes*. He got good reviews but did not win worldwide fame until he left England for the United States in 1913, at age 24, when he began his spectacular career as a movie comedian, writer, director, and producer. (See page 413.)

Jackie Coogan (1914–1984): Jackie was born in Los Angeles, California, where both of his parents were actors. He made his own stage debut at age three, in an act with his father. In

1921, at age six, he costarred with Charlie Chaplin in *The Kid* and was an overnight sensation (see page 414). No other child star had ever received such immediate attention and adulation. He made a dozen other films later, including *Oliver Twist, Tom Sawyer, Huckleberry Finn,* and *Peck's Bad Boy,* all before the age of 16, and became one of the youngest people ever to earn $4 million. In World War II he became a glider pilot; after the war he continued to act, but never again to the old acclaim.

Jackie Cooper (1922–): Born in Los Angeles, this Jackie made his movie debut when three years old. At seven he joined the *Our Gang* company. In 1930, when he was eight, he starred in *Skippy*, based on a popular comic strip, and a year later costarred with Wallace Beery in *The Champ*. At 12 he starred in *Treasure Island*. During World War II he served in the Navy and then returned to Hollywood, going on to adult roles and also working as a director and producer.

Carlotta Crabtree, also known as **"Little Lotta"** (1847–1924): Carlotta was born in New York City and in 1852 when she was five she became the rival and East Coast counterpart of "Little Cordelia" (see page 410), playing Little Eva on the stage in *Uncle Tom's Cabin*. She was only six when she began singing and dancing gracefully and moved out West where she again rivaled Cordelia, enchanting audiences, especially in San Francisco. She was called "The California Diamond" and "The Pet of the Miners." In 1867, at age 20, she played Little Nell in a stage version of Charles Dickens's *Old Curiosity Shop*. By age 17 she was almost as rich as she was popular. She went on to play Little Nell in New York and London and elsewhere for 25 years. On her forty-fifth birthday she retired, the most popular and wealthiest actress in America at the time.

Sammy Davis, Jr. (1925–1990): Davis's parents were dancers in vaudeville, and he spent his first birthday in a crib in the dressing room of the New York City Hippodrome. At two he was already a talented mimic, a gift he never lost. One sideline of his entertainment career was that he could sing in almost anybody's voice and style, as he demonstrated on many phonograph records. At four he joined his parents' act, and at five he appeared in two movies. In the years after that, in spite of the handicap of losing one eye, he became a much loved personality, as well as a gifted actor, singer, dancer, and comic on stage, TV, and in films and nightclubs.

Deanna Durbin, real name **Edna Mae Durbin** (1922–): Deanna made her debut as a singer on the Eddie Cantor radio program and then, because her face was as pretty as her voice, was snapped up for the movies. She won an honorary Oscar in 1938, at age 16, and earned $2 million in 10 years, retiring at 27. Later, commenting on her career in an interview, she said,

> My fans sat in the dark, anonymous and obscure, while I was projected bigger than life on the screen. . . .How can a young unformed girl fight this publicized image of herself while still groping for her own personality? I represented an idealized daughter to millions of frustrated fathers and mothers. They could, with their tickets, purchase twice a year new stocks of sweetness and innocence.

Edith Fellows, known as **"Little Edith"** (1923–): Edith's mother deserted her when she was two and she was raised by her grandmother in Atlanta, Georgia. She took up dancing to cure pigeon toes. At four she starred in a stage production as a singer and ballet and tap dancer. She made her Hollywood movie debut at five, and became one of the regular players in the *Our Gang* series, until she retired from the group at age 10.

W. C. Fields, real name **William Claude Dunkinfield** (1880–1946): Comedian, juggler, film writer, and producer born in Philadelphia, Pennsylvania. Fields had an unhappy childhood, with only four years of school. At age nine he sneaked past the ticket taker at a local vaudeville house and became entranced watching a juggling act. He resolved then and there to become a great juggler and practiced on the fruits and vegetables he and his father sold for a living, thereby ruining many and often getting beaten. At 11, after a bitter fight with his father, he ran away from home and for the next few years lived in poverty and hunger, stealing and going to jail between getting a few low-paying jobs. One job was delivering ice daily at 3 A.M. for $3 a week. One job was as an elephant water boy in a circus. Finally, at 15 he got a job as a juggler in an amusement park, and by 19 he was a success, billed as "The Distinguished Comedian." In his first stage role, as *The Tramp Juggler*, Fields was so skillful that he juggled 25 cigar boxes balanced end on end with a rubber ball on top. By age 23 he was touring Europe as an international star, getting top billing at the Folies Bergères. From the Ziegfeld Follies of 1915 he went on to other musicals, and then to movies, writing and starring in many unforgettable comedies.

Eddie Foy, real name **Edward Fitzgerald** (1856–1928): Born in New Rochelle, New York, Eddie was only six when his father died, and he began singing, dancing, and doing acrobatics in saloons in New York City to help support his impoverished family. Later he was a mimic, pantomimist, eccentric dancer, and clown in pubs, circuses, and minstrel shows all over the United States. He married four times; his wives died; he was never divorced. His third wife, Madeline, had 11 children, four of whom died, but the survivors ranging from two years old on up became famous along with their dad in an enormously popular vaudeville act as *Eddie Foy and the Seven Little Foys*. For more than a decade the family sang, danced, and made people laugh in what one critic called "a humanitarian effort to bring more cheer into the world." After Eddie's death, a delightful movie was made about the Foys.

Judy Garland, real name **Frances Gumm**, also known as **"Baby Frances"** (1922–1969): Born in Grand Rapids, Minnesota, Judy started in a vaudeville song and dance act at age two, with her two sisters Jane and Virginia. When she was four her family moved to Hollywood, where she studied singing and dancing, and she became world famous after being chosen to appear in the perennially favorite film, *The Wizard of Oz*. Other enormously popular films that she made while still a child were the *Andy Hardy* series with Mickey Rooney and *Meet Me in St. Louis*. Her career continued with concert tours and recordings after she became an adult, and some of her films are still shown every year on TV.

Lillian Gish, also known as **"Baby Lillian"** (1893–1993): Born in Springfield, Ohio, Lillian made her stage debut at the age of three. She, her sister Dorothy Gish (1898–1968), and their mother, who had been deserted by her husband, moved to New York where they shared an apartment with the Smiths, whose daughter Gladys later became the legendary star Mary Pickford. Lillian and Dorothy were child models until 1909 when they got movie roles with D. W. Griffith. They went to Hollywood in 1914 when Lillian was 15 and Dorothy was 13, where they played many leading roles in silent and talking movies, as well as on the stage. At first they often performed together, but gradually Lillian's career eclipsed Dorothy's. Lillian made 105 films, never ceasing to be a magical star for more than 90 years. She received an honorary Oscar in 1971 and the American Film Institute's Life Achievement Award in 1983.

Joseph Grimaldi (1778–1837): English comic actor, pantomimist, and clown. Regarded as the greatest of all clowns, he got an early start. His first role was as a baby clown with his family in 1781, at age two. In later life, his white-faced character "Joey" strongly influenced the whole development of the circus clown.

June Havoc, real name **June Havich**, also known as **"Baby June," "The Pocketsize Pavlova,"** and **"Dainty June"** (1926–): June made her vaudeville debut at age two, featured in an act with her older sister, striptease performer Gypsy Rose Lee. She left her family to marry at 13, and as an adult she became an excellent serious actress and author.

Helen Hayes, real name **Helen Hayes Brown** (1900–1993): Often called "The First Lady of the American Theater," Helen was the only actress ever to have won Oscar, Emmy, Tony, and Grammy awards. Born in Washington, D.C., she made her professional stage debut at age five in a stock company. Her Broadway debut was at age nine in *Old Dutch*. After a successful career as a child star, pushed by a possessive and ambitious "stage mother," she made a graceful transition to ingenue roles. She left her mother when she married playwright Charles MacArthur, whom she met at a party when he strolled over to her and poured some peanuts into her lap, saying "I wish these were diamonds." She moved on to adult leading roles, her most memorable being the part of Queen Victoria in which she managed to age from a teenager to an old woman as successfully as she later did in her own life. After she was too old to play heroines, she became outstanding in cameo roles and character parts on both stage and screen and was an active sponsor and generous supporter of charities.

Cordelia Howard, also known as **"Little Cordelia"** (1848–1941): She was the first of the really big little stars, making her debut at age four in 1852, in the role of Little Dick, an inmate of the workhouse in a stage adaptation of Charles Dickens's *Oliver Twist.* She was instantly acclaimed. Her father promptly wrote and produced a stage version of *Uncle Tom's Cabin* (see 403), starring her as Little Eva, in September 1852, and she went on to national fame as she toured in the production year after year after year. As she aged she continued to appear in the play, graduating from the role of Little Eva to those of older characters. This was the only play she performed in, but neither she nor the play lost their popularity during her lifetime and she lived to be 91.

Elsie Janis, real name **Elsie Janet Bierbauer,** also known as **"Little Elsie"** (1889-1956): This American actress began her career at age four in the role of Little Willie in a road show production of the melodrama, *East Lynne*. From age 9 to 14 she performed as Little Elsie in vaudeville. Then she changed her name to Elsie Janis and had a long career as an international musical comedy star. During World War I "Elsie Janis and Her Gang" was presented and she was much admired for performing in a show written by her at the front for the allied troops.

Buster Keaton, also known as **"The Human Mop"** (See page 405.)

"Baby Le Roy," real name and age unknown: This child was a costar with W. C. Fields while still in a baby carriage. This cute baby was a natural foil for child-hater Fields, maintaining an angelic look of childish innocence as he swatted Fields over the head with a milk bottle or a sledgehammer. There was only one problem. The producers wanted to have a baby boy in the part, so they gave the infant a boy's name, and audiences were quite upset when they learned that Le Roy was really a baby girl. They were unforgiving about the deception and his/her career was over before she was two years old.

Margaret Montgomery, known as **"Baby Peggy"** (1918–): Her Hollywood film debut was made at the age of 20 months, in a two-reel comedy filmed in five days called *Playmates* in which she costarred with Brownie, a dog. She was such a hit that she was immediately signed to a seven-year contract. When she was four, her salary was raised to a then-unheard-of $10,000 a week. She made four Baby Peggy comedy films and at five starred in *Captain January* and *Helen's Babies*. Her fifth birthday was celebrated with much aplomb during a nationwide tour, and a New York newspaper reporter noted that "her mother holds a contract by which the baby makes as much in the next five years as all the presidents since Lincoln have drawn from the Treasury of the United States." In 1924, at age six, Baby Peggy was the official mascot at the Democratic National Convention. From ages seven to 10 she toured in vaudeville, invariably to sold-out houses. Yet at 10 she was unemployed and unemployable. In 1979, many years after she had left Hollywood, married, and become a mother living in Mexico, she wrote a delightful book about the child star era called *Hollywood's Children*.

Margaret O'Brien, real name **Angela Maxine O'Brien** (1937–): Born in San Diego, California, Margaret made her screen debut when she was four, in the movie *Babes on Broadway*. At age five she starred as a war orphan in the title role of *Journey for Margaret*, and at age seven she was in the 1944 version of Oscar Wilde's witty story, *The Canterville Ghost*, with Charles Laughton (1899–1962) as the ghost. That same year she was awarded a special Oscar as the outstanding child actress of the 1940s.

Our Gang, also known as **"The Little Rascals"**: In the 1920s, 1930s, and 1940s this series of motion picture comedies produced by Hal Roach was a favorite feature in movie theaters every Saturday afternoon. More than 175 children played feature roles in the series, chosen out of 140,000 applicants from all over the United States. Among the rejects, surprisingly, were Mickey Rooney and Shirley Temple. These films were not only surefire attractions in movie houses but also in merchandising of breakfast cereals, school lunch boxes, coloring books, shoes, caps, roller skates, chewing gum, and so forth. The Rascals were resurrected in the 1990s as a regular series on television.

Anna Pavlova (1882–1931): Russian ballerina. Anna entered the Imperial Ballet School in St. Petersburg when she was nine and rapidly became the most famous and most exquisite ballet dancer in the world in her era. In her twenties she toured Europe and the United States with her unique dance creations, the best known of which were "The Butterflies" (*Papillons*), "Autumn Bacchanal" and above all "The Death of the Swan" (*Le Cygne*), a ballet composed especially for her by Michel Fokine. Even though it was over 70 years ago, no one who was lucky enough to see her dying swan would ever be able to forget how exquisite it was.

Mary Pickford, real name **Gladys Smith**, also known as **"Baby Gladys"** (1893–1979): Born in Toronto, Canada, Gladys and her mother soon moved to New York, where she made her vaudeville debut at age five in a one-act play called *The Littlest Girl*. Her Broadway debut was at age nine, when she took over the part of another child actress, her friend Lillian Gish, who was ill, in *The Little Red School House*. For this performance the

411

producer changed her name to Mary Pickford and on opening night he rewarded her for her fine performance by giving her a doll, the first one she had ever had. She first achieved fame in the theater as Little Eva in *Uncle Tom's Cabin*. Movies were just beginning then, and she made her first ones in New York, starting at age 13. She worked for the director David Griffith (1875–1948), who was so impressed by her natural charm, expressive face, and acting skills that he persuaded her mother to move with her to California where he was opening a new movie studio.

Mary made her Hollywood film debut at 17, but she kept her age a secret because she was still playing child roles. Among films in which she played were *Little Annie Rooney, Little Lord Fauntleroy, Rebecca of Sunnybrook Farm,* and *Pollyanna*. To maintain the illusion of the child characters she played year after year, her sets were built a little out of scale, with chairs, tables, windows, and doors all a trifle larger than life so that she seemed smaller and younger than she was. This ploy worked and she became the best loved of all silent film stars; she was known as "America's Sweetheart." In later years she became a successful film producer and continued to star in films for most of her 84 years.

Mickey Rooney, real name **Joe Yule, Jr.** (1920–): He was nicknamed "Sonny" until the movie moguls changed his name to **Mickey McGuire,** the name of a cartoon character he portrayed in several films, and later to Mickey Rooney. His parents were in vaudeville; he spent his first year sleeping in a wardrobe trunk and was on the stage by age two. When he was four his mother took him to Hollywood, and at five he got a role as a child character actor in *The Us Bunch*, a rival to the *Our Gang* comedies. His first movie role as Mickey Rooney was that of a midget in a film called *Orchids and Ermine*, made when he was five. He starred in 14 *Andy Hardy* films. At 15 he was in *Ah, Wilderness!* and starred in *The Adventures of Huckleberry Finn*. At 17 he costarred with Freddie Bartholomew and Spencer Tracy in *Captains Courageous*. At 18 he starred with Spencer Tracy in *Boys' Town* and played the title role in *Tom Sawyer*.

But his adult life became difficult. He had earned $12 million during his childhood but went bankrupt in 1966. He married seven times and had six children; one of his wives was murdered. His comment on his life, in his autobiography, was:

> I was a child actor making money before I went to school. . . .Then I was in my teens. That's supposed to finish the child actor. . . .Jackie Coogan and the rest went downhill after puberty. But not me. . . .I became bigger than I'd ever been and the money came faster than 10 children could spend it. Finally I was a man. . . .I could vote. I could marry. But in manhood, in my immature manhood, I made my childish mistakes. It was almost as if, never having been a child, I turned childish as a man.

However, with his buoyant, scrappy personality Mickey always bounced back. In 1979 he received an honorary Oscar for Lifetime Achievement in Films, and in the 1980s his career took off again with a highly praised performance starring in a hit Broadway musical.

Gloria Swanson, real name **Gloria May Josephine Swensson** (1899–1983): Movie star born in Chicago, Illinois. In elementary school Gloria appeared in school plays and looked forward to being a singer. Her formal education ended with her first year in high school when, at age 14, she was given parts in two films, *Elvira Farina* and *The Meal Ticket*. Six months later, changing her name to Gloria Swanson, she went to California, and immediately got leading roles in slapstick comedies produced by Keystone. She soon graduated from these and played glamorous leading ladies under the direction of Cecil B. DeMille, becoming one of the biggest box office attractions in silent films. Among her firsts, she was the first famous Hollywood actress to have a child, to adopt a baby, to become a grandmother, and to make a picture in France and a talking picture in England. She was the first Hollywood celebrity to have her own television show (in 1948). She was also the only silent film star to dare to come out of retirement and make a talking film that spoofed herself as a faded egocentric star, in *Sunset Boulevard*. She became a successful business woman and maintained her health and vitality for 90 years, spending her last decades married happily to a much younger man and writing articles and books about nutrition, as well as an entertaining and candid autobiography.

Elizabeth Taylor (1932–): Born in London, England, Elizabeth made her first public appearance at age three, in a Royal Command Performance dancing with her ballet class before King George V and Queen Mary in 1935. Her first movie, made in 1940 was *Man or Mouse*. At 10 she was in *There's One Born Every Minute*. At 11 she starred in *Lassie Come Home*, at 13 in *National Velvet*, and at 17 in *Father of the Bride*. Nobody who saw her in *National Velvet* could ever forget how amazingly beautiful she was. She was one of the few actresses to make a painless transition from sweet child star to charming ingenue to dramatic adult roles, and, as everyone knows, she never retired, in spite of having to leave the screen temporarily from time to time because of frequent illnesses and some scandals and tragedies in her personal life. Her perseverence has been as outstanding as her beauty.

Shirley Temple, full name **Shirley Jane Temple** (See page 415.)

Jane Withers (1927–): Born in Atlanta, Georgia, Jane headed her own radio program in Atlanta at age four, billed as "Dixie's Dainty Dewdrop." When she was 15 she went to Hollywood, and her first movie, *Handle with Care* was made in 1932. In 12 years she made 47 movies, almost always in humorous parts where she was the sassy girl. She has continued to act occasionally in TV commercials and movies.

Natalie Wood, real name **Natasha Gurdin** (1938–1981): Movie actress born in San Francisco. Natalie's first role was in *Happy Land* at age five. At eight she had her first featured role, in *Tomorrow Is Forever*, with Claudette Colbert and Orson Welles. The perennially beloved film, *Miracle on 34th Street*, was made when she was nine. This added to her fame and she became a top star, managing gracefully the transition from cute child to popular leading lady until her sudden, tragic death by drowning in 1981.

The Little Tramp and the Kid
Charlie Chaplin (1889–1977)

Chaplin's lovable character of the homeless tramp, who always bounced back optimistically in spite of constant bad luck and rejection, was an extension of his own personality and poverty as a child. The childhood of Charlie and his brother Sydney was worthy of a novel by Dickens. Their parents were talented and attractive music hall singers, but the father was irresponsible, deserting his family, getting arrested for nonsupport, and dying of alcoholism when Charlie was 12. And their mother, whom Charlie adored, also began making frequent and frightening disappearances into mental hospitals when he was only six years old. Later she was hospitalized permanently. Even so, Charlie said later that she was "one of the greatest pantomime artists I have ever seen. . .the most splendid woman I ever knew. . . .If I have amounted to anything, it is because of her."

For years the two boys were shunted off to workhouses and orphanages, and "there was never enough to eat in the orphanage, never enough to wear," he said. "The children were always cold and hungry. There were floggings, deprivations, and solitary confinements."

When Charlie was not in an institution he was out on the streets. "As a child I made little boats out of newspaper and sold them on the streets so as not to die of hunger." He also used to sing and do a clog dance on the street, passing the hat to onlookers, and he ran errands, and lathered customers' faces in a barbershop. Yet "even when I was in the orphanage and when I was roaming the streets trying to find enough to eat to keep alive, even then I thought of myself as the greatest actor in the world! I had to feel that exuberance that comes from utter confidence in yourself. Without it you go down to defeat."

It was appropriate that Charlie's first acting role on the London stage, other than short parts in children's pantomimes, was that of a street urchin in *Jim, A Romance of Cockayne*, when he was 14. But it was not until 12 years later, in 1915, that he developed the character of the tramp with whom he became permanently identified, in a short film comedy called *The Tramp*. That was the first time he made his classic exit waddling away sadly up a country road, the picture of dejection, and then suddenly shaking himself, giving his cane a twirl and perking up into a jaunty step as the film ends.

The craze for the Little Tramp, *Charlot* as he was fondly called in France, swept the world, with Chaplin dolls, toys, books, and songs. Children everywhere bought derbies, canes, and false mustaches, and tried to imitate his inimitable walk. Once, in New York, he was amused, as he told a friend, when he saw some youngsters pretending to be him, and he stopped and said to them, "I'll show you how to do that." He did and they scornfully said, "You don't do it right."

In 1919, long after he had surmounted his childhood poverty and become a famous and wealthy movie star, he faced another tragedy. His firstborn son died when only three days old, and Chaplin was shattered. While still reeling from the emotional shock he decided to make a movie about an abandoned infant, called *The Waif*. It was later to become renowned when renamed *The Kid*.

Jackie Coogan (1914–1984)

Ten days after the death of his infant son, Charlie Chaplin went to the theater and saw an act by Jack Coogan, an eccentric dancer, who brought his four-year-old son out at the end of the act to give an impersonation of his dancing. Jackie Jr. was a brilliant mimic, and Chaplin was enchanted. He went backstage to ask the boy what he did, and the four-year-old solemnly replied, "I am a prestidigitator who works in the world of legerdemain." Chaplin was totally smitten, saying Jackie was "the most amazing person I ever met in my life."

He promptly hired him to play the part of the waif. Between Chaplin's touching script and his portayal of the Tramp who befriends the Kid, and Jackie's performance as the Kid, they made one of the world's most memorable movies. David Robinson, in his biography of Chaplin, wrote that "no child actor, whether in silent or in sound pictures, has ever surpassed Jackie Coogan's performance as The Kid, in its truthfulness and range of sentiment."

The film opened in New York in January l92l to an instant and huge success and within three years it had been distributed in more than 50 countries. It made little Jackie into a world figure, partly as a symbol of all orphans of the recent war. In l924 he undertook a World Crusade in aid of Near East Relief, which raised more than $1 million worth of food and clothing. He was decorated by the Pope and adulated by the public and by heads of state.

Jackie made a few more movies, of which a notable one was *Oliver Twist*, but when the Kid ceased to be a kid his movie career also ceased. As a Hollywood commentator said, "Senility hit him at l3."

Disaster struck him again when his father died in a car crash five months before Jackie's twenty-first birthday. Jackie had earned $4 million as a child actor, which he expected to have access to when he became 2l, but all of his father's estate went to his mother, and she said there was almost no money left.

Postscript

Shortly after Jackie's father's death, his mother married Jackie's business manager. They denied the existence of any trust fund and asserted the legal right of parents to all money earned by their children while they were minors. In l938 an embittered Jackie sued his mother and stepfather. The only happy outcome of the case, which was too late to help him, was that it led to the passage of the *Child Actors Bill* in l939, ever since known as the *Coogan Act*, which provides that the guardian of a child artist must set aside half of the child's earnings for a trust fund or an equivalent form of savings for the child's benefit.

During World War II Jackie became a glider pilot, and he must have been the envy of every other service man when he married Betty Grable, America's glamorous "pin up girl" whose photo brightened almost every soldier's locker and whose legs were insured for $1 million by Lloyd's of London. But the marriage soon ended as did Jackie's several other brief marriages. He continued to live in Hollywood and appeared in a few more pictures, but never again to the acclaim he had previously known.

Chaplin's film career as the Tramp, on the other hand, went on from triumph to triumph, in wonderful movies like *The Gold Rush, City Lights, Modern Times*, and *The Great Dictator*. There were a few years when he was vilified as pro-Communist and he was persona non grata in the United States, so he finally retired from the movies and moved to Switzerland. But the Motion Picture Academy greeted him with a tumultuous welcome and a special Lifetime Achievement Award when he paid a visit back to the United States near the end of his life. And during his last years, despite having had as sad a marital history as Jackie had, he found personal happiness. At 54 he married his fourth wife, 18-year-old Oona O'Neill, against the strenuous objections of her father, playwright Eugene O'Neill, who disowned her for going ahead with the wedding. Against the odds they had a happy marriage that lasted more than 30 years and produced l0 children, in addition to his three from previous marriages.

Shirley Temple, the Greatest of All Child Stars

Born in 1928, Shirley Temple made her film debut at age four in a two-reel film, *Glad Rags to Riches,* in l932. The audience response was so terrific that she was immediately signed up to make other films. At age five her full-length movie *Stand Up and Cheer* made her a major star. It was followed by *Little Miss Marker* and five other enormously popular films. She did not yet know how to read, so each evening her mother would read the next day's script to her and by the next day she knew not only her own lines but those of everyone else in the scene. Her IQ was tested when she was five and it was 155—20 points above genius level. This added fuel to a rumor that even the Pope asked about: Since she was such a mature performer, not only as an actress but as an accomplished singer and dancer, was she actually a midget pretending to be a child?

In 1934, at age six, she made 10 films and was receiving 4,000 fan letters a week. On her birthday, April 23, she received from fans an enormous number of birthday presents which she wasn't allowed to keep; they were sent to an orphanage. And that year she became the youngest person ever to win an Oscar. Her salary was raised from $150 a week to $1,000 a week, with her mother getting $250 a week as her advisor. Each year her salary kept getting raised, until by the age of 10 she had become the world's youngest millionaire.

All through the 1930s Shirley was the number one box-office attraction in movies, making five or six pictures a year, every one a huge hit. Major adult movie stars were delighted to appear in her films. In one film, the great tap dancer Bill "Bojangles" Robinson and Shirley did a delightful dance up and down a flight of stairs as the movies' first interracial dancing couple. In 1938 when the *Wizard of Oz* was going to be made into a movie, the producers wanted Shirley to play the lead, but instead she made *The Little Princess*, her first color film.

At 19 she played her first romantic role, in *That Hagen Girl* (opposite Ronald Reagan). The public proved fickle and did not accept her in teenage roles, so she retired from acting in her early twenties. She married one of her leading men, John Agar, at 17, but they were divorced several years later, and she married again at 22. She and her second husband, Charles Black (who was one of the very few people who had never seen her in movies) had two children, and she replaced her screen career with others: as a wife and mother, as a writer of books for children, and as a distinguished public servant.

In the 1970s Shirley was appointed as a delegate to the United Nations, where she had to live down some ruthless ridicule when she first showed up, from people who could not take her seriously. They snickered when she walked down the hall and handed out lollypops in memory of her song *"The Good Ship Lollypop,"* which she sang in *Bright Eyes*. But her unflappable friendliness, and her obvious intelligence and sincerity overcame their prejudice and won Mrs. Black, as she was now known, great respect. She later served successfully as U.S. Ambassador to Ghana and Czechoslovakia.

Other Child Performers

Julie Andrews, real name **Julia Wells** (1935–): Singer and actress born in Walton-on-Thames, England. She made her debut on the London stage at age 12, singing operatic arias in a revue, *Starlight Roof*. She was a soprano with an amazing vocal range of more than four octaves. After she sang and acted in Christmas pantomimes for children, her career flourished as she grew from a child into a children's governess in the musical film *Mary Poppins* in 1964, when she won an Oscar for her "supercalifragilisticexpialidocious" performance in the title role. In 1965 she starred as another governess in the musical film about the Von Trapp family, *The Sound of Music*. In 1965 and 1966 she had a triumphant success on Broadway in a stage adaptation of the film. She has remained a shining star ever since.

Fred Astaire, real name **Frederick Austerlitz** (1899–1987): Dancer, singer, actor, and choreographer born in Omaha, Nebraska. Fred and his sister Adele toured in vaudeville when he was seven and she was six. The road led inevitably to Broadway, where they performed together brilliantly in several successful musicals. Their partnership ended when Adele retired to marry an Englishman, and Fred moved to Hollywood where he achieved even more spectacular success as the leading man in a large number of musical films. In 1978, the Kennedy Center for the Performing Arts in Washington, D.C. created its Honors Awards program to recognize outstanding lifetime achievements of five distinguished artists every year, and Fred Astaire was the first person to be honored in the triple categories of actor, dancer, and singer. In 1981 The American Film Institute repeated the compliment by giving him its own Life Achievement Award.

George Burns (1896–1996): Burns's remarkable 93-year career in show business began in New York City when he was a school dropout at age seven and he and three other boys formed the Pee-Wee Quartet. They sang in saloons and on the Staten Island ferry where, he said, the only way for people to avoid them was to jump overboard. Burns soon went on his own and added dancing, roller-skating, and even a seal to his act. At 13 he and a friend opened B-B's College of Dancing. He was a successful song-and-dance man in vaudeville and from 1922 to 1959 was famous as the writer and straight man for his comedy act with his delightfully zany wife Gracie Allen (1906–1964) on the stage and in radio, movies, and television. Their standard sign-off was for him to tell her, "Say goodnight, Gracie," to which her obedient reply was "Goodnight, Gracie." After her death in 1964 his fame as a wit became legendary. He wrote 10 books and was a star attraction in nightclubs and movies, in three of which he played the role of God. "Why shouldn't I?" he asked. "At my age anything I do is a miracle." In his eighties he said, "I've reached a point where I get a standing ovation just for standing." In 1988 at age 92 he received a John F. Kennedy Center Arts Award for lifetime achievement, but his life was far from over. He aspired to live to 100, and he made it.

Maurice Chevalier (1888–1972): Singer and actor born in Paris. After making his debut as a Parisian café singer at age 13, helping to support his mother and siblings after his father had deserted them, Maurice became and remained a great international star in movies and theaters. He was romantic, amusing, and charming for over 60 years.

Noel Coward (1899–1973): Playwright, actor, and songwriter born in Taddington, England. Noel had a difficult childhood, deserted by an alcoholic father and living with a devoted but mentally ill mother. Nevertheless, his love of the theater combined with *A Talent to Amuse*, the title of his autobiography, was evident very early. His first public performance was in a school concert where he brought down the house singing "Coo" from *The Country Girl*, accompanying himself on the piano. His first professional appearance in London was at age 10 in what was billed as *The Goldfish: A Fairy Play* in 3 Acts with a STAR CAST OF WONDER CHILDREN." The reviewer for *The London Times* wrote: "Performances by children are usually boring and last night's was no exception [but] great success was scored by Master Noel Coward as Prince Mussel." At 11 he was in *Where the Rainbow Ends*, produced by a children's theater company that included three children who also later became stars and lifelong friends of his: Brian Aherne, Hermione Gingold, and Gertrude Lawrence. At 13 he played a mushroom in *An Autumn Idyll* set to music by Chopin. At 15 he played the role of Slightly in *Peter Pan* and at 16 the role of Charley in *Charley's Aunt*. Also at 16 he wrote the lyrics and music of his first song, "Forbidden Fruit." He was well on his way to one of the greatest careers ever in show business.

Macaulay Culkin (1980–): American child movie star. His first movie, *Home Alone*, made when he was l0, was a fabulous hit. It was about a little boy who accidentally got left behind when his parents and siblings flew to Paris on a vacation. The scrapes he got into and the ingenious ways in which he managed to survive until his frantic family came back were funny, and his own quirky personality and wild energy made him overnight the world's biggest juvenile star. The film was the sixth highest money maker in movie history, grossing over $140 million in the United States and $507 million worldwide. After that, he appeared in a Michael Jackson video called *Black or White* and another, less successful, movie, *My Girl*, which was set in a mortician's home; in it he was laid out in a little white coffin after being stung to death by bees. But he came back with a vengeance in the sequel to his first hit, *Home Alone 2: Lost in New York*, another huge success, and this became the fifteenth all-time highest money maker, earning $102 million for its producers. When it was distributed as a rental film in 1992 it was the year's top money maker, earning another $102 million.

His career was managed by his father Kit Culkin, whose aggressive negotiations and what some people in the film industry considered exorbitant demands for control angered many people but made the boy incredibly successful: his reputed salary for filming "Home Alone 2" was $45 million. In 1995, however, the boy's mother, who had seven children but had never married their father, sued Kit in an unusually bitter custody fight, saying his methods were ruining the children's careers in films.

Patty Duke, real name **Anna Marie Duke** (1947–): Stage and screen actress born in New York City. In 1962 at age 15 Patty won an Academy Award for her performance as the deaf-blind child Helen Keller in the movie version of *The Miracle Worker*, a very demanding role in which she had also starred on Broadway when she was 10.

Annette Funicello (1942–): Singer, dancer, and actress born in Los Angeles. Annette starred in the movie version of the Victor Herbert operetta *Babes in Toyland*, the first live action musical made by Walt Disney, in her teens. She remained a professional "teenager" for many years, making many movies featuring teenagers and appearing on television as the leading "Mouseketeer" on Disney's *Mickey Mouse Club* show. When she was truly grownup, she became an invalid, a victim of multiple sclerosis, but she never lost her engaging cheerfulness. In 1994 she published a highly praised autobiography, recalling her earlier years with charm and humor.

Savion Glover (1974–): Savion Glover's mother enrolled him in tap classes at New York City's Broadway Dance Center when he was seven. He was so precocious that at age 12 he landed the title role in *The Tap Dance Kid* on Broadway. At 14, he costarred with Sammy Davis, Jr. and Gregory Hines in the movie *Tap*. At 15 Savion returned to the stage in *Black and Blue* and became the youngest performer ever to win a Tony nomination. Between the years 1991 and 1995 he was a regular performer on *Sesame Street*. While doing that, he costarred in 1992 with Gregory Hines in the Broadway musical hit *Jelly's Last Jam*. Hines, who is no mean tap dancer himself, says, "Savion is the best tap dancer that ever lived. He was doing things as a dancer at 10 that I couldn't do until I was 25. He has steps, speed, clarity, and an invention that no one else ever had. He's redefined the art form."

In 1996 at 22, Glover had his greatest success to date, winning his first Tony Award for choreography in the sensational hit show, *Bring in 'da Noise, Bring in 'da Funk*, a chronicle of tap dancing by Black Americans, for which he receives nightly standing ovations. *The New York Times* critic hailed him as "today's answer to Fred Astaire, with the same prodigious inventiveness and nimble elegance."

Cary Grant, real name **Archibald Alexander Leach** (1904–1986): Motion picture super-star, born in Bristol, England. He was born to Cockney parents who were poor, and when he was 10 his mother was committed to a mental hospital. Nobody explained this to Archie and he did not see her again for 21 years. At 13 he left home and joined a troupe of comedians and acrobats. His father made him go back to finish school, but at 14 he was expelled for peeking into the girls' bathroom, and that was the end of his education. He got a job backstage at the London Hippodrome, and then became a member of Pender's Knockabout Comedians. When he was 16 the troupe had a chance to perform in New York and when they left he stayed there, earning a meager living by advertising an amusement park on stilts and selling ties from sidewalk displays. One day an actors' agent, Jean Dalrymple, saw him and was so impressed by his good looks that she decided to represent him despite his heavy Cockney accent. She got him a screen test, but he was rejected because he had bowlegs and a thick neck. In the next few years he appeared in several Broadway musicals, but it was not until he was 28 that he was finally given a movie contract, by Paramount, who told him to change his name; thus "Cary Grant" was born. He said later, "I patterned myself on a combination of Jack Buchanan [the reigning English musical comedy star in those days] and Noel Coward. I pretended to be somebody I wanted to be, until I finally became that person." In fact, he became the man nearly every woman was in love with and nearly every man wanted to be like: suave, handsome, witty, and romantic clear into his eighties. He was the leading man in 72 films, but he said his best production was his daughter Jennifer. After retiring in his eighties, he was given an Academy Award and a Kennedy Center award for a lifetime of achievement.

Rita Hayworth, real name **Margarita Cansino** (1918–1987): Film actress and dancer known as "The Love Goddess" in the 1940s, Rita started dancing on the New York stage at age six with her Spanish father as a partner. Her film career was very glamorous, but her personal life was not. She had a number of unhappy marriages, including to Orson Welles and to Aly Kahn; she suffered from Alzheimer's disease for years before she died.

Gregory Hines (1946–): American dancer and actor born in New York City. Gregory started tap dancing at age three and began dancing in small town nightclubs at nine with his 11-year-old brother Maurice. "I can't remember ever not dancing," he says. In the 1980s and 1990s he became a major star, both on the Broadway stage and in motion pictures.

Lena Horne (1917–): Popular singer and actress born in Brooklyn, New York. Lena began her long career at age 16 in a Harlem Cotton Club review. Billie Holiday taught her to sing the blues. She included these with standard pop songs in the varied repertoire she featured in her nightclub, radio, stage, and concert hall performances. Her concert debut was made while she was still in her teens in the first jazz concert ever given at Carnegie Hall. Lena was strikingly beautiful and also a good actress, but Hollywood had not yet decided to give glamor girl roles to black women, so her acting career never rose to the heights it should have reached. In 1981 she produced an autobiographical show on Broadway called *Lena Horne, The Lady and Her Music,* in which she vented her rage over the years she had spent as a victim of Hollywood's racism. She proved that in her sixties she was more electrifying than ever, and that year she was recognized for a lifetime of achievements as a Kennedy Center honoree. But her lifetime was not yet over. In 1994 at age 76

419

she produced one of her finest record albums, called "We'll Be Together Again," which the liner called "a prayer, a private, sacred promise to a lost love." The lost love was Billy Strayhorn, who died in 1967, a fine jazz composer and collaborator with Duke Ellington.

Janet Jackson (1966–): Rock star born in Gary, Indiana. The younger sister of the famous Jackson Five family of rock singers, she began performing on television on her own at age nine and soon afterwards began producing hit records that rivaled those of her brother Michael (see below) in popularity. With one of her records *(Rhythm Nation 1814),* made when she was still in her teens, she made another kind of record: It was in the Top Five on the popularity charts seven times and remained high on the charts for a year and a half. She and Michael were the first brother-sister pair to earn individual number one pop hits. And in 1991 she signed an unprecedented deal with Virgin Records reported to be worth $60 million.

Michael Jackson (1958–): Rock star born in Gary, Indiana. At 11 Michael was the lead singer of the Jackson Five, the youngest performer in this phenomenally successful musical group made up of five brothers. In his teens he broke with his family and became a solo performer whose sensational popularity both on records and on concert tours never waned. His albums *Thriller* and *Bad* were the two best-selling albums of the 1980s, with combined sales of 54 million. In 1991, just after his sister had obtained her fabulous record contract, he outdid her, signing with Sony Records with substantial upfront cash, the highest royalty rate of any recording artist, potential money from films and music videos, and his own record label. The total deal was said to be worth a billion dollars. He ran into trouble in the 1990s when he was accused of child abuse and nearly had a nervous breakdown, from which he recovered, at least temporarily, in 1994 when he married Lisa Marie Presley, the daughter and heiress of Elvis Presley. The marriage lasted only two years, however, when Presley filed for divorce, citing irreconcilable differences. She seemed to confirm the previous accusations against Michael claiming he would have loved her more if she was a young boy. He was evidently dismayed by her leaving him and had to cancel a scheduled stage appearance because of renewed illness. Although the Jackson family was indignant at Presley's "betrayal" and begged her to reconsider, Lisa returned to live with her two children by her previous marriage.

Tina Majorino (1985–): American child actress. "When I was little," this still little girl told Kate Meyers, who interviewed her for *Entertainment Weekly* magazine, "I used to watch lots of movies and I always wanted to be on the screen, so I asked my mom. She thought I was joking and she laughed." But Tina had the last laugh. Her mother agreed to enroll her in dance and voice classes, and she made several commercials and did a stint on a short-lived TV sitcom, *Camp Wilder.* Then, at age nine, she got her first big break, winning critical praise for her performance as the daughter of Meg Ryan in the hit movie *When a Man Loves a Woman,* and right after that she won more acclaim playing the role of Cupid for Whoopi Goldberg and Ray Liotta in another hit film, *Corrina, Corrina.* Following those successes, later in 1994 Tina went to Hawaii to film *Waterworld* with Kevin Costner and then spent the rest of her summer vacation performing with Keith Carradine in *Andre.* "I love everything that's happened to me, every single bit," she told an interviewer.

Andrea McArdle (1963–): American singer and actress. In 1977, at age 14, Andrea was the first and the best of the actresses who played the title role in *Annie,* the long-running musical hit that had to keep changing its cast because the child actors kept growing up.

Hayley Mills (1946–): Film actress born in London. Daughter of the distinguished British actor John Mills, Hayley made her movie debut as her father's daughter in a British film, *Tiger Baby*, when she was 12. Walt Disney, visiting her father on the set, was so impressed by her that he immediately signed her to a contract. Her first Disney role was *Pollyanna* at age 14, in 1960, for which she won an Oscar. Other Disney films followed: a dual role playing identical twins in *The Parent Trap* in 1961, when she was 15; *In Search of the Castaways*, a Disney version of *The Swiss Family Robinson* in which again she played her own real-life father's daughter, in 1962; *Summer Magic* made in 1963; and *The Moon Spinners* in 1964. As a grownup she has not appeared in as many films, but whenever she has she has been equally impressive.

Tatum O'Neal (1963–). Film actress born in Los Angeles. At age 10 she won an Academy Award for her role in the film *Paper Moon* costarring with her father Ryan O'Neal. Three years later she had become the highest paid child star in the history of movies up to that time, but she walked away from her career when she married tennis champion John McEnroe and became the mother of their three children. They divorced in 1995 when she attempted to resume her acting career.

Dolly Parton (1946–): Country western singer, composer, and movie actress born in Locust Ridge, Tennessee. Born and raised in a two-room shack, the fourth of 12 children of a struggling farmer and laborer, Dolly helped raise her younger brothers and sisters. "We had absolutely nothin'. . .we wore rags," she has said, but they "had the best mama and daddy in the world" and had "fun. . .love. . .and music—all my people was musical." Even before she could recite the alphabet she was creating songs, with her mother transcribing the lyrics until Dolly learned to write. Her first musical instrument was "a busted-up mandolin," which she began playing when she was six. At eight she was given a guitar and began playing and singing gospel music in church, believing in "makin' a joyful noise unto the Lord." At 11 she got some radio bookings in Knoxville, Tennessee. In high school she played the snare drum in the marching band.

The day after her high school graduation Dolly took a bus to Nashville, the capital of country music, and there got contracts to make records. By now over 400 of her songs have been recorded, and she says "thousands and thousands more" fill trunks and boxes in her home. She claims she has written and sung into a tape recorder up to 20 sets of lyrics almost every day for years. According to the *Guinness Book of World Records* she is one of the world's highest paid entertainers, earning $400,000 for one live concert. She has also in recent years become an admired comedienne in motion pictures.

Ginger Rogers, real name **Virginia Katherine McGrath** (1911–1995): Movie actress and dancer born in Independence, Missouri; she changed her name to Rogers when her mother remarried. Ginger received her first offer of a motion picture contract at age six, but her mother felt she was too young to accept it. At 11 she appeared in public as a pianist, but in spite of encouraging audience response she switched from piano to concentrate on acting and dancing. Her stage debut was in Fort Worth, Texas, at age 13, in a play written and produced by her mother. At 14 she performed briefly in vaudeville with the famous Eddie Foy troupe and that same year she won a Charleston dancing contest; the prize was a month-long vaudeville tour. She named her tour "Ginger and her Redheads" and it was such a hit that it ran for almost two years. She continued in vaudeville touring the South and Midwest until she was 17. At 18 she made her debut in musical comedy, and at 19 made her first full-length movie, *Young Man of Manhattan*, and was signed to a movie contract. That same year, playing a leading role in a Gershwin musical, *Girl Crazy*, on Broadway, she first met Fred Astaire, who was helping to stage the production, neither of them dreaming that in the future they would become linked together as partners in a series of movies that are now legendary. In addition to being Astaire's most frequent and most popular dancing partner, she acted in non-musicals, and in 1940 won an Oscar for her portrayal of *Kitty Foyle*. In 1992 Ginger was a recipient of Kennedy Center honors for a lifetime of achievement.

Sabu, real name **Sabu Dastagir** (1924–1963): Indian film actor born in Karapur, India. When he was a 12-year-old penniless and illiterate elephant helper in the stables of an Indian maharajah, Sabu was discovered by a visiting Hollywood producer and made the star of a major feature film called *Elephant Boy*, which led him to worldwide fame. A comic book called *Sabu, Elephant Boy*, was written about him and published in 1950. Sabu's last film was Disney's *A Tiger Walks*, released in 1964 after he had died.

Brooke Shields (1965–): Model and film actress born in New York City. Her first job, at age one, was modeling for Ivory soap commercials. Her first major film role was a shocker. She was still a child and she played a child prostitute in *Pretty Baby*, a movie about Storyville, the red light district of New Orleans that thrived in the years before World War I before the government closed it down. Produced by the talented French director Louis Malle, it was a serious and sensitive film despite its sensational subject matter, and Brooke's acting was exquisite. She became a celebrity overnight and moved on to teenage roles, notably in *Blue Lagoon*, a movie about a boy and girl who grow up together on a deserted island. Somehow Brooke managed to maintain her career while she was a full-time student at Princeton University, from which she graduated with honors. In 1995 she appeared in the musical *Grease*, her first Broadway role, and got excellent reviews.

Ellen Terry, full name **Ellen Alycia (or Alice) Terry** (1848–1928): Stage actress born in Coventry, England. Her 70-year-long career began at age nine, in a production of *A Winter's Tale*. She was the most famous English actress of her era, and Henry Irving's leading lady in Shakespearean roles for 24 years. She was also the mother of an illegitimate son, the brilliant stage designer Gordon Craig, and for many years she maintained through correspondence a romantic but never consummated relationship with George Bernard Shaw.

Orson Welles, real name **George Orson** (1915–1985): Actor, director, and producer on stage and radio, and in motion pictures, born in Kenosha, Wisconsin. Orson produced, directed, and acted in school productions of Shakespeare, Marlowe, and Ben Jonson at age 11. After school, when he continued producing, directing, and acting, he was hailed as a boy wonder. He founded an excellent repertory company, the Mercury Theater, after World War II with a government subsidy of WPA (the Works Project Administration) and was much admired. However, he had a catastrophe when he produced a radio program about a supposed invasion from outer space that was so realistic that listeners took it literally; it nearly caused a nationwide panic. He produced many fine movies over the years, including *Citizen Kane* (1941), and the quality and quantity of his work made some of his admirers consider him a near rival to Shakespeare.

WALT DISNEY (1901-1966)

Few children in the world have not been entertained by Walt Disney. Born in Chicago, Illinois, he spent his childhood in many places as his father searched for work to support his family of five children. When Walt was nine, his father bought a newspaper delivery service and Walt and his 17-year-old brother Roy Disney got up every morning at 3:30 A.M.to begin deliveries. As an adult he recalled that "in the winters there'd be as much as 3 feet of snow—I was a little guy and I'd be up to my nose in snow. I still have nightmares about it."

To amuse himself, he began to draw at an early age, and when 14 enrolled in a class at the Kansas City Art Institute. While there he got part-time work as a newspaper cartoonist.

At 16 Walt enlisted in the Red Cross Ambulance Corps and served as a driver in England during World War I. Returning to America in 1919, he got his first job with a commercial art studio at age 17—but was fired.

He then went to work with the Kansas City Film Ad Company which made animated commercials shown in local theaters. At night he and a colleague, Ub Iwerks, made their own short animated cartoons, which they sold to the Newman Theater, naming them "Newman Laugh-o-Grams." They were so successful that he left his regular job and opened his own studio. Soon thereafter he moved to Hollywood where the Walt Disney Studios grew bigger and bigger along with his greater and greater success, until he had a staff of 1,100 people working for him and for the world's children.

His first big hit was Mickey Mouse (see page 424), whose debut was in 1928, the same year that his first *Silly Symphony* cartoon appeared. In 1932 a *Silly Symphony* called *Flowers and Trees*, the first Disney cartoon photographed in color, won an Academy Award, and in 1933 *The Three Little Pigs*, another *Silly Symphony*, was another award winner. In fact, Disney films continued to win Academy Awards every single year through 1940, and many additional times in the '40s, '50s, and '60s.

In 1934 Donald Duck made his screen debut in *The Wise Little Hen*, and before long he was nearly as popular all over the world as Mickey Mouse was.

Disney's first full-length animated cartoon was made in 1937. It was *Snow White and the Seven Dwarfs*. Dubbed into 10 languages, it was popular in France and Germany but censored in England, the Netherlands, and South Africa because of scenes considered too frightening for young children.

Disney frequently used classical music in his films, as in *Sleeping Beauty*, a 75-minute animated cartoon with Tchaikovsky's ballet music, and in 1940 he produced the ambitious extravaganza *Fantasia*, in which music by Bach, Beethoven, Mussorgsky, Stravinsky, Tchaikovsy, and others was conducted by Leopold Stokowski and interpreted by animated cartoons. Another of his musical ventures was a cartoon version of Prokofiev's *Peter and the Wolf*.

In the 1940s Disney began making educational films. He called the animated cartoon "the most flexible, versatile, and stimulating of all teaching facilities" and schoolchildren who saw *Our Friend the Atom* and *Donald in Mathemagic Land* enthusiastically agreed.

He made many educational films during the next two decades. In 1949 he produced *Seal Island*, the first of his *True Life Adventure* films and another Academy Award winner. From then on he expanded his educational films to include magnificent photography with astonishing closeups of real animals in *Beaver Valley, Jungle Cat, Niki, Wild Dog of the*

North, Olympic Elk, Survival in Nature, The African Lion, The Coyote's Lament, The Legend of Lobo, The Miracle of the White Stallions, Yellowstone Cubs, and his series of short films called People and Places: Lapland, Nature's Half Acre, Samoa, Seven Cities of Antarctica, Switzerland, The Alaskan Eskimos, The Vanishing Prairie, White Wilderness, and Wonders of the Water World. These became staples on the school circuit.

In the l950s Disney also plunged into the production of full-length, live-action feature films. Comedies were Almost Angels, Flubber, Save That Tiger, The Absent-Minded Professor, The Shaggy Dog, and others. His film versions of children's classics, many of which were big hits, featured well-known actors and actresses.

Starting in 1954 the seemingly inexhaustible Disney became a performer as well as a producer, the host of a weekly hour-long TV show called Disneyland, which coincided with the opening of the first Disney amusement park in California. In l959 the show's name was changed to Walt Disney Presents and in l961 changed again to Walt Disney's Wonderful World of Color, because from then on it would be seen in color, still a novelty on television at that time. After he died in l966 the program continued, under the new name of The Wonderful World of Disney.

Since his death the Disney Studios have continued to produce many films and TV shows. They added new illustrated books and magazines for children in many languages to their output. In 1995 they bought the CBS-TV network and in 1996 established the Disney network to feature children's entertainment. Many of their productions are available for rental or purchase on l6-millimeter film and on video cassettes for individuals and for schools. As Walt's brother Roy, his lifelong colleague, said, Walt Disney had succeeded in building such a strong organization that it could outlive him. He had not accomplished it all by himself, of course; characters were sometimes sketched by as many as 50 different animators. But it was he who inspired and supervised them for more than 30 years, thinking up, initiating, and producing hundreds of cartoons and live-action short subjects, many public service films, hundreds of TV shows, and more than 80 feature films.

In l987 The Museum of Cartoon Art, founded in the United States in l974 with a permanent collection of more than 60,000 pieces of original cartoon art dating back to l860, held a special exhibition on "The Art of the Walt Disney Studio." The museum's curator said that of all the forms of cartoon art, Disney animation had the largest impact on the public and the culture. His enormous creativity and innovative imagination had enriched the lives of children not only in his own era but also of countless children not yet born.

Mickey Mouse

One day in l927 Walt Disney saw a little mouse nibbling crumbs near his drawing board, and he was inspired to create a cartoon mouse. At first he called him Mortimer, but his wife renamed him Mickey.

The first animated cartoons featuring Mickey were silents: Plane Crazy and Gallopin' Gaucho, both made in 1928. They were rereleased with sound added in 1929 after the third Mickey Mouse film, Steamboat Willie, had come out with sound effects. Disney's own voice was used for Mickey's.

In 1929, he produced l2 other Mickey Mouse cartoons, and nine more in l930, the year in which the first Mickey Mouse comic strip appeared.

Mickey was by now established as an international star. In Germany, *Steamboat Willie* was chosen as one of the 10 best films released there in 1930, and the Russians liked it so much they sent Mickey an antique cut-glass bowl from the first Soviet Cinema Festival.

In 1931 Disney produced 12 more animated Mickey Mouse cartoons, and 14 in 1932. And now he branched out from films into merchandising and publishing. Mickey Mouse toys, bookends, thermometers, toothbrushes, and watches all became best sellers. And a 120-page book, *Mickey Mouse Annual,* was published for the first time; in Florence, Italy, it was called *Topolino* (Mickey's name in Italy). This was the beginning of a worldwide network of foreign language Disney comics.

Mickey Mouse Magazine, an American monthly, was launched in 1933. In October 1934, *Le Journal de Mickey* started in Paris. In March 1935, a magazine called *Mickey* began publication in Barcelona, Spain. In 1936, *Mickey Mouse Weekly,* a 12-page full-color magazine, was first published in London. In January 1937, *Mickey Maus Zeitung* began publication in Zurich.

The year 1939 was special: one of the nine Mickey films produced that year was the first to be produced in technicolor. It was *The Band Concert*, in which Mickey frantically conducted the *William Tell Overture* while Donald Duck sabotaged him with a contrapuntal saxophone rendition of *The Turkey in the Straw*.

That same year a *New York Times Magazine* critic wrote, in bewilderment: "Mickey Mouse is the best known and most popular international figure of his day," and he tried to figure out why, asking the following questions:

> What is the secret of his appeal? How has an imaginary creature only 6 years old, going on 7, captured the interest of almost every tribe on this terrestrial ball? Why is it that university presidents praise him, the League of Nations recommends him, *Who's Who* and the *Encyclopedia Brittanica* give him paragraphs, learned academics hang medals on him, art galleries turn from Picasso and Epstein to hold exhibitions of his monkeyshines, and the King of England won't go to the movies unless Mickey is on the bill?

In 1940 Mickey appeared in one of Disney's most ambitious and imaginative projects, *Fantasia*, in which animated cartoons were used to illustrate classical music conducted by Leopold Stokowski. Mickey gave an unforgettable performance in this as "The Sorcerer's Apprentice."

Another achievement of Mickey's in 1944 was that he became a war hero. His name was the Allies' password on D-Day.

Later he became a TV star as well as a movie star. In 1955 a daily half-hour variety show on television called *The Mickey Mouse Club* made its debut. It was phenomenally successful, featuring a likeable group of children called the "Mouseketeers," who wore black hats with Mickey Mouse ears and sang, danced, joked, acted in skits and serialized productions of children's stories, and watched old Disney cartoons along with their television audience.

Ever since 1955 a larger-than-mouse-sized Mickey and his girl friend Minnie Mouse—and his dog Pluto as well as Donald Duck have been star attractions at Disneyland in California and Disney World in Florida, and since 1992 at EuroDisney in France (also Tokyo).

The questions asked by the *Times* critic back in 1939 seem even more unanswerable today, now that Mickey has outlived his creative creator.

Disneyland(s)

"I want this to be the happiest place on earth," Walt Disney said in 1955 when he opened Disneyland in Anaheim, California. It has remained such a happy and popular place that since his death the happiness has proved contagious and has spread to other places. There is now a Walt Disney World in Orlando, Florida, a Disney Leisure Park in Tokyo, and a fourth Disney park in France, near Paris, called EuroDisney.

Within each Disneyland there are other lands, such as "Adventureland," "Fantasyland," "Frontierland," and "Tomorrowland," all of which have fascinating features: fairy tales that come to life; vivid scenes of the wilderness and the Wild West; movies including 3D ones; amazing laser shows and holographs; exciting aerial rides and tours, not only through different countries but back in time to see dinosaurs, and forward in time through outer space. In all Disneylands gala parades are led daily by a friendly Mickey, Minnie, Pluto, and Donald Duck, with balloons, marching bands, and fireworks. Each is indeed a very happy place for literally millions of children. . .and for the former children who accompany them.

One of the many rides in California's Disneyland is "It's a Small World," featuring charming music and cute puppets of children in varied national costumes from around the globe. Disney originally created these to honor UNICEF and the world's children at the New York World's Fair of 1965, but they are now a permanent part of Disneyland.

Florida's Walt Disney World also contains Epcot Center, where a vision of the twenty-first century is seen and the future is being helped along through research in agriculture, environmental problems, oceanography, and space technology.

Two attractive features of the French Disneyland expected to be big attractions when it opened were an "Island of Discovery," based on the adventure tales of Jules Verne, and a panoramic display of famous scenes from French history. However, EuroDisney ran into trouble. Not as many people thronged to it as its planners had expected, and it was the first Disneyland not to make a profit. Apparently the price of admission was considered too high, and there was unexpected antagonism from people who objected to the "Americanization" of European culture.

The Disney corporation also ran into unforeseen opposition in 1994 when it purchased land near Washington, D.C., where it intended to construct another Disneyland that would reproduce and reenact important events in American history. Local landowners objected vociferously to the traffic jams and other problems that would occur if this commercial enterprise invaded their peaceful rural area, and historians were equally emphatic in objecting to what they considered would be an inevitable falsification of history resulting from an entertainment approach to serious subjects such as the history of slavery and the Civil War. They maintained that it would inevitably trivialize the subjects it depicted, and also that it was inappropriate because of its closeness to the center of government, where there were already many authentic memorials to American history.

Eventually these critics succeeded in getting the Disney organization to drop this project, but this defeat has by no means ended Disney's continuing enormous influence on children's art and entertainment.

RADIO AND TELEVISION

Children today can hardly believe that life was worth living before television existed. They have no idea how entertaining radio was, nor do they know how much fun they are missing now that nothing is left to their imagination. Back then, they could make up their own pictures, fantasize about what their heroes or heroines looked like, and thrill to dramatic and humorous sound effects that made up for the lack of pictures.

An outstanding example of how interactive radio was, long before interactive TV and computers took over, is a popular program called *Story to Order.* It ran from 1945 to 1951 on NBC and local stations. Lydia Perera, its creator, was called the "story cook" because she lured listeners into her story kitchen where she cooked up unique tales based on listeners' ideas.

As a reviewer in the March 19, 1945 *Time* magazine wrote,

> she has a sense of humor and a sense of children's dignity that keep her from acting either cute or brimful of fake wonder. For her novel program, listeners send in lists of "any three things in the world" and around the three things she writes her Story to Order. Sometimes they come out fantasies, sometimes realistic dramas, sometimes burlesques. . . .Sample story ingredients: a milk bottle, a violin, and a rake; a jockey, some snow, and a duck; an egg, a towel, and a light— all about an egg that almost cracks under the strain of modern living.

Each week the "story cook" received about 1,500 letters suggesting topics, and she would pick the combination that seemed the hardest. Although this was a children's program, even adults could not resist the challenge. Her devoted listeners ranged in age from two to 80, and they all racked their brains trying to think up unrelated topics to stump her. One eager youngster thought he had done it when he requested a story about "nothing, nobody, and nowhere," but she managed to come through with a good tale built around his negative thesis.

One of Perera's stories was about a cake of ice; the ice was an ice carving made for a great banquet, but it began to melt because the dinner was so late.

Another, about a cactus, a starfish, and a suit of armor, dealt with competition among three museums in the same town.

A foxhole, a keyhole, and an armhole were featured in a story about a fox who leapt through a window of a southern mansion, to escape from dogs who chased him; he hid in a closet pretending to be the fur collar of a coat, so the fox hunters never caught him.

Often *Story to Order* made inanimate objects into live characters, but Perera tried never to have an inanimate object or an animal do anything that was not in character. She played all the parts herself, changing her voice to suit the characters. She had the assistance of a talented organist who wrote music for the show, and of some of the top sound effects men in the business, who outdid themselves making sounds such as a winding road unwinding itself, or a dentist's drill, or a roller coaster sailing into the air and landing.

Perera proved that stories do not have to have crime or cruelty to be suspenseful. Today people wonder why so few shows appropriate for children are being broadcast. She says, "It is only because producers have the unreal idea that one can't hold a child's interest with a 'tame' story. That is nonsense, because the great and lasting children's tales—from *Peter Rabbit* to *Charlotte's Web*—are real 'cliff hangers.'"

Children's Entertainment in the Early Years of TV

Television was invented in 1927 but was still a novelty rather than an obsession in the 1930s and 1940s, and most children rarely watched it. Many children were satisfied when told they could watch one show a week providing it was one their parents approved. When they did watch, what they usually saw was a comedy, game show, or sports program designed for adults. Some of these appealed to kids, but it was not until 1947 that a program specifically designed for children caught on.

Howdy Doody: Created by Bob Smith in 1948, this was the show that weaned young American children from the radio to TV. It ran on NBC until 1960, and its opening greeting, "It's Howdy Doody Time!," was the signal for thousands of youngsters to drop whatever they were doing and move to sit in front of the family's television set for a happy hour. The title role was played by a puppet, whose comical and cheerful face was reproduced on a popular toy and his rompers and matching shirt were copied in children's sizes and sold to fans in clothing stores—the earliest instances of a children's TV show being used in merchandising spinoffs.

The program made an indelible impression on its young viewers. Even years after it went off the air its devoted fans still cherished the memory of the delight they experienced back then. One rabid fan, Neil Sakow, has (sort of) grown up into an equally rabid collector of relics from his childhood, and now runs the three-story "Neil's American Dream Museum" in Hartford, Connecticut. The museum, which is open to the public by appointment, free of charge, contains a Howdy Doody room full of the program's paraphernalia, an unopened bottle of Howdy Doody Welch's grape juice from 1953, and a Howdy Doody cardboard general store. Sakow is writing a book called *Living in a Howdy Doody World*. His vast collection also contains Hopalong Cassidy and Roy Rogers memorabilia along with many other toys and games from the 1950s and 1960s and almost anything one can think of related to baseball.

Television's First Children's Shows and Stars

Milton Berle (1908–): After a childhood career as an actor in silent films, vaudeville, and musical comedies such as "The Zeigfield Follies," Berle moved to television and became known as "Uncle Milty," the host on a television variety show, *Texas Star Theatre*. He was so popular with both children and adults that he earned the title "Mr. Television." The program ran from 1948 to 1956, and *The Cambridge Dictionary of American Biographies* says Berle "helped change the television set from a toy for the wealthy into a family fixture."

Bozo the Clown: First appearing on the air in 1959, this comedy show for children produced by Larry Harmon Pictures has since broadcast more than 150,000 individual episodes on 150 television stations in the United States and abroad. According to the 1996 *Guinness Book of Records*, this is the greatest number of episodes ever shown on any TV program. Bozo was one of the first entertainers to visit UNICEF projects overseas where he cavorted with the needy children they were helping, often turning tears into gleeful giggles.

Robert James ("Bob") Keeshan (1927–): It almost seems prophetic that Bob Keeshan was born in the year that TV was invented, because for nearly 40 years his life revolved around television. He played the role of Clarabell on *Howdy Doody* from 1947 to 1952 and then appeared on another children's program called *Time for Fun* on ABC from 1953 to 1955. In 1955 he began producing and starring in his own children's show called *Captain Kangaroo*. This was a highly praised and enormously popular show during its 30-year run, until CBS finally dropped it. After that it moved to public television for seven seasons, but due to limited funding Keeshan was unable to tape new material for the show, and in 1992 it finally went off the air.

On it Keeshan played a grandfather named for the two large pockets in his coat, and he always combined education with entertainment through humorous antics of puppets and by chatting about many subjects with his amiable folksy assistant "Mr. Green Jeans." They discussed such things as gardening, good manners, protecting the environment, doing one's school work, and other upbeat practices, and kids did not object to the moralizing because it was always good natured and mixed with humor.

In his autobiography, *Growing Up Happy*, published in 1989 by Doubleday, Keeshan wrote that the characters on his show were designed to give children positive male role models because in the 1950s most children spent their days being cared for by their mothers. He also said, "If I had one piece of advice to give new parents, I'd urge them to do everything they can to build their child's self-esteem. And that's what we strived to do on the show." Peggy Charron, the children's media consultant who for 20 years was president of Action for Children's Television (see page 438), said "Captain Kangaroo was a breath of fresh air, the kind of program caring parents looked for on that screen. Children who watched Captain Kangaroo came away thinking, 'This program cares about me, so therefore I'm worth caring about.'"

Since his program left the air, Bob Keeshan has found a new career as an ardent child advocate, deeply concerned about the problems of today's children. Because so many are now growing up in fragmented families, he says we have lost he ability to deal with children's problems in everything from immunizations to psychological care, and "we have allowed children to become the principal underclass in our society." He has served on the boards of colleges, hospitals, the National Committee for Prevention of Child Abuse, and the National Council for Children and Television. In 1991 he also helped organize the Coalition for America's Children, a voter education group that boasts 200 member organizations.

Today, he says, "not every child has a functioning family, but every child has a school," so he believes that teachers must step in and play the role the family used to play. Admitting that expecting teachers to act as social workers is asking a lot, he says, "But it's a lot cheaper than paying for remedial programs—or prison terms—for kids who don't get help. If we deal with the problems facing children in an effective way, we will build a quite wonderful society. But we have to start dealing with them while children are still in the crib. . . . Where do problems like drug use come from? These kids have been kicked around and told they're no good, told they're losers. So they get a chance to take a drug that makes them feel good, and our society tells them 'just say no.' It's ludicrous."

Fred Rogers (1928–): Rogers was an only child until he was 11, and he always felt lonely. His parents were over-protective and would not let him go outdoors alone until he was nearly a teenager. He was also sickly, getting, as he says, "every disease that came down the pike," including scarlet fever and such severe hay fever that all during the ragweed season he was confined to his room. Perhaps these years of solitude explain his affection for a friendly neighborhood, which characterizes his famous TV show for children, *Mister Rogers' Neighborhood*.

During the 1950s Rogers produced a local children's TV program in Pittsburgh called *The Children's Corner*. While working on the show he also studied at a Presbyterian seminary and at the same time trained in child psychology at Pittsburgh's Arsenal Family and Children's Center, co-founded by such luminaries as Dr. Benjamin Spock and Erik Erikson. In 1963 he was ordained, and in 1965 took his ministry to children as "Mr. Rogers" on National Educational Television. Like Bob Keeshan (see above) he taught kids wholesome values and managed to make his viewers like both the messengers and the messages. His friendly and gentle manner, as he talks, sings, plays the piano (he learned to play on a toy organ at age five), and uses amusing puppets to help preschoolers express their feelings on serious issues, have made him a durable national institution.

Rogers does not call his show a show, saying it is a service, because each week he takes up a different important theme, calmly telling small children what they need to know to handle their problems, such as nighttime fears, toilet training, when parents go to work, illness, and even death. In 1967 he dealt with international relations, taking the program to Moscow where he did a joint production with a Soviet children's program, *Spokoinoi Nochu, Malyshi* (Good Night, Kiddies).

By 1990, Mr. Rogers' neighborhood program was being shown on 290 stations across the U.S., and as of 1996 it was the longest-running children's show on PBS and one of the longest-running shows of any kind of television. Rogers maintains a staff of 16 people at his nonprofit production company, Family Communications, Inc. but he does most of the work for each episode himself. He is the executive producer, writer, composer, lyricist, chief puppeteer, and star. Over the years he has also published books and record albums related to the program. And he still receives an average of 100 fan letters a week from children. He personally answers each one twice, one letter to the child who wrote him and one to the parents.

Romper Room: Romper Room was one of the first programs on TV that used children as participants. It was performed on a set resembling a model nursery school, and its juvenile guests, selected from the studio audience, played games, heard stories, and learned lessons from a friendly young kindergarten teacher. The teachers were played by different young ladies over the years, but the program's concept and format remained the same for decades.

Educational Television

The four most popular television programs for children are produced by the Children's Television Workshop (CTW), founded in 1968 by Joan Ganz Cooney, a producer of TV documentaries. They all grew out of a dinner party at Mrs. Cooney's home in February, 1966, when the subject of television came up and one of her guests asked if she would be interested in studying the possible use of television in preschoool education. Several months later she submitted a report to the Carnegie Corporation in which she noted the following:

- In America 96 percent of all families owned TV sets.
- In homes with children, the sets were on for as many as 60 hours each week.
- There was a growing consensus among educators concerning the great need to start schooling before the age of five.

- Since so many young children were watching TV, this was definitely a medium that should be used to help educate them.

On the strength of her report, Mrs. Cooney was granted $8 million to develop an experimental educational TV program. The Federal government provided half the money, a cheap investment in comparison with the $210 million it spent in 1967 to fund its Project Head Start, which had reached only 215,000 children. It was estimated that it would cost the government $3 billion to put all four-year-olds in regular classrooms, whereas for a fraction of that sum, according to Joan Cooney, many more children could be brought together in a "classroom without walls."

CTW, The Children's Television Workshop

Mrs. Cooney gathered a group of educators, child psychologists, and writers, who set about observing and interviewing children to find out what they liked to watch on TV, instead of what experts thought they ought to watch. They found that almost all youngsters watched and easily memorized TV commercials and jingles and enjoyed fast action, music, humor, and brevity. After all, the attention span of young children is short. So they decided to use the brisk, humorous, and varied techniques that were successful on commercials to "sell" education.

Their curriculum goals were basic: recognition of letters of the alphabet; recognition of numbers 1 through 10 and simple counting ability; beginning language skills and vocabulary; increased awareness of self and of the world; and values such as cooperation, tolerance, fairness, self-esteem, and curiosity. All were designed to help children get off to a good start when they entered school. In later years their curriculum goals were expanded to include additional skills such as learning to follow directions, knowledge about libraries, hospitals, police, fire, safety messages, disabled children, illness, and even childbirth and death.

Sesame Street

This program, the first project of CTW, was aimed primarily at children from deprived backgrounds whose families did not expose them to books and stimulating play activities. It was therefore set on a racially integrated lower-class urban street where an assortment of neighbors mingled. It featured a mixture of actors, including some children, and large comical puppets (sometimes joined by famous visitors, movie stars, comedians, athletes, musicians and singers). It featured lively music, silly jokes, and imaginative graphics to get its messages across.

The felt puppets designed and animated by Jim Henson quickly became famous as the Muppets and are now right up there with characters from Mother Goose and other children's classics in universal popularity. They include Big Bird, who delights children by making hilarious mistakes, Oscar "the Grouch," and Kermit the Frog, who teaches racial tolerance by explaining that it is not easy being green.

When the Workshop first presented its plans for the program to a TV channel they were greeted with skepticism but allowed to try it out as an experiment. To the skeptics' surprise, as soon as it was broadcast it became an instant and sensational hit. Playgrounds and supermarkets emptied during the hours when it was on the air, as parents and children stayed home to watch, parents enjoying the show almost as much as their children did.

During its very first season a research survey in a New York slum area found that the program was reaching 91 percent of its potential three- to five-year-old audience, and that poor children watching it made gains in letter recognition, counting, and reasoning two-and-a-half times greater than poor children of the same age who did not watch the show.

Sesame Street is often called the "Longest Street in the World." In the many years since it has been on the air it has maintained a regular weekly audience in the United States of more than 9 million children under age six, reaching more children than all other children's TV shows combined. It has also been seen in more than 90 countries and territories. Furthermore, it has the distinction of having won 59 Emmy awards, which the 1996 *Guinness Book of Records* says is almost double the number of those any other television program has ever received.

The Electric Company

Two years after the debut of *Sesame Street*, CTW followed it with a series of half-hour programs starring Morgan Freeman and Rita Moreno, for children aged 7 to 10, designed to provide supplementary instruction in basic reading skills for children experiencing difficulty in learning to read. It distributes teaching guides to help elementary schoolteachers incorporate the program's contents into their classwork. Over 100,000 teachers have used this program to help them with their remedial reading courses, and more than 3 million pupils regularly watch it in school. A study of its impact, conducted by the Educational Testing Service, reported that the program improved reading scores of its target-age viewers compared with nonviewers in 19 out of 21 reading skills tested. It doubled the use of TV in schools and helped increase the number of TV sets in classrooms. A 1983 study by the Corporation for Public Broadcasting found that it was the most widely used instructional series in American schools.

It has also been used in 26 other countries, including Japan, where teachers use it as a supplement to classroom studies in English.

3–2–1 Contact

In 1980 the CTW launched a third program, an introduction to science and technology for children between 6 and 11. It used a magazine format, which included live action documentaries, interviews, and animated cartoons, with three teenage hosts as commentators. A different theme was explored each week: babies, earth, farms, flight, light, sports, water, and so forth.

During its first season it attracted 23 million viewers and was used in 500,000 classrooms. Viewership increased substantially after the first year; in homes with children aged 12 to 17 it rose 16 percent and even rose 35 percent in homes where the children were below age six. A booklet was developed linking the Girl Scouts' science merit badge to the series. In the first year of broadcast 2,000 Scout leaders were trained in use of the program and 10,000 Scouts earned their science badges. Other projects were developed with science museums and teachers' guides, and reference books were published to supplement the show. It too has been successful outside the United States, in 32 countries. France, Germany, and Spain have coproduced their own versions, drawing on the contents of the American original but featuring local casts and newly produced film elements.

Square One TV

The CTW continues to work hard on its policy of "educating through pleasure." In 1987 it produced a fourth half-hour series called *Square One TV,* which tackled the difficult task of making mathematics fun and developing mathematical problem-solving skills in elementary school children from 8 to 12 years old.

Television Specials and Theater Productions

The Workshop has produced a large number of spinoffs, too, including several outstanding TV specials.

Big Bird in China, a 90-minute show that was the first ever U.S.–China TV coproduction, was shown in both countries and won an award from the National Association of Television Arts and Sciences as the best children's program of 1983.

Don't Eat the Pictures: Sesame Street at the Metropolitan Museum was produced in 1984 to introduce children to the wonders of art museums.

Two touring companies called "Sesame Street Live," each featuring 20 young performers costumed as Muppet characters in a two-hour musical show, started touring the United States in 1980, playing to nearly 4.5 million children and parents in 80 cities each year. Featuring arithmetic, music, and original stories in their shows, these troupes have also covered Australia, New Zealand, Hong Kong, and the Philippines.

And for the The Electric Company, the Workshop has developed "Power Stations," which are after-school clubs with organized activities built around development of skills in reading and languages.

The Man Behind the Muppets

Jim Henson (1936–1990), the creator of the puppets that became such a phenomenally popular part of the television show *Sesame Street,* as well as other TV programs, maintained the playfulness of a child all his life.

He began making comical puppets in the 1950s while attending the University of Maryland, where he met Jane Nebel, another student there. Together they produced a late-night TV show, *Sam and Friends,* which was aired over a Washington, D.C. station and became a big local hit. A year after its inception he created the character of "Kermit the Frog" out of a cast-off coat of his mother's, a bisected ping-pong ball, and a sock.

Three years later he and Jane married. They had five children, whose childhoods in a happily chaotic household were shared with both life-sized and miniature puppets, and who all grew up to become film makers, designers, artists, producers, or puppeterers.

Sam and Friends ran for seven years, then in 1969 Jim was hired by the producers of *Sesame Street,* whereupon he promptly became famous as the creator of the "Muppets": Kermit the Frog, Big Bird, Oscar the Grouch, Grover, Bert, Ernie, the Cookie Monster, Waldorf the Chef, and others.

His great innovation in puppetry was to emphasize the puppets' faces, because on television closeups are important. After seeing the Muppets, few children ever again preferred traditional stiff, dangling marionettes. His characters' frowns and smiles and eyes, even their eyebrows, eyelashes, and nostrils, were uncannily expressive, and their mouths moved in perfect synchronization with their words.

Some of them, like Kermit, were small and could be operated by a single puppeteer, but the more complicated characters required teamwork. One "Muppeteer" would move the left arm and another the right arm and head, synchronizing their movements by watching their composite creature on a hidden video monitor. Muppeteers had to be tall enough to hoist the creatures into the camera's view above a built-up stage set, and agile enough to endure the cramped and contorted postures often required for staying out of sight. The work was hard and required great skill, but all the people who worked with Jim agreed that it was tremendous fun.

His characters were produced with the aid of a large and devoted staff, some of whom worked with Jim for more than 25 years, in a large former mansion in New York City. His company, Henson Associates, had the appropriate logo of HA!

In 1976, while continuing to work on *Sesame Street*, Jim decided to launch his own TV program, *The Muppet Show*. It was turned down by all three American commercial TV networks, but Lord Grade, a British producer, enthusiastically took it on; 120 episodes were produced in England and dubbed into five languages. In two years the Muppets became international celebrities, with 235 million people, adults as well as children, watching them every week in 106 countries. The program also launched the career of a new international star, the glamorous and amorous "Miss Piggy," who later joined the *Sesame Street* cast and fell in love with Kermit.

When Jim Henson died in 1990, the whole world grieved. He was only 53 and his death was unexpected. He had caught a strep infection that he did not think was serious enough for a visit to the doctor, but it led to pneumonia and in just three days he was dead. However, his puppets were—and are—so alive that his spirit definitely lives on.

A week after he died a unique memorial service was held in the imposing Cathedral of St. John the Divine in New York, attended not only by human family and friends and fans but by Big Bird, who sang Kermit's theme song, "It's Not Easy Being Green." Several years before, Jim had planned part of the service himself, asking that no one wear black and saying he would appreciate it if there was a Dixieland Band there to play "When the Saints Go Marching In." Both requests were honored.

He had also written letters to his children to be opened after his death, and his son Brian read parts of them aloud. Jim's advice to his children, and by extension to all children, was: "Please watch out for each other and love and forgive everybody. It's a good life; enjoy it."

One happy development during 1996 was that Jim Henson's group of puppets outlived their imaginative creator's death. Thanks to *Jim Henson's Creature Shop*, his family and former co-workers were still appearing on the air every morning, both to entertain and to teach children. They are also featured in a primetime spot, evidence of the desirable and age-defying charm of their characters.

Later Examples of Children's TV

By 1995, 98 percent of American families owned at least one television set, and children were spending on the average almost seven hours a week watching its programs, according to Neilsen Media Research. And today's TV is very different from yesterday's.

Whole networks now specialize in "kidvid" and a great diversity in types of children's shows exists: mostly cartoons, but also lots of rock music, TV versions of children's books and fairy tales, science programs, and many boisterous audience participation shows, in addition to the ubiquitous *Sesame Street* and its offshoots. Today's children are of course also exposed to an avalanche of varied children's and adults' programs with the result that millions of them would look down on the unsophisticated shows their parents enjoyed when they were kids as boring and corny.

The Federal Communications Commission (FCC), which regulates the licensing of television stations, requires all stations to devote a certain percentage of their schedules to educational programs for children. Many stations have evaded the rule by defining the term "educational" extremely loosely, for example calling *The Flintstones,* that amusing but utterly inaccurate depiction of life during the Stone Age, "educational." But the late 1990s, responding to growing protests from Congress and parents, an effort has been made to tighten up enforcement of the rule, and it is now required that every station air educational programs at least three hours a week.

Shari Lewis and Lamb Chop: A ventriloquist who works in closeups so successfully that no one can see her lips move, Shari Lewis's (1934–) television career began with a group of little hand puppets she designed. Her first TV show, *Learn Facts 'n' Fun*, aired in 1953. Lamb Chop was by far the most beloved puppet so that by the 1990s it was the only one she continued to feature regularly. She used this appealing little character primarily for children's amusement, and in 1996 the two of them have appeared regularly on public television in *Lamb Chop's Play Along*. Lewis interjects educational material into their conversations and also occasionally produces and stars in TV specials on serious subjects handled with a light touch, such as one in December, 1995, on Hanukkah, in which she explained the origin, meaning, and customs associated with the Jewish holiday.

Nickelodeon: Owned by MTV (Music Television), Nickelodeon is a cable network devoted to children's entertainment. It concentrates on competitive games, jokes, and often rowdy audience participation, stories both scary and comical, and loud music. Its material is definitely not designed for adults' tastes, but many children enjoy its shows. A few of its programs are genuinely educational, such as *Think Fast, Make the Grade*, and the excellent award-winning *Mr. Wizard's World*, which proves that learning can be fun as it demonstrates complicated scientific information with excellent graphics and witty commentary. Among its other worthwhile programs is *Don't Just Sit There*, designed to build kids' self-confidence by putting them in charge—hosting, starring, even making the music for the program. The network claims that it also promotes independent thinking, with its programs *Eureeka's Castle* and *You Can't Do That On Television*, which teach kids how to evaluate a problem, make decisions, and resist peer pressure.

The Disney Channel: The Disney Corporation's cable channel features its animated cartoons, other special programs, and films. On a typical month in 1996 it showed *Alice in Wonderland, Charlie Brown, Donald Duck, Dumbo, Kids, Inc., The Adventures of the American Rabbit, Muppet Treasure Island, The Baby-Sitters Club, The Little Mermaid, The Magical World of Disney, The Making of Pochahontas, The Mickey Mouse Club*, and *Winnie the Pooh*, among others. This is good news for children, who get a chance to see again many of their favorite movies.

Barney and Friends: Barney, seen on the PBS network, is considered a beguiling and virtuous role model by many children and inane and cloyingly saccharine by many adults. Parents who complain about too much TV violence should welcome him warmly. Many adults regard his show as a throwback to TV's earlier "age of innocence." Barney is a "do-gooder." In addition to his daily appearances on public television, he makes many personal appearances at children's toy stores, charities, hospitals, and birthday parties.

Barney defies its critics and is not ashamed of stressing moral values. Its producers have teamed up with others on "Kids for Characters," working with the Josephson Institute of Ethics, a nonprofit foundation devoted to character development. In 1993 the foundation launched the Character Counts Coalition aimed at imparting to young people "a core set of 6 pillars of character": trustworthiness, respect, responsibility, fairness, caring, and citizenship. It has attracted support from leaders of both U.S. political parties and more than 60 national organizations, including the Boys and Girls Clubs of America, 4-H, YMCA, Little League, and the American Federation of Teachers. It has big plans to produce, in conjunction with Universal Studios in Florida, entertaining and educational videos on character development aimed at preschoolers, starring Barney and many other children's characters such as Babar, the Cat in the Hat, Fred Flintstone, Garfield, Lamb Chop, Madeline, Ronald McDonald, and Peter Rabbit.

Michael Josephson, founder of the Institute of Ethics, realizes that unless parents collaborate in teaching values the programs will not help much. He says parents can help through what he call "TAME," which stands for four elements. The first is to TEACH, by explaining why such things as honesty and fairness are better than their opposites. The second is to ADVOCATE good behavior, so that children will see what is acceptable and what is not. The third letter stands for MODEL, with parents showing their children that they themselves practice what they preach. And the fourth is to ENFORCE the rules.

Barney, like *Sesame Street*, also publishes a magazine for children and one for parents called *Family*, which is packed with suggestions for family recreation and child guidance.

These efforts, augmented with record albums, personal appearances, and concert tours, indicate a new trend, returning to the earlier years of children's TV. This seems much needed today when so many children are growing up without adequate guidance, as is sadly demonstrated by the large numbers who are increasingly antisocial and violent. Perhaps it is not naive to make TV genuinely educational; it was evidently very naive not to do so.

TELEVISION AND VIOLENCE

Back in the 1950s and 1960s when television was just beginning, Dr. Frederic Wertham, a psychiatrist, received a lot of press, though little agreement, when he warned that if programming trends continued the way they were going the children then growing up would see during their childhood more murders and other acts of violence than any children had ever even heard of in previous generations, and he predicted serious psychological and social harm as a result. He was widely ridiculed as an alarmist, but were his fears justified?

In 1966 Wertham wrote a book called *A Sign for Cain: An Exploration of Human Violence*, which was published by Macmillan. It surveyed violence throughout history and revealed in gruesome detail how much frightful violence has always been a large part of human life and death. In its introduction he wrote: "The fact that the idea that violence can be greatly diminished and eventually eliminated is still considered so controversial shows how much we have let ourselves be conditioned to accept a social evil as part of our inescapable destiny. But human violence is not ordained by immutable laws of nature or of human existence. It is amenable to scientific research and remedy."

By the time this book appeared, Wertham's views were becoming more widely accepted, and the book was universally praised by psychologists, sociologists, historians, and literary critics. One wrote that "history may well accord Dr. Wertham a role as one of the more important men of the twentieth century. . . . What he has to say is important for the survival of civilization." This is ironic since today hardly anyone remembers him, even though there is more evidence now than when he wrote an article for *Ladies Home Journal* in 1965 about the dangerous effects of violent television on children.

> Can anyone reasonably argue that the kind of intelligence and imagination one needs to survive in today's highly complex world is wholesomely nourished or trained in a child by his sitting in front of a screen and being 'entertained' by violence hour after hour? With the progress of civilization we have learned— slowly and painfully—that violence is not the best way to settle human differences. But we seem to be using the marvelous technical media of movies and television to teach children that it is the only way.

One child who seemed to have gotten that message was the young son of David Susskind (1920–1987), a prominent American television producer in the 1960s. One day, when he was describing to his family an upsetting argument he had had with a colleague, his son, trained in the gangster and western morality he had watched on TV, piped up with what he thought was a helpful suggestion: "Why don't you kill him, Daddy?" Susskind was so shocked that he made a big change in his career: from then on he produced only talk shows and documentaries instead of dramatic fiction.

In 1975 Michael B. Rothenberg in the *Journal of the American Medical Association*, wrote that "By the time an average American child graduates from high school, he or she will have viewed some 18,000 murders, and countless highly detailed incidents of robbery, arson, bombing, forgery, smuggling, beating and torture."

Anne R. Sommers, a Canadian community health speacalist, in a Report of the Royal Commission on Violence in the Communications Industry in 1976, concluded that programs of violence cause "pollution of the mind which has contributed to an epidemic of youthful violence that seriously threatens the health of American youth." She cited statistics showing that 75 percent of street crimes were committed by people under 25 years of age and 45 percent were by those under 18.

Violent outbursts and physical aggression among children kept on rising during the 1980s and 1990s, as many schoolteachers began complaining that they were having to spend more time disciplining their pupils than teaching them.

Dr. George Gerbner, dean of the School of Communications at the University of Pennsylvania, was another person who made serious studies of TV programming. He found that violence occurred 10 times more often on television than in real life, and that children who watched a lot of TV regarded the world as more violent than less frequent viewers. In detailed analyses of the contents of more than 280 dramatic TV shows appearing on prime time over a three-year period, he found that about eight out of every 10 programs contained violence and that the occurrence of violent incidents was at the rate of almost eight per hour.

From 1979 to 1983 in the United States the average time that TV stations allotted to children's programming dropped from 11.3 to 4.4 hours a week, but the advertisers of children's toys did not correspondingly reduce their output. *Advertising Age* magazine reported that more than $40 million were spent in 1986 on ads supporting terrorism-related toys. After-school TV turned into a war zone, with high-tech weapons and teams of "good guys" fighting "bad guys" and with nuclear weapons and hostile aliens and the total destruction of our planet becoming just one more exciting adventure.

Jane E. Brody, health editor of *The New York Times*, wrote in January 1987 that "American children between the ages of two and 12 watch an average of 25 hours of television every week, and by the time they graduate from high school each will have spent approximately 15,000 hours watching TV in comparison with only 11,000 hours in the classroom."

TV programs specifically aimed at children can be divided into five main types: educational programs, usually scheduled at inconvenient nonpeak viewing hours; daily action adventure shows featuring superheroes; bland and sentimental specials aimed at little girls; Saturday morning network programs specializing in cartoons, rock music, and characters based on commercial toys; and advertisements for toys, candy, and fast foods, sprinkled among which are a few public service messages about brushing one's teeth, being kind to others, and so forth.

But of course most children who are television addicts do not watch only children's programs. Children whose TV viewing is unsupervised by parents see a great many programs not designed for children: news broadcasts saturated with graphic scenes of war, terrorism, corruption, and crime; soap operas where glamorous men and women pop into bed, often without any emotional commitment to each other and almost never mentioning AIDS or birth control but rarely getting sick or producing babies—unlike the teenagers who watch and imitate them. They also see action programs where people are mugged and murdered, but they are rarely shown the tragic consequences, such as a family's bereavement. Also, people killed on TV tend to die neatly and quickly, without hours or days of agony, screaming, vomiting, and wetting their pants, and reality is further distorted because the scene soon shifts to a jolly commercial or an unrelated event.

More than 3,000 studies have linked TV violence to increased aggression and violent behavior in children and adolescents. At the very least, according to the American Academy of Pediatrics, TV violence "promotes a proclivity to violence and a passive response to its practice."

Opinions about Constructive Television for Children

Peggy Charren (1928–) founded Action for Children's Television (ACT) in 1968. While home caring for her preschoolers, she began to watch a lot of children's TV, and she did not like what she saw: lots of shows geared mainly to selling toys. She gathered some neighbors at her home in Newton, Massachusetts, and formed ACT. During the next 24 years this watchdog group grew until it had more than 15,000 members, and it became the most effective and vocal champion of worthwhile TV fare for kids. Charren lobbied Congress, regulatory agencies, and broadcasters to help bring intelligent, informative children's programming to the airwaves.

Unlike many advocacy groups that rely on moral persuasion, ACT's chief weapon was the law. In 1970 ACT petitioned the Federal Communications Commission (FCC) and the Federal Trade Commission (FTC) for more regulation of children's programming. Soon after, broadcasters began creating more science, news, drama, and art shows for children. Other gains were rules against misleading advertising, a limit on commercial time, and bans on sales pitches by program hosts.

438

In the 1980s the FCC deregulated commercial television, which was a bitter blow for ACT. "All the advances made in the seventies were undone in the eighties," Charren said. The decline in children's programming was not only due to deregulation but to such things as cost-cutting and a "new Hollywood breed of manager" with little interest in educational shows. By 1987 there were as many as 70 toy-based programs on the air until ACT won a court ruling ordering the FCC to review deregulation. As a result the number of these "30-minute ads" dropped significantly. In 1990 Congress passed the Children's Television Act, which set limits on advertising on children's programs and required TV stations to air some quality programs for children or lose their licenses. With the passage of this act, Charren felt her goal had been achieved ("We now have Congress on our side," she said) and she disbanded ACT in 1992.

> This instrument [television] can teach, it can illuminate. Yes, and it can even inspire. But it can do only to the extent that humans are determined to use it to those ends. Otherwise, it is merely lights and wires in a box.
>
> —*Edward R. Murrow (1988–1965, pioneer television newscaster*

Following are excerpts from a special report written by Peggy Charren in 1994 for the Harvard University's Graduate School of Education about the possibilities she foresees for better television for children:

> The choices on TV should be as diverse as the books in a good children's library. Instead the choice is narrow. Commercial television has generally abdicated an educational role. . .often showcasing the violence, sexual innuendo, and raunchy behavior prevalent in popular culture. Many adults, frustrated, angry, and deeply concerned about TV's role in modeling murder and mayhem, wish the government would ban television violence. But government censorship is not the answer. Tolerating offensive speech is the price we pay for freedom of political expression—a freedom too precious to lose. . . .
>
> Ultimately, TV's influence on our children is regulated at home. We parents have to teach our youngsters that violence is not the best solution to any problem, and we must monitor what our kids watch and use the off button more often.
>
> In the future, a television industry offering 500 channels may pose an even greater challenge to parents, but it could also provide opportunities for an abundance of worthwhile new programming choices.
>
> Tomorrow's TV sets will be interactive and linked by computer to libraries and other educational resources around the world. The new national information infrastructure will be wired into every school and library. . . .We must demand that the government ensures affordable access to programs and services designed to support families. There should be parenting channels offering instruction in how to raise healthy and happy children, and noncommercial children's channels featuring the best in kids' shows from around the world, including programs produced by youngsters. . . .

When it comes to improving the lives of children at risk, television can be part of the solution. TV shows can enrich a child's education and help kids develop self-esteem and coping skills. Television can empower young people to involve themselves in improving their neighborhood, their city, their planet. It can help our children understand the rights and responsibilities of citizenship.

The International Children's Day of Broadcasting

Since 1992 the second Sunday of each December has been set aside by members of the television industry to concentrate all day long on airing programs for and about children. In 1993 after it was inaugurated almost 1,000 television and radio stations in 112 countries took part, producing programs especially for that day. In more than 50 of these countries, TV and radio producers involved children in planning, promoting, and celebrating the day, and in 16 countries there was some level of government involvement, with national leaders and heads of state participating.

Participants included leading broadcast unions and producers and professional groups and organizations, all forming a unique partnership to show their concern for children. Even a war-torn country, Somalia, took part, with local radio stations belonging to rival clans airing a special message sent to UN troops and the local population across the entire Somali territory, and two Somali children went live via satellite on BBC's Radio Five, talking to children in the United Kingdom about the situation in their country.

Tom Johnson, the president of Cable News Network (CNN), wrote an article that was circulated to producers in the television industry saying why he strongly supported the day. He cited a recent poll that showed 43 percent of Americans believe the media play the most important role in determining issues on our national agenda. He said

> This poll demonstrates the tremendous impact of the media. . . .Our power carries with it heavy responsibilities to the publics we serve. . . .

> Children form a large part of the viewing audience, yet their opinions on what they see and what they would like to see are largely ignored. . . .Children usually are not part of the programming process. . . .There are many untold stories to which the media could turn its attention. I believe the most compelling of these, the ones around which we can all most easily unite, are those that involve children, the issues that concern them today, their hopes, their dreams for the future. The needs of children can help raise our sights above politics, above war. Beyond our responsibility to report on their concerns and take heed to their views, we should learn from children. . . .

> To help us focus on children's needs, UNICEF and the International Council of the National Academy of Television Arts and Sciences initiated the International Children's Day of Broadcasting. . . .I join them in asking every television and radio station around the world to take part.

CHILDREN'S THEATER

Since the demise of vaudeville, live theater has undergone many changes. At the beginning of this century in the U.S. professional productions of plays were usually seen only in four American cities. They included: Chicago, New Haven, and Philadelphia where shows aiming for Broadway in New York were usually first rehearsed and tried out. But today there are repertory companies in most major cities and amateur theater groups almost everywhere. Some, such as The Paper Bag Players in New York, specialize in putting on plays for children. However, for most children live theater is no longer such an exciting event as it was for their parents and grandparents. There is too much competition from movies, television, radio, rock concerts, sports events, museums, and even from libraries, which often put on free programs for youngsters.

One thriving exception, however, is *The Nutcracker,* which has been produced with children in the cast during every Christmas season for more than 100 years. Its premiere performance was in 1892 in St. Petersburg, Russia, and since then it has been performed all over the world. The music is by Tchaikovsky, but it is not a concert nor an opera, and the choreography is by Balanchine, yet it is not a ballet. It is a romantic story about a young girl's dream at Christmastime, told through young actors as well as dancers and singers. In New York City it is always performed with young boys and girls who are not professionals in many of the parts, and its popularity with young audiences is undying.

Another outstanding stage tradition is the Children's Theatre Company (CTC) in Minneapolis, which brings the best of children's literature to the stage each year in eight elaborate, magnificently designed and acted productions. The casts are made up largely of professional actors, but children also perform with the company. It employs 90 professionals and 300 part-time employees, has 28,000 subscribers and plays to more than 400,000 people annually in Minneapolis and St. Paul and on tour. Many of the children who perform in its productions also attend afternoon acting classes at CTC. When they travel with the company on its tours, tutors and chaperones are supplied.

Over the years CTC has produced dramatic versions of *Beauty and the Beast, Little Women, The Little Match Girl, Robin Hood,* and the first nine chapters of *Jane Eyre.* Playwrights whose works it has shown include Shakespeare (*A Midsummer Night's Dream*) and Thornton Wilder (Our Town). Dr. Seuss's stories have been adapted to the stage by CTC, which owns exclusive performance rights to them, and authors Beverly Cleary and Madeleine L'Engle have likewise given their blessings to CTC productions of their works. Original works are also regularly commissioned from playwrights to join the classics.

Jon Cranny, the company's artistic director, has explained his guiding principles in a brochure this way:

> We do not have a culture that supports the arts even halfway as much as sports. We want to create an atmosphere that shows how performance art can be a significant part of your life. So we do all kinds of performing arts, not just drama. Children need to experience, they need to know, to inquire, to take those journeys art takes you on, and be brought back having learned something of value. . . .If you start attending performances at age six or seven and you stay until you're 12, you will have seen all kinds of theatrical styles and techniques. You will already be a sophisticated theatergoer. . . .Our work has to be substantive, so people will learn at a young age that you go to the theater because something important happens there and you will come out the richer for it.

Stage Productions in Other Countries

The performing arts are featured extensively in some countries, even more than in America. In Russia many children's theaters have been launched since the first one, Moscow's Music Theatre, opened in 1918. England, as part of its unusually rich theatrical tradition, puts on Christmas "pantomimes" for children every year, and during school vacations other plays for children are always produced.

In Asia, ballet is a centuries-old tradition that is held in high esteem. In Bali, dancing is associated with religion, and children from an early age are trained to dance and sing. Their exquisite performances are a major tourist attraction in that country. In Thailand young girls become professional dancers while very young, and their style is unique and very demanding. Their traditional postures and hand gestures require great skills and stamina. In Korea, child dancers are an important part of their nation's culture. The Little Angels Children's Folk Ballet of Seoul, Korea, consisting of girls from seven to 15 years old, tours other countries regularly, performing to admiring audiences in places like Carnegie Hall and the Kennedy Center in Washington. Not only are the children charming but they are dressed in a wide variety of colorful costumes and as they glide, dip, and spin in mini-spectacles based on Korean legends and regional dances, they inspire awe. At time they dance exuberantly, at other times with great dignity, and they end their performance with genuinely lovely choral singing by the children.

The Children's Music Theatre in Moscow

The civil war in Russia, which culminated in the Bolshevik Revolution of 1917, had a sad by-product: thousands of *bezprizorni* (homeless orphans). Many people were sorry for these pitiful children, and one, a 15-year-old girl named Natalya Sats, who headed the children's art department at the Moscow City Soviet, decided to do something special for them. She began organizing shows at the Bolshoi Theater for these youngsters, believing that children who had lived through famine and fear were in need of entertainment to cheer them up as well as of food and housing, even at a time when Moscow was short of firewood and bread. In 1918, on the first anniversary of the October Revolution, Natalya opened a children's theater, assembling a group of composers, artists, and actors who shared her ideas. This eventually led to the first permanent Children's Music Theatre, which blended two powerful educational elements capable of touching a child's heart and soul: pageantry and music.

By 1986 the theater had been established in a special building of its own. The architects designed the building so that little children found themselves in a festive atmosphere the moment they crossed the threshold. At the entrance they were greeted by heroes of the best-known children's books, among them Tom Sawyer and Becky Thatcher, who made the young visitors feel like honored guests and that something beautiful and exciting was in store for them.

The second story of the two-tiered foyer had a large birdcage, a round lacy structure where children listened to stories and background music. Next to the birdcage was a music room with a grand piano. This was where children were encouraged to ask any questions they had about music.

In addition to a children's theater museum, the building had a Little Brothers and Sisters Room, where children who did not want to see the show for some reason, either because they were overtired or overexcited, could sit it out, watched over and entertained by teachers on the theater's staff. There were 450 people on the staff, including 60 actors and 74 orchestra musicians.

The theater's Grand Hall had three stages, whose sizes could be changed in accordance with the requirements of different productions. There was also a Small Hall for chamber music that required an intimate setting. This was also a good setting for an evening lecture on Russian folk instruments, followed by a virtuoso balalaika concert. The next day it might feature a talk from the "Birth of an Opera" cycle, which would have the young audience listening spellbound to an account of the life of Mozart and to his rarely performed one-act *Bastien and Bastienne*.

The theater's purpose was to educate children with excitement, without preaching. Tickets were inexpensive and it continually played to full houses.

The Repertoire

By the 1980s the theater had built up a repertoire of 15 operas, ballets, cantatas, and symphonic works.

The Blue Bird of Happiness was made the official emblem of the Children's Music Theatre, as the Seagull has long been the symbol of the celebrated Moscow Art Theatre, and a statue of the Blue Bird holding a harp crowned the theater's roof. A regular production of the theater was *The Blue Bird*, a ballet based on a mystical story by the famous Belgian playwright and poet Maurice Maeterlinck (1862–1949), set to music by Mikhail Raukhverger and Ilya Sats (Natalya's father). The ballet's libretto is a fairy tale, so the sets were fantastic. Joining hands, a boy named Tyltyl and a girl named Mytyl set out on a journey in search of happiness. They travel not only in space but also in time, visiting the past and the future. They also find themselves in a fantastic land where they learn the language of animals. They meet many hardships on the way, reminding audiences that happiness is elusive and not always easy to find, but friendship and love help them overcome all obstacles. Tyltyl and Mytyl do not manage to catch the Blue Bird, but at the end of the performance when the lights go on in the auditorium and the audience is applauding, the Bird flits through the air over the children's heads like a promise of happiness for all of them.

Enchanted Music by Mark Minkov is one of the most popular operas the theater has produced. It is an opera about opera. With the help of the orchestra and singers, clowns describe a duet, a trio, and a chorus. They also tell the audience what a libretto is and explain all about the action in an opera. After that, they set out on a merry journey to Foolsland, which is ruled by King Chatterbox XIV and Queen Yawn. Both the Queen and her daughter, Princess Tearsabeth, are dying of boredom until the clowns and two wandering minstrels bring Dame Music into the palace, and the reign of Boredom and Malice is overthrown under the influence of a melody that is the show's chief musical theme. In the finale the audience gets to join in singing the song, "Thank You, Music!"

Peter and the Wolf by the great Soviet composer Sergei Prokofiev (1891–1953), written in 1936 at the request of Natalya Sats, has been another perennial favorite. Its purpose is to teach children to recognize the different instruments in a symphony. Before the beginning of a performance, a master of ceremonies acquaints the youngsters in the audience with each instrument in the orchestra. "The flute plays the role of the bird," he explains. "Now listen to the sound." At this point the flutist plays the opening bars of his theme song. Then the narrator says, "The oboe has the role of the duck," and the oboe plays the duck's theme. Next, "The clarinet plays the cat" and the clarinetist performs.

"And the bassoon is the grumpy grandfather." The first sounds of the bassoon usually draw loud laughter. "Three French horns are the wolf" and again there are appreciative cheers. "And the hunters' shots are, naturally, played on the drum and kettledrum." Finally, it is explained that "the role of Peter, being the most important and complex, is played by the whole orchestra."

After this introduction, the musical narrative is performed about the bird who cannot swim so he is jealous of the duck, and the duck who cannot fly so he is jealous of the bird, but their fates are joined when the wolf swallows the poor duck while the frightened cat and bird, former enemies, hide together in a tree until brave Peter rescues everybody by catching the nasty wolf with his lasso, and they all become friends. The story's mixture of humor and suspense invariably brings the delighted children to their feet with tumultuous applause.

Other Children's Theater Productions

After Natalya Sats's brainchild opened in Moscow, children's theaters sprouted all over Russia. Theaters were started even at the most difficult times. The Kazakh Children's Theater, for instance, was opened in 1944 during World War II. It is impossible to give an exact count of the number of children's theaters in the former Soviet Union because new ones kept opening one after another. By the late 1980s the number had approached 200, and an International Association of Children's and Youth Theatres had united more than 38 national companies.

But Moscow's Music Theatre was the first and is unique. American audiences saw its productions of "Enchanted Music" and "Peter and the Wolf" when the company toured the U.S. and Canada in 1986. The tour was a sensational success. One review in the Canadian press was appropriately entitled "A Theatre That Overcomes Language Barriers." Natalya Sats's long life was a triumph. She lived into her nineties, dying in 1995, and she well deserves the honorific she has been given as "The Mother of Children's Theatre."

12

Children and Literature

COMMENTS ABOUT CHILDREN AND LITERATURE

This is the sort of thing that glees my heart.
—A little girl describing Alice in Wonderland

I started reading at 4 and I've kept at it for over three-quarters of a century with occasional interruptions for eating, sleeping and a few other matters. Within that vast stretch of years my most enjoyable reading was done between 4 and 14 . . . . That's the best time . . . . I read for the same reason we all like to open Christmas gifts. Each book was a surprise package stuffed with things I had no idea ever existed. I grew bug-eyed over the miracle of language. How could a few punctuation marks plus words made out of 26 letters be put together so as actually to make (inside my head) people, animals, stories, landscapes, streets, towns, and even ideas? Here I was, a rather dull boy looking at an unopened book. Then within a short time the dull boy found he was entertained, amused, saddened, delighted, mystified, scared, dreamy, puzzled, astonished, held in suspense—all depending on what was in those pages . . . . It's good to get such feelings at an early age . . . .

Understand the basic difference between reading and watching most of TV: reading makes the mind and imagination do some interesting work or play, and most of TV simply doesn't . . . . there's a chapter from Louise Fitzhugh's *Harriet the Spy*. Harriet sits down to read. "How I love to read," she thought. "The whole world gets bigger." If you don't get the habit when you're young, you may never get it. And if you don't get it, you may grow up to be just as dull as most adults are. For they're the ones for whom, as Harriet would say, the world never got bigger.
—Clifton Fadiman, in the introduction to his anthology
The World Treasury of Children's Literature *(1985)*

Of all people children are the most imaginative. They abandon themselves without reserve to every illusion. No man, whatever his sensibility may be, is ever affected by *Hamlet* or *Lear* as a little girl is affected by the story of poor *Red Riding Hood*. *—Thomas Babington Macaulay (1800–1859)*

Shall we simply allow our children to listen to any story anyone happens to make up, and so receive into their minds ideas often the very opposite of those we shall think they ought to have when they are grown up?
—Plato (427–347 B.C.)

In my judgment, the divine Plato struck the right note when he advised nurses to exercise careful choice even in telling stories to children, so that their minds should not at the outset be filled with foolishness and vice.
—Plutarch (46–120 A.D.)

I conceive that the right way to write a story for boys is to write so that it will not only interest boys but will also strongly interest any man who has ever been a boy. *—Mark Twain (1835–1910)*

446

In my experience, the only difference [between writing for children and for adults], save for a very slight modification of vocabulary, is in one's state of mind. Children are a wonderful audience—they are so eager, so receptive, so quick . . . . I rather suspect that it is a great help if one has managed never really to grow up. Some writers, I have noticed, have a tendency to write down to children. That way lies disaster.   —*E. B. White (1899–1986)*

MOTHER GOOSE: WHO WAS SHE?
Candidates

Bertha, La Reine (?–783): She was the mother of Charlemagne and was called *Berthe aux grands pieds* (Bertha of the big feet) and "Queen Goosefoot" or "Goose-footed Bertha." In French legends she is pictured as incessantly spinning, with hordes of children around her, listening to her stories.

Bertha of Burgundy (962–1031): She was the cousin and second of three wives of King Robert II of France, who despite being known as "Robert the Pious" was excommunicated by the Pope for marrying her. At that time the Church considered marriages between cousins to be incest, so it prohibited them; the child Bertha and Robert had was "therefore" born a "monster" and described in legends as a creature with the head of a goose . . . making Bertha the "mother of a goose."

Elizabeth Foster Goose (1665–1757): Elizabeth Foster Goose is buried in the historic old Granary Burying Ground in Boston, and her tombstone identifies her as "Mother

Goose." In 1692, at the age of 27, she married Isaac Goose, aged 55. Her husband had been married before, and she immediately became stepmother of 10 children and then had six children of her own. By her daughter and namesake Elizabeth Goose Fleet she also had seven grandchildren. It is said that Elizabeth Foster Goose "lulled" her grandchildren to sleep with rhymes and that her son-in-law Thomas Fleet, who was a printer, decided to publish them in 1719 under the title *Songs for the Nursery, or Mother Goose's Melodies.*

With 23 children in her household, some people have identified her as "the old woman who lived in a shoe and had so many children she didn't know what to do." (The shoe has long been a symbol of fertility; hence the custom of tying a shoe to the vehicle in which a bride and groom leave together after their wedding.) However, this rhyme, even if it could be applied to her, was actually born before she was. Also, no copies of the book said to have been published by Thomas Fleet have been found, whereas we know of earlier books that include the name "Mother Goose," so even if this book did exist, he may just have appropriated the name, which would make Elizabeth Goose a mother but not *the* Mother Goose. It is also possible that she was the first Mother Goose to compose nursery rhymes rather than fairy tales.

A highly entertaining musical play for children called *The Strange Case of Mother Goose,* written in 1954 by Pamela and Edward Borgers, won the Aline Bernstein Award for that year and had its premiere performance at the Junior Theatre of Columbia, South

Carolina, the following year. It set out to solve the mystery of why Thomas Fleet's book of Mother Goose rhymes has never been found. It does so in a fanciful way, with magic tricks, unusual sound and lighting effects, and cheery music and witty dialogue, but it makes a serious and pretty logical case.

The play's action takes place in 1720 in the Fleets' home where Thomas's print shop is located. The president of Boston's Selectmen, Solomon Grundy, comes to visit and sees the books, which have just come off the press. He is a notorious prig with no sense of humor and is shocked by the light-hearted nonsense of the verses. He orders Thomas to destroy them. When Thomas refuses, Mr. Brundy storms out in anger and proceeds to organize a mob to come to the house and burn Mother Goose as a witch (this is taking place only eight years after the notorious witch trials in Salem.) She escapes, so then the mob seizes the books and burns them and after that proceeds to smash the printing press. Since Thomas has no money to buy a replacement that is the end of his career as a printer.

Something of that kind is very probably what happened. It would be neither the first nor the last time puritanical censors in Boston have acted in that manner. But the play ends on a happy note, with Mother Goose comforting the children who are crying because they cannot get copies of her book. She tells them they do not need them because "you'll sing these songs to your children and they'll sing them to their children forever."

In a program note, the play's authors wrote, "Some of the rhymes ascribed by tradition to Mother Goose were surely created before Mrs. Isaac Goose was born. But that she did write many of them, and that she was a lively, original personality, the record makes quite clear. Mother Goose remains one of those universally appealing people who, by their timeless qualities of compassion and humor, give meaning to our lives."

Earliest Known Publications

The name "Mother Goose," as a teller of nursery tales rather than of nursery rhymes, goes back to the year 1650 when *La Muse Historique* was published in France, with a volume containing the line, "Comme un conte de la Mère de l'Oye" (like a story by Mother Goose). In Germany, around this same time, stories were published by *Fru Gode* and *Fru Gosen.*

Charles Perrault (1628–1703), a dignitary at the Court of Versailles in France, published in 1697, under the name of his 10-year-old son Perrault d'Armancourt, a collection of fairy tales called *Les Contes de la Mère l'Oye* (Tales of Mother Goose).

In 1729 in England, a book of *Fairy Tales by Mother Goose* was published by J. Pate of Charing Cross. This was the first printing in English of Charles Perrault's tales.

Hear What Ma'am Goose Says

The following "Letter to Children from Ma'am Goose" appeared in an early American edition of nursery rhymes:

My dear little Blossoms, there are now in this world, and always will be, a great many grannies besides myself, both in petticoats and pantaloons, some a deal

448

younger to be sure; but all monstrous wise, and of my own family name. These old women, who never had chick nor child of their own, but who always know how to bring up other people's children, will tell you with very long faces, that my enchanting, quieting, soothing volume, my all-sufficient anodyne for cross, peevish, won't be comforted little babies, ought to be laid aside for more learned books, such as they could select and publish. Fudge! I tell you that all their banterings can't deface my beauties, nor their wise pratings equal my wiser prattlings; and all imitators of my refreshing songs might as well write a new Billy Shakespeare as another Mother Goose—we two great poets were born together, and we shall go out of the world together.

> No, no, my melodies will never die,
> While nurses sing or babies cry.

Two centuries later a distinguished literary critic confirmed what "Ma'am Goose" said on this subject:

Nursery rhymes will live forever. Or at any rate as long as there are small children who like to laugh, sing, and dream—and I hope that means forever.
> —*Clifton Fadiman*

Leading Authors and Collectors of Fairy Tales and Fables

Aesop (c. 620–560 B.C.): Greek fabulist. Born a slave and deformed, Aesop had such wit and charm that his master, Iadmon, freed him and he gained a reputation not only as a wit but as a sage. Croesus, King of Lydia from 560–546 B.C., believed knowledge was power and gathered around him people who had attained a reputation for wisdom. When Aesop came to his court, he was already famous as a storyteller whose tales contained shrewd comments on the morals and politics of the day. He quickly gained favor with Croesus by his good humor and genial way of imparting knowledge. His travels also led him to Corinth and Athens where he was equally well received, and to Delphi, where he was not. The Delphic oracles felt their own reputation for wisdom, the source of their income, was threatened by him, so they killed him by hurling him from a precipice. Later they repented and offered financial compensation for his death to anyone who could prove a title to their self-imposed fine, but none appeared and it was finally awarded to Iadmon, the grandson of Aesop's old master.

The first printed collection of *Aesop's Fables* was published 200 years after his death. It included some that have been traced to earlier stories as well as some that actually originated after he had died. Among the more than 500 that have been attributed to him the most famous are: "The Ant and the Grasshopper," "The Boy Who Cried Wolf," "The Country Mouse and the City Mouse," "The Dog in the Manger," "The Fox and Sour Grapes," "The Father, Son and Ass [or Mule]," "The Shepherd Turned Merchant," "The Tortoise and the Hare," and "The Wind and the Sun."

Hans Christian Andersen (1805–1875): Danish author. He wrote three novels, but his claim to immortal fame is his 172 *Fairy Tales*. Among the most popular are: "Little Claus

449

and Big Claus," "The Fir Tree," "The Red Shoes" (later made into a ballet and a movie), "The Snow Queen," "The Swineherd," "The Tinder Box," and "The Ugly Duckling."

Jon Arnason (1819–1888): Icelandic writer and collector. Arnason is known for his collections of his country's traditional tales: *Folk Tales of Iceland* (1862–1864) and *Icelandic Folktales and Legends* (1872).

Contesse Marie Catherine d'Aulnoy (1650–1705): French author. The Contesse is best known for her *Diverting Works*, a collection of fairy tales that includes "L'Oiseau Bleu" (Bluebird) and "La Belle aux Cheveux d'Or" (Goldilocks).

Sir Richard Burton (1821–1890): British explorer and Orientalist. He produced an English translation of *A Thousand and One Nights,* which he titled *Arabian Nights,* in 16 volumes published between 1885 and 1888.

Jean de La Fontaine (1621–1695): French fabulist. A favorite at the illustrious court of Versailles under King Louis XIV (1638–1715) where Racine and Moliere were also celebrated writers, Fontaine wrote, among other books, 12 for children: *Fables choisies, mises en vers* (Selected Stories Told in Verse), which he dedicated to the king's children and to their governess, Mme. de Montespan. They were published in 1668, 1679, and 1694.

The Brothers Grimm—Jacob Ludwig Grimm (1785–1863) and **Wilhelm Karl Grimm** (1786–1859): German scholars. These two professors, who specialized in philology and mythology, published both individually and jointly many scholarly books on early literature, but they are best remembered for their collaboration on a two-volume work, *Kinder und Hausmärchen* (Children and Household Tales), published in 1812 and 1815. These included more than 80 traditional folk tales they had collected, These stories were translated and published in English in 1823 under the title *German Popular Stories;* they are best known in English today as *Grimms' Fairy Tales.*

Nathaniel Hawthorne (1804–1864): American author. The literary success of this distinguished novelist and short story writer was first established by books he wrote for children: *Twice-Told Tales* (two series, the first published in 1837, the second in 1842), followed by *The Snow Image and Other Twice-told Tales* in 1851, *A Wonder Book for Girls and Boys* in 1852, and *Tanglewood Tales for Girls and Boys* (a retelling of Greek legends) in 1853. Among his most famous stories was "The Little Match Girl."

Edward William Lane (1801–1876): English scholar. Lane specialized in Arabic studies and was, in 1840, the first translator into English of *Arabian Nights' Entertainments,* or *A Thousand and One Nights.* Later there were other translations, notably the one by Burton (see above). The original source of these stories is unknown, but it is believed they were collected in Egypt by a professional storyteller some time during the fourteenth to sixteenth centuries. The most famous of the stories are "Sinbad the Sailor" and "Aladdin and the Lamp."

Andrew Lang (1844–1912): Scottish poet and scholar. Lang considered folklore the foundation of mythology and wrote a book in 1888, *Perrault's Popular Tales*, in which he discussed the origins of many nursery tales. When he was not busy writing historical studies, biographies, and novels, he wrote collections of nursery tales and added some new ones of his own in 12 volumes of *The Fairy Books*, with each volume named after a different color, for example, *The Red Fairy Book. The Blue Fairy Book,* published in 1889, contains "East of the Sun and West of the Moon," a popular Norwegian fairy tale.

Marie, Queen of Romania (1875–1938): English author. Marie was the eldest daughter of Alfred, Duke of Edinburgh, and her baptismal name was **Marie Alexandra Victoria.** At 18 she married Ferdinand who became King of Romania in 1914. She served her adopted country well and was much beloved by its people, but she had another unusual distinction for a Queen: she was the author of several books, all in English, both fiction and nonfiction, including a collection of beautiful Romanian fairy tales.

Iona and **Peter Opie** (1918–1982): English scholars. The lifework of this married couple has been to collect material about children. All their books have been published by the Oxford University Press. They have compiled volume after volume on children's games, songs, nursery rhymes, poems, as well as *The Classic Fairy Tales,* published in 1974.

Charles Perrault (1628–1703): French writer. Perrault's collection of great fairy tales (mentioned on page 000), *Les Contes le la Mère l'Oye (Tales of Mother Goose),* and subtitled *Histoires ou contes de temps passée, avec des moralités,* published in 1697, included seven stories and their morals: "Cinderella," "Diamonds and Toads," "Hop o' My Thumb," "Little Red Riding Hood," "Puss in Boots," "Sleeping Beauty" and "Three Wasted Wishes."

Gustav Schwab (1792–1850): German author. Schwab published his own verse as well as anthologies of German prose and poetry. These included volumes in 1836 of *Deutsche Volksbücher* (*German Folk Books*) and in 1845 *Gods and Heroes: Myths and Epics of Ancient Greece.*

Oscar Wilde, full name **Oscar Fingal O'Flahertie Wills Wilde** (1854–1900): Irish author. The acid wit and cynicism characteristic of Wilde's plays and conversation was replaced by sweetness and idealism in his beautiful *The Happy Prince and Other Tales* (1888).

AESOP'S FABLES ABOUT CHILDREN

Most of Aesop's fables used animals as characters who could teach humans how to, and how not to, behave. But in a few fables he used children to teach morals, for example, in the following versions from *Fables of Aesop and Others, with Instructive Applications by Samuel Croxall D.D., and Other Moralists* (1876):

> **"Fortune and the Boy."** A boy was sleeping by the side of a well. Fortune saw him, and came and waked him, saying, "Pr'ythee, good child, do not lie sleeping here, for if you should fall in, nobody would impute it to you, but lay all the blame to me, Fortune."

> *The Application*: Poor Fortune has a great deal thrown upon her indeed, and often times very unjustly too. Those of our actions that are attended with success, though often owing to some accident or other, we ascribe, without any scruple, to some particular merit or good quality in ourselves; but when any of our doings miscarry, though probably through our own insufficiency or neglect, all the ill consequences are imputed to Fortune, and we acquit ourselves of having contributed anything towards it.

"The Brother and the Sister." A certain man had two children, a son and daughter. The boy beautiful and handsome enough, the girl not quite so well. They were both very young, and happened one day to be playing near a looking glass, which stood upon their mother's toilet; the boy, pleased with the novelty of the thing, viewed himself for some time, and in a wanton, roguish manner, took notice to the girl how handsome he was. She resented it, as if he had intended it for a direct affront to her. Therefore she ran immediately to her father, and complained of her brother, for having acted so effeminate a part as to look in a glass, and meddle with things which belonged to women only. The father, embracing them with much tenderness and affection, told them that he should like them both to look in the glass every day. "To the intent that you," says he to the boy, "if you think that face of yours handsome, may not disgrace and spoil it by an ugly temper and a foul behavior. You," says he, speaking to the girl, "that you make up for the defects of your person, if there be any, by the sweetness of your manners and the agreeableness of your conversation."

The Application: It is good to study ourselves carefully.

"The Shepherd's Boy," better known today as "The Boy Who Cried Wolf." A certain shepherd's boy kept his sheep upon a common, and in sport and wantonness would often cry out, "The Wolf, the Wolf!" By this means he sometimes drew the husbandmen in an adjoining field from their work, who, finding themselves deluded, resolved for the future to take no notice of his alarm. Soon after, the wolf came indeed. The boy cried out in earnest. But no heed being given to his cries, the sheep were devoured by the wolf.

The Application: He that is found once to be a liar, besides the ignominy and reproach of the thing, will not be credited even when he speaks the truth.

BOOK PUBLISHING FOR CHILDREN
John Newbery (1713–1767)

The first publisher of books specifically for children was John Newbery (1713–1767), who also wrote for children and in 1745 opened a children's bookshop in London, described in *The Vicar of Wakefield* by Oliver Goldsmith (1728–1774). The first book Newbery published was called *A Little Pretty Pocket Book* and subtitled "for the instruction and amusement of little Master Tommy and pretty Miss Polly." Before this time, some children had, of course, read books, but they were usually books written for adults that children discovered and borrowed.

Newbery was also the first merchandiser of gimmicks to help promote the sales of children's books. Along with his *Little Pretty Pocket Book* he sold "an agreeable Letter to read from Jack the Giant Killer, and also a Ball and a Pincushion, the use of which will infallibly make Tommy a good Boy and Polly a good Girl." And he published many special gift editions such as *The Christmas Box, The Twelfth Day Gift* (promoted as *Plum Cake for Ever*), and *The New Year's Gift*. These were called "gilt books" because they were covered in fancy shiny papers.

In 1751 Newbery published the *Lilliputian Magazine*, or "The Young Gentleman's and Lady's Golden Library, being an attempt to establish the Plainness, Simplicity, Virtue and Wisdom of the Golden Age so much celebrated by Poets and Historians." He believed in amusing children as well as educating them, so the magazine contained riddles, songs, and illustrations as well as edifying stories.

In 1760 he published *Mother Goose's Melody, or Sonnets for the Cradle* and in 1766 *The History of Little Goody Two Shoes*, a story about an orphan who, through virtue and wisdom, achieved prosperity. It was dedicated "to all young Gentlemen and Ladies who are good or intend to be good" and

> "Who from a State of Rags and Care
> and having Shoes but half a Pair
> Their Fortune and their Fame would fix
> and gallop in a Coach and six."

Newbery's own fortune and fame have been commemorated since 1921 by the Newbery Medal awarded annually to the author of the most distinguished contribution to literature for children published in America during the preceding year.

AUTHORS OF CHILDREN'S BOOKS IN PREVIOUS CENTURIES

Jacob Abbott (1803–1879): American author. His *Little Rollo* (1834) was the first book to portray a genuine American child character in fiction. It launched the Rollo series of 28 volumes: *Rollo at Play; Rollo at Work; Rollo Learning to Read; Rollo's Travels*; and so forth. Abbott had a higher regard for children's intelligence than many twentieth-century teachers. In his "Notice to Parents" in *Rollo Learning to Read*, he said, "The difficulty with most books intended for children just learning to read is that the writers make so much effort to confine themselves to words of one syllable that the style is quaint and uninteresting and far more unintelligible than the usual language would be." He was a Congregational minister and founder of a school for girls, but after the success of *Little Rollo* he retired from the ministry to devote himself to writing juveniles, including *Harper's Story Books* (36 volumes). He also wrote children's books about historical characters, and he was the favorite author of Abraham Lincoln.

Louisa May Alcott (1832–1888): American author. While still in her teens she wrote stories in order to make money to help her family. In 1867 she edited a magazine for children, *Merry's Museum*. Later she wrote novels for children, some based on her own childhood in Concord, Massachusetts: *Little Women* (two volumes, in 1868 and 1869), *An Old-Fashioned Girl* (1870), *Little Men* (1871), *Jo's Boys* (1886), *Under the Lilacs* (1878), and *Eight Cousins*. All of them are still popular and widely translated. *Little Women* has been successfully adapted to film numerous times, most recently in 1995.

Thomas Bailey Aldrich (1836–1907): American author and editor. His children's books are *The Story of a Bad Boy* about his own childhood (1870) (by today's standards he was an extremely good boy) and *Marjorie Daw* (1873). His childhood home has been preserved as a museum in the city of Portsmouth, New Hampshire.

Horatio Alger (1832–1899): American writer. This Unitarian minister wrote more than 100 hugely popular books for boys: *Ragged Dick* (1867), *Luck and Pluck* (1869), *Tattered Tom*

(1871), *Phil the Fiddler*, and others. Of all the authors of series of books for boys, he is the best remembered. His books bore different titles and the heroes different names, but they were really each the same book and the same hero, rising from rags to riches through hard work, virtue, and courage. Alger deserves credit for having helped bootblacks, fiddlers, beggar boys, and other poor street children; in some of his books he portrayed their plight so vividly that public indignation was aroused against their exploitation.

Arnaud Berquin (1749–1791): French writer. Known as "The Children's Friend," he wrote 24 volumes, all translated into English and popular in both France and England. One of his most endearing and enduring stories was "Androcles and the Lion" which George Bernard Shaw adapted into a play in 1912.

Lewis Carroll (See page 460.)

Collodi, real name **Carlo Lorenzini** (1826–1890): Italian writer. He took the name of Collodi from the town where his mother was born. He came from a poor family and ran wild through the streets of Florence and was a terror in school. Later, however, he became a government official and took an interest in improving education. He wrote several books on education and then wrote a story for children about a wooden puppet who, like himself, had trouble at school but who eventually learned the error of his ways. The book was *Le Avventure di Pinocchio,* first published in *The Children's Journal of Rome*, and then issued as a book (1882). Before long a million copies of the book had been sold. Since then it has been translated into many languages, and was made into a delightful Disney animated cartoon film. It has also taught many children not to tell lies for fear their noses will grow long like Pinocchio's.

Susan Coolidge, real name **Sarah Chauncey Woolsey** (1835–1905): American writer. She wrote several entertaining books for girls about a young heroine called Katy: *What Katy Did* (1873), *What Katy Did at School* (1874), *What Katy Did Next* (1886). One of the things Katy did at school was to become a member of SSUC (The Society for the Suppression of Unladylike Conduct.), a girls' secret society.

John Cotton (1584–1652): American writer. This Puritan preacher wrote the first children's book published in the United States, printed in Cambridge, Massachusetts in 1646. Its title was literally quite a mouthful: *Spiritual Milk for Boston Babes Drawn from the Breasts of Both Testaments for Their Souls' Nourishment.*

Thomas Day (1748–1789): English author. An ardent follower of Jean Jacques Rousseau, he wrote *The History of Sanford and Merton,* three popular volumes published in 1783, 1787, and 1789. All the poor people in his books are suffering saints, and his rich people are all idle, vain, dissolute, and useless. But he himself was not entirely useless; he was one of the first authors to inveigh against cruel sports and unkindness to animals.

Daniel Defoe (1660–1731): English journalist and novelist. He did not turn to writing fiction until he was nearly 60 years old, when he wrote the immortal *Robinson Crusoe* (1719). This adventure story is based on the real experiences of a Scottish sailor, Alexander Selkirk (1676–1721), who was a castaway shipwrecked on an uninhabited island off the coast of Chile for four years. Defoe also wrote *The History of Colonel Jack* and *Moll Flanders* (1721) and *The Highland Rogue, Rob Roy* (1723). He has been said to be the first writer of fiction to write realistic portrayals of children. Whether dealing with the childhood of poor little Moll who, at age eight, prays not to be sent into service in a great house where she will be beaten and overworked, or the childhood of his gutter hero, Colonel Jack, he is equally convincing. When Charles Dickens published *Oliver Twist* in 1837–1839 he was acclaimed as the first great author to describe poor children, but his readers must have forgotten that more than 100 years earlier Defoe had described the homeless children of London. Defoe is still a worldwide bestselling author; there were 50 translations of his books published in the International Year of the Child (1979), and in 1995 *Rob Roy* was made into a Hollywood film.

Charles Dickens (See page 459.)

Mary Mapes Dodge (1831–1905): American writer and editor. To support her two children after her husband died, she wrote *Irvington Stories,* based on American history. Next, her publisher asked her to write a novel about the Civil War, but instead she wrote *Hans Brinker, or the Silver Skates* in 1865, set in Holland where she had never been, although her family background was Dutch. Within 30 years the book went into 100 editions in six languages, and the Dutch even built a statue to honor it. In 1873 she became the first editor of *St. Nicholas Magazine* for children, where, for 32 years, she published outstanding stories.

Alexandre Dumas (Père) (1802–1870): French playwright and novelist. Among his most famous works are the swashbuckling adventure stories that have been reproduced many times in the movies: *The Count of Monte Cristo* (1844), *The Three Musketeers* (1844), and *The Man in the Iron Mask* (1848). For a long time his books were on the Vatican's Index of Forbidden Books because of their anticlericalism and romanticization of illicit love and of dueling, but nothing could persuade people, particularly children, not to read and enjoy them.

Maria Edgeworth (1767–1849): English author. She wrote 20 adult novels and a collection of short stories for children called *The Parents' Assistant* (1796). "It seems no very easy task to write books for children," she wrote in her preface to this book, but she was outstandingly successful at it. She wrote didactic tales with a sense of humor and a strong sense of character. Her stories were always tried out on her many brothers and sisters, who listened to "Lazy Lawrence," "Simple Susan," "Waste Not, Want Not," "The Birthday Present," "The False Key," and others. Through her stories they learned the evils of laziness, affectation, dishonesty, and the like, while being thrilled by her ingenious plots.

Martha Farquharson, married name **Martha Farquharson Finley** (1828–1909): American author. She wrote under her maiden name many books for girls, including *Elsie Dinsmore* (26 volumes, the first in 1868), *The Mildred Series* (7 volumes), and *Pewit's Nest Series* (12 volumes).

Oliver Goldsmith (c. 1730–1774): English poet, dramatist, and novelist. Although he is best known today for his adult writings, including the Restoration comedy *She Stoops to Conquer* (1773) and the novel *The Vicar of Wakefield* (1776), Goldsmith was a constant writer of children's literature for the publishing house of John Newbery between 1762 and 1767, editing and writing the preface to *Mother Goose's Melody* and many of its jesting notes and maxims. Newbery called him "the Very Great Writer of Very Little Books." It is believed that he was the anonymous author of *Little Goody Two Shoes.*

Lucretia Peabody Hale (1820–1900): American writer. She wrote *The Peterkin Papers* (1880) and *The Last of the Peterkins* (1886). Until these books came along, mothers in most children's books were towers of strength to their families, but Mrs. Peterkin was as scatterbrained as the rest of her family. Perhaps that is why children who were beginning to doubt the nineteenth-century dogma about the infallibility of parents were so very fond of her.

Nathaniel Hawthorne (1804–1864): American novelist. His father died when he was only four and he took it very hard; there is a tinge of melancholy in much of his writing. Nevertheless, Hawthorne had many good friends at Bowdoin College in Maine, where his roommate was Henry Wadsworth Longfellow, and he also had a happy marriage and family life. He was the author of several adult novels; the best known is *The Scarlet Letter.* He also wrote books for children that became classics: *The House of the Seven Gables* (1851), a novel about a young girl; and several collections of lovely fairy tales (see page 450). The actual house of seven gables in Salem, Massachusetts, is now a popular tourist attraction—a combined museum, souvenir shop, and tea room.

Ernst Theodor Amadeus Hoffmann (1776–1822): German composer, fiction writer, and illustrator. He wrote operas and novels that have made generations of children, both child performers and children in the audience, happy with his "Nutcracker" fantasy set to music by Tchaikovsky and performed every year at Christmas time. For children who cannot get to the theater, or who want to relive the experience, *The Story of the Nutcracker* has also been published as a book, illustrated by Maurice Sendak (see page 484).

Mary Howitt (1799–1888) and her husband **William Howitt** (1792–1879): English authors. Despite bearing and rearing 12 children, Mary found time to be an author, poet, editor, and translator of more than 100 books. She translated the fairy tales of Hans Christian Andersen and introduced them to the English-speaking world. William produced almost as many books as his wife did, including *The Boy's Country Book* in 1839, a memoir of his childhood.

Thomas Hughes (1822–1896): English jurist, social reformer, and writer. He is best remembered for his novels, *Tom Brown's School Days,* first published in 1856 anonymously by "An Old Boy" (and in the 1980s presented in an excellent adaptation on British television), and its sequel *Tom Brown at Oxford* (1861). His hero Tom is a bright boy from a poor family befriended by a patron who gets him admitted to a posh school where, because of his shabby clothes and lower-class accent, he is sneered at and bullied by the other boys and by a snobbish teacher. When the teacher holds him up to ridicule in front of his fellow students for mispronouncing a word, Tom sticks up for himself, saying he's not ashamed that he has read more words than he has heard spoken. Through well-drawn characters, especially his appealing young hero, and a compelling story, Hughes shows, without preaching, how cruel and unjust class prejudice can be, and his books had considerable impact in bringing about reforms in important aspects of British schools.

Victor Hugo (1802–1885): French poet, novelist, and dramatist. He wrote several novels, most notably *Les Miserables* (1862), as well as other works. Despite its great length, *Les Miserables,* a 10-volume novel about poverty and injustice, still fascinates children and adults, and its hero Jean Valjean is a favorite even among 10-year-olds. Abridged versions are available for less ambitious readers, as well as movie versions and the sensationally successful musical version first staged in 1980 by the Royal Shakespeare Company in England and brought to Broadway in 1987 where it became one of New York's longest-running shows. Productions of the musical version have been staged in major cities worldwide. With its French music and libretto, its English adapters, directors, and produc-ers, and with local casts in 22 countries, it seems to have signaled the internationalization of a new theatrical art form beyond its author's wildest dreams.

Washington Irving (1783–1859): American essayist, biographer, and historian. His *Sketch Book* contained two immortal stories loved by youngsters: "The Legend of Sleepy Hollow" and "Rip Van Winkle."

James Janeway (1636–1674): English author. He wrote an inspirational book for children called *A Token for Children, Being an Exact Account of the Conversion, Holy and Exemplary Lives and Joyful Deaths of Several Young Children*. Editions of it continued to be printed into the nineteenth century.

Annie Fellows Johnston (1863–1931): American author. She wrote several novels for girls, but the one that enjoyed the most lasting success was *The Little Colonel,* written in 1895 about a young Southern belle during the American War of Independence. The "Little Colonel" was a wealthy aristocrat with Tory sympathies and a close friend of an English spy, Major John André, but American girls fell in love with the book anyway. It was similar to *Gone with the Wind* with its vivid evocation of a glamorized South mingled with fascinating historical details about this exciting time. They read and reread the book, reveling in the glittering ballroom scenes and weeping over the death of the handsome major. In real life Major John André was a loyal English patriot who negotiated with the American traitor Benedict Arnold for the betrayal of West Point to the British, yet he was respected as such a gracious and brave foe that even his captors regretted hanging him, and today he is honored at the site of his death by a statue with a laudatory epitaph in Tarrytown, New York.

Charles Kingsley (1819–1875): English clergyman, novelist, poet, and history professor at Cambridge University. He wrote many novels as well as scholarly essays and sermons, and three books that children enjoyed. *Westward Ho!* (1855), his most successful novel, was not written for children, but they eagerly adopted it. It is a fast-moving adventure story set during the reign of Queen Elizabeth I, full of action with episodes of betrayal, naval warfare, persecution by the Spanish Inquisition, revenge, and romance. *The Heroes* (1856) was written for young readers to acquaint them with the Greek legends about Perseus, Theseus, and the Argonauts. *The Water Babies, A Fairy Tale for a Land Baby* (1863) is a humorous story for young children about a chimney sweep who ran away from a bully and fell into a river, where he was turned into a water baby and made friends with all sorts of delightful aquatic creatures.

Jan Ámos Komensky (1592–1670): Czechoslovakian. According to teachers in the Czech and Slovak Republics, this man was the author of the first book ever written for children: *Orbis Sensualium Pictus* ("The Visible World in Pictures"), a pocket-sized textbook published in 1658. It was filled with woodcut illustrations because Komensky thought children would find it easier to remember words if they were represented with pictures. Today Czech and Slovak children honor this innovator's birthday every year on "Teacher's Day," March 28, by bringing flowers and other gifts to their teachers.

Charles Lamb (1775–1834) and his sister **Mary Ann Lamb** (1764–1847): English authors. For W. Godwin's Juvenile Library they wrote *Tales from Shakespeare* (1807), designed to make Shakespeare's works familiar to the young, with Charles writing the tragedies and Mary doing the comedies; *Bible Stories for Children,* and *The Adventures of Ulysses*

457

(1808). Charles also wrote poetry, with many verses both for and about children, including a touching elegy "On an Infant dying as soon as born" (1827). It was extraordinary that he managed to write so many fine essays and articles and poems, because his life was difficult. Sickness and madness ran in the family; his sister Mary killed their invalid mother in 1796, in a fit of insanity, and all her life she was subject to periodic seizures. He gave up a planned marriage in order to take care of his sister, and throughout his life there were financial as well as emotional problems.

George Macdonald (1824–1905): Scottish theologian, novelist, and poet. He wrote two classics for children, *The Princess and the Goblin* and *At the Back of the North Wind* (1871) in which delightful fantasies teach moral lessons.

Karl May (1842–1912): German author. After a bad start in life, a childhood spent in poverty and seven years in prison, May became the most popular author of books for boys in Germany during the last half of the nineteenth century. He wrote numerous adventure stories set in the American West, the Near East, and South America, using first-person narrative in order to give the impression of actual experiences. His popularity did not end in the nineteenth century and was not confined to Germany; 22 translations of his books were published during the International Year of the Child (1979).

Oliver Optic, real name **William Taylor Adams** (1822–1897): American author and educator. As a teacher and principal in public schools in Boston, Massachusetts, Adams knew much about boys and what they liked. He wrote 1,000 stories for boys for magazines and newspapers and 116 books for boys in different series.

Peter Parley, real name **Samuel Griswold Goodrich** (1793–1860): American writer. Goodrich was the first person in the United States to write novels just for children. His *Tales of Peter Parley about America* came out in 1827, followed by *Tales of Peter Parley about Europe* and so on, until there were about 170 small volumes; five million copies were sold by 1850. Peter Parley's stories were concerned with children discovering "fact and fancy" about the world. Goodrich called the books "intellectual plum pudding." No one today reads him, but he and Jacob Abbott (see page 453) started something that is still popular today: the series.

Edgar Allan Poe (1809–1849): American poet and story writer. He wrote many fine poems, such as "Annabelle Lee," "The Raven," "Ulalume," and "The Bells." Poe is considered the founder of the mystery story because of such stories as "The Fall of the House of Usher," "The Gold Bug," "The Murders in the Rue Morgue," "The Pit and the Pendulum," "The Telltale Heart," and others. These are still scary and titillating even for today's children, hardened by horror movies.

Anna Sewell (1820–1878): English author. She wrote *Black Beauty: The Autobiography of a Horse.* It would be impossible to count the number of children who have wept and learned to be kind to animals through this beloved book, first published in 1877 and still read in more than 20 languages after more than 100 years.

Johanna Spyri, maiden name **Johanna Heusser** (1827–1901): Swiss writer. She was one of six children of a country doctor. After she was married she started writing short stories for children based on memories of her own childhood in the Alps. These were so popular that she combined them into a single novel called *Heidi* (1881). The book was an immediate success and went through 13 editions in 10 years. It is still one of the world's most popular children's books, and translations have been published in more than 20 languages. *Heidi* has also been made into several successful motion pictures (in 1937, 1952, 1965, and 1993) and in 1996 a 225-minute *Heidi* video set was issued of two of the films.

Robert Louis Stevenson (1850–1894): Scottish essayist, novelist, and poet. He was frail in health from infancy and a victim of gastric fever; he had to spend much of his childhood at home in bed. An imaginative child, he pretended that his sheets were sailboats and battlefields, and made up fanciful adventures for himself, which later became the basis of *A Child's Garden of Verses* (1885). His first popular book, *Travels with a Donkey in the Cévennes* (1879), was about a trip to France taken to improve his health. Once, while on a vacation, he drew a treasure map for his young stepson Lloyd, and then made up a story around it which grew into the book *Treasure Island,* published serially in *Young Folks* magazine in 1883. This was followed by another adventure story for children, *Kidnapped,* and by *Dr. Jekyll and Mr Hyde* (both published in 1886), *The Merry Men* (1887), and *The Black Arrow* (1888). Today his books for children are better known than his many distinguished poems, travel writings, and essays.

Margaret Sidney, pseudonym of **Harriet Mulford Lothrop**, née **Harriet Mulford Stone** (1844–1924): American writer. Her book *The Five Little Peppers and How They Grew* (1881) was the first in a series about a poor but resourceful and delightful family of five children. It practically made its child readers wish they were equally poor so they could have as much fun as Ben, Polly, Joel, David, and little Phronsie had. Theirs was not the grim, crime-ridden poverty known in slums today; it simply meant they did not have meals in restaurants or fancy store-bought clothes and had to make up their own amusements instead of having expensive toys to play with. They had enough high spirits and imagination to make up for the lack of possessions, and they helped to expand young readers' appreciation of simple pleasures, too. Sidney also wrote some charming historical novels for girls: *A Little Maid of Concord Town* (1898), *A Little Maid of Nantucket,* and others.

Mark Twain (See page 462.)

Charles Dickens (1812–1870)

This amazingly prolific and masterful English writer triumphed over a bitter childhood. He had little education and lived in insecurity and poverty; his father was at one time imprisoned for bankruptcy. In adult life he was frequently worried about providing for his own ten children. These facts greatly influenced his novels, in which the problems of the poor are so vividly portrayed that they helped to bring about important legislative reforms in regard to child labor, bankruptcy laws, prisons, asylums, and orphanages.

Dickens's unique career began in his early twenties when he became a reporter for several periodicals on debates in the House of Commons. These articles were later republished as *Sketches by Boz, Illustrative of Every-Day Life and Every-Day People.* They were so witty that "Boz" gained a large following, and soon after that he followed them with the humorous series, "Posthumous Papers of the Pickwick Club," published in 20 monthly magazine installments, and later known as *The Pickwick Papers,* his first published book.

His first novel, *Oliver Twist,* was published when he was 25 years old. In 1842, when he was 30, he traveled to America on a lecture tour advocating international copyright laws and the abolition of slavery. After returning home he wrote another book, *American Notes.* Other travels included a long visit to Italy in 1844 and one to Switzerland in 1846, where he wrote the novel *Dombey and Son,* and a second, highly successful tour of America in 1867 during which he read excerpts from some of his by then internationally famous novels.

Most of his books were not written specifically for children, but almost all contained children as characters and most are now considered children's classics. Many were first published in serial form in weekly or monthly magazines, so their publication dates often extend over more than one year. He was paid by the word, which also helps to explain why some of them were so long.

In chronological order the publication dates of his major works are: *The Pickwick Papers* (1836–1837); *Oliver Twist* (1837–1839); *Nicholas Nickleby* (1838–1839); *The Old Curiosity Shop* (1840); *Barnaby Rudge* (1841); *A Christmas Carol* (1843); *The Cricket on the Hearth* (1845); *The Battle of Life* (1846); *Dombey and Son* (1848); *The Haunted Man* (1848); *David Copperfield* (1849–1850), his most autobiographical novel; *Bleak House* (1852); *A Child's History of England* (1852–1854); *Hard Times* (1854); *Little Dorrit* (1855–1857); *A Tale of Two Cities* (1859); *Great Expectations* (1860–1861); *Our Mutual Friend* (1864); and *The Mystery of Edwin Drood.* (Edwin Drood was incomplete when he died in 1870, but in the 1990s a Broadway producer had it adapted into play form with three different endings and with the members of the audience at each performance voting on which ending they preferred).

Dickens also wrote a book privately for his own children, *The Life of Our Lord,* which was not published during his lifetime.

Although his books dealt with contemporary problems in Victorian England, their appeal is universal and undiminished, with their mixture of humor, sentimentality, melodrama, the supernatural, passionate concern about right and wrong, and unforgettable characters. They have continued to grow in popularity in numerous languages, with sales beyond computation, and in a number of highly successful movie versions and stage productions. All this in spite of the following comment by a book critic in the May 8, 1858, issue of London's *Saturday Review:* "We do not believe in the permanence of his reputation . . . . Fifty years hence, most of his allusions will be harder to understand than the allusions in The Dunciad, and our children will wonder what their ancestors could have meant by putting Mr. Dickens at the head of the novelists of his day."

Lewis Carroll (1832–1898)

Carroll was an English author whose real name was Charles Lutwidge Dodgson; he wrote *Alice's Adventures in Wonderland* (1865), *Through the Looking Glass* (1872), *The Hunting of the Snark* (1876), and other nonsense verses. He had seven sisters and as a child provided them with much entertainment: a marionette theater, magic lantern shows, a family magazine, conjuring tricks, and many games, puzzles, and playthings. All his life he enjoyed nonsense based on ambiguity, logic, and word play. He coined many words that have become part of the English language, such as *chortle,* and made what he called *portmanteau words* by combining two others; his imaginary animal the *snark,* for example, was a combination of a snake and a shark. Since his day others have borrowed his technique to make up new words such as *brunch* (breakfast and lunch) and *smog* (smoke and fog).

Despite his lifelong love of fun Carroll was a serious person: a clergyman and professor of mathematics at Christ Church, Oxford University, an author of treatises on mathematics, a poet, and a fine photographer. He was one of the first people to create works of art with cameras and film when these were new inventions.

On July 4 in 1862 he took Alice Liddell, the 10-year-old daughter of a friend, on an outing on the river Thames, and to amuse her made up some stories about "Alice's Adventures Underground." She loved them and begged for more. After he had made up a lot of stories about Alice, which included Mr. Dodgson himself as one of the characters, the "Dodo," she said, "There ought to be a book about that there ought." So Dodgson wrote the stories down for her, with his own sketches for illustrations, and gave them to her as a Christmas gift in 1864 with a note saying, "To a Dear Child in memory of a Summer's day."

Friends who saw the book, including the writer of children's books George MacDonald, urged Dodgson to publish it. They managed to persuade him, but to protect his dignity as a clergyman and Oxford don, he used a pseudonym. And instead of using his own charming but amateurish drawings, he engaged John Tenniel, an artist who worked for *Punch* magazine and who had illustrated a book of Aesop's fables, as illustrator. Dodgson had 2,000 copies printed and expected to lose money; he published it "not for money, and not for fame, but in the hope of supplying, for the children whom I love, some thoughts that may suit those hours of innocent merriment which are the very life of Childhood."

Despite an unfavorable review published in *Children's Books* in 1865 saying, "We fancy that any real child might be more puzzled than enchanted by this stiff, overwrought story," by the time Dodgson died, 180,000 copies of the book had sold and since then millions more, with translations into many languages.

Dodgson sent Alice a copy of the first published edition on July 4th, 1865, exactly three years after the outing when he had made up the first story.

In 1871 he published a sequel, *Through the Looking Glass (And What Alice Found There),* dedicating it to Alice Liddell, who was now 19, as follows:

> Child of the pure unclouded brow
> And dreaming eyes of wonder!
> Though time be fleet, and I and thou
> Are half a life asunder,
> Thy loving smile will surely hail
> The love-gift of a fairy-tale.
> I have not seen thy sunny face
> Nor heard thy silver laughter;
> No thought of me shall find a place
> In thy young life's hereafter—
> Enough that now thou wilt not fail
> To listen to my fairy-tale.

In 1885 Dodgson borrowed Alice's personal handwritten copy of the first Alice book, and had a facsimile edition published with his own illustrations. He inscribed it, "to Her whose children's smiles fed the narrator's fancy and were his rich reward."

In 1932, at the age of 80, Alice, now the widowed Mrs. Reginald Hargreaves, attended Lewis Carroll Centenary Celebrations and, when awarded an honorary degree for having inspired two great literary works, she said, "I wonder how many stories the world has missed, because he never wrote anything down until I teased him into doing it."

A lovely British film, *Dreamchild*, was made in 1985, with characters from the Alice books depicted by puppets made by Jim Henson, creator of the Muppets, and with Australian actress Coral Browne portraying Alice herself from childhood through old age.

Mark Twain (1835–1910)

Mark Twain's real name was Samuel Langhorne Clemens, and he was born when Halley's comet was in the sky. He often called himself and the comet "unaccountable freaks" which, having arrived together, must also go out together. His prediction came true; he died in April 1910 when the comet was again in the sky.

He spent most of his childhood in a town about 100 miles north of St. Louis: Hannibal, Missouri, on the Mississippi River, which is more than half a mile wide at that point. Twain loved the river and for four years, in his twenties, was a river pilot. When he began writing books he took his pen name from the sailors' cry "mark twain," which means two fathoms deep, or safe water.

At the age of five Twain was already making up stories to entertain his brother and sisters. He began his writing career in his teens with articles for his brother's newspaper, one of six that Hannibal supported in the 1850s, but he did not start writing books until he was 32. His first book, *The Celebrated Jumping Frog of Calaveras County, and Other Sketches* (1867) was an instant success.

Of the 22 books he wrote, that one and the following are children's favorites: *The Adventures of Tom Sawyer* (1875), made into a Hollywood picture with Mickey Rooney in 1937 and a Russian TV film in 1985 with child star Fedya Stukow; *The Prince and the Pauper* (1882), also made into a film; *The Adventures of Huckleberry Finn* (1884), also made into a movie several times; *The Tragedy of Puddin' Head Wilson* (1894); *Tom Sawyer, Detective* (1896); and *A Connecticut Yankee in King Arthur's Court* (1889). Twain's books have been translated into more than 60 languages.

In the past, many parents did not share children's enthusiasm for Twain's boy heroes, and some librarians have kept Tom and Huck on shelves too high for children to reach. The books have actually been banned from some libraries and schools. Nevertheless, so many people love these books that Hannibal now attracts hundreds of tourists every year who come to visit its Mark Twain Museum and to celebrate the town's "Tom Sawyer Days" with jumping frog contests. Also, as the author said,

> Huckleberry was cordially hated and dreaded by all mothers of the town, because he was idle and lawless and vulgar and bad—and because all their children admired him so, and delighted in his forbidden society, and wished they dared to be like him. Tom was like the rest of the respectable boys, in that he envied Huckleberry his gaudy outcast condition, and was under strict orders not to play with him. So he played with him every time he got a chance.

On the other hand, many authors have acknowledged their debt to Twain and Huckleberry. Hemingway claimed that Huckleberry Finn became the foundation of modern American literature with Twain's decision to write in Huck's own voice and from his own limited viewpoint, and Faulkner and Salinger have also acknowledged their debt to Clemens for his use, in Huckleberry Finn, of natural rather than formal dialogue.

A new controversy over Huckleberry Finn arose in 1992 when Shelley Fisher Fishkin, an associate professor of American studies at the University of Texas in Austin, published articles about a surprising discovery she claimed to have made. Twain's book has often been under attack for its supposed racism because the word *nigger* appears on so many pages, ignoring the fact that Huck rescues "Nigger Jim," an escaping slave, even though he fears he may go to hell for breaking the law. Professor Fishkin claimed that a black boy rather than a white one had served as "the model for the voice with which Twain would change the shape of American literature."

Professor Fishkin claimed that the boy was 10-year-old Jimmy, who was carrying trays in a midwestern hotel where Twain was staying one night. They got into a conversation and Twain was so captivated by Jimmy that in November 1874, a little more than a year before he started writing *Huckleberry Finn*, he published an article in the *New York Times* called "Sociable Jimmy," describing the boy as "the most artless, sociable and exhaustless talker I ever came across" and saying he listened to him "as one who receives a revelation." In the article he transcribed Jimmy's monologue, and Professor Fishkin compared its figures of speech, grammatical errors, mispronunciations, and subject matter line for line with dialogue in the book. (Each finds a dead cat, and each is bravely nonchalant about his drunken father who beats him.) She also turned up an unpublished letter Twain wrote his wife in which he said, "I think I could swing my legs over the arms of a chair and that boy's spirit would descend upon me and enter into me."

She followed her articles by writing a book called *Was Huck Black?* Some scholars do not find her argument convincing. But others do. Huckleberry Finn is evidently doomed to stay controversial. Perhaps the best comment on it was made by an Englishman who once startled Twain by saying, "Mr. Clemens, I would give ten pounds not to have read your *Huckleberry Finn*." When Twain looked puzzled, the Englishman smiled and said, "so that I could have again the great pleasure of reading it for the first time!"

SOME AUTHORS OF CHILDREN'S BOOKS IN THE TWENTIETH CENTURY

Joan Aiken (1924–): English author. One of Britain's favorite writers for children, Aiken's books include *A Necklace of Raindrops, All You Have Ever Wanted, Harp of Fishbones, Night Birds on Nantucket, Nightfall, Small Pinch of Weather, The Cuckoo Tree,* and *The Wolves of Willoughby Chase*. In 1969 she won the Guardian Award for children's fiction for her novel *The Whispering Mountain* and in 1971 her *Kingdom under the Sea* was awarded the Kate Greenaway Prize for its illustrations by Jan Pienkowski. She has also written two plays for children, *The Mooncusser's Daughter* and *Winterthing*.

Sir James Barrie (1860–1937): Scottish novelist and dramatist. He first wrote about Peter Pan, the boy who never grew up, in 1902 in *The Little White Bird*, a collection of short stories. The following year he wrote four plays: *Little Mary, Quality Street, The Admirable Crichton,* and *Peter Pan,* an expansion of his earlier story. In 1911 he rewrote *Peter Pan* as a novel called *Peter and Wendy* and later followed it with another: *Peter Pan in Kensington Garden*. The play has been performed repeatedly, delighting generations of children and actresses; the title role of Peter has always been played by an actress: Maude Adams, Eva Le Gallienne, Mary Martin, and Sandy Duncan, among others. In a silent film version the English actress Betty Bronson played the role. Mary Martin said that the scenes when she was flying through the air, even over the audience at times, attached to invisible wires, and having to take out life insurance before being allowed to perform, were scary at first but more fun than anything else she ever did on the stage.

After the play's 1904 debut Barrie got into trouble with parents whose children had accepted Peter's word that they too could fly if they believed strongly enough. Some children did believe and hurt themselves, so Barrie added to the play a cautionary statement that they could fly only if they had first been sprinkled with "fairy dust."

One of the reactions to the play that Barrie most enjoyed was that of a small boy who had been watching it from a box seat. When he was asked which bits he liked best, the child replied, "What I think I liked the best was tearing up the program and dropping the bits on people's heads."

Agniia Lvovna Barto (1906–1981): Russian author. The children's books by this prolific award-winning author include *Wang Li, the Chinese Boy* (1925); *Little Thief Misha* (1925); *Little Brothers* (1928); *Back to Front Boy* (1935); *The Toys* (1936); *Over a Sea of Stars* (1937); *You and I* (1937); *The Chatterbox* (1939); *There Goes the Schoolboy* (1944); *Girl in the First Grade* (1945); *He is Fourteen* and *Of People Big and Small* (1958); *To School* (1966); *Tamara and I* (1966). She also wrote poetry for children that has been translated into English, and scripts for films about children.

Lyman Frank Baum (1856–1919): American writer. Strange as it seems almost a century after *The Wonderful Wizard of Oz* was first published in 1900, Baum's concept of "an American fairy story" was rejected by a number of publishers until he finally found one who agreed to publish it if Baum and W. W. Denslow, his illustrator, would pay all printing costs and also turn over to him all royalties from *Father Goose,* a book they had published the year before. They thought this new book "might sell as much as 5,000 copies." It was published in August, and by October 25,000 more copies had to be printed, and 20,000 more in November. It has never been out of print since. Over 5 million copies have been published, making it one of the biggest best sellers of all time. There have been at least 30 editions, and it has been translated into many languages. In Russia it is used to teach English to school children. Versions of it have also been made into highly successful musical comedies for the stage, the first one in 1901, and in 1983 a black version with rock music called *The Wiz* became the twenty-first longest run hit in Broadway history. And the 1939 musical movie version with Judy Garland is still so popular that it has become an annual special event on television during every Christmas season.

Baum also wrote many other books for children: *American Fairy Tales; Dot and Trot of Merryland; Father Goose: His Book; John Dough and the Cherub; Mother Goose in Prose,* which in 1897 was the first book ever illustrated by Maxwell Parish; *Queen Zixi of Ix; Sea Fairies; Sky Island; The Enchanted Island of Yew; The Life and Adventures of Santa Claus.* But he received so many letters from children begging for more Oz books that he wrote 13 sequels to the first one, including *Dorothy and the Wizard of Oz, Ozma of Oz, The Emerald City of Oz, The Marvellous Land of Oz, The Patchwork Girl of Oz,* and *The Road to Oz,* to please his "loving tyrants" as he called his fans. And because children could not bear to believe there would be no more, the series was continued even after his death, by other writers: Rachel Cosgrove, Eloise McGraw, John Neill, Jack Snow,

Ruth Plumly Thompson, and Laurie Wagner. But Baum's originals still outsell their successors by six to one. (See also page 141.)

Stan and Jan Berenstain (1923–): American authors. Their books have consistently been among the top 80 best sellers of all time among paperback books for children: *The Berenstain Bears' Nursery Tales* (published in 1973*); The Berenstain Bears' New Baby* (1974); *The Berenstain Bears and the Sitter, The Berenstain Bears Visit the Dentist* and *The Berenstain Bears Visit the Doctor* (all three in 1981); *The Berenstain Bears Get in a Fight* and *The Berenstain Bears in the Dark* (both 1982), *The Berenstain Bears and the Messy Room* and *The Berenstain Bears and the Truth* (both 1983*); The Berenstain Bears and Too Much T.V.* (1984); and *The Berenstain Bears and Too Much Junk Food* (1985). Judging by the titles, this couple is very familiar with the kinds of typical problems that beset small humans and their parents (as well, evidently, as bears), which no doubt explains why so many little and big people enjoy these books.

Margery Williams Bianco, maiden name **Margery Williams** (1881–1944): English author. She wrote more than 30 books. Her classic *The Velveteen Rabbit* was published in 1922 under her maiden name, but she continued writing children's books under her married name. Most of them were about playthings she had loved in her own childhood and still remembered fondly, such as *All about Pets, The Little Wooden Doll,* and *The Skin Horse,* which was exquisitely illustrated by her daughter Pamela Bianco.

Judy Blume (1938–): American author. She is a writer of children's books with a remark-able knack for getting on best-seller lists. She had nine books in *Publishers Weekly*'s 1989 list of over 80 all-time best-selling children's paperback books. *Are You There, God? It's Me, Margaret* (1974) was the second all-time best-seller. The other titles that appeared in the list were *Tales of a Fourth Grade Nothing* (1976), *Superfudge* (1981), *Freckle Juice* (1978), *Blubber* (1976), the 12th; *Then Again, Maybe I Won't* (1973), *Deenie* (1974), *Iggie's House* (1976), and *Tiger Eyes* (1982).

Enid Blyton (1897–1968): English author. Blyton wrote the humorous *Noddy* series. Both her books and the toys based on the character of the cute little boy Noddy were phenom-enally popular not only with English children but also in other countries. In 1980 alone 64 translations of her books were published.

Michael Bond (1926–): English writer. *A Bear Called Paddington* (1936) was Bond's book in a very popular series including *More about Paddington* and *Paddington Helps Out,* about "a very rare sort of bear" from Peru who turned up at a railway station in London wearing a sign saying "Please take care of this bear" and who was adopted by a family of three English children. Paddington managed as both the hero in books and as a toy to rival the well-established place of Winnie-the-Pooh in the hearts of far more than three children, and not only English ones. More than 16 translations of Paddington books have been published.

Margaret Wise Brown (1910–1952): American writer. By far the most prolific author of children's books in the 1940s, she wrote more than 100 of them, including the enduring classics *Goodnight Moon; The Runaway Bunny; The Noisy Books;* and *The Little Fur Family. The Little Fur Family* was originally published in 1946 as a tiny, three-inch-tall book charmingly illustrated by Garth Williams and bound in real rabbit fur, until some moths in the publisher's warehouse proceeded to nibble away at the covers, so that later editions have been sold in a cloth binding with synthetic fur. Brown started to write while she was a student teacher at the Bank Street School in New York, a nursery school run by the Bureau of Educational Experiments, which was studying children's speech development. Lucy Sprague Mitchell, the director, believed that stories about real things and children's own experiences were a better introduction to reading for the very young than traditional fairy tales, and Brown began making up stories for the children in the school. Soon she was going strong and became the first editor at a new children's book publishing company, W. R. Scott. She became its most prolific author and wrote for numerous other publishers as well, turning out about eight books a year; to avoid monopolizing the market she wrote some of them under pseudonyms.

Children cannot get enough of Brown's books. They are read aloud to them over and over again as bedtime stories. The children get to know them by heart, and will not allow the reader to change or leave out a single word. The appeal is not just the fact that the books are about real-life things to which children can relate but the way they are written. The sing-song cadence of Brown's rhythmic prose, full of alliterations and rhymes, weaves a potent spell.

Frances Hodgson Burnett (1849–1924): English-born American novelist and playwright. Burnett wrote extremely successful children's books in the last half of the nineteenth century and on into the twentieth: *Little Lord Fauntleroy* (1886), which was twice made into a movie, first with Mary Pickford in the title role, and later, in 1936, starring Freddie Bartholemew; *Editha's Burglar* (1888); *Sara Crewe* (1888); *The Pretty Sister of Jos* (1889); *Little Saint Elizabeth* (1890); *The Secret Garden* (1911); and the delightful *Racketty Packetty House (as told by Queen Crosspatch)*. Her stories seem a bit dated today, because they are sentimental and moralistic. For instance, the heroine of *Editha's Burglar* is an almost too-good-to-be-true little girl who, by befriending rather than fearing and hating a burglar who enters her house, reforms him. *Sara Crewe* is about a pathetic, ill-treated child in a boarding school whose heroic patience in adversity is in the end rewarded; in a later edition, it was titled *The Little Princess*. And when *The Secret Garden* was adapted into a play in the 1990s many people predicted it would be a flop because they thought it was too sentimental for sophisticated audiences, but to their surprise its charm and tenderness were so genuine that audiences loved it.

Henry (Harry) Castlemon, pseudonym for **Charles Austin Fosdick** (1842–1915): American author. He wrote 50 books for boys, including: *Frank on the Lower Mississippi* (1869), *The Buried Treasure* (1877), *The Boy Trapper* (1878), *Oscar in Africa* (1894), *Carl the Trailer* (1900), *The Floating Treasure* (1901), *Frank Nelson in the Forecastle* (1904), as well as books in the *Gunboat, Rocky Mountain, Sportsman Club,* and *Pony Express* series. He was not bothered by literary critics, saying, "Boys don't like fine writing. What they want is adventure."

Beverly Cleary (1916–): American writer. This extremely popular author, whose career began in the 1950s and continued to thrive through the 1990s, was influential in starting the modern trend toward books about children who are not unbelievably virtuous but who are normal and have children's ordinary experiences. She felt strongly that there was a need for stories about children who were neither princes nor princesses. With her memories of her own childhood and her gift for getting inside the minds of children, she produced delightful, realistic stories.

Cleary has written 37 books, all wonderfully funny and touching. They have sold 75 million copies in 20 countries in 14 languages, and have won many prizes, including the

Newbery Medal for Children's Literature awarded for *Dear Mr. Henshaw,* about a boy of divorced parents who wrote sad and funny letters to a favorite author.

Henry Huggins, Cleary's first book, written for third graders, was published in 1950 and was an instant best seller. In 1955 she wrote the first of six books about Ramona, a precocious, stubborn, incorrigible child prone to tantrums because, to quote her, great big noisy fusses were often necessary when a girl was the youngest member of the family and the youngest person on her block. The perennial favorite in this series is *Ramona the Pest,* which describes Ramona's difficult adjustment to kindergarten and her disgrace as a temporary school dropout. In later books, as Ramona grew older, she faced other real problems and discovered that even parents have problems, which, Cleary says, "is part of growing up." Ramona's father lost his job and she worried about whether his smoking would kill him and how the family would pay its bills, until she had to make a new adjustment when her mother went to work. The series ended in 1984 with *Ramona Forever* in the eighth grade and happy because she was "winning at growing up."

Over the years there have been plays and some television shows and a Ramona doll based on these books. Cleary has received offers from Hollywood but turned them down because studios would not give her script approval.

In October, 1995, there was a ceremony in Portland, Oregon, where Beverly Cleary had spent her childhood and which was the setting for the adventures of her two most famous creations, Henry Huggins and Ramona Quimby. A professor at Portland State University, Eric A. Kimmel, felt that the city should celebrate this fact by having a permanent monument to honor what were two of the most comical and authentic characters in American children's literature, just as London's Kensington Gardens has *Peter Pan* and the Boston Commons has its *Make Way for Ducklings.* One of his students, Heather Johnson, organized a grassroots campaign to raise money for such a tribute, and "A Beverly Cleary Sculpture Garden for Children" with a wading pool and fountain and bronze statues of Ramona, Henry, and Henry's dog, was constructed. On the day of its dedication, Beverly was escorted by 200 librarians on a tour of her old neighborhood and then brought to Grant Park for a celebration where a crowd of 1,000 children and adults had gathered to pay tribute to her.

Cleary now lives in Carmel Valley, California. She still writes for three or four hours on most days, between breakfast and lunch. Her latest book is *My Own Two Feet,* the second volume of an autobiography.

Paul Gallico (1897–1976): American journalist and short story writer. He is now remembered primarily for his two exquisite children's books, *The Snow Goose* and *Thomasina,* both made into superior films.

Howard R. Garis (1873–1962): American writer. Garis was astonishingly prolific and popular, producing more than 160 books for children during his long life. His first novel, written in 1889 when he was 16, was called *A World without Women* because he had just been rejected by a girl and hated all women; he was rejected by the publisher too, but the following year changed his mind about women and married Lilian McNamara, who later wrote the famous *Bobbsey Twins* series. Garis's most famous books grew out of his *Uncle Wiggily* series about a jolly long-eared rabbit, which was a daily newspaper feature on the *Newark News* where he had worked as a reporter. The first of these stories appeared in January 1910 and, from that month on, a daily story by Garis appeared six days a week for more than 50 years. They were syndicated in many other newspapers and then published in book form, the first in 1912, followed by 48 others through 1947, and reprinted many times since then. The stories became even more popular when he began to read them aloud over the radio, and in 1917 he invented an Uncle Wiggily game that for a while became the largest selling children's game in the world.

Besides the Uncle Wiggily series Garis wrote 14 others: *A Great Newspaper* series (5 books between 1907 and 1912); *The Campfire Girls* (two volumes under the pseudonym of Marion Davidson, published in 1913); a *Daddy* series (10 volumes, in 1916); *Venture Boys* (two books, in 1917 and 1918); a *Rick and Ruddy* series (10 books from 1920 through 1930); a *Curlytops* series (13 books, from 1923 through 1932); *Two Wild Cherries* (a series of four books in 1924 and 1925); a *Happy Home* series (six books, in 1925, 1926, and 1927); *Tom Cardiff's Circus* (five books from 1926 through 1929); a *Buddy* series (21 books published between 1929 and 1930); *Dick and Janet Cherry* (four books, in 1930); an *Outboard Motor Boat* series (four books, under the pen name of Clarence Young, in 1933 and 1934); a *Rocket Riders* series (four books, in 1933 and 1934); a *Teddy* series (seven books, from 1936 through 1941); and the *Tom Swift* series, under the pen name of Victor Appleton. Even this was not enough. He also wrote 14 other individual children's books, and stories for the children's magazine, *St. Nicholas*.

Rumer Godden, pseudonym of Mrs. Lawrence Foster (1907–): English novelist. Godden's most famous book is *The River,* a beautiful memoir about her childhood in India, but she also wrote many other wonderful books for young children including: *An Episode of Sparrows, Mr. McFadden's Halloween* (1975), *The Doll's House* (1976), *The Rocking Horse's Secret* (1978), *A Kindle of Kittens* (1979), *The Dragon of Og* (1981), *The Valiant Chatti Maker* (1981), *The Mousewife* (1982), *Four Dolls* (1984), and *The Story of Holly and Ivy* (1985).

Kenneth Grahame (1859–1932): Scottish author. His most famous and perennially admired book, *The Wind in the Willows* (1908), was based on bedtime stories he first made up for his seven-year-old son and then continued in letter form. Later it was made into a children's play, *Toad of Toad Hall* by A. A. Milne, who admired the book so much that he said,

> One does not argue with *The Wind in the Willows*. The young man gives it to the girl with whom he is in love, and if she does not like it, asks her to return his letters. The older man tries it on his nephew, and alters his will accordingly. The book is a test of character. We can't criticize it, because it is criticizing us.

Still later the book was made into a Disney film entitled *The Adventures of Mr. Toad*. Grahame also wrote *The Golden Age* (1895), *Dream Days* (1898), and *The Reluctant Dragon,* which too was later made into an entertaining Disney film.

Joel Chandler Harris (1848–1908): American journalist and author. He wrote *Uncle Remus, His Songs and Sayings* (1880); *Nights with Uncle Remus* (1883); *Uncle Remus and His Friends* (1892); *The Tar Baby* (1904); *Uncle Remus and Brer Rabbit* (1906); and *Uncle Remus Returns* (1918). These books were enormously popular during Harris's lifetime because each contains a wise moral via a humorous story, supposedly told by a kind old black man who is entertaining and teaching a group of delighted children. They are an ethnic variation of the Aesop's fables tradition. However, few people read them today because the thick dialect in which they are written is hard to understand, and also because the narrator is a lovable old "darkie" who no longer presents the image that today's African Americans want to represent their race. Yet despite the difficulty presented by the local dialect, a Russian translation of Uncle Remus was published in the Soviet Union in 1980.

Erich Kastner, real name **Robert Neuner** (1899–1974): German author. He wrote *Emil and the Detectives,* a children's novel that was as popular when translated into English as it was in its original language. In 1931 it was made into a German motion picture; it was adapted to the stage in 1962, and in 1964 it became a Walt Disney film. Another of Kastner's successful books for children was *Das Doppette Lottchen* (Lisa and Lottie), which was also made into a Disney film, *The Parent Trap,* in 1961.

Carolyn Keene: American author. This is the pseudonym of the author of a series of mystery stories for girls about *Nancy Drew, Girl Detective,* published by the Stratemeyer Syndicate, which also published the *Bobbsey Twins, The Hardy Boys, The Rover Boys, Tom Swift,* and *Uncle Wiggily* series. The first book in the Nancy Drew series was *The Secret of the Old Clock* written by Edward Stratemeyer (see page 472). After he died in 1930, his daughter Harriet Adams became "Carolyn Keene" and wrote more than 70 sequels. After her death in 1982, Nancy Axelrod, who had been working for the syndicate for almost 20 years, succeeded her, turning out three more books each year. Today the books are written by a committee of more than 12 writers, who issue one new volume every month. Thus Nancy Drew has been a popular teenage heroine for almost 60 years. Millions of girls have adored the stories; those whose parents thought they were junk devoured them avidly anyway, often borrowing them from libraries and reading them secretly under their bed covers with a flashlight. Finally, librarians and teachers who had scorned the books decided that if they were so popular they at least helped to develop the habit of reading, and they began to recommend them. Today, by virtue of its longevity, the series has assumed almost the status of a classic; all of them are still in print and more than 27 translations have been published.

Rudyard Kipling (1865–1936): English novelist, poet, and short story writer. Born in India of English parents, Kipling was sent to England to be educated at the age of six. He had a lonely and unhappy childhood in a foster home and at school. At 17 he returned to India to work as a journalist instead of going to college. He became a Nobel Prize-winning author of many books, short stories, and poems. His books for children included: *Wee Willie Winkie* (1889); two *Jungle Books* (in 1894 and 1895) about Mowgli, an orphaned boy brought up by wolves, the spiritual descendent of Romulus and Remus and precursor of Tarzan; *Captains Courageous,* which he wrote while he was living the United States, and which was made into a great movie; *Stalky and Co.* (1899); *Kim* (1901); *Just So Stories for Little Children* (1902); *Puck of Pooh's Hill* (1906); *Rewards and Fairies* (1910).

Kipling's colorful and comical use of language entertains young children, in spite of the theories of those educators who insist on "vocabulary norms" in books for children, failing to recognize most children's "'satiable curiosity" (the adjective is Kipling's) about words. When Kipling has the Bi-Colored-Python-Rock-Snake say to the Elephant's Child,

Rash and inexperienced traveler, we will now seriously devote ourselves to a little high tension, because if we do not, it is my impression that yonder self-propelling man of war with the armor-plated upper deck (and by this, O Best Beloved, he meant the crocodile), will permanently vitiate your future career.

469

Small children do not understand all the words, of course, but they squeal with delight at the sounds as the story is read aloud to them again and again.

Eric Mowbray Knight (1897–1943): English-born American writer. In World War I he was an army private in Canada, and in World War II he entered the U.S. Army a year before his death, dying in an airplane crash while on an official mission. Between the two world wars he became a successful novelist for adults, but the book that endures in children's hearts is the one he wrote last, *Lassie Come Home* (1940), forerunner of the enormously popular movies and television series.

Ruth Krauss (1911–1993): American author. She has the wackiest sense of humor of any writer for children, and it is no wonder that children love her. Her most quoted book is *A Hole Is to Dig: A First Book of First Definitions*, with illustrations by Maurice Sendak that are a perfect accompaniment to the text. Here are just a few samples of her definitions:

A face is so you can make faces.
A face is something to have on the front of your head.
A nose is to blow.
A lap is so you don't get crumbs on the floor.
Snow is to roll in.
Cats are so you can have kittens.
A book is to look at.
Children are to love.

She and Sendak have collaborated on several other delightful books, but this remains the favorite.

Selma Lagerlöf, full name **Selma Ottiliana Lovisa Lagerlöf** (1858–1940): Swedish novelist, poet, and schoolteacher. She was the first woman to win the Nobel Prize for Literature (1909) and the first woman member of the Swedish Academy. She wrote nine full-length novels, a trilogy, and several collections of short stories, but her most famous work was a children's book, which almost immediately became a classic. It grew out of a request by a group of fellow teachers that she write about the geography and lore of Sweden. After several years of research she invented a tiny boy who understands animals and birds and who flies all over Sweden on the back of a wild goose: *The Wonderful Adventures of Nils* (2 volumes, 1906 and 1907).

Munro Leaf (1905–1976): American humorist, illustrator, and author. He wrote several excellent children's books, *Manners Can Be Fun, Metric Can Be Fun, Safety Can Be Fun*, but he is best remembered for *Ferdinand the Bull* (1936), about a "little bull who would rather just sit and smell the flowers than fight." Why he was chosen to appear in a bullfight and what happened when he got there is not only very funny but made him a "role model" to pacifists and to all mothers who want to teach their children not to fight.

C. S. Lewis, full name **Clive Staples Lewis** (1898–1963): British author. Like his close friend J.R.R. Tolkien (see page 474), Lewis was a scholar and an Oxford University professor who wrote several much-admired books for children in addition to many books for adults. One of his books, *The Screwtape Letters* (1942) is sort of a cross between the two. It teaches morality by teaching its opposite through an imagined correspondence between an old and experienced devil who is tutoring a young devil on how to take advantage of human weaknesses, and it is so funny that even though it was written for grownups and its irony has a serious purpose, some children have thoroughly enjoyed it. The books Lewis wrote specifically for children also teach moral lessons. They are *The Chronicles of Narnia,* seven volumes beginning with *The Lion, The Witch and the Wardrobe* (1950), all containing adventures of children in Narnia, an imaginary but believable magical world.

Jack London (1876–1916): American author. He wrote many short stories and 44 books. Those with the most appeal to young readers are his adventure stories such as *The Son of the Wolf* (1900), *The Call of the Wild* (1903), *The Sea Wolf* (1904), and *The Cruise of the Snark* (1911).

A. A. Milne, full name **Alan Alexander Milne** (See page 475.)

L. M. Montgomery, married name **Lucy Maude Macdonald** (1874–1942): Canadian novelist. She wrote her first juvenile, *Anne of Green Gables,* in 1908, using "unisex" initials so that no one could tell if the author was a man or a woman. But after her marriage two years later, she wrote other books using her married name: four more "Anne" books, *Anne of Avonlea, Chronicles of Avonlea, Anne of Ingleside, Anne of the Island,* as well as *Emily of New Moon* (1923), *The Blue Castle* (1926), *A Tangled Web* (1931), *Jane of Lantern Hill* (1937), and several others. *Anne of Green Gables* is still the favorite and was made into an appealing television series in 1986.

E. Nesbit, married name **Edith Nesbit Bland** (1858–1924): English novelist and poet, Nesbit was one of the founders of the Socialist Fabian Society, along with her husband Hubert Bland, whom she married in 1880 and with whom she collaborated on a novel, *The Prophet's Mantle* (1885). Despite her seriousness and strong social conscience, she had her greatest success after 1890 with a series of amusing juvenile novels about the "Bastable children": *The Story of the Treasure Seekers* (1899), *The Wouldbegoods* (1901), *New Treasure Seekers* (1904), *The Railway Children* (later made into a film) and *The Five Children.* Here is an excerpt from the child narrator of *The Treasure Seekers:*

> I have often thought that if the people who write books for children knew a little more, it would be better. I shall not tell you anything about us except what I should like to know about if I was reading the story and you were writing it. Albert's uncle says I ought to have put this in the preface, but I never read prefaces, and it is not much good writing things just for people to skip. I wonder other authors have never thought of this.

Scott O'Dell (1898–1989): American author. He wrote many books for children and received a spectacular number of awards for them. *The Island of the Blue Dolphins* (1960) was based on a true story about two children abandoned and marooned on a tropical island; it won the Rupert Hughes award in 1960, the Newbery medal in 1961, the Hans Christian Andersen award of merit in 1962, and the William Allen White award and the German Juvenile International award in 1963. It was later made into a movie with Brooke Shields. *The King's Fifth* (1966) won the Newbery medal in 1967 and the German Juvenile International award in 1969. Other books of his were *The Black Pearl,* which was awarded the Newbery medal in 1968; *The Park Canoe* (1968); *Journey to Jericho* (1969); *Sing Down the Moon,* the Newbery award winner in 1971; *The Treasure of Topo el Bampo* (1972);

The Cruise of the Arctic Star (1973); *Child of Fire* (1974); and *The Hawk That Dare Not Hunt by Day* (1975).

In 1981 O'Dell established the Scott O'Dell Award for Historical Fiction for Children or Young People. Its $5,000 cash prize is the largest in the United States for children's literature.

Eleanor H. Porter (1868–1920): American novelist. Her novel *Pollyanna* (1913) was made into a silent film in 1920, with Mary Pickford in the title role, and into a Walt Disney film in 1960 with Hayley Mills. The book's spirited young heroine, who gradually managed to tame her nasty aunt and other villains through her unwavering optimism, invented "the glad game" many years before Norman Vincent Peale promoted "the power of positive thinking" in 1952.

Frank Richards, pseudonym of **Charles Harold St. John Hamilton** (1875–1961): English writer. According to the Guinness Book of Records, this writer's lifetime output has been calculated as between 72 million and 75 million words, making him the most prolific author in history. He was the creator of a series of stories for boys, *Billy Bunter*, and in his peak years from 1915 to 1926 he wrote up to 80,000 words a week for three British boys' school weeklies, *Gem, Magnet,* and *Boys' Friend.*

J. D. Salinger, full name **Jerome David Salinger** (1919–): American novelist and short-story writer. His book *The Catcher in the Rye* (1951) and its follow-up *Franny and Zooey* (1961) have enjoyed continuing popularity among preteens and teenagers for their realistic depictions of the torments of being young. Among their torments are the fact that, according to the American Library Association, *The Catcher in the Rye* is "a perennial No. 1 on the censorship list" because of its irreverent language. Prudish parents continually try to get it banned from libraries, oblivious of the fact that the way the book's hero Holden Caulfield speaks is the way his peers in real life actually do speak, and they ignore the fact that 17-year-old Holden is an extremely loving, generous, and kind boy, "as moral a character as has ever appeared in American fiction," according to an editorial in the *New York Times*. Of course, every time someone demands that the book be banned, this creates an increased demand for it among other people.

Controversies over the book are whetted by the mysterious personality of its author, who has lived in hermit-like isolation in New Hampshire for more than 30 years, publishing nothing and refusing to be interviewed or quoted.

Alvin Schwartz (1927–1992): American author. The writing career of this best-selling author began as a sideline to help support his family; he had two sons and two daughters. It soon became much more than a sideline. He published more than 50 books and sold more than three million of them during his lifetime. His last one, *And the Green Grass Grows All Around,* a collection of folk poetry, was published the month he died. The previous year he produced two best sellers for children: *Ghosts* and *Scary Stories 3*. While many of his books were lighthearted, drawing on jokes and folklore, others were criticized as being much too scary for young readers, with troubled ghosts, ghouls, witches, and sinister zombies. One of them, *In a Dark Dark Room* (1984) was described by a reviewer as "the stuff nightmares are made of." Yet Schwartz received both critical and popular acclaim, and student polls often voted his books as favorites. His first volume of tongue twisters, *A Twister of Twists, a Tangle of Tongues* (1972), was described by a *New York Times* reviewer as "one of the most delightful children's books I've come across in years."

A sample of his ingenious tongue twisters is "The sixth sheik's sixth sheep's sick." In 1974 he wrote *Cross Your Fingers, Spit in Your Hat,* debunking superstitions. In 1980 he wrote a book of silly riddles, *Ten Copycats in a Boat and Other Riddles* (such as "When is a car not a car? When it turns into a parking lot").

He also wrote serious, informative books for children, such as *The People's Choice* (1968) to show how government works, and *Stores* (1977), describing how stores operate. And he wrote two books for parents: *How to Fly a Kite, Catch a Fish, Grow a Flower, and Other Activities for You and Your Child* (1965) and *To Be a Father* (1967).

Isaac Bashevis Singer (1904–1991): Polish-born American author. A winner of the Nobel Prize for Literature in 1978, he was the author of *When Shlemiel Went to Warsaw* and other witty stories for children, written in Yiddish and based on his childhood and on philosophical Jewish folklore. When he gave his acceptance speech at the Nobel ceremonies in Stockholm, he made some amusing comments about the reading habits of little boys and girls. Saying there were 500 reasons why he enjoyed writing for young children, he then cited a few:

> Children read books, not reviews. They don't give a hoot about the critics . . . . They love interesting stories, not commentary, guides or footnotes . . . . When a book is boring they yawn openly, without any shame or fear of authority . . . . They don't expect their beloved writer to redeem humanity. Young as they are, they know that is not in his power. Only adults have such childish illusions . . . . They still believe in God, the family, angels, devils, witches, goblins, logic, clarity, punctuation and other such obsolete stuff . . . ."

Burt L. Standish, real name **William Gilbert Patten** (1866–1945): American writer. He wrote 209 books of adventure stories for boys, all about the same hero, Frank Merriwell. In 1896 he started writing 20,000 words a week about Frank: *Frank Merriwell's Chums, Frank Merriwell Down South, Frank Merriwell's Courage,* [His] *Daring, Faith, Foes,* and so forth. They were innocuous fare to which boys succumbed as to a recurrent contagious fever.

Danielle Steele (1947–): American author. One of the modern world's bestselling novelists, she is also the mother of nine children and in 1989 published *The Max and Martha Books: Six Stories for Children,* dealing with both problems and joys of childhood: *Martha's Best Friend, Martha's New Daddy, Martha's New School, Max and the Babysitter, Max's Daddy Goes to the Hospital* and *Max's New Baby.*

Edward Sylvester Stratemeyer (1863–1930): American writer. He founded the Stratemeyer Syndicate which specialized in publishing juvenile serials in newspapers and magazines. It published *The Bobbsey Twins* by Lilian McNamara and the many books by Howard Garis, her husband (see page 467). Under the pseudonym of Carolyn Keene (also see page 469), Stratemeyer wrote the first book in the *Nancy Drew* series, and as Arthur M. Winfield wrote the *Rover Boys* (1899–1926) who roved *On the Ocean, Out West, In the Jungle, On Land and Sea, In the Air,* until it seemed there was no place left for them to explore.

Albert Payson Terhune (1872–1942): American writer. He wrote extremely popular books about his collie *Lad: a Dog* (1919), *Lad of Sunnybank, Further Adventures of Lad;* and about other dogs, *Bruce,* who performed heroically in World War I and *Treve; Dog of the*

Note: Although for centuries no books were written especially for children, according to the trade magazine *Publishers Weekly,* children's books are now the fastest growing sales sector in book publishing. So even these long lists of books for children are bound to be woefully incomplete. We apologize to authors and readers whose favorite books have been omitted.

High Sierras. The farm where he and his dogs lived in Pompton Lakes, New Jersey, is maintained today as a monument.

J. R. R. Tolkien, full name **John Ronald Revel Tolkien** (1892–1973): English author. As a professor at Oxford University, Tolkien was grading papers one day and came across a "hole," a page in an exam book that a student had accidentally skipped. He suddenly wondered what kind of creature would live in a hole and invented the *hobbit.* Soon he was making up stories for his children and eventually published them as *The Hobbit* (1937), followed later by *The Fellowship of the Rings, The Two Towers,* and *The Return of the King.* He created not merely imaginary creatures but a whole world and civilization for them, and his many fans, both childen and adults, practically formed a cult around them. His stories had happy endings, in which virtue triumphed through providence, which he called eucatastrophes.

P. L. Travers, full name **Pamela L. Travers** (1906–1996): Australian author. She claimed she never wrote for children, but the world's children would emphatically disagree. She wrote about their ideal nanny in *Mary Poppins* (1934), *Mary Poppins Comes Back* (1935), *Mary Poppins Opens the Door,* and *Mary Poppins in the Park.* The movie in which Julie Andrews starred as Mary Poppins, was Walt Disney's biggest hit.

E. B. White, full name **Elwyn Brooks White** (1899–1985): American writer. "I took to writing early, to assuage my uneasiness and collect my thoughts, and I was a busy writer long before I went into long pants," White once wrote, but his professional writing career did not begin until he was 28. Primarily an essayist, he wrote three distinguished books for children: *Stuart Little* (1945), about a mouse; *Charlotte's Web* (1952), about a spider and a pig, inspired by a spider's web in his barn; and *The Trumpet of the Swan* (1970), about a swan who charms the guests at the Ritz Carlton Hotel in Boston, Massachusetts, by playing his trumpet in the lobby. Since 1970 the hotel has answered letters from more than 1,500 children asking about the book. To honor White, since his death the hotel has given away a copy of the book to each child guest.

Kate Douglas Wiggin (1856–1923): American writer. She organized and opened the first free kindergarten in the American West, in San Francisco, and also helped her sister, Nora Archibald Smith, found a training school for kindergarten teachers. She began writing children's books in order to raise money for her school. Among her many books, her most famous were *Rebecca of Sunnybrook Farm* (1903); *Fairy Ring* (1906); *Magic Casements* (1907); *The New Chronicles of Rebecca* (1907); *Tales of Laughter* (1908); *Tales of Wonder* (1909); *Mother Carey's Chickens* (1911); *The Library of Fairy Literature,* a collection of 100 folk tales and fables compiled and edited with her sister; and *Talking Beasts* (1911). She and her sister also wrote several works on children's education. Her heroine Rebecca has been described as "the nicest child in American literature." Her story was dramatized and filmed with success in 1937, with Shirley Temple playing Rebecca.

474

Laura Ingalls Wilder (1867–1957): American author. During her long life she wrote many semihistorical and semiautobiographical stories about her childhood and home life during the pioneer days in the American Middle West*: By the Shore of Silver Lake; The First Four Years; The Long Winter; These Happy Golden Years;* and four others: *Little House on the Prairie,* which Michael Landon made into a television series which ran from 1979 to 1982; *Little House in the Big Woods, On the Banks of Plum Creek,* and *Farmer Boy.* She did not begin writing her *Little House* books until she was in her sixties, and much of the writing was actually done by her collaborator, her daughter Rose Wilder Lane, based on her mother's recollections. Each of these books has sold more than 2.5 million copies since they were published in paperback with illustrations by Garth Williams in 1971. They are among the top 15 in sales of children's paperback books of all time.

Margery Williams (See **Margery Bianco,** on page 465.)

Boris Zakhoder (1918–): Russian poet, author, and translator. His book *The Crocodile's Toothbrush* has been translated into English and he repaid the compliment by translating Lewis Carroll's *Alice in Wonderland,* James Barrie's *Peter Pan* and A. A. Milne's *Winnie-the-Pooh* and *House on Pooh Corner* into Russian. In 1985 the Pooh books sold more than 3.5 million copies in the Soviet Union. *Vinnie Pookh,* as Pooh is known in Russia, has even had his own radio show, in which he taught grammar to Russian children.

A. A. Milne (1882–1956) and Christopher Robin Milne (1920–1996)

The literary career of the English writer, Alan Alexander Milne, ranged over five decades and included humorous essays, light verse, political pamphlets, novels, and plays. For eight years he was an editor on the British humor magazine *Punch.* He was well known as a successful poet and a playwright of sparkling comedies, but his immortality stems from the stories and poems he wrote for and about children: two books of verse, *When We Were Very Young* (1924) and *Now We are Six* (1927); and two books of stories, *Winnie the Pooh* (1926) and *The House at Pooh Corner* (1928). The books about Pooh consisted of bedtime stories he made up at the suggestion of his wife about their son Christopher Robin and his stuffed animals.

Most people, both children and adults, love these stories, the notable exception being the famous cynic Dorothy Parker who used to review books for the *New Yorker* magazine under the pseudonym of "Constant Reader"; her reaction to Winnie-the-Pooh was "Constant Weader fwowed up." Hers was definitely a minority opinion. The book has sold over 2.5 million copies in the United States alone, and it is the fifteenth of the best-selling children's books of all time. It sells more than 100,000 copies annually in the United States and has been translated into at least 20 languages, even into Latin by a classics professor who thought his students would enjoy it more than Caesar's Wars. And Benjamin Hoff, a Buddhist philosopher, wrote two books called *The Tao of Pooh* and *The Tao of Piglet,* in which he used the characters in the books to explain elusive principles of Taoism. Through witty stories and dialogues he showed that while Eeyore frets, Piglet hesitates, Rabbit calculates, and Owl pontificates, Pooh just is and thus achieves the state of tranquility.

The country home of A. A. Milne was about an hour from London in Hartfield, a charming village in Sussex next to 500 acres of scenic woods, Ashdown Forest, which was the model for the books' "Hundred Acre Wood" where "Once upon a time, a very long time ago now, about last Friday, Winnie-the-Pooh lived in a forest." Today there is a shop at "Pooh Corner" in Hartfield with an adjoining tea room. The Corner contains a "Christopher Robin's Sweet Shop" with all kinds of hard candies that Christopher Robin loved as a child, and the main shop sells a large number of Pooh items, such as stuffed animals and coloring books. This commercialism would probably have distressed Milne and Pooh's illustrator, Ernest H. Shepard, who both eventually got heartily sick of the lovable bear they had created.

The Ashbara Forest Center provides maps indicating particular sites that appear in the books, for example, the bridge where Pooh invented "Poohsticks," the game where friends drop sticks on one side of a bridge and then rush to the other side to see whose stick drifts through first. At the top of a hill in the middle of the forest there is an enclosure with a plaque set into a large rock, saying

> And by and by they came to an enchanted place on the very top of the Forest called Galleon's Lap. Here at Gills Lap are commemorated A. A. Milne (1882–1956) and E. H. Shepard (1879–1976) who collaborated in the creation of Winnie-the-Pooh and so captured the magic of Ashdown Forest and gave it to the world.

Shepard's illustrations not only added enormously to the books' appeal but they were also very accurate in showing what the Forest looks like.

In 1939 Milne wrote an autobiography called *It's Too Late Now*. It concentrated primarily on his own childhood. In an echo of the words of Wordsworth, "The Child is father of the Man," he explained his belief that most of what we become we already are as children. In a way he did remain a child all his life, which helps to explain why he was so good at writing about childhood.

Milne was a happy and precocious child, the third of three boys, reading at age two and soon showing an unusual flair for advanced mathematics. His literary career began at Cambridge University, where he edited and wrote for the student magazine *Granta*. In 1913 he married Dorothy de Sélincourt whom he called Daphne or Daff, and their only child, Christopher Robin, was born seven years later, in 1920.

His life has been further described in *A. A. Milne: The Man behind Winnie-the-Pooh* by Ann Thwaite. Her book is an engrossing study of a complex man, full of charm but also of contradictions, as is made even clearer in the books written by his son after both of his parents were dead. Christopher Robin wrote two autobiographical books: *The Enchanted Places* (1974) about his early life, and *The Path through the Trees* (1979), describing his upbringing and its effects upon his adult life.

He said he was much closer to his nanny than to his parents when he was little. As he grew up, he gradually discovered that he was more famous than the father who wrote about him. At first he enjoyed his fame, but later it embarrassed him terribly, especially when he was sent away to school. He was unhappy there because his parents gave him a girlish haircut and dressed him in little frocks instead of trousers. He was a shy boy and had to endure a lot of teasing about the image everyone had of him always playing with babyish toys or on his knees at bedtime ("Hush, hush, whisper who dares; Christopher Robin is saying his prayers"). He developed an agonizing stutter when he was eight, which did not leave him until his father died.

Despite the impression one gains from the books, it was not until Christopher was 10 that he and his father became close. They shared a love of math, cricket, crossword puzzles, and other word games. But his father was manipulative and discouraged the boy's desire to write. His university education was cut short by World War II. He failed his army physical, saying excitement made him tremble, but his father pulled strings and got him into the engineers corps as a carpenter. In the army Christopher began to find his own identity, delighting in being called Robin instead of Christopher Robin and in his new freedom from family. He even delighted in war itself because it matured him and he developed from being a shy, immature youth into a resourceful and courageous officer who could handle crises well.

After the war he got married, and he and his wife Lesley, a first cousin, escaped from their contentious families; Robin's mother had not spoken to her maternal uncle, who was Lesley's father, for years. They moved to Dartmouth, a remote seaside town, where they made a living for 21 years running the Harbor Bookshop and supplementing profits from books with prints, picture framing, cards, working for the preservation of the area, es- pousal of education, and working on behalf of various causes now that he was no longer hampered by a stutter. His long marriage was a happy one, except for the fact that their only child, a daughter Clare, was severely disabled and confined to a wheelchair.

But her needs were a welcome challenge to his skills; thinking about how unfair it is that most people can have all kinds of attractive and comfortable chairs to sit on while she was stuck with a single hideous one, he designed and made for her a large choice of handsome wheelchairs.

The death of his mother, with whom he had not been in touch for 15 years (since his daughter was born) gave him his first share in the royalties from his father's books. He did not want them at first because, he said, "I prefer to walk . . . . To be offered a lift by anybody would therefore have been bad enough . . . . But to be offered a lift by, of all people, my fictional namesake, to have to travel the rest of my way in his company—this was the final insult to my injured pride!" However, for the sake of his daughter who could never walk, he accepted the income, and used it in part to free himself to become the writer he had once wanted to be in spite of his father telling him not to.

The story of this conflicted family is in sad and perplexing contrast to the sunniness and affection shown in Milne's books.

Some Authors Who Are Also Illustrators

Helen Bannerman (1862–1946): Scottish. She began thinking up a story about a little Indian boy and doing accompanying sketches for it, while on a train in India. The result was *Little Black Sambo* (1899). Because of its deft use of infectious rhythm and repetition and the story's mixture of suspense and comedy, it was for many years one of children's favorite read-aloud stories. But in recent times it has been condemned as racist and removed from some libraries.

Ludwig Bemelmans (1898–1962): Austrian-born American. While in a hospital after a bicycle accident in France, Bemelmans was inspired by the nuns with their starched white hats that looked like butterfly wings and by a little girl in an adjoining room who had just had her appendix out. A year later, back in New York City, he created a mischievous

French heroine, naming her for his wife and modeling her after his daughter, writing and drawing on the backs of menus in Pete's Tavern, a restaurant well known as a writer's hangout. The first book about "Madeline" with pictures of her dressed in a bright yellow school uniform and a big yellow sailor hat was published in 1939 and was so popular that it resulted in a series: *Madeline and the Bad Hat, Madeline and the Gypsies, Madeline in London, Madeline in the Hospital, Madeline's Christmas, Madeline's House* and *Madeline's Rescue*. On the fiftieth anniversary of the publication of the first book, six of them were collected, along with some never-before-published drawings, in one big volume, *Mad about Madeline: The Complete Tales,* by the Book of the Month Club, in a set that included a Madeline doll with red yarn hair, a blue felt coat, a wide-brimmed hat—and an appendectomy scar! The book contained an introduction by the Pulitzer Prize-winning columnist and novelist Anna Quindlen, who explained why Madeline appealed to her so much: "When I was a girl, girl characters who were outspoken, smart, strong, and just a bit disobedient were the primary way I found to define and discover myself."

Bemelmans also wrote and illustrated other books for children, including *Hansi* in 1934, *Donkey Inside* (1941), and *I Love You, I Love You, I Love You* (1942), but none came close to rivaling the books about the spunky little Madeline.

William P. du Bois, full name **William Pene du Bois** (1916–1993): American. Born into a family of artists, his father was a painter and teacher; he learned art from his father and also studied and lived in France. Du Bois illustrated many books and magazines and in his early twenties began creating dozens of children's books and continued doing this for the rest of his life. He was known for both whimsy and serious themes. In 1948 the American Library Association honored him with its Newbery Medal for the best children's book of the year, *The Twenty-One Balloons.* In 1951 a *New York Times* review of his book *Bear Party,* about how some squabbling koala bears learned to live in harmony, said, "Children will want to hear and see it over and over—which will work no hardship on the adults who share the fun." In 1971 the *New York Times Book Review* named his *Bear Circus* one of the 10 best children's works of the year, calling him "a rare artist-author, one of the most talented and stylistic" and calling the book "a genuine comedy, a work of literary merit where pictures and text control and sustain more serious undertones."

> "What is the use of a book," thought Alice, "without pictures . . . . "
>
> —*from* Alice's Adventures in Wonderland *by Lewis Carroll*

Among other praised children's books by Du Bois were *Lion* (1956), *Porko von Popbutton* about the trials and eventually the triumph of a fat boy (1969), *Gentleman Bear* (1986), and *Otto and the Magic Potatoes* (1970).

Jean de Brunhoff (1899–1937) and his son **Laurent de Brunhoff** (1925–): French. Jean's first book, *The Story of Babar, the Little Elephant* (1931), launched a series about Babar the King, his wife Celeste, his cousin Arthur, their friend the Old Lady, and other characters. They were based on bedtime stories that Jean's wife, Cécile de Brunhoff, made up for her two little sons. The detailed and humorous illustrations, and the size of the books, three times larger than most children's books were when they were first published, as well as the amusing stories, made them stand out from crowded bookshelves in stores, and they quickly became known all over the world. The seven stories published before Jean's death were so popular that nine years later his son Laurent resumed the series, producing 30 more tales about Babar, successfully imitating both the tales and the illustrations.

In France the kindly elephant became "a national hero" and on the sixtieth anniversary of the first book's publication, Paris celebrated the occasion with an amazing fashion show at the Musée en Herbe. Jean de Brunhoff was the son of a designer who had helped to found the French *Vogue,* and his elephant family was always well dressed, so he would no doubt have considered the exhibit appropriate. The idea for this exhibit was born in 1987 when the French Ministry of Foreign Affairs asked Carol Mann, a British art historian, to devise a traveling exhibit that would illustrate something typically French. She thought of Babar, and 27 top fashion designers rose to her challenge to make clothes for elephantine figures. Hubert de Givenchy gave Céleste a dress with slimming vertical stripes; Babar acquired a leather suit by Hermès. Accessories included jewels, lambskin gloves, and crocodile handbags; Philippe Model, owner of three fashionable millinery shops, even made them tiny sunglasses.

It is not only in France that Babar's popularity is phenomenal. There has been a full-length Babar movie, a Babar animated cartoon series on Home Box Office, Babar cassettes and videos, and a literally elephantine array of Babar products on sale throughout the world, often produced by companies without the permission of the copyright owners: backpacks, balloons, bath towels, blackboards, a card game, figurines, fruit drinks, gift wrap, lunch boxes and thermos bottles, mugs, pajamas, paper dolls, pencil boxes and pens, perfume, puppets, puzzles, shoes and slippers, a toy car, a trunk, and wallpaper. In the 1990s, however, this kindly African King, the world's most famous elephant, was condemned by some advocates of "political correctness" as a colonialist, and there were calls to make him join the ranks of Holden Caulfield, Doctor Doolitttle, Huckleberry Finn, Little Black Sambo, Robin Hood, Tom Sawyer, Uncle Remus, and Uncle Tom, and be banned from children's libraries.

Wilhelm Busch (1832–1908): German. *Max und Moritz,* his first book for children, may have been the first ever that gave an inkling that children are not always good. It is considered the first story to be told in pictures and thus the forerunner of comic books, and it was followed by about 60 similar books, all of which met great success.

Randolph Caldecott (1846–1886): English. This artist contributed to *Punch* and other periodicals and did the illustrations for Washington Irving's *Old Christmas* (1876); he also illustrated children's favorites, such as *The House That Jack Built.* Maurice Sendak (see page 484) says that Caldecott was one of his great heroes and that the fun and inventiveness and poignancy of his work helped to provide him with the basis of his own style. Every year an illustrator of a children's book is honored as the year's best with the prestigious Caldecott Award, and Caldecott himself is immortalized and honored by the fact that the award is given in his name.

Wanda Gág (1893–1946): American. She was the eldest of seven children, and her parents died when she was 14. Just before he died her father called her to his bedside, took her hands in his and said, "What Papa could not do, Wanda will have to finish." He had been a part-time painter, and all his children had learned to draw as soon as they could hold a pencil. When Gág grew up she said she was surprised to find that "to many people drawing is not as important as sleeping and eating." She had a hard time taking care of her brother and sisters. They were very poor, and for two years all the girls skipped breakfast so that their young brother would have enough to eat. At one time she supported her family by painting lampshades for 25¢ an hour. For a while she worked for a family whose two children begged her for stories. Her books grew out of stories she made up for them and for her younger siblings. They were all delightful: *Millions of Cats* (1928), *ABC Bunny, Snippy and Snappy* and *The Funny Thing* (posthumous, 1957).

John (Johnny) Gruelle (1880–1938): American. Primarily a professional cartoonist and originator of the comic strip "Brutus," which was the winner of a *New York Herald Tribune* competition in 1910, Gruelle was also the author and illustrator of many books for children. The one with the most enduring fame is *Raggedy Ann.*

Will James, full name **William Roderick James** (1892–1942): American. Born in Montana, James grew up to become an unusually talented cowboy. He worked as a ranch hand on ranges in both the western United States and in Canada, and he wrote two books based on his experiences, which he illustrated himself: *Cowboys, North and South* (1924) and *Smoky* (1926). The latter, a sensitive and exciting story about the taming of a wild horse, was the one that children loved. It was awarded the Newbery Medal as the best children's book of its year.

Dorothy Kunhardt (1901–1979): American. In 1940 she published a unique, highly original little book for children too young to read, called *Pat the Bunny.* It contained a soft cotton bunny that a child could pat, a shiny mirror to look in, as well as other things to do, and it promptly became the first book for people to give to babies. It sold approximately 5 million copies in its first 50 years and became the second best-selling children's book of all time. It will undoubtedly continue to be a best seller for as long as new babies continue to be born.

Hugh Lofting (1886–1947): English. Enlisting in the British Army in 1916, Lofting saw nothing pleasant in the trenches to write about in letters to his children. He was concerned, too, over the cruel fate of defenseless animals in wartime. In his letters home, therefore, instead of describing his experiences he began writing stories, with accompanying pictures, about an imaginary figure, Doctor Doolittle, who was, he said, the best animal doctor in the world and who had learned animal language from Polynesia, a parrot. The doctor's first patient was a horse that had left a veterinarian who was treating him for spavin when all he needed was glasses. Doctor Doolittle, understanding every word that came from the horse's mouth, fitted him with a fine pair of spectacles, and from then on the doctor's reputation was made, with children as well as with patients. After the war, the *Doctor Doolittle* series was published (1922, 1926, 1933). They were best sellers, going into 45 printings and more than 13 translations. Later, some of the stories were made into a motion picture, with Rex Harrison playing the title role. Of all the doctor's feathered, furred, and four-footed friends, the "pushmipullyu" is most children's favorite; he has two heads, one for talking, and one for eating, "so that I can talk while eating without being rude."

Robert McCloskey (1914–): American. This author and illustrator specializes in producing humorous stories for young children about American rural life. He illustrated six books written by other authors and eight written by himself: *Lentil* (1940); *Make Way for Ducklings,* the Caldecott Medal winner in 1941; *Homer Price,* in which one of the characters is a friendly skunk named Aroma (1943); *Blueberries for Sal,* inspired by a day when his daughter Peggy was picking blueberries and he heard "kuplink, kuplank, kuplunk" as she dropped the berries into her bucket (1948); *Centerburg Tales* (1951); *One Morning in*

Maine, about a little girl who lives on a small island in Maine, and loses her first tooth in the mud while digging for clams but who gets the wish she made on it anyway (1952); *Time of Wonder,* which shows Maine's beautiful pine trees, green-blue water, and differently shaped islands in colorful paintings that it took him three years to complete (1957); and *Burt Dow: DeepWater Man* about a boy who makes friends with a whale, hides from a storm in its stomach, and puts a peppermint-striped band-aid on its tail (1963). Like his characters, Bob McCloskey lives on a small island in Maine.

All the books, with their mixture of real things, made-up things, noises, and smells as well as pictures, have great charm, but the children's favorite for more than 55 years has been *Make Way for Ducklings.* It is about a line of ducklings following Mrs. Mallard, their proud mother, as she takes them on an excursion to the Boston Public Garden, with the police stopping traffic so they can waddle across the street in safety.

Dhan Gopal Mukerji (1890–1936): Indian. This distinguished author-artist from Calcutta moved to the United States and wrote several books for adults, but he was best known for his extraordinarily beautiful books for children: *Kari the Elephant* (1923) and *Gay Neck: the Story of a Pigeon.* The latter won the Newbery Award in 1927.

Beatrix Potter (See page 482.)

Howard Pyle (1853–1911): American. Primarily a successful illustrator of other people's books, Pyle also wrote several of his own for young readers, with large colorful illustrations: *The Merry Adventures of Robin Hood* (in 1883), *Howard Pyle's Book of Pirates, Legends of King Arthur* and *Men of Iron.*

H. A. Rey (1898–1977): American. Children are very fond of Rey's stories and the pictures accompanying them about the wild misadventures of Curious George, a cute little monkey whose curiosity is always getting him into trouble. Perhaps the books might warn children about being too curious except that, happily, George always manages to get out of trouble and the things that happen to him are funny rather than scary.

Antoine de Saint-Exupéry, full name **Antoine Marie Roger Saint-Exupéry** (1900–1944): French. A commercial and wartime pilot who wrote philosophical novels about the beauty, joys, and excitement of flying: *Night Flight; Wind, Sand and Stars; Flight to Arras.* He is best known for one book he wrote and illustrated, *The Little Prince,* published just a year before his death. He was declared missing in action in 1944 after a flight to North Africa during World War II, so he never knew that he had produced a classic. It is a mysterious fable that seems almost prophetic, because it is set in the North African desert after his airplane has crashed there. The book's dedication sets its tone of combined humor and seriousness and indicates his attitude toward children:

With its thought-provoking but enigmatic story, this book became an immediate best seller; it is still much loved today, almost as much for the 40 whimsical watercolors that are an essential part of the story as for the character of the charming little prince. The publisher wrote about the book: "There are a few stories which in some way, in some degree, change the world forever for their readers. This is one."

Maurice Sendak (See page 484.)

Dr. Seuss: (See page 483.)

James Thurber (1894–1961): American. A famous cartoonist, essayist, and editor of the *New Yorker,* Thurber was also the author of many books. His works include *My Life and*

Hard Times (1934), hilarious memoirs about his days as a schoolboy who suffered from poor vision so that he never saw in the microscope what he was supposed to see and whose scientific experiments always came out wrong; and *The Secret Life of Walter Mitty*, about an impractical dreamer. This was made into a film with Danny Kaye. His children's books, published in the 1950s, were *Fables for Our Time; Many Moons; The Thirteen Clocks;* and *The Last Flower*, a touching tale about how world war destroys almost everything on earth, except for one sign of hope for future renewal: one tiny, beautiful, and sturdy flower smiling up at the sun.

Beatrix Potter (1866–1943)

Born in England, Beatrix Helen Potter was a lonely only child, and never went to school; she was educated by governesses. She had few toys and no playmates; her only companions were her governesses and a few pet animals: a tortoise, a white rat, and a rabbit she named Peter. She loved animals and taught herself to draw and paint them, along with plants and other natural objects.

In 1893, when Beatrix was 27, Noel Moore, the five-year-old son of Mrs. Moore who, as Miss Annie Carter, had been Beatrix's governess for German, got ill, and she wrote him a letter. To cheer him up she enclosed a little story she made up, with anecdotes and pictures of four bunnies, whom she named Flopsy, Mopsy, Cottontail, and Peter. Eight years later she got the idea of making a little book out of the story and, fortunately for all children, Noel had saved it. She copied the drawings, added others, made the story a little longer, called it *The Tale of Peter Rabbit*, and in 1902 published it, at her own expense because she could not find any publisher who was interested in it. The following year she published a second book, *The Tailor of Gloucester*. After that a commercial publisher took over, and later in 1903 *Squirrel Nutkin* appeared, her first financial success.

Two years later Beatrix bought a farm, which became her home and the setting for more of her books. The books have been translated into more than 20 languages, and their enormous popularity has never diminished. It is possibly due as much to their format and diminutive size, which makes them pleasant for tiny readers' hands to hold, and to their exquisite drawings, as it is to their amusing stories. In the United States alone, *The Tale of Peter Rabbit* has sold more than nine million copies, not counting book club or international sales, more than any other children's book ever published.

Year after year Potter kept writing and drawing. In alphabetical order, the titles of her 21 other books are: *Appley Dapply's Nursery Rhymes; Cecily Parsley's Nursery Rhymes; The Story of a Fierce Bad Rabbit; The Story of Miss Moppet; The Tailor of Gloucester,* which she said was her favorite; and *The Tale of Benjamin Bunny; Ginger and Pickles;* the self-important *Jemima Puddle-Duck; Johnny Town-Mouse; Little Pig Robinson;* the gentlemanly frog *Mr. Jeremy Fisher; Mr. Tod; Mrs. Tiggy-Winkle;* the polite but nervous *Mrs. Tittlemouse; Pigling Bland; Samuel Whiskers;* the reckless *Squirrel Nutkin; The Flopsy Bunnies; The Pie and the Patty-Pan; Tom Kitten; and Two Bad Mice.* A few years ago all 23 of her books were collected and sold together by the Book of the Month Club in their original size, with the original color and black-and-white drawings, and with introductions by Potter explaining the origin of each tale, in a handsome slipcase under the title *The World of Peter Rabbit.* All of them have also been reprinted in one soft-cover volume by another book club, Quality Paper Backs, under the title *The Complete Tales of Beatrix Potter.*

Potter felt that her books were more appreciated in America than in her native country, even though they were very popular in Britain, but she said Americans took children's literature more seriously than the English. Yet she herself could not take some of the praise for her books as seriously as some critics did. She disagreed emphatically when people compared her drawings of nature with those of John Constable (1776–1837) and could not believe it when the novelist Graham Greene (1904–1991) in his capacity as a literary critic wrote about her in the *London Mercury* in 1933, comparing her with E. M. Forster (1879–1970) and Henry James (1811–1882) and even finally with Shakespeare (1564–1616). He described her influence on his own writing and that of H. G. Wells (1866–1946). Her reaction to his remarks was "Bosh!" and she wrote him an acrimonious letter. She was also indignant at what she considered his "Freudian" analysis of her later work, which he said showed she had become more pessimistic between 1907 and 1909 after her fiancé suddenly died.

One aspect of her writing that deserves mention is her vocabulary. Like Rudyard Kipling and Robert Louis Stevenson and other successful writers for children, Potter did not hesitate to use big words even though she was writing little books for little people. Although she had great rapport with children, she wrote as an adult, using words such as *soporific, affronted, resourceful, disdainful,* and *superfluous.* Even though the tiny size of her books showed that she wanted them to be comfortable in children's hands, she obviously expected the stories to be read aloud by adults. Her phrasing, the development of her narratives, the cadences and rhythms of her prose, and her love of alliteration and onomatopoeia, were certainly part of her appeal to both adults and youngsters.

Dr. Seuss (1904–1991)

This American writer and illustrator, whose real name was Theodore Seuss Geisel, began his career as editor of his college humor magazine. He then became a cartoonist in advertising and in newspapers. In 1951 he did an animated cartoon about an imaginary character, *Gerald McBoing-Boing,* which won an Academy Award. His first book was *And to Think That I Saw It on Mulbery Street;* it was turned down by 27 publishers before being accepted, but as soon as it was published children loved it and launched Seuss on his unique career of what he called his "logical insanity."

Seuss claimed that he made up his imaginary creatures, such as the Befts, Flummoxes, Foons, Frumms, the Greeches, Grinches, Gootches, Gussets, the Mop-Noodled Finches, the Tufted Mazurkes, Yooks, Zans, and many others, because he did not really know how to draw very well: "If I draw what I think a kangaroo looks like, that seems to turn out all right, but if I go to the zoo and look at a real kangaroo and try to figure out what his legs do, it comes out all wrong."

He wrote several beginner books to try to make it fun for children to learn to read, using vocabulary lists supplied by teachers but putting the words into combinations no one had dreamed of before. *The Cat in the Hat* (1957), his first beginner book, consists of only 220 words, rhymed in funny combinations, which tickled young readers bored with *Dick and Jane* and other bland primers; it immediately sold 2 million copies, and later ranked fourth among all-time sales of children's books. In 1958 he followed this up with *The Cat in the Hat Comes Back* and this too broke records, becoming the thirteenth all-time best seller among children's books. His alphabet book, published in 1963, *Dr. Seuss's ABC,* was another top seller, twelfth among all-time children's book sales. For another

483

alphabet book, called *Beyond Zebra*, he invented wild examples: for instance, instead of Z is for Zebra it was Z is for Zizzer Zazzer Zuzz, and he made up extra letters, too.

Among his other huge hits are *Green Eggs and Ham*, which reached fifth place among all-time best-selling books for children, with over 36 million copies sold as of 1988; *One Fish, Two Fish, Red Fish, Blue Fish*, ninth children's best seller of all time; *Hop on Pop* (10th all-time best seller); *The 500 Hats of Bartholomew Cubbins; Horton Hatches the Egg; Horton Hears a Who*, made into a TV film; *How the Grinch Stole Christmas*, about the Grinch who is such a grouch that if he sees anyone having fun he gets so angry he bites himself (the film version of this story, with Boris Karloff as narrator, has played on television every Christmas since 1978); *The Butter Battle Book* about nuclear confrontation, a subject most people thought could not be used in a book for young children, but it too has been a best seller, in the United States, Britain, Japan, and Israel; *The Lorax,* about another serious subject, the environment, which the United Nations and environmental groups distribute regularly in many languages; it too has been made into a film.

People think that Seuss's books are such nonsense that they must have been easy to produce, but actually they were the result of hard work. It took Seuss a year to write *The Cat in the Hat.* "You try telling a pretty complicated story using less than 250 words," he said once in an interview.

> No, don't, not unless you're willing to rewrite and rewrite and rewrite. To get a 60-page book, I may easily write 1,000 pages before I'm satisfied. The story has to develop clearly and logically with a valid problem and a valid solution. The characters, no matter how weird, have to be vivid and believable and consistent. Fantasy must be logical, inside its own dream world. Then I have to get illustrations that fit the text and don't destroy the mood. The whole effect has to be just right—because children are tough critics. You can't kid kids. They have a relentless sense of logic, and know instantly if you violate the law of simplicity and consistency, or if you condescend or write down to them. That's been the trouble with children's books and elementary textbooks for years, this 'now, my little man' approach. The kids don't like it. Why should they? The old tellers of fantastic fairy tales, Grimm and Andersen, never talked down to their audiences.

Someone once called Dr. Seuss the greatest moralizer since Elsie Dinsmore. His response was: "Could be. In any story things happen and characters have motives that are good or bad. So every storyteller is a moralist whether he knows it or not. Children have a strong ethical sense. They want to see virtue rewarded and arrogance or meanness punished. You don't want to hit them over the head with the moral, of course; you have to work it in sideways. But it has to be there."

P.S. Dr. Seuss even wrote one book for adults, whom he called "obsolete children." Titled *You're Only Old Once!,* it too has a moral. Through his characteristically wacky rhymes and illustrations, he showed that getting older is a special cause for celebration.

Maurice Sendak (1928–)

Probably the best-known illustrator of his day, Sendak has illustrated more than 55 books, some written by him and others by other writers, including Robert Graves, Isaac Bashevis Singer, and Leo Tolstoy. His books have appeared on the *New York Times* lists of the best-illustrated children's books more than 14 times. In 1964 he won the Caldecott Award for *Where the Wild Things Are*, a book he both wrote and illustrated, and he was runner-up for the Caldecott Award for five other books. Michel di Capus, one of his editors, said some people were horrified when Sendak got the Caldecott Award. They claimed to object to the monsters in the book, but what they really objected to, said di Capus, was that "the book acknowledged that children get angry at their mothers; these are the people who tend to sentimentalize childhood, to be overprotective. Maurice had almost singlehandedly opened a door on another world."

In his books, children are often combative, stubborn, pugnacious, unhappy. He thinks most children's books fail to confront the realities of childhood, offering "a gilded world unshadowed by the least suggestion of conflict or pain, a world manufactured by those who cannot—or don't care to—remember the truth of their own childhood." He says his mission is "involvement with this inescapable fact of childhood—the awful vulnerability of children and their struggle to make themselves king of all wild things." Max, the hero of *Where the Wild Things Are*, whom he calls "my truest and therefore my dearest creation," gets so mad at his mother that he runs away and spends a wild time with "the wild things" until he finally becomes lonesome and realizes he wants "to be where someone loves him best of all," so he returns home and finds his supper waiting for him.

In 1962 Sendak published *Nutshell Library*, a set of four books only 2½ x 4 inches, packaged in a slipcase. One of them is *Alligators All Around*, a delightful alphabet book; instead of such trite definitions as "A is for Apple," A is for Alligators who have problems. Other examples: H is for Having Headaches, P is for Pushing People, Q is for Quite Quarrelsome, and T is for Throwing Tantrums.

In 1974 he became the first American to win the Hans Christian Andersen Award, the highest international honor for excellence in children's book illustration. When he received it he jokingly called it the Hans Jewish Andersen Award. In his acceptance speech in Bologna, Italy, when receiving the award, he said,

> As a child I felt that books were holy objects to be caressed, rapturously sniffed and devotedly provided for. I gave my life to them. I still do. I continue to do what I did as a child: dream of books, make books and collect books.

Sendak was born in 1928, the third child of Philip Sendak, a Jew from Poland who had emigrated to America. His father was a born storyteller who often entertained his children by extending his improvisations for many nights. Jack Sendak, his oldest son, imitated his father and was always writing and illustrating books, and Maurice just naturally copied his big brother. When they grew up they both became writers and illustrators.

During World War II, Jack was in the army but Maurice was still in high school where he studied art and worked afternoons and weekends for All American Comics, filling in backgrounds and extending the story lines of such comic strips as *Mutt and Jeff*. In 1948 he and Jack started constructing animated wooden toys. They took them to the toy store F.A.O. Schwartz, but were told they would be too expensive to market in quantity. Jack took a job in the electronics industry, but Maurice got a job in the window display department at Schwartz, while attending evening classes at the Art Students League.

The Schwartz book buyer Frances Christie introduced him to Ursula Wordstrom, an editor at Harpers' publishing house, who was so impressed by his sketches that she invited him to illustrate *The Wonderful Farm* by Marcel Ayme. That was his first published book

(1951). Wordstrom was also looking for an illustrator for a new book by Ruth Krauss, *A Hole Is to Dig*, and decided Sendak would be perfect for it. He was. It came out in 1952 and promptly established him as a brilliant and unique illustrator. From then on he not only illustrated many books for children but also began writing his own books, digging into his own childhood for ideas, characters, and favorite toys, and remembered experiences that were emotionally authentic while being permeated with fantasy. An example is Jennie, his Sealyham terrier, who appears often and to whom he dedicated one of his books.

In 1988 Sendak illustrated a previously undiscovered story by Wilhelm Grimm, *Dear Mili*, about a little girl who is sent by her mother into a forest to hide from a terrible war. She is lost and afraid, but an unseen guardian angel guides her, and she meets an old hermit whom she serves faithfully for three days. She is then sent back to her mother for a happy reunion, though the three days in the forest have somehow stretched into 30 years in the outside world. Loneliness, despair, terror, the sense of being abandoned yet also the sense of being protected, the gulf between parent and child, reconciliation, acceptance of death—the story includes all these themes. Both the story and Sendak's pictures were highly praised as true works of art. In commenting on the book, Sendak told an interviewer that he hoped readers would experience through it

> something of what happened to me, which was a kind of transcendence, a happiness above and beyond the story. After all, Wilhelm wrote this not to depress somebody but to elate somebody, give hope. There's something touching and sweet in the way children will persist despite everything, despite all calamity. Creative work is a catharsis in that it retrieves that feeling for me. I get it back in painting and writing. And I think that's why I work all the time, because it makes me happy.

Charles Monroe Schultz (1922–)

Schultz is the creator, artist, and writer of the famous comic strip *Peanuts*, which features a group of young children including the hapless Charlie Brown, crotchety and bossy Lucy, timid Linus, and vain Violet, along with Charlie's lovable dog Snoopy. The strip has appeared in over 2,000 newspapers in 56 countries. And Snoopy won a special place in history when a shuttle in the U.S. space program was named for him.

This strip has been translated into numerous languages and is read by approximately 80 million people a day! Book collections of *Peanuts* have been published in Belgium, Brazil, Denmark, England, France, Germany, Iceland, Japan, Sweden, Switzerland, South Africa, and the United States.

It is hard to believe that these eternally young "Peanuts" (i.e., children) are now actually more than 40 years old, but this ageless strip appeared for the first time on October 2, 1950, in a grand total of nine American newspapers. During the first year the number of papers carrying the strip increased to 35, and there were 45 the following year.

Peanuts first appeared on television on December 9, 1965, in a TV special called "A Charlie Brown Christmas," produced by Lee Mendleson and animated by Bill Melendez. The show won an Emmy and a Peabody Award, and is repeated every year during the Christmas season. Since then there have been more than 20 more *Peanuts* specials on TV. The voices used in them are those of very young children. New boys and girls are auditioned every two years because as these child actors grow, their voices change and become too mature. One exception to this rule, however, is the voice of Snoopy, which has always been done by Bill Melendez.

On March 7, 1967, a musical, *You're a Good Man, Charlie Brown*, opened in New York, starring Gary Burghoff as Charlie Brown. The play ran for four years in New York and there were nine touring companies, both in the United States and abroad.

The *Peanuts* characters also appeared in a feature-length film, *A Boy Named Charlie Brown*, which opened at Radio City Music Hall in New York on December 11, 1969. Since then, four other feature-length movies of *Peanuts* have been made.

Schultz claims that he did not base the strip on his own or his children's childhood, but there is at least one instance when he did use a real child's experience for a series of cartoons. He had Lucy get *strabismus* and *amblyopia*, eye problems that can cause cross-eye and eventual loss of vision and facial paralysis if not detected and taken care of in time, because a little girl he knew had these problems and was cured. He wanted to publicize these conditions in order to alert parents to the importance of early diagnosis and treatment. He donated the original drawings for this part of his strip to the New York Eye and Ear Infirmary, which had saved the eyesight of his young friend.

He also designed a special poster, which he donated to UNICEF, showing Linus and his security blanket—to help bring more security to children all over the world.

POETS WHO WROTE FOR CHILDREN

Hilaire Belloc (1870–1953): English author. In addition to his larger output of series essays and books on religion, Belloc wrote humorous verses for children, such as the following "Dedication on the Gift of a Book to a Child":

> Child! do not throw this book about!
> Refrain from the unholy pleasure
> Of cutting all the pictures out!
> Preserve it as your chiefest treasure.
> Child, have you never heard it said
> That you are heir to all the ages?
> Why, then, your hands were never made
> To tear these beautiful thick pages!
> Your little hands were made to take
> The better things and leave the worse ones;
> They also may be used to shake
> The massive Paws of Elder Persons.
> And when your prayers complete the day,
> Darling, your little tiny hands
> Were also made, I think, to pray
> For men that lose their fairylands.

A Bad Child's Book of Beasts, a collection of his nonsense verse, was so popular that the first edition (1896) sold out in four days. He also wrote *More Beasts for Worse Children* (1897), and *Cautionary Tales for Children* (1907).

William Blake (1757–1827): English mystical poet. He produced *Songs of Innocence*, "happy songs every child may joy to hear" (1789), which he wrote, illustrated, engraved, printed, and sold all by himself.

Robert Browning (1812–1889): English poet. *The Pied Piper of Hamelin* (1842), a narrative poem that Browning wrote to amuse Willie, a friend's young son, was based on a 13th-century German legend and, as a result of the poem's fame, the town of Hamelin has become a major tourist attraction.

Gelett Burgess (1866–1951): American writer. Published *Goops and How to Be Like Them* (1900); he was also the author of the following famous nonsense poem "Purple Cow," which appeared in the magazine *Lark* that he edited from 1895 to 1897:

> I never saw a purple cow.
> I never hope to see one,
> But I can tell you anyhow
> I'd rather see than be one.

Lewis Carroll (1832–1898): English author. His books about Alice contain many verses that children and adults love: "The Walrus and the Carpenter," "Jabberwocky," "Father William," and so on.

Nathaniel Cotton (1705–1788): English physician. He treated mental diseases in an asylum, but he was also a poet; he wrote *Visions in Verse, for the Entertainment and Instruction of Younger Minds* (1751) and short poems that are still included in anthologies.

Walter de la Mare (1873–1956): English poet. He wrote *Songs of Childhood* (1902); *Peacock Pie* (1913); and *Poems for Children* (1930).

T. S. Eliot (1888–1965): American-born English poet. His book of verse for children, *Old Possum's Book of Practical Cats* (1939), was transformed in the 1980s into *Cats*, a highly successful musical revue for adults that ran for more than 10 years on Broadway.

Eugene Field (1850–1895): American homespun poet. Most of his work, a mixture of whimsical stories, wit, and children's verse, appeared in "Sharps and Flats," a column in the *Chicago Record,* a newspaper he edited from 1883 to 1895. Among the most famous of his poems for children are "The Duel (The Gingham Dog and the Calico Cat)," "Little Boy Blue," "Wynken, Blynken and Nod," and "Over the Hills and Far Away." In addition to his own lullabies and jingles he adapted a number of Armenian, Dutch, Japanese, Jewish, Norwegian, and Sicilian lullabies and folk songs.

Robert Frost (1874–1963): American poet. For his adult poems he won the Pulitzer Prize in 1923, 1930, 1936, and 1942. He later issued a selection of his poems that he made especially for children called *You Come Too: Poems for Young People.*

Sarah Josepha Hale (1788–1879): American author, editor, and poet. A young widow with five children to support, Mrs. Hale wrote novels, poems, and cookbooks and edited magazines, including *Godey's Lady's Book.* In 1830 she was editor of a magazine for children, *The Juvenile Miscellany,* and published a book, *Poems for Our Children Designed for Families, Sabbath Schools, and Infant Schools.* The immortal "Mary Had a Little Lamb" appeared in both the magazine and the book, and it became famous after 1857 when it was included in *McGuffey's Second Reader,* as McGuffey's Readers were the standard textbooks in American schools for 50 years. Mrs. Hale said the poem was based on an actual incident in her own childhood when she cared for a lamb on her father's farm, but in 1928 Mr. and Mrs. Henry Ford published *The Story of Mary's Little Lamb as*

Told by Mary and Her Neighbors and Friends; they collected 200 documents to prove that Mary Sawyer Tyler of Sudbury, Massachusetts, was the original Mary and they restored her old schoolhouse as a memorial to her. However, as Mrs. Hale had pointed out, there were probably many occasions when rural children were accompanied to school by pet animals, including lambs.

Rudyard Kipling (1865–1936): English author. In addition to his many stories and books for both adults and children, Kipling wrote poems, including *Wee Willie Winkie* (1889) and *Rewards and Fairies* (1910), a book that contained his famous poem "If," giving advice to boys. (See also page 469.)

Charles Lamb (1775–1834) and his sister **Mary Lamb** (1764–1847): English authors. In addition to their other books, they published *Poetry for Children*, entirely original (1809).

Edward Lear (1812–1888): English inventor of the limerick. By profession Lear was an artist, but he wrote and illustrated many books of "nonsense" verses for children including *The Book of Nonsense* (1846), *Nonsenses, Songs, Stories, Botany and Alphabets* (1871), *More Nonsense* (1872), and *Laughable Lyrics* (1877). His earliest poems and drawings of animals were written to amuse some children whose father owned a menagerie. His most famous poem is "The Owl and the Pussycat."

> Teach your children poetry;
> it opens the mind, lends
> grace to wisdom, and makes
> the heroic virtues hereditary.
>
> —*Mohammed (570–632)*

Henry Wadsworth Longfellow (1807–1882): American poet. Among his many poems, those which have special appeal to children are "The Village Blacksmith" (1841); "Evangeline: A Tale of Acadia" (1847); "The Golden Legend" (1851); and "The Song of Hiawatha" (1855), which he wrote in the meter of the epic *Kalavala*, a compilation of folk verses from Finland. Another still popular poem of his, which he never expected to be published, was:

> There was a little girl
> Who had a little curl,
> Right in the middle of her forehead,
> And when she was good,
> She was very, very good,
> But when she was bad she was horrid.

He wrote this about his daughter Edith one day after she had had a tantrum. In its original version it said she was a little "dirl" who had a little "turl," and he was so embarrassed when somehow the poem got circulated outside his amused family that at first he tried to disavow its authorship.

Clement Clarke Moore (1779–1863): American clergyman. He wrote "A Visit from St. Nicholas (The Night before Christmas)" in 1822 to amuse one of his six children, who was sick in bed. It was published anonymously by a friend the following year, but Moore, a dignified minister and professor, did not acknowledge its authorship until it appeared in *The New York Book of Poetry* in 1837. It forever transformed America's conception of Santa Claus, and it remains one of the favorite poems of American children today.

Ogden Nash (1902–1971): American humorist. In addition to this prolific poet's many humorous verses that entertained adults, he also wrote *The New Nutcracker Suite and Other Innocent Verses, a Children's Album* (1962), containing verses written to accompany piano pieces from the *Nutcracker Suite* by Tchaikovsky.

John Newbery (1713–1767): English publisher. One of the earliest books of poetry ever written for children was his *A booke in English metre, of the great Marchaunt man called Dives Pragmatious, very preaty for children* (1563).

Laura Elizabeth Richards (1850–1943): American poet. One of six children of the poet Julia Ward Howe, the composer and author of "The Battle Hymn of the Republic," Mrs. Richards wrote many verses and jingles for *St. Nicholas* magazine; she said she used the back of her firstborn baby for a writing desk, as the baby lay across her knees. She also published two books of children's poems, *In My Nursery* (1890) and *Tirra Lirra* (1932).

James Whitcomb Riley (1849–1916): American "Hoosier poet." Among his large output of verses were several books for children: *The Old Swimmin' Hole and 'Leven More Poems,* published under the pseudonym "Benj. F. Johnson, of Boone" in 1883; *Rhymes of Childhood* (1890); *Book of Joyous Children* (1902); and *The Little Orphant Annie Book* (1908).

Michael Rosen (1946—): English poet, performer, and anthologist. One of Britain's most successful poets, Rosen writes poems for children and visits schools all over the country, entertaining children with stories and readings of his poems. He also appears regularly on children's television programs, always conveying his message that one can have a good time by reading, singing, or writing about, and sharing, thoughts, dreams, and ideas through poetry. His own poems can be found in his books, among which are *You Can't Catch Me* and *Quick, Let's Get Out of Here,* and an anthology he compiled and published in 1985, called *The Kingfisher Book of Children's Poetry.* It contains 250 poems including ballads, limericks, rhyming riddles, and nonsense verse both by and for children, some by 56 famous writers, others by unknown people, some contemporary, some from ancient Egypt and Rome, and some which have been translated from Chinese, French, and Russian.

Robert Louis Stevenson (See page 144.)

Rabindranath Tagore (1861–1941): Indian author. Winner of the Nobel Prize for Literature in 1913, he wrote thousands of poems and songs, many of them for children, in addition to his plays, novels, short stories, and essays. Two of his poems became the lyrics of national anthems, for India and Bangladesh. His books are the first that Indian children learn to read, and children celebrate his birthday (May 9) every year with recitals of his works.

Ann Taylor (1782–1866) and her sister **Jane Taylor** (1783–1824): English poets. They collaborated on *Original Poems for Infant Minds,* two volumes (1804 and 1805) that became extremely popular. Other volumes followed, including *Rhymes for the Nursery* (1806) which contained "The Baby's Dance" and the still famous "Twinkle Twinkle Little Star."

Louis Untermeyer (1885–1977): American anthologist. He was an editor and a part-time poet but was primarily known as an anthologist; among other books, he published *The Golden Treasury of Poetry, an anthology of poems for children.*

Isaac Watts (1674–1748): English theologian. It is said that when this theologian and composer of hymns was a child he had such a propensity for speaking in rhyme that he could not avoid it even when he wished. Once, when his annoyed father threatened to whip him to break him of this habit, the child burst into tears and on his knees cried, "Pray, Father, do some pity take, And I will no more verses make." Obviously, however, he continued: during his life he wrote more than 600 hymns. He also wrote *Divine and Moral Songs Attempted in Easy Language for the Use of Children* (1715).

Charles Wesley (1707–1788): English composer of hymns. He was an even more prolific writer of hymns than Isaac Watts, creating 6,500 of them. Some were collected in a book, *Hymns for Children* (1763). When Wesley was a student his classmates called him a "methodist" because he was so methodical in his studies, and later when his brother John Wesley appropriated the name and founded the Methodist church, Charles worked with him, although he did not always agree with John's strict views.

John Greenleaf Whittier (1807–1892): American poet. Among his numerous books of verse several had special appeal to children: *Ballads* (1838), *Home Ballads* (1860), *School Days*, and the individual poem, "The Barefoot Boy."

LITERARY PRODIGIES

Dante Alighieri (1265–1321): Italy's greatest poet. He started writing sonnets at age nine, the same year he met eight-year-old Beatrice Portinari, whose angelic image remained with him throughout his life and inspired him to write *The Divine Comedy* long after she had died at age 24.

Daisy Ashford (1882–1972): English novelist. She wrote her first book, a full-length novel, *The Young Visiters; or Mr. Salteena's Plan*, at the age of nine. It was published in 1919, with spelling, punctuation, and arithmetic mistakes included, under the sponsorship of Sir James Barrie. It brought her sudden and lasting fame.

An excerpt from *The Young Visiters*

So now that all our friends are marrid I will add a few words about their familys.

Ethel and Bernard returned from their honeymoon with a son and hair a nice fat baby called Ignatius Bernard. They soon had six more children, four boys and three girls, and some of them were twins, which was very exciting. The earl only got two rather sickly girls called Helen and Marie because the last one lookeed slightly french. Mr. Salteena and a large family of 10, five of each, but he grew very morose as the years rolled by and his little cottage was very noisy and his wife was a bit annoying at times, especially when he took to dreaming of Ethel and wishing he could have married her. Still he was a pius man in his way and found relief in prayer.

Jane Austen (1775–1817): English novelist. She never knew she would go down in history as one of the world's greatest and most beloved authors. She wrote six novels that have given her lasting fame, but none did so during her lifetime. Four were published anonymously: *Sense and Sensibility* in 1811; *Pride and Prejudice* in 1813; *Mansfield Park* in 1814; and *Emma* in 1816. Two, *Northhanger Abbey* and *Persuasion*, were not published until a year after her death.

Her first novel, written when she was 14, was *Love and Freindship* (that is not a typographical error; she spelled it that way). She subtitled it *A Novel in a Series of Letters. Deceived in Freindship & Betrayed in Love.* It was a brilliant parody of popular eighteenth-century fiction, with swooning ladies and avid husband-hunters, and it revealed a precocious awareness of human weaknesses and affectations. It was "inscribed by Her obliged Humble Servant The Author" to a girlhood friend.

Jane kept a copy of it in one of three notebooks, along with her other "Juvenalia," written before she was 17 for her own amusement and that of her family. She read them aloud; her brother Henry said her works "were never heard to so much advantage as from her own mouth; for she partook largely in all the best gifts of the comic muse."

Her other juvenalia were *The Three Sisters,* dedicated as follows: "A Novel, to Edward Austen Esqre The following unfinished Novel is respectfully inscribed by His obedient humble servt The Author); *A Collection of Letters,* inscribed "To Miss Cooper Cousin Conscious of the Charming Character which in every Country, & every Clime in Christendom is Cried, Concerning you, with Caution & Care I Commend to your Charitable Criticism this Clever Collection of Curious Comments, which have been Carefully Culled, Collected & classed by your Comical Cousin The Author"; *Lesley Castle,* "An Unfinished Novel in Letters" dedicated to her brother "Henry Thomas austen Esqre Sir I am now availing myself of the Liberty you have frequently honoured me with of dedicating one of my Novels to you. That it is unfinished, I greive; yet fear that from me, it will always remain so; that as far as it is carried, it Should be so trifling and so unworthy of you, is another concern to your obliged humble Servant The Author." But evidently her brother did not consider it so unworthy, because he paid her 100 guineas for it; and *The History of England*, "by a partial, prejudiced, & ignorant Historian. To Miss Austen eldest daughter of the Revd George Austen, this Work is inscribed with all due respect by The Author. N.B. There will be very few Dates in this History." Here is a sample of this prejudiced and amusing history, from the last section, about the reign of Charles I:

> This amiable Monarch seems born to have suffered Misfortunes equal to those of his lovely Grandmother; Misfortunes which he could not deserve since he was her descendant. Never certainly was there before so many detestable Characters at one time in England as in this period of its History; Never were amiable Men so scarce. The number of them throughout the whole Kingdom amounting only to five. . . .

All these manuscripts showed signs of her future talent: her vivid characterizations, brilliant ear for dialogue, gift for irony, charm, and delicious humor, the qualities that have caused so many people in every generation since to read and reread her books with delight.

Thomas Chatterton (1752–1770): English poet. Called the "marvelous boy," from his early years Chatterton was fascinated by antiquities and at age 12 began to write imitations of ancient writers: poems, satires, political tracts, and essays assuming the styles of Gray, Pope, Smollet, and others, some of which he pretended were authentic. At 14 he published a romance in prose and verse supposedly by Thomas Rowley, an imaginary fifteenth-century monk. He also produced a purported transcript of a 1469 treatise on painting by T. Rowley, and an "Excellent Balade of Charitie" as if from a parchment of the same priest. When these were challenged as forgeries and he was unable to sell poetry under his own name, he committed suicide at 18 and was buried in a pauper's grave.

For 80 years thereafter there was a heated controversy over the Rowley poems, which were admired but finally proved to have been Chatterton's own inventions. They had been archaized with the help of the *Dictionarium Anglo-Britannicum* by John Kersey, but after the indignation at the fraud died down Chatterton was finally acknowledged to have been a poet of great originality, dramatic power, imagination, and lyric beauty.

Hilda Conkling (1910–): American child poet. This daughter of a teacher of literature at Smith College started making poems at age two, which her mother wrote down. Many were published in magazines and in 1920, when she was 10, a collection of 107 of them was published in a book called *Poems by a Little Girl.* When she was 12 a second volume called *Shoes in the Wind* was published. The eminent poet Amy Lowell wrote a preface for the first volume in which she said, "I know of no other instance in which such really beautiful poetry has been written by a child. One has stumbled upon that flash of personality which we call genius. . .the oldest poet in the world could not improve upon them." She praised Hilda's mother for unobtrusively cultivating and stimulating Hilda's imagination, appreciating and not stifling the child's originality of expression, feelings, and cadence. As Hilda said in her book's dedication to her mother:

> I have found a way of thinking
> To make you happy.
> If I sing, you listen;
> If I think, you know.

John Evelyn (1620–1706): English government official and diarist. Evelyn began a diary at age 11 and continued it all his life until his death at age 84, leaving a valuable and entertaining record of English seventeenth-century life.

Eleanor Farjeon (1881–1965): English author. She wrote as many books, mostly juveniles, as the 84 years she lived, starting when she was seven years old. She never went to school even for one day, but in her father's library there were 8,000 books that educated her. Eleanor came from an unusual family. Her grandmother was one of 26 sisters. Her mother was the daughter of a famous actor, Joseph Jefferson, who for years played Rip Van Winkle on the stage. Her father was a novelist. Two of her brothers were playwrights and a third was a music critic and composer. Their friends were artists, writers, playwrights, and musicians. She herself was plain, nearsighted, and bookish. In her childhood she had poor health yet somehow was always entertaining people, writing stories, plays, verses, nursery rhymes, jokes, and many volumes of fairy tales. Among her most popular stories were "Elsie Piddock Skips in Her Sleep" and "Martin Pippin in the Apple Orchard."

Anne Frank (1929–1945): German refugee living in Holland during the Nazi occupation; a diarist. On June 12, 1942, on her thirteenth birthday, she made her first entry in a diary, which she called "the nicest of all" the birthday presents she received. Less than a month later she and her family went into hiding because the Nazis were planning to arrest her father. She continued writing in her diary during the two years the family lived in hiding, until August 1944 when they were discovered and shipped to concentration camps in Germany. Anne died in captivity of typhus in 1945, just two months before the war in Europe ended, and three months before her sixteenth birthday. Later her diary was discovered and published. Its humor, charm, idealism, honesty, and simple wisdom contrasted so eloquently with Anne's tragic fate that the book became an international best seller. (For more information on Anne, see page 549.)

493

Johann Wolfgang von Goethe (1749–1832): Germany's greatest poet and dramatist. Most of his success was in later life, but Goethe started writing poetry at age six and wrote his first play when he was 10. By age 16 he had already learned English, French, Greek, Italian, and Latin.

William Hazlitt (1778–1830): English author, essayist, critic, and lecturer. At age 14 he wrote *A New Theory of Criminal and Civil Legislation.*

Amy Lowell (1874–1925): American poet. She started writing verse at age nine, and became one of the foremost experimental exponents of *vers libre* (free verse), which she preferred to call "unrhymed cadence."

Mikhail Luryevich (1814–1841): Russian poet and novelist. Orphaned in his early childhood, he began writing poetry at age 13 and finished his first cycle of love poems at 16.

Edgar Allan Poe (1809–1849): American poet and short-story writer. At age 15 he wrote a distinguished poem "To Helen," the mother of a school friend he was visiting. His own mother died when he was young and he was adopted by the Allan family in Richmond, Virginia. After one term at the University of Virginia, when he was 17, Poe ran away from home and returned to Boston, his birthplace, where he published *Tamerlane and Other Poems.* His financial resources were soon exhausted, so he enlisted in the army that year and served until his foster father secured his release two years later. His adult life was a mixture of great writing produced by his genius and of misery produced by poverty, alcoholism, and periodic bouts of insanity.

Alexander Pope (1688–1744): English poet. He wrote his "Ode to Solitude" when he was 12 years old, the same year that he became ill, permanently crippled, and deformed. By age 16 he had produced a large output of poems that attracted the attention of the prominent playwright William Wycherly (1640–1716), who helped him get them published. Pope was a brilliant poet and wit but a contentious enemy and savage satirist of many influential people due to his strong opinions. He was an ardent Catholic in an ardently anti-Catholic society, so he was frequently embroiled in controversies, but his poetry has outlived them.

Dorothy Strait (1958–): American writer. At age four she became the world's youngest-ever commercially published author when Pantheon Books published her *How the World Began.*

Nika Turbina (1974–): Russian child poet. She wrote her first poem at age four and published her first book, called *First Draft,* at 10. Translations of the book have been published in England, France, and Italy, where it won that country's Gold Lion of Venice Award for Poetry. In November, 1987, when Nika was 12, she visited the U.S. and gave dramatic readings of her poetry in New York and Boston. She also spent a few hours shopping and bought two dolls, Barbie and Elvis. A recording of her recitations has sold more than 30,000 copies in the former Soviet Union, where poetry is more popular than anywhere else in the world, with large crowds filling football stadiums to hear poets read from their works. Nika once said in an interview for *Soviet Life* magazine:

> Poetry has no nation and no age. I write for all people. Somewhere people are being killed, somewhere children are dying, and with my poems I want to help remove the blocks that currently divide the world.

494

Lope de Vega (1562–1635): Spanish poet, dramatist, and priest. He started writing poetry at the age of 12, and plays soon after. Extraordinarily prolific, Vega wrote about 1,800 plays. He was the founder of Spain's national drama.

The Children's Express
A News Service by Children for Children

In 1975 a lawyer named Robert H. Clampitt (1927–1996) founded an ambitious and original project: a news service "by children for children." Skeptics who thought children would not have the skills or perseverence to produce such a service have been amazed. For over 20 years under his guidance more than 3,500 children have taken part in Children's Express (CE). It now runs bureaus in the U.S., Australia, England, New Zealand, and Japan.

Its reporters (maximum age: 13) and editors (maximum age: 18) who work on a volunteer, after-school basis, have published newspapers, magazines, and a book, conducted national and international hearings on important issues, carried out overseas assignments for major publications, taped interviews and discussions on subjects ranging from divorce and suicide to national politics and international affairs and have produced segments for television news programs.

At first they just wrote about children's activities, but at the 1976 Democratic Presidential Convention they began to focus on adult politics. One young reporter came up with a scoop that put the Children's Express on the map: Jimmy Carter's choice of Walter Mondale as his vice-presidential candidate.

Since then the group has covered every Democratic and Republican national convention, where they have presented to delegates findings and recommendations on child health and welfare, education, youth employment, juvenile justice, and other topics.

In 1977 the first CE newspaper column appeared in the *New York Times*, and a CE magazine achieved a regular national distribution of 200,000 in 50 states; however, the magazine had to be discontinued after seven issues for lack of funds, and since then the reporters and editors have concentrated primarily on the children's news service.

In 1979 CE produced a book called *Listen to Us: The Children's Express Report*, published by Workman Press. They were honored at a White House reception, put out a special magazine for the International Year of the Child, and conducted hearings in New York on institutionalized children.

In 1980 CE began producing three columns a week, distributed nationally by the Field Syndicate with more than 60 newspaper subscribers. That year, accompanied by Clampitt, they also sent a news team to Thailand and Cambodia, and were among the first journalists to visit the areas' refugee camps, interviewing doctors, nurses, and refugees.

In 1981 CE was nominated for a Pulitzer Prize in commentary, and it held hearings on disabled children.

In 1982 the first CE news bureau was opened in Salem, Massachusetts.

In 1983 a series of CE news reports was featured on the Today Show on NBC. Also twice-weekly distribution of the CE news column, featuring interviews and discussions, began over the United Press International wire service to 2,500 newspapers worldwide.

In 1984 CE news bureaus were opened in four additional cities—Newark, New Jersey; San Francisco; Tokyo; and Melbourne, Australia. Its Tokyo columns appear in the Saturday Supplement of *Yoiuri Shimbun*, a newspaper with a circulation of 9 million.

Members of CE have appeared on network TV shows, and its series on Public Television won both an Emmy and a Peabody award.

In 1985 CE celebrated its tenth anniversary by publishing a special journal and holding a banquet at which Jim Grant, executive director of UNICEF, was the keynote speaker. Mayor Ed Koch of New York City declared November 26, 1985, to be Children's Express Day "to recognize the importance of exploring and strengthening media coverage of children's issues" and, he said, to acknowledge the fact that

> during the past decade, CE reporters, working with teenage assistant editors, have examined a wide variety of subjects ranging from foster care to hunger, from health care to education. . . .CE is the only nationally distributed newspaper column dealing regularly with a variety of issues affecting children.

In 1986, their second decade began with two major events: an international conference in Japan attended by almost 50 CE reporters and editors from seven bureaus, and a symposium on the media and children's issues attended by many top news media executives and journalists.

During their third decade CE continued its tradition of going wherever the hot news stories are and several of its reporters and editors visited Sarajevo.

One hopes that the imagination, inspiration, and guidance of the late Robert Clampitt, which is no longer available to these children except in honored memory, will continue to enable the Children's Express to train many more bright young journalists in the future.

13

Children and Poverty and Violence

THE CHILDREN OF KARL MARX

Karl Marx (1818–1883), the philosophical father of Communism and co-author with Friedrich Engels (1820–1895) of *The Communist Manifesto* (1847) and *Das Kapital* (three volumes, 1867, 1885, 1894), married at age 25, in 1843. He and his wife had seven children in the next 12 years: Jenny, born in 1844; Laura, born in 1845; Edgar, nicknamed Musch, born in 1847; Heinrich, whom they called Guido, born in 1849; Franziska, born in 1851; Eleanor, nicknamed Lene, born in 1855; and an unnamed child who died right after birth in 1856.

Poverty, Illnesses, and Early Deaths

The bitter indignation with which Marx reacted to the existence of poverty, which influenced political and economic thought with such momentous worldwide consequences in the twentieth century, must have been strongly reinforced by his agony over how poverty made his family suffer.

"Misfortune was a permanent guest at Marx's home," according to Fritz J. Raddatz, editor of the published correspondence between Marx and Engels. "His son Guido, born 1849, died after a year. In 1852 his daughter Franziska also died at the age of one year. No sooner was his daughter Eleanor born in January 1855 than his dearly loved son Edgar, called Musch, died on 6 April. Marx was totally crushed."

Excerpts from his letters vividly reveal the worries and griefs of a father watching his children die:

27 February 1852:

> For a week now . . . for a lack of coats, stored at the pawnshop, I no longer leave the house, and for lack of credit can no longer eat meat.

8 September 1852:

> My wife is ill, little Jenny is ill, little Lene has a kind of nervous fever. I could not and cannot call the doctor because I have no money for medicine. For 810 days I have kept the family going on bread and potatoes, and it is even doubtful whether I can get these today. That diet of course was not conducive to health. . . . I've written no articles because I did not have the penny to go to read newspapers. . . . Then there are the baker, the milkman, the tea fellow, the greengrocer, and an old butcher's bill. How am I to cope with all this diabolical mess. . . . My house is a hospital, and the crisis is getting so disruptive that it compels me to give it my all highest attention. What's to be done?

3 June 1854:

> I am up to my ears in trouble. During my wife's illness, in the midst of a crisis, the good Dr Freund stays away and sends me a bill for 26f., desiring to arrive at a "clear understanding concerning his medical relationship" with me. As my wife's condition was dangerous—and still gives rise to concern—I was of course forced to capitulate and to promise him in writing that I would pay 8f. at the end of the month and the rest every 6 weeks . . . one cannot change doctors in the middle of an illness, as one does shirts . . . the pharmacy alone swallowed up a considerable budget . . . . At the end of this week, when my wife feels strong

enough, she will spend two weeks with the children in Edmonton. Perhaps the country air will restore her . . . I can assure you that these last few troubles have made me a very morose fellow. Happy the man who has no family.

3 March 1855:

Today just these few lines to explain to you the reason for my silence: (l) Musch has a dangerous gastric fever . . . (2) The baby (Eleanor) grew every day worse, disturbed the whole house . . . (3) My wife, although childbed passed splendidly, developed a so-called whitlow on the index finger of her right hand . . . very intensive and irritating. The thing was operated on yesterday . . . (4) The whole house was and largely still is a hospital.

16 March 1855:

I don't believe that dear Musch will overcome his illness. You will understand what effect this prospect is having here at home. My wife is quite low again . . .

27 March 1855:

For the past few days Musch has been visibly improving, and the doctor is voicing the best hopes. If everything goes well Musch must get out into the country at once. He is of course terribly weak and thin. . . . The main question is now merely whether his constitution is strong enough to get through the whole of the treatment . . .

30 March 1855:

I've been putting off sending you medical bulletins from one day to the next because the illness has had such ups and downs . . . hope seems to have been abandoned even by the physician. My wife for the past week has been more sick than ever before, from mental distress. As for me, my heart is bleeding and my head is burning although of course I must keep up a brave appearance. Not for a moment has the child during his illness denied his innate good tempered and yet independent character.

6 April 1855:

Poor Musch is no more. He passed over in his sleep in my arms between 5 and 6 o'clock today. . . . My wife sends you her warmest regards. . . . I must find a way of helping her over these first days.

12 April 1855:

Our home of course is totally deserted and orphaned since the death of our dear child who had been its life-giving soul. It is indescribable how we miss the child everywhere. I have been through all kinds of bad luck but it is only now that I realize what real misfortune is. I feel broken down. . . . I have had such a furious headache since the day of the funeral that I am incapable of thinking or hearing or seeing.

8 July 1857:

My wife has given birth. The child, however, was not viable and died at once.

15 July 1858:

> My wife is nervously debilitated . . . she is haunted by the daily pressures and the specter of an inevitable final catastrophe. This latter, however, cannot be long postponed, and even a remission for a few weeks will not put an end to this intolerable daily struggle about the mere necesssaries, and will leave the general situation such that everything must come to grief because of it.

30 November 1868:

> My wife—understandably so, in the circumstances, but not therefore more agreeable—has for many years lost her mental equilibrium, and with her lamentations and irritability and bad humor plagues the children virtually to death, although no children could take it all in a more cheerful way.

After repeated and painful illnesses during most of the 39 years of her marriage, Mrs. Marx died at the age of 67 in December 1881.
And two more blows came to Marx when Jenny, their firstborn and his wife's namesake, became ill early in January 1883, and died on 11 January at the age of 38, just before her own daughter, also named Jenny and Marx's only grandchild, died, when she was just four years old. Eleanor, Marx's third daughter, said she hardly knew how to tell him: "I felt that I was bringing my father his death warrant. On the long sad journey I had tortured my brain to discover how to break the news to him. I did not have to break it to him, my face betrayed me. He said at once: 'Our little Jenny is dead!'" Marx lost his will to live and died two months later.

CHILD LABOR

Child Labor in Nineteenth-Century Britain

The nineteenth century, with its rapid industrialization, had a brutal effect on children. The English social critic E. P. Thomson (1878–1917) called the exploitation of child labor in that century "one of the most shameful events in our history." To the Victorians, child labor was viewed as cheap and inexhaustible. Only gradually did it come to be seen as morally offensive.

Although children had always worked, they faced in the new factory system the tyranny of regimentation and inhuman demands of the new machinery. Poor families forced off the land, either by enclosure laws or grinding poverty, moved to industrial towns and introduced their children to factories at a very early age. It was said that "anyone big enough to stand up is big enough to work."

Local authorities in East Anglia, where there was much poverty in the 1820s and 1830s, had agreements with mill owners to send them families of widows and orphans. Local authorities thus saved money they would have had to spend on their poor, and factory owners obtained a compliant labor force. Children might be paid two or three shillings a week for over 72 hours of work.

Conditions were even worse in the mines, where children from four years of age spent upwards of 14 hours a day underground. And girls and young women were exploited throughout the century in London sweatshops and in domestic service.

Gradually, however, from the 1830s onwards various laws helped to control the worst excesses of the employment of children. These were instituted by the House of Commons in the face of fierce opposition from business interests. In 1832 Michael Sadler spoke about child labor conditions in which he described children working longer hours than slaves and being beaten to be kept awake. He said legislation was necessary because children could not negotiate with employers on equal terms.

Reforms proceeded slowly, in several stages. First, the working day was shortened, though not by much, and age limits were set for workers. In 1802, the hours of work per day were limited to 12, and in 1833 the *Factory Act* prohibited employment of children under nine. Regulations were passed to improve working conditions and inspectors were appointed to visit work places to see that the rules were followed. But there was generally a lapse of decades between the institution of reforms and their enforcement. The power of expanding industry was stronger than legal or government measures. Children were told by their supervisors to lie about their ages, and inspectors were frequently willing to overlook infractions of the law to cooperate with mill owners and local magistrates.

The introduction of compulsory full-time schooling after 1870 was what finally destroyed the widespread use of child labor in England. Trade unions and other working class organizations did not campaign against child labor itself, but they placed great importance on the struggle to achieve universal compulsory schooling, because education was seen as a means of escape from a life of drudgery and poverty.

Throughout the latter part of the century, pressure kept growing to protect children from the worst excesses of the industrial system, but there were other problems, too. Swarms of children lived on the streets of London and other cities, beyond the reach of any laws. Henry Mayhew, a nineteenth-century researcher of London life, said children were "flung onto the streets through viciousness, or as outcasts from utter destitution." Once on the streets, Charles Dickens observed, "they hop about like wild birds, pilfering the crumbs which fall from the table of the country's wealth." But these children showed great resourcefulness by running errands, passing out handbills, polishing shoes, sweeping the streets, entertaining, guarding horses, and prostituting themselves.

Perhaps the greatest tragedy of all was that so many children lost their childhood. One eight-year-old girl testified to this, when she remarked to Mayhew that because she was taking care of herself she was no longer a child.

Friedrich Engels on Child Labor

Friedrich Engels (1820–1895) was the son of a prosperous German manufacturer of textiles. One day, when he was six years old, his father, to familiarize him with his future inheritance, showed him through the factory. Instead of being impressed, as his father expected, the little boy was profoundly shocked by the miserable working conditions under which children hardly older than himself had to labor. Before his stern father he disguised his feelings, but on his return home, in great agitation, he asked his mother, "Must I too go to work soon in the factory?"

"No, my dear," she assured him. "Thank God you won't have to. You can be glad that the factory belongs to us."

"And how about the children? Are they glad?"

"No, Friedrich, not like you. But it's better for you not to trouble your little head about it. No one can change things, even you."

The boy slept little that night. In the morning he said to his mother. "Mother, suppose I want to change things — then what?"

He did want to, so much that when he grew up he became a socialist leader and political philosopher who collaborated with Karl Marx on *The Communist Manifesto*, published in 1848, a year in which revolutionary ferver erupted all over Europe. This was one of the most influential pamphlets ever written. It urged the workers of the world to unite and take over the means of production from the owners because "you have nothing to lose but your chains."

He moved to England and spent most of his adult life collaborating with Marx, translating and editing his works, and helping Marx financially. He also wrote several scholarly books about the history of slavery and oppression, including *The Origin of the Family*, which dealt with the oppression of women and children. He published another book, *The Condition of the Working Classes in England*, in its German edition in 1845; the English translation appeared in 1897.

Engels's influence on the labor movement in Europe, the United States, and Russia, and on three generations of the intelligentsia in those countries, cannot be overestimated.

Child Labor Today

The International Labor Organization (ILO), a specialized agency associated with the United Nations, is concerned with social and economic progress and human rights in the world of work. Through its programs it hopes to improve economic and social conditions, and thus eliminate the need for child labor. The following analysis of child labor is taken from ILO posters produced during the International Year of the Child (1979) and follow-up reports in the 1980s and 1990s.

Why Should We Be Concerned about Child Labor?

Earnest efforts are being made by governments and employers' and workers' organizations around the world to reduce or eradicate child labor, but in many places it still persists. It is not a thing of the past, nor is it confined to poor countries.

Because of their dependent position, children are the most easily exploited of all workers. They do many kinds of work and are particularly vulnerable to exploitation; they are casually hired, and just as casually fired. They are not even figured in official labor force statistics; when they grow up to reach that stage, the chances are that they will be counted among the unemployed.

They are the cheapest type of labor and do not organize themselves to demand better health and safety at work, or any other protections that trade unions have fought for over the years. Increasingly, children are doing the work of adults, while being paid as children. The number of children involved is apt to increase in times of economic recession and depression, when children become especially attractive to some employers. Like other weak groups within the labor force, such as migrants and women homeworkers, children are used by unscrupulous employers to reduce wage costs and avoid legal obligations.

Trade unions, therefore, have a strong interest in abolishing child labor. But even if this interest did not exist, child labor is opposed because of the negative effects it has on the personal development of children.

Destructive Consequences of Child Labor

It is increasingly recognized that the effects of child labor on the welfare of children and the development of their personalities are essentially negative from many points of view, the most important of which are

- Lack of harmonious family life, particularly when children work outside the home, which prevents them from receiving adequate care and attention from their parents.

- Insufficient free time for play or for sporting or cultural activities appropriate to their age.

- Exposure to social hazards or even delinquency (drugs or prostitution), particularly when work is done outside the home or in the street.

- Health risks: the endurance and muscular strength of growing children are less than those of adults, and they tire more quickly. Children are, therefore, particularly susceptible to occupational diseases (for example, tuberculosis from exposure to dust in the textile industry) and accidents at work. Moreover, long-term health problems may occur: malnourished children use up scarce energy and become susceptible to infectious diseases; young girls working in electronics factories for 12–14 hours a day joining fine wires suffer damage to their eyesight; children may be exposed to dangerous machinery or to chemicals used in agriculture, or may be forced to undertake such hazardous tasks as creeping under moving parts of machinery; heart failure can arise in the medium or long term owing to overstrain in the early years of life. The list of health and safety dangers appears endless.

- The impossibility in most cases of benefiting from educational and training facilities that can provide the basic general and vocational knowledge necessary for normal mental and intellectual development and enable children to acquire skills and to lead a successful occupational and social life later on. Their futures are jeopardized by the fact that they cannot go to school because they are working, or by the need for them to leave school early or make an uneasy compromise between school and work. Moreover, too frequently no training is given, even in the case of apprentices.

- Children are discriminated against financially. In most cases working children are either unpaid or receive negligible wages. In family undertakings, particularly in agriculture, children receive no wages. In many cases where they work outside the home, they are employed in exchange for bed and board and occasionally receive a little pocket money.

- The living conditions of most working children, particularly when they belong to the poorest sections of the population and live in the least developed regions, often verge on destitution. They are lodged in makeshift accommodations devoid of all

503

comforts, often sleeping in the corner of the shop or workplace, and they get insufficient food of poor quality.

How Many Children Are Involved in Child Labor?

Economists' estimates of the number of children under 15 years of age who are employed worldwide as laborers range from 52 million to nearly 100 million children, 96 percent of them in poor countries. At least 38 million children between the ages of seven and 15 work in Asia; 10 million in Africa; 3 million in Latin America; 1 million in developed countries.

Why Do Children Work?

Not all children work out of necessity, although the great majority do. These work for their own and their families' survival: survival is the motivation and poverty is the cause. Income from child workers, small as it may be, contributes to the primary needs of the family. For many children, too, the absence of educational opportunity or lack of access to it makes work the only alternative to idleness.

Laws in the countries of the northern hemisphere have progressively required more schooling for children. At the same time, children have been excluded from more and more types of adult work, which has extended the period known as childhood, but these changes have also meant that children in northern countries have become an economic burden to their parents, rather than an economic asset.

In the southern hemisphere, many poor children are much more a part of the adult world. Their experience of childhood can be brief. In poorer countries the children help their families with household and farming tasks and with small industries. Although children employed outside the family are often paid very low wages for work that can be hard and dangerous, the child's labor helps poor families to survive—and may be vital, so in that sense having children is seen by parents as a sound investment. Children may also be the only support that poor parents can depend on in their old age.

Child labor is a highly complex problem because of the variety of factors that give rise to it: massive poverty; changes in industrial production; mass migration to urban centers; types of family structure; cultural values concerning the roles of women and children; government social policies. Given this complexity, it is impossible to legislate child labor out of existence overnight. To eliminate child labor without social and economic changes would leave poor families worse off than ever. Therefore policies aimed at promoting adult employment, raising incomes, and improving living standards must be the basis for long-term action to abolish child labor. The adoption and implementation of regulations can be successful only as part of effective policies on national development and the elimination of poverty.

Is Working Always Bad for Children?

Most people would agree with the ILO when it states not all work is necessarily harmful for children. Some activities under regulated conditions may have positive effects for the child and society. In practice we tend to talk of *child work* where it is a positive experience and *child labor* when it is harmful. Although we may agree that no child should be forced to work, we may also question a society that prevents children from working.

But if children are to work, how is this best organized, and in particular how can education and work experience be combined? These are still unresolved issues worldwide.

The ILO's Concern for the Special Needs of Children

The ILO's constitution names the protection of children as a basic prerequisite for the improvement of overall conditions of work for all workers, and it is committed to promoting child welfare among all nations.

The child is not a "small adult" but a fragile personality to be nurtured into the mature citizen and worker of tomorrow. The child needs the protection of a statutory minimum age for admission to employment, and needs schooling, training, and guidance—gateways to personal fulfillment in adult life. The young worker needs a fair wage, strict limitation of working hours, improved working and living conditions and environment; and he or she needs to be shielded from exposure to arduous, unhealthy, and dangerous work and needs a fair and effective apprenticeship system. The child also needs revision of medical safeguards and of vocational guidance and training, as well as the outlawing of night work.

A Modern Form of Slavery: The Childhood of Lin-Lin

This material is based on a Human Rights Watch report, "A Modern Form of Slavery: Trafficking of Burmese Women and Girls into Brothels in Thailand."

Lin Lin was 13 years old in 1980 when she was recruited by an agent for work in Thailand. Her father took $480 from the agent with the understanding that his daughter would pay the loan back out of her earnings.

The agent took Lin Lin to Bangkok, and three days later she was taken to Ran Dee Prom brothel. Lin Lin did not know what was going on until a man came into her room and forced her to have sex.

For the next two years Lin Lin worked in various parts of Thailand in four different brothels, all but one owned by the same family. The owners told her she would have to keep prostituting herself until she paid off her father's debt. Her clients, who often included police, paid the owner $4 each time.

On January 18, 1993, the Crime Suppression Division of the Thai police raided the brothel in which Lin Lin worked. She was 15 years old, had spent over two years of her young life in compulsory prostitution, and tested positive for HIV.

Unfortunately, Lin Lin's case is not an isolated one. The South Asian Coalition on Child Servitude (SACCS) estimates that today over 200 million young children in the world are victims of servitude.

> Child servitude is the ugliest blot on the face of mankind. It is a challenge to those who value liberty, childhood, and humanity. . . . You and I can wait for tomorrow, or a decade, but not the children whose childhoods are robbed. **CHILDHOOD IS JUST TODAY AND TODAY ALONE. They must be saved TODAY AND NOW!**
>
> —*Kailash Satyarthi, founder of the* South Asian Coalition on Child Servitude

Here is how one young victim described his almost unbelievable experience in SACCS's newsletter:

A man appeared in my village one day and asked "Come with me. I teach you how to read and write and to weave. I'll give you 300 rupees (US $19) a month. I'll bring you back to your home once a fortnight or whenever you like." He gave my father 300 rupees and took me away but afterwards he never gave my father anything and when I got there he said to me "Now we'll never let you leave. We keep children here until they rot." We were very badly fed. What they fed us was only half cooked. We had diarrhea. They did not give us any medicine. They would beat us if we wanted to go to the toilet. They would say "Weave your rugs" and at the same time beat us until we bled. They kicked us and for sleeping we were given ripped rags and at night we were locked in. I didn't know what was happening to me and why I was held prisoner. I cried. I was desperate.

India alone accounts for 55 million of the victims. SACCS seeks out slavery camps, raids them, frees the children, and works to alleviate the misery, physical afflictions, illiteracy, and other problems of scores of bonded children, kindling their hope and increasing their strength at a rehabilitation-cum-vocational training-cum-social education center named Mukti Ashram near New Delhi, and in 14 schools in various child-labor-prone areas.

SACCS is run by Kailash Satyarthi, a man who has been honored with several prestigious awards from international human rights groups. By direct action and through courts of law, he has helped to rescue more than 28,000 bonded children in the past 15 years. Although that is a small percentage of all the country's bonded children, he says he sees a silver lining in the dark clouds because the government used to deny the existence of child servitude, but now, aware of the overwhelming and undeniable evidence, it cooperates with SACCS. Satyarthi is also encouraged by a nonprofit organization called Friends at Home, Inc. (P.O. Box 66, Springfield, VA USA 22150), which has been organized as a fund-raising wing for SAACS.

THE IMPORTANCE OF HELPING POOR CHILDREN—QUOTES

The suffering of children is not in itself what is revolting, but the fact that it is undeserved. . . . If we cannot make a world in which children no longer suffer at least we can try to reduce the number of suffering children.
—*Albert Camus (1913–1960) in* L'Homme Revolte

Poverty is a threat to peace—particularly poverty of opportunity. We simply won't have the kind of world we want until every child born into it has the opportunity to realize in full his capacities for material, intellectual and spiritual growth.
—*Paul Hoffman (1891–1974), former Director of the World Bank*

Children are the world's most valuable resource and its best hope for the future. It is a real tragedy that in an era of vast technological progress and scientific achievement millions of children should still suffer from lack of medical care,

proper nutrition, adequate education, and be subjected to the handicaps and uncertainties of a low income, substandard environment.
—*John Fitzgerald Kennedy (1917–1963) U.S. President*

In an era where the words "reaching for the moon" no longer mean striving for the impossible, but simply describe a practical possibility, there is no longer any excuse for the world to permit its children to go hungry in mind or body, to be deprived of the essentials of life—food, medical care and educational opportunities.
—*Henry Labouisse (1904–1987) former executive director of UNICEF*

It is customary, but I think it is a mistake, to speak of happy childhood. Children are often over-anxious and acutely sensitive. Man ought to be man and master of his fate, but children are at the mercy of those around them.
—*John Lubbock, Lord Avebury (1834–1913), in* The Pleasure of Life

"We can discuss many things, but not this great shame that is a naked and hungry child. The child did not ask to be born, and begs without any other plea than his puny body which reveals undernourishment, an unhealthy environment, and poverty. We are guilty of many errors and as many sins, but our worst crime is the abandonment of children.
—*Gabriella Mistral (1889–1957), Nobel Prize-winning poet from Chile*

Banish the tears of children! Continual rains upon the blossoms are hurtful.
—*Jean Paul (1763–1825), German philosopher*

We are not yet able to remove poverty from everywhere, but at least we can say, all right, we will take care of the children to begin with. We will start with the children, and then we will be able to move forward.
—*Chiadambaram Subramanian, Minister of Planning in India in 1969*

A child is, by nature, a dependent being who relies on adults to care for him. Because he did not come into the world of his own free choice, because he is unable to provide for his own needs, and because he embodies mankind's past and present achievements and its future aspirations, the child is our most sacred responsibility. The child is the most poignant victim of men's failures in achieving social justice, economic stability and peace. The deprivation, discrimination and humiliation which society so often inflicts upon helpless, innocent children is intolerable and must be remedied if the world is ever to have peace and prosperity.
—*U Thant Secretary-General of the United Nations from 1961 to 1972*

It is the poorest who bear the brunt of any insufficiency in available resources for development or for children. The poorest survive by drawing on their own, often unsuspected, resources or ingenuity, perseverance, courage and the will to live. It is incumbent on UNICEF as the humanitarian conscience of the international community to place the children of the very poor at the top of its concerns.

—Father Joseph Wresinski (1917–1988),
Secretary-General of the Fourth World Movement

Rivers do not drink their own water. Trees do not eat their own fruit. Clouds do not swallow their own rain. What great ones have is always for the benefit of others.

Who does kindly deeds becomes rich. *—Hindu Proverbs*

Kindness is the beginning and the end of the law.

It is no disgrace to be poor—which is the only good thing you can say about it.
—Jewish Proverbs

God is merciful to those who are kind. *—Moroccan Proverb*

Do not refuse a kindness to anyone who begs it, if it is in your power to perform it.
—Old Testament Proverbs 3:27

Caption of a cartoon over the Xerox machine in the office of the New York Mission Society:

"Sometimes I get very mad at God, and want to ask Him why He doesn't do more to help the poor. But of course I don't."

"Why not?" asks a friend.

"Because I'm afraid He might ask me the same question."

"A Modest Proposal" to End Poverty

In 1729 an Irish cleric, Jonathan Swift (1667–1745) who had become famous three years earlier as the author of *Gulliver's Travels*, received even more fame and became a popular hero in Ireland as a result of a satirical essay he wrote to express his indignation at British callousness during a severe famine in Ireland. In this essay, called "A Modest Proposal," he suggested a "fair, cheap, and easy method" of ending the miserable plight of the poor.

"I have been assured by a very knowing American," he wrote, "that a young, healthy child well nursed is at a year old a most delicious, nourishing, and wholesome food." He suggested that poverty-stricken Irish mothers should be given 10 shillings per child to provide English gourmets with culinary delights, and to spare Dubliners the sad sight of "beggars of the female sex followed by three, four or six children, all in rags and importuning every passerby for alms." Understandably, this essay created a furor, and the proposal was never adopted, but to this day it has remained a classical example of wit wedded to social conscience.

CHILDREN'S REACTIONS TO POVERTY AND RACISM

Ethel Waters, a Child Who Triumphed Over Racism and Poverty

Few children have started out in worse circumstances than Ethel Waters (1900–1977). She was born as the result of her mother being raped at the age of 12, and her mother never fully recovered from the experience. Her family consisted of her, her frail mother, two alcoholic aunts, and her grandmother who supported them as best she could by working as a maid. They lived in what Ethel called a "vermin-infested rickety shanty in the bloody red-light district of Philadelphia." This background threatened the child's very survival and certainly gave no indication that she would ever rise in the world to become a great and famous artist. All she had going for her at first was that she enjoyed singing and dancing.

She seemed destined for a life of crime. In her autobiography called *His Eye Is on the Sparrow* she says, "I just ran wild as a little girl. I was bad, always a leader of the street gang in stealing and general hell-raising. By the time I was seven I knew all about sex and life in the raw. I could out-curse any stevedore and took a sadistic pleasure in shocking people." She became the ringleader of a gang of poor neighborhood kids who stole food to eat and to sell, and she ran errands and served as a lookout for those she called the area's "sporting people," bursting into innocent children's songs to warn prostitutes and petty criminals about the presence of vice squads in the area. And in elementary school she distressed her teachers with her "roughness and profanity."

How She Began to Change

But her life began to change when her grandmother sent her, over her mother's objections, to a Catholic school for two years, where she said she blossomed "under the patience and kindness of the nuns," felt protected and encouraged for the first time in her life, and began to develop a sense of right and wrong.

She got her first paying job, at $5 a week, in her early teens when her mother got sick and Ethel took over her job as a hotel chambermaid. She loved it. She later told an interviewer, "I had about a half-hour to clean up each room but I'd hurry and get them done in about 10 minutes, and that left me 20 minutes to act. I'd get in front of the mirror and the show would begin. I'd get so carried away with whatever part I was making up for myself that I'd act all over the room and I'd even whistle and applaud for myself when I got through, and then I'd come back and take a bow."

In spite of this early indication that she enjoyed performing, it did not occur to her at this point that she might actually make a career of it. As singer Susannah McCorkle pointed out in an informative and insightful article in 1994 in *American Heritage* magazine, Ethel was so battle-scarred from her childhood on the streets that at this time her highest aspiration was to get a job as a lady's maid for a wealthy woman who would travel around the world, and she had so little self-confidence that at every stage in her future career she had to be pushed ahead.

She was first discovered by two black vaudevillians who offered her $10 a week to join their tour, on which she became the first woman ever to sing "St. Louis Blues." For security she held onto her chambermaid job by sending in substitutes whenever she went on a tour. Conditions on the black vaudeville circuit were very uncomfortable, but no worse than they were at home.

After a few jobs in all-black stage shows she began singing on *race records.* In those days racial segregation was so complete that black singers could not normally appear on records issued by companies that produced recordings of white singers. But a Harlem showman, Earl Dancer, heard her and considered her so exceptional that he urged her to appear in *white time.* She was sure she would be a flop, but he got her a booking in Chicago and to her enormous surprise she was a hit, suddenly hailed by white critics as "the greatest artist of her race and generation." Bobby Short, who later became a leading cabaret artist, saw and met her at the RKO Palace Theater when he was a child performer in Chicago, and says, "She was the greatest black performer I have ever seen. . . . I was awestruck."

After that Ethel began working regularly in nightclubs where, for the first time in her life, she made friends with white people, mostly artists who lived in Greenwich Village in New York, and theatrical celebrities including Eugene O'Neill, Cole Porter, and Noel Coward. "These bohemians were like my own people, and I liked them. Your color or your bank account made no difference to them."

Then she was booked into the Cotton Club, "the class spot in Harlem that drew the white trade," and her dramatic interpretation of the song "Stormy Weather" became the talk of the show business world and led to another turning point in her career. Irving Berlin came to hear her and the next day offered her a featured role in his new Broadway revue, *As Thousands Cheer,* written in collaboration with the playwright Moss Hart. "Supper Time," one of the songs Berlin wrote for her, was the quiet lament of the wife of a lynching victim as she wondered how to break the news to her children. The show's top stars wanted it dropped as too depressing, but with that song and three others that Berlin wrote for her, Ethel stole the show, which was a smash hit. A few months later she became the highest-paid female performer on Broadway, and when the show went on the road she became the first black ever to be given equal billing with white stars south of the Mason and Dixon line.

By now she was no longer poor, and she owned a 10-room penthouse apartment in New York. She was becoming increasingly religious, and turned one room into a chapel. Ever since she had money to spare she had been contributing to various Catholic charities. She also befriended several illegitimate children and adopted a goddaughter whom she took on a long trip to Europe, but as soon as she returned to the United States and took up her career again, the girl was struck with infantile paralysis. After she recovered her natural mother reclaimed her.

As Ethel Waters grew older, she lost her good looks and was no longer a pretty ingenue, so she went on to a new stage in her career. She began starring in dramatic roles in serious dramas. And here again she was a great success, getting rave reviews.

However, in 1957 she was at a low point in her life. She was tired and out of work and in serious debt, and she had become more than 200 pounds overweight. Only religion made her feel that life was still worth living. She met Billy Graham and joined his Crusade, singing in his chorus.

How had she gone into debt after making so much money? She told the press, "Where I come from, people don't get close enough to money to keep a working acquaintance with it, so I don't know how to keep it."

She was still much admired by most people, but not by everyone. She was angry when other blacks criticized her for portraying maids in plays and on TV. Her grandmother had been a maid all her life, and she and her mother had also been maids; she said this was a reality of black life and that she saw nothing disgraceful in it.

By the time she became matronly her "mammy" roles angered the black power movement and these became all she was remembered for. Forgotten was the fact that she had been the first black artist to break through racial barriers in music, theaters, nightclubs, radio, films, and television, opening doors for everyone who came after her.

She died at age 77, 20 years after telling a reporter for the *Los Angeles Mirror*, "I'm not afraid to die, honey. In fact, I'm kinda looking forward to it. I know that the Lord has his arms wrapped around this big fat sparrow."

How and Why Different Children React to Problems Differently

Children who live in poverty and/or encounter racism are apt to become bitter and give up hope. But not all do. General Colin Powell said his response to racism was to decide that if he was placed in a segregated part of society he would at least make sure that he was successful in that part. Which he certainly was. And he is by no means the only example of someone triumphing over prejudice.

In 1960 a six-year-old girl named Ruby Bridges faced a frightening challenge with so much courage that she unwittingly inspired a witness, the psychiatrist Dr. Robert Coles, so much that, he says, she changed his life.

One morning when Dr. Coles was in New Orleans he saw an angry crowd of cursing, screaming people near a school. Wondering what was causing the fury, he hung around, and a few minutes later he saw a little girl walking between two U.S. marshals. When they started going up the steps to the school entrance, the crowd went berserk. They were white men and women, and little Ruby was black. The U.S. government had just declared an end to segregated schooling for black children, so Ruby was being escorted by federal marshals as she arrived at this school, which had never before had a Negro pupil.

Almost every day after that, Coles returned there in the morning, watching the small, poised, neatly dressed girl arrive at the school, seemingly ignoring the noisy crowds that hissed, yelled, spat at, and threatened her.

Then her teacher told Dr. Coles that one morning Ruby had suddenly paused before entering the building, turning towards the mob and speaking softly. Coles contacted her later to ask what she had said to them, and she replied, "I wasn't talking to them. I was talking to God. I was praying for them."

Stunned, he asked how she could pray for these people who wanted to hurt her.

"Don't you think they need praying for?" she asked. "I prayed, 'Dear God, help these people because they don't know what they're doing.'"

He was impressed not only because she had shown such calm and moral courage each morning under the extreme stress of the vicious hatred shown her but because she was not in the least ostentatious about it, or bragging. She was just quietly witnessing on behalf of her people, neighborhood, city, and American law.

"If this were a better America," he says, "Ruby Bridges would be as well known as our famous politicians."

After she grew up, Ruby became a teacher and established a foundation to help poor children.

Curious to learn the source of her moral strength, Dr. Coles made a point of getting to know her well, and found that it came from her strong, loving family and their community's church.

After meeting Ruby, Coles decided to get to know, study, and help many other children, both those who like her were strong and lived with supportive families and others who were not that lucky. Ever since then he has traveled, meeting, talking with, and listening to children, those who live in poverty, those in ghettos where brothers and other family members have been murdered, children of migrants and sharecroppers, Chicanos, Eskimos, Indians, Mexicans, and also children in affluent and wealthy families who have problems with divorced or abusive parents.

Finding that many children have great difficulty identifying or verbalizing their problems, he, like many other child psychologists, has encouraged them to express their feelings in art. Their pictures reveal a lot about their view of the world—their fears, angers, and wishes—by the ways in which they portray themselves, their families, and homes.

One teenage boy in Massachusetts had become full of hatred, including self-hatred, at a very early age. He told Dr. Coles, "My real father left home before I was born. It was because he knew I'd be a bad kid, I think."

The boy's mother was a heavy drinker who did not know how to cope with him, and his stepfather distanced himself, spending hardly any time with him. When he was three or four years old the boy was fragile, but he felt almost superhuman when he gave vent to his anger. He choked and kicked his mother, hit a teacher, fought with schoolmates, broke his TV set, messed up his room, punched a hole through the window, and finally got charged with hitting a police officer and was sent to a home for juvenile offenders. That was where Dr. Coles met him, listening and talking and having him draw pictures of himself and his home.

The boy's drawings showed a mother with huge hands; she sometimes clubbed him with them, telling Dr. Coles that "sometimes we had to hurt him, just to calm his down." The pictures were drawn entirely in black, with no color except for his own contorted face, which was bright red representing rage, and his figure was separated from the others, enclosed inside thick, black prisonlike walls.

Dr. Coles says the only way to solve a problem is to identify it, admit it, and then tackle it honestly, and the boy began to realize this. He told Dr. Coles he now understood that he must learn to conquer his inclination to violence, because he knew that when he returned home "nothing is going to change—except me."

Dr. Coles also says "the moral creativity and energy of children is a strong force." And sometimes it is strong enough to turn a "bad" (e.g., extremely troubled) child into a moral one. However, he thinks loving parents are by far the most important factor in producing a happy and moral child.

In suggesting guidelines to parents on how to help a child grow up to be a good person, he says it is as important to say No to them as to say Yes, in order to teach them the difference between right and wrong, and that if one fails to do this their children are in extreme jeopardy. Children who are given everything they want, he tells parents, have nothing to aspire to.

He also says teachers share responsibility with parents. Although schools are often afraid to discuss morals, they must do so because there is no such thing as value-free education. "All of us," he claims, "are part of the story, and share complicity when children don't learn the difference between right and wrong."

THE GROWTH OF POVERTY IN THE UNITED STATES

In October 1994 the U.S. Census Bureau released a report revealing that the typical American household saw its income decline by 7 percent during 1993, and that more than a million Americans fell into poverty during the year. (A family of four is considered poor if its income is lower than the national median). Average per capita income was up by 1.8 percent, but most of the benefits flowed to the wealthiest Americans. The census report showed record levels of inequality, with the top fifth of American households earning 48.2 percent of the nation's income while the bottom fifth earned just 3.6 percent.

"America is in danger of splitting into a two-tiered society," according to Secretary of Labor Robert B. Reich. The trend toward inequality had been apparent for most of the previous two decades, and according to Mr. Reich, "America now has the most unequal distribution of income of any industrialized nation in the world. We cannot have a prosperous or stable society if these trends continue."

At one time poverty was most prevalent in rural areas, but a decline in the farm population reduced the numbers of rural poor. In 1959, 56 percent of the poor in the United States lived in rural areas, but 20 years later only 38 percent did, while most of the poor lived in metropolitan areas. This trend has continued to accelerate. Children living in a city, especially the very young ones, were more likely to be poor than those who lived in a suburb, especially if they were black instead of white. Years of racial segregation and white flight to the suburbs produced large urban ghettos inhabited only by poor blacks.

Black families are disproportionally poor, although in absolute numbers there are more white poor people than black. But in cities, according to surveys, 34.3 percent of black residents are poor, almost three times as high a proportion as the 12.7 percent of white city residents. Especially disturbing is the fact that almost half of all black children in cities come from poor families, and rates for various inner city subpopulations are higher still.

The gender of the head of a household is another important factor in America's increased poverty. Families headed by females are particularly vulnerable. Department of Labor studies show that the connection between unemployment status and poverty depends on the composition of the family. For workers in families headed by a married couple, low earnings by one adult do not necessarily lead to poverty, but the poverty rate has reached 51 percent for families headed by women who could only find part-time employment. By 1980, 6.2 percent of all U.S. families headed by a married couple were poor, compared to 11 percent of male-headed families with no wife, while 32.7 percent of female-headed families with no husband were poor.

Since the 1960s the perception of the poor has been that they are mired in a *culture of poverty*. This theory attracted and eased the conscience of people who saw that poor blacks and Appalachian whites did, indeed, seem different from the rest of the population. The label *culture of poverty* gained great usage as a way of blaming what used to be called *the undeserving poor* for their condition. As the Protestant theologian Reinhold Niebuhr (1892–1971) once said, "It has always been the habit of privileged groups to deny oppressed classes every opportunity for the cultivation of innate capacities and then to accuse them of lacking what they have been denied the right to acquire."

Certainly poverty does shape the quality of life of its victims. The poor and near poor are less apt to receive the same quality of medical care and nutrition that others do. Education in poor neighborhoods is usually inadequate, and has been for many years, and many families have to live in overcrowded and rat-infested, untended buildings, in neighborhoods where gangs and drug pushers and addicts make life very dangerous.

Some 60,000 children are never going to be told to clean their room, take out the garbage, bring in the mail, mow the lawn, help with the dishes, weed the garden, or stop tying up the phone. Why? Because according to the National Alliance to End Homelessness, that is the number of American children who are now growing up homeless. If you think of the homeless as an unattractive mass of lazy, dirty, middle-aged, and elderly derelicts, you are mistaken. The National Alliance says that in New York City *the average age of a homeless person is nine years old!*

Since the environment plays such an influential part in forming one's character, many children become so used to poverty that they are psychologically unready to take full advantage of changing conditions or improved opportunities that may develop in their lifetime.

Living on welfare, even though it does not provide affluence, provides a sense of security and entitlement, and often becomes a "normal" way of life to such an extent that some take it for granted as their permanent fate, as one schoolteacher in a New York City public school learned to her dismay when she gave a fourth-grade boy an A for a paper he had written and he begged her to change the mark. She asked, "Why? It was a very good paper and you deserved an A." He said, "But I don't want you to give it to me because then people might think I'm smart and start expecting things of me." "Don't you want them to?" she asked. "Don't you want to go on to college and be able to improve your life?" "No," he replied, "what for? I already have everything I need—my family's on welfare." She was horrified and almost decided there was no point in trying to teach poor kids, if even bright ones lacked all ambition.

A child who feels hopeless may seem resigned to his fate but almost always, simmering below the blasé noncaring attitude, there is anger and resentment, which is fueled by people who convince him that he is a victim of a cruel society. Jealousy and resentment of other people's success and wealth may produce a combustible mixture of apathy and anger that embitters a child permanently.

The Biography of Robert "Yummy" Sandifer (1983–1994)

His mother called him "an average 11-year-old." But neither he nor his family were "average."

This was a cute-looking black boy who lived in Chicago where he had committed murder in September 1994 and three days later was murdered in turn, when he was only 11 years old. The nation was horrified, first by the crimes he committed, and then, as information about his short life was published, by the crimes that had been committed against him. As Patrick Murphy, public guardian in Cook County, Illinois, said: "If ever there was a case where a kid's future was predictable, it was this case. What you've got here is a kid who was turned into a sociopath by the time he was three years old."

When he was even less than three, a child abuse worker at a hospital, where he was being examined because of suspicious bruises, said something he didn't like, and he yelled "F—you, you bitch! I'm gonna cut you!" and grabbed a toy knife, putting its blade against her arm.

Yummy was a young career criminal, yet many people could not help liking him. He received his nickname because he was so fond of cookies and Snickers bars. He stole them so often from a local grocer that he was barred from the store; the grocer called him a "crooked son of a bitch, always in trouble. He stood out there on the corner and strong-armed other kids. No one is sorry to see him gone." But Lulu Washington, who sold discount candy out of her home just across the street from his grandmother's house, told a *Time* magazine reporter, "He just wanted love. He'd say thank you, excuse me, pardon me." And 12-year-old Kenyata Jones agreed, telling interviewers, "Everyone thinks he was a bad person, but he respected my mom, who's got cancer. He used to come to our house several times a month for sleep-overs. We'd bake cookies and brownies and rent movies like the old Little Rascals in black and white. He was my friend. I just cried and cried at school when I heard about what happened. And I'm gonna cry some more today! and I'm gonna cry some more tomorrow too."

Yummy loved not only cookies. He loved animals (he had a pet frog), basketball, bicycles, and big automobiles. He often hung out at the local garage, learning about them. Micaiah Peterson, a 17-year-old who knew him, said, "He could drive real well. It was like a midget driving a luxury car." In fact, he loved cars so much that he took to stealing them. Carl McClinton, another neighbor, told reporters, "When he wasn't stealing cars he was throwing things at them or setting them on fire. What could you do? Tell his grandmother? She'd yell at him, and he'd be right back on the street. If the police picked him up, they'd just bring him back home because he was too young to lock up. He was untouchable, and he knew that."

His Family

His mother, Lorena Sandifer, was the third of 10 children from four fathers, and she never knew her own father. When she was 15 she had her first son, Lorenzo, then Victor, then Robert, and eventually three more children. She dropped out of tenth grade, went on welfare and found an apartment, and became a crack addict. Yummy's father, Robert Akins, was convicted on drug and weapons charges. They soon split up, and he was later given a long prison sentence.

In 1984 Lorena was for the first time charged with child neglect when she failed to follow doctor's orders for treating her two-year-old Victor's eye condition; he eventually went blind. In 1985, 22-month-old Yummy was brought to Jackson Park Hospital covered with scratches and bruises. And a few months later his sister, with second- and third-degree burns on her genitals, was brought there; Lorena claimed that the toddler had fallen on the radiator, but a nurse in the hospital testified that the injuries did not match the story and it looked as if someone had held the child against the heater.

Another year went by, and the next time Yummy was admitted to the hospital he had long welts on his left leg. Police suspected that he had been beaten with an electric cord; there were also cigarette burns on his shoulders and buttocks. A psychiatrist reported to the juvenile court, "There is no reason to believe that Lorena Sandifer will ever be able to adequately meet her own needs, let alone to meet the needs of her growing family." So in 1986 the court took the children away from her, after neighbors told police that the children were routinely being left at home alone. By 1994 Lorena, then 29 years old, had been arrested 41 times, mostly for prostitution.

Yummy and his brothers and sister were placed with their grandmother, Janie Fields, in spite of the fact that her psychiatric report was just as unfavorable as that of her daughter, describing her as "a very controlling, domineering, castrating woman with a rather severe borderline personality disorder." Her own 10 children and 30 grandchildren lived with her at one time or another, and her neighbors once unsuccessfully launched a petition to drive her out of the area, saying "all those kids are little troublemakers, they are dirty and noisy, and they are ruining the neighborhood."

When he was 10, Yummy was moved to a juvenile center after a Cook County probation officer testified that young women were working as prostitutes from the grandmother's home.

Yummy's Strange Life as a Career Criminal

Chicago authorities had known about Yummy for years. As a student he was such a frequent truant that he missed more days of school than he attended. His first arrest was for shoplifting, when he was eight. Later arrests were for damage to property, robbery, and armed robbery. Yet many people had a hard time believing he was so vicious. Ann O'Callaghan, an attorney assigned to him in December 1993, said, "He was adorable. I thought no way this little pumpkin could be in a gang."

The police arrested him again and again, but the most they could do under Illinois law was detain him for 30 days and then put him on probation. Thirteen local juvenile homes refused to take him because he was too young. But in November 1993, he was given a psychiatric evaluation. The examiner asked him to complete the sentence "I am very . . ." and his reply was "sick." The examiner's report was that he was "a child full of self-hate, lonely, illiterate, wary; Robert is emotionally flooded. His response to the flooding is to back away from demanding situations and act out impulsively and unpredictably. He has a sense of failure that has infiltrated every aspect of his inner self. His lack of education has left him so stunted that he couldn't complete written questionnaires. Asked to add 3 and 4 he answered 'Zero.'" Yet, incredibly, when asked what his ambition was, he said he wanted to be a policeman.

At last Yummy was placed with the Lawrence Hall Youth Services, which runs homes for troubled teenagers, though he was still two years short of becoming one. He didn't stay long, however. He ran away after five months and went back to his grandmother. Within days he was arrested again, this time for burglarizing a school. And again he spent two weeks in a detention facility.

In the last year and a half of his life Yummy was arrested for 23 felonies and five misdemeanors, an average of a felony a month. He had made a fateful decision when he was nine, joining the local branch of the Black Disciples, a gang that has several thousand members in Chicago. The gang is led by "ministers" in their 30s and 40s who recruit children, using the little ones as arsonists, car thieves, drug runners, extortionists, and hit men because they are too young to be seriously punished if they are caught. Yummy proudly wore the gang's insignia as one of three tattoos.

In July 1994 Yummy and his cousin Darryl went on a church trip to an amusement park, but Yummy was not amused: he was humiliated and frustrated because he was so small that he was not allowed on most of the rides. On another day, Ida Falls, a neighbor, took Yummy and 12 other kids to the local police station to see a film on crime. But the cops asked her not to bring him back again because he got into fights with the other children.

The Final Days

In August 1994, Yummy committed another burglary, and in September he was ordered by his gang, in what police believe was a test of loyalty, to fire on a rival gang member . . . but instead he sprayed bullets with a semi-automatic weapon into a crowd of kids playing football. He shot two boys in the hand and a stray bullet hit a 14-year-old girl, Shavon Dean, in the head. (She lived around the corner from Yummy's grandmother and he had known her for years; her mother said she used to carry him as a young boy to church, where he and Shavon sang in the choir together.) Shavon died within minutes.

Yummy spent the next three days on the run. Gang members shuttled him between safe houses and abandoned buildings as police and reporters hunted for him. Gang leaders felt the heat, and so did he. He got so frightened that he went to a neighbor's porch asking the people inside to say a prayer for him and to telephone his grandmother so he could turn himself in. They went inside to phone, and when they returned he had disappeared. Derrick Hardaway, 14 years old, and his 16-year-old brother Cragg, two fellow gang members (both honor students!) had found Yummy and promised to help him get out of town. Instead, they drove him to a railroad viaduct, a dark tunnel covered with gang graffiti. Three days later his body was found there, lying face down amid blood and mud and broken glass, with two bullet wounds in the back of his head. Police theorized that gang members wanted the boy silenced before officers could get to him.

The entire community where these children lived was in shock. Mothers brought their children to the funeral to see the scrawny corpse of Yummy in his coffin, next to his stuffed animals, at last harmless. The Reverend Willie James Campbell said to the children, "Cry if you will, but make up your mind that you will never let your life end like this."

Yummy's tragic life and death brought the problems of juvenile crime to the attention of the public in a dramatic way. It also raised questions difficult to answer: Although his criminal behavior could perhaps be explained by the fact that he was raised in a dysfunctional family, the two boys who murdered him were children who were honor students and who had good parents. Obviously the parents had not been able to counteract the harmful environment with its gangs and drugs and guns.

An editorial in the *New York Times* in 1994 said,

> Robert's story is as complicated as America's urban disaster. More certain punishment—and, yes, more police and more jail cells—might help to counter the atmosphere of impunity in which urban gangs operate. But just as clearly, city children need a community in which to grow up, some adult structure that will chasten them for doing wrong and show them how to do something right. Too many American children of all races lack functional families. Boys need career paths other than the drug business, girls need choices other than teenage motherhood that produces more neglected children.

Part of what makes this social chemistry volatile is the gun culture. People too young to comprehend death's finality have easy access to death's machines. These confer status and power. No formula for change will work without a plan to reduce the number of guns on America's streets and in children's hands.

Robert Sandifer's short life and pitiful death—along with the strangers who mourned beside his coffin—illustrate the awful state of America' s cities, where even loving parents cannot save children. If they cry out for anything, it is to abandon the demagoguery and partisanship that have characterized the crime debate so far, and to focus some real resources on the neglected cities where these children struggle every day to survive."

A l9-year-old neighbor of Yummy's on Chicago's South Side pointed out how many children lose out in the struggle for survival. He said, "If you make it to l9 around here, you are a senior citizen. If you live past that, you're doing real good."

YOUTH GANGS

Before the Twentieth Century

Severe poverty and its offshoots, juvenile criminals and gangs, are not new phenomena, although the enormous numbers of them (there are more than 100,000 young gang members today in the Los Angeles area alone) and their extreme violence (many children become killers by the time they are 12) are something new.

Extreme poverty was so great in the middle of the nineteenth century that no family below the middle class could afford to support children past the age of 12. Few could support them past the age of eight, and many not past infancy. So the children were abandoned. Girls went to work as early as the boys, but few means of support were open to them. If they were employed as pieceworkers in a factory or as shop girls, they were seldom paid more than a dollar and a half a week, not enough to pay for lodgings above the flophouse level. Many of the girls, particularly orphans, became prostitutes, and many of the boys stayed alive by becoming criminals.

In New York City there was what then seemed like a very large youthful underworld. Teenage street gangs recruited younger children. Among their trainees were the gangs called the Forty Little Thieves, the Little Dead Rabbits, and the Little Plug Uglies. Children as young as five or six were enrolled in schools led by the American equivalent of Charles Dickens's Fagin to learn how to pick pockets, snatch purses, and rob from carts, all tasks at which they could outdo their seniors. They all served well as lookouts and decoys. Those who worked on the waterfront (the Little Daybreak Boys) were important because of their ability to crawl through ships' portholes.

The Reverend Lewis Morris Pease was one of the first people to realize the extent of this youthful underworld, and in 1850 he opened a Five Points House of Industry in an effort to reform the youngsters. He had one notable success: he claimed to have converted Wild Maggie Carson, the leader of the Forty Little Thieves, and supervised her first bath at the age of nine. Later he taught her to sew buttons, and still later he managed to marry her off to the scion of a pious family.

But the crime wave continued. In the 1890s the major Fagin was a man called Crazy Butch, who had begun his own criminal career when he was very young. He first proved his skill as a teacher by training his dog, Rabbi, to snatch purses, and then he went on to coach kids. His pupils were called Squab Wheelmen. They were most notable for the following trick: one member would hit a pedestrian, preferably an old lady, with his bike and then dismount and start screaming at the victim, and as a curious throng gathered, the other members of the gang would infiltrate the crowd and pick their pockets while they were too distracted to notice.

The pleasures of adult gangsters—sex, gambling, drinking, extortion, racketeering, and fraud—were all emulated by these child gangsters. There were saloons for boys with glasses of whiskey for three cents, and with little girls in the back rooms. They wanted to experience everything quickly because their average life expectancy was only 15 or 20 years, when they succumbed to disease, malnutrition, exposure, stab wounds, or gunfire. However, the crimes the children committed seem like pranks when compared to those that occur today.

Youth Gangs Today

The growing number of juvenile criminals in today's society is scary enough, but when they organize into gangs they are even more frightening. And their crimes often go unpunished because witnesses and victims are afraid to accuse them, knowing they risk reprisals. Gang members band together to take care of each other, and if one member gets in trouble they promise to "take care of it," their euphemism for getting revenge. So when police try to get tough and put a gang member in jail, this does not end the gang's crimes; it may actually result in additional crimes.

To most people today gangs seem to be something akin to cancer, a killer disease against which people are helpless. Increasingly, in inner cities and even in some suburbs, people are afraid to go out at night, afraid to be alone, even afraid when they are "safely" at home because gang members can and do break into houses or apartments to steal, rape, or murder. Being in a gang makes it easier for criminals to commit crimes, because the members help each other, serve as lookouts, drive getaway cars, set up alibis, and bolster each other's courage.

Attempts to foil gangs have been made in many cities but without much effect. Curfews are sometimes established so that youngsters cannot be out on the streets after nine or 10 at night, but they can still terrorize people indoors, and especially in public housing in poor neighborhoods they frequently do. The number of police may be increased, but even cops can be scared of violent criminals, and shoot-outs often result, sometimes with disastrous results, injuring or even killing innocent bystanders. Heavier jail sentences and threats of the death penalty do not help much, if at all, because in addition to their code of courage, most gang members share two other traits: fatalism and despair. "I'm gonna die some day," they say, "so what the hell. Who cares?"

Surprisingly, a few people do care, and actually try to help gang members instead of wanting to incarcerate them.

Mothers against Gangs

Since most members of gangs are unemployed school dropouts who have never learned good work habits, this organization, with local branches in some cities, hosts "career nights" inviting children to meet artists, doctors, electronics technicians, firefighters, photographers, police officers, secretaries, and social workers, with the goal of encouraging the kids to learn about the various occupations and discuss their educational requirements and employment opportunities. These sessions may succeed in capturing the interest of some kids who might otherwise drop out of school and join a gang, but hardened gang members would, unfortunately, not even bother to attend such meetings.

Mothers against Gangs also tries to do more than this. The founder of their Chicago chapter, Frances Sandoval, gets many tearful phone calls from parents with kids who are too scared to leave a gang but even more scared of staying in and she tries to advise and help them. "Unfortunately," she says, "there is very little I can offer them. In most cases it's hopeless unless they can literally pack up and leave. And we're talking about moving to another state."

Dan Korem

This investigative journalist in Dallas, Texas, is a nationally known expert on gangs, cults, and issues and trends affecting young people. He has written several books, including *Suburban Gangs: The Affluent Rebels* (1994), and frequently speaks to university, corporate, and professional audiences in the U.S. and Europe. He was a volunteer with a community group in Dallas that worked with more than 500 youths from 1986 to 1992, and to the best of his knowledge not one of these youths ever joined a gang.

In 1993 Korem went to Budapest to do a survey on skinhead gangs. These vicious groups first sprang up in England in the 1970s, but by mid-1980 they had become an ugly and frightening force in such diverse countries as Austria, the former East Germany, Hungary, Poland, and the United States. In Hungary their activities had grown as family conditions deteriorated nationwide; Hungary has a chronically high divorce rate and the world's highest teenage suicide rate.

Getting close to these belligerent and secretive youths is hard and can be dangerous, but with the help of a teacher who had attended one of Korem's lectures, some skinheads from different gangs agreed to be surveyed as long as only their first names were used. Their frank responses to Korem's questions confirmed what he had learned from studying gangs in the U.S. All but two said their parents were either divorced or separated.

Hatred of gypsies and "foreigners" prompted two-thirds of those taking the survey to join skinhead gangs. The rest said they joined because they hated Jews and blacks and "idolized Hitler."

Here are excerpts from a report entitled "Why Kids Join Neo-Nazi Skinhead Gangs," which Korem prepared in 1994 for the Southern Poverty Law Center in Montgomery, Alabama, an organization that works courageously and tirelessly to prevent hate crimes and publishes "Teaching Tolerance," an excellent quarterly guide that it distributes free to more than 50,000 schoolteachers.

Korem wrote:

> In most cases, the desire to belong to a skinhead gang (or any other type of gang for that matter) is the result of trouble at home. Virtually every gang member I have interviewed came from a family with one or more of the following factors: divorce, separation, physical and/or sexual abuse, and dysfunctional parents. These conditions are further compounded by joblessness, poverty, lack of education, language barriers, academic deficiencies, and destructive elements from popular cultures, such as violent themes in music, television and films. . . .

For some youths, gangs are the distraction that diverts their attention from what is really bothering them. This is particularly true for youths who have a lot of idle time. Time spent with their gang fills the void so they don't have to think about their pain. . . . In some neighborhoods and some schools, if you aren't a member of a gang you are exposed to the whim of the streets, seemingly without protection. . . .

The most expedient way to disengage the majority of youths from a gang is to first discover the reason or reasons for the youth's involvement, the payoff he or she seeks from gang membership, and the specifics of that youth's environment and personality. Then, after carefully considering these factors, the most likely reasons for disengagement are used as a foundation for building a strategy for permanently separating a youth from the gang.

Law enforcement officers in the United States and Europe have told me that when implemented by a qualified juvenile officer, youth pastor, social worker, or caring adult, this strategy for disengagement is one of the best they have encountered. In fact . . . they believe this strategy cuts through the political rhetoric and can more quickly isolate a youth from a manipulative adult leader who hides behind a political agenda. Sometimes a youth will quit a gang after just a few days of discussion, while for some it may take months or, in extreme cases, even years.

The major trouble with this approach is that trying to quit a murderous gang can be even more dangerous than staying in it Take the case of Jimmy T. (Names here are changed to protect people's identity.) At age 14 he was a semiliterate high school dropout and like most kids in his west side neighborhood in Chicago, he joined a gang called the Vice Lords. He enjoyed the companionship at first, but one night fellow members told him it was time for him to do some work for them. "Here's the gun, there's the car. Get up and go, boy. Time to prove your stuff by shooting some rivals. Try not to hit someone's mama or baby, but mainly just pull the trigger bang bang bang—and don't lose the damned gun."

Jimmy was terrified. He drove around in the stolen car with a gun under the seat for 40 minutes, carefully obeying every traffic signal as he furiously worked through his options. He definitely did not want to be stopped by the police, really did not want to fire the gun but also definitely did not want to disappoint the gang. Finally he drove toward a group of teenagers hanging out on a corner in rival turf and blasted seven rounds of bullets into the crowd, wounding three of them. When asked later why he did this, he said, "Damn, man, don't you know what would happen to me if I just told my gang I want out? That I'm scared?"

Keith Smith, a minister's son in Waukegan, Illinois, could tell you. He called it quits in August, 1992, after eight months in a gang called Latin Lovers. When he told them he wanted to leave, a de-initiation ceremony took place at night in a local park. The ground rules were four against one for three minutes, with no weapons. Keith, who was then 15, collapsed after the first minute, and he remained in a coma for 58 days. Another example: Thomas R., an 18-year-old former Crip in Los Angeles who tried to leave the gang in April, 1992, says, "They did me pretty bad," leaving him with a broken arm, a broken wrist, two teeth knocked out, lots of cigarette burns on his face, and a few dozen bruises.

Project Freedom

It seems that the safest way to leave a gang is to move away, but that is not a feasible option for many. However, in May, 1992, a 12-year-old boy in Wichita, Kansas, who was being forced to work as a drug courier for a gang that was threatening him and his family was rescued when he and the entire family and all its belongings were whisked away to a safe house by members of the congregation of Pastor Chuck Chipman who descended on the boy's neighborhood before gang members could react. And that evacuation prompted a local group called Project Freedom to construct a network, which they call the underground railroad, to carry gang members and their families to safety in cases where all else fails. They are shuttled to safety through a chain of churches both in and out of the state. This remarkable group pays for the initial move, while local congregations agree to assume housing costs and arrange for jobs and education for as long as two years.

Operation Fresh Start

Membership in a gang is considered a lifelong commitment, so if ex-members are ever tracked down or recognized by the tattoos they wear they are never out of danger. Tattoos not only pose a danger to former gang members; they also make it hard to start a new life and find work. But Dr. Jay Rosenberg, a plastic surgeon in Elgin, Illinois, is doing something about that problem. He founded Operation Fresh Start to remove identifying tattoos from former gang members. Once a month, with the help of another doctor, a registered nurse, and hospital volunteers, he uses a penlike laser to trace the shape of the tattoos, erasing the evidence of the past. Dr. Rosenberg tells his patients, "You were dumb for doing it. Now you want it off, and that's wonderful—but it's going to hurt."

This program was launched in January, 1995, with the help of former Chicago Bears football player Roland Harper, who was a gang member in Louisiana (where he says his worst offense was throwing eggs at houses). Harper volunteered to be the first to have his tattoos erased. Since then Operation Fresh Start has removed 440 tattoos from 140 patients, and there is a waiting list of 3,500 men and women. "I'll be here for the next seven years if I'm the only one doing this," Dr. Rosenberg says. The director of the Advanced Surgery and Laser Center at the hospital wishes they could do more, but the procedure is very expensive. The hospital absorbs the cost, which is about $12,850 a month.

Father Greg Boyle, S.J.

This priest sympathizes with gang members' desire and need to be part of a group that fills the emotional hole caused by their dysfunctional families. Instead of trying to persuade them to leave a gang, he tries to get all of them to change their behavior while still belonging to it, in the process transforming the gang into a group of friends who will prefer legal, constructive activities to illegal ones.

Boyle himself grew up in Los Angeles in a strong Irish-American family with eight brothers and sisters. As a child he never knew what a gang was, so he was never even tempted to join one. "But that doesn't make me morally superior," he says; it just means that he was formed by an entirely different environment from that which today's gang members have experienced. He deplores the fact that "most people demonize these kids. These are human beings, our sons who are in trouble."

In 1986, at age 32, he came to Dolores Mission Church in a poor Latino neighborhood in East Los Angeles, one of the most violent areas of the city. His work was described in a book called *Father Greg & the Homeboys* (1995).

Boyle says that all the gang members he knows, whose ages range from 12 to their 20s, "have been raised in poverty without rules" and their common characteristic is "a crippling, paralyzing, pervasive despair." He sees his task as giving them "an infusion of hope" by loving them unconditionally, the way God loves. "They can't imagine a future for themselves. All of them expect to be dead or in jail within the next five years, so threats of prison or the death penalty don't deter them. Some of them deliberately put themselves in harm's way hoping they won't come out alive. Some commit suicide." But he tells them, "You can't see it, but I can see a future for you, and I'll help you walk into it." He lets them know that, no matter what, he will always be there for them. And gradually they begin to trust him.

Boyle says the government's current policy of trying to scare kids straight with threats of increased punishments will not work with gangs because threats are already such a big part of their lives. The only virtues they admire are bravery, "what they think it means to be a man," and loyalty to their gangs. Local teachers and probation officers with whom Father Greg works say that what each of these kids needs is at least one caring and reliable adult. Father Greg *is* that adult for them, and the nuns and other women in Dolores Mission Church, who were aghast and scared at first when he took the daring step of hiring some of the boys to work for him in the church, have now become other caring adults for them as well.

Idleness and joblessness are a big part of their problems, so Father Greg has organized "Home Boy Industries" and "Jobs for a Future" to provide jobs for them in bakeries and merchandising. He also works to educate the general public and persuade employers to hire gang members. Because the boys have had no experience of showing up on time, taking orders, finishing tasks, or dressing neatly, he goes along with them when they start their jobs. Some boys have had their lives completely altered by these work experiences.

Many of the boys have children (Boyle says, "I'm forever baptizing") so he gets them only jobs that pay more than minimum wage. "These aren't middle-class kids working to supplement an allowance. They need to support themselves so they need jobs that pay decently, and I've never known one of them to turn such a job down when it was offered."

But Boyle admits there are limits to what he can do: "I can walk them to the door to adulthood but I can't walk through it for them." He has had encouraging successes but many failures too. He has buried 49 kids, who died in shoot-outs or who committed suicide. He himself got in the middle of a shoot-out once when he was riding his bike, but some of his Home Boys threw themselves on top of him to save him.

Once a gang member killed a boy to sabotage a peace treaty that was about to be signed with another gang that claimed turf two blocks away. "These gangs are mirror images of each other," Boyle says. "I knew the kid who was killed. I loved that kid—*and* I love the kid who killed him! I personally know everybody in these fights. But I was enraged, and said so at the funeral. I have to be clear and honest, telling them what I think, but I try to dole rage out in bite-size bits."

Father Greg sets rules and tells the boys that if they violate them they will be "counted out," their term for being forced to leave the gang. And if he finds a gun he tells them it's his, even though they protest. He says, "I won't give it back."

One time after a 15-year-old was killed, the members of the boy's gang were so sorry that they organized a car wash to earn money to give to his mother. She refused to take it though, saying, "If it weren't for you my son would still be alive." Father Greg says, "This was the equivalent of splashing cold water on them, and really made them think."

When asked how much his friendly and compassionate approach really accomplishes, he says, "It's for someone else to decide if what I do is effective, as long as I know I'm doing what I feel called to do and think is right."

Celeste Fremon and the Home Boys' Mothers

Freelance writer Fremon met Father Greg in 1990 when she was doing research for her book, *Father Greg & the Homeboys.* She has worked closely with him as well as with the boys' mothers ever since, and at the request of one of the mothers with whom she became a close friend, she is the committed godmother of one of the mother's daughters.

One of the first things Father Boyle did when he came to East Los Angeles was to organize the women into study groups. They grew from what Celeste calls "three anemic gatherings" to 10 energetic groups who met weekly to discuss ways to reshape themselves and their surroundings. They live in Pico Gardens and Aliso Village, a mile-square twin housing project that forms the largest public housing complex west of the Mississippi and, according to the Los Angeles Police Department, the most violent neighborhood in the city. Drug use and drug dealing are rampant. Small craters pockmark the walls of stores and apartment buildings, reminders of the times when people have been shot or killed.

Most of the women in this community never finished high school and many are unable to read. But Celeste became impressed by them when she learned that, in rotating shifts, they made dinner every night for 125 or more homeless men who slept in the church.

One day she saw 64 of the women walking in a procession towards the church, singing hymns in Spanish, while inside the rectory five other mothers were holding a meeting with members of a street gang known as The Mob Crew (TMC). A few days earlier, these mothers had met with a rival gang, Cuatro Flats. A week before that, the war between these two gangs had taken the lives of two boys, Johnny, a 12-year-old Cuatro member, and Joseph, a 13-year-old who was mistaken for his 16-year-old TMC brother. The gangs' enmity, she says, was particularly shocking and tragic because the members lived only two blocks apart, had grown up together, and even shared a set of brothers.

These deaths spurred the mothers into action and they organized marches and meetings with the hope of working out a lasting truce. Every weekend they walked through the community's streets in what came to be called Love Walks, telling the gang members by their presence and words, "You are our sons. We love you and don't want you to kill each other."

All these women face innumerable problems. The husband of one is serving time in prison, convicted of a drug-related theft; she had three children, but her middle son was killed in a gang-related shooting, shot by boys he had known all his life. Another mother is raising four grandchildren and a boy in a gang as well as a drug-addicted girl whose birth mother died locked up in the Los Angeles County Jail. Her own daughter, who is both beautiful and bright, became pregnant by a gang member named Stranger and in 1991 gave birth to a daughter when she was only 15; a year later Stranger was convicted of murder and sentenced to life without the possibility of parole, and the girl talked about killing herself. But the resilience of some of these people is amazing; she managed to turn her life around, got married, and became a kindergarten teacher.

The mother of an 18-year-old who was killed in a gang-related fight at first sobbed, "I don't want to live any more. I don't care about nothing." But her son's death transformed her. Instead of rejecting the boys who had killed him, she befriended them even going into the aartments where they hang out. The astonished boyds would watch her in awe, not sure how to react. She began walking the streets with the other mothers' *Comité Pro Paz en el Barrio,* a women's organization that struggles to keep peace in the barrio, In just a few months she learned enough English to give talks in public, and in 1994, after becoming president of the Comité, she left the area to help other Los Angeles communities organize their own mother-based activism.

However, as Celeste says, the grief continues. The peace process is derailed again and again. "Doesn't it sometimes seem hopeless?" she once asked. "Yes, it does," was the reply, "but we can't stay that way, because if we do, it means we are hopeless and our children are hopeless. No. We are going to make this peace work."

In response to most of the community's tragic aspects, the women have continued to launch programs, usually with Father Boyle's help. There is now a community owned and operated day-care center, built by a construction crew of local gang members; a women's leadership training program; and a mentor program for the area's junior high and high school girls; as well as the *Comité Pro Paz en el Barrio.* So they obviously have not given up the struggle.

The Tariq Khamisa Foundation

In January, 1995, 20-year-old Tariq Khamisa was shot to death by a 14-year-old gang member named Tony Hicks during a botched holdup. That may seem a minor news item these days, but what happened afterwards was unusual. Tony became the youngest person in California's history to be charged with murder as an adult. He pleaded guilty and was sent to jail—where he will become eligible for parole in the year 2017.

Tariq's grief-stricken father, while mourning the death of his only son, says, "That night America was robbed of both children; there were victims at both ends of that gun." He got in touch with Tony's family and developed a close relationship with Ples Felix, Tony's grandfather and guardian. He found the sadness and sense of desolation that he felt over his own son's death mirrored in the feelings experienced by Felix when he learned that his grandson had committed murder and all his future plans for the boy had crumbled.

Khamisa decided to react to this crime in a way that would help save children *before* catastrophe strikes. Believing strongly that hatred, bitterness, and policies that embrace only punishment will not prevent future tragedies, he established the Tariq Khamisa Foundation, which Tony's grandfather immediately joined, dedicated to the prevention of youth violence rather than to revenge.

This effort may seem remarkably forgiving and generous, with a goal that will be hard to achieve, but it has reminded some people of a quixotic campaign to save the lives of three whales that were trapped in Arctic ice in Alaska back in October, 1988. Saving the whales became a national obsession, as heroic rescuers volunteered to brave bitter cold and long odds to try to free the trapped whales. Everyone agreed with President Ronald Reagan when he told the rescuers, "Our hearts are with you," even though the total cost of the rescue efforts, according to government officials, was "embarrassing." A letter to the editor of the *New York Times* during that memorable month, by Marylin B. Meyers, was printed under the headline "Children, Like Whales, Are in Need of Rescue." It said, "Every day millions of children are trapped in the Arctic ice of poverty, chaos, hopelessness, and helplessness. Are they any less worthy of the heroic efforts and support offered to the whales? The drama of the whales is very, very touching, but so is that of the children." One can only hope and pray that rescue efforts like those of Khamisa on behalf of children will inspire strong support from the public and eventually be as successful as the campaign to save the whales was.

Adults' Violence against Children

Horrifying as the growth of juvenile violence is, there is an equally disturbing causative factor that must not be forgotten. Behind almost every child murderer there is a child abuser, and behind that abuser there is apt to be another abuser.

Susan Smith was the single mother of two little boys. One day in 1994 she strapped them into their car seats, opened the windows, released the brakes, got out and locked the car door, and then pushed the car downhill into a lake. She listened until their screams stopped. She then called the police and said that a black man had stolen her car and kidnapped her children. For over a week she kept appearing on television, tearfully begging people to help her get her children back, causing a tremendous outpouring of sympathy and making everyone look with fear and suspicion at every black man in the area. Finally, discrepancies in her story having aroused police suspicions, she broke down and admitted what she had done.

People were so appalled that they demanded she get the death penalty. However, her lawyer looked into her past and found that Smith's mother had been neglectful while she was growing up, and her stepfather admitted that he had sexually abused her for years. A jury decided she was too deranged as a result to be fully responsible for her actions and sentenced her to life in prison instead of death. This was probably a more severe sentence than death would have been, because it is said that she is unable to forget what she did and cries every day.

Unfortunately this incident, while extreme, is not unique. Almost every week newspapers describe other cases of children who are maltreated, battered, even murdered by mothers, fathers, nannies, baby sitters, friends, teachers, even priests, as well as by strangers. Babies are thrown into trash cans. Emergency calls come in to 911 from children who are petrified and hungry because they have been left alone for days. A two-year-old girl is raped in a park. A nine-year-old is kidnapped by a "family friend" and held prisoner in a small underground room for over a week before being discovered. A kindergartner is beaten to death by her adopted father while the mother watches and does nothing about it. And it is not happening just in the U.S. In February, 1996, 16 five- and six-year-old kindergartners were killed and 12 others wounded by a crazed gunman in a primary school in a village in Scotland.

One little boy in New York was so badly beaten that he had welts and bruises from the top of his back to his waist; his wrist, with which he had tried to deflect the blows was fractured. His injuries were reported to a Child Welfare caseworker yet never investigated until the boy was dead. His father was finally arrested and admitted that he had repeatedly tied his son's arms and legs together and beaten him with sticks and electrical cords. He told prosecutors that he had beaten the boy so that "he would not turn out like me."

In September, 1992, a television documentary called *Scared Silent,* narrated by Oprah Winfrey, was broadcast on three commercial television networks and the Public Broadcasting System. It reported the conclusions of the U.S. Advisory Board on Child Abuse and Neglect that labeled child abuse a "national emergency." Reported incidents, long ignored as a national issue, had risen from 60,000 in 1974 to 2.7 million in 1991. It said that as many as 5,000 children die annually because of abuse, half of them before age one. Family members are guilty of 88 percent of the abuse, and most experts assume that if unreported cases were added the total number would double.

Teachers, neighbors, and nurses in hospitals frequently see suspicious bruises and cigarette burns on children, but either fail to report them to authorities or, if they do, there is often no follow-up. Caseworkers are too busy to try to handle every rumor, and there are so many instances of brutality against children that the public becomes numb. But every now and then a case is so extreme that it arouses special indignation because the child care authorities failed to protect the child involved by not investigating obvious signs of abuse.

Adam Mann and His Brothers

In 1990, when Adam was five years old, he was beaten to death. His teeth were knocked out, he suffered numerous broken bones, and he endured rectal abuse. At one point, in the attack that finally killed him, he was hung from a coat hook and beaten. He had three brothers and an infant sister who were removed from the parents' custody, and the parents were both sent to prison. Plans were made to try to have the youngsters adopted. End of case? By no means!

In April, 1996, Bob Herbert, a columnist for the *New York Times,* reported that Terry Weiss, an assistant deputy commissioner in the city's child welfare agency, had changed the plans. She believes strongly in keeping families intact, and decided that, although adoption proceedings were under way for the now six-year-old girl, the long-term goal for the boys should be to return them to their parents. "The question arises," Herbert wrote:

> How many of their children's bones do parents have to break, and how many children do they have to kill, before a decision is made by the authorities that they are no longer eligible for custody? Obviously, in the view of certain key child welfare officials, Rufus Chisolm (who is still in prison) and Michelle Mann (who was released in 1994) have not achieved the necessary threshold of horror that would bar them from further considerations of custody. Perhaps if they kill one more child.

Marcia Robinson Lowry, director of Children's Rights, Inc., an advocacy group, says the city cannot be trusted to protect children any more, and

> there are consequences for ignoring these children and failing to act responsibly, and the consequences to the city are harsh. . . . The Mann case is exceptional only because the abuse was so extreme, but except for the horrible circumstance under which these kids came in, this kind of lack of planning, and totally unrealistic goal, is very typical of how they treat all kids.

Lowry filed a multi-million dollar lawsuit that accused the city of repeatedly failing to investigate credible charges of child abuse, and of failing to manage properly the cases of children placed in its care.

Elisa Izaquierdo

On the day before Thanksgiving in 1995 an ambulance driver summoned to a project on the lower east side of Manhattan discovered the horribly scarred and lifeless body of six-year-old Elisa.

Elisa's father, who was divorced from her mother, had doted on her, working overtime to provide for her and making sure she was always immaculately dressed. She looked like a princess and when a real prince, Michael of Greece, once visited her school and said he would like to sponsor a child in need, one of the school's administrators recommended Elisa; he met her and offered to underwrite the cost of her education.

But in late 1991 Awilda Lopez, Elisa's mother, who had recently emerged from a drug rehab center, won the right to have Elisa spend every other weekend with her. The child always returned from these visits anxious and depressed. Her father and teachers suspected she was being abused, but after warning Lopez against hitting the child, a family court judge allowed the visits to continue. And then in May, 1994, Elisa's father died and Lopez was given full custody.

Soon afterwards Elisa began to exhibit symptoms of emotional disturbance, but because Lopez's other children seemed to be well cared for, caseworkers did not believe she or her new husband could be to blame. Over the next year there were many indications of trouble. Lopez removed Elisa from the YWCA school in Brooklyn, despite Prince Michael's readiness to pay her fees, and placed the child in kindergarten. Then in April 1995 she took her out of school altogether. Concerned neighbors reported to the Child Welfare Administration that after this they never saw the child. Later it was found that the mother kept Elisa in a locked room and forced her to urinate and defecate in a cooking pot. The mother was convinced that devils inhabited the girl's body, so she repeatedly beat her, tortured her with a stiff hairbrush, and pushed objects up her rectum.

An emergency room doctor at one point reported treating Elisa for a four-day-old shoulder injury. Then Elisa's stepfather was arrested for stabbing his wife seven times, and a grand jury tried to investigate why the Child Welfare Administration had failed to act in view of these developments. Because the records were protected as confidential, its efforts were blocked.

Public revulsion at the bungling of this case emboldened the state legislature at last to relax the confidentiality laws, and a new law called "Elisa's Law" was passed that made records more accessible. This flagrant cycle of ineptitude by the Human Resources Administration, which operated with a billion-dollar budget, also caused New York's mayor to examine the bureaucracy closely, and in January, 1996, he announced that he was removing child protection services from the HRA. He appointed Nicholas Scoppetta, a former president and chairman of the Children's Aid Society, as commissioner of a new children's agency that he created in response to Elisa's brutal death. "I can't think of anything more important to do," Scoppetta said.

On taking office the commissioner said, "I think that poor child's death has been a catalyst for an enormous amount of public support—demand, really. It's a tough problem to get at because it happens in people's homes, but I don't think it's a problem we can't get a lot better at." But when asked how soon reforms would be made, he said he expected it would take at least two years to reshape the agency and even longer to accomplish everything he wanted done.

Mr. Scoppetta asked to see all the files on Adam Mann and his brothers. Bob Herbert's comment was that when this man who "is supposed to bring a semblance of sanity to the lunacy that passes for child protection in New York" reviews them, "the bulging, stomach-turning files should give him a pretty good idea of how much work he has to do."

One hopeful sign was a new National Committee to Prevent Child Abuse, with a telephone hot line (1-800-CHILDREN). It advertised that "For years, child abuse has been a problem to which there were few real answers. But now there's an innovative new program that can help stop the abuse before it starts. A program that reaches new parents early on, teaching them how to cope with the stresses that lead to abuse. It's already achieving unprecedented results."

Racists' Threats to Children

Child abuse transcends racial, cultural, economic, and geographical distinctions, but there is one particularly vicious form that is not directed at individual children but at large groups of them. The Southern Poverty Law Center (SPLC) in Montgomery, Alabama, founded in 1971, maintains a "Klanwatch" that keeps track of hate crimes committed by the well-known Ku Klux Klan and by a growing number of smaller but equally bigoted and dangerous organizations that threaten children in two ways: by terrorism, persecuting and attacking those they dislike, and by corrupting children and recruiting them to help do their dirty work.

The 1996 edition of Klanwatch's Intelligence Report gave a chilling picture of these terrorist groups, listing all those known to be active in 1995 and describing their activities. A map of their locations showed only six out of the 52 states in the U.S.—Alaska, Hawaii, Maine, New Mexico, South Dakota, and Wyoming—where there were no known hate groups. These groups run camps that keep stockpiles of rifles and machine guns and material with which to build explosives like those used in the Oklahoma City bombing, and they train their members to use these in ways that threaten everyone, not just children. One group in Ohio was arrested for illegally obtaining vials of freeze-dried bubonic plague culture. Another group in Minnesota was found to have enough ricin, a deadly toxin, to kill 1,400 people.

In addition to holding marches, rallies, and meetings, and publishing literature, their activities involving children included bias incidents that range from insults and harassment, robbery and assaults, to stabbing and murder.

Among the hate crimes listed in Klanwatch's 1996 survey were anti-Semitic graffiti and swastikas smeared in a school bathroom, a gymnasium, and a lunch room. A school yearbook was defaced with racist insults, and racist graffiti was scrawled on student artwork in a high school and spray-painted in a toy store, on an Indian family's fence, and on playground equipment in a park. It was also scratched onto a high school boy's car and onto families' homes.

Black teenagers have beaten up whites, and vice versa. Both have attacked Asians and Hispanics. Children have assaulted old people and, again, vice versa. And it gets worse. A Jewish boy was shot in the face with a pellet gun by a teen who shouted an anti-Semitic slur at him.

Crosses have been erected and burned at elementary and high schools and at Catholic and Jewish private schools, in parks and playgrounds, in synagogues, churches and mosques, in front of Jewish and black families' homes. Threatening letters and phone calls are common.

Hate crimes are felonies, so these activities can ruin, at least temporarily, the lives of the perpetrators as well as of their victims. A 14-year-old boy and a 17-year-old boy were both arrested for beating a gay man; the younger one was sent to boot camp and the older one to prison. In August 1995 three white boys, 14, 15, and 17, were arraigned on attempted murder charges in connection with the fire-bombing of a southeast Asian family's home.

Teaching Tolerance

To counteract these hate-mongers and reduce their influence on children, the Southern Poverty Law Center (SPLC) decided in 1992 that it was not enough to deal with the consequences of hatred, but that it should also attack its causes. It decided to publish a magazine, *Teaching Tolerance*, for teachers, to help them guide their pupils toward positive attitudes that could inoculate them against bigotry. The magazine has a distinguished advisory board, headed by child psychiatrist Robert Coles, and it is mailed twice a year to educators free of charge. All a teacher has to do to receive it is to ask for it, by contacting SPLC, P.O. Box 548, Montgomery, Alabama 36177-9621. More than 200,000 teachers were receiving it in 1996.

When the magazine was first announced, some people were skeptical about how effective it could be. They thought SPLC should just stick to what they knew it was good at, alerting people to the hate groups and helping to get offenders arrested and convicted. But the skeptics were pleasantly surprised. It is an extremely attractive publication, with colorful graphics including a lot of children's art, and with varied articles on many subjects, designed to break down stereotypes about people in minority groups, from handicapped children to members of different races and religions. It describes effective teaching methods and activities and recommends useful books and other resources.

To supplement the magazine, SPLC has produced two curriculum kits, each containing text and video: *America's Civil Rights Movement* and *The Shadow of Hate: A History of Intolerance in America.* The latter 40-minute video was nominated in 1996 for an Academy Award in the short documentary category. (Another documentary produced for SPLC, *A Time for Justice,* was the Oscar winner in 1995.)

In addition to producing films, SPLC publishes books. Morris Dees, the center's cofounder and executive chairman, has published three: *A Season for Justice*, an account of the early days of SPLC; *Hate on Trial*, a gripping description of the courtroom drama that resulted in a $12.5 million judgment against the White Aryan Resistance for the murder of an Ethiopian student in Portland, Oregon; and *Gathering Storm: America's Militial Threat*, written shortly before the Oklahoma City bombing and warning the U.S. Attorney General that militia violence was threatening to erupt.

Sara Bullard, the editor of *Teaching Tolerance,* has also written three books. The text components of the magazine's teaching kits have been published in hardcover library editions by Oxford University Press. A third book is aimed at parents: *Teaching Toler-*

ance: Raising Open-minded, Empathetic Children, published by Doubleday in 1996. This one explores the roots of intolerance in human nature and helps readers recognize the traits of intolerance in themselves. It also provides practical guidelines for parents and caregivers who want to help children overcome prejudice and practice respect for all people. Extensive lists of suggested activities and resources are included.

Producing high-quality publications and distributing so many free to so many people is very ambitious and expensive. It is made possible by financial contributions from almost 300,000 individuals who support the nonprofit SPLC. The work is also dangerous. The life of Morris Dees is under constant threat from the hate groups that would like nothing better than to destroy him and his center, which has to maintain tight security at all times. He and the rest of the 55 staff members are true heroes, seemingly fearless and totally dedicated to their work. His courage and brilliance as a trial attorney have been a challenging inspiration to the young law students he helps to train.

THE WORLD'S VIOLENCE EPIDEMIC

There have always been a few psychopaths in the world: rapists, serial killers, child abusers. And as horrifying as the crimes they have committed are, they have at least been rare. But in the 1990s the number of crimes has increased, and the age of the criminals has decreased. It used to be that most criminals were adults, whereas in recent years one of the saddest and most alarming facts about crime is that so many children have become not only victims but criminals.

On a typical day in 1993, approximately 100,000 juveniles were in jail in the United States. More American children are committing crimes than ever before, and their crimes are more serious than ever before. In 1986 most cases of juvenile offenders brought before Family Court in New York City were misdemeanors, but in 1994 more than 90 percent were felonies: murder, rape, robbery, and aggravated assault. In Los Angeles during the years 1991 to 1994, boys under 18 committed 450 homicides, and 17 of them were done by children 14 or younger. Criminologist James Alan Fox of Northeast University says, "not only are violent teens maturing into even more violent young adults, but they are being succeeded by a new and larger group of teenagers." Since the mid-1980s, juvenile violence has grown far faster than the juvenile population, and arrests of youths under 18 for murder have more than doubled.

Although the nationwide homicide rate has not increased in several years, adolescents are killing and being killed in sharply rising numbers. A study released in October, 1994, by the Centers for Disease Control and Prevention, showed that from 1985 to 1991 the annual rate at which boys 15 to 19 years old were being killed jumped 154 percent, far surpassing the rate changes in any other age group. Homicide rates among men over age 25 have been declining since 1985 while rising among adolescents.

Why Has This Happened?

The crime epidemic stems partly from increasing hopelessness among the young. Some children express their despair by hurting other people; others turn it on themselves: another alarming fact is that suicide has become one of the major causes of death among children, according to the World Health Organization. More than one in five American children now live below the poverty line, a rate that edged upward in recent years. And children raised by single parents are among the most likely to get into trouble. Continuing a long trend, 30 percent of all births in 1991 were out of wedlock, and the figure was expected to hit 40 percent by the year 2000. So there has been an increase in the number of children poorly raised by poor mothers, many of whom are immature, uneducated, and neglectful, even abusive.

Well-meaning laws passed in the early part of this century that were meant to protect youngsters have also backfired, in accordance with what Malcomb Muggeridge described as "the law of unintended consequences." Young offenders are now tried in Family Courts, where they receive shorter sentences than are given to older criminals tried in the regular courts. In New York, for example, since 1978 the maximum sentence for criminals between the ages of 13 and 15 has been 18 months, regardless of the seriousness of the crime. Youngsters know this and take advantage of it. Many of them figure they can get away with breaking the law because "it's no big deal." Even if they are caught they will receive only a reprimand or a short sentence until they are older when they may join gangs, which lure younger kids into doing their dirty work. A child under 16 knows he cannot be executed for murder, even for multiple murders, and if sent to jail he will get out at age 25.

Also, when children are convicted of a crime it is not put into the public record; it is kept confidential to protect the child's reputation, so judges often do not know that a child is a habitual offender. For example, a judge who had to decide on appropriate punishment to give to 12-year-old Percy Campbell, who was arrested in September 1994 for attempted burglary in Fort Lauderdale, Florida, did not know that Percy had already been arrested more than 30 times for 57 crimes, some of them felonies. Not too surprising: his mother was in jail for murder, his grandmother had just been arrested for shoplifting, and an uncle was the person who had taught him how to steal cars.

Furthermore, if children are sent to jail, the time they spend there is not conducive to encouraging reform. Often the children eat better and get better health care and feel safer while in jail than they do on the outside. But in most cases they do not get any drug counseling, job training, or schooling, and they associate with older criminals who teach them even worse behavior. And then, when they are released, they are put back on the streets, untrained and jobless, and with a felony conviction that makes it even harder for them to find a new job. As a 17-year-old criminal, in prison for auto theft and aggravated assault, told a reporter, life on the outside is an open invitation to go bad again: "They send you straight back into the same situation. The house is dirty when you left it, and it's dirty when you get back."

The Dangerous Combination of Drugs and Guns

When studying the statistics about the growth of crime among juveniles, Professor Alfred Blumstein of Carnegie Mellon University noticed that the sudden marked increase in homicides among young people took place in the mid-1980s along with the coming of crack. He explains that the drug markets recruit kids, and then the drug dealers give the kids guns, which are "the tools of their trade." Once this process had started, youths dealing drugs began carrying their guns around with them, in school and in their neighborhoods, and then other teenagers began copying them. Dr. Mark Rosenberg of the National Center for Injury Prevention and Control pointed out, when analyzing an October 1994 study of juvenile crime, "Virtually all of the increase in homicides, 97 percent, was attributable to the use of guns." The use of crack among teenagers lessened in the 1990s but by then the process of younger and younger people arming themselves had become self-perpetuating, and Rosenberg said that the wave of extreme violence that has so alarmed Americans "is not an epidemic of some vague evil, or immorality; it is specifically a problem of firearms' deaths."

While drug abuse overall has held steady in the 1990s, inner-city addiction remains high and, in order maintain a drug habit, addicts need lots of money. And kids who want money find it far more profitable to sell drugs, even if they do not use drugs themselves, than to mow lawns or sell newspapers or lemonade. Therefore, they want guns in order to protect themselves from older kids who might steal their money. It is possible to rent a gun on the streets for $20 an hour, although a new crime law passed by Congress in 1994 made it a crime for juveniles to possess a handgun or for any adult to transfer one to them except in certain supervised situations. But the guns are already out there, and even supervision does not guarantee safety, as has been proved by the cases where children, out of curiosity, have played with their parents' guns and have accidentally killed a playmate or themselves. No gun is safe from an impulsive child. Even toy guns are not safe any more; children have waved them at people who did not realize they were toys and who therefore shot back.

The people who drew up the child protecting laws did not foresee the widespread availability of drugs and guns that has resulted in so much dangerous behavior. But nowadays, even in places where teenagers commit crimes no more often than they used to, when tempers flare the results can be lethal. Fights that used to be settled with fists are now settled with guns.

Shootings over seemingly minor slights have become increasingly frequent in recent years. Such cases are typically difficult to solve because they often involve people who do not know each other.

What Can Be Done to Change Things?

One thing that is being done is that schools are becoming less "user friendly." School systems have installed metal detectors and surprise locker searches and have begun to enact strict anti-gun regulations to try to eliminate weapons from schools. In many schools, a student caught with a firearm is now automatically suspended for up to a year—yet children continue to bring them to school.

In San Diego, California, to eliminate what school officials say are the most common hiding places for guns, new school buildings no longer have lockers where pupils can keep their lunch boxes, coats, and books. In Charlotte, North Carolina, students in some schools are no longer allowed to carry book bags from class to class because they might conceal weapons in them. In Corpus Christi, Texas, trained dogs have been brought into the schools to sniff children when they arrive in the morning, and to check lockers for alcohol, drugs, and guns.

In 1994 Ramon C. Cortines, then chancellor of the public schools in New York, was asked by the mayor to develop detailed school safety proposals after the accidental shooting of a student in a Brooklyn high school by a 15-year-old friend. Both students had been transferred into their new high school after disciplinary problems at other schools, and both had lengthy criminal records. The chancellor came up with a proposal to establish disciplined academies for students apt to endanger other students, which would provide "a highly structured alternative setting for youngsters" and would offer a full curriculum and feature computer labs as well as programs offering credit for community service. The new schools would be mandatory for any student caught at school with a gun or illegal knife or one who uses any weapon in an aggressive act, and would focus on building self-esteem, long- and short-range goal setting, and improving peer and authority relationships. The academies would resemble part-time reform schools with rigorous academic programs. He urged the city to use funds from the federal crime bill to establish one academy for intermediate and another for high school students in each of the city's five boroughs. The schools would each have a capacity of 1,350 students. It was suggested that judges might be willing to enroll students convicted of felonies in these schools as an alternative to incarceration. The mayor of the city and the governor of the state both endorsed the proposal, although some people thought it would be better to set up boarding schools where such children would be isolated from the environment that had fueled their misbehavior.

But these various measures to make schools safer, necessary as they seem to be, can be only partial cures, since schools are not the only places where violence occurs. Must all parks and playgrounds be turned into fortresses? What about city streets and country roads? And what about apartments and private homes?

U.S. Attorney General Janet Reno believes that crime has its roots among neglected children. She stresses the need for "a continuum" of government attention beginning with prenatal care and including the school system, housing authorities, health services, and job training, while also realizing that in some cases the continuum will have to end in an early jail cell. "It's imperative," she says, "for serious juvenile offenders to know they will face a sanction. Too many of them don't understand what punishment means because they have been raised in a world with no understanding of reward and punishment." Under current laws, it takes forever to punish kids who are hardened criminals and who have seriously broken the law, while wayward kids who might still be turned around are neglected.

Mike Easley, the attorney general of North Carolina, agrees with Reno, saying, "We can't look a kid in the eye and tell him that we can't spend a thousand dollars on him when he's 12 or 13 but that we'll be happy to reserve a jail cell for him and spend a hundred grand a year on him later. It's not just bad policy, it's bad arithmetic."

Punishment or Prevention?

Statistics indicate that only 6 percent of the boys in a community will be responsible for at least 50 percent of the serious crimes committed by all boys of that age. More than 50 percent of all kids in long-term juvenile institutions in the United States have immediate relatives who have also been incarcerated. A low IQ is another characteristic of these incurable criminals, and from an early age they drink and get high. They usually start showing troublesome behavior as early as the third grade. Yet even some of these kids can be, and have been, saved.

Peter Reinhyarz, head of the Family Court Division in New York, says that having the worst kids stand trial as adults will not solve the problems, any more than more and more already overcrowded jails will. It will still load too many desperate characters into a system that is under-equipped to deal with them. "I don't know what the solution is," he told an interviewer for *Newsweek* magazine, "but I can tell you what it isn't. You're looking at it."

Some proposed solutions will not solve anything. Giving more and more criminals longer and longer jail sentences is like locking the barn door after the horses are gone, because murder victims cannot be brought back to life no matter how long their murderer stays in jail. By sitting in a cell a murderer is at least prevented from killing another victim, but unless he is kept there for life, the day will come when he finally gets out, and he will not be in a very nice mood because prison life is inherently degrading, dehumanizing, and brutalizing.

According to Robert Drinan, S.J., a professor at the Law Center of Georgetown University and former chairman of the Subcommittee on Criminal Justice of the Judiciary Committee in the House of Representatives, America already has the highest incarceration rate of any nation in the entire world. And although people in a panic over escalating crime may feel relieved to think that more and more criminals are locked up, he points out that the cost of jailing people is astronomically expensive. Even now states cannot meet the financial obligations of the prisons they have built. South Carolina, which has the nation's third highest incarceration rate, spent $80 million on new prisons that it has not opened because it cannot afford the operating costs.

Drinan is also distressed by the way women prisoners are treated, pointing out that 80 percent of them are mothers; two-thirds of them had children before they were 18 years old, and about 10 percent of them are pregnant when they are sent to prison. Almost all of them were the sole support of their children, so the incarceration is very destructive of the relationship between the mothers and their children, which needs to be helped and strengthened rather than weakened or destroyed.

Clearly, instead of giving in to fear and panic or a fierce desire for revenge, it would be far wiser for society to concentrate on the *prevention* of crime. An excellent study of the subject by Ted Gest and Dorian Friedman, published in *U.S. News and World Report* in September 1994, produced many constructive proposals. Here are some excerpts:

1. **Beginning early**. A child's first memories can shape habits and notions of right and wrong for a lifetime. The earlier a youngster gets positive reinforcement—through preschool and nutrition programs like Head Start, for example—the better. Some promising efforts begin even before birth. In Elmira, New York, nurses visited many women during pregnancy and for two years afterwards to teach them parenting skills; mothers who were counseled were five times less likely to abuse their kids than those who were not. That is significant because children exposed to violence are the most likely to turn violent themselves.

2. **Involving schools.** Traditionally, schools have shunned crime-prone youths, but many of today's educators are working with students in elementary school or even earlier to teach conflict-resolution skills, stress firearm safety, or offer adult mentors. The payoff is evident, says Judge Allen Nelson, who handles juvenile crime cases in Flint, Michigan: "You can see it in the way these kids relate to their peers and resolve the smallest conflicts."

3. **Involving communities.** "Communities That Care," a model designed by two Seattle sociologists now being tested in 100 cities, preaches that anti-violence messages need to be reinforced from *all* quarters: home, school, peer groups, church, and the media. They argue that youth violence can be curbed only by "changing community norms, values, and policies." That's a tall order that cannot be accomplished by government alone. "You need people who are driven to work with kids," says Michael Agopian, a California criminologist and ex-Justice Department official.

4. **Family intervention.** Even under the best circumstances, parents can't do the whole job. But experts say many young offenders are better off getting intensive counseling at home than in lockups. In the "Choice Program" of the University of Maryland in Baltimore County, caseworkers visit each of 650 troubled kids three to four times daily. The youngsters, ages 9 to 17, must follow strict rules set by their families and the social worker. A study showed 73 percent of them had avoided further trouble six months later—a record better than that of most traditional corrections programs.

5. **Simple and effective ideas.** Chris Jackson, when he was 18, joined a basketball league in Glenarden, Maryland, in suburban Washington, D.C. Late one night, after spraining his ankle making a lay-up, Jackson sat in an emergency room as three friends were rushed in, victims of a drive-by shooting. "If not for midnight basketball," he told his coach, "I would have been out there, too." League director Nelson Standifer says Jackson's "whole attitude turned around." Jackson now attends college. Crime in the area has dropped substantially since the program started. Recreation and counseling offered by Boys and Girls Clubs of America also appear to keep kids out of trouble. Housing projects with such clubs report 13 percent fewer juvenile crimes and 25 percent less crack cocaine.

6. **Long-term planning.** The best crime prevention strategies take years of follow-up. "Single-shot inoculations are not going to be successful," warns Harvard public health professor Stephen Buka, who helps direct an eight-year study of a central Chicago neighborhood to determine why some kids commit crimes while others resist. Like many experts, Buka believes violence prevention must be instilled from the preschool years into a young adult's working life. Finishing school and getting a job are potent safeguards against engaging in crime.

So it seems that there are some practical, realistic ways in which to fight crime. These are not as dramatic as locking people up, and they require a lot of time and patience, but they are more effective.

The New York Police Athletic League (PAL), which works with young children organizing constructive activities to keep them happy and out of trouble, has an appropriate slogan: "In order to change the world you have to start small."

NEW HOPE FOR POOR CHILDREN

Tapori

The term *Tapori* means "poor children." It comes from Marathi, a language spoken in Bombay, India. It is the name of the children's branch of the Fourth World Movement, and its slogan is "We want all children to have the same chances."

The term "Fourth World" refers to the poorest people in the world, wherever they are. They can be found in rich countries as well as in poor Third World countries. The term originated during the French Revolution, when society in France was organized into three orders. The first in prestige and power were the nobles; the second order was the clergy; the third was lay people who knew how to read and write. This structure left out the large majority of people who were extremely poor and illiterate and were not included in the government. During the Revolution they rose up, calling themselves the Fourth World, and demanded representation.

Today's Fourth World Movement is a nongovernmental organization that has consultative status at the United Nations. It grew from a camp for homeless people created in 1957 in a French shantytown, with a handful of friends and volunteers brought together by a priest, the late Father Joseph Wresinski (1917–1988), who himself grew up in poverty and who chose the name "Fourth World" as a positive identity for poor people. He initiated October 17 as a day to honor the world's poorest and to promote international solidarity among them. In 1992 the UN General Assembly adopted the date as an annual World Day for Overcoming Extreme Poverty.

Other people joined them over the years, building up an organization that now has many thousands of supporters and a nucleus of several hundred deeply committed long-term, full-time volunteers who live and work with poor families in Africa, Asia, Central America, Europe and, since 1964, in the United States.

"We cannot forget that the goal is still in front of us and still far away. . . . To eliminate poverty requires an encounter with the poorest men and women, seeking them out wherever they are, to learn from them who they are and what they expect from us," said Father Wresinski. Families who live in deep poverty, ignored or rejected by others, are remarkable for their courage, he added; they struggle every day to survive, to be respected, and to be able to give a future to their children. "Such families, whose poverty often has extended over many generations, are present in all countries, left out of the progress of the society around them," he said. "Our societies will be immeasurably richer when these poor people are allowed to participate."

What Do the Members of the Fourth World Movement Do?

Supporters and volunteers work together so that the voices of the poorest will be heard, their courage and dignity recognized, and their full and free participation in society encouraged. Supporters' work includes:

- family vacation centers "for families who are exhausted and close to despair because of their poverty"

- research projects on poverty, which have resulted in fact sheets providing useful information about particular needs of the poor

- an international center called "An Alternative for Youth," founded in France in 1971, which has sponsored trips for young people from French slums to meet and make friends with their counterparts in other countries

- advocacy campaigns, which have increased public awareness of the needs of the poorest of the poor

More important than any specific projects, however, is the continuing presence of full-time volunteer workers among needy families, offering them literacy and training programs, not only teaching them but learning from them, acting as a bridge, and bringing isolated people together in friendship and cooperation.

The Creation and Growth of Tapori

As a result of sharing the lives of these people, Fourth World volunteers became especially concerned about the children in these deprived families, so in Europe (in 1971) and in the United States (in 1974) they started an affiliated organization just for children: Tapori.

This grew into an international network, building friendship among children, starting with the poorest.

Examples of Tapori projects:

- It publishes monthly newsletters to which children contribute stories, pictures, questions, jokes, and ideas for activities that bring poor children together with others across the barriers of languages, oceans, national boundaries, races, and social classes.

- It runs *street libraries* and *field libraries*, with volunteers going once a week into slums, ghettos, and isolated rural areas, bringing books, toys, games, paints, pencils, puzzles, and paper, to read with the children, to teach them games, and to encourage correspondence with children in other countries. Some of the most popular and inspiring books in these libraries were written and illustrated and donated for children by children.

- At the United Nations, in 1984, a children's mural was displayed, which later traveled to other areas to introduce communities to Tapori and to inspire more children and their parents to commit themselves to its ideals.

- In the United States, high school students have participated in a work camp preparing puppet theaters, puppets, and plays for summer street libraries. In 1986, American members of Tapori held a Penny Portrait Campaign, distributing cards that featured portraits drawn by children surrounded by 100 circles on which they placed pennies collected for UNICEF. A delegation of children and parents presented 237 portraits, with 237 dollars, to UNICEF's Executive Director James Grant during an exhibition on "Working Together for Children," organized by nongovernmental organizations to mark UNICEF's fortieth anniversary. Mr. Grant invited the children and their parents to meet the delegates at the UNICEF Executive Board, which was then in session, introducing them by saying, "The Fourth World Movement has spread around the world. . . . It really does show what people can do to help each other, and the fact that poor people in one country can help poor people in other countries."

1994 Observance in Honor of the Victims of Extreme Poverty

In 1994, designated by the UN as the International Year of the Family, the Fourth World Movement brought 300 delegates from 40 countries to the United States for its fourth Family Congress, to raise world awareness of the strengths of poor families. On October 17, the International Day for the Eradication of Poverty, they gathered at the UN. American signers of a letter to the U.S. President described the delegates to the Congress as "international faces of hope—Christians, Jews, Muslims, and Buddhists from Africa, Asia, Europe, and the Americas . . . who will give Americans the chance to support the efforts of the world's poorest parents, for whom the family is key to overcoming poverty." As the delegate from Burkino Faso said, "Hunger doesn't worry us that much; what worries us is whether we can educate our children."

It was quite a day. The delegates walked from the Fourth World Movement's original U.S. headquarters on Fourth Street in Manhattan to the UN Headquarters on Forty-Sixth Street, as a symbol of the poor families everywhere who have finally emerged from an excluded neighborhood to a forum of the world's peoples—Father Wresinski's great ambition. The ceremony at the UN began with a message from children. The director of UN Conference Services announced that this Congress carried with it "the hopes of 10,000 children who have written, painted, drawn, embroidered, or sewn their names to make the beautiful Tapori banners you can see displayed here. Tapori is a network of friendship among children from all backgrounds, and today children tell us 'Together we are stronger than poverty.'"

The official ceremony was very colorful, with delegates dressed in traditional clothing from many lands, appearing before a backdrop of banners from various countries. One banner from Senegal read, "All children should have a home and shoes." They spoke of their riches: their families and children. A delegate from Scotland said, "We are people who exhaust ourselves doing undeclared and irregularly paid work on rubbish dumps, factories and farms and in mines. Our children are our only wealth. It is especially for them that we want a different life." They quoted their founder, Father Wresinski, who said, "The world will change because we have listened to children."

Delegates presented the UN with an 8- by-10-foot quilt dubbed the "Patchwork of Lives," made of pieces of cloth donated by poor people from 28 countries, bearing the words of Father Wresinksi: "Wherever men and women are condemned to live in extreme poverty, human rights are violated. To come together to ensure that these rights be respected is our solemn duty." The quilt was then scheduled to travel through all the UN member states.

The Family Congress's final message at the end of the ceremony was,

> We are a people that resists the misery that eats away at the hearts of our children, that destroys our families and communities and comes between us and our future. Yet we do all we can to keep our families going hour by hour, day by day, year in and year out, generation after generation. We are a people that believes that tomorrow things will be different. In a few days we will go back to our families and communities, knowing that it will not be easy. But our paths have crossed yours, and we have dared to take the time to get to know one another, to face one another without shame. We have confidence in you, knowing the future will be both in your hands and in ours.

The ceremony was followed by a reception at UNICEF House, during which the delegate from Canada, Raymond Desrochers, spoke about his country: "Canada is rich, and the Government is generous to the poor, but sometimes its policies break families apart. We wonder why those who want to help us don't ask our opinions. Who understands that nothing replaces love? Can't we help parents to take better care of their children?"

In the evening there was an interfaith service at the Cathedral of St. John the Divine, "a time of hope, prayer, music, and testimony to celebrate the courage of the poor and to renew commitment with them."

Two days later the delegates were received at the White House. Before leaving Washington, they issued the following declaration:

> We do not pretend to know everything about how to put an end to poverty and exclusion, but we do know that we can sit, think, and act, together with others, in order to free the world from extreme poverty. What we have had the privilege of experiencing here, no one can ever take from us. But our march forward is not over. It will be continued with new strength that will enable us to believe that we can make friends and take our places everywhere that our children's future is being decided, everywhere that our countries' and regions' development is being planned. We will be like water that flows to fill every opening, every crevice.

In the 1990s, many people became contemptuous of poor people, even afraid of them, considering them repulsive, lazy, dirty, and prone to antisocial behavior, who increasingly expected handouts but did not deserve them. They felt that efforts to help the poor were useless, because they were ungrateful and hostile, blaming all their troubles on those who had more money. In many cases this was true, but it seems possible that Father Joseph Wresinski had hold of a very important concept, that instead of isolating rich and poor into enemy camps, neither of them could constructively improve society by themselves, so they must get to know each other. Tarzi Vittachi (1921–1993), a UNICEF executive and a brilliant journalist who was raised in Sri Lanka by a very poor (but happy and loving) family, used to say, "The only experts on poverty are the poor, but the politicians and bureaucrats think they know what the poor need, and never ask them about what they themselves know they need. So they concoct welfare programs that increase dependency and destroy family life." It is to be hoped that the Fourth World Movement can bring people, both poor and well-off, together in constructive cooperation.

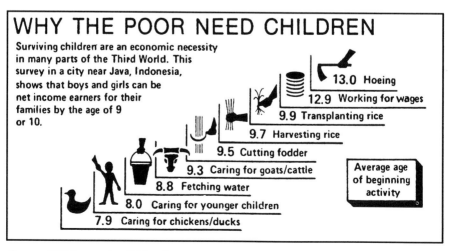

Source: IYC Secretariat, Sri Lanka

HOW TO LIVE ON $100 A YEAR

(Two people meet. B looks downcast.)

A: Hey, friend, you look troubled. What's your problem?

B: Money.

A: Can't make ends meet, huh?

B: Meet? I can't even get them in shout-ing distance. The way prices are going up. . .

A: (interrupts) Friend, have I ever got the program for you! It's called "How to live on $100 a year."

B: One hundred dollars a year? Is that possible?

A: Sure. Half the people in the world do it all the time.

B: How do I start?

> This is a short skit that is used by some advocacy groups as a fund raiser, following it with passing the hat for offerings or pledges for future contri-butions. It has only two characters, requires no costumes, scenery, or props, a nd can be performed in a classroom, meeting, house, church, or anywhere.

A: First, get rid of all your furniture except one table and one chair. That cuts down not only on payments, but also on cleaning supplies.

B: Cuts down on guests, too. But where do I sit to watch TV?

A: No TV, no radio, no books or magazines. You're cutting down, remember.

B: Yeah, but. . .well, I guess I have to go out for my entertainment?

A: If you like. But give away all your clothes except one outfit—your oldest. And keep one pair of shoes for the head of the family.

B: You mean everybody else goes barefoot? The kids might like that for a while, but I don't know about making it a regular practice. What else?

A: Shut off your electricity, water, and gas. Think of all the money you'll save! And discon-nect the phone—don't forget that.

B: How will we run the dishwater, toaster, hair dryer?

A: Send those to Goodwill. You can't afford them on $100 a year. And as for baths, use the rain.

B: How will we cook?

A: Gather scraps of wood and things that will burn. It's amazing how much waste wood you can find if you try. But donate most of your food to a crisis center. Keep only a small bag of flour, some sugar and salt, a few moldy potatoes or some rice, a handful of onions, and some dried beans. Meal planning becomes a breeze!

B: (doubtfully) But is that a balanced diet?

A: Friend, on $100 a year, you can't have everything.

B: But what if I get sick? I can't even call a doctor—no phone.

A: Use the midwife in a clinic about ten miles away. Half the world does. And if you need a doctor, there's one further down the road.

B: How long would it take to get to a doctor—driving, I mean?

A: Driving? Oh—I forgot. You'll need to give up your car. They eat up your income.

B: (sarcastic) What'll we do with the garage—rent it out?

A: No—live in it. Get rid of the house, too. Of course your garage is larger than the ordinary house allowed in this program, but since you don't have a tool shed. . .

B: Hey, this isn't living, it's. . .What do I do about my job? (or school?) I can't walk there on an empty stomach, in my oldest clothes without a bath, and expect them to let me stay very long. I suppose this program thought of that?

A: Sure. Your best bet is to become a tenant farmer. With three acres and a good year, you can expect from one to three hundred dollars' worth of cash crops. Pay the landlord a third and the moneylender 10 percent, and you get what's left.

B: Moneylender? Oh, come on. Why do I need a moneylender?

A: Well, some years there'll be a drought, or maybe a flood. Then you won't get a hundred dollars. And you *need* a hundred dollars to live on this program effectively.

B: Yeah, I can see I do. What about saving for my old age?

A: Well, there's bad news and good news. You can't afford insurance, pension plans, or savings accounts, which is bad news. But the good news is that you won't need them.

B: Yeah? Why not?

A: Because under this program you can count on living 25 to 30 years less.

B: Oh, that's great. Hey, look, forget it, okay? I really appreciate your trying to help and all, but suddenly I don't think I need help after all. My bills look pretty small. (He walks away and mutters to himself.) That's not living. It's barely existing, in fact. I'm not sure people can live like that. (Exit)

A: (turning from B to the audience and addressing them) Millions of people do. As I said before, half the people in our world live on this program, year in and year out. They didn't choose it, but they're stuck with it. In our economy we can't really live on $100 a year. But could we live on a hundred dollars a year *less*? That's about nine dollars a month, or two dollars a week. Would that require sacrifice? Would we even miss it? Yet think what could be done for the world's hungry, if each person or even each family in this room gave a hundred dollars a year to fight hunger . . . Shall we?

14

Children of Peace and War

COMMENTS ABOUT CHILDREN AND WARFARE

In peace the sons bury their fathers and in war the fathers bury their sons.
—*Francis Bacon (1561–1626), in* Apophthegms New and Old *(1624)*

Men under 35 should be exempt from military service, and warriors must be at least 40. And if that doesn't work, then wars can be started only with the consent of the mothers.
—*Jamil M. Baroody, Saudi Arabian Ambassador
to the United Nations in 1970*

Youth is the first victim of war; the first fruit of peace. It takes twenty years or more of peace to make a man; it takes only twenty seconds of war to destroy him.
—*King Baudouin I of Belgium (1930–),
in a speech to the U.S. Congress in 1959*

It is ironical that in an age when we have prided ourselves on our progress in the intelligent care and teaching of children we have at the same time put them at the mercy of new and most terrible weapons of destruction.
—*Pearl Buck (1892–1973), noted author*

In front of us a curious figure was standing, a little crouched, legs straddled, arms held out from his sides. He had no eyes, and the whole of his body, nearly all of which was visible through tatters of burnt rags, was covered with a hard black crust speckled with yellow pus. A Korean woman by his side began to speak, and the interpreter said: 'He has to stand, sir, cannot sit or lie.' He had to stand because he was no longer covered with a skin, but with a crust like crackling which broke easily.
—*Rene Cutforth, in* Korean Reporter *in 1952*

War is one of the constants of history, and has not diminished with civilization or democracy. In the last 3,421 years of recorded history only 268 have seen no war. . . . The causes of war are the same as the causes of competition among individuals: acquisitiveness, pugnacity, and pride; the desire for food, land, materials, fuels, mastery. The state has our instincts without our restraints.
—*Will (1885–1981) and Ariel Durant (1898–1981)
in* The Lessons of History *(1968)*

Every gun that is made, every warship launched, every rocket fired signifies, in the final sense, a theft from those who hunger and are not fed, those who are cold and are not clothed.

This world in arms is not spending money alone. It is spending the sweat of its laborers, the genius of its scientists, and the hopes of its children.

The cost of one modern heavy bomber is this: a modern brick school in more than 30 cities. It is two electric power plants, each serving a town of 60,000 population. It is two fine, fully equipped hospitals. It is some 50 miles of concrete highway. We pay for a single fighter plane with a half million bushels of wheat. We pay for a single destroyer with new homes that could have housed more than 8,000 people. This is the best way of life to be found on the road the world has been taking. This is not a way of life at all, in any true sense. Under the cloud of threatening war, it is humanity hanging from a cross of iron. . . .

I like to believe that people in the long run are going to do more to promote peace than governments. Indeed, I think that people want peace so much that one of these days governments had better get out of their way and let them have it.
—*Dwight D. Eisenhower (1890–1969), U.S. President*

[In a speech to parents:] If we are to reach a real peace in this world and if we are to carry on a real war against war, we shall have to begin with children; and if they will grow up in their natural innocence, we won't have to struggle, we won't have to pass fruitless, idle resolutions, but we shall go from love to love and peace to peace.

[In a letter to four young children:] Yes, it is little children like you who will stop all war. This means that you never quarrel with other boys and girls, or among yourselves. You can't stop big wars, if you carry on little wars yourselves.
—*Mohandas K. (Mahatma) Gandhi (1869–1948), Indian reformer*

We shall never stop war, whatever machinery we may devise, until we have learned to think always, with a sort of desperate urgency and an utter self identification, of single human beings.   —*Sir Victor Gollancz (1893–1967), English author*

The basic human needs of the overwhelming majority of men, women and children on earth could be realized by devoting as much each year to the task of achieving them as is now devoted every six weeks to the task of maintaining and increasing the world's military capacity.
—*James P. Grant, executive director of UNICEF from 1980 to 1995*

I can send the flower of German youth into the hell of war without the slightest pity.   —*Adolf Hitler (1889–1945), German dictator*

Older men declare war. But it is youth that must fight and die.
—*Herbert Hoover (1874–1964), U.S. President*

At the heart of the fight for peace is the development of the mind, beginning with the child. What we are now beginning to recognize as the vital process of human resource development is also the development of generations that can positively nurture peace between nations. . . .Peace is created within each individual. It is necessary above all, to create a peaceful world, to begin with the children, the children who are the coming generation.
—*Gunnar Jahn, Chairman of the Nobel Peace Prize Committee in 1965*

All wars are wars against children.
—*Eglantine Jebb (1876–1928), Founder of Save the Children*

O my people, hear me. I am tired of fighting. Our chiefs are killed. . . .The old men are dead. . . .It is cold and we have no blankets. The little children are

freezing to death. . . .I want to have time to look for my children and see how many of them I can find. Maybe I shall find them among the dead. Hear me, my chiefs. I am tired. My heart is sick and sad. From where the sun now stands I will fight no more forever.
—*War Chief Joseph (c. 1840–1904), chief of the Nez Percé tribe*

I became very different in the war. I grew up very fast. . . .I know what war is. Many adults do not know what war means, the way it not only kills people but hurts the soul.   —*Jasmina Kapic, 16-year-old girl in Sarajevo (1994)*

I look upon the whole world as my fatherland and every war has to me the horror of a family feud. I look upon true patriotism as the brotherhood of man and the service of all to all. The only fighting that saves is the one that helps the world toward liberty, justice and an abundant life for all.
—*Helen Keller (1880–1968)*

The suffering and privations of children do not ennoble. They frustrate and embitter. The longer the world tolerates the slow war of attrition that poverty and ignorance now wage against the millions of children in developing countries, the more likely it becomes that our hope for lasting peace in the world will be the ultimate casualty
—*Henry Labouisse, Executive Director of UNICEF from 1965 to 1979*

We will stop fighting when we love our children more than we hate our enemies.
—*A father in Lebanon in 1978*

When the young people of all nations of the world understand each other, then we shall indeed have peace on earth.
—*Gabriela Mistral (1889–1957), Nobel Prize winner for Literature*

As I watched, two things that looked like great big hideous lizards crawled in slowly, making croaking, groaning sounds. I was paralyzed with horror for minutes. Then the light got a little stronger and I could see they were human beings—skinned alive by fire or heat, their bodies all smashed where they had been thrown against something hard. . . . After a few minutes I saw something coming up the road that looked like a parade of roast chickens. . . .They were skinned. The skin of their hands had been torn away at the wrists. It was hanging from their fingertips just behind the nails, turned inside out like a glove. In the dim light I saw many other children lying all about the yard.
—*Takashi Nagai, in* We of Nagasaki *(1945)*

It will be very difficult to maintain peace as long as the gap continues to grow which separates wealthier nations from those which often have not even the minimum required for survival. We must ask ourselves whether there will continue to accumulate over the heads of this new generation of children the threat of common extermination. . . .Are the children to receive the arms race from us as a necessary inheritance?

Amplified by historic grievances and exacerbated by the manipulations of the unscrupulous, the fear of 'difference' can lead to a denial of the very humanity of 'the other', with the result that people fall into a cycle of violence in which no one is spared, not even the children. *—Pope John Paul II (1920–)*

You can no more win a war than an earthquake!
*—Jeanette Rankin (1880–1973), the only member
of the U.S. Congress to vote against declaring war in 1941*

Nothin's worth killing someone.
*—Paul Rome, 13-year-old boy in Belfast, Ireland,
when asked why he didn't want his father's murder by the IRA avenged*

I have seen war. I have seen children starving. I have seen the agony of mothers and wives. I hate war. . . .The motto of war is: "Let the strong survive; let the weak die." The motto of peace is: "Let the strong help the weak to survive."
—Franklin D. Roosevelt (1882–1945), U.S. President

We are mad, not only individually but nationally. We check manslaughter and isolated murders; but what of war and the much vaunted crime of slaughtering whole peoples? *—Seneca (54 B.C.–A.D. 39), in* Ad Lucilium

War is cruelty and you cannot refine it . . . . There is many a boy here today who looks on war as all glory, but, boys, it is all hell.
*—William T. Sherman (1820–1891),
Union general in the U.S. Civil War*

It will be a great day when our day care centers have all the money they need and the Navy has to hold a bake sale to buy battleships. *—Peter Ustinov (1921–)*

Is there any man here or any woman—let me say, is there any child—who does not know that the seed of war in the modern world is industrial and commercial rivalry? *—Woodrow Wilson (1856–1924), U.S. President*

MISCELLANEOUS ITEMS ABOUT WAR AND PEACE

Abraham and Other Fathers

Almost everyone on earth claims to hate war, yet almost every generation of fathers seems strangely willing to sacrifice the younger generation for wars they believe in. The English poet Wilfred Owen (1892–1918) was one of the 10 million boys and young men who died in World War I; he was killed in action one week before the Armistice, at age 25.

One of his poems was called "The Parable of the Old Man and the Young." It retold the story of Abraham, the patriarch of Judaism, Christianity, and Islam, about to sacrifice his son with a knife when he heard an angel call out to him from heaven saying, "Lay not thy hand upon the lad, neither do anything to him. . . .Offer the Ram of Pride instead of him."

The poet then changed the story's ending, with these words:

> But the old man would not so,
> but slew his son,
> And half the seed of Europe,
> one by one.

Abraham Lincoln and His Sons

One day, hearing the anguished cries of children in the street, one of Lincoln's neighbors in Springfield, Illinois, rushed out of his house in alarm. There he found Lincoln with two of his sons, both of whom were sobbing bitterly.

"Whatever is the matter with the boys, Mr. Lincoln?" he asked.

"Just what's the matter with the whole world," replied Lincoln resignedly. "I've got three walnuts, and each wants two."

. . .and His Enemies

Another time, towards the end of the Civil War, a group of ladies called on President Lincoln and berated him for planning a reconciliation settlement instead of determining to destroy the Union's enemies. Lincoln replied, "Am I not destroying our enemies when I change them into friends?"

Source of a Famous Antiwar Slogan

Carl Sandburg (1878–1967) was describing a battle in the Civil War to a little girl. After hearing about it, she said to him, "Supposing they gave a war and no one came?"

War Is Often Welcomed— Though This Is Not Usually Admitted

When people's lives are boring, they consciously or unconsciously welcome war. Mild-mannered, sensible Harold Macmillan, though gravely wounded and disabled in World War I, was in North Africa in 1942 and 1943 and said, "I enjoy wars. Any adventure's better than sitting in an office."

The Cost of World Armaments

UNESCO reported in 1967 that if a dollar coin were dropped each second, it would take 5,750 years, or 1,000 years more than the age of the Egyptian pyramids, for the last coin to drop of the $182 billion the world spent on armaments in one year. The United States spends nearly $1 billion every day on defense. That is like paying for the total cost of World War II every single month.

Children's Comments on the United Nations

The United Nations Association has collected letters received from school children. Among some of the choicest comments were these:

I get A's in French and so I want to be either a UN guide or an interrupter.

I am a 6th grade boy writing a report on Japan. Iwould like some odds and ends on this country. I would also like some information.

I have long admired the UN and its methods. I am l0 years old.

I am very interested in the UN because I hear so much bad material on it that I know there has to be another side to it.

Our room plans a UN Bazaar. I represent the United States. We are making objects to sell to represent our countries. I made 3 missiles.

THE DIARY OF ANNE FRANK
Anne (Annaliesa) Frank, 1929–1945

A few days after receiving a diary as a gift on her thirteenth birthday, Anne (Annaliesa) Frank (1929–1945) wrote in it:

It's an odd idea for someone like me to keep a diary, not only because I have never done so before but because it seems to me that neither I—nor for that matter anyone else—will be interested in the unbosomings of a 13-year-old schoolgirl.

How wrong she was. Less than a month after starting the diary on July 8, 1942, it contained an unexpectedly dramatic entry: "The SS [the special Nazi task force responsible for concentration camps and the principal enforcers of Hitler's policy to exterminate Jews] have sent a call-up notice for Daddy."

The family hastily went into hiding in the empty top floor of a large building that was a combination office and warehouse. Dutch friends, recently married Jan and Miep Gies, who worked in the building, hid them and one other family there at great personal risk, bringing them food and occasional gifts and news; the couple was later imprisoned as a reward for their courage and generosity.

Days stretched into weeks, weeks into months, and months into years, as Anne and her parents and several other people who joined them had to stay very quiet ("as quiet as baby mice," Anne wrote), conversation conducted rarely and only in whispers durng the day when the offices below were occupied. They were able to move around relatively freely only at nighttime—but in darkness so that no lights would show in the windows to reveal their presence. And they were never able to go outdoors even once, for two whole years.

It is surprising they were able to keep sane, and there were times when claustrophobia and boredom, personal tensions and perpetual fear took their toll on everyone, including young Anne. She was energetic and high-spirited, chafing at her confinement, longing to go outdoors and be with friends her own age, and deeply worried about the future—yet she had remarkable psychological and spiritual strength, a saving sense of humor, an affectionate nature in spite of normal teenage resentment aboutrules laid down by her mother, and an unquenchable basic idealism that shines through her diary. She shared two frequent traits of youth, an invincible love of life and an ability to have fun even during very sad circumstances. Her diary is by no means an unrelieved horror story. It is full of amusing and touching comments about herself, her parents, her friends, and thoughtful observations on the meaning of life.

Anne had been born in Frankfurt, Germany. When she was four years old her family left Germany for Holland because of the Germans' increasingly cruel persecution of Jews. For six happy years in what Anne called "this beautiful country," starting in kindergarten, Anne was a pupil in Amsterdam's Montessori School, which has since been renamed in her honor as the Anne Frank School. But in May 1940, when Hitler invaded Holland, she had to leave this school and switch to the Jewish Lyceum because the occupying Nazis forbade Jewish children to associate with non-Jewish children.

On August 4, 1944, her family's hiding place was discovered. The Dutch informant who revealed their "secret annex" to the Nazis was never identified but was probably an employee in the warehouse who received the standard reward of 60 guilders (approximately $1.40) for each person he betrayed.

Anne and her parents were in the last shipment of 1,000 Dutch Jews deported from Holland by the Nazis; in all, 100,000 were deported, jammed into freight cars and shipped to concentration camps. Her parents were held at Auschwitz, where her mother died in January 1945, less than a month before her father was freed by Russian soldiers who liberated the camp. Anne and her sister Margot were transferred to another camp at Bergen-Belsen where their sufferings finally ended when they both died in March 1945 from typhus and starvation.

It was providential that the diary survived her death. Its handwritten pages aroused no interest among the men who arrested her. They were too busy looking for money and other valuables that they could steal, so they ignored the little handwritten notebooks. But a few days later, Miep Gies went up to the apartment and discovered the diary. As a result, Anne's quiet voice became a loud one. Ernest Schnabel, author of *Anne Frank: A Portrait in Courage,* published in New York in 1958, wrote that "her voice was preserved out of the millions that were silenced, this voice no louder than a child's whisper . . . it has outlasted the shouts of the murderers and has soared above the voices of time."

The worldwide and enduring success of Anne's diary is particularly interesting in view of two entries she made in 1944. In one she said, "I want to go on living even after my death," and on May 11, 1944, just three months before she was captured and taken to the concentration camp where she died, she was particularly specific. She wrote to Kitty (her nickname for her diary), "You've known for a long time that my greatest wish is to become a journalist some day and later a famous writer. In any case, I want to publish a book entitled *Het Achterhuis* (The Secret Annex) after the war." It was only three years later that this book was published under the title Anne had chosen and her "greatest wish" came true.

When Otto Frank returned to Amsterdam after the war and learned that he was the sole survivor of the group that had shared life in the Annex (he was liberated from Auschwitz by the Russian army in Janurary, 1945, and lived to the age of 91), he read his daughter's diary and was so moved by it that he circulated it to some friends, as a private memoir. A Dutch publisher saw it and decided it deserved a wider readership. It was published in Holland under the title *Het Achterhuis* (The Secret Annex) in 1947 and immediately went into several printings. In 1950 it was translated and published in France and Germany, and in 1952 in England and the United States. In later years it was translated into more than 50 languages.

In 1955 a play called *The Diary of Anne Frank,* by Frances Goodrich and Albert Hackett, was produced on Broadway and received the Pulitzer Prize among other prestigious awards. In 1956 a Dutch version of the play opened in Amsterdam and a German version was performed in many German cities, to unexpected and universal acclaim. In 1959 the play was made into a motion picture. And in 1996 another movie called *Anne Frank Remembered* was produced. It was awarded an Oscar as the best documentary feature of the year. The movie critic of *The New Republic* said "this film deepens our connection with the story" and the critic of the *Seattle Intelligence* called it "a rare piece of history that virtually comes alive, taking your breath away with its immediacy."

Anne's father had carefully edited the diary and omitted passages he thought were indiscreet or embarrassing or too personal to publish. These include passages in which Anne recounted her emotional battles with her strict mother and worshipful ones about her adored Papa, who stuck up for her and sympathized with her. Her mother didn't understand, she complained to her diary, "that I am simply a young girl badly in need of some rollicking fun." Otto Frank also expurgated her ecstatic descriptions of her first and subsequent kisses.

The family that shared life in the Annex with the Franks included a boy about two years older than Anne, Peter Van Pels; Anne gave his family the false name of Van Daan in her diary, for their protection in case of the diary's discovery. It was inevitable that the two teenagers isolated from any other friends their age should find comfort in each other. Despite both families' vigilant efforts to chaperone them she managed to sneak into his room at times and share unsupervised confidences and eventually to become emotionally, though shyly and tentatively, involved with him. Their mutual affection grew until finally Anne's father, who felt that a 14-year-old girl was too young to be romantically involved with a boy, forbade her to spend time alone with Peter. Anne refused to obey, saying, "he loves me, and I love him." This seems to have been the only time Anne ever defied her father.

After Otto Frank died an unexpurgated edition of the diary was published, which was even more fascinating than the first edition, revealing as it did not just a youthful philosopher but a normal youngster who, in spite of her unique life in hiding, shared the warm human feelings, from teenage rebelliousness to curiosity about sex, of her age group. Deep thanks are owed to Miep Gies not only for having helped the Franks so courageously but also for having preserved the entire diary intact and finally releasing all of it to the world.

Today the building in which Anne and her family hid is a museum sponsored by the Anne Frank Foundation. Dedicated to preserving Anne's ideals of tolerance and optimism, it is visited every year by approximately 600,000 people and is the headquarters of an International Youth Center, where lectures and conferences are held. In 1993 the Foundation published another book on Anne called *Anne Frank beyond the Diary, A Photographic Remembrance*, with an eloquent introduction by Anna Quindlen. It contains a wealth of family photographs, with many charming pictures of a happy Anne playing and laughing with childhood friends and her family in the years before they had to go into hiding, plus photos of their "secret annex" revealing more than words can do just how confined they were while living there "as quietly as baby mice." One cheerful touch, however, is the wall of Anne's room, which she decorated with photos of movie stars.

In 1944 Anne had written in her diary, "I want to go on living even after my death." The circumstances of her death when she was only 15 were tragic, but at least this wish of hers has beautifully come true.

Excerpts

In the following excerpts from her diary, Anne discussed the problems of young people growing up in a world where the Nazis and war were destroying dreams of a good life.

July 6, 1944—People who have a religion should be glad, for not everyone has the gift of believing in heavenly things. You don't necessarily even have to be afraid of punishment after death; purgatory, hell and heaven are things that a lot of people can't accept, but still a religion, it doesn't matter which, keeps a person on the right path. It isn't the fear of God but the upholding of one's honor and conscience. How noble and good everyone could be if, every evening before falling asleep, they were to recall to their minds the events of the whole day and consider exactly what has been good and bad. Then, without realizing it, you try to improve yourself at the start of each new day; of course, you achieve quite a lot in the course of time. Anyone can do this, it costs nothing and is certainly very helpful. Whoever doesn't know it must learn and find by experience that: "A quiet conscience makes one strong!"

July 8, 1944—We all live, but we don't know the why or the wherefore. We all live with the object of being happy. Our lives are all different and yet the same. . . . We have the chance to learn, the possibility of attaining something, we have reason to hope for much happiness but . . . we must earn it for ourselves. And that is never easy. You must work and do good, not be lazy and gamble, if you wish to earn happiness. Laziness may *appear* attractive, but work *gives* satisfaction.

July 15, 1944—We have a book from the library with the challenging title of *What Do You Think of the Modern Young Girl?* I want to talk about this subject today. The author of this book criticizes the youth of today from top to toe without, however, condemning the whole of the young brigade as "incapable of anything good." On the contrary she is rather of the opinion that if young people wished, they have it in their hands to make a bigger, more beautiful and better world but that they occupy themselves with superficial things, without giving a thought to real beauty. In some passages, the writer gave me very much the feeling she was directing her criticism at me.

"In its innermost depths youth is lonelier than old age." I read this saying in some book and I've always remembered it and found it to be true. Is it true that grownups have a more difficult time than we do? No. I know it isn't. Older people have formed their opinions about everything, and don't waver before they act. It's twice as hard for us young ones to hold our ground, and maintain our opinions, in a time when all ideals are being shattered and destroyed, when people are showing their worst side, and we do not know whether to believe in truth and right and God.

Anyone who claims that older people have a more difficult time certainly doesn't realize to what extent our problems weigh down on us, problems for which we are probably much too young but which thrust themselves upon us continually until, after a long time, we think we have found a solution, but the solution doesn't seem able to resist the facts which reduce it to nothing again. That's the difficulty in these times: ideals, dreams and cherished hopes rise within us, only to meet the horrible truth and be shattered.

It's really a wonder that I haven't dropped all my ideals, because they seem so absurd and impossible to carry out. Yet I keep them, because *in spite of everything I still believe that people are really good at heart*. I simply can't build up my hopes on a foundation consisting of confusion, misery, and death. I see the world gradually being turned into a wilderness. I hear the ever approaching thunder which will destroy us too. I can feel the sufferings of millions and yet, if I look up into the heavens, I think that it will all come right, that this cruelty too will end, and that peace and tranquillity will return again.

LEGACY OF THE VIETNAM WAR: AMERASIAN CHILDREN

It is no secret that many American soldiers during the Vietnam War comforted themselves by having amorous relationships with Vietnamese girls. Many of the girls got pregnant, and when their men finished their tours of duty, in a modern update of the opera *Madame Butterfly*, they went away and left the mothers alone with the living reminders of their romances. It has been estimated that 30,000 children were fathered and abandoned by American servicemen and civilian workers. Many of the children were not the result of one-night stands but of longstanding family relationships. Yet when the men had a chance to go back home, they left their women and children, often walking away without a backward glance, sometimes promising to stay in touch but forgetting the promises after they were back in the States.

Thus thousands of single mothers were left behind, and they had extra problems in addition to raising their children alone. In Vietnam children who are half-American (Amerasian) are usually considered inferior. They are scorned and hounded by other Vietnamese.

Since 1982 about 3,000 Amerasians and their relatives had emigrated to the United States, primarily for economic reasons, but 8,800 more have applied for—and not been given—exit visas. Few have any hope of finding their natural fathers, and only a handful of U.S. servicemen have tried to get in contact with their Vietnamese children. In December 1987, the first group since January 1986 was permitted to leave, and U.S. State Department officials said that all those who wanted to emigrate would be resettled in the United States by 1990.

The sympathies and conscience of at least two prominent American women were deeply touched by the plight of these children, and they did something about it. Following are their stories.

Pearl Buck, Best-selling Author (1892–1973)

Pearl Buck was American, but she spent her childhood and part of her adult life in China. Her parents were missionaries and she was raised by a devoted *amah,* the Chinese word for a nanny. Her first novel, *The Good Earth*, written in 1931 and set in China, won her the unusual dual distinction of a Pulitzer Prize and a Nobel Prize. When the Vietnam war began to involve the United States she was torn in her sympathies as an American who still felt a close affinity with Asians. And she was horrified as she began hearing about how many American servicemen were cohabiting with Vietnamese girls and producing babies whom they left behind when they returned home. She knew how people in Asia feel about "half-breeds," so she worried about these children who were sure to face both poverty and discrimination.

Buck did not know what she could do about it, however, until one day she saw in a newspaper a photograph of a little Amerasian girl, and fell in love! She decided to try to find the child and adopt her. She wrote a lovely, honest poem, admitting that she had tried to find excuses not to get involved, but ending with the line, "Too late, too late! I've looked into your eyes." She found the girl, brought her to America, and made her part of her family. And then she did more. She wrote another poem to urge other people to help those she called "outcasts and half-persons and children of the dust."

> The years between birth and
> adulthood are swift and few.
> Whatever way you choose to help,
> let it be now, I beg of you.

She then established the Pearl S. Buck Foundation at her farm in Green Hills, Perkasie, Pennsylvania, which arranged to bring Amerasian children to America, keeping them with her until she could place them with other families. And she made out a will to guarantee that the foundation's work would continue after she died. With the support of many people, including Alan Alda, whose work on the TV show *M.A.S.H.* had made him aware of and sympathetic to the problems of children in Korea who had been fathered and deserted by Americans, it has continued to help Amerasian children after her death.

Kitty Kelly and "Those Kids I Couldn't Forget"

Kelly was a news commentator on NBC when she made a trip to Saigon in 1988 out of curiosity about the country that had played such a painful part in America's history. And when she got there she could not help noticing the blonde, fair-skinned, and sometimes blue-eyed children, whom she said could have been in Norman Rockwell paintings but instead were living on the streets or in ramshackle buildings. She spent days with them and saw how curious and eager they were to speak English and learn about America's geography and history, although a local official told her they were stupid and not worth bothering with.

When Kelly returned to New York and her glamorous and high-paying job on television, she found she could not get those kids out of her mind. Before working on TV she had been a teacher, so she decided to go back to Vietnam and teach them. She nearly choked on all the red tape she encountered as she tried to find a classroom to use, until one day she met an Amerasian teenager named Jim. Jim's life story was sadly typical: his father, a helicopter mechanic, had lived with Jim's mother Lan for five years before leaving without a word when the Communists swept down on Saigon in 1975 and helicopters airlifted out the last remaining Americans. Jim, then four years old, ran outside, crying "Daddy, Daddy! I'm here, come get me!" but he and his mother never saw or heard from him again.

Jim took Kelly to his home, a small, shabby apartment, and Lan pointed out a small corner, saying she could use that for a classroom. For five hours a day that corner was school for up to a dozen or more youngsters. Sometimes the kids said they had headaches and stomachaches; then Kelly realized they were hungry. So at mealtime she took them out to street stands and bought them rice and chicken or, if there were not too many of them, she continued the classes in a sit-down restaurant.

Kelly marveled at the generosity of this family who it seemed had nothing to give. When they discovered a young homeless Amerasian boy abandoned by both parents and sleeping on the street, Lan did not hesitate to take him into her already crowded home. "He can stay here. He good boy. No problem." Kitty felt that across the miles and the years, a kinship linked her with these people, because she too had grown up in poverty in Nebraska, in a house that did not have indoor plumbing and sometimes no heat. She had worn cast-off clothes sent by a cousin in California. Yet, as part of a big family that included some wonderful relatives, she had a very happy childhood. Her parents were always as generous as Lan was, sharing whatever they had with people who needed help.

By the end of the year, because of the Amerasian Homecoming Act, many of the kids Kelly had become close to were at last being resettled in America by the U.S. government. She knew they would need help adjusting, so she moved back to New York and sponsored some of them. Some moved in with her until they were resettled in other parts of the country. She wrote a book called *A Year in Saigon* and donated the proceeds from it to St. Rita's Asian Center and other groups that were helping Amerasians. St. Rita's was a resettlement agency working with Vietnamese refugees in the New York City area, which offered an alternative high school for Amerasians, job training and placement, and a clothing bank. Kitty worked there three or four days a week after discovering it, tutoring and helping to organize activities.

Other People Who Have Also Befriended These Children

It would be unfair to imply that these two women were the only people who have helped Amerasian children. For example, William Fero, a wounded combat veteran who lost both of his legs in the war and had to spend the rest of his life in a wheelchair, returned home in 1971 and by 1988 had taken 49 Vietnamese refugees into his home in the United States.

In 1987 a group of American veterans returned to Vietnam to try to exorcise their nightmares of their times there. They made friends with the Amerasian children they met as crowds of them walked together on the street in Ho Chi Minh City. They had imagined them as small children and were startled to realize how much time had passed; after all these years, the children were no longer children but young adults, some of them with children of their own.

A reporter and photographer who was traveling with the ex-soldiers remembers how the "children" ran to her side, grabbed her hand, and through their tears said, "You my mother, you my sister." She looked in their eyes and felt very sad: "So this is what we left behind." Bombed-out buildings had been rebuilt, bomb craters had been filled, but these children, more than 15,000 of them, were daily reminders of those years of war.

The reporter learned that many of these young people lived on the streets without any home or parents, and made their living begging from foreigners or selling small trinkets and chewing gum. Their only dream was to go to the United States, and every morning dozens of them gathered in front of the city's Foreign Affairs Office to wait there until sundown, hoping that today would be the day that their exit papers would come through.

Then the reporter learned that not all of these young people wanted to leave Vietnam. One boy named Tuan, who had been abandoned by both his father and his mother at birth, told her a town had taken him in and "raised me as one of their own," and he was happy to stay just where he was. She was happy to realize that the generalizations she had heard about how all Amerasians were treated badly were exaggerated. She was also comforted to realize that most Vietnamese, despite years of hardship and pain, had managed to put the war behind them. Tunnels, which during the war had been a vast underground supply network for the Viet Cong and one of the most fearful places for American soldiers, were now a tourist attraction where young children played hide-and-seek.

One night in a small town outside Hanoi, the reporter and the American soldiers met a former North Vietnamese army regular who had been stationed at the same place and the same time as one of the visiting veterans. When they realized they had fought each other in 1969 and survived, they hugged and kissed, and then the Vietnamese man, who was there with his young daughter, placed the girl on the American's lap and the two men cried. Enemies can become friends.

REPORTING FROM THE FORMER YUGOSLAVIA

Edith Simmons spent a year working as information and liaison officer in the office of the UNICEF special representative to the republics of the former Yugoslavia. During that time, she traveled throughout Croatia, Serbia, and Bosnia-Herzegovina on a regular basis and undertook 12 missions to the besieged city of Sarajevo. Simmons initiated the "I Dream of Peace" project, which encouraged children in schools and refugees to use writing or drawing as a means of expressing their emotions. She later conceived the idea for the book *I Dream of Peace*, a collection of writings and drawings by these children, with a preface by the author-illustrator Maurice Sendak, who says, "Who better than children to sum up, without artifice or sentimentality, the monumental stupidity of war!" Here are her observations:

The war in the former Yugoslavia is not my first. The first was in Lebanon, in 1982, a month after the notorious Sabra and Chatila massacre. As I came face to face, for the first time, with the brutal reality of war, I realized that there is one aspect of a conflict that television can never convey to viewers: the pervasive smell of fear, of helplessness, of hate, and of destruction—a smell as unforgettable as the putrid stench of decaying bodies trapped under destroyed buildings or rotting in shallow graves.

Whether wars happen in the Middle East, in Africa, or in Europe, they all present the same horrific picture of vulnerable civilians—mostly women and children unable to protect themselves—being terrorized, humiliated, forced to abandon their homes, or being wounded or killed.

The war in the former Yugoslavia really challenged some of my thinking and shattered a few assumptions. I had never imagined for a moment that another war in Europe would ever be allowed to erupt with such force. As a child who grew up in the aftermath of World War II, I trusted the promise of my elders when they vowed "Never again."

If the majority of contemporary wars—there are 32 taking place in the world at the time of this writing [summer of 1994] can in the main be blamed on lack of information, lack of education, and extreme poverty, one of the most chilling factors of the war in the former Yugsolavia is that the worst violence is often orchestrated by well-informed and highly educated individuals, who use both modern and medieval tactics to terrorize the civilian populations, to maim, and to kill—all in the name of a very virulent strain of nationalism. "It begins with the desire to save your own culture, and it ends with the hatred of others," says a friend who has been a witness to the volatile struggle for some time.

From the outset, no one seemed able to stem the violence. The hatred quickly reached epidemic proportions, pitting neighbor against neighbor, erasing every last trace of normal existence, and destroying children's lives and their hopes for the future. Many ethnically mixed families have separated since the start of the war, and the children, confused and depressed, do not know which way to turn any more.

The majority of the victims of the notorious practice of "ethnic cleansing" (which has now forced nearly 4 million people, mainly women and children, into exile) were totally taken by surprise and are still completely bewildered as to the causes of the hatred or the reason for the war. Now they cannot see how the conflict and the hate will be resolved. "Do you think our neighbors will be able to look at us when we return?" asked one litle girl who saw her house being burned and her father beaten by their former friends and neighbors.

During my year in the former Yugoslavia, I encountered some of the most evil people, blinded by rage and hatred, and some of the most heroic, dedicated, and peace-loving individuals. While some people are still bent on destroying, others are sparing no effort to rebuild shattered lives—bringing in humanitarian aid, repairing broken bodies and broken minds, and helping children to overcome their worst pains: their traumas and their psychological nightmares.

UNICEF estimates that some 1.5 million children are now psychologically war-traumatized. The closeness of the violence—when the perpetrator is the neighbor, the friend, the work colleague, or even a family member—has seldom been seen before, at least not in contemporary wars. But hundreds of thousands of children in the former Yugoslavia know the violence that originates close to home only too well. They have seen it all: their house being burned down, their father being beaten, their relatives being raped, tortured, taken away to camps, or killed.

Tormenting Flashbacks

Many of these children do not believe they will make it to adulthood. They are full of sorrow and fear; they have nightmares, they cannot concentrate, and some have become very aggressive. These children need to talk to someone they can trust, who is prepared to listen, who understands, and who can put the pieces together for the healing to start. UNICEF has taken on this challenge and is training local psychologists, teachers, social workers, and parents to recognize the children's symptoms and to help them, through relaxation, group discussions, and art therapy, to overcome some of their worst experiences.

"Before the war, we were just like any other school," says the headmistress of a school close to one of the frontlines, where such a program is in place. "But now, after talking together openly about the war, our pain, and our losses, we are so close—just like a family."

Often children remain silent about the tormenting flashbacks, and it is easy for the adults, themselves traumatized and fearful, to think that the children may not have understood everything that happened. But nothing could be further from the truth.

"Children have the most sensitive antennae," says Professor Magne Raundalen, a Norwegian child psychologist. "When I sit down with a child, I think, 'You have so heavy a burden, give it to me. I can carry it for you.' And I open my hands like that." (He cups his hands together like a vessel ready to be filled.) "So I show the children that I will take some of the pain, some of this heavy burden, for them."

I learned a lot from listening to the children's experiences, as I often had the privilege of accompanying Magne Raundalen or Rune Stuvland, the UNICEF psychologist for the former Yugoslavia, on their visits to refugee camps, schools, and hospitals. The children's names, their faces, their voices, and especially what the war has done to them, I shall remember to the end of my life.

Sadly for humanity, the struggle in the former Yugoslavia demonstrates clearly that our civilization is still in the Dark Ages when it comes to respecting humanitarian conventions. The hatred and violence that fuel the conflict are as raw and as primitive as the face of unleashed chaos. Children have seen that malevolence, and they have experienced it; many have been wounded and killed by grenades and snipers' bullets deliberately aimed at them.

But no one should be allowed to sabotage the children's future with such impunity. That is why the UNICEF program to help war-traumatized children is so crucial. The process will lead, gradually, to tolerance education and I hope will afford children the choice they need to have—between more violence or peace—when they themselves reach adulthood.

"Goodness Will Win at the End"

As part of the psychological program for war-traumatized children, the UNICEF I Dream of Peace project asked children in over 50 schools and refugee camps in the former Yugoslavia to draw and write about their situation and their hopes for the future. In the drawings, pain and creativity have united to produce works of art. Some children used colors with passion, to show destruction and fear; others drew in black only, a reflection of their mourning and deep sorrow. Where the children have chosen words rather than pictures to express their feelings, the images strike a chord inside everyone who knows—without personal experience of the war—the burning pain of injustice, the fear of violence, or the anxiety of waiting for news of a loved one.

Despite their trauma and their sorrow, the children have two wishes: the first is for the war to end and for peace to return to their homeland; the second is that no other children in the world should have to experience what they have gone through.

In one of the drawings, filled with some of the ugliest sights of the war—bombs falling from the sky, houses pockmarked by bullets, people lying wounded or dead on the ground—a nine-year-old boy has put himself in the picture, a tiny figure on the edge of the drawing. The caption reads: "Goodness will win at the end."

I pray that nothing will ever force him to change his mind.

Zlata's Diary: A Vivid Account of How War Affects Children

In September 1991, an 11-year-old girl named Zlata Filipovic who lived in Sarajevo, in Bosnia-Herzegovina, began keeping a diary. She was the only child of a middle-class couple of mixed Muslim, Croat, and Serb descent. She had just ended a happy summer vacation in the country with her father, a lawyer, and her mother, a biochemist, and her close-knit family of grandparents, aunts, and cousins, and was getting ready for a new year at school. She was an *A* student who took tennis and piano lessons and had a passion for pizza, MTV, and Michael Jackson. She said, "I wanted to have a happy memory from a happy childhood. I wanted 20 years after to open that funny book and read about the things that happened."

The first entries in Zlata's diary were about movies, parties, school, music, vacation trips, and visits with friends, but soon an ominous note intruded. In parts of the land that used to be Yugoslavia war had broken out, and on television she saw scary news broadcasts showing how the lovely city of Dubrovnik was being destroyed; people were starving, being injured, and killed. Zlata asked "Why? For what? Politics, it seems, but I don't understand politics."

Later in her diary, she said,

> I've been thinking about politics again. No matter how stupid, ugly and unreasonable I think this division of people into Serbs, Croats and Muslims is, these stupid politics are making it happen. . . maps are being drawn up, separating people. . . Those 'kids' [a local slang term for politicians] really are playing around with us. Ordinary people don't want this division, because it won't make anybody happy. . . . But who asks ordinary people?

While worrying about the troubles in Dubrovnik, Zlata wondered if "the winds of war" could blow from there to Sarajevo, but decided, "No, that's impossible."

In April 1992, however, the impossible happened. Sarajevo was bombed. On April 5 she wrote: "I'm trying to concentrate so I can do my homework but I simply can't. Something is going on in town. You can hear gunfire from the hills . . . my stomach is still in knots. . . ."

Zlata continued her diary throughout 1992 and ended it in October 1993, writing that she wished "THAT THIS STUPID WAR WOULD END!"

Originally the diary was published by UNICEF in Croat. The English language version, *Zlata's Diary: A Child's Life in Sarajevo*, published by Viking Press, includes an eloquent introduction to the many color photographs of Zlata, her family, and friends, plus reproductions of pages from the diary with delightful drawings by Zlata.

Janine di Giovanni, a French journalist who worked in Sarajevo and met Zlata and her parents in 1993, and a French photographer, Alexandra Boulat, took copies of the diary to a French publisher, Laffont/Fixot, who agreed to publish it and also to help Zlata and her parents escape from Sarajevo. On December 23, 1993, they at last got away, transported from their home in armored vehicles by the French UN contingent, and were taken to Paris in a French government plane. Di Giovanni says she once asked Zlata about her dreams, and Zlata said, "I used to dream about the beach, somewhere warm, but when there is shelling, I only think about being safe." So it was good news that she and her parents were now safe at last—but this was not yet a truly happy ending, not only because they had to leave beloved friends and relatives behind, but also because they learned that just two days after their arrival in Paris—on Christmas Day—five more children in Sarajevo were killed when the Serbs shelled a kindergarten.

Zlata, in an interview, said this was "a war between idiots, not between Serbs and Croats and Muslims. They're crazy. Even when they're signing a cease-fire, we could hear the boom of shells landing." And she reminded reporters that there were 70,000 or so children under the age of 15 who were still in Sarajevo. Among them were children who had lost parents, brothers, sisters, and friends, children still sitting in the dark, hungry and terrified by the continued shelling, and that it was for these children that her diary had been published. The publisher and Zlata had both agreed to contribute some of their royalties to relief agencies that were helping Sarajevo's children.

The French edition of the book, published in December 1993, immediately went to the top of France's list of nonfiction best sellers. Rights to the book were soon sold to 25 other countries, and Universal Studios in Hollywood paid $1 million for film rights. A few weeks after coming to Paris, Zlata traveled to Germany, Holland, and Italy to publicize the book, and in March 1994, she arrived in the United States for a promotional tour. As one reporter on the tour, Alan Riding, wrote,

> The diary's instant success suggests that even in a world numbed by television
> images of daily atrocities in Sarajevo, in a Western Europe racked by guilt over
> its failure to halt the 21-month-old conflict in Bosnia and Herzegovina, the
> voice of an innocent child still carries special weight.

Girls Face Special Terrors in Wartime: Rape

In l992, in the former Yugoslavia, girls faced another special terror in addition to bombs and shells. It seems that the Serbs, as part of their determination to subdue their enemies, instituted a systematic campaign of sexual abuse, ordering their soldiers to rape girls in the areas they conquered.

No one knows how many victims there have been, but estimates have ranged from 30,000 to 50,000. There were reports of repeated rapes of girls as young as six and seven, including rapes of young girls performed in front of their fathers, mothers, siblings, and other children. Some gang rapes were so brutal that the victims died.

The UN Security Council, citing "massive, organized, and systematic detention and rape," voted unanimously in December 1992 to condemn "atrocities committed against women, particularly Muslim women, in Bosnia and Herzegovina." But as so repeatedly happened in this bitter war, verbal condemnations probably had little effect in changing behavior.

Among all the horror stories, however, three revealed a glimmer of humanity in at least three soldiers. A Muslim virgin reported that she was rounded up with 400 other women, then picked out of the crowd along with one other girl, also a virgin, by two soldiers, who took turns raping them both. Afterwards the soldiers laughed at them and told them they were pretty and that they were glad they had saved themselves for them. The men then dumped them in a yard, but one of them came back to bring her to his commander, who told her to take off her clothes and lie down on his bed. He started to kiss and caress her—when she looked into his eyes and asked him if he had a wife. He said no. She then asked if he had a sister. He said he had one. Then she said, "How would your sister feel if somebody did the same thing to her that you are doing to me?" At that he jumped up and told her to get dressed and leave.

Another girl also told a story indicating that a few men were not as evil as the others. She was grabbed by a soldier who took her away and lay down next to her, and then whispered, "I'm only going to pretend, but don't let anyone know."

In October, 1992, a Muslim schoolgirl, Rahima Siladzic, described to a reporter how a group of Serb soldiers who had been drinking taunted her and some friends, saying, "How many rapes today? How many good Serbian babies are we going to make?" One of the soldiers then led her to a nearby house. She was stunned by what happened next. He said, "Look, I don't want to hurt you. But I have to pretend to rape you and you have to pretend you were raped."

Land Mines

When wars are over they are not really over, because during every modern war APMs (antipersonnel mines) are planted in the ground and stay there until they are accidentally stepped on when they explode and someone promptly loses an arm or a leg or is blinded or has his head blown off. According to the U.S. State Department, nearly 2,000 people are killed or injured by land mines each month, and 90 percent of them are civilians.

Ostensibly, these vicious little weapons are meant to harm enemy soldiers, but they are also intended to prevent the cultivation of fields, so every time peasants go to work they are risking their lives, and so is every child who runs out to play in an open field.

Up to 110 million active mines are believed to be scattered in 64 countries. In sub-Saharan Africa, 20 years of war have left about 15 million mines in Angola, at least one for every man, woman, and child in the area. In East Asia, 23 million mines are known to have been planted, 10 million in Cambodia alone. In Latin America, approximately 240,000 mines are in the region, with thousands on the disputed border between Ecuador and Peru. And in Eastern and Central Europe, seven million mines exist, including about three million of an especially deadly high-tech type in Bosnia.

They are called "the classic poor man's weapon" because they are inexpensive. Small mines costing as little as 3 dollars each, the ones that most often cripple civilians, are therefore favorite weapons of guerillas in countries like Afghanistan, Eritrea, Ethiopia, Mozambique, Somalia, and Sudan. But though cheap to purchase and install, they are difficult and expensive to destroy. Most of them cannot be located by metal detectors, and they have a long life, except for a new type that is designed to self-destruct after a set time. The cost of clearing one land mine ranges between $300 and $1,000. The cost of ridding the world of them would be $33 billion in 1996 but even more in future years, because more are constantly being put down. In 1994 two million new mines were planted, 20 times as many as were removed.

In 1989 the Women's Commission for Refugee Women and Children was founded. This is the only organization in the U.S. that specifically targets the needs of women and children affected by war, violence, persecution, and famine. It got involved in efforts to ban land mines after some of its representatives visited Cambodia and interviewed women and children who had suffered from contact with mines. It has joined with several hundred relief, religious, and veterans' groups and other nongovernmental organizations to launch, in 1992, an International Campaign to Ban Landmines. At its headquarters in Palo Alto, California, the Women's Commission has a resource office to serve as a base for petitions, letter writing, and poster campaigns to outlaw these weapons.

In 1996 the Vietnam Veterans of America Foundation was joined by at least a dozen retired U.S. generals, including former Joint Chiefs of Staff chairman David Jones, Desert Storm commander Norman Schwarzkopf and former NATO commander John Galvin, in calling for an immediate ban on production and use of AMPs. They are manufactured and sold by 36 countries, but 24 countries were now joining the demand to outlaw these weapons forever.

What Is It Like to Try to Help These Children?

Even though it is amazing how wars bring out the darkest, most ruthless and violent tendencies in people, it seems equally—or even more—amazing that anyone not personally involved in a war would be willing to risk getting involved in an effort to help the victims. We read about the constant tortures and killings and wonder if or how members of organizations such as CARE, Doctors without Boundaries, Human Rights Watch, the International Rescue Committee, the Red Cross, Save the Children, UNICEF, and others who ask us to help them help other people can actually do anything to alleviate such violence. Do real people actually go voluntarily into danger zones, risking their own lives in order to help total strangers? And even if they are that generous and that brave, are they actually able to make any difference amidst the mayhem? What are these people like, and what enables them to keep going in such ghastly circumstances?

Here are excerpts from a report called *Sarajevo Journal* by Mia Drake Brandt, director of communications for the U.S. Committee for UNICEF, which describes what life is like for some of these relief workers:

> In late October l993, I traveled to Sarajevo in order to film a TV spot to fundraise for the children and women victims of war in the former Yugoslavia. Rather than using the usual approach—general footage of the conflict's horrors, with a professional narrator speaking to the audience—we wanted the UNICEF workers who work there day after day to describe the desperate situation in their own words . . . .

I flew in on a UN military plane with about 20 soldiers and relief workers. Half an hour outside Sarajevo, we were told to put on our flak jackets and helmets because the planes are regularly shot at. My excitement at entering a war zone was quickly muted with apprehension and a touch of dread. As a news producer, I had been in combat situations before in Nicaragua and the Middle East. But now, as the mother of two young children, I had not allowed myself to focus on the risk I was taking because I so much wanted to complete this assignment. Looking at the unsmiling, tense face of the soldier next to me, I wondered if this time I'd gone a little too far.

The atmosphere was extremely tense around the airport because the Bosnian Army and the Serbs were positioned on either side of the runway with weapons trained on each other....(During the three weeks after my visit, two people in separate incidents were hit getting on and off this plane.)

The drive between the airport and the UNICEF office was through a decimated no man's land where shelling was common. Right before my visit, a woman from a European relief organization had gotten out of her car on that route to take a picture and had been killed instantly by a shell.

A Thousand Shells

UNICEF's offices are in the same building that houses the UN troops and I had told myself that I'd be safe staying there, but the barracks seemed to be under fire as much as any place else, and almost every window was broken from being hit . . . . there was sniper activity in the parking lot that I and my colleagues walked in and out of many times a day, and you could still see the holes in the ground from shells that had killed two people there in recent months.

Generally, the atmosphere in the office was one of intense focus, as well as tension and fatigue. For the four days I was there, we could hear constant gunfire and shelling as we went about our work. During one of those days, more than a thousand shells fell on Sarajevo, not to mention a constant barrage of automatic weapons fire. There were signs all over the walls to stay away from the windows, and sandbags were piled near every possible opening.

Many of the UNICEF staff are Bosnians, and nearly all have stories of being separated from their husbands, wives, children, or parents. The staff work on the water supply, coordinate nutrition and health programs, and run counseling programs for traumatized children. Many UNICEF staff slept on the floor of the office because it was safer than other places and allowed them to avoid traveling around the city.

The streets were empty of running vehicles except those of the relief and military effort, with rows and rows of destroyed cars lining the main road. We drove everywhere in Sarajevo at about 80 miles an hour, not just to make it harder for the snipers to hit us, but because if they did, the aerodynamics would deflect the bullets upward once we were speeding. UNICEF uses bulletproof vehicles, but the staff joke that they would prefer not to test their effectiveness. Of course in any case, they would be useless protection against shells . . . .

The town was eerily devoid of the sounds of human life. Small groups of adolescent boys roamed about, thin as rails beneath their baggy clothing from a subsistence diet of stale white bread, plus whatever they can beg from the relief workers.

The only place large groups of people gathered was around the town's few water sources. The grey, grim facial expressions are what I remember most about Sarajevo, as people hauled water, jogged through the streets to avoid snipers, dug in the city parks for roots to eat, or talked in hushed tones in doorways. The only, and rare, smiles were from children, who seemed quietly mature and kind with each other.

On my second day, we headed downtown for our first interview. We stopped and set up our equipment where the camera crew said we would be relatively safe because the rubble from shelled buildings had collapsed to form a wall between us and the snipers just across the river. We had been out of the car just three minutes when two shells whizzed past us about 400 yards away. I'll never forget that sickening high-pitched squealing sound and how we all cowered helplessly together.

A Precariously Cruel World

We moved locations to what used to be the university library and was now a protected but destroyed pile of rubble, where we did our first interview with a UNICEF worker. The moment after we finished filming, we turned around to see a small gang of thugs running towards us, all armed with guns. They attacked us, roughly ripping our flak jackets off our bodies, yanking our helmets off our heads, and then sauntering away . . . .

My last night in Sarajevo was spent at the Holiday Inn. Half of it was literally blown away, and there was no electricity, water or elevator service. It was surreal: a handful of guests wandering around this huge luxury hotel with flashlights, while homeless families gathered outside on the street hoping to go through the garbage.

The next day I left, flying out on the military plane with a French UN soldier, who had been shot in the head, writhing in pain on a stretcher at my feet.

The amazing thing to me was not that wartime conditions were so brutal, but that I acclimated to them and that they so quickly became my norm. It's when you leave the war zone that some depression and aftershock set in, and you more fully understand the suffering you have just witnessed.

But of course the magic of seeing UNICEF's work firsthand is that you are left with years of extra motivation and inspiration. Sharing four days of vulnerability and terror with the people of Sarajevo left me with deep questions about good and evil and made me face the fact that I cannot protect even my own two children in such a precariously cruel world. But it has also made me more determined and energetic than ever and has filled me with gratitude that I can spend my days working to protect and nurture children who need us so much.

1965: THE YEAR WHEN CHILDREN WON THE NOBEL PEACE PRIZE

On October 25, 1965, Henry R. Labouisse, who was then the executive director of UNICEF, issued a statement to the press announcing that he had just received a telegram from Oslo stating that the Nobel Committee of the Norwegian Parliament had awarded the Nobel Peace Prize for 1965 to the United Nations Children's Fund. Pandemonium broke out at UNICEF's headquarters on the eighteenth floor of the UN Secretariat Building.

That afternoon one small boy in New York ran to his father, a newspaper correspondent at the UN, with the excited announcement, "Hey, Dad! We just won the Nobel Prize!" By "we" he meant his classmates and himself, who went "trick or treating" for UNICEF every year. He could just as easily have extended this "we" to include all the other children around the world who have helped UNICEF or who have been helped by it. This was truly their prize. Fostering universal friendship among these children was what gave UNICEF its right to the prize, because, according to the terms of Alfred Nobel's will, the Peace Prize is to be awarded each year to the person or organization that "shall have done the most or the best work for brotherhood among nations. . ."

UNICEF's specific task has always been to strengthen the foundations of peace by providing a better life for the world's children, and its working philosophy has always been that any child in need, anywhere, deserves help, regardless of his or her race, color, creed, political persuasion, or nationality. But an equally important aspect of its work has been the creation of a bond between needy children and those who are more fortunate.

UNICEF's National Committees have sent lecturers and exhibits into schools to inform children about the needs of those in developing nations and to tell them what UNICEF does to help them. Study guides, wall charts, photo exhibits, maps, posters, quizzes, special songs and recordings, films and filmstrips, books and booklets, stories and plays written to be performed for, or by, schoolchildren have brought knowledge of suffering children to the attention of luckier ones. This information has become part of children's studies of history and geography, and the interest aroused has met a generous response from children who have organized many special projects, including fund-raising.

The first nongovernmental contribution to UNICEF came from a group of grade-school children in Carson, Washington, who donated $2.19 in 1947. Who but children would have thought they could do anything important to improve the world with just $2.19? But these children did. Their contribution quickly inspired many other contributions, both individually and from groups such as the Scouts organizations, schools, and youth clubs.

In 1950 another group of naive children in a small Sunday school class, following a suggestion from the Reverend Clyde M. Allison of the Presbyterian Church in Bridesburg, Pennsylvania, went out on Halloween and collected $17 for UNICEF. This was the first "trick or treat for UNICEF" program, which surprisingly transformed the night of Halloween from its tradition of the one night of the year when children felt free to engage in mischievous, often destructive, pranks like slashing tires and breaking windows, into an evening when they found it just as much fun to do something generous. The example of these children spread like a forest fire. By 1965 over 3 million children in more than 13,000 communities were "trick or treating for UNICEF" and they collected $2 million.

The idea caught on in Canada, too; its first Halloween collection raised $15,000 and the amount grew each year to over $400,000 by 1965. "Nobel Prize winners in disguise," as the children were often called, looking like goblins, witches, clowns, fierce monsters, and anything else a childish imagination could invent, held parties or went door-to-door seeking financial contributions to help support UNICEF's work.

These children knew that the pennies and dimes they collected on Halloween helped UNICEF save the lives of other children. As President John Kennedy said, "UNICEF has caught the imagination of our people—especially our children, whose Halloween collections have become a symbol of concern and an expression of tangible aid."

Ambassador Hambre of Norway at a meeting of the twenty-first General Assembly in 1966, saying he was speaking on behalf of his own country and also of Denmark, Finland, Iceland, and Sweden, made a speech in which he said that UNICEF's gifts to "all the healthy, happy, and robust children in the world" were as valuable as the help it gave underprivileged children, because through UNICEF these more fortunate children "learn the joy of giving—this is a precious gift UNICEF has given these children." By making possible "concrete individual action" UNICEF is teaching them "the profound importance of personal contributions" and of "good deeds." The members of the next generation will be "nearer neighbors to each other than the people of our generation," he said, and "the future of the race depends on their being good neighbors."

The Worldwide Response to the Award

The world's press spread the good news quickly and enthusiastically, with headlines, pictures, articles, and editorials. For once, people everywhere agreed. Whether the writers were capitalists or communists, Arabs, Jews, Christians, agnostics, or atheists, from the West or from the East, from the North or from the South, in every language the words were similar: "wonderful news," "hearty congratulations," "we are overjoyed," "never was an award so aptly made," and so forth.

Why were so many people, in so many countries, so thoroughly pleased? They gave many reasons. It was because the award recognized work on behalf of children, "the innocent victims of mankind's oldest enemies—disease, hunger and ignorance"; and "because every child in the world is important" and UNICEF "maintains the dignity and worth and value of the individual"; and because the work is nonpartisan, "a difficult but vital task" meeting "a need which has no measure and knows no politics"; and because the effort was unprecedented, "the unparalleled accomplishments of UNICEF, unique in history, saved a whole generation of children," succeeding "in the face of seemingly insurmountable obstacles"; and because UNICEF's work is not merely idealistic but extremely concrete and "a practical way to search for a durable peace."

Norway's "Minor Peace Prize"

Inspired by the action of their Parliament in giving 1965's Nobel Peace Prize to UNICEF, a spontaneous grassroots movement was launched to raise funds for an extra gift from the Norwegian people themselves. Schools, private organizations, and individuals began urging the United Nations Association of Norway to do "something extra." The challenge caught on and the campaign spread through the press, radio, and television.

Pan Gathe Strand, press secretary of Norway's UNA in 1965, issued a press release that described what happened:

> Everyone was asked to make a contribution to UNICEF—or more exactly, to make a contribution to the millions of children all over the world who suffer from disease and hunger and malnutrition. People raised money in a variety of ways—there was no lack of imagination or dedicated effort: the students in teacher training colleges in Oslo and Bergen all got a few days off from school in order to sell UNICEF cards and seals. Some put loudspeakers in their cars and drove through the streets; others set themselves up on street corners with phonographs and played sentimental chorales as they requested donations. Even in the 16 degree below zero weather, people stopped and opened their purses. Some elementary school classes gave benefit performances and invited parents. Others baked cakes and sold them. The first amount given to the "minor peace prize" was 1,000 Kroner (U.S. $140) raised at a meeting of a youth association in Oslo. A successful lyric poetry performance was arranged in the University of Oslo by the organization "En Verden Ungom" (One World Youth) and by the Youth Group of the United Nations Asssociation.

When delegates from UNICEF arrived in Oslo on December 8, they were greeted by the sight of students and teachers standing in strategic parts of the city selling UNICEF seals and cards. At this time of year Norway shows the reverse side of its fame as "the Land of the Midnight Sun." In contrast to its long sun-filled summer days and nights, the days in winter are dark and cold and brief. The sun was already setting at two o'clock in the afternoon, but even in the dark, in a freezing snowstorm, people were out on the streets helping UNICEF.

On the evening of December 9 a gala benefit show was held for UNICEF in the Norwegian Opera House, donated rent-free for the occasion; the entire staff of the Opera House and a large group of Norway's most important artists had all agreed to perform without fee.

Danny Kaye, the American comedian who was UNICEF's world-famous "Ambassador at Large," arrived just in time to perform in the last act of the show. He had flown to Oslo direct from his television studio in Hollywood, piloting his own airplane emblazoned with the name "UNICEF." This was the same plane he flew across the United States each October greeting children at every major airport, to publicize and recruit kids for "trick or treat for UNICEF." A small boy had been assigned to come forward on the stage to present Danny with a miniature Viking ship, but the youngster was suddenly overcome with stage fright and was unable to utter a word of his prepared welcome speech. Danny, who had a magical touch with children, took him on his knee, whispered in his ear, and managed to make him giggle, but still the boy could not speak. Finally, Danny presented the ship to himself, playing both parts. The audience roared with laughter and gave him a standing ovation. Nearly 40,000 kroner (U.S. $5,620) were raised for UNICEF at this performance.

The result of the Norwegian people's generous drive to supplement the Nobel Prize with a "minor peace prize" of their own was overwhelming. How big this "minor" prize would finally be was not yet known at the time of the Oslo ceremonies, but it was already clear that it would at least equal the cash value of the Nobel Prize itself (U.S. $54,000).

The presentation speech was given by Mrs. Aase Lionaes representing the Nobel Committee of the Norwegian Storting (Parliament). She recalled how UNICEF was set up

567

by a UN resolution in December 1946 and, although the resolution passed unanimously, she said,

> I well remember that in United Nations circles in New York that autumn we had a great many discussions with various politicians as to whether the UN really ought to organize a children's fund. The UN, many of them maintained, was a political forum which was not justified in dealing with such 'minor' peripheral problems as aid to children.

Mr. Labouisse, in his acceptance speech, also referred to Nobel's childhood, saying

> We know from Alfred Nobel's own childhood what care and tireless effort can mean in enabling a fragile, sickly boy to attain great heights in later life . . . . He lived, and his name today is associated with mankind's highest achievements. Had Alfred Nobel been born, not in 1833 but even in 1965, in a steamy, isolated village in Asia, Africa, Latin America, what would be his chances of survival and of success? The hard reality is that, in more than 100 developing countries of the world, the odds that confront the average child today—not to say a sickly one—are still overwhelming. They are four to one against his receiving any medical attention, at birth or afterwards. Even if he survives until school age, the chances are two to one that he will get no education at all. If he does get into school, the chances are about three to one that he will not complete the elementary grades. Almost certainly he will have to work for a living by the time he is 12. He will work to eat—to eat badly and not enough. And his life will, on the average, end in about 40 years.

> Such statistics make us face the staggering waste of human energy and talent which drains, year in, year out, the very nations which need them the most . . . . The developing countries are making a courageous effort to catch up with the industrial ones . . . . One of the crucial factors in the progress of a country is the development of the child, the adult of tomorrow—tomorrow's engineers, doctors, progressive farmers, teachers, scientists, social leaders. That is the great task in which UNICEF is taking a share.

> UNICEF aid comes marvelously alive in the field when you see, for instance, a whole pilot region raising its standards simultaneously in education, nutrition, sanitation and health, with everyone lending a hand, from the local teachers and doctors to the poorest families of the jungle villages—all this with the help of our supplies and of advice from United Nations experts.

> The "fraternity of nations" that Alfred Nobel, in his will, dreamt to see promoted is truly there in action. On our UNICEF staff we have men and women of 171 different nationalities and, on our Board, 30 nations; 121 governments contribute on a purely voluntary basis to our budget, and 118 countries receive our assistance while, in turn, doing their share of the financing and of the work. Such worldwide cooperation contributes, in itself, to a better understanding within the family of men.

Secretary-General U Thant confirmed in his 1965 message for Universal Children's Day that UNICEF was now perceived not only as an organization working for children but as a potent force for peace. After warning that the gap between standards of living in the rich and poor countries is accompanied by "a dangerous lack of understanding between peoples," he said, if all the children of the world could grow up regarding themselves as members of a single—though wonderfully diversified—family, if this was made a vital part of every child's preparation for life, then international understanding would no longer be the elusive ideal it has too often proved to be in the past.

CHILDREN WHO HAVE WORKED FOR PEACE
Samantha Smith and Her Friends

In 1982 a 10-year-old American schoolgirl from Maine unexpectedly became world famous. After reading a newspaper article that upset her, Samantha Smith wrote a bold and naive personal letter to Yuri Andropov, who was then the leader of the Soviet Union, asking him, "Why do you want to conquer the world or at least the United States?" To everyone's surprise, Andropov wrote her back saying, "We want nothing of the kind. . . . We want peace for ourselves and for all people of the planet, for our own children and for you, Samantha." He then invited Samantha and her parents to visit the Soviet Union as his guests. These two letters were hailed by the international press as "a dialogue unprecedented in diplomatic history," and Samantha was called "the girl diplomat."

The following summer Samantha and her parents, Arthur and Jane Smith, went to the USSR for two weeks. With her openness and warmth she quickly made many friends, especially during a stay at the Young Pioneer Camp Artek, a summer camp for children in the Crimea, on the coast of the Black Sea. She also visited Moscow and Leningrad (now St. Petersburg).

Samantha held many press conferences both during and after her visit to Russia. She made 30 appearances on television, wrote a book about her trip, and won a leading role on a popular American TV network series, but in August 1985, on her way from filming in London, the plane on which she was traveling with her father crashed, and they were both killed. The whole world mourned.

After this tragic accident, well-wishers sent Samantha's mother $4,000 in spontaneous expressions of sympathy. Jane Smith decided to use the money to start a Samantha Smith Foundation based in Washington, D.C. It produced a children's newsletter and in 1986 sponsored a trip to the USSR for Samantha's classmates. In 1987 it sponsored a reciprocal trip for a group of Soviet teenagers to visit Washington, Boston, and a summer camp in Maine.

Samantha's memory was also kept alive in the USSR. A commemorative six-kopek postage stamp issued in 1985 featured a photograph of her. A ship on the Black Sea was named the Samantha Smith. A flower hybridizer in Lithuania named a violet after her. A cedar was planted in the People's Druzhba (Friendship) Park in Dushanbe, and it was named for her. A huge (32.7-carat) diamond "of rare beauty," found in the Siberian town of Mirny, which means "peaceful" in Russian, was named for her and sent to the diamond treasury in the Moscow Armory, where it was placed on permanent exhibit. In the state of Uzbekistan, a street in the city of Chichik was renamed Samantha Smith Street and in the city of Tashkent, Secondary School 122 established a Samantha Smith International Friendship Club. In the Artek children's camp a lane lined with palm trees was named Samantha Smith Lane, and a monument to her was built there.

"Samantha was an ordinary child," her mother says. Not everyone would agree: she had extraordinary charm, enthusiasm, and poise, a radiant smile, and a special gift for friendship. But she became a symbol of every ordinary child. And her mother carried on her mission because, she said, "I'm convinced that children should meet, get acquainted, and learn to trust each other." The last question Samantha was asked by a Soviet reporter before she left the Soviet Union was: "What would you like to wish all children?" Her reply was: "To live without worrying about war."

Follow-up: Children as Peacemakers

In March 1986 an organization based in San Francisco called Children as Peacemakers sponsored a two-week trip to the United States by a Soviet schoolgirl in memory of Samantha Smith. The founder and executive director of the organization, Patricia Montandon, said she hoped more and more children would join Samantha in working for peace: "Children have purity, honesty and integrity," she said, "and they are very worried about their future. They are afraid of not growing up because of a nuclear war. By working for peace, the children can eliminate that fear." In extending its invitation, the organization made two conditions: the Soviet girl who would be selected for the peace tour had to be active in the peace movement and was to be no older than Samantha was. Katerina ("Katya") Lycheva, 11 years old, was selected. She had taken part in antiwar productions and recitals at her school theater and was an active member of the International Friendship Club at the Palace of Young Pioneers in Moscow. At her school she had organized a Samantha Smith exhibit that she hoped would be transformed into a permanent museum. "I never met Samantha Smith," she told American reporters, "but I saw and heard her on television. Her visit to the Soviet Union inspired me with the hope that children can make a big contribution to the cause of peace, to the maintenance of peace on earth."

Katya, accompanied by Star Rowe, a 10-year-old girl from San Francisco, went to Chicago, Houston, Los Angeles, New York, and Washington, D.C., and visited Disneyland, NASA's Space Center, the Statue of Liberty, and the United Nations, as well as many schools. In the schools they were greeted with warm smiles, colorful balloons, and posters saying "Welcome" in Russian, and by choruses of children singing the song, "Let There Be Peace on Earth, and Let It Begin with Me." Katya gave the children she met paper doves that had been made by Soviet school children especially for her visit. On one side of each dove the children had written their names and addresses. The mayors of Chicago and Washington called the time she spent in their cities "Days of Children as Peacemakers" and in New York and Los Angeles they were proclaimed "Days of Katya Lycheva."

A joint US-USSR publishing venture, a book with an initial run of 75,000 copies, chronicled the trip of Moscow's Katerina and San Francisco's Star. The title of the book, which was published in August 1987, was *Making Friends: We Wish You to Be Happy.*

In August 1986 Katya and another group of Soviet and American schoolchildren took part in an unusual television production called "We Wish You to Be Happy" and dedicated it to Samantha Smith's memory. The idea for the program was proposed by another American organization, The Children's Peace Fund, and backed by the Minnesota state government; Governor Rudy Perpich visited the Soviet Union especially to arrange for the broadcast which was to take place simultaneously at the Ostankino TV Studio in Moscow and the Children's Theater in Minneapolis, with singer John Denver hosting the American part of the show and a Russian star, Vladimir Pozner, hosting the Soviet part.

The culmination of the program was a meeting of two symbolic characters, Katya representing Russia and an American boy, Bobby, representing the U.S. Bobby had

570

appeared the year before in a musical called *Peace Child,* produced by the Peace Child Foundation, written by playwright David Wollcomb and composer Steve Rifkin, and performed by both Soviet and American children; this had been a hit at the twelfth World Festival of Youth and Students held in Moscow in August 1985.

Sequences from a film on Samantha Smith were shown during the program, but the climax came when Katya and Bobby took part in an unprecedented dialogue. Though separated by the Atlantic Ocean and two continents, they chatted together and, along with other Russian and American children, sang together, and at the end of the show actually held hands across the miles. The American children brought bags full of hundreds of letters onto the stage and the children exchanged views. "Can we teach anything to the grownups?" asked one American girl. The answer from a Russian child was, "Of course we can! We can teach them how to communicate and smile and live in peace!" Questions and answers on both sides were numerous, both serious and funny, naive and wise.

The tremendous technical advances of twentieth-century communications had enabled these children to be together via satellite in a 90-minute event that thrilled them. Although it could not fully satisfy their interest in each other, it helped to launch further contacts by correspondence. The Russian children wrote down the address where they could write to their new American friends at WCCO Company, Minneapolis, and in turn supplied their peers with their own address: International Friendship Club, Young Pioneers Palace, Moscow.

Are Children Effective as Peace Advocates?

Many hawks during the Cold War considered children like these to be ignorant dupes of hypocritical Soviet politicians, almost an unpatriotic fifth column. But as one participant in the play *Peace Child*, a 16-year-old boy from Leningrad, said: "I asked my mother and father what prevents us from being friends with Americans. They said it was because of politics. Politics are over my head, but I think nothing can stop people from being friends if they really want to be." An American boy was equally apolitical, saying, "I like wind surfing and wanted to train all summer. But I came to the Soviet Union because if we do nothing I'll end up wind surfing not on the water but on a nuclear cloud."

Children like these did not consider themselves sentimental or unrealistic. They thought they were more realistic than grownups who seemed not to mind the horrible waste of human life caused by warfare. In a dramatic effort to convince people that war should not be part of any government's practical policies, the Children as Peacemakers Foundation in San Francisco embarked on a special project to provide vivid documentation of the ghastly results of war in a banner ironically called "The Banner of Hope."

It took two years for children in 40 countries to produce this banner, under the foundation's auspices. It stretched for half a mile and had 240 silk panels memorializing a geography of death: Auschwitz, Beirut, Cambodia, Gaza, Hiroshima, and other blood-stained areas, and 90 blood-red panels. It was a sort of counterpart of the Vietnam Memorial in Washington, with the individual names and ages, painted in children's lettering in black on white doves, of 13,000 of the approximately 18 million children who were killed by war and war-related violence between 1930 and 1988. As Pat Montandon, who founded Children as Peacemakers in 1982, said: "No one really knows exactly how many children have died, been wounded or displaced in adult conflicts. It's as though we can't admit to ourselves that we've done such a terrible thing." But after seeing panel after panel honoring victims like Solomon Goldfarb, two years old, Federico Cortez, three, Maria Goering, four, it was hard to dismiss the dead as mere statistics.

The banner was unfurled publicly for the first time in September 1988 from street lamps in Moscow. After two days on display before a changing honor guard of Soviet children, it was taken to Leningrad where it was draped across the Siege Memorial where more than 1 million of the 20 million Russians who died in World War II are buried in mass graves. It was then taken to Germany where it was paraded through both East and West Berlin, and then through Belfast in Northern Ireland. After that it was flown to New York for the opening of the United Nations General Assembly on September 20.

Six children who had worked on panels accompanied the banner on its international tour. One of them, 11-year-old Angela Staehle of Vernon, New Jersey, explained her hope for what the banner might accomplish: "Sometimes I think about everything we could do if we didn't have to worry about bombs. We don't have to change the world in three weeks on this trip. But if we can get just one person to really imagine a world without war, then we've done something."

The Children of War Program

Children who have actually experienced the horrors of war, oppression, and torture cannot possibly be called naive or unrealistic in their hatred of war. A group of such children was brought together in 1984 to meet across cultural lines and national boundaries. Their meeting was organized by an interfaith coalition of groups working on issues of social justice and disarmament called The Religious Task Force. It had decided to launch an idealistic and ambitious project, "The Children of War Program," in an effort to uproot fear, bitterness, and hatred and in their place plant the seeds of a truly cooperative global society. The program was based on the belief that young people are deeply concerned about the world and that they have an undiscovered power to transform this concern into effective action, working to build peace within themselves, their neighborhoods, their towns, states, countries, and the world.

The Task Force conducted its first annual Children of War tour in 1984 with 40 teenagers from war-torn countries (Cambodia, El Salvador, Germany, Guatemala, Israel, Lebanon, the Marshall Islands, Namibia, Nicaragua, Northern Ireland, South Africa, and Vietnam). They visited more than 200 public institutions—150 high schools, churches, synagogues and community centers—in the United States. More than 135 prominent national and international newspapers ran articles about the tour, and the participants also appeared on prime-time network news and many other television programs, asking for partners in their mission to conquer demoralization and cynicism among young people by involving them in an active crusade for worldwide peace and justice. Since then they have reached more than 250,000 kids in face-to-face meetings, with contacts in 60 cities throughout the United States reaching more than 450 high schools and 200 community-based organizations.

The friendships they have developed amid frank exchanges of opinion, and their willingness to overcome the violence and despair that robbed them of a normal and safe childhood, allowed them to gain hope for themselves and to inspire it in others. During their first tour they met with Nobel Peace Prize-winner Archbishop Desmond Tutu of South Africa, who told them, "When you return home to your countries and are walking down the street and someone looks at you and says 'Who's that?' you tell them, 'I am a sign of hope!'"

Following the 1984 tour, participants were contacted to serve as consultants for a newly formed UNICEF Committee on Children in Armed Conflict. This committee marked an important new step for UNICEF in the area of child advocacy, out of which it developed the concept of Children as Zones of Peace. This concept later accomplished cease-fires between rebels and governments in several countries torn by civil war and also managed to bring medicines and food to children in Iraq during and after the Gulf War.

Several children from the tour, along with the directors of the Children of War Program, were invited to brief a high-level gathering of UNICEF's field personnel along with members of the International Red Cross and the International Commission on Human Rights in March 1985.

In addition to its annual tours, the Children of War Program has worked to empower young people from areas of war, oppression, racism, underdevelopment, and famine through many other activities aimed at establishing an international ongoing network of young people working as healers and leaders in their communities. Their activities have included study groups, intensive leadership training courses, work camps, publication of a monthly international newsletter, a youth speakers bureau, rehabilitation, and housing programs. The heart of all their work is to extend peer-to-peer empowerment and to provide continual witness to local, national, and international leaders, making young people's voices heard. They call this a struggle against *agism*, which they define as "the disrespect by the adult world toward the intelligence, abilities, judgment, emotional life, leadership, and physical being of young people." They say the adult world "cannot seem to trust young people's ability to make creative solutions for the issues affecting their lives."

> The deepest values of most families are what the Children of War program is all about: creating deep, unbreakable bonds; loving and protecting each other; standing by each other through sorrow and hardship; rejoicing in each others' good fortune; and helping each other to achieve our most cherished dreams. This kind of a family implies unity, strength, honesty, intimacy, tears, and laughter. A world order based on these values could not contain warfare and violence. There would be no more children of war. This, of course, is our hearts' deep desire.
> —*Love and Peace, John Bell, the editor of* Imagine,
> The Children of War Program's "Family Newsletter"

A Harrowing Description of Children as "Hostages of the Madness of Adults"

Arn Chorn, a refugee from Cambodia living in the United States, was the student advisor and initial inspiration behind the first Children of War tour. He was also the keynote speaker at the annual convention of Amnesty International two years in a row, 1984 and 1985, and one of the speakers invited to brief UNICEF's staff following the first Children of War tour. His words on that occasion, describing his childhood experiences, were particularly powerful:

> The movie *The Killing Fields* brought the chilling tragedy of my country's genocide to the front of many people's minds. But the dark secret is that even that movie does not come close to telling it like it is . . . . All of my family was executed. In fact, I saw thousands die.

573

The smell and sight of blood decorated the Children's Center houses. The children were abandoned and made to be hostages of the madness of adults . . . .

I lived through the terror of seeing a student disembowelled and his kidney eaten while he was still alive, watching on in terror and agony. That story is so unbelievably brutal it can't be told in pictures. It is a nightmare for me that literally destroys my nights. I am in the middle of a field. On one side is the Khmer Rouge with all their madness, killing and murdering. They are calling to me and they have guns. On the other is a child who calls for my help. If I go to the child I will be shot or tortured. But if I don't go I will never be alive inside. Maybe the child is actually a symbol of all children, of all the people of my country . . . .

But because of the Children of War tour I feel that the world cares and is doing something to help us. It converted my despair into hope.

A few months after this talk, Arn demonstrated how his spirit had constructively managed to survive and transcend the horrors he had experienced.

No other tragedy since the Holocaust has equalled the level of human suffering that occurred during the Khmer Rouge genocide in Cambodia from 1975 to 1979. Up to 3 million people died as a result of inhuman brutality inflicted upon them by the Khmer Rouge, a group of rebels who overthrew the Lon Nol regime shortly after the end of the Vietnam war.

Most children were immediately separated from their parents and taken to child labor camps where they performed arduous manual labor in the rice fields, with only one bowl of watery rice a day. If they were unable to produce enough they were tortured or killed while others were forced to witness . . . .

Arn helped to design and implement a new Cambodian Youth Peace Project which brought together inside Cambodia (now officially called Kampuchea) young people living there along with those in refugee camps along the border and others, like Arn, who have been resettled in other countries. They began a process of dialogue aimed at building trust and cultural reconstruction and healing of the deep wounds of their traumatic collective experience.

INTERNATIONAL YEAR OF PEACE EARTH RUN

In the autumn of 1986 an amazing event took place: a three-month-long relay race called the First Earth Run (FER). It circled our planet, with runners carrying a torch to the earth's highest point, Mount Everest, and lowest point, the bottom of the ocean. It began on September 16, the first day of the 1986 UN General Assembly session, which was proclaimed the International Day of Peace, and ended on December 11, UNICEF's 40th anniversary. The run was funded by private and corporate donations and through the sales of T-shirts and sweatshirts. All proceeds went to UNICEF. The runners wore T-shirts and carried banners bearing the slogan "Give the World a Chance—Children Need Peace."

The original organizer of this global race was David Gershon, who had organized a 1976 Bicentennial relay race across the United States and also a torch relay from Athens,

Greece, to Lake Placid, New York, which opened the 1980 Olympics. He said, "The idea is that for one moment in time a substantial part of the world will be connected and focused on one thought: that as human beings we can make a better world by demonstrating a spirit of cooperation."

The concept received a hearty endorsement from President Reagan with the following message:

> The First Earth Run, commemorating 1986 as the International Year of Peace and UNICEF's fortieth anniversary, is a compelling global initiative for peace that will touch the lives of people throughout the world and inspire enthusiastic participation. Carrying the torch of peace around the world is stunning in both its rich symbolism and utter simplicity. Because of this, it has the strength to evoke a powerful response and inspire mature reflection about the future. Everyone can play a part in some way and benefit the children of the world . . . . I extend personal congratulations and best wishes to the organizers of the First Earth Run, to those in the private sector who are lending it their support, to the international community, to the multitude of participating volunteer groups, and to each person who will hold the torch aloft and move it closer to the finish line.

The Inspiring Send-off

At dawn on September 16, representatives from six Native American tribes started a fire with sparks from flints and held a traditional Fire Creating Ceremony in keeping with an ancient Indian belief that if a sacred fire is carried around the world, it will help to bring world peace. In the meantime 100 lively children followed by a truck festooned with flowers and banners were running 6 kilometers through New York City. When they reached the United Nations building, UNICEF's "Ambassador to Children," actor Danny Kaye, led them to the front lawn where they watched the secretary-general ring the peace bell donated by Japan; the bell was cast in metal from coins contributed by Japanese children.

Then, using a flame kindled by the Native American's fire, 12-year-old Brian Noodt, star of the Broadway musical *Oliver,* ignited the FER torch and passed it to the secretary-general who in turn passed it through a row of ambassadors and Olympic athletes to nine-year-old Valentino Avana, a Special Olympics champion, who carried it on the first lap of the marathon, escorted by Olympic decathlon gold medalist Bruce Jenner. Valentino in turn passed it to a member of the United Nations Athletic Club, which had two teams all set to go, with runners from 14 countries. They sped along highways and through towns in Connecticut, Rhode Island, and Massachusetts, and 32 hours later, at 7:00 P.M. the next evening, they arrived in Boston where the next team took over, running up through New England to Canada.

Along the torch's global route there were many candlelight processions with people lighting their candles from the FER flame, and prayer services with children's choirs in churches and temples, educational programs in schools, public ceremonies in town squares, launchings of balloons carrying peace messages, and parades of thousands of children and parents. In Rio de Janeiro, later in the tour, 60,000 men, women, and children paraded through the streets. The runners everywhere were greeted by prime ministers and presidents, kings and queens, and blessed by the Pope.

Even Enemies Participated

The runners made stunning peace news as they passed the torch to groups who were at war. In El Salvador, for example, the prime minister lit 14 torches from the FER flame for each of the provinces in his war-torn country, and after lengthy negotiations and through efforts of local church leaders and UNICEF, the FER torch was provided safe passage as it was carried by two children, one from each side of the civil war. In Ireland this was the first-ever relay to link Dublin and Belfast; the event was described as "a breath of fresh air blowing across the country." In Korea the demilitarized zone became for a few moments a true "zone of peace" as a South Korean runner passed the torch to one from North Korea. And the torch was carried from the historic Buddhist palace—the largest building in the world—of the Dalai Lamas in Tibet to China where it lit up the Great Wall. It was also carried to Red Square in Moscow and to 65 other cities in the USSR, and to Jerusalem and Damascus.

Among other places where the torch was welcomed were England at Buckingham Palace, France at the Eiffel Tower, and India at the Taj Mahal. All in all, it passed through 99 major cities in 61 countries.

Other Special Goals of the Earth Run

In addition to its peace message, FER wanted to commend and publicize outstanding local projects along its worldwide route, through the "What's Working in the World" program. Projects that had effectively solved local problems were the centerpieces of ceremonies held when the torch passed through communities. Information about them had been stored in a data bank and were available to communities around the world through the United Nations University for Peace in Costa Rica and its affiliated educational organizations.

On the final day of the run, the torch, accompanied by lusty cheers from schoolchildren, was carried back to the UN building, and used to light an eternal flame within the General Assembly building. To honor its years of work on behalf of children and peace, a gala birthday party for UNICEF followed, hosted by actress Liv Ullmann, at which the executive director of UNICEF said, "For the people of the world, the First Earth Run has offered an opportunity to collectively express their most fervent prayer—indeed their demand—for a more peaceful, healthier world for their children. Our children need peace."

THE WAR PRAYER BY MARK TWAIN

These are excerpts from an unfinished story by Mark Twain called "The Mysterious Stranger." It was discovered among his papers and only published after his death in 1910.

> It was a time of great and exalting excitement. The country was up in arms, the war was on, in every breast burned the holy fire of patriotism . . . . the church was filled—the service proceeded; "Bless our arms, grant us the victory, O Lord our God, Father and Protector of our land and flag!" An aged stranger entered . . . ascended to the preacher's side . . . took his place . . . then in a deep voice he said:

"I come from the Throne . . .bearing a message from Almighty God . . . . He has heard the prayer of His servant, your shepherd, and will grant it if such shall be your desire after I, His messenger, shall have explained to you its import . . . . Is it one prayer? No, it is two . . . one uttered, the other not. Both have reached the ear of Him who heareth all supplications . . . . I am commissioned of God to put into words the other part of it . . . the part which the pastor, and also you in your hearts, fervently pray silently. And ignorantly and unthinkingly? God grant that it was so! When you have prayed for victory you have prayed for many unmentioned results which follow victory:

"O Lord our God, help us to tear their soldiers to bloody shreds with our shells; help us to cover their smiling fields with the pale forms of their patriot dead, help to drown the thunder of the guns with the shrieks of their wounded, writhing in pain; help us to lay waste their humble homes with a hurricane of fire; help us to wring the hearts of their unoffending widows with unavailing grief; help us to turn them roofless with their little children to wander unfriended the wastes of their desolate land in rags and hunger and thirst, sports of the sun flames of summer and the icy winds of winter, broken in spirit, worn with travail, imploring Thee for the refuge of the grave and denied it . . . for our sakes who adore Thee, Lord, blast their hopes, blight their lives, protract their bitter pilgrimage, make heavy their steps, water their way with their tears, stain the white snow with the blood of their wounded feet! We ask it in the spirit of love, of Him who is the Source of Love and who is the ever-faithful refuge and friend of all that are sore beset and seek His aid with humble and contrite hearts."

It was believed afterward that the man was a lunatic, because there was no sense in what he said.

UNICEF/94-0158/Betty Press

577

15

Advocates for Children

SOLDIERS WHO BECAME ADVOCATES FOR EUROPE'S CHILDREN

Soon after peace was declared after World War II members of a United States Signal Corps Film Unit were asked if they would be willing to stay on in Europe to make a documentary film for the United Nations Relief and Rehabilitation Administration (UNRRA) to record the impact of the war on children. Captain David Miller, a movie director for MGM who was the head of the unit, had been in the army almost five years and was tired and eager to go home, but instead he went to Paris and managed to recruit a volunteer crew of eight cameramen. They were all Hollywood professionals who had served throughout the war and were also eater to get home. He persuaded them by saying, "The shooting war is over, but the war itself is not. Now we have to go out there and save the children."

Miller assigned Sergeant Art Arthur, a freelance Hollywood screenwriter also with the Film Unit, to write the script. General Dwight D. Eisenhower authorized them to visit displaced persons' camps, hospitals, and war-devastated areas, and for the next 10 weeks the crew focused their cameras on children in 11 countries: Albania, Belgium, Czechoslovakia, Egypt, England, France, Germany, Greece, Holland, Italy, and Yugoslavia.

Arthur named the film they were making *Seeds of Destiny* to emphasize that "children are the makers of tomorrow" and "to make viewers wonder what tomorrow will be like if we continue to let so many children grow up sickly, neglected, and bitter." In his script he quoted something Hitler said just before his death, that his revenge for defeat would be that "we shall leave an inheritance of ruins, stone heaps, rats, epidemics, hunger and death and thereby Western civilization shall decline," and a Nazi general who said, "We can best accomplish this through systematic malnutrition, in the end far superior to machine guns, especially among the young."

It looked as if Hitler and the Nazi general would achieve their objective. The sights the film crew saw were so ghastly that these tough, war-hardened cameramen frequently burst into tears after taking pictures of wounded, crippled, blinded, orphaned, terrorized, and starving children shivering and slogging in freezing mud, often without shoes, or even feet, standing in long lines waiting for food or foraging for scraps of food in garbage cans, living in ruins, caves, cattle sheds, among rats and lice, many of them begging, stealing, or selling black market cigarettes to stay alive. They saw one woman blown 50 feet into the air after stepping on a land mine, and one child died on camera.

Everywhere the film crew went, they faced horror: "We went into an improvised hospital somewhere in Italy," Miller reported to Eisenhower,

> where ill children were being treated. The stench was so terrible in the children's ward that we had to cover our mouths and noses with wet handkerchiefs while we filmed. We took turns going outside to vomit. During the two to three hours it took us to shoot 100 feet of film, three children died. We found conditions like this in many countries. This was a heartbreaking film to make.

They were very glad they had made it, though. Years later Miller told a friend he was prouder of it than of anything else he had ever done in his life.

When their task was completed, they returned home on the U.S.S. *Enterprise*, the first time the Navy had ever been willing to transport an Army unit. Back in the States the film was edited, with actor Ralph Bellamy narrating, ending with a plea that every country contribute one percent of its gross national product (GNP) to help these children. In February, 1946, a private showing was arranged at the White House. One person who saw it there and wept was Fiorello LaGuardia, former Mayor of New York City and newly appointed director of UNRRA, who wrote Miller saying, "It will be a tragedy if this film is not shown in every moving picture theater in this country." An article in *The Hollywood Reporter* praised the film and its eloquent and important message and urged its wide distribution. However, the American Theaters Association refused to distribute it, saying it had a "sock message" but was "too depressing" and "entirely too gruesome, not a fit subject to show children. . .not even a fit subject for theaters generally. People want to forget about the war."

Then hundreds of individual advocates for children came to the rescue. *Mademoiselle* and *Look* magazines organized appeals to their readers, based on the film, asking them to contribute to emergency food collections. Screenings were held by churches, unions, parent-teacher associations, service clubs, and other private groups in Australia, Britain, Canada, France, and the United States. Within three years some 11 million people saw the film and were so moved that they donated more than $200 million to children's welfare, making *Seeds of Destiny* the biggest moneymaker for charity of its day. And despite never having been shown in movie theaters, it became the first documentary ever to win an Oscar at the 1947 Academy Awards ceremony.

In August 1947 it was sent to Geneva where Lord Philip Noel-Baker (1889–1982), UK delegate to UNRRA, arranged for it to be shown daily to members of UNRRA's governing council. UNRRA had been set up as a temporary postwar emergency operation and was about to disband. Its council now voted unanimously to propose that an international children's emergency fund be created out of UNRRA's unspent funds, and many maintained that this film convincingly showed the importance of such a proposal. Later the proposal was accepted, and UNICEF was created.

When the Marshall Plan came before the U.S. Congress in 1947 another special showing of *Seeds of Destiny* helped gain support for its passage. The film had become what some people called "the most powerful editorial ever written."

HERBERT HOOVER (1874–1964) AND MAURICE PATE (1894–1965)

During the difficult years of the First World War and the chaotic years that immediately followed, these two Americans, who were to become the most influential and successful advocates for children in their time, worked closely together in London, occupied Belgium, Poland, and other parts of Eastern Europe. Hoover was chairman of the Commission for Relief in Belgium and food administrator of the American Relief Commission. Pate, his 20-years-younger assistant, was inspired by the older man and profited from his tutelage, and together they gained a wide reputation for remarkable efficiency. Due to their tact and determination, they sometimes even succeeded in obtaining the cooperation of governments that were actively fighting each other, in order to get shipments of food and medicines through to devastated areas.

In 1943, when World War II was in its fourth year, the exiled Government of Poland asked Hoover to establish a Polish Relief Commission. Hoover took on the challenge and appointed Pate as his assistant. Hoover also created a Finnish Relief Commission and ordered that both agencies emphasize relief to child victims of the war. Hoover received additional requests for help from the exiled governments of Belgium, Free France, Holland, and Norway. Hoover and Pate worked hard but they were often frustrated when their relief efforts were stopped by combatant governments' blockades, until May 1945 when the European war ended with the surrender of Germany and Italy.

What Hoover and Pate managed to achieve in spite of formidable obstacles caused President Truman, who had seen *Seeds of Destiny* and learned that an estimated 800 million Europeans were facing starvation, to call again on Hoover in 1945 to head a famine commission to coordinate world food supplies to relieve the famine.

In February of that year Hoover made a public statement from Washington announcing that this commission would visit 38 countries, and that he had recruited "the invaluable Maurice Pate for the specific duty of investigating the condition of the children in each of the 38 countries."

In April, Pate gave his first report to Hoover, telling him there were more than 20 million children seriously underfed and 11 million orphans in Europe and that the death rate for children less than one year old was in many places 200 per 1,000, which is higher than in any developing country today. He said, "The most poignant human problem in Europe today" was that "the parental instinct of Europeans is no less strong than in our own country but their wherewithal to fulfill this instinct toward their children is far less."

Hoover issued public statements, including a radio speech from Cairo saying,

> If Europe is to have a future, something must be done about the children. Unless they are better fed, many will die and others will grow up with stunted bodies and distorted minds. They will furnish more malevolence in the world . . . . The reconstruction of children is more precious than factories or bridges. They will determine the good or evil future of Europe.

In May, Hoover and Pate returned from their 50,000-mile trip and reported to President Truman, the U.S. Government's Famine Emergency Committee, and to delegates from 30 nations at a meeting called by the United Nations: "Special feeding and medical care of physically subnormal children should be organized systematically and should be the sole charitable contribution of governments. That is the most needed reconstruction effort in the world."

In June, Hoover made his most important speech to the Canadian Parliament in Ottawa, summing up his views on why helping children is so vital to civilization.

His advocacy was instrumental in persuading the United Nations to establish an International Children's Emergency Fund. He recommended that Maurice Pate serve as its executive director. On December 10, 1946, Pate sent a personal letter to a friend that revealed how concerned he was about the welfare of *all* children regardless of their nationality or the politics of their parents. In it he wrote,

> A minor item in the news, which may grow larger in time, is the establishment of the International Children's Fund under the UN. I had been asked to take an active part in it, to which I agreed on one condition, namely that it include all children of ex-enemy countries, Japanese, Finnish, Austrian, Italian, and German. This was accepted so I may soon be at work again.

When the three years the UN had approved for UNICEF's life-saving work expired and the European situation was no longer urgent, the General Assembly was about to terminate its mandate. Pate sought out Hoover's advice explaining that recommendations had been made for UNICEF to extend its work in the field of assistance to include economically underdeveloped countries. He was concerned about whether this was a logical step for an emergency organization that had been set up with the primary purpose of aiding war victims. Hoover's simple answer was: "The children in underdeveloped countries have been and still are existing in a dire state of emergency. You should go right ahead." Soon afterwards the General Assembly voted to continue and expand the work of UNICEF indefinitely, and Pate undertook his new tasks with characteristic enthusiasm and determination.

In 1962 Hoover made the following public statement: "It is my conviction that UNICEF is ably and honestly conducted. To me it is the major beneficial service of the United Nations."

On Hoover's ninetieth birthday Dr. Howard Rusk was one of many people who paid homage to him, saying to reporters that among his accomplishments he had

> made one of extreme importance that is not generally known. He had the original idea of establishing the United Nations Children's Fund. . . .UNICEF is held in high repute throughout the world and has a reputation for concrete action. . . .Mr. Hoover is a man who believes in concrete action [and] his vision has laid one of the solid foundation stones of the United Nations itself.

Pate served as UNICEF's executive director for 18 years until his death, and it was his administration that led to ever-growing respect and won the organization the Nobel Peace Prize, which he never knew, because he died 10 months before it was announced.

Among the millions of tributes paid to Pate were these:

- The Riverside Church in New York gave him its Charles Evans Hughes Award posthumously, a plaque praising him for having "faith without credulity, conviction without bigotry, charity without condescension, courage without pugnacity, self respect without vanity, humility without obsequiousness, love of humanity without sentimentality, and meekness with power."

- In his Nobel acceptance speech, Henry Labouisse, who was appointed as UNICEF's second Executive Director following the death of Maurice Pate in January 1965, said, "How very much we wish that my predecessor, Maurice Pate, could be here with us. This great practical idealist was UNICEF's architect and builder."

Many people had called him a "practical idealist" but Herbert Hoover had described him more originally and vividly when he said, "Maurice Pate is the most efficient and dedicated human angel I have ever known."

Hoover's Report on World Famine, June 28, 1946

This historic speech, delivered to the Canadian Parliament in Ottawa, was the catalyst that led to the creation of UNICEF. Here is an excerpt:

> Disease and mortality among the little ones are ever the sensitive barometers of starvation and poverty. Several nations have done the best they could by giving the children priority in their meager dairy products; some extra food is given in

some schools; and the scattered charitable agencies are doing the best they can in limited areas. But in all, they are only touching the fringe of the problem.

Millions of mothers are today watching their children wilt before their eyes. The proof of this is an annual mortality rate in many cities as high as 200 per 1,000 among children under one year of age. The further proof is that there are somewhere from 20 to 30,000,000 physically subnormal children on the continent of Europe. There are other millions in Asia. . . .

Civilization marches forward upon the feet of healthy children. We cannot have recovery of civilization in nations with a legacy of stunted bodies or distorted and embittered minds. . . .

I would like to suggest that the redemption of these children be organized at once. . .and that all nations be called upon to contribute to this cost. The job could be done with three or four hundred million dollars—a charge beyond any organized private charity but not a great sum from the world as a whole. . . .

The world has ended a bloody and horrible era of killing of even women and children. The jeopardy to mankind by famine gives to us an opportunity to change the energies of the world from killing to saving life. These months can bring the glow of a new faith and a new hope for the dawn of a new era to mankind. To succeed is far more than a necessity to economic reconstruction of the world. It is far more than the path to order and peace. It marks the return of the lamp of compassion to the earth. And that is part of the moral and spiritual reconstruction of the world.

Helenka Pantaleoni, UNICEF's "Godmother" (1900–1987)

A World War II widow, charming mother of five and grandmother of 14, Helenka Pantaleoni was also "godmother" to millions of children, involved with UNICEF in 1945 even before it existed, enthusiastically encouraging her friend Maurice Pate when he was considering starting a new agency for children's relief.

In 1950, Pantaleoni was alarmed because another friend, Eleanor Roosevelt, who was then the influential head of the U.S. delegation to the UN General Assembly, on the advice of the U.S. State Department wanted to reduce UNICEF's role to providing technical advice instead of supplying direct aid to children. But Ahmed Bokhari, the representative from Pakistan, swayed everyone with his passionate appeal on behalf of the children in his part of the world, and Mrs. Roosevelt became one of UNICEF's most loyal advocates, frequently speaking and writing about it and even giving it royalties from her books.

In 1952, Pantaleoni was elected president of the newly formed U.S. Committee for UNICEF, with the job of educating the American public to an awareness that UNICEF was not, as she put it, "a Lady Bountiful dispensing the equivalent of lollipops to poor children overseas" but was doing serious work in health care, disease control, nutrition, and training. And an important contribution she made was not just educational—she involved people, feeling strongly that individual people should be a part of UNICEF, that they had opinions about what governments and UNICEF should do and were willing to help pay for it. While she was president of the committee, it raised more than $113 million for UNICEF. But she did more than raise funds and lobby the government on its policies toward children. She recruited hundreds of volunteers besides herself and her friends. Jim Grant, UNICEF's executive director at the time of her retirement in 1982, said that "in working unstintingly for children, she, perhaps more than any other individual, made UNICEF the 'people to people' arm of the UN."

Pantaleoni said her job was easy because "we have such an ally in the children and in the fact that UNICEF really works. It's a unique thing—Arabs and Jews, Indians and Pakistanis, Americans and Russians working together on the same Executive Board. As long as you keep politics out of it, kids draw people together."

When asked how she could have worked continuously and full time for UNICEF for 30 years without ever having been paid, Pantaleoni replied, "Oh, I have been paid—but in a different currency: in satisfaction!"

DANNY KAYE (1913–1987)
The First "Ambassador to the World's Children"

In 1954 Danny Kaye was sitting in an airplane next to a man he had never met before—Maurice Pate. Pate introduced himself, saying he was the executive director of a fairly new organization, UNICEF, and he described its work. Their chat led the comedian on the first stage of a 34-year journey that transformed his life.

Pate and Kaye kept in touch, and a few months after that first meeting, Pate asked Kaye, who was about to take a trip to Asia, if he would be willing to visit some UNICEF projects there and upon his return talk about them on the radio or write a magazine article. "I'll do a little better than that," Kaye responded. "I'll try to do a documentary." With that promise, Dag Hammarskjold, who was then secretary-general of the UN, presented Kaye with a scroll officially appointing him as the UN's Ambassador at Large "charged with making known the needs of children throughout the world." Kaye felt pleased and honored, saying, "This is kind of a new role for me, but one with an objective that is important to me—kids. We'll try to get as good a record as we possibly can. We'll try to get it all on film and come back and see that people have a fuller and greater realization of what UNICEF is doing."

The outcome of Kaye's trip was a 20-minute technicolor film called *Assignment Children*. Kaye directed and appeared in it, mixing his infectious humor with scenes of children in Burma, India, Japan, Korea, and Thailand, showing how UNICEF protected them from disease and hunger. In 1954 Paramount Pictures produced the film in 19 languages and donated the proceeds to UNICEF. Eventually the film was seen by over 100 million people and netted UNICEF more than $100,000.

His Travels on Behalf of Children

Kaye's first trip to Asia was followed by 126 other trips, visiting children in 34 countries. On these global travels, language barriers meant nothing to him. With his fantastic gift for mimicry he put children and adults at ease by double-talking in fake Finnish, Hindi,

Japanese, Swedish—whatever languages they spoke. And as he said, laughter is a universal language.

On UNICEF's fifteenth anniversary in 1961, Kaye went to Japan and other Asian countries and was reunited with "Sam," a boy in Thailand who as a little child had had a severe case of yaws, a dreadful tropical skin disease, but who was cured in two weeks by one dose of penicillin supplied by UNICEF, a fact that was featured in *Assignment Children*.

In November 1966 Kaye flew to Paris to join a gala party called "Rendezvous with Danny Kaye," a celebration of UNICEF's twentieth anniversary. It was telecast to 20 countries and raised $45,000 for UNICEF. The show's stars included Marlon Brando, Leslie Caron, Louis Jourdan, Shirley MacLaine, James Mason, Michele Morgan, and Maurice Chevalier—who greeted Danny with a kiss, calling him "the most brilliant comedian of our age. . .a man who has helped UNICEF do so much for the children of the world."

In June 1967 Danny flew to Israel and went on an international fund-raising tour; as part of it he conducted the Israel National Youth Symphony.

In May 1970 Kaye went again to Japan, representing UNICEF on United Nations International Children's Day, visiting Expo 70, and appearing as the main star and emcee of a two-hour variety show at the Festival Plaza, where he conducted the famous Suzuki violinists and then led a procession of children to the U.S. Pavilion to unveil a plaque to the memory of Maurice Pate, who had died in 1965.

In 1971 after a heavy flood in India had destroyed many homes, Kaye was even able to bring laughter to families huddled in misery in flimsy, overcrowded, nonsheltering shelters that were unable to protect them from cold, hunger, and disease. Kaye was at first criticized for wanting to visit these refugee camps; people thought it inappropriate to make jokes in such places. But he went anyway and afterwards the Indian government thanked him for bringing the children there the only happiness they had known in months. And Danny demonstrated that he was not merely a clown. The anguish in his face as he held a dying baby left no viewer of the film made about this trip unmoved.

Kaye also traveled widely in the United States. For several years to promote "trick or treat for UNICEF" on Halloween, he flew his own plane to cities where he was met by the press and cheering children at airports, staying just long enough to refuel, to encourage, and to thank the children for raising money to help other children.

"I tell you it's the most exciting thing in the world," he told a reporter at one of these stops.

> I say to a child, "I'm going to make you an ambassador for UNICEF. You're going to take this little orange box and go to somebody's house, and they're going to put in a nickel or a dime or a penny or a quarter or a dollar and that money in this box is going to save a child's life somewhere in the world." Kids are really very moved by the fact that they can do something to influence a child's life somewhere in the world. I think it's a remarkable beginning of people learning to live with each other.

Kaye made the first of these flights in October 1965. He and Henry Labouisse started out in Danny's plane, now dubbed the "Trick or Treat Special," to visit eight cities. But there was an unexpected, though welcome, interruption. In Philadelphia they got a phone call telling them UNICEF had just won the Nobel Peace Prize. Danny did a memorable "Victory Ballet" with other elated volunteers at the airport. He then flew on to Washington, D.C., for a press conference and to meet more youngsters.

At the end of the trip Kaye took time off in Los Angeles to start production on a new weekly CBS-TV program. And then, on December 9, he made an even longer trip, piloting his plane across the continent and the Atlantic Ocean, to Oslo, Norway. He arrived there late at night, just in time to perform in the last act of a gala benefit show being held for UNICEF in the Norwegian Opera House, where he got a standing ovation. The next day he was among the 600 honored guests at the official Nobel Prize ceremonies.

Kaye summed up his feelings about his UNICEF work most eloquently when he said,

> Children die quietly because they have no political force and no voice to present before the world. UNICEF has become their voice. . . .Wherever I can do the most good, there will I go and there will I wander.

Some Final Words from Danny Kaye about Children and Childhood

The most precious natural resource that any country can have is its children. They are more important than oil, more beautiful than rivers, and more determined that the world shall exist. . . .

Children are the same the world over. Their behavior is exactly the same. Customs and traditions and color and background may be different. Some children may be shy and withdrawn, others aggressive, some may be unhappy and hungry and diseased, but they all respond to the same treatment. They all respond to one lovely little four-letter word—love. . . .

A lot of adults spend most of their lives trying to bury the child within them somewhere, but you don't become an adult simply by putting on long pants, and I think they would be a lot better off if they admitted that a great part of them was still the remaining child, and to embrace it and make friends with it. If they would recognize that some of our behavior and our motivation stems from what we've experienced as children, they wouldn't fight it so much. . . .

I think the United Nations Children's Fund is doing a remarkable job in seeing that the children of the world have a chance to grow into some kind of healthy maturity, to take their place in society and to be contributing forces to what I hope will eventually be world peace. . . .

I wish everyone could see the difference UNICEF makes to a child. . .the difference between a child's hope and despair. To see sick, needy and hungry children actually flower before your eyes is one of the most rewarding things I've ever seen in my life. UNICEF's swift response to the suffering children of the world is one of the sources of the deep pride I have in my long association with the agency. It's exciting to go back to a place and see progress. Some of the kids who were helped in the Far East 13 or 15 years ago have taken their place in the community and are helping other kids to grow up. My great hope is that all of these kids will some day realize that many people of many nationalities, faiths and colors have banded together to make their lives palatable. . . .

PETER USTINOV (1921–)

Peter Ustinov, whose full name and title is Sir Peter Alexander Ustinov, is a world-famous actor, director, and producer for the stage, screen, and television, a playwright, novelist, storyteller, a pianist, cartoonist, master mimic, and witty raconteur, with many devoted friends all over the world. He was born in London in 1921 and made his stage debut at age 17, then interrupted his career to serve in the British Army in World War II. Since then he has made more than 50 films and numerous stage appearances in plays he has written and produced, always satirical comedies with serious theme.

Ustinov is the son of "White Russian" parents; his paternal grandfather was exiled from Russia in the 1860s for becoming a Protestant. His maternal grandmother was of French parentage; he explains that "they had followed a French duke into exile after the Russian revolution, my great-grandfather being his pastry cook." His father was a half-Russian, half-German journalist, and his mother was a painter of Russian-French-Italian ancestry. He adds that "being the eventual result of these two intersecting migrations, I am well situated to understand the problems of displaced children."

Knighted by Queen Elizabeth II, Ustinov is one of the great figures in show business and recipient of its most coveted awards—two Oscars, three Emmys, and a Grammy—he has also received the UNICEF Award for Distinguished Service at the International Level. That award is a golden statuette of an adult and a child with interlocking arms, designed by artist Kurt Plowitz. It was instituted in 1976 by Henry Labouisse, then UNICEF's executive director, who emphasized that the dedicated contribution of UNICEF's volunteers is a cornerstone of the agency's effectiveness. The award's first recipient was Danny Kaye, the second Professor Robert Debré, President of the International Children's Center in Paris, and Ustinov was the third, in 1978.

Peter Ustinov is as funny a man as Danny Kaye and at the same time as deeply serious. As Mr. Labouisse pointed out when presenting the award to him,

> Peter Ustinov is a great star but he doesn't act like a star. He has a concern for other people and is a wonderful, intelligent, compassionate, talented and sensitive man. All of us at UNICEF are very proud to have him here. A lot of people speak of the problems of the world but Peter Ustinov's compassion goes beyond just deploring the injustices of the world. He believes in trying to change things, doing something, particularly doing something about the problems of children. It is this special quality of his that first brought him to help UNICEF.

Ustinov had earned the award by working as one of UNICEF's Goodwill Ambassadors for nine years, and he has continued to do so ever since. He makes numerous public appearances and media appeals to raise money for UNICEF. He travels widely speaking on behalf of the children of the developing world whom UNICEF serves.

But Ustinov disarmed everyone present at his award ceremony by saying he didn't feel he deserved the award. "It's quite normal," he said,

> for actors, who are often adversely criticized and ignored by the public, to feel this is unjust. Equally, when we are given awards we feel that we don't deserve them. This helps us to maintain a balance within ourselves and somehow eradicates from your memory any contribution you've made and you feel the whole time that some hideous mistake has been made and that somebody else's name will be inscribed on the award.

He then grinned and added, "But now that I've got this award, I can go away and start beginning to deserve even a portion of it. In the meantime, however," he joked, "I'm delighted to be the joker in your pack."

Ustinov's advocacy for children had gained him another unique honor the year before he received UNICEF's "Oscar." He was made a member of "The Order of Smile" and received a medal showing a child's picture of a smiling sun. This is the only Order in the world given to adults by children "in recognition of good heart, friendliness, goodness and patience given to young ones." Established in Poland, children and teenagers transmit their proposals to the chapter of the Order of Smile situated in Warsaw. The chapter selects laureates from the candidates named by the children and decorates them with the sunny medal. They have described it as

> the only Order awarded in the name of children, irrespective of the color of their skin, habitat, nationality or religion; the only distinction born out of the initiative of children, designed by them and awarded solely on the basis of children's recommendations; and proof that the youngest citizens of all countries are able to reward friendly attitudes and gifts of the heart.

Ustinov smiled when he received the smiling medal, and said, "The idea of establishing the Order of Smile awarded to adults by children deserves recognition, too. . . . The very idea is beautiful and I hope it stays so, provided adults do not interfere and turn it into a dead-earnest affair."

Ustinov's family history and his own observations gave him a distrust of narrow nationalism, and since he has a creative imagination he invented an imaginary country of his own. He says it became very real to him, and "having one's own country to react through relieves one of an awful lot of pointless frustration over international situations in which the individual has no part." He told Tony Hewitt, during an interview for UNICEF, that "Ustinovia" has been growing over the years. "My country is fairly large, too large for my comfort nowadays." Casting an appraising eye at his own ample girth, he chuckled and added, "But then, so am I." He enjoyed this joke heartily, but then turned serious, saying,

> Whatever we do for children, we're really doing what all governments of the world should be doing, but despite the impressive contributions of some countries like Sweden, it's not enough. The only thing to do is to nag continually at people's consciences. Sooner or later, I think, there must be governments which take a more enlightened view and realize that although the results of generosity are not immediately tangible, they are certainly extremely important.

Hewitt said Ustinovia sounded like a nice place to visit. "You're very welcome," said Ustinov graciously, but then his voice instantly changed and he was suddenly what Hewitt called "that maddening creature, the Universal Passport Official" saying, "Of course I'll need an application, in triplicate." This was the quintessential Ustinov, a man whose imagination and talent can play the benign monarch and the petty bureaucrat within the same sentence.

In his autobiography called *Dear Me*, published in 1977, Ustinov described how his association with UNICEF began in 1969 when he was asked to be master of ceremonies at a gala in Paris. "I was tremendously impressed by the number of people who had got together. We had Polish violinists and Soviet singers—all sorts of people that you could never have got together for a commercial evening. . . .I thought to myself, what is this organization that can inspire this kind of trust and confidence in so many diverse people? I began to wonder what UNICEF was all about, and I made inquiries and found out. After that I was as hooked as anybody can be on a drug, because if you happen to have children yourself, who are not bad looking, not unintelligent, not vile, then I think you have to pay your debt for that."

Ustinov narrated a film called *All Our Futures* as part of his contribution to UNICEF's twenty-fifth anniversary, showing its work across the years and across the globe. It was described as an exciting adventure story about a new type of war being waged on many fronts by soldiers from many countries—a war being fought with medicine instead of guns, food instead of bullets, education instead of bombs, love instead of hatred.

When asked why he was so interested in working on this film, Ustinov explained that he enjoys a happy life but feels guilty. "Guilty of what?" he was asked. "Guilty of happiness, guilty of comfort, guilty of knowing." Of knowing what? "That there are so many millions of unfortunate children in this world and that I am an adult." He said he wants everyone to share his concern, so that they will join him in helping UNICEF help these children. Why? "That's simple. Because a child is a child. And because helping children is a sound and lasting investment in people, in world peace, and in all our futures."

LIV ULLMANN (1938–)

To the movie-going public Liv Ullmann is the beautiful, talented, and internationally acclaimed Norwegian actress who starred in many distinguished films produced by the Swedish director Ingmar Bergman. But to the world's children she became well known as UNICEF's first woman Goodwill Ambassador. Explaining why she took on this new type of role, she said, "I wanted to do something else. . .all my life I have been made up to be other people, spoken other people's lines. . . .Now I am the one speaking."

Once she undertook this role, Ullman gave it complete dedication. She became an indefatigable traveler, visiting countries in Africa, the Americas, Asia, and Europe. She met with government officials and field workers but spent most of her time making friends with local people in rural areas, urban slums, and refugee camps, always promising to bring their messages about their problems and needs back to the outside world.

After each trip, Ullman reported on what she had seen and learned to UNICEF and many of its national committees in Europe, Australia, and the United States. Through television and radio programs, press conferences, personal appearances, newspaper and magazine interviews, she helped mobilize the world community with her personal touch and vivid descriptions that turned depressing statistics about famine and poverty, of which the public was tired of hearing, into human interest stories about appealing individual children. She brought a warm, motherly quality to her advocacy that touched hearts, and she had the ability to make people see and feel what she had personally seen and felt and to share her sense of urgency.

Not all her reports were sad or alarming. She also joyously wrote about progress that was being made. For example, here are excerpts from an article she wrote in 1984 about her UNICEF experiences entitled "A Miracle That Will Never Make the Headlines":

It was the smallest baby I had ever seen. . .smaller than the doctor's hand even. It clung with its puny strength to the mother to which it was strapped, naked body against naked body. I carefully put out a finger to touch the tiny infant— and suddenly a wrinkly little hand darted out and grabbed it with incredible strength. The doctor laughed and said, "There aren't many places in the world where you'd see a child as small as this one outside of an incubator." He covered the baby lovingly with his hand. What a miracle to see and feel life throbbing with such vitality in so small a being.

I was in Colombia, studying UNICEF-related programs, and meeting with a group of pediatricians at Bogotá's Mother and Child Institute of San Juan de Díos Hospital. These doctors had embarked on a revolutionary project to think of ways to sustain life in prematurely born babies without the use of incubators. Under the leadership of Dr. Edgar Rey. . .they instituted new procedures in which the premature infants obtain the warmth they desperately need from their own mothers' bodies; they are "packed" close to the mother's chest, under her blouse or sweater right next to the breast, to allow them to suck at it any time they wish.

"When the baby is breast-fed it has the immunological protection of the mother through her milk," Dr. Rey said. "In addition, this eliminates the infection dangers a baby is exposed to when it is suddenly taken out of the incubator's sterile environment and placed in the generally unhygienic surroundings of a poor home. [Also] in an incubator the baby is too quiet. It is not stimulated in any way. No voice, no sounds, no touch—just glass."

Before Dr. Rey introduced this technique in 1979, all premature babies born in the hospital weighing less than two pounds died. Now three out of four are saved. . . .The initial results indicate a success that is absolutely phenomenal. Although the death rate for premature babies in the poor areas and slums of Colombia is still alarming, the mortality rate of those born in this hospital has dropped from more than 70 percent before 1979 to an incredible five percent now. At the same time, no expensive technology was needed.

Dr. Rey touched the little baby again, caressing it in the most beautiful way saying, "Love, affection and stimulus are very important for the newborn child, and one of the reasons my program is so successful is that the mother easily learns these simple things."

. . . .Colombia is a developing country with limited resources—but this simple miracle was in fact only one of the many advances demonstrated to me. It is part of the national effort there to make the children the country's first priority. . . .

In addition to her speeches and articles Liv Ullmann wrote two books about her experiences as an advocate for children, one called *Choices* and one called *Tides*. She said they were not memoirs but the product of her travels "for UNICEF and for love."

Like Mother, Like Daughter

When Liv's daughter Linn Ullmann was in her late teens she was appointed Youth Ambassador by UNICEF, to spread the word about children's needs and UN activities among her peers. But she had been involved with UNICEF before that. When she was 16 she accompanied her mother on several trips and became anxious to be an advocate for children. In an interview with Lelei LeLaulu for the *UN Secretariat News* when she finally received her official appointment, she said that as a little girl she was "a spoiled brat" until she got interested in UNICEF and Third World issues; she was 10 years old in fourth grade at a school in Norway.

> Our class was divided up one day into three unequal parts. I was put in the "Africa-Asia" part while my best girlfriend was sitting in the "Europe" part. We'd been promised a surprise, and in comes the teacher bringing plates full of newly baked muffins. Half of them quickly went to Europe; the other 45 percent quickly went to North America, and left for us—the majority sitting in the "Asia-Africa" and "South America" sections—were three little muffins to be shared by 15 children. I said, "This isn't fair! I didn't choose to sit in this group!" "I remembered those words several years afterwards when my mother had gone on her first UNICEF trip and she was talking about people's lack of choice, and I just decided that I *can* choose, I can make a choice. And for me, that choice is to do something for people with no choice.

Linn was eager to talk to her peers because she felt that in many schools in America and Europe there is a lack of awareness about the plight of children in other parts of the world. She said she thought the "me, me, me" concerns of her contemporaries about "my grades, my success, my Mercedes" were twisted values and that it was as if "everybody is knocking on the wrong door."

On her first trip with her mother, at 16, they visited the Philippines and then took a tour through Europe. They had press and TV interviews in Finland. Then, near Cologne in Germany, they were invited to visit a high school in Trossdorf, to describe what they had seen of children in developing countries to some 500 students who listened attentively and asked many questions. The students' interest was strong because they had been working for these children through door-to-door collections and the sale of UNICEF greeting cards and a small fund-raising event; they had raised close to $25,000 for UNICEF in only two years. Linn congratulated them and shared her own information and fund-raising ideas with them while her mother addressed parliamentarians and recorded some TV spots for UNICEF.

Later Linn took a trip to Africa, expecting to see a continent of beggars and skeletons but instead saw the faces of real and proud people who wanted to make a new life for themselves. Not that she didn't see any who were starving. In her UN interview she recalled a child who had just been admitted to a UNICEF feeding camp, hopelessly hungry and dehydrated. They wanted to weigh and measure him and she tried to hold him because he was so emaciated that he could not stand up alone on the scales, weighing only 16 pounds even though he was four years old. She said she could still recall his cries, because there was no hope in them. He had no home, no parents, no future. "I think a hopeless cry is beyond sadness," she said. "It's a cry that no child, anywhere, should have to know." She added,

> I also remember a child I saw in Mali, who had not been immunized. He had polio and was like a dog. He was maybe seven or eight years old, condemned to walk on all fours for the rest of his life. He couldn't stand up, so he had to use his hands to walk on the ground. One shot for very few dollars could have saved him from that.

But I also remember a child who had not lost hope. He came up to me and said, through a translator, "I want to dance for you." He was just saying, "Let me give you something, I can't give you much else, but I can give you a dance." That was the message I got all over the African countries: "Let me give you something." Why can't we, in this industrial world, learn from that? Why can't we say, "Let me give you something, let me share of myself." Even if it's just a word, or a raising of awareness. Maybe you can't give money but give something. That's what I learned in Africa. The culture shock really was in coming back to New York. A young girl, my own age, saying the next day, "God! I've got a pimple on my face! I'm going to die! My life is over!" That was the culture shock, and somebody complaining about the cheesecake at lunch.

It's so simple, really, if we could just start to realize how simple it is, to share of ourselves.

AUDREY HEPBURN (1929–1993)

Certainly one of the most famous and beloved of all children's advocates was this elegant and glamorous movie star. Hepburn's first involvement was a humble one, as years ago she became one of the millions of unsung volunteers who generously devote time every year to selling UNICEF greeting cards.

Hepburn's concern for children in need undoubtedly grew out of her own troubled childhood. She was born in Brussels, Belgium. Her real name was Edda van Heemstra Hepburn-Ruston and she was the daughter of a Dutch baroness and a British banker. Her father abandoned his family when Audrey was six. She lived through the German occupation in the Netherlands during World War II, and her courage and strong social conscience were demonstrated when as a teenager she carried coded messages for the Resistance. The winter of 1944–1945 she called the "hunger winter," when she and her mother and brother Jan were so poor and hungry that they actually survived by eating tulip bulbs. A single white tulip was placed on her coffin at her funeral.

Severely malnourished, Hepburn was among those who received food and medical relief at the end of the war from UNRRA and from the Red Cross. In 1989 she told a U.S. congressional committee on foreign affairs that she would carry the memory of her needed relief always, and spoke of the "courage and determination that hope can bring."

UNICEF/Victoria Brynner

As a youngster Hepburn studied ballet and expected to be a dancer, but her destiny took another turn when she became an overnight sensation in her very first film, *Roman Holiday*. Gregory Peck was its star, but after the film was made he insisted that she get star billing too, although she was then an unknown. After her death he commented, "It was my good luck to be her first screen fellow, to hold out my hand and help her keep her balance while she made everybody in the world fall in love with her."

Hepburn became UNICEF's second woman Ambassador of Goodwill in 1988, working tirelessly for children until her own death. In 1989 Hepburn spoke to a group of school children in New York whom she visited because they had helped raise funds for UNICEF. She described to them a recent trip she had made to the Sudan, during its civil war. UNICEF was a lead agency in Operation Lifeline Sudan, the aim of which was to help some 2.2 million people in need of relief, 100,000 of whom might otherwise die that year of starvation, the majority of them children.

Describing what it was like to go there, Hepburn explained that her tour would have been cut in half were it not for her team's resourcefulness. Through international negotiations, eight "corridors of tranquillity" had been created to bring food and medical supplies to areas in need, but when entrance to rebel-held territory could not be gained from the Sudan, her group entered it by crossing the northern frontier of Kenya. Still, the organization's problems underlined some of Sudan's own. It didn't seem that all the relief would reach stricken areas, and the timetable was critical because heavy rains in May would make all but inaccessible a countryside where roads are rare. Even in dry weather, those that exist are in very poor condition. To compound these problems, there was no cease-fire. Because of all these factors, Hepburn thought the relief effort might have to rely more on airdrops of food and supplies.

"I think there has to be positive thinking," she said, "and a lot of encouragement as we support the people who are out there, risking their lives for those other people who are so in need."

Hepburn concluded her speech by telling the children,

> You are our future and we depend on you. You must learn from our mistakes, and we've made plenty. We've been slow in reacting to our mistakes. People, and especially children, are the victims of war. . . .Now, all over the Sudan there are hundreds of camps with starving people and sick and starving children. Peace is not acquired through hatred, nor through wars. . . .It's only peace that can give us a normal life, allow us to live with our parents and not suffer. How many times have I said to myself, especially in the Sudan, "How can this be? How can the world allow this to happen?" But the world will not let this go on, because pretty soon the world will be in your hands.

In 1992, even though she was already ill with cancer, Hepburn traveled to more than a dozen countries to observe the condition of children and to comfort them, and to meet with high government officials. Later in the year she retired to her home in Switzerland. But as the pastor who delivered the eulogy at her funeral pointed out, calling her "an angel in the biblical sense" as his voice broke, "Even in her illness, she visited those children of Somalia, and in their faces was a light reflected from her smile."

Her son Sean spoke after the eulogy:

> Even on the day she died, her thoughts were with the children. She rallied for the last time and wanted to know if there had been any messages from UNICEF about the children in Somalia.

Sean added a personal note that revealed a clue to her character:

> Last Christmas Eve, Mummy read a letter to us written by a writer she admired. . . . "Remember," it said, "if you ever need a helping hand, it's at the end of your

arm. As you get older, you must remember that you have a second hand. The first one is to help yourself, the second one is to help others."

An Audrey Hepburn Memorial Fund has been established to benefit specific projects for African children who are in especially difficult circumstances.

OTHER ADVOCATES FOR UNICEF

Renato Aragao, UNICEF's Special Representative for Brazilian Children since September 1991: He is a very popular entertainer and singer in Brazil who does a yearly Telethon for UNICEF.

Lord Richard Attenborough, Goodwill Ambassador since October 1987: This well-known British film actor, producer, and director donated proceeds from his film *Gandhi*, which in 1982 won three Academy Awards for the year's best picture, best director, and best actor, to UNICEF. This raised a lot of money; the film was also used as the basis of an educational program in many schools. Since then Attenborough has produced other films and donated part of their profits to UNICEF.

Harry Belafonte, Goodwill Ambassador since March 1987: This popular American entertainer—a recording artist, concert singer, movie, Broadway, and television star and producer—was the first member of the entertainment industry to be named by President Kennedy as a cultural advisor to the Peace Corps. As vice-president and spokesman for United Support of Artists for Africa (USA for Africa), Belafonte's enthusiasm and support in 1985 led to the creation and recording of the song "We Are the World," which raised millions of dollars for children. Convinced that artists and intellectuals can "help change the course of human history as it relates to children," he chaired a four-day UNICEF symposium in Dakar, Senegal, to enlist the support of African artists, writers, and educators in mobilizing people behind child survival and development policies and to help bridge the gap between life-saving techniques such as vaccinations and oral rehydration therapy and the actual use of them by African families. Since then he has frequently appeared on TV and radio programs, speaking on behalf of UNICEF. And in 1995 he made a fact-finding trip to Rwanda to see what he could do to help the child victims of that terrible civil war.

Sir Edmund Hillary, Special UNICEF Representative for the Children of the Himalayas since March 1991: After conquering Mount Everest, this New Zealander became determined to conquer some of the severe problems of children in the surrounding area, particularly iodine deficiency disorders, mental illness, and Down's Syndrome. He has also built several schools in the area.

Julio Iglesias, UNICEF's Special Representative for the Performing Arts since March 1989: This Spanish singer of romantic music, one of the two or three most popular singers in the world, regularly gives benefit concerts for UNICEF.

Imran Khan, Special Representative for Sports since December 1988: He is the world's best known cricket player, with a huge number of fans in Pakistan, his native country, and in Australia, Bangladesh, India, New Zealand, Sri Lanka, and the United Kingdom. He continually promotes the cause of UNICEF and children in connection with his matches.

Johann Olav Koss, another Special Representative for Sports since December 1994: This Norwegian speed skater, who won three gold medals in the 1994 Winter Olympics, is a generous man who loves children. A Children's Olympics was held in Norway alongside the official Games and children were also prominently featured during the Games' opening and closing ceremonies. Koss decided to add to his personal victories by achieving victories for the world's children, volunteering to become their advocate by helping to promote interest in UNICEF among athletes and sports fans.

Mario Kreutzberger, Special Representative for UNICEF since March 1994: As "Don Francisco" he is host of a TV show in Chile that has more than 10 million viewers in his own country, other Latin American countries, and among Spanish-speaking people elsewhere. He produces two telethons a year on *Sabado Gigante* (Big Saturday), raising money to help children.

Tetsuko Kuroyanagi, Goodwill Ambassador since February 1984: One of the best-known television personalities in Japan and a best-selling author of children's books, Kuroyanagi was chosen because of her commitment to helping children, including the disabled, to develop to their full potential. She described her new role as an "honor and privilege," saying, "I'll do what I can to bring home the situation of children and mothers of the developing world to the people of Japan who enjoy the lowest infant mortality rate in the world and the highest life expectancy." Among the books she has written for children is *Totto Chan* (The Little Girl at the Window), an autobiographical account of her experiences in school; she donated the proceeds from it to projects assisting disabled children. She is also active in the theater for the deaf in Japan and abroad. She gets only two weeks' vacation a year, and since her appointment she has spent them visiting UNICEF projects and producing documentaries about her trips. Each one has resulted in contributions of approximately $1 million, and over the years she has raised $11 million for UNICEF.

Leon Lai, Youth Ambassador since July 1994: This young singer from Hong Kong gives concerts there and in China that have special appeal to young teenagers. He hopes to get them to pay as much attention to his message about needy children as they do to his music.

Roger Moore, Special Representative for the Film Arts since August 1991: When this British actor, best known for his portrayals of "The Saint" and the famous spy "James Bond," was appointed to this new role, Deputy Executive Director Richard Jolly announced at a press conference that "Now 007 is pledging double efforts for the under 7s through UNICEF." Moore said he became aware of the plight of displaced children when he was stationed in Germany during World War II, and that he had followed UNICEF's work through the years. His first direct association with it was in the early 1980s when he promoted its greeting cards in radio spots. He was UNICEF spokesperson at a song festival in Bologna, Italy, and cohosted with Audrey Hepburn the 1990 and 1991 Danny Kaye International Children's Award TV program from the Netherlands. He told the press that he admired Danny Kaye for his ability to make children smile, and that he too wanted to be able to do that.

Youssou N'Dour, Special Representative for the Performing Arts since April 1991: This singer, musician, and band leader from Senegal works with and for children in French-speaking Africa.

National Committees: UNICEF is unique among UN agencies in its need for support from the public. It receives no financing from the UN and even the support governments provide, on which it depends for 75 percent of its revenue, is voluntary. This disadvantage forced it to turn to the public for support, which in turn forced it to explain the needs of children to people. To arouse public support, national UNICEF committees were formed. Now in more than 35 countries, these committees play a crucial role by providing a direct link between UNICEF and the general public. They work with teachers and publishers to produce educational materials; they give lectures, conduct seminars, hold essay and poster competitions, and organize special fund-raising events.

One of the largest committees, and the oldest, is the U.S. Committee, and it has organized a National Support Council and Corporate Friends of UNICEF, who serve as advocates and fund-raisers in the business community. Hugh Downs, Emmy-award-winning television commentator, who is also an author, sailor, explorer, aviator, and humanitarian, is the best known of the U.S. committee's members, having served for many years as the committee's chair.

Nongovernmental Organizations (NGOs): In addition to all these individual advocates, there is an active liaison committee of 300 national and international NGOs officially affiliated with UNICEF. They represent thousands of private and nonprofit organizations in more than 100 countries, whose professional staffs and volunteers work to help youngsters around the world in many different ways. Their programs supplement the projects of governments, and they are often more flexible and innovative. They operate locally, nationally, regionally, and internationally.

UNICEF Greeting Cards: The national committees are the main sales agents for UNICEF's cards. Approximately 2,500 artists have donated designs for these, following the example of little Jitka Samokova, the Czechoslovakian seven-year-old. Her picture of a smiling sun and dancing children, drawn to thank UNICEF for the emergency aid it had given her and so many other European children, became the first UNICEF Christmas card. The profit on just one box of these cards enables UNICEF to buy enough Vitamin A to protect 100 children from blindness or enough vaccine to immunize 36 children against tetanus, diphtheria, and whooping cough. When UNICEF introduced these cards, they were the only noncommercial cards available, but they proved so popular that many other charities and child advocates now produce greeting cards, too.

MARIAN WRIGHT EDELMAN (1939–)

Founder and President of the Children's Defense Fund

One of the most passionate of all child advocates, Marian Wright grew up in a loving family that cared for its neighbors as well as its children. She is the happily married mother of three sons, and her children understand that she cannot ignore other people's children who are in greater need. As her son Jonah Martin Edelman wrote in his foreword to a book she wrote in 1992, *The Measure of Our Success: A Letter to My Children and Yours*, she "has carried on the values of her father and mother, dedicating her life to helping others as a child advocate. . . .she is tirelessly devoted to both her children and her cause."

A graduate of Spelman College and of the Yale Law School, Edelman was the first black woman ever to be admitted to the bar in Mississippi, where she worked as a private civil rights lawyer in 1964 and 1965. She came to realize that she could have only limited impact on meeting children's needs in that poor state without coherent national policies and strategies to complement community actions. She says she also learned that critical civil and political rights do not mean much to a hungry, homeless, illiterate child and family if they lack the social and economic means to exercise them. So she founded the *Children's Defense Fund*, which publicizes children's needs and lobbies for them as a national organization with headquarters in Washington, D.C.

Edelman has won numerous major awards for her work for the fund, including a MacArthur Prize and the Albert Schweitzer Humanitarian Award. In 1983 she gave a memorable commencement address to the graduating class at Milton Academy, one of New England's oldest and most respected preparatory schools.

Edelman told her audience about a study conducted by the Department of Human Services in Maine that said poor children in America die at a rate three times that of nonpoor children, and that poverty is the ultimate cause of death for 11,000 American children each year—more deaths in five years than the total number of American deaths in battle during the Vietnam War. She also cited a World Health Organization estimate that 10 children die each minute of infectious diseases that are preventable, because only 10 percent of the 80 million children born each year in the developing world are immunized against these diseases. Furthermore, more than 40 percent of poor black urban children in the United States between five and nine years old are not immunized either, even though it costs only $3 to vaccinate a child. She said:

> It is my strong view that the American people have been sold a set of false choices by our national leaders, who tell us we must choose between jobs and peace, between filling potholes in our streets and cavities in our children's teeth, between day care for 5 million latchkey children and home care for millions of senior citizens living out their lives in the loneliness of a nursing home. There are other choices—fairer choices—that you and I must insist our national leaders make. While slashing programs serving the neediest children, the President and Congress found $750 billion to give untargeted tax cuts mostly to nonneedy corporations and individuals. . .we are spending $28 million an hour on defense. The House Democratic leadership wants to spend $27 million an hour, and they are being labelled soft on defense.
>
> Just one hour's worth of proposed increases in military spending would pay for free school lunches for 19,000 children for a school year, she said, and she asked her listeners whether they would rather spend $100 million a year on 100 military bands or put that money into teaching 200,000 educationally deprived children to read and write as well as their more privileged peers can, and whether they would rather build 100 B-1 bombers, at a cost of $250 million each, or build nine fewer and finance a year's Medicaid for all pregnant women and children living below the poverty level.

"As you leave Milton Academy," she told them, "I hope you will care deeply—as citizens and as parents—about the choices those who represent you make, about the needs of those who lack a voice in our society, and about our national mission in a world plagued by hunger, joblessness, and militarism." She urged them to "try to keep your eye on the human bottom line," to become involved in making necessary changes in our society. She explained that in addition to caring about the problems of preserving peace and fighting poverty it was necessary for them to achieve focus by picking a piece of the problem they can help solve, studying it thoroughly, and following up to make sure that changes, once instituted, are kept, never forgetting that "each of us—as individuals—can make a critical difference if we simply care enough and bring to that caring skill, targeted action, and persistence." And they shouldn't let fear of failure hold them back.

She then told them about Sojourner Truth (1797–1883), a slave who could neither read nor write but never gave up talking or fighting against slavery and second-class treatment of women. Once a heckler told Sojourner that he cared no more for her antislavery speech than for a flea bite. "Maybe not," she answered, "but the Lord willing, I'll keep you scratching." Mrs. Edelman said that today we should keep those scratching who would turn their backs on the social outcasts of our society, and who would threaten world peace.

> Enough fleas, biting strategically, can make even the biggest dog—biggest community institutions or government— mighty uncomfortable. If they flick some of us off and others of us keep coming back, we will begin to get the needs of our children and the poor heard and attended to, and oil the creaks of our institutions that may no longer work. It is you and I who must make them work. Democracy is not a spectator sport.

Her audience responded with a standing ovation.

If her views sound radical, here are reactions from two eminent nonradicals. Republican Senator Orrin Hatch has endorsed her work, saying, "I think the Children's Defense Fund is one of the most effective organizations for child care in America today. They are strong, formidable, and forceful advocates who are very good, very effective, and know what they are talking about." Democratic Senator Bill Bradley agreed, saying, "There is no stronger or clearer national voice for children than Marian Wright Edelman and the Children's Defense Fund. They have relentlessly focused national attention on the plight of our children so that all of America's children can grow up to be the best that they can be."

Yet in spite of the praise Edelman has received for her eloquence and hard work, most of the problems she mentioned in 1983 have not been solved, and frightening new ones have arisen. In 1994 she wrote, "We are losing our children" and gave horrifying statistics about what she called "an ugly and malignant tumor" growing in America, the violence that is not only killing many children but turning some of them into killers. She wants to keep guns out of children's hands and wants government regulation of the sale and possession of all nonsporting firearms as the dangerous products they are. But her national strategy for crime prevention goes deeper; it includes an "Ounce of Prevention Fund" that would provide summer employment; after-school, weekend, and summer recreation; and other programs to help idle inner-city and rural youths. She is also working to provide information and educational materials to religious and community leaders to help them offer antiviolence programs that teach values such as respect for one another and self-esteem.

Edelman strongly endorses a new child advocacy group working for black children called the Black Community Crusade for Children (BCCC) whose mission is to "leave no child behind." The Children's Defense Fund and BCCC have set five fundamental goals: To give every child:

1. A Safe Start—"We can't do anything else for our children if they are afraid of dying in their schools, their neighborhoods, and their homes."

2. A Healthy Start—"If we want to save our children we must give them healthy bodies and healthy minds. This means that all mothers must have prenatal care, and remain drug- and alcohol-free. We must ensure that our children get well-baby care, are immunized, and are educated about and protected against too early pregnancy."

3. A Head Start—"High quality early childhood programs have been proven to get children ready for school and to help poor children get better grades, higher graduation rates, lower crime rates, and decreased incidence of teenage pregnancy. . .but despite this remarkable success story, Head Start still reaches only about one out of three of all eligible children."

4. A Fair Start—"Children should grow up in families and communities that are economically secure. . .we are endorsing welfare reforms that move families back into the economic mainstream by providing recipients with job opportunities, child care, education and training, and other supports that can lead to self-sufficiency and a life of dignity."

5. Strengthened Families—"BCCC strongly emphasizes moral values, strong families, and love, as well as jobs and quality education. We must give our children positive role models, attention by caring adults, and a sense of a future worth striving for."

In the appeal letter she mailed to supporters she wrote, "You may think these goals are ambitious. They have to be. . . .Our mission is to save children and restore the joy and innocence of childhood to a generation of children who are growing up in deprivation and fear. None of us can turn from this responsibility."

In 1996 Edelman undertook her most ambitious act of child advocacy, criss-crossing the nation to recruit people to come to Washington, D.C., for a mobilization to be held at the Lincoln Memorial on the first of June, called "Stand for the Children." She told them:

> We have got to come to grips with who we are and what we value, and stop the people who mouth family values and yet don't support the things families need to do a good job raising their children. . . . If there are families that are worried about whether their child is going to get sick and not be able to see a doctor because they don't have health insurance, they should come stand with us. Parents and grandparents who are concerned about the 211 million guns in circulation, and whether their children are safe walking in their neighborhoods or going back and forth to school, should come stand with us.

Edelman said she is pleased that the U.S. can boast the largest number of millionaires and billionaires of any industrialized country, "but I am not pleased that we allow our children to be the poorest group of Americans." Although the U.S. leads industrialized nations in health technology, she pointed out that 17 of those nations do better than the U.S. in their rates of infant mortality.

The response to her invitation was encouraging. More than 1,200 national, state, and local organizations—including the American Nurses Association, the American Pediatrics Society, the Easter Seal Society, the Girl Scouts, the Harvard School of Public Health, dozens of Junior Leagues, the March of Dimes, the National Council of Jewish Women, the National Council of

STAND FOR CHILDREN

June 1, 1996
Lincoln Memorial
Washington, DC

Negro Women, Outward Bound, Project HELP, the United Way, and the Urban League—signed on as cosponsors. And when the day arrived, 200,000 individuals showed up, arriving in cars, buses, trains, and planes from all over the country.

The message Edelman delivered to them was not new. In her rapid-fire way (journalist Bob Herbert describes her as "a long-distance runner maintaining a sprinter's pace") she repeated what she has said before, that "we are losing our children." She cited the latest statistics: every nine seconds a child drops out of school; every 14 seconds a child is arrested; every 25 seconds a baby is born to an unmarried mother; every 15 minutes a baby dies; every two hours a child is killed by a firearm; every four hours a child commits suicide; every seven hours a child dies from abuse of neglect.

Saying she was deeply moved by the numbers who had come to Washington in response to her call, she urged the vast audience to return to their communities and actively work to change these statistics.

In spite of the grave problems that concern her, Marian Edelman appears undaunted. Somehow she never seems to lose hope:

> We can reverse this course. We have a historic opportunity to rescue our children from the forces of poverty, dependency, violence and despair. The steps we must take to change the world in which our children grow up are now getting real consideration. . . .These are no pipe dreams. These are the building blocks of a different future for all of our children.

DR. ROBERT COLES (1929–)

Another passionate advocate for children is the famous psychiatrist, author, and Harvard University professor, Robert Coles. After four decades of teaching in many of the university's schools, including the law school, medical school, Kennedy School of Government, and the undergraduate college, in 1995 Coles was named to a newly created position as the James Agee Professor of Social Ethics in the Graduate School of Education at Harvard. Social ethics and public service have always been central to his writing and teaching. For example, for three summers before this new appointment he helped Harvard undergraduates run academic youth camps for families in the Boston area.

Coles is best known for his work with children. Like Jean Piaget (1896–1980) and Erik Erikson (1902–1994) he has spent almost an entire lifetime learning about the inner life of the child.

For more than 30 years Coles traveled around the United States, Canada, South America, and Europe, visiting schools and making friends with families, getting to know their children so that he could understand and help them cope with their problems, and also helping parents and teachers to understand and meet their children's needs.

Coles is seemingly tireless and endlessly creative, managing to do all this year after year in addition to his work at Harvard, and somehow he has found time to write more than 50 books, many of them best sellers. The majority of the books are about children; the others are biographies or oral histories of outstanding people who have responded to *The Call of Service* (the title of one of his books).

Coles wrote a five-volume series called *Children of Crisis: A Study of Courage and Fear* (1967–1978), which won him a Pulitzer prize. Among his other books are *Uprooted Children, Teachers and the Children of Poverty, The Call of Stories: Teaching and the*

Moral Imagination, Erik Erikson: The Growth of His Work, The Child in Our Times, The American Teenager, Drugs and Youth, The Moral Life of Children, The Political Life of Children, and *The Spiritual Life of Children.* The latter book is particularly moving, as it reveals feelings and thoughts that we can all relate to: as one young girl from a destitute family in Brazil said to him about God, "I'm either upset with Him or I'm praying for Him to tell me why the world is like it is."

Coles also frequently gives lectures to groups of parents and teachers, and appears on television, urging them to realize how pivotal their roles are in raising children. He believes the future of American civilization depends on how we raise our children. "Children," he says, "are a moral challenge to us. Children are us handed on to another generation, and our very citizenship is at stake."

(For more information about Coles's work on behalf of children, see page 267.)

OTHER BENEFACTORS OF CHILDREN

It is unjust that so many people who deserve to be included among these child advocates have been left out. It certainly is not because what they have done to help children has not been valuable. In fact, many have done invaluable work. Each has been inspired to help and has in turn inspired other people, in a beautiful chain reaction. The problem is simply that there is not enough room in one volume to include all the people who have helped needy children.

The beautiful Eglantine Jebb (1876–1928) lived by two mottos, "We must get something done" and "I can, I will." She drafted the world's first Declaration on the Rights of the Child in Geneva in 1926 and founded the International Union for Child Welfare and its many now independent national branches, Save the Children. These all act as effective children's advocates in their own countries and undertake important life-saving field work for children in more than 50 other countries.

Father Edward Flanagan (1886–1948), an idealistic Irish priest, founded Boys' Town in Omaha, Nebraska. He was regarded as somewhat daft when he maintained that "there is no such thing as a bad boy" and set out on what people considered a quixotic dream to rescue and raise a few homeless boys, including some who were in trouble with the law. But his "impractical" project grew and has thrived for over 50 years, and now it also helps girls.

The people who founded and live in the Children's Villages in Europe and Asia make loving homes for otherwise homeless children.

Covenant House with its volunteer Faith Community is made up of people who give up secure jobs, cheerfully committing themselves for at least a year to work for $12 a week, to provide havens and help for millions of frightened, cold, hungry, desperate street children from broken families, runaways or throwaways, in six American cities. They also provide housing, counselling, and training for teenage mothers.

Mother Hale (1907–1994) for more than 50 years, even in her late eighties, was an ardent advocate for unwanted children, welcoming them into her home in Harlem and raising them as lovingly as if they were her own. Widowed at 27, with three children to rear whom she did not want to leave alone while she worked as a domestic, she started taking in other children for two dollars a week and eventually became a licensed foster parent. Between 1941 and 1968 she successfully raised more than 40 children, all of whom graduated from high school, though she was 87 years old before she herself won a high school equivalency diploma. Many went on to college; they rewarded her with 60 children of their own, whom she regarded as her grandchildren. In 1969 she opened "Hale House," which became the first program in New York City to care for heroin-addicted babies. In 1980 she opened her home to its first baby with AIDS and showed people that it was okay to hug, kiss, and love such infants. In 1982 she welcomed her first crack baby. Over the years she and a dedicated staff and volunteers inspired by her provided home, security, love, and healing for nearly 1,000 children, helping them when their mothers were unable or unwilling to do so.

In 1990 when Mother Hale needed money to keep going, she appealed to the public and more than 90,000 people contributed money, toys, diapers, clothing, food, baby bottles, and children's furniture so that she could continue, which she did until a few weeks before she died in 1994. Since then her daughter, Dr. Lorraine Hale, who, in order to help her mother, earned doctorates in child development and psychology, has kept up her work.

The International Starlight Foundation and the Make a Wish Foundation make hospital stays happier for sick children by arranging parties and bringing mobile "fun centers" to their rooms, with videocassettes and games, many donated by Nintendo, rolled up to their beds so they can play. For children who are critically or chronically or terminally ill, they make arrangements to have dreams come true, answering requests for trips or to meet favorite celebrities or to receive special toys their parents cannot afford.

Speaking of dreams, the remarkably generous Eugene Lang founded an "I Have a Dream" program to help inner-city kids get a good education; he not only promises to pay for their college if they stay in school but takes a personal and prolonged interest in each child who agrees not to become a dropout. The schoolchildren he has helped have achieved a 90 percent high school graduation rate and in 1991 a Hispanic girl who went on to Bard College became his first college graduate. Inspired by his example, many other individuals and corporations have launched similar projects all around the United States.

Other generous people are the Big Brothers and Sisters of America, who volunteer to give warm personal attention to kids whose parents are too busy, too poor, or for other reasons are unable to give their children the amount of quality time they need.

An enormous number of actors, actresses, artists, athletes, musicians, and singers have also contributed time, talent, and money, appealing to the public to help poor children in their own countries and overseas. Many practice what they preach, in many cases adopting or sponsoring children in need.

Since 1938 the March of Dimes has financed research to learn the causes of birth defects so more of them can be prevented. It also helps to save children who are born with defects and helps their families.

All over the world there are international and national nongovernmental organizations (NGOs) actively working on behalf of children. Their sheer numbers make it impossible to give credit to all of them. In addition to those affiliated with UNICEF, it has been estimated that more than 3,000 others around the world assist children in various ways.

The League of Red Cross and Red Crescent Societies, which have an international membership of 230 million volunteers and health professionals, launched a Child Alive program in 1984 to promote child survival. More than 20 national societies are running this program and have played a key role in many immunization campaigns. Rotary International, through its Polio Plus program, has allocated millions of dollars to protect millions of children against polio in more than 30 countries.

There are many religious groups, particularly the Josephites, who have worked for black children for over l00 years. Maryknoll trains families who volunteer to spend a year or more in other countries, helping poor families there and living among them, and it publishes a monthly magazine to inform the public of the many needs of poor children in these countries. The Medical Mission Sisters are both nuns and physicians serving the poor worldwide. The Salesians provide homes, schooling, and job training to poor children and orphans. The Salvation Army also has a special concern for the health, education, and welfare of children.

And one must never forget the heroic sacrifices of people who voluntarily do difficult and dangerous work to rescue children whose lives are threatened by famine or by war, selflessly putting their own lives at grave risk. Doctors without Borders, the largest private medical relief organization in the world is but one of the organizations that acts as an advocate for people the world has abandoned. It brings these people critically important moral and psychological support as well as desperately needed medical and surgical care. For example, it sent 30 brave volunteers to work in Sarajevo, where they discovered that snipers with a lust for killing had developed cruel specialties; some killed only children. By the time the doctors arrived snipers had killed 4,000 children and wounded l5,000 more, many of whom the doctors were able to save. They found the hospitals in a shambles, overcrowded and lacking water and electricity, so the volunteers became repairmen as well as doctors.

There are special individuals, as well as organizations, who have contributed to children's well-being in many ways. For example, Claude Perret of Paris won a prize of $200,000 in l967 and, instead of keeping it, donated the money to UNICEF, and after that became a leading seller of its greeting cards. Another prize winner with great generosity was Bernard Winkler, an architect who in 1970 won a significant award for urban design by creating a "joyous environment," a pedestrian zone in the old part of Munich. When he learned about the award he immediately asked that the monetary part of it ($20,000) be turned over directly to UNICEF.

Hundreds of volunteers who work at Disneyland and other places bring happiness to children, such as the delightful "Story Land, Where Fantasy Comes to Life" in Glen, New Hampshire, and "where no frowns, no tears, or other fears are allowed." The Fresh Air Fund is active in over 300 communities and has given more than l.6 million boys and girls living in inner-city slums summer vacations with rural host families or at one of its five camps. It is one example of how oak trees grow from tiny acorns: In l877 a rural minister in Pennsylvania persuaded his parishioners to invite some urban children into their homes for a brief summer respite. Today the fund's "alumni" and their families can be found in all 50 states, and they are happy to describe how a few summer weeks in their childhoods away from abject poverty and terrifying violence were enough to give them hope and change their lives.

And for year-round help for urban children, there are the nonprofit Boys' and Girls' Clubs that are active in many big cities. They provide supervised sports and recreation programs, tutoring and help with homework, dental care, and pleasant oases from the dangerous streets.

Last but by No Means Least

Innumerable teenagers and children have also worked as advocates and fund-raisers to help other children. They may not be able to turn over huge amounts of money, but their contributions certainly add up. Many have given what they could—their weekly allowances and money given them on their birthdays or at Christmas, profits from recitals and exhibits that they have put on, or taken up collections in school.

The U.S. Committee for UNICEF once received a letter from an eight-year-old girl, Theresa La Fountaine, living in the small town of Weybridge, Vermont, who described what the 78 pupils in her elementary school were doing. She wrote,

> You won't believe this! Our small school has just saved over 140 lives! Even though my school is small, we think we can make a big difference in the world. In the beginning of the year, our hot lunch program had a lot of wasted food. We heard that kids in some countries don't have as much food to eat as we were wasting each day, so we decided to make a waste watch resolution. We try to have the whole school waste less than a pound of food at each lunchtime. Each day we do that, people from all over Addison County have pledged money to us. We send the money we get to UNICEF so they can buy a mixture called KMix II. One pound of it will save a kid's life! If we don't waste a pound of food, then we can buy them a pound of KMix II. Now do you see how it works? This is great news because our school is really saving children's lives!

Other children in a fourth-grade class in Bernardsville, New Jersey, were among many people who responded to a 1982 UNICEF report saying that "Far from being priceless, a child's life was worth less than $100 in 1981. Many millions of children's deaths could have been prevented last year at the cost of $100 per child." These elementary school children managed to collect $100 by doing chores; they sent "the price of a life" to UNICEF.

Students in a New York City school gave UNICEF a "Mile of Pennies." They collected pennies by holding exhibits, a block party where they served national dishes, volleyball games, and sales of homemade sweets and crafts. They put the pennies into 62-foot-long strips of sticky tape and rolled them into wheels of $10 each. A scroll in the school lobby honored each student who contributed one foot or more. If you wonder how many pennies there are in a mile, the answer is 848,800.

Students have held art, essay, and poetry contests, athletic competitions, spelling bees, and beauty contests to raise money for children. One group of college students in Ohio was original: they put on costumes and masks and held an entertaining "Ugliness Contest."

In Australia teenagers have dressed in costumes from different countries and performed in children's plays, puppet shows, magic acts, pantomimes, and other theatrical productions for children in schools, orphanages, hospitals, community centers, theaters, and public parks.

In addition, some children do focussed work on projects and give personal help in emergencies. Some 25 million Scouts and Guides all over the world have increasingly become involved in working for child survival. The Boy Scouts have project "Scoutreach," in which they have worked in poverty-stricken urban areas, with earthquake victims in Guatemala, and at summer camps for disabled youngsters. Girl Scouts and Girl Guides have undertaken in many lands projects concerned with child health and education. In America, the Junior League began as a social club but now undertakes many projects to help underprivileged children. In England, the Child-to-Child organization has been very successful in training children to help other children by teaching them about good nutrition, teaching them to read, and working with their handicapped contemporaries.

Others have thought up extremely ingenious and original ways to raise money in support of their favorite children's advocates. Some teenage farmers in England sold eggs as usual but gave the money for every twelfth egg to UNICEF to help finance one of its nutrition projects. John Bers, a student at Yale University, organized a Yale Food for India Drive, in which 2,000 students gave up their evening meal one night to help feed the hungry in the villages of India. The university dining halls agreed to turn over the money they saved to UNICEF's Applied Nutrition Project in Asia. Bers was pleased, though he said this "one-meal 'fast' was a gesture of conscience and involvement but to say our contribution is even a drop in the bucket is a gross exaggeration. Yet what if every student in every college did the same thing?" The idea caught on in Belgium, Canada, England, the United States, and other countries, where many college students made the same sacrifice.

In Vancouver, Canada, l00 high school students held a "Starvathon," living for three days on CSM, a corn-soya-milk flour developed by UNICEF to combat child malnutrition.

Students have not only fasted but have held "walkathons," getting sponsors who paid them for each mile they walked. In Canada l00,000 teenagers, even some in wheelchairs, took part in a Miles for Millions campaign, a lengthy march in which they said they raised blisters and money for UNICEF, led by two boys holding a large poster saying, "Hi there! We're those rotten teenagers."

"Thons" have been an especially popular way of raising money. There have been "bike-a-thons," "walkathons" and "singathons," "danceathons," "readathons," and "talkathons," and their opposites, where children are paid for the number of minutes they can keep quiet; some Boy Scouts in Scotland raised $ll6 in one night with a Sponsored Silence. They got people to pay them for each minute they could refrain from talking, shouting, laughing, playing records, answering the phone, or engaging in any other noisemaking. And l0 American girls held an astonishing "rockathon," giving a new meaning to rock and roll. They actually sat in rocking chairs and rocked for 24 hours to raise money.

Every Little Bit Helps

Knowing about all these people and their activities is encouraging. To help such people realize how useful they are even if all they can do is merely "a drop in the bucket," here are some proverbs that show the value of even small drops:

- From China: Enough shovels of earth, a mountain; enough pails of water, a river.
- From the Congo: Little by little grow the bananas.
- From England: From little acorns great oak trees grow.
- From Ethiopia: When spider webs unite, they can tie up a lion.
- From France: Drop by drop fills the tub.
- From Germany: Little and often fills the purse.

- From India: Joined together, even little things are strong. A mad wild elephant can be bound with a few straws if the straws are formed into a rope.

- From Japan: Daylight will peep through a very small hole.

- From Liberia: A little rain each day will fill the rivers to overflowing.

- From Nigeria: Little is better than nothing.

- From Russia: A small hole can sink a big ship.

- From the Sudan: A little shrub may grow into a tree.

- From Tanzania: A little and a little, collected together, become a great sea; the heap in the barn consists of single grains, and drop and drop makes the flood.

Helen Keller once said, "Science may have found a cure for most evils, but it has found no remedy for the worst of them all—the apathy of human beings." As far back as the eighteenth century two wise men spoke about this problem. Edmund Burke (1729–1797) wrote that "all that is necessary for the forces of evil to win in the world is for enough good men to do nothing," and Sidney Smith (1771–1845) said, "It is the greatest of all mistakes to do nothing because you can only do a little. Do what you can."

When someone does that, and other people learn about it, the results can be remarkable. A good example of this is what happened in December 1983 when a 10-year-old boy, Trevor Ferrell, who lived in a suburb near Philadelphia, saw on TV some scenes of homeless people living on the streets. He could not believe his eyes and ran to ask his parents, "Is this really happening?" When they said yes, he asked them to take him out that night so he could give a pillow and a blanket to a homeless person. His father told him, "You're better off going back and doing your homework," but Trevor nagged and pleaded until his parents gave in. From that night on, the boy began collecting pillows, blankets, clothing, and food for the homeless and taking these to them each night. Soon his efforts drew national attention. TV programs and newspapers told about him and enough private donations flowed in so that he and his family were able to start Trevor's Campaign for the Homeless, a charity that converted a 33-room house into a shelter called "Trevor's Place."

In 1987 when he was 14, Trevor received the Christopher Award for his continued commitment and dedication. He said he did not deserve an individual award, because "it just takes one person to start it, but then others will continue. We now have more than 700 volunteers in the Philadelphia area" with three vans that take food to about 150 homeless people and, he said, "they haven't missed a single night in three years." He also claimed that the homeless deserved an award for "living out there in the cold weather, sleeping in the streets, having pavement for a pillow." But he thanked Father John Catoir, the head of the Christophers, for honoring his work because "it encourages me to help out more," and "helping people gives me a natural high." He added that another advantage of helping people was that it had taught him to be more appreciative of all the comforts so many people take for granted. "It's made me think twice when I get in the shower sometimes just knowing that water is going to come out, and going into a bed at night, being able

> Never doubt that a small group of thoughtful, committed citizens can change the world; indeed it is the only thing that ever has.
>
> —*Margaret Mead (1901–1978), anthropologist*

to turn on the electricity, having a garage to park your car, having a car."

Isn't it wonderful that people like Trevor Ferrell and so many others are not apathetic and are doing whatever they can to help others? As Sam Levenson (1911–1980), the American humorist and essayist, wrote in a letter to his children: "To my parents freedom meant, above all, 'Live and let live.' They were willing to settle for tolerance as a way of life. For the world in which you are going to live, tolerance will not be good enough. We are now in the 'Live and help live' era."

This is the true joy in life, the being used for a purpose recognized by yourself as a mighty one. I am of the opinion that my life belongs to the whole community and as long as I live it is my privilege to do for it whatever I can. Life is no brief candle to me. It is a sort of splendid torch which I have got hold of for the moment, and I want to make it burn as brightly as possible before handing it on to future generations.

—*George Bernard Shaw (1856–1950), playwright and essayist*

What Can the Rest of Us Do to Help Children?

There are many, many ways that anyone can help in the fight to make a better world for children. Here are some suggestions, and remember, every little bit helps.

First, stop thinking of "junk mail" as junk. Instead of tossing out letters that you know are asking for money at least read them before you do. Perhaps you will learn about a program you would enjoy supporting. If you are short of funds, send just a tiny amount because even the smallest show of support can help. And if you cannot manage to give any money at all, remember that conversation costs nothing. Pass the information along by enthusiastically telling other people about the good work this or that organization does; maybe some of them would contribute.

Money is not the only thing we can contribute. Instead of throwing out clothes, books, or toys, we can contribute these to children who could make good use of them. Look in the telephone book for names and addresses of local thrift shops, churches, synagogues, schools, libraries, or other charitable organizations where we can drop these things. Or call the local St. Vincent de Paul Society or Salvation Army, who will probably be glad to come and pick up at least some of your items.

There is also something even more valuable than things that many of us could contribute. Hospitals, nursery schools, school boards, day care centers, shelters for the homeless, and many other institutions need volunteers. Many people hesitate to volunteer because they are afraid their efforts will take more time than they are really willing to spend. Before starting, we should explain exactly how much time we will contribute, whether once a week or once a month, and for how long we expect to be able to continue.

In New Hampshire in April, 1996, Governor Stephen Merrill, after nearly four years as one of the state's most popular politicians, announced that he was quitting elective politics because he wanted to spend more time at home with his two children. In an emotional news conference, he said, "You know, public life in the 1990s is difficult when you have children under three years of age. I am really saying I want to spend time with my children, go to their school plays and be there as a dad, and read to them. It's hard to shut the door again and again and listen to my son cry."

So not everyone should try to be an active advocate for children. Those who are willing and able to are to be greatly admired, and we should lend them our warm support in whatever ways we can, but we should not feel guilty if we cannot always emulate them. Charity really does begin at home, and by doing our best for our own children, we are actually following the advice of the organizations that tell us to "think globally but act locally." Every parent who helps his or her children grow up into healthy, good people is helping children. Setting a good example as a "role model," keeping a watchful eye on your kids and encouraging their talents, teaching them sound values are all ways parents can help their own members of the next generation. The day will come almost before you expect it when they no longer need your full-time attention or protection, and *then* you can extend your love to help other people's children.

Doug Brunner

16

Children and the Future

COMMENTS ABOUT CHILDREN AND FUTURE PROGRESS—QUOTES

Progress begins with the belief that what is necessary is possible.
—*Norman Cousins (1912–1990), American editor and essayist*

The long ages of infancy and childhood through which the human race had to pass, have receded into the background. Humanity is now experiencing the commotions invariably associated with the most turbulent stage of its evolution, the stage of adolescence, when the impetuosity of youth and its vehemence reach their climax, and must gradually be superssxeded by the calmness, the wisdom and the maturity that characterize the stage of manhood. Then will the human race reach that stature of ripeness which will enable it to acquire all the powers and capacities upon which its ultimate development must depend.
—*Shoghi Effendi (1899–1957), Baha'i spiritual leader, c. 1922*

I believe that the sum total of the energy of mankind is not to bring us down but to lift us up. . . . If we are to make progress we must not repeat history but make new history. . . .If we may make new discoveries and inventions in the phenomenal world, must we declare our bankruptcy in the spiritual domain?. . .Hope in the future I have never lost and never will. . . .When I despair, I remember that all through history truth and love have always won. There have been tyrants and murderers—and for a time they can seem strong. But in the end they always fall. Think of it—always . . . .When you are in doubt that that is God's way, the way the world is meant to be. . .think of that. . . .
—*Mohandas (Mahatma) Gandhi (1869–1948),*
Indian spiritual leader and social reformer

This is a crucial moment in history. . . .The world's present and future needs both cry out with one voice. Each decade in the future will see magnification of either the success or the failures of the world community's response to the needs of today's children.

In the acquisition of their needs and in defense of their rights, children are relatively powerless. . . they have no unions, and no votes. Usually it is the parents who are empowered to protect and provide. But if parents are deprived of that power, then the responsibility falls to the community of which the child is part. In the very earliest human societies . . .average life expectancy was probably little more than 20 years and many children were deprived of both their parents before they were of an age to provide for themselves. The survival of the child and the continuing survival of the community therefore depended upon the assumption of that responsibilty by that community.

However large and complex the community may have grown, that special relationship of responsibility to its children is still an indispensable ethic of civilization. Indeed, it is an increasingly relevant ethic as science and technology increasingly invest the earth with the attributes of a global village. . .if a local community is unable to meet the needs of its children then the responsibility

sibility extends to the nation and the international community. That special relationship of conscientious concern for children is essential for future progress.

—James P. Grant (1980–1995), Executive Director of UNICEF, 1981

The child is at the heart of everything and very especially at the heart of the question of the peace, the happiness and the prosperity of the world of tomorrow.

—John Grun, Special UNICEF officer during 1979,
the International Year of the Child

We must come to see that human progress never rolls in on the wheels of inevitability. It comes through the tireless efforts and persistent work of men willing to be coworkers with God, and without this hard work time itself becomes an ally of the forces of social stagnation. . . . I have a dream that one day men will rise up and come to see that they are made to live together as brothers. . .and every man will respect the dignity and worth of human personality. . .I have a dream that one day on the red hills of Georgia sons of former slaves and the sons of former slave owners will be able to sit down together at the table of brotherhood. I have a dream that my four little children will one day live in a nation where they will not be judged by the color of their skin but by the content of their character. I have a dream that one day little black boys and black girls will be able to join hands with little white boys and white girls as sisters and brothers.

—Martin Luther King, Jr. (1929–1968),
American minister and civil rights leader

Neglect of children will produce a hungry, ignorant and resentful world that, of necessity, will create societies that are unstable and prone to violent upheaval.

—Indalecio Lievano, President of the UN General Assembly
during the International Year of the Child, 1979

If we do not prepare children to become good citizens, if we do not develop their capacities, if we do not enrich their minds with knowledge, imbue their hearts with love of truth and duty, mankind must sweep through another vast cycle of sin and suffering before the dawn of a better era can arise upon the world.

—Horace Mann (1796–1859), American educator

Somehow the fact that ultimately everything depends upon the human factor gets rather lost in our thinking of plans and schemes of national development in terms of factories and machinery and general schemes. It is all very important and we must have them, but ultimately, of course, it is the human being that counts, and if the human being counts, well, he counts much more as a child than as a grownup. . . .I have always felt that the children of today will make the India of tomorrow, and the way we bring them up will determine the future of the country. . . .Children are one the world over, and they could become a unifying factor in a world that is torn apart by strident and narrow nationalism.

—Jawaharlal Nehru (1889–1964), first Prime Minister of India

611

I have end-of-century jitters. It's a big thing when a century ends, a time of fate and foreshadowing . . . . The 1890s were a pleasant time, a beautiful epoque, and a prelude to the most killing century in the history of man. Start out on a bicycle built for two, wind up at Verdun. . .start out at Sarajevo, wind up at Sarajevo. . . .Henry Ford changed our lives more than the women's movement has. Kids have no one home now. Many of them are going through life with a parent-sized hole inside. We are the inheritors of a coarsened country, and Hollywood is partly to blame.

—*Peggy Noonan in 1994, interviewed in connection with her book* Life, Liberty and the Pursuit of Happiness

My biggest hope is that the day will come when so many people everywhere will be gainfully employed that they themselves will be able to feed and protect their children and provide them with education. Then there will be no need for UNICEF.

—*Maurice Pate (1894–1965), founder and first Executive Director of UNICEF*

Development demands bold transformaton, innovations that go deep. . . .We must also begin to work together to build the common future of the human race. . . .Advanced nations have a very heavy obligation to help the developing peoples. . . .At stake are the survival of so many innocent children and, for so many families overcome by misery, the access to conditions fit for human beings. At stake are the peace of the world and the future of civilization. It is time for all men and all peoples to face up to their responsibilities.

—*Pope Paul VI (1898–1978),* Encyclical on the Development of Peoples, *1967*

It has become fashionable today to mock or to treat with suspicion anything which looks like faith in the future. If we are not careful, this skepticism will be fatal, for its direct result is to destroy both the love of living and the momentum of mankind. . . .Love is the most universal, formidable and mysterious of cosmic energies. . . .Some day, after mastering the winds, the waves, the tides and gravity, we shall harness for God the energies of love, and then, for the second time in the history of the world, man will discover fire.

—*Pierre Teilhard de Chardin (1881–1955)*

The attitude towards children is a reflection of the attitude towards the future of mankind. If we are to build a world of peace, friendship, equality and social justice we must, first of all, start to work already now towards securing such a world for our children. We must not allow the injustices of the world of today to be primarily felt by the youngest generation. Today millions of children are deprived of the most elementary conditions essential to life and growth, not to mention those who have perished in flames of war. . . .There is nothing as noble as working for the child's welfare and for his happiness, not only in one's own country but in every corner of our planet. The care for children, their protection and well-being are an integral part of the struggle for progress, for better understanding and friendship among peoples, for happiness and prosperity of all nations.

—*Josip Broz Tito (1892–1980), President of the former Yugoslavia*

Development means giving people fair access to conditions in which they may grow physically, mentally, spiritually and materially to their full capacity. . . . The challenge of removing the worst aspects of global poverty in the next 20 years is awesome. So are the opportunities for digging out new knowledge, devising new techniques, trying out new ideas, making new networks of young and old who want to work with and for children. There are enough material resources, skills and willing heads and hands to put a floor under hunger by the end of this decade. The trick is to bring it all together. Can we pull it off? Maybe not, but we cannot avoid the responsibility of trying.

—Tarzie Vittachi (1921–1993),
Sri Lankan journalist and UNICEF Executive

PREDICTIONS—ACCURATE AND INACCURATE

Most People are irresistibly tempted to sum up a decade that is just ending and to predict how the next decade will differ from it for better or worse, and this temptation is never greater than just before the end of a millennium.

Many people used to believe in the inevitability of progress, assuming that every decade would improve on the one before. When this turned out not always to be true, pessimism became more fashionable, and many people today are alarmists. Journalist Alistair Cooke (1906–) once said "I'd be astonished if this planet is still going 50 years from now. I don't think we will reach 2000. It would be miraculous." In saying this, he was echoing the belief of Nostradamus, the sixteenth-century astrologer who predicted that the world would come to an end in A.D. 1999.

> Far from offering a short cut to clairvoyance, history teaches us that the future is full of surprises and outwits all our certainties.
>
> —Arthur M. Schlesinger, Jr., American historian (1917–1966)

Below are some examples of predictions made in the past that turned out to be so laughable that today it is hard to believe anybody considered them seriously. Thee were not concerned directly with the future of childhood, but they were serious analysis of the possibilities of technological progress and other matters that would produce the kind of world in which children would be living in the future—with (or without) new inventions, methods of transportation, types of recreation, changes in the urban environment, in racial and international harmony, in medical care, and in population growth or decline. Reading about these prophecies made with confidence by respected authorities should warn us about how mistaken prophets can be, so as the next millenium approaches we will not take too seriously the frightened doomsayers who will undoubtedly arise.

Incorrect Prophecies by Past Experts

By the second half of the twentieth-century most differences among races will be extinct and the citizens of the world will be speaking one universal language.
—Felix Bodin, French futurologist, 1834

The [flying] machines will eventually be fast; they will be used in sport, but they are not to be thought of as commercial carriers.
—*Octave Chanute, Aviation pioneer, 1904*

Atomic energy might be as good as our present-day explosives, but it is unlikely to produce anything very much more dangerous.
—*Winston Churchill, 1939*

Everything that can be invented has been invented.
—*Charles H. Duell, Director of the U.S. Patent Office, 1899*

The problem with television is that the people must sit and keep their eyes glued to a screen; the average American family hasn't time for it. . . . For this reason, if no other, television will never be a serious competitor of [radio] broadcasting.
—*Orrin E. Dunlap, Jr., New York Times reporter assigned to evaluate the new technology being introduced at the New York World's Fair in March 1939*

The phonograph . . . is not of any commercial value.
—*Thomas Edison, 1880, Three years after he invented it*

Heavier-than-air flying machines are impossible. . . . X-rays will prove to be a hoax. . . . Aircraft flight is impossible. . . . Radio has no future.
—*Lord William Kelvin, President of the Royal Society of Science, eminent nineteenth-century engineer and physicist, c.1895*

Television won't matter in your lifetime or mine.
—*Rex Lambert in* The Listener *magazine, 1936*

The ordinary horseless carriage is, at present, a luxury for the wealthy, and although its price will probably fall in the near future, it will never come into as common use as the bicycle.
—Literary Digest, *1899*

The population of the earth decreases every day, and if this continues, in another 10 centuries the earth will be nothing but a desert.
—*Baron de la Brède et de Montesquieu, French philosopher, 1743*

Time and money spent on airship experiments are wasted.
—New York Times *editorial, 1903*
(seven days before the Wright brothers first flew a powered heavier-than-air ship)

Cities will become sanitary—no dirt, dust, or smoke will be possible.
—*Charles Steinmetz, American electrical engineer, 1915*

Even if the propeller had the power of propelling a vessel, it would be found useless in practice, because with the power being applied in the stern it would be impossible to make the vessel steer.
—*Sir William Symonds, British Navy surveyor, 1837*

Any general system of conveying passengers at a velocity exceeding 10 miles per hour or thereabouts is extremely improbable.
—*Thomas Tredgold, British railroad designer, 1835*

Who the hell wants to hear actors talk?
> —*Harry M. Warner, Head of Warner Brothers Pictures, c.1927*

I think there is a world market for about five computers.
> —*Thomas J. Watson, President of IBM, 1958*

Men will not fly for 50 years.
> —*Wilbur Wright, 1901, two years before he and his brother flew their first airplane*

Between 1924 and 1932, nearly 100 British intellectuals wrote a book apiece speculating about the future. Not one of the books was about the possibility of overpopulation. J. B. S. Haldane (1892–1964), a celebrated geneticist, predicted that the population of the United States would level off at 145 million—in fact, by 1985 it had reached 237.2 million.

A pithy put-down of predictors was made by Will Rogers (1879–1935) when he said, "It's not what you don't know that bothers me. It's what you know for certain that ain't so." And Arthur C. Clarke, in his book *Profiles of the Future*, analyzed the problem with predictions this way: "When a distinguished but elderly scientists states that something is possible, he is almost certainly right. When he states that something is impossible, he is very probably wrong."

In a period of changes as rapid and earthshaking as our own, accurate predictions are even more difficult to make than at other times. Watching the astounding changes that took place in the Soviet Union and Eastern Europe beginning in 1989 and the unexpected changes that followed, we must agree with the philosopher Ralph Waldo Emerson (1893–1882) who said, "Progress is achieved through impossibilities surmounted," and with Mark Twain (1835–1910) when he said, "Truth is stranger than fiction, because fiction has to content itself with possibilities and truth does not."

If he were alive when the USSR was breaking up, William Shakespeare (1564–1616) would probably have been cheering the people who were trying to improve their society, as well as reformers in other parts of the world trying to tackle and topple tyrants and end poverty, war, and injustice. He said, "There is a tide in the affairs of men which, taken at the flood, leads on to fortune. Omitted, all the voyage of their life is bound in shallows and in miseries." But the political strategist Niccolò Machiavelli (1467–1527) in his famous book *The Prince* had words of caution for people seeking to bring about social change:

> There is nothing more difficult to carry out nor more doubtful of success, nor more dangerous to handle, than to initiate a new order of things. For the reformer has enemies who profit by the old order, and only lukewarm defenders in all those who would profit by the new order. This lukewarmness arises partly from fear of their adversaries, who have the law in their favor, and partly from the incredulity of mankind, who do not truly believe in anything new until they have had actual experience of it.

The euphoria most people felt at the end of November 1989 when freedom was on the march in Eastern Europe did indeed give away to new troubles and confusion. People learned that it was not enough to get rid of repressive governments. The hardest task was replacing them without violence and chaos, particularly in countries that had no experience in democratic government. Expectations of a wonderful new life quickly bumped into the reality that food shortages existed and that the new rulers were not at all sure how to govern. People's disillusionment and frustration gave way in many cases to rage, so they found and persecuted new scapegoats in orgies of bigotry, nationalism, and "ethnic cleansing."

Edward S. Cornish, a futurist who is neither an optimist nor a pessimist, wrote in his book *Welcome to the Future*:

> Whether we are on the threshold of a Golden Age or on the brink of a global cataclysm that will extinguish our civilization is, I believe, not only unknown and unknowable, but also undecided. The decision will emerge through what we do in the years ahead, for reach of us will create a little piece of the common future of all mankind.

This is a reminder of an important thing to realize about the future. It is not something "out there" waiting to pounce on us and that we can do nothing about. On the contrary, it is something that we ourselves are creating right *now*, and we—not a blink, inexorable, impersonal fate—are deciding what it will be like. If we do certain things, certain results will follow. If we do other things, other results will follow.

For example, if we feed children enough nourishing food, they will not die from malnutrition. If we do not, they will. If we educate children well, they will not grow up ignorant. If we do not, they will. These are predictions that are safe to make, because they are self-evident.

Two Uncannily Correct Prophets

Not all prophecies are inaccurate, of course. And there are at least two outstanding examples worth noting where the prophets' accurate predictions were even more surprising than the inaccuracy of the majority,

In the year 1448, an extremely mysterious prophecy was made, five centuries before such things as movies and television, submarines and airplanes, or world wars existed. The following strange lines are on an ancient tombstone in the village of Kirby in Essex, England:

> When pictures look alive with movements free
> When ships like fishes swim beneath the sea
> When men like birds do skim the sky
> Then half the world deep drenched in blood shall lie.

And in 1863, a young writer named Jules Verne wrote a novel called *Paris au XXe Siecle* (*Paris in the Twentieth Century*). It was rejected by the publisher he sent it to, who said, "My dear Verne, if you were a prophet no one would believe your prophecies today."

Among his prophecies for the year 1963 he imagined a place where people communicate by telegraph and telephones, use calculators and computers, and where "electronic concerns" are heard (using synthesizers in which 200 pianos are linked by electric current to a single piano played by one musician). In this future city people travel by subways and in gas-driven cars that are simple to handle ("the mechanic, sitting in his seat turning a steering wheel, with a pedal at his foot that allows him to change the speed of the vehicle instantly")—though the first such car was not built until 1889, 26 years after Verne had foreseen it. Stock exchanges across Europe are linked by telegraph. "Further," he wrote, "the photographic telegraph permits the dispatch over long distances of the facsimile of any writing, signature, or design." He predicted electricity, even describing street advertisements in lights, and furthermore forecast the electric chair (which did not make its appearance until 1888); "people are no longer being beheaded" he said; "they are being electrocuted."

Paris in the twentieth century would also, Verne foresaw, be an overcrowded city in which everyone can read but where Latin and Greek are no longer taught in schools, and where society is dominated by money but destitute homeless people roam the streets.

Despite this book's rejection, Verne later became famous as a prophet-novelist, or as we would call him today, a science fiction writer, through other books like *20,000 Leagues under the Sea* in which he predicted submarines and *Around the World in 80 Days* in which he predicted air travel. But this handwritten manuscript was put aside and forgotten. It remained undiscovered until his great-grandson Jean Jules Verne came across it 131 years later. In 1994 it was finally published, causing a sensation, both because of its amazingly accurate predictions about technology and it pessimism about the quality of twentieth-century education and culture.

THE STATE OF THE WORLD AND ITS CHILDREN

The two books quoted to the right are updated and published every year. They are the social equivalent of annual medical checkups.

The special concern of the Worldwatch Institute is the environment. It is the most complete and reliable guide first to our world's physical resources and how they are being managed—or mismanaged— and it makes practical proposals on how to protect and preserve the world's physical resources while at the same time developing the sustainable future we all want. It is used in more than 800 college and university courses, and is a standard reference for journalists, editors, and writers.

The other book, *State of the World's Children,* is published by the Oxford University Press as well as by UNICEF, and is obviously concerned with what has often been called "the world's most valuable resource," its children.

The emphasis in each book is different yet they overlap to some extent. Both discuss the dangerous impact of increasing poverty, waste, population growth, the costs of wars and of demilitarization, the problems of refugees, and the need to revamp international institu-

> Our generation is the first to be faced with decisions that will determine whether the Earth our children inherit will be habitable. . . . we're at a crossroads in human history.
>
> —State of the World, 1995, *published annually by the Worldwatch Institute*

> The world will not solve its major problems until it learns to do a better job of protecting and investing in the physical, mental, and emotional development of its children.
>
> —State of the World's Children, *1995, published by UNICEF*

617

tions in order to meet human needs. Each volume examines how present world problems will affect the future.

Since the issues involved are global in extent, both are published in many languages. Both books are important, but because the special concerns of the book you are now reading are childhood and children, excerpts from UNICEF's report are those given below and on the following pages.

The 1995 edition was the last one supervised by James Grant, UNICEF's executive director who died later that year. The 1996 edition was unique in two ways. It was the first to be issued by the new executive director, Carol Belamy, and 1996 was UNICEF's fiftieth anniversary, so instead of focusing primarily on the current year as previous issues had done, it presented an overview of the past 50 years.

First, the Bad News: The Impact of Modern Warfare

The opening chapter of the 1995 of the *State of the World's Children* edition began on "a note of anger and sadness" about an

> increasingly frequent series of catastrophe for children. . . .All of these conflicts, made the more devastating by weapons exported from the industrialized nations, have brought not only short-term suffering to millions of families but long-term consequences. . . .What kind of adults will they be, these millions of children who have been traumatized by mass violence. . .denied the opportunity to develop normally in mind and body. . .deprived of homes and parents, of family and community, of identity and security, of schooling and stability?

The 1996 edition updated this report's "statistic of shame," saying that

> between 1945 and 1992 there were 149 major wars. . . .On an average yearly basis, the number of war deaths in this period was more than double the deaths in the nineteenth century and seven times greater than in the eighteenth century. . . .During the last decade, child victims have included:
>
> - 2 million killed;
> - 4–5 million disabled;
> - 12 million left homeless;
> - more than 1 million orphaned or separated from their parents;
> - some 10 million psychologically traumatized.

> In the wars of the eighteenth, nineteenth, and early twentieth centuries, only about half the victims were civilians. In the later decades of this century the proportion of civilian victims has been rising steadily: in World War II it was two thirds, and by the end of the 1980s it was almost 90 percent. . . .

> Most civilian casualties are children. But one of the most deplorable developments in recent years has been the increasing use of young children as soldiers. . . .Recently, in 25 countries, thousands of children under the age of 16 have fought in wars. In 1988 alone, they numbered as many as 200,000.

The report described UNICEF's new Anti-war Agenda that contains specific goals in regard to child soldiers, land mines, war crimes, children as zones of peace, sanctions, emergency relief, rehabilitation, and education for peace.

Finally, Some Good News

The report concluded, however, with some dramatic statements describing real progress that has been made despite the problems that remain. Among other examples, it said, "Health conditions across the world have improved more in the past 40 years than in all of previous human history."

Chapter two of the 1996 report also ended on a hopeful note. After describing "Fifty Years for Children" with concrete examples of constructive work in such matters as village water supplies, community-based health care, and other medical advances, it said,

> As a result of this century's vast improvements in child survival and development, parents have greater hopes for their children. . . .And society is investing much more in their education and training.

> This is no accident. As we come to the end of the decade, the education of children, especially girls, has become one of the centerpieces of international development. The principle that education brings empowerment, and with it the opportunity to transform life, has been affirmed strongly, by the global conferences at Cairo, Copenhagen, and Beijing. Seldom has the international community been so united as it is on the priority for universal primary education.

> That is precisely what makes the future for children a realm of optimism rather than a crucible of despair. For the complex of reasons spanning 50 years, as set out in this report, it is now possible—in spite of the wars and the poverty—to believe that, ultimately, the world will not abandon, marginalize, or depreciate children.

> It has been a long struggle to have the lives of children taken seriously; it has consumed half a century to put children at the center of the international development and human rights agenda. But they are there, and nothing will now dislodge them. It is therefore possible to say, even amid the horrors of conflict and deprivation, that the twenty-first century will belong to children. It then remains to shape the policies and the programs, the principles and the resources to give meaning to what has been achieved.

THE POPULATION EXPLOSION
And Its Implications For the Future

The current rate of population growth is entirely new in history. At the time of Julius Caesar (c. 100–44 BC) the earth's total population was approximately 100 million, but in the twentieth century the total population is increasing by 150 million every two years.

It took one million years for the world to reach a population of one billion people, in 1800 . . . and then,

in 1930	it reached	2 billion
in 1960		3 billion
in 1974		4 billion
in 1985		5 billion
in 2000	estimates are	7 billion

619

Demographers estimate that every minute 100 people die and 240 are born—so the world's population is increasing by 140 people per minute. An hour from now probably more than 14,000 children will have been born, and by the end of this week more than two million, over 70 percent of them in poor countries that are least able to provide the social services they will need. Will food supplies, uncontaminated water, and housing and schools be able to increase rapidly enough to keep up with all these newcomers?

Population Distribution

Half the world's people live in just four countries: China, India, Russia, and the United States. China's population increases by more than 35,000 per day. By 1994 its population was larger than that of the entire world 150 years previously.

The most densely populated country is little Holland, with 920 people living in every square mile. England has 600 people per square mile, China 280, and the United States only 65. But of course these people are not scattered evenly. For instance, the state of New Jersey in the U.S., with only half the area of Holland, beats it; it has 966 people per square mile. And New York City has a whopping 23,494 people per square mile. Yet it is not the most crowded place on earth. According to the 1996 edition of the *Guinness Book of World Records,* the tiny Portuguese province of Macau as of 1994 had an estimated population of 416,000 in an area of 6.9 square miles, giving it a density of 60,290 people per square mile.

In some African and Asian countries, children account for 50 percent of the population. In most of the world, however, they are a minority. According to demographers, in 1900 children under 18 accounted for 40 percent of the United States' population, but by 1995 only 26 percent of Americans were under 18 (that is still a lot of children: approximately 60.9 million, and for the first time in history the most rapid population increase was among people over age 75.

According to James D. Weill, general counsel of the Children's Defense Fund, "a majority of voters do not live with children," and since children do not vote or make campaign contributions to political parties, this may be why U.S. politicians are more willing to allocate government funds for highways, large corporations, and other institutions that serve adults than they are to invest in schools, child care services, and aid to dependent children.

Professor Timothy M. Smeeding of Syracuse University, an economist who is director of the Luxembourg Income Study, says, "Other countries have more programs that help families, a better safety net. European countries, while cutting back many social programs for adults in recent years, have expanded programs for single parents and low-income families."

Donald J. Hernandez, a demographer at the U.S. Bureau of the Census, says it is against a nation's self-interest to neglect programs to help children, because "our investment in children will determine how productive they are, how much they can contribute to the retirement income of the baby-boom generation," and "the productivity of those workers will, in turn, depend on the quality of the education, training, and health care received by members of minority groups when they are children." According to U.S. Census Bureau projections, the proportion of all children who are members of racial and ethnic minority groups will reach 50 percent by the year 2030, doubling from 25 percent in 1980.

THE WORLD SUMMIT FOR CHILDREN

The World Summit for Children was a historic event so unprecedented that it was written up in *The Guinness Book of World Records* and attracted enormous media coverage; more than 3,000 journalists were accredited to cover the meetings.

It was nothing new, of course, for politicians to express love and concern for children. In fact, candidates for public office kissing and hugging children is a political cliché, yet many of the same politicians regularly vote against educational and nutritional programs needed by children. So it remained to be seen if these 72 heads of government would actually put their money where their mouths were and give priority in their budgets to children's needs.

Although this summit was child advocacy on a vaster scale than had ever been attempted before, what did it actually achieve? Would its words actually be translated into effective actions, or would the summit be "no more than two days of well-intentioned talk," as Senator Bill Bradley of New Jersey feared?

The primary goal of the summit was child advocacy and consciousness-raising, and it most certainly did achieve that, if only temporarily. In the week before the summit, thousands of churches, synagogues, and mosques held special services and prayers for children. In more than 80 countries 2,600 candlelight vigils were held. City-wide activities and town meetings in support of the summit were held all across the United States. The thirtieth of September through the seventh of October was officially declared "New York City Children's Week" with the theme "Make a Difference; Get Involved." Some 300 children representing countries from around the world took part in a Children's International Congress, an all-day program called "Kids Meeting Kids Can Make a Difference," with delegates from organizations such as Children of War, Child Hope, and Global Kids, to discuss problems facing children, and two days later representatives from this congress reported to a four-hour Children's Outdoor International Forum on the north lawn of the United Nations, where 4,000 children, along with teachers; government representatives; news media; well-known personalities; a group from Canada, the Rainbow Kids; and the Peace Child Foundation, a dance troupe from India; and Smokey Mountain, a soft rock group of youngsters from the Philippines performed. This Children's International Congress presented letters, petitions, and a large mural depicting the rights and needs of children to be displayed at the UN during the summit.

At 8 P.M. on the summit's opening day church bells throughout New York rang and the lights of the city's Great White Way, Broadway, were darkened in memory of the thousands of children who would die during the two days of the summit.

The *Plan of Action for the Protection, Survival and Development of Children* issued in the summit's concluding session was intended as a practical guide for national governments, international and non-governmental organizations (NGOs), bilateral aid agencies, and other sectors of society to meet the challenges, tasks, and opportunities that lie ahead. It specified seven major goals:

- Between 1990 and the year 2000, reduction of the under-five child mortality rate by one third or 70 per 1,000 live births, whichever is less;

- Reduction of the maternal mortality rate by half;

- Reduction of severe and moderate malnutrition among under-five children by half;

- Universal access to safe drinking water and to sanitary means of excreta disposal;
- Universal access to basic education and completion of primary education by at least 80 percent of primary school-age children;
- Reduction of world illiteracy to at least half of its 1990 level with emphasis on female literacy;
- Improved protection of children in especially difficult circumstances.

Other Activities Inspired by the Summit

Although the World Summit for Children was the most highly publicized of the child advocacy activities that took place in September, 1990, many private groups also got into the act, recognizing that meeting the needs of children cannot and should not be left to governments alone but requires mobilization of all sectors of society. From September 15 to 18 a Youth Round Table in Geneva, on the theme "Children First," was attended by young people from all over the world to launch a "Youth NGO World Initiative for Children."

Also in September in New York, NGOs, recognizing that their help would be vital if the goals of the World Summit for Children were to be met, held a summit of their own. Over eleven hundred people from 60 countries representing more than 600 nongovernmental organizations examined their own roles in making "A World Safe for Children: Meeting the Challenge in the 1990s." Concrete actions and long-term strategies were planned, and specific recommendations were proposed. This conference stated the "doability" of measures that could be taken to alleviate many problems. It acknowledged that the knowledge and technology exists to provide solutions that can roll back world rates of infant, child and maternal deaths and give universal access to food, clean water, and safe sanitation, and that the only thing lacking is the sustained, coordinated will to put the solutions into practice. Insisting that "children must no longer be the victims of the follies of their elders," the conference pointed out that less than one day's military expenditure per year is all that is needed to prevent the deaths of 50 million children over the coming decade.

Post-Summit Progress

Early in 1995 UNICEF issued the following report:

It is clear that a majority of the goals set for 1995 are going to be met by a majority of the developing nations. More than 100 of the developing nations, with over 90 percent of the developing world's children, are making significant practical progress towards the goals that were set four years ago. . . .

Malnutrition has been reduced; immunization levels are generally being maintained or increased; measles deaths are down by 80 percent; large areas of the developing world, including all of the western hemisphere, have become free of polio; iodine deficiency disorders are being eliminated; vitamin A deficiency is in retreat; the use of oral rehydration therapy is rising (preventing more than 1 million child deaths a year); guinea worm disease has been reduced by some 90 percent and complete eradication is in sight; thousands of major hospitals in developing and industrialized countries are now actively supporting breastfeeding;

progress in primary education is being resumed; and the Convention on the Rights of the Child has become the most widely and rapidly ratified convention in history.

Such progress means that approximately 2.5 million fewer children will die in 1996 than in 1990. It also means that tens of millions will be spared the insidious sabotage wrought on their development by malnutrition. And it means that at least three quarters of a million fewer children each year will be disabled, blinded, crippled, or mentally retarded.

Amid the constant flow of bad news about the developing world, these achievements deserve wider recognition. They have been brought about by the largely unrecognized efforts of thousands of organizations and individuals, inside and outside government, who have believed in those goals for children and who have worked to see them achieved.

All of these achievements are a suitable reply to those who believe that international gatherings produce only fine words and forgotten promises, or that there is only disaster and failure to report from the developing world, or that the United Nations family of organizations is not effective in helping to make the world a better place. . . .

Tomorrow's Global Village—Quotes

The world has become so interdependent that no one part can get away without needing the rest or being needed by it. There is no safety for some when others are in misery.   *—Isaac Asimov (1920–1992), American science writer*

The illusion of separateness is the greatest heresy.
     —Gautama Buddha (c.563–483 B.C.)

I dipt into the future, far as human eye could see,
Saw the vision of the world, and all the wonder that would be,
Till the war-drum throbbed no longer, and the battle flags were furled,
In the Parliament of man, the federation of the world.
Then the common sense of most shall hold a fretful realm in awe,
And the kindly earth shall slumber, lapt in universal law.
For I doubt not through the ages one increasing purpose runs
And the thoughts of men are widened with the process of the suns.
    —Charles Dickens (1812–1870), English novelist

God grant that not only the love of liberty but a thorough knowledge of the rights of man may pervade all the nations of the earth, so that a philosopher may set his foot anywhere on its surface and say: This is my country.
    —Benjamin Franklin (1706–1790), American statesman

My nationalism is intense internationalism. I am sick of the strife between nations and religions. All humanity is one undivided and indivisible family. . .It is not nationalism that is evil, it is the narrowness, selfishness, exclusiveness which is the bane of modern nations which is evil. Each wants to profit at the expense of and to rise on the ruin of the other. . . .If we believe in God, not merely with our intellect but with our whole being, we will love all mankind without any distinction of race or class, nation or religion. We will work for the unity of mankind. *—Mahatma Gandhi (1869–1948), Indian social reformer*

Having traveled across the face of our beautiful planet, having traversed all its oceans and its continents, having shared deep human hopes with my brothers and sisters of every nationality, religion, color, and race, having broken bread and found loving friendship and brotherhood everywhere on earth, I am prepared to declare myself a citizen of theworld, and to invite everyone everywhere to embrace this vision of our interdependent world, our common humanity, our noblest hopes and our common quest for justice in our times, and, ultimately, for peace on earth, now and in the next millenium. . . .It is easy to scoff at this vision of our humanity, our oneness, our common task as fellow passengers on a small planet. The great and powerful of this earth can easily sniff cynically and return to their game of power politics. . . .But somehow I believe there is enough good will in our country and in the world to expect millions of people. . .to say that we do want all men and women to be brothers and sisters, that we do believe in justice and peace, and that we think homes, fields of grains, schools, and medicine are better than guns, tanks, submarines, ABMs and MIRVs.
—Theodore M. Hesburgh (1917–),
former president of Notre Dame University

With the hope of the world resting on the coming generation, the problem of caring for the children is international in scope and its solution must be found on an international basis.
—Trygve Lie (1896–1968), first secretary-general
of the United Nations, 1947

For the first time in all of time men have seen the earth; seen it not as continents or oceans from the little distance of a hundred miles or two or three, but seen it from the depths of space; seen it whole and round and beautiful. . . .The medieval notion of the earth put man at the center of everything. The nuclear notion of the earth put him nowhere—beyond the range of reason even—lost in absurdity and war. This latest notion may have other consequences, formed as it may remake the minds of mankind. No longer that preposterous figure at the center, no longer that degraded and degrading victim off at the margins of reality and blind with blood, man may at last become himself. To see the earth as it truly is, small and blue and beautiful in that eternal silence where it floats, is to see ourselves as riders on the earth together. . . brothers who know now they are truly brothers. *—Archibald MacLeish (1892–1982), American poet*

A Village with Five Billion Neighbors

This is difficult to imagine. To realize what the world is really like it helps to think of it as a village, a village of 5,000 people, with each person representing one million of the people on earth.

One-third of the people in this world-village live in the wealthier section. Two-thirds live in slums or on poor farms.

About 400 people in the wealthy part of town are children, healthy and well cared for, who go to school. In the poorer parts of town there are about 1,700 children, most of them undernourished and in poor health. Only five out of 10 children in the poor parts of town get a chance to go to school, and only three go for more than a few years. This means that seven out of every 10 are growing up illiterate and will be poor all their lives.

There are not enough doctors or nurses to take care of the people in the poor parts of this village. Out of every 10 children who live there, only three get any medical care from trained people. In some parts of town almost half the children die before reaching the age of five, and many of those who survive will be sickly all their lives.

The average person's income in the poor parts of town is less than $700 a year, and in some sections less than $100. They cannot afford nice homes, clothes, toys, automobiles, television sets, vacations, or most of the other pleasant things that people in the rest of town take for granted.

Most of the people who live in the rich section of town do not give even one percent of their annual incomes to help the poor people. Furthermore, even though there are not nearly as many of them as there are of the poor, the rich people use up 85 percent of the town's energy resources and material supplies, including food.

In about 20 years there will be twice as many people living in this town as there are now, which means they will need twice as much food, twice as many doctors, nurses, schools, teachers, homes, water and sanitation supplies, everything, not to improve the town but just to keep it from getting worse.

This village is not an imaginary one. It is a small-scale image of the one we all live in: the planet Earth—our home town.

We will have to do more than we are now doing to help each other if we want our village to be a decent and happy place. We will have to learn to share and stop wasting. Right now we spend much more money producing guns than we do building schools and hospitals and homes.

The terrible thing is that we are wasting not only our material possessions but our most valuable asset: people. People who never get educated and who are in poor health are wasted, because they can never do the useful work they could do otherwise. They are a burden on the town instead of a help to it. But people who are healthy, energetic, well-trained, intelligent, hard-working, and generous can solve problems instead of adding to them.

Our village is very beautiful and could be a wonderful place to live in, if every child in it had enough to eat and enough good medical care and schooling, and if all of us were friendly neighbors and helped each other. Then our global village would be a very happy place, both today and tomorrow.

Some Advice to Today's Young People

Actor Alan Alda is an adult who has great sympathy for today's young people. He showed this with his characteristic mixture of humor and seriousness when he gave the commencement address at Connecticut College where one of his daughters was in the graduating class. He showed his sympathy, but he also gave them some advice. Here are excerpts from his speech:

You are being flung into a world that's running about as smoothly as a car with square wheels....If you feel a little off balance it's understandable....But keep laughing—I've noticed that when people are laughing they are generally not killing one another. And if you can get other people to join in your laughter you may help keep this shaky boat afloat.

We live in strange times....Here's my Golden Rule for a tarnished age: be fair with others, but then keep after them until they're fair with you.

Life is meaningless unless you bring meaning to it....It is up to us to create our own existence. Unless you do something, unless you make something, it's as though you aren't there....Learn skills....You can use them to dig into the world and push it into better shape....

The soup of civilized life is a nourishing stew, but it doesn't keep bubbling on its own. Put something back in the pot as you leave, for the people in line behind you. Do good when you can. . .laugh and enjoy yourself. . . .Love your work. If you put your heart into everything you do you can't lose. . .whether you wind up making a lot of money or not, you will have had a wonderful time and no one will ever be able to take that away from you.

In May 1994 Garrison Keillor wrote a column for the *New York Times* Op Ed page, pretending to deliver a commencement address to "Exhausted Faculty, Anxious Graduates, Weepy Parents and Angry Taxpayers." In it he deplored the fact that there is more self-pity these days than ever before, that too many people feel dysfunctional, abused, addicted, dependent, disabled, and in pain. He said more self-pity is available these days than there was during the Great Depression when many people lived in houses with newspaper stuffed in the cracks and worked so hard their bodies ached at night but they did not complain much because they thought that if you smile, you will feel better. So they threw big parties. They sang and danced and told jokes. "But nowadays, people are always complaining about sexual harassment and child abuse and weeping over their painful memories."

He worries about our lack of humor:

Laughter is what proves our humanity. When Moses came down from the mountain with the clay tablets, he said, "Folks, I was able to talk Him down to 10. Unfortunately, we had to leave Adultery in there, but you will notice that Solemnity was taken out. . . ."

He ended with

Get together with people you like a lot, dance, be romantic, be silly....Satire, kids, is your sacred duty. . . ."

THE FUTURE BELONGS TO OUR CHILDREN

Your children are not your children.
They are the sons and daughters of Life's longing for itself.

They come through you but not from you.
And though they are with you yet they belong not to you.
You may give them your love but not your thoughts,
For they have their own thoughts.
You may house their bodies but not their souls,
For their souls dwell in the house of tomorrow, which you cannot enter, not even in your dreams.
You may strive to be like them, but seek not to make them like you,
For life goes not backward nor tarries with yesterday.
You are the bows from which your children as living arrows are sent forth.
Let your bending in the archer's hand be for gladness.
—Kahlil Gibran, "On Children" in *"The Prophet"*, 1923

Abraham Lincoln (1809–1865) expressed these thoughts less poetically but just as truthfully when he said "A child is a person who is going to carry on what you have started. . . . He will assume control of your cities, states, and nations. He is going to move in and take over your churches, schools, universities and corporations. . . .the fate of humanity is in his hands."

In short, life is a relay race, with each generation handing the torch to the next one. Tomorrow literally belongs to today's children because they are the people who are going to live in it.

It is therefore in their self-interest for young people to learn how to become productive citizens and to work together to build a future in which the world will be a safer and happier place than it is now, and it is the duty and privilege of their elders to prepare them for this task.

One reason children should be encouraged and given opportunities to work on behalf of society's future is that they are in some ways better qualified to do so than older people are. Without the curiosity and adventurousness and energy of youth the world would long ago have died of mental hardening of the arteries.

On the other hand, it is obvious that children need guidance. Wisdom, like the quality of good wine, increases with age. This is why good education is so vitally important. There are skills that must be acquired.

So in life's relay race, teamwork is as important as in any other relay race. Cooperation between the younger members of society and older ones is necessary. Youngsters must listen to their elders with respect and benefit by their greater experience. And older people must treat younger ones with respect and be open to new ideas.

The French have a saying that "if you aren't a radical when you're young, you have no heart, and if you're not a conservative when you're older you have no brains." In India people also think that different attitudes are appropriate at different ages. The Hindu ethical system divides life into segments, ascribing different virtues to different stages. In childhood, they say, the most important virtue is docility, the willingness to be taught. In youth, the most important thing is to apply what one has learned, to establish a career according to one's talents and interests. In maturity, the main virtue, they believe, is to create and take care of a family, or to be a teacher, passing on what one has learned to the next generation. Whereas in old age, it is time to let go, to turn over such responsibilities to the next generation and, through prayer and meditation, to prepare oneself for death.

What the world's future will be like does not depend so much on the growth of technology, computers, factories, and highways, all the things we think are so important, as it does on how children are raised. As the English author John Galsworthy (1867–1933) once said, "In the child of today, tomorrow has its beginning. They are from year to year the human harvest, good or bad according as we men and women till the field of child life." And as Aase Lionaes, member of the Norwegian Parliament said when she presented the Noble Prize for Peace to UNICEF in 1965, "The children of today are the history of the future."

There is a long-honored rule for emergencies at sea: "Women and children first." The world today is facing a serious emergency, so it should act on a similar rule. Children before guns. Children before highways. Children before everything else.

A Crisis Can Be a Challenge to Improve

Today's juvenile delinquents and suicides are giving the world a wake-up call. There is a character in Chinese calligraphy for the word *crisis*, which is made up of the characters of two other words: *danger* and *opportunity*. Perhaps today's crisis has become so dangerous that the world will wake up and seize the opportunity to react to it soon enough and constructively enough to end it.

Not that we can ever expect to have a world that is free of crises. Here is a complaint about the state of the United States that sounds rather familiar:

> It is a gloomy moment in the history of our country. Not in the lifetime of most men has there been so much grave and deep apprehension; never has the future seemed so incalculable as at this time. The domestic economic situation is in chaos. Our dollar is weak throughout the world. Prices are so high as to be utterly impossible. The political cauldron seethes and bubbles with uncertainty. It is a solemn moment of our troubles. No man can see the end.

Many would agree that this is an accurate description of things today. But it was published in *Harper's Weekly* in October 1857.

And here is an even earlier comment about the world's problems. Back in the fourth century Saint Augustine wrote,

> We must not grumble. . .Is there an affliction now endured by mankind that was not endured by our fathers before us? What sufferings of ours can bear comparison with what we know of their sufferings, and yet you hear people complaining about this present day and age because things were so much better in former times. I wonder what would happen if they could be taken back to the days of their ancestors—would we not still hear them complaining? You may think past ages were good, but it is only because you are not living in them.

Is it any consolation to realize that "the good old days" were actually even worse than our own? It is not the selfish idea that misery loves company, but the answer should be a resounding YES, because it means that there actually is such a thing as progress. In most parts of the world today cannibalism, slavery, infanticide, legal prostitution of children, dueling, trial by ordeal, physical torture, and superstitious, cruel, and ineffectual medical practices have been abolished, and there are now laws against many other evils that were once not even considered evil.

To cite Saint Augustine again: "Hope has two beautiful daughters. Their names are Anger and Courage: anger at the way things are, and courage to see that they do not remain the way they are." Crises are opportunities as well as dangers that can be overcome. In our era we have faced horrendous crises caused by two world wars, the Depression, Hitler, and Stalin, and they were overcome. With courage and determination we can conquer today's problems, too, and help to provide our children with a future worth having.

So we should count our blessings as well as our worries. Man cannot live by dread alone. There are some good things happening nowadays along with many terrible things, but both good and bad things happen to all people all the time. And although worrying too much can lead to apathy and despair, following the advice and examples of the many wise and good people who have graced our planet through the centuries will enable us to surmount present problems.

Not that we will not then encounter new ones, but as Chiadambaram Subramanian, minister of planning in India in the 1970s, once explained to an interviewer,

> When you start to change things you are asking for trouble, but that is how progress has always been made. Otherwise, we would never have left our caves and would all have stayed primitive human beings. By asking for trouble we are able to go on improving. . . .Human wisdom is such that, even though there might be setbacks here and there, we will go on progressively improving our world because man has the capacity to learn. . . .I get concerned when we are struggling with the same old problems, because that means we are not making progress. But when we are confronted with a new, more difficult and complex problem, then I am satisfied! Because that is a sure sign that we are achieving progress.

Our Paradoxical Century

The twentieth century began with high hopes. People believed in the inevitability of progress and most thought that science had reached such an enlightened stage that it was about to transform the world, abolishing superstition, disease, racial and religious hatred, wars, severe poverty, and ignorance, so that everyone was going to live happily ever after. They had no foreknowledge that huge numbers of children were going to die in gas chambers and as military targets in bombing raids. That there would be two world wars and a depression in between. That something called juvenile delinquency was going to erupt and produce more young and violent criminals and terrorists, drug addicts and suicides than history had ever seen before. That broken families and homelessness were going to increase and a terrible new disease called AIDS would take many lives. Or that modern inventions, combined with human wastefulness and greed and a tremendous population explosion, would produce such devastating pollution of air, earth, and water that all life on our planet would be threatened.

Dear Posterity,

If you have not become more just, more peaceful, and generally more rational than we are (or were)—why then, the Devil take you.

Having with all respect, given utterance to this pious wish, I am (or was)

Your
Albert Einstein
(1879–1955), written c. 1936

But these evil things are only part of our century's story. The century's remarkable inventions, labor-saving devices, the telephone and telegraph, the automobile and the airplane, radio and movies and television, the computer, and amazing medical advances have been even greater blessings than the early optimists foresaw and have brought luxuries beyond the imagination of the wealthiest kings and queens of ancient times to millions of people. And many more people than ever before are working to bring these blessings to those who lack them.

Father William J. Leonard, S.J., a professor at Boston College at the end of World War II when many of his students were weary war veterans studying under the G.I. Bill, tried to inspire them with his vision of what the world could be like in the future. He said in his autobiography, *The Letter Carrier,*

> The society we shall erect must be in very truth a commonwealth. Away then with any caste system, any upper or lower or middle class, fabricated on wealth, education, or other privilege. We shall be members of a social body, in which every member shall have respect for the contribution he makes to the well-being of the whole, in which the weak shall be shielded and assisted, not ground down and exploited. . . .No slums, then, in our Commonwealth! No ghettos where some citizens are segregated because their color or creed differs from that of the majority. No dehumanizing drudgery, in which some lose self-respect and are degraded to the level of machines for production, that others may grow rich. . . . In all your studies here, keep this Commonwealth before you. Draw the blueprint for it as completely as you can. Write its constitutions and plan how they may be implemented. People will call you mad. Well, we want a few mad people now; see where the sane ones have landed us.
>
> . . . it is better and holier to have dreamed in vain for the good of one's fellowman than never to have dreamed at all. . . . We, your teachers, shall not regret your folly in so high a cause; we shall praise and point to you as an inspiration. We have only one fear, that in this critical hour, when the one thing needful has been laid before you, you will not be equal to the quest. You will turn from it in cynicism or in selfishness. You will quail, like Hamlet, before the holy task. "The time is out of joint: O cursed spite, that ever I was born to set it right." Indeed, the time is sadly out of joint, but we were born to set it right and, God helping us, we will.

And, as U.S. Senator Hubert Humphrey (1911–1978), said, "The good old days were never that good, believe me. The good new days are today, and better days are coming tomorrow. Our greatest songs are still unsung."

Every Child Has the Right

to affection, love and understanding

to adequate nutrition and medical care

to free education

to full opportunity for play and recreation

to a name and nationality

to special care if handicapped

to be among the first to receive relief in times of disaster

to learn to be a useful member of society and to develop individual abilities

to be brought up in a spirit of peace and brotherhood

to enjoy these rights, regardless of race, color, sex, religion, national or social origin

630

Bibliography

Note: Sources used for information found in more than one chapter are listed in the "General Bibliography" section, beginning on page 653.

Chapter 1

Ancient Civilizations: Sollberger, E.: *Babylonia.* Drower, Margaret: *Egypt.* Finley, M.I.: Crete. Allchin, F.R.: *India.* Twitchett, D.C.: *China.* Parry, J.H.: *Mexico and Peru.* London: British Broadcasting Corporation, 1963.

Bayne-Powell, Rosamond. *The English Child in the Eighteenth Century.* New York: E. P. Dutton & Co., 1939.

Bettmann, Otto L. *The Good Old Days—They Were Terrible!* New York: Random House, 1974.

Bishop, Morris. *The Middle Ages.* New York: American Heritage Press, 1970.

Bonnard, André. *Greek Civilization from the Iliad to the Parthenon.* Translated from French by A. Lytton Sells. London: Allen & Unwin, 1957.

Boswell, James. *Life of Samuel Johnson.* London, England, 1791. Reprint, with commentaries by John A. Vance. Athens, Ga.: University of Georgia Press, 1985.

Boswell, John. *The Kindness of Strangers: The Abandonment of Children in Western Europe from Late Antiquity to the Renaissance.* New York: Pantheon Books, 1988.

Boyle, John, ed. *The Concise Encyclopedia of World History.* New York: Hawthorne Books, 1958.

Bronowski, J. *The Ascent of Man.* Boston: Little, Brown & Co., 1973.

Cannon, John, and Ralph Griffiths. *The Oxford Illustrated History of the British Monarchy.* Oxford, England: Oxford University Press, 1988.

A Century of Childhood: 1820–1920. Rochester, N.Y.: The Margaret Woodbury Strong Museum, 1984.

Deanesly, Margaret. *A History of the Mediaeval Church, 590–1500.* Cambridge, Mass.: Cambridge University Press, 1985.

Delort, Robert. *Life in the Middle Ages.* Translated by Robert Allen. New York: Crown Publishers, 1983.

DeMause, Lloyd, ed. *The History of Childhood.* New York: Harper & Row, 1974.

Eban, Abba. *Heritage: Civilization and the Jews.* New York: Simon & Schuster, Summit Books, 1984.

Einhard. *The Life of Charlemagne.* Forward by Sidney Painter. Ann Arbor, Mich.: University of Michigan Press, 1979.

Everyday Life in Ancient Times. Washington, D.C.: National Geographic Society, 1958.

Grun, Bernard. *The Timetables of History.* New York: Simon & Schuster, 1982.

Guhl, E., and W. Koner. *The Life of the Greeks and Romans.* Translated by F. Hueffer. London: Chapman & Hall, 1875.

Hawkes, Jacquetta. *Prehistory.* New York: Harper & Row, 1965.

Heaton, E. W. *Everyday Life in Old Testament Times.* London: B. T. Batsford, 1956.

Hourani, Albert. *A History of the Arab Peoples.* Cambridge, Mass.: Harvard University Press, 1991.

Johnson, Paul. *Modern Times: The World from the Twenties to the Eighties.* New York: Harper & Row, 1985.

Joy, Charles R. *Young People of the British Isles.* New York: Sloan & Pearce, 1965.

Kirchner, Walther. *Western Civilization to 1500.* New York: Barnes & Noble Books, 1960.

Kramer, Samuel Noah. *History Begins at Sumer.* Garden City, New York: Doubleday, 1959.

Miller, Kenneth D., and Ethel Prince Miller. *The People Are the City: 150 Years of Social and Religious Concern in New York City.* N.Y.: Macmillan, 1962.

Miller, Shane. *The Egyptians in the Middle Kingdom.* Life Long Ago Series. New York: Coward-McCann, 1963.

———. *The Romans in the Days of the Empire.* Life Long Ago Series. New York: Coward-McCann, 1963.

Montague, Ashley. *Man: His First Million Years.* New York: New American Library, 1958.

Payne, George Henry. *The Child in Human Progress.* Preface by Dr. A. Jacobi. New York: G. P. Putnam's Sons, 1916.

Peart, Jane. *The Orphan Train Trilogy.* Carmel, New York: Guideposts Books, 1994.

Power, Eileen. *Medieval People.* New York: Doubleday, 1924.

Powers, Richard M. *The Cave Dwellers in the Old Stone Age*. Life Long Ago Series. New York: Coward-McCann, 1963.

Quennell, Marjorie, and C. H. B. Quennell. *Everyday Life in Prehistoric Times*. New York: G. P. Putnam's Sons, 1959.

Rowling, Marjorie. *Life in Medieval Times*. New York: G. P. Putnam's Sons, 1968.

Schlesinger, Jr., Arthur M. *The Almanac of American History*. New York: G.P. Putnam's Sons, 1983.

Scott, Martin. *Medieval Europe*. New York: Dorset Press, 1964.

Shenkman, Richard. *Legends, Lies & Cherished Myths of World History*. New York: HarperCollins, 1993.

Stewart, Robert, ed. *The Illustrated Almanac of Historical Facts*. New York: Simon & Schuster, 1992.

Tapsell, R.F., comp. *Monarchs, Rulers, Dynasties, and Kingdoms of the World: An Encyclopedic Guide from 3000 B.C. to the 20th Century*. New York: Facts on File, 1983.

Todd, Malcolm. *Everyday Life of the Barbarians: Goths, Franks and Vandals*. New York: Dorset Press, 1972.

Toynbee, Arnold. *A Study of History*. 2 vols. London: Oxford University Press, 1987, 1974.

Ullmann, Walter. *A Short History of the Papacy in the Middle Ages*. London: Metheun & Co., 1972.

Van Loon, Hendrik. *The Story of Mankind*. Garden City, N.Y.: Garden City Publishing Co., 1938.

Weir, Alison. *The Princes in the Tower*. New York: Ballantine Books, 1992.

Weisgard, Leonard. *The Athenians in the Classical Period*. Life Long Ago Series. New York: Coward-McCann, 1963.

Wood, Michael. *In Search of the Dark Ages*. New York: Facts on File, 1987.

Wood, Tim. *What They Don't Teach You About History*. New York: Dorset Press, 1992.

CHAPTER 2

Armstrong, Karen. *Muhammad: A Biography of the Prophet*. New York: HarperCollins, 1992.

Beebe, Catherine. *Saints for Boys and Girls*. Milwaukee, Wis.: Bruce Publishing Company, 1959.

Beevers, John. *Storm of Glory: The Story of St. Thérèse of Lisieux*. Garden City, N.Y.: Doubleday, Image Books, 1955.

————. *St. Joan of Arc*. Garden City, N.Y.: Doubleday, Image Books, 1962.

————. *St. Teresa of Avila*. Garden City, N.Y.: Doubleday, Image Books, 1961.

Bernanos, Georges. *Sanctity Will Out; an Essay on Saint Joan*. London: Sheed & Ward, 1947.

Black, Naomi, ed. *Celebration: The Book of Jewish Festivals*. New York: Dutton, 1987.

Bonfanti, Leo, comp. *Strange Beliefs, Customs, & Superstitions of New England*. Wakefield, Mass.: Pride Publications, 1980.

The Book of Saints. Benedictine Monks of St. Augustine's Abbey, comps. Rausgate, N.Y.: Macmillan Co., 1944.

Buchanan, Donald. *Santa Claus, His Full Story in a Children's Book for the First Time*. London: Inncourt Press, 1961.

Bushman, Richard L. *Joseph Smith and the Beginnings of Mormonism*. Chicago: University of Illinois Press, 1984.

Campbell, Joseph. *The Masks of God*. 4 vols. New York: Penguin, 1959–1968

Chagnolleau, Jean. *Lourdes*. Paris: N. Arthaud, 1953.

Chamberlain, Alexander Francis. *The Child and Childhood in Folk-Thought*. New York: Macmillan Co., 1896.

Chaplin, Dora P. *Children and Religion*. New York: Scribner's, 1948.

Cole, W. Owen, and Piara Singh Sambhi. *The Sikhs: Their Religious Beliefs and Practices*. London: Hemley, 1978.

Coles, Robert. *The Spiritual Life of Children*. Boston: Houghton Mifflin, 1990.

Connell, Janice T. *The Visions of the Children: The Apparitions of the Blessed Mother at Medjugorje*. Introduction by Robert Faricy. New York: St. Martin's Press, 1992.

Coulson, John. *The Saints: A Concise Biographical Dictionary*. Introduction by C.C. Martindale, S.J. New York: Hawthorne Books, 1958.

De Marchi, John. *Fatima, The Facts*. Translated by I.M. Kingsbury. Cork, England: The Mercer Press, 1950.

————. *The Shepherds of Fatima*. Retold in English by Elisabeth Cobb. Illustrated by Jeanyee Wong. New York: Sheed & Ward, 1952.

Emrich, Marion Vallat, and George Korson. *A Child's Book of Folklore*. New York: Dial Press, 1947.

Fadden, Marie Celeste. *Martin de Porres and His Magic Carpet*. St. Meinrad, Ind.: St. Meinrad's Abbey, 1951.

Fitch, Florence Mary. *One God: The Ways We Worship Him*. New York: Lothrop, Lee & Shepard, 1944.

Ghosh, Oroon. *The Dance of Shiva and Other Tales from India*. Boston: New American Library, 1965.

Great Religions of the World. Washington, D.C.: National Geographic Society, 1971.

Haughton, Rosemary. *Six Saints for Parents*. London: Burns & Oates, 1962.

Hearn, Lafcadio. *Japanese Fairy Tales*. Mount Vernon, New York: Peter Pauper Press, 1958.

History of the Church of Jesus Christ of Latter-day Saints. Salt Lake City, Utah: Deseret, 1967.

Jones, E. Michael. *Medjugorje: The Untold Story.* South Bend, Ind.: Fidelity Press, 1993.

Kinsley, David R. *The Sword and the Flute: Kâalâi and Kòròsòna, Dark Visions of the Terrible and the Sublime in Hindu Mythology.* Berkeley, Calif.: University of California Press, 1975.

Kolatch, Alfred J. *The Jewish Book of Why.* New York: Jonathan David Publishers, 1981.

La Salette, La Sainte Montagne. Lyon, France: M. Lescuyer & Fils, 1947.

Larousse Encyclopedia of Mythology. Introduction by Robert Graves. New York: Prometheus Press, 1959.

Lorie, Peter. *Superstitions.* New York: Simon & Schuster, 1992.

Mahadevan, T. M. P. *Ten Saints of India.* Bombay, India: Bharatiya Vidya Bhavan, 1965.

Martindale, C.C., S.J.. *Blessed Bernadette Soubirous.* London: Catholic Truth Society.

McGinley, Phyllis. *Saint-Watching.* Chicago: Thomas More Press, 1982.

Moore, Clement C. *The Night before Christmas.* Philadelphia: Porter & Coates, 1883.

Newland, Mary Reed. *The Year and Our Children: Planning the Family Activities for Christian Feasts and Seasons.* New York: P. J. Kennedy & Sons, 1956.

Opie, Iona, and Moira Tatern, eds. *A Dictionary of Superstitions.* Oxford: Oxford University Press, 1989.

Peers, E. Allison, ed. and trans. *The Complete Works of Saint Teresa of Jesus.* New York: Sheed & Ward. 1846.

Piaget, Jean. *The Child's Conception of the World.* Paterson, N.J.: International Library of Psychology, Philosophy and Scientific Method, Littlefield, Adams, 1960.

Piburn, Sidney, comp. and ed. *The Dalai Lama, an Anthology of Writings by and about the Dalai Lama.* With a Foreword by Clairborne Pell. Ithaca, New York: Snow Lion Publications, 1990.

Pickthall, Mohammed Marmaduke. *The Meaning of the Glorious Koran: An Explanatory Translation.* Boston: New American Library, 1954.

The Prophet: Joseph Smith's Testimony. Salt Lake City, Utah: Deseret, 1981.

Rouse, W. H. D. *Gods, Heroes and Men of Ancient Greece.* New York: New American Library, 1957.

Saint Maria Goretti, by Her Mother. Translated by Rev. D. Novarese. Glasgow: John S. Burns & Sons, 1951.

Sandhurst, B. G. *We Saw Her. Accounts of Eye Witnesses of Bernadette during Her Visions.* Introduction by C.C. Martindale, S.J. London: Longmans, Green, 1953.

Sayings of Buddha. New York: Peter Pauper Press, 1957.

Shaw, George Bernard. *Preface to Saint Joan.* Garden City, N.Y.: Doubleday, 1951.

Shivkumar, K. *Krishna and Sudama.* New Delhi, India: The Children's Book Trust, 1967.

Singh, Kartar. *Stories from Sikh History.* New Delhi, India: Heemkunt Press, 1976.

Smart, Ninian and Richard D. Hecht, eds. *Sacred Texts of the World: A Universal Anthology.* New York: Crossroad, 1982.

Spiegelman, Judith. *UNICEF's Festival Book.* New York: U.S. Committee for UNICEF, 1966.

Steinzaltz, Adin. *The Essential Talmud.* New York: Bantam Books, 1976.

Thérèse of Lisieux. *The Story of a Soul.* Lisieux, France: Carmelites, 1898.

Thubton Jigme Norbu. *Tibet Is My Country* (autobiography of the Dalai Lama's brother, as told to Heinrich Harrer). New York: E. P. Dutton, 1961.

Ulanov, Barry. *The Making of a Modern Saint: A Biographical Study of Thérèse of Lisieux.* Garden City, N.Y.: Doubleday, 1966; London: Jonathan Cape, 1967.

Unset, Sigrid. *Saga of Saints.* London: Sheed & Ward, 1935.

Weiser, Francis X. *The Holyday Book: The Story of the Observance in Liturgy and Folklore of the Pentecost Season and the Feasts of Saints throughout the Year.* New York: Harcourt, Brace, 1956.

Werfel, Franz. *The Song of Bernadette.* New York: Amereon, 1941.

Williamson, Hugh Ross. *The Challenge of Bernadette.* London: Burns & Oates, 1958; Westminster, Maryland: Newman Press, 1958.

Woodlock, Francis, S. J. *Lourdes and Modern Miracles.* New York: Paulist Press.

Yoors, Jan. *The Gypsies.* New York: Simon & Schuster, 1967.

Zaehner, R C., trans. and ed. *Hindu Scriptures.* London: J. M. Dent & Sons, 1977.

Zimmer, Heinrich. *Myths and Symbols in Indian Art and Civilization.* Edited by Joseph Campbell. New York: Bollingen Foundation, 1963.

CHAPTER 3

Andereson, C., and Mary M. Aldrich. *Babies Are Human Beings.* New York: Macmillan Co., 1938.

Anderson, Karen, and Jo Robinson. *Full House: The Story of the Anderson Quintuplets.* Boston: Little, Brown, 1986.

Baird, Jane. *This Starry Stranger: An Anthology of Babyhood.* London: Frederick Muller, 1951.

Bel Geddes, Joan. *Small World: A History of Baby Care from the Stone Age to the Spock Age.* New York: Macmillan, 1964; London: Heinemann, 1965.

Brazelton, T. Berry, M.D. *What Every Baby Knows.* New York: Ballantine Books, 1987.

Cawthorne, N. *The Sex Lives of the Kings and Queens of England.* London: Prion, 1995.

A Child Is Born: Photographs of Life before Birth and Up-to-Date Advice for Expectant Parents. Photos by Lennart Nilsson. Text by Mirjam Furuhjelm, Axel Ingelman-Sundberg, and Claes Wirsénn. New York: Delacorte Press, 1978.

Culpepper, Nicholas. *Directory for Midwives.* London, 1653.

Galton, Francis, Sir. *Hereditary Genius: An Inquiry into Its Laws and Consequences.* New York: St. Martin's Press, 1978.

Gesell, Arnold, and Katherine Gesell Walden. *How a Baby Grows, A Study in Pictures.* New York: Harper & Brothers, 1945.

Graham, Harvey, M.D. *Eternal Eve: The Mysteries of Birth and the Customs That Surround It.* London: Hutchinson, 1960.

Guttmacher, Alan F., M.D. *Pregnancy and Birth.* New York: Viking Press, 1956.

Johnson, Robert V., ed. *Mayo Clinic Complete Book of Pregnancy & Baby's First Year.* New York: William Morrow, 1994.

Kingsley, David R. *The Sword and the Flute.* New Delhi, India: Motilal Bunarsidass, 1979.

La Barre, Weston. *The Human Animal.* Chicago: University of Chicago Press, 1954.

Leach, Dr. Penelope. *Babyhood: Stage by Stage from Birth to Age Two—How Your Baby Develops Physically, Emotionally, Mentally.* New York: Alfred A. Knopf, 1983.

Leman, Kevin. *The Birth Order Book: Why You Are the Way You Are.* New York: Dell Publishers, 1985.

Montague, Ashley. *Human Heredity.* New York: New American Library, 1959.

Morris, Desmond. *Babywatching.* New York: Crown Publishers, 1991.

———. *Intimate Behavior.* New York: Random House, 1972.

———. *The Naked Ape.* New York: Random House, 1967.

The Notebooks of Leonardo da Vinci. Arranged, Rendered into English and Introduced by Edward MacCurdy. New York: Reynal & Hitchcok, 1939.

Polo, Marco. *Travels.* A.D. 1300. Reprint, translated by Marion Koenig. New York: Golden Press, 1966.

Read, Grantly Dick. *Childbirth without Fear.* New York: Harper & Brothers, 1954.

Ribble, Margaretha A. *The Rights of Infants: Early Psychological Needs and Their Satisfaction.* New York: Columbia University Press, 1943.

Savage, Beverly, and Diana Simkin. *Preparation for Birth: The Complete Guide to the Lamaze Method.* New York: Ballantine Books, 1987.

Stern, Daniel N., M.D. *Diary of a Baby: What Your Child Sees, Feels and Experiences.* New York: HarperCollins, Basic Books, 1990.

Waddington, C. H. *Principles of Embryology.* London: Allen & Unwin, 1960.

Wilson, Bradford, and George Edington. *First Child, Second Child. . . Your Birth Order Profile.* New York: McGraw-Hill, 1981.

Winn, Marie, editor. *The Baby Reader: The World's Most Famous Authors, Past and Present, Celebrate the Joys and Frustrations of Being a Parent.* New York: Simon & Schuster, 1973.

CHAPTER 4

Atkinson, Donald T., M.D. *Magic, Myth and Medicine.* New York: Fawcett World Library, 1958.

Baker, Susan, Roberta R. Henry, and David Estridge. *Parents' Guide to Nutrition.* Boston: Boston Children's Hospital, 1986.

Bancroft, Corinne, Bessie Cutler, and Elizabeth Pierce. *Pediatric Nursing.* New York: Macmillan, 1923.

Bartlett, Frederic H., M.D. *Infants and Children, Their Feeding and Growth.* New York: Farrar & Rinehart, 1932.

Bell, Albert J., M.D. *Feeding, Diet and the General Care of Children.* New York: Davis, 1923.

Bergenstein, Erik. *Alfred Nobel, The Man and His Work.* Translated by Alsan Blair. London: Thomas Nelson & Sons, 1962.

Bowlby, John. *Maternal Care and Mental Health.* Geneva, Switzerland: World Health Organization (WHO), 1951.

Brown, Christy. *My Left Foot.* London, 1954. Reprint. New York: Simon & Schuster, 1975.

Burton, Josephine. *Crippled Victory.* New York: Sheed & Ward, 1956.

Cutler, Bessie, R.N., Elizabeth Pierce, R.N., and M. Corrine Bancroft, R.N. *Pediatric Nursing.* New York: Macmillan, 1932.

D'Ambrosio, Richard. *No Language But a Cry.* New York: Dell Publishing, 1971.

Doman, Glenn. *What to Do about Your Brain-Injured Child—Or Your Brain-Damaged, Mentally Deficient, Cerebral-Palsied, Spastic, Flaccid, Rigid, Epileptic, Autistic, Athetoid, Hyperactive Child.* Garden City, N.Y.: Doubleday, 1974.

Dunn, Courtney. *The Natural History of the Child.* London: Sampson, Low, Marston, 1919.

Freeman, Margaret B. *Herbs for the Mediaeval Household, for Cooking, Healing and Divers Uses.* New York: Metropolitan Museum of Art, 1943.

Gesell, Arnold, M.D. *Vision: Its Development in Infant and Child.* New York: Harper & Brothers, 1949.

Gibson, William. *The Miracle Worker and Monday after the Miracle.* New York: Doubleday, 1984.

Global Pollution and Health. Geneva, Switzerland: World Health Organization (WHO), 1987.

Gronowicz, Antoni. *Bela Schick and the World of Children.* New York: Abelard-Schumann, 1955.

Haggard, Howard W., M.D. *Devils, Drugs and Doctors.* New York: Pocket Books, 1959.

Jarvis, D. C., M.D. *Folk Medicine.* New York: Henry Holt, 1959.

Keller, Helen. *The Story of My Life.* New York: Doubleday, 1954.

———. *Teacher: Anne Sullivan Macy.* Introduction by Nella Brady Henney. Garden City, N.Y.: Doubleday, 1955.

Killilea, Marie. *Karen.* New York: Prentice Hall, 1953.

———. *With Love from Karen.* New York: Dell Publishing, 1974.

Larson, David E., editor. *Mayo Clinic Family Health Book.* New York: Morrow, 1991.

MacCracken, Mary. *Turnabout Children: Overcoming Dyslexia and Other Learning Disabilities.* Boston: Little, Brown, 1986.

Mallison, Vernon. *None Can Be Called Deformed; Problems of the Crippled Adolescent.* New York: Roy Publishers, 1957.

Melton, David. *When Children Need Help: A Handbook of Guidance and Help for Parents of Children Who Have Been Diagnosed as Braininjured, Mentally Retarded, Cerebral Palsied, Learning Disabled, or as Slow Learners.* New York: Thomas Y. Crowell, 1972.

Schmitt, Barton. *Your Child's Health: A Pediatric Guide for Parents.* New York: Bantam Books, 1991.

Soddy, Kenneth. *Mental Health and Infant Development.* New York: Basic Books, 1956.

Swindell, Larry. *Spencer Tracy, A Biography.* New York: World Publishing, 1969.

Walker, Lou Ann. *A Loss for Words: The Story of Deafness in a Family.* New York, Harper & Row, 1986.

Wark, David, M.D. *The Practical Home Doctor for Women and Children: A Woman's Medical Handbook.* New York: Gay Brothers, 1882.

Weiner, Florence. *Help for the Handicapped Child.* New York: McGraw-Hill, 1973.

Williams, Donna. *Nobody Nowhere: The Extraordinary Autobiography of an Autistic.* New York: Random House, 1992.

The Womanly Art of Breastfeeding. Franklin Park, Ill.: La Leche League, 1961.

Woodham-Smith, Cecil. *Florence Nightingale (1820–1910), A Biography Based on Papers and Letters Never before Made Public.* New York: McGraw-Hill, 1951.

CHAPTER 5

Brazleton, T. Berry. *Touchpoints: Your Child's Emotional and Behavioral Development.* Reading, Mass.: Addison Wesley, 1992.

Crystal, David, ed. *Cambridge Encyclopedia of Language.* Cambridge, England: Cambridge University Press, 1987.

De Kay, James T. *The Left-Hander's Handbook.* Camp Hill, Penn.: Quality Paperback Book Club, 1995.

Elkin, Frederick. *The Child and Society: The Process of Socialization.* New York: Random House, 1963.

Fincher, Jack. *Lefties: The Origins and Consequences of Being Left-handed.* New York: G. P. Putnam's Sons, 1980.

Gardner, Howard. *Frames of Mind: The Theory of Multiple Intelligences.* New York: Basic Books, 1983.

———. *The Unschooled Mind: How Children Think and How Schools Should Teach.* New York: Basic Books, 1991.

Gesell, Arnold, M.D. *Infancy and Human Growth.* New York: Macmillan, 1928.

———. *A Guide to the Study of the Preschool Child.* New York: Harper & Row, 1940.

———. *The First Five Years of Life.* New Haven: Yale University Press, 1940.

———. *The Child from Five to Ten.* New York: Harper & Row, 1977.

———. *The Mental Growth of the Pre-School Child: A Psychological Outline of Normal Development from Birth to the Sixth Year.* Grosse Pointe Woods, Michigan: Scholarly Press, 1968.

Gesell, Arnold, M.D., et al. *Child Development: An Introduction to the Study of Human Growth.* New York: Harper & Row, 1949.

———. *Infant and Child in the Culture of Today.* New York: Harper & Brothers, 1951.

Gesell Institute. *Child Behavior.* New York: Dell Publishing, 1958.

Giles, F. T. *Children and the Law.* London: Penguin, 1959.

Goleman, Daniel. *Emotional Intelligence: Why It Matters More Than IQ.* New York: Bantam Books, 1995.

Grant, Joe, and Dick Huemer. *Baby Weems.* New York: Doubleday, 1941.

Greene, Margaret C.L. *Learning to Talk: A Parents' Guide to the First Five Years*. Illustrations by Jill Hassell. New York: Harper & Brothers, 1960.

Hernstein, Richard J., and Charles Murray. *Intelligence and Class Structure in American Life*. New York: Free Press, 1994.

Howard, Marion. *How to Help Your Teenager Postpone Sexual Involvement*. New York: Continuum Publishing, 1988.

Ilg, Frances L., M.D., and Louise Bates Ames. *Child Behavior*. Foreword by Arnold Gesell, M.D. New York: Harper & Brothers, 1956.

International Child Development Centre. *Essays, Global Reports, Monographs* and *Occasional Papers*. Florence, Italy: Spedale degli Innocenti Centre, 1994.

Jespersen, Otto. *Language: Its Nature, Development and Origin*. New York: Henry Holt, 1925.

Kelly, Marguerite. *The Mother's Almanac II: Your Child from Six to Twelve*. New York: Doubleday, 1989.

Kelly, Marguerite, and Elsa Parson. *The Mother's Almanac*. Revised edition, New York: Doubleday, 1992.

Leach, Penelope. *Your Baby and Child: From Birth to Age Five*. Rev. ed. New York: Alfred A. Knopf, 1989.

——. *Your Growing Child: From Babyhood through Adolescence*. New York: Alfred A. Knopf, 1986.

——. *The Child Care Encyclopedia: A Parents' Guide to the Physical and Emotional Well-being of Children from Birth through Adolescence*. New York: Alfred A. Knopf, 1984.

Montessori, Maria. *The Secret of Childhood*. London: Orient Longmans, 1936.

Morris, Desmond. *The Book of Ages*. New York: Viking Press, 1984.

Morse, John Lovett, M.D., et al. *The Infant and Young Child: Its Care and Feeding from Birth Until School Age*. Philadelphia: W. B. Saunders, 1923.

Pinker, Steven. *The Language Instinct: How the Mind Creates Language*. New York: William Morrow, 1994.

Richter, Irma. *The Notebooks of Leonardo da Vinci*. Oxford: Oxford University Press, 1980.

Soddy, Kenneth: *Mental Health and Infant Development*. New York: Basic Books, 1956.

Tsanoff, Radoslav A. *The Ways of Genius: An Investigation of the Sources, Nature and Working of Genius in the Arts and Sciences*. New York: Harper & Brothers, 1949.

CHAPTER 6

Bombeck, Erma. *Family—The Ties That Bind. . .and Gag!* New York: McGraw-Hill, 1987.

Boswell, John. *Same-Sex Unions in Premodern Europe*. New York: Villard Books, 1994.

Burton, Elizabeth. *The Elizabethans at Home*. London:Secker & Warburg, 1958.

Cahill, Susan, ed. *Mothers: Memories, Dreams and Reflections by Literary Daughters*. New York: New American Library, 1988.

Calhoun, Arthur W. *A Social History of the American Family*. New York: Barnes & Noble, 1945.

Cosby, Bill. *Fatherhood*. New York: Doubleday, 1986.

Crump, Lucy. *Nursery Life 300 Years Ago*. London: George Rutledge & Sons, 1929.

Cunningham, Bess B. *Family Behavior, a Study of Human Relations*. Philadelphia: W. B. Saunders, 1936.

De Boer, Robby. *Losing Jessica*. New York: Doubleday, 1995.

Edelman, Marian Wright. *The Measure of Our Success: A Letter to My Children and Yours*. Boston: Beacon Press, 1992.

Everyday Life in Ancient Times. Washington, D.C.: National Geographic Society, 1958.

Gies, Frances, and Joseph Gies. *Marriage and the Family in the Middle Ages*. New York: Harper & Row, 1987.

Goertzel, Victor, and Mildred Goertzel. *Cradles of Eminence: A Study of the Childhoods of over 400 Famous Twentieth-Century Men and Women*. Boston: Little, Brown, 1962.

Grollman, Earl A. *Talking about Divorce: A Dialogue between Parent and Child*. New York: Beacon Press, 1995.

Hale, Christina. *The English Housewife in the Seventeenth Century*. London: Chatto & Windus, 1948.

Highbaugh, Irma. *Family Life in West China*. New York: Agricultural Missions, 1948.

Hillman, Eugene, C.S.Sp. *Polygamy Reconsidered: African Plural Marriage and the Christian Churches*. Maryknoll, N.Y.: Orbis Books, 1975.

Hirshon, Stanley P. *The Lion of the Lord, A Biography of Brigham Young*. New York: Alfred A. Knopf, 1969.

Hostetler, John A. *Amish Society*. Baltimore, Maryland: Johns Hopkins University Press, 1980.

Hunt, David. *Parents and Children in History: The Psychology of Family Life in Early Modern France*. New York: Basic Books, 1970.

Jones, Evan. *The Father: Letters to Sons and Daughters*. New York: Rinehart, 1960.

Knox, Sarah T. *The Family and the Law*. Chapel Hill, N.C.: University of North Carolina Press, 1941.

Langford, Laura Carter Holloway. *The Mothers of Great Men and Women*. New York: Funk & Wagnalls, 1883.

Leman, Kevin. *Keeping Your Family Together When the World Is Falling Apart*. New York: Delacorte Press, 1992.

Mace, David, and Vera Mace: *The Soviet Family: Love, Marriage, Parenthood, and Family Life under Communism.* Garden City, New York: Doubleday, 1964.

McCoy, Bill. *Father's Day.* New York: Times Books, 1995.

Mead, Margaret. *Culture and Commitment: A Study of the Generation Gap.* Garden City, New York: Doubleday, 1970.

Mill, John Stuart. *The Subjection of Women.* 1869. Reprinted in Harvard Classics. New York: P.F. Collier & Son, 1936.

Muller-Lyer. *The Family.* Translated from German by F. W. Stella Browne. New York: Alfred A. Knopf, 1912.

Pearson, Lu Emily Hess. *Elizabethans at Home.* Stanford, California: Stanford University Press, 1957.

Price, Christine. *Happy Days: A UNICEF Book of Birthdays, Name Days and Growing Days.* New York: United States Committee for UNICEF, 1969.

Read, Mary L. *The Mothercraft Manual.* Boston: Little, Brown, 1917.

Renoir, Jean. *Renoir, My Father.* London: Collins, 1963.

Roper, William. *The Life of Sir Thomas More.* 1851. Reprint. London: J. M. Dent & Sons, 1938.

Russell, Bertrand. *Marriage and Morals.* New York: Bantam Books, 1959.

Salk, Lee. *Familyhood, Nurturing the Values That Matter.* New York: Simon & Schuster, 1992.

———. *What Every Child Would Like His Parents to Know.* New York: David McKay, 1973.

Salzman, L. F. *English Life in the Middle Ages.* London: Oxford University Press, 1926.

Sasson, Jean P. *Princess: A True Story of Life behind the Veil in Saudi Arabia.* New York: William Morrow, 1992.

Schmiedeler, Edgar, O.S.B. *An Introductory Study of the Family.* New York: Appleton Century-Crofts, 1947.

———. *Parent and Child.* New York: Paulist Press, 1932.

Scott, Nora E. *The Home Life of the Ancient Egyptians.* New York: Metropolitan Museum of Art, 1958.

Silverstone, Marilyn, and Luree Miller. *BALA, Child of India.* London: Methuen, 1966.

Sulzberger, C. L. *Fathers and Children.* New York: Arbor House, 1987.

Truxell, Andrew G., and Francis E. Merrill. *Marriage and the Family in American Culture.* New York: Prentice Hall, 1947.

Van Straalen, Alice. *The Book of Holidays around the World.* New York: E. P. Dutton, 1986.

Victor, Joan Berg, and Joelle Sander. *The Family: The Evolution of Our Oldest Human Institution.* New York: Bobbs-Merrill, 1978.

Wallerstein, Judith S., and Sandra Blakeslee. *Second Chances: Men, Women and Children a Decade after Divorce: Who Wins, Who Loses—and Why.* New York: Tickner & Fields, 1989.

Westermarck, Edward. *The History of Human Marriage.* New York: Macmillan, 1922.

Wylie, Philip. *Generation of Vipers.* New York: Rinehart, 1955.

Wilson, Bradford, and George Edington. *First Child, Second Child.* New York: McGraw-Hill, 1981.

Women's Co-operative Guild. *Maternity: Letters from Working Women.* Preface by the Right Hon. Herbert Samuel, M.P. London: G. Bell and Sons, 1915.

CHAPTER 7

Bainton, Roland H. *Here I Stand: A Life of Martin Luther.* New York: New American Library, 1952.

Bayne-Powell, Rosamond. *The English Child in the Eighteenth Century.* New York: E. P. Dutton, 1939.

Beekman, Daniel. *The Mechanical Baby: A Popular History of the Theory and Practice of Child Raising.* London: Dennis Dobson, 1977.

Bel Geddes, Joan. *How to Parent Alone.* New York: Seabury Press, 1974.

Bettelheim, Bruno. *A Good Enough Parent: A Book on Child-Rearing.* New York: Alfred A. Knopf, 1987.

Bowlby, John. *Child Care and the Growth of Love.* London: Pelican Books, 1953. Reprint, Baltimore, Maryland: Penguin Books, 1963.

Bush, Barbara. *A Memoir.* Carmel, N.Y.: Guidepost Books, 1994.

Carpenter, Charles H. *History of American Schoolbooks.* Philadelphia: University of Pennsylvania Press, 1963.

Clark, Kate Upson. *Bringing Up Boys: A Study.* New York: Thomas Y. Crowell, 1899.

Cobb, Lyman. *The Evil of Corporal Punishment as a Means of Moral Discipline in Families and Schools.* New York: Mark A. Levinan, 1847.

Cutt, M. Nancy. *Mrs Sherwood and Her Books for Children: A Study.* London: Oxford University Press, 1974.

Dodson, Fitzhugh. *How to Discipline with Love, from Crib to College.* New York: New American Library, 1978.

Doman, Glenn. *How to Teach Your Baby to Read.* New York: Random House, 1964.

Elson, Ruth Miller. *Guardians of Tradition: American Schoolbooks of the Nineteenth Century.* Lincoln, Nebraska: University of Nebraska Press, 1964.

Erasmus. *De Civilitate Morum Puerilium.* Translated from Latin by Robert Whittinton, as *A Lytle Booke of Good Manners for Children.* London, 1532.

———. *In Praise of Folly.* Harvard Classic, Reprint. New York: P. F. Collier, 1956.

————. *The Whole Familiar Colloquies of Erasmus of Rotterdam*; Translated from Latin by Nathan Bailey. Glasgow, Scotland: Alexander Campbell, 1877.

Erikson, Erik. *Young Man Luther*. New York: Norton, 1958.

Eyre, Linda, and Richard Eyre. *Teaching Your Children Values*. New York: Simon & Schuster, 1993.

Froebel, Friedrich. *Educational Laws for All Teachers*. Edited by James L. Hughes. New York: D. Appleton, 1907.

Frost, John. *Historical Sketches of the Indians*. Hartford, Conn.: E. Hunt & Sons, 1854.

Fulghum, Robert. *All I Really Need to Know I Learned in Kindergarten*. New York: Villard Books, 1988.

Gardner, James. *The Paston Family Letters*. Westminster, England: Constable, 1895.

Ginott, Haim G. *Between Parent and Child*. New York: Macmillan, 1965.

Gore, Tipper. *Raising PG Kids in an X-Rated Society*. Nashville, Tenn.: Parthenon Press, 1987.

Gutek, Gerald Lee. *Pestalozzi and Education*. New York: Random House, 1968.

Heroard, Jean. *Journal de Jean Hâeroard*. Paris. Fayard, 1989.

Holt, John. *How Children Fail*. New York: Delta, 1964.

Hughes, James L. *Froebel's Educational Laws for All Teachers*. New York: D. Appleton, International Education Series, 1907.

Leach, Penelope. *The Child Care Encyclopedia: A Parents' Guide to the Physical and Emotional Well-Being of Children from Birth through Adolescence*. New York: Alfred A. Knopf, 1984.

Leman, Kevin. *Making Children Mind without Losing Yours*. New York: Dell Publishing, 1987.

Lesser, Gerald S. *Children and Television: Lessons from Sesame Street*. New York: Random House, 1974.

Luther, Martin. *Table Talk*. c. 1540. Reprinted in Harvard Classics, edited by Charles W. Eliot. New York: P. F. Collier, 1956.

Mann, Horace. *On the Crisis in Education*. Introduction by Louis Filler. Yellow Springs, Ohio: Antioch Press, 1965.

Manning, Anne. *The Household of Sir Thomas More*. London: J. M. Dent & Sons, 1938.

McGuffey, William. *Pictorial Eclectic Primer for Young Children; Eclectic Primer; Eclectic First Reader for Young Children; Eclectic Second Reader; Eclectic Third Reader; Eclectic Fourth Reader; Eclectic Progressive Spelling Book*. Reprinted by Mott Media, 1987. Distributed by Conservative Book Club, Harrison, New York, 1987.

Mill, John Stuart. *Autobiography*. 1873. Reprint, preface by John Jacob Coss. New York: Columbia University Press, 1960.

Miller, Nathan. *The Child in Primitive Society*. New York: Brentano's, 1928.

Miller, Perry. *The American Puritans: Their Prose and Poetry*. Garden City, N.Y.: Doubleday, Anchor Books, 1956.

Montessori, Maria. *The Secret of Childhood*. London: Orient Longmans, 1936.

————. *Dr. Montessori's Own Handbook*. London: William Heinemann, 1914.

Pascal, Blaise. *Pensées*. 1663. Reprinted in Harvard Classics, edited by Charles W. Eliot. New York: P. F. Collier & Son, 1956.

Patterson, Gerald R., and M. Elizabeth Gillion. *Living with Children: New Methods for Parents and Teachers.* Champaign, Ill.: Research Press, 1971.

Pestalozzi, Heinrich. *The Education of Man: Aphorisms*. New York: Philosophical Library, 1951.

Plato. *Republic*. c. 350 B.C. Reprint, translated and edited with an introduction and notes by Robert Waterfield. Oxford: Oxford University Press, 1994.

Rambusch, Nancy McCormick. *Learning How to Learn: An American Approach to Montessori*. New York: 1962.

Read, Mary L. *The Mothercraft Manual*. Boston: Little, Brown, 1917.

Sanders, Charles. *The Schoole Reader, First Book*. New York: Ivison, Blakeman, Taylor & Co., 1858.

Schachtel, Ernest G. *Metamorphosis: On the Development of Affect, Perception, Attention and Memory*. New York: Da Capo Press, 1984.

Sears, Robert R., Eleanor E. Maccoby, and Harry Levin. *Patterns of Child Rearing*. White Plains, N.Y.: Row, Peterson, 1957.

Segar, Francis. *The Schoole of Vertue, a Booke of Good Nourture for Chyldren and Youth to Learn Their Dutie by*. London: 1557.

Speare, Elizabeth George. *Child Life in New England, 1790–1840*. Sturbridge, Mass.: Old Sturbridge Village, 1961.

Spock, Benjamin, M.D. *Common Sense Book of Baby and Child Care*. New York: Duell, Sloan & Pearce, 1946. Reprints. *Baby and Child Care*. New York: Pocket Books, 1959–1984.

Spock, Benjamin, and Mary Morgan. *Spock on Spock, A Memoir of Growing Up with the Century*. New York: Pantheon, 1989.

Spock, Benjamin, and Michael B. Rothenberg, M.D. *Dr. Spock's Baby and Child Care*: Revised edition and updated for the 1980s. New York: Pocket Books, 1985.

Standing, E. M. *Maria Montessori, Her Life and Work*. London: Hollis & Carter, 1957; New York: New American Library, 1962.

Watson, John B. *Behaviorism*. Chicago: University of Chicago Press, Phoenix Books, 1939.

Willison, George F. *Saints and Strangers*. New York: Reyaal & Hitchcock, 1945.

Zimmer, Heinreich. *Philosophies of India*. Cleveland, Oh.: World Publishing, 1965.

CHAPTER 8

Arnold, Arnold. *How to Play with Your Child*. New York: Ballantine, 1955.

Batten, Lindsey W. *The Single-Handed Mother*. Preface by H. G. Wells. London: Allen and Urwin, 1939.

Bengtsson, Arvid. *The Child's Right to Play*. Sheffield, England: International Playground Association, Tartan Press, 1974.

Bragdon, Allen D. *Joy through the World: Holidays and Toys*. New York: Dodd, Mead, 1985.

Fournier, Edouard. *Histoire des Jouets et des Jeux d'Enfants*. Paris: Dentu, 1889.

Gordon, Lesley. *Peepshow into Paradise: A History of Children's Toys*. New York: John de Graff, 1954.

History of Bicycles. London: Central Office of Information Reference Pamphlet, Her Majesty's Stationery Office, 1932.

Johnson, June. *Home Play for the Preschool Child*. Introduction by Frances I. Ilg, M.D. New York: Harper & Brothers, 1957.

Joseph, Joan. *Folk Toys around the World*. New York: Parents' Magazine Press, 1972.

Kenward, James. *The Suburban Child*. Cambridge, England: Cambridge University Press, 1955.

Kepler, Hazel. *The Child and His Play, A Planning Guide for Parents and Teachers*. New York: Funk & Wagnalls, 1952.

Mathes, Ruth E., and R. C. Mathes. *The Decline and Fall of the Wooden Doll*. Doll Collectors of America, 1964.

Toys and Games. London: London Museum Picture Book, Her Majesty's Stationery Office, 1959.

CHAPTER 9

Ashe, Arthur, and Arnold Rampersad. *Days of Grace, A Memoir*. New York: Alfred A. Knopf, 1993.

Collins, John W. *My Seven Chess Prodigies*. New York: Simon & Schuster, 1975.

Eales, Richard. *Chess: The History of a Game*. New York: Facts on File, 1985.

Grey, Jayne. *Party Games for Young Children*. London: Ward, Lock, 1961.

Grunfeld, Fredric V. *Games of the World: How to Make Them, How to Play Them, How They Came to Be*. Zurich, Switzerland: Swiss Committee for UNICEF and Plenary Publications International, 1982.

Hyun, Peter, ed. *It's Fun Being Young in Korea*. Korea: Saem Toh Sa Publishing, 1978.

Lloyd, Chris Evert, with Neil Amdur. *Chrissie, My Own Story*. New York: Simon & Schuster, 1982.

Locke, Raymond Friday, ed. *The Human Side of History: Man's Manners, Morals and Games*. Los Angeles: Mankind Publishing, 1970.

Mesesrole, Mike, ed. *The 1994 Information Please Sports Almanac*. Boston: Houghton Mifflin, 1994.

Miedzian, Myriam. *Boys Will Be Boys: Breaking the Link between Masculinity and Violence*. New York: Doubleday, 1991.

Miller, Carl S., comp., ed., and arr., et al. *Sing, Children, Sing: Songs, Dances and Singing Games of Many Lands and Peoples*. Introduction by Leonard Bernstein. New York: Chappell, 1972.

Nelson, Mariah Burton. *The Stronger Women Get, the More Men Love Football: Sexism and the American Culture of Sport*. New York: Harcourt Brace, 1994.

The Sports Illustrated 1996 Sports Almanac. Boston, New York, London, and Toronto: Little, Brown, 1996.

Wallace, Amy. *The Prodigy*. New York: E. P. Dutton, 1986.

Wood, Clement, and Gloria Goddard. *The Complete Book of Games*. Garden City, N.Y.: Doubleday, 1940.

Woolum, Janet. *Outstanding Women Athletes: Who They Are and How They Influenced Sports in America*. Phoenix, Ariz.: Oryx Press, 1992.

Zaharias, Babe Didrikson. *This Life I've Led*. New York: A. S. Barnes, 1955.

CHAPTER 10

Anderson, Emily. *Letters of Mozart and His Family*. London: Macmillan, 1938.

Ariès, Philippe. *Centuries of Childhood*. Translated by Robert Baldick. New York: Alfred A. Knopf, 1962.

Armke, Ken. *Hummel: An Illustrated Handbook and Price Guide*. Indianapolis, Indiana: Literary Guild, 1995.

Burn, Barbara. *Metropolitan Children*. New York: Metropolitan Museum of Art/Harry N. Abrams, 1984.

Chase, Alice Elizabeth. *Famous Paintings*. New York: Platt and Munk, 1951.

Clark, Kenneth. *Leonardo da Vinci, An Account of His Development as an Artist.* Introduction by Martin Kemp. New York: Penguin, 1971.

Daiken, Leslie. *The Lullaby Book.* London: Edmund Ward, 1959.

Dali, Salvador. *Diary of a Genius: The Secret Life of Salvador Dali.* New York: Prentice Hall, 1986.

DePree, Mildred. *A Child's World of Stamps.* New York: Parents' Magazine Press, 1973.

Descharnes, Robert, and G. Neret. *Salvador Dali: The Work, the Man.* New York: Barnes & Noble, 1995.

Di Leo, Joseph. *Young Children and Their Drawings.* New York: Brunner/Mazel, 1970.

Ehemann, Eric. *Hummel: The Complete Collectors' Guide and Illustrated References.* Huntington, N.Y.: Portfolio Press, 1976.

Grady, Terence. *The Beatles—A Musical Evolution.* Boston: Twayne Publishers, 1983.

Hertsgaard, Mark. *A Day in the Life: The Music and Artistry of the Beatles.* New York: Delacorte Press, 1994.

Holmes, Kenneth, and Hugh Collinson. *Child Art Grows Up.* London: The Studio Publications, 1952.

Janson, H. W., and Dora Jane. *The Story of Painting for Young People.* New York: Harry N. Abrams, 1952.

Kagan, Pauline Wright. *From Adventure to Experience through Art.* San Francisco: Chandler Publishing, 1959.

Kellogg, Rhoda, and Scott O'Dell. *Psychology of Children's Art.* New York: Random House, 1967.

Kerst, Friedrich, composer and editor. *Mozart: The Man and the Artist Revealed in His Own Words.* Translated from German by Henry Edward Krehbiel. New York: Dover, 1965.

Lindstrom, Miriam. *Children's Art: A Study of Normal Development in Children's Modes of Visualization.* Los Angeles: University of California Press, 1957.

M. I. Hummel, the Golden Anniversary Album. New York: Portfolio Press, Robert Campbell Rowe Books, 1984.

Mendelowitz, Daniel M. *Children Are Artists.* Stanford, California: Stanford University Press, 1954.

Merejkowski, Dmitri. *The Romance of Leonardo Da Vinci.* Translated by Bernard Guilbert Guerney. New York: Random House, 1931.

Miller, Carl S., comp. and ed. *Rockabye Baby.* New York: Chappell, 1975.

———. *Songs, Dances and Singing Games of Many Lands and Peoples.* With an Introduction by Leonard Bernstein. New York: Chappell, 1972.

Morris, Desmond. *The Biology of Art.* London: Methuen, 1962.

Plato. *Republic.* c. 350 B.C. Reprint, translated by H. D. Lee, London: Penguin, .

Read, Herbert. *Education through Art.* New York: Pantheon Books, 1958.

———. *The Meaning of Art.* London: Faber & Faber, 1972.

Rondes et Chansons Pour les Enfants Sages. Paris: Librairie Gründ, 1947.

Scott, A. C. *Literature and the Arts in Twentieth Century China.* New York: Doubleday, 1963.

Ulanov, Barry. *Duke Ellington.* London: Musicians Press, 1946.

———. *A History of Jazz in America.* New York: Viking Press, 1952.

———. *A Handbook of Jazz.* New York: Viking Press, 1957.

Vasari, Giorgio. *Lives of the Greatest Italian Painters, Sculptors and Artists.* Rome: 1550. Reprint, Lives of the Artists. Edited by Betty Radice and C. A. Jones. Translated by George Bull. Baltimore, Maryland: Penguin, 1975.

Chapter 11

Blesh, Rudi. *Keaton.* New York: Macmillan, 1966.

Cary, Diana Serra. *Hollywood's Children.* Boston: Houghton Mifflin, 1979.

Deschner, Donald. *The Films of W. C. Fields.* New York: Citadel Press, 1966.

Everson, William K. *The Art of W. C. Fields.* New York: Bobbs-Merrill, 1967.

Franklin, Joe. *Classics of the Silent Screen.* New York: Bramhall House, 1959.

Funicello, Annette, with Patricia Romanowski. *A Dream Is a Wish Your Heart Makes: My Story.* New York: Hyperion, 1994.

Hedrick, Joan D. *Harriet Beecher Stowe: A Life.* Oxford: Oxford University Press, 1994.

James, Clive. *Fame in the 20th Century.* New York: Random House, 1993.

Keaton, Buster, with Charles Samuels. *My Wonderful World of Slapstick.* New York: Doubleday, 1960.

Leslie, Cole. *The Life of Noel Coward.* New York: Penguin Books, 1976.

Maltin, Leonard. *The Disney Films.* New York: Crown Publishers, 1984.

Maltin, Leonard, ed. *Movie Encyclopedia.* New York: Dutton, 1994.

Maltin, Leonard, and Richard Bann. *The Little Rascals: The Life and Times of Our Gang.* Camp Hill, Penn.: Quality Paperback Book Club, 1995.

Robinson, David. *Chaplin: His Life and Art.* New York: McGraw-Hill, 1985.

Speaight, George. *Punch and Judy, A History.* Boston: Plays, Inc., 1970.

Stowe, Harriet Beecher. *Uncle Tom's Cabin, or Life among the Lowly.* 1851. Reprint. New York: Braziller, 1966 .

Ulanov, Barry. *The Incredible Crosby.* New York: McGraw-Hill, 1948.

CHAPTER 12

The Aesop for Children. New York: Checkerboard Press, 1947.

Arbuthnot, May Hill, comp., et al. *Children's Books Too Good to Miss: International Year of the Child.* New York: University Press Books, 1979.

Ashford, Daisy. *The Young Visitors or Mr. Salteenas' Plan.* Preface by J. M. Barrie, 1919. Reprint. London: Chatto Windus, 1936.

Austen, Jane. *Love and Freindship and Other Early Works.* Introduction by Geraldine Killalea. New York: Harmony Books, 1981.

Baring-Gould, William S., and Ceil Baring Gould. *The Annotated Mother Goose.* New York: Clarkson N. Potter, 1962.

Batey, Mavis. *Alice's Adventures in Oxford.* London: Pitkin Pictorials, 1980.

Bennett, William J., ed. *The Book of Virtues: A Treasury of Great Moral Stories.* New York: Simon & Schuster, 1993.

———. *The Children's Book of Virtues.* Illustrations by Michael Hague, New York: Simon & Schuster, 1995.

Bettelheim, Bruno. *The Uses of Enchantment: The Meaning and Importance of Fairy Tales.* New York: Random House, Vintage Books, 1976.

Bonfani, Leo. *The Witchcraft Hysteria of 1692.* New England Historical Series. Wakefield, Mass.: Pride Publications, 1971.

Borges, Pamela, and Edward Borges. *The Strange Case of Mother Goose: A Musical Play in Two Acts.* Anchorage, Kentucky: The Children's Theatre Press, 1954.

Burgess, Gelett. *The Purple Cow and Other Poems.* Pasadena, California: Grant Dahlstrom/The Castle Press, 1968.

Carpenter, Humphrey, and Mari Prichard. *The Oxford Companion to Children's Literature.* London: Oxford University Press, 1994.

Carroll, Lewis. *The Annotated Alice.* New York: Clarkson N. Potter, 1960.

———. *More Annotated Alice: Alice's Adventures in Wonderland and Through the Looking Glass and What Alice Found There.* Notes by Martin Gardner. New York: Clarkson N. Potter, 1960.

Croxall, Samuel. *Fables of Aesop and Others.* New York, World Publishing House, 1876.

Fadiman, Clifton. *The World Treasury of Children's Literature.* New York: Little, Brown, 1984.

Field, Eugene. *Poems of Childhood.* New York: Airmont Publishing, 1970.

Fishkin, Shelley Fisher. *Was Huck Black? Mark Twain and African-American Voices.* London: Oxford University Press, 1994.

Garner, James Finn. *Politically Correct Bedtime Stories.* New York: Macmillan, 1994.

Hearn, Lafcadio. *Japanese Fairy Tales.* New York: Peter Pauper Press, 1958.

Hoff, Benjamin. *The Tao of Pooh: What Pooh Can Tell Us About Ourselves.* New York: Penguin. 1982.

———. *The Tao of Piglet: What Piglet Can Tell Us About Ourselves.* New York: Penguin, 1982.

Kelen, Emery. *Mr. Nonsense: A Life of Edward Lear.* London: Thomas Nelson, 1986.

Levi, Peter. *Edward Lear, A Biography.* New York: Scribner's, 1995.

Milne, A. A. *The World of Christopher Robin.* New York: E. P. Dutton, 1958.

Nandris, Mabel, trans. *Folk Tales from Rumania.* London: Routledge & Kegan Paul, 1952.

Norton, Mary. *The Borrowers.* New York: Harcourt, Brace, 1953.

Lang, Andrew, ed. *Olive Fairy Book.* New York: Longmans, Green, 1956.

Opie, Iona, and Peter Opie, eds. *The Oxford Dictionary of Nursery Rhymes.* London: Oxford University Press, 1952.

———. *The Lore and Language of Schoolchildren.* London: Oxford University Press, 1959.

———. *The Oxford Book of Children's Verses.* London: Oxford University Press, 1973.

———. *The Classic Fairy Tales.* London: Oxford University Press, 1994.

Paine, Albert Bigelow. *Mark Twain, A Biography.* New York: Harper & Brothers, 1912.

Perrault, Charles. *Fairy Tales.* 1697. Reprint, translated from French and introduction by Geoffrey Brereton. London: Penguin, 1957.

Rosen, Michael. *The Kingfisher Book of Children's Poetry.* London: Grisewood & Dempsey, Kingfisher Books, 1991.

Schulz, Charles M., with R. Smith Kiliper. *Charlie Brown, Snoopy and Me.* New York: Doubleday, 1980.

Shepard, Ernest R. *Drawn from Memory.* Philadelphia: J. B. Lippincott, 1957.

Singer, Isaac Bashevis. *Stories for Children.* Toronto: Collins Publishers, 1984.

This Singing World: An Anthology of Modern Poetry for Young People. Illustrations by Florence Wyman Ivins. New York: Harcourt, Brace, 1923.

Thomas, Katherine Elwes. *The Real Personages of Mother Goose.* London: Lothrop, Lee & Shepard, 1930.

Wood, L. S., ed. *A Book of English Verse on Infancy and Childhood.* London: Macmillan, 1921

CHAPTER 13

America's Original Sin: A Study Guide on White Racism. Washington, D.C.: Sojourners Resource Center, 1992.

Angelou, Maya. *I Know Why the Caged Bird Sings.* New York: Random House, 1969.

Branch, Taylor. *Parting the Waters: America in the King Years, 1954–1963:* New York: Simon & Schuster, 1988.

Cagen, Seth, and Philip Dray. *We Are Not Afraid: The Story of Goodman, Schwerner and Chaney and the Civil Rights Campaign for Mississippi.* New York: Macmillan, 1988.

Coles, Robert. *Children of Crisis.* Boston: Little, Brown, 1973.

———. *The Moral Life of Children.* New York: Houghton Mifflin, 1991.

de Alba, Joaquin, *Violence in America: De Tocqueville's America Revisited.* Foreword by Chester Burger. Washington, D.C.: Acropolis Books, 1969.

De Tocqueville, Alexis. *Democracy in America.* Brussels: 1835.

De Waal, Frans. *Peacemaking among Primates.* Cambridge, Mass.: Harvard University Press, 1989.

Dershowitz, Alan M. *The Abuse Excuse: And Other CopOuts, Sob Stories and Evasions of Responsibility.* Boston: Little, Brown, 1994.

Douglass, Frederick. *Narrative of the Life and Times of Frederick Douglass, 1845. An American Slave.* Reprint, edited by Houston A. Baker, Jr. New York: Penguin.

Drinan, Robert F., S. J. *Cry of the Oppressed: The History and Hope of the Human Rights Revolution.* San Francisco: Harper & Row, 1987.

Edelman, Marian Wright. *Families in Peril: An Agenda for Social Change.* Cambridge, Mass.: Harvard University Press, 1987.

Engels, Friedrich. *The Lives of the Upper Classes in England.* 1845.

Fanelli, Vincent. *The Human Face of Poverty.* New York: Bootstrap Press, 1990.

Fyfe, Alec. *All Work and No Play: Child Labour Today.* London: Committee for UNICEF, 1986.

Fremon, Celeste. *Father Greg & the Homeboys: The Extraordinary Journey of Father Greg Boyle and His Work with Latino Groups of East L.A.* New York: Hyperion, 1995.

Gates, Henry Louis, Jr. *Colored People: A Memoir.* New York: Alfred A. Knopf, 1994.

Giles, F. T. *Children and the Law.* London: Penguin, 1959.

Gordon, Linda. *Pitied But Not Entitled: Single Mothers and the History of Welfare, 1890–1935.* New York: Free Press, 1994.

Grubb, W. Norton, and Marvin Lazerson. *Broken Promises: How Americans Fail Their Children.* New York: Basic Books, 1982.

Haley, Alex. *Roots: The Saga of an American Family.* New York: Doubleday, 1976.

Hearth, Amy Hill. *Having Our Say: The Delany Sisters' First 100 Years.* New York: Kodansha America, 1993.

Hechinger, Grace. *How to Raise a Street Smart Child: The Complete Parents' Guide to Safety on the Street and at Home.* New York: Facts on File, 1984.

Hentoff, Nat. *Free Speech for Me—But Not for Thee.* New York: HarperCollins, 1992.

Hollenbach, David. *Justice, Peace, & Human Rights: American Catholic Social Ethics in a Pluralistic Context.* New York: Crossroad Publishing, 1988.

Jacobs, Jane. *Death and Life of Great American Cities.* New York: Random House, 1961.

Judson, Stephanie, comp. and ed. *A Manual on Nonviolence and Children.* Philadelphia: Friends Committee on Nonviolence and Children, 1984.

Keneally, Thomas. *Schindler's List.* New York: Simon & Schuster, 1982.

King, Martin Luther, Jr. *Stride Toward Freedom: The Montgomery Story.* New York: William Morrow, 1958.

Leach, Penelope. *What Our Society Must Do—and Is Not Doing—for Our Children Today.* New York: Alfred A. Knopf, 1994.

Lorenz, Konrad. *On Aggression.* Translated from German by Marjorie Kerr Wilson. New York: Harcourt, Brace & World, 1971.

Mannix, Daniel P. *The History of Torture.* New York: Dell Publishing, 1964.

Marx, Karl. *Correspondence: The Personal Letters, 1844–1877, A Selection.* Ed by Fritz J. Raddatz. London: Weidenfeld and Nicolson, 1981.

Mathabane, Mark, and Gail Mathabane. *Love in Black and White: The Triumph of Love over Prejudice and Taboo.* New York: HarperCollins, 1992.

McGeady, Mary Rose. *"Am I Going to Heaven?" The Shocking Story of America's Street Kids.* New York: Covenant House, 1994.

———. *God's Lost Children: The Shocking Story of America's Homeless Kids.* New York: Covenant House, 1991.

Miller, Alice. *For Your Own Good: Hidden Cruelty in Childrearing and the Roots of Violence.* New York: Farrar, Straus & Giroux, 1983.

Mones, Paul. *When a Child Kills: Abused Children Who Kill Their Parents.* New York: Simon & Schuster, Pocket Books, 1991.

Moreira, Neiva, ed. *Third World Guide.* The Hague, Netherlands: Novib Publishing House, 1984.

Paul VI, Pope. *Populorum Progressio* (Development of Peoples). Vatican City: Papal Encyclical, 1967.

Perella, Frederick J., Jr. *Poverty in American Democracy: A Study of Social Power.* Washington, D.C.: Campaign for Human Development, U.S. Catholic Conference, 1974.

Quinnett, Paul G. *Suicide: The Forever Decision—For Those Thinking about Suicide, and for Those Who Know, Love, or Counsel Them.* New York: Continuum Publishing, 1987.

Siegler, Ava L. *What Should I Tell the Kids: A Parent's Guide to Real Problems in the Real World.* New York: E. P. Dutton, 1994.

Steele, Shelby. *The Content of Our Character: A New Vision of Race in America.* New York: St. Martin's Press, 1990.

Swift, Jonathan. *A Modest Proposal.* London: 1729. Edited by Charles W. Eliot. Reprinted, Harvard Classics. New York: P. F. Collier & Son, 1956.

Trevelyan, G. M. *English Social History.* New York: Longmans, Green & Co., 1942.

The Wresinski Report: Chronic Poverty and Lack of Basic Security. Landover, Md.: Fourth World Movement, 1994.

Urban Basic Services: Reaching Children and Women of the Urban Poor. New York: UNICEF, 1984.

Washington, Booker T. *Up from Slavery.* New York: Penguin, 1901.

Waters, Ethel, with Charles Samuels. *His Eye Is on the Sparrow.* Garden City, N.Y.: Doubleday, 1951.

Wright, Richard. *Native Son.* New York: Harper's, 1966.

Young, James J., C.S.Sp. *Prejudice.* New York: Paulist Press, 1966.

Chapter 14

Erikson, Erik. *Gandhi's Truth: On the Origins of a Militant Nonviolence.* New York: W.W. Norton, 1969.

Fahey, Joseph, and Richard Armstrong, eds. *A Peace Reader: Essential Readings on War, Justice, Nonviolence and World Order.* New York: Paulist Press, 1989.

Filipovic, Zlata. *Zlata's Diary: A Child's Life in Sarajevo.* Translated, with notes, by Christina Pribichevich-Zoric. Introduction by Janine Di Giovanni. New York: Penguin, 1994.

Flower, Kelsey. *Children of Deerfield.* Deerfield, Mass.: 1952.

Fogelman, Eva. *Conscience & Courage: Rescuers of Jews during the Holocaust.* New York: Doubleday, Anchor Books, 1994.

Frank, Anne. *The Diary of a Young Girl.* Edited by Otto H. Frank. Translated by B. M. Moyaart. New York: Doubleday, Pocket Books, 1952.

Gies, Miep, with Alison Leslie Gold. *Anne Frank Remembered: The Story of the Woman Who Helped to Hide the Frank Family.* New York: Simon & Schuster, 1987.

Hollins, Harry B., Averill L. Powers, and Mark Sommer. *The Conquest of War: Alternative Strategies for Global Security.* New York: Westview Press, 1989.

Howard, Helen Addison, and Dan L. McGrath. *War Chief Joseph.* Lincoln, Neb.: University of Nebraska Press, 1967.

John XXIII, Pope. *Pacem in Terris* (Peace on Earth). Vatican City: Papal Encyclical, 1961.

Kelly, Kitty. *A Year in Saigon: How I Gave Up My Glitzy Job in Television to Have the Time of My Life Teaching Amerasian Kids in Vietnam.* New York: Simon & Schuster, 1992.

Kincade, William H., and Priscilla B. Hayner, eds. *The Access Resource Guide: An International Directory of Information on War, Peace, and Security.* Cambridge, Mass.: Ballinger Publishing, 1988.

Krieger, David, and Frank Kelly, eds. *Waging Peace II: Vision and Hope for the 21st Century.* Chicago: Noble Press, 1993.

McGinnis, Kathleen, and Barbara Oehlberg. *Starting Out Right: Nurturing Young Children as Peacemakers.* Oak Park, Ill.: Meyer-Stone Books, 1988.

O'Connell, Robert L. *Of Arms and Men: A History of War, Weapons and Aggression.* Oxford: Oxford University Press, 1991.

Rosenblatt, Roger. *Children of War.* Garden City, N.Y.: Doubleday, Anchor Press, 1983.

Sayegh, Juliette. *Child Survival in Wartime: A Case Study from Iraq, 1983–1989.* Baltimore, Maryland: Johns Hopkins School of Hygiene and Public Health, Department of Population Dynamics, 1992.

Urquhart, Brian. *A Life in Peace and War.* New York: Harper & Row, 1989.

Van der Rol, Ruud, and Rian Verhoeven. *Anne Frank: Beyond the Diary: A Photographic Remembrance.* Introduction by Anna Quinlen. Translated by Tony Langham and Plym Peters. New York: Viking Press, 1993.

Weiner, Florence, comp. *Peace Is You and Me: Children's Writings and Paintings on Love and Peace.* New York: Avon Books, 1971.

CHAPTER 15

Aarons, Audrey, and Hugh Hawes, eds., with Juliet Gayton. *Child to Child*. London: Macmillan, 1979.

Black, Maggie. *The Children and the Nations: The Story of UNICEF*. Sidney, Australia: P.I.C., 1986.

Caming, William. *Story Land*. Glen, N.H.: Morrell Family Attractions, 1992.

Coles, Robert. *The Call of Service: A Witness to Idealism*. Boston: Houghton Mifflin, 1993.

Edelman, Marian Wright. *The Measure of Our Success: A Letter to My Children and Yours*. Boston: Beacon Press, 1992.

———. *Guide My Feet*. New York: Farrar, Strauss & Giroux, 1996.

Fernandez, Harry Craven. *The Child Advocacy Handbook*. Pilgrim Press, 1980.

Gaan, Margaret. *His Name Is Today: The Early Years of the United Nations Children's Fund in Southeast Asia*. Sacramento, Calif.: Self-published, 1992.

Gross, Beatrice, and Ronald Gross, eds. *The Children's Rights Movement: Overcoming the Oppression of Young People*. Garden City, N.Y.: Doubleday, Anchor Books, 1977.

Hale, Lorraine. *The House That Love Built*. New York: Hale House, 1991.

Hughs, Ina. *A Prayer for Children*. New York: William Morrow & Co., 1995.

Jeal, Tim. *The Boy-Man: The Life of Lord Baden-Powell*. New York: William Morrow & Co., 1990.

Keeny, Sam. *Half the World's Children*. New York: UNICEF & Association Press, 1957.

Kenny, Father Kevin. *It Only Hurts When I Grow: Stories from Covenant House for Hurting Kids*. New York: Paulist Press, 1988.

Melton, David. *When Children Need Help*. New York: Thomas Y. Crowell Co., 1972.

Shusterman, Neal. *Kid Heroes: True Stories of Rescuers, Survivors, and Achievers*. New York: Tor, Tom Doherty Associates, 1991.

Simon, Arthur. *Bread for the World*. New York: William B. Eerdmans Publishing Co., 1975.

Soman, Shirley Camper. *Let's Stop Destroying Our Children*. New York: Hawthorne Press, 1974.

Ward, Barbara (Lady Jackson). *A New Creation: Reflections on the Environmental Issue*. Vatican City: Pontifical Commission on Justice and Peace, 1973.

CHAPTER 16

Asimov, Isaac. *Earth: Our Crowded Spaceship*. New York: John Day Co., 1974.

Beitz, Charles, and Michael Washburn. *Creating the Future: A Guide to Living and Working for Social Change*. New York: Bantam, 1974.

Berry, Thomas. *The Dream of the Earth*. California: Sierra Club Books, 1989.

Callahan, Daniel: *Ethics and Population Limitation*. Bridgeport, Conn.: The Population Council, 1971.

Danesh, Hossain. *The Violence-free Society: A Gift for our Children*. Toronto: Canadian Association for Studies on the Baha'i Faith, 1979

Ferencz, Benjamin B., in cooperation with Ken Keyes, Jr., . *PlanetHood: The Key to Your Survival and Prosperity*. Coos Bay, Oregon: Vision Books, 1989.

50 Simple Things Kids Can Do to Save the Earth. Berkeley, Calif.: Earth Works Press, 1990.

Flugel, J. C. *Population, Psychology and Peace*. Introduction by C. E. M. Joad. London: Watts & Co., 1947.

Hollender, Jeffrey A. *How to Make the World a Better Place: A Guide to Doing Good*. New York: William Morrow 1990.

Huxley, Aldous. *Brave New World*. New York: Doubleday, 1932.

Jones, Landon Y. *Great Expectations: America & the Baby Boom Generation*. New York: Coward, McCann & Geoghegan, 1980.

Kidder, Rushworth N. *An Agenda for the 21st Century*. Cambridge, Mass.: MIT Press, 1989.

———. *Reinventing the Future: Global Goals for the 21st Century*. Cambridge, Mass.: The MIT Press, 1989.

Lappé, Frances Moore. *Rediscovering America's Values: A Dialogue that Explores our Fundamental Beliefs and How They Offer Hope for America's Future*. New York: Ballantine Books, 1989.

Leonard, William J., S. J. *The Letter Carrier*. Kansas City: Sheed & Ward, 1993.

MacEachern, Diane. *Save Our Planet: 750 Everyday Ways You Can Help Clean Up the Earth*. New York: Dell Publishing, 1990.

Making Reality of Children's Rights. Radda Barnen (Save the Children). Stockholm, Sweden: 1989.

Malthus, Thomas Robert. *Population*. 1789. Reprint. With a foreword by Kenneth E. Boulding. Ann Arbor, Mich.: University of Michigan Press, 1959.

Naar, John. *Design for a Livable Planet: How You Can Help Clean Up the Environment*. Foreword by Frederic D. Krupp. New York: Harper & Row, 1990.

Nash, Roderick Frazier. *The Rights of Nature: A History of Environmental Ethics.* Madison, Wis.: University of Wisconsin Press, 1990.

Planting Seeds for the Future. New York: Edward S. Cornish Press, 1979.

State of the World: A Worldwatch Institute Report on Progress Toward a Sustainable Society. Project Director: Lester R. Brown. New York: W. W. Norton & Co., published annually.

————. *Vital Signs: The Trends That Are Shaping Our Future,* published annually.

Theilard de Chardin, Pierre. *The Phenomenon of Man.* Translated by Bernard Wall. New York: Harper & Row, 1959.

Thomas, Lewis: *The Fragile Species.* New York: Macmillan, Collier Books, 1992.

Thompson, Sir George. *The Foreseeable Future: What Will the World be Like a Hundred Years From Now? What Will Science Have Done for Us or to Us?* New York: Viking Press, 1955.

Toffler, Alvin. *Future Shock.* New York: Bantam Books, 1971.

Toffler, Alvin, and Heidi Toffler. *Creating a New Civilization: The Politics of the Third Wave.* Introduction by Newt Gringrich. Washington, D. C. : Progress & Freedom Foundation, 1994.

Ulanov, Barry. *Seeds of Hope in the Modern World.* New York: P. J. Kennedy & Sons, 1962.

UNICEF. *Children and Agenda 21: A Guide to UNICEF Issues for Development and Environment into the 21st Century.* Geneva: UNICEF, 1992.

UNICEF. *The Progress of Nations: The Nations of the World Ranked According to Their Achievements in Child Health, Nutrition, Education, Family Planning, and Progress for Women.* Peter Adamson, editor. Wallingford, England: Oxford University Press, published annually.

UNICEF. *The State of the World's Children.* New York: UNICEF. Oxford: Oxford University Press, issued annually.

United Nations Population Fund (UNFPA). *Population and the Environment: The Challenges Ahead.* London: Banson Publications, 1990.

Verne, Jules. *Paris au XXe Siecle.* Paris: Hachette Livre, 1994.

Vittachi, Anuradha. *Earth Conference One: Sharing a Vision for Our Planet.* Foreword by James Lovelock. Boston: Shambhala Publications, New Science Library, 1989.

World Commission on Environment and Development. *Our Common Future.* Introduction by Gro Harlem Brundtland. Oxford: Oxford University Press, 1989.

GENERAL BIBLIOGRAPHY

Asimov, Isaac. *Isaac Asimov's Book of Facts.* New York: Bell Publishing, 1979.

Auden, W., and Louis Kronenberger, eds. *The Viking Book of Aphorisms: More Than 3000 Selections from More Than 400 Authors.* New York: Viking Press, 1966.

Augarde, Tony, ed. *The Oxford Dictionary of Modern Quotations.* New York: Oxford University Press, 1991.

Augustine of Hippo, Saint. *Confessions.* A.D. 397. Translated with introduction and notes by Henry Chadwick. Oxford: Oxford University Press, 1991.

Australia. Library of Nations Series. Alexandria, Virginia: Time-Life Books, 1985.

Balsham, A.L. *The Wonder That Was India.* New York: Grove Press, 1954.

Bartlett, John. *Familiar Quotations.* Christopher Morley and Louella D. Everett, editors. Boston: Little, Brown & Co., 1942.

Bowman, John S, ed. *The Cambridge Dictionary of American Biography.* Cambridge, Mass.: Press Syndicate of the University of Cambridge, 1995.

Britain. Library of Nations series. Alexandria, Virginia: Time-Life Books, 1986.

Byrne, Robert, comp. and ed. *1,911 Best Things Anybody Ever Said.* New York: Ballantine Books: 1988.

Castle, Anthony P. *Quotes and Anecdotes for Preachers and Teachers.* London: Kevin Mayhew, 1979.

Cerf, Christopher, and Victor Navaslky. *The Experts Speak: The Definitive Compendium of Authoritative Misinformation.* New York: Pantheon Books, 1984.

Chinese Proverbs from Olden Times. Mount Vernon, N.Y.: Peter Pauper Press, 1956.

Collier's Encyclopedia. New York: P.F. Collier & Son, 1959.

Collins Dictionary of People and Places. London: William Collins Sons & Co., 1975.

Crystal, David, ed. *The Cambridge Encyclopedia.* Cambridge, England: Cambridge University Press, 1992.

Durant, Will, and Ariel Durant. *The Lessons of History.* New York: Simon & Schuster, 1968.

Eliot, Charles W., ed. *The Harvard Classics* (50 vols.). New York: P. F. Collier & Son, 1956.

Emerson, Ralph Waldo. *Essays.* Reprinted in *Harvard Classics.* New York: P. F. Collier & Son, 1956.

Erasmus. *The Esssential Erasmus.* Selected and translated with introduction and commentary by John P. Dolan. New York: New American Library, 1964.

Erikson, Erik H. *Childhood and Society.* New York: W. W. Norton, 1950.

Evans, Bergen. *Dictionary of Quotations*. New York: Delacorte Press, 1978.

Fadiman, Clifton, ed. *The Little, Brown Book of Anecdotes*. Boston: Little, Brown & Co., 1985.

Fairservis, Walter A., Jr. *India*. Cleveland, Ohio: World Publishing Co., 1961.

Falladay, George. *Erasmus*. New York: Stein & Day, 1970.

Farrow, John. *Pageant of the Popes*. New York: Sheed & Ward, 1942.

Ferrell, Robert H, ed. *The Twentieth Century, an Almanac*. Introduction by Averill Harriman. New York: World Almanac Publications, Ballantine Books, 1984.

Foy, Felician A., O. F. M., and Rose M. Avato, eds. Huntington, Ind.: Our Sunday Visitor, 1989.

Franklin, Benjamin. *A Biography in His Own Words*. Edited by Thomas Fleming. Introduction by Bell Whitfield, Jr. New York: Newsweek Book Division, 1972.

Fuller, Edmund, ed. *Thesaurus of Anecdotes*. New York: Crown Publishers, 1942.

Geddie, William, and Uddell Geddie, eds. *Chamber's Biographical Dictionary*. London: W. & R. Chambers, 1929.

Gershoon, Andrew. *Russian Proverbs*. London: Frederick Muller, 1941.

Good News for Modern Man: The New Testament; Today's English Version. New York: American Bible Society, 1966.

Grigson, Geoffrey, and Charles Harvard Gibbs-Smith. *PEOPLE: A Volume of the Good, Bad, Great and Eccentric Who Illustrate the Admirable Diversity of Man*. New York: Hawthorne Books, 1957.

Guinness Book of Records. London: Guinness Publishing; New York: Facts on File, published annually.

Herodotus. *The Histories*. 450 B.C. Reprint. Garden City, N.Y.: Doubleday, 1929.

Holland, Saba. *A Memoir of the Reverend Sydney Smith by His Daughter*. New York: Harper & Brothers, 1855.

The Holy Bible, containing the Old and New Testaments (commonly called *The King James Bible*). London: 1611.

Hourant, Albert. *A History of the Arab Peoples*. Cambridge, Mass.: Harvard University Press, 1991.

Information Please Almanac. New York: Information Please Publishing, published annually.

James, William. *The Writings of William James: A Comprehensive Edition*. Edited, with an introduction and preface by John J. McDermott. Chicago: University of Chicago Press, 1977.

The Jerusalem Bible.

Josephus, Flavius. *Antiquities of the Jews*. c. A.D. 100. Reprint, with notes. New York: Viking Press, 1974.

Joy, Charles R. *Young People of the British Isles*. New York: Duell, Sloan & Pearce, 1965.

Kane, Joseph Nathan. *Famous First Facts*. New York: H. W. Wilson, 1950.

Kempe, Ruth S., and C. Henry. *Child Abuse*. Cambridge, Mass.: Harvard University Press, 1978.

Khushwant Singh's India. Bombay, India: IBH Publishing, 1970.

Leslau, Charlotte, and Leslau Wolf, comps. *African Proverbs*. Mount Vernon, N.Y.: Peter Pauper Press, 1962.

Machiavelli, Niccolò. *The Prince*. 1532. Reprint, edited and translated by J.R. Hale. London: Oxford University Press, 1988.

MacGregor, Forbes, comp. *Scots' Proverbs and Rhymes*. Edinburgh, Scotland: Moray Press, 1948.

Mathelssen, F. O. *The James Family: Including Selections from the Writings of Henry James, Senior, William, Henry, and Alice James*. New York: Alfred A. Knopf, 1947.

Matthew, Helen G. *Asia in the Modern World*. New York: New American Library, Mentor Books, 1963.

McCann, Sean. *The Wit of Oscar Wilde*. New York: Dorset Press, 1969.

McDermott, John J., ed. *The Writings of William James*. Chicago: University of Chicago Press, 1977.

Mencken, H. L. *A New Dictionary of Quotations on Historical Principles from Ancient and Modern Times*. New York: Alfred A. Knopf, 1966.

Mexico. Library of Nations series. Alexandria, Virginia: Time-Life Books, 1986.

Mieder, Wolfgang. *Yankee Wisdom: New England Proverbs*. Shelburne, Vermont: New England Press, 1989.

Miller, Perry. *The American Puritans, Their Prose and Poetry*. Garden City, N.Y.: Doubleday, 1956.

Montaigne, Michel de. *Essays*. c. 1595. Reprinted in Harvard Classics, edited by Charles W. Eliot, LLD. New York: P. F. Collier & Son, 1956.

Moyers, Bill. *Listening to America*. New York: Doubleday, 1971.

———. *A World of Ideas*. New York: Doubleday, 1989.

Neil, William, ed. *Concise Dictionary of Religious Quotations*. Grand Rapids, Mich.: William B. Eerdmans Publishing, 1974.

New York Public Library. *Book of 20th-Century American Quotations*. New York: Warner Books, 1992.

———. *New York Public Library Desk Reference*. New York: Prentice Hall, 1993.

The Old and New Testaments, translated and edited by Catholic scholars under the patronage of the Episcopal Committee of the Fraternity of Christian Doctrine. Paterson, N.J.: St. Anthony Guild Press, 1941.

The Oxford Dictionary of Quotations. Oxford: Oxford University Press, 1979. 4th ed., edited by Angela Partington. Oxford: Oxford University Press, 1994.

People: A Volume of the Good, Bad, Great and Egocentric Who Illustrate the Admirable Diversity of Man. New York: Hawthorn Books, 1957.

Piaget, Jean. *The Language and Thought of the Child.* New York: Meridian Books, 1955.

Pliny the Elder. *Natural History.* c. A.D. 70. Reprint, edited by J. Nesome. Translated by Philemon Holland. Oxford: Clarendon Press, 1964.

Plutarch. *Opera Moralia* (Essays). c. 110 A. D. Reprint, translated by Robin Waterfield. Introduction and annotations by Ian Kidd. London: Penguin, 1992.

———. *The Parallel Lives of the Noble Greeks and Romans.* c. 110 A. D. Reprint of 12 of the Lives edited and abridged with an introduction by John W. McFarland and Pleasant and Audrey Graves. New York: Random House, 1966.

Powis Smith, J. M., ed. *The Old Testament, An American Translation.* Chicago: University of Chicago Press, 1947.

Prabhu, R. K. and Shewak Bhojraj ("Dada"), comps. and eds. *Bapu and Children.* Ahmedabad, India: Navajivan Press, 1964.

Proverbs to Live By: Truths That Live in Words. Kansas City, Missouri: Hallmark, 1968.

Ravitch, Diana, ed. *The American Reader: Words That Moved a Nation.* New York: HarperCollins, 1990.

Roper, William. *The Life of Sir Thomas More,* 1851. Reprint. London: J. M. Dent & Sons, 1938.

Rosten, Leo. *Leo Rosten's Treasury of Jewish Quotations.* New York: McGraw-Hill, 1972.

Sann, Paul. *Fads, Follies and Delusions.* New York: Crown Publishers, 1967.

Sethi, Narendra, comp. *Hindu Proverbs and Wisdom.* Mount Vernon, New York: Peter Pauper Press, 1962.

Soghikian, Juanita Will. *Lands, Peoples and Communities of the Middle East.* Waverly, Mass.: Middle East Gateway Series, 1963.

Springs of Hope: Goethe, Seneca, Shakespeare, Shelley, Tagore. New York: Herder and Herder, 1971.

Springs of Indian Wisdom. New York: Herder Book Center, 1965.

Springs of Oriental Wisdom. New York: Herder Book Center, 1964.

Tagore, Rabindranath. *Whisperings: The Inspirational Writings of Rabindranath Tagore on Nature, Love, and Life.* Selected by Lois Huffmon. Kansas City, Missouri: Hallmark, 1973.

THINGS: A Volume of Objects Devised by Man's Genius Which Are the Measure of His Civilization. New York: Hawthorn Books, 1957.

Trager, James. *The People's Chronology: A Year-by-Year Record of Human Events from Prehistory to the Present.* New York: Henry Holt, 1992.

Tripp, Rhoda Thomas. *The International Thesaurus of Quotations.* New York: Thomas Y. Crowell, 1970.

Troop, Minam. *Children around the World.* New York: Grosset & Dunlap, 1958.

Walker, J. B. R. *The Comprehensive Concordance to the Holy Scriptures, based on the Authorized Version.* New York: Macmillan, 1948.

Wallechinsky, David, and Irving Wallace. *The People's Almanac.* Garden City, New York: Doubleday, 1975.

Webster's Biographical Dictionary. Springfield, Mass.: G. & C. Merriam, 1957.

Weiss, Irving, and Anne D. Weiss. *Reflections on Childhood: A Quotations Dictionary.* Santa Barbara, Calif.: ABC-CLIO, 1991.

Wertham, Frederic. *A Sign for Cain: An Exploration of Human Violence.* New York: Macmillan, 1966.

West, Rebecca. *Saint Augustine.* Chicago: Thomas More Press, 1982.

White, Emmons E., translator. *The Wisdom of India.* Mount Vernon, N.Y.: Peter Pauper Press, 1968.

Wise Sayings from the Orient. Mount Vernon, N.Y.: Peter Pauper Press, 1963.

The World Almanac and Book of Facts. New York: Newspaper Enterprise Association, published annually.

647

Index

by Virgil Diodato

660

661